THE PAPERS OF
THOMAS JEFFERSON

THE PAPERS OF
Thomas Jefferson

Volume 27
1 September to 31 December 1793

JOHN CATANZARITI, EDITOR

EUGENE R. SHERIDAN, SENIOR ASSOCIATE EDITOR

J. JEFFERSON LOONEY, ASSOCIATE EDITOR

ELIZABETH PETERS BLAZEJEWSKI AND LINDA MONACO,
EDITORIAL ASSISTANTS

JEAN-YVES M. LE SAUX, CONSULTING EDITOR

PRINCETON, NEW JERSEY
PRINCETON UNIVERSITY PRESS

1997

Library of Congress Cataloging-in-Publication

ISBN 0-691-01585-6

This book has been composed in Monticello

Princeton University Press books are printed on
acid-free paper and meet the guidelines for permanence
and durability of the Committee on Production
Guidelines for Book Longevity of the
Council on Library Resources

Printed in the United States of America
by Princeton Academic Press

DEDICATED TO THE MEMORY OF

ADOLPH S. OCHS

PUBLISHER OF THE NEW YORK TIMES

1896-1935

WHO BY THE EXAMPLE OF A RESPONSIBLE

PRESS ENLARGED AND FORTIFIED

THE JEFFERSONIAN CONCEPT

OF A FREE PRESS

ACKNOWLEDGMENTS

As INDICATED in the first volume, this edition was made possible by a grant of $200,000 from The New York Times Company to Princeton University. Since this initial subvention, its continuance has been assured by additional contributions from The New York Times Company and The New York Times Company Foundation; by grants of the Ford Foundation, the National Historical Publications and Records Commission, and the National Endowment for the Humanities; by grants of the Andrew W. Mellon Foundation, the Pew Charitable Trusts, The John Ben Snow Memorial Trust, and the L. J. Skaggs and Mary C. Skaggs Foundation to Founding Fathers Papers, Inc.; by benefactions from the Charlotte Palmer Phillips Foundation, Time Inc., the Dyson Foundation, the Lucius N. Littauer Foundation, and the Florence Gould Foundation; and by gifts from James Russell Wiggins, David K. E. Bruce, and B. Batmanghelidj. In common with other editions of historical documents, THE PAPERS OF THOMAS JEFFERSON is a beneficiary of the good offices of the National Historical Publications and Records Commission, tendered in many useful forms through its officers and dedicated staff. For these and other indispensable aids generously given by librarians, archivists, scholars, and collectors of manuscripts, the Editors record their sincere gratitude.

FOREWORD

THIS volume concludes the publication of Jefferson's papers as Secretary of State. In addition to documenting the busy final months of his climactic year in that office, it includes a supplement that prints, summarizes, or notes some 270 documents for the period 1764-93 that have come to light or been reclassified since the appearance of the first supplement in Volume 15 (1958).

Three appendices round out the documentation for the State Department volumes. Appendix I lists more than 100 letters that were written to or intended for Jefferson as Secretary of State during the last four months of 1793 and the early months of 1794, but which he did not receive after he left office and which had no impact on him. Two other appendices fulfill Julian P. Boyd's expressed intention to account for the some 475 routine, formulaic, and trivial documents that, in accordance with the design of the edition, were not intended for publication, summary, or even brief digest in the annotation in the State Department volumes (see Vol. 16: ix-x). Appendix II includes brief descriptions of miscellaneous appointment papers, Jefferson's routine letters transmitting laws to the states and the acknowledgments he received from state officials, and papers relating to passports, copyrights, and patents. Appendix III describes and illustrates a small but representative selection from a large number of official documents—commissions, laws, passports, patents, and the like—that Jefferson signed ex officio as Secretary of State. Both of these appendices are presented in the summary form employed for analogous documents pertaining to Jefferson's governorship of Virginia (Vol. 6: 640-6 and illustrations following 668).

It is the Editors' pleasant duty to record their gratitude to the many historians, librarians, and archivists who have assisted them in ways too numerous to mention as they prepared this and the previous volume for the press: Eugenio F. Biagini, Charles C. Gillispie, Anthony T. Grafton, William C. Jordan, Stuart Leibiger, Stanley J. Stein, Jochen R. Twele, and Alexander D. Wainwright of Princeton University; Donald L. Singer and Timothy Connelly of the archival staff of the National Historical Publications and Records Commission; Louis L. Tucker, Peter Drummey, Virginia H. Smith, and the staff of the Massachusetts Historical Society; James H. Hutson and his staff at the Manuscript Division of the Library of Congress, especially Fred Bauman, Ernest Emrich, Jeffrey Flannery, Gerard W. Gawalt, Charles Kelly, Michael Klein, Kathleen C. McDonough, Paul H. Smith, and Mary Wolfskill; James Gilreath of the Rare Book and Special Collections Division at the Library of Congress;

FOREWORD

Lucia C. Stanton, Douglas L. Wilson, Kristen Onuf, Ann Lucas, and Mindy Black of the Thomas Jefferson Memorial Foundation at Monticello; Michael Plunkett of the Special Collections Department at the University of Virginia; Mary Ann Hawkins of the Federal Records Center in East Point, Georgia; John Van Horne of the Library Company of Philadelphia; Mark Frazer Lloyd of the University of Pennsylvania; Monique Bourque of the Balch Institute for Ethnic Studies; Stephen Crook of the New York Public Library; Jane Segal of Columbia University Library; Eric Holzenberg of the Grolier Club; Christine Nelson of the Pierpont Morgan Library; Margaret Heilbrun of the New-York Historical Society; Robert L. Scribner and Minor T. Weisiger of the Virginia State Library and Archives; Celeste Walker of The Adams Papers at the Massachusetts Historical Society; Dorothy W. Twohig, Philander D. Chase, Mark A. Mastromarino, and John Warren of The Papers of George Washington at the University of Virginia; Barbara B. Oberg, Ellen R. Cohn, Jonathan R. Dull, and Kate M. Ohno of The Papers of Benjamin Franklin at Yale University; Elizabeth M. Nuxoll and Mary A. Gallagher of The Papers of Robert Morris at Queens College of the City University of New York; Ene Sirvet of The Papers of John Jay at Columbia University; Charles F. Hobson of The Papers of John Marshall at the College of William and Mary; Nancy Kane of the Circuit Court of York County, Yorktown, Virginia; Michael La-Forest, Stephen J. Kindig, and Linda Rowe of Colonial Williamsburg; Robert Egleston of the New Haven Colony Historical Society; Dianne M. Gutscher of Bowdoin College Library; Denison Beach of the Houghton Library at Harvard University; Betsy Tyler of the Nantucket Historical Association; Susan Brady and Diane E. Kaplan of Yale University Library; Debra A. Fillos of the Lyme Historical Society; David Fowler of the David Library of the American Revolution; Cindy Palmer of the American Swedish Historical Museum; Gregory A. Stiverson of the Maryland Hall of Records; Margaret Cook of the Earl Gregg Swem Library at the College of William and Mary; Nathalie Auerbach of Stanford University Library; Susan Raveden of Bowdoin College Library; John J. McCusker of Trinity University; Christer Wijkström of the Royal Swedish Academy of Sciences; Pedro González Garcia and Blanca Yrazusta of the Archivo General de Indias; Nicholas Smith of Cambridge University Library; and Whitfield J. Bell, Jr., Debra Gianulis, John D. Gordan III, Wanda S. Gunning, Charles M. Harris, Williard F. King, Stephanie A. Longo, Christopher Mills, Pamela Scott, and Barbara Stein. To these and other colleagues the Editors tender their cordial thanks.

The Editors also wish to acknowledge their particular indebtedness to the many loyal friends of the enterprise who over the last three decades contributed or helped locate documents for the supplement: Henry F. Bedford of The Phillips Exeter Academy; Christopher Bickford of the Connecticut Historical Society; James C. Bradford of Texas A & M University; Beth Carroll-Horrocks of the American Philosophical Society; Timothy Connelly, Donald L. Singer, and the late Oliver W. Holmes of the National Historical Publications and Records Commission; Stephen Crook of the New York Public Library; Philip N. Cronenwett of Dartmouth College Library; Charles T. Cullen of the Newberry Library; Elizabeth A. Falsey and Jennie Rathbun of the Houghton Library at Harvard University; David Fowler of the David Library of the American Revolution; Gerard W. Gawalt, Paul H. Smith, and Mary Wolfskill of the Manuscripts Division at the Library of Congress; Lori E. Gilbert of the Pierpont Morgan Library; Mary A. Hackett of The Papers of James Madison at the University of Virginia; Jane G. Hartye of the Stevens Institute of Technology; Philip A. Hayden of the New Jersey Historical Society; Tony Jenkins of Duke University; Robin Kaller of Kaller Historical Documents, Inc.; Jon Kukla of the Historic New Orleans Collection; Stuart Leibiger of Princeton University; Alfred E. Lemmon of the Historic New Orleans Collection; Claude A. Lopez of The Papers of Benjamin Franklin at Yale University; Laura V. Monti of the Boston Public Library; Roxanne M. Morris and Tonette J. Morris of the Albemarle County Circuit Court Clerk's Office, Charlottesville, Virginia; F. P. O'Neill and Jennifer Sharkey of the Maryland Historical Society; Elaine W. Pascu of The Papers of Albert Gallatin at Baruch College of the City University of New York; Kermit J. Pike of the Western Reserve Historical Society; Michael Plunkett and Barbara Fehse of the Special Collections Department at the University of Virginia; John Powell of the Madison County Courthouse in Madison, Virginia; John H. Rhodehamel of the Huntington Library; Randy Roberts of the State Historical Society of Missouri; May E. Robertson of Yale University Library; Richard A. Ryerson of The Adams Papers at the Massachusetts Historical Society; Robert L. Scribner of the Virginia State Library and Archives; E. Lee Shepherd of the Virginia Historical Society; Richard Shrader of the University of North Carolina Library; Donald C. Skemer of Princeton University; Linda Stanley of the Historical Society of Pennsylvania; Lucia C. Stanton of the Thomas Jefferson Memorial Foundation at Monticello; Saundra Taylor of the Lilly Library at Indiana University; John Van Horne and Lauren A. Goldberg of the Library Company of Philadelphia; Alexander D.

FOREWORD

Wainwright of Princeton University Library; Jane E. Ward of the Peabody and Essex Museum; Minor T. Weisiger of the Virginia State Library and Archives; George Wise of Yale University Library; and Milton L. Grigg, Mary-Jo Kline, Mrs. A. Slater Lamond, and Lucius Wilmerding, Jr. Though the passage of time has undoubtedly put many other documentary contributors beyond the reach of our memories, we are no less in their debt.

JOHN CATANZARITI

30 April 1996

GUIDE TO EDITORIAL APPARATUS

1. TEXTUAL DEVICES

The following devices are employed throughout the work to clarify the presentation of the text.

[. . .], [. . . .]	One or two words missing and not conjecturable.
[. . .]¹, [. . . .]¹	More than two words missing and not conjecturable; subjoined footnote estimates number of words missing.
[ ]	Number or part of a number missing or illegible.
[roman]	Conjectural reading for missing or illegible matter. A question mark follows when the reading is doubtful.
[*italic*]	Editorial comment inserted in the text.
⟨*italic*⟩	Matter deleted in the MS but restored in our text.

2. DESCRIPTIVE SYMBOLS

The following symbols are employed throughout the work to describe the various kinds of manuscript originals. When a series of versions is recorded, *the first to be recorded is the version used for the printed text.*

Dft	draft (usually a composition or rough draft; later drafts, when identifiable as such, are designated "2d Dft," &c.)
Dupl	duplicate
MS	manuscript (arbitrarily applied to most documents other than letters)
N	note, notes (memoranda, fragments, &c.)
PoC	polygraph copy
PrC	press copy
RC	recipient's copy
SC	stylograph copy
Tripl	triplicate

All manuscripts of the above types are assumed to be in the hand of the author of the document to which the descriptive symbol pertains. If not, that fact is stated. On the other hand, the following types of manuscripts are assumed *not* to be in the hand of the author, and exceptions will be noted:

FC   file copy (applied to all contemporary copies retained by the author or his agents)

Lb   letterbook (ordinarily used with FC and Tr to denote texts copied into bound volumes)

Tr   transcript (applied to all contemporary and later copies except file copies; period of transcription, unless clear by implication, will be given when known)

3. LOCATION SYMBOLS

The locations of documents printed in this edition from originals in private hands and from printed sources are recorded in self-explanatory form in the descriptive note following each document. The locations of documents printed from originals held by public and private institutions in the United States are recorded by means of the symbols used in the National Union Catalog in the Library of Congress; an explanation of how these symbols are formed is given in Vol. 1: xl. The symbols DLC and MHi by themselves stand for the collections of Jefferson Papers proper in these repositories; when texts are drawn from other collections held by these two institutions, the names of those collections will be added. Location symbols for documents held by institutions outside the United States are given in a subjoined list. The lists of symbols are limited to the institutions represented by documents printed or referred to in this volume.

CSmH   The Huntington Library, San Marino, California
CSt   Stanford University Library, Stanford, California
CtHi   Connecticut Historical Society, Hartford
CtY   Yale University Library
DeHi   Historical Society of Delaware, Wilmington
DLC   Library of Congress
DNA   The National Archives, with identifications of series (preceded by record group number) as follows:

      AL   American Letters
      CD   Consular Dispatches
      DCI   Diplomatic and Consular Instructions
      DCLB District of Columbia Letter Book
      DD   Diplomatic Dispatches
      DL   Domestic Letters
      LGS   Letters from the Governors of the States
      MD   Miscellaneous Dispatches
      MDC   Miscellaneous Duplicate Consular and Diplomatic Dispatches
      MLR   Miscellaneous Letters Received

MTA	Miscellaneous Treasury Accounts
NFC	Notes from Foreign Consuls
NL	Notes from Legations
PBG	Public Buildings and Grounds
PC	Proceedings of the Board of Commissioners for the District of Columbia
PCC	Papers of the Continental Congress
SDC	State Department Correspondence: Copy books of George Washington's Correspondence with the Secretaries of State
SDR	State Department Reports: A Record of the Reports of Thomas Jefferson, Secretary of State for the United States of America
SWT	Southwest Territory Papers
TR	Transcribed Reports

DNCD	National Society of the Colonial Dames of America, Washington, D.C.
DP	United States Patent Office, Arlington, Virginia
FMU	University of Miami Library, Coral Gables, Florida
GEpFAR	Federal Archives and Records Center, Atlanta Region, East Point, Georgia
GU	University of Georgia Library, Athens
ICHi	Chicago Historical Society
ICN	Newberry Library, Chicago
IHi	Illinois State Historical Library, Springfield
IU	University of Illinois Library, Urbana
InU	Indiana University, Bloomington
M-Ar	Massachusetts Secretary of State, Archives Division, Boston
MB	Boston Public Library
MBFM	Massachusetts Grand Lodge, F. and A.M., Boston
MH	Harvard University Library
MHi	Massachusetts Historical Society, Boston
MSaE	Essex Institute, Salem, Massachusetts
MWA	American Antiquarian Society, Worcester, Massachusetts
MdAA	Maryland Hall of Records, Annapolis
MdHi	Maryland Historical Society, Baltimore
MeB	Bowdoin College Library, Brunswick, Maine
MiU-C	William L. Clements Library, University of Michigan, Ann Arbor

MoHi	Missouri State Historical Society, Columbia
MoSHi	Missouri Historical Society, St. Louis
NHi	New-York Historical Society, New York City
NN	New York Public Library
NNC	Columbia University Library
NNP	Pierpont Morgan Library, New York City
Nc-Ar	North Carolina State Department of Archives and History, Raleigh
NcD	Duke University Library, Durham, North Carolina
NcU	University of North Carolina Library, Chapel Hill
NhD	Dartmouth College Library, Hanover, New Hampshire
NhExP	Phillips Exeter Academy, Exeter, New Hampshire
NhPoS	Strawbery Banke, Portsmouth, New Hampshire
NjHi	New Jersey Historical Society, Newark
NjHoS	Stevens Institute of Technology, Hoboken, New Jersey
NjP	Princeton University Library
OClWHi	Western Reserve Historical Society, Cleveland, Ohio
OT	Toledo-Lucas County Public Library, Ohio
PHarH	Pennsylvania Historical and Museum Commission, Harrisburg
PHi	Historical Society of Pennsylvania, Philadelphia
PPAmP	American Philosophical Society, Philadelphia
PPL	Library Company of Philadelphia
PWacD	David Library of the American Revolution, Washington Crossing, Pennsylvania
R-Ar	Rhode Island State Archives, Providence
RPAB	Annmary Brown Memorial Library, Providence, Rhode Island
ScHi	South Carolina Historical Society, Charleston
Vi	Library of Virginia, Richmond
ViHi	Virginia Historical Society, Richmond
ViU	University of Virginia Library, Charlottesville
ViW	College of William and Mary Library, Williamsburg, Virginia

The following symbols represent repositories located outside of the United States:

AGI	Archivo General de Indias, Seville
AHN	Archivo Histórico Nacional, Madrid
AMAE	Archives du Ministère des Affaires Étrangères,

Paris, with identification of series as follows:

    CPEU   Correspondance Politique, États-Unis

PRO   Public Record Office, London, with identification of series as follows:

    FO   Foreign Office

RSAS   Royal Swedish Academy of Sciences, Stockholm

4. OTHER SYMBOLS AND ABBREVIATIONS

The following symbols and abbreviations are commonly employed in the annotation throughout the work.

Second Series   The topical series to be published as part of this edition, comprising those materials which are best suited to a topical rather than a chronological arrangement (see Vol. 1: xv-xvi)

TJ   Thomas Jefferson

TJ Editorial Files   Photoduplicates and other editorial materials in the office of *The Papers of Thomas Jefferson*, Princeton University Library

TJ Papers   Jefferson Papers (applied to a collection of manuscripts when the precise location of an undated, misdated, or otherwise problematic document must be furnished, and always preceded by the symbol for the institutional repository; thus "DLC: TJ Papers, 4: 628-9" represents a document in the Library of Congress, Jefferson Papers, volume 4, pages 628 and 629. Citations to volumes and folio numbers of the Jefferson Papers at the Library of Congress refer to the collection as it was arranged at the time the first microfilm edition was made in 1944-45. Access to the microfilm edition of the collection as it was rearranged under the Library's Presidential Papers Program is provided by the *Index to the Thomas Jefferson Papers* [Washington, D.C., 1976])

RG   Record Group (used in designating the location of documents in the National Archives)

SJL   Jefferson's "Summary Journal of Letters" written and received for the period 11 Nov. 1783 to 25 June 1826 (in DLC: TJ Papers). This register, kept in Jefferson's hand, has been checked against the TJ Editorial Files. It is to be assumed that all outgoing letters are recorded in SJL unless there is a note to the contrary. When the date of receipt of an incoming letter is recorded in SJL, it is incorporated in the notes. Information and discrepancies revealed in SJL but not found in the letter itself are also noted. Missing letters recorded in SJL are, where possible, accounted for in the notes to documents mentioning them or in related documents.

A more detailed discussion of this register and its use in this edition appears in Vol. 6: vii-x

SJPL   "Summary Journal of Public Letters," an incomplete list of letters and documents written by TJ from 16 Apr. 1784 to 31 Dec. 1793, with brief summaries, in an amanuensis's hand. This is supplemented by six pages in TJ's hand, compiled at a later date, listing private and confidential memorandums and notes as well as official reports and communications by and to him as Secretary of State, 11 Oct. 1789 to 31 Dec. 1793 (in DLC: TJ Papers, Epistolary Record, 514-59 and 209-11, respectively; see Vol. 22: ix-x). Since nearly all documents in the amanuensis's list are registered in SJL, while few in TJ's list are so recorded, it is to be assumed that all references to SJPL are to the list in TJ's hand unless there is a statement to the contrary

V   Ecu
ƒ   Florin
£   Pound sterling or livre, depending upon context (in doubtful cases, a clarifying note will be given)
s   Shilling or sou (also expressed as /)
d   Penny or denier
₶   Livre Tournois
℔   Per (occasionally used for pro, pre)

5. SHORT TITLES

The following list includes only those short titles of works cited frequently, and therefore in very abbreviated form, throughout this edition. Since it is impossible to anticipate all the works to be cited in very abbreviated form, the list is appropriately revised from volume to volume.

Adams, *Diary*   L. H. Butterfield and others, eds., *Diary and Autobiography of John Adams*, Cambridge, Mass., 1961, 4 vols.

Adams, *Works*   Charles Francis Adams, ed., *The Works of John Adams*, Boston, 1850-56, 10 vols.

AHA   American Historical Association

AHR   *American Historical Review*, 1895-

Ammon, *Genet Mission*   Harry Ammon, *The Genet Mission*, New York, 1973

Ammon, *Monroe*   Harry Ammon, *James Monroe: The Quest for National Identity*, New York, 1971

Annals   *Annals of the Congress of the United States: The Debates and Proceedings in the Congress of the United States . . . Compiled from Authentic Materials*, Washington, D.C., Gales & Seaton, 1834-56,

42 vols. All editions are undependable and pagination varies from one printing to another. The first two volumes of the set cited here have "Compiled . . . by Joseph Gales, Senior" on the title page and bear the caption "Gales & Seatons History" on verso and "of Debates in Congress" on recto pages. The remaining volumes bear the caption "History of Congress" on both recto and verso pages. Those using the first two volumes with the latter caption will need to employ the date of the debate or the indexes of debates and speakers.

APS   American Philosophical Society

Archives Parlementaires   *Archives Parlementaires de 1787 à 1860: Recueil Complet des Débats Législatifs & Politiques des Chambres Françaises*, Paris, 1862- , 222 vols.

ASP   *American State Papers: Documents, Legislative and Executive, of the Congress of the United States*, Washington, D.C., Gales & Seaton, 1832-61, 38 vols.

Barnby, *Prisoners*   H. G. Barnby, *The Prisoners of Algiers: An Account of the Forgotten American-Algerian War, 1785-1797*, London, 1966

Bear, *Family Letters*   Edwin M. Betts and James A. Bear, Jr., eds., *Family Letters of Thomas Jefferson*, Columbia, Mo., 1966

Bemis, *Jay's Treaty*   Samuel Flagg Bemis, *Jay's Treaty: A Study in Commerce and Diplomacy*, rev. ed., New Haven, 1962

Bemis, *Pinckney's Treaty*   Samuel Flagg Bemis, *Pinckney's Treaty: America's Advantage from Europe's Distress, 1783-1800*, rev. ed., New Haven, 1960

Betts, *Farm Book*   Edwin M. Betts, ed., *Thomas Jefferson's Farm Book*, Princeton, 1953

Betts, *Garden Book*   Edwin M. Betts, ed., *Thomas Jefferson's Garden Book, 1766-1824*, Philadelphia, 1944

Biog. Dir. Cong.   *Biographical Directory of the United States Congress, 1774-1989*, Washington, D.C., 1989

Bowman, *Neutrality*   Albert H. Bowman, *The Struggle for Neutrality: Franco-American Diplomacy During the Federalist Era*, Knoxville, Tenn., 1974

Brant, *Madison*   Irving Brant, *James Madison*, Indianapolis, 1941-61, 6 vols.

Brigham, *American Newspapers*   Clarence S. Brigham, *History and Bibliography of American Newspapers, 1690-1820*, Worcester, Mass., 1947, 2 vols.

Butterfield, *Rush*   L. H. Butterfield, ed., *Letters of Benjamin Rush*, Princeton, 1951, 2 vols.

Childs, *French Refugee Life*   Frances S. Childs, *French Refugee Life in the United States, 1790-1800: An American Chapter of the French Revolution*, Baltimore, 1940

Cooke, *Coxe*   Jacob E. Cooke, *Tench Coxe and the Early Republic*, Chapel Hill, 1978

Correspondance   [Edmond Charles Genet], *Correspondance entre le Citoyen Genet, Ministre Plenipotentiaire de la Republique Française pres les Etats-Unis, et les Membres du Gouvernement Féderal, Precedee des Instructions données à ce Ministre par les Autorités constituées de la France*, Philadelphia, 1794

Correspondence   [Edmond Charles Genet], *The Correspondence between Citizen Genet, Minister of the French Republic, to the United States of North America, and the Officers of the Federal Government; to which are Prefixed the Instructions from the Constituted Authorities of France to the Said Minister. All from Authentic Documents*, Philadelphia, 1793

Counter Case   *The Counter Case of Great Britain as Laid before the Tribunal of Arbitration, Convened at Geneva, under the Provisions of the Treaty between the United States of America and Her Majesty the Queen of Great Britain, Concluded at Washington, May 8, 1871*, U.S. House of Representatives, Executive Documents, 42d Cong., 2d Sess., Vol. XVI, No. 324, Washington, D.C., 1872

CVSP   William P. Palmer and others, eds., *Calendar of Virginia State Papers . . . Preserved in the Capitol at Richmond*, Richmond, 1875-93, 11 vols.

DAB   Allen Johnson and Dumas Malone, eds., *Dictionary of American Biography*, New York, 1928-36, 20 vols.

DeConde, *Entangling Alliance*   Alexander DeConde, *Entangling Alliance: Politics & Diplomacy under George Washington*, Durham N.C., 1958

DHRC   Merrill Jensen, John P. Kaminski, Gaspare J. Saladino, and others, eds., *The Documentary History of the Ratification of the Constitution*, Madison, Wis., 1976- , 10 vols.

DNB   Leslie Stephen and Sidney Lee, eds., *Dictionary of National Biography*, 2d ed., New York, 1908-09, 22 vols.

DSB   Charles C. Gillispie, ed., *Dictionary of Scientific Biography*, New York, 1970-80, 16 vols.

Evans   Charles Evans, Clifford K. Shipton, and Roger P. Bristol, comps., *American Bibliography: A Chronological Dictionary of all Books, Pamphlets and Periodical Publications Printed in the United States of America from . . . 1639 . . . to . . . 1820*, Chicago and Worcester, Mass., 1903-59, 14 vols.

Extracts, ed. Adams   Dickinson W. Adams and Ruth W. Lester, eds., *Jefferson's Extracts from the Gospels*, Princeton, 1983, *The Papers of Thomas Jefferson*, Second Series

Fitzpatrick, *Writings*   John C. Fitzpatrick, ed., *The Writings of George Washington*, Washington, D.C., 1931-44, 39 vols.

Foner, *Paine*   Philip S. Foner, ed., *The Complete Writings of Thomas Paine*, New York, 1945, 2 vols.

Ford   Paul Leicester Ford, ed., *The Writings of Thomas Jefferson*, Letterpress Edition, New York, 1892-99, 10 vols.

Freeman, *Washington*   Douglas Southall Freeman, *George Washington*, New York, 1948-57, 7 vols.; 7th volume by J. A. Carroll and M. W. Ashworth

Gaines, *Randolph*   William H. Gaines, Jr., *Thomas Mann Randolph: Jefferson's Son-in-Law*, Baton Rouge, 1966

Geggus, *Slavery*   David P. Geggus, *Slavery, War, and Revolution: The British Occupation of Saint Domingue, 1793-1798*, Oxford, 1982

Hardie, *Phila. Dir.*   James Hardie, *The Philadelphia Directory and Register . . .*, Philadelphia, 1793

HAW   Henry A. Washington, ed., *The Writings of Thomas Jefferson*, New York, 1853-54, 9 vols.

Hening   William Waller Hening, ed., *The Statutes at Large; Being a Collection of All the Laws of Virginia*, Richmond, 1809-23, 13 vols.

Henry, *Henry*   William Wirt Henry, *Patrick Henry, Life, Correspondence and Speeches*, New York, 1891, 3 vols.

Hunt, *Madison*   Gaillard Hunt, ed., *The Writings of James Madison*, New York, 1900-10, 9 vols.

JAH   *Journal of American History*, 1964-

JCC   Worthington C. Ford and others, eds., *Journals of the Continental Congress, 1774-1789*, Washington, D.C., 1904-37, 34 vols.

Jefferson Correspondence, Bixby   Worthington C. Ford, ed., *Thomas Jefferson Correspondence Printed from the Originals in the Collections of William K. Bixby*, Boston, 1916

JEP   *Journal of the Executive Proceedings of the Senate of the United States . . . to the Termination of the Nineteenth Congress*, Washington, D.C., 1828

JHD   *Journal of the House of Delegates of the Commonwealth of Virginia* (cited by session and date of publication)

JHR   *Journal of the House of Representatives of the United States*, Washington, D.C., Gales & Seaton, 1826, 9 vols.

JS   *Journal of the Senate of the United States*, Washington, D.C., Gales, 1820-21, 5 vols.

JSH   *Journal of Southern History*, 1935-

Keller, "Genet Mission"   William F. Keller, "American Politics and the Genet Mission, 1793-1794," Ph.D. diss., University of Pittsburgh, 1951

Kimball, *Jefferson, Architect*   Fiske Kimball, *Thomas Jefferson, Architect*, Boston, 1916

King, *Life*   Charles R. King, ed., *The Life and Correspondence of Rufus King*, New York, 1894-1900, 6 vols.

Kinnaird, *Spain*   Lawrence Kinnaird, ed., *Spain in the Mississippi Valley, 1765-1794: Translations of Materials from the Spanish Archives in the Bancroft Library*, American Historical Association, *Annual Report*, 1945, 3 vols.

Knox, *Barbary Wars*   Dudley W. Knox, ed., *Naval Documents Related to the United States Wars with the Barbary Powers*, Washington, D.C., 1939-45, 7 vols.

L & B   Andrew A. Lipscomb and Albert E. Bergh, eds., *The Writings of Thomas Jefferson*, Washington, D.C., 1903-04, 20 vols.

LCB, ed. Wilson   Douglas L. Wilson, ed., *Jefferson's Literary Commonplace Book*, Princeton, 1989, *The Papers of Thomas Jefferson, Second Series*

Library Catalogue, 1783   Jefferson's MS list of books owned or wanted in 1783 (original in Massachusetts Historical Society)

Library Catalogue, 1815   *Catalogue of the Library of the United States*, Washington, D.C., 1815

Library Catalogue, 1829   *Catalogue: President Jefferson's Library*, Washington, D.C., 1829

List of Patents   *A List of Patents granted by the United States from April 10, 1790, to December 31, 1836*, Washington, D.C., 1872

Madison, *Papers*   William T. Hutchinson, Robert A. Rutland, J. C. A. Stagg, and others, eds., *The Papers of James Madison*, Chicago and Charlottesville, 1962-   , 22 vols.

Malone, *Jefferson*   Dumas Malone, *Jefferson and his Time*, Boston, 1948-81, 6 vols.

Marshall, *Papers*   Herbert A. Johnson, Charles T. Cullen, Charles F. Hobson, and others, eds., *The Papers of John Marshall*, Chapel Hill, 1974-   , 8 vols.

Mayo, *British Ministers*   Bernard Mayo, ed., "Instructions to the British Ministers to the United States 1791-1812," American Historical Association, *Annual Report*, 1936

Mays, *Pendleton*   David J. Mays, ed., *The Letters and Papers of Edmund Pendleton, 1734-1803*, Charlottesville, 1967, 2 vols.

MB   James A. Bear, Jr., and Lucia C. Stanton, eds., *Jefferson's Memorandum Books: Accounts, with Legal Records and Miscel-*

lany, 1767-1826, Princeton, forthcoming in *The Papers of Thomas Jefferson*, Second Series

Message   *A Message of the President of the United States to Congress Relative to France and Great-Britain. Delivered December 5, 1793. With the Papers therein Referred to. To Which Are Added the French Originals. Published by Order of the House of Representatives*, Philadelphia, 1793

Miller, *Treaties*   Hunter Miller, ed., *Treaties and other International Acts of the United States of America*, Washington, D.C., 1931-48, 8 vols.

Minnigerode, *Genet*   Meade Minnigerode, *Jefferson, Friend of France, 1793: The Career of Edmond Charles Genet . . .*, New York, 1928

Mitchell, *Hamilton*   Broadus Mitchell, *Alexander Hamilton*, New York, 1957-62, 2 vols.

Morris, *Papers*   E. James Ferguson, John Catanzariti, and others, eds., *The Papers of Robert Morris, 1781-1784*, Pittsburgh, 1973- , 8 vols.

MVHR   *Mississippi Valley Historical Review*, 1914-64

Notes, ed. Peden   Thomas Jefferson, *Notes on the State of Virginia*, ed. William Peden, Chapel Hill, 1955

NSP   Eileen D. Carzo, ed., *National State Papers of the United States, 1789-1817. Part II: Texts of Documents. Administration of George Washington, 1789-1797*, Wilmington, Del., 1985, 35 vols.

OED   Sir James Murray and others, eds., *A New English Dictionary on Historical Principles*, Oxford, 1888-1933

Parl. Writings, ed. Howell   Wilbur S. Howell, ed., *Jefferson's Parliamentary Writings*, Princeton, 1988, *The Papers of Thomas Jefferson*, Second Series

Peterson, *Jefferson*   Merrill D. Peterson, *Thomas Jefferson and the New Nation*, New York, 1970

PMHB   *Pennsylvania Magazine of History and Biography*, 1877-

Prager, *Fitch*   Frank D. Prager, ed., *The Autobiography of John Fitch*, Philadelphia, 1976

Pub. Recs. Conn.   Charles J. Hoadly and others, eds., *Public Records of the State of Connecticut*, Hartford, 1894- , 9 vols.

Randall, *Life*   Henry S. Randall, *The Life of Thomas Jefferson*, New York, 1858, 3 vols.

Randolph, *Domestic Life*   Sarah N. Randolph, *The Domestic Life of Thomas Jefferson, Compiled from Family Letters and Reminiscences by His Great-Granddaughter*, 3d ed., Cambridge, Mass., 1939

Scott and Rothaus, *Historical Dictionary*   Samuel F. Scott and Barry

Rothaus, eds., *Historical Dictionary of the French Revolution, 1789-1799*, Westport, Conn., 1985, 2 vols.

Selby, *Revolution*   John E. Selby, *The Revolution in Virginia, 1775-1783*, Williamsburg, 1988

Setser, *Reciprocity*   Vernon G. Setser, *The Commercial Reciprocity Policy of the United States*, Philadelphia, 1937

Shipton-Mooney, *Index*   Clifford K. Shipton and James E. Mooney, comps., *National Index of American Imprints through 1800: The Short-Title Evans*, [Worcester, Mass.], 1969, 2 vols.

Sowerby   E. Millicent Sowerby, comp., *Catalogue of the Library of Thomas Jefferson*, Washington, D.C., 1952-59, 5 vols.

Stein, *Worlds*   Susan R. Stein, *The Worlds of Thomas Jefferson at Monticello*, New York, 1993

Syrett, *Hamilton*   Harold C. Syrett and others, eds., *The Papers of Alexander Hamilton*, New York, 1961-87, 27 vols.

Taxay, *Mint*   Don Taxay, *The U.S. Mint and Coinage: An Illustrated History from 1776 to the Present*, New York, 1966

Terr. Papers   Clarence E. Carter and John Porter Bloom, eds., *The Territorial Papers of the United States*, Washington, D.C., 1934- , 28 vols.

Thomas, *Neutrality*   Charles M. Thomas, *American Neutrality in 1793: A Study in Cabinet Government*, New York, 1931

Thorne, *Parliament*   R. G. Thorne, *The History of Parliament: The House of Commons, 1790-1820*, London, 1986, 5 vols.

TJR   Thomas Jefferson Randolph, ed., *Memoir, Correspondence, and Miscellanies, from the Papers of Thomas Jefferson*, Charlottesville, 1829, 4 vols.

Tucker, *Life*   George Tucker, *The Life of Thomas Jefferson*, Philadelphia, 1837, 2 vols.

Turner, *CFM*   Frederick Jackson Turner, "Correspondence of French Ministers, 1791-1797," American Historical Association, *Annual Report*, 1903, II

U.S. Statutes at Large   Richard Peters, ed., *The Public Statutes at Large of the United States . . . 1789 to March 3, 1845*, Boston, 1855-56, 8 vols.

VMHB   *Virginia Magazine of History and Biography*, 1893-

Washington, *Diaries*   Donald Jackson and others, eds., *The Diaries of George Washington*, Charlottesville, 1976-79, 6 vols.

Washington, *Journal*   Dorothy Twohig, ed., *The Journal of the Proceedings of the President, 1793-1797*, Charlottesville, 1981

Washington, *Papers*   W. W. Abbot, Dorothy Twohig, and others, eds., *The Papers of George Washington*, Charlottesville, 1983- , 24 vols.

White, *Federalists*   Leonard White, *The Federalists: A Study in Administrative History*, New York, 1948

WMQ   *William and Mary Quarterly*, 1892-

Woods, *Albemarle*   Edgar Woods, *Albemarle County in Virginia*, Charlottesville, 1901

CONTENTS

1793

CONTENTS

CONTENTS

CONTENTS

CONTENTS

CONTENTS

CONTENTS

CONTENTS

CONTENTS

[xxxiii]

CONTENTS

CONTENTS

CONTENTS

CONTENTS

CONTENTS

CONTENTS

CONTENTS

SUPPLEMENTARY DOCUMENTS

CONTENTS

1775

1777

1778

1779

1780

CONTENTS

·⤙⟨ **1781** ⟩⤚·

CONTENTS

CONTENTS

1785

1786

1787

1788

CONTENTS

·◁ᘒ **1789** ᘓ▷·

·◁ᘒ **1790** ᘓ▷·

CONTENTS

$$\cdot\text{«}\big\{\quad 1791 \quad\big\}\text{»}\cdot$$

CONTENTS

1792

1793

CONTENTS

APPENDICES

ILLUSTRATIONS

Following page 394

MORTALITY TABLE ON THE YELLOW FEVER EPIDEMIC

The yellow fever epidemic that gripped Philadelphia from August to November 1793 created a health crisis of major proportions in the national capital. Before the epidemic ran its course, at least 5,000 of the city's population of 57,000 people (including 2,000 French refugees recently arrived from Saint-Domingue) succumbed to the disease, several thousand others were infected but survived, and another 17,000 to 20,000 fled the city to avoid contagion. Unaware that yellow fever was transmitted by the *Aëdes ægypti* mosquito, a discovery that Dr. Walter Reed did not make until the beginning of this century, medical opinion in Philadelphia was divided between contagionists, who believed that the disease was transmitted by visitors or immigrants, especially from the West Indies, and climatists, who thought that it was caused by the foul air resulting from the city's unsanitary conditions. As his 1 Sep. 1793 letter to James Madison shows, Jefferson accepted the climatist explanation for the origin of yellow fever. The mortality table, which Jefferson annotated, was clipped from an unidentified newspaper and is now mounted on the press copy of his letter to George Washington of 15 Sep. 1793. It appeared in somewhat different form in "A Desultory Account of the Yellow Fever prevalent in Philadelphia, and of the present state of the city," a 16 Oct. 1793 essay by Mathew Carey that was printed in the 19 Oct. 1793 issue of the *New-York Daily Gazette* and the 26 Oct. 1793 issue of the Philadelphia *Independent Gazetteer, and Agricultural Repository*. (*Courtesy of the Library of Congress*)

ELI WHITNEY'S MODEL OF HIS COTTON GIN

"There is probably no other instance in the history of invention of the letting loose of such tremendous industrial forces so suddenly as occurred with the invention of the cotton gin," one Whitney biographer has observed (DAB). Jefferson himself was quick to recognize Whitney's application of 20 June 1793, supplemented by supporting documents enclosed in a letter of 15 Oct. 1793, as the most significant patent request received during his tenure as Secretary of State. The patent itself was not issued until after Jefferson left office because of a delay in completion of the model. While the original patent model was destroyed in a Patent Office fire in 1836 and any prototypes Whitney might have retained were lost in a conflagration at his New Haven workshop in 1795, the model depicted here follows the patent specification closely and was one of several that he prepared shortly after the workshop fire for use in the numerous patent-infringement lawsuits with which he doggedly defended his invention from a host of competitors. (*Courtesy of the New Haven Colony Historical Society*)

JEFFERSON'S NOTES ON ALEXANDER HAMILTON AND ON TWO
CABINET MEETINGS

This page from Jefferson's private record of political transactions during his tenure as Secretary of State, which posthumously became known as the "Anas," illustrates the deep conflicts over foreign affairs that split the Cabinet in November 1793. In a brief entry of 15 Nov. Jefferson continued his practice of documenting what he regarded as the heretically pro-British views of his chief antagonist, Secretary of the Treasury Alexander Hamilton. Then, in a lengthy account which extended to a second page, he described meetings of 8 and 18 Nov. at which the Cabinet split evenly and heatedly over the vexed issue of whether to suspend the functions of French minister Edmond Charles Genet and expel him without waiting for France to respond to the administration's request that he be recalled for repeated instances of disrespectful challenges to American neutrality policy. At the later meeting the Cabinet also began considering how the President should inform the new Congress of recent events and immediately proved unable to agree on how to justify the Proclamation of Neutrality. Stymied by the continuing standoff among his advisors, Washington lamented that "we had left him exactly where we found him." (*Courtesy of the Library of Congress*)

GEORGE WASHINGTON TO THE SENATE AND THE HOUSE OF REPRESENTATIVES

In this executive message on relations with France and Great Britain, completed by Jefferson on 2 Dec. 1793 and finally dated three days later, the President first made public his administration's demand that French minister Edmond Charles Genet be recalled. Jefferson's first and second drafts illustrate the difficult task faced by the Secretary of State as he sought to balance the revelation of Genet's misdeeds with a recounting of British misconduct, in the face of both Cabinet opposition and unwelcome reports of new French maritime provocations. Jefferson's first draft initially stressed that the French minister's insulting challenges to American executive authority contrasted sharply with his nation's uniformly friendly conduct, while emphasizing that Britain's failure to honor its treaty commitment to turn over to the United States the forts it occupied within American territory or to respect American neutrality on the high seas seemed to be a matter of settled policy. In the face of strenuous objections from Alexander Hamilton and Henry Knox at a 28 Nov. Cabinet meeting, Jefferson emended the first draft to tone down some of the language more obviously favorable to France without changing the basic thrust of the document. Shortly thereafter he learned that France was countering British acts against American vessels trading with the French Republic by adopting similar measures to undermine the American neutral carrying trade with Britain. In the page from the first draft shown here, Jefferson accordingly reworked the message to say that France as well as Great Britain was violating American neutrality on the high seas. In the page from the second draft he took the unusual step of copying out fair the paragraph most affected by the change as it stood after the Cabinet meeting and then intentionally lining it out lightly and interpolating his proposed substitution so that the President could review it. (*Courtesy of the Library of Congress*)

PUBLICATION OF JEFFERSON'S CORRESPONDENCE ON FRANCE AND GREAT BRITAIN

This pamphlet, published by order of the House of Representatives, reflects Jefferson's effort to prevent Federalists from capitalizing on the Washington administration's request for the recall of Edmond Charles Genet as the French Republic's minister to the United States. Although the administration had initiated the request in August 1793, it did not publicly announce it until the President's 5 Dec. 1793 message to Congress on relations with France and Great Britain described above. Washington's message was accompanied by a voluminous selection of Jefferson's correspondence with Genet bearing on the French minister's defiance of American neutrality, with George Hammond on longstanding British violations of the Treaty of Paris, and with Thomas Pinckney on recent British infringements of American neutral trade. Jefferson had favored making all of this correspondence public, thereby balancing French infractions with British transgressions, in order to reduce the impact of Genet's recall on domestic public opinion. Alexander Hamilton and Henry Knox sought to frustrate this effort by arguing in the Cabinet that Congress should be enjoined to treat the correspondence with Hammond and Pinckney as state secrets, and to Jefferson's consternation Edmund Randolph lent his partial support to their argument by recommending that the Pinckney correspondence be withheld. Washington, however, strongly sided with Jefferson and decided to submit all three categories of correspondence to Congress, thereby marking the first occasion when the President acted against the opinion of a majority in the Cabinet. (*Courtesy of the Library of Congress*)

JEFFERSON'S REPORT ON COMMERCE

Nearly three years in the making, Jefferson's report on commerce was his last attempt as Secretary of State to reduce British dominance of the American economy. Submitted to Congress on 16 Dec. 1793, this state paper catalogued comprehensively the restrictions other nations imposed on American trade and recommended the adoption of a program of commercial discrimination as a means of retaliation. Under the leadership of James Madison, House Republicans reacted to the report early in 1794 by launching a major legislative attack on the British navigation system. But this effort foundered in the face of determined Federalist opposition, thereby frustrating Jefferson's dream of fundamentally reordering the new nation's political economy. Reflecting Jefferson's characteristic attention to detail, the report went through at least two drafts, scrutiny by members of the mercantile community, selective review by foreign ministers in the United States, and many revisions before its submission to Congress two weeks before his resignation from office. The extent of Jefferson's labors is apparent in the two pages of the first state of the report illustrated here, the first of which was completed in largely unrevised form before 23 Aug. 1791 and the second of which was one of two pages that he substituted after 13 Apr. 1792. (*Courtesy of the Library of Congress*)

JEFFERSON'S CHART ON THE RATIFICATION OF THE BILL OF RIGHTS

As Secretary of State, Jefferson kept a tally of state actions on the twelve amendments to the Constitution proposed by Congress and submitted to the states by President Washington on 2 Oct. 1789. His chart, proceeding from north to south, must have been drawn before the admission of Vermont to the Union on 4 Mch. 1791—by which time nine states had already ratified the ten amendments known to contemporaries as the Bill of Rights—for Jefferson recorded Vermont's actions on the line between the columns for Connecticut and

New York. He did not learn until 30 Dec. 1791 and 18 Jan. 1792, respectively, that Virginia and Vermont had also ratified, thus providing the constitutionally mandated three-fourths majority for the amendments. There are no entries in the columns intended for Massachusetts, Connecticut, and Georgia because they did not ratify the Bill of Rights until 1939. The first two amendments proposed, the only ones not ratified contemporaneously by three-fourths of the states, dealt with the apportionment of members in the House of Representatives and with compensation for members of the House and the Senate. Jefferson enclosed a pamphlet recording the state-by-state ratification of the Bill of Rights in a 1 Mch. 1792 circular letter to the governors printed in the supplement to this volume. (*Courtesy of the Library of Congress*)

THE GREAT CLOCK AT MONTICELLO

With this imposing mechanism, still hanging in the Entrance Hall at Monticello, Jefferson sought further to extend his zeal for chronological precision and control to his family and slaves. The seven-day clock included the interior face shown here, an exterior face on the East Portico with an hour-hand only, and a gong specially imported from China which struck on the hour and could be heard all over the estate. Power for the instrument has been supplied since 1804 by a set of fourteen cannonball-like weights of eighteen pounds each, which descend from the top corners of the Entrance Hall flanking the clock past wall markers for the days of the week through the floor into the cellar below. Jefferson himself often used a key to rewind the clock on Sundays while standing on an ingenious folding stepladder constructed at his joinery and still at Monticello. Documentary evidence for the Great Clock begins with Jefferson's undated directions for construction of the instrument, written in 1792 or 1793 and printed in the supplement to this volume, and with his letter of 13 Nov. 1792 asking Henry Remsen to help him acquire a gong. The mechanism was evidently complete by 27 Apr. 1793, when Jefferson paid Philadelphia clockmaker Robert Leslie for it, but when Jefferson set it up at his residence at Gray's Ferry just outside Philadelphia in the summer of 1793, it developed that Leslie's journeyman Peter Spurck, the actual builder, had bungled the work and was obliged to re-do the striking movement "on the common plan" in order to make the clock run. Brought to Monticello when Jefferson retired as Secretary of State, the Great Clock was installed by September 1794 and with occasional modifications and repairs has remained in use ever since. (*Courtesy of the Thomas Jefferson Monticello Foundation, Inc.*)

Volume 27

1 September to 31 December 1793

JEFFERSON CHRONOLOGY

1743 · 1826

1743	Born at Shadwell, 13 Apr. (New Style).
1760	Entered the College of William and Mary.
1762	"quitted college."
1762-1767	Self-education and preparation for law.
1769-1774	Albemarle delegate to House of Burgesses.
1772	Married Martha Wayles Skelton, 1 Jan.
1775-1776	In Continental Congress.
1776	Drafted Declaration of Independence.
1776-1779	In Virginia House of Delegates.
1779	Submitted Bill for Establishing Religious Freedom.
1779-1781	Governor of Virginia.
1782	His wife died, 6 Sep.
1783-1784	In Continental Congress.
1784-1789	In France as Minister Plenipotentiary to negotiate commercial treaties and as Minister Plenipotentiary resident at Versailles.
1790-1793	Secretary of State of the United States.
1797-1801	Vice President of the United States.
1801-1809	President of the United States.
1814-1826	Established the University of Virginia.
1826	Died at Monticello, 4 July.

VOLUME 27

1 September to 31 December 1793

1 Sep.	Writes of yellow fever epidemic in Philadelphia for the first time.
5 Sep.	Additional rules for restoring or compensating for certain French prizes.
7 Sep.	Admonishes French consular officials to respect American neutrality.
7 Sep.	Informs Edmond Charles Genet of the American government's request for his recall.
7 Sep.	Instructs Thomas Pinckney to protest British violations of American neutral rights.
17 Sep.	Leaves home on Schuylkill to visit Monticello.
22 Sep.	Protests to George Hammond about British violations of American neutral rights.
3 Oct.	Revocation of Antoine Charbonnet Duplaine's exequatur.
15 Oct.	Eli Whitney sends descriptions and drawing of cotton gin.
17 Oct.	Advises President not to change meeting place of Congress.
30 Oct.	Edmond Charles Genet invokes guarantee clause of treaty of alliance.
30 Oct.	Edmond Charles Genet seeks American support for French expeditions against Louisiana and Canada.
1 Nov.	Arrives at Germantown.
6 Nov.	Instructs Isaac Shelby to oppose French expedition against Louisiana.
8 Nov.	Provisional definition of American maritime limits.
10 Nov.	Rules for prizes captured in American waters.
18-28 Nov.	Cabinet debates President's address and messages to Congress.
30 Nov.	Arrives in Philadelphia.
14 Dec.	Report on Morocco and Algiers.
16 Dec.	Proposed Public Statement on Edmond Charles Genet.
16 Dec.	Report on Commerce.
18 Dec.	Orders first nailrod for Monticello nailery.
30 Dec.	Supplementary Report on Commerce.
31 Dec.	Submits accounts and resigns as Secretary of State.

THE PAPERS OF
THOMAS JEFFERSON

·《═══════》·

To James B. M. Adair

SIR   Philadelphia Sep. 1. 1793.

I have been favored with your letter from New York, [and I] am very thankful for your care of the letters from Mr. Pinckney and particularly so also for your attention to the threshing machine, which, if it answers what I have heard of it will be a vast acquisition to the states of Virginia and North Carolina. If you should not be coming on yourself to Philadelphia in the course of the present week, and could take the trouble of finding some careful gentleman coming in the stage, and who would be so kind as to take charge of the machine, or if you will be so good as to deliver it to Mr. Remsen, of the bank, with the same request, it will oblige me. It should come in the body of the stage, and not on the trunk board behind, where I presume it would be rattled to pieces. If it is too large to come within the stage, Mr. Remsen knows a line of conveyance almost wholly by water, and will be so good as to send it by that. Whenever you come to Philadelphia I shall be happy to see you, and to render you any services which may be agreeable to yourself and prove my respect to Professor Stewart and Mr. Vaughan, for both of whom I have very high esteem. Mr. Pinckney informs me you propose to go to Virginia, in which case I can probably be useful to you. If the workman who has come with you will go on immediately to Virginia, he may quickly make a fortune by building threshing machines in that state. A very peculiar circumstance in all the country South of the Patowmac, the finest wheat country in America, renders such a machine as valuable as the discovery of the grain itself. If wheat is not threshed out there within 3. or 4. weeks after it is cut, it is destroyed all of a sudden by the weavil. If threshed immediately after harvest and kept in it's chaff, it is secure against that insect. To thresh out a crop by hand at that season, or to tread it out with horses, which is the practice, is so slow a process that it loses the season for getting the next year's crop into the ground. So that very frequently we are in the dilemma of sacrificing either the crop of the present, or of the next year. I mention these circumstances to shew that a machine, which relieves them from this dilemma, which exists only in Virginia and N. Carolina, must bring the workman into more rapid demand in those states, than any where else. If he chuses to go there, I will give him letters, and he shall have the benefit of exhibiting my model at Richmond so as to get himself into business at once. He is now in time to work for the present crop, and a main object with me in sending for the machine was to save the labours of my countrymen. He can pass from hence to Richmond in the stage in 5. days.

The affidavit you were pleased to prepare in the case of the Ship Jay, is quite sufficient to ground an application on. I write to Mr. Ward by this post. I have the honour to be respectfully Sir Your most obedt. servt. TH: JEFFERSON

PrC (DLC); faded; at foot of first page: "Dr. Adair."

To J. P. P. Derieux

Philadelphia Sep. 1. 93.

Th: Jefferson with his compliments to Mr. Derieux sends him a letter from Mde. Bellanger. The duplicate (which came with it) shall come by next week's post, as also he believes assuredly Mr. Vaughan's account and balance, which he has promised for next post.

PrC (DLC). Tr (ViU: Edgehill-Randolph Papers); 19th-century copy. Enclosure not found.

From David Humphreys

SIR Lisbon Septr. 1st. 1793.

On the 28th. of last Month a Packet arrived from Falmouth; in which Captn. Cutting came passenger, and delivered to me your several letters of the 21st., 22nd. of March and 12th. of April, together with the official and other Papers accompanying them. Of those of a private nature I notice the Contents, and will comply with your intimations. As to the public Dispatches, I entreat the Executive may be assured, that I shall exert my utmost powers to justify the confidence reposed in me, without wasting unnecessarily one moment of time. I hope either to find a safe passage, or charter a neutral vessel for Gibralter, so that I may leave this in about ten days from this date. At least, if I do not set out as soon as that, or sooner, it shall not be owing to want of arrangement, or exertion on my part.

The Portuguese Ship of war which was sent to convoy the Moorish Princesses (mentioned in some of my late letters) after going with them to Tangier, has returned.

The British and French channel fleets, of nearly the same force, have been in sight of each other, but have had no action.

Nothing very remarkable seems to have occured in the Armies since the capture of Valenciennes and Mentz. . . . . In France, the Mountain still prevails—the Queen's trial has commenced, and it was expected She would have been executed on the 10th. of August; but, that being past, some expectations are now entertained that She will be saved . . . or at least, that her fate may depend on the approach of the German Armies towards Paris. Custine is on his trial—Biron superseded—Dillon and Miranda again arrested. Yet in the midst of these, and an infinity of other violences, the Insurrections appear to be rather subsiding, and the Constitution to be adopting as a new rallying point. By a Packet which arrived yesterday, I find Exchange in London, was becoming considerably more favorable than it had been for Paris, Bourdeaux &c. tho' it is still very low.

The report in the English Gazettes, that Perpignan is taken, is false.

On the Spanish side, Mr. Short writes thus, in a letter just received: "The last Courier from the Army in Roussillon, informs us that the Spanish General, by advices from Deserters, had every reason to believe he should be attacked in force about the 25th. of this month (August)— Preparations for that purpose being in train on the French side."

The Portuguese Troops are to sail for the Mediterranean in a short time, as their Commander himself informs me.

I expect to have an opportunity of writing to you again in a few days, and in the mean while, I have the honour to be, with every sentiment of respect & esteem, Sir Your most obedient & Most humble Servant

D. HUMPHREYS

RC (DNA: RG 59, DD); at head of text: "(No. 80.)"; at foot of text: "The Secretary of State &c. &c. &c."; ellipses in original; endorsed by TJ as received 4 Nov. 1793 and so recorded in SJL. Tr (Lb in same). Enclosed in TJ to George Washington, 5 Nov. 1793.

From James McHenry

SIR   Fayetteville near Baltimore 1st Sepr. 1793

I shall communicate to the merchants of Baltimore your official letter addressed to them which I have reason to believe will be very welcome agreeable and satisfactory. I shall also recommend to them to appoint a committee of their own body to extend its contents to those whom it concerns and to carry the object it contemplates into effect.

The french fugitive from St. Domingo whose application you forwarded some time since had experienced the same degree of attention and relief as his fellow sufferers, as however his age gives him some claims which may be peculiar only to a few others I shall obtain for him some part of the succour he solicits. I am D Sir with sincere respect Your most obt st. JAMES MHENRY

RC (DNA: RG 59, MLR); at foot of text: "Thomas Jefferson Eqe"; endorsed by TJ as received 4 Sep. 1793 and so recorded in SJL.

YOUR OFFICIAL LETTER: Circular to American Merchants, 27 Aug. 1793. FRENCH FUGITIVE: M. Lentilhon (see TJ to McHenry, 26 Aug. 1793).

To James Madison

Sep. 1. 93.

My last was of the 25th. Since that I have received yours of the 20th. and Colo. M's of the 21st. Nothing further has passed with Mr. Genet, but one of his Consuls has committed a pretty serious deed at Boston, by going with an armed force taken from a French frigate in the harbour, and rescuing a vessel out of the hands of the marshal who had arrested her by process from a court of justice. In another instance he kept off the Marshal by an armed force from serving a precept on a vessel. He is ordered consequently to be arrested himself prosecuted and punished for the rescue, and his Exequatur will be revoked.—You will see in the newspapers the attack made on our commerce by the British king in his *additional instructions* of June 8. Tho' we have only newspaper information of it, *provisional* instructions are going to Mr. Pinckney to require a revocation of them and indemnification for all losses which individuals may sustain by them in the mean time. Of the revocation I have not the least expectation. I shall therefore be for laying the whole business (respecting both nations) before Congress. While I think it impossible they should not approve of what has been done disagreeable to the friendly nation, it will be in their power to soothe them by strong commercial retaliations against the hostile one. Pinching their commerce will be just against themselves, advantageous to us, and conciliatory towards our friends of the hard necessities into which their agent has driven us. His conduct has given room for the enemies of liberty and of France to come forward in a stile of acrimony against that nation which they never would have dared to have done. The disapprobation of the agent mingles with the reprehension of his nation and gives a toleration to that which it never had before. He has still some defenders in Freneau's and Greenleaf's papers. Who they are I know not: for even Hutcheson and Dallas give him up. I inclose you a Boston paper which will give you a specimen of what all the papers are now filled with. You will recognise Mr. A——— under the signature of Camillus. He writes in every week's paper now, and generally under different signatures. This is the first paper in which he has omitted some furious incartade against me. Hutcheson says that Genet has totally overturned the Republican interest in Philadelphia. However, the people going right themselves, if they always see their republican advocates with them, an accidental meeting with the Monocrats will not be a coalescence.—You will see much said and gainsaid about G's threat to appeal to the people. I can assure you it is a fact.—I received yesterday the MS. you mentioned to me from F____n. I have only got a dozen pages into it, and never was more charmed with any thing. Profound arguments presented in the simplest point of view entitle him really to his antient signature. In the papers received from you I have seen nothing which ought to be changed, except a part of one sentence, not necessary for it's object, and running foul of something of which you were not apprised.

A malignant fever has been generated in the filth of Water street which gives great alarm. About 70. people had died of it two days ago, and as many more were ill of it. It has now got into most parts of the city and is considerably infectious. At first 3. out of 4. died. Now about 1. out of 3. It comes on with a pain in the head, sick stomach, then a little chill, fever, black vomiting and stools, and death from the 2d. to the 8th. day, every body, who can, is flying from the city, and the panic of the country people is likely to add famine to disease. Tho becoming less mortal, it is still spreading, and the heat of the weather is very unpropitious. I have withdrawn my daughter from the city, but am obliged to go to it every day myself.—My threshing machine is arrived at New York. Mr. Pinckney writes me word that the original from which this model is copied threshes 150 bushels of wheat in 8. hours with 6. horses and 5. men. It may be moved either by water or horses. Fortunately the workman who made it (a millwright) is come in the same vessel to settle in America. I have written to persuade him to go on immediately to Richmd. offering him the use of my model to exhibit, and to give him letters to get him into immediate employ in making them. I expect an answer before I write to you again. I understand that the model is made mostly in brass, and in the simple form in which it was first ordered, to be worked by horses, it was to have cost 5. guineas, but Mr. Pinckney having afterwards directed it to be accomodated to a water movement also, it has made it more complicated, and costs 13. guineas. It will thresh any grain from the Windsor bean down to the smallest. Adieu.

P.S. The market, was the last winter from 25. to 50 percent higher than it was in the winter preceding. It is now got to from 50. to 100. percent higher. I think by the winter it will be generally 100 per cent on the prices of 1790. European goods are also much risen. Of course you must expect a rise in the boarding houses compounded of these two. In the mean time the produce of the farmer, say wheat, rice, tobacco has not risen a copper. The redundancy of paper then in the cities is palpably a tax on the distant farmer.

P.S. Sep. 2. I have made great progress into the M.S. and still with the same pleasure. I have no doubt it must produce great effect. But that this may be the greatest possible, it's coming out should be timed to the best advantage. It should come out just so many days before the meeting of Congress as will prevent suspicions of it's coming with them, yet so as to be a new thing when they arrive, ready to get into their hands while yet unoccupied, before the panic of the culprits shall be over, or any measures for defeating it's first effect may be taken. I will direct it to appear a fortnight before their meeting unless you order otherwise. It might as well be thrown into a church yard, as come out now.

RC (DLC: Madison Papers); unsigned; endorsed by Madison. PrC (DLC); last line of text frayed. Tr (DLC); 19th-century copy consisting only of first postscript, with two passages canceled, and all but last line of second postscript.

For the ADDITIONAL INSTRUCTIONS, see Enclosure No. 1 listed at Thomas Pinckney to TJ, 5 July 1793. TJ sent Pinckney PROVISIONAL INSTRUCTIONS in a letter dated 7 Sep. 1793. The BOSTON PAPER was the *Columbian Centinel*, 24 Aug. 1793, which contained an essay in which CAMILLUS attacked French minister Edmond Charles Genet for threatening to appeal decisions made by the President directly to the Amer-

ican people, denied that France's support of American independence had been motivated by anything but self-interest, asserted that America thus owed the French nation no gratitude, and claimed that despite its protestations to the contrary France was trying to force the United States to enter the European war. Rather than MR. A—presumably a reference to John Adams—the author may have been Federalist congressman Fisher Ames of Massachusetts, who had used the same pseudonym in 1787 (Madison, *Papers*, xv, 91n). For the manuscript which CHARMED TJ, see note to James Monroe to TJ, 21 Aug. 1793; and note to Madison to TJ, 11 Aug. 1793.

To Thomas Pinckney

Dr Sir   Philadelphia Sep. 1. 1793

The inclosed affidavit will inform you of the capture of the ship Jay, an American vessel, laden with flour &c. alledged to be American property, bound to Havre de grace, taken by the armed brig Orestes and carried into Plymouth. Though nothing is yet known of the further proceedings against her, yet I have thought it well, not to lose time, to inclose you the affidavit, and to desire that if the owners should not be able to obtain justice through the ordinary channel of the courts, you will then interfere on their behalf, as far as their evidence will justify, to procure from the government the redress to which you shall find them entitled. The unworthy deception practised by the commander of the armed vessel will surely more than obliterate all the effects of the declarations into which he frightened or decoyed the master of the Jay. I send this to the persons concerned to be used or not as they shall find necessary. I have the honor to be with great esteem Dr. Sir your most obedt. servt   TH: JEFFERSON

PrC (DLC); at foot of text: "Thomas Pinckney esq. Min. Pleny. of the US. at London." FC (Lb in DNA: RG 59, DCI). Enclosure listed at Elias Vanderhorst to TJ, 4 July 1793. Enclosed in TJ to Samuel Ward, 1 Sep. 1793.

To David Meade Randolph

DEAR SIR   Philadelphia Sep. 1. 1793.

I should with great satisfaction have complied with the desire of Mr. Gregorie, patronised by yourself and Mr. Barksdale, by recommending him for the appointment of Consul at Dunkirk, but that it has been decided to have three consulships only on the Atlantic coast of France, to wit, at Bordeaux, Nantes and Havre. Under this arrangement Dunkirk is within the Consulate of Havre, and the business of the US. at Dunkirk has been done by a Mr. Coffyn, an American, appointed by Dr. Franklin, ever since the beginning of the revolution war. He has done it well, and I am confident it was no part of Mr. Gregorie's view to wish that appointment. I will ask the favor of you to communicate this to the other two gentlemen, and am with great esteem, Dr. Sir Your friend & servt   TH: JEFFERSON

PrC (DLC); at foot of text: "D. M. Randolph. esq." Tr (ViU: Edgehill-Randolph Papers); 19th-century copy.

For the correspondence which elicited this letter, see John Gregorie to TJ, 20 Mch. 1793, and note.

To Abraham Runnels

SIR   Philadelphia Sep. 1. 1793.

I thought I had clearly and sufficiently answered your former application, by telling you personally, as I did also to Mr. Soderstrom, Consul, that, by the laws of this country, the Judiciary was the branch charged with the care of redressing wrongs of the nature that you complain of, our courts being open to nations at peace, tho' they cannot interpose between those at war: and wherever the courts can give a remedy, the Executive do not intermeddle. I had the reason to suppose you understood the proper line of redress, on being informed by Mr. Randolph that you were prosecuting your case by the courts. I am Sir Your most obedt. servt   TH: JEFFERSON

PrC (DLC); at foot of text: "Mr. Runnels." FC (Lb in DNA: RG 59, DL).

To George Taylor, Jr.

Sunday Sep. 1. 1793.

Th: Jefferson will be obliged to Mr. Taylor to wait immediately on Mr. Hammond, Mr. Van Berkel, and Messrs. Viar and Jaudenes, and present them the inclosed letters. If the request of the charitable committee of Baltimore be admissible, Th:J. would be very glad to recieve any passports or letters they may be pleased to give, in time to send by tomorrow's post.

PrC (DLC). Tr (ViU: Edgehill-Randolph Papers); 19th-century copy. Enclosed in TJ to James McHenry, Robert Gilmor, and Samuel Sterett, 2 Sep. 1793.

The INCLOSED LETTERS were probably Robert Gilmor and Samuel Sterett to TJ, 29 Aug. 1793, and the missing letter of 18 Aug. 1793 from the same pair noted at TJ to James McHenry, Gilmor, and Sterett, 22 Aug. 1793.

From Elias Vanderhorst

Bristol, 1 Sep. 1793. He wrote from Plymouth on 4 July—but was unable to copy—an acknowledgment of TJ's 21 Mch. letter because the ship by which he sent it, the *Amsterdam Packet* bound for New York, was then on the point of sailing. He went to Falmouth and found several American ships detained there on pretexts similar to those used against the *Eliza* and the *Jay* at Plymouth. He encloses a copy of the Court of Admiralty decree on the *Portland* and a copy of instructions to captains of men of war and privateers that explain the object of these detentions. Messrs. Fox of Falmouth conclude that the government plans to purchase the *Portland*'s cargo from the governmental orders they have received to superintend its landing and render an account of it. He has communicated everything to Pinckney, who has reportedly submitted a remonstrance to the ministry, the result of which is not known, demanding redress for this incident and everything injurious to American commerce that has lately happened here. The war with France grows daily more unpopular, and it would not do to add to it an American war, which people here deprecate most of all. He hopes for peace and for France to be rightfully left to settle her internal affairs. Because of the derangement of French affairs he has been unable to do anything about the indigo belonging to his friends Smiths, De Saussure & Darrell taken from the American ship *Commerce* by Captain Desgue and the crew of the *Tyger*, a French privateer from St. Malo. He hopes the United States government will obtain satisfaction for this from the French minister. The French executive have no doubt taken from those concerned in the *Tyger*, who are reportedly men of very considerable property, the security usually given by owners and masters of privateers. In view of this unwarrantable act, it would not be unreasonable to add at least 25 percent to the invoice for damages, making £316 sterling the amount due Smith & Company, to whom he has written for proof of ownership of the indigo. With TJ's aid he hopes the matter will soon be resolved to their satisfaction. The grain crops in this country, most of which have been harvested, are promising, the weather having been favorable. Wheat especially is very good, though not as abundant as in some years. Because no corn will be wanting here before next season and he is informed that the general harvest in Europe is also abundant, British ports will probably soon be shut to foreign grain. He has sent Pinckney a bond as requested and if TJ does not approve it he will execute and forward the one TJ lately sent him. The Commissioners of the Customs have not replied to his letter, but, their officers being interested, have sent it to the collector here, from whom he has obtained no satisfaction even though he offered to pay the clerks for the information required. Consequently in future it will be proper and necessary for masters of all American ships to be required under penalties to show their registers and manifests to the consuls so that they can furnish the accounts expected from them. Would it not be proper for collectors to require receipts from returning masters to prove they furnished these documents? Some masters supply them upon request, but many others have absolutely refused, citing the lack of a legal requirement. There has been no material change in the price of American produce since the 3 Aug. account dispatched in his absence by his son by the *Roebuck* bound for Philadelphia. Many houses lately building in the environs of the city are being taken down and their materials put up for sale—the sad effects of war that should be an instructive lesson to this nation and others. He gives an extract of a letter just received from Hawker at Plymouth stating that Doctors Commons has issued commissions for the delivery of the cargoes of the *Eliza*, *Jay*, and *Cato*, addressed to agents of the captors and claimants, who are directed to put separate locks on the warehouses; that the property of the captains and mates is restored and the *Eliza* has just left for Bordeaux; that all of the *Jay*'s cargo except 50 barrels of flour, 550 hides, and a barrel of tar is ordered to be delivered to the victualling office and the *Cato*'s cargo of naval stores to the royal dockyard; that the produce is to be lodged in the Registry Court until matters are tried and a commission of appraisal and sale for the hides has been sent to Hawker and Lloyd; and that in several cases there is every reason to believe the captors have tried to bribe American masters and crews to help them secure the condemnation of their cargoes. He refers to the enclosed newspapers for current news. [P.S.] He encloses dispatches for TJ just received from Pinckney. He has just been advised that today British ports were shut to foreign wheat, etc. Because some of the packets in the dispatches from Pinckney are bulky and have his name on the covers, he has decided instead to entrust them to Captain Jameson of the brig *Grange*, bound for New York, who promises to deliver them as soon as possible after arrival.

RC (DNA: RG 59, CD); 5 p.; endorsed by TJ as received 4 Nov. 1793 and so recorded in SJL. Enclosures (1) Additional instructions to captains of British warships and privateers, 8 June 1793 (Tr in same; see Enclosure No. 1 listed at Thomas Pinckney to TJ, 5 July 1793). (2) Decree of High Court of Admiralty, 31 July 1793, ordering Harding Shore, commander of the privateer *Thought*, and all other custodians to restore the *Portland*, Captain Thomas Robinson, to the claimant Philip Sansom for its owners and proprietors, "with freight, and expences, to be a charge on the Cargo"; reserving the question of the cargo for further adjudication; and stipulating that the provisions in the cargo were to be sold to the British government and the proceeds therefrom held by the court's registry until further order by the court (Tr in same). Enclosed in TJ to George Washington, 5 Nov. 1793.

To Samuel Ward

SIR   Philadelphia Sep. 1. 1793.

I duly received your favor of Aug. 30. on the capture of the ship Jay by the British armed brig the Orestes. The circumstances mentioned in the affidavit of the Captain were certainly such as would justify the carrying the vessel into port for examination. However we must hope that he would be able to establish the property both of the ship and cargo to be American, in which case it is presumed that the courts of the country will do justice. In case however they should not, I have written to Mr. Pinckney (and now inclose to you the letter) desiring his patronage of their rights so far as the evidence shall establish them, and that he will endeavor to obtain from the government indemnification for the loss. Of this letter you will of course have no occasion to make use, but in the event of a denial of justice by the courts. I am respectfully Sir your most obedt. servt   TH: JEFFERSON

PrC (DLC); at foot of text: "Mr. Samuel Ward." FC (Lb in DNA: RG 59, DL). Enclosure: TJ to Thomas Pinckney, 1 Sep. 1793.

Ward's FAVOR OF AUG. 30 was actually dated 29 Aug. 1793.

To Wilson, Potts & Easton

GENTLEMEN   Philadelphia Sep. 1. 1793.

The President having referred to me your petition on the capture of your vessel by the French privateer the Sans pareil, I consulted thereon with the Attorney general, well knowing that if the laws of the land give you any redress at all, it will be surer and quicker than any by negociation. The advice given you by Mr. Lee appears to be perfectly solid, and if you were in time in pursuing that, we presume it's effect will be certain. If the vessel and cargo are no longer in the reach of legal process, the purchasers probably may be come at, and will we presume be deemed liable for a property which they possessed without title, for the condemnation by the French Consul was a mere nullity, he having no such jurisdiction. We had depended that Mr. Genet had taken measures to restrain the Consuls from arrogating this jurisdiction, application having been made to him for that purpose in the first case which came to the knolege of the government; but this not having been done, more effectual measures are now taking to restrain them. Should you fail of obtaining redress at law, be so good as to give me information of it, and the best means shall be taken for obtaining redress from the government of France. I have the honor to be gentlemen Your most obedt. servt

TH: JEFFERSON

PrC (DLC); at foot of text: "Messrs. Wilson, Potts & Easton." FC (Lb in DNA: RG 59, DL).

Thomas Jefferson and Edmund Randolph to George Wythe

DEAR SIR   Philadelphia Sep. 1. 1793.

Your favor of Aug. 17. was received, and the address it covered was immediately delivered to the President. We are sincerely & affectionately Your's   TH: JEFFERSON

PrC (DLC); entirely in TJ's hand; at foot of text: "George Wythe, Chancr. of Virginia." Tr (ViU: Edgehill-Randolph Papers); 19th-century copy. Recorded in SJL as a letter from "Th:J. & E.R."

To Christopher Gore

SIR   Philadelphia Sep. 2. 1793.

The President is informed through the channel of a letter from yourself to Mr. Lear, that Mr. DuPlaine Consul of France at Boston, has lately, with an armed force, seized and rescued a vessel from the officer of a court of justice by process from which she was under arrest in his custody: and that he has in like manner, with an armed force, opposed and prevented the officer, charged with process from a court against another vessel, from serving that process. This daring violation of the laws requires the more attention, as it is by a foreigner, clothed with a public character, arrogating an unfounded right to Admiralty jurisdiction, and probably meaning to assert it by this act of force. You know that by the law of nations, Consuls are not diplomatic characters, and have no immunities whatever against the laws of the land. To put this altogether out of dispute, a clause was inserted in our Consular Convention with France, making them amenable to the laws of the land as other inhabitants. Consequently Mr. Duplaine is liable to arrest, imprisonment, and other punishment, even capital, as other foreign subjects resident here. The President therefore desires that you will immediately institute such a prosecution against him, as the laws will warrant. If there be any doubt as to the character of his offence, whether of a higher or lower grade, it will be best to prosecute for that which will admit the least doubt, because an acquittal, though it might be founded merely on the opinion that the grade of offence with which he is *charged*, is higher than his *act* would support, yet it might be construed by the uninformed to be a judiciary decision against his amenability to the law, or perhaps in favor of the jurisdiction these consuls are assuming. The process therefore should be of the surest kind, and all the proceedings well guarded. In particular, if an arrest, as is probable, be the first step, it should be so managed as to leave room neither for escape nor rescue. It should be attended with every mark of respect, consistent with safe custody, and his confinement as mild and comfortable also as that would permit. These are the distinctions to which a Consul is entitled, that is to say, a particular decorum of deportment towards him, indicative of respect to the sovereign whose officer he is.

The President also desires you will immediately obtain the best evidence it shall be in your power to procure, under oath or affirmation, of the transaction stated in your letter, and that in this you consider yourself as acting as much on behalf of Mr. Duplaine as the public, the candid truth of the case being exactly that which is desired, as it may be the foundation of an act, the justice of which should be beyond all question. This evidence I shall be glad to receive with as few days or even hours of delay as possible.

I am also instructed to ask the favor of you to communicate copies of any memorials, representations or other written correspondence which may have passed between the Governor and yourself with respect to the privateers and prizes which have been the subject of your letters to Mr. Lear. I have the honor to be with great respect Sir Your most obedt servt Th: Jefferson

PrC (DLC); at foot of first page: "Mr. Gore." FC (Lb in DNA: RG 59, DL).

Gore's LETTER to Tobias LEAR is described in note to Cabinet Opinions on the *Roland* and Relations with Great Britain, France, and the Creeks, 31 Aug. 1793. For the relevant CLAUSE . . . IN OUR CONSULAR CONVENTION WITH FRANCE, see Vol. 14: 172.

TJ submitted this letter to the President, who approved it this day (Washington, *Journal*, 236).

To James McHenry, Robert Gilmor, and Samuel Sterett

GENTLEMEN   Philadelphia Sep. 2. 1793.

Your favor of Aug. 29. was brought to me in the country yesterday. I immediately sent to town by express in hopes of being able to procure what you desired to be sent by the post of this day. Mr. Van Berkel however was out of town, as also the Spanish Commissioners, and not to be in town soon. I inclose you my note to Mr. Taylor, my chief clerk, and his pencilled statement of what Mr. Hammond requires. I am sorry so simple a business should meet such delay, but I have not lost a moment that could be avoided. I hope your next will enable to obtain your wish. I am with great respect Gentlemen Your most obedt. servt.

TH: JEFFERSON

PrC (DLC); at foot of text: "Messrs. Mc.Henry, Gilmer & Sterritt." Enclosures: TJ to George Taylor, Jr., 1 Sep. 1793, and Taylor's missing response.

The FAVOR OF AUG. 29 was from Gilmor and Sterett only.

From James Madison

DEAR SIR   Sepr. 2. 93

I write this by your servant on his way to George Town with a Horse. He applies to me for his best route. I advise the circuitous one by Fredg., in preference to the shorter one, in which he would probably lose more by mistakes than would be equal to the difference between the two in point of distance. I left Monroe's yesterday. My stay was spun out by waiting for Mr. D. R., who did not arrive at Monto: till Friday evening. Your letter by him was duly received. On getting home last night I found your subsequent one of the 18th. inst: I have not yet read the paper inclosed in it. I shall write you in the course of the day by another opportunity for the post[1] which will afford me time to say what I could not say now without detaining the Servant.

RC (DLC: Madison Papers); unsigned; endorsed by TJ as received 8 Sep. 1793 and so recorded in SJL.

D. R.: David Meade Randolph. YOUR LETTER BY HIM: TJ's second letter to Madison

of 11 Aug. 1793. TJ's letter OF THE 18TH. INST: was actually dated 18 Aug. 1793.

[1] Preceding three words interlined.

From James Madison

I dropped you a few lines this morning by the servant going to George Town with your horse. I had not time, without detaining him to say more than that I had your two favors of the 11th. Ult: by Mr. D. R. and of the 18th. by post. The former was communicated to Monroe, as shall be the latter in case of opportunity. The conduct of Genèt as developed in these, and in his proceedings as exhibited in the newspapers, is as unaccountable as it is distressing. The effect is beginning to be strongly felt here in the surprize and disgust of those who are attached to the French cause, and viewed this minister as the instrument for cementing instead of alienating the two Republics. These sensations are powerfully reinforced by the general and habitual veneration for the President. The Anglican party is busy as you may suppose in making the worst of every thing, and in turning the public feelings against France, and thence, in favor of England. The only antidote for their poison, is to distinguish between the nation and its Agent, between principles and events; and to impress the well meaning with the fact that the enemies of France and of Liberty are at work to lead them from their honorable connection with these, into the arms and ultimately into the Government of G. B. If the genuine sense of the people could be collected on the several points comprehended in the occasion, the calamity would be greatly alleviated if not absolutely controuled. But this is scarcely possible. The Country is too much uninformed, and too inert to speak for itself; and the language of the towns which are generally directed by an adverse interest will insidiously inflame the evil. It is however of such[1] infinite importance to our own Government as well as to that of France, that the real sentiments of the people here should be understood, that something ought to be attempted on that head. I inclose a copy of a train of ideas sketched on the first rumour of the war between the Ex. and Genet, and particularly suggested by the Richmond Resolutions, as a groundwork for those who might take the lead in county meetings. It was intended that they should be modified in every particular according to the state of information and the particular temper of the place. A copy has been sent to Caroline with a hope that Mr. P. might find it not improper to step forward. Another is gone to the District Court at Staunton in the hands of Monroe, who carried a letter from me on the subject to A. Stuart; and a third will be for consideration at the District Ct. at Charlottesville. If these examples should be set, there may be a chance of like proceedings elsewhere: and in themselves they will be respectable specimens of the principles and sensations of the Agricultural,[2] which is the commanding part of the Society.

I am not sanguine however that the effort will succeed. If it does not, the State Legislatures, and the federal also if possible, must be induced to take up the matter in its true point of view. Monroe and myself read with attention your despatch by D.R. and had much conversation on what passed between you and the P. It appeared to both of us that a real anxiety was marked to retain you in office, that over and above other motives, it was felt that your presence and implied sanction might be a necessary shield against certain criticisms from certain quarters; that the departure of the only counsellor possessing the confidence of the Republicans would be a signal for new and perhaps very disagreeable attacks; that in this point of view the respectful and conciliatory language of the P. is worthy of particular attention; and that it affords a better hope than has existed of your being able to command attention, and to moderate the predominant tone. We agreed in opinion also that whilst this end is pursued, it would be wise to make as few concessions as possible that might embarrass the free pursuit of measures which may be dictated by Republican principles and required by the public good. In a word we think you ought to make the most of the value we perceive to be placed on your participation in the Ex: Counsels. I am extremely glad to find that you are to remain another quarter. The season will be more apropos in several respects; and it will prevent any co-operation which a successor might be disposed to make towards a final breach with France. I have little hope that you will have one whose policy will have the same healing tendency with yours. I foresee, I think, that it will be either King, if Johnson is put at the Treasy: or E. Rutlege, if Walcot should be put there. I am glad the President rightly infers my determination from antecedent circumstances, so as to free me from imputations in his mind connected with the present state of things. Monroe is particularly solicitous that you should take the view of your present position and opportunities above suggested. He sees so forcibly the difficulty of keeping the feelings of the people as to Genèt distinct from those due to his Constituents, that he can hardly prevail on himself absolutely, and *openly*, to abandon him. I concur with him that it ought to be done no further than is forced upon us, that in general silence is better than open denunciation and crimination; and that it is not unfair to admit the apologetic influence of the errors in our own Government which may have inflamed the passions which now discolor every object to his eye: such as the refusal in the outset of the Government to favor the commerce of F. more than that of G. B. the unfortunate appointment of G. M.[3] to the former: the language of the proclamation—the attempts of Pacificus to explain away and dissolve the Treaty, the notoriety of the Author, and the appearance of its being an informal manifestation of the views of the Ex. &c.

I paid a short visit to Mr. W. N.[4] as I proposed. He talks like a sound Republican, and sincere friend to the French cause in every respect. I collected from him that E. R. had admitted to him that he drew the Procln: that he had been attacked on it at Chatham by Mr. Jos: Jones, that he reprobated the comment of Pac–f–s–&c. W. N. observed that H.[5] had taken the Ex. in by gaining phrases of which he could make the use he has done. The circumstances which derogate from full confidence in W. N. are 1st. his being embarked in a variety of projects which call for money, and keep him in intercourse with the merchants of Richd. 2d. his communication and intimacy with Marshal of whose *disinterestedness* as well as understanding he has the highest opinion. It is said, that Marshal who is at the head of the great purchase from Fairfax, has lately obtained pecuniary aids from the Bank or people connected with it. I think it certain that he must have felt, in the moment of the purchase an absolute dependence on the monied interest, which will explain him to every one that reflects, in the active character he is assuming. I have been obliged to write this in great haste, the bearer impatiently waiting the whole time.[6]

I hope you have received the five Nos. of Hel–v–d–s. I must resume the task I suppose, in relation to the *Treaty*—and *Gratitude*. I feel however so much awkwardness under the new posture of things, that I shall deliberate whether a considerable postponement at least may not be adviseable. I found also on my return a House full of particular friends who will stay some weeks and receive and return visits from which I can not decently exclude myself. If I should perceive it impossible or improper to continue the publication so as to avail myself the channel used to the press, I shall suspend it till I see and talk with you on the whole matter. Adieu—

RC (DLC: Madison Papers); unsigned; consisting of one sheet folded to form four pages; endorsed by TJ as received 14 Sep. 1793 and so recorded in SJL.

Madison prepared the enclosed TRAIN OF IDEAS reiterating support for French-American friendship in collaboration with James Monroe to serve as model resolves for Virginia Republicans wishing to counter the 17 Aug. 1793 RICHMOND RESOLUTIONS and similar manifestos approved at other Federalist meetings (George Wythe to TJ and Edmund Randolph, 17 Aug. 1793, and note). They had completed the resolutions by 27 Aug. 1793, when Madison informed TJ that he had sent a copy to John Taylor in CAROLINE County, urging him to see if MR. P.—Edmund Pendleton—MIGHT FIND IT NOT IMPROPER TO STEP FORWARD. But because Madison was unable to decipher the encrypted portions of TJ's letter of 3 Aug., he and Monroe did not learn until 30 Aug., when the account in TJ's second letter of 11 Aug. arrived, that the Washington administration had decided to demand the recall of French minister Edmond Charles Genet and that TJ was urging his political allies to abandon him—a delay that put Republican efforts to neutralize Federalist initiatives in Virginia at a disadvantage. With this news in hand, Madison and Monroe moved on 1 Sep. to influence events in STAUNTON, whither Monroe carried a version of their resolutions and a LETTER from Madison to Archibald STUART. Resolutions adopted by Republican-dominated meetings in Staunton (with Stuart serving as secretary) on 3 Sep., in Caroline County at a meeting chaired by Pendleton on 10 Sep.,

and in CHARLOTTESVILLE on 10 Oct., all
followed the lead of the Madison-Monroe
prototype, though in the first two meetings
the resolves coupled criticism of the French
diplomat's interference in American politics with a censure of Federalist attempts to
capitalize on it for the purpose of weakening French-American friendship. No surviving evidence links Madison and Monroe
to these changes, but Monroe's extreme
reluctance to disavow Genet ABSOLUTELY,
AND OPENLY, may account for the silence
of the Albermarle resolutions on that score.
In any event, the effort by Madison and
Monroe to inspire LIKE PROCEEDINGS ELSE-
WHERE enjoyed only mixed success in
Virginia, where victories in some locales
were balanced by standoffs (as in Petersburg and Fredericksburg) and Federalist
triumphs in others, and virtually none in
other states, where Republican leaders had
weaker contacts than their Federalist rivals
and the suspension of newspaper publication in Philadelphia during the yellow fever
epidemic hindered dissemination of the resolutions (Madison to TJ, 27 Aug. 1793,
and note; Monroe to TJ, 3 Sep. 1793, and
note; Thomas Griffin Peachy to TJ, 3 Sep.
1793, and note; Memorandum to George
Washington, 22 Sep. 1793; Monroe to TJ,
14 Oct. 1793, and note; Editorial Note in
Madison, *Papers*, xv, 76-9n; Madison to
Archibald Stuart, 1 Sep. 1793, same, 87-8;
broadside of the Staunton resolutions, 3
Sep. 1793, Evans, No. 26204; Mays,
Pendleton, II, 608-13; Nicholas Lewis to

George Washington, 24 Oct. 1793, enclos-
ing Albemarle County resolutions of 10
Oct. 1793, in DLC: Washington Papers;
Harry Ammon, "The Genet Mission and
the Development of American Political
Parties," JAH, LII [1966], 725-41; Ammon,
Genet Mission, 132-46; Richard R. Bee-
man, *The Old Dominion and the New Nation*
[Lexington, Ky., 1972], 126-34).

John Marshall was the prime mover,
though an unnamed partner, in THE GREAT
PURCHASE in February 1793 of more than
200,000 acres of land in Virginia's Northern Neck from the Reverend Denny Martin
FAIRFAX, the heir of Thomas, Sixth Lord
Fairfax. Marshall had hoped to pay for his
share of the purchase with profits realized
from the sale of bank stock he had contracted to buy from Arthur Lee, but it was
not until 1806 that he and other partners
overcame formidable legal and financial obstacles to complete the purchase (Marshall,
Papers, II, 138-9, 140-56, 254-8).

[1] Preceding three words interlined in
place of "of."
[2] Madison here canceled "interest."
[3] At a later date Madison expanded the
abbreviation to "Gour. Morris."
[4] At a later date Madison expanded the
abbreviation to "W. C. Nicholas."
[5] At a later date Madison expanded the
abbreviation to "Hamilton."
[6] Remainder of text written lengthwise
in the margin between the fourth and first
pages.

ENCLOSURE

Resolutions on Neutrality and Friendship with France

[ca. 27 Aug. 1793]

It being considered that, 'tis at all times the right and at certain periods the
duty of the people to declare their principles and opinions on subjects which
concern the Natl. interest; that at present conjuncture this duty is rendered the
more indispensable by the prevailing practice of declaratory resolutions in
places where the inhabitants can more easily assemble and consult than in the
Country at large, and where interests views and political opinions different from
those of the great body of the people, may happen to predominate, whence there
may be danger of unfair and delusive inferences concerning the true and general
sense of the people; It being also considered that under the disadvantage a great
proportion of the people labor in their distant and dispersed situation from the
want of timely and correct knowledge of particular incidents and the conduct of
particular persons connected with public transactions, it is most prudent and

safe, to wait with a decent reserve for full and satisfactory information in relation thereto, and in public declarations to abide by those great principles, just sentiments and established Truths which can be little affected by personal or transitory occurrences.

Therefore as the sense of the present Meeting

Resolved

That the Constin. of the U. S. ought to be firmly and vigilantly supported against all direct or indirect attempts that may be made to subvert or violate the same.

That as it is the interest of U. S. to cultivate the preservation of peace by all just and honorable means, the Ex. Authy. ought to be supported in the exercise of its constitutional powers and functions for enforcing the laws existing for the purpose.

That the eminent virtues and services of our illustrious fellow Citizen G.W. P. of U.S. entitle him to the highest respect and lasting gratitude of his Country, whose peace liberty and safety must ever remind it of his distinguished agency in promoting the same.

That the eminent and generous aids rendered to the U. S. in their arduous struggle for liberty, by the Fr. Nation, ought ever to be remembered and acknowledged with gratitude, and that the spectacle exhibited by the severe and glorious Contest in which it is now engaged for its own liberty, ought and must be peculiarly interesting to the wishes, the friendship and the sympathy of the people of America.

That all attempts which may be made in whatever form or disguise to alienate the good will of the people of Amera. from the cause of liberty and Republican Government in F. have a tendency to weaken their affection to the free principles of their own Government and manifest designs which ought to be narrowly watched and seasonably counteracted.

That such attempts to disunite nations mutually attached to the cause of liberty, and viewed with unfriendly eyes by all who hate it, ought more particularly to be reprobated at the present crisis, when such vast efforts are making by a combination of Princes and nobles to crush an example that may open the eyes of all mankind to their natl. and political rights.

That a dissolution of the honorable and beneficial connection between the U. S. and F. would obviously tend to forward a plan of connecting them with G.B. as one great leading step towards assimilating our Government to the form and spirit of the British Monarchy; and that this apprehension is greatly strengthened by the active Zeal displayed by persons disaffected to the Amn. Revn. and by others of known Monarchical principles, in propagating prejudices against the French Nation and Revolution.

MS (DLC: Madison Papers); entirely in Madison's hand; undated, but assigned to 27 Aug. 1793 on the basis of Madison to TJ of that date; at head of text in an unidentified hand: "Sketch of Resolutions referred to in Letter of 2nd Sept. 1793."

To Thomas Mann Randolph, Jr.

DEAR SIR   Philadelphia Sep. 2. 1793.

I wrote to you on the 26th. Ult. since which I have received yours of the 14th. Ult. Maria is well, and is with me on the Schuylkill. A malignant fever has been generated in the filth of the docks of Philadelphia which has given great alarm. It is considerably infectious. At first 3 out of 4. died, at present not more than one out of three. Three days ago (my latest information) about 70. had died and about that number were ill of it. It is called commonly a yellow fever, but by the physicians Typhus gravior. Begins with a pain in the head, sickness at the stomach, then a slight rigor, fever, black vomitings and fæces, and death from the 2d. to the 8th. day. At first it was confined to Water street, but is now in many parts of the city. It is still spreading, tho become less mortal. Every body, who can, is flying from the city, and the country people, being afraid to come to the market, there is fear of a want of supplies. Tho there is some degree of danger, yet, as is usual, there is much more alarm than danger; and knowing it to be usual also to magnify these accounts in proportion to distance, I have given you the particulars, that you may know exactly what the case is.—My threshing machine is arrived at New York, and will be here this week. Mr. Pinkney writes me that the original from which my model is taken, gets out 150. bushels of wheat in 8. hours with 6. horses and 5. men. It will thresh any grain, from the Windsor bean to the smallest, and may be moved by horses or water. It happens that the workman who made it (a millwright) is come over in the same vessel, I have written to advise him to go to Virginia, and commence building these machines, offering him the use of my model to exhibit in Richmond if he chuses, in order to get himself into work.—Your letter of the 14th. does not mention the receipt of any of mine on the subject of sending on the horse. Still however presuming some of them will have got to hand, I have sent off a servant with Tarquin so that he will arrive at Georgetown the day after tomorrow. He has orders to wait there a week if necessary.—The character you give of Giovannini is a just one. He is sober, industrious and honest. He lived with me as gardener some time before I went to Europe. However I shall find it necessary to have a gardener constantly at his business, and think to teach a negro at once.—Our last accounts from France are of a very mixed complexion. The combined armies had made no progress. The insurgents of Brittany had obtained a signal victory, and had afterwards been more signally defeated, but not suppressed.—My love to my dear Martha and am Dear Sir Yours affectionately & constantly

Th: Jefferson

RC (DLC); at foot of first page: "Mr. Randolph"; endorsed by Randolph as received 10 Sep. 1793. PrC (DLC). Erroneously recorded in SJL as a letter of 1 Sep. 1793.

TJ's letter to Randolph of THE 26TH. ULT. was actually dated 25 Aug. 1793.

From John Vaughan

2 Sep 1793

M. Vaughan takes the liberty of enclosing to Mr. Jefferson a Copy of a Contract for Land, made by a worthy French Family. M. Vaughan wishes Mr. Jefferson would favor him with any information in his power on the subject of these Lands—Which The family would I believe wish to dispose of. If you can communicate your opinions to Mr. Priestly, I shall be Still more obliged. Yours sincerely

JN VAUGHAN

RC (MHi); endorsed by TJ as received 2 Sep. 1793 and so recorded in SJL. Enclosure not found.

To George Washington

[ca. 2-4 Sep. 1793]

Th: Jefferson has the honor to inclose to the President his letter of Aug. 7. to Mr. Hammond, which was confined to the special cases of three vessels therein named. The object of Mr. Hammond's letter of Aug. 30. is to obtain from the government a declaration that the principle of those special cases shall be extended to all captures made within our waters or by the proscribed vessels, whether *before* or *after* the 7th. of Aug. and to establish, as a general rule, *restitution*, or *compensation*. The forming a general rule requires great caution. Th:J. in preparing the draught of an answer to Mr. Hammond, has endeavored to establish what he thinks the true grounds on which a general rule should be formed. But, if the President approves of it, he would wish to send the draught to the Secretaries of the Treasury and war, and Atty. Genl. for their consideration and amendments, or to meet on the subject, when an answer to the latter part of the letter might also be agreed on.

RC (DNA: RG 59, MLR); undated, but see note below; addressed: "The President [. . .]"; endorsed by Bartholomew Dandridge, Jr., at a later date as a letter of the "beginning of Septr 1793." PrC (DLC). Tr (Lb in DNA: RG 59, SDC); at foot of text: "N.B. This letter was wrote about the begining of Sept." Erroneously recorded in SJPL under 30 Aug. 1793, evidently on the basis of George Hammond's 30 Aug. 1793 letter, which TJ did not receive until the following day. Enclosures: (1) TJ to Hammond, 7 Aug. 1793. (2) Draft of TJ to Hammond, 5 Sep. 1793.

Despite TJ's entry in SJPL, he probably wrote this letter sometime between 2 Sep., when he submitted to the President Hammond's 30 Aug. letter, and 4 Sep. 1793, when the Cabinet approved the DRAUGHT of his reply (Washington, *Journal*, 236; Notes on Cabinet Meetings, 4 Sep. 1793).

From Nathaniel Cutting

Sir   Lisbon, 3d. Septr. 1793.

From the date of this Letter, compared with the time of my departure from Philadelphia, you might possibly imagine I had visited the place of my destination, and was thus far on my return: no such thing. I conceived the object of my mission to be of so much importance, that I was loth to expose myself and the dispatches with which I was entrusted to the probability of being intercepted and subjected to the impertinent examination of Persons who had no business to be acquainted with either. I consider'd that an occurrence of this kind would inevitably occasion great delay in the execution, if not entirely frustrate the intention of my mission. Add to this the consideration of personal safety. If a British Packet falls in with a French Cruiser, when the former can not escape by sailing, she must engage her Enemy so long as there exists a chance that she may beat her off. Now, I am not invulnerable; and a ball issuing from the deadly cavity of a Cannon by the force of Gunpowder, is, like God, "no respecter of Persons"; So that, notwithstanding every precaution I could take, perhaps I should get a broken head, or be a limb out of pocket; and who would make me compensation for that? I do not think much of sacrificing the prospect of great personal advantage when it comes in competition with the service of my Country; but the trivial stipend which I am allow'd for my present services is not adequate to the risk of life and limb in battle; especially where there is not the consolation of gaining honor neither. These reasons, therefore, induced me to wait so long as I did in London for an opportunity of coming hither in a neutral Ship. I was flatter'd from time to time with the prospect that two American Ships in particular, would be dispatch'd directly from London to this Port; but at length they were both Charter'd for other voyages; my patience was exhausted, and after having from time to time acquainted Mr. Pinckney with the reasons of my delay, in the propriety of which he apparently acquiesced, I took the resolution, with his approbation of proceeding by the British Packet from Falmouth, which I might have done a fortnight after my arrival in England. The Packet in which I took passage sail'd under peculiar advantages; being convoy'd clear of the Channel Cruizers by a two-deck'd Frigate which was conveying Lord Dorchester and family to Canada.

After we parted company with the Frigate and several Packets that also come out under her Convoy, we were frequently alarm'd, and sometimes put out of our route, by Vessels which did not appear to be *Quakers*; but favorable breezes, and *thick weather, which* also was favorable, enabled us to reach this place in safety, after nine days passage.

Colonel Humphreys has given directions to charter a neutral Vessel to convey us to the place of our destination, provided the price demanded is not too exorbitant. Though the price may be high, and the fund appropriated to the object of our mission and for defraying expences is very small, I conceive, vastly inadequate to the business, yet I think it will prove good economy to have a vessel whose motions we may direct in preference to one whose convenience must direct us; therefore I am strenuous for chartering in the first instance, in preference to taking our chance as passengers in any vessel whatever. Perhaps the delay I have met with, has prevented our going [on][1] a longer voyage that we had in contemplation, "*to t'other world*," as 'tis commonly exprest—for Colonel Humphreys has intelligence that the Plague raged at _____ with great violence in course of the last spring. We hope that by this period its ravages have ceased. I have the honor to be, with the greatest respect, sir, Your most obedient humble servant,

NAT. CUTTING

RC (DNA: RG 59, CD); at foot of first page: "The Secretary of State for the U.S.A."; endorsed by TJ as received 24 Oct. 1793 and so recorded in SJL.

TJ submitted this letter to the President on 2 Nov. 1793, and Washington returned it the same day (Washington, *Journal*, 243).

[1] Word supplied.

From David Humphreys

SIR   Lisbon Septr. 3d. 1793.

In addressing a letter to you the day before yesterday, and announcing the arrival of Captn. Cutting, I promised to write to you again by an opportunity which would occur in a few days. Determining there would be no sufficient compensation for the delay of going by Madrid, my hope was that you would have been informed, at this time, of our having at least secured a passage to Gibralter. This we have not yet been able to effect. I fear we shall be obliged to give a high price, as the demand for neutral vessels is great. But you may be assured I shall leave no effort untried, to make dispatch and security consist with economy as much as possible.

I have just this moment received letters from Mr. Short, dated at St. Ildefonso the 23d. of August, giving the substance of a Treaty which has been negotiated by Lord St. Helens on the part of Great Britain with Spain—as Mr. Short's letter, received at the same time, goes to you by the same conveyance as this, I presume he has furnished you with the same and perhaps more particulars than he has me.

In my letter, No. 73. I advised you of some dangerous propositions, which, I had good reason to believe, had been made by the Court of

Spain to the Court of England, respecting the U.S. of America. The same Person, who gave me the original intelligence, sent for me yesterday, to assure me he had a confirmation of it, and that the same overtures had been made by Spain to Portugal, and that probably the Portuguese Ambassador, just returned from Madrid to Lisbon, was charged with something on that subject. He added that the Court of Portugal had not listened to those overtures, that he could not without a violation of confidence enter into a farther disclosure, but that he gave me this information (which might be absolutely depended upon) in order that the U.S. might be on their guard. With sentiments of great esteem & respect I have the honour to be, Sir Your most obedient & most humble Servant   D. HUMPHREYS

RC (DNA: RG 59, DD); at head of text: "(No. 81.)"; at foot of text: "The Secretary of State &c. &c. &c."; endorsed by TJ as received 8 Nov. 1793 and so recorded in SJL. Tr (Lb in same).

TJ submitted this letter to the President on 9 Nov. 1793, and Washington returned it the same day (Washington, *Journal*, 250).

From Thomas Sim Lee

Anns. Sepr. 3. 1793

I have the Honour to enclose Copies of two Letters lately received from Citizen Moissonier Vice-Consul of the french Republic at Balt. and of my Answers[1] thereto—which you will be pleased to make known to[2] the President of the United States.

For an explanation of the principal subject of those representations, I beg leave to refer to a letter and enclosures which I have this day forwarded to the Secy. of War. I have the honor &ca   T S L

Dft (MdAA: Maryland State Papers); with second paragraph added in a clerk's hand; endorsed in part: "The Honble Thos. Jefferson Sey. of State." FC (MdAA: Letterbooks of Governor and Council). Recorded in SJL as received 11 Sep. 1793. Enclosures: (1) Lee to F. Moissonnier, Annapolis, 31 Aug. 1793, stating in reply to his letter of 25 Aug. 1793 that his representation should be directed to the President of the United States, the governor being unauthorized to make a determination in the matter, that the proceedings respecting the brig *Maxwell* were undertaken by order of the Council in consequence of instructions from the federal government, and that the actions of the admiralty and customs officers presumably were in accordance with judicial process or directions from the federal executive, in neither of which he could interfere (FC in same). (2) Moissonnier to Lee, Baltimore, 1 Sep. 1793, complaining that his letter of 25 Aug. 1793 protesting against the threatened seizure of French prizes has not been answered and that since then the state has turned over the *Maxwell* to the British consul and taken possession of the prize *Betsy* in order to restore it to its owners, insisting that these actions violated France's treaties with the United States, demanding reparations, and requesting an answer to transmit to the French minister (RC in MdAA: Scharf Papers, in French; Tr in same, in English). (3) Lee to Moissonnier,

3 Sep. 1793, stating that he had answered his 25 Aug. representation without delay, repeating that all steps taken by the state executive respecting prizes sent into Baltimore by French privateers had conformed to instructions from the federal government, "in which the interpretation of treaties is exclusively vested," and declining any discussion of the matter, which he has no authority to regulate (FC in MdAA: Letterbooks of Governor and Council). Moissonnier's 25 Aug. 1793 letter has not been found.

For the LETTER and two of the ENCLOSURES informing the SECY. OF WAR that

pursuant to his orders the *Maxwell* of Kirkcudbright, a prize sent into Baltimore by the privateer *Sans Culotte*, had been taken from its captors and delivered to British Vice-Consul Edward Thornton for restoration to its owners, see Lee to Henry Knox, 3 Sep. 1793, and James Brice, President of the Council of Maryland, to the Collector of the Customs for the Port of Baltimore, 21, 24 Aug. 1793, MdAA: Letterbooks of Governor and Council.

[1] FC: "answer."
[2] Preceding four words interlined by Lee in place of "to *submit to the Consideration of.*"

To Samuel Miller

Sep. 3. 1793.

Th: Jefferson has the honor to present his respectful compliments and thanks to the reverend Mr. Millar for the copy he was so kind as to send him of his very excellent and patriotic discourse preached on the last anniversary of independance, an occasion worthy of a good theme, and a theme worthy of it's occasion.

RC (NjP: Samuel Miller Papers); addressed: "The Revd. Samuel Millar New York"; franked, stamped, and postmarked. PrC (DLC). Tr (ViU: Edgehill-Randolph Papers); 19th-century copy.

Samuel Miller (1769-1850) had been ordained as a Presbyterian clergyman in New York City earlier this year and officiated in that city until 1813, after which he served on the faculty of Princeton Theological Seminary until his death (DAB).

The DISCOURSE Miller had sent TJ was his first publication, *A Sermon, Preached in New-York, July 4th, 1793. Being the Anniversary of the Independence of America: at the request of the Tammany Society, or Columbian Order* (New York, 1793), which among other things criticized slavery and defended the French Revolution. See Sowerby, Nos. 2815, 4681.

From James Monroe

DEAR SIR   Staunton Sepr. 3. 1793.

I parted from Mr. Madison three days past at my house. He was so kind as shew me your letter to him by Mr. Randolph. The state into which the conduct of an indiscreet man on the one part, and some very wicked men on the other, has thrown us in respect to France fills me with extreme concern. That he should not have implicitly followed your advice in all the affairs of his country is to me astonishing, as well from your known attachment to that nation and her cause as his having mentioned that fact in Richmond on his way to Phila. With respect to him he must follow the fortune he has carved out for himself. It remains for us to prevent the ill effects which menace us from that quarter, by appeasing France by every possible explanation &ca in our power; and counteracting at home the views of the party who have brought the subject to the publick view.

That the object of this party is to seperate us from France and ultimately unite us with Engld. is what I am well assured of—and that the certificate of Messrs. Jay and King was concerted at Phila. as the means of bringing the subject before the publick is likewise what I believe. Tis likewise to be presumed that they had made their arrangments for taking the subject up through out the continent so as to give the proceeding a face that would be highly disgusting to France. I consider the whole however as a mere trick and which will ultimately recoil on the authors of it. The people will soon perceive they have been abused and hurried into excesses they will be ashamed of as soon as they become cool.

The party in Richmond was soon set in motion, and from what I have understood here have reason to believe they mean to produce the most extensive effect they are capable of. Mr. Marshall had written G. Jones on the subject and the first appearances threat'ned the most furious attack on the French minister, the press &ca. b[ut] it has ended in a manner honorable to the parties concerned (the mention of that character alone excepted) and he is only classed with Messrs. Jay and King. I am persuaded the subject will likewise be taken up in Albemarle and other parts of the State, and apprehend there is some danger these latter gentlemen may be presented by the Grand jury for their improper interference in the affairs of the Executive. Satisfied I am that in a publick discussion, the sense of the community will be found, in the proportion of 9. to 1. in favor of the French cause and in reprobation of any effort to lessen its merits and interest here. I doubt not your sense of the conduct of the individual is confined to a very narrow circle, for the experiment of seperating him from his country, in every view, is of that delicate nature, that its consequences cannot be for'seen. Many here, and since his letter, and the certificate alluded to have been seen, applaud him for his zeal in pressing the cause of his country. But if they believed that you really thought him culpable, it would create a desponden[cy] that would complete the triumph of the enemies to his country and her cause.

I have been long sensible that your departure, and especially since the publick mind has been so much agitated, would be sincerely felt and vehemently opposed by a particular character. If I mistake not he fears to be left exposed, in the society of those who would be left behind with him after your departure. If your opinions had more weight upon the questions agitated, I should believe the desire for your continuance was not dictated by self-love. Permit me to add that I consider your situation, the most important and interesting that can be conceived. Its importance is felt by the opposit party in such a degree that altho' in one view they would be gratified by your retreat, yet they fear greater injury to themselves, from that event than your continuance, and therefore wish it. They know the solidity of your principles founded on reason and reflection, and in case the republican party should pass that boundary, count upon your restraining them; because they well know that that party repose an unlimited confidence in you. Your friends indeed will be happy in your continuance because they will be greatly aided by your councils. I write you in great hurry, not having indeed leasure to read it over, so that you will find an apology for any impropriety it may contain, knowing the sincerity with which I am yr. affectionate friend and servant   JAS. MONROE

RC (DLC); torn and faded in part; endorsed by TJ as received 14 Sep. 1793 and so recorded in SJL.

INDISCREET MAN: Edmond Charles Genet. Federalists John MARSHALL and Gabriel JONES had hoped the citizens of Staunton would pass resolutions similar to those approved in Richmond on 17 Aug. 1793; for the results of the Staunton meeting, see note to James Madison to TJ, 2 Sep. 1793 (second letter). PARTICULAR CHARACTER: George Washington.

From Thomas Griffin Peachy

SIR   Virginia, Petersburg, Septr. 3d. 1793.

The paper, inclosed, contains certain Resolutions of the Inhabitants of this Town and its vicinity, respecting the President's late Proclamation; they have desired me to transmit them to you, with a request that you'll be so obliging as to communicate them to the President of the United States. I am, with great respect, Sir Yr. most obt hble Servant
                                              T: G: PEACHY

RC (DLC); endorsed by TJ as received 12 Sep. 1793 and so recorded in SJL. Enclosure: Proceedings of Meetings of the Inhabitants of Petersburg and Vicinity, 31 Aug., 2 Sep. 1793, at the first of which a committee of seven, including Peachy, was chosen to draft resolutions on the Proclamation of Neutrality and the government's neutrality policy, and at the second of which the committee's resolutions expressing support for American neutrality and the Proclamation—while condemning interference by foreign powers or ministers in American internal affairs as well as any attempts to undermine confidence in the President—were unanimously approved, after which the meeting continued and adopted a resolution stating that it considered "the Combination of the despots of Europe against the Liberties of France" as tending "to destroy the political happiness of Mankind" and wished, despite its support for neutrality, that "Liberty and the Rights of Man may be the prevailing principle's throughout the Universe" (MS in DLC: Washington Papers; undated; signed by Peachy as chairman; endorsed by Bartholomew Dandridge, Jr.).

Thomas Griffin Peachy (1734-1810), clerk of Amelia County, Virginia, from 1757 to 1791, was an alderman and former mayor of Petersburg. In December 1792 he participated in an abortive effort to found a bank at Richmond (WMQ, 1st ser., I [1892], 26, III [1894], 112; CVSP, IV, 572, VI, 480-2; Hening, XIII, 599).

The context of the Petersburg meetings is described in notes to George Wythe to TJ and Edmund Randolph, 17 Aug. 1793, and James Madison to TJ, 2 Sep. 1793 (second letter).

From Elias Vanderhorst

Bristol, 3 Sep. 1793. Contrary to his 1 Sep. letter by this conveyance, in which he reported advice from Messrs. Hellicar, the most considerable corn factors here, that British ports were to have been closed to foreign wheat, they just now inform him of an announcement in the last Gazette that they will be permitted until 30 Nov. at the second low duty of six pence per quarter. This seems to be a sudden resolution by the Privy Council contrary to what it apparently first intended. He has had little trouble here with the press gangs because the regulating master Captain Hawker has always acted "with great politeness" and given up every impressed man who appeared to be American. But in Plymouth and Falmouth every means have been used to impress and detain American seamen, not only by offering them "petty offices" on ships of war, but also by confining them on receiving ships and claiming the bounty would expire if they did not enter service by a certain time, by which means many have entered contrary to inclination. He has informed Pinckney of these circumstances and everything in their power is being done to prevent a recurrence, but his agents at those ports write that they still have a good deal of trouble on this head, though less than before. People here fear a rupture with America, and he wishes he could think there were no indications of one. He will enclose one of the last newspapers if the London post arrives before he seals the letter. *4 Sep.* He quotes an extract from a 2 Sep. letter from London stating that by a proclamation of the king in council in the last Gazette the port is shut to foreign wheat until 16 Nov.; that the export of English wheat with bounty is also forbidden until then, though the port is open to all other kinds of foreign grain until 30 Nov.; and that English wheat is 38/ to 48/ and foreign wheat 32/ to 45/ per quarter. Having seen the Gazette, he vouches for the correctness of this account. Messrs. Hellicar were right in the first information they gave him but not in the second, owing they say to an ambiguity in part of the proclamation. He encloses three of the last newspapers.

RC (DNA: RG 59, CD); 2 p.; at foot of text: "The Secretary of State. Philadelphia"; endorsed by TJ as received 4 Nov. 1793 and so recorded in SJL. Enclosed in TJ to George Washington, 5 Nov. 1793.

The last consular letter TJ received from Vanderhorst, written on 12 Sep. 1793 and recorded in SJL as received 26 Nov. 1793, has not been found. Later consular letters from Vanderhorst are listed in Appendix I.

To Thomas Chittenden

Philad[elphia] 4. Sep. 1793.

The letter of July 8. which you did me the honor of writing was duly recieved, and I immediately delivered to the President that which it covered, recommending to him Mr. Knight as successor to Mr. Chipman in the office of Judge for the district of Vermont. The circumstances you stated in favor of Mr. Knight, and your own and your council's testimony on his behalf placed him on ground as favorable as it was doubtless just. The President, feeling it his duty, however to make enquiry into the comparative fitness of different persons proposed for the office, took time for that purpose, and after the best enquiries in his power to make, the qualifications of Mr. Hitchcock, the Attorney General of your state, appeared to him to preponderate, and consequently to make it his duty to nominate him, which he has accordingly done; and he has no doubt that the justice of yourself and your council will approve the motives by which he has been governed. A just sense of Mr. Knight's merit, and of the respectability of the recommendation on which he was brought forward, has rendered him anxious that these motives should be understood. I have the honor to be with great respect Your Excellency's Most obedient servt.   TH: JEFFERSON

PrC (DLC); faded, with date overwritten in ink by Benjamin Bankson; at foot of text: "H. E. Govr. Chittenden." FC (Lb in DNA: RG 59, DL).

Neither Chittenden's LETTER OF JULY 8, recorded in SJL as received from Windsor on 15 July 1793, nor the enclosed letter TO THE PRESIDENT has been found. A missing letter to TJ of 10 Aug. 1793 from Vermont Senator Moses Robinson, recorded in SJL as received from Bennington on 24 Aug. 1793, had recommended Samuel HITCH-COCK for the judgeship (Washington, *Journal*, 230). Unlocated letters from Vermont Senator Stephen R. Bradley of 24 June and from Vermont Representative Israel Smith of 2 July 1793, recorded in SJL as

received from Westminster and Rutland on 29 July 1793, may also have related to the vacant post. On 9 Sep. 1793 TJ sent Hitchcock a note enclosing his interim commission as Judge for the District Court of Vermont (PrC in DLC, in Benjamin Bankson's hand, signed by TJ, with "Samuel Hitchcock. Vermont" at foot of text and endorsement in ink by Bankson on verso; FC in Lb in DNA: RG 59, DL; not recorded in SJL). The commission is dated 3 Sep. 1793 (MS in DLC: Ethan Allan Hitchcock Papers; in a clerk's hand, with date completed by Washington; signed by Washington and countersigned by TJ). The Senate confirmed the appointment on 30 Dec. 1793 (JEP, I, 143-4).

Memorial from George Hammond

The undersigned, his Britannic Majesty's Minister Plenipotentiary to the United States, has the honor of representing to the Secretary of State—that since the 12 of July last, a very considerable French fleet has arrived in the ports of the United States—that of this fleet several ships are now cruizing in the adjacent seas—but that the principal part of it, consisting of two ships of 74 Guns each, two frigates of 36 Guns each, one ship of 20 Guns and a brig of 16 Guns is *stationed* in the port of New-York—that thence a regular succession of some of them appears to be appointed, to cruize on the coasts in the vicinity, for the purpose of annoying or intercepting, any vessels which they may happen to encounter, and which may be the property of the subjects of the powers now engaged in war with France—and that in the above mentioned city a species of jurisdiction has been established, by the person representing the actual rulers of France, which *avowedly* arrogates to itself, all the authority and functions, exercised by the directors of the marine and by the admiralty tribunals of France.

It is unnecessary for the Undersigned to observe that this situation not only presents to the Commanders of the French vessels a convenient station, from which they can direct their attacks against their enemies, but that (added, to the facility, which this government has granted them of disposing by sale in its ports of any captures they may make, and to the exclusion of privateers and even of ships of war, hostile to the ruling party of France, "*coming with their prizes*" into the American ports) it also affords them every possible advantage which they could enjoy in ports of their own country.

The undersigned has to this moment been induced to preserve the strictest silence on all these circumstances, by the hope, which he entertained, that the government of the United States would have conceived such a state of things, which he asserts is of a nature unprecedented, except in the case of Nations in alliance and acting *offensively* against a common enemy, to be incompatible both with the system of neutrality it has professed and with all its real interests. But as he has perceived with the most profound concern that these transactions have remained unnoticed, he now esteems it a duty, which he owes to the interests of the country he represents, to remonstrate against them, and to request respectfully to be informed, whether the existence of them has come to the knowledge of the executive government of the United States, or whether it be its intention to continue indefinitely to the commander of the French ships of war, those benefits, which they have hitherto enjoyed in its ports, and which they have manifested every disposition to abuse.   GEO. HAMMOND

Philadelphia 4th: September 1793

RC (DNA: RG 59, NL); in a clerk's hand, signed by Hammond; at foot of first page: "The Secretary of State"; docketed by TJ: "French ships of war cruizing from our ports"; endorsed by TJ as received 4 Sep. 1793 and so recorded in SJL. FC (Lb in PRO: FO 116/3). Tr (same, 5/1) Tr (Lb in DNA: RG 59, NL). Tr (AHN: Papeles de Estado, legajo 3895); in Spanish; attested by Josef Ignacio de Viar and Josef de Jaudenes.

The FRENCH FLEET that was STATIONED at New York had carried refugees from the Saint-Domingue slave revolt (see note to Notes of Cabinet Meeting on Edmond Charles Genet, 23 July 1793).

TJ submitted this letter to the President on 5 Sep. 1793, and Washington returned it the same day (Washington, *Journal*, 238).

Notes on Cabinet Meetings

Sep. 4. 1793. At a meeting held some days ago, some letters from the Govr. of Georgia, were read, with a consultation of officers, and a considerable expedition against the Creeks was proposed. We were all of opinion no such expedition should be undertaken. My reasons were that such a war might bring on a Span. and even an English[1] war, that for this reason the aggressions of the Creeks had been laid before the last Congress and they had not chosen to declare war, that therefore the Executive should not take on itself to do it, and[2] that according to the opinions of Pickens and Blount it was too late in the season. I thought however that a temperate and conciliatory letter should be written to the Govr. in order that we might retain the disposition of the people of the state to assist in an expedition when undertaken. The other gentlemen thought a strong letter of disapprobation should be written. Such a one was this day[3] produced, strong and reprehendatory enough, in which I thought were visible the personal enmities of Kn. and Ham. against Telfair, Gun and Jackson, the two last having been of the council of officers. The letter past without objection, being of the complection before determined.

Wayne's letter was read, proposing that 600. militia should set out from Fort Pitt to attack certain Miami towns while he marched against the principal towns. The Presidt. disapproved it because of the difficulty of concerted movements at 600. miles distance, because these 600. men might and probably would have the whole force of the Indns. to contend with, and because the object was not worth the risking such a number of men.[4] We all concurred. It appeared to me further that to begin an expedition now from Fort Pitt, the very 1st. order for which is to be given now when we have reason to believe Wayne advanced as far as Fort Jefferson would be either too late for his movements or would retard them very injuriously.—Note the letters from the Commrs. were now read, announcing the refusal of the Indns. to treat unless the Ohio were made the boundary and that they were on their return.

A letter from Govr. Clinton read, informing of his issuing a warrant to arrest Govr. Galbaud at the request of the French Consul, and that he was led to interfere because the judge of the district lived at Albany. It was proposed to write to the judge of the district that the place of his residence was not adapted to his duties, and to Clinton that Galbaud was not liable to arrest. Ham. said that by the laws of N.Y. the Govr. has the powers of a justice of peace, and had issued the warrant as such. I was against writing letters to judiciary officers. I thought them independent of the Executive, not subject to it's coercion, and therefore not obliged to attend to it's admonitions. The other three were for writing the letters, they thought it the duty of the President to see that the laws were executed, and if he found a failure in so important an officer, to communicate it to the legislature for impeachment. E.R. undertook to write the letters and I am to sign them as if mine.

The Presidt. brought forward the subject of the posts, and thought a new demand of answer should be made to Mr. Hammond. As we had not Mr. Hammond's last answer [of June 20.] on that subject, agreed to let it lie over to Monday.

Ham. proposed that on Monday we should take into consideration the fortification of the rivers and ports of the US. and that tho' the Exec. could not undertake to do it, preparatory surveys should be made to be laid before Congr.—to be considered on Monday.

The letters to Genet covering a copy of mine to Gov. Mor. [of   ][5] to the Fr. consuls threatening the revocation of their Exequaturs, to Mr. Pinckney on the additional instructions of Gr. Br. to their navy for stopping our corn, flour, &c. and to Govr. Mor. on the similar ord. of the French Natl. assembly are to be ready for Monday.

My letter to Mr. Hammond in answer to his of Aug. 30. was read and approved. Ham. wished not to narrow the ground of compensation so much as to cases after Aug. 7. Knox joined him, and by several observations shewed he did not know what the question was. He could not comprehend that the letter of Aug. 7. which promised compensation [because we had not used all the means in our power for restn.] would not be contradicted by a refusal to compensate in cases after Aug. 7. where we should actually use all the means in our power for restn., and these means should be insufficient. The letter was agreed to on R's opinion and mine, Ham. acquiescing, Knox opposing.

MS (DLC); entirely in TJ's hand; brackets in original except where noted. Included in the "Anas." Entry in SJPL: "Notes of consultn on a war against the Southern Indns. & Northern. arrest of Govr. Galbaud.—detention of posts—fortificns.—compensn."

The MEETING HELD SOME DAYS AGO took place on 31 Aug. 1793 (see Cabinet Opinions on the *Roland* and Relations with Great Britain, France, and the Creeks, 31 Aug. 1793, and note). GUN AND JACKSON: Georgia Senators James Gunn and James Jackson.

General Anthony WAYNE'S LETTER to Henry Knox, written from "Hobson's Choice Near Fort Washington" on 2 July 1793, charged British Indian agent Alexander McKee with encouraging the Western Indians to delay talks with the American peace commissioners and aspiring to unite them and the Southern Indians in a concerted effort to obtain territorial concessions from the United States, especially an Ohio River boundary; predicted that the Southern and Western Indians would hold a conference at McKee's residence at the "rapids of the Miami," where he distributes arms, ammunition, clothing, and provisions to hostile tribes; proposed to obtain 600 or 700 mounted militia volunteers from Pennsylvania's frontier counties and Ohio County, Virginia, and to send them to attack the Indian towns "at the rapids of the Miami of the Lake, (being the place where the stores and supplies for the Indians are always issued)"; suggested that the expedition would entail little risk since most Indian warriors would be collected to oppose his own army; and asked for presidential approval of his enclosed drafts of letters concerning this proposal to General John Gibson and the inspectors or county lieutenants of Washington, Westmoreland, Fayette, and Allegheny counties, Pennsylvania, and Ohio County, Virginia (PHi: Wayne Papers; see Washington, *Journal*, 217).

The LETTERS FROM THE COMMRS. who had been sent on a peace mission to the Western Indians consisted of a letter to Henry Knox dated 21 Aug. 1793 and related documents (ASP, *Indian Affairs*, I, 359-60).

The letter from Governor George Clinton of New York to the President concerning GOVR. GALBAUD is described in note to TJ to James Duane, the federal JUDGE OF THE DISTRICT of New York, 10 Sep. 1793, which Attorney General Edmund Randolph prepared and TJ signed AS IF MINE, along with a letter to Clinton of the same date. For more on the Galbaud controversy, see Edmond Charles Genet to TJ, 6 Sep. 1793, and note.

THE SUBJECT OF THE POSTS, deferred until MONDAY, was actually considered, along with drafts of TJ's letters to GENET, the FR. CONSULS, and Thomas PINCKNEY, at a meeting held on Saturday, 7 Sep. 1793 (see Cabinet Opinions on Relations with France and Great Britain, 7 Sep. 1793, and note). TJ evidently did not prepare the contemplated letter to Gouverneur Morris. TJ's letter to British minister George Hammond IN ANSWER TO HIS OF AUG. 30. was dated 5 Sep. 1793.

¹ Preceding four words interlined.
² Remainder of sentence, with "opinions" in the singular, initially written after "My reasons were" above.
³ TJ here canceled "approv."
⁴ MS: "me."
⁵ Closing bracket supplied.

From Jeremiah Wadsworth

SIR   Hartford Septr 4 1793

This mornings Post brought me your favor covering a letter to the Merchants of this place. They assembled this Evening and I here inclose a reply. I have the honor to be with great respect Your obedt Hum Sevt   JERE WADSWORTH

RC (DNA: RG 59, MLR); at foot of text: "The Hon Thos Jefferson"; endorsed by TJ as received 9 Sep. 1793 and so recorded in SJL. Enclosure: see the following document.

LETTER TO THE MERCHANTS: Circular to American Merchants, 27 Aug. 1793.

From Jeremiah Wadsworth

SIR   Hartford, September 4, 1793.

The Merchants of this place have desired[1] me to assure you they have entire confidence in Governments taking the best measures to procure redress for the injuries they have or may sustain, from the privateers of the powers at war, and to prevent their being repeated. They will lose no time in making known your communications to all whom they may concern in this state. I have the honor to be, with great respect, Your most obedient servant,   JERE. WADSWORTH

MS not found; reprinted from the Hartford *Connecticut Courant*, 9 Sep. 1793; at foot of text: "The Hon. Thomas Jefferson, Secretary of State." Also printed in the

Hartford *American Mercury*, 9 Sep. 1793. Enclosed in preceding letter.

[1] *American Mercury*: "directed."

From Tench Coxe

Northern Liberties Septr. 5th[1] 1793

Mr. Coxe takes the liberty of suggesting to Mr. Jefferson the expediency of appointing Consuls in such of the ports of the British American islands as have partaken most in the privateers, which have carried in the vessels of the U. S. vizt. St. Kitts, (with an extension of power to all the British Islands lying to Windward of porto Rico) Jamaica, New Providence (with an extension of power to all the Bahamas) and Bermuda for the whole of that Island and the little Isles or Keys around it.

Mr. Coxe requests that Mr. Jefferson will do him the honor to send him a very summary statement of the Census of the U.S. as last made. The Name of each *State*, and each *territorial Government*, with *the free persons* and *the slaves* in each, will be sufficient. An informal minute, without date or signature, extracted from the records of the Department by one of the Gentlemen in the Office will be sufficient.

RC (DLC); endorsed by TJ as received 6 Sep. 1793 and so recorded in SJL.

CENSUS OF THE U.S.: see Report on Census, 24 Oct. 1791.

[1] Digit written over "4."

To George Hammond

SIR   Philadelphia, September 5.[1] 1793.

I am honored with yours of August 30th. Mine of the 7th. of that month assured you that measures were taking for excluding, from all further asylum in our ports, vessels armed in them to cruize on nations with which we are at peace, and for the restoration of the prizes the Lovely lass, Prince William Henry, and the Jane of Dublin, and that should the measures for restitution fail in their effect, the President considered it as incumbent on the United States to make compensation for the vessels.

We are bound by our treaties with three of the belligerent[2] nations, by *all the means in our power*, to protect and defend their vessels and effects in our ports, or waters, or on the Seas near our shores and to recover and restore the same to the right owners when taken from them. If all the means in our power are used, and fail in their effect, we are not bound, by our treaties with those nations, to make compensation.

Though we have no similar Treaty with Great Britain, it was the opinion of the President that we should use[3] towards that nation the same Rule which, under this article, was to govern us with the other nations; and even to extend it to captures made *on the high Seas* and brought into our ports, if done by vessels which had been armed within them.

Having, for particular reasons, forborne to use *all the means in our power* for the restitution of the three vessels mentioned in my letter of August 7th. the President thought it incumbent on the United States to make compensation for them: and though nothing was said in that letter of other vessels taken under like circumstances, and brought in[4] after the 5th. of June, and *before the date of that letter*, yet, where the same forbearance had taken place, it was and is his opinion that compensation would be equally due.

As to prizes made under the same circumstances[5] and brought in *after the date of that letter*, the President determined that all the means in our power should be used for their restitution. If these fail, as we should not be bound by our treaties to make compensation to the other powers, in the analogous case, he did not mean to give an opinion that it ought to be done to Great Britain.[6] But still, if any cases shall arise subsequent to that date, the circumstances of which shall place them on similar ground with those before it, the President would think compensation equally incumbent on the United States.

Instructions are given to the Governors of the different States to use all the means in their power for restoring prizes of this last description[7] found within their ports.[8] Though they will of course take measures to be informed of them,[9] and the general Government has given them the aid of the custom house officers for this purpose, yet you will be sensible of the importance of multiplying the channels of their information as far as shall depend on yourself, or any persons under your direction, in order that the governors may use the means in their power, for making restitution. Without knowledge of the capture, they cannot restore it. It will always be best to give the notice to them directly: but any information which you shall be pleased to send to me also, at any time, shall be forwarded to them as quickly as distance will permit.

Hence you will percieve, Sir, that the President contemplates *restitution* or *compensation* in the cases *before* the 7th. of august, and, *after* that date, *restitution*,[10] if it can be effected by any means in our power: and that it will be important that you should substantiate the fact that such prizes are in our ports or waters.

Your list of the privateers, illicitly armed in our ports, is, I believe correct.

With respect to losses by detention, waste, spoliation, sustained by vessels taken as beforementioned between the dates of June 5. and Aug. 7. it is proposed, as a provisional measure, that the Collector of the Customs of the district, and the British Consul, or any other person you please, shall appoint persons to establish the value of the vessel and Cargo, at the times of her capture, and of her arrival in the port into which she is brought, according to their value in that port.[11] If this shall be agreeable to you and you will be pleased to signify it to me, with the names of the prizes[12] understood to be of this description,[13] instructions will be given accordingly[14] to the Collectors of the Customs where the respective vessels are. I have the honor to be with great respect, Sir, Your most obedient and most humble servant

PrC (DLC); in the hand of George Taylor, Jr., unsigned, with dateline completed by him (see note 1 below); at foot of first page: "The minister plenipotentiary of Great Britain." Dft (DLC); entirely in TJ's hand, except for date added by Taylor; unsigned; only the most important emendations have been recorded below. Tr (DNA: RG 46, Senate Records, 3d Cong., 1st sess.). FC (Lb in DNA: RG 59, DL). Tr (Lb in PRO: FO 116/3). Tr (same, 5/1). Tr (same). Tr (same); extract consisting of paragraphs 2-4. Tr (MiU-C: Melville Papers). Tr (NNC: John Jay Letterbook); misdated 5 Sep. 1794. Recorded in SJPL. Printed in *Message*, 74-5.

On the previous day TJ had submitted this letter to a meeting of the President and the Cabinet, a majority of which approved it (Notes on Cabinet Meetings, 4 Sep. 1793). A text was annexed to the Jay Treaty in order to clarify the section of Article 7 of that agreement dealing with compensation for British merchant ships captured by French privateers fitted out in the United States (Miller, *Treaties*, II, 253, 265-6).

[1] Day inserted in ink by Taylor in space left blank in manuscript.

[2] In Dft TJ here canceled "parties."

[3] In Dft TJ first wrote "it was the intention of the President to use" and then altered it to read as above.

[4] Preceding three words interlined in Dft.

[5] Preceding four words interlined in Dft in place of "by vessels armed in our ports."

[6] Remainder of paragraph written in the margin of Dft.

[7] Preceding five words interlined in Dft in place of "vessels."

[8] In Dft TJ here canceled "which have been taken on the high seas by vessels armed in the US. or which have been taken within our waters or on our coasts by any vessels."

[9] Word interlined in Dft in place of "such prizes within their respective limits."

¹⁰ In Dft TJ here canceled "only."

¹¹ In Dft TJ wrote in the margin next to this sentence: "The Collector of the customs and the Consul by themselves or persons of their appointment to fix the value of the vessel and cargo at the times of the capture and of her arrival in the port into which she is brought, according to the prices current in that port. This to be provisory only."

¹² Word interlined in Dft in place of "vessels."

¹³ In Dft TJ here canceled "orde."

¹⁴ Word interlined in Dft.

From Edmund Randolph

SIR   German Town Sepr. 5. 1793.

The interruption, which the contagious disorder now prevailing in Philadelphia, has given to my residence there, is the cause of the delay, which has occurred in my examination of Mr. Hammonds last memorial on Pagan's case.

I beg leave to refer you to my former communications on this head; that I may not repeat them here unnecessarily.

It is true, that I considered an application to the Supreme fœderal court, indispensable; and that it has been unsuccessful. Whether it was pressed in the most advantageous form, I undertake not to decide; but while I shall ever acknowledge the abilities and integrity of Pagan's counsel, I still adhere to my former representation.

It is no less true, that the refusal of a writ of error[1] evinced the sense of the judges, that the case was not of a nature susceptible of relief by process of law,[2] issuing from the Supreme court of the U. S.

It is then reduced to its original State; namely, a question began in the courts of Massachusetts, where it has run thro' all the forms of proceeding, and has been decided against a British Subject. He complains of injustice; but of no conduct in the judges[3] founded on impure motives. To this point my quotation from the argument[4] on the Silesia loan is applied; and farther I must remark, that[5] if the judges have erred, and there be an appeal, it is the business of Mr. Pagan to appeal; if there be no appeal according to the laws of Massachusetts, no fœderal authority can give one,[6] and therefore no relief can be had in our courts.

Such, sir, is the state of our jurisprudence with respect to this case; and as Mr. Hammond seems now to make it an affair of negotiation, upon the ground, that the American courts ought not to have assumed a jurisdiction over it, and that, if they might, the Armistice was misinterpreted, the subject is no longer[7] within the Sphere of my office. If however you mean to discuss these two questions, and my aid can be useful, it is at your command. I have the honor &c

EDMD. RANDOLPH

RC (DNA: RG 59, Letters from and Opinions of the Attorneys General); at head of text: "To the Secretary of State"; with penciled notation by TJ: "to be copd. &

press copd."; endorsed by TJ as received 7
Sep. 1793 and so recorded in SJL. PrC of
Tr (DLC); in a clerk's hand. Tr (Lb in
DNA: RG 59, DL). Tr (Lb in PRO: FO
116/3). Tr (same, 5/1). Enclosed in TJ to
George Hammond, 13 Sep. 1793.

HAMMOND'S LAST MEMORIAL: Hammond
to TJ, 19 Aug. 1793. ARGUMENT ON THE
SILESIA LOAN: see Randolph to TJ, 12 Apr.
1793. See also note to Hammond to TJ, 26
Nov. 1791.

[1] Preceding four words interlined in
place of "relief."
[2] Randolph here canceled "But by what
process of law? By process."
[3] Preceding three words interlined.
[4] Sentence through "argu" interlined in
place of "The [. . .] is made to correct."
[5] Preceding six words interlined in place
of "for."
[6] Remainder of sentence inserted.
[7] Randolph here canceled "of a judicial
nature."

George Taylor, Jr., to Bartholomew Dandridge, Jr.

Thursday 5 Septr. 1793

G. Taylor Jr. presents his respectful Compliments to Mr. Dandridge—and informs him that Mr. Jefferson desired the Commissions to be filled up agreeably to the Presidents desire on the day the present ones should determine, which will be on the 26. of the present Month. This has accordingly been done having all been commissioned on that day in 1789.

Will Mr. Dandridge be so obliging as to send 100 Blank Sea letters? We want that number to make up the 500 per Month with which we furnish the Treasury.

RC (DNA: RG 59, MLR); addressed:
"B. Dandridge Esqr."; endorsed by Dandridge. Tr (Lb in same, SDC).

The COMMISSIONS were for Federal marshals, who served four-year terms at the pleasure of the President (White, *Federalists*, 411-15).
On 4 Sep. 1793 TJ had written a brief circular letter to certain marshals announcing the President's desire to continue their services and enclosing their commissions (RC to Allan McLane in NHi, in Benjamin Bankson's hand, signed by TJ, addressed to "Allen McLean"; FC in Lb in DNA: RG

59, DL, with the following recipients listed at foot of text: Robert Forsyth of Georgia, Isaac Huger of South Carolina, Samuel McDowell, Jr., of Kentucky, Thomas Lowrey of New Jersey, Philip B. Bradley of Connecticut, Nathaniel Ramsay of Maryland, and Allan McLane of Delaware; not recorded in SJL). Bradley acknowledged his reappointment in a brief letter to TJ of 15 Sep. 1793 (RC in same, MLR; endorsed by TJ as received 24 Oct. 1793 and so recorded in SJL). See also Washington, *Journal*, 236; Memorandums to Bankson, [15 Sep. 1793].

From Anonymous

SIR   [ca. 6 Sep. 1793]

In presence of John Samuel Sherburne Esqr. of New Hampshire, it was mentioned that you was a Deist. The pleasure with which he received the Intelligence, leads the writer of this to mention the fact—that you may early see whether he will not indeavour by artfully playing with such an idea—to warp you to his purposes.

The truth or falsehood of the assertion, is not hereby intended to be credited or disbelieved.

RC (DLC); undated and unsigned; addressed: "The Honble. Mr Jefferson Secretary of State In The United States"; postmarked: "Charlestown Sept. 6. 93."; franked; endorsed by Benjamin Bankson as received 16 Sep. 1793; endorsed by TJ as a letter from "Anonymous" received 2 Oct.

1793 and so recorded in SJL. Enclosed in Bankson to TJ, 23 Sep. 1793.

SHERBURNE was a Republican member of the United States House of Representatives from New Hampshire, 1793-97 (*Biog. Dir. Cong.*).

From John Barret, Benjamin Harrison, Jr., and James Heron

SIR   Richmond 6th Sepr 1793

The Mayor of this City has handed to us your favor of the 27th. Ulto., we have had a meeting to day and taken the proper Steps to communicate your Information to the different trading Towns of this State. That meeting have directed us (their Committee) to make our acknowledgements to Government for it's Attention to our Interests, and to thank you for the Polite communication, these Orders we most cheerfully and cordially, obey, for we are Sir with the highest sentiments of Respect your most Obedt Serts

JNO BARRET
BENJ HARRISON JR
J HERON

RC (DNA: RG 59, MLR); endorsed by TJ as received 12 Sep. 1793 and so recorded in SJL.

John Barret (1748-1830), Benjamin Harrison, Jr. (ca. 1751-99), and James

Heron (1754-1829) were Richmond merchants. Barret served as mayor of Richmond in 1791, 1793, and 1798 (Marshall, *Papers*, I, 356n, 399n, 408n; VMHB, XXXV [1927], 89-92).

From James Currie

DR SIR   Richmond. Sepr. 6th. 1793

It is sometime since I had the honor of a line from you. In your last, I was inform'd that, my suit versus Griffin would probably be determin'd last April Court. Not having heard since leaves me in doubt whether any thing has been done in it. Will be glad to be inform'd when you are at leisure its situation and still continue to sollicit your friendly attention to it. We were in hopes of the pleasure of seeing you in this country during the Fall, but I have lately been inform'd you are not expected so soon. From what the news papers inform us you seem to be surrounded with tumultuous Politecians in no small number. It is much to be wished and greatly hoped that Europe will soon terminate their Wars that we may enjoy peace in Reality. With best Wishes for your health & happiness I have the honor to subscribe myself Dr Sir Your most Ob & V. H. Servt. JAMES CURRIE

RC (MHi); endorsed by TJ as received 12 Sep. 1793 and so recorded in SJL.

From Edmond Charles Genet

MR. Newyork le 6. 7bre. 1793.

Je viens De Decouvrir la plus affreuse[1] conspiration qui ait été formée contre le Succès Des armées de la republique francaise.[2] Je viens de Decouvrir tous les fils et toutes les preuves De la trame infernale qui, depuis deux mois, tenait dans vos ports l'escadre française dans un etat de nullité; De cette trame[3] qui menaçait non Seulement la Sûreté De nos vaisseaux, mais encore celle De nos possessions coloniales. Les traitres galbaut tangui et plusieurs autres scelerats,[4] non contents D'avoir fait verser à St. Domingue le Sang d'un peuple immense, non contents D'y avoir causé à la republique[5] la perte D'un milliard, concertaient ici, à baltimore, et à philadelphie le projet de faire concourir nos forces[6] à l'affreux plan que meditaient des hommes que leurs crimes ont fait chasser De leur patrie, De retourner à St. Domingue[7] pour y renouveller les horreurs et les massacres[8] qu'ils y ont déjà fait commettre. J'ai été informé que le Succès que Se promettaient les colons de ce plan[9] n'était rien moins que fondé, ainsi que l'avait été celui dont on vient de tenter l'execution aux îles du vent,[10] Sur l'alliance qu'on Se proposait De faire avec les ennemis, actuellement en guerre avec la republique,[11] les anglais, et les espagnols.

La france, Monsieur, Dans Des circonstances pareilles, a exigé, en europe, Des puissances qui l'avoisinent, qu'elles S'opposassent à tout préparatif qui pourroit Se faire chez elles, par les emigrés, contre Sa Sûreté. Elle espère d'un gouvernement ami et allié[12] qu'il Suffira[13] de lui Denoncer[14] les complots qui Se forment contr'elle Sur Son propre territoire, pour obtenir de lui tous les moyens propres à les déjouer.[15] J'ai effectué le Desarmement Du vaisseau qui etait dans l'etat De la rebellion la plus allarmante: mais les éxcitateurs[16] Se Sont enfuis, et j'apprends qu'ils Se repandent Sur le continent où ils ne peuvent être que très nuisibles, tant à la tranquillité du pays qu'aux interets de leur patrie.[17] Je demande en conséquence au gouvernement fédéral de prendre les me-sures les plus actives et les plus efficaces pour les faire arreter et prévenir ainsi les attentats aux quels ils pourraient Se porter.

Le gouverneur et les magistrats De New york ont delivré des War-rants contre tangui galbaut conscience et bonne:[18] mais l'un et l'autre ont echappé à l'activité des[19] personnes envoyées pour les arreter. Les traitres fuyent le Supplice qui était reservé à leurs forfaits[20] et sans doute ils vont S'occuper de nouveaux moyens d'executer les complots qu'ils ont formé contre la france. J'ai des renseignemens positifs qu'ils Sont encore Sur les terres des etats unis, et comme l'effet des Warrants de New york Se borne aux limites de cet etat, je Demande Specialement au[21] gouvernement fédéral, contre les nommés galbaut, tangui, cons-cience, et bonne, dont je joins ici le Signalement, des ordres d'arresta-tion[22] dont l'effet puisse S'étendre à toute la partie Du continent Dépendante des etats unis. Je lui Demande encore[23] d'exercer la Sur-veillance la plus active Sur les complots que je lui dénonce.[24]

Puisse cet acte eclatant, ne laissant pas de doute Sur la Sincerité Des voeux que fait[25] le gouvernement des etats unis pour les Succès De[26] la republique française, faire trembler tous les traitres[27] que[28] mon éstime pour votre pays m'a fait peut être trop mépriser et qui se servent de l'accès que leur offre[29] la bonté et l'hospitalité de votre nation pour cons-pirer[30] dans son sein même et dans le cercle de ses personnages les plus[31] élevés[32] contre la france et contre la liberté generale des peuples.[33]

2d Dft (DLC: Genet Papers); in the hand of Jean Baptiste Cassan, unsigned, with dateline, salutation, and revisions by Genet; above salutation in Genet's hand: "Le Cit genet &c ⟨au Cit⟩ à Mr Jefferson se-cretaire d'Etat des Etats unis"; only the most significant emendations have been re-corded below. Dft (same); undated; en-tirely in Cassan's hand; lacks final para-graph and otherwise varies from 2d Dft (see notes below). FC (same). FC (same). Tr (AMAE: CPEU, xxxviii); certified by Genet. Tr (same, xxxix); signed by Genet; with minor variations. Tr (DNA: RG 46, Senate Records, 3d Cong., 1st sess.); in En-glish. Recorded in SJL as received 11 Sep. 1793. Printed with translation in *Message*, 24 (App.), 79-80; translation printed in ASP, *Foreign Relations*, i, 177. The enclosed descriptions have not been found, but pre-sumably they were similar either to the ones included in Enclosure No. 1 listed at TJ to James Duane, 10 Sep. 1793, or to the vari-ant texts included in Genet to an unidenti-fied correspondent, 30 Aug. 1793 (DLC: Genet Papers). Enclosed in TJ to George Washington, 15 Sep. 1793.

Thomas François GALBAUD, the recently ousted governor of Saint-Domingue, his aide de camp CONSCIENCE, and the French corporal BONNE were among the refugees from the slave revolt on that island who had arrived at New York City early in August with a French fleet. Genet soon became con-vinced that the three men were conspirators against the French Republic; after they es-caped from confinement aboard the French fleet and fled to Canada, he enlisted New York State authorities in his efforts to arrest them as deserters under the consular con-vention of 1788 between France and the United States (see TJ to George Clinton, and TJ to James Duane, both 10 Sep. 1793, and notes). Galbaud subsequently denied Genet's charge that he was involved in a counterrevolutionary conspiracy with Claude Corentin Tanguy de la Boissière, a refugee journalist from the slave revolt on that island who later this month began pub-lication in Philadelphia of the *Journal des Révolutions de la Partie Française de Saint-Domingue*, a newspaper that was sharply critical of the French minister (Keller, "Ge-net Mission," 343-8, 359-63; Ammon, *Ge-*

net Mission, 121-5; Childs, *French Refugee Life*, 51-5).

According to SJL, TJ received another letter of 6 Sep. 1793 from Genet on the "tonnage of vessels" that was delivered by Bournonville on 11 Sep. 1793 but has not been found.

[1] Dft: "horrible."

[2] In Dft Cassan here canceled "et ⟨*l'etablissement du gouvernement republicain qu'elle vient de Se donner*⟩ l'affermissement de son nouveau gouvernement."

[3] Dft reads "de cette trame infernale qui tenait dans un etat de nullite l'escadre francaise qui Se trouve en ce moment dans vos ports et."

[4] Preceding four words interlined by Genet.

[5] Dft: "à la france ⟨*dans l'incendie du cap*⟩."

[6] Dft: "les forces de la republique."

[7] Dft: "qui Se meditait entre des hommes que leurs crimes ont fait expulser de St Domingue, De retourner dans cette colonie."

[8] Remainder of sentence interlined in place of "qu'ils viennent d'y commettre." In Dft Cassan here added "du 20 juin dernier et jours Suivants."

[9] Sentence to this point in Dft interlined in place of "L'execution de ce plan."

[10] Preceding clause written in the margin by Cassan in place of a heavily canceled and illegible passage.

[11] In Dft Cassan first wrote "les ennemis de La republique Française" and then altered it to read as above.

[12] Cassan first wrote "d'un peuple ami" and then altered it to read as above.

[13] Genet here canceled "à Son ministre."

[14] Preceding two words interlined in place of "de denoncer au gouvernement De ce peuple."

[15] Remainder of paragraph lacking in Dft.

[16] Word interlined by Genet in place of "Deserteurs."

[17] Preceding two words interlined by Cassan in place of "la france."

[18] Cassan first wrote "tanqui et galbaut" before Genet revised the passage to read as above.

[19] Cassan here canceled "connestables."

[20] Remainder of sentence lacking in Dft.

[21] Preceding two words interlined by Cassan in place of "au."

[22] In Dft Cassan first wrote "Je vous demande des ordres d'arrestation contre ces deux individus" and then altered it to read as above.

[23] Sentence to this point in Dft reads "Je demande aussi au gouvernement federal au nom de l'amitié et de l'alliance qui unissent ⟨*les deux peuples*⟩ la France et les etats unis."

[24] Cassan here canceled "et de revêtir de son Sceau tous les warrants déjà delivrés ou à delivrer par les gouverneurs Des Different états contre les personnes qui leur ont été ou qui ⟨*pourraient leur être*⟩ leur seront denoncés par les agens francais, afin que cet acte eclatant fasse trembler les traîtres qui conspirent ici contre leur patrie, et ne leur laisse pas de doute Sur les voeux Sinceres que font les etats unis pour les Succès de la republique francaise."

[25] Clause to this point interlined by Cassan in place of "dissipant tout doute sur les voeux Sinceres que font les etats."

[26] Cassan here canceled "l'armée."

[27] Genet here canceled "qui conspirent ici contre leur patrie" and wrote the remainder of the text.

[28] Before this word Genet canceled "Car J'ai la certitude que des hommes."

[29] Genet here canceled "un peuple bon."

[30] Genet here canceled "dans le sein même d'un peuple libre et notre allie."

[31] Genet here canceled "distingués."

[32] Genet here canceled "en dignités."

[33] This paragraph lacking in Dft.

From George Hammond

SIR   Philadelphia 6th September 1793

I have had the honor of receiving your letter, dated yesterday, and I request you to accept my acknowledgements for the full exposition which you have given me of the intentions of this government, relative to prizes taken by privateers fitted out in ports of the United States.

Should any future captures be made by armed vessels of this description, I shall certainly employ every exertion in my power to obtain the evidence, requisite to substantiate the facts of any such captures. In the mean time, Sir, I esteem it an act of justice on my part, to offer my testimony to the scrupulous fidelity and vigilance, with which the collectors of the Customs have discharged the duty, imposed on them by the President's directions, in regard to this object: Since no instance has yet occurred, in which those officers do not appear to have pursued the most effectual means for conveying, to the Governors of the respective States, the earliest intelligence of the arrival in their districts of vessels, that had been captured by any of the privateers in question.

With respect to the mode you have prescribed of ascertaining the value of "losses by detention, waste, or spoliation, sustained by vessels taken, as before mentioned, between the dates of June 5th.[1] and August 7th."[2]—it appears to me perfectly just and satisfactory: And I shall in consequence thereof communicate it to his Majesty's Consuls, in order that they may arrange with the Collectors of the customs, in the districts in which they reside, the measures necessary to carry it into immediate operation.

In addition to the list of privateers, illicitly fitted out in ports of the United States, which accompanied my letter of the 30 ulto., I have lately received information that another, named the Industry, has within the last five or six weeks been armed, manned and equipped in the port of Baltimore. I have the honor to be with sentiments of great respect Sir, Your most obedient humble Servant   GEO. HAMMOND

RC (DNA: RG 59, NL); in a clerk's hand, signed by Hammond; at foot of first page: "Mr Jefferson"; with notation by TJ: "manner of fixg damages by spoliation &c"; endorsed by TJ as received 7 Sep. 1793 and so recorded in SJL. FC (Lb in PRO: FO 116/3). Tr (same, 5/1). Tr (Lb in DNA: RG 59, NL).

[1] RC and all other texts: "7th."
[2] Quotation mark supplied.

Memorial from George Hammond

The undersigned, his Britannic Majesty's Minister plenipotentiary to the United States, has the honor of submitting to the Secretary of state the accompanying papers, relative to the capture, by the French brig le Cerf, of the British brigantine the William Tell, which, with its cargo, is the property of subjects of Great Britain, resident in the island of Dominica.

From these papers it is manifest, that this vessel was taken at the distance of about half a mile from the shore of the American coast, and consequently under the protection of the American territory, and that the Marshal of the district of New-York was prevented, by the menaces of the principal agent of the actual rulers of France, from taking it into his custody, and from thereby subjecting the validity of the capture to the decision of a Court of judicature in the United States. In its present situation therefore, the restitution of this vessel, and of its cargo, can be only effected by the intervention of the executive government of this country.

It would certainly be improper for the undersigned to offer any observations on the various aggressions on the sovereignty of the United States, which a review of this single case presents—in the particulars of the capture itself—in the extent of the powers arrogated by the pretended tribunal of the French Consul—and in the nature of the threats thrown out by the person representing, in this country, the ruling party of France. At the same time he conceives it to be strictly within the line of his duty, to express the solicitude, which, from a consideration of the last mentioned circumstance, he naturally feels, to obtain as early and explicit a knowledge of the determination of this government, as may be convenient, on the subject of the memorial, which he had the honor of presenting on the 4th. of this month. For if, added to the establishment of a regular succession of cruizers from New-York, and to the facility, which this government has afforded them of disposing of their prizes, the Commanders of the French ships of war exercise the right also of opposing their force to the functions, of a judicial officer acting under the authority of the United States, exerted for the purpose of procuring justice to British subjects, it is become more and more important for the undersigned to learn with as little delay as possible—whether it be the intention of the executive government of the United States to grant to the French ships of war the permission of an *indefinite* continuance within its ports.

Philadelphia 6th September 1793   GEO. HAMMOND

RC (DNA: RG 59, NL); in a clerk's hand, signed by Hammond; at foot of first page: "The Secretary of State"; with penciled notation by George Taylor, Jr.: "to be filed with the other letters"; endorsed by TJ as received 7 Sep. 1793 and so recorded in SJL. FC (Lb in PRO: FO 116/3). Tr (same, 5/1). Tr (Lb in DNA: RG 59, NL). Enclosures: (1) Extract from the Protest of Charles Choler, New York, 3 Sep. 1793, stating, as master of the Dominican brigantine *William Tell*, that on 29 Aug., while "nearly opposite to the Light House on Sandy Hook and not farther from the shore than one Mile and he verily Beleives Scarcely more than half a mile," which he supposed to be within the jurisdiction and under the protection of the United States, his vessel was fired at and boarded by armed men from the French ship-of-war *Cerf*, Captain Emeriau, with 10 guns and 2 swivels mounted; that the boarding party took possession of the *William Tell*, as well as its cargo and papers, in the name of the French Republic, and brought him, all but three members of his crew, and two Negroes belonging to the ship's owners to the *Cerf* as prisoners; and that, despite his repeated protests that these actions violated the law of nations, the *Cerf* took the *William Tell* to New York, where it was being held as a prize and where the day before he was allowed to go ashore after giving security that he would return on demand. (2) Deposition of Isaac Sears, New York, 4 Sep. 1793, stating that, after learning on 31 Aug. that the brig *Cerf* had captured the *William Tell*, owned by Samuel Chollet and Peregrine Bourdieu of Dominica, within the territorial limits and protection of the United States—about half a mile from Sandy Hook—he and Paschal N. Smith, New York City merchants and agents for the owners, on advice of counsel, informed Hauterive, the French consul, that they intended to notify the executive authority of the United States of the capture and requested his assurance that the ship would remain in his custody until it had acted; that after Hauterive, with Edmond Charles Genet present but silent, insisted that the case must be decided by his consular tribunal, they filed a libel in the District Court of New York seeking restitution of the ship, cargo, and two slaves, and obtained a precept authorizing the marshal of the New York district to take custody of the ship and cargo pending the outcome of the suit; and that when the marshal went with him this day to serve the order on Hauterive, "Mr.

Genet assumed the Business and observed that an Agreement having taken Place between him and the President by which the Consuls of France had a Right to keep Possession of all Prizes taken by French Vessels, he would not permit the Marshal to have any Thing to do with the said Brig William Tell—that he had given Orders to the Squadron in Hudson's River to prevent any Person taking the said Brig from the Protection she was then under—and that he *hoped* no Person would attempt it" (MSS in same, in clerical hands, with No. 1 bearing subjoined notarization of 4 Sep. 1793 by John Wilkes of New York, before whom the original was made, and No. 2 signed by Sears and attested by Mayor Richard Varick; Trs in Lb in same; Trs in PRO: FO 5/1; Trs in DLC: Genet Papers, in French).

TJ submitted this memorial to the President and the Cabinet on 7 Sep. 1793 (Cabinet Opinions on Relations with France and Great Britain, 7 Sep. 1793).

Henry Knox's Report on Defense, with Opinion by Jefferson and Edmund Randolph

The Secretary of War humbly reports to the President of the United States

That the following measures appear necessary to be taken in order in some degree to place the United States in a situation to guard themselves from injury by any of the belligerent powers of Europe.

1st. To have all the small arms of the United States put in order for immediate use.

2dly. To have all the cannon in possession of the United States whether for the field or for batteries, either new mounted or repaired as the case may require.

3d. To purchase one hundred tons of Lead.

4th. To purchase one hundred tons of Saltpetre or the equivalent in Gun powder.

5th. To have the useless brass cannon in the arsenal at Springfield cast into field pieces, and to have the same mounted.

6th. To engage one thousand rifles to be made.

7th. To remove the surplus arms and stores from Philadelphia to Trenton.

8th. To remove the surplus stores from west point to Albany.

9th. To make certain repairs at Forts Putnam, and Clinton at[1] west point on Hudson's river, so as to prevent its being surprized or insulted

Most of these measures have been put in train in pursuance of certain verbal directions from the President of the United States, but the subscriber humbly conceives it proper to submit a connected view thereof for his approbation, as it will be necessary to prepare estimates of the expences attendant thereon, in order to be laid before the next session of Congress.

All which is respectfully submitted.

War Department   H KNOX
September 6. 1793.   Secy of War

We are of opinion that the preceding measures should be carried into effect.   TH: JEFFERSON
                                                               EDM: RANDOLPH

MS (DLC: Washington Papers); in a clerk's hand, revised and signed by Knox, with subjoined opinion in TJ's hand signed by TJ and Randolph; endorsed by Bartholomew Dandridge, Jr.

[1] Preceding five words interlined by Knox.

To David Rittenhouse

Sep. 6. 93.

Th: Jefferson presents his friendly respects to Mr. Rittenhouse. He has two young ladies at his house whose time hangs heavily on their hands, and the more so, as their drawing master cannot attend them. If Mr. Rittenhouse then does not take his Camera obscura with him into the country, Th:J. will thank him to permit them the use of it a few days, that they may take a few lessons in drawing from nature.

RC (PWacD: Feinstone Collection, on deposit PPAmP); addressed: "Mr. Rittenhouse"; with unrelated calculations by Rittenhouse on address cover. Not recorded in SJL.

The TWO YOUNG LADIES were probably TJ's daughter Mary and her friend and schoolmate Sarah Corbin Cropper (TJ to Mary Jefferson, 15 Dec. 1793; Jennings C. Wise, *Col. John Wise of England and Virginia [1617-1695]: His Ancestors and Descendants* [Richmond, 1918], 96). On 3 Jan. 1794 TJ purchased this or another CAMERA OBSCURA from Rittenhouse (MB, 3 Jan. 1794; Stein, *Worlds*, 426-7).

Memorial from F. P. Van Berckel

Le Soussigné Resident de Leurs Hautes Puissances les Seigneurs Etats Géneraux des Provinces-Unies a l'honneur de representer à Monsieur le Secretaire d'Etat: Que depuis l'arrivée d'une Flotte Françoise dans les ports des Etats-Unis, un nombre de Ces Vaisseaux, Consistant en deux de 74 Canons et plusieurs Fregates ont pris poste dans le port de New York, dans le dessin d'etablir une Croisiere reguliere Sur la Cote adjacente, afin d'intercepter les bâtimens appartenans aux Sujets des Puissances actuellement en Guerre avec la France; et que la personne gerant les affaires du parti dominant en France vient d'Établir dans la Ville de New York une espèce de Jurisdiction, S'arrogeant toute l'autorité et les fonctions exercés par les tribunaux d'Amirauté de France.

Le Soussigné ne Se permettra aucune remarque Sur les avantages que le Gouvernement des Etats Unis a jugé à propos d'accorder aux Vaisseaux François par dessus Ceux des autres Nations; il Se Contentera d'observer, que la faculté qui leur a été donnée de vendre leurs prises dans les ports des Etats Unis, Sans aucune forme de procès, a occasionné des pertes Considerables à quelques Negocians Hollandois, en Ce que les moyens leur ont été ôtés de faire valoir leurs droits Contre l'illégalité des prises; et que la disposition que les Agens François ont déjà trop manifestée d'abuser de l'indulgence accordée à leurs Vaisseaux, laissant peu de doute Sur leurs intentions futures, le Soussigné Croiroit manquer à Son devoir, S'il négligoit de fixer l'attention du Gouvernement Sur un ordre de Choses, par lequel les interets de la Nation qu'il représente Sont Compromis. Il Se fonde Simplement Sur le Système de neutralité, que le Gouvernement des Etats Unis a adopté; Système dont le but est d'agir impartialement vis-à-vis de toutes les Puissances en Guerre, et qu'il Conçoit être incompatible avec les avantages décidés dont la Flotte Françoise jouit dans le port de New York, au préjudice d'autres Nations non moins Amies des Etats Unis, et parmi les quelles Celle, qu'il représente, a été une des premières à donner les marques non equivoques de Son Amitié envers Eux.

Le Soussigné Se flatte que le Gouvernement des Etats Unis daignera gracieusement reflêchir Sur Ce qui dessus, et Le prie respectueusement de vouloir le mettre à même d'informer Son Souverain des intentions du Gouvernement à Cet egard.

Fait à Philadelphie Ce 6e. Septembre 1793.   F. P. van Berckel

RC (DNA: RG 360, PCC); endorsed by TJ as received 7 Sep. 1793, but recorded in SJL as a document of 7 Sep. 1793 received that date.

Cabinet Opinions on Relations with France and Great Britain

At a meeting at the Presidents Sep. 7. 1793.

A circular letter from the Secretary of state to the Consuls and Vice Consuls of France, informing them that their Exequaturs will be revoked if they repeat certain proceedings, also one to Mr. Genet covering a copy of the letter of the Secretary of state to Mr. Gouverneur Morris desiring the recall of Mr. Genet, were read and approved.

A letter from the Governr. of Georgia to the Secy. of state dated Aug. 21. 1793. was read, communicating the demand by the Vice Consul of France in Georgia of certain individuals under prosecution in a court of justice. It is the opinion that he be answered that the law must take it's course.

A Memorial from Mr. Hammond dated Sep. 6. complaining of the capture of the British brig the William Tell by the French brig le Cerf, within the limits of the protection of the US. and the refusal of the French minister and Consul to have the prize delivered into the hands of a marshal charged with process from a court[1] to arrest her, was read. It is the opinion that a letter be written to Mr. Genet calling for evidence in the cases of the vessels heretofore reclaimed and not yet finally decided on, and which were permitted to remain in the hands of the French Consuls in the meantime, informing him that the letter of June 25. was not intended to authorize[2] opposition to the officers, or orders, of courts respecting vessels taken within the limits of our protection, that therefore the brig William Tell ought to be delivered into the hands of the officer charged to arrest her, and that in the event of the court's deciding that it has no jurisdiction of the case, as in that of the ship William whereon the letter of June 25. was written, she may again be replaced in the Consul's hands till the Executive shall have decided thereon.

A letter from Lt. Govr. Wood dated Aug. 29. stating that the French vessel the Orion was arrived in Norfolk and had brought in the Sans Culottes as a prize, and doubting whether from the particular circumstances of this prize she came within the general orders heretofore given. It is the opinion that the situation of the Sans culottes is the same in respect to England and France as any other French vessel not fitted in our ports, and therefore that the Orion is within the 17th. article of our treaty, and the rules heretofore given on that subject.

A Memorial from Mr. Hammond dated Sep. 4. was read complaining of the long stay of a French fleet in New York, that a regular succession of them appears to be appointed for cruizing on the coasts, that a jurisdiction over prizes is exercised by the French Consuls, and desiring to be informed whether it be the intention of the Executive to permit this indefinitely. It is the opinion that Mr. Hammond be informed that effectual measures are taken to put an end to the exercise of admiralty jurisdiction by the French Consuls, that the French have by treaty a right to come into our ports with their prizes, exclusively, that they have also a right by treaty to enter our ports for any urgent necessity, that this right is exclusive as to privateers but not so as to public vessels of war[3] and has therefore not been denied to British ships of war[4] nor has the Executive as yet prescribed to either any limits to the time they may remain in their ports.

A letter from Mr. Bordman at Boston dated Sep. 4. was read complaining of the capture of the schooner Flora an American vessel by the Roland, one of the illicit privateers. It is the opinion he must seek redress in the courts of law.

The draught of a letter to Mr. Pinckney on the Additional instructions of the court of St. James's dated June 8. 93. was read and approved.

A Question was proposed by the President Whether we ought not to enquire from Mr. Hammond if he is prepared to give an answer on the subject of the inexecution of the treaty? It is the opinion that it will be better to await the arrival of the next packet, then to make the application to Mr. Hammond, and if he be not prepared to answer, that Mr. Pinckney be instructed to remonstrate on the subject to the British court.

TH: JEFFERSON

H KNOX

EDM: RANDOLPH

MS (DLC: Washington Papers); in TJ's hand, signed by TJ, Knox, and Randolph; endorsed by George Washington. Dft (DLC: TJ Papers, 92: 15840); undated; entirely in TJ's hand; consists of slightly variant version of last sentence of fifth paragraph written on a small sheet containing on verso TJ's Notes for Replies to Edmond Charles Genet and George Hammond, [7-9 Sep. 1793].

CIRCULAR LETTER: Circular to French Consuls and Vice-Consuls, 7 Sep. 1793. ONE TO MR. GENET: TJ to Edmond Charles Genet, [7 Sep. 1793].

THAT HE BE ANSWERED: see TJ to Edward Telfair, 9 Sep. 1793. THAT A LETTER BE WRITTEN TO MR. GENET: see TJ to Genet, 9 Sep. 1793.

The ORION was actually a British warship. The 17TH. ARTICLE OF OUR TREATY of commerce with France is described in notes to Genet to TJ, 27 May 1793, and to Document II of a group of documents on

the referral of neutrality questions to the Supreme Court, at 18 July 1793. RULES HERETOFORE GIVEN: Rules on Neutrality, 3 Aug. 1793.

THAT MR. HAMMOND BE INFORMED: see TJ to George Hammond and F. P. Van Berckel, 9 Sep. 1793.

The letter from William BORDMAN, written from Boston on 29 Aug. and recorded in SJL as received 4 Sep. 1793, has not been found.

DRAUGHT OF A LETTER TO MR. PINCKNEY: see TJ to Thomas Pinckney, 7 Sep. 1793.

[1] Preceding five words interlined.

[2] Word interlined in place of "produce."

[3] TJ here canceled what appears to be "to which therefore the same right has."

[4] TJ first wrote "that this right not being exclusive, has not been denied to the british vessels," and then altered it to read as above.

Circular to French Consuls and Vice-Consuls

Sir   Philadelphia, September 7th. 1793.

Finding by the protests of several of the Consuls of France, by their advertisements in the public papers, and other proceedings, and by other sufficient testimony, that they claim, and are exercising, within the United States a general admiralty jurisdiction, and in particular assume to try the validity of prizes, and to give sentence thereon as Judges of Admiralty; and moreover that they are undertaking to give Commissions within the United States, and to enlist, or encourage the enlistment of men, natives or inhabitants of these States, to commit hostilities on nations with whom the United States are at peace, in direct opposition to the laws of the land; I have it in charge from the President of the United States to give notice to all the Consuls and Vice Consuls of France in the United States, as I hereby do to you, that if any of them shall commit any of the acts beforementioned, or assume any jurisdiction not expressly given by the Convention between France and the United States, the Exequatur of the Consul so transgressing,[1] will be immediately revoked, and his person be submitted to such prosecutions and punishments as the laws may prescribe for the case. I have the honor to be, with respect Sir, Your most Obedient and most humble servant.   TH: JEFFERSON

RC (CtY); in Benjamin Bankson's hand, signed by TJ; at foot of text: "Citizen Francois Dupon[t], Consul for France in Philadelphia." RC (Dr. Max Thorek, Chicago, 1946); in Bankson's hand, signed by TJ; at foot of text: "Citizen Moissonier, Vice Consul for France in Maryland." Dft (DLC); in TJ's hand, unsigned, with dateline by George Taylor, Jr.; at head of text: "Circular to the French Consuls." PrC to Alexandre Maurice d'Hauterive (DLC); in Taylor's hand, unsigned; at foot of text: "The Citizen Hauterive Consul from the Republic of France at New York"; with four lines, one partly torn, added by Taylor in ink below complimentary close:

"Citizen Francois du Pont Consul Phila.
Citizen Moissonier—Vice C. Maryland
⟨Citizen du plaine [Vice C.] N. Hamp. Mass. & Rh. Isld.⟩
Mangourit. Consul Charleston." Tr (DNA: RG 46, Senate Records, 3d Cong., 1st sess.). FC (Lb in DNA; RG 59, DL).

Tr (AMAE: Correspondance Consulaire, New York, III); certified by Cassan. Tr (same); in French; at foot of first page: "Citoyen hauterive consul de la rpqu. fse. a New york"; certified by Bournonville. Tr (same, CPEU, XXXIX); in French; dated "le   Sept. 1793." Tr (DLC: Genet Papers); in French. Tr (same); in French; incomplete. Recorded in SJPL. Printed in *Message*, 75. Enclosed in TJ to Edmond Charles Genet, [7 Sep. 1793].

This circular was approved by the Cabinet (Cabinet Opinions on Relations with France and Great Britain, 7 Sep. 1793). For the controversy over the right claimed by French consuls to exercise exclusive ADMIRALTY JURISDICTION over prizes brought by French ships into American ports, see Thomas, *American Neutrality*, 206-20.

[1] Word altered in Dft from "offending."

From Robert Were Fox

Falmouth, 7 Sep. 1793. Since his last, the principal occurrence affecting American shipping is the capture by a Liverpool privateer of the sloop *Aurora* bound from New York to Le Havre with a cargo of coffee, pearl ash, etc. He sees not the least pretense for the detention of this cargo and concludes that it will be returned with damages. At the request of the captors, the English government has taken the cargo of flour, beef, pork, sugar, and staves carried by the American ship *Portland*, Captain Robinson, and the Victualing Board has asked Robinson to submit his demand for the cargo, including freight and charges. The gentleman in London acting for the owner does not appear inclined to compromise and will consult the minister there on how to act. He has secured the release of some impressed American seamen upon proper application and expects this will be the case in the future.

RC (DNA: RG 59, CD); 2 p.; in a clerk's hand, signed by Fox; at foot of text: "Thomas Jefferson Esqr London"; endorsed by TJ as received 7 Nov. 1793 and so recorded in SJL. This is the last consular letter TJ received from Fox. See Appendix I.

To Edmond Charles Genet

SIR   [7 Sep. 1793]

The correspondence which has taken place between the Executive and yourself, and the acts which you have thought proper to do, and to countenance, in opposition to the laws of the land, have rendered it necessary in the opinion of the President to lay a faithful statement of them before the government of France, to explain to them the reasons and the necessity which have dictated our measures, to renew the assurances of that sincere friendship which has suffered no intermission during the course of these proceedings, and to express our extreme anxiety that none may be produced on their part. This has accordingly been directed to be done by the Min. Pleny. of the US. at Paris, in a letter a copy of which I now inclose to you. And in order to bring to an end what can[1] not be permitted to continue, there could be no hesitation to declare in it the necessity of their having a representative here disposed to respect[2] the laws and authorities of the country, and to do the best for their interest which these would permit. An anxious regard for those interests, and a desire that they may not suffer, will induce the Executive[3] in the mean time to recieve your communications in writing, and to admit the continuance of your functions so long as they shall be restrained within the limits of the law as heretofore announced to you, or shall be of the tenor usually observed towards independant nations by the representative of a friendly power residing with them.

The President thought it respectful to your nation as well as yourself to leave to yourself the restraining certain proceedings of the Consuls of

France within the US. which you were informed were contrary to the laws of the land, and therefore not to be permitted. He has seen with regret however, that you have been far from restraining these proceedings, and that the duty has devolved on him of suppressing them by the authority of the country. I inclose to you the copy of a letter written to the several Consuls and Vice consuls of France, warning them that this will be done if any repetition of these acts shall render it necessary. To the Consul of France at Boston no such letter has been written. A more serious fact is charged on him, which if proved, as there is reason to expect, will render the revocation of his Exequatur an act of immediate duty. I have the honor to be with great respect Sir your most obedt. servt

Dft (DLC: TJ Papers, 92: 15992); entirely in TJ's hand, unsigned; undated, but assigned on the basis of the dated translations listed below; at foot of text "Mr. Genet. Min. Pleny. of France"; in pencil on verso: "to be copd & press cop[d]." FC (Lb in DNA: RG 59, DL); undated; with marginal note by Timothy Pickering: "This letter to Mr. Genet being without date, it may be convenient to note, that the receipt of it is recognized in his letter to Mr. Jefferson dated the 18th of Septr. 1793. (published with the other letters from Mr. Genet) and that the letters to the Consuls to which Mr. J. refers, is dated Sept. 7th. T.P." Tr (DLC: Genet Papers); in French; dated 7 Sep. 1793; draft translation. Tr (AMAE: CPEU, xxxix); in French; dated 7 Sep. 1793; certified by Genet. Not recorded in SJL. Enclosures: (1) TJ to Gouverneur Morris, 16 Aug. 1793. (2) Circular to French Consuls and Vice-Consuls, 7 Sep. 1793.

This letter was approved by the Cabinet this day (Cabinet Opinions on Relations with France and Great Britain, 7 Sep. 1793). According to George Hammond, who wrote apparently on the basis of information provided by Alexander Hamilton, the Cabinet decided to delay sending Genet a copy of the enclosed letter to Gouverneur Morris requesting the French minister's recall so as to avoid having the ship carrying the dispatch to France intercepted by a French vessel (Hammond to Lord Grenville, 17 Sep. 1793, PRO: FO 5/1).

[1] Word interlined in place of "could."
[2] TJ first wrote "capable of respecting" and then altered it to read as above.
[3] Word interlined in place of "⟨Executive⟩ President."

To Dennis Griffith

Sir   Philadelphia Sep. 7. 1793.

I have duly received your favor of Aug. 31. and am sorry it is not in my power to give you any satisfactory answer, as the papers which served for my information in writing the Notes on Virginia were left in that state when I went to Europe and are still there. Ten or eleven years having elapsed since writing that work, and my mind totally withdrawn in the mean time to other objects, my memory does not enable me to say upon what information I stated the latitude of the dividing line of Virginia and Maryland on the Eastern shore. But I suspect it was on a

Report from Commissioners appointed by Virginia to examine that boundary. I know there was such a report, and I either have it, or had the use of it, and I believe it was made either a little before or after the commencement of the Revolution war. The original must be in the office of the house of delegates of Virginia. A copy of it must be among the papers of the late Colo. G. Mason, who was too curious in things of this kind not to have had a copy of it. The difference between Mason and Dixon's computation of a degree of Latitude, adopted by you, viz. 68.896 Miles (I take this from your letter and suppose it to be decimal notation) and Cassini's which I adopted to wit 68 Miles–864 feet, or in miles and decimals of a mile 68.1636 miles would account for between one and two seconds of our variation.—Should you not have occasion to decide this matter before February or March next I shall be able to answer you from an inspection of my papers in Virginia, and will examine into it for you with pleasure. I am Sir Your most obedt. servt.

Th: Jefferson

PrC (DLC); at foot of text: "Mr. D. Griffith." Tr (ViU: Edgehill-Randolph Papers); 19th-century copy.

On 10 Dec. 1777 the Virginia General Assembly appointed George Mason, Thomas Ludwell Lee, and James Henry COMMISSIONERS to meet with a delegation from Maryland "to adjust and confirm the rights of each, to the use and navigation of, and jurisdiction over, the bay of Chesapeake, and the rivers Potomac and Pocomoke." No agreement was reached at this time, and the Virginia report which TJ consulted has not been found (JHD, Oct. 1777,

1827 ed., p. 64-5, 73-4; Edward B. Mathews and Wilbur A. Nelson, *Report on the Location of the Boundary Line along the Potomac River between Virginia and Maryland In accordance with The Award of 1877* [Baltimore, 1928], 3-4). TJ presumably obtained CASSINI'S figure for the length of a degree of latitude from César François Cassini de Thury, *Relation de deux Voyages Faits en Allemagne . . . Par Rapport a La Figure de la Terre, Pour déterminer la grandeur des degrés de longitude . . .* (Paris, 1763). See Sowerby, No. 3806; *Notes*, ed. Peden, 3-4.

From James Maury

Liverpool, 7 Sep. 1793. He encloses a price current. On 3 Sep. the *Sisters*, Captain William Provoost, bound from New York to Le Havre, was brought here under suspicion of carrying French property—the fourth American ship brought here on that pretext. The courts have not determined the fate of any of their cargoes, though the ships *Aerial* of Philadelphia and *George* of Baltimore have been restored.

RC (DNA: RG 59, CD); 1 p.; at foot of text: "The Secretary of State to the United States Philadelphia"; endorsed by TJ as received 22 Nov. 1793 and so recorded in SJL. A missing duplicate is recorded in SJL as received 28 Nov. 1793. Enclosure: Price current of American produce at Liverpool, 6 Sep. 1793, with subjoined extracts

from Lloyd's list of quotations for stock, exchange with Paris, and gold and silver, 3 Sep. 1793 (printed form in same; signed by Maury, with date, prices, and comments entered in a clerk's hand).

This is the last consular letter TJ received from Maury. See Appendix I.

Notes for Replies to Edmond Charles Genet and George Hammond

[7-9 Sep. 1793]

29. Ship Wm.
      no power in this country could take out of custody of court
29. brig Fanny.
July 12. Lovely Lass and Pr. W. H.
      Wm. Tell.
desire the Lovely Lass and Pr. W. Henry to be restored.

[*Notes for reply to Hammond:*]
Consular jurisdiction.
   Brig Wm. Tell will be delivered to court
                  or reclaimed by executive.
   both parties right to cruize.
   Fr. has secured to herself 2. rights
      1st. XVIIth. to bring in prizes. exclusive
         Gr. Br. and Fr. same
      2d. XIX to come in for urgent necessity
        XXII. makes it exclusive as to privateers.
       not so as to public vessels of war.

MS (DLC: TJ Papers, 92: 15840); entirely in TJ's hand; undated; consists respectively of notes for letters of 9 Sep. 1793 to Genet and Hammond written upside down from each other at opposite ends of a small sheet containing on verso Dft of Cabinet Opinions on Relations with France and Great Britain, 7 Sep. 1793.

To Thomas Pinckney

SIR   Philadelphia, September 7th. 1793.[1]

We have received through a channel, which cannot be considered as authentic, the copy of a paper stiled "Additional instructions to the Commanders of his Majesty's Ships of war and privateers &c" dated at St. James' June 8th. 1793. If this paper be authentic, I have little doubt but that you will have taken measures to forward it to me. But as your communication of it may miscarry, and time, in the mean while be lost, it has been thought better that it should be supposed authentic, that on that supposition I should notice to you it's very exceptionable nature, and the necessity of obtaining explanations on the subject from the British Government; desiring at the same time that you will consider this letter as provisionally written only, and as if never written, in the event that the paper, which is the occasion of it be not genuine.

The 1st. article of it permits all vessels laden wholly or in part, with corn, flour or meal, bound to any port in France to be stopped, and sent into any British port to be purchased by that Government, or to be released only on the condition of security given by the Master that he will proceed to dispose of his Cargo in the ports of some country *in amity with his Majesty.*

This article is so manifestly contrary to the law of nations, that nothing more would seem necessary than to observe that it is so. Reason and usage have established that when two nations go to war, those who chuse to live in peace retain their natural right to pursue their agriculture, manufactures and other ordinary vocations, to carry the produce of their industry, for exchange, to all nations, belligerent or neutral, as usual, to go and come freely without injury or molestation, and in short, that the war among others shall be for them as if it did not exist. One restriction on their natural rights has been submitted to by nations at peace, that is to say, that of not furnishing to either party implements merely of war for the annoyance of the other, nor any thing whatever to a place blockaded by it's enemy. What these implements of war are, has been so often agreed, and is so well understood, as to leave little question about them at this day. There does not exist perhaps a nation, in our common hemisphere, which has not made a particular enumeration of them in some or all of their treaties, under the name of contraband. It suffices for the present occasion to say that corn, flour and meal are not of the class of contraband, and consequently remain articles of free commerce. A culture which, like that of the soil, gives employment to such a proportion of mankind, could never be suspended by the whole earth, or interrupted for them, whenever any two nations should think proper to go to war.

The state of war then existing between Great Britain and France, furnishes no legitimate right to either to interrupt the agriculture of the United States or the peaceable exchange of it's produce with all nations; and consequently the assumption of it will be as lawful hereafter as now, in peace as in war. No ground, acknowledged by the common reason of mankind, authorizes this act now, and unacknowledged ground may be taken at any time and all times. We see then a practice begun, to which no time no circumstances, prescribe any limits, and which strikes at the root of our agriculture, that branch of industry which gives food, clothing, and comfort to the great mass of the inhabitants of these states. If any nation whatever has a right to shut up, to our produce, all the ports of the earth except her own, and those of her friends, she may shut up these also, and so confine us within our own limits. No nation can subscribe to such pretensions, no nation can agree, at the mere will or interest of another, to have it's peaceable industry suspended, and it's Citizens reduced to idleness and want. The loss of our produce destined for foreign markets,[2] or that loss which would result from an arbitrary restraint of our markets,[3] is a tax too serious for us to acquiesce in. It is not enough for a nation to say, we and our friends will buy your produce. We have a right to answer that it suits us better to sell to their enemies as well as their friends. Our Ships do not go to France to return empty— they go to exchange the surplus of one produce which we can spare, for surplusses of other kinds which they can spare and we want; which they can furnish on better terms, and more to our mind, than Great Britain or her friends. We have a right to judge for ourselves what market best suits us, and they have none to forbid to us the enjoyment of the necessaries and comforts which we may obtain from any other independent country.

This act too tends directly to draw us from that state of peace in which we are wishing to remain. It is an essential character of neutrality to furnish no aids (not stipulated by treaty) to one party, which we are not equally ready to furnish to the other. If we permit Corn to be sent to Great Britain and her friends, we are equally bound to permit it to France. To restrain it, would be a partiality which might lead to war with France; and between restraining it ourselves, and permitting her enemies to restrain it unrightfully, is no difference. She would consider this as a mere pretext, of which she would not be the dupe, and on what honorable ground could we otherwise explain it? Thus we should see ourselves plunged, by this unauthorized act of Great Britain, into a war, with which we meddle not, and which we wish to avoid if justice to all parties, and from all parties,[4] will enable us to avoid it. In the case where we found ourselves obliged by treaty to withold from the enemies of France the right of arming in our ports, we thought ourselves in justice bound to withold the same right from France also; and we did it. Were we to withold from her supplies of provisions, we should in like manner be bound to withold them from her enemies also; and thus shut to ourselves all the ports of Europe where Corn is in demand, or make ourselves parties in the war. This is a dilemma which Great Britain has no right to force upon us, and for which no pretext can be found in any part of our conduct. She may indeed feel the desire of starving an enemy nation: but she can have no right of doing it at our loss, nor of making us the instrument of it.

The President therefore desires that you will immediately enter into explanations, on this subject, with the British government. Lay before them in friendly and temperate terms all the demonstrations of the injury done us by this act, and endeavour to obtain a revocation of it, and full indemnification to any Citizens of these States who may have suffered by it in the mean time. Accompany your representations[5] with every assurance of our earnest desire to live on terms of the best friendship and harmony with them, and to found our expectations of justice on their part on a strict observance of it on ours.

It is with concern however I am obliged to observe that so marked has been the inattention of the British Court to every application which has been made to them, on any subject, by this government, (not a single answer I believe having ever been given to one of them except in the act of exchanging a Minister) that it may become unavoidable, in certain cases, where an answer of some sort is necessary, to consider their silence as an answer. Perhaps this is their intention. Still however, desirous of furnishing no color of offence, we do not wish you to name to them any term for giving an answer. Urge one as much as you can without commitment, and on the 1st. day of December be so good as to [6] give us information of the state in which this matter is, that it may be received during the session of Congress.

The 2d. article of the same instruction allows the armed vessels of Great Britain to seize, for condemnation, all vessels on their first attempt to enter a blockaded port, except those of Denmark and Sweden, which are to be prevented only, but not seized, on their first attempt. Of the nations inhabiting the shores of the Atlantic Ocean and practising it's navigation, Denmark, Sweden and the United States, alone are neutral. To declare then all *neutral* vessels (for, as to the vessels of the *belligerent* powers, no order was necessary) to be legal prize, which shall attempt to enter a blockaded port, except those of *Denmark and Sweden*, is exactly to declare that the *vessels of the United States* shall be lawful prize, and those of Denmark and Sweden shall not. It is of little consequence that the article has avoided naming the United States, since it has used a description applicable to them, and to them alone, while it exempts the others, from it's operation, by name. You will be pleased to ask an explanation of this distinction: and you will be able to say, in discussing it's justice, that in every circumstance, we treat Great Britain on the footing of the most favored nation; where our treaties do not preclude us, and that even these are just as favorable to her, as hers are to us. Possibly she may be bound by treaty to admit this exception in favor of Denmark and Sweden. But she cannot be bound by treaty to withold it from us. And if it be witheld merely because not established with us by treaty,[7] what might not we, on the same ground have witheld from Great Britain [8] during the short course of the present war, as well as the peace which has preceded it?

Whether these explanations with the British government shall be verbal, or in writing, is left to yourself. Verbal communications are very insecure: for it is only to deny them, or to change their terms, in order to do away their effect at any time. Those in writing have many and obvious advantages, and ought to be preferred unless there be obstacles of which we are not apprized.[9] I have the honor to be with great & sincere esteem Dr. Sir, Your most Obedt servant   TH: JEFFERSON

RC (William M. Elkins, Philadelphia, 1945); in Benjamin Bankson's hand, signed by TJ; at foot of first page: "Mr. Pinckney"; endorsed by William A. Deas. PrC (DLC). Dft (DLC); entirely in TJ's hand, unsigned; only the most significant emendations are recorded below. PrC (DLC: James Madison Papers); lacks some emendations (see notes 1, 2, 3, 5, 8, and 9 below); last page torn. Tr (DNA: RG 46, Senate Records, 3d Cong., 1st sess.). FC (Lb in DNA: RG 59, DCI). Letter and enclosure printed in *Message*, 107-10. Enclosed in TJ to Henry Remsen, 11 Sep. 1793.

On 31 Aug. 1793 the Cabinet considered an unauthenticated copy of the ADDITIONAL INSTRUCTIONS TJ had received from James Maury, the United States consul in Liverpool, and authorized the dispatch to Pinckney of provisional instructions calling for their revocation and indemnification for all losses suffered by American citizens in consequence of them (Cabinet Opinions on the *Roland* and Relations with Great Britain, France, and the Creeks, 31 Aug. 1793). This day it approved TJ's draft of the letter printed above (Cabinet Opinions on Relations with France and Great Britain, 7 Sep. 1793). Less than a week later TJ received authenticated copies of the additional instructions from Pinckney and George Hammond (Pinckney to TJ, 5 July 1793, and enclosure; Hammond's second letter to TJ, 12 Sep. 1793).

TJ's protest against the additional instructions proved to be ineffectual in the short run. In December 1793 Pinckney submitted to Lord Grenville a formal representation against them that to a large extent was based almost verbatim on the above letter. While praising Pinckney's "moderate and conciliatory language," Grenville responded by instructing Hammond in January 1794 to notify the United States government that Britain rejected American objections to the instructions. Three months later Hammond defended the instructions at length in a letter to Secretary of State Edmund Randolph, but in August 1794 the British government relented to the point of exempting neutral grain ships bound for France from capture and preemption (Pinckney to TJ, 25 Nov., 17 Dec. 1793, listed in Appendix I; ASP, *Foreign Relations*, I, 448-50; Mayo, *British Ministers*, 45-7; Josiah T. Newcomb, "New Light on Jay's Treaty," *American Journal of International Law*, XXVIII [1934], 685-92).

[1] Dateline inserted in Dft. Emendation not in PrC of Dft.

[2] In Dft TJ first wrote "the produce of the year" and then altered it to read as above. Emendation not in PrC of Dft.

[3] Remainder of sentence interlined in Dft in place of "would be a heavier tax, than even the state of war which we are so much endeavoring to avoid." Emendation not in PrC of Dft.

[4] Preceding four words interlined in Dft.

[5] Word altered from "recommendations" in Dft. Emendation not in PrC of Dft.

[6] Preceding five words interlined in Dft.

[7] Preceding two words interlined in Dft.

[8] Remainder of paragraph interlined in Dft. Emendation not in PrC of Dft.

[9] Remainder of text interlined in Dft. Emendation not in PrC of Dft.

From George Washington

Sir   Philadelphia 7 Septr. 1793

I have received your letter of yesterday's date, and approving the measures suggested therein, desire you will make arrangements for carrying them into effect with as little loss of time as may be.

Go: Washington

FC (Lb in DNA: RG 59, SDC); at head of text: "The Secretary of State."

TJ's letter of yesterday's date has not been found.

To Joseph Yznardi, Jr.

Sir   Philadelphia Sep. 7. 1793.

I have duly received your favor of Aug. 25. from Boston, and am sensible of the candor of your proposition on the subject of Algiers: but our matters with them have been for some short time past in a train of settlement, the result of which however is yet unknown, and uncertain.

Captn. Roger Robbins arrived here about the middle of last month. I knew he had been detained several days at Algeziras, but I have not learnt from him the particulars.

I shall be obliged to you for a pipe of good dry Sherry, ready for drinking, such as you have perhaps seen at the house of Messrs. Viar and Jaudenes, and as you I think informed me was of the quality frequently sent to London.

Having nothing at this moment for Madrid, I have only to add my wishes for a good voyage, & assurances of the regard with which I am Sir Your most obedt. servt   Th: Jefferson

P.S. The wine to be sent to Richmond in Virginia.

PrC (DLC); at foot of text: "Mr. Yznardi junr."

Joseph Yznardi, Jr., the scion of a Cadiz mercantile family who had come to the United States in January 1793 in quest of a consular appointment in that city, obtained the post the following month on the strength of letters of recommendation from William Carmichael and Nathaniel Cutting stressing his mercantile experience, his fluency in English, and his family's influence with the Spanish court (Nathaniel Cutting to TJ, 30 Jan. 1793, and note; Memorandum on Consuls and Consular Appointments, 15 Feb. 1793). Yznardi remained in America until he embarked for Spain in March 1794; he supplied wine to TJ for many years thereafter. During much of his term as consul Yznardi was away from Cadiz, and he deputed his father, Joseph Yznardi, Sr., to act in his behalf. In February 1801 the Senate approved John Adams's nomination of Henry Prebble to the post, but TJ did not issue a commission and instead appointed Yznardi's father as consul later the same year (Yznardi, Sr., to Edmund Randolph, 2 Sep., 12 Nov. 1794, and to Timothy Pickering, 3 Apr. 1800, Vindication of Yznardi, Sr., [10 Nov. 1800], and Alexander J. Dallas to [Levi Lincoln?], 31 Mch. 1801, all in DNA: RG 59, CD; MB, 19 Nov. 1794, and note; JEP, I, 381, 385, 403, 405).

From George Hammond

Sir   Philadelphia 8 September 1793

I have the honor to inform you that I have received the inclosed copy of Mr. Shoolbred's commission, as his Majestys Vice-Consul for the states of North Carolina, South Carolina and Georgia, which he has forwarded under a presumption that a copy would be competent to the purpose of obtaining the recognition of the President of the United States.

The particular cases of exigency, which have lately arisen, and of which some actually exist in Charleston, require the immediate exertion of Mr. Shoolbred's official duties; and as a considerable time must necessarily elapse before the original commission could be thence obtained, I flatter myself, Sir you will be pleased upon this occasion to dispense with its production, and interpose your good offices for obtaining a speedy recognition of Mr. Shoolbred's appointment under the inclosed copy of his commission to which I am ready to add any authenticity that my official situation can enable me to give it. I will also procure from Mr. Shoolbred the original commission, which can at any future period be substituted in the place of the Copy. I have the honor to be, with sentiments of great respect, Sir, your most obedient, humble Servant,

Geo. Hammond

RC (DNA: RG 59, NL); at foot of text: "Mr Jefferson"; endorsed by TJ as received 9 Sep. 1793 and so recorded in SJL. Tr (Lb in same). Enclosure: James Shoolbred's commission from George Miller as British vice-consul in North Carolina, South Carolina, and Georgia, 17 June 1793 (Trs in same and in Lb in same).

Owing to the need to examine Shoolbred's original commission, the President did not sign his exequatur until 8 Feb. 1794, but in the meantime he was allowed to exercise his consular functions (TJ to Hammond, 10 Sep. 1793; Washington, *Journal*, 283).

To James Madison

Sep. 8. 93.

I have received and am charmed with No. V. I thought the introduction an useful lesson to others as I found it to myself, for I had really, by constantly hearing the sound, been led into a pretty free use of it myself. I struck out the passage you desired in the last page. I struck out also the words 'and neutrality' in the following passage 'taking the proclamation *in it's proper sense* as reminding all concerned that as the US. were at peace, the laws of peace *and neutrality* were still obligatory.' Also a paragraph of 4. lines that a minister from France was hourly expected when the proclamation issued.—There was one here at the time—the other did not arrive in 6. weeks.—To have waited that time would have given full course to the evil.

I went through Franklin with enchantment; and what peculiarly pleased me was that there was not a sentence from which it could be conjectured whether it came from N. S. E. or West. At last a whole page of Virginia flashed on me. It was in the section on the *state of parties*, and was an apology for the continuance of slavery among us. However this circumstance may be justly palliated, it had nothing to do with the state of parties, with the bank, encumbered a good cause with a questionable argument; many readers who would have gone heart and hand with the author so far would have flown off in a tangent from that paragraph.—I struck it out. Justify this if you please to those concerned, and if it cannot be done say so and it may still be reestablished.—I mentioned to you in my last that a Fr. Consul at Boston had rescued a vessel out of the hands of a marshal by military force. Genet has at New York forbidden a marshal to arrest a vessel and given orders to the French squadron to protect her by force. Was there ever an instance before of a diplomatic man overawing and obstructing the course of the law in a country by an armed force?—The Yellow fever increases. The week before last about 5. a day died. This last week about 11. a day have died; consequently from known data about 33. a day are taken, and there are about 330. patients under it. They are much scattered through the town, and it is the opinion of the physicians that there is no possibility of stopping it. They agree it is a non-descript disease, and no two agree in any one part of their process of cure. The Presidt. goes off the day after tomorrow as he had always intended. Knox then takes flight. Hamilton is ill of the fever as is said. He had two physicians out at his house the night before last. His family think him in danger, and he puts himself so by his excessive alarm. He had been miserable several days before from a firm persuasion he should catch it. A man as timid as he is on the water, as timid on horseback, as timid in sickness, would be a phaenomenon if the courage of which he has the reputation in military occasions were genuine. His friends, who have not seen him, suspect it is only an autumnal fever he has. I would really go away, because I think there is rational danger, but that I had before announced that I should not go till the beginning of October, and I do not like to exhibit the appearance of panic. Besides that I think there might serious ills proceed from there being not a single member of the administration in place. Poor Hutcheson dined with me on Friday was sennight, was taken that night on his return home, and died the day before yesterday. It is difficult to say whether the republican interest has suffered more by his death or Genet's extravagance. I sometimes cannot help seriously believing the latter to be a Dumourier, endeavoring to draw us into the war against France as

Dumourier, while a minister, drew on her the war of the empire.—The Indians have refused to meet our Commissioners unless they would make the Ohio a boundary by preliminary condition. Consequently they are on their return and we may suppose Wayne in movement.— Since my last which was of the 1st. your's of the 22d. Aug. and 2d. Sep. are received. Adieu.

RC (DLC: Madison Papers); unsigned; endorsed by Madison. PrC (DLC). Tr (DLC); 19th-century copy; consists of mutilated text of last thirteen sentences only.

TJ was editing Madison's "Helvidius" essay NO. V., which appeared in the *Gazette of the United States* on 18 Sep. 1793. AN USEFUL LESSON: Madison's criticism of "Pacificus," for "the application of the term *government* to the *Executive authority alone*" (Madison, *Papers*, xv, 114). For the passage in which TJ deleted 'AND NEUTRALITY,' see same, 119. FRANKLIN: John Taylor of Caroline, who agreed to the removal of the APOLOGY FOR THE CONTINUANCE OF SLAVERY from the draft of his pamphlet cited in note to Madison to TJ, 11 Aug. 1793 (same, 121, 123).

From James Madison

[after 8 Sep. 1793]

The want of opportunity has left me in debt for 3 favors those of Aug. 18. 25. and Sepr. 8th. which I now acknowledge by one which is too precarious for any thing confidential. I have long been uneasy for your health amidst the vapors of the Schuylkil. The new and more alarming danger has made me particularly anxious that you were out of the sphere of it. I cannot altogether condemn your unwillingness to retire from your post under the circumstances you describe; but if your stay be as unessential as I conceive it to be rendered by the absence of the P. and the fever does not abate, I pray you not to sacrifice too much to motives which others do not feel. As I intimated in my last, my time has been *totally* diverted from my object. I have scarcely been able to turn it even in my thoughts. It is probable therefore that you will not hear further from me in relation to it before you leave P. In fact the temper of the present moment and the uncertainty of many things seem to advise a postponement if nothing more. All the liberties you have taken will I am sure be approved. I have neglected hitherto to comply with your request as to a rotation farm. In the main it appears to be judicious and unobjectionable. Of this opinion are those with whom I have conferred. One or two alterations not very material occurred; but as they may be doubtful, and if proper, can be made at any time, I do not now trouble you with them. I have tried the patent plow amended by fixing the Colter in the usual way. It succeeds perfectly, and I think forms the plow best suited to its object. I am happy at the arrival of your Threshing Model. What will be about the cost of the Machine? Will it be removeable from one to another part of an extensive farm? Adieu. Yrs. always & affy.

The other Newspapers in my next.

RC (DLC: TJ Papers, 96: 16503); undated and unsigned; endorsed by TJ as received 2 Dec. 1793 and so recorded in SJL.

A letter from Madison to TJ of 16 Sep. 1793, not found, is recorded in SJL as received 2 Dec. 1793.

To Martha Jefferson Randolph

MY DEAR MARTHA   Schuylkill Sep. 8. 93.

I received this day Mr. Randolph's letter of Aug. 31. with the horse, rather thin, having performed his journey in 7. days. However I shall hope to recruit him before I set out. The servant gives a very good account of him. The President sets out the day after tomorrow for Mount Vernon, and will be back about the last of the month. Within 4 or 5. days or a week after his return I can set out. The yellow fever, of which I wrote Mr. Randolph last week still encreases. The last week about twice as many have died as did the week before. I imagine there are between 3. and 400. persons ill of it. I propose after the President's departure to remove my office into the country so as to have no further occasion to go into the town. I was just about ordering some few stores to be got and sent off to Richmond for Monticello: but I think it too unsafe now, and shall therefore write to Colo. Gamble to send up some from Richmond.—Tell Mr. Randolph that the box for me in the Custom house at Bermuda must be a small Orrery, cost 2½or 3 guineas.— If Mrs. Beverley Randolph is still with you tell her that the Indians having refused to meet our Commissioners, we expect Mr. Randolph her spousy[1] here in the course of a week on his way back. Present my respects to her and your other friends with you. My best affections to Mr. Randolph, yourself and dear little ones. Adieu my dear dear Martha.   TH:J.

RC (NNP); at foot of text: "Mrs. Randolph"; endorsed by Mrs. Randolph. PrC (MHi).

[1] Preceding two words interlined.

From Samuel Sterett

SIR   Baltimore 8. Sept. 1793

Your letter of the 2d. inst. was received by the Committee and communicated to the Vice-Consul of the French Republic.

At a late hour of the Evening and when I despair of a meeting of the Committee, I am solicited to request you to forward a letter of that nature which the British Minister will please to grant. The unfortunate people, whom it is intended to protect, if it can carry protection with it at all, are extremely chagrined at the treatment they experience from the Representative of a Nation that professes to support their principles and conduct; for they are all of them the avowed enemies of the French Revolution and of every Government that is not monarchical. The Recommendation that is offered to them, I am myself fearful will not be accepted, and the expedition is probably at an end. But still it will depend very much on the tenor of the Minister's letter. Many of the unfortunate Exiles experience too keen a misery in their present situation, not to wish for a Change, and they are willing to risque any fate that can be inflicted by a people of Humanity. The Ladies particularly love cleanliness and comfort. But the means of both have been cruelly and unfeelingly torn from them by British Cruisers in their passage here, in every instance that they were exposed to such treatment. If they can be persuaded to have a little confidence in the British Minister's proposed favor, they may be induced still to go, and the Charity of the Town will be relieved from a Burthen of 600 or 800 Dollars, weekly, which is the present expenditure for their support, and much too heavy to be of very long continuance. If this plan cannot be effected, the poor Wretches must soon be exposed to a misery infinitely surpassing their present feelings.

The numbers already entered and for whom a provision has been made at a heavy expence to the French Republic and the Inhabitants of this Town, are as follow—

In the Marianne, Capt. Ardouin, 250 persons

In the Nouvelle Rosalie, Capt. Dupouy 180. persons, in all 430.

It is not without great pain and reluctance that I have consented to write this letter. My scruples have been overcome by the solicitation of a people, who have strong claims to our pity and compassion. I have the honor to be, with great respect, Sir, Your Humb. Ser

SAMUEL STERETT

RC (DNA: RG 59, MLR); at foot of text: "Tho. Jefferson, Esq.—Sec. of State"; endorsed by TJ as received 11 Sep. 1793 and so recorded in SJL.

TJ's LETTER OF THE 2D. INST. was addressed to James McHenry, Robert Gilmor, and Sterett. A missing letter from Sterett to TJ of 4 Sep. 1793 is recorded in SJL as received from Baltimore on 7 Sep. 1793.

From James B. M. Adair

I had the honour of receiving your favour in course of post, and as I did not know of any person going to Philadelphia, with whom I could entrust your model, I delivered it to Mr. Remsen, informing of the precautions necessary to be observed in forwarding it, and I hope that before this time you have received it in perfect safety. The greatest care was taken, on board the Ship, to put it into a dry place, so that I have the greatest reason to flatter myself that it has totally escaped rust. This I should certainly have taken the liberty to ascertain by inspection had not Mr. Pinckney inclosed the key in a sealed packet.

I communicated, Sir, to William Hutton, the Millwright, Your very kind offer, of recommendations to Richmond, and of the use of the Model as an introduction to immediate employment. I own, it appears to me, that the most sanguine wishes could not possibly have pictured out to him, a more excellent introduction to business or a circumstance more likely to be productive of solid and permanent advantage. Of this he seemed perfectly sensible, but he had rashly entered into a sort of verbal engagement, with an old Scotch acquaintance here, to superintend the erection of a Cotton Mill at Newhaven in Connecticut. To this person he thought himself obliged to apply for advice on the subject, and he promised, before this time to communicate to me the result of his inquiries. This I am much surprised that he has not done, as I made him fully sensible of the necessity of forming an immediate determination, it not being probable, that you, Sir, would allow the model of so important a machine to remain long unemployed. Should he determine to accept your very generous proposal, I shall send him on immediately to Philadelphia.

By this post, Sir, you will receive a packet from Sir John Sinclair, with the delivery of which to you he did me the honour to intrust me. I have reason to believe it contains the Plan, since approved and executed, of a board of Agriculture to be established in Britain. At the same time, I shall take the liberty to forward copies of two pamphlets, several of which he has given me to distribute, and some queries respecting breeds of sheep and the quality of wool. Statistical inquiry, and the improvement of wool, are objects which Sir John has greatly at heart. He has commissioned me to transmit to the board of Agriculture the result of my inquiries respecting the latter, as well as other branches of Œconomics practised in the United States, and has charged me to endeavour to promote Statistical inquiries in America. The admirable example of such investigations, which, permit me Sir to say, you have given in your Notes on Virginia, leads me to hope, that you will do me the honour to assist me in these inquiries, by pointing out the persons from whom I shall be likely to receive the best information. Allow me, Sir, to add, that nothing but my ardent wish for the prosperity of the United States, and my conviction that nothing can enable a government to promote the interests of its people, so effectually as accurate information respecting their real situation, could embolden me to address you on the subject, or to occupy a single moment of your time, which is sacred to the honour and happiness of your country.

I am just about to set out on a short tour to the Eastward, and shall on my arrival at Philadelphia have the honour, with your permission to pay my respects to you. I have the honour to be, with the highest respect, Sir, Your most obedient & faithful Servant   JAS. M. ADAIR

RC (DLC); at foot of first page and of text: "The Secretary of State"; endorsed by TJ as received 11 Sep. 1793 and so recorded in SJL.

The PACKET FROM SIR JOHN SINCLAIR, dated 15 June 1793, is recorded in SJL as received from London on 11 Sep. 1793, but has not been found. PLAN . . . OF A BOARD OF AGRICULTURE: [Sir John Sinclair], *Plan for establishing a Board of Agriculture and Internal Improvement . . .* ([London], 1793). The TWO PAMPHLETS and the QUERIES RE-

SPECTING . . . SHEEP AND . . . WOOL have not been identified. See also enclosure to Enoch Edwards to TJ, 16 Aug. 1793, and note.

On 11 Sep. 1793 Sinclair sent George Washington "Copies of the additional Papers printed by the Board of Agriculture, since he last had the Honor of writing to His Excellency, which he begs may also be communicated to Mr. Adams and Mr. Jefferson" (DLC: Washington Papers).

A missing letter of 10 Oct. 1793 from Adair to TJ is recorded in SJL as received from New York on 24 Oct. 1793.

To Edmond Charles Genet

SIR   Philadelphia September 9th. 1793.

In my letter of June 25th. on the subject of the Ship William, and generally of vessels suggested to be taken within the limits of the protection of the United States by the armed vessels of your nation, I undertook to assure you it would be more agreeable to the President that such vessels should be detained under the orders of yourself or the Consuls of France than by a military guard, until the government of the United States should be able to enquire into and decide on the fact. In two separate letters of the 29th. of the same month, I[1] had the honor to inform you of the claims lodged with the Executive for the same ship William and the brig Fanny, to inclose you the evidence on which they were founded, and to desire that if you found it just you would order the vessels to be delivered to the Owners, or if overweighed in your judgment by any contradictory evidence which you might have, or acquire, you would do me the favor to communicate that evidence, and that the Consuls of France might retain the Vessels in their custody in the mean

time[2] until the Executive of the United States should consider and decide finally on the subject.[3]

When that mode of proceeding was consented to for your satisfaction, it was by no means imagined it would have occasioned such delays of Justice to the individuals interested. The President is still without information either that the vessels are restored, or that you have any evidence to offer as to the place of capture. I am therefore, Sir, to[4] repeat the request of early information on this subject, in order that if any injury has been done those interested, it may be no longer aggravated by delay.

The intention of the letter of June 25th. having been to permit such vessels to remain in the custody of the Consuls, instead of that of a military guard, (which in the case of the Ship William[5] appeared to have been disagreeable to you) the indulgence was of course to be understood as going only to cases where the Executive might take or keep possession with a military guard, and not to interfere with the authority of the Courts of Justice[6] in any case wherein they should undertake to act. My letter of June 29th. accordingly, in the same case of the Ship William, informed you that no power in this country could take a Vessel out of the custody of the Courts, and that it was only because they decided not to take cognizance of that case that it resulted to the Executive to interfere in it. Consequently, this alone put it in their power to leave the vessel in[7] the hands of the Consul. The Courts of Justice exercise the sovereignty of this country in judiciary matters, are supreme in these, and liable neither to controul nor opposition from any other branch of the Government. We learn however from the inclosed paper that the Consul of New York in the first instance, and yourself in a subsequent one,[8] forbid an officer[9] of Justice to serve the process with which he was charged from his Court on the British brig William Tell, taken by a French armed vessel within a mile of our Shores, as has been deposed on oath and brought into New York, and that you had even given[10] orders to the French Squadron there to protect the vessel against any person who should attempt to take her from their custody. If this opposition were founded, as is there suggested, on the indulgence of the letters before cited, it was extending that to a case[11] not within their purview: and even had it been precisely the case to which they were to be applied,[12] is it possible to imagine you might assert it within the body of the country by force of arms?[13]

I forbear to make the observations which such a measure must[14] suggest, and cannot but believe that a moment's reflection will evince to you the[15] depth of the error committed in this opposition to an officer of Justice, and in the means proposed to be resorted to[16] in support of it. I am therefore charged to declare to you expressly that the President expects and requires that the officer of justice be not obstructed in freely and peaceably serving[17] the process of his Court, and that in the mean time the Vessel and her Cargo be not suffered to depart till the Judiciary, if it will undertake it, or himself if not, shall decide whether the seizure has been made within the limits of our protection. I have the honor to be with great respect, Sir Your most obedient and most humble servant

PrC (DLC); in Benjamin Bankson's hand, unsigned; at foot of first page: "M Genet, Minister pleniy. of the Republic of France." Dft (DLC); in TJ's hand, unsigned; with marginal note by Henry Knox: "Approved H Knox"; on verso of final page by TJ in pencil: "to be copd & press copd"; only the most significant emendations have been recorded below. Tr (DNA: RG 46, Senate Records, 3d Cong., 1st sess.). FC (Lb in DNA: RG 59, DL). Tr (DLC: Genet Papers); in French. Tr (AMAE: CPEU, xxxix); in French; certified by Genet. Recorded in SJPL. Printed in *Message*, 75-6. For enclosures, see those listed at Memorial from George Hammond to TJ, 6 Sep. 1793. Draft enclosed in TJ to George Washington, 9 Sep. 1793.

The Cabinet agreed to the outlines of this letter on 7 Sep. 1793 after considering George Hammond's memorial to TJ of the preceding day. TJ then secured approval of his draft from the President and Secretary of War Henry Knox before dispatching the final text (Cabinet Opinions on Relations with France and Great Britain, 7 Sep. 1793; TJ to Washington, 9 Sep. 1793).

[1] In Dft TJ here canceled "informed you."

[2] Preceding four words interlined in Dft.

[3] In Dft TJ here canceled "And in a letter of July 12. you were ⟨desired⟩ informed that the President would expect that the Lovely Lass and Prince Wm. prizes to the Citoyen Genet should not depart until his ultimate determination on them should be made known."

[4] In Dft TJ here canceled "ask the favor."

[5] In Dft TJ here canceled "which (occasioned [by?] that letter)."

[6] Preceding two words interlined in Dft.

[7] In Dft TJ first wrote "and consequently to put the vessel into" and then altered it to read as above.

[8] Preceding three words interlined in Dft in place of "the next.

[9] In Dft TJ here canceled "of a court."

[10] In Dft TJ first wrote "as has been sworn, and told him you had given" and then altered it to read as above.

[11] In Dft TJ here canceled "never meant to be."

[12] In Dft TJ ended the sentence with "is it possible you could conceive yourself justified to assert it by force of arms?" before altering it to read as above.

[13] In Dft TJ here canceled "The XIXth. article of our treaty which permits your vessels when forced by stress of weather, pursuit of enemies or other urgent necessity to come into our harbors, says it shall be to refresh, and provide what is needful for their sustenance and reparation."

[14] Preceding two words interlined in Dft in place of "conduct would."

[15] In Dft TJ here canceled "consequences."

[16] Remainder of sentence interlined in Dft.

[17] In Dft TJ first wrote "be admitted freely and peaceably to serve" and then altered it to read as above.

To George Hammond and F. P. Van Berckel

Sir   Philadelphia September 9th.[1] 1793.

I have the honor to acknowledge the receipt of your[2] two Memorials of the 4th. and 6th. instant, which have been duly laid before the President of the United States.

You cannot be uninformed of the circumstances which have occasioned the French Squadron now in New York to seek asylum in the ports of the United States. Driven from those where they were on duty by the superiority of the adverse party in the Civil war which has so unhappily afflicted the colonies of France, filled with the wretched fugitives from the same scenes of distress and desolation, without water or provisions for the shortest voyage, their vessels scarcely in a condition to keep the sea at all, they were forced to seek the nearest ports in which they could be received and supplied with necessaries.[3] That they have ever been out again to cruise, is a fact we have never heard, and which we believe to be impossible from the information received of their wants and other impediments to active service.[4] This case has been noted[5] specially to shew that no inconvenience can have been produced to the trade of the other belligerent powers by the presence of this Fleet in our harbors. I shall now proceed to more general ground.

France, England[6] and all other nations have a right to cruise on our coasts; a right not derived from our permission,[7] but from the law of nature. To render this more advantageous, France has secured to herself by treaty with us, (as she has done also by a treaty with Great Britain, in the event of a war with us or any other nation[8]) two[9] special rights. 1st. Admission for her prizes and privateers into our ports.[10] This by the XVIIth. and XXIId. articles[11] is secured to her exclusively of her enemies[12] as is done for her in the like case by Great Britain were her present war with us, instead of Great Britain. 2d. Admission for her publick vessels of war into[13] our ports in[14] cases of stress of[15] weather, pirates, enemies, or other urgent necessity, to refresh, victual, repair &c. This is not exclusive.[16] As then we are bound by treaty to receive the public armed vessels of France, and are not bound to exclude those of her enemies, the Executive has never denied the same right of assylum in our ports to[17] the public armed vessels of your nation. They, as well as the French are free to come into them in all cases of weather, pirates, enemies, or other urgent necessity, and to refresh, victual, repair &c: and so many are these urgent necessities to vessels far from their own ports, that we have thought enquiries into the nature as well as the degree of the necessities which drive them hither as endless as they would be fruitless, and therefore have not made them. And the rather, because there is a 3d. Right, secured to neither by treaty, but due to both on the principles of hospitality between friendly Nations, that of coming into our ports, not *under the pressure of urgent necessity*, but whenever their comfort or convenience induces them. On this ground also[18] the two nations are on a footing.

As it has never been conceived that either would detain their Ships of war in our ports when they were in a condition for action, we have never conceived it necessary to prescribe any limits to the time of their stay.[19] Nor can it be viewed as an injury to either party to let their enemies be idle in our ports from year's end to year's end, if they chuse it. Thus then the public ships of war of both nations injoy a perfect equality in our ports. 1st. in cases of urgent necessity. 2d. in cases of comfort or convenience—and 3d. in the time they chuse to continue; and all a friendly power can ask from another is, to extend to her the same indulgencies which she extends to other friendly powers. And tho' the admission of the prizes and privateers of France is exclusive, yet it is the effect of treaty, made long ago, for valuable considerations,[20] not with a view to the present circumstances, nor against any nation in particular, but all in general; and may therefore be faithfully observed without offence to any; and we mean faithfully to observe it.[21] The same exclusive article has been stipulated[22] as was before observed, by Great Britain in her treaty with France, and indeed is to be found in the treaties between most nations.

With respect to the usurpation of Admiralty jurisdiction by the Consuls of France within these States, the honor and rights of the States themselves were sufficient motives for the Executive to take measures to prevent its continuance, as soon as they were apprized of it. They have been led by particular considerations to await the effect of these measures, believing they would be sufficient: but finding at length they were not, such others have been lately taken as can no longer fail to suppress this irregularity completely.

The President is duly sensible of the character of the act of opposition made to the Service of legal process on the Brig William Tell, and he presumes the Representations made on that subject to the Minister of France, will have the effect of opening a free access to the officer of Justice when he shall again present himself with the precept of his Court.[23] I have the honor to be with great respect, Sir, Your most obedient and most humble servant

PrC (DLC); in Benjamin Bankson's hand, unsigned, with dateline completed in ink; at foot of first page: "Mr. Hammond, Minister pleniy. of Great Britain." PrC (DLC); in Bankson's hand, unsigned; at foot of first page: "Mr Van Berckel, Resident of the United Netherlands"; identical except for variations described in notes 2, 6, 8, 12, 16, 21, and 23 below. Dft (DLC); in TJ's hand, unsigned, with "Sepr. 9th." dateline added by Bankson; marginal notation by Henry Knox: "Approved H Knox";

with variations for letter to Van Berckel inserted in brackets (see note 2 below); only the most significant emendations are recorded below. Tr (DNA: RG 46, Senate Records, 3d Cong., 1st sess.); addressed to Hammond. Tr (same); addressed to Van Berckel. FC (Lb in DNA: RG 59, DL); addressed to Hammond. FC (same); addressed to Van Berckel. Tr (Lb in PRO: FO 116/3); addressed to Hammond. Tr (same, 5/1); addressed to Hammond. Recorded in SJPL: "Th:J. to foreign ministers. circular. general principles." Both letters printed in *Message*, 76-9. Draft enclosed in TJ to George Washington, 9 Sep. 1793.

This letter began as a response to George Hammond's memorials of 4 and 6 Sep. 1793. The Cabinet considered them the following day, agreeing to the outlines of a reply, and TJ secured approval of his draft letter to the British minister from the President and Secretary of War Henry Knox before dispatching the final text (Cabinet Opinions on Relations with France and Great Britain, 7 Sep. 1793; TJ to Washington, 9 Sep. 1793). At some point TJ modified the letter to serve as a reply to F. P. Van Berckel's memorial of 6 Sep. 1793 (see note 2 below).

[1] Day inserted in ink in space left blank in manuscript.
[2] Remainder of paragraph in PrC to Van Berckel reads "Memorial of the 5th. [i.e. 6th] instant." This and the other variations recorded in notes 6, 8, 12, 16, 21, and 23 below were added by TJ in the margins of the Dft, all except those recorded in notes 8 and 23 being in a different ink than the body of that text.
[3] In Dft TJ here canceled "So far from being in a condition and when they."
[4] In Dft TJ first wrote "to action" and then altered it to read as above.
[5] Word interlined in Dft in place of "stated."
[6] PrC to Van Berckel: "Holland."

[7] Preceding two words interlined in Dft in place of "us."
[8] Preceding four words interlined in Dft. Parenthetical passage omitted in PrC to Van Berckel.
[9] In Dft TJ here canceled "parti."
[10] In Dft TJ first wrote this sentence as "To bring her prizes into our ports" and then altered it to read as above.
[11] Preceding six words and digits interlined in Dft.
[12] Remainder of sentence in PrC to Van Berckel reads "and there is a salvo of it in her favor in our treaty with the United Netherlands."
[13] Preceding eight words interlined in Dft in place of "by the XVIIth. and XXIId. articles to enter."
[14] In Dft TJ here deleted "all."
[15] Preceding two words interlined in Dft.
[16] Sentence interlined in Dft in place of "This is exclusive for her privateers, but not for her public ships of war. Those of the latter description." The sentence is continued in PrC to Van Berckel with "and is secured also to the United Netherlands by our treaty with them and their publick armed vessels are accordingly free to come into our ports"—at which point it joins the passage beginning with "in all cases" two sentences below.
[17] Remainder of sentence interlined in Dft in place of "British ships of war."
[18] In Dft TJ here canceled "the public vessels of."
[19] In Dft TJ here canceled "And it can scarcely be."
[20] Preceding three words interlined in Dft.
[21] Remainder of paragraph in PrC to Van Berckel reads "and this has been expressly admitted as was before observed, in our treaty with the United Netherlands."
[22] Word interlined in Dft in place of "copied."
[23] Preceding sentence omitted in PrC to Van Berckel.

From Henry Knox

S<small>IR</small>   War Department September 9th. 1793

Will you be so good as to inform the British Minister that the privateers Petit Democrate and Caramagnole sent into New London as a prize the Brig Nancy of Jamaica, That the Governor of Connecticut having possess'd himself of the said Brig by a party of Militia was ready to deliver her up to her Master or Owner at the time of her capture, but that no such persons have appear'd, and that in this case the Governor will deliver her to the Owner or the Minister. I have the honour to be with great Respect Sir Your Humble Servant   H. KNOX

Secy of War

RC (DLC); in a clerk's hand, signed by Knox; at foot of text: "The Secretary of State"; endorsed by TJ as received 11 Sep. 1793 and so recorded in SJL.

The BRIG NANCY, Captain Barry, was captured on 12 Aug. 1793 on a voyage from Jamaica to Philadelphia and seized by orders of the GOVERNOR OF CONNECTICUT on 28 Aug. 1793 (Melvin H. Jackson, "The Consular Privateers; an account of French Privateering in American waters, April to August, 1793," *American Neptune*, XXII [1962], 93).

From John Langdon

SR   Portsmouth. 9th. Septemr. 1793

I was honor'd with your favo'r of the 27th. Ult. by last post Incloseing your letter, directed to the Merchants of this place, which I laid before them at their Insurance Office, on the same evening that it came to hand; the gentlemen, Merchants were much pleased, and gratified with the attention of government to their Commerce, and are determined to pay particular attention, in procuring all the proof and information in their power, Relative to the Injurys or Insults, offer'd to our Trade, by the Belligerent Powers. I have the honor to be with the highest sentements of Esteem and Respect Sr. your most Obt. Servt

JOHN LANGDON

RC (DNA: RG 59, LGS); at foot of text: "Honl. Mr. Jefferson"; endorsed by TJ as received 2 Oct. 1793 and so recorded in SJL. Enclosed in Benjamin Bankson to TJ, 23 Sep. 1793.

To Edward Telfair

SIR   Philadelphia Sep. 9. 1793.

I have been honored with your Excellency's letter of Aug. 21. inclosing the demand of Joseph Riviere to be delivered out of the hands of justice because he bears a commission in the service of France. This demand is made by a John Brickell, subscribing himself Vice-Consul for the French republic in Georgia, and it is supported by Mr. Mangourit the Consul of France at Charleston, and even extended to two other persons of the names of Hunt and Seymore. These papers have been duly laid before the President.

In the first place, I have the honor to inform your Excellency, speaking from the records of my office, that no Exequatur has been issued to any such person as John Brickell to permit his exercise of the functions of either Consul or Vice-Consul of France in any part of the US. and I leave to your Excellency's good judgment to determine how far it may be necessary for you to call on him to shew his Exequatur, if any he has.

As to the three persons demanded, they are in the possession of the Judiciary department, and the law must take it's course. If they have not transgressed the laws of the land, the judges will discharge them; if they have transgressed, they ought to be punished. It is not to your Excellency that I need observe that in our country the Judiciary is sovereign in it's department, and can neither be controuled nor opposed by the Executive. I have the honour to be with perfect respect & esteem, your Excy's most obedient servant   Th: Jefferson

RC (PWacD: Feinstone Collection, on deposit PPAmP). PrC (DLC); at foot of text: "H.E. the Govr. of Georgia." FC (Lb in DNA: RG 59, DL).

To George Washington

Sep: 9. 1793.

Th: Jefferson with his respects to the President has the honor to inclose him draughts of letters to Mr. Genet and Mr. Hammond, as agreed on Saturday. If Genl: Knox and the Atty. Genl. should wait on the President to-day, it would be well they should see them. Th:J. will have that honour before he leaves town.

RC (DNA: RG 59, MLR); addressed: "The Preside[. . .]"; endorsed by Bartholomew Dandridge, Jr. Tr (Lb in same, SDC). Not recorded in SJL. Enclosures: (1) TJ to Edmond Charles Genet, 9 Sep. 1793. (2) TJ to George Hammond, 9 Sep. 1793.

George Washington to the Commissioners of the Federal District

Gentlemen   Philadelphia Sep. 9. 1793.

I have duly recieved your letter of Sep. 5. and in consequence thereof have authorised Mr. David Ross of Bladensburg, and Colo. Robert Townshend Hooe of Alexandria, to examine the accounts and vouchers of the expenditure of the monies appropriated to your trust as Commissioners of the public buildings of the federal territory, and to certify to me the result.

Dft (DLC: Washington Papers); entirely in TJ's hand, unsigned; endorsed by Bartholomew Dandridge, Jr. The letter Washington sent followed the Dft (Fitzpatrick, *Writings*, XXXIII, 85).

On 1 Aug. 1793 the Commissioners had requested the President to have their accounts and expenditures examined, and he proposed Captain Richard Conway of Alexandria and Major John Ross of Bladensburg for this task four weeks later. In their LETTER OF SEP. 5. the Commissioners noted that Washington had evidently mistaken John for David Ross and suggested a number of Alexandria residents, including HOOE, as alternates to Conway, who they suspected would probably decline the appointment in order to attend to his private business affairs (Commissioners to Washington, 1 Aug., 5 Sep. 1793, DNA: RG 42, DCLB; Washington to Commissioners, 29 Aug. 1793, Fitzpatrick, *Writings*, XXXIII, 74-5).

This day TJ also drafted a letter for the President notifying Ross and Hooe of their appointment and duties (Dft in DLC: Washington Papers; in TJ's hand, with revisions by Dandridge to change the text from a circular to individual letters for each; at foot of text: "Mr. David Ross. Bladensburgh. Colo. Robert Townshend Hooe. Alexandria"; endorsed by Dandridge; the FC in Lb in same follows TJ's wording). Ross and Hooe made their report to the President on 31 Oct. 1793 (DNA: RG 42, PC).

To George Clinton

SIR   Philadelphia September 10th,[1] 1793.

The President of the United States has received the letter, which Your Excellency addressed to him on the second instant.

He considers it as a fresh proof of your disposition, to prevent the exercise of state authorities from clashing with those of the[2] fœderal Government.[3]

The event which Your Excellency has communicated, is indeed, what you express it to be, of national concern, and the power of arresting, derived from[4] the 9th: article of the consular convention with France, is capable of great abuse. For altho' some degree of security may arise from the character of Consuls and Vice-Consuls, who alone are designated as intitled to demand deserters; and a person unjustly apprehended be ultimately discharged;[5] yet the facility which is afforded by that instrument, for obtaining the interposition of the Magistracy, merely by exhibiting the register of a vessel, or a ship's roll, may often expose to a temporary imprisonment those, who never constituted a part of any crew whatsoever. The President therefore feels an assurance, that by the cautions which Your Excellency will prescribe to yourself on such occasions, you will save the United States from every possible embarrassment. I have the honor to be with sentiments of great respect Sir, Your most obedient and most humble servant

TH: JEFFERSON

RC (Irving Coopersmith, New York, New York, 1955); in a clerk's hand, signed by TJ; date completed after PrC was made (see note 1 below), at foot of text. "His Excellency the Governor of the State of New York." PrC (DLC); unsigned; date completed in ink. Dft (DLC: TJ Papers, 93: 16017); entirely in the hand of Edmund Randolph; undated; only the most important emendations are noted below; at head of text: "Draught of a letter, proposed to be written by the Secretary of state to the Governor of New-York"; conjoined to Dft of TJ to James Duane, 10 Sep. 1793. FC (Lb in DNA: RG 59, DL). Described in SJL as "drawn by E.R."; draft recorded in SJPL under 5 Sep. 1793: "E.R's draught of a lre from Th:J. to Govr. of N.Y. arrest of Galbaud."

For the background to this letter and Edmund Randolph's authorship of it, see Notes on Cabinet Meetings, 4 Sep. 1793, and note; and TJ to James Duane, 10 Sep. 1793, and note.

[1] Day inserted in space left blank in manuscript; day inserted in ink on PrC.

[2] In Dft Randolph here canceled "United Stat."

[3] In Dft Randolph here canceled "[or] its stipulation."

[4] Preceding two words interlined in Dft in place of "under."

[5] In Dft Randolph first wrote "and a person apprehended will be be discharged, if he be unjustly seized" before altering the phrase to read as above.

To Tench Coxe

Sep. 10. 1793.

Th: Jefferson presents his compliments to Mr. Coxe. He directed a Census to be sent him in the moment of receiving his note of the 5th. With respect to the placing Consuls in the British islands, we are so far from being permitted that, that a common mercantile factor is not permitted by their laws. The experiment of establishing Consuls in the Colonies of the European nations has been going on for some time, but as yet we cannot say it has been formally and fully admitted by any. The French colonial authority has received them, but they have never yet been recognised by the national authority.

PrC (DLC). Tr (ViU: Edgehill-Randolph Papers); 19th-century copy.

To James Duane

SIR   Philadelphia September the 10th.[1] 1793.

The inclosed papers relate to an event of national importance and they are transmitted to you by the direction of the President of the United States: the district judges being the officers contemplated by law, as best suited to the execution of the 9th. article of the consular convention he thinks it[2] desirable, that all such information, should, if possible be acted upon by the judicial power. I have the honor to be with sentiments of great respect Sir, Your most obedient and most humble servant

PrC (DLC); in a clerk's hand, unsigned; date completed in ink (see note 1 below); at foot of text in ink: "The honorable Judge Duane." Dft (DLC: TJ Papers, 93:

16017); in Edmund Randolph's hand, undated; with emendations, only the most important being noted below; at head of text: "Draught of a letter, proposed to be written by the Secretary of state to the district-judge of New-York"; subjoined to Dft of TJ to George Clinton, 10 Sep. 1793. FC (Lb in DNA: RG 59, DL). Described in SJL as "drawn by E.R." Enclosures: (1) Edmond Charles Genet to Governor George Clinton, New York, 30 Aug. 1793, reporting that General Galbaud, his aide-de-camp Conscience, and Corporal Bonne escaped last night from custody on board the *Jupiter*, asserting that they were deserters and that as such the French had a right to reclaim them, requesting that warrants be delivered to the French consul so that they could be arrested and brought to one of the vessels in the fleet, supplying descriptions of the three men, and adding in a postscript that the men did not speak English and that the consul would show the mayor of New York the *Jupiter's* muster roll to prove they were crew members. (2) Clinton to Genet, New York, 30 Aug. 1793, stating that in response to Genet's request he had instructed state judges and officials to give all the aid and assistance for capturing the deserters consonant with Article 9 of the Consular Convention, but adding that although the ship's roll was a proof sufficient to justify this measure, the convention also permitted those proceeded against to prove that they were not deserters, and that if they did so to a judge's satisfaction they might be released. (3) Proclamation of Clinton, 1 Sep. 1793, instructing New York judges and officials, pursuant to Article 9 of the Consular Convention—since Genet had shown from the roll of the French warship *Jupiter* that Galbaud, Conscience, and Bonne were crew members and asserted that they had deserted—to aid in the trio's capture and imprisonment until they could be returned to the ship, provided that such detention did not exceed three months. (4) Clinton to Galbaud, 31 Aug. 1793, inferring from Galbaud's letter of this date that he had seen No. 3, observing that he had acted as the Consular Convention stipulated and that if a deception regarding the ship's roll had been practiced, those responsible were answerable, confirming that his proclamation had been misdated, though the mistake was immaterial since the directions would take effect from

the time they were issued and were the duty of magistrates even without the formality of an order, and stating that Galbaud's claim of protection and hospitality from the state would be honored in all cases but the present one. (5) Clinton to George Washington, 2 Sep. 1793, enclosing Nos. 1-4; stating that the French consul general's application placed him in "a very delicate situation" where his refusal to interfere might lead to charges of undue denial of aid stipulated by the Consular Convention and of not having done his duty, that the United States District Attorney had agreed that his proclamation was proper, that though the April 1792 federal statute concerning consuls appeared to commit such cases to the exclusive jurisdiction of federal district judges and marshals, the rigorous application of this interpretation would render the convention article respecting the return of deserters a dead letter from the remote residence of the district judge, and that the alleged deserters had been pursued and overtaken in Westchester County but had escaped there and evidently fled the state; relating that he had been unable to detain the *Republican*, a prize of the English frigate *Boston*, because it sailed away before he received the relevant letter from Secretary of War Henry Knox; and reporting that the French privateers *Carmagnole* and *Petite Démocrate* arrived here yesterday and that appropriate measures will be taken immediately to cause their departure (Trs of Nos. 1-4 in DNA: RG 59, LGS, No. 1 in French, with Nos. 1, 3, and 4 in DeWitt Clinton's hand, all being endorsed on a separate sheet by George Taylor, Jr., in part: "inclosed in Gov. Clinton's 2 Sep. 93"; RC of No. 5 in same, in DeWitt Clinton's hand, signed by George Clinton, endorsed by TJ and Taylor).

For the background to this letter and Edmund Randolph's authorship of it, see Notes on Cabinet Meetings, 4 Sep. 1793, and note.

According to the 9TH. ARTICLE OF THE CONSULAR CONVENTION with France, which TJ had helped to negotiate in 1788, consuls and vice-consuls could have crew members who deserted from vessels of their respective nations arrested and repatriated if they petitioned the competent magistrate in writing and proved from the ship's roll, subject to proof to the contrary by the men in question, that those demanded were part of the crew. The consuls were to be given all aid and assistance in searching for and seizing the deserters, who could be incarcerated for up to three months after their arrest at the expense of the consuls while arrangements were made to send them out of the country (see Vol. 14: 176). The April 1792 law carrying this convention into effect made United States district judges the "competent judges" for carrying out this article and designated United States marshals and their deputies to serve as the "competent executive officers" stipulated by the convention to assist French consular officials (*Annals*, III, 1360).

[1] Day inserted in ink in space left blank in manuscript.

[2] In Dft Randolph here canceled "probable, that the information, now forwarded, may suggest the propriety of forming [. . .], which."

From Edmond Charles Genet

New york le 9. [i.e. 10] 7bre. 1793. l'an 2e.

Le Citoyen Johanene, Capitaine de la Goëlette le Citoyen Genet armé à charleston en vertu des traités entre la france et les etats unis Sous l'autorisation du Gouvernement francois et avec l'assentiment du gouvernement local de la Caroline du Sud[1] après avoir eprouvé mille obstacles depuis le Commencement de son expédition en Course vient d'être arreté[2] ainsi que son nav[ire] par l'amirauté des Etats unis dans la delaware au moment ou il alloit se soumettre aux ordres qui lui avoient été donnés par le gouvernement:[3] Comme il est évident,[4] d'après les traittés, que les Cours d'amirautés n'ont aucun droit Sur nos prises et sur nos batimens armés et qu'il est probable que des ordres particuliers[5] emanés du Gouvernement federal ont autorisée a agir celle des Etats unis[6] Je vous prie M. de donner les ordres nécessaires[7] pour que la Goëlette le Citoyen Genet[8] que le Capitaine ne veut plus employer à la Course et qu'il destine à servir d'aviso à la Republique soit relaché.

Le Citoyen Johanene Officier de marine de la république francaise employé à bord du Jupiter, ayant agi d'après des autorisations légales, ne peut etre arrete pour cause resultant de cet armement. Il est donc de la plus grande Justice que les poursuittes contre lui cessent également.[9]

Dft (NHi: Genet Family Papers); in a clerk's hand, unsigned, with dateline and revisions by Genet; above salutation by Genet: "Le Citoyen genet Mtre. à Mr. Jefferson." FC (DLC: Genet Papers); in English. Recorded in SJL as a 10 Sep. 1793 letter received 12 Sep. 1793.

Concerning Captain Johanene and the *Citoyen Genet*, a French privateer commissioned by Genet in Charleston in April 1793, see George Washington to TJ, 19 Aug. 1793, and note.

[1] Preceding thirteen words interlined by Genet in place of "local."

[2] Preceding four words altered by Genet from "S'est vu arreter." Remainder of sentence to "gouvernement" interlined by Genet in place of "en vertu des Varrans pour causes relatives à cet affaire: il m'informe, en même tems, que l'amirauté des Etats-unis vient de faire saisir sa goelette."

[3] Genet here canceled "de sortir de cette" but neglected to cancel "sans."

[4] Genet here canceled "incontestable."

[5] Word interlined by Genet in place of "superieurs."

[6] Preceding four words interlined by Genet.

[7] The clerk first wrote "Je viens vous de-

mander un ordre" and then Genet altered it to read as above.

[8] Remainder of paragraph interlined by Genet in place of "soit relachée."

[9] Word inserted by Genet.

To Alexander S. Glass

SIR   Philadelphia. Sep. 10. 1793.

I have duly received your memorial praying that your sloop Betsey, a prize to the Citoyen Genet, might be delivered to you, by the Executive. As this is done by the interposition of a military force only, I have inclosed the memorial and documents to the Secretary at war, with whom it will rest to consider whether it can be done, and to give you an answer. I am with regard Sir Your most obedt. servt

TH: JEFFERSON

PrC (DLC); at foot of text: "Mr. Alexander S. Glass." FC (Lb in DNA: RG 59, DL).

Glass's MEMORIAL of 7 Sep., recorded in SJL as received 7 Sep. 1793, and the enclosed DOCUMENTS have not been found.

From Christopher Gore

SIR   Boston Septr 10. 1793

Yesterday morning I receiv'd your favor of the 2d. instant, and this day preferr'd a complaint to Judge Lowell against Mr. Duplaine for wilfully and Knowingly opposing and obstructing the Deputy Marshal in an attempt to serve and execute a writ of the United States. This complaint was supported by the oaths of several witnesses. Mr. Duplaine was arrested, and brought before the judge who has recogniz'd him in the sum of 1000 dollars, with two sureties in the sum of 500 dollars each, for his appearance before the next circuit court, and answering to what may then be objected against him in behalf of the United States, especially to the subject of this complaint. I did not apprehend that Mr. Duplaine or any consul enjoy'd the privilege of a diplomatic character—but always consider'd persons of his quality amenable to the laws.

At the time this opposition to law took place, the judge of the district was absent, and I did not think it expedient to hazard an enquiry in a matter of this importance before a common justice of the peace. When the judge return'd the vessels were in possession of the Governor. The grand jury being soon, viz on the 12th. October, to attend the circuit court in Boston I thought it adviseable the process shoud originate

[79]

there. Having doubts whether the action of replevin woud lie in cases of this nature, I considerd the argument in favor of Duplaine drawn from this supposition at least plausible—and thinking there was no danger that Mr. Duplaine woud leave the district before the 12 Octr., I had concluded prior to the receit of your favor to delay any prosecution till the sitting of the Circuit Court. These reasons will shew why I did not make complaint against Mr. Duplaine at an earlier day.

I enclose evidence of the conduct of Mr. Duplaine in this transaction, which was taken in his presence and when he had counsel to cross examine the witnesses. These depositions were taken at the time of the enquiry into the truth of the complaint—thus they were taken with every advantage to Mr. Duplaine, thô he did not Know the purpose for which they were taken. Enclosed are copies of the representations made by me to Governor Hancock, my letter to Mr. Duplaine and note to Mr. Avery Secretary of the Commonwealth, also a copy of the writ under which the deputy marshal acted. I am sir with the greatest respect your most obed servt   C. GORE

RC (DNA: RG 59, MLR); endorsed by TJ as received 2 Oct. 1793 and so recorded in SJL. Enclosures: (1) Memorial of Gore to John Hancock, [3 Aug. 1793], requesting the governor to prevent from putting out to sea a 27-ton American-built and lately American-owned sloop now in the "gut of Nantucket" that had been fitted out as a French privateer in Boston and Charlestown, as indicated by the enclosed affidavits, and was planning to set sail this evening or tomorrow morning; with note by Gore stating that the memorial and enclosed affidavits were presented on 3 Aug. 1793 to Hancock, who, according to Secretary John Avery, sent the affidavits to the "Executive of the United States." (2) Gore to Avery, 6 Aug. 1793, asking whether Hancock had issued any orders concerning the French privateer *Roland*; with note by Gore stating he had received no written answer to this inquiry (Trs in same; each with subjoined note in Gore's hand). (3) Writ of replevin of the United States District Court of Massachusetts, Boston, 21 Aug. 1793, ordering the federal district marshal of Massachusetts or his deputy to replevy the schooner *Greyhound*, John Henry Hilt master, owned by Alexander Brymer and Andrew Belcher of Halifax, Nova Scotia, and its cargo of mackerel, now detained in Boston by Lewis Guillaume Felix Laumosne of that city, and to summon Laumosne to appear before the United States Circuit Court of Massachusetts on 12 Oct. 1793 to answer Brymer and Belcher's plea of replevin (printed form in same with blanks filled, the names of John Jay and N. Goodale being inserted as witness and clerk respectively, attested by Deputy Marshal Samuel Bradford; Tr in DNA: RG 46, Senate Records, 3d Cong., 1st sess.; Tr in Lb in DNA: RG 59, DL; Tr in DLC: Genet Papers). (4) Gore to Antoine Charbonnet Duplaine, 22 Aug. 1793, demanding that the French vice-consul remove the armed men who yesterday by his direction had forcibly taken possession of the *Greyhound* after the marshal had replevied and assumed custody of it (Tr in DNA: RG 59, MLR, with subjoined note in Gore's hand, 10 Sep. 1793, stating that Duplaine had not replied to this letter; Tr in same, lacking Gore's note; Tr in Lb in DNA: RG 46, Senate Records, 3d Cong., 1st sess., lacking Gore's note; Tr in Lb in DNA: RG 59, DL, lacking Gore's note; Tr in DLC: Genet Papers, lacking Gore's note). (5) Memorial of Gore to Hancock, [26 Aug. 1793], requesting the governor to take into custody the *Roland*, the French privateer complained of in No. 1 and now refitting in Boston, as well as the two prizes it brought into that port on 21 Aug. 1793; with a subjoined note by Gore, 10 Sep. 1793, stating that after Bradford delivered the memorial to Hancock on [26] Aug.

1793 the governor told Bradford that he had ordered the adjutant general to take possession of the two prizes and to direct the *Roland* to leave port, which led to the dismantling of the privateer and the prizes coming into the governor's custody (Tr in DNA: RG 59, MLR; with note in Gore's hand). (6) Deposition of Samuel Bradford, 10 Sep. 1793, stating that at about 7:00 P.M. on 21 Aug. 1793 he received a writ of replevin to serve on Laumosne, prize master of the *Greyhound*; that accompanied by Captains Lyde and Hagman he went aboard the *Greyhound*, read the writ to Laumosne in the presence of the captain of the *Roland*, explained the nature of the legal action, claimed possession of the prize, and offered assurances that a bond had been given to cover any damages arising from his taking possession of the vessel; that later that evening M. Jutau from the nearby French frigate *Concorde* came aboard the *Greyhound* in response to Laumosne's request and declared that the prize was the property of the French Republic and could not be attached; that within ninety minutes after Jutau's subsequent return to the *Concorde* a lieutenant and twelve armed marines from the frigate took possession of the *Greyhound*, ignoring his protest, and that the lieutenant, in accordance with his orders from the captain of the *Concorde*, had the prize stationed near the frigate and the *Roland*; that he dismissed the men who had come with him to help serve the writ after being informed by the lieutenant that he was under express orders to use force to prevent the removal of the *Greyhound*; that he was advised by Duplaine, who boarded the prize with Chancellor Jutau and M. Nancrede about midnight, after the lieutenant had returned to the *Concorde* leaving a corporal and four marines on the *Greyhound*, that he was free to return to the prize the next morning even though Duplaine intended to keep possession of it; that he is certain the captain of the *Concorde* was acting under Duplaine's orders; that about noon on 24 Aug. the corporal and the guard left the *Greyhound* and returned to the *Concorde* just before it left for sea and were replaced by a Frenchman from the *Roland*; and that an hour later he took possession of the *Greyhound*, had it moved to a wharf, and legally executed the writ, to Duplaine's apparent surprise (Tr in same, with subjoined note by Gore that the deposition was sworn be-

fore United States District Court Judge John Lowell on 10 Sep. 1793, being endorsed by George Taylor, Jr., with reference to all the enclosures: "Evidence in the Case of Consul Duplaine—of the Repub. of France at Boston"; Tr in DNA: RG 46, Senate Records, 3d Cong., 1st sess.; Tr in Lb in DNA: RG 59, DL; Tr in DLC: Genet Papers). (7) Deposition of Marshal John Brooks, 10 Sep. 1793, stating that on 22 Aug. 1793, having learned that Bradford had been prevented from serving a writ of replevin on the *Greyhound* by an armed force acting under orders from Captain Van Dogen, commander of the *Concorde*, he went aboard the *Concorde* and, in the presence of Duplaine, Justice Cooper, and Thomas Amory, Jr., demanded that Van Dogen restore the prize; that Van Dogen was angry over the removal of some Americans from a French vessel and Bradford's effort to take possession of a vessel flying the French flag and under the protection of a French warship; that Van Dogen refused to surrender the *Greyhound*, claiming that he was acting under orders from Duplaine; that after he met privately with Duplaine on the 22d and 23d the French consul stated that he would keep possession of the *Greyhound* and that unless Hancock did something about it he would advertise the prize in the newspapers and in six days condemn it to the captors if no one else proved a claim to it; that according to a statement Van Dogen made to him in Duplaine's presence the laws of the French Republic required French naval commanders to obey orders in foreign ports from French consuls, who "were Admirals, or had the power of admirals"; and that, while Duplaine stated that he would order the armed guard to leave the *Greyhound* and would protest the measures of the United States government, he subsequently refused to withdraw the guard (Tr in DNA: RG 59, MLR, with subjoined notes by Gore, 10 Sep. 1793, that the deposition was sworn before Judge Lowell and that "Then Thomas Amory junr. Rufus Greene Amory, Nathaniel Byfield Lyde and John Brooks Esqr. made Oath to the Truth of the annexed Depositions by them respectively subscribed, in the Presence of Antoine Charbonnet Duplaine and declared that they did not recollect any Other material Circumstance relative to the Matter in Enquiry and the annexed Deposition of Samuel Bradford is

Transcript of his Deposition taken under like Circumstances"; Tr in DNA: RG 46, Senate Records, 3d Cong., 1st sess.; Tr in Lb in DNA: RG 59, DL; Tr in DLC: Genet Papers). (8) Deposition of Thomas Amory, Jr., 10 Sep. 1793, of the same import as No. 7, but adding that on 22 Aug. 1793 Duplaine asserted that any vessel flying the French republican flag was entitled to his protection; that Van Dogen claimed, in answer to a hypothetical case posed by Brooks, that he would feel duty-bound to protect a French merchant ship attached in Boston harbor by an American citizen; that Van Dogen noted he had written to Hancock and would give up the *Greyhound* if the governor demanded and forward copies of his letter and Hancock's reply to Edmond Charles Genet; that during a meeting at Duplaine's lodgings the consul assured him and Brooks that he would under protest order Van Dogen to give up the *Greyhound*, an assurance he abruptly contradicted after Jutau joined the meeting and spoke a few words to him in French; that upon being pressed by Brooks, Duplaine stated that he did not wish to use force against American legal officials and promised a final answer the next morning about the *Greyhound*; that on the morning of the 23d Duplaine informed Brooks and him that he would keep possession of the vessel, whereupon Brooks stated that he would notify the government and he himself handed Duplaine No. 4, which the consul read without making a reply, and then left with Brooks. (9) Deposition of Rufus G. Amory, 10 Sep. 1793, of the same import as No. 6 with respect to Van Dogen's refusal to return the *Greyhound*, but adding that he himself had obtained the writ of re-

plevin as attorney for Brymer and Belcher; that Van Dogen had considered the *Greyhound* to be under his protection as soon as it entered Boston harbor as a prize flying French colors; and that Van Dogen had complained to Hancock about the American attempt to take possession of this ship without his permission. (10) Deposition of Nathaniel B. Lyde, 10 Sep. 1793, of the same import as No. 6, but adding that Bradford had remained aboard the *Greyhound* throughout the period it was in the custody of armed French guards (Trs in DNA: RG 59, MLR, each with subjoined note by Gore that the depositions were sworn before Judge Lowell on 10 Sep. 1793; Trs in DNA: RG 46, Senate Records, 3d Cong., 1st sess.; Trs in Lb in DNA: RG 59, DL; Trs in DLC: Genet Papers). Enclosures Nos. 3-4 and 6-10 printed in *Message*, 83-8. Enclosed in Benjamin Bankson to TJ, 23 Sep. 1793; Enclosures Nos. 3-4 and 6-10 enclosed in TJ to Bankson (second letter), TJ to Antoine Charbonnet Duplaine, TJ to Edmond Charles Genet, TJ to Gouverneur Morris, and TJ to George Washington (fifth letter), all 3 Oct. 1793.

After receiving this evidence of Duplaine's defiance of federal authority, TJ promptly informed him, in accordance with a previous decision by the Cabinet, that the United States government was revoking his exequatur as French vice-consul for New Hampshire, Massachusetts, and Rhode Island (Cabinet Opinions on the *Roland* and Relations with Great Britain, France, and the Creeks, 31 Aug. 1793, and note; TJ to Duplaine, 3 Oct. 1793).

To George Hammond

Sir   Philadelphia Sep. 10. 1793.

I received yesterday, and laid before the President your letter of the 8th. instant, desiring that James Shoolbred should have an Exequatur on the copy of a consular commission inclosed in that letter. But it appears so material in law that our records should be founded on an inspection of the original, that the President, on account of the distance, thinks it more convenient that Mr. Shoolbred should be permitted to act for a while without an Exequatur, I am therefore authorized hereby to declare his permission to him to exercise the functions of Vice-Consul for his Britannic majesty in the states of North Carolina, South Carolina, and Georgia, without the formality of an Exequatur, until there shall have been full time to produce the original of his commission to be exhibited to the President. I have the honor to be Sir Your most obedt. servt   TH: JEFFERSON

PrC (DLC); at foot of text: "The Minister Pleny. of Gr. Britain." FC (Lb in DNA: RG 59, DL).

From Alexandre Maurice d'Hauterive

New york Le 10. Sepre. 1793. L'an deux de la république française.

J'ai Envoyé, Monsieur, votre Lettre au ministre plénipotentiaire de la république à qui elle auroit dû être adressée, car accredité auprès du Gouvernement de L'Etat de New york, je n'ai de relations officielles avec Le Gouvernement général que par la médiation du Gouvernement Local, ou par celui du Ministre plénipotentiaire de la République. J'ai encore Moins du M'attendre aux reproches que votre Lettre Exprime. J'ai protesté auprès du Gouvernement Local et auprès de vos Cours pour maintenir les droits nationaux; J'ai invité au Soutien de la Cause de la Liberté les Français Soldats, matelots et amis de la Liberté: car tous les français qui ne Sont pas Soldats ou Matelots et amis de la Liberté, ont besoin qu'on les avertisse qu'ils n'ont accès ni au Consulat, ni sur les Vaisseaux de la République; Si ces actes qui Sont dans la Ligne, je ne dis pas de mes droits, mais de mes Devoirs m'attirent la Disgrace du Gouvernement de ce Paÿs, Je suis obligé de vous Declarer, Monsieur, qu'aucun avantage, qu'aucun inconvenient personnels n'entrent dans les Motifs qui me Determinent. Quant aux Menaces qui terminent votre Lettre, il m'est impossible d'y répondre: car elles attentent à L'honneur d'une puissante République qui m'a imposé une Loi que je trouve bien facile à Suivre, celle de ne rien Craindre au monde, que le malheur de transiger Sur Ses droits ou Sur mes Devoirs. J'Espere, Monsieur, que Je n'aurai jamais ce reproche à me faire. Dureste, Monsieur, Je recevrai Sur cet objet les ordres du ministre de le république française et J'y obeïrai.   HAUTERIVE
                                                                        Consul

RC (DNA: RG 59, NFC); in a clerk's hand, signed by Hauterive; at head of text by Hauterive and Edmond Charles Genet: "Le Consul de la république fse. à New york à Mr. Jefferson Secretaire d'etat"; endorsed by TJ as received 12 Sep. 1793 and so re-corded in SJL. Tr (DLC: Genet Papers). Tr (AMAE: Correspondance Consulaire, New York, III). Tr (same: CPEU, XXXIX).

Alexandre Maurice Blanc de Lanautte d'Hauterive (1754-1830), born into a mod-est noble family, became a minor official in the French diplomatic service and served as French consul in New York from May 1793 to March 1794, when he was relieved of his duties by the commissioners who succeeded Edmond Charles Genet as the French Republic's representatives in the United States. After remaining in America three more years for reasons of health, Hauterive returned to France in 1797 and went on to hold a series of increasingly responsible positions in the French foreign ministry (Frances S. Childs, "The Hauterive Journal," *New-York Historical Society Quarterly*, XXXIII [1949], 69-70, 83-5; Jean Tulard,

ed., *Dictionnaire Napoléon* [Paris, 1987], 865-6).

VOTRE LETTRE: Circular to French Consuls and Vice-Consuls, 7 Sep. 1793. In transmitting TJ's circular to Genet, Hauterive described it as the work of the temporary minister of a republic that owed its birth to France, criticized TJ for daring to speak to representatives of the most powerful nation on earth in the language of ancient tyrants, and left it up to Genet to determine whether French consular officials should comply with TJ's demands (Hauterive to Genet, [10] Sep. 1793, DLC: Genet Papers).

To Henry Knox

SIR   Philadelphia Sep. 10. 1793.

The inclosed memorial of Alexandr. S. Glass praying the exertion of the publick force to deliver to him his sloop the Betsey, prize to the Citoyen Genet, belonging to your department, I have the honor of inclosing it to you, & of being with great respect, Sir, Your most obedt. servt   TH: JEFFERSON

P.S. I inclose the letter of Mr. Soderstrom, who communicated the papers to me.

PrC (DLC); at foot of text: "The Secretary at War." FC (Lb in DNA: RG 59, DL). Enclosures not found.

To Adam Lindsay

SIR   Philadelphia Sep. 10. 1793.

Your favor of the 27th. came duly to hand, and I have to thank you for the intelligence it contained. I meant to have asked the continuance of it, but that I am likely to leave this place a little sooner than I had intended. You will have heard of an infectious and mortal disease which has broken out in this city. There was a hope till lately that it might have been prevented spreading. However it is now beyond all expectation of that, and the deaths which had increased from 5. to 10. a day, were the last two days probably risen to 25. a day. It happened that the President had made his preparations to visit Mt. Vernon, having some time ago fixed on this day for his departure. He is accordingly gone. Colo. Hamilton is ill of the fever tho' on the recovery. The people of business in the line of government are mostly gone or going: so that I think it probable I shall go to Virginia myself within a week or ten days, uncertain as to the time of my return. I am Sir Your obedt. servt   TH: JEFFERSON

PrC (DLC); at foot of text: "Mr. Adam Lindsay." Tr (ViU: Edgehill-Randolph Papers); 19th-century copy.

To David Meade Randolph

DEAR SIR   Philadelphia Sep. 10. 1793.

I learn from Mr. Randolph that there is a box from England lodged for me in the custom-house at Bermuda. I presume it contains a small orrery, as I know that such an one has been sent out for me. The cost was $2\frac{1}{2}$ or 3. guineas, I do not remember which, and my letters are packed so that I cannot turn to the one mentioning this. I do not know what the duty is, but as it cannot be much I will take the liberty of asking you to pay it, and contrive the box to me, and I will take care to have the duty reimbursed. If you will send the box to Colo. Gamble he will readily forward it to me.

The yellow fever is spreading so fast in this city, that the President being gone, Genl. Knox going, and Colo. Hamilton ill of it, I believe I shall go also within a few days though I had not intended to set out till the beginning of next month. My best respects to Mrs. Randolph & am Dear Sir Your friend & servt   TH: JEFFERSON

PrC (DLC); at foot of text: "D. M. Randolph. esq." Tr (ViU: Edgehill-Randolph Papers); 19th-century copy.

To Richard Söderström

SIR   Philadelphia Sep. 10. 1793.

I have the honor to acknolege the receipt of your letter of the 7th. inst. accompanying the application of Mr. Glass for the delivery of his sloop Betsey, a prize to the Citoyen Genet. If the case admits of redress by the Executive, it will be only by the interposition of an armed force, and cases of that class belonging to the department of war, I have inclosed the memorial and other papers to the Secretary at war, with whom it rests to consider whether delivery can be made in that way and to give an answer. I have the honor to be Sir Your most obedt. servt

TH: JEFFERSON

PrC (DLC); at foot of text: "Mr. Soderstrom." FC (Lb in DNA: RG 59, DL).

The Swedish consul's LETTER OF THE 7TH. INST., recorded in SJL as received 7 Sep. 1793, has not been found.

To St. George Tucker

DEAR SIR   Philadelphia Sep. 10. 1793

Your favor of June 14 came to hand some time ago, and nothing but a load of business has prevented my sooner acknoleging it. No person on earth heard with more sincere regret the tales which were the subject of it, no body lamented more the torture thro' which their victim must have passed. For myself, when placed under the necessity of deciding in a case where on one hand is a young and worthy person, all the circumstances of whose education and position in life pronounce her virtuous and innocent, and on the other, the proneness of the world to sow and spread slander, there is no hesitation in my mind. I needed no evidence therefore on this question, and could at any time have conscientiously appeared as one of her compurgators.—What an ocean is life! And how our barks get separated in our passage[1] thro it! One of the greatest comforts of[2] the retirement to which I shall soon withdraw will be it's rejoining me to my earliest and best friends, and acquaintance. I shall hope to be in your way in some of your tacks, and to be able to assure you personally of the sincere respect & esteem with which I am Dear Sir Your friend & servt   TH: JEFFERSON

RC (ViW: Tucker-Coleman Collection); addressed: "The honble St. George Tucker. Richmond"; franked, stamped, and postmarked. PrC (DLC); with alteration by TJ in ink (see note 1 below). Tr (DLC); 19th-century copy.

Tucker's FAVOR OF JUNE 14, recorded in SJL as received from Richmond on 21 June 1793, has not been found, but it must have contained a defense of Ann Cary Randolph,

the VICTIM of allegations of adultery with her brother-in-law, Tucker's stepson Richard Randolph, who was accused of infanticide in connection with the same scandal (TJ to Martha Jefferson Randolph, 28 Apr. 1793, and note).

[1] In PrC TJ substituted "beating" in ink for the preceding two words. Tr follows PrC.

[2] TJ here canceled "my."

From George Washington

DEAR SIR   Chester Septr 10th. 1793.

I return, from this place, the Papers which you put into my hands on the Road, to day.

The unpromising state of the Negotiation at Madrid, and the opinion of the Commissioners that their Commission should be withdrawn, and matters at that Court placed in Statu quo, deserve very serious consideration. I pray you to give it; and if it rests altogether with the Executive (after the Agency the Senate has had in the business) let me know the result.

Mr. Carmichael must not be the person left there; for, from him we should never hear a tittle of what is going forward at the Court of Madrid. I am Your Affecte   Go: Washington

RC (DLC); at foot of text: "Secretary of State"; endorsed by TJ as received 12 Sep. 1793 and so recorded in SJL. Dft (DNA: RG 59, MLR); in the hand of Bartholomew Dandridge, Jr. FC (Lb in same, SDC); with a minor variation. Recorded in SJPL.

Enclosure: William Carmichael and William Short to TJ, 6 June 1793. Other enclosures not identified, though one of them—perhaps the only other one—may have been the missing extract, received by TJ the day before, of Short's 7 June 1793 letter.

To Benjamin Bankson

Sep. 11. 1793.

Th: Jefferson will be obliged to Mr. Bankson as soon as he has finished the letters left with him yesterday, to go on with the Duplicate of those Aug. 16. and 23d. to Mr. Gouverneur Morris and the documents, taking therein the assistance of the other gentlemen. The press copy is to be sent to Mr. Morris, that on writing paper being wanting for another purpose. When it is ready, Mr. Bankson will be pleased to exert himself particularly to find some vessel going to France, and if possible a trusty passenger to whom he can commit it. Th:J. is authorised to refund the reasonable [1] expences from the port of *landing* to Paris, of any trusty person who will undertake to deliver it. The letter now inclosed is to be sent with the other.

PrC (DLC). Tr (ViU: Edgehill-Randolph Papers); 19th-century copy. Enclosure not identified.

FOR ANOTHER PURPOSE: probably for inclusion among the documents pertaining to the recall of Edmond Charles Genet that the President submitted to Congress in December 1793 (ASP, *Foreign Relations*, I, 141-88).

This day TJ also wrote a brief note to Bankson inclosing "the return of a Senator for Delaware, which he desires him so to dispose of as that it may be certainly delivered to the Secretary of the Senate when in town" (RC in DNA: RG 59, MLR, address being largely torn away, with note at foot of text by Robert Heyzham—"Received October the 26th. 1793 of Mr. Benjamin Bankson the Commission of John Vining Esqr. as a Senator of the United States from the State of Delaware. For Samuel A. Otis Secy of the Senate of the United States Rob: Heyzham Chf Clk"—and endorsement by George Taylor, Jr.; PrC in DLC; recorded in SJL as a letter of 12 Sep. 1793). SJL records a missing letter of 6 Sep. 1793 from Governor Joshua Clayton of Delaware received 11 Sep. 1793 dealing with the "return of Senator."

On 2 Nov. 1792 Governor Thomas Sim Lee of Maryland had written a brief note to TJ from Annapolis transmitting an election certificate for members of the House of Representatives from that state (FC in MdAA: Maryland State Papers; recorded in SJL as received 6 Nov. 1792).

[1] Word interlined.

From John Bringhurst

[11 Sep. 1793]

John Bringhurst informs his friend TJ. that he is very sorry it is not in his power to come in the country to see him, as he departs for New York in the early stage of tomorrow, nevertheless any particular business respecting the notes or otherwise will be punctually attended to. If TJ leaves an order for the money on the treasury, he (JB) will gett the money when due and pay the notes as he will not be absent more than 3 weeks. Any Letter or orders left at my brothers Store No. 131 South front Street will meet due attention. The note sent Last was informal the word to (or order) being omitted prevented my getting it done, and expect the banks will shut to day. I will leave orders with my brother to pay the remainder of money due in Cash.

RC (MHi); undated; addressed: "Thomas Jefferson Esqr *Present*"; endorsed by TJ as received 11 Sep. 1793 and so recorded in SJL, which describes it as a letter of that date.

MY BROTHERS STORE: the establishment of James Bringhurst, Jr., an ironmonger (Hardie, *Phila. Dir.*, 15). THE NOTE SENT LAST has not been found.

To William Carmichael and William Short

GENTLEMEN   Philadelphia Sep. 11. 1793.

My last letters to you were of the 12th. and 16th. of July. Since that I have recieved yours of Apr. 18. May 5. and June 6. The present occasion does not admit of my entering into particulars on the subject of your letters: I will only inform you therefore generally that the President approves of your proceedings and views. Proceed in the plan your letter of June 6. expresses; we make no other alterations in our instructions. The negociation was fixed at Madrid at the express desire of that court delivered to me verbally by their Chargés here, and on which some explanations in writing took place.—The Indians on our North West have refused to meet our Commissioners unless they would fix the Ohio as our boundary by a Preliminary article. This being impossible on account of the army locations and sales to individuals North of that river, the war goes on, and we expect Genl. Wayne is now in motion.— An infectious, putrid and mortal fever has broken out here. The week before last the deaths were about 40. the last week about 80. and this week they will probably be 200. and it is increasing. Every body who can is flying. We hope the approaching cold will stop it. The President sat out for Mount Vernon yesterday, according to arrangements made sometime since. Colo. Hamilton is ill of the fever, but is on the recovery. The Secretary at war is setting out Northwardly, and I shall in a few days set out for Virginia. Our reassembling will depend on the course of this malady, and on that will depend the date of my next letter to you. I have the honor to be with great & sincere esteem, Gentlemen, your most obedt. servt.   TH: JEFFERSON

PrC (DLC); at foot of text: "Messrs. Carmichael & Short." FC (Lb in DNA: RG 59, DCI).

This day TJ wrote a brief note to Joseph Yznardi, Jr., who at this time was preparing to leave America to take up his post as consul at Cadiz, asking him to take charge of this letter (PrC in DLC; FC in Lb in DNA: RG 59, DCI).

To George Hammond

SIR   Philadelphia Sep. 11. 1793.

According to your desire I wrote to the Committee of Baltimore to inform me of the passengers to France who ask your passport. The following is an extract from their letter, of Sep. 8. 'The numbers already entered and for whom a provision has been made at a heavy expence to the French republic and the inhabitants of this town are as follow. In the Marianne, Capt. Ardouin 250. persons. In the Nouvelle Rosalie, Capt. Dupouy 180. persons, in all 430.'

I have also the honor to inclose you the names of 330. the roll of which was sent to me on the part of these unhappy persons themselves. This was the whole number then inscribed, but it was mentioned that they were daily increasing.

To the favor of giving the most effectual protection you can to them, will you be so good as to add that of putting it under cover to Mr. Samuel Sterritt, Baltimore, and have it put in the post-office that it may go off immediately. Otherwise my residence out of town may delay it a day or two which I understand is of great importance to these poor people. I write to Mr. Sterrett that I have asked this favor of you. I have the honor to be with great respect Sir Your most obedt. servt

TH: JEFFERSON

PrC (DLC); at foot of text: "Mr. Hammond." Tr (ViU: Edgehill-Randolph Papers); 19th-century copy. Enclosure not found.

The letter TO THE COMMITTEE OF BALTIMORE is TJ to James McHenry, Robert Gilmor, and Samuel Sterett, 2 Sep. 1793. The EXTRACT is taken from Sterett to TJ, 8 Sep. 1793.

To David Humphreys

Philadelphia Sep. 11. 1793.

I have to acknolege yours of May 19. 29. and July 20. being Nos. 72. 73. and 76. It is long since I wrote to you, because I knew you must be where you could not receive my letters: and perhaps it may be sometime before I write to you again on account of a contagious and mortal fever which has arisen here, and is driving us all away. It is called a yellow fever, but is like nothing known or read of by the Physicians. The week before last the deaths were about 40. the last week about 80. and this week I think they will be 200. and it goes on spreading. All persons who can find asylum elsewhere are flying from the city: this will doubtless extend it to other towns, and spread it through the country unless an early winter should stop it. Colo. Hamilton is ill of it, but is on the recovery.—The Indians have refused to meet our Commissioners unless they would agree to the Ohio as our boundary, by way of Preliminary article. This being impossible because of the army locations and sales to individuals beyond the Ohio, the war is to go on, and we may soon expect to hear of Genl. Wayne's being in motion. The President sat out for mount Vernon yesterday, according to an arrangement of some time ago. Genl. Knox is setting out for Massachusets, and I think to go to Virginia in some days. When and where we shall reassemble will depend on the course of this malady. I have the honour to be with great & sincere esteem & respect Dr. Sir Your affectionate friend & servt

Th: Jefferson

RC (NjP: Andre deCoppet Collection); at foot of text: "Colo. Humphreys"; endorsed by Humphreys as received 25 Jan. and as answered 30 Jan. 1794. PrC (DLC). FC (Lb in DNA: RG 59, DCI).

From Henry Knox

Sir War Department Septemb. 11. 1793

The Swedish neutral Vessel having been brought into our ports before the fifth of August, is not comprehended in the rule to restore Vessels taken by the illicit privateers after that period.

It would appear to me, that the appeal to the Circuit Court should be prosecuted. If the event should then be unfavorable, and it should be proper to interfere with force, it must I conceive be by virtue of a special rule, and orders from the President of the United States.

If I err in this opinion, I shall be much obliged to you to point out the mode of procedure. I have the honor to be with great respect Sir Your obedt. hble servant H Knox

RC (DLC); in a clerk's hand, signed by Knox; at foot of text: "The Secretary of State"; endorsed by TJ as received 11 Sep. 1793 and so recorded in SJL.

To Gouverneur Morris

DEAR SIR   Philadelphia Sep. 11. 1793.

My late letters to you have been of Aug. 16. 23. and 26: and a dupli-cate of the two first will accompany this. Yours lately received are Apr. 4. 5. 11. 19. May 20. and June 1. being Nos. 26. to 31. I have little particular to say to you by this opportunity which may be less certain than the last.—The North Western Indians have refused to meet our Commissioners unless they would agree to the Ohio as our boundary by way of preliminary article; and this being impossible on account of the army locations and particular sales on that side the river, the war will go on. We may shortly expect to hear that Genl. Wayne is in motion.—An infectious and mortal fever is broke out in this place. The deaths under it the week before last were about 40. the last week about 80. This week they will probably be about 200. and it is increasing. Every one is get-ting out of the city who can. Colo. Hamilton is ill of the fever, but is on the recovery. The President, according to an arrangement of some time ago set out for Mt. Vernon yesterday. The Secretary at War is setting out on a visit to Massachusets. I shall go in a few days to Virginia. When we shall reassemble again may perhaps depend on the course of this malady, and on that may depend the date of my next letter. I have the honor to be with great & sincere esteem & respect Dr. Sir your most obedt. servt.   TH: JEFFERSON

PrC (DLC); at foot of text: "Mr. Morris." FC (Lb in DNA: RG 59, DCI).

To Thomas Pinckney

DEAR SIR   Philadelphia Sep. 11. 1793.

Your letters of May 11. and 15. June 14. and 20. are recieved. My last to you have been of Aug. 20. and 29. and Sep. 1. The first of these covered a bill of exchange drawn by John Wilcocks in your favor on Edward Mc.Culloch & Co. London for £1077–11–9 sterl. cost here 5000.D. of which I now inclose a duplicate. I am endeavoring to pro-cure a remittance of 10,000. Dollars more to London or Amsterdam. I now inclose you the following papers.

1793. Apr. 18. a letter of Messrs. Carmichael and Short to me.
    May. 5. do.
June 18. a letter of Messrs. Viar and Jaudenes to me.
    30. a letter of mine to Messrs. Carm. and Short.

July 11. a letter of mine to Messrs. Viar and Jaudenes.

    11. a letter of theirs to me.

    13. another do.

    14. a letter of mine to them.

    a note of the policy of Spain as to the Missisipi, from good authority.

These are communicated merely for your information, and to govern your discretion in any occurrence which may arise where this information may enable you to do good or avoid evil. You mention that when proposing arrangements for the regulation of impressments of seamen, so as to shelter our seamen from them, you were told that Mr. Bond was to make enquiries here for a final arrangement. He has been long arrived, and we have never heard of any enquiries.—You must have received the President's proclamation by Lesley who was the bearer of it, whose arrival you mention in your last. The North-Western Indians have refused to meet our Commissioners unless they would agree as a preliminary article to make the Ohio our boundary. This was impossible on our part, on account of the lands sold on the other side to Individuals: consequently the war goes on, and we may expect very shortly to hear of General Wayne's advance towards them.—A very contagious and mortal fever has made it's appearance here lately. The week before last there were about 40. deaths under it, the last week about 80. This week they will be about 200. and it goes on increasing. The city is thrown into the utmost consternation by it. All descriptions of people are flying from it, as far as any asylum can be found. This endangers the spreading it through the country and in other large cities. All the public offices are shutting. The President went to M. Vernon yesterday according to an arrangement of long standing. Colo. Hamilton is ill of the fever, though on the recovery. General Knox is going away. I think to go also in some days. When or where we shall re-assemble will depend on the course this malady takes, and on that will depend the date of my next letter to you. I have the honor to be with great & sincere respect & esteem Dr Sir your friend & servt   Th: Jefferson

RC (CtY); at foot of first page: "Mr. Pinckney." PrC (DLC). FC (Lb in DNA: RG 59, DCI). Enclosure: Bill of exchange payable to Pinckney drawn by John Wilcocks on Edward MacCulloch & Company of London, Philadelphia, 31 July 1793 (printed form with blanks filled, signed by Wilcocks, in CtY; consisting of second set of exchange). Enclosed in TJ to Henry Remsen, 11 Sep. 1793.

TJ's letter of aug. 20. was actually dated 22 Aug. 1793. note of the policy of spain: see Enclosure No. 1 printed at first Memorandum to George Washington, [11 July 1793]. president's proclamation: the Proclamation of Neutrality.

To Henry Remsen

DEAR SIR   Philadelphia Sep. 11. 1793.

Your favors of July 29. and Aug. 1. are now before me, and the inkpot was duly received, for which I return you a thousand thanks, for it is to me a great convenience. You did not mention the price, but I suppose it to be about 3. dollars (judging from the former one) and will not fail to replace it by the first person I can find passing. Schneider's price is high. I must do the less in his way; but still I must employ him when I am ready. I go home to live decidedly at the beginning of the new year. Can I get the favor of you to watch for a trusty passenger to send the inclosed letter to Mr. Pinckney by. It is of an extreme confidential nature, and moreover covers a bill of exchange.—You will have heard much of the contagious and mortal disorder broke out here. It is really formidable. During the last three weeks the deaths have more than doubled weekly, and it is still spreading. I think the deaths this week will be 200 at least. Colo. Hamilton is ill of it, but on the recovery. The President went to Virginia yesterday according to an arrangement of long standing. Genl. Knox is going off. I believe I shall also go to Virginia in a few days. When and where we shall reassemble will depend on the course this malady takes.—Command my services always freely, as I am sincerely and affectionately your friend & servt.

                                                                TH: JEFFERSON

RC (PWacD: Feinstone Collection, on deposit PPAmP); at foot of text: "Mr. Remsen"; endorsed by Remsen in part: "Sent the letter for Mr. Pinckney by Capt. Hervey of the Ellice who was to deliver it personally— H. R." PrC (DLC). Tr (ViU: Edgehill-Randolph Papers); 19th-century copy. En-closures: TJ to Thomas Pinckney, 7 and 11 Sep. 1793 (see also Remsen to TJ, 1 Oct. 1793).

The INKPOT—a silver inkstand—cost 2 dollars (MB, 5 Jan. 1794).

To Samuel Sterett

SIR   Schuylkill Sep. 11. 1793.

I this moment recieve your favor of the 8th. and have sent to Mr. Hammond the numbers for whom the passports are asked. Besides this I was enabled by Mr. Bournonville to inclose him a roll of the names of 330. of them. I have desired him to put his passports under cover to you and send them to the post office; otherwise my residence in the country might occasion the loss of a post. I have the honor to be with great esteem Sir Your most obedt. servt   TH: JEFFERSON

PrC (DLC); at foot of text: "Mr. Sterrett." Tr (ViU: Edgehill-Randolph Papers); 19th-century copy.

From George Taylor, Jr., with Jefferson's Note

DEAR SIR   Philadelphia Septr. 11th. 1793.

On shewing the Note you were so kind as to give me, to Mr. Kean Cashier of the Bank of the U.S. he told me that it would be thrown out by the direction on account of it's want of form. I therefore take the liberty to enclose it and the one he proposed, and to request the favor of you to direct it's amount to be paid to Mr. Benjn. Bankson, who has promised to forward the same to me in Post notes. I have the honor to be with much respect and sincere attachment, Dear Sir, Your mo. obt. & very humble servant.   GEO: TAYLOR JR.

[Note by TJ:]
Endorsed a note in due form for Mr. Taylor, and destroyed the first.

RC (DLC); with TJ's undated note below signature; at foot of text: "Mr. Jefferson"; endorsed by TJ as received 11 Sep. 1793 and so recorded in SJL. Enclosures not found.

The day before TJ had endorsed a sixty-day note for 200 dollars to THE BANK OF THE U.S. for Taylor (MB, 10 Sep. 1793).

From George Washington

SIR   Elkton 11 Septr. 1793.

I will thank you to have made out and forwarded to me a Commission for the Collector of Annapolis, in place of ⸻ Davidson,[1] leaving the name of the person blank to be filled up by me.

You will please to have the U: States seal affixed thereto, and countersigned by you, so that it may be sent directly from me to the person who shall be appointed. With much esteem, I am, Sir, Your mo: hble Servt.   GO: WASHINGTON

RC (DLC); in the hand of Bartholomew Dandridge, Jr., signed by Washington; internal address at foot of text clipped; endorsed by TJ as received 12 Sep. 1793 and so recorded in SJL. Dft (DNA: RG 59, MLR); entirely in Dandridge's hand and endorsed by him. FC (Lb in same, SDC). Recorded in SJPL.

On 23 Nov. 1793 Washington FILLED UP the blank with the name of Robert Denny, who declined. The post was then given to John Randall (Washington, *Journal*, 257; JEP, I, 143-4).

[1] Clause interlined in Dft.

To Willing, Morris & Swanwick

Sep. 11. 1793.

Th: Jefferson presents his compliments to Messrs. Willing, Morris, & Swanwick, and notwithstanding the hope given in the above extract that their bill will be paid, thinks it his duty to communicate it to them.

PrC (DLC); subjoined to extract described below. FC (Lb in DNA: RG 59, DL).

ABOVE EXTRACT: a slightly edited text of that part of the last paragraph of Thomas Pinckney's 20 June 1793 letter to TJ from London relating to the bill of exchange for £3,000 drawn by Willing, Morris & Swanwick on John & Francis Baring.

Willing, Morris & Swanwick evidently responded to TJ in a letter of 12 Sep. 1793, which is recorded in SJL as received the same date but has not been found.

Circular to Certain Consuls and Vice-Consuls

SIR   Philadelphia Sep. 12. 1793.

The object of the present is chiefly to acknolege the receipt of your favors of Dec. 30. Apr. 10. June 10. and July 4. and to express our satisfaction with your attention to the cases of the ships Commerce and Jay.

The US. persevere[1] in their line of peace with all nations,[2] and will, we hope, by a just conduct to all, be enabled to preserve it. We think it best that our vessels should take passports in our own ports only, and renew them every voyage, as the surest[3] means of[4] avoiding the difficulties produced to ourselves by the usurpation of our flag, to which we desire[5] your particular attention.

A kind of jail or camp-fever has lately[6] broken out in this city, where being unusual it has excited considerable alarm. It is but little infectious and we hope that more experience in it's treatment, and the cool weather now commencing will soon stop it. I am with great respect Sir Your most obedt servt   TH: JEFFERSON

PrC (DLC); at foot of text: "Mr. Vanderhorst." FC (Lb in DNA: RG 59, DCI); at head of text: "Messrs. Vanderhorst, Maury, Auldjo, Fox, Saabye and Church." In addition to the letter sent to Elias Vanderhorst, the consul at Bristol, the FC lists at foot of text the different introductory paragraphs substituted in the texts sent to the other five recipients mentioned in it. TJ also included variant opening paragraphs in the letters he sent to five other consuls and vice-consuls listed below, as well as to C. W. F. Dumas. With the exceptions recorded below, and apart from minor differences in the complimentary closes, all the letters contain the same last two paragraphs printed above, the variations in the first paragraph being as follows:

(1) *To Thomas Auldjo, vice-consul at Poole*: PrC in DLC, consisting of last two paragraphs only with variant opening sentence recorded in note 1 below, at foot of

[95]

text: "Mr. Auldjo"; FC in Lb in DNA: RG 59, DCI, consisting of variant part of opening sentence. Auldjo's last consular letter to TJ as Secretary of State, dated 3 Sep. 1793, is recorded in SJL as received 7 Nov. 1793 from Cowes but has not been found.

(2) *To Stephen Cathalan, Jr., consul at Marseilles*: "The object of the present is chiefly to acknolege the receipt of your favors of Feb. 27. Mar. 19. May 23. and 25. Your attention to the cases of Capt. Burgoin and Robbins meets entire approbation" (PrC in DLC, containing variant version of second paragraph recorded in notes 2-4 below, with "M. Cathalan" at foot of text; FC in Lb in DNA: RG 59, DCI).

(3) *To Edward Church, consul at Lisbon*: "By a letter lately received from Colo. Humphreys I learn your arrival at Lisbon" (PrC in DLC, at foot of text: "Mr. Church"; FC in Lb in DNA: RG 59, DCI, consisting of extract of sentence quoted).

(4) *To Henry Cooper, consul at Santa Cruz*: "I have to acknolege your favor of July 10." (PrC in DLC, at foot of text: "Mr. Cooper"; FC in Lb in DNA: RG 59, DCI).

(5) *To Delamotte, vice-consul at Le Havre*: "The object of the present is chiefly to acknolege the receipt of your favors of Jan. 15. Mar. 9. 12. 14. and June 2. We have seen with much approbation the interest you took in the enlargement of our commerce with France and her colonies, by the application you made to Mr. Monge; as also your attention to the case of the ship Laurence. Be pleased to acknolege for me to Mr. Coffyn the receipt of his well detailed statements relative to the whale fishery" (PrC in DLC, containing variant version of second paragraph recorded in note 4 below, with "M. de la Motte" at foot of text; FC in Lb in DNA: RG 59, DCI). Delamotte later wrote a consular letter which TJ did not receive. See Appendix i.

(6) *To Joseph Fenwick, consul at Bordeaux*: "The object of the present is chiefly to acknolege the receipt of your favors of Jan. 20. Feb. 10. 25. 28. Apr. 4. June 28. and to thank you for your intelligence from time to time. Your attentions to the case of the brig Sally are entirely approved" (PrC in DLC, containing variant version of second paragraph recorded in note 4 below, at foot of text: "Mr. Fenwick"; FC in Lb in DNA: RG 59, DCI).

(7) *To Robert W. Fox, consul at Falmouth*:

"I have duly received your favor of June 8. The error in your Christian name shall be duly attended to for correction at the next session of Congress" (PrC in DLC, at foot of text: "Mr. Robert Weare Fox"; FC in Lb in DNA: RG 59, DCI, consisting of extract of sentences quoted).

(8) *To James Maury, consul at Liverpool*: "The object of the present is chiefly to acknolege the receipt of your favors of Mar. 16. June 3. and July 4. and to thank you for your intelligence which is sometimes of considerable utility to us" (PrC in DLC, at foot of text: "Mr. Maury"; FC in Lb in DNA: RG 59, DCI, consisting of extract of sentence quoted).

(9) *To Benjamin H. Phillips, consul at Curaçao*: "The object of the present is chiefly to acknolege the receipt of your favors of June 7. July 28. and Aug. 8. and to approve of your attention to the circumstance of a Dutch vessel taking slaves out of a schooner from Baltimore on suspicion that they were French property. That circumstance does not justify a Dutch vessel committing such an act, because our treaty with the United Netherlands expressly agrees that free bottoms shall make free goods. The owner therefore has a full right to pursue his property" (PrC in DLC, at foot of text: "Mr. B. H. Phillips"; FC in Lb in DNA: RG 59, DL).

(10) *To John M. Pintard, consul at Madeira*: "I have to acknolege the receipt of your favors of Mar. 21. 27. July 4. and 23. and to assure you that we are well pleased that you availed yourself of an opportunity of serving the French prisoners carried into your port, as we wish on all occasions to shew our sincere friendship for that nation. I have also to inform you that there is nothing incompatible with your present office in undertaking to act as Consul or Agent for that republick. I observe what you say on the subject of fees, and I await Colo. Humphrey's report thereon" (PrC in DLC, at foot of text: "Mr. Pintard"; FC in Lb in DNA: RG 59, DCI).

(11) *To Hans Rodolph Saabije, consul at Copenhagen*: "The object of the present is chiefly to acknolege the receipt of your favors of Dec. 22. and Jan. 5. and to express to you our satisfaction at your attention to the cases of the ship Hamilton and Brig Betsey" (PrC in DLC, at foot of text: "Mr. Saabye"; FC in Lb in DNA: RG 59, DCI, consisting

of extract of sentence quoted). Saabÿe later wrote a consular letter which TJ did not receive. See Appendix I.

(12) *To C. W. F. Dumas, agent at The Hague:* "The object of the present is chiefly to acknolege the receipt of your favors of Jan. 29. Feb. 3. Apr. 5. 14. May 1. 25." (PrC in DLC, containing variant version of second paragraph and rearranged third paragraph recorded in notes 2 and 6 below, with "M. Dumas" at foot of text; FC in Lb in DNA: RG 59, DCI).

TJ enclosed six of these circulars in a note of this date to Thomas Pinckney: "Th: Jefferson with his respects to Mr. Pinkney incloses letters to Messrs. Vanderhorst, Maury, Auldjo and Fox, into which he will be pleased to stick wafers and forward them. He also asks his care of those to Messrs. Saabye and Church" (PrC in DLC; FC in Lb in DNA: RG 59, DCI, with marginal note: "This with the Letters to the Consuls, forwarded to Mr. Heny. Remsen [N. York]"). On the same day he also wrote a brief note to Henry Remsen enclosing the letter to Pinckney and its enclosures and asking him "to give the same passage to the inclosed letter to Mr. Pinckney as to the former" (PrC in DLC). The "former" letter was TJ to Pinckney, 11 Sep. 1793.

[1] Sentence to this point in PrC to Auldjo: "The object of the present is chiefly to inform you that the US: continue to persevere."

[2] Preceding three words omitted in PrC to Cathalan. Remainder of paragraph in PrC to Dumas: "To preserve it, is not without difficulty; but a just conduct will we hope do it. We think it best that our vessels shall take passports in our own ports only, and that they shall be renewed every voyage, in order to prevent injury both to our friends and ourselves by the usurpation of our flag."

[3] PrCs to Auldjo, Cathalan, Church, Delamotte, Fenwick, Fox, Maury, and Saabÿe: "best."

[4] Remainder of paragraph in PrCs to Cathalan, Delamotte, and Fenwick: "preventing injury both to our friends and ourselves by the usurpation of our flag, against which we wish every attention to be paid," with "used" instead of "paid" in the last two.

[5] PrCs to Auldjo, Church, Cooper, Fox, Maury, Pintard, and Saabÿe: "we shall desire."

[6] Remainder of PrC to Dumas: "broke out in this city, which being unusual has given considerable alarm. More experience in the treatment of it, and the cool weather now commencing will we hope soon stop it. It appears to be but little infectious."

To Edmond Charles Genet

Sir   Philadelphia, September 12th. 1793.

I have the honor of your letter of the 6th. instant, and can assure you with real truth of the readiness and zeal with which the Executive will concur in preventing within the limits of the United States any preparation of hostilities against France or her Colonies, as far as this can be effected by the exertion of that portion of the public power with which they are invested by the laws. Your letter requires the arrest and delivery of Tanqui, Galbaud, Conscience and Bonne, escaped from the ship Jupiter and from the punishment of crimes committed[1] against the Republic of France, and also that[2] necessary measures be taken to prevent the carrying into execution certain plots formed by them and others against their country. These two requisitions stand on different ground. The laws of this Country take no notice of crimes committed out of their jurisdiction. The most atrocious offender coming within their pale is

[97]

viewed by them as an innocent man, and they have authorized no one to seize or deliver him. The evil of protecting malefactors of every dye is sensibly felt here as in other countries, but until a reformation of the criminal Codes of most Nations, to deliver fugitives from them would be to become their accomplices—the former therefore is viewed as the lesser evil. When the Consular Convention with France was under consideration, this subject was attended to: but we could agree to go no further than is done in the IXth. article of that instrument where we agree mutually to deliver up 'Captains, Officers, Mariners, Sailors, and all other persons being part of the Crews of vessels' &c. Unless therefore the persons before named be part of the Crew of some vessel of the French Nation no person in this country is authorized to deliver them up, but on the contrary they are under the protection of the laws. If they are part of the Crew of a vessel, they are to be delivered up,[3] but then it happens that the District Judge of each State is by the law of Congress made the competent person to execute this article of the Convention, and consequently each within his own State, and no one over all the States. So that as Criminals they cannot be given up, and if they be of the Crew of a vessel, the act of Congress has not given authority, to any one officer to send his process through all the States of the Union.

The other branch of your request is more completely provided for by the laws, which authorize coercions as to[4] expeditions formed in the territory of the United States against nations with whom they are at peace. If therefore you will be pleased to give me such information as to persons and places as may indicate to what points the vigilance of the officers is to be directed, proper measures will be immediately taken for preventing every attempt to[5] make any hostile expedition from these States against any of the dominions of France. The stronger the proofs you can produce, and the more pointed as to persons, the stronger will be the means of coercion which the laws will allow to be used.

I have not yet laid this matter before the president, who is absent from the seat of Government: but to save delay which might be injurious, I have taken the liberty as the case is[6] plain, to give you this provisory answer. I shall immediately communicate it to the President, and if he shall direct any thing in addition or alteration, it shall be the subject of another letter. In the mean time, I may venture to let this be considered as a ground for your proceeding. I have the honor to be with great respect, Sir, your most obedient Servant.   TH: JEFFERSON

PrC (DLC); in Benjamin Bankson's hand, signed by TJ in ink; at foot of first page: "Mr Genet"; with clerical corrections interlined in ink by TJ. Dft (DLC); entirely in TJ's hand, unsigned; on verso in pencil: "Copy & press copy"; only the most significant emendations are recorded below. Tr (DNA: RG 46, Senate Records, 3d Cong., 1st sess.). FC (Lb in DNA: RG 59, DL). Tr (AMAE: CPEU, xxxix); in French. Recorded in SJPL. Printed in *Message*, 80. Enclosed in TJ to George Washington, 15 Sep. 1793.

ACT OF CONGRESS: see TJ to James Duane, 10 Sep. 1793, and note.

[1] Preceding six words interlined in Dft in place of "guilty of crimes."

[2] In Dft TJ here canceled "the gov."
[3] Clause written in margin of Dft, the next word being omitted there.
[4] In Dft TJ first wrote "authorize proper coercions against" and then altered it to read as above.
[5] In Dft TJ here canceled "equip."
[6] Word interlined in Dft in place of "was."

To Alexander Hamilton

SIR   Philadelphia Sep. 12. 1793.

I have the honor to inclose you a paper delivered me by Mr. Bournonville on the part of the Minister of France reclaiming against the demand of tonnage on the vessels which came hither from the West Indies in their late calamity. It is urged that they were driven out of their harbours by superior force, obliged to put to sea without water or stores, and therefore to make the first ports where they could be relieved, which constitute in their opinion those circumstances of distress and necessity which exempt vessels from the payment of tonnage. This case belonging to your department, I take the liberty, in the absence of the President and to save time, to transmit it to you directly, for your consideration. I have the honor to be with great respect Sir your most obedt. servt   TH: JEFFERSON

PrC (DLC); at foot of text: "The Secretary of the Treasury." Tr (DNA: RG 46, Senate Records, 3d Cong., 1st sess.). FC (Lb in DNA: RG 59, DL). Printed in *Message*, 81. Enclosed in TJ to Oliver Wolcott, Jr., 12 Sep. 1793.

The PAPER in question has not been identified, but it may have been the "Memorial in favour of the Captains of french vessels arrived in the harbours of the United States in July 1793," which claimed, on the basis of Section 37 [i.e., 38] of the 4 Aug. 1790

Tonnage Duty Act and Articles 19 and 26 of the 1778 treaty of commerce with France, that the circumstances in Saint-Domingue which drove French merchant ships to take refuge in American ports entitled them to an exemption from the payment of American tonnage duties (Tr in DLC: Genet Papers; undated, unaddressed, and unsigned; with copy of subjoined certification by Alexandre Maurice d'Hauterive). For the rejection of the French claim, see Hamilton to TJ, 30 Nov. 1793.

To George Hammond

SIR   Philadelphia Sep. 12. 1793.

I have the honor to inform you that the privateers Petite Democrate and Caramagnole sent into New London as a prize the Brig Nancy of Jamaica: that the Govr. of Connecticut, having possessed himself of the said brig by a party of militia, was ready to deliver her up to her master or owner at the time of her capture, but that no such persons have appeared, and that in this case the Governor will deliver her to the owner or to your order. I have the honor to be with great respect Sir your most obedt servt   Th: Jefferson

PrC (DLC); at foot of text: "The Min. Plen. of G. Britain." FC (Lb in DNA: RG 59, DL).

From George Hammond

Sir   Philadelphia 12 September 1793

I have this day had the honor of receiving your letter, dated the 9th. curt., in answer to my memorials of the 4th. and 6th. of this month.

As there appears to subsist an essential difference between us, on a matter of fact, I esteem it necessary for my justification, to assure you that my statement, of the *establishment of a regular succession of cruizers*, from the French fleet stationed at New-York, was founded on information, which at the time I knew to be authentic, and was particularly intended to apply to the Favorite of 20 Guns and the brig Cerf of 16 Guns, both of which were *successively* detached from the fleet at New-York, and have sent British prizes into that port. They are now reinforced by the frigate Concorde of 40 Guns and le Normand of 20 Guns, all, or at least the principal part, of which vessels are, as I have the greatest reason to believe, at this moment employed in cruizing on the American coasts in the vicinity of New-York. I have the honor to be with sentiments of great respect Sir, your most obedient humble Servant   Geo. Hammond

RC (DNA: RG 59, NL); in a clerk's hand, signed by Hammond; at foot of text: "Mr Jefferson"; with notation by TJ: "French cruizers on our coasts"; endorsed by TJ as received 13 Sep. 1793 and so recorded in SJL. Tr (PRO: FO 5/1). Tr (Lb in DNA: RG 59, NL). Enclosed in TJ to George Washington, 15 Sep. 1793.

From George Hammond

Sir   Philadelphia 12th September 1793

I have the honor of transmitting to you, a copy of an additional instruction, given by his Majesty's order in council, to the Commanders of the British armed vessels, respecting the commerce of neutral nations with France in the article of grain, and also with regard to such French ports as may in the course of the war be blocked by the vessels of his Majesty, or of the other powers engaged in the war.

In communicating to you this paper, it is necessary for me to remark that, by the law of nations, as laid down by the most modern writers, it is expressly stated that all provisions are to be considered as contraband and as such liable to confiscation, in the case where the depriving an enemy of these supplies, is one of the means intended to be employed for reducing him to reasonable terms of peace. The actual situation of France is notoriously such as to lead to the employing this mode of distressing her by the joint operations of the different powers engaged in the war: And the reasoning, which in these authors applies to *all* cases of this sort, is certainly much more applicable to the *present* case, in which the distress results from the unusual mode of war employed by the enemy himself—in having armed almost the whole labouring class of the French nation, for the purpose of *commencing* and supporting hostilities against all the governments of Europe. But this reasoning is most of all applicable to the circumstances of a trade, which is now in a great measure entirely carried on by the actually ruling party of France itself; and which is therefore no longer to be regarded, as a mercantile speculation of individuals, but as an immediate operation of the very persons who have declared war, and are now carrying it on against Great Britain. On these considerations therefore the powers at war would have been perfectly justifiable, if they had considered all provisions as contraband, and had directed them as such to be brought in for confiscation.

But the present measure pursued by his Majesty's government, so far from going to the extent, which the law of nations and the circumstances of the case would have warranted, only has prevented the French from being supplied with *corn*, omitting all mention of *other* provisions, and even with respect to corn, the regulation adopted is one, which, instead of confiscating the cargoes, secures to the proprietors, supposing them neutral, a full indemnification for any loss they may possibly sustain.

With respect to the rule that has been adopted relative to ports blockaded—it is conformable to the general law and practice of all nations, and the exception, there mentioned as to Denmark and Sweden, has reference to existing treaties with those powers, and cannot therefore give any just ground of umbrage or jealousy to other powers, between whom and Great Britain no such treaties subsist.

Before I conclude this letter, I deem it proper to express my hope that you, Sir, will perceive in the communication itself of this paper a proof of my willingness, to furnish this government with any intelligence that may be interesting to it, and thereby to anticipate the necessity of enquiries on the subject: And I cannot avoid farther adding my conviction[1] that the explanation I have now given of this measure, will satisfactorily evince the propriety of recurring to it in the present instance. I have the honor to be, with Sentiments of great respect, Sir, Your most obedient humble Servant, GEO. HAMMOND

RC (DNA: RG 59, NL); in a clerk's hand, signed by Hammond; at foot of first page: "Mr Jefferson"; with notation by TJ: "seizure of corn on high seas"; endorsed by TJ as received 13 Sep. 1793 and so recorded in SJL. FC (Lb in PRO: FO 116/3). Tr (same, 5/1). Tr (DNA: RG 46, Senate Records, 3d Cong., 1st sess.). Tr (Lb in DNA: RG 59, NL). Enclosure: Enclosure No. 1 listed at Thomas Pinckney to TJ, 5 July 1793. Printed in *Message*, 110. Enclosed in TJ to George Washington, 15 Sep. 1793.

Hammond had recently received the ADDITIONAL INSTRUCTION enclosed with a 5 July 1793 letter from Lord Grenville (Mayo, *British Ministers*, 40-2). With the exception of the final paragraph, his letter is taken almost verbatim from the British foreign minister's dispatch.

[1] Preceding two words interlined.

To James Madison

Sep. 12. 1793.

The fever spreads faster. Deaths are now about 30. a day. It is in every square of the city. All flying who can. Most of the offices are shut or shutting. The banks shut up this day. All my clerks have left me but one: so that I cannot go on with business. I shall therefore set out in 3. or 4. days and perhaps see you before you get this. H. had truly the fever, and is on the recovery, and pronounced out of danger.

PrC (DLC); unsigned and unaddressed.

From Henry Remsen

DR SIR   New York Septr. 12. 1793

A few days ago a gentleman called upon and informed me, that he had a small box containing a model, which you had desired him to leave under my care until a safe conveyance for Philadelphia should offer, when I should send it. I accordingly received it from him, and have now the pleasure to forward it by Capt. Elkins of one of the packets between this and Philadelphia, who is a very careful man and will have it in the cabin under his own eye. He proposes after arriving at Philadelphia, to lye at one of the wharves just below Penrose's shipyard, to avoid as much as possible the malignant fever prevailing there. I mention this, that Crosby may be at no loss in enquiring for him. He sails from here tomorrow.

I sincerely hope, Sir, that neither you, Miss Jefferson nor any of your family have, or may be attacked with the fever which now rages so much at Philada., and which, from the daily accounts we have from there, resembles more a pestilence than any of the diseases to which we in this country are liable. I have the Honor to be with great respect and esteem, Dr Sir Your most obt. and h'ble servt.   HENRY REMSEN

RC (DLC); at foot of text: "Thomas Jefferson Esqr."; endorsed by TJ as received 15 Sep. 1793 but recorded in SJL as received a day earlier.

The GENTLEMAN was James B. M. Adair (Adair to TJ, 9 Sep. 1793).

To Oliver Wolcott, Jr.

Sep. 12. 93.

Th: Jefferson, being obliged for form's sake to direct the inclosed to the Secretary of the Treasury, notwithstanding his known illness, puts it, open, under cover to Mr. Wolcott with his compliments, and a desire that he will do any thing in it which under present circumstances can be done. Not acquainted with the line of division between Mr. Wolcott's and Mr. Coxe's offices, should he have mistaken in addressing this to the former, he begs the favor of him to send it to the other.

PrC (DLC). FC (Lb in DNA: RG 59, DL). Enclosure: TJ to Alexander Hamilton, 12 Sep. 1793.

Oliver Wolcott, Jr. (1760-1833), the son of the perennial lieutenant governor of Connecticut, was educated at Yale and studied law with Tapping Reeve. A staunch Federalist for most of his political career, Wolcott served under Alexander Hamilton in the Department of the Treasury as Auditor from September 1789 to June 1791 and then as Comptroller. Upon Hamilton's resignation in January 1795, Wolcott succeeded him as Secretary of the Treasury and held this office until he resigned in December 1800. Although Wolcott was appointed a United States Circuit Court judge by John Adams in 1801, his position was abolished by the Judiciary Act of 1802. Wolcott retired to private life for the next fifteen years, engaging in a number of commercial and banking ventures, but capped his career of public service with his election to the governorship of Connecticut in 1817 as the candidate of the Toleration Party, a victory which helped end Federalist control of the state. Annually reelected until 1826, Wolcott also presided over the convention that framed the constitution of 1818, which disestablished the Congregational church in Connecticut and introduced other reforms (DAB).

From Edmond Charles Genet

MONSIEUR

Newyork le 13.[1] 7bre 1793.
l'an 2e. de la république française

J'ai reçu la lettre que vous m'avés fait l'honneur de m'ecrire le 9 de ce mois et Je m'empresse de vous assurer que depuis longtems Je presse le Consul de la république à Philadelphie de me mettre à portée de vous communiquer les informations que vous m'aves demandées sur les prises des Corsaires, le Citoyen Genet et le Sans culotte,[2] nommees le William et la Fanny; mais que ses occupations extremement multipliées depuis l'arrivée de l'escadre et une maladie[3] qu'il vient d'essuyer l'ont empeché Jusqu'a present de me fournir Ces materiaux; au surplus, Monsieur, Je doute que nous puissions en faire un usage utile tant qu'il n'aura pas été défini de part et d'autre ce que l'on entend par la ligne de protection que les Agens de nos ennemis reclament sans cesse auprès de vous pour faire servir vos mains à nous depouiller des foibles dédomagemens[4] que nous recueillons de la guerre de la tirannie contre la liberté. Presque tous les gouvernemens presque tous les Jurisconsultes ont une maniere differente de voir sur cet objet et Je crois, Monsieur,[5] que C'est aux Corps legislatifs de nos deux païs qu'il appartient de Juger la question: quant à moi Je penserais qu'il ne faudrait reclamer le droit de protection et de Jurisdiction que lorsque par la nature des choses on pourrait proteger et rendre Justice avec effet. Si ce principe etait etabli il ne s'agirait plus que de trouver une mesure invariable et la moyenne proportionnelle de la portée de Canons[6] d'un calibre et d'une charge determinées me paroitrait propre à remplir cet objet.

Il me reste à repondre, Monsieur, à la seconde partie de votre lettre Je veux dire aux reproches très amers que vous me faittes d'avoir opposé quelque resistance à l'ordre donné par un tribunal de cette ville à un de ses marechaux de s'emparer à la réquisition des négotians[7] anglais,[8] d'une prise faitte par un Vaisseau de le République et vous me demandés au nom de Mr. Le President de faire remettre ce batiment entre les mains de la ditte Cour. Je prens la liberté de vous observer, Monsieur, que cette requisition implique une double contradiction puisque 1°. le traitté statue de la maniere la plus positive[9] qu'aucune Cour ne prendra connoissance de nos prises et, 2° que les decisions renfermées dans votre lettre du 25 Juin ont etabli que les prises[10] supposées avoir été faittes dans la ligne (indéfinie) de protection resteront Jusqu'a leur Jugement entre les mains du Consul de la république.[11]

Par respect pour nos traittés, qui sont aussi des loix et pour les decisions du gouvernement fœderal J'ai du agir comme Je l'ai fait: Je vais d'ailleurs préscrire au Capitaine du Cerf de se conformer aux intentions de Mr. le President[12] aussitôt que le tribunal qui requiert[13] la saisie du Guillaume Tell aura produit ou cité la loi en vertu de la quelle il se propose de faire son exploït: Je sais tout ce qui est du Monsieur, aux tribunaux qui exercent une partie de la Souveraineté du Peuple; mais Je sais aussi que ces tribunaux crées par la loi n'ont d'action que par elle et que lorsqu'ils s'ecartent des limites qu'elle leur a tracées ils tombent dans l'arbitraire et:[14] Je vais en consequence, Monsieur, faire requerir le Juge qui a osé lancer un decrêt de prise de corps[15] contre Guillaume

Tell de nous produire la loi ou l'autorisation [16] d'après laquelle il agit et si se refusant à nous [17] satisfaire sur ce point ïl nous prouve que les lois du païs l'autorisent à rendre [18] arbitrairement des Warrans et a violer des traittes existans et des décisions du pouvoir éxécutif des Etats unis [19] Je lui ferai remettre [20] la prise et J'exprimerai à mon tour au gouvernement [21] fœderal toute ma sensibilité sur l'erreur dans laquelle [22] nous a fait tomber la Constitution des Etats unis qui dit que les traités sont au nombre de leurs lois les plus sacrées et les décisions qui ont été le resultat des arrangements relatifs aux prises [23] supposées faites dans la ligne de protection des Etats unis.   GENET

2d Dft (DLC: Genet Papers); consists of fair copy of Dft in a clerk's hand, with revisions and signature by Genet; date altered (see note 1 below); above salutation: "Le Citoyen Genet Ministre plenipotentre de la république française à Monsieur Jefferson secretaire d'Etat des Etats unis." Dft (same); entirely in Genet's hand, unsigned; dated 11 Sep. 1793 (see note 1 below); the most significant variations and emendations are noted below. Tr (AMAE: CPEU, xxxix); dated 13 Sep. 1793; with minor variations. FC (DLC: Genet Papers); in English; dated 13 Sep. 1793; follows 2d Dft. Recorded in SJL as received 2 Oct. 1793. Enclosed in Benjamin Bankson to TJ, 23 Sep. 1793, and TJ to George Washington, 3 Oct. 1793 (fifth letter).

Genet's letter was an important link in the chain of events that led to a historic definition of the maritime limits of the United States. Hitherto the United States government had confined itself to asserting its maritime jurisdiction over Delaware Bay (see note to Memorial from George Hammond, 2 May 1793). By raising the question of the LIGNE DE PROTECTION the federal government intended to offer to the shipping of countries at peace with the United States but at war with France, Genet led the Washington administration in November 1793 to proclaim provisionally a three-mile limit for the nation's maritime jurisdiction (TJ's fifth letter to George Washington, 3 Oct. 1793; TJ to Genet, 8 Nov. 1793).

[1] Date altered, possibly from "11." Date altered in Dft from "10" to "11."

[2] In Dft Genet first wrote "la prise du Citoyen Genet" and then altered it to read as above.

[3] In Dft Genet first wrote "l'Escadre et l'eruption des laves méphétiques et d'autres ca" and then altered it to read as above.

[4] Preceding two words interlined in Dft in place of "propriétés."

[5] In Dft Genet here canceled "qu'il ne dépend pas de nous d'établir."

[6] 2d Dft: "Canon." Dft: "canons."

[7] Word interlined in Dft.

[8] Preceding nine words written in the margin in Dft.

[9] In Dft Genet first wrote "puisque notre traité et les propres décisions renfermées dans votre lettre du 25. Juin établit de la maniere la plus positive premierement" and then altered it to read as above.

[10] In Dft Genet here canceled "contestées en vertu."

[11] In Dft Genet here canceled "et à leur défaut."

[12] Genet here canceled an interlined passage that appears to read "mais J'⟨attends⟩ espere, Mr., ⟨qu'il⟩ que ce Magistrat vous a bien" and wrote the next six words in the margin.

[13] Clause to this point altered by Genet from "Je suis pret d'ailleurs à me conformer aux intentions de Mr. le President lorsque le tribunal qui requiert."

[14] Genet here canceled "autorisent la résistance à l'oppression."

[15] Passage reworked by Genet from "faire sommer le Juge qui a lancé un Warrans."

[16] Preceding three words written in the margin in Dft.

[17] Word interlined by Genet in place of "me" here and later in this sentence.

[18] Word interlined by Genet in place of "lancer."

[19] Preceding nine words written in the margin by Genet.

[20] Preceding three words interlined by

Genet in place of "le laisserai s'emparer de."

[21] Preceding two words interlined in Dft in place of "les plaintes les plus."

[22] Remainder of sentence altered by Genet from "il m'a fait tomber par ses propres decisions," the words with which the Dft ends.

[23] Genet here canceled "contestées."

To George Hammond

SIR   Philadelphia, September 13th. 1793.

I have now the honor to enclose you the copy of a letter from the Attorney General of the United States in the case of Hooper and Pagan, in consequence of your last to me on that subject. It is still to have been wished that no efforts had been spared on the part of Mr. Pagan to bring his case before the Supreme Court of the United States. However supposing the Court of Massachusetts to be the Court of last resort in this case, it is then to be observed that the decision has been pronounced by the Judges of the land entrusted for their learning and integrity with the administration of justice to our own Citizens, that all the proceedings in the case have been marked with candor and attention towards Mr. Pagan, and that their decision can in no wise be charged with gross and palpable error. On the contrary, the interpretation they have given to the armistice (which entered into this question) is precisely that which has been given by every Court in the United States where it has come into question, and which was pronounced in this very instance in the British Court of Admiralty in Nova Scotia, where the question began. None of those strong features therefore of partiality and wilful injustice is to be seen in this case, which render a nation responsible for the decisions of it's Judges, and which the United States would have been perfectly disposed to rectify, as I hope you will have been satisfied by the attention and care which has been bestowed on the complaint. I have the honor to be, with great respect, Sir, Your most obedient Servant.

PrC (DLC); in Benjamin Bankson's hand, unsigned; at foot of text in ink by George Taylor, Jr.: "Mr Hammond." FC (Lb in DNA: RG 59, DL). Tr (Lb in PRO: FO 116/3). Tr (same, 5/1). Tr (MHi); 19th-century copy. Enclosure: Edmund Randolph to TJ, 5 Sep. 1793.

From David Humphreys

SIR   Lisbon Septr. 13th. 1793.

We have chartered a Swedish vessel at the rate of 340 Millrees per Month for two Months certain, and as much longer as we shall have occasion for it. This was the only expedient left for us, and the best terms we could make, and at all events will prove œconomical in case of our success at the place of destination. We shall have our Money, Passport, and every thing provided, and I hope we shall meet with no impediment to our going out the day after tomorrow. My zeal for the service will not permit us to be detained one moment longer than absolutely necessary: for the circumstances strongly urge our departure, and render the business more critical and the success more doubtful every day.

Since my last we learn, that the Algerines have taken another of our vessels near Malaga—the Crew fortunately escaped or the prospect of our success would have been utterly at an end. The vessel taken sometime ago off Cape de Gat has been converted into a Cruizer, and made this last capture. The last appears to be, by the Cadiz Marine list and other informations, the Schooner Laurel, Captn. John Daniel, from Philadelphia. This will also probably be turned into a Cruizer.

The Dutch are about sending a great Embassy to treat with the Algerines. Vice Admiral Melvil is appointed Ambassador, and is expected here very soon with several Ships of the line and frigates under his orders. He is to leave his Convoy, and proceed directly with the fleet to the Mediterranean. No body can appreciate more highly than I do the advantage of getting the start of the Dutch negotiator. A comparison between our means and his, almost precludes us from the least gleam of expectation of success. In fine, if, with our limitations, and under all the views, we should happily succeed, I shall esteem it almost a miracle. It will, at least, be one of the happiest days of my life.

I write the general News, which is of great importance, to the President; and hasten to conclude with assurances of the sentiments of perfect respect & esteem, with which I have the honour to be Sir Your most obedt & Most humble Servant   D. HUMPHREYS

P.S. I could not obtain an interview with Mr. Pinto until last Evening, when I introduced Mr. Church to him as remaining in charge with the affairs of the U.S. during my absence. I have left with Mr. Church a letter to be delivered to Mr. Pinto in case of war between this Country and France.

RC (DNA: RG 59, DD); at head of text: "(No. 82.)"; at foot of text: "The Secretary of State"; endorsed by TJ as received 18 Nov. 1793 and so recorded in SJL. Tr (Lb in same).

TJ submitted this letter to the President on 19 Nov. 1793, and Washington returned it the same day (Washington, *Journal*, 255).

To Patrick Kennan

SIR   Philadelphia Sep. 13. 1793.

Being authorised by a power of Attorney to act for Mr. William Short, who had some property in the hands of Mr. Alexr. Donald of London, I have just received a letter from Mr. Donald informing me that he has written to you by the same packet which brought his letter to me to account to me for what you have in your hands of this property. I shall be obliged to you for an exact statement of it, as it is my wish during a visit I am making to Virginia, to settle Mr. Short's affairs, in order to give him a clear statement of them. I am Sir Your most obedt servt   TH: JEFFERSON

PrC (DLC); at foot of text: "Mr Patrick Kennon. New York."

Patrick Kennan was a merchant at 34 Hanover Square, New York City (William Duncan, *The New-York Directory, and Reg-*ister, *for the Year 1792* [i.e. *1793*] [New York, 1793], 81).

The LETTER FROM Alexander DONALD of 4 July 1793, recorded in SJL as received from London on 12 Sep. 1793, has not been found.

To Thomas Sim Lee

SIR   Philadelphia Sep. 13. 1793.

I am honoured with your Excellency's favor of the 3d. inst. The answers given to the French Consul are so perfectly proper that no further observation on the subject is necessary. It is really unfortunate that the agents of the French republic should be conducting themselves as if their object was to disgust and alienate all the friends of their nation. It is but an act of justice however to distinguish between the conduct of their nation, which is replete with affection to us, and that of those gentlemen themselves, to which it is difficult to give a proper and yet temperate appellation. I have the honor to be with the highest esteem & respect Your Excellency's Most obedient servt.   TH: JEFFERSON

RC (MoSHi); addressed: "His Excellency Governor Lee Annapolis"; franked, stamped, and postmarked. PrC (DLC). Tr (ViU: Edgehill-Randolph Papers); 19th-century copy.

To Stephen Moylan

SIR   Philadelphia Sep. 13. 1793.

The President, on his departure, left in my hands a commission for a Marshal of this district with a blank for the name to be inserted. It was his wish that your's should be inserted if you should think the office would suit you. I must ask the favor of you to say whether you would accept of the commission, and to do it in a letter to Mr. Benjamin Bankson at my office, as I set out for Virginia within two or three days. Should you decline it I must still ask you to notify it to him, that he may proceed to follow the instructions given him in that case. The office will be vacant on the 20th. inst. by the resignation of Colo. Biddle, and I can with truth express the satisfaction it would give me personally to have it filled again by a person to whose merits I am less a stranger than to his person. I am with great respect Sir Your most obedt. servt

TH: JEFFERSON

PrC (DLC); at foot of text: "Genl. Moylan." FC (Lb in DNA: RG 59, DL).

Stephen Moylan (1737-1811), a native of Ireland educated in Paris, established himself as a merchant at Philadelphia in 1768. He served in the Continental Army throughout the Revolution, beginning with terms as muster-master general and quartermaster general, but spent most of the war commanding contingents of cavalry. He turned down the post of United States MARSHAL but later this year accepted Washington's appointment as commissioner of loans for Pennsylvania (DAB; Moylan to TJ, 19 Sep. 1793; JEP, I, 140).

To Oliver & Thompson

GENTLEMEN   Philadelphia Sep. 13. 1793.

The present is to acknolege the receipt of your favor of the 10th. inst. and to assure you it shall be duly attended to as soon as other matter shall be received of the same nature, which is expected shortly to be recieved. I have the honor to be Gentlemen Your most obedt servt

TH: JEFFERSON

PrC (DLC); at foot of text: "Messrs Oliver & Thompson Baltimore." FC (Lb in DNA: RG 59, DL).

Robert Oliver (ca. 1757-1834) and Hugh Thompson (1760-1826) were natives of Ireland who immigrated to Baltimore in 1783 and 1784, respectively. They formed a mercantile partnership in 1785 and dissolved it eleven years later, after which Oliver entered into a very successful partnership with his brothers (Stuart W. Bruchey, *Robert Oliver, Merchant of Baltimore, 1783-1819* [Baltimore, 1956], 19-20; *Maryland Historical Magazine*, L [1955], 332).

Oliver & Thompson's FAVOR OF THE 10TH. INST., recorded in SJL as received 12 Sep. 1793, has not been found.

To Thomas Griffin Peachy

SIR   Philadelphia Sep. 13. 1793.

I received by the last post your favor of the 3d. covering the resolutions of the inhabitants of Petersburg and it's vicinity respecting the President's late proclamation. I shall have the honor of forwarding them by the first post to Mount Vernon to which place the President is gone.

He will certainly receive with great satisfaction this testimony from the inhabitants of Petersburg and it's vicinity of their approbation and support of the line of conduct he is pursuing for the preservation of the peace of our country, and of the respect which is due to it. I have the honor to be with great regard Sir Your most obedt. servt

TH: JEFFERSON

PrC (DLC); at foot of text: "T. G. Peachy esq." Tr (ViU: Edgehill-Randolph Papers); 19th-century copy.

To John Ross

DEAR SIR   Schuylkill Sep. 13. 1793.

As all the world is flying, I think to fly too in two or three days. But I am *money-bound*. I shall have 215. dollars free out[1] of monies to be recieved for me at the Treasury between two and three weeks hence. But, to pay some matters to people in want, and to carry me home also, I have occasion for 100. Doll. more. Having never had any money connection at Philadelphia, I take the liberty of applying to you rather than any other person, to enable me to receive immediately the amount of the inclosed order on Mr. Bankson (one of my clerks who is to receive the money at the treasury for me) and of my own note for 100.D. which I cannot get by discount from the bank till Wednesday next, and my wish is to go on Sunday or Monday. I expect to be absent 7. weeks, but for fear any accident might delay me a few days, I have left the date of my note blank to be filled on the day it shall be lodged in the bank, that I may be the less hurried by this circumstance in my return. I will assuredly see that it be taken up in time. If you can, for this paper, furnish me a check on the bank or it's amount otherwise, you will enable my wheels to get into motion, which otherwise stand still. I have the honor to be with great esteem & respect Dr. Sir, your most obedt. servt

TH: JEFFERSON

RC (PHi: Society Collection); addressed: "John Ross esquire at his country seat"; endorsed by Ross as received and answered the same day. PrC (DLC). Tr (ViU: Edgehill-Randolph Papers); 19th-century copy. Enclosures: (1) TJ's order on Benjamin Bankson, 13 Sep. 1793, in Ross's favor, for 215 dollars payable at 21 days' sight "out of the monies to be recieved for me from the treasury." (2) TJ's promissory note to Ross, dated "Sep. 1793," for 100 dollars payable in 60 days (PrC in DLC, both documents being letterpressed on one sheet, with "Mr. Bankson at the Secretary of state's office" at foot of No. 1; Tr in ViU: Edgehill-Randolph Papers, 19th-century copy). Presumably TJ separated the two instruments before sending the originals to Ross.

[1] TJ first wrote "I have 215. dollars free at" before altering the phrase to read as above.

From John Ross

DEAR SIR   Philadelphia Say Grange 13 Septr. 1793.

I have before me your favour of this date, Am much pleased when I can Serve a friend, and without troubling You with further occurrence's on the Subject, Receive a Check for the Amount of the two Notes Sent to me, vizt. one of 215. Drs.

and 1 other of <u>100</u> Say 315 Dollars. I wish it had been convenient for You to have done my Family the pleasure to have Spent a day with us here, but under the present Unfortunate Situation of the City, it is certainly prudent to get out of the Way as Soon as possible. Wishing You an Agreeable Jaunt, Believe me with Sincerity to be very truely Dear Sir Your Most Obedt Servt   JNO ROSS

RC (MHi); at foot of text: "The Honble Thomas Jefferson Esqr."; endorsed by TJ as received 13 Sep. 1793 and so recorded in SJL. Enclosure not found.

To Arthur St. Clair

DEAR SIR   Philadelphia Sep. 13. 1793.

I received yesterday your favor of Aug. 9. Your having endeavored to avail the public of my agency in convening your legislature needed no apology. I did it with pleasure, as a public servant, and as one willing to serve yourself. Judge Symes however was at a distance, and Judge Turner gone from hence.[1] With respect to the question to whom you should send your observations on the laws relating to your government, I can answer with more disinterestedness, as before they can come I shall be no longer in my office. All the business of the government is divided into 3. departments, to wit, of war, finance and state. To some one of the heads of these every possible matter belongs. As to whatever you have to do in your military capacity, you refer yourself to the Secretary at war. I do not know that you can ever have any thing to do in the line of finance. Every thing else falls into the department of state, to the head of which it should be addressed. To him the general report, given every six months, is referred, and if there are matters in it proper for the other departments he reports them to the President who sends the extracts to the proper department.—Whether in or out of office I shall ever be happy to render you any service I can, being with sincere respect Dear Sir Your most obedt. servt   TH: JEFFERSON

PrC (DLC); at foot of text: "Govr. Sinclair." FC (Lb in DNA: RG 59, DL).

A letter from St. Clair of 1 Nov. 1793, recorded in SJL as received from Cincinnati on 18 Dec. 1793, has not been found, but the journal of the President, to whom TJ sent it on 18 Dec. and who returned it the same day, describes it as a letter of 7 Nov. 1793 relating "to an Expedition said to be in contemplation against the Spanish on the Mississipi. Genl. Clarke, who is to command it has received, thro' Mr. Genet, a Commission under the Govt. of France. Extract of a letter of Dr. O'Fallon's relative to the same—thinks it will take with the people of Kentucky &c." (Washington, *Journal*, 269). The extract from James O'Fallon's letter has not been found, though the letter itself has been identified elsewhere as one from O'Fallon to Captain Francis Her-

ron, Louisville, 18 Oct. 1793 (same, 270n; see also John C. Parish, "The Intrigues of Doctor James O'Fallon," MVHR, XVII [1930], 258-9n). For the failure of this enterprise, see Editorial Note on Jefferson and André Michaux's proposed western expedition, at 22 Jan. 1793; see also note to TJ to Isaac Shelby, 28 June 1793.

[1] Preceding sentence interlined.

Circular to Foreign Ministers in the United States

Sep. 14. 93.

Th: Jefferson presents his compliments to [Mr. Genet] and being about to be absent from this city for a few weeks begs the favor of him to write his name on the outside of all letters he shall do him the honor to write to him before his return, that, being sent to his office, they may receive the particular attention for which he leaves instructions in order to shorten as much as possible the delay of answer which may be occasioned by his absence.

Dft (DLC); entirely in TJ's hand; brackets in original; at foot of text: "A copy of the above to Mr. Genet

Mr. Hammond
Mr. Van Berckel
Messrs. Viar & Jaudenes

leave a blank for my name
in the beginning, that,
inserting it myself, it may
answer for a signature." Recorded in SJPL.

From Edmond Charles Genet

New york le 11. [i.e. 14] 7bre. 1793.
M.   l'an 2e. de la Republique françoise.

Les affaires multipliées dont J'ai été accablé depuis que Je suis ici ne m'ont point encore permis de vous accuser la reception de la lettre que vous m'avés écrite le 5.[1] août. Elle m'est parvenue dans son tems et comme les décisions qu'elle renferme ne sont qu'une conséquence de celles contre les quelles Je vous avois déja fait les representations les plus fortes et les plus fondées J'ai pensé que Je devois laisser au gouvernement federal le soin de les éxécuter,[2] parcequ'il ne m'appartenoit en aucune maniere de donner aux Consuls de la République des ordres contraires au sens de nos traités, de leur préscrire de ne point se conformer[3] relativement aux armements et aux prises de[4] nos batiments aux instructions qui leur ont été données par des autorités superieures à la

[112]

mienne et de leur enjoindre de suspendre l'éffet des Commissions que nos armateurs[5] tiennent du Conseil éxécutif et non de[6] son délégué. À l'égard des Indemnités promises par Mr. le President des Etats unis au Ministre d'Angleterre en vertu des principes qu'il a établi Il n'est pas plus en mon pouvoir d'y consentir que d'après ma maniere de voir il n'est au sien de le promettre puisque pour operer cette appropriation nouvelle des fonds des Etats unis ou de la france[7] l'aveu des Corps legislatifs des deux parties est indispensable.

Au surplus, M., quoique Je n'aie point le droit de retirer d'autorité les Commissions dont nos armateurs sont nantis, quoique Je ne puisse point non plus les contraindre de se soumettre à des décisions que nos traités d'alliance et de Commerce ne sanctionnent point et que des Jugements rendus par plusieurs tribunaux des Etats unis que des négociations entamées avec vous même semblent contredire Vous devés être assuré cependant qu'après avoir défendu aussi longtems que Je l'ai pu les droits et les interêts[8] du peuple françois Je ne néglige rien pour engager par les voies de la persuasion nos armateurs à suspendre leur course[9] et à Changer leur déstination: L'objet pour lequel nous avons encouragé l'armement de tous ces petits batiments étoit de détruire le Commerce de nos énnemis et de bloquer leurs marins dans vos ports afin[10] d'accelerer le retour de la paix en diminuant leurs forces.[11] Ce plan étoit[12] bon et malgré tous les obstacles qu'il a rencontré il a réussi au point de faire tomber entre nos mains une cinquantaine[13] de leurs batiments et de condamner à l'inaction un nombre[14] infiniment plus grand. Actuellement cet objet est rempli. Des forces Superieures achéveront le reste et si J'ai eu le malheur par mon aveugle[15] obeissance à mes instructions par mon opiniatreté à ne reconnoitre que les lois et les traités des Etats unis[16] de déplaire à quelques Anglophobes[17] J'ai au moins la satisfaction d'avoir rendu un service important à ma patrie dont la politique aujourdhui est entiérement dirigée vers la guerre.

Je suis très sensible, Mr., aux mesures que vous avés prises pour faire avorter les projets odieux de quelques[18] réfugiés[19] de St. domingue et il seroit à souhaiter que l'on put éxpulser entierement cette race[20] ainsi que celle des émigrés aristocrates d'Europe bien plus dangereux pour la paix la liberté et l'Indépendance des Etats unis que tous les corsaires du monde.

Dft (DLC: Genet Papers); unsigned; above salutation: "Le Cit Genet Ministre plenipotentiaire &c à Mr Jefferson secretaire d'Etat des Etats unis"; only the most significant emendations are recorded below. Tr (AMAE: CPEU, xxxix); dated 11 Sep. 1793; with variations, the most important being noted below (see note 1); certified by Genet. FC (DLC: Genet Papers); in English. Tr (DNA: RG 46, Senate Records, 3d Cong., 1st sess.); in English; dated 14 Sep. 1793; with correction by TJ. Recorded in SJL as a letter of 14 Sep. 1793 received 2 Oct. 1793. Printed as a letter of 14 Sep. 1793 with variations and translation in *Message*, 24–5 (App.), 24–5; translation printed in ASP, *Foreign Relations*, I, 184-5. Enclosed in Benjamin Bankson to TJ, 23

Sep. 1793, and TJ to George Washington, 3 Oct. 1793 (fifth letter).

The LETTRE from TJ in question was actually dated 7 Aug. 1793.

¹ In AMAE Tr "7" is written over "5."
² Genet here canceled "⟨mes pouvoirs n'allant p⟩ C'est en vertu."
³ Preceding five words interlined in place of "de ⟨spen⟩ revoquer."
⁴ Message: "prises faites par."
⁵ Genet first wrote "ces mêmes armateurs" and then altered it to read as above.
⁶ Genet here canceled "moi."
⁷ Message: "la République."
⁸ Preceding three words written in the margin.
⁹ Preceding four words altered from "à se désaisir de leurs lettres de marque à se desarmer."
¹⁰ Preceding two words written in the margin in place of "ports non dans la vue de vous attirer la guerre; mais celle."

¹¹ Genet here canceled "et d'augmenter chés eux le nombre ⟨de leurs⟩ des mécontents."
¹² Genet here canceled "assés."
¹³ Preceding two words interlined in place of "50."
¹⁴ Genet here canceled "très grand."
¹⁵ Word omitted in Message.
¹⁶ Preceding fifteen words written in the margin.
¹⁷ Message: "Anglophobes ou Anglomanes."
¹⁸ Word interlined in place of "⟨des emigrés et Je souhaiterois qu'il fut au pouvoir de votre gouvernement⟩ Colo."
¹⁹ Message: "émigrés refugiés."
²⁰ Preceding eight words reworked from a heavily emended passage which, with some intermediate cancellations restored, reads "⟨que vous pussiés⟩ que ⟨le gouvernement federal put donner des à présent quelque⟩ l'on put faire donner aussi une décision ou loi provisoire pour éxpulser entierement cette race."

To John Kean

SIR   Philadelphia Sep. 14. 1793.

I have recieved your favor of yesterday, and am to thank the Directors of the bank for their assistance in the purchase of bills of exchange. I will therefore ask the favor of you to procure, on account of the Secretary of state, bills of the value of ten thousand dollars, on London or Amsterdam. The remittance [being] finally to be made to the latter place, that circumstance will decide between offers otherwise equal. As I shall be absent from this place some weeks, and our ministers abroad must be nearly in want, I will ask the further favor of you to send the London bills to Mr. Pinckney our minister there, to whom they should be payable, and the Amsterdam bills to the bankers of the US. *on account of the Secretary of state.* These bills are to be paid for out of the funds of my department lodged in the bank. I have the honor to be with great esteem & respect, Sir, Your most obedt. servt   TH: JEFFERSON

PrC (DLC); torn, with bracketed word supplied from FC; at foot of text: "John Kean esquire. Cashier of the bank of the US." FC (Lb in DNA: RG 59, DL).

John Kean (1756-95), who represented South Carolina in the Confederation Congress, 1785-87, and had just completed his

service as one of the Commissioners of Accounts for the States, was cashier of the Bank of the United States from its formation in 1791 until his death (*Biog. Dir. Cong.*; George Washington to the Commissioners of Accounts for the States, [22 June 1793], and note).

In his brief FAVOR OF YESTERDAY, Kean

transmitted a resolution passed that day by the directors of the Bank of the United States ordering him "to purchase for account of the United States such amount in Bills of exchange as may be directed by the Secretary of State" and indicated that he stood ready to receive TJ's instructions (RC in MWA; addressed: "Thomas Jefferson Esqr. Secy. of State &ca."; date of letter and resolution reworked from 12 Sep.; endorsed by TJ as received 13 Sep. 1793 and so recorded in SJL).

To Thomas Pinckney

DEAR SIR   Philadelphia Sep. 14. 1793.

In my letter of Aug. 20. I inclosed you the 1st. of John Wilcocks' bill on Messrs. Edwd. Mc.Culloch and Co. of London for £1077–11–9 sterl. (cost here 5000. Dollars) payable to yourself at 60. days sight to be applied to the use of our diplomatic gentlemen abroad. In my letter of the 11th. inst. I inclosed the 2d. and now the 3d. of the same bill. I have also engaged the bank of the US. to purchase bills for 10,000 Dollars more, either on London or Amsterdam. Those on the former place will be forwarded to you, those on the latter to our bankers at Amsterdam, where it is best the deposit should finally be made. Mr. Kean, cashier of the bank is charged with the purchase and remittance of the bills.

Your letter of July 5. is now recieved, and a communication of the paper, which was the subject of it, has been recieved from Mr. Hammond. He was answered that the measure was new and deeply interesting to us, and that instructions were sent to you to make representations on the subject of it, which of course rendered it's discussion here unnecessary. I have the honor to be with great esteem & respect Dear Sir your friend & servt.   TH: JEFFERSON

P.S. Messrs. Willing, Morris & Swanwick assure me their bill, tho' noted, will be paid.

RC (CtY); at foot of text: "Mr. Pinckney." PrC (DLC). FC (Lb in DNA: RG 59, DCI). Enclosure: Bill of exchange payable to Pinckney, consisting of third set of exchange otherwise identical to enclosure to TJ to Pinckney, 11 Sep. 1793 (printed form with blanks filled, signed by Wilcocks, in CtY).

This day TJ wrote a brief letter to Samuel Sterett asking him to give "a safe conveyance" to this letter and enclosure, as well as his "important" letter of the same date to Willink, Van Staphorst & Hubbard, both of "which he prefers sending at present from Baltimore" (PrC in DLC; FC in Lb in DNA: RG 59, DCI).

MY LETTER OF AUG. 20: see TJ to Pinckney, 22 Aug. 1793.

To Willink, Van Staphorst & Hubbard

GENTLEMEN   Philadelphia Sep. 14. 1793.

Your last favor recieved was of the 4th. of April. My last explained to you that the critical position of Holland, at that moment had induced me to prefer for that occasion remittances to London for the use of our diplomatic gentlemen. Since that other remittances to the same place have been made from the impracticability of getting bills on Amsterdam. Mr. Pinckney however would forward the proceeds to you, in whose hands it is my wish the deposit should rest. Mr. Kean, cashier of the bank of the US. is now charged to procure bills to the amount of 10,000. Dollars, on London or Amsterdam, but preferably the latter, and to remit them to yourselves if on Amsterdam, or to Mr. Pinckney if on London, to be by him remitted to you. Being to be absent from hence some weeks, I have thought it proper to advise you of this. On my return I shall hope to find your account here to the 1st. of July 1793. I have the honor to be with great esteem, Gentlemen your most obedt. servt

TH: JEFFERSON

PrC (DLC); at foot of text: "Messrs. Willinks, V. Staphorsts & Hubbard." FC (Lb in DNA: RG 59, DCI).

Memorandums to Benjamin Bankson

[15 Sep. 1793]

Memorandums for Mr. Bankson.

Mr. Bankson will receive for me at the Treasury 875. Dollars. He will in the first place pay 600. Dollars of it to the bank of North America, and take up a[1] note of mine for that sum endorsed by J. Bringhurst and due the 3d. or 4th. of October.

There will then remain free money	275. Dol.
also Mr. Bringhurst's note now delivd. to Mr. Bankson for	48.
	323

Out of this Mr. Bankson will be pleased to pay

	Dol	
My note in the hands of Mr. John Ross payable Oct. 4.	215.[2]	(say 215)
Mrs. Fullerton, the acct. now delivd.	66.67	
Mr. Ker. do.	41.20	322.87

[116]

Bringhurst's note is payable at sight, and Crosby will collect it. It may[3] furnish the payment to Mr. Ker.

The blank commission for a Marshal of this district in the room of Colo. Biddle, who means to resign at the expiration of his term, is offered to Genl. Moylan, who is desired to write to Mr. Bankson, if he accepts it. In that case his name is to be inserted. If he does not accept, it is then to be offered to Majr. Lenox, and his name inserted. If he will not accept Mr. Bankson will be pleased to write to the President informing him of it, and asking his orders. I think Colo. Biddle's commission expire's about the 20th. inst. so there is no time to be lost.

Forward all letters to me 'at Monticello near Charlottesville' by the post of every[4] Monday morning. It goes through but once a week.[5]

Forward Freneau's and Fenno's papers and the Leyden gazette. But no other newspapers. Keep back also all foreign[6] packets appearing to have newspapers in them, and all packets appearing to have books or pamphlets.

After Monday the 21st. of October send nothing more to me, as before their arrival at my house, I shall be set out on my return to Philadelphia.

Send by post to the President all the Sea letters countersigned by me and not yet signed by him. As fast as they are sealed, let them be sent to the Treasury.

I have desired Mr. Genet, Mr. Hammond, Mr. Van Berckel and Messrs. Viar and Jaudenes to indorse their names on the letters they write to me in my absence. Forward them with my other letters till the President's return, but after his return send them to him instead of me.

PrC (DLC: TJ Papers, 94: 16107-8); undated; endorsed by TJ. Recorded in SJL under 15 Sep. 1793 as "memms" to Bankson. Enclosures not found.

Clement BIDDLE declined another four-year term as marshal for the Pennsylvania district, and after Stephen MOYLAN turned down the appointment, David LENOX accepted it and was confirmed by the Senate in December 1793 (*Annals*, II, 2249; Moylan to TJ, 19 Sep. 1793; JEP, I, 143, 144).

[1] TJ here canceled "bill."
[2] Digits reworked from illegible numbers.
[3] TJ here canceled "be paid to Mr."
[4] Word interlined.
[5] TJ here canceled a new line: "Retain all newsp."
[6] Word interlined.

To Nicholas Collin

DEAR SIR   Schuylkill Sep. 15. 1793.

Having had very certain accounts that a threshing machine was at length invented in Scotland, and got into use in England, which furnished the farmer with that great desideratum, I wrote to England for a model. It arrived in N. York (cost 13. guineas) and is now on it's way from that place, which it left the 13th. inst. for Philadelphia, by one of the packets plying between the two places, commanded by Capt. Elkins, who is to lye at one of the wharves just below Penrose's shipyard. As this is near your house and I am to be absent, I must beg the favor of you to be on the lookout for this vessel, and prevent the possibility of my losing this precious machine by the captain's not finding me. Your love of the useful arts as well as your goodness to me will, I am sure, induce you to take this trouble and either to keep the machine at your own house till my return, or to lodge it at my office. I am with sincere esteem & respect Dr. Sir Your friend & servt   TH: JEFFERSON

RC (RSAS: Collin Papers). PrC (DLC); at foot of text: "Dr. Collin."

From Tench Coxe

Septr. 15th. 1793.

Mr. Coxe has the honor to enclose to the Secretary of State a letter from the Attorney Genl. of the Bahamas to Mr. C's brother, who had written to him upon some business of the Vessels of the U.S. taken into Providence. Mr. J. D. Coxe wishes, that a knowledge of Mr. Franks's communication may be confined to the principal Officers of the Government, and that the letter may be returned in the course of the Month—also that no copy of it may be taken.

Mr. C. had the honor to receive Mr. Jefferson's Note relative to the Appointment of West India Consuls.

RC (DLC); at head of text: "(Private)"; dateline above postscript; endorsed by TJ as received 2 Oct. 1793 and so recorded in SJL. Enclosure not found. Enclosed in Benjamin Bankson to TJ, 23 Sep. 1793, and TJ to George Washington, 3 Oct. 1793 (fifth letter).

To James Currie

DEAR SIR   Schuylkill Sep. 15. 1793.

I have duly recieved your favor of the 6th. and immediately wrote to Mr. Serjeant, your lawyer. I inclose you his answer, by which you will perceive that the fatal fever of this place has not been without it's effect on you also. I had intended to go to Monticello a fortnight hence; but the suspension of all business by the malady, renders it more convenient that I should be absent now. I think therefore to set out in one, two, or three days. My stay there will be short, and not much longer here when I return, as I mean decidedly to retire about the close of the year. This will give me time to wind up your affair here, to which I will give every attention. When I look back to the time of it's commencement, and consider that it has been in the commercial city of Philadelphia that such a delay has taken place, I am filled with astonishment. My best compliments to Mrs. Currie and am with sincere esteem Dr. Sir Your friend & servt   TH: JEFFERSON

PrC (DLC); at foot of text: "Dr. Currie." Tr (ViU: Edgehill-Randolph Papers); 19th-century copy.

TJ's letter to Jonathan Dickinson Sergeant, who would die of yellow fever in Philadelphia on 8 Oct. 1793, is not recorded in SJL and has not been found. Sergeant's ANSWER of 14 Sep. 1793, recorded in SJL as received the same day, is also missing.

To J. P. P. Derieux

DEAR SIR   Schuylkill Sep. 15. 1793.

I find myself on the eve of my departure for Virginia without being able to finish your matter. The contagious fever in the city has prevented my going there for a week past. I had been in daily expectation of receiving the account and balance from Mr. Vaughan who had repeatedly promised it, and excused himself by the multiplicity of his business. I have now written him a letter which I hope will produce an immediate remittance either to yourself or me in Albemarle, where I shall probably arrive as soon as this letter. I am, with respects to Mrs. Derieux Dr. Sir Your most obedt. servt.   TH: JEFFERSON

PrC (DLC); at foot of text: "Mr. Derieux." Tr (ViU: Edgehill-Randolph Papers); 19th-century copy.

Agreement with James Hemings

Having been at great expence in having James Hemings taught the art of cookery, desiring to befriend him, and to require from him as little in return as possible, I do hereby promise and declare, that if the said James shall go with me to Monticello in the course of the ensuing winter, when I go to reside there myself, and shall there continue until he shall have taught such person as I shall place under him for that purpose to be a good cook, this previous condition being performed, he shall be thereupon made free, and I will thereupon execute all proper instruments to make him free. Given under my hand and seal in the county of Philadelphia and state of Pennsylvania this 15th. day of September one thousand seven hundred and ninety three.   TH: JEFFERSON

Witness
Adrien Petit

PrC (MHi); in TJ's hand except for Petit's signature; endorsed by TJ in ink: "James."

James Hemings (1765-1801), the sixth of twelve children of the slave Elizabeth (Betty) Hemings who can be documented from TJ's papers, and the second of six she is alleged to have had by TJ's father-in-law, John Wayles, was one of two bondsmen TJ formally freed during his lifetime, the other being his brother Robert Hemings, who in 1794 arranged to purchase his freedom. TJ freed five other slaves in his will—one outright and the others after various terms of service—all men with trades who belonged to the Hemings family, a clan he had inherited through marriage from the Wayles estate. James Hemings was the only slave who in 1784 accompanied TJ to France, where he learned the ART OF COOKERY well enough to serve as TJ's chef starting in late 1787, and continued in that capacity at New York, Philadelphia, and Monticello. Hemings must have taught his replacement, possibly his brother Peter Hemings, TO BE A GOOD COOK by February 1796, when TJ signed an indenture TO MAKE HIM FREE and paid his expenses to Philadelphia. Although negotiations in 1801 to persuade

Hemings to become his chef at the President's House broke down, TJ employed him at Monticello for a month and a half in the summer of that year, but Hemings left his service and later committed suicide in Baltimore, reportedly as a result of "drinking too freely" (Thomas Jefferson Memorial Foundation, *Report of the Curator*, [1977], p. 10-20; James A. Bear, Jr., "The Hemings Family of Monticello," *Virginia Cavalcade*, XXIX [1979], 78-87; Elizabeth Langhorne, *Monticello: A Family Story* [Chapel Hill, 1987], 25, 26, 27, 33, 34-5, 46, 75, 76, 104-8; MB, 28 Sep. 1778, 26 Feb. 1796, 19 Sep. 1801; Deed of Manumission to Hemings, 5 Feb. 1796; TJ to William Evans, 22 Feb., 31 Mch. 1801; Evans to TJ, 27 Feb., 5 Nov. 1801). For three other members of the Hemings clan whom TJ either "allowed" to run away or made no forceful efforts to recapture, see Lucia Stanton, " 'Those Who Labor for My Happiness': Thomas Jefferson and His Slaves," in Peter S. Onuf, ed., *Jeffersonian Legacies* [Charlottesville, 1993], 152-3, 174n). The argument that the present agreement was not a benevolent act on TJ's part is developed in Paul Finkelman, "Jefferson and Slavery: 'Treason Against the Hopes of the World,' " in same, 204-5.

To James Kerr

Sep. 15. 1793.

Th: Jefferson presents his compliments to Mr. Ker. He has put into the hands of Mr. Bankson a note of Mr. J. Bringhurst's payable at sight, out of which Mr. Bankson will pay Mr. Ker's account. It has been impossible for Th:J. to go to town to recieve and deliver the money to Mr. Ker. He will be back again in seven weeks, proposing to set out tomorrow.

PrC (DLC); conjoined to PrC of TJ to Valeria Fullerton, 16 Sep. 1793. Tr (ViU: Edgehill-Randolph Papers); 19th-century copy; conjoined to Tr of TJ to Fullerton, 16 Sep. 1793.

James Kerr was a coachmaker at 297 High Street, Philadelphia (Hardie, *Phila. Dir.*, 77).

To James Madison

Schuylkill Sep. 15. [1793]

I have to acknolege yours of Aug. 27. and Sep. 2. The fever in town is become less mortal, but extends. Dupont the Fr. Consul is dead of it. So is Wright the painter. His wife also. Lieper is said to be dead, but that is not certain. J. Barclay ill. Ham. and his wife recovered. Willing on the recovery. The banks are not shut up, as I had been falsely informed when I wrote you last. I have some expectation to set out tomorrow, and shall make it eight days to your house; but it is very possible I may yet be detained here two or three days.—The arrangement on which I had consented to remain another quarter was that the President was to be absent three weeks, and after that I was to be absent 6. weeks. This got me rid of 9. weeks of the 13. and the remaining 4. Congress would be setting. My view in this was precisely to avoid being at any more councils as much as possible, that I might not be committed in any thing further. This fever by driving me off sooner, will bring me back sooner, and so far counteract my view.—But I need not take the trouble of writing on this subject, as I shall see you as early as you will get this letter. Adieu.

RC (DLC: Madison Papers); partially dated; unsigned. PrC (DLC). Tr (ViU: Edgehill-Randolph Papers); 19th-century copy.

To Thomas Mann Randolph, Jr.

DEAR SIR   Schuylkill Sep. 15. [1793]

Your's of the 4th. to Maria arrived last night. Mine of last week mentioned a contagious fever which had broke out in Philadelphia. Since that it is so much spread, as to have driven every body off, who can get out of the town, and to have suspended business of every kind. I have never been into the town since the President's departure on the 10th. But I find it impossible to keep my servants from going; and as my clerks have all gone off except one, so that the business of my office cannot be carried on, I have determined to go also. I think to leave this in one, two, or three days, and shall be nine days on the road. Probably

I shall be with you before you recieve this, and therefore I shall add nothing more than assurances of sincere affection to you all. Adieu Dear Sir Your's &c   TH: JEFFERSON

RC (DLC); partially dated; addressed: "Thomas M. Randolph junr esq. at Monticello near Charlottesville"; franked, stamped, and postmarked. PrC (DLC). Tr (ViU: Edgehill-Randolph Papers); 19th-century copy.

TJ's letter OF LAST WEEK, addressed to Martha Jefferson Randolph, was dated 8 Sep. 1793.

To John Vaughan

DEAR SIR   Philadelphia. Sep. 15. 1793.

I received some time ago from you the inclosed paper, but not being certain of the precise point of the enquiry intended, I meant to have had the pleasure of seeing you. In the mean time the malady of the town prevents it, and occasions my setting off for Virginia tomorrow. I presume it might be to know something of the value of the lands: but on this subject a more ignorant person could not have been applied to, as I never was beyond the mountains, nor ever interested to know the value of an acre of land there in my life.

The situation of my friend Mr. Derieux, obliges me to become importunate on his account. I must therefore entreat for the remittance of his balance immediately, as he informs me that he has staved off some demands on the weekly expectation of that till they say they will be put off no longer. I know he will be au desespoir on seeing me arrive without his money. I am with much esteem Dr. Sir Your most obedt. servt

                                                   TH: JEFFERSON

RC (MHi: Waterston Autographs); addressed: "Mr. John Vaughan Philadelphia"; endorsed by Vaughan in part:
    "relative to Derieux
        Money Sent him
        Ansd by Sending Money
        2 Jany 1794." PrC (DLC).

Tr (ViU: Edgehill-Randolph Papers); 19th-century copy. Enclosure not found.

Vaughan's endorsement on the letter suggests that he may have sent part or all of the BALANCE due to Derieux in his missing letter to TJ of 2 Jan. 1794, which is recorded in SJL as received the same day.

To George Washington

DEAR SIR   Schuylkill Sep. 15. 1793.

I have duly received your two favors from Chester and Elkton, and have now the honor to inclose you an address from the town and vicinity of Petersburg, which in a letter from Mr. Peachey I was desired to deliver you.

I also inclose you a letter from Mr. Genet on the subject of Galbaud, and his conspiracies, with my answer sent to him. My hurry of business has prevented my translating the former, but if it cannot be done in your family, I shall be in time to do it myself.

I inclose also Mr. Hammond's reply to my letter of the 9th. Mr. Pinckney's letter of July 5. Mr. Hammond's letter of Sep. 12. communicating the English instructions for the seizure of corn, and the answer I propose to send to him if approved by you. I expect also to recieve from the office the blank commission for the collector of Annapolis in time to inclose it herein.

Having found on my going to town, the day you left it, that I had but one clerk left, and that business could not be carried on, I determined to set out for Virginia as soon as I could clear my own letter files. I have now got through it so as to leave not a single letter unanswered, or thing undone, which is in a state to be done, and expect to set out tomorrow or next day. I shall hope to be at Mount Vernon on the 5th. day to take your orders. The fever here, is still diffusing itself. It is not quite as fatal. Colo. Hamilton and Mrs. Hamilton are recovered. The Consul Dupont is dead of it. So is Wright.   The Consul Hauterive has sent me an answer to my circular letter, as proud as could have been expected, and not very like a desisting from the acts forbidden. As I shall probably be with you as soon as this letter, I shall add nothing further than assurances of the high respect & esteem with which I have the honor to be sincerely Dear Sir Your most obedt & most humble servt

Th: Jefferson

P.S. Sep. 16. I find I shall not be able to get away to-day. Since writing the above I have more certain[1] accounts from the city. The deaths are probably about 30. a day, and it continues to spread. Saturday was a very mortal day. Dr. Rush is taken with the fever last night.

RC (DNA: RG 59, MLR); at foot of first page: "The President"; endorsed by Bartholomew Dandridge, Jr. PrC (DLC); lacks postscript; with newspaper clipping listing deaths in Philadelphia from the yellow fever epidemic, bearing TJ's notations, pasted on second page opposite signature (see illustration). Tr (Lb in DNA: RG 59, SDC). Tr (DLC); 19th-century copy; lacks postscript. Enclosures: (1) Thomas Pinckney to TJ, 5 July 1793. (2) Enclosure listed at Thomas Griffin Peachy to TJ, 3 Sep. 1793. (3) Edmond Charles Genet to TJ, 6 Sep. 1793. (4) TJ to Genet, 12 Sep. 1793. (5) George Hammond to TJ, 12 Sep. 1793 (last two letters). (6) Draft of TJ to Hammond, 22 Sep. 1793.

The letter from HAUTERIVE is dated 10. Sep. 1793.

[1] Preceding two words interlined in place of "good."

To Valeria Fullerton

Sep. 16. 1793.

Th: Jefferson presents his compliments to Mrs. Fulle[rton,] whose account he has received and left in the hands of Mr. Bankson, at his office, with an order to pay it out of monies he will receive at the treasury for Th:J. in the course of the week after next. The present difficulty of money transactions in the city, on account of the absence of so many people and his own journey, has put it out of his power to be more immediate in the discharge of Mrs. Fullerton's account. [He?] begs her to accept assurances of his high respect & esteem for her.

PrC (DLC); with some text lost in right margin; subjoined to PrC of TJ to James Kerr, 15 Sep. 1793. Tr (ViU: Edgehill-Randolph Papers); 19th-century copy; subjoined to Tr of TJ to Kerr, 15 Sep. 1793. Recorded in SJL as a letter of 15 Sep. 1793.

Valeria Fullerton, a widow, kept a boarding school at 113 Mulberry Street, Philadelphia. TJ placed his daughter Maria there in October 1792 and withdrew her around the beginning of September 1793, presumably to safeguard her from the yellow fever epidemic (James Hardie, *The Philadelphia Directory and Register . . .* [Philadelphia, 1794], 54; TJ to Thomas Mann Randolph, Jr., 12 Oct. 1792, and note; MB, 20 Nov. 1792, 20 Feb., 25 Nov. 1793; TJ to David Rittenhouse, 6 Sep. 1793, and note).

To Edmond Charles Genet

SIR   Philadelphia Sep. 16. 1793.

I am honoured with your letter of the 10th. inst. on the subject of the arrest of Capt. Johannene and his vessel the Citoyen Genet, which you supposed to have been by order of the Executive. This I knew could not be; because the Judiciary being sovereign within their department, they would no more act under an order from the Executive or Legislature, than these would presume to give one. I was satisfied also that the impediment to their departure could not be purely from the Executive; because their will had been expressed to be that the vessel should depart. I recommended therefore to Mr. Bournonville to enquire into the fact; and he finds that the arrest is from a court of justice at the suit of an individual, for damages sustained; and security being given to perform the judgment of the court, he has reason to expect that the captain and his vessel are free to depart. Mr. Bournonville was to make still further enquiry, and I am in hopes he is able to inform you by this post that there exists no obstacle to the departure of the vessel and her commander. I have the honor to be with great respect Sir your most obedt. servt   TH: JEFFERSON

PrC (DLC); at foot of text: "The Minister Plenipy. of France." FC (Lb in DNA: RG 59, DL). Tr (DLC: Genet Papers); in French. Tr (same); in French.

From David Humphreys

Sir   Lisbon Septr. 16th. 1793.

We are this moment embarking, and I would not take my departure without just informing you of it. The wind prevented, or we should have sailed yesterday, as I had proposed. It is even now uncertain whether we shall be able to get over the bar to-day.

The Portuguese Troops destined for Spain are beginning to embark this day, and will sail about the 20th. instant.

Yesterday a Packet arrived from Falmouth. The intelligence brought by it does not confirm the numerous and vague reports we have had, of a great battle fought near Paris, and of the consequent capture of that City by the Prince of Cobourg. On the contrary all these seem to have been premature—and there is nothing very important. I am forced to conclude in haste, with assurances of the great esteem & consideration, with which I have the honour to be, Sir Your Most obedient & Most humble Servant   D. Humphreys

RC (DNA: RG 59, DD); at head of text: "(No. 83.)"; at foot of text: "The Secretary of State"; endorsed by TJ as received 18 Nov. 1793 and so recorded in SJL. Tr (Lb in same).

TJ submitted this letter to the President on 19 Nov. 1793, and Washington returned it the same day (Washington, *Journal*, 255).

To Moses Cox

Sir   Schuylkill Sep. 17. 1793.

The malady prevailing in the city, and which has nearly suspended all business, has induced me to take a trip to Virginia, and as the season for the country will be nearly over before I return (which will be about the end of next month) I have had my furniture here packed, so as to be out of the way if you would chuse to occupy the house in order to secure yourself against the prevailing infection. I have been obliged to place my boxes of furniture in the passages below and above stairs, and to leave 4 or 5. trunks piled on one another in one of the rooms. I would have put them in the room below ground but on account of the [damp,] or would gladly have sent them to the city, but on account of the infection to which I would not expose them, as they are to go on to Virginia. I have also left a pipe of wine in the small cellar. I am sorry that these things will be somewhat in your way. There are between 2 and 3. dozen chairs not packed, which may be useful to your family, and save the trouble of bringing chairs. The same circumstance of infection has put it out of my power to have workmen from town to mend 5 or 6. broken panes of glass, fill up screw holes made by the clock, cover with tin a small hole made in the trap door for the bell wire of the clock, and plane out a scratch in the passage floor made in moving a heavy box of books. These are all the repairs I know of which should have been made by me, and if you will be so good as to have them done and make a bill of them, I will pay them with my rent on my return. I leave a servant to finish packing my furniture as soon as he can get 2 or 3 more boxes from town. I shall be happy if my early departure shall be an accomodation to you, as it is certainly a moment when refuge in the country is desireable. I am Sir Your most obedt servt   TH: JEFFERSON

PrC (DLC); faded. Tr (MHi); 19th-century copy. Not recorded in SJL.

From David Humphreys

SIR   On board the Postillion, Lisbon Harbour, Septr. 17th 1793.

We are now under way with a fair breeze, to go over the bar, in company with the vessel which will carry this letter.

Since my letter of yesterday we have nothing new, except an account from Spain (which is depended upon) that the Spanish Camp near Perpignan commanded by Genl. Ricardos, has been surprised by the French, and that the Spaniards have lost three thousand men in the affair.

The Portuguese Troops, who began to embark yesterday, are still embarking.

I have letters from Gibralter, which treat of the affairs of Morocco; but not of those of Algiers. By other channels, I have been informed that the Plague still rages at Algiers, insomuch that 60 Persons die of a day. The British Consul, destined for that place, is yet at Gibralter. With perfect respect & esteem, I have the honour to be, Sir, Your Most obedient & Most humble Servant   D. HUMPHREYS

RC (DNA: RG 59, DD); at head of text: "(No. 84.)"; at foot of text: "The Secretary of State &c. &c. &c."; endorsed by TJ as received 18 Nov. 1793 and so recorded in SJL. Tr (Lb in same).

TJ submitted this letter to the President on 19 Nov. 1793, and Washington returned it the same day (Washington, *Journal*, 255).

From Edmond Charles Genet

MONSIEUR

Newyork le 18 septembre 1793.
l'an 2e. de la République Française.

Persuadé que la souveraineté des Etats-unis reside essentiellement dans le Peuple et sa representation dans le Congrès; Persuadé que le pouvoir éxécutif est le seul qui ait été confié au President des Etats-unis; Persuadé que ce magistrat n'a point le droit de décider des questions dont la Constitution reserve particulierement la discussion au Congrès; Persuadé qu'il n'est point le maitre de faire plier, des traités éxistans, aux circonstances et d'en changer le sens; Persuadé que la ligue formée par tous les Tirans pour aneantir les principes républicains fondés sur les droits des hommes sera l'objet des plus serieuses déliberations du Congrès; J'avais differé, dans la seule vuë de maintenir la bonne harmonie entre les Peuples libres d'amerique et de france de communiquer à mon gouvernement avant l'epoque à laquelle devaient s'assembler les representans du Peuple les pièces originales de la correspondance qui s'est etablie par écrit entre vous et moi sur les droits politiques de la France en particulier, sur les interets de la liberté générale et sur les actes proclamations et decisions de Mr. Le President des Etats unis relativement à des objets qui necessitent par leur nature la sanction du Corps legislatif. Cependant instruit que les messieurs qui m'ont été peints si souvent comme des aristocrates partisans de la monarchie, partisans de l'angleterre, de sa constitution et par consequent ennemis des principes que tous les bons français ont embrassés avec un enthousiasme religieux, alarmés de la popularité que faisait rejaillir sur le Ministre de france l'affection du Peuple américain pour la république française et pour la cause glorieuse qu'elle defend, alarmés également de mon inébranlable et incorruptible attachement aux maximes severes de la démocratie, travaillaient à me perdre dans ma patrie après avoir réuni tous leurs efforts pour me Calomnier dans l'esprit de[1] leurs concitoyens; J'allais commencer à rassembler ces tristes materiaux et Je prenais des mesures pour les faire passer en France avec mes rapports lorsque la dénonciation que ces mêmes hommes ont excité Mr. Le President à faire porter contre moi par Mr. Morris m'est parvenuë. Fort des principes qui ont dirigé ma conduite, a l'abri de tout reproche fondé, Je croyais néanmoins y trouver des allegations graves; mais quel a été mon étonnement lorsque J'ai vu que le Peuple americain y etait plus outragé que moi, que l'on supposait que J'exerçais sur lui une influence souveraine, que l'on pretendait que Je lui faisais prendre part à la guerre de la liberté pour la deffense de ses freres de ses alliés contre les intentions de son gouvernement; que des Jugemens favorables à nos interets rendus au milieu des acclamations des Citoyens de Philadelphie par des Jurés et par des tribunaux independans n'ont pas été l'expression d'une Justice severe; enfin que J'étais une puissance dans une autre puissance. D'aussi étranges accusations prouvant seulement que le Peuple américain aime et soutient nos principes et notre cause en depit de ses nombreux ennemis et que la puissance que l'on me fait l'honneur de m'at tribuer n'est que celle de la reconnoissance qui lutte contre l'ingratitude, de la verité qui combat l'erreur, Je n'enverrai point d'autre Justification de ma conduite. Je Joindrai Seulement à l'appui des opinions que Je devais professer quelques ecrits qui ont été publiés ici, tels que ceux de *veritas* et d'*Helvidius*, &c. Quant aux outrages personnels, quant aux doutes que vous insinués sur mon devouement à l'union des Peuples, J'ai lieu de croire qu'ils ne feront point une grande impression lorsqu'on relira mes réponses aux nombreuses adresses que vos concitoyens ont daigné me présenter; lorsqu'on se rappellera que placé à l'age de 12 ans dans le bureau des affaires etrangeres c'est moi qui ai eu l'avantage de contribuer a pénétrer les Français de l'esprit de 1776. et de 1777. en traduisant dans notre langue sous la direction de mon Pere, alors chef de Bureau, la plupart de vos loix et des ecrits de vos politiques; que depuis cette époque, toujours fidèle à la cause de la liberte, J'ai rendu aux américains dans les differens emplois que J'ai occupés tous les services qui ont dépendu de moi et qu'enfin, chargé de representer le peuple français auprès du premier peuple qui ait proclamé les droits de l'homme, sachant à quel point notre ancien gouvernement avait mis d'entraves liberticides au commerce et à l'intimité de nos deux nations, Je n'ai rien négligé pour obtenir d'une part les bases liberales sur les quelles doivent se négocier les nouveaux liens que la république française desire contracter avec les Etats unis, pour faire sentir de l'autre au gouvernement fœderal combien il etait instant de S'occuper promptement de la conclusion de ce veritable pacte de Famille qui doit unir à Jamais les interets politiques et commerciaux de Deux peuples également en but à la haine de tous les tirans. Au surplus, Monsieur quel que soit le resultat de l'exploit dont vous venés de vous rendre le généreux instrument, après m'avoir fait croire que vous etiés mon ami, après m'avoir initié dans des misteres qui ont enflammé ma haine contre tous ceux qui aspirent au pouvoir absolu; Il est un acte de Justice que le Peuple americain, que le Peuple français, que tous les peuples libres sont interessés à reclamer, c'est qu'il soit Fait une enquete particuliere dans le prochain congrès des motifs d'après lesquels le chef du pouvoir éxécutif des Etats-unis à pris sur lui seul de demander la destitution d'un Ministre public que le Peuple souverain des Etats-unis avait recu fraternellement et reconnu avant que les formes diplomatiques eussent été remplies à son égard à Philadelphie.

C'est au nom du Peuple français que Je suis envoyé auprès de ses frères; auprès d'hommes libres et Souverains, C'est donc aux representans du Peuple américain[2] et non à un seul homme à porter contre moi un acte d'accusation si Je l'ai mérité. Un despote peut seul se permettre de demander à un autre despote la destitution de son representant et ordonner en cas de refus son expulsion; c'est ce que l'imperatrice de

russie à fait à mon egard vis-à-vis de Louis XVI; mais dans un etat libre
il ne peut point en etre ainsi, à moins que l'ordre ne soit entierement
interverti, à moins que le Peuple dans un moment d'aveuglement ne
veuille river ses fers en faisant à un seul individu l'abandon de ses droits
les plus precieux. Je vous prie donc, Monsieur, de mettre sous les yeux
du President des Etats unis la demande que Je lui fais, *au nom de
l'équité*, de presenter à la discussion du congrès à l'époque ou il s'assem-
blera par la loi, si les grands événemens qui occupent l'univers ne paroissent pas encore suffisans pour accelerer Sa convocation 1°. toutes les
questions relatives aux droits politiques de la france dans les Etats-unis.
2°. les differens cas resultans de notre etat de guerre avec les puissances
dont Je vous ai Fait connoitre les actes d'agression: 3°. les chefs d'accusation que le Ministre des Etats-unis auprès de la République française
est chargé de porter contre moi et contre les Consuls dont le caractere se
trouve compromis et outragé de la maniere la plus scandaleuse, pour
avoir obéi a des ordres superieurs qu'il n'etait ni en leur pouvoir, ni au
mien de révoquer. Dans cette attente, Monsieur, Je ne considere point
la dignité de la Nation francaise comme compromise par la position
extraordinaire dans laquelle Je me trouve ainsi que les Consuls et Je n'ai
a me plaindre que des formes que vous avés employées. Le Conseil
éxécutif de la republique française avait aussi des plaintes d'une éspece
bien differente que celles que l'on allegue contre moi à porter contre Mr.
Morris votre ambassadeur à Paris; mais pénétré d'un Juste sentiment de
respect pour la Souveraineté du Peuple americain il m'a recommandé de
ne vous Faire que des observations confidentielles sur la necessité de
rappeller ce Ministre plenipotentiaire accusé par la voix publique sur
des Faits constatés, mais non par les representans du Peuple, après une
enquete réguliere, d'avoir favorisé autant qu'il a pu les projets contre
revolutionnaires de Louis XVI. de lui avoir fait parvenir des mémoires
dans les quels il lui conseillait de ne point accepter la Constitution, de
n'avoir eu de liaisons qu'avec des hommes suspects, d'avoir affecté le
plus grand mepris pour tous ceux qui servaient loyalement la cause du
Peuple; d'avoir été le Canal des Conseils qui ont conduit Lafayette dans
les cachots de la Prusse; d'avoir abusé du respect que le peuple francais
portait à l'envoyé du Peuple americain pour faciliter plus surement la
correspondance et les conspirations de tous ses ennemis; de n'avoir
montré que de l'aigreur dans ses relations avec les ministres de la république; d'avoir affecté en leur ecrivant de n'employer en parlant de
l'exécutif des Etats-unis que de ces mots *au nom de sa cour* si choquants
pour des oreilles républicaines; d'avoir demandé un passeport le 10
aoust 1792 pour passer en angleterre avec l'ambassadeur de George III.
et d'avoir dit publiquement avec une confiance que l'evenement actuel

Justifie que si l'ambassade de la république etait recuë à Philadelphie son éxistance et celle des Consuls républicains en Amerique[3] n'y serait pas de longue durée.

Je vous ai deja Fait part, Monsieur, de quelques unes de ces imputations; mais comme Je vous l'ai deja dit par respect pour la souveraineté des Etats-unis, J'ai cru devoir laisser à leur sagesse le soin de prendre les mesures les plus convenables pour concilier leur dignité avec ce que peut éxiger leur prudence.

Ne doutant point, Monsieur, que la Justice que Je reclame ne me soit renduë ainsi qu'à mes cooperateurs; Je dois vous prevenir que Je vais faire imprimer toute ma correspondance avec vous, toutes mes instructions et toutes celles des Consuls, afin que le Peuple americain, dont l'estime m'est plus chere que la vie, Juge si Je me suis rendu digne ou non de l'accueil fraternel qu'il a daigné me Faire, si dans tous mes offices Je n'ai point exprimé mon respect pour cette nation vertueuse et ma confiance dans la pureté de ses sentimens; si J'ai insiste Sur un seul principe qui n'ait ete soutenu depuis par des décisions des Jurés et des tribunaux du païs; si en agissant et en m'exprimant avec la franchise et l'energie d'un républicain J'ai attaqué la Constitution; si J'ai meconnu une seule loi, enfin si en reclamant avec toute la fermete qui m'etait prescrite l'execution fidele de nos traittés Je n'ai point cherché a encourager le gouvernement fœderal a employer les seuls moyens qui conviennent à un grand Peuple pour conserver la paix et Jouïr de tous les avantages attachés à la neutralité; objet utile qui ne s'acquiert pas par des demarches timides et incertaines, par des proclamations prématurées qui semblent arrachées par la peur par une impartialité partiale qui aigrit vos amis sans satisfaire vos ennemis; mais par une attitude ferme et prononcée qui annonce à toutes les Puissances que le desir très légitime de Jouïr des douceurs de la paix n'a point fait oublier ce que l'on doit à la Justice, à la reconnoissance et que sans cesser d'etre neutres on peut remplir des engagemens publics contractés avec ses amis dans un moment ou l'on etait soi même en danger.

Je repondrai plus en detail lorsqu'il en sera tems, Monsieur, à votre violente diatribe mais elle renferme un fait sur lequel Je dois à present vous donner des explications. L'on vous ordonne de me reprocher d'avoir imprimé inopinement à mes demarches officieles un ton de Couleur qui a Fait imaginer que l'on n'avait connu en france ni mon Caractere ni mes manieres; Je vous en dirai la raison, Monsieur, c'est qu'un sang pur et chaleureux coule avec rapidité dans mes veines, que J'aime passionement ma patrie, que J'adore la cause de la liberté, que Je suis toujours pret à lui sacrifier ma vie, qu'il me parait inconcevable que tous les ennemis de la Tirannie que tous les hommes vertueux ne marchent point avec nous au Combat et que lorsque Je trouve que l'on

Fait une injustice à mes Concitoyens ou que l'on ne prend point leurs interets avec le zèle qu'ils méritent aucune consideration au monde n'empecherait ni ma plume, ni ma bouche de tracer,[4] d'exprimer ma douleur: Je vous dirai donc sans detour que J'ai été éxtremement blessé Monsieur, 1° que le President des Etats-unis se soit haté avant de savoir ce que J'avais à lui transmettre de la part de la République française de proclamer des Sentimens sur lesquels la decence et l'amitié auraient au moins du Jetter un voile. 2°. qu'il ne m'ait parlé dans ma premiere audience que de l'amitié des Etats unis envers la france sans me dire un mot, sans énoncer un seul sentiment sur notre révolution, tandis que toutes les villes, tous les villages depuis charleston Jusqu'à Philadelphie venaient de faire retentir les airs de leurs voeux les plus ardens pour la République française. 3°. qu'il ait recu et admis à une audience particuliere avant mon arrivée Noaïlles et Talon agens connus des contre revolutionnaires français qui depuis ont eu des relations intimes avec deux membres du gouvernement fœderal. 4°. que ce premier magistrat d'un Peuple libre ait decoré son sallon de certains medaillons de Capet et de sa Famille qui servaient à Paris de signes de ralliement. 5°. que les premieres plaintes qui ont été faittes à mon predecesseur sur les armemens et les prises qui ont eu lieu à Charleston lors de mon arrivée n'aient été, pour ainsi dire, que la paraphrase des notes du Ministre d'angleterre. 6°. que le secretaire de la guerre auquel Je Fis part du desir qu'avaient nos Gouvernemens des Isles du vent de recevoir promptement quelques fusils et quelques canons qui les missent en etat de deffendre des possessions garanties par les Etats-unis, ait eu le front de me repondre avec une insouciance ironique que les Principes etablis par le President ne lui permettaient pas de nous pretter même un pistolet. 7°. que le secretaire de la tresorerie que J'entretenais sur la proposition que J'avais Faitte de convertir presque toute la dette américaine au moyen d'une opération de finance autorisée par la loi, en farines, en ris, en grains, en salaisons et en autres objets dont la France avait le plus pressant besoin, ait ajouté au refus qu'il avait déja Fait officielement de favoriser cet arangement la déclaration positive que dans le cas même ou il serait praticable les Etats unis ne pourraient point s'y pretter vû que l'angleterre ne manquerait pas de considerer ce remboursement extraordinaire fourni à une nation avec la quelle elle est en guerre comme un acte d'hostilité. 8°. que d'après les instructions du President des Etats unis des Citoyens americains qui s'etaient rangés sous les bannieres de la france ayent été poursuivis et arretés, attentat inoui contre la liberte dont un Jury vertueux et populaire a vengé avec éclat les deffenseurs de la plus belle des causes: 9°. que l'on ait souffert que des tribunaux incompetens aient pris connoissance de Faits relatifs aux prises dont les traittés leur interdisent expressement le pouvoir de s'emparer; que sur l'avoeu de leur incompetence l'on nous ait enlevé ces propriétés acquises par le droit de la guerre, qu'on ait trouvé mauvais que nos consuls aient protesté contre Ces actes arbitraires et que pour prix de son devouement à ses devoirs celui de Boston ait été emprisonné comme un malfaiteur: 10°. que le Président des Etats-unis ait pris sur lui de donner à nos traittés des interpretations arbitraires absolument contraires à leur veritable sens et que par une serie de décisions que l'on voudrait nous faire recevoir comme des loix, il n'ait laissé d'autre dédomagement à la France, pour le sang qu'elle a repandu, pour les tresors qu'elle a dissipés,[5] en combattant pour l'indépendance des Etats-unis; que l'avantage[6] illusoire d'amener dans leurs ports les prises faittes sur ses ennemis sans pouvoir les y vendre: 11°. que l'on n'ait pas encore répondu à la notification que J'ai Faitte du decret de la convention nationale, qui ouvre tous nos ports dans les deux mondes aux Citoyens americains en leur accordant les mêmes faveurs qu'aux citoyens français avantages qui cesseront si l'on continuë à nous traitter avec la même injustice. 12° que l'on ait differé malgré mes respectueuses insinuations de convoquer immediatement le Congrès pour recueillir les veritables sentimens du Peuple pour Fixer le sisteme politique des Etats-unis et decider s'ils veulent rompre, suspendre ou resserer leurs liens avec la france, marche loyale qui aurait evité au gouvernement fœderal bcaucoup de contradictions et de subterfuges, à moi beaucoup de peines et de degouts, aux Gouvernemens locaux des embarras d'autant plus grands qu'ils se trouvent placés entre les traittés qui sont des loix et les decisions du gouvernement fœderal qui n'en sont point; Enfin aux tribunaux des devoirs d'autant plus penibles a remplir qu'ils les ont souvent mis dans la necessité de rendre des Jugemens contraires aux intentions du gouvernement.

Il resulte de tous ces Faits, Monsieur, que J'ai du etre profondement affecté de la conduite du gouvernement fœderal envers ma patrie; conduite si contraire à tout ce que la volonté de son souverain a tout ce que les procedés du mien me donnaient lieu d'attendre et que si J'ai montré de la fermeté c'est qu'il etait indispensable que ma résistance fut égale à l'oppression, aux injustices auxquelles se trouvaient en but les interets qui m'etaient confiés; c'est qu'il n'était pas dans mon caractère de parler comme beaucoup de gens d'une maniere et d'agir d'une autre, d'avoir un language officiel et un language confidentiel. J'ai Fait strictement mon devoir, J'ai deffendu mon terrein et Je ne laisserai prescrire contre aucun des droits du peuple français tant qu'il me restera un souffle de vie, tant que nos deux républiques n'auront point changé les Fondemens de leurs rapports politiques et Commerciaux, tant qu'on n'aura pas persuadé au peuple americain qu'il est plus avantageux pour lui de redevenir insensiblement l'esclave de l'angleterre,[7] le tributaire passif de Son Commerce, le jouet de sa Politique,[8] que de rester l'allié de la seule

puissance qui soit interessée a deffendre sa souveraineté et son indépendance,[9] à lui ouvrir ses Colonies, et à offrir à toutes ses richesses, des
débouchés qui en doublent la valeur. Si c'est la que tendent toutes les
machinations que l'on Fait agir contre les républicains francais et contre
leurs amis dans les Etats-unis, si c'est pour y parvenir plus commode-
ment que l'on veut avoir ici au lieu d'un ambassadeur démocrate un
ministre de l'ancien régime, bien complaisant, bien doux, bien disposé
à faire sa Cour aux gens en place à se conformer aveuglement à tout ce
qui peut flatter leurs vuës et leurs projets,[10] et à préferer surtout à la
Société modeste et Sure des bons fermiers, des simples citoyens, des
honnêtes artisans, celle de ces personnages distingués qui spéculent si
patriotiquement sur les fonds publics, sur les terres et sur les Papiers
d'Etat. J'ignore si la république française vous trouvera aujourd'hui un
pareil homme dans son sein; mais dans tous les cas Mr., Je puis vous
certifier que Je presserai vivement son gouvernement de me sacrifier
sans balancer si cette injustice presente la moindre utilité. Agréés mon
respect.   GENET

Dft (DLC: Genet Papers); consists of fair copy in a clerk's hand of a missing earlier draft, with complimentary close and signature by Genet, as well as revisions by Genet and a second clerk, only the most important being noted below; above salutation: "Le Citoyen Genet Ministre plenipotentre. de la République française près les Etats unis à Monsieur Jefferson secretaire d'Etat des Etats-unis." Tr (AMAE: CPEU, XXXVIII); certified by Genet; with variations, only the most important being noted below. FC (DLC: Genet Papers); in English. Tr (DNA: RG 46, Senate Records, 3d Cong., 1st sess.); in English; on verso in the hand of George Taylor, Jr.: "Note. This letter was one among several others which were received at the Secretary of State's Office, in Philadelphia, there formed into a packet Sept. 30th. addressed to him and forwarded by Post to Virginia. By some accident of the post they did not get on to him in Virginia, were returned to Philadelphia, and there received by him only the 2d. day of December." Recorded in SJL as received 2 Dec. 1793. Printed with translation and Taylor's note in *Message*, 25-8 (App.), 69-73; translation with Taylor's note printed in ASP, *Foreign Relations*, I, 172-4. Enclosed in Benjamin Bankson to TJ, 30 Sep. 1793.

Genet's belatedly received letter was his reply to TJ's official notification that the United States was requesting his recall by the French government (TJ to Genet, [7 Sep. 1793]). DÉNONCIATION . . . CONTRE MOI PAR MR. MORRIS: see TJ to Gouverneur Morris, 16 Aug. 1793. Genet evidently cited the VERITAS newspaper essays—which he mistakenly believed TJ himself had written and which, like those of HELVIDIUS, criticized American neutrality policy—in order to highlight what he believed to be the discrepancy between TJ's private and public views on the subject (Turner, *CFM*, 241, 245; Notes on Alexander Hamilton and "Veritas," 12 June 1793, and note; Madison, *Papers*, XV, 66-73, 80-7, 95-103, 106-10).

VERITABLE PACTE DE FAMILLE: see Genet to TJ, 23 May 1793, and note. M'AVOIR INITIÉ DANS DES MISTERES: a reference to conversations between TJ and Genet in which, as described by the latter, the Secretary of State allegedly portrayed himself as the only friend of France in the Cabinet and supposedly claimed that the President was decisively influenced by the pro-British views of Alexander Hamilton and Robert Morris. As a result, Genet consistently attributed to the President rather than the Secretary of State primary responsibility for the criticisms of his diplomatic conduct in TJ's 16 Aug. 1793 letter to Gouverneur Morris cited above (Turner, *CFM*, 232, 241, 242-3, 245, 247).

Genet's expulsion by the IMPERATRICE

DE RUSSIE in 1792 for enthusiastically supporting the French Revolution while serving as chargé d'affaires of the French embassy in St. Petersburg is described in William L. Blackwell, "Citizen Genet and the Revolution in Russia, 1789-1792," *French Historical Studies*, III (1963), 72-92. For the PLAINTES of the Provisional Executive Council against Gouverneur Morris, see notes to Morris to TJ, 10 June, 19 Sep. 1792; and enclosure to TJ to George Washington, 20 Feb. 1793.

Although Genet had been planning for more than a month to vindicate himself by publishing TOUTE MA CORRESPONDANCE AVEC VOUS, in the end he confined himself to publishing in December 1793 a carefully selected collection in English of the letters he exchanged with TJ. This publication, a French edition of which was printed early in 1794, also included partial texts of his INSTRUCTIONS from the Provisional Executive Council, but it omitted TOUTES CELLES DES CONSULS (see note to Genet to TJ, 16 May 1793; Genet's third letter to TJ, 20 Dec. 1793, and note; Turner, *CFM*, 241).

DE PROCLAMER DES SENTIMENS: a reference to the Proclamation of Neutrality, which was issued on 22 Apr. 1793, while Genet was still on his way from Charleston to Philadelphia. Louis Marie, Vicomte de NOAÏLLES, the brother-in-law of the Marquis de Lafayette, and Omer Antoine TALON, a former judge and member of the National Assembly, had both arrived in Philadelphia early in May 1793 seeking refuge from the French Revolution. There is no supporting evidence for Genet's belief that at that time Noailles and Talon presented to the President "des lettres du prétendu Régent, que ce Vieillard a eu la foiblesse d'ouvrir." Hamilton and Henry Knox were undoubtedly the DEUX MEMBRES DU GOUVERNEMENT FŒDERAL with whom the two refugees were allegedly friendly (Turner, *CFM*, 218, 246; *Windham Papers*, I, 121, 124-5; AHR, XXXVIII [1933], 633; Childs, *French Refugee Life*, 31-3).

LES PREMIERES PLAINTES: see TJ to Jean Baptiste Ternant, 15 May 1793. DE RECEVOIR PROMPTEMENT QUELQUES FUSILS ET QUELQUES CANONS: on 8 June 1793

Knox, in Hamilton's presence, informed the President that Genet had informally asked to be furnished with "a supply of Arms . . . from the public Arms of the U.S. for the French . . . in such a way as to give an appearance of their being furnished by individuals." With TJ's concurrence, the President and the three Cabinet members agreed the same day that Knox should inform Genet that it would be "highly improper" to comply with his request, pointing out the imprudence of reducing the surplus of arms then in American arsenals "in case the War between the Indians & the U.S. continued, or any circumstances should make it necessary to put this Country in a general state of defence" (Washington, *Journal*, 164, 165n). PROPOSITION . . . DE CONVERTIR PRESQUE TOUTE LA DETTE AMÉRICAINE: see Genet to TJ, 22 May 1793 (third letter), and note.

UN JURY VERTUEUX ET POPULAIRE: a reference to the acquittal of Gideon Henfield, on which see note to Memorial from Genet, 27 May 1793. TRIBUNAUX INCOMPETENS: the United States District Courts, which thus far had refused to assume jurisdiction over French prizes captured from nations with which the United States was at peace. DECRET DE LA CONVENTION NATIONALE: see note to Joseph Fenwick to TJ, 25 Feb. 1793.

[1] Preceding three words not in AMAE Tr.

[2] AMAE Tr: "Souverain."

[3] Preceding two words interlined by Genet in place of "à Philadelphie."

[4] Preceding two words not in AMAE Tr.

[5] Here "le sang qu'elle a repandu" is canceled.

[6] Here "presqu' " is canceled.

[7] The clerk first wrote "redevenir l'esclave des rois d'angleterre" before it was altered to read as above.

[8] Preceding two clauses written in the margin by second clerk.

[9] Remainder of sentence written in the margin by second clerk.

[10] Remainder of sentence written in the margin by second clerk.

From Henry Lee

SIR   Richmond September 18th. 1793.

It has been deemed proper by this Government to direct Vessels coming from Philadelphia, the Grenades and Tobago to perform quarantine.

The officers of the Customs might contribute to the due execution of the regulations prescribed by giving to the Superintendants of Quarantine every information which may reach them concerning the apprehended disorder on the Arrival of Vessels from the infected ports.

I am induced on this ground to mention the matter to you for the information of the President who can give the requisite directions if he pleases. I have the honor to be sir With great respect Your Ob: h: ser.

HENRY LEE

RC (DNA: RG 59, MLR); in a clerk's hand, with complimentary close and signature by Lee; at foot of text: "The secretary of State"; endorsed by TJ as received 2 Dec. 1793 and so recorded in SJL. FC (Vi: Executive Letterbook); dated 17 Sep. 1793.

From Michael Morphy

Málaga, 18 Sep. 1793. He confirms what he wrote on 30 July, since which there has been nothing in this consulate worth mentioning. On 16 Aug. the Algerine cruisers, which are constantly on this coast, captured the *Laurel*, a small empty Philadelphia sloop bound for here from Cádiz, whose master and crew escaped and landed safely. By virtue of a private treaty in train for some time with Admiral Hood, the people of Toulon have proclaimed Louis XVII, hoisted the white flag, and surrendered the port to the British and Spanish fleets under whose protection they will remain until order is restored in France. Twenty-eight French ships of the line and nine frigates were reportedly in that port, from which Admiral Truguet and many of his officers have retired to France. Troops are heading to Toulon from most Spanish ports, including about 2,000 who will leave here in three or four days and reportedly three British regiments from Gibraltar. He encloses a copy of a treaty of alliance beween Great Britain and Spain, the original printed text in both languages having only arrived yesterday from Madrid. Political divisions and royalism are growing so strong in France that it is generally thought there will be a suspension of arms before the year ends—a welcome prospect for trading nations. Few American ships appear here; the only two now loading for America are the *Augusta*, Benjamin Richards, for New York, and the brigantine *Joseph*, Thomas Dissmore, for Boston. Because of the penchant for secrecy among merchants and ship masters, who conceal the destinations, quantity, and quality of their cargoes from each other, he cannot keep a register and furnish the accounts required by the United States until the subjects are ordered to produce their manifests and swear to the contents after the English practice, which is a sure method to prevent smuggling.

RC (DNA: RG 59, CD); 4 p.; at head of text: "No. 3"; at foot of first page: "Honble Thomas Jefferson &ca. &ca."; endorsed by TJ as received 8 Nov. 1793 and so recorded in SJL. Enclosure: Treaty of alliance between Great Britain and Spain, 25 May 1793, with 5 July 1793 note on the exchange of letters of ratification (Tr in same).

TJ submitted this letter and its enclosure to the President on 9 Nov. 1793, and Washington returned them the same day (Washington, *Journal*, 250).

From Benjamin H. Phillips

Curaçao, 18 Sep. 1793. He last wrote on 8 Aug. In contrast to the account given in his 8 June letter, it appears from Captain Ross's protest that he went of his own accord to Aruba, where an armed vessel took "the Negroes &ca." from his American schooner. Upon arriving here, Ross received back the Negroes who were his property, but the French property found in the Dutch harbor has been kept, though Ross was allowed freight on it. A high-ranking officer and pretended friend to America is displeased because he unsuccessfully urged the court to condemn the property and then, changing sides, was unable to persuade Ross and himself to file what would have been a tedious and unsatisfactory suit. Since the officer will probably address the President on this subject, he is obliged to report that he has been informed that the Dutch ambassador will be furnished with such papers as will fully explain the affair. Not being received in a consular capacity, his situation is peculiar in regard to Ross, though he has advised him to receive back his property and let "the point of Honour be referred to the two Courts."

RC (DNA: RG 59, CD); 2 p.; at foot of text: "Thomas Jefferson Esqr."; endorsed by TJ as received 9 Nov. 1793 but recorded in SJL as received 4 Nov. 1793.

A 2 Nov. 1793 letter from Phillips to TJ recorded in SJL as received on 2 Dec. 1793 has not been found.

From Tench Coxe

SIR   Sept. 19. 1793.

I learn from the gentlemen in my office that two hundred Sea letters have been sent thither. They were accompanied by a Note from Mr. Bankson. Immediate Measures were taken for their distribution among the Collectors, for which purpose I presume they were sent. Any others which shall be received will also receive immediate Attention. I have the honor to be with great respect, Sir, yr. mo. obedt. Servant

TENCH COXE

RC (DLC); endorsed by TJ as received 7 Nov. 1793 and so recorded in SJL.

From Patrick Kennan

Sir   New York September 19. 1793

Yours of the 13 I received on the 17th. by which I find you are Authorized to Act for Mr. Short which is confirmed to me by a letter of the 4th. July from Mr. Donald and in order to comply with your request I have here inclosed you Copy of my A/Ct. with them balance in their favor 50.17 Dollars and by the first of next month their will be to receive a quarters Interest due then on 6 and 3 ℔Cents equal to 59.66 Dollars. If I receive that I shall have in my hands $109\frac{83}{100}$ Dollars. Besides that I hold 2800 Drs. 6 ℔Cents. 2356.1 Drs. 3 ℔Cents and 2150 Drs. of Deferred Debt all of which stands registered in my name. You will therefore be so good as Send me a copy of your Power and by Power of Attorney Appoint Some Person here to receive the Stock and what money may be in my hands So that I may receive a discharge for the Same, and with respect I remain Sir Your most obdt hue Servt

PATR. KENNAN

RC (MoSHi: Bixby Collection); endorsed by TJ as received 2 Oct. 1793 and so recorded in SJL. Enclosure: Account Current between Alexander Donald, on behalf of William Short, and Kennan, New York, 18 Sep. 1793, listing debit entries from 10 Nov. 1791 to 18 Sep. 1793 and credit entries from 1 July 1792 to 1 July 1793 (MS in same, entirely in Kennan's hand and signed by him). Letter and enclosure enclosed in Benjamin Bankson to TJ, 23 Sep. 1793.

From Stephen Moylan

Sir   West Chester Sepr. 19th 1793

I this day received your Letter of the 13th. inclosed in one from Mr. Bankson of the 17th. instant. To the Later I returned an Answer which was my Non Acceptance of the Kind Offer made me thoro You by the President to fill the Office of Marshal for this District vacant by the Resignation of Colonel Biddle. After makeing my most respectfull and grateful Acknowledgements to the President for his wish to Serve me and to you Sir for the very polite manner of communicating his intention, I must confess that nothing but the narrowness of my Circumstances makes me decline accepting this honorable Office. I had but little time to gain information respecting its income, if I thought the emoluments of it were at present Such, that with a rigid Oeconomey I coud mentain my familly I most certainly woud accept of it, but from the little information I can procure the income does not exceed 400 dollars ℔ annum. I hold an Office under the state which brings me about that Sum, which with the produce of a Small farm enables me to rub thoro Life in this Country with decency, it woud not do in the City. Pardon me sir for troubling you with my privat affairs the Subject necessarily led to it. Be So good as to Lay this before the President, who has not a more sincere freind than the writer of it, and believe me with great respect and perfect esteem Sir Your obedient and Very humble Servant

STEPHEN MOYLAN

RC (DNA: RG 59, MLR); at foot of text: "The Honorable Thomas Jefferson Esqr"; endorsed by TJ as received 4 Nov. 1793 and so recorded in SJL. Tr (DLC: Washington Papers, Applications for Office); in Moylan's hand; at head of text: "Copy." Enclosed in TJ to George Washington, 5 Nov. 1793.

Moylan later sent a copy of this letter to the President, explaining that in light of the disruption of communications caused by the yellow fever epidemic he was unsure that it had ever reached TJ (Moylan to George Washington, 21 Oct. 1793, DLC: Washington Papers, Applications for Office).

From John Parish

Hamburg, 20 Sep. 1793. He sent a duplicate of his 19 July letter by Captain Dryburgh of the *Polly*, since which a number of American ships have been drawn here by the high freight given to the American flag. They have all been dispatched, but notwithstanding a temporary stop to that trade because of a reported misunderstanding between America and England that has made underwriters unwilling to sign risks except for exorbitant premiums, he is confident that commerce and harmony between the two courts will continue and that ships coming here will find good employment. Because in a month about 20 American ships have taken aboard wheat for Lisbon at a freight charge more than double that given to other neutral ships headed there, the suspicion arises that the captains are privately instructed to land their cargoes in a French port, which may lead to their detention by English cruisers because of Britain's declaration that corn destined for France is contraband. Having warned the captains of this danger, they all swore to their destinations, and he gave them certificates affixed to their manifests that he hopes will be respected. Advice from London today reports that the Court of Admiralty has decided that Captain Earl will be paid freight, demurrage, etc., with the sum to be fixed by arbitrators, which is all the more pleasing because the court dismissed the cause of Hambrô and the Danish ships brought to England at the same time, absolving the captors of any freight or demurrage claims. Appearances indicate that the present bloody campaign will not settle the dispute.

RC (DNA: RG 59, CD); 3 p.; in a clerk's hand, signed by Parish; at foot of text: "The Right Honorable The Secretary of State for the United States of America"; endorsed by TJ as received 11 Nov. 1793 and so recorded in SJL. A Dupl recorded in SJL as received 5 Dec. 1793 has not been found.

TJ submitted this letter to the President on 11 Nov. 1793, and Washington returned

it the same day (Washington, *Journal*, 251).

Parish also wrote a brief letter to TJ on 24 Sep. 1793, enclosing a duplicate of the above letter, which had gone on the 21st by the *Jean*, Captain Daniel McPherson, noting that underwriters still hesitated to sign the risk for an American ship headed for Cádiz, which was a "great drawback" on the trade, and hoping for the arrival of news for him to disseminate that the American flag was under no danger (RC in DNA: RG 59, CD; in a clerk's hand, signed by Parish; at foot of text: "The Right Honorable The Secretary of State for the United States of America at Philadelphia"; endorsed by TJ as received 5 Dec. 1793 and so recorded in SJL). This is the last consular letter TJ received from Parish. See Appendix I.

From Edward Church

SIR   Lisbon 22d Septr. 1793

Coll. Humphreys with Mr. Cutting embarked the 17th. Instt. on board a Swedish Vessel called the Postillion commanded by Abm: Herbst bound first for Gibralter. The Algerine Corsairs are (unfortunately for Us) more at liberty just at this time than heretofore, the Portugueze Ships of War, which were stationed on that Coast, being obliged to quit it, to follow the orders of *their masters* the English; it is therefore to be feared that this circumstance may increase the difficulties of the proposed negociation, as the Algerines only wanted this obstacle removed to have become Masters long ere this of many of our Vessels and fellow-Citizens. Coll. H. has probably informed You that an American Vessel was taken by the Algerines the 18th. Ulto. and that the Men fortunately escaped in their boat to the opposite Shore near Malaga. Had the Men been taken, it is more than probable that the great object in view would have been defeated. The Algerines were in an American Vessel which they had taken some time before and armed for the purpose. The Crew of this Vessel had also effected their escape in the same way. An American Vessel from Boston sailed from this Port last Week bound for Malaga, it is of the utmost importance that She also should escape, for should one other American Crew fall into the Dey's hands, *our Friend's* means would be totally inadequate, and his mission of course fruitless. Under the most favourable circumstances, with his present means, We have no great reason to be very sanguine of his success. The extreme ignorance and imprudent conduct of one of the Precursors on the same errand, have greatly magnified the expectations and demands of the Dey, and the tribute paid by other Nations far exceeds the Sum prescribed by the U.S. Fortunately for America She has every thing possible to hope from the present Agent, Who goes with a heart tremblingly alive to the Sufferings of the unfortunate Captives, and who also possesses every other requisite conducive to the success of such an Enterprize; but when we consider that he has to treat with a rapacious Despot, who is probably actuated solely by self-interest, and restrained only by fear; that it is palpably for the interest of all the European maritime Nations that We should be excluded from a share in the mediterranean trade, and therefore that all the Barbary Powers should be our

Enemies; I would hope, whatever may be the issue of this negociation, that my Countrymen will give Coll. Humphreys all the credit due to a Man who has done all that Man can do. No man is more thoroughly convinced than I am of the importance, and vast commercial advantages to the U.S. of Amca. of a free mediterranean Navigation, but I am by no means convinced that these advantages can possibly be secured to Us *in our present Situation*; the faith of Pirates—whose only support is plunder, and who have hitherto contemned all those ties and obligations which clash with their interest, and which sometimes bind more civilized Despots, seems to me to be but a feeble dependence on which to place a large Stake.

When we can appear in the *Ports* of the various Powers, or on the *Coast*, of Barbary, with Ships of such force as to convince those nations that We are able to protect our trade, and to compel them if necessary to keep faith with Us, then, and not before, we may probably secure a large share of the Meditn: trade, which would largely and speedily compensate the U.S. for the Cost of a maritime force amply sufficient to keep all those Pirates in Awe, and also make it their interest to keep faith.

We are here almost as ignorant of what the belligerent Powers are doing as if we were in the moon, being excluded from all communication with France, and having only the garbled accounts in the London papers, calculated in general to tickle the ears, and drain the pockets of that duped, and *almost ruined* Nation.

This Nation seems in general extremely averse to engaging in the War, both Nobles and People, but the Prince Regent is said to be under the absolute guidance and controul of one Man, *Martin de Mello*, who is the Creature and Idolator of the English. 6000 Troops are just embarked to join the Spanish Army, and the Portugze. have sometime since furnished their Quota of Ships to the English, but it seems the French still consider this nation as not involved in the War against them, as a Portugueze Ship is lately arrived from Bayonne in France laden with pitch, tar, and paper. All the portugueze vessels lately arrived, as well as many Americans, complain bitterly of the insults and pillage of the *british* privateers which they meet at Sea, and of the politeness of the *french*—but it is probably more wise and prudent for both, to pocket the abuses at present, than to resent them. The following very recent event will give you some idea of the power of the present Minister of State, of the blindness and ignorance of the P__e, and of the extreme Servility of his Court; I give it to you from the most unquestionable Authority. A Ship richly laden from Brazil bound to Lisbon was lately captured by a french Privateer, the Ship was ransomed, and hostages given for the payment of the ransom on condition that War had been declared by either nation prior to the Capture; the Vessel arrived here, and the Prince being informed of the circumstance when a very large number of his Courtiers were present, expressed great surprize and resentment on the occasion, and as no one present spoke on the subject, a By-stander would have concluded they were all struck dumb with astonishment, but the fact was, they all knew that six weeks prior to this event, the Governour of Madeira had seized a french East India Ship that touched at that Island on her Return from the East, with a Cargo valued at £80,000 Sterling, and had confined the Capt., Passengers, and Crew, and that he had also detained an American Vessel in that Port near a month, for no cause assigned, but Mr. Pintard who had chartered her, supposes it was because She was bound to Bordeaux. Such is the Power of Martin de Mello and his Creatures, and such are the blessings of a *wise* and *absolute* Prince. I was greatly affected on seeing the Troops embark for Spain, their prejudices it is well known are violent against the Spaniards. It is also said that far the greater number are married and have families, be that as it may—they cried like Children, loudly murmured, and insisted that they were sent to be sacrificed, and that none of them would ever return. The Prince was present, and made a short speech, which I am informed was intended to animate and console them and seemed to have such an effect—what a strange Machine is Man!

Herewith I take the liberty to send you Copy of a Letter which I had the honor to write you soon after my arrival here under date of 31st: July on the subject of the Consular functions &ca.—since which Mr. Cutting has arrived here, and delivered me your favor of the 21st. March, accompanied with a blank bond, which shall be filled up as soon as one of the Sureties (whom I have named, and who with the Other is approved by our Minister at this Court) arrives from Oporto, whither he is gone on a Visit, and it shall be forwarded without delay; Sorry I am to inform you, that I cannot look forward with any promising prospect of even an indemnification for what I have already unavoidably expended in consequence of my consular appointments, and the delay and disappointment attending the first, unless Congress should grant a Salary adequate to the importance and utility of the Office, and in consideration of the great sacrifice which every Citizen of the U.S. must necessarily make who expatriates himself, particularly those who have families—but I beg pardon for troubling You with matters which have no direct claim to your attention. Those which have, shall never pass unnoticed, while I consider it my duty to attend to them, which I do more particularly at this time, as the Minister is absent, and as prior to his departure, he did me honor to introduce me to the Portugueze Minister and Secretary of foreign Affairs, as Chargé des affaires of the Ud. States during his Absence—if therefore, (as the time of our Minister's Return is at present uncertain) there should be any thing requiring immediate attention at this Court, in which I may be thought worthy to be employed, you will be pleased to honour me with your Commands.

No safe Opportunity has yet offered to convey your letter to Mr. Short, and those to Messrs. Carmichael and Short, at Madrid, and my instructions from Coll: Humphreys are, not to hazard a doubtful conveyance; nor has any thing yet transpired from Messrs. C. and S. relative to the object of their joint Commission. With Sentiments of the most perfect esteem & respect I have the Honor to be Sir Yor. most humble & devoted Servant   EDWD. CHURCH

P.S. Coll. Humphries (from whom I received the information) has doubtless aquainted you, that England and Spain seem to be plotting in what way they can most effectually clip our Eagle's Wings. They are both extremely envious of her soaring; this may probably be one cause that retards the conclusion of the business which occupies our Commissioners at the Spanish Court.

Septr. 23d. It is whispered that there has been a second severe action near Perpignan between the French and Spaniards in which the latter have been greatly worsted. The best voucher which I can produce at present in confirmation, is the sombre visages of almost all the English here but this may proceed more from their fears, than from their knowledge of the truth of the report.

RC (DNA: RG 59, CD); above postscript: "Honble. Thomas Jefferson Esqr. Secretary of State for the Und. States of Amca. Or to His Successor in the Office"; endorsed by TJ as received 25 Nov. 1793 and so recorded in SJL. Dupl (same, MD); in a clerk's hand, unsigned; at head of text: "Copy" and "Original Pr. Brig Maria Captn. James Parsons Via Boston"; endorsed by TJ in part: "Duplicate." Enclosure: Church to TJ, 31 July 1793.

This day Church also wrote a brief letter to TJ dealing with the death and burial of Captain William Denney of Baltimore, who had died of consumption, intestate, exactly a week before in Lisbon, a day after his return from a voyage to Fayal (RC in DNA: RG 59, CD; at foot of text: "Honble. Thomas Jefferson Esquire Secy. of State for

the Und. States of America Or to His Successor in the Office"; endorsed by TJ as received 25 Nov. 1793 and so recorded in SJL). TJ submitted both letters to the President on 25 Nov. 1793, and Washington returned them the next day (Washington, *Journal*, 257-8).

ONE OF THE PRECURSORS: John Lamb, who, having been authorized in 1785 by TJ and John Adams to offer the Dey of Algiers a ransom of $200 each for the 21 American mariners then in Algerine captivity, had grossly exceeded his instructions and offered $48,300 in an unsuccessful effort to obtain their release (Barnby, *Prisoners*, 72-81). PRINCE REGENT: John Marie Joseph Louis, Prince of Brazil, who was governing Portugal in place of his incapacitated mother, Queen Maria I, did not actually assume the title of Prince Regent until

1799 (H. V. Livermore, *A New History of Portugal* [Cambridge, 1966], 244). MARTIN DE MELLO: Martinho de Melo e Castro, the former Portuguese foreign minister (same, 239).

To George Hammond

SIR   September 22.[1] 1793.

I have yet to acknowledge the receipt of your favor of the 12th. instant covering an additional Instruction, to the Commanders of British armed vessels, and explaining it's principles, and I receive it readily as a proof of your willingness to[2] anticipate our enquiries on subjects interesting to us. Certainly none was ever more so than the instruction in question, as it strikes at the root of our agriculture, and at the means of obtaining for our Citizens in general the numerous articles of necessity and comfort, which they do not make for themselves, but have hitherto procured from other nations by exchange. The paper had been before communicated to the President, and instructions immediately sent to our Minister at London to make proper representations on the subject, in the effect of which we have all that confidence which the justice of the British Government is calculated to inspire. That 'all provisions are to be considered as contraband in the case where the depriving an enemy of these supplies is one of the means *intended to be employed*' or in any case but that of a place *actually blockaded*, is a position entirely new. However, the discussion having been transferred to another place, I forbear to enter into it here.

We had conjectured, but did not before certainly know that the distinction which the instruction makes between Denmark and Sweden on the one hand, and the United States on the other, in the case of vessels bound to ports blockaded was on the principle explained by you, that what was yielded to those countries by treaty it is not unfriendly to refuse to us, *because not yielded to us by treaty*. I shall not contest the right of the principle, as a right to it's reciprocity necessarily results to us. I have the honor to be with great respect, Sir, Your most Obedient servant   TH: JEFFERSON

PrC (DLC); in Benjamin Bankson's hand, unsigned; with dateline completed in ink by TJ (see note 1 below); at head of text: "Mr. Hammond." Dft (DLC); written and signed by TJ ca. 15 Sep. 1793; with "Mount Vernon" in dateline; on verso in pencil: "[to be] copd [and] press copd." Tr (DNA: RG 46, Senate Records, 3d Cong., 1st sess.). FC (Lb in DNA: RG 59, DL). Tr (Lb in PRO: FO 116/3); with "Mount Vernon" in dateline. Tr (same, 5/1); with "Mount Vernon" in dateline. Recorded in SJPL. Printed in *Message*, 111. Draft enclosed in TJ to Washington, 15 Sep. 1793.

TJ secured Washington's approval of this letter while visiting Mount Vernon this day and no doubt promptly dispatched the missing recipient's copy. In forwarding a copy of TJ's letter to the British foreign minister, Hammond called attention to "the avidity, with which he seizes on the distinction made in favor of Danish and Swedish ships, as offering a justification of the United States in continuing to France those advantages which that country de-rives from existing treaties" (Hammond to Lord Grenville, 12 Oct. 1793, PRO: FO 5/1).

[1] Digits added in ink by TJ in space left blank by Bankson.
[2] In Dft TJ here canceled "furnish us."

From Thomas Pinckney

SIR   London 22d. Septr. 1793

Mr. Miller the bearer hereof is an English Gentleman of science and good reputation who was recommended to me by the Marquis del Campo. He is now going on business to Canada, and as in the present state of warfare between his Country and France it is not impossible that he may be captured and carried into one of our ports, I rely upon your love of science and general philanthropy to excuse the liberty I take in requesting that you will in that case extend to Mr. Miller those good offices which may tend to alleviate any unpleasant circumstances attending his situation. I have the honor to be with the utmost respect Sir Your most obedient Servant   THOMAS PINCKNEY

PrC (ScHi: Pinckney Family Papers); at foot of text: "Mr. Jefferson."

Memorandum to George Washington

Heads of answer to the Caroline resolutions.

Taking them up in their order, they appear susceptible of answer in the following way.

The 1st. and 2d. by a concurrence of sentiment for the maintenance of the constitution, and preservation of peace, and the pleasure with which the President recieves their assurances of support in these objects.

3. Notice of the expressions of their personal respect.

4. Approbation of their expressions of gratitude to the French nation for aids extended in a time of need, and the honorable trait evidenced in the National character by a strong remembrance of it, even in the moment when the justice due to others imposes laws on the manifestation of it. That being firmly persuaded that the interest and happiness of all the parties engaged in the present contests of Europe will be most promoted by their obtaining every one what is right, and no more, we may innocently and justly pray to heaven that such may be the result of these afflicting contests.

5.6.7. to express a firm attachment to the free principles of our government, and a confidence that the virtue and good sense of our citizens will counteract and defeat all measures which might tend to weaken their affection to these principles, to alienate them from the republican government they have established for themselves, or to innovate on it's character.

8. it would seem more delicate and dignified to pass over this altogether.

Sep. 22. 1793.

MS (DLC); entirely in TJ's hand. Entry in SJPL: "draught of answr. from G.W. to Caroline resolns."

The CAROLINE RESOLUTIONS on French-American relations had been approved by a 10 Sep. 1793 meeting of citizens of Caroline County, Virginia, chaired by Edmund Pendleton, who transmitted them to the President in a letter dated a day later. The first seven followed the order, substance, and in large measure the wording of sample resolves drafted by James Madison and James Monroe to guide Republicans seeking to respond to Federalist resolutions approved in Richmond on 17 Aug. 1793. The eighth resolution, the connection of which to Madison and Monroe is unclear, condemned any attempt by foreign diplomats to bypass the executive and appeal to the people directly, but suggested that if French minister Edmond Charles Genet was indeed guilty of this offense his conduct should not be attributed to France unless that nation defended his conduct. TJ had received a copy of the draft by Madison and Monroe that inspired the Caroline resolutions eight days before Washington asked him for help in composing a response when he stopped at Mount Vernon on the way to

Monticello (Madison to TJ, 2 Sep. 1793, and enclosure; George Wythe to TJ and Edmund Randolph, 17 Aug. 1793, and note; Caroline Resolutions, 10 Sep. 1793, enclosed in Pendleton to Washington, 11 Sep. 1793, DLC: Washington Papers, the former printed in Mays, *Pendleton*, II, 608-10, from a newspaper text containing one important error).

The President's 23 Sep. 1793 answer to Pendleton departed in several ways from TJ's suggestions. Washington moved his thanks for the EXPRESSIONS OF THEIR PERSONAL RESPECT to the end of the letter and dropped any mention of the PRESENT CONTESTS OF EUROPE, although he retained a sentence approving the grateful remembrance of past French aid. He followed closely TJ's formula for responding to the fifth, sixth, and seventh resolutions until the end, when he replaced the hostile allusion to those who might INNOVATE ON the government's CHARACTER with a reference to the "unequalled prosperity and happiness" hitherto enjoyed by Americans under their republican government. As TJ suggested, Washington chose to PASS OVER the final resolution (Fitzpatrick, *Writings*, XXXIII, 91-2).

From Benjamin Bankson

SIR   Philadelphia, Septemr. 23d. 1793.

The Letters which you will receive herewith are all that have come to the Office since your departure.

I have not yet received an answer from Genl. Moylan. His residence is in Chester County 30 miles from this City, and out of the post road, so that I fear your Letter and one I have written him have miscarried. Mr. Biddle's Commission will expire the 26th. inst.—and from your instructions "that no time be lost"[1] in ascertaining the acceptance or non acceptance of the Office by him or Major Lenox—I hope I shall be in the line of my duty in sending an Express.

Crosby left Town yesterday for a week or [ ] days—he said with your permission.

No opportunity has yet offered for Europe from this place—and as all communication is cut off between this City, New York and Baltimore, it is uncertain when one will present itself. I have the honor to be very respectfully Your most obed Servt.   B BANKSON

RC (DLC); torn at seal; at foot of text: "Mr. Jefferson"; endorsed by TJ as received 2 Oct. 1793 and so recorded in SJL. Enclosures: (1) Jean Antoine Gautier to TJ, 25 May 1793. (2) Grand & Cie. to TJ, 25 May 1793 (two letters). (3) William Lyall and Others to TJ, 30 June 1793. (4) Willink, Van Staphorst & Hubbard to TJ, 1 July 1793. (5) George Nicholas to TJ, 25 Aug. 1793 (not found, but see note to TJ to Nicholas, 15 July 1793). (6) Anonymous to TJ, [ca. 6 Sep. 1793]. (7) John Langdon to TJ, 9 Sep. 1793. (8) Christopher Gore to TJ, 10 Sep. 1793. (9) Edmond Charles Genet to TJ, 13, [14] Sep. 1793. (10) Genet to TJ, 14 Sep. 1793 (noted at TJ to Genet, 2 Oct. 1793). (11) Tench Coxe to TJ, 15 Sep. 1793. (12) Thomas Russell to TJ, and Russell and Others to TJ, both 15 Sep. 1793 (noted at Circular to American Merchants, 27 Aug. 1793). (13) Charles François Bournonville to TJ, 18 Sep. 1793 (noted at TJ to Bournonville, 3 Oct. 1793). (14) Patrick Kennan to TJ, 19 Sep. 1793.

[1] Quotation mark supplied.

From Joret de Longchamps

SIR   Lyme 23 September 1793

Elapsed as so many poor inhabitants of hispaniola who have lost here their fortune. I am about purchasing a little settlement in the Connecticut's state. Would you Sir Do me the favor to answer me if I Can Depend upon the protection of united States after my naturalisation. In that Case I would return to hispaniola for 6 or 8 months at most, and bring with me the revenue of my plantation and other goods I Can yet have in that unhappy Country. I am with the most profound Respect your mos obedient servant   JORET DE LONGCHAMPS
at Capne. wait

RC (DNA: RG 59, MLR); at head of text: "The honorable Thom Jefferson Secretary of State"; endorsed by TJ as received 2 Dec. 1793 and so recorded in SJL.

After purchasing a farm in Lyme, M.F. Joret de Longchamps, by his own account a native of France who had fled HISPANIO-LA, petitioned the Connecticut General Assembly for naturalization or the capacity to hold lands and in October 1793 was granted permission to buy and secure title to lands in that state on the same footing as citizens of Connecticut (*Pub. Recs. Conn.*, VIII, 121-2).

From Edmond Charles Genet

Newyork. le 23. [i.e. 24] Septembre 1793
l'an 2e de la République

Monsieur

Je suis chargé de vous communiquer le decret rendu par la Convention nationale le 13 du mois d'avril dernier par lequel elle declare "que le Peuple français ne s'immiscera en aucune manière dans le gouvernement des autres puissances, mais qu'il ne souffrira qu'aucune puissance s'immisce dans le régime interieur de la République et prononce la peine de mort contre quiconque proposerait de négocier ou de traitter avec les Puissances ennemies qui n'auraient pas reconnu solemnellement l'independance et la souveraineté de la république française."

Lorsque les Citoyens français à l'exemple des Citoyens americains ont voulu etablir un gouvernement fondé sur les droits des hommes, Ils devaient s'attendre a trouver des ennemis dans tous les ambitieux, avides de l'autorite, dans tous les Cabinets ou le machiavelisme est en honneur, et lorsque le Peuple français, indigné fatigué des[1] machinations tenebreuses de ses ennemis, de leurs attaques publiques, des insultes contenuës dans les offices des cours despotiques,[2] des gouvernements tendants à la monocratie à voulu repousser ces perfidies par des actes marqués au coin de la loyauté, de la grandeur, de la philosophie a l'instant même ses vils ennemis ont repandu qu'il voulait aneantir tous les gouvernemens, détruire toutes les autorités, repandre le trouble et la confusion partout, comme si repondre a une provocation n'etait pas de droit naturel, comme si un grand peuple victime de la haine particuliere du gouvernement d'un autre Peuple n'avait pas le droit de lui faire connoitre ses craintes, de l'eclairer sur Ses erreurs, et de tenter par ces moyens doux et Justes d'empecher de très grands malheurs, de prévenir même[3] la guerre: quoiqu'il en soit la Convention nationale a cru devoir pour rassurer les amis de l'humanité et fermer la bouche à ses ennemis proclamer les intentions du Peuple francais et ses agens montreront dans toutes les Circonstances qu'ils savent aussi bien respecter les lois[4] des autres Peuples que deffendre celles de la nation française[5] et maintenir ses droits.

Dft (DLC: Genet Papers); in a clerk's hand, unsigned, with revisions by Genet; above salutation: "Le Citoyen Genet Ministre plenipotentiaire de la République francaise à Monsieur Jefferson secretaire d'Etat des Etats-unis." Tr (AMAE: CPEU, xxxix); with minor variations; misdated 13 Sep. 1793. FC (DLC: Genet Papers); in English; dated 23 Sep. 1793. Tr (DNA: RG 46, Senate Records, 3d Cong., 1st sess.); in English; dated 24 Sep. 1793. Recorded in SJL as a letter of 24 Sep. 1793 received 2 Dec. 1793. Enclosure: Decree of the National Convention, 13 Apr. 1793, declaring that it would neither interfere with the government of any other power nor tolerate any other power's interference with France's internal affairs, and providing the death penalty for anyone proposing to treat with an enemy power that had not recognized the French Republic's independence, sovereignty, indivisibility, and unity, founded on liberty and equality (*Archives Parlementaires*, 1st ser., LXII, 3). Printed as a letter of 24 Sep. 1793 with translation in *Message*, 28-9 (App.), 81; translation printed in ASP, *Foreign Relations*, I, 178.

[1] Genet here canceled "effets funestes des."

[2] The clerk here first wrote "des injures de Burke non pas comme particulier, mais comme membre d'un gouvernement des intrigues de Mr. Morris à Paris." Genet canceled the passage and interlined "dans les intrigues de quelques Agens é" before canceling the addition and interlining the next six words.

[3] Preceding three words interlined by Genet in place of "et enfin."

[4] Word interlined by Genet in place of "droits."

[5] Remainder added by Genet.

From Edmond Charles Genet

New york. le 24. 7bre 1793.
M.
l'an 2e. de la Repe. francoise une et indivisible.

J'ai l'honneur de vous adresser un éxemplaire des nouveaux congés maritimes décrétés pour nos batiments de commerce par une loi de la Convention nationale en date du 22. Janvier dernier et dont Je Joins également ici un éxemplaire. Le Conseil m'a fait passer avec le modele de ces Congés des modeles de lettres de marque absolument conformes M. à ceux dont J'ai déja eu l'honneur de vous donner Communication et J'apprens par le Citoyen dennery Consul de la Republique à Boston que le Conseil éxécutif étoit tellement persuadé que nos armements dans les ports des Etats unis ne rencontreroient aucun obstacle qu'il a cru devoir le charger de faire parvenir à tous nos Consuls plusieurs paquets de lettres de marque indépendament des trois Cents que J'avois reçu l'ordre de leur distribuer.

Dft (DLC: Genet Papers); unsigned; above salutation: "Le Cit Genet Ministre plenipre. de la Repe. francoise près les Etts. unis à Mr Jefferson secretaire d'Etat des Etats unis." FC (same); in English. Recorded in SJL as received 2 Dec. 1793. Enclosure: Decree of the National Convention, 22 Jan. 1793, stating that the old forms of "congés et passeports" for French trading ships would be valid until 1 June 1793, after which new forms would be used (*Archives Parlementaires*, 1st ser., LVII, 540-1). Other enclosure not found.

From Edmond Charles Genet

24. 7bre. [1793] l'an 2e.

Edmond Charles Genet a reçu la note que Mr. Jefferson lui a écrite le 14. de ce mois et il se[1] Conformera à l'avis qu'il a bien voulu lui donner.

Dft (DLC: Genet Papers); partially dated. Recorded in SJL as received 2 Dec. 1793.

The NOTE in question was the Circular to Foreign Ministers in the United States, 14 Sep. 1793.

[1] Genet here canceled "bornera à l'avenir dans sa Correspondance a ne lui."

From Edward Church

Lisbon, 25 Sep. 1793. He wishes to provide a more authoritative account of two actions between the French and the Spanish that his accompanying letter of 22 Sep. mistakenly described as having taken place near Perpignan. On 28 Aug. General Dagobert's army surprised and defeated a Spanish force of about 3,000 men, commanded by General La Penha and camped near Montlouis, killing 700 to 800 of them, taking almost all the rest prisoner, capturing eight artillery pieces and all the baggage, and entering and garrisoning Puycerda, reportedly the key to Catalonia. On 5 Sep. an army of 6,000 chosen Spanish troops, commanded by General Vasques and situated so as to sever all communication between Dagobert's army and France, was attacked and completely defeated by the French, reportedly with a third of the men slaughtered in battle, the rest taken prisoner, and thirteen cannon, all baggage, and many mules fallen into French hands, the loss of the mules being especially regretted. The English have raised their costly siege of Dunkirk. The allied forces will probably need another campaign but may not be able to afford it. *26 Sep.* He has received a polite and unequivocal letter from Luís Pinto de Sousa stating that orders have been sent this day to the governor of Madeira to make full compensation to Pintard, the consul there, for detaining his vessel bound for Bordeaux.

RC (DNA: RG 59, CD); at foot of text: "Honble. Thomas Jefferson Esquire Secy. of State for the U. S. of Amca: Or to His Successor in the Office"; endorsed by TJ as received [25] Nov. 1793 and so recorded in SJL.

TJ submitted this letter to the President on 25 Nov. 1793, and Washington returned it the next day (Washington, *Journal*, 258).

From Thomas Pinckney

DEAR SIR   London 25 Septr. 1793

No alteration has taken place since my last in the conduct of this Government towards the neutral powers, they still assert the propriety of preventing the provisions specified in their additional instructions from being sent to French ports, and of making prize of their enemy's property in whatever Vessels it may be found—the execution of these measures of course creates much uneasiness among our citizens whose commerce is much injured thereby. I receive assurances that their courts will amply redress the irregularities which may be committed by their cruizers upon proper application, but these are frequently of a nature to be with difficulty brought under the cognizance of the judiciary and I find our seafaring people in general rather inclined to submit to the first inconvenience than risk the event of a lawsuit: The Court of Admiralty in the begining of the present month adjudged freight, demurrage and expences to an American Vessel whose cargo was condemned. I am hopeful since this precedent that it will be allowed in all other cases which will of course prevent so many of our Vessels from being brought in. The protection afforded our seamen remains also on the same footing, they profess a willingness to secure to us all real American seamen when proved to be such, but the proof they will not dispence with—our Consuls are allowed to give protections where the master of the Vessel and the Mariner swear that the party is an American native and citizen, which protections in general are respected, though some irregularities occasionally take place: So many objections are made to the arrangement we propose on this subject that I see no prospect of its taking place.

The Vessel which conveys this will also carry out the remainder of the Copper for the Mint, the first parcel was sent by the Pigou Captn. Loxley.

I inclose my account up to 1st. July last; as I have not yet received all the Consuls accounts for settlement and several articles in those which are rendered must be referred for your determination I would detain it no longer for them. I remain with great and sincere respect Dear Sir Your most obedt & most faithful Servt.   THOMAS PINCKNEY

RC (DNA: RG 59, DD); at foot of first page: "The Secretary of State"; endorsed by TJ as received 28 Nov. 1793 and so recorded in SJL. PrC (ScHi: Pinckney Family Papers); lacks page with signature; at foot of text: "Mr. Jefferson." Dupl (DNA: RG 59, Duplicate Diplomatic Dispatches); in the hand of William A. Deas except for abbreviated complimentary close, unsigned; at head of text: "(Duplicate)"; conjoined to RC of Pinckney to TJ, 27 Sep. 1793. Tr (Lb in same, DD). Tr (DNA: RG 46, Senate Records, 3d Cong., 1st sess.); final two paragraphs omitted. Enclosure not found. Printed without final two paragraphs in *Message*, 115. Enclosed in TJ to George Washington, 29 Nov. 1793.

A decree of the British COURT OF ADMIRALTY of 3 Sep. 1793 set forth the circumstances under which masters of neutral ships were entitled to payment for freight, reasonable expenses, demurrage, and the seizure of corn, provisions, and naval stores (Tr in DNA: RG 59, DD).

From Thomas Pinckney

DEAR SIR   London 25th. Septr. 1793

In consequence of your favor of 15 March concerning M. La Fayette I renewed to the Prussian Minister here in an authorised stile the application I had before unofficially made to him in behalf of our unfortunate friend, declaring the interest taken by the United States in his welfare and suggesting the obligation his liberation would confer. I was hopeful that before this time I should have been able to communicate an answer but none has yet been received. I had previously obtained permission through the same channel for a correspondence by open letters to be carried on between Mr. Lafayette and his wife which however was not to extend beyond information of their respective healths nor to be *trop suivie*. I am happy to find that of late his confinement is not altogether so rigorous as it was at first He being now allowed to walk an hour in the day in the open-air. The money lodged for him by Mr. Morris supplies his expences.[1] He lately drew on me through a confidential person for six thousand livres expressing in the draft that it was to assist him to emerge from captivity. I paid the bill from the contingent fund, but wish for particular instructions specifying what money may be advanced to him and his family and for what purposes.

You may rest assured, Sir, that a more pleasing task could not be assigned me than that of endeavoring to alleviate the misfortunes of one to whom we owe so much. I correspond with Mr. Morris on this subject when occasion offers and will not fail to give you information if any favorable prospect should arise. I have the honor to be with great & sincere respect Dear Sir Your most obedt & most faithfull Servant

THOMAS PINCKNEY

I sounded Lord Grenville some months past without success.[2]

RC (DNA: RG 59, DD); with two sentences and postscript written in code; decoded interlinearly in part by TJ (see note 1 below) and by the Editors (see note 2 below); at foot of text: " Mr Jefferson"; endorsed by TJ as received 28 Nov 1793 and so recorded in SJL. PrC (ScHi: Pinckney Family Papers). Tr (Lb in DNA: RG 59, DD); with portion decoded by TJ written *en clair* in brackets; lacks postscript. Enclosed in TJ to George Washington, 29 Nov. 1793.

[1] Remainder of paragraph written in code, the text being supplied from TJ's decipherment and verified by the Editors using partially reconstructed Code No. 16.
[2] Postscript written in code, the text being deciphered by the Editors using partially reconstructed Code No. 16.

To Robert Gamble

SIR   Monticello Sep. 26. 1793.

In passing through Baltimore I received the Skipper's reciept for the 14. cases of wine, which having been shipped from thence on board the sloop Polly, James Fibbett master, on the 7th. inst. is I hope arrived at Richmond by this time, in which case I shall be happy to receive them, or a part of them by the first waggon. I took the liberty of desiring a box of books from Baltimore to be also addressed to you. They will come to hand later. The receipt for the wine is inclosed. I have the honor to be Sir Your most obedt. servt   TH: JEFFERSON

PrC (DLC); at foot of text: "Colo. Robert Gamble." Tr (ViU: Edgehill-Randolph Papers); 19th-century copy. Enclosure not found.

From David Humphreys

SIR   Gibralter Septr. 26th. 1793.

After a very favorable passage, we landed at this Garrison on Sunday last; and the next day proceeded with all the dispatch and diligence in our power to unpack the different articles of public property left here by the late Mr. Thos. Barclay, and to select such as might be proper for the object you propose. We have not as yet made such progress as to enable me to give you the result.

I have seen Mr. Matra, the British Consul for Morocco, who informs me, there is very little change in the state of Affairs since last winter. The harvest was good. The exportation of wheat has been allowed: but is prohibited on the remonstrance of the People, who have been so much distressed by scarcity as to dread the consequences of farther extraction.

Mr. Mace the new British Consul for Algiers is still here. All the intelligence I can gain from that Place is contained in a letter of an old date from Mr. Logie to him. At the time when that letter was written the Plague still continued to rage, and ten of the Dutch Captives had died of it. The Plague has absolutely cut off all intercourse, so that nothing has been heard from the Americans in captivity there, since I was here last winter.

The Frigate, which escorted Mr. Lucas to Tripoli, returned here yesterday. Mr. Tulley the former Consul, who came in it, I understand, reports rebellion and confusion to exist in a dreadful degree, in that Country.

The wind came round yesterday to the Eastward, so as to enable the

Convoy from Leghorn to sail from this Port for England. This is a rich fleet, and the first Convoy from the Mediterranean since the War.

I have concluded to go to Alicant, and hope (for many reasons) to be able to sail in company with the Portuguese fleet mentioned in my late letters, and which may be expected whenever the wind becomes fair.

It is confidently asserted, that the Project for the Surrender of Marseilles has miscarried, and that the Republicans have made an amazing slaughter of the Royalists.

Had not the cession of Toulon taken place on the very day it did, it would almost certainly have been prevented the next day by the arrival of Troops in the Town. Lord Hood's conduct appears to be considered here as almost rash, tho' successful; and the issue somewhat dubious, tho' in some way or another it must be important.

The Commanding Officers of the combined forces at Toulon have sent to all quarters for succours. The Spanish, English and Royalist forces in that Town amount to nearly 10,000. The former, an indifferent Corps; the second, weak in number (2000); both suspicious of the latter. In several little actions on the outside of the Town, the combined troops have had the worst of it. A valuable English Officer (belonging to this Garrison) of my acquaintance, was killed in one of them. Yesterday three Ships of war arrived here from Toulon, to solicit and transport a reinforcement from this Garrison. The Governor has already named Officers of Engineers and Artillery for that service; and I think he will send some troops, without waiting for orders from his Court.

General O'Hara, with whom I dined yesterday, informed me, an intelligent Correspondent wrote him from Toulon, "there is no news from Paris, except that of the death of the Queen." This, however, coming through no other channel, seems doubtful.

Admiral Gell, and other Officers of high rank write pressingly for all manner of eatables and drinkables. If we had but the free navigation of the Mediterranean, what an extensive market would be opened for our Produce? With Sentiments of perfect respect & esteem I have the honour to be Sir Your most obedient & Most humble Servt

D. HUMPHREYS

RC (DNA: RG 59, DD); at head of text: "(No. 85.)"; at foot of text: "The Secretary of State &c. &c. &c."; endorsed by TJ as received 11 Dec. 1793 and so recorded in SJL; with penciled notation by George Taylor, Jr.: "to go with algerine Business." Dupl (same, Duplicate Diplomatic Dispatches); at head of text: "(Duplicate)"; at foot of text: "N B The original goes under Cover to Mr Church Lisbon—the Duplicate by Cadiz"; endorsed by TJ as received 26 Dec. 1793 and so recorded in SJL. Tr (DNA: RG 46, Senate Records, 3d Cong., 1st sess.). Tr (Lb in DNA: RG 59, DD). Enclosed in James Simpson to TJ, 26 Sep. 1793, and Report on Morocco and Algiers, 14 Dec. 1793.

TJ submitted this letter to the President on 11 Dec. 1793, and Washington returned it the same day (Washington, *Journal*, 266).

From Robert Leslie

Sɪʀ   London September 26th 1793

Since I wrote you last, your frend Mr. Cutting has arived from Irland, in whos aquantince I find a great deal of pleasure, and am very much obliged to you, for your Introduction to him.

I find my improvements much better recived here than I expected, so much so, that several of the most eminent watch and Clock makers, have offered to be at all the expence of getting patents here, and alow me half of all the profits, which I should have thought very avantageous proposals, if better had not offered, as the patents will cost one hundred guines each, but I have now agreed with one who is very largely in business, he is to be at all the expence of the patents, and furnish any some of money I wish, under fifteen thousand pounds, to work on, so that I shall have one half of all the profits, and not be under the necessity of useing any of my own money, this is a contract by which I cannot loose, and may perhaps gain some thing handsom.

I have now begun business on the above plan, and hope by spring you will see som of our performance, which I have no doubt will give satisfaction, as we have engaged some of the best workmen in London. The watch you was pleased to order, shall be among the first.

I am now in the very situation I have allways wished for, as the gentleman I am conected with, has giv me the intier direction the business, and wishes to indulge me with every experiment I choose to make at his expence.

I find your Report on Weighs and measures, is very well known here, and very generaly approved of, so that if it is adopted by Congress, I have no doubt but the Parliment here will follow the example. I have by the asistence of Mr. Pinkney, got permison to viset the Royal Observatory at greenwich, and think it a very convenient place to try the Pendulum Rod, as I can have the use of the best instruments to reagulated it by. I know of no convenient place in America, that is in Lat. 45, and Greenwich is as near it, as Philadelphia, and perhaps the tables showing the lenght of Pendulums in different Lat., will show what it would be in 45, so that an alowence might be made.

If you find no objection to the above plan, I shall be glad to have the honour of making the experiment and bring it over with me, on my return, or send it, if it should be wanted sooner.

I hope you will always look on me as an American and every thing I do, as the productions the United States. I am Sir with the highest respect your much obliged and very Humble Sert   Rᴏʙᴇʀᴛ Lᴇꜱʟɪᴇ

RC (DLC); endorsed by TJ as received 6 Dec. 1793 and so recorded in SJL.   TJ's ɪɴᴛʀᴏᴅᴜᴄᴛɪᴏɴ of Leslie to John Brown Cutting was dated 25 Apr. 1793.

At some point TJ also received Leslie's printed circular letter of 26 Aug. 1793 giving his address as 12 Aldersgate Street or 4 Merlin's Place, near the New River Head, London, and announcing that he would sell "Plated, Silver, and Jewellery; Japanned, Cutlery, and Hard Wares; of the best Quality, and newest Fashions" at five percent above cost (RC in DLC).

From Michael Morphy

Málaga, 26 Sep. 1793. Since his 18 Sep. letter, sent to New York by the *Augusta*, Benjamin Richards, the Spanish court has officially published news of the entry on 29 Aug. of the British and Spanish fleets into the harbor of Toulon, where they were joyously greeted by the chiefs and the people of that strong garrison. A force from both fleets immediately took possession of the strong posts in the port and city, and at a meeting between French governmental chiefs and principal allied naval commanders a preliminary agreement was reached to restore the town to Louis XVII "with its fortifications and Stores, as well as the Arsenal Ships, and every thing belonging thereto." The keys of the city were accordingly delivered to the new governor, Rear Admiral Samuel Granston Goodall Esq., commander in chief of the civil line, and Rear Admiral Don Federico Gravina of the military line. Seventeen French ships of the line in the bay and all batteries posing any danger to the allies were immediately disarmed. Admiral St. Julien, the second in command for the French, was taken prisoner to Barcelona because of his alleged treacherous designs. Essential reinforcements and provisions are daily going to Toulon from Spain and Gibraltar, and a report of an attempt to prevent this by a French army has proven to be false. Pilots have gone from here to convey to Barcelona 6,000 Portuguese troops expected at Gibraltar, and an army of equal force from Naples is to go there, both to reinforce Spain in Roussillon. There is little expectation that the recently reinforced French garrison at Perpignan will surrender this campaign. Letters from Cádiz report that two American ships, reportedly with rich cargoes loaded at Bordeaux for St. Thomas but suspected of being destined for some of the French settlements, were last week brought to Cádiz by a Spanish frigate of war. William Carmichael reports that many American vessels in England have been released and allowed damages for detention.

RC (DNA: RG 59, CD); 4 p.; at head of text: "N. 4"; at foot of first page: "Honble Thomas Jefferson &ca. &ca. &ca."; endorsed by TJ as received 26 Nov. 1793 and so recorded in SJL.

This is the last consular letter TJ received from Morphy. See Appendix I.

From James Simpson

Gibraltar, 26 Sep. 1793. Inclosing a copy of his letter of 25 Aug. sent to New York by the brig *Ann*, he acknowledges TJ's 22 Mch. letter, received a few days ago from Humphreys, and will comply with the directions about the public money and effects left in his charge by Thomas Barclay. What he has done with those articles will be explained by the enclosed letter from Humphreys. He is pleased that TJ has accepted his offer to report news about this country or the adjacent African states, but for now there is nothing to communicate.

Tr (DNA: RG 59, CD); 1 p.; unsigned; at head of text: "Copy"; at foot of text: "The Honble Thos. Jefferson Esqr."; conjoined to RC of Simpson to TJ, 8 Oct. 1793; recorded in SJL as received 18 Dec. 1793. Dupl (same); endorsed by TJ as a duplicate received 26 Dec. 1793. Enclosure: David Humphreys to TJ, 26 Sep. 1793.

TJ submitted this letter to the President on 18 Dec. 1793, and Washington returned it the same day (Washington, *Journal*, 269).

From Edmond Charles Genet

MR.   A Newyork &. &. Le 27. 7bre.[1] [1793] l'an 2e & . . . &.

Je vous envoye le Decret rendu par la convention nationale le 9 mai De la presente année relatif à la conduite, que Doivent tenir Les vaisseaux armés De la france envers les batimens Des puissances neutres. Je vous adresse en même tems celui Du 23 Du même mois que j'ai été chargé De vous communiquer et qui renferme Des Dispositions particulieres en faveur Des batimens americains.

Tous les amis De l'humanité rendront sans doute hommage, Monsieur, aux Dispositions Du Decret Du 9 mai. Par cette loi, les principes De la justice la plus sévère envers les particuliers Neutres Se trouvent conciliés avec les mesures De rigueur qu'a exigées De la france[2] l'odieuse tyrannie exercée Sur les nations neutres par les gouvernemens qui l'ont forcée à la guerre: Dans le cinquieme article, La convention manifeste Solemnellement un voeu Dont l'execution est Depuis long tems sollicitée par la raison et la justice; c'est De voir les puissances neutres jouir De tous les avantages que doit leur assurer la neutralité, même par rapport aux marchandises ennemies chargées à bord De leurs batimens. L'expression De ce voeu et l'engagement qu'a pris la convention De retirer les mesures de rigueur ordonnées par Son decret aussitôt que les puissances avec qui elle est en guerre auront adopté la même Disposition Sont bien faits pour lui attirer la reconnoissance Des nations neutres, pour les interresser De plus en plus à Ses Succès, et concilier aux principes généraux[3] qui Dirigent sa Diplomatie, touts les peuples De l'univers.

Le Decret Du 23 mai prononce en faveur Des americains une exception aux mesures De rigueur que la france a été contrainte d'ordonner par celui Du 9 mai contre les batimens Des nations neutres. Les considérations qui ont Déterminé ce Decret ont été D'un côté, la fidelité religieuse avec laquelle la france est Disposée à observer dans toute Sa latitude le traité qui la lie avec les etats-unis; et De l'autre, la confiance intime où elle est que les americains n'abuseront pas De ce privilege pour porter à Ses ennemis Des produits par lesquels ils doivent concourir à la défense d'une cause qui est autant la leur que la Sienne même; elle espère qu'elle ne Sera pas trompée Dans l'attente qu'elle a fondée à cet égard Sur les principes et l'amitié De Ses frères D'amerique.

J'ai été instruit que le gouvernement anglois[4] avait annoncé la résolution de faire[5] conduire dans les ports anglais tous les Batimens américains chargés De comestibles pour les ports De france. La republique française attend, Monsieur, que le gouvernement Des etats unis, tant par attachement pour elle que par égard pour Son propre commerce et pour la Dignité qu'il Se doit, S'empressera De faire des Demarches énergiques pour faire revoquer cette Decision[6] qui est une Suite bien Digne de l'audacieuse Diplomatie à laquelle cette cour pretend Depuis long tems assujettir toutes les autres nations. Si les Démarches que vous ferez à cet egard, Démarches qui Sont dans l'esprit Si elles ne Sont pas la lettre De nos traités, Sont insuffisantes ou infructueuses, et que votre neutralité, ainsi qu'elle l'a été jusqu'ici, ne puisse qu'être utile aux ennemis De la france et funeste à elle même, vous Sentirez Sans doute qu'elle exercera un droit bien naturel en prenant Des mesures propres à en arrêter une qui lui est Si contraire et qui annulle l'effet Des principes Sur lesquels ont été fondés les traités passés entr'elle et les etatsunis. En attendant, je Suis autorisé à vous annoncer que les vaisseaux français qui Sont en ce moment maitres De la manche et Du golphe De gascogne, ont ordre De protéger les batimens américains Destinés pour france, et d'assurer leur arrivée[7] jusqu'aux ports pour lesquels ils seront expediés, De manière que les negocians américains peuvent, Malgré la tyrannie exercée Sur eux par l'angleterre[8] Diriger avec Securité leurs Speculations vers nos ports, et nous donner Des preuves De leur attachement pour nous et pour la cause[9] De la liberté.

Dft (DLC: Genet Papers); partially dated; in Jean Baptiste Cassan's hand, unsigned, with date and address completed by Genet and with revisions by him; above salutation: "Le Cen genet &. &. à Mr. Jefferson secretaire"; ellipsis in original; only the most significant emendations are noted below. Tr (AMAE: CPEU, xxxix); signed by Genet. Recorded in SJL as received 2 Dec. 1793. Enclosures: Decrees of the National Convention, 9 and 23 May 1793 (see note to Gouverneur Morris to TJ, 20 May 1793; and Enclosure No. 2 listed at Morris to TJ, 1 June 1793). Translations of letter and enclosures printed in *Correspondence*, 19-21; printed with variations in *Correspondance*, 23-6.

[1] Date inserted by Genet in space left blank by Cassan.

[2] Preceding three words not in *Correspondance*.

[3] *Correspondance:* "généreux." *Correspondence:* "generous."

[4] Preceding three words interlined by Genet in place of "le ministre Du Roi D'angleterre vous."

[5] Preceding two words interlined by Genet in place of "De Sa cour, D'après la quelle les vaisseaux De cette majesté ont ordre De," the first and last words being inadvertently left uncanceled.

[6] Passage altered by Genet from "De faire auprès De cabinet De St. james toutes les Demarches nécessaires pour obtenir la revocation De cette mesure."

[7] Preceding four words interlined by Cassan in place of "de les escorter."

[8] Preceding eight words interlined by Cassan in place of "les Dispositions de l'angleterre."

[9] Cassan here canceled "que nous Defendons."

From Thomas Pinckney

DEAR SIR   27 Septr. 1793

The above is the duplicate of my last by the Mohawk. I omitted to mention therein that I have directed insurance to be made on the whole of the copper against the dangers of the seas only. I have no instructions on this head but have acted as I should have done for myself. By desire of the correspondents of the Owners I inclose a statement of the case of the Ship Laurens concerning which there appears to be some unjustifiable proceedings on the part of the Captors, I believe Mr. Morris has made some representation on the subject but hitherto without success. Four Regiments of infantry are now said to be under sailing orders for Canada, but the events of the campaign so far determine the destination of the troops of this Country that untill they have actually sailed nothing concerning it is certain. I remain with the utmost Respect My dear Sir Your faithful & most obedt Servant   THOMAS PINCKNEY

RC (DNA: RG 59, Duplicate Diplomatic Dispatches); subjoined to Dupl of Pinckney's first letter to TJ, 25 Sep. 1793; at foot of text: "The Secretary of State"; endorsed by TJ as received 28 Nov. 1793 and so recorded in SJL. PrC (ScHi: Pinckney Family Papers). Tr (Lb in DNA: RG 59, DD). Enclosure: Bird, Savage & Bird and other English consignees of the *Laurens* to Pinckney, London, 12 Sep. 1793, stating that the *Laurens*, Captain Thomas White, owned by Smiths, DeSaussure & Darrell of Charleston, all American-born, and carrying a cargo of rice and indigo worth about £30,000 sterling belonging to the ship's owners and other American citizens, was seized by the French privateer *Sans Culottes* while on its way from Charleston to London and brought to Le Havre on 23 Mch. 1793; that on 16 Apr. the Court of Admiralty there decreed that the capture was illegal and in violation of the French-American treaty, ordered the ship and cargo to be restored to White, and directed the captors to pay costs, interest, damages, and demurrage for the delay; that while the captors were appealing this decree, the National Convention on 9 May passed a decree, retroactive to the beginning of the war, authorizing the capture of neutral ships carrying neutral-owned provisions to enemy ports or enemy-owned merchandise, a decree it alternately exempted United States ships from and resubjected them to in decrees of 23 and 29 May and 1 and 27 July; and that if the *Laurens* and its cargo were condemned at Le Havre, the underwriters would refuse to pay the insurance the consignees had taken out on the assurance that the ship and cargo were both American property—in consequence of which they sought Pinckney's assistance on behalf of the American owners in recovering the ship and cargo wrongfully held in violation of the neutrality of the American flag and the treaty between the United States and France (RC in same). Enclosed in TJ to George Washington, 29 Nov. 1793.

For further information on the LAURENS, see Gouverneur Morris to TJ, 19 Apr. 1793, and note.

This is the last ministerial letter from Pinckney that TJ received as Secretary of State. See Appendix I.

From George Washington

SIR Mount Vernon Septr. 27. 1793.

The enclosed Letter and Memorial came to my hands yesterday, to which I returned an answer of which the enclosed is a copy.

GO:WASHINGTON

RC (DNA: RG 76, French Spoliations); in the hand of Bartholomew Dandridge, Jr., signed by Washington; at foot of text: "Thos. Jefferson Esqr. Secy. of State"; endorsed by TJ as received 9 Oct. 1793 and so recorded in SJL. Dft (DLC: Washington Papers photostat); written and signed by Washington. FC (Lb in DNA: RG 59, SDC). Enclosures: (1) Joseph Harper to Washington, Philadelphia, 10 Sep. 1793, stating for himself and the company that they were enclosing a memorial they believed, upon inquiry, to concern a case so special as to render any decision on a previous case submitted to the President inapplicable, and that therefore they hoped he would provide them with the relief they were justified in expecting as his fellow citizens (RC in DNA: RG 76, French Spoliations; endorsed by TJ as received 9 Oct. 1793). (2) Memorial to Washington from James King, Henry Pratt, Joseph Harper, and Isaac Snowden as owners of the *Andrew* and a considerable part of its cargo, and from William Bell in his own right and Henry Pratt and George C. Schroeppel as administrators of the estate of the deceased William Starman, owners of the rest of the cargo, Philadelphia, 9 Sep. 1793, stating, as American citizens, that the *Andrew*, Samuel Makins master, left Charleston on or about 28 Feb. 1793, unaware that France had declared war on any foreign power, with 875 whole casks of rice, 202 half-tierces of rice, and 57 bags of pimento consigned to their respective correspondents in Amsterdam; that on 10 Apr. the French privateer *Ambitieux*, Captain John Pontevin, captured the *Andrew*, imprisoned Makins and six seamen on the privateer, and brought them to Brest on 19 Apr.; that upon being released three days later Makins and his men proceeded to L'Orient, where the *Andrew* had been taken and where on 25 Apr. the Chamber of Commerce ruled that as American property the capture of the ship and cargo was illegal and declared both to be free; that on the following day, in consequence of a decree passed by the L'Orient General Council in the presence of two commissaries deputed by the Department of Finisterre and Morbihan and by the National Convention, Makins was forced, despite his protest, to deliver his cargo to the French Republic "(they being in great Want)" in return for the payment of freight by the Ordonnateur of the Marine at L'Orient; that on 17 June, the cargo having in the meantime been unloaded between 14 and 24 May, the efforts by Makins to obtain from various L'Orient officials satisfaction for the detention of his ship and payment for his cargo and freight led the Deputy Paymaster of the Marine to pay him 51,328 livres, 9 sols, and 1 denier in assignats, the amount of the freight as reckoned by these officials minus a deduction of 1,290 livres for a deficiency of 5 casks of rice in the cargo; that after further fruitless efforts to obtain payment, Makins left L'Orient with the *Andrew* in ballast on 3 July—after receiving from its mayor and municipal officers a certificate attesting that he had delivered 1,070 hogsheads or half-hogsheads of rice weighing 589,030 pounds gross for the Marine and War Departments, as well as 57 bags of pimento weighing 8,987 pounds—and arrived in Philadelphia on 29 July; and that because the capture and detention of the *Andrew*, the imprisonment of its captain and crew, and the forced disposal of its cargo, for which they had authentic proofs, all violated the treaty with France, they asked the United States government to compensate them for their losses, "which they believe can be more readily done, as it has it at this time in its Power to do it, by an appropriation to which with submission we Concieve there Can be no reasonable Objection either by our Own Government or that of France" (MS in same; in a clerk's hand, signed by King, Pratt, Bell, Harper & Snowden, and Schroeppel). (3) Washington to Harper & Company, 27 Sep. 1793, stating that he had received Nos. 1 and 2 only yesterday and would transmit them to the Secretary of State, to whom they should have been sent in the first place, and who would need proofs to render a full report to the President, provided the American minister in Paris had not already taken action (Tr in same; FC in Lb in DLC: Washington Papers).

From Joshua Johnson

London, 28 Sep. 1793. Since writing on 24 Aug., he has received no favors from TJ, who will be informed of public affairs by Pinckney. There has been no change in the Admiralty's treatment of American seamen; they are still detained and he receives no answer. American ships captured and brought in are perishing while awaiting a court decision. At Pinckney's request, he encloses a bill of lading and invoice for nine cases of copper for the United States Mint.

RC (DNA: RG 59, CD); 2 p.; at head of text: "Thomas Jefferson Esqr."; with notation by TJ at foot of text: "invoice sent to Mr Rittenhouse." FC (same); in Johnson's hand. Recorded in SJL as received 26 Nov. 1793. Enclosure not found.

This is the last consular letter TJ received from Johnson. See Appendix I.

From Henry Marchant

SIR   Newport State of Rhode Island Sepr. 28th. 1793.

As the Appointments to the fœderal Offices were honored by Your Communication of them, I presume it proper, that through the Secretary of State, the President of the United States should be informed of any Vacancies. Mr. Channing the United States Attorney for the District of Rhode Island departed this Life on Saturday the twenty second Instant. In Him the Publick sustain the Loss of an active, vigilant Officer, and a firm Patriot. In His Profession He was of the first Rank. As a Gentleman Society feel His departure: A Wife and nine Children are left inconsoleable.

Sir, I know not but I may have transgressed in the mode of my Communication to the President of the 3d. of August last, respecting the Conduct of Wm. Davis, Commander of the Ship Catherine, the Steps taken therein, and the Circumstances which arose thereon. Upon Reflection afterwards I was led to suspect, I ought to have transmitted them through You. If I was wrong I should wish to be set right. You may rely upon it my Errors will never arise from any disrespect either to the President or to the Secretary of State, for I am with sincere Esteem and high Respect Your most obedient and very humble Servt.

HENRY MARCHANT

RC (DNA: RG 59, MLR); at foot of text: "The Honble Thomas Jefferson Esqr. Secretary of State for the United States"; endorsed by TJ as received 24 Oct. 1793 and so recorded in SJL.

Henry Marchant (1741-96), a Newport lawyer who was attorney general of Rhode Island, 1771-76, a delegate to the Continental Congress, 1777-79, and a state legislator, 1784-90, led the supporters of the federal Constitution at the Rhode Island ratifying convention and received an appointment as judge of the United States District Court for that state, a post he held from 1790 until his death (DAB).

TJ's COMMUNICATION enclosing Marchant's judicial commission was dated 6 June 1790 (FC in Lb in DNA: RG 59, PCC; at head of text: "To Henry Merchant Esquire"; not recorded in SJL). Marchant's missing response of 19 July 1790 is recorded in SJL as received from Newport on 24 July 1790.

From William Carmichael and William Short

SIR   Sn Lorenzo Septr. 29. 1793

The despatches which you forwarded by Mr. Blake having been delivered to us we think it proper to make use of the first conveyance to announce it to you. This being by the ordinary post we shall send two copies of this letter by to-morrow's mail being the first for Cadiz and Lisbon. Mr. Blake arrived at Madrid on the 24th. inst. The Court was to come the next day from St. Ildefonso to this place. Mr. Carmichael's indisposition prevented his proceeding here in company with Mr. Blake until the day before yesterday when he arrived and found the other commissioner who had come directly to this place from St. Ildefonso. We immediately proceeded to take a joint communication of your several letters of May 31. June 30. July 12. and 16. and the papers they respectively inclosed, and have since then been employed in weighing them with the most anxious care and attention.

It is with a mortification which you will easily concieve, that we have observed that none of our letters had been recieved by you so low down as the departure of Mr. Blake. Those written Feb. 19. April 18. and May 5. we might have hoped would certainly have got to your hands before that time, and possibly that of June 6th. The three first were sent by duplicates and the fourth by triplicate. They were prolix in the extreme and gave you a full account of all that had taken place and of all we knew or expected. Nothing has since occurred to change our opinions or expectations on those subjects nor can we yet add any thing of importance to what we then said. Taking it for granted that some of the copies of those letters will have been recieved, we think we cannot do better by this conveyance than to confirm what we then said.

Although nothing new occurred after the first conference of which we rendered you a full account in our letters of April 18. and May 5. yet we should have written more often merely to have repeated their contents, had such conveyances as we could with propriety have made use of, occurred more often. This however was not the case; and as the conveyances did not depend on us the two letters abovementioned were delayed thereby after having been written.

Nothing in the bosom of futurity appeared to us more inevitably certain than that you would consider it indispensable to write to us after having recieved information which we knew would get to you from others previous to the reciept of our letters, and that expectation had the influence on us which we have formerly mentioned to you. Until Mr. Blake's arrival however we have not had the honor of recieving a single line from you since your letter of Nov. 3. 1792. We recieved the gazettes as low down as Jany. 1st. and three of the month of April—except which we have remained in an ignorance of what was passing in the U.S. to a degree which added beyond measure to our embarassment.

We had the honor of writing to you also on the 15th. of August inclosing copies of letters which had passed between M. de Gardoqui and ourselves. The intention which we then announced to you for St. Ildefonso was changed after our arrival, for the reasons which we shall mention by another conveyance. Those matters therefore remain in statu quo.

We shall immediately proceed to lay before M. de Gardoqui the substance of your letters and will endeavour to get his answer in time to despatch Mr. Blake by the middle of October. Our experience however of the delay generally used by no means allows us to be sure of it. An answer to the subject contained in your letters is all that you can expect by him. Nothing new will be known with respect to the subjects of our former letters to you, or at least nothing more favorable than what we then mentioned to you.

Colo. Humphreys wrote us some time ago that he had recieved from you two letters for us, which you desired he might entrust to some person of confidence and that not having found such an one to forward them by he should leave them on his departure with Mr. Church the Consul, to forward them if a proper conveyance should present itself, or if not, to take our orders thereon. As you did not direct Colo. Humphreys to send a special messenger with them, we feared to do it being unacquainted with the nature of their contents and the expense being considerable. We know not therefore when or how we shall recieve those letters, but hope Mr. Church will find out some means of conveying them to us by some person of confidence coming from thence.

You will have[1] recieved the convention between England and Spain. We think you may be assured it will be interpreted in its most extensive sense, and that a rupture with either party for any cause however different from those expressed would be made common to both.

Naples has joined the league against France by a convention of the month of July. It is thought that their succours and the Piemontese troops are by this time at Toulon. We have the honor to be with the most profound respect Sir, your most obedient &c. &c.

WM. CARMICHAEL

W SHORT

P.S. The treaties alluded to in your letter of May 31. were not inclosed as announced by you.

FC (DLC: Short Papers); in Short's hand, signed by Carmichael and Short; at head of text: "(Copy)"; at foot of first page: "The secretary of State for the United States." Tr (DNA: RG 46, Senate Records, 3d Cong., 1st sess.). Tr (Lb in same, TR). Recorded in SJL as received 11 Dec. 1793.

This is the last letter from Carmichael and Short that TJ received as Secretary of State. See Appendix I.

TJ submitted this letter to the President on 11 Dec. 1793, and Washington returned it the same day (Washington, *Journal*, 266).

[1] According to a marginal note by Short, the remainder of the paragraph was written in code in the original; clerical notes in the Trs, however, indicate that the entire paragraph was encoded.

From Benjamin Bankson

SIR   Philadelphia, September 30th. 1793.

The inclosed Letters and papers from Mr. Dumas were received last Wednesday—a number of French News papers and a pamphlet accompanied them, which I have retained agreeably to your instructions.

The Letter with Mr. Genet's name on the outside was taken from the post office last Saturday, and is the only one from any of the foreign Ministers that has come to my hands.

I did not receive an answer from Genl. Moylan until the 25th. on which day the Express I had sent returned with one, a copy of which is enclosed. I immediately forwarded a Letter to Major Lenox whose residence is about 10 miles from the City—and expect his answer to morrow.

The Documents to accompany Mr. Morris' Letter I hope to finish this day, and shall exert myself in finding an opportunity to transmit them—none as yet has offered. Not a word from any of the Gentlemen of the Office since your departure. I have the honor to be with great respect Sir, your most Obed servt.   BENJN. BANKSON

NB: Fenno did not print last week.

RC (DLC); at foot of text: "Th: Jefferson Esq."; endorsed by TJ as received 2 Dec. 1793 and so recorded in SJL. Enclosures: (1) C. W. F. Dumas to TJ, 1 May 1793 (two letters), (2) Dumas to TJ, 22 June 1793 (recorded in SJL as received 2 Dec. 1793, but not found). (3) Stephen Moylan to Benjamin Bankson, Goshen, 25 Sep.

1793, declining a commission as federal marshal for the district of Pennsylvania and noting that a letter he had written on 20 Sep. explaining his decision was not forwarded by his brother because of the "fatal disorder prevailing in the City" (Tr in DLC; in Bankson's hand).

The letter with Edmond Charles GE-NET'S NAME ON THE OUTSIDE must have been one of those the French minister wrote on 24 or 27 Sep. 1793. Later this day Bankson wrote a brief note to David LENOX enclosing his commission as "marshal for Pennsylvania District" in response to a 28 Sep. letter from him accepting the appointment (Tr in DLC; in Bankson's hand). DOCUMENTS TO ACCOMPANY MR. MORRIS' LETTER: presumably the enclosures to TJ's 16 Aug. 1793 letter to Gouverneur Morris requesting Edmond Charles Genet's recall.

From Edmond Charles Genet

Newyork Le 30 7bre. 1793.
L'an 2e. de la République française

MONSIEUR

Je Suis Chargé de vous communiquer un nouveau décrèt de la Convention Nationale rendüe le 26. mars[1] relatif au Commerce des Etats unis avec nos Colonies. Vous y trouverez de nouvelles preuves de l'attachement que porte la france aux americains Et de l'Interêt qu'elle prend à leur prospérité. Non contente d'accorder[2] à leur commerce d'Europe tous les avantages qu'ils pouvaient désirer pendant la guerre présente, elle leur confirme par[3] le decret que je vous envoye, l'ouverture de Ses ports Coloniaux pour la consommation de tous les produits de leur Sol et de leur Industrie, pour l'Importation dans les Etats unis d'une partie de Ses Sucres et de ses cafés, Et pour l'Exportation de toutes Espéces de denrées Coloniales pour les ports de france aux mêmes conditions que les francais. Cette loi Interprétative de celle du 19 fevrier[4] me parait telle que Je ne crois pas que les Etats unis puissent En désirer une plus favorable. J'ai été chargé d'Enjoindre à tous les consuls Et autres agens de la République francaise de suivre les armements qui pourront se faire dans les divers ports des Etats unis pour les colonies francaises Et d'Empêcher qu'il ne se commette aucune contravention aux dispositions des articles 1 et 3. du décrèt cijoint; j'ai lieu de croire que le gouvernement fédéral voudra bien prendre Sans délai les mesures nécessaires pour que les ordres que Je vais donner à cet Egard n'eprouvent pas de difficulté dans leur Exécution.

Jusqu'ici, Monsieur, ma correspondance ne vous a présenté En grande partie[5] que des détails affligeants pour un Philosophe: la déclaration de guerre faite par la tirannie à la france libre ne m'a permis de vous Entretenir[6] que des rapports militaires qu'a etablis entre votre nation Et la mienne l'alliance qui les unit: Et Je trouve un veritable plaisir à[7] vous occuper aujourdhui de détails plus consolants, de détails qui ne peuvent pas manquer d'Exciter en vous le plus vif Interêt[8] puisqu'ils n'ont pour objet que les occupations paisibles et naturelles de l'homme Social, de L'homme Sur qui Seul la Philosophie aime à fixer Ses regards.

Pressée par les convulsions qu'Excite dans son Sein l'Etablissement d'une constitution qui annéantit tous les priviléges, qui Etouffe tous les préjugés, entourée de toutes les forces qu'ont appellées contr'elle de tous les points de L'Europe la Tirannie Et Le fanatisme, la france Tenant d'une main la lance de la liberté Et de l'autre les foudres de la guerre trace déjà par Son génie, ces vastes entreprises dont l'Exécution doit assurer au retour de la paix le bonheur des francais, celui de leurs alliés et préparer la régénération de tous les habitants du Globe.

Parmi ces Entreprises, celles qui les premieres ont fixé Son attention ont été les relations commerciales de la République avec les autres nations. [9] La convention nationale a éprouvé ces mouvements délicieux que fait goûter [10] le Spectacle de Cette Institution qui annullant les distances, réunit sur le même point les productions Et les Jouissances de tous les climats et qui liant tous les hommes Epars Sur le globe devrait n'en faire qu'une même famille perpetuellement animée par les Echanges que nécessitent leurs besoins réciproques. Elle a vu avec douleur tous les peuples gémissant sous des loix commerciales aussi absurdes que Tyranniques, victimes partout de L'Erreur et de l'avidité fiscale; elle les a vus avec peine après avoir franchi les mers, les montagnes, les déserts et toutes les barieres que la nature paroissait avoir élevées entr'eux, arretées au moment où leur courage allait être Couronné, par des réglements et des Combinaisons ministerielles qui [11] mettent à leur communication des Entraves plus Insurmontables que celles que la nature elle même paroissait avoir crées.

La france, Monsieur, a apperçu le moment ou toutes les nations Seront affranchies de ces obstacles, elle a apperçu le moment où tous les peuples régis par les mêmes loix, guidés par les mêmes Interêts et promenant librement leur activité Sur la surface du globe, n'y trouveront d'autres loix commerciales que celles de leur génie; elle a fixé Ses regards Sur cette heureuse époque et elle a résolu de l'accelerer. Persuadée que le moyen le plus propre à y parvenir etait de présenter l'Exemple de deux peuples Jouissant de tous les avantages d'une Communication parfaitement libre, elle a tourné Ses yeux Sur les americains. Ce peuple gouverné comme elle Sans Roy et dont les principes constitutionnels ont de l'affinité avec [12] les siens; ce peuple dont les lumieres ont, comme Chez elle, étouffé ou Sont prêtes à Etouffer tous les préjugés de l'Ignorance; ce Peuple enfin dont le génie s'irrite, comme le Sien, contre les obstacles qu'opposent à Son activité commerciale, les Sistêmes corrupteurs des Cours; [13] ce Peuple lui a paru être celui qu'elle devait s'associer pour [14] effectuer le grand projet qu'elle medite. C'est avec ce peuple qu'elle a résolu de Conclure un nouveau [15] Traité qui, fondé Sur les principes Immuables de la nature,[16] puisse devenir un objet d'Envie pour les autres nations, les Inviter à y participer, et Servir de modèle à tous ceux qui Se feront à l'avenir entr'elles. Au lieu de l'Interêt reciproque des nations contractantes, elle n'a vu dans tous les traités faits Jusqu'icy que le resultat des combinaisons d'un fisc avide ou Ignorant, que le calcul perfide de quelques Individus, et le rafinement d'un regime[17] que condamnent également la raison, l'Equité et la saine Politique. C'est dans le vice de ce regime qu'elle a reconnu L'Instabilité, Et la cause de la violation Si fréquente de tous les traités qui ont été faits Jusqu'icy Entre Les gouvernements: aussi, la france veut aujourd hui avec le peuple americain non un traité, Le mot seul en annonce la nullité, mais un pacte[18] accepté par les deux peuples et dont la durée ait pour base[19] non l'Interêt du moment, non les combinaisons de deux cabinets, mais l'Interêt vrai et Immuable des deux peuples.[20]

C'est dans cette vüe que la Convention nationale s'est faite rendre compte des rapports commerciaux qui Se Sont Etablis entre les deux nations[21] depuis les traités passés sous notre dernier gouvernement. Elle a vu avec peine que ces relations avaient été presque nulles,[22] que[23] le maximum des Importations annuelles des américains dans les ports français s'etait à peine[24] élevé à onze millions;[25] que leurs Exportations etaient à peine de deux millions et demi, et que les huit millions[26] de Surplus d'Importations payés en numeraire n'avaient eu pour destination que d'aller alimenter les manufactures anglaises: La france a vu avec regret[27] que depuis qu'elle appelle de toutes parts l'Introduction des comestibles Sur son Territoire, les americains[28] ont fourni à peine le Seizieme des grains et farines qui y ont été Introduits, et que les quinze Seiziemes y ont été portés par les nations Etrangéres, même par celles dont le gouvernement l'a forcée à la guerre.[29] On a vu avec peine dans ce compte qu'après avoir réduit considérablement les droits Imposés Sur votre tabac, qu'après avoir admis dans Ses marchés[30] votre morue et vos huiles de poisson, ce qui la[31] force[32] de Conserver des primes aux Etablissements de la Pêche de la morue Et de la Baleine, nous ne jouissions ches vous d'aucune Espèce de faveur pour nos Importations Et Exportations, enfin[33] qu'après avoir affranchi du droit de fret les batimens de votre nation, vous ayéz imposé les notres à un droit exorbitant de Tonnage. La Convention nationale a été Instruite par ce même Compte que depuis la derniere guerre, l'admission des américains dans nos Colonies a fait passer dans leurs mains l'argent Immense, qu'y avait laissé cette guerre; celui qu'y a Introduit depuis ce tems le gouvernement français pour les frais d'administration; celui enfin qu'y ont répandu les relations tant directes qu'Indirectes avec les colonies Espagnoles Et anglaises: elle a été Instruite qu'ils en avoient Exportés tous les sirops et melasses, la plus grande partie des Rums et des Tafias, et une quantité Immense de sucre de Caffé Et d'autres productions Coloniales,[34] surtout depuis que la révolution y a fait negliger les moyens de prohibition. La france, Monsieur, a vu Sans regret qu'une partie de ces immenses produits avait Contribué à La prospérité d'un peuple dont elle a secondé les efforts pour la liberté, mais elle a vu avec la plus vive douleur que la plus grande partie de ces richesses n'ait[35] Servi qu'a payer vos relations avec les Anglais et à enrichir Ses propres Ennemis;[36] elle a vu avec sensibilité[37] que Ses liaisons avec votre nation n'avaient fait que ruiner Son Commerce colonial[38] sans procurer le moindre Encouragement à Ses manufactures, Sans fournir le moindre débouché aux produits Superflus de Son sol.

La france malgré ce tableau facheux[39] est bien éloignée de Songer à retirer les faveurs qu'elle vous a accordées, elle désire au contraire les accroitre et Ses décrèts en Sont la preuve, mais elle vous demande une Juste réciprocité; elle entend que la part qu'elle vous céde à Ses richesses, loin d'être transportée à une puissance qui est autant votre ennemie que la sienne ait Son effet naturel, celui de perfectionner nos rapports mutuels; elle veut[40] que L'Immense débouché qu'elle offre à toutes vos denrées[41] en procure un à Ses manufactures et aux produits que la nature a refusés Jusqu'ici à votre Sol: elle veut enfin que cette part qu'elle vous donne à ses richesses de toute espéce, Surtout à Ses[42] richesses coloniales vous fournisse des objets d'Echange, non avec vos anciens Tyrans, mais avec vos alliés, avec vos amis les plus Sinceres.

Sans doute, Monsieur, la france sollicite avec répugnance contre l'angleterre des loix dont elle condamne le principe: Sans doute Son voeu le plus chéri Seroit de voir la nation anglaise, ainsi que toutes les autres nations unies par un commerce libre, par un commerce qui n'eut d'autre règle et d'autres bornes que leur activité; mais Jusqu'a ce que cette nation Se soit affranchie du Sistème fiscal Sous lequel elle gemit, Jusqu'a ce qu'elle ait renoncé à Son projet de domination sur les mers Et de commerce universel, Jusqu'a ce qu'elle ait consenti à l'abandon d'un Sistème aussi Impolitique pour elle que revoltant pour les autres nations, la france est obligée d'apporter une réaction egale aux efforts[43] que fait Son ministere pour un Commerce Exclusif; elle est obligée de Suivre vis à vis d'elle un sistème qu'elle reprouve mais que l'Interêt des francais rendra nécessaire tant qu'il sera la base de la conduite[44] du gouvernement De St. james.

C'est d'après ces considérations que J'ai été Chargé, ainsi que J'ai déjà eu l'honneur de vous en informer[45] plusieurs fois,[46] d'ouvrir avec vous une nouvelle négociation dont les bases Soient la Candeur et la loyauté, dont la regle Soit l'amitié sincere qui unit les deux peuples,[47] dont le but Soit L'Interêt reciproque Et bien Entendu des deux nations. Je me promets que Je trouverai pour cette grande opération, dans le gouvernement des Etats unis, la même franchise que Je suis chargé d'y mettre: Je me promets que vous Seréz egalement empressé de concourir à la conclusion d'une convention qui honorera l'humanité,[48] et dont les bases fondées sur la nature même la rendront Imperissable. Il me Seroit bien douloureux, Il Seroit bien affligeant pour la france, Si J'étais trompé dans cette attente; ce serait avec bien du regret que Je me verrois forcé de vous communiquer la seconde partie de mes Instructions Tendantes à vous annoncer, en cas de refus ou de détour, la révocation des loix qu'ont dictées l'attachement des francais pour les americains, Et le désir de resserrer de plus en plus les liens qui les unissent.[49] Mais Je ne Saurois craindre d'opposition de votre part, en considerant la vaste carriere que Je Suis chargé d'offrir à vos négocians; En considérant l'activité que ce nouveau pacte commercial[50] va répandre dans vos champs, dans vos pêches, dans l'Education de vos bestiaux, dans la coupe de vos bois; en considerant la source Intarissable de richesses que vous offrira l'ouverture Libre des Colonies françaises; en Considerant Surtout que la france ne vous demande en retour de ces grands bienfaits, que de tirer de chés les francais, au lieu d'aller chercher chés nos Ennemis communs, le Drap Et Le vin necessaires à votre consommation. Fort de cet Espoir, heureux du grand objet que nous allons remplir, J'attends que vous me fixiés un mode de négociation qui nous conduise dans le plus court délai possible à la fixation d'un projet de Pacte national[51] qui puisse bientôt être presenté à la ratification des représentans des deux peuples, et dont la Simplicité egale la grandeur du but que nous devons nous proposer. Agréés mon respect.

GENET

3d Dft (DLC: Genet Papers); consisting of initial RC in a clerk's hand, with complimentary close and signature by Genet, then endorsed by TJ as received 24 Oct. 1793 and so recorded in SJL, after which it was returned to Genet in TJ's 5 Nov. 1793 letter, though not before being laid before the President on 7 Nov. 1793 (Washington, *Journal*, 248), and then subsequently revised by Jean Baptiste Cassan to serve as draft of missing second RC; above salutation: "Le Citoyen Genet, Ministre plenipotentiaire de la République française près les Etats unis de l'amerique à Mr Jefferson Secretaire d'Etat des Etats unis." 2d Dft (same); in Cassan's hand, with revisions by Genet; at head of text: "A copier"; only the most significant emendations are recorded below. Dft (same); heavily emended text in Cassan's hand; only a few of the many revisions are noted below. FC (same); in a clerk's hand, with two minor corrections by Genet; wording follows unrevised 3d Dft. Tr (AMAE: CPEU, xxxix); wording follows unrevised 3d Dft with variations, the most important of which is recorded in note 22 below; certified by Genet. The second RC, enclosed in Genet's first letter to TJ of 14 Nov. 1793 and recorded in SJL as received the following day, has not been found. Enclosure: Decree of the National Convention, 26 Mch. 1793 (see translation in Supplementary Report on Commerce, 30 Dec. 1793). Translations of letter (following 3d Dft as revised) and enclosure printed in *Correspondence*, 13-18; printed in *Correspondance*, 17-23.

LOI . . . DE CELLE DU 19 FEVRIER: see note to Joseph Fenwick to TJ, 25 Feb. 1793. UN NOUVEAU TRAITÉ: see Genet to TJ, 23 May 1793, and note, for the Washington administration's response to Genet's first overture for a new commercial treaty between France and the United States. COMPTE DES RAPPORTS COMMERCIAUX . . . ENTRE LES DEUX NATIONS: the 12 Mch. 1793 Committee of Commerce report to the National Convention on the state of French-American trade since the Revolutionary War that recommended passage of the enclosed decree liberalizing United States trade with France and the French West Indies (*Archives Parlementaires*, 1st ser., LX, 113-16).

[1] *Correspondence*: "20th March." Remainder of sentence interlined in 2d Dft by Genet.

[2] Sentence to this point inserted by Cassan in place of "Après avoir assure par les décrêts précédents."

[3] Remainder of clause inserted by Cassan in place of "celui-ci."

[4] Preceding five words and digits interlined in 2d Dft by Genet.

[5] Preceding three words interlined in 2d Dft by Genet.

[6] In 2d Dft Genet here canceled "jusqu'a ce jour."

[7] Clause to this point interlined in 2d Dft by Genet in place of "j'ai à."

[8] Altered in Dft from "D'exciter le plus vif interet dans un ami de l'humanité."

[9] In 2d Dft Genet here canceled "de l'univers."

[10] In 2d Dft Genet here canceled "a tout ami de l'humanité."

[11] Here and in 2d Dft Cassan canceled "etouffant le génie."

[12] Preceding five words interlined in 2d Dft by Genet in place of "Sont les mêmes que."

[13] Altered in 2d Dft by Genet from "les Systèmes ministeriels des malheureuses nations."

[14] In Dft Cassan here canceled "procurer à l'humanité le plus grand des bienfaits."

[15] Word written in the margin of 2d Dft by Cassan.

[16] Dft: "liberté."

[17] In Dft Cassan here canceled "⟨aussi impolitique que destructeur de la prosperité publique⟩ que condamne la prospérité reciproque des peuples."

[18] Word interlined in 2d Dft by Genet in place of "une convention mutuelle."

[19] In 2d Dft Cassan first wrote "non la foi D'un engagement." Genet then interlined "vaine promesse" in place of "foi" before canceling the entire passage and writing the remainder of the sentence through "cabinets" in the margin.

[20] Altered in 2d Dft by Genet from "Des Deux nations."

[21] Dft: "entre le peuple français et le peuple americain."

[22] AMAE Tr and FC: "Très foibles."

[23] In response to TJ's request for a clarification of this passage at the top of page 7 of the unrevised 3d Dft (see TJ to Genet, 5 Nov. 1793), Cassan inserted the sentence to this point in place of "Il en est résulté de cette recherche que nos relations ont été presque." In 2d Dft Genet had interlined this unfinished passage in place of "La Stérilité De leurs relations l'a vivement affligée; elle a vu avec peine."

[24] Preceding four words inserted by Cassan in place of "ne S'est point," the first word being inadvertently left uncanceled.

[25] Dft: "ne S'elevaient pas à plus de dix millions."

[26] Dft: "les Sept millions et demi."

[27] Preceding two words inserted by Cassan. In 2d Dft Genet here canceled "avec etonnement."

[28] In 2d Dft Genet here canceled "ce peuple Sur lequel elle comptait le plus."

[29] Next sentence written in the margin of 2d Dft by Cassan with revisions recorded in notes 32-33 below.

[30] Preceding three words inserted by Cassan.

[31] Word inserted by Cassan in place of "nous."

[32] In 2d Dft Genet interlined "nous force" in place of "la tient dans la necessité."

[33] Word inserted by Cassan in place of "et," which was interlined in 2d Dft by Genet in place of "elle a vu Surtout avec etonnement."

[34] Preceding five words interlined in Dft in place of "de cottons et de cacaos."

[35] Altered by Cassan from "n'avait."

[36] In Dft Cassan here canceled "en portant la vie dans leurs atteliers."

[37] Preceding five words written in the margin of 2d Dft by Cassan.

[38] In Dft Cassan here canceled "et surtout Ses raffineries."

[39] Word interlined in 2d Dft by Genet in place of "effrayant."

[40] Word inserted by Cassan in place of "Se persuade."

[41] Dft: "que le debouché qu'elle offre a vos bois, à vos peches, a toutes vos denrées territoriales."

[42] Preceding seven words not in Dft.

[43] Dft: "efforts tyranniques."

[44] Remainder of sentence altered by Cassan from "de Son gouvernement." Dft: "de Sa conduite ministerielle."

[45] Clause to this point interlined in 2d Dft by Genet.

[46] Preceding two words inserted by Cassan. Preceding clause not in Dft.

[47] In 2d Dft Cassan here canceled "et qu'il convient d'affermir de plus en plus entre les Deux peuples."

[48] Dft altered from "je me promets que je trouverai dans le gouvernement des etats-unis le même empressement que desire mettre le gouvernement des français à conclure entre les deux peuples ⟨un traité⟩ une convention qui honore l'humanité."

[49] In Dft Cassan here keyed for insertion an uncanceled and unfinished passage he had written on the first page: "Je Serois faché de vous annoncer que la purification qui S'est effectuée du regime intérieur De Ses colonies."

[50] Preceding four words inserted by Cassan in place of "cette convention."

[51] Preceding two words interlined in 2d Dft by Genet in place of "convention."

From Moissonnier

MONSIEUR   [September 1793]

Lorsque la Republique francaise a Envoyé dans les Etats unis de L'amerique des officiers Consulaires, elle leur a donné les mêmes pouvoirs qu'ils ont de tout temps Exercé dans tous les Etats ou Royaumes où Ils Se Sont trouvés, c'est à la puissance qui les employe à les restraindre S'ils Sont trop Etendus Et *Je n'ai Jamais pu croire que les agens d'une nation quelconque puisse recevoir d'autres loix que de leur Commettans*. Le bonheur des Etats unis Est si Intéressé, Monsieur, au pouvoir qu'ont les consuls francais de représenter L'amirauté, de Juger les prises Et de les faire vendre, à qui les Etats unis doivent Ils S'adresser, au ministre qui représente un peuple libre, à la nation elle même; mais les Pouvoirs que Je tiens de la nation francaise Sont In-dépendants des pouvoirs de l'Exécutif des Etats unis, L'Exequatur qui m'a été remis ne renferme aucune Restriction, Et si vous vous rap-prochés des Conventions Consulaires, vous y verrés, Monsieur, qu'elles n'ont aucun rapport avec ce que vous me prescrivés par votre lettre. Peut être, Monsieur, blamerés vous ma franchise. Si J'ai tort de vous répondre vous avés eu tort de m'ecrire. Subordonné à des chefs qui ne Sont point, vous, ni Monsieur le Président des Etats unis, c'est d'eux que Je reçois mes ordres Et Si mon Exequatur vous fait plaisir, Je Suis prêt à vous la renvoyer, En attendant, Monsieur, Je ferai mon devoir. J'ai l'honneur d'Etre &c.   Signé MOISSONNIER

Tr (AMAE: CPEU, xxxviii); undated; at head of text: "Copie de la Lettre du Ci-toyen Moissonnier Consul à Baltimore à Mr. Jefferson secretaire d'Etat des Etats unis."

F. Moissonnier, Edmond Charles Genet's secretary in Russia and one of the three secretaries the French minister brought with him to the United States, had been serving as French vice-consul for Maryland since June 1793 (Exequatur for Moissonnier, 5 June 1793, FC in DNA: RG 59, Exequaturs, with George Washington and TJ as signatory and countersignatory; Minnigerode, *Genet*, 118, 156). There is no evidence that TJ ever received Moissonnier's letter, a response to TJ's 7 Sep. 1793 circular to French consuls and vice-consuls that was presumably written in the same month.

From James Barry

Baltimore, 1 Oct. 1793. Since he will be delayed in coming to Philadelphia, he forwards by a safe hand two enclosed letters which he received from Montgomery of Alicante a few days before sailing from Falmouth on 14 July with directions to deliver them to TJ.

RC (DNA: RG 59, MLR); 1 p.; at foot of text: "The Honble: Mr: Jefferson"; endorsed by TJ as received 24 Oct. 1793 and so recorded in SJL. Enclosures: (1) William Carmichael and William Short to TJ, 6 June 1793. (2) William Short to TJ, 7 June 1793.

James Barry, a Baltimore merchant, had been serving since July 1791 as vice-consul for Portugal in Maryland and Virginia (William Thompson and James L. Walker, *The Baltimore Town and Fell's Point Directory* . . . [Baltimore, 1796], 6; Exequatur for Barry, 11 July 1791, FC in Lb in DNA: RG 59, Exequaturs, with George Washington as signatory and TJ as countersignatory).

From Edmond Charles Genet

M.   New york le [1][1] 8bre. 1793. l'an 2e. de la Repe.

J'ai l'honneur de vous adresser les premieres informations relatives à la prise faite par la Corvette de la Republique le Cerf du Navire le Guillaume Tell qui est actuellement sous la garde[2] du Consul de la Repe. à N.y. En attendant que le gouvernement federal[3] ait défini la ligne[4] de protection et de Jurisdiction des Etats unis et déterminé si guillaume Tell y a été pris ou non, Je dois vous observer, M., que[5] ce Navire est dans un état de déperissement caracterisé et qu'il est instant de le vendre pour conserver la propriété[6] de ceux à qui il se trouvera définitivement appartenir. Une autre prise de la Concorde faite en pleine mer se trouve dans le même cas et le Consul sera obligé d'en autoriser la vente en vertu de nos lois en vertu de nos traités en vertu de ses instructions. Ces actes, Mr., ne sont point comme vous vous êtes si souvent plu à le supposer un empiètement[7] sur les tribunaux du pays et l'usurpation d'une Jurisdiction souveraine, mais l'exércice très légitime que font nos officers Consulaires du droit qui leur est donné par nos conventions de recevoir en dépôt les propriétés francoises et d'en autoriser la vente droit qui doit partlculierement avoir Son effet pour des propriétés acquises par la guerre dont les tribunaux du pays ne peuvent prendre aucune Connoissance.[8] Agréés mon respect.

Dft (DLC: Genet Papers); partially dated; unsigned; above salutation: "Le Cit Genet Ministre &c à M. Jefferson &c."; only the most significant emendation are recorded below. Tr (AMAE: CPEU, xxxix); dated 1 Oct. 1793; with one variation (see note 4 below); docketed by Genet. Recorded in SJL as a 1 Oct. 1793 letter received 24 Oct. 1793.

For further information on the capture of the *William Tell* by the CERF, see Memorial from George Hammond, 6 Sep. 1793, and note. CONSUL DE LA REPE.: Alexandre Maurice d'Hauterive.

[1] Supplied from Tr; space left blank by Genet.

[2] Preceding three words interlined in place of "entre les mains."

[3] Word interlined.

[4] AMAE Tr here adds: "de démarcation et."

[5] Genet here canceled "dans tous les cas."

[6] Genet first wrote "conserver les droits" and then altered it to read as above.

[7] Preceding two words interlined in place of "des Jugements."

[8] Genet here canceled "sans épouser la querelle de l'une ou de l'autre des parties belligérentes ce qui n'est pas tout à fait dans l'esprit de la proclamation de Mr. le President."

From Edmond Charles Genet

MONSIEUR

Newyork le 1er. octobre 1793.
l'an 2e de la République française

Les Circonstances qui ont améné dans les Ports des etats-unis le Convoi de St. domingue ont interessé le Cœur de tous les americains. La perte que le Commerce de france éprouve à ce Sujet est d'autant plus considerable que plusieurs batimens ont été obligés pour echapper aux dangers qui les menaçaient de Fuïr sur leur lest. Ils sont venus dans vos ports chercher des secours et un asile et sans doute la France entendra avec reconnoissance le rapport de l'accueil qu'ils y ont reçu de leurs Freres.

Après avoir obtenu du Peuple americain des marques signalées de l'interet qu'il a pris individuellement a leur position, ils en sollicitent une de leur Gouvernement qui parait fondée Sur une loi portée dans la seconde session du Congrés en 1790. chapitre 35. section 35: cette Faveur est la remise du droit de tonnage et la loi qui Justifie leur demande est ainsi concuë *and be it further enacted that if any Ship or vessel from any foreign port or place compelled by distress of Weather or other necessity.* Il ne peut y avoir certainement de cas auquel le bénéfice de cette loi puisse s'appliquer plus Justement qu'a celui qui a amené dans vos ports le Convoi français. Je me promets que le Ministere américain prendra dans la plus serieuse consideration la demande que Je lui fais de la part de tous les Agens du Commerce de france interessés dans ce convoi: J'ai lieu de croire qu'il aura égard aux circonstances malheureuses qui les ont mis dans la nécéssité exprimée par la loi de relacher ici—qu'il considerera le dédomagement pour le Fisc des Etats-unis et le bénéfice pour le commerce Americain qui resulteront de la vente des objets qu'on dechargera si on peut compter sur la remise reclamée.

Le Commerce Français est d'autant plus fondé a l'esperer que les batimens americains sont affranchis de cet impot dans les ports de france et[1] J'ai lieu de croire d'après ces motifs que le gouvernement Fœderal s'empressera de donner aux preposés des douanes de Norfolk de Baltimore, de Newyork et autres ports ou se sont retirés les batimens Français, l'ordre de ne pas exiger de leurs capitaines le droit de tonnage, ou au moins d'en suspendre la perception Jusqu'a la tenüe du Congrès.

Dft (DLC: Genet Papers); in a clerk's hand, unsigned, with salutation and revisions by Genet; above salutation: "Le Citoyen Genet Ministre plénipotentiaire de la République française près les Etats-unis à Mr Jefferson secretaire d'Etat." Tr (AMAE: CPEU, xxxviii); certified by Genet. FC (DLC: Genet Papers); in English. Recorded in SJL as received 24 Oct. 1793.

In response to a previous request made on Genet's behalf by Charles François Bournonville, a secretary in the French legation at Philadelphia, TJ had already submitted to the Secretary of the Treasury the issue of granting an exemption from American tonnage duties to French ships that had left Saint-Domingue in June 1793 on account of the slave revolt on the island (TJ to Alexander Hamilton, 12 Sep. 1793, and note).

[1] Genet here canceled "qu'il la demande dans un moment ou il se voit ruiné par les loix que vient de prononcer la convention nationale en Faveur du Commerce des Etats unis."

From Henry Remsen

DEAR SIR   NewYork October 1st. 1793

I have had the Honor to receive your favor of the 11th. Ult: enclosing two letters for Mr. Pinckney, and one from Mr. Taylor of the same date enclosing a third; also a note from you of the 12th. with a fourth letter for Mr. Pinckney. These letters I put under a cover, and delivered to Capt. Harvey an american, and commanding the Ship Ellice a constant trader from here to London. I thought this a preferable conveyance to the English packet, as there were several french cruisers out when she sail'd some days ago. Capt. Harvey was recommended to me by one of the owners of the ship, as a person in whom the greatest confidence might be placed.

Just before I received your's of the 11th. abovementioned I had the pleasure to write informing you, that I had put on board one of the Philadelphia packets a box containing a model, which a gentleman by your direction left with me. This gentleman was Dr. Adair. The vessel still remains here with the box onboard, the captain having expected to sail from day to day; but as he now says it is uncertain when he shall go,

I shall take it out and keep it until she does sail, or I meet with some earlier conveyance equally safe. This vessel has been detained on account of the malady in Philadelphia, as another vessel the same property and in the same trade, which had been sent there some time ago remains unloaded, no person applying for the effects and merchandize she carried.

The contagious and mortal disorder which broke out some time ago in Philadelphia, still rages with great violence. Every day we receive accounts of it's progress, and of it's victims. Some think it was engendered in Philadelphia, but others, more justly perhaps, suppose it to have been imported; and this latter idea is confirmed by the circumstance of the arrival there of a vessel from Barbadoes, while the disorder was unknown, the Captain of which and three of the crew died on the passage, and the greater part of the rest soon after they had gone into lodgings in water street. It is also now ascertained, that some months ago a very mortal fever prevailed in some of the English islands. But from whatever cause it may have originated, it's effects have been dreadful. It is conjectured that at least half the people of Philadelphia have left it, and that the number of persons who have died is not much short of 3,000. This shocking event has alarmed the continent. At Boston every person who comes from the southward, tho' no farther south than this, must undergo an examination and a purification by smoke. At Albany they must be also examined. The inhabitants here have taken every possible precaution to prevent it's introduction, but still some people from Philadelphia who arrived in seeming good health, have been attacked with it and died. These deaths amount to 6 or 7, and among the persons dead is a Mr. Carnes, the brother of Burrell Carnes. None of our people, even those who were about these sick persons, as physicians, nurses &c. have taken the infection. A Committee of Citizens and our Physicians (and they are supported by the police of the City) now require that all coming from Philadelphia shall perform quarantine for 14 days before they can be admitted; and have forbidden masters of vessels, river-craft, &c. from places lying in the route from Philadelphia landing any passengers until the visitation and report of the inspecting physicians. Patroles of citizens are on the look-out every night to see that these regulations are not transgressed. Col. Hamilton after his recovery came on to Powles hook, but understanding his crossing the river would be disagreeable to the inhabitants, went up to Albany on the west side of the river. He was examined by physicians after he got there; and indeed before he was suffered to go to Gen. Schuylers, consented to certain restrictions they thought it prudent to impose on him. Gen. Knox having performed his quarantine at Elizabeth-town and Blackpoint, was expected here this day.

As there is little expectation that Philadelphia will be sufficiently purified of the infection of, or even free from the fever, by the time Congress is to meet, it is possible that after assembling there, they will adjourn either to Baltimore or New York. The former will be the place probably, as it will be saving the travel at a future day.

I beg, Sir, you will not trouble yourself about remitting me the price of the inkstand—it was two dollars only, and as it is possible I may have an opportunity of paying my respects to you before you retire from public business, it will be as well to postpone it for the present. If you should want another, or any thing else that can be procured here please to let me know, and I shall with pleasure attend to your directions or wishes. I defered writing you 'till now, as I had understood you had left Philadelphia, and was uncertain where my letter would find you had I written before. I concluded therefore to wait till you had time to reach Monticello, where I hope, my dear Sir, you are now in good health. I take the liberty to enclose a few of the latest newspapers, as they contain interesting european information and as you may not have been lately in the regular receipt of any—and subscribe myself with great respect & esteem—Dear Sir Your grateful & obedt. Servt.   HENRY REMSEN

RC (DLC); at foot of text: "Thomas Jefferson Esquire Secretary of State"; endorsed by TJ as received 24 Oct. 1793 and so recorded in SJL.

The letter from George TAYLOR, Jr., probably enclosed TJ to Thomas Pinckney, 26 Aug. 1793. For the NOTE FROM YOU OF THE 12TH, see note to Circular to Certain Consuls and Vice-Consuls, 12 Sep. 1793. Remsen's hope that the SHIP ELLICE would escape from harassment by FRENCH CRUISERS proved ill-founded. A list of documents concerning French spoliations evidently compiled in 1795 described a "cer-

tificate signed by Captain Harvey of the American ship Ellice and several of the passengers of insults and ill treatment the captain received from the commandant of the French Fleet whilst his Ship laid at Anchor at Sandy Hook, which certificate has [been] transmitted to M. Jefferson by a letter from the Committee of the Chamber of commerce of New York" (Fulwar Skipwith to James Monroe, 18 Jan. [1795], DNA: RG 76, France, Miscellaneous Records). Neither the transmittal letter, which is not recorded in SJL, nor the certificate has been found.

To Edmond Charles Genet

SIR   Monticello in Virginia Oct. 2. 1793.

I was honored yesterday with your letter of the 14th. of Sep. covering the commission of the citizen Dannery to be Consul of the republick of France at Boston. I now lay the same by letter before the President to obtain his Exequatur, which will be forwarded to you with the Commission. The Exequatur is made exactly commensurate with the commission; but I apprehend that neither is so with the intentions of the Executive council, who probably did not mean to confine the functions of Mr. Dannery to the township of Boston. Should this be the case, you will be sensible of the expediency of obtaining for him as early as possible a new commission defining the limits of his office as extensively as they mean he shall exercise them, to which, a new Exequatur being adapted, their intentions will be fulfilled.

Satisfied that errors in the address of their commissions proceed from a want of intimacy with our constitution, no difficulty has been made on that account in the case of the present commission. But it is my duty to remark to you that by our constitution all foreign agents are to be addressed to the President of the US. no other branch of the government being charged with the foreign communications. I have no doubt you will draw the attention of your government to this circumstance of form in future commissions. I have the honor to be with great respect & esteem, Sir your most obedient & most humble servt

Th: Jefferson

PrC (DLC); at foot of text: "The Minister Pleny. of France." Tr (DNA: RG 46, Senate Records, 3d Cong., 1st sess.). FC (Lb in DNA: RG 59, DL). Tr (DLC: Genet Papers). Tr (Mrs. Francis H. Smith, Charlottesville, 1946); 19th-century copy. Tr (DLC: Genet Papers); in French; with corrections by Genet. Tr (AMAE: CPEU, xxxviii); in French. Printed in Message, 81-2. Enclosed in TJ to Benjamin Bankson, 3 Oct. 1793 (first letter), and TJ to George Washington, 3 Oct. 1793 (first letter).

Genet's letter of the 14th. of sep., written from New York and recorded in SJL as received 2 Oct. 1793, has not been found. The Provisional Executive Council's commission to Thomas dannery, dated 19 Dec. 1792, appointed him to serve as French consul in Boston (DNA: RG 360, PCC; in French). See also Dannery to Samuel Adams, 4 Nov. 1793, in NN: Samuel Adams Papers.

The President approved the above letter on 10 Oct. 1793 (Washington, Journal, 241).

From Josef de Jaudenes and Josef Ignacio de Viar

Muy Señor nuestro   Nueva-York 2. de Octubre de 1793

Con relacion al perverso proyecto contra la Luisiana que tubimos la honrra de comunicar à V. S. en nuestro Oficio de 27. de Agosto ultimo, han salido esta mañana en el Carruage que conduce la mala del Sur los quatro Franceses siguientes Monsr. Lachaise, Charles Delpeau, Malhurin, y Gignoux.

Los mencionados van autorizados por el Ministro de Francia Monsieur Genet para dirixirse à Kentuckey haciendo quantos Proselitas puedan en todo el camino de Americanos, y Franceses por todos los medios que les sea posible, sin pararse en el dinero, pues à este fin van bien provistos de especie, y credito.

En Kentuckey deben embarcarse y por el Ohio, y Mississipi pasar à la Luisiana, y atacar los primeros puestos de aquella Provincia con la Gente que huviesen levantado, y proceder hasta la Nueva-Orleans si les fuese practicable con la ayuda que les debe proporcionar la Esquadra que se halla en los Puertos de los Estados Unidos, y que devuelta de Terranova para donde va à partir, debe pasar à la boca del Mississipi y con Buques pequeños desembarcar Tropas, piezas de Campaña, y demas pertrechos en la expresada Provincia.

Con el mismo objeto nos consta se han ofrecido Comisiones de orden del precitado Ministro à varios Americanos, y quando sepamos de cierto si las han acceptado lo comunicaremos à V. S. con sus nombres.

En atencion à quanto va expuesto, y à que en ello no cabe duda; pasamos à pedir à V. S. informe de todo al Presidente de los Estados Unidos para que con acuerdo à la buena disposicion y amistosa correspondencia que subsiste entre el Rey nuestro Amo, y los Estados Unidos, y arreglado à los principios de Neutralidad que tan sabiamente desea guardar el Govierno de V. S. se sirva dar las ordenes que Juzgase oportunas con la energia, y actividad que requiere el caso para evitar el que los consavidos Franceses revoltosos, seduzcan los animos de los habitantes Americanos, ô de qualquiera otra Nacion en terreno de los Estados Unidos; y se les aprese à los citados, apoderandose de sus Papeles que van en una maleta.

Para este objeto incluimos à V. S. adjuntas las señales de los tres Capatazes en el Idioma Frances mismo en que nos las han dado.

Al mismo tiempo confiamos que los Estados Unidos encargaràn à los Gefes que mandan sus Provincias, y Puestos den avisos à los de las Posesiones de S. M. de qualquiera proyecto que descubriesen contra ellas, y de los medios que adoptasen para ponerlos en execucion, cooperando de igual suerte con sus disposiciones à quanto prescrive la reciproca buena correspondencia la humanidad, el buen orden, y los Dictados de Neutralidad.

Con referencia a esta permitanos V. S. representar contra varios hechos de que hemos sido testigos, y otros de cuyos informes no debemos dudar, que nuestros enemigos los Franceses han practicado, y estan continuando en los Puertos, y terreno de los Estados Unidos sumamente perjudiciales al interes de España, y de algunas de las Potencias sus Aliadas, sinque les sean permitidos por el Tratado entre Francia, y los Estados Unidos.

El Tratado no autoriza à los Franceses à hacer Reclutas en el territorio de los Estados Unidos, y por disposicion del mencionado Monsieur Genet se han hecho, y estan haciendo en esta Ciudad, y es dable suceda lo mismo en varias otras.

El mismo tiene empleado un Bote Americano de Piloto por ciento, y cinquenta Libras al mes que sirve de traerle los avisos de quantos Barcos de las Potencias aliadas se descubren sobre la Costa, para proporcionarle su presa.

Los Buques de Guerra, y Corsarios Franceses entran, y salen à discrecion de los Puertos de los Estados Unidos, y dan vela tan frequente como les acomoda en sequito de los de sus enemigos conforme lo hemos visto practicar desde que residimos en esta Ciudad sin guardar las quarenta, y ocho horas de espera que son generalmente permitidas en los Puertos neutrales, mientras el Articulo 19. del Tratado solo expresa tomar asilo en los Puertos de los Estados Unidos y proveerse de quanto puedan necesitar en caso de hallarse persequidos del enemigo, desastre û otro caso urgente.

Todos estos acaecimientos Juntamente con el osado proyecto que llevamos referido al principio, son circunstancias tan opuestas al interes de nuestra Nacion y de las Potencias nuestras aliadas, y se apartan de una estrecha neutralidad en terminos, que Juzgamos de nuestra obligacion exponerlas à V. S. para que lo haga al Presidente de los Estados Unidos esperanzados en que se servirà adoptar los medios mas eficazes à fin de precaver los repetidos perjuicios que se siguen à las Potencias aliadas, (y particularmente à la que tenemos la honrra de representar) de los diferentes abusos cometidos por los Franceses, y tolerados en los Estados Unidos. Nuestro Señor gue à V. S. como deseamos. B. l. mo. de V. S. Su mas recondos. y obedtes. servs.

JOSEF DE JAUDENES   JOSEF IGNACIO DE VIAR

EDITORS'   TRANSLATION

OUR VERY DEAR SIR   New York 2 October 1793

In connection with the perverse scheme against Louisiana that we had the honor to communicate to you in our note of 27 August last, this morning in the coach that carries the mails for the South the following four Frenchmen departed: Messrs. Lachaise, Charles Delpeau, Malhurin, and Gignoux.

These persons are under authorization from the French Minister, Monsieur Genet, to head for Kentucky and make as many recruits as they can along the way, of Americans and Frenchmen, by whatever means they may find possible, without consideration of money, for they are well provided with both cash and credit for this purpose.

In Kentucky they are supposed to take ship and go by the Ohio and Mississippi to Louisiana, and to attack the first posts in that province with such forces as they may have raised, and to proceed to New Orleans, should it prove possible, with help they are supposed to receive from the fleet which is stationed in the ports of the United States, and which, back from Newfoundland, must, to reach its destination, continue to the mouth of the Mississippi and with small craft unload troops, field pieces, and other equipment in the aforesaid province.

With the same objective, it is evident to us that commissions have been offered by the aforementioned Minister to several Americans, and when we know if they have accepted them, we shall communicate this to you with their names.

In view of everything we have explained, and the matters about which there is no doubt, we proceed to request that you inform the President of the United

States so that he may, in accord with the favorable attitude and friendly relationship that subsists between the King our master and the United States, and in conformity with the principles of neutrality which your government so wisely desires to maintain, be pleased to issue such orders as he may deem appropriate, with the energy and force required by this case, so as to prevent the obviously obstreperous Frenchmen from seducing the spirits of the American inhabitants, or those of any other people on United States soil, and from impressing such persons by taking their papers kept in traveling cases.

To this end we enclose for you descriptions of the three operatives in the French language just as they were given to us.

At the same time, we trust that the United States will instruct the officials in charge of its provinces and posts to warn the authorities in His Majesty's possessions of any scheme they may uncover against them and the means to be used for its execution, and to cooperate likewise in their actions in accord with the prescriptions of mutually good relations, humaneness, good order, and the rules of neutrality.

With reference to neutrality, permit us to protest against several acts of which we have been witnesses, and others, the reports of which give us no reason to doubt that our enemies the French have carried them out and are continuing to carry them out in ports and territories of the United States, actions extremely harmful to the interests of Spain and certain of her allies, and not allowed under the treaty between France and the United States.

The treaty does not authorize the French to engage in recruiting in United States territory, and by the disposition of the aforementioned Monsieur Genet persons have been recruited, and are being recruited in this city, and it is to be supposed that the same thing is going on in several other cities.

He has himself hired an American pilot boat for one hundred and fifty pounds a month whose function is to bring him reports of whatever ships belonging to the allied powers are to be found along the coast so that he may take them as prizes.

French warships and privateers enter and leave United States ports at will, and put to sea whenever they please in pursuit of their enemies, as we have seen happen since we have been residing in this city, without observing the forty-eight hours of delay generally permitted in neutral ports, whereas Article 19 speaks only of taking asylum in United States ports and of taking on such provisions as may be needed in case of pursuit by the enemy, of a disaster, or of some other urgent situation.

All these events together with the daring scheme we recounted at the beginning are circumstances so contrary to the interests of our nation and those of powers that are our allies, and so depart from a strict neutrality, that we deem it obligatory for us to put them before you so that you may put them before the President of the United States, in the hopes that he will be pleased to take the most effective measures for preventing the repetition of damages to the allied powers (and particularly to the power that we have the honor of representing) caused by the different abuses committed by the French and tolerated in the United States. May Our Lord preserve you as we desire. Respectfully yours, Your most grateful and obedient servants

JOSEF DE JAUDENES   JOSEF IGNACIO DE VIAR

RC (DNA: RG 59, NL); in Viar's hand, signed by Jaudenes and Viar; at foot of text: "Senor Don Thomas Jefferson &ca."; endorsed by TJ as received 24 Oct. 1793 and so recorded in SJL. Dupl (same); in Viar's hand, signed by Jaudenes and Viar; at head of text: "Duplicado"; endorsed by TJ as received 24 Oct. 1793. Tr (AHN: Papeles de Estado, legajo 3895); attested by Jaudenes and Viar. Tr (same, legajo 3895 bis); attested by Viar and Jaudenes.

Jaudenes and Viar derived their latest information about Edmond Charles Genet's projected invasion of Louisiana from one of the four agents they listed as having been dispatched to Kentucky by the French minister to facilitate this plan. In a report written in New York the previous day and addressed to the Spanish ambassador to the United States, an obvious misunderstanding of the positions held by the two Spanish agents, the otherwise obscure GIGNOUX, who signed himself as Pis Gignouse, revealed that Auguste LACHAISE (a native of Louisiana who had recently come to New York after having served as a private in Louis XVI's bodyguard and as a captain on Saint-Domingue), Charles DELPEAU (actually Charles De Pauw, a Kentucky merchant of Huguenot ancestry who reportedly came to America with Lafayette during the American Revolution), and one MALHURIN (in fact a carpenter named Mathurin) were leaving for Kentucky at Genet's behest in two days at the latest and described the tasks Genet had assigned them in preparing the assault on Louisiana. Although Gignouse professed to be horrified by the proposed attack on Louisiana, the Spanish diplomats' inclusion of him as one of Genet's agents suggests that they were not entirely sure of his trustworthiness (AHA, *Annual Report*, 1896, p. 1002-7). For further information about these agents and their subsequent activities in Kentucky, see same, 977-82, 1023-4, 1026, 1032, 1040, 1046, 1051-2, 1102-6; ASP, *Miscellany*, I, 931; and DAB, s.v. "De Pauw, Washington Charles").

Gignouse himself provided the physical descriptions of the TRES CAPATAZES printed below (AHA, *Annual Report*, 1896, p. 1006). For the decision by the federal government determining how long privateers and warships had to wait in the PUERTOS DE LOS ESTADOS UNIDOS before they could pursue departed belligerent vessels, see note to Genet to TJ, 15 June 1793. For ARTICULO 19 of the 1778 commercial treaty between France and the United States, see Miller, *Treaties*, II, 17-18.

ENCLOSURE

Descriptions of French Agents

Le signalement du Sieur Lachaise;
Taille de cinq pieds, neuf pouces et demie, figure alongée, cheveux rond, grand favoris, taille bien faite.
Signalement de Delpeau.
Taille de cinq pieds neuf pouces, figure alongée, les yeux enfoncés, grand cheveux, alonge un peu blonden, palle de figure.
Signal de Gignoux.
Taille de cinq pieds, six pouces, cheveux et sousis chaten, nes gros, bouche mogenne, manton rond.

Tr (DNA: RG 59, NL); undated; in Viar's hand, attested by Jaudenes and Viar. Tr (same). PrC of another Tr (DLC); in TJ's hand; enclosed in TJ to Isaac Shelby, 6 Nov. 1793.

To Benjamin Bankson

Monticello Oct. 3. 1793.

Mr. Bankson will recieve herein an original commission for Mr. Dannery to be Consul of France at Boston, an Exequatur signed by the President and myself, and a letter from me to Mr. Genet meant to accompany both. He will be pleased to retain in the office a copy of the original commission, then to inclose the commission itself with the Exequatur (to which he will first affix the seal of the US.) and my letter to Mr. Genet.
TH: JEFFERSON

PrC (DLC). Tr (ViU: Edgehill-Randolph Papers); 19th-century copy. Enclosures: (1) Provisional Executive Council's Commission to Thomas Dannery, 19 Dec. 1792 (see note to TJ to Edmond Charles Genet, 2 Oct. 1793). (2) TJ to Genet, 2 Oct. 1793. Other enclosure printed below.

ENCLOSURE

Exequatur for Thomas Dannery

George Washington President of the United States of America.
To all whom it may concern.
The Citizen Dannery having produced to me his commission as Consul for the Republick of France at Boston, I do hereby recognize him as such, and do declare him free to exercise and enjoy such functions, powers, and priviledges, as are allowed to Consuls of the French Republick by the laws, treaties, and conventions, in that case made and provided.

In testimony whereof I have caused these letters to be made patent, and the seal of the United States to be hereunto affixed.

Given under my hand the   day of   [1] in the year of our Lord one thousand seven hundred and ninety three, and the Independence of the United States of America, the eighteenth.

By the President
TH: JEFFERSON

PrC (Pierce W. Gaines, Fairfield, Connecticut, 1965); in George Pfeiffer's hand, except for last line and signature added in ink by TJ, and day and month later added in ink, possibly by George Taylor, Jr., sometime after 10 Oct. 1793 (see note 1 below); with space left for Washington's signature; endorsed by Taylor. Tr (DNA: RG 46, Senate Records, 3d Cong., 1st sess.); lacks day and month. FC (Lb in DNA: RG 59, Exequaturs); with Washington as signatory and TJ as countersignatory; dated 10 Oct.

1793. Printed with blanks for day and month in *Message*, 82. Enclosed in TJ to George Washington, 3 Oct. 1793 (first letter).

The President signed and dated Dannery's exequatur on 10 Oct. 1793 (Washington, *Journal*, 241).

[1] Blanks later completed with "10" and "Octr.," respectively.

To Benjamin Bankson

Monticello Oct. 3. 1793.

Mr. Bankson will find herein inclosed the following papers, to wit

1. Letters patent revoking the Exequatur of the Vice Consul, signed by the President and countersigned by myself. He will affix to it the seal of the US.
2. a letter from me to Mr. Duplaine.
3. another to Mr. Genet.
4. another to Mr. Morris.
5. the original evidence on which the whole is founded. Of these he will make up and forward three dispatches, consisting of the following papers.

1. to Mr. Duplaine.   my original letter to him ⎫
                           a copy of the Letters patent ⎬
                           a copy of the Evidence ⎭

2. to Mr. Genet.   my original letter to him ⎫
                     a copy of the Letters patent ⎬
                     a copy of the Evidence. ⎬
                     a copy of my letter to Duplaine ⎭

3. to Mr. Morris   my original letter to him ⎫
                     a copy of the Letters patent. ⎬ press copies
                     a copy of the Evidence ⎬ will do for
                     a copy of my letter to Duplaine ⎬ this if good.
                     a copy of my letter to Mr. Genet ⎭

Mr. Bankson will also have the Letters patent published in Fenno's and Freneau's papers as usual.   TH: JEFFERSON

PrC (DLC). Tr (ViU: Edgehill-Randolph Papers); 19th-century copy. Enclosures: (1) TJ to Antoine Charbonnet Duplaine, 3 Oct. 1793, and enclosures. (2) TJ to Edmond Charles Genet, 3 Oct. 1793. (3) TJ to Gouverneur Morris, 3 Oct. 1793. Letter and enclosures enclosed in TJ to George Washington, 3 Oct. 1793 (third letter).

The LETTERS PATENT revoking Antoine Charbonnet Duplaine's exequatur as French vice-consul in New Hampshire, Massachusetts, and Rhode Island were published in the *National Gazette*, 26 Oct. 1793. They were not published in the *Gazette of the United States*, which suspended operations between 18 Sep. and 11 Dec. 1793 because of the yellow fever epidemic in Philadelphia.

To Benjamin Bankson

SIR   Monticello Oct. 3. 1793.

I have duly received by post your favor of Sep. 23. and the letters accompanying it. I now inclose you a returned commission to be filed in the office.—Crosby mentioned to me that he had some interests, of moment to himself and his wife, to settle in Delaware, which would require an absence of a week, and I thought he could not take a better time than during the suspension of our business. Indeed I was in hopes that yourself as well as him would retire a little way from the city, where the risk is serious and unnecessary. I therefore desired him to tell you that Mr. Grey would let you make use of a very agreeable room, separated from his other houses, if you should chuse to retire to it.—I shall be obliged to you in your letters to give me an exact statement of the progress and state of the fever in and about Philadelphia. I think it probable we shall re-assemble as near there as will be safe about the end of October.— Having given some particular directions in separate packets, I have only to add assurances of the esteem of Sir your most obedt. servt

TH: JEFFERSON

PrC (DLC); at foot of text: "Mr. Bankson." Tr (ViU: Edgehill-Randolph Papers); 19th-century copy. Enclosure: Commission to George Nicholas as District Attorney for Kentucky (not found, but see TJ's fifth letter to George Washington, 3 Oct. 1793, and note).

To Bournonville

SIR   Monticello in Virginia. Oct. 3. 1793.

I recieved yesterday your favor of Sep. 18. stating that the vessel the Industry, armed at St. Domingo, having taken and sent into Baltimore the English vessel the Rochampton, the same had been arrested by order of the government, and guards put on board, and I shall immediately communicate it to the President. Should he not in the mean time have recieved information of this seisure, whether it has been by any agent of the Executive authority, and on what grounds, the enquiry will be immediately ordered. Should it turn out to have been under that authority, and on improper grounds, you may be assured the President will have the vessel immediately liberated. Should the arrest, on the other hand, have been made under the Judiciary authority, I have equal confidence that that branch of the government will exercise it's powers with equal exactness for the liberation of the vessel, if she has been unjustifiably arrested, and the correction of any error committed therein by it's agents.

On this and every other occasion, I may venture to assure you of the concurrence you desire in arranging, with the cordiality and good understanding of free, friendly, and allied nations, whatever matters may arise of mutual concern, and in proving the price we set on these motives of attachment by every friendly act which justice to others will permit. I beg you to accept personally of the sentiments of esteem & respect with which I have the honor to be Sir your most obedt. servt

TH: JEFFERSON

PrC (DLC); at foot of text: "Monsr. de Bournonville." FC (Lb in DNA: RG 59, DL). Tr (MHi); 19th-century copy. Enclosed in TJ to George Washington, 3 Oct. 1793 (second letter).

Charles François Bournonville, a boyhood friend of Edmond Charles Genet, was second secretary of the French legation in Philadelphia during Genet's tenure as minister to the United States (AMAE: CPEU, XXXIX, 193; Minnigerode, *Genet*, 156). Neither his letter of SEP. 18, recorded in SJL as a letter from "[Genet] by Bournonville" received from Philadelphia on 2 Oct. 1793, nor one of 9 Aug. 1793, recorded in SJL as received 10 Aug. 1793, has been found.

To Tench Coxe

Monticello Oct. 3. 1793.

Th: Jefferson presents his compliments to Mr. Coxe and returns him Mr. Franks's letter with thanks for the perusal of it. His situation has permitted him to communicate it to the President, but no further. The oppressions of our commerce in the West Indies are really grievous: but it seems best to take no small measure, but to wait for the mass of matter we expect from the merchants and to require indemnification for the whole, fortifying our claim to it by observing the most exact justice towards them in the mean time.

PrC (DLC). Tr (ViU: Edgehill-Randolph Papers); 19th-century copy. Enclosure not found, but see Coxe to TJ, 15 Sep. 1793. Enclosed in TJ to George Washington, 3 Oct. 1793 (fourth letter).

To Antoine Charbonnet Duplaine

SIR   Octob. 3. 1793.

Authentic information being recieved that under colour of your office as Vice-Consul of the republic of France, you have with an armed force, opposed the course of the laws of the land, and rescued out of the hands of an officer of justice a vessel which he had arrested by authority of a precept from his court, the President of the United States has considered it as inconsistent with the authority of the laws and the respect which it is his office to enforce to them, that you should any longer be permitted to exercise the functions, or enjoy the privileges of Vice Consul in these United States; and has therefore thought proper by the letters patent of which I inclose you a copy, to revoke the Exequatur heretofore granted you, and to make the same publick. I have the honor also to inclose copies of the evidence whereon this measure is founded, and to be with due respect Sir Your most obedt. servt: TH: JEFFERSON

PrC (DLC); at foot of text: "Mr. Duplaine Vice Consul of France. Boston." Tr (DNA: RG 46, Senate Records, 3d Cong., 1st sess.). FC (Lb in DNA: RG 59, DL). Tr (DLC: Genet Papers). For enclosures, see Enclosures Nos. 3-4 and 6-10 listed at Christopher Gore to TJ, 10 Sep. 1793. Other enclosure printed below. Letter and enclosures printed in *Message*, 83-8. Letter and enclosures enclosed in TJ to Benjamin Bankson (second letter), TJ to Edmond Charles Genet, TJ to Gouverneur Morris, and TJ to George Washington (third letter), all 3 Oct. 1793.

Antoine Charbonnet Duplaine (d. 1800) came to the United States ca. 1787 and taught French at 124 North Third Street in Philadelphia, where he acquired a reputation as "a man of worth, and a very sincere republican." Commissioned by Edmond Charles Genet on 4 June 1793 to reside at Boston as French vice-consul for New Hampshire, Massachusetts, and Rhode Is-

land, Duplaine returned to Philadelphia after the revocation of his exequatur, resuming his former occupation, and remained there until his death (Commission to Duplaine, 4 June 1793, DNA: RG 59, NFC; TJ to John Hancock, 28 June 1793; Hardie, *Phila. Dir.*, 39; same, [Philadelphia, 1794], 43; Philadelphia *Aurora*, 1 Jan. 1801; Syrett, *Hamilton*, XVI, 464; PMHB, XXIX [1905], 404; Abraham P. Nasatir and Gary E. Monell, *French Consuls in the United States: A Calendar of their Correspondence in the Archives Nationales* [Washington, D.C., 1967], 375).

The President approved this letter on 10 Oct. 1793, the same day he also signed and dated the enclosed letters patent (Washington, *Journal*, 241). For the events leading up to the revocation of Duplaine's exequatur, see Cabinet Opinions on the *Roland* and Relations with Great Britain, France, and the Creeks, 31 Aug. 1793, and note, and Christopher Gore to TJ, 10 Sep. 1793, and note.

ENCLOSURE

Revocation of Duplaine's Exequatur

George Washington President of the United States of America.
To all whom it may concern.
The Sieur Antoine Charbonet Duplaine heretofore having produced to me his Commission as Vice Consul for the Republick of France, within the States of New Hampshire, Massachussets, and Rhode Island, and having thereon received from me an Exequatur bearing date the fifth day of June 1793. recognising him as such, and declaring him free to exercise and enjoy such functions, powers, and priviledges as are allowed to Vice Consuls of the French republick by the laws, treaties, and conventions in that case made and provided, and the said Sieur Duplaine having under colour of his said office, committed sundry encroachments, and infractions on the laws of the land, and particularly having caused a vessel to be rescued, with an armed force out of the custody of an officer of justice, who had arrested the same by process from his court, and it being therefore no longer fit nor consistent, with the respect and obedience due to the

laws, that the said Sieur Duplaine should be permitted to continue in the exercise and enjoyment of the said functions, priviledges, and powers, these are therefore to declare that I do no longer recognise the said Antoine Charbonet Duplaine as Vice Consul of the republick of France in any part of these United States, nor permit him to exercise or enjoy any of the functions, powers, or priviledges, allowed to the Vice Consul of that nation, and that I do hereby wholly revoke and annul the said exequatur heretofore given, and do declare the same to be absolutely null, and void from this day forward.

In testimony whereof I have caused these Letters to be made patent, and the seal of the United States of America to be hereunto affixed.

Given under my hand this   day of   in the year of our Lord 1793. and the Independence of the United States of America the Eighteenth.

By the President
TH: JEFFERSON

PrC (DLC: TJ Papers, 93: 16027-8); partially dated; in George Pfeiffer's hand, signed by TJ, with minor corrections added by him, and with space left for Washington's signature. Tr (DNA: RG 46, Senate Records, 3d Cong., 1st sess.); partially dated, with TJ alone as signatory. FC (Lb in DNA: RG 59, DL); dated 10 Oct. 1793, with Washington as signatory and TJ as countersignatory. Tr (DLC: Genet Papers); dated 10 Oct. 1793; lacks names of signatories. Printed with blanks for day and month, and with Washington as signatory and TJ as countersignatory, in *Message*, 88; also printed widely in newspapers. Enclosed in TJ to Benjamin Bankson (second letter), TJ to Edmond Charles Genet, TJ to Gouverneur Morris, and TJ to Washington (third letter), all 3 Oct. 1793.

To Edmond Charles Genet

SIR   Monticello in Virginia. Oct. 3. 1793.

In a former letter which I had the honor of writing you, I mentioned that information had been recieved that Mr. Duplaine, Vice-Consul of France at Boston, had been charged with an opposition to the laws of the land, of such a character, as, if true, would render it the duty of the President immediately to revoke the Exequatur whereby he was permitted to exercise the functions of Vice-Consul in these United States. The fact has been since enquired into, and I now inclose you copies of the evidence establishing it, whereby you will perceive how inconsistent with peace and order it would be to permit any longer the exercise of functions in these United States by a person capable of mistaking their legitimate extent so far as to oppose by force of arms the course of the laws within the body of the country. The wisdom and justice of the government of France, and their sense of the necessity, in every government, of preserving the course of the laws free and unobstructed, render us confident that they will approve this necessary arrestation of the proceedings of one of their agents; as we would certainly do in the like case, were any Consul or Vice Consul of ours to oppose with an armed force the course of their laws within their own limits. Still however indispensable as this act has been, it is with the most lively concern the President has seen that the evil could not be arrested otherwise than by an appeal to the authority of the country. I have the honor to be with great esteem & respect Sir Your most obedt. & most humble servt

TH: JEFFERSON

PrC (DLC); at foot of text: "The Min. Pleny. of France." Tr (DNA: RG 46, Senate Records, 3d Cong., 1st sess.). FC (Lb in DNA: RG 59, DL). Tr (DLC: Genet Papers). Tr (same); in French. Tr (AMAE: CPEU, xxxviii); in French; misdated 13 Oct. 1793. Enclosures: TJ to Antoine Charbonnet Duplaine, 3 Oct. 1793, and enclosures. Letter printed in *Message*, 89. Enclosed in TJ to Benjamin Bankson (second letter), TJ to Gouverneur Morris, and TJ to George Washington (third letter), all 3 Oct. 1793.

FORMER LETTER: TJ to Genet, [7 Sep. 1793].

The President approved this letter on 10 Oct. 1793 (Washington, *Journal*, 241).

From David Humphreys

Gibraltar, 3 Oct. 1793. Having announced in his last their arrival here with the hope of sailing to Alicante with the Portuguese fleet, they have been detained and probably will not leave in less than five or six days. The Portuguese fleet passed through the straits the day before yesterday, part of it coming into this harbor and part falling eastward of the Rock, before taking advantage of the current and resuming its voyage that evening. The fleet left Lisbon a day after they did with a fine body of troops much wanted by the Spanish, who by their own account were repulsed with considerable loss but who, from private letters by the last post, suffered even more severely. As hinted in his last, two infantry regiments and an artillery detachment set out from this garrison for Toulon without waiting for orders from England. A Swedish vessel that arrived yesterday brought news that the French minister had been sent from Naples and that 6,000 troops were embarking for Toulon when it sailed. Reports say that Lyons is totally destroyed and that, having completely vanquished the Royalists, the Republicans are marching in force on Toulon. There is no other news from France and nothing important from Barbary since his last. P.S. Three Dutch warships from Genoa arrived here to join Admiral Melvill's squadron, which is soon expected. By the last marine list from Málaga, six or seven American vessels were there, some having been very far up the Mediterranean. Mace has received letters from Algiers and reports that the Algerines have rapidly increased their cruisers. A Swedish 74-gun ship and frigate have just arrived in the Mediterranean from the Baltic. The French commanding officer of a ship of the line, three frigates, and a corvette at Tunis has promised the Bey to make no captures on his coast. English merchant vessels bound for Tunis are unmolested.

RC (DNA: RG 59, DD); 3 p.; at head of text: "(No. 86.)"; above postscript: "The Secretary of State &c. &c. &c."; endorsed by TJ as received 23 Dec. 1793 and so recorded in SJL. Tr (Lb in same).

To Gouverneur Morris

Dear Sir   Octob. 3. 1793.

Mr. Duplaine, Vice-Consul of France at Boston, having by an armed force, opposed the course of the laws of this country within the same, by rescuing out of the hands of an officer of justice a vessel which he had arrested by authority of a precept from his court, the President has thought it necessary to revoke the Exequatur by which he had hitherto permitted him to exercise his functions here. I inclose you copies of the act, and of the evidence on which it has been founded; as also of the letters written to him and Mr. Genet, and you are desired to communicate the same to the government of France, and to express to them the very great concern with which the President has seen himself obliged to take a measure with one of their agents, so little in unison with the sentiments of friendship we bear to their nation, and to the respect we entertain for their authority. But conscious we should deem it an act of friendship in them to do the like in the like case, and to prove their confidence in our justice and friendship by instantaneously[1] disabling from a repetition of the act any Consul or Vice Consul of ours who should once have been guilty of such an aggression on their authority, we rely on the same friendly construction, on their part, of the disagreeable measure now forced on us. I have the honor to be with great esteem & respect Dear Sir Your most obedt. & most humble servt

Th: Jefferson

PrC (DLC); at foot of text: "G. Morris esq." Tr (DNA: RG 46, Senate Records, 3d Cong., 1st sess.). FC (Lb in DNA: RG 59, DCI). Tr (Mrs. Francis H. Smith, Charlottesville, 1946); 19th-century copy. Enclosures: (1) TJ to Antoine Charbonnet Duplaine, 3 Oct. 1793, and enclosures. (2) TJ to Edmond Charles Genet, 3 Oct. 1793. Letter printed in *Message*, 89. Enclosed in TJ to Benjamin Bankson (second letter) and TJ to George Washington (third letter), both 3 Oct. 1793.

The President approved this letter on 10 Oct. 1793 (Washington, *Journal*, 241).

[1] Word interlined.

To George Washington

Monticello. Oct. 3. 1793.

Th: Jefferson with his respects to the President has the honor to inclose him a commission from the French Executive council to Mr. Dannery to be Consul for them at Boston, also an Exequatur, countersigned by himself, which will want the President's signature, and then the seal of the US. With these is a letter to Mr. Genet, and a cover to Mr. Bankson directing him what to do. Should the whole be approved by the President, he will be so good as to sign the Exequatur and then stick a wafer in the cover of the whole to Bankson.

RC (DNA: RG 59, MLR); addressed: "The President of the United States at Mount Vernon"; notation by TJ next to address: "Dannery's Exequatur"; endorsed by Washington. PrC (DLC). Tr (Lb in DNA: RG 59, SDC). Tr (ViU: Edgehill-Randolph Papers); 19th-century copy. Enclosures: (1) TJ to Edmond Charles Genet, 2 Oct. 1793. (2) TJ to Benjamin Bankson, 3 Oct. 1793 (first letter), and enclosure.

To George Washington

Monticello Oct. 3. 1793.

Th: Jefferson has the honor to inclose to the President a letter he has received from Mr. Bournonville, and his answer. He is in hopes Mr. Dandridge will be able to translate the letter to the President, and if he approves of the answer he will be pleased to stick a wafer in it, as well as in the cover to Mr. Bankson.

RC (DNA: RG 59, MLR); addressed: "The President of the United States at Mount Vernon"; notation by TJ next to address: "Bournonville's letter and answer"; endorsed by Washington. PrC (DLC). Tr (Lb in DNA: RG 59, SDC). Tr (ViU: Edgehill-Randolph Papers); 19th-century copy. Enclosure: TJ to Bournonville, 3 Oct. 1793. Other enclosure not found.

To George Washington

DR SIR   Monticello Oct. 3. 1793.

I received from Mr. Gore by yesterday's post the evidence on the aggression committed by Mr. Duplaine Vice Consul of France at Boston, and it appears fully to establish the fact against him. I have therefore prepared and countersigned a Revocation of his Exequatur, with letters on the subject to him, to Mr. Genet, and Mr. Morris; as also instructions to Mr. Bankson in what way to make up their several packets. Although I know of no circumstance which might change the determination with respect to Mr. Duplaine, yet I have prepared these papers separately and unconnected with any other business, and put them under a separate cover and instructions to Mr. Bankson, so that if you should chuse it, the whole will be completely suppressed by your stopping this packet. Should you on the other hand think, as I confess I do, that an example of authority and punishment is wanting to reduce the Consuls within the limits of their duties, and should you approve of the papers prepared for that purpose, I must trouble you to stick a wafer in the cover to Mr. Bankson, and forward it by post. I have the honor to be with the most perfect respect & esteem Dear Sir Your most obedt. & most humble servt   TH: JEFFERSON

RC (DNA: RG 59, MLR); addressed: "The President of the United States Mount Vernon"; notation by TJ next to address: "Duplaine's Exequatur"; endorsed by Washington. PrC (DLC). Tr (Lb in DNA: RG 59, SDC). Enclosures: TJ to Benjamin Bankson, 3 Oct. 1793 (second letter), and enclosures.

To George Washington

Monticello Oct. 3. 1793.

Th: Jefferson has the honor to inclose to the President a Note to Mr. Coxe and a letter which is the subject of it. When perused he will ask the favor of the President to stick a wafer into the cover and forward it by post. Mr. Coxe's note to Th:J. is put into a separate packet among papers to be returned to Th:J.

RC (DNA: RG 59, MLR); addressed: "The President of the US. Mount Vernon"; notation by TJ next to address: "Letter from Nassau. for perusal"; endorsed by Washington. PrC (DLC). Tr (Lb in DNA: RG 59, SDC). Tr (ViU: Edgehill-Randolph Papers); 19th-century copy. Enclosure: TJ to Tench Coxe, 3 Oct. 1793, and enclosure.

To George Washington

DEAR SIR   Monticello Oct. 3. 1793.

I have the honor to inclose herewith the following papers.

1. a Note from Mr. Coxe which covered a letter from Nassau.
2. a letter from George Nicholas which covered his commission, returned.
3. a letter from Mr. Gore, relating to Mr. Duplaine, and the communications between him and Govr. Hancock, which I asked at the desire of the Secretary at war, and which are for him.
4. a letter from Mr. Genet of Sep. 14. which, being merely an answer to one of mine, requires no reply.
5. a letter from Mr. Genet of Sep. 13. This is an answer to the written and verbal applications made to him on the subject of the William and the Fanny. After being in his hands between two and three months, the Consul at Philadelphia is still too busy to furnish the information I had desired. He is since dead, which of course furnishes a new excuse for delay. This indicates clearly enough that Mr. Genet does not mean to deliver them up. However he adds that the information would be useless until we settle what is to be deemed the extent of *the limits of our*

protection. As this has never yet been decided, I am not able to answer him until you shall be pleased to determine what shall be proposed on that subject. I think my self that these limits are of great consequence, and would not hesitate the sacrifice of money to obtain them large. I would say, for instance, to Great Britain, 'we will pay you for such of these vessels as you chuse; only requiring in return that the distance of their capture from the shore shall, as between us, be ever considered as within our limits: now, say for yourself, which of these vessels you will accept payment for.' With France it might not be so easy to purchase distance by pecuniary sacrifices: but if by giving up all further reclamation of the vessels in their hands, they could be led to fix the same limits (say 3. leagues) I should think it an advantageous purchase, besides ridding us of an article of account which they may dispute. I doubt on the whole whether any thing further can be effactually done on this subject until your return to the seat of government, or to the place where you will fix for the time.

Mr. Genet's answer with respect to his opposing the service of process on a vessel is singularly equivocal. I rather conjecture he means to withdraw the opposition, and I am in hopes my letter to Mr. Hammond will have produced another effort by the Marshal which will have succeeded. Should this not be the case, if military constraint cannot be used without endangering military opposition, this vessel also may become a subject of indemnification.

Mr. Bankson writes me word that Genl. Moylan's residence being off the Post road, he had been obliged to send an express to him, which was not yet returned. Besides the duplicate dispatches for Gouvernr. Morris, I had left in his hands letters for all our foreign ministers and Consuls. He writes me that the communications with Philadelphia had been so much intercepted that he had not yet obtained conveyances.

The death of Wright will require a new nomination of an engraver. If it be left to Mr. Rittenhouse, I think he would prefer Scott.

Just before I left Philada. I received from Mr. Genet a claim of exemption from tonnage for their vessels which quitted the Cape in distress and made the first ports in the US. and particularly as to those which came to Baltimore, the tonnage of which amounted to a large sum. As you were come away, I thought it would shorten the business to send his claim in a letter addressed to the Secretary of the Treasury, but (as he was sick) under cover to Mr. Wolcott, in hopes they would make a report thereon to you for your consideration. The necessity of these abridgments of formalities in our present distant situations requires that I should particularly suggest to you the expediency of desiring Genl. Knox to communicate to the foreign ministers *himself directly* any matters relative to the interpositions of his department through the governors. For him to send these to me from Boston to this place merely that I may send them back to the ministers at Philadelphia or New York,[1] might be an injurious delay of business.

I shall hope to have the honor of a line from you whenever you shall have fixed on the time and place at which you shall decide to reassemble us. I have the honor to be with sentiments of the most perfect respect & attachment Dear Sir Your most obedt. & most humble servt

TH: JEFFERSON

RC (DNA: RG 59, MLR); at foot of first page: "The President of the US."; endorsed by Washington. PrC (DLC). Tr (Lb in DNA: RG 59, SDC). Enclosures: (1) Tench Coxe to TJ, 15 Sep. 1793. (2) George Nicholas to TJ, 25 Aug. 1793 (not found, but see note to TJ to Nicholas, 15 July 1793). (3) Christopher Gore to TJ, 10 Sep. 1793, and Enclosures Nos. 1 and 5 listed there. (4) Edmond Charles Genet to TJ, 13 and [14] Sep. 1793.

For the Washington administration's decision on the EXTENT OF THE LIMITS OF OUR PROTECTION, see Circular to Certain Foreign Ministers in the United States, 8 Nov. 1793. MY LETTER TO MR. HAMMOND: apparently a reference to TJ to George Hammond, 5 Sep. 1793.

The death of Joseph WRIGHT, the en-graver of the United States Mint, during the yellow fever epidemic in Philadelphia led the President on 23 Nov. 1793 to commission Robert Scot, an English-born engraver and watchmaker who had been Virginia's engraver during TJ's governorship, as his successor (Washington, *Journal*, 257; Taxay, *Mint*, 105-6). In a brief covering note of the same date TJ sent Scot a commission for this office (TJ to Scot, 23 Nov. 1793, PrC in DLC, in the hand of George Taylor, Jr., unsigned, with day added in ink, at foot of text: "Robert Scot"; FC in Lb in DNA: RG 59, DL). The Senate confirmed his appointment on 30 Dec. 1793 (JEP, I, 143, 144). LETTER ADDRESSED TO THE SECRETARY OF THE TREASURY: TJ to Alexander Hamilton, 12 Sep. 1793.

[1] TJ here canceled "would."

From John Harriott

HONOURABLE SIR   New Port, Rhode Island Octr: 4th, 1793

The Capt: of a Vessell from Spain that arrived in this Port yesterday, reports, that all the American Vessells which were at Bourdeaux and other neighboring Ports, were detain'd there by the French. How far his information may be depended on, I can not say, but some respectable Merchants here, beleive it true, possibly you have better intelligence. But I would not neglect an Opportunity of evincing my sence of the Duty every One owes, who lives under protection of the Laws of the Country he resides in as a Citizen, by giving the earliest information of what comes to his knowledge, which he thinks material to the interests of the Country.

Will you pardon my troubling you with Thoughts that occurred at New York, while looking on the French Ships of Warr laying there so long. It struck me, should the present Government in France declare Warr against America (as well as the rest of the World,) how easy it would be for these Ships to lay New York under a heavy Contribution &c. The best, and as it appear'd to me, the only remedy against such Evil, would be to provide a sufficient number of small Fire Ships both above and below the Town. And the present critical situation of this Country either with England, or France, would justify the guarding against such Insult from either Nation.

I receiv'd your much esteem'd favor of the 5th. of Augst: just as I was embarking with my Family onboard a Sloop from Baltimore to this Port. I have been tolerably busy since, in visiting parts of *this*, and New York, the Jerseys, and Connetticut States, the result, I find myself much mistaken in the opinion I entertain'd and flatter'd myself with, of being able to farm Lands in this Country on a large Scale, in an improved manner. Certainly there is room enough for improvement (I have not yet seen five Acres of Arable Land in a tolerable condition,) but the scarcity, and dearness of Labor, join'd to an inveterate obstinacy, appears an insurmountable objection, so much so, that I have now partly determin'd giving over the pursuit, at least on so large a Scale as I was in hopes might have enabled me to provide better for my Children here, than in England. Consequently the only motive left to induce a continuance in this Country, is a preference to its Laws and Government. Whether this will counter-ballance old Friends and Connections, I have not as yet resolved on.

Had not the melancholy state of Philadelphia prevented, I should have extended my Journey (when in the Jerseys) to have paid my Personal Respects, with a hope of receiving fuller information about the Southern Co[untry] you were pleas'd to recommend to my notice. My re[asons] for not extending my views so far Southerly, were the Heat of the Climate, and my ignorance of the management of Negroes which I conceive requires a long habit to manage to advantage, and if severity is necessary, I should not like to attempt it.

Having been twice in Turkey while the Plague raged violently (We had four Men died onboard with it) I take the liberty of observing that those European families who took the precaution to live in the upper parts of their Houses, (and even on the Tops,) escaped the Infection, while those who neglected it suffered nearly as much as the native Turks. Possibly it may be of service to those unhappy Inhabitants of Philadelphia, who are oblig'd to remain [there?] to be acquainted with this Circumstance. Thanking you Sir, for your kind Wishes and a[. . .] to a Stranger, I remain Your Devoted, & faithful Hble Servant

JOHN HARRIOTT

RC (DLC); torn; addressed: "The Right Honble; Thos: Jefferson Esqri Secretary of State Philadelphia"; franked and postmarked; endorsed by TJ as received 9 Nov. 1793 and so recorded in SJL.

From David Howell

Dear Sir Providence Octo, 4. 1793

DEAR SIR

I wrote you a few days ago by private conveyance: but fearing miscarriage of that Letter I now write by Post. You will have been informed before this can be put into your hands of the death of Mr. Channing, the Atty. for this District. The most respectable Gentlemen in this place have been pleased to recommend me for that place. Flattering myself of your good opinion from the notice you have on former occasions, been pleased to take of me I take the Liberty to request your interest with the President in my favour for that appointment.

Ever since I left Congress I have with unremitting assiduity applied myself to the study and practice of the Law—and have studiously avoided political life and have no expectations but in the line of my profession. For my zeal in adopting the new Constitution the good people of this State did me the Honor to leave me out of the place of Atto. General which I then held.

I know of no Competitor on this occasion excepting a Young Gentleman D. L. B. who has not resided more than a year in this State—of this fact, as relative to him, I wish the President to be informed.

My Situation in this Town is at present agreeable and easy. I am furnished with, I presume, the best Library that ever was in N. England—and it is my expectation to devote my life to the business of my profession. *Sat verbum sapienti.*

I expect a *temporary* appointment will be made immediately. With great esteem I remain Dr Sr Your affectionate friend

DAVID HOWELL

RC (DLC); endorsed by TJ as received 24 Oct. 1793 and so recorded in SJL.

TJ submitted this letter on 2 Nov. 1793 to the President, along with a letter from THE MOST RESPECTABLE GENTLEMEN in Providence supporting Howell's pretensions, describing him as the professor of law at the College of Rhode Island and a former justice of the state Superior Court, and confirming that he had lost his bid for reelection as ATTO. GENERAL of Rhode Island because of his "decided opinion officially given in spirited addresses to both houses of our Legislature in favour of a convention for adopting the fœderal constitution" (John Brown, John Francis, George Benson, Welcome Arnold, Jabez Bowen, Joseph Nightingale, Thomas Arnold, and

William Peck to TJ, Providence, 2 Oct. 1793, RC in DLC; erroneously endorsed by TJ as received 24 Sep. 1793 but recorded in SJL as received 24 Oct. 1793). Washington returned both letters the same day (Washington, *Journal*, 243). TJ did not show the President the letter of A FEW DAYS AGO from Howell, actually dated 3 Oct. 1793, which was shorter but of the same purport as the one printed above (RC in DLC; endorsed by TJ as received 24 Oct. 1793 and so recorded in SJL). D. L. B.: Providence attorney David Leonard Barnes (Syrett, *Hamilton*, xv, 357-8). Howell and Barnes were both passed over in favor of Ray Greene, whom the Senate confirmed in January 1794, but TJ appointed Howell to the office in 1801 (JEP, I, 147, 401, 405).

From Henry Lee

SIR   Richmond October 4th. 1793.

The intelligence contained in the letter from the British Consul at Norfolk of the 26th. ultimo, was repeated to me in letters of the same date from the Collector at that Port and from the Commandant of the Militia. They were submitted to the United States Attorney for this district, who did not consider the Privateer Republic as violating the established Neutrality.

His opinion was forwarded by me to the respective parties with out delay, but from the last letter from Mr. Hamilton it seems that the Captain of the Privateer did not wait the reply although it had been Stipulated on his part so to do—and that material changes were made in the Vessel as well as additional force received on board. I have &c.

                                                    HENRY LEE

FC (Vi: Executive Letter Book); at head of text: "To the Secretary of State." Recorded in SJL as received 24 Oct. 1793.

The enclosed LETTER to Lee from John Hamilton, the BRITISH CONSUL AT NORFOLK, actually dated 20 Sep. 1793, stated that the French privateer schooner *Republicaine*, refitted since its arrival in Portsmouth and about to set sail on a cruise according to information he had received, should be prohibited from departing under the Proclamation of Neutrality; recounted that he had written to the collector for Norfolk and to Colonel Wilson, the commander at Portsmouth, requesting them to detain the ship if it fit the above description, and that Wilson had replied that he was in need of instructions, since the owner, Mr. Isdril, had not only produced a commission, dated at Cap-Français 26 May 1793, and other papers which convinced him that the privateer was legally commissioned, but had also indicated that only some rotten plank had been replaced and that some six pound cannon would be exchanged for an equal number of four pounders; and asked the Virginia Executive to determine whether the ship could depart and proceed on its cruise in view of rule 7, adopted by the President of the United States and annexed to the Treasury Secretary's circular letter, which declared equipments adapted solely for war unlawful, and of Articles 18 and 19 of the treaty between the United States and

France, the exceptions to which did not comprehend this case, since the ship had entered with the French fleet from Cap-Français and been in the harbor since then (RC in Vi: Executive Papers; printed in CVSP, VI, 539-40). For confirmation of the earlier date, see Lee to Hamilton, 25 Sep. 1793, Vi: Executive Letterbook.

The letters to Lee from Norfolk and Portsmouth COLLECTOR William Lindsay and Norfolk County COMMANDANT Willis Wilson, actually dated 21 and 19 Sep. 1793 respectively, emphasized that the *Republicaine* had arrived in Virginia in distress and had reduced rather than augmented its cannon (Vi: Executive Papers; printed in CVSP, VI, 539, 540-1). District ATTORNEY Alexander Campbell informed Lee on 25 Sep. 1793 that he DID NOT CONSIDER the *Republicaine* to be in violation of neutrality because it did not meet the description of an illegal privateer under the Proclamation of Neutrality and the rules prescribed by the President, "the Exchange of military armament under such circumstances being perfectly permissible" (same, 548). Hamilton's LAST LETTER to Lee, dated 27 Sep. 1793, complained that, before sailing in violation of the owner's promise to the commandant, the privateer had added to its cannon and small arms, augmented its crew by twenty or thirty men, and replaced its bottom and sails, all of which he regarded as unauthorized by the Proclamation of Neutrality, the French treaty, or the President's rules (Vi:

[195]

Executive Papers; printed in CVSP, VI, 551). See also Rules on Neutrality, 3 Aug. 1793. On 2 Nov. 1793 TJ submitted this letter and its enclosure to the President, who returned them the same day (Washington, *Journal*, 243).

From Isaac Shelby

SIR   Kentuckey Octr. 5th. 1793

I have just now been Honoured with Your favour of the 29 of August wherein you Observe, that the Spanish Commissioners have Complained to the President of the United States, that certain persons are taking Measures to excite the inhabitants of Kentucky to join in an interprise against the Spanish Dominions on the Mississippi. I think it my duty to take this early oppertunity to Assure you that I shall be perticularly Attentive to prevent any Attempts of that Nature from this Country. I am well perswaded at present none such is in Contemplation in this State. The Citizens of Kentucky possess too just a Sence of the Obligations they owe the General Government, to embark in any interprise that would be so injurious to the United States. I have the Honour to be with very great respect & Esteem Sir Your Most Obedient servt.

ISAAC SHELBY

RC (DNA: RG 59, LGS); at foot of text: "The Honble. Thomas Jefferson Esqr. secy. of State." PrC of Tr (DLC); in Benjamin Bankson's hand; at foot of text: "Copy." Tr (DNA: RG 46, Senate Records, 3d Cong., 1st sess.). Tr (Lb in same, TR). Tr (Lb in DNA: RG 59, DL). Tr (AHN: Papeles de Estado, legajo 3895 bis); in Spanish; attested by Josef de Jaudenes and Josef Ignacio de Viar. Recorded in SJL as received 9 Nov. 1793. Enclosed in TJ to Viar and Jaudenes, 10 Nov. 1793.

TJ submitted this letter to the President on 9 Nov. 1793, and Washington returned it the same day (Washington, *Journal*, 250). It is the last letter from Shelby that TJ received as Secretary of State. See Appendix I.

From David Humphreys

SIR   Gibralter Octr. 6th. 1793

A dispatch boat has just arrived from Algiers, which brings authentic[1] intelligence, that a Truce for 12 months is concluded between Portugal and that Regency. In consequence of which eight Algerine cruizers, viz. four frigates, one brig and three Xebeques, have just passed through the Streights, into the Atlantic. Our vessels will now be exposed to the most eminent hazard of capture, as it was the Portuguese squadron alone which hitherto prevented the Algerines from cruising in the Atlantic against them. I have thought it of so much importance to put our Countrymen immediately upon their guard, as to justify me in dispatching Expresses with the News to our Consuls at Cadiz, Malaga and Lisbon. And I lose not a single instant in communicating it to you, in order that such use shall be made of it, as may be deemed expedient in the United States. With sentiments of perfect respect & esteem I have the honour to be Sir Your Most obedt & Most humble Servt

D. HUMPHREYS

P.S. The Portuguese had no public Character at Algiers—in a future letter I shall explain by whose instrumentality the Truce was made.

RC (DNA: RG 59, DD); at head of text: "(No. 87.) ⟨(*fourth Copy*)⟩"; at foot of text: "The Secretary of State &c. &c. &c."; endorsed by TJ as received 11 Dec. 1793 and so recorded in SJL. Dupl (same, MDC); at head of text: "(No. 87.) (duplicate)." Tripl (same, Duplicate Despatches); at head of text: "(No. 87.) (first Copy)." Tr (Lb in same, DD). Enclosed in Bartholomew Dandridge, Jr., to TJ, 11 Dec. 1793.

The TRUCE Great Britain arranged between Algiers and Portugal in September 1793 accentuated a growing crisis in Anglo-American relations and spurred the renaissance of the defunct United States Navy. Since late in 1785 American merchant ships trading with southern Europe had been the beneficiaries of a Portuguese naval blockade of the Straits of Gibraltar, which confined Algerine corsairs to the Mediterranean in order to prevent them from attacking the economically vital Brazilian convoys. In April 1793, however, the Portuguese government informed the British and Spanish courts of its willingness to make peace with Algiers so that the Portuguese navy could take part in the war against France. Acting under instructions from the English government—which did not inform Portugal in its eagerness to obtain that nation's naval support against France—Charles Logie, the British consul at Algiers, prevailed upon the Dey of Algiers to agree on 12 Sep. 1793 to a twelvemonth truce with Portugal, assuring him that Portugal was willing to pay a huge sum (over 2,400,000 dollars according to one report) for a peace treaty. As a result of this truce Portugal ended its blockade, thereby allowing Algerine corsairs to sail into the Atlantic, where in October and November 1793 they captured eleven American merchant ships, sharply driving up insurance rates on American shipping and increasing

the number of Americans in Algerine captivity from 13 to 117. But late in November 1793, after learning how much a peace treaty with Algiers would cost, Portugal repudiated the truce, reinstituted its naval blockade, and provided naval protection against Algerine corsairs for American ships bound to or from Portuguese ports (TJ to John Paul Jones, 1 June 1792; James Simpson to TJ, 8 Oct. 1793; Edward Church to TJ, 12 Oct. 1793; Mayo, *British Ministers*, 50; Barnby, *Prisoners*, 97, 103, 110-11; Ray W. Irwin, *The Diplomatic Relations of the United States with the Barbary Powers, 1776-1816* [Chapel Hill, 1931], 57-60; Marshall Smelser, *The Congress Founds the Navy, 1787-1798* [Notre Dame, Ind., 1959], 35-8, 40, 44, 51).

The arrival in Philadelphia in December 1793 of news of the Algerine-Portuguese truce unleashed a storm of public criticism of the British role in effecting this agreement that cut across party lines. Coming in the wake of British efforts to halt the American grain trade with France, the truce was widely viewed by Americans as a deliberate British attempt to strike back at a commercial rival by subjecting American merchant shipping to the depredations of Algerine corsairs—a conviction that was merely strengthened early in March 1794 when news began to reach the United States of the British capture of hundreds of American trading vessels in the West Indies. TJ, who privately shared this view of British motives, gave official notice of the truce in a report on Morocco and Algiers that the President submitted to Congress on 16 Dec. 1793. After several months of debate, during which various members regularly excoriated British motives for bringing about this agreement, Congress late in March 1794 authorized the construction of six warships for the express purpose of protecting American shipping from Barbary piracy. TJ had long favored the use of American naval power for this purpose, but though he did not mention it in his Report on Morocco and Algiers, or in his 16 Dec. 1793 Report on Commerce, he privately expressed the hope that Congress would adopt a program of commercial retaliation as the proper response to this perceived British assault on American trade. In any event, this act of Congress marked the rebirth of the United States Navy, which TJ as President was to use to such good effect against the Barbary state of Tripoli (Report

on Morocco and Algiers, 14 Dec. 1793; TJ to Martha Jefferson Randolph, 22 Dec. 1793; James Madison to TJ, 9 Mch. 1794; Bemis, *Jay's Treaty*, 214-17; Peterson, *Jefferson*, 312-14, 422; Smelser, *Congress Founds the Navy*, 48-59, 60-1).

TJ submitted this letter to the President on 11 December 1793 (Washington, *Journal*, 266).

¹ Word interlined in Dupl in place of "official," but omitted in Tripl and Tr.

From Benjamin Bankson

SIR   Philadelphia, October 7th. 1793

The inclosed Letter and account from Mr. Dumas as also the Letter from Mr. Remsen were taken from large packets of News papers which are deposited in the office.

I yesterday received a Letter from a Mr. J. Mason dated Georgetown, the 26th. ultimo—covering a Bill of Lading for a Cask of Macarony expected to arrive in the Ship Salome Capt. Watson from Havre. No such vessel has entered in this City since you left it—upon her arrival I shall pay the necessary attention.

Your note which was lodged in the Bank of N.A., as also the one drawn in favor of John Ross, are taken up. Bringhurst is still in the Country. I will discharge Kerr's account this day, and wait his, or your return for a reimbursement.

The Salary of the Gentlemen of the office (who are all absent) I have deposited in the Bank of the United States, payable to their order.

No opportunity presenting, and seeing in the New York papers several vessels advertised for Havre and other parts of France, I forwarded the dispatch for Mr. Morris as also the Letters to the American Consuls to Mr. Henry Remsen, with a Letter, a Copy of which is inclosed. I have the honor to be with great respect Sir, your most obedient serv.

B. BANKSON

RC (DLC); at foot of text: "The Secretary of State"; endorsed by TJ as received 24 Oct. 1793 and so recorded in SJL. Enclosures: (1) C. W. F. Dumas to TJ, 22 June or 13 July 1793 (both recorded in SJL as received 24 Oct. 1793 but not found). (2) Henry Remsen to TJ, 1 Oct. 1793. (3) Bankson to Remsen, 2 Oct. 1793: "The inclosed packet for Mr. Morris the American

Minister at Paris, I am directed to forward with all possible dispatch. Business of all kinds being at a stand owing to the Fever prevailing here which continues to rage with great violence, it is uncertain when an opportunity may offer for its transmission. Will you permit me to solicit your exertions to forward it by the first vessel which may sail from your port to France. The following is an extract from Mr. Jefferson's Instructions to me. 'T. Jefferson desires Mr. Bankson to get if possible a trusty passenger or Captain of a vessel to be the Bearer of the Duplicates to Mr. Morris, and even, if necessary, to engage to reimburse the reasonable expences of the Journey from the place of landing to Paris and back.' The three Letters to American Consuls in France, you will please put under cover to the Consul of the port where the vessel may be bound" (Tr in DLC; in Bankson's hand; at foot of text: "Mr. Henry Remsen New York"; paraphrasing TJ to Bankson, 11 Sep. 1793;

mistakenly endorsed by TJ as a letter from Bankson to him received 24 Sep. 1793 but recorded in SJL as received 24 Oct. 1793).

DISPATCH FOR MR. MORRIS: duplicates of TJ to Gouverneur Morris, 16 and 23 Aug. 1793 (see TJ to Bankson, 11 Sep. 1793). LETTERS TO THE AMERICAN CONSULS: the texts addressed to Stephen Cathalan, Jr., Delamotte, and Joseph Fenwick of TJ's 12 Sep. 1793 Circular to Certain Consuls and Vice-Consuls (see also Enclosure No. 3 listed above).

From David Humphreys

SIR   Gibralter Octr. 7th. 1793.

I wrote to you, under yesterday's date, letters to be forwarded by four different conveyances, containing information that a Truce for twelve months was concluded between Portugal and Algiers; and that a Fleet of eight Algerine Cruizers had gone through the Streights into the Atlantic.

I observed in a Postscript, that I should afterwards explain by whose instrumentality the Truce was made. I have now to inform you it was effected by Mr. Logie, Consul of G. Britain at Algiers: but I am very happy to add, there are strong circumstances to induce me to believe, it was without the authority or even knowledge of his own Court—from which (I am most credibly assured) he has not received any direct official communications for fourteen months past . . . this was owing to his having been recalled, and a Successor appointed for that residence. By what I have learned in a confidential manner, from good authority, Mr. Logie wishes to remain at Algiers until the final negotiation between that Regency and Portugal be concluded.

The strong easterly wind, called the Levanter, has prevented the Portuguese Convoy, mentioned in my late letters, from proceeding any distance up the Mediterranean. The same cause still detains the English ships with Troops on board in this harbour, tho' a second vessel has arrived with Dispatches from Lord Hood to accelerate their departure. In consequence of this last arrival, some more Artillerists, with field Artillery, have been detached from this Garrison—and Genl. O'Hara (the Leiutenant Governor) is going to take the Chief Command at Toulon.

By yesterday's mail we have nothing but an account of the Duke of York's repulse with the loss of his Cannon and Baggage—and a considerable advantage gained by the Spaniards over the French near Perpignan. With sentiments of great respect & esteem I have the honour to be Sir Your most obedient & most humble Servant   D. HUMPHREYS

P.S. I shall prosecute my former Plan of proceeding to Alicant, the moment the wind will permit.

RC (DNA: RG 59, DD); ellipsis in original; at head of text: "(No. 88.)"; at foot of text: "The Secretary of State"; endorsed by TJ as received 22 Dec. 1793 and so recorded in SJL. Tr (DNA: RG 46, 3d Cong., 1st sess.). Tr (Lb in DNA: R6 59, DD). Enclosed in addendum to Report on Morocco and Algiers, 14 Dec. 1793, Bartholomew Dandridge, Jr., to TJ, 23 Dec. 1793, and George Washington to the Senate and the House of Representatives, 23 Dec. 1793.

TJ submitted this letter to the President on 23 Dec. 1793 (Washington, *Journal*, 272).

From Henry Remsen

DR. SIR   New York October 7th. 1793

Two days ago I received a letter from Mr. Bankson of your Office dated the 3d., enclosing a packet for Mr. G. Morris, one letter for Mr. Fenwick, one for Mr. Cathalan and one for Mr. dela Motte; and this day, having previously put them under cover to Mr. de la Motte, sent them by the Brig Rebecca owned in this port and bound to Havre. The Capt. promised to deliver the dispatch to Mr. de la Motte himself; and from what Mr. Bankson wrote me respecting Mr. Morris letter, I thought it proper to write a few lines to Mr. de la Motte, informing him it was your desire that that letter should be sent to Paris *only* by a confidential conveyance.

Mr. Bankson says the fever continues to rage with great violence; but our accounts, 'tho still very distressing, were more favorable by this day's post than they were the last week.

I have taken from on board the vessel to my own chamber the box containing the model, where it will remain in perfect safety. At present it would be impossible to get it to Philadelphia, there being few or none going thither either by land or water, except the post.

Messr. Brothers, Coster & Co. tell me they have received answers to several letters they sent by the Brig Sion, whence they infer that the letter bag of that vessel has at last got to Amsterdam. You may recollect, Sir, that some important dispatches you sent me for Mr. Short remained long unaccounted for—they were sent by this vessel, which foundered soon after she sailed; but the Capt: Crew and letter bag were picked up by another vessel, and carried into Newfoundland. It must be satisfactory to you, knowing the letters were preserved, should they have reached Mr. Short without inspection, even should they now be useless. I hope, Sir, you either have had, or soon will have an acknowledgment of their receipt.

I enclose a few of the latest papers, in one of which vizt. that of the 3d., is a list of the american vessels captured by the new Providence privateers, and carried in and detained there. I have the Honor to be with great respect and esteem, Dr. Sir Your most obt. & most h'ble servt.   HENRY REMSEN

RC (DLC); at foot of text: "Thomas Jefferson esquire"; endorsed by TJ as received 24 Oct. 1793 and so recorded in SJL.

The LETTER FROM MR. BANKSON was actually dated 2 Oct. 1793 (see note to Benjamin Bankson to TJ, 7 Oct. 1793). For the IMPORTANT DESPATCHES, see Van Staphorst & Hubbard to TJ, 26 July 1793, and note.

From William Short

DEAR SIR   The Escurial Oct. 7th. 1793

I have had the pleasure of recieving by Mr. Blake your kind and friendly letter of July. 11th. I cannot too warmly express my grateful feelings on the subjects it treats of, and particularly for the new proofs it gives me of your friendship. The intelligence with respect to my funds in Mr. Browne's hands was agreeable and satisfactory beyond measure and the more so as it was so much more than I had expected. His reprehensible silence to me since the year 91. was of an ominous nature which left me little to hope, and much to fear under such circumstances.

The information you give me with respect to the commencement of tenanting lands in Virginia gave me a double pleasure—both as a proof of the increasing prosperity of my country, and of the practicability of placing one's fortune, in that solid, substantial and patriotic way. If lands could be tenanted in the manner you mention I should be exceedingly happy to have my funds or at least the greater part of them say $\frac{2}{3}$ or $\frac{3}{4}$ placed in that way. As it is impossible at this distance to give a precise instruction on such a subject, viz. fix on the precise spot or manner in which I wish it to be vested, I will indulge myself in giving my ideas, relative thereto and ask the favor of you to draw from thence the conclusion according to circumstances in America.

I shall go on the idea of my funds in Mr. Browne's hands being safe, which your friendly letter of July seems to warrant me in, and on that of Mr. Kennon of New York, (Mr. Donald's agent) having delivered you for me the funds he had of mine as mentioned in former letters. These funds amounted to I think 6000 dollars of various descriptions, with the interest accruing thereon and vested from time to time in more funds. Mr. Browne was to have followed the same method with those in his hands—and of which he has rendered no account since the year 91.

I have or ought to have besides this 1000 acres of land near Norfolk on the grean sea—and $\frac{2}{3}$ of 15000 acres of military lands. It seems to me that much too great a part therefore of my estate is in paper. I have only been tempted hitherto to keep it in that form from the convenience of the property during my absence, and from the inconvenience of our landed estates in Virginia, during the absence of the owner. And also from the difficulty of fixing on a proper investment in lands without being present. I am sorry however at present not to have directed a part to have been placed in some of the ways which now occur to me, so as to have varied the kind of my fortune as much as possible.

Two modes have long existed of doing this and since your letter a third—namely 1. Lots producing rent in towns. 2. shares in the canal companies—and now 3. in tenanted lands. I have formerly thought a good deal on this subject and should have desired it to be executed if I had not experienced how little I could rely on Colo. Skipwith's taking any trouble about it—and if I had not been without any other person in that part of the country to whom I could apply. Nor should I now have ventured to have troubled you on such a subject but for your former letter encouraging me to hope that being retired to a private life, you would have more leisure to serve an absent friend. I still fear it will give you too much trouble of the kind to which you are not accustomed and in that case I hope you will have no scruple in dispensing yourself from it. But to proceed with my ideas.

In these investments I would wish three things to be considered. 1st. The solidity of the investment. 2dly. the convenience of the rent and security of its being recieved—and 3dly. the facility of disposing of the investment when I shall return to America, in order that I may place it if I should chuse it in some estate of land to settle on. It seems to me that well chosen lots in some flourishing town and whose prosperity depends on the nature of its position and the country around it, say Philadelphia, Baltimore—(Geo. Town on Potowmac, I suppose the lots are now at an advanced price on the contingency of the seat of government coming there and Alexandria perhaps exposed to some degree of uncertainty also as connected therewith) Richmond or Norfolk—I mean lots which are leased on a ground rent and which are built on—so that the property is in the land only, the houses belonging to the lessee; and which are a security for the regular payment of the rent—or lots with houses on them, the houses being insured against fire and other accidents. I should prefer the former however—and it should be observed that in the case of the latter the rent should be considerably higher (viz.

the interest of the money invested) because of the repairs and final decay of the houses, which must be rebuilt by the owner—whereas this is not the case with lots on a ground rent—and of course I think the interest accruing on the money laid out is generally calculated so as that it should be double or nearly double to put it on a par. However the solidity of the buildings—the price of insurance against fire and other accidents, are to be taken into the account in order to form a proper estimation.

From my idea of the profits of stock in the U.S.—and of course the general interest of money, I imagine no persons who have their property in ground rents can recieve less than 5. p. cent annually on the value of the ground of those lots—and if I could place my money at that rate I should be satisfied—and think it better than to keep it in the funds at six—that is to say, I should be satisfied, supposing I have 20,000 dollars 6. p. cents for instance which bring me in annually 1200 dollars to vest them in the ground of lots, which are leased out on a ground rent (being built on by the lessee) and which bring in 1000 dollars annually, supposing better could not be done; and that it should seem probable that I should be able to dispose of this property again with facility for the price I pay for it, should I chuse on my return to dispose of it, in order to purchase a landed estate to settle on. As these lots would not be to live on, but merely to derive a rent from their geographical position would be more indifferent, except that *caeteris paribus*, I should prefer them the least removed from Virginia.

2. Stock in the canal companies also seems to me an agreeable kind of property after the canal shall have been finished, and some idea can be formed of the clear profits to be counted on. In all countries the price of labor, the profits of stock, and the interest of money unavoidably bear a certain proportion to each other—of course the profits arising from money vested in this way must be considerable, since it is so in all others, in the U.S. It should and must be greater here than on ground rents, because there are more contingencies—and all these things, though they operate insensibly, operate however infallibly to establish a proper level. I know not how far the James River or Potowmac canals are advanced—nor in what train they are—but should either be so far advanced as to shew what will be the probable clear profits I imagine it will be the Potowmac and therefore I should prefer being concerned therein, as far as I can judge from here—or if they are both advanced sufficiently I should have no objection to be concerned a little in both—always having a view to the circumstances abovementioned viz. the security and rate of interest arising on the money vested there and the facility (which will depend a good deal on those circumstances) of disposing of my capital therein if I should chuse it in order to vest it in lands to settle on. I cannot say what should be the clear annual profits of

this kind of stock in order to put it on a level with other vestments—this must depend on circumstances of which a person on the spot and in the way of judging can alone decide—and which I must leave to you. My general idea being given to you, viz to place a part of my funds in some convenient and sure way, so as to be able to change that placement if I should chuse it hereafter and in the mean time to derive a proportionable interest therefrom—I would add also to vest more or less in this way in proportion as the canal should be finished or not, and the rate of clear profit ascertained. [1]

3. Could lands be tenanted in Virginia it would certainly be to me the most agreeable of all kinds of property. This system will unquestionably be adopted in time—but I should apprehend as yet that lands were too cheap and too easily to be procured in property for laborers to content themselves with taking them on lease—leases can not be valuable until the farmers are rich, and those who are rich will necessarily and with reason prefer laying out a part of their capital in the property of lands to taking them on lease. If by tenanting you mean that humane and philanthropic system of letting them to the slaves, in the way of metairies then it seems to me that it would not answer my present purpose—because not to mention that it is an experiment to be made (although I believe firmly it would answer with proper care)—the capital to be laid out in the purchase of slaves would be too considerable to admit of any reasonably adequate revenue. Still I think those who have the misfortune to own slaves, should for the sake of humanity make the experiment. When I shall return to America it is my intention to preach this not only by precept but by example—and for this purpose I intend purchasing a small number—it is a subject my mind goes much on—I have already formed the rules to be observed for exciting in these people the idea of property and the desire to acquire it, which I think would be easily done, and which when done, I think would insure the success of the experiment—this should be done gradually, and in the mean time a part of the estate should be kept as at present—where might be retained and employed such as were found unworthy of being employed in another way. Several of the present generation who have grown up in slavery and to whom the care and foresight necessary to take care of themselves, their families, and their property would be worse than slavery itself, might be found of this description—but there would be many of a different character even among the present generation—and I take it all their children grown up and formed in a different way would be capable of being at least metayers—and some of them farmers if proper advances should be made to them or at least such of them as should be judged trustworthy. It seems to me therefore that there should be those three gradations of *slaves—metayers* and *farmers*—to secure the business.

The two last exist in France and indeed all the civilized part of Europe almost may be divided into them. In many parts there exist also what may be compared to our slaves. Let any person examine the situation of Russia and Poland for instance and compare those countries with France or England and he may form some idea of what our southern states would be could our slaves be made free tenants, compared with what they are now. This is one of the most pleasing reveries in which I indulge myself. It seems to me to unite the very ideas which are formed to give the most heartfelt satisfaction to a pure and virtuous mind—viz. an union of the purest principles of humanity with the prosperity of one's country. These reflexions have insensibly drawn me off from my subject, to which I now return.

If it were possible to vest my funds in lands yielding a clear rent of 5. p. cent, I should think it a desirable mode—and if there seemed a certainty of disposing of them after my return to America, so as to purchase lands to settle on, if these should not suit me, then their geographical position would be less important—but as there would be always some inconvenience probably in alienating this kind of property it would be desirable to consult the geography a little, and the other considerations with respect to a proper place of settlement—this however it would be difficult for me to do well at this distance, and without a later view of the ground than I have had. There was a time when my enthusiasm and inexperience of the affairs of this world was such that I should have preferred being settled on a few acres on the top of Montalto to any other position—and even now the being your neighbor would have infinite weight with me as it will during all my life, and under every circumstance of my life. I like also the climate of Albemarle—but the soil and position of any estate immediately round Monticello, do not seem to me to admit of such a grazing, meadowy farming establishment as I should like. No part of E. Carter's land for instance seems to me to have water in proportion to the thirstiness of the soil—it is excellent for planting—but not suitable for farming according to my mind—and that stiff-red clayey soil is disagreeable in other respects—at least my examination of these subjects here—and my recollection of those things whilst there leave me this impression. J. Cole's tract to the south and Thos. Walkers to the North of Monticello, were those which pleased me most. I never shall forget the fine *gazon* of Cole's yard when we fled there. I know not how these tracts are as to water—but except the yard Thos. Walker's possession presents itself the most agreeably to me at present—as being less red and argillous I think, more level—and nearer market—but I remember that both these tracts were of those privileged kind which in the midst of cheap lands were carried to an exorbitant height in the estimation of their owners and particularly the latter.

Instead of meddling with over-rated tracts I should imagine it would be better to think of such as being sold for particular and inevitable reasons present always considerable advantage to the holder of ready money, which I should be in this case by means of my funds. It seems to me good opportunities of this sort might be found by a person on the spot among our *ci-devant* James river Nabobs. Lands thereabouts also would be more easily tenanted I should imagine. If I were rich enough to have a farming establishment there, then I should like a small country seat as near as possible to Monticello to spend the hot months at—but such things are beyond my capital I fear, and to be indulged only in idea. What person on earth would be as happy as I should be if I were with such a partner of domestic enjoyments as I have an idea of, rich enough to be settled on such a place as Curls, suppose (or any other place capable of being converted into a profitable, and prosperous farm) and with a summer retreat on the mountains in your neighborhood. It is then that Montalto would have all its charms—or Collé—or something thereabouts.

Whilst Gov. Morris was employed by Mr. R. Morris at Paris, and even after he became the Min. Plenipo: of the U.S.—he had several tracts of land to dispose of for him, on the terms of Mr. R. Morris's engaging to take them as lessee for a given number of years at a given rent, which amounted as well as I remember to at least 5. p. cent on the sum paid. He wished to dispose of the famous Dover tract (formerly Griffin's) in that manner. He communicated this to me as knowing the tract, that I might give information respecting it, in the case of being applied to by any of those to whom he should offer it. I do not recollect the number of acres, or whether there were slaves with it, or indeed any of the other particulars—but the sum demanded I remember was £20,000 stlg. or thereabouts. It is possible also he might have meant 500,000. livres tournois which according to the then exchange would have been only about half of the sum. I know not whether he sold it—though I remember he sold a small tract near Philadelphia, to his friend Poor Segur, who purchased it absolutely *de confiance* for about £5000 stlg.—and was induced thereto absolutely from the persuasion that he was placing his money in land at the rate of 5. p. ct. I don't doubt he will find this to be really the case as Mr. Morris knew he was dealing with his friend who knew nothing of the matter and proceeded blindly on his word—but with any other than a person of M. Morris's character and delicacy, the bargain might turn out a very different one to Segur—for a person might very well agree to give a 5. p. cent rent, for a few years on a sum double the real value of the land, in order to engage him to purchase that land in fee for the double of its value.

If however the price paid was really no more than the value of the land, then in my case it would be a very agreeable circumstance that a responsable seller should bind himself to lease it for a given number of years at a rent of 5. p. cent on the money—but it should be seen that the price paid was really no more than the worth of the land.

Not venturing to hope that my fortune will ever be sufficient to admit of the plan abovementioned I must confine myself I imagine to one residence and I have therefore for some time been revolving in my mind this subject to find what place would most probably unite all the desiderata, of climate, soil, health, profit, *agrément* &c. It seems to me with the map in my hand, and all other considerations in my mind—that that region lying on the Potowmac or on some of the waters falling into it on its south side and above the falls, must possess several inducements to preference for me. The lands there I believe are dearer than further south— but they would be more easily tenanted also. I should like as much water and as much level land as possible except an height for an house and other conveniencies—places capable of giving mill seats and other means of facilitating labor in the ruder manufactures would be also desirable—and unless a too great increase of price should oppose it, the lower down and the nearer the Potowmac the better. Too near the falls I should apprehend lands would have felt the influence and been raised in price on account of the contingency of the seat of federal government coming there—and, as I have said above, I don't like contingencies whenever they can be avoided.

Having been obliged to deal so much in generalities I cannot be sure of having given you a sufficient knowlege of my ideas on the subject, to induce you to act for me: and indeed I rather apprehend the contrary unless some particular case should present itself of so desirable and advantageous a vestment of my funds as should leave no room in your mind for doubt. This I take the more likely to happen with respect to lots on ground rent, (where the title is clear and beyond all possibility of dispute) or with respect to canal shares than with respect to land, because being more merchantable objects and their neat rent being more accurately ascertained, their true value is known with greater exactitude, and shew more clearly whether the bargain is an advantageous one. Should you find no such opportunity of placing my funds, as you should chuse to make use of, I should be much obliged to you to write to me on these subjects and to inform me, what would be practicable in this way, Viz. the price of some lots—canal shares—and tracts of land, and as nearly as may be the clear rent they produce. I mean this as nearly as you may know it, without giving yourself too much trouble about it.

Should any opportunity present itself of making an investment as abovementioned then I should prefer my six p cent funds being employed in that way, as far as they may go—the relative prices of the deferred and 3. p. cents, at the time of the sales, should decide which of them it is best to dispose of. There is one thing also which I fear will be productive of still further doubt and uncertainty. The funds viz. the 6. p. cents I observe are considerably below par—and the rest in proportion. Now it would be hard to dispose of them with that loss after their having been already whittled down by the $\frac{1}{3}$ and $\frac{2}{3}$ and $\frac{1}{3}$ of $\frac{2}{3}$ system—which was as unequal as it was unjust in its operation and which I never would have subscribed to if Mr. Browne had consulted me. And yet as long as they are selling under par in the market I can't expect to get par for them, and I should be unwilling to dispose of them at a lower rate, unless indemnified by the bargain made—as for instance take 10,000 doll. of 6. p. cents which yield an annual interest of 600 dollars—if they could be placed in lots yielding a ground rent of 300 dollars, and of which there was a good likelihood of their appreciating so as to command in a short time 10,000 dollars in money, then it would be immaterial what was the nominal rate at which the 6. p. cents were disposed of, whether 19. shillings 18. shgs. or any other rate, in the pound. Such a case might happen from the owner of the lots or other property wishing to recieve the cash for them and of course selling them low. Such cases however must be rare, and rarely to be found except by persons on the spot and hackneyed in the ways of business. I can hardly expect therefore that a *bonne fortune* of the kind should fall to our lot. This is all I can say on the business, and indeed in order to say so much I have been obliged to have constantly in my mind that you would be before the arrival of my letter retired from public life.

In your letter recieved by Mr. Blake you do not inform me whether any of the letters I have written to you since my arrival have got to your hands except the two of April 2. Besides those I wrote to you previously as Sec. of State—Feb. 3. and March. 6.—and Mr. Carmichael and myself: Feb. 19. None of these letters are acknowleged by you so low down as July 16th. the date of your last to us. I wrote to you also a private letter of April. 5. in answer to yours of Jany. 3d. It was so long, so voluminous and so prolix, that I was really and in conscience ashamed of it. Still I hope on account of its contents being a complete and satisfactory statement of every thing that had passed that it will have got to your hands. I repeated the same subject also more abridged and by duplicate the 23d. of June.

Mr. Carmichael and myself wrote to yøu also jointly and fully and sent our letters by duplicates and triplicates after the conferences opened—April 18. May. 5. and June 6: We have been as much surprized as mortified to learn that none of them had arrived before the departure of Mr. Blake. On his arrival here we immediately announced it to the Sec. of State by post via Cadiz and Lisbon four copies and mentioned the several letters we had written up to the present time.

In my No. 124. (March 6:) I confirmed by examples as to this court in particular what I had mentioned on former occasions in my private letters to you, respecting the usages of courts in general as to diplomatic characters. As you tell me in your letter you suppose what you formerly mentioned as to me would take place, I find my letter even if it should have arrived has produced no effect. I must own that it seems to me a little odd that our government in paying this third grade nearly as much as some powers pay the second, should persist with so much inveteracy in withholding the single word of *Plenipo*: which produces certainly two effects inevitably and which have been stated—namely to disable the agent from speaking with the minister of foreign affairs except by shifts and starts, and when he is quite exhausted—and to expose the agent to daily humiliations in his own eyes, and also in the eyes of others at most courts, and particularly at the Hague and still more particularly here. It is different I learn at Lisbon, or at least much less so—as the usage there is to go to court two or three times the year only—and to see the foreign minister by appointment only when business requires it, so that a chargé des affaires has an equal chance with an Ambassador. As to Ministers Rest. I believe they are obsolete except in old rusty books and on our diplomatic establishment.

I recollect as to this court what happened to Mr. Carmichael and myself and which made me feel somewhat and laugh at the ridiculousness of the position in which this system or no system placed us. After the minister had lost and made us lose some time in finding out what to do with us or how to present us under our mongrel character, he settled it in a way that Mr. Carmichael observed to him it was useless he should be presented a second time having already been presented in that way—viz. in being kept in an out antichamber until all the ministers of the second order have done, and until the King having left them goes to dine and gets up from dinner—whilst he is picking his teeth and the public are standing around him understrappers are brought in and shewn to him—the *corps diplomatique* go away before dinner. As I never had been shewn to the King, it seemed that I could not well dispense myself as Mr. Carmichael did. Accordingly on the day appointed we went to the Palace—we were stopped of course in the first antichamber—whilst there, the members of the first and second order passed by us to go into the next antichamber to wait until the King was ready to recieve them. Among them I remember passed the Secretary of the English embassy, a young man of three or four and twenty. He as other Secretaries of the embassy, is made Min. Plenipo:—the British ministry having more regard it seems for the feelings of the persons they employ, and for the estimation in which they wish them to be held by others, than our government has. It is impossible to describe the triumph which was painted on the countenance of this young Englishman to pass by and see two *soi-disant diplomates* from America waiting in an out antichamber among the vulgar. Rebels in fact deserve no better treatment—and it would seem as if our government was conspiring with them to humiliate our national respectability in the eyes of foreigners. This might be done with impunity if we had a large fleet and army to establish our respectability, but as it is, the policy is as bad as it is inexplicable, on any principle resulting from a knowlege of Europeans and European courts. As the Prest. has been happy enough for himself, never to have been among them, and as the same may be the case with your successor I hope it will not be considered as blasphemy to say that he must be unacquainted with the details of this business—and that it would not be very wrong for you simply to give him your opinion thereon—though I can hardly expect it now as it seems you must have thought it improper whilst having that department. If I had not seen this to be your way of thinking I should have thought it a real duty in a person situated as you were. I have said so much on this head really more from a regard to the interest and character of the U.S. than to my own. For it has become to me a matter which will probably be of little importance. I shall not remain here after affairs get somewhat settled in France, longer than may be thought indispensable—so that my accepting what may be offered will depend more on this circumstance than the grade they give. I do not like the climate or any thing else here well enough to be tempted to remain, and most certainly will not remain a moment after France becomes travellable and habitable, in the humiliating (and uselessly expensive) grade of Min. Rest. I say uselessly expensive because really in it no business can be done with the Minister of foreign affairs, or no business which could not be just as well done, by some young clerk in a good banking house who might be employed (and would consider himself liberally paid at £100 stlg. p. Ann.) to write news to government, send newspapers, edicts cedules &c.—and on occasion be the agent of such American citizens as might have lawsuits or other contestations, adjourned to the capital. And at this court particularly it would be the case, as really nothing can be more useless than the expence of £1000 stlg. a year, for a person who is only a daily monument of our country treating this court with less respect than they do France or England, and of course a daily source of ill humour here; this country being more than any other jealous of its own dignity of the respect shewn by others—to which by way of compensation also it is exceedingly sensible when satisfied—and this you may consider as one of the strongest traits in their national character. I have been so convinced of this that I have endeavored to smooth over the subject whenever it has been mentioned to me, as it has been frequently and sometimes with warmth—by observing that America had begun by sending a Min: Plenipo: who had not been recieved—and that Spain had never sent one as yet—to this it was observed that great allowances should be made for Spain at the time of Mr: Jay's coming—and that Spain had since sent a Minis: Plenipo: for that M. de Gardoqui, (as he has observed on several occasions) had that commission in his pocket and was always ready to unfold it if America would have named one of the same grade.

He now wishes much that this grade should be adopted—not only from the national considerations abovementioned, but particularly I believe because he wishes to send his son to America in that character. I should have no doubt of his succeeding therein as he has since his return from America been constantly in that line and employed at Vienna and Florence, if I did not know he had a dangerous rival in a person who desires the place much and who is very much in the personal confidence of the Duke de la Alcudia whose will would be without control. The persons now in America would in that case be provided for elsewhere, and which would not be a misfortune as I apprehend their correspondence does not produce the most favorable effect, being of the old school of G. and conformable to the ideas he took up whilst in America, and which are certainly far from being just particularly as applicable to our present government.

After all whatever may be decided on as to the permanent establishment here I shall never cease reflecting on the kind of fortune which has always pursued and persecuted me in this line. After being kept in that suspended, and anxious way at Paris for so long a time and being succeeded there in so humiliating a way—I am sent to the Hague and placed there where the corps diplomatique, may be considered constantly as raked to publick view—and where the English faction domineering, would view with devouring pleasure whatever would tend to humiliate or mortify an *insurgent* and particularly an *insurgent diplomate*—my grade there is such as no other person has, and I am excluded thereby from admission to a diplomatick society and subjected to such treatment at what they call the court, and which they think the thermometer, of the respect due to any member of the *corps diplomatique*, as became the food for all the commerage of the place to the great amusement of all the *Anglomen*. Whilst thus situated, and ostensibly treated I was employed by our government in a way which required more responsibility, and would have argued more confidence, than any thing they could have shewn, by the large sums of money which were put under my control. So that whilst I was apparently and ostensibly an underling character and employed in a grade in which other countries employ the lowest sort of clerks, I was subjected in fact to all the weight, anxiety and responsability of the most dignified and confidential agents. A business is then to be conducted at Madrid it is thought of so much importance as to require a particular commission being formed and a person being sent there at a very considerable expence to the public— this honor is destined to me. I pack off during the rigorous season, in a bad state of health—through a vast country where there might be every day a thousand inconveniences and I arrive after a journey of 400 leagues, to be kept a considerable time without the ministers giving any sign of acknowleging me, because he did not know in what manner our new character should be acknowleged, and at length admitted to an out antichamber, to remain there in the mob, until the corps diplomatique should have passed and repassed—the King have dined—and been ready to see the vulgar. As in Spain the U.S. are still called and considered *las Colonias*, we were and could only be considered by the Spaniards as the counterpart of their agents from Mexico, Peru &c.—sent to reside near the court to sollicit the affairs of those colonies—and as we were the first instance of Plenipotentiaries treated in that way, being the first who had ever been seen here without letters of credence, we were and could only be considered by the *corps diplomatique* as representing a country not entitled to what is called in their language *the perfect rights of sovereignty*. If the President supposed that under these circumstances we were to enjoy a proper degree of respect in the eyes of the Spaniards or of the *corps diplomatique*, or that the representations or arguments of persons in our humiliating situation would have the same weight with any Spanish minister, as they would have done if we had been placed on the same footing with the *corps diplomatique*, he must know little indeed of the one or the other. In this instance no argument from economy can be pleaded—nothing was wanted but a single letter of credence. Mr. Carmichael would have asked no augmentation of salary, and as my expences are to be borne, they would have come to the very same. I can account for it therefore only on the principle of the destiny which has constantly pursued me since I have had the now irremediable misfortune not to have followed your friendly advice of abandoning this infernal and for me pernicious and humiliating career. It will embitter the rest of my days. I never was destined certainly for it—for with respect to everything that has occurred to me in it, I can compare it only to what is seen in some animals of whom I have read to whom the most wholesome food becomes poison as soon as they touch it. To any other than myself in a diplomatic career, special commissions are always honorable and the most desirable incidents—and insure their advancement—to me they become sources of pain anxiety and humiliation. What could be apparently more honorable and more likely to insure advancement, than being employed as I was in the affair of Holland, with a degree of confidence as to the sums under my disposition of which there is no example to any public agent in Europe, whether Ambassador Envoy or any other foreign missionary. Well I undertake it, and with all the aversion that instinct could supply and which nothing but necessity in the first instance arising from the fear of disappointing government if I declined it—and aided also by an hope that if well executed, I should be advanced at Paris, there being no older diplomatick American that seemed to have a preference. I execute it to the full satisfaction of government, and with a zeal which I never have felt since I have seen the issue and never shall feel again. I am even fondled and flattered into a continuance, by government, who find I act so well that they say they can't think of adding any other person to me in so delicate a commission, notwithstanding my earnest sollicitations. To any other than myself this would have been a sure source of promotion—to me it is only one of pain, anxiety and mortification. The same with respect to the Spanish mission—honorable and flattering as it might have been—with me it has only produced trouble and anxiety before arriving here and humiliation since. Thus circumstanced—thus treated by the President my mind is made up—I abandon all hopes of advancement in a line under his control and am ready to abandon it should my fortune in Mr. Browne's hands be safe as I trust after your friendly letter, I thank God that I have enough to live on for myself and independent of the frowns or favors of any body. I never desired indeed that any unmerited favor should be shewn to me by government. I respect the unquestionable right of the President to give his confidence under our constitution, to any persons he may please and the Senate approve—it is not certainly for those who are supplanted to criticise—they can never be supposed sufficiently impartial—but I feel they have a right to require that they should be treated with a sufficient degree of confidence by government, to know what they may expect—and not be kept in an uncertain condition during years for the meer personal convenience of those destined to supplant them. I feel they have a right to ask the same degree of impartiality which is shewn to their more fortunate rivals and particularly by a person who *affiches* such a perfection of reserve and indifference to all—and such a distance from all sorts of favoritism. Was this practised with respect to Mr. Morris and myself? You know and every body except the Prest. must have known that Mr. Morris had rendered himself famous at Paris for ridiculing the principles of the French revolution—and as to the new constitution accepted by the King he had not confined himself to meer words—and bons mots, which had been doated on as food by all the Aristocrats—and the cause of scandal and displeasure to the friends of the revolution. The Prest. remained deaf and blind to these words and deeds—although M: Morris had been attacked on their account in the journals printed in Paris—and this was during a continuance of years. I go to the Hague. I remain there only six months—and immediately the President becomes all eyes and all ears as to me, and hears at once all I say—and what is still more extraordinary hears and believes all I do not say, with respect to this same French revolution—his usual caution deserts him and he adds faith to what must have come at least through a suspected chanel, and for purposes which must have been obvious to the Prest. had it related to any other than myself. I have written to you already on these subjects. I should not have renewed them here but for a letter which I have found respecting me in the Newspapers just recieved from America. I must premise however that this letter is published long after the Prest. has heard of what I said at the Hague—and of course that it is not from thence that he could have derived his information.

This letter is said to be written from Rotterdam by a respectable merchant of that place dated Dec. 20th. It seems to have been first printed in a Baltimore paper and copied from thence in others. I find it in Freneau's and also in [Davis's][2] of Richmond. I am there accused by this respectable merchant generally of conducting myself not as the envoy of a republic but as a minion of despotism and particularly of two things, of being the first to treat the French minister with disrespect—and of being under the counsels, and the friend—or as Mr. Davis[3] has inserted it, the *humble* (in Italics) friend of Ld. Auckland. As to general accusations I know not how to refute them except by general denials—and those I give here in the most solemn and unreserved manner. Without recollecting every particular circumstance of my conduct, I feel myself so purely a republican—I love and cherish so much the excellent constitution of our country, I venerate so much the principles of my fellow-citizens, and above all I ever have had and still have such a perfect abhorrence of despotism, and such a sovereign contempt for all its minions of every description, that I do not hesitate to affirm that I have never in any instance of my life swerved from the line which the envoy of a republic ought to pursue—or given any foundation, by word or deed, for the reproach of Conducting myself like a minion of despotism. As to being the first to treat the French minister with disrespect that charge is more particular and admits of a more particular answer. As M. de Maulde was the only French minister at the Hague whilst I was there it must allude to him. You will see whether it is founded or not. On my arrival at the Hague, and presenting my credentials I paid the usual visit and in the customary way to all the *corps diplomatique* and among them M. de Maulde. This was returned by them in the same manner as by M. de Maulde. He came once to see me afterwards and I went also to see him. He certainly experienced nothing but civility from me—our visits were not renewed, probably because we did not suit each other enough to court each others society—but I do not know that I was bound from any respect to make advances to M. de Maulde, more than he was to me—and I respect the dignity of my country sufficiently to consider its representatives in foreign courts on a level and entitled to the same respect with any foreign minister—and by no means bound to make advances to any. There were others of the corps diplomatique also with whom I kept up no more communication than with M. de Maulde—but I never supposed that this was treating them with disrespect. To such as were civil to me, I replied by civility and did not imagine that any thing more would be required. I was not there long enough to have formed an intimacy with any of them. I did not consider my country far enough advanced in the politics and intrigues of Europe (and God grant that she never may be) to render it necessary that her agents abroad should render their society and visits subordinate thereto. I meddled with no intrigue and had none (I thank God) to meddle with. My object was so to conduct myself as not to give any cause of dissatisfaction to the country where I was sent to reside—and to acquire sufficiently their confidence, by meriting it, to be useful to my own country in such business as I might have to transact there for them. This was not only conformable to general and obvious rules of propriety, but to your official instructions to me. To have acted otherwise would have been a violation of the confidence reposed in me. Had the government of the United Provinces supposed any particular intimacy between M. de Maulde and myself, I should have immediately forfeited all pretensions to so much of their confidence as is necessary in conducting business. On what ground I know not they had taken up an idea that M. de Maulde was actively employed in fomenting disturbances in their country—they supposed that he held meetings with those who are known by the appellation of the patriotic party[4] and that he was endeavoring to bring on a general insurrection. In the situation in which things then were suspicions became certainties in the mind of that government—and for all I know they may have entertained those suspicions or those certainties, unjustly with respect to M. de Maulde—but be that as it may, such were the impressions that it excited, that neither M. de Maulde or any person who was intimately connected with him could expect to be considered in the light in which alone a foreign minister can hope to serve his country to advantage in that character. Had any circumstance placed me in that position with that government I should have thought it my duty to acquaint our government with it and to have owned to them frankly that I considered myself incapable of managing their interests against the torrent of such prejudices. These circumstances however did not require that I should affect any singularity in my conduct with respect to M. de Maulde. I behaved to him as to others when we met—

nothing contrary to civility ever passed between us—and I cannot concieve therefore in what this writer from Rotterdam (if it is really from thence that the letter is written) can suppose I shewed disrespect to the French minister. It would be something like despotism, thus to pry into and denounce my private conduct even if it were conformable to truth and to exact, that without any object I should be forced to cultivate the society of a person, who for all this writer knows, might be disagreeable to me, or who might find my society disagreeable to him. And after all if the reproach of disrespect is founded on our visits not being kept up, then I insist that he should make the same reproach of disrespect also to M. de Maulde; as I paid him as many visits as he did me. He must be liable to the same reproach unless it should be proved that a minister from the U.S. is not on a level with a minister from France or any other country—and this it would take all the writers in Rotterdam and the seven United Provinces together to convince me of. The second accusation against me is being the *friend* or according to Mr. Davis, the *humble* friend of Ld. Auckland. If I had the honor of being better known to Mr. Davis, I trust he would soon satisfy himself that I never was and never shall be the *humble* friend of any body. And I am much at a loss to know on what this Rotterdam gentleman can have founded his idea of my being at all the friend of Ld. Auckland, or led by his counsels. Luckily I had not occasion for the counsels of any body whilst at the Hague, and if I had had it would not certainly have been to Ld. Auckland that I should have addressed myself. He is not a man I believe to inspire confidence very readily and still less so to an American than any other. The fact is that I never in my life recieved a counsel of any sort from Ld. Auckland, and do not remember ever to have seen him except in public companies. His house was open twice a week not only to the *corps diplomatique*, but to all the Hague and to all foreigners who passed. As there was little resource at the Hague every body went there as to the only rendezvous of the place, if it were meerly to hear the news. I went there generally and passed an hour with the others. M. de Maulde went there also for some time, and discontinued it afterwards I imagine because he had other business, or because it did not amuse him. I never gave myself the trouble to enquire about the cause of it. It was never understood I believe that all those who went to the public assemblies of an Ambassadors were his friends and further than that I certainly never recieved any kind of civility from Ld. Auckland which could warrant the supposition of my being his friend—nor was there ever any circumstance which could give rise to an idea of my being under his counsels—and if I had been they would not probably have induced my treating M. de Maulde with disrespect, as there was certainly more communication between M. de Maulde and him than M. de Maulde and any other person of the *corps diplom:.* I cannot quit this subject without observing that whatever the Rotterdam writer may have thought of my conduct towards M. de Maulde, it would seem as if the inhabitants of the Hague did not view it in the same light. It was there constantly reported on the contrary that the greatest intimacy prevailed between us—that we had meetings together and with the discontented party which we were exciting—that the place of our rendezvous with these people, was particularly at Ryswick a small village near the Hague &c &c. These things came to my knowlege from different sources. I never took pains to contradict them, supposing the government were sufficiently acquainted with the proceedings of all the foreign ministers residing there—and as to busy chattering idle individuals I always despised their reports too much to take notice of them and hope I always shall whether they confine themselves to private slander, or exhibit in the more formidable garb of public print—though I own this latter mode makes a deeper impression on me, being less accustomed to it in that way, and above all its coming from my country and through my countrymen, to whom it is said to have been handed from a respectable merchant of Rotterdam. For my part however I can see but little mercantile respectability in a traffic of infamous falsehoods of this kind—and I am sorry to say it, still less candor and propriety in Printers inserting and copying an atrocious and anonymous libel against a fellow citizen absent from his country and devoting his whole time to her service. It is somewhat hard to be thus considered at the Hague, leagued with M. de Maulde, for the purpose of propagating revolutionary principles—to be looked on there in every society where strangers are admitted, for I can speak of no other, as a real Jacobin, to be ill regarded by many on that account, and at the same time to be denounced from Rotterdam and believed in America, to be the first to treat this same French minister with disrespect, and to have conducted myself as a minion of despotism.

I observe that M. Morris is denounced in the same paper and under the same head on a still more serious account, and I don't doubt with as little foundation—however I am not uneasy as to him as I suppose the public will pass it over, and the proper person be blind and deaf to it as hitherto. I should not have troubled you with so much of this on my own account, but from knowing what prompt credit was given by the same person to what had formerly come from the Hague on my account, and through chanels if I don't mistake, still more subject to caution than the present.

I have used every effort since my arrival in Spain, and hitherto in vain to procure Cortez's letters. The Booksellers assure me that the book is not to be found unless by the greatest accident Having learned that the Archbishop of Toledo gave copies of the work, with pleasure, I applied to a friend of his to make the request of him. He told me that to his knowlege he had not a copy left, having distributed them all. I see little hopes of procuring it, but I have spoken to two booksellers to endeavor to find it, and they have written to their correspondents in the case of accident throwing it in their way and you may rest assured of having it if it is to be got.

I find no satisfactory information with respect to the history of the Mexican dollar. M. de Gardoqui tells me there is no book which treats of it—and seems ignorant of it himself, although at the head of the mint. I have spoken with others in his department who should be informed, but I learn nothing from them of the nature I wished. I shall ever remain my dear Sir your friend as sincere as I am troublesome and tedious.

W Short

P.S. You never answered my public letter with respect to correcting the title given the States General in my letter of credence[5] although I wrote to you twice respecting it. I will thank you to let me know the cause of it—and what is to be expected as they really make a point of this article. I hope I shall often hear from you if you have leisure. WS.

PrC (DLC); at head of text: "(Private)"; at foot of first page: "Mr. Jefferson—Monticello"; endorsed by TJ as received 23 Dec. 1793 and so recorded in SJL. RC (PHi: Gilpin Collection); not sent, as explained in Short's attached note: "*NB*—the press copy of this letter sent as a duplicate having been acknowleged before the original was sent (on acct. of Mr. Blakes delay), the original is substituted here to the 2d press copy kept."

The LETTER . . . RESPECTING ME IN THE NEWSPAPERS, a translated extract of a 20 Dec. 1792 letter from a "respectable merchant at Rotterdam" to a friend in Baltimore, charged that as minister to the Netherlands Short had "conducted himself not as an envoy of a republic, but as a minion of despotism," that he had been one of those who had shown the "most disrespect" to

FRENCH MINISTER Max Maulde-Hosdan, and that he had been unduly influenced by William Eden, Baron AUCKLAND, the British ambassador at The Hague. An accompanying editorial commentary claimed that letters recently received from France by Baltimore merchants indicated that the "British cabinet are tampering" with Gouverneur MORRIS "for the purpose of drawing these States into a coalition of the rulers of Europe against France" (*National Gazette*, 26 June 1793).

[1] Preceding sentence inserted.
[2] Supplied from RC, where it was substituted for "Dixon's."
[3] Word interlined in ink in place of "Dixon." Correction also made in RC.
[4] Remainder of sentence interlined.
[5] Remainder of sentence interlined.

From George Washington

DEAR SIR   Mount Vernon Oct 7th: 1793

It appearing to me that the public business will require the Executive Officers to be together some time before the meeting of Congress, I have written to the Secretaries of the Treasury and War to meet me at Philadelphia or vicinity—say Germantown—by the first of November, and should be glad to see you there at the same time. The Attorney General is advised of this also.

In a letter from General Knox of the 24th. Ulto. who was then at Elizabeth Town performing quarantine before he could be admitted into New York is the following paragraph. "The french fleet is still in New York, in a wretched state of disorganization, which prevents its Sailing. Mr. G___t has been low spirited for ten days past. The fleet have been told by him that the Executive of the United States prevent their selling their prizes, and citizen Bompard who belongs to a Club in France as well as all his Sailors, say that they shall represent the matter[1] in its proper colours. I do not find that Mr. G___t has promulgated the last letter of the Secretary of State, excepting as to the effect of the measures with the Consuls, which prevent their selling their prizes—Would to God it had been thought proper to publish the letter to Mr. Morris—The minds of our own people would have been convinced of the propriety of the measures which have been adopted, and all caval at the meeting of Congress prevented."

I should be of this opinion likewise if there is danger of the public mind receiving unfavourable impressions from the want of information on one hand, whilst the insiduous attempts to poison it are so impudently and unweariedly practiced on the other.

In another letter from Genl. Knox dated the first instant at the same place after having lain quarantine from the 19th. of September to that date, he says "The french fleet excepting the Ambuscade will sail to morrow from New York upon some cruise unknown. The Surviellant sailed on the 29th. ult. for France with dispatches from Mr. G___t and such is his desire that they should arrive safely, that he will in a day or two dispatch the Ceres, an armed Brig with duplicates."

If our dispatch boat should fail, and duplicates are not sent, he will play the whole game[2] himself.

General Knox expects to be back by the 25th. of this Month.

We are sustaining at this Moment, a drought, which if of much longer continuance, will I fear, prove fatal to the Wheat now in the ground—much of[3] which is come up badly, and is diminishing every day for want of Rain. I am sincerely & Affectionately yours

Go: WASHINGTON

PS. The enclosed from Mr. Leslie you will know best what to do with—and say to him. G W—n

RC (DLC: TJ Papers, 94: 16089-90); at foot of first page: "Mr. Jefferson"; endorsed by TJ as received 15 Oct. 1793 and so recorded in SJL. Dft (DNA: RG 59, MLR); dated 6 Oct. 1793, with day added in different ink, but endorsed by Washington as a letter of 7 Oct. 1793; only the most significant variations and emendations are noted below. FC (Lb in same, SDC); dated 6 Oct. 1793; wording follows Dft. Recorded in SJPL. Enclosure: Robert Leslie to Washington, London, 24 July 1793, reporting that he expects to stay in London three or four years; that before leaving Philadelphia he was unable to complete the clock and pendulum he had proposed to him but brought it to London and expects to complete the necessary experiments this winter for fixing a standard of weights and measures; that although TJ's report proposes a rod vibrating seconds in latitude 45, the United States has no convenient place in that latitude and at 51 London is as close to it as Philadelphia; that he therefore proposes to adjust the rod here, Greenwich's latitude being universally known, and he can use some of the best timekeepers to regulate it and send it over ready for immediate use; and that if Washington approves he may be able to complete the work by the time Congress passes the act regulating weights and measures (RC in DLC; addressed: "The President of the United States Philadelphia").

Washington's letters to the SECRETARIES OF THE TREASURY AND WAR were dated 25 Sep. 1793, that to the ATTORNEY GENERAL 30 Sep. 1793; he had notified the Secretary of State of the date he wished the Cabinet to reassemble during TJ's 22 Sep. 1793 visit to Mount Vernon (Fitzpatrick, *Writings*, XXXIII, 102, 103-4, 107-9). Washington edited the paragraph from the letter from Henry KNOX OF THE 24TH. ULTO. to remove a report that French sailors in New York intending to massacre Laurent François Le Noir, Marquis de Rouvray, and his son had attacked the nobleman's house and fled to Elizabethtown (DLC: Washington Papers). LAST LETTER: TJ to Edmond Charles Genet, [7 Sep. 1793]. LETTER TO MR. MORRIS: TJ to Gouverneur Morris, 16 Aug. 1793.

[1] Dft and original Knox letter cited above here add "upon their return."
[2] In Dft Washington wrote "will have the game" before altering the phrase to read as above.
[3] Preceding two words interlined in Dft.

From Edward Church

SIR   Lisbon 8th October 1793

I had the honor to write you on the 22nd. Ulto. since which nothing material has occurred here. I have been diligent in my Enquiries concerning the Views of the belligerent Powers with regard to the U.S. and have solid grounds to believe that it is the determined purpose of England and Spain sooner or later to unite their Endeavours to Crush Us, I mean of the Courts and Kings of those Nations. It is probably a very fortunate circumstance with respect to Us that the combin'd Powers have not succeeded as they expected against France. It should seem that nothing else has prevented their Active operations against Us. Our fate may therefore at this time be considered as more intimately involved with that of France than is generally supposed, at the same time I anticipate, and feel alarmed at, the probable Effects of the present Mania of the French Democrats, who are crouding into the U.S. lest it should create in those of not the greatest discernment such a disgust and dread of the like excesses prevailing Among Us, as to produce effects similer to those consequent on the insurrection of Shays and his party in New England, where a Majority of the moderate Men, among whom were many good Patriots, on the quelling the insurgents, seemed disposed in order to avoid a similar extreme to plunge head long into a more fatal one, and to wish to draw the Cords of Government so close as to strangle all the blessings resulting from the Revolution.

In conversing on the Subject of the intentions of England and Spain towards America, with a Portugueze Gentleman of great erudition, and of the purest Democratical principles, he observed, that when the Pope established and supported the King of Naples against the Duke of Suabia, the latter in an attempt to recover his right, was taken prisoner by the King of Naples, who wrote to the Pope for advice how he should dispose of him, when the Pope return'd this answer, "the Life of the Duke is the death of the King,"—"and vice versa,"' by this we may judge of the opinions and jealousy of those powers, and how seriously they consider themselves interested in our destruction.

The Portugueze have no treaty with the English or any other Nation for the Article of Bacallão or dried Cod-fish, and small pickled fish of all kinds; The Encouragement of that fishery, and a good market, is of the greatest importance to the U.S. as on these will greatly depend our future Naval Strength. A large Portion of Spain is supplied through Portugal by land, in addition to the vast consumption of these Articles in this Country. A mode might be adopted to secure to the U.S. a monopoly of the Sale in this kingdom without any great loss or sacrifice on our part, let the U.S. reduce the duty on the Wines of Portugal, and the same per Centage I am led to believe will be allowed by this Government on our fish, and as the Amount of the Exports from America wou'd far exceed the Imports of Wines from this Country, the advantage of such a Contract wou'd be palpably in our favor, and woud exclude all competition. In this reduction of the Duty of Portugal Wines, I do not include those imported from the Island of Madeira, but only the Wines imported from Lisbon and Oporto into the U.S., the duty on these wou'd be but a trifling object compared to the advantages of encouraging our fishery, and of securing the Monopoly of this Market for our fish, which must be the result of a large reduction on the duty on Wines, this wou'd go far to annihilate the English Newfound-land Fishery which is now thought to be on the decline. The Portugueze grow daily more and more impatient of their dependence on the English, and wish to shake of the Yoke, even Martin de Mello I am told would not be averse if he had a plausible pretence to turn the course of Portugueze Gold into a different Channel, or at least a part of it; I have asked, supposing a War between the U.S. and England if the Portugueze woud conceive themselves obliged to take an Active part on the side of great Britain, The same well informed Portugueze Gentleman seemed to think that this Nation were not disposed to Quarrel with Us, or to aid the English Against Us, but Personal safety, their opinion and dread, of the power of Britain, and our supposed weakness, might possibly drive them to act against their own inclination, but this he seemed to think rather doubtful, though he is painfully sensible of the present servile state of dependence of this Nation, they Ask me where is your Strength? you have no Ships of War, what therefore can you do against the Naval force of Britain? I have said all I could to obviate these objections, which could not be much; but shou'd nevertheless be glad to see something like an American Fleet, though it shou'd be but small, it wou'd sound large in Europe, and might be greatly magnified and multiplied in crossing the Atlantic. The British it is true have many Ships but they want Men, particularly to Act against Us, which wou'd be the most unpopular measure in England that could be adopted by the british Minister.

It would be very dangerous to publish the object of the proposed reduction of the duty on Portugal Wines, for if the English had any Idea of our design to obtain this Market exclusively for our Fish, they would infallibly defeat Us with their Gold, but if I cou'd promise a reciprocity on our part, I have every reason to think I could bind the Bargain secretly and irrevocably (War excepted) for a certain term of Years. With perfect esteem & Respect I have the honor to be Sir Yor. faithful & mo: obedt. Servt.   EDWD. CHURCH

N.B. There were two Vessels sailed for Boston the day before the News arrived of the Algerines being on this Coast, by one of which I sent the Original of this Copy. The Betsy Capt. Atkins and The Violet Capt. Babson were the names of the two that sailed.

Dupl (DNA: RG 59, CD); in a clerk's hand, with part of complimentary close, signature, and postscript by Church; at head of text: "No. 1." and "(Copy)"; at foot of text: "Honble. The Secretary of State—for the United States of America at Philadelphia";

endorsed by TJ as received 11 Dec. 1793 and so recorded in SJL.

TJ submitted this letter to the President on 11 Dec. 1793, and Washington returned it the same day (Washington, *Journal*, 266).

From David Humphreys

SIR   Gibralter Octr. 8th. 1793.

I have already forwarded for you five copies of Dispatches, to inform you, that a Truce for twelve Months was concluded between Portugal and Algiers; and that a fleet of Algerine Cruizers had gone through the Streights into the Atlantic, on Saturday night last. They were reported to me by an officer of a Portuguese frigate who spoke with them, to consist of eight sail; I believe, however, there were but three frigates, two Xebecks and a brig. This morning another Algerine frigate was in this harbour, and has gone through the Streights to the westward.

To multiply the chances of getting early information to you, I am sending off to order neutral vessels to be chartered at Cadiz and Lisbon to carry my Dispatches to you, if they cannot otherwise be transmitted by the most expeditious and certain conveyances: and those vessels will be ordered to put into the first Port in the U.S. they can reach. With Sentiments of great esteem, I have the honour to be Sir Your most obedient & Most humble Servant   D. HUMPHREYS

RC (DNA: RG 59, DD); at head of text: "(No. 89.)"; at foot of text: "The Secretary of State &c. &c. &c."; with penciled notation by TJ beneath signature: "to be copd & press copd twice for Congress"; endorsed by TJ as received 11 Dec. 1793 and so recorded in SJL. Tr (DNA: RG 46, Senate Records, 3d Cong., 1st sess.). Tr (Lb in DNA: RG 59, DD). Enclosed in Bartholomew Dandridge, Jr., to TJ, 11 Dec. 1793, and addendum to Report on Morocco and Algiers, 14 Dec. 1793.

TJ submitted this letter to the President on 11 Dec. 1793 (Washington, *Journal*, 266). It is the last letter from Humphreys that TJ received as Secretary of State. See Appendix I.

From John M. Pintard

Madeira, 8 Oct. 1793. In his 23 July letter he informed TJ that the island's governor had detained an American vessel he had chartered here at £65 a month to go to Bordeaux and that he had sent Humphreys documents proving the detention. A few days ago he received a 14 Sep. letter from Lisbon in which Humphreys stated that he was to sail the next day for Gibraltar, that he only had time to write to the Secretary of State on this subject, and that Lisbon Consul Edward Church would transmit that official's answer. He encloses a copy of Humphreys's letter to the Secretary of State and a copy of Church's letter received by the brig *Washington*, Captain Lemuel Goddard, who arrived here three days ago. Yesterday evening an aide-de-camp to the governor informed him that he was to remain under house arrest until further orders and refused to explain why or to give the order in writing. He can write no more because a vessel is just about to depart for America, but he will write again by a vessel leaving tomorrow.

Tr (DNA: RG 59, CD); 2 p.; unsigned; at head of text: "The Honble. Thomas Jefferson Esqr."; at foot of text: "Copy"; conjoined to Pintard to TJ, 9 Oct. 1793 (see below). Recorded in SJL as received 19 Dec. 1793. Enclosures: (1) David Humphreys to Luís Pinto de Sousa Coutinho, Lisbon, 14 Sep. 1793, protesting, as diametrically opposed to commercial principles and "the usages of Nations at peace," the detention by the governor of Madeira of the American brigantine *Minerva*, chartered by Pintard to go to Bordeaux, the details of which will be found in the enclosed petition to and dispatch from the governor, and requesting him to send notice of the Portuguese government's response to the redress and indemnification he requests for Pintard to Edward Church, who will be in charge of American affairs at the Portuguese court after he leaves for Gibraltar tomorrow or the day after (Tr in same; at head of text: "Copy"). (2) Church to Pintard, Lisbon, 26 Sep. 1793, stating that he has just received a note from Pinto in answer to one of his own informing him that Pinto had this day sent an order to the governor of Madeira to make full compensation to Pintard for the detention of the *Minerva* (Tr in same; at foot of text: "Copy"). Enclosed, with 9 Oct. 1793 letter noted below, in Pintard to TJ, 15 and 29 Oct. 1793.

Pintard wrote a brief letter to TJ on 9 Oct. 1793, in which he enclosed a copy of the above letter, stated that the governor of

the island had set him at liberty without an explanation, and promised to write again when he received the one he planned to demand of the governor on the 9th or the 10th (Tr in DNA: RG 59, CD; unsigned; at foot of text: "Copy"; subjoined to Pintard to TJ, 8 Oct. 1793; recorded in SJL as received 19 Dec. 1793).

TJ submitted this letter and the one mentioned above to the President on 19 Dec. 1793, and Washington returned them the same day (Washington, *Journal*, 271).

From James Simpson

Gibraltar, 8 Oct. 1793. He encloses a copy of his last dispatch and reports that there is nothing new in West Barbary. He is extremely concerned to see the Algerine fleet sail into the Atlantic; under such an unpleasant circumstance, he is glad to see Humphreys in Gibraltar and promises to continue to assist him in conveying prompt news of this event wherever necessary for American citizens. By a letter from the English consul at Algiers it appears that Portugal agreed to the truce on 12 Sep. for twelve months by his mediation, but the conditions are still unknown. The ship that passed the Straits of Gibraltar this morning is one of two corvettes France gave the Algerines to replace one of two xebecs destroyed by Neapolitan cruisers near Toulon in 1791. Pierced for 22 guns on the main deck, it has a small figurehead and ports that open in halves fore and aft and lay high.

RC (DNA: RG 59, CD); 3 p.; at foot of text: "The Honble Thomas Jefferson Esqr Secretary of State &ca"; endorsed by TJ as received 18 Dec. 1793. Tr (same); unsigned; at head of text: "*Copy*"; conjoined to Tr of Simpson to TJ, 21 Oct. 1793 (see Appendix I). Enclosure: Simpson to TJ, 26 Sep. 1793.

TJ submitted this letter to the President on 18 Dec. 1793, and Washington returned it the same day (Washington, *Journal*, 269). It is the last consular letter TJ received from Simpson. See Appendix I.

A letter from Simpson of 12 Feb. 1794, recorded in SJL as received from Gibraltar on 11 Apr. 1794, has not been found.

To George Washington

DEAR SIR   Monticello Oct. 9. 1793.

I have the honor of answering, by the return of post, your favor of Sep. 27. recieved this day, inclosing the letter and memorial of Messieurs King, Pratt and others, owners of the ship Andrew, and her cargo, desiring the interposition of the Executive on account of the cargo of rice taken by a decree of the general council of L'orient, and of the freight and detention of the vessel. The memorialists seem to expect that an indemnification may be made them by this government out of the monies due from us to France. But this would be an act of reprisal, which the usage of nations would not justify until justice has been required from France, and formally denied. Their money in our treasury can no more be taken for this purpose, nor under any other forms, than their vessels in our harbors. It is necessary therefore that the Memorialists make application to the government of France for indemnification, exhibiting the fullest and most authentic proofs. If they will at the same time furnish me with a copy of these, I will instantly write to our minister at Paris, and desire him to give to their claim that firm support which it's justice calls for. The conduct of that government in other cases communicated to us by Mr. Morris, gives every reason to presume they will do ready and ample justice in the present one. I have the honor to be with great & sincere respect & attachment Dear Sir your most obedt. & most humble servt   TH: JEFFERSON

RC (DNA: RG 59, MLR); at foot of text: "The President of the US."; endorsed by Washington. PrC (DLC). Tr (Lb in DNA: RG 59, SDC). Tr (ViU: Edgehill-Randolph Papers); 19th-century copy.

To John Hopkins

SIR   Monticello Oct. 10. 1793.

In consequence of a power of Attorney from Mr. Short to act for him in all his affairs here, Colo. Hamilton was so kind as to furnish me with copies of your letters to him of Apr. 29. and July 18. containing a statement of Mr. Short's property in the public funds transferred by Mr. Brown. Being much unacquainted with this kind of business I am obliged to ask your information What sums of interest are due on this property? Where and by whom it is to be paid? Whether it can be paid at Philadelphia? And whether any particular form of order is requisite? If you will be so good as to favor me with an answer by the return of the post, which leaves Richmond on the Monday morning for this place, it will find me still here, and particularly oblige Sir Your most obedt. servt

TH: JEFFERSON

PrC (DLC); at foot of text: "Mr. Hopkins. Commissioner of loans." Tr (ViU: Edgehill-Randolph Papers); 19th-century copy. Recorded in SJL as a letter of 9 Oct. 1793.

John Hopkins (ca. 1757-1827), a Richmond merchant and director of the Bank of Richmond, was appointed federal commissioner of loans for Virginia in 1790 (Walter L. Hopkins, *Hopkins of Virginia and Related Families* [Richmond, 1931], 211-14; William Armistead to TJ, 20 May 1780; Madison, *Papers*, III, 325-6n; JEP, I, 57).

For Hopkins's LETTERS to Alexander Hamilton, the latter actually dated 16 JULY, see note to Hamilton to TJ, 26 July 1793.

From Tobias Lear

DEAR SIR New York October 10th: 1793

I shall embark at this place for London in the early part of November, from whence I shall go to Holland and other parts of Europe to make arrangements for carrying into effect the commercial establishment which I have made in the City of Washington. You had the goodness to tell me in Philadelphia that you would favor me with letters to such of your friends and acquaintances in Europe as might be able to give me useful information on the subject of my tour—and to add thereto a few notes respecting the rout, the best mode of travelling &c. through such parts of Europe as you had passed and which it might be useful for me to visit. If, my dear Sir, you can make it convenient to transmit these letters and notes to me before the 10th. of November they will probably find me here, and should I have sailed their being recommended to the care of Mr. James Greenleaf would ensure their reaching me in London or Amsterdam by the next Vessel sailing after they get here.

As we have it in contemplation to engage in the Levant Trade, beleiving it to be a commerce that may be carried on very beneficially with the part of the Country where our principal establishment is made, You will add much to the obligation I shall feel for the other letters &c. if you will have the goodness to give me letters to or Notes respecting the southern parts of Europe that may tend to give the necessary information which it will be my object to acquire if I extend my tour to that quarter. Wishing you every blessing that health and an honest mind can give I have the honor to be with very sincere attachment & respect Your Obliged friend & Obed Servt TOBIAS LEAR

RC (DLC); at foot of text: "Thomas Jefferson Esqr."; endorsed by TJ as received 24 Oct. 1793 and so recorded in SJL; with penciled notes for reply subjoined by TJ: "Hague. Dumas
Havre. La Motte
Bordeaux. Fenwick
Marseilles. Cathalan
Paris. Heraut de Sechelles
Cadiz. Yznardi.
Lond. Havre. Paris. Amstdm. Coblentz. Cologne. Frankfort. Strabg. Lyons. Marseilles. Cette. Bordeaux. Lisbon. Cadiz."

From Thomas Paine

MY DEAR SIR Paris Oct. 10th. 1793 2d. year of the republic

As far as my Judgement extends I think you cannot do better than send Commissioners to Europe; and so far as the freedom of Commerce may become a subject of Conference it ought to be done. It may be a means of terminating the war for it is necessary that some power should begin. England is in a wretched condition as to her Manufactures and her public and private credit. The combined Armies make no progress. My opinion is that they cannot agree among themselves, and that the object of the English Government is to get possession of both sides the channel, which certainly cannot be consented to by the Northern powers. It is not the English alone that has possession of Toulon, the Spaniards have landed more troops than the English as if to keep an Eye upon them. Holland does nothing. She must wish to be out of the war. If you send Commissioners Holland will be the best place for them to arrive at—they can there make known their Credentials to all the resident Ministers. It will not do to appoint Gov: Morris upon that business. His appointment here has been unfortunate. He has done more harm than good. All the Americans will give you the same account. I wish much to be in America were it only to press the sending Commissioners. I think it is a plan in which all parties among you will unite. Were you to appoint two or three Comsss. from America and direct them to call Mr. Pinckney to their Councils, I think it would have a good effect. I suppose you know the person that wrote the enclosed American letter. The contents show there are many subject for conference that does not appear at first sight. It either has or will be published in London in a few days. Remember me to the President and all my friends. Your's affectionately   THOMAS PAINE

RC (DLC); at foot of text: "Thomas Jefferson Secretary of State United States of America"; endorsed by TJ as received 31 Mch. 1794 and so recorded in SJL. Enclosure: [Thomas Paine], *A Citizen of America, to the Citizens of Europe* [Paris, 1793], calling upon the allied coalition to abandon its goal of restoring the Bourbon monarchy and instead make peace with the French Republic—an appeal that Paine cast in the form of a letter written from Philadelphia on 28 July 1793 in order to conceal his authorship, and that he based upon the mistaken supposition that Congress at its next session was to consider a proposal to send commissioners to Europe to confer with other neutral powers about negotiating preliminary peace terms between France and the coalition (pamphlet in AMAE: CPEU, xxxviii; printed in Foner, *Paine*, ii, 561-5).

From Philip Freneau

[*Ed. Note*: This 11 Oct. 1793 letter was printed in Vol. 20: 759 as part of a group of documents on Jefferson, Freneau, and the founding of the *National Gazette*.]

In Vol. 20: 752n the Editors accounted for a 7 Nov. 1793 letter from Freneau based on a mistaken reading of SJL. No documentation for such a letter has been found.

From George Washington

Dear Sir   Mount Vernon October 11. 1793.

Your dispatch of the 3d. with it's several enclosures, reached Alexandria on Wednesday evening, and got to my hands yesterday morning.

This afternoon I shall send to the post office the Letters for Mr. Bankson, with my signature to the Exequatur for Mr. Dannery, and Letters patent revoking that of Mr. Duplane. Your letter to the latter, two to the French Minister, one to his Secretary Mr. Bournonville and another to Mr. Morris, being approved are also forwarded.

To a Letter written to you a few days ago I refer for the time and place mentioned for the meeting of the Heads of Departments, and hope it will be convenient for you to attend. If I do not take a circuitous rout by Frederick-town in Maryland &c. I shall not leave this before the 28—and in that case should be glad of your company, if it is not inconvenient for you to call.

Since writing that letter, however, I have received the enclosed from the Attorney General which may make a change of *place* necessary; but I shall wait further advices before this is resolved on. I have also received a letter from the late Speaker, Trumbull; and as I understand sentiments similar to his are entertained by others—query, what had I best do? You were of opinion when here, that neither the Constitution nor Laws gave power to the President to convene Congress at any other place than where the Seat of Government is[1] fixed by their own act. Twelve[2] days since I wrote to the Attorney General for an official opinion on this head, but have received no answer. If the importance and[3] urgency of the case, arising from a supposition that the fever in Philadelphia should not abate,[4] would justify calling together the Legislature at any other place—where ought it to be? This, if German town is affected, with the malady, involves[5] the Executive in a serious and[6] delicate decision. Wilmington and Trenton are equidistant, in opposite directions, from Philada. both on the great thoroughfare, equally dangerous[7] on account of the infection being communicated to them, and would, I presume, be equally obnoxious to one or the other set of[8] members; according to their situations. Annapolis has conveniences— but it might be thought I had interested and local views in naming this place. What sort of a town then is Reading, and how would it answer?[9] Neither Northern nor Southern Members would have cause to complain of its situation. Lancaster would favor the Southern ones most.

You will readily perceive, if any change is to take place, not a moment is to be lost in the notification—whether by a simple statement of facts (among which, I presume, the House intended for them in Philada. will be unfit for their reception[10])—and an intimation that I shall be at a certain place   days before the first of December, to meet them in their legislative capacity,[11] or to advise with them on measures proper to be taken in the present exigency. If something of this sort should strike[12] you favorably, draw (and if necessary sign) a proper Instrument to avoid delay, leaving the name of the place blank, but giving your opinion thereon. German town would certainly have been the best place for them to have met in the first instance, there to have taken ulterior resolutions without involving the Executive.

I have no objection to the Director of the Mint, with your concurrence, chusing an Engraver in place of Mr. Wright.

No report has been made to me relative to the Tonnage of the French ships from St. Domingo.

Major Lenox, I perceive by the papers, is marshall for the District of Pennsylvania.

Limits of jurisdiction and protection must lie over till we meet, when I request you will remind me of it. I am Your Affecte. Servant

Go: Washington

RC (DLC); in the hand of Bartholomew Dandridge, Jr., signed by Washington; at foot of text: "Thomas Jefferson Esqr. Secretary of State"; endorsed by TJ as received 16 Oct. 1793 and so recorded in SJL. Dft (DNA: RG 59, MLR); entirely in Washington's hand; signature and part of complimentary close clipped; only the most significant variations and emendations are noted below. FC (Lb in same, SDC); wording follows Dft. Recorded in SJPL. Enclosures: (1) Edmund Randolph to Washington, 3 Oct. 1793, advising that the yellow fever epidemic had claimed victims in Germantown, where Washington had instructed his Cabinet to meet him at the beginning of November (not found; but see Fitzpatrick, *Washington*, xxxiii, 125). (2) Jonathan Trumbull to Washington, Lebanon, Conn., 2 Oct. 1793, reporting that the fatal sickness continues to rage in Philadelphia and that it was more than probable the city cannot be rendered healthful and convenient for business for several months; and suggesting that "the Occasion exists, sufficiently extraordinary, to warrant the Presidents interposing his discretionary power of making a *special Call* of Congress, to convene *at some other place*, than that to which they now stand adjourned," that this "may be constitutionally done, under the urgency of existing Circumstances," the date to be fixed a few days prior to the first Monday in December, that otherwise a majority of both houses would have to convene at Philadelphia no matter what the danger before Congress could adjourn to a place of safety and convenience, and that his suggestion was motivated soley by "anxiety for the Health and Safety of the Executive and Legislative of the Union" and of the government departments (RC in DLC: Washington Papers).

[1] Reworked in Dft from "where they were."

[2] Word interlined in place of "ten" in Dft.

[3] Preceding two words interlined in Dft.

[4] Dft: "arising from the unabating fever in Philada."

[5] In Dft Washington here interlined and then canceled "a delicate."

[6] Preceding seven words interlined in Dft in place of "is a case of difficulty and delicacy."

[7] Preceding two words interlined in Dft, which omits the remainder of the clause.

[8] Preceding six words (except "the") interlined in Dft in place of "the."

[9] Preceding five words interlined in Dft, with remainder of paragraph added in margin.

10 Dft: "be unfinished."

11 In Dft Washington first wrote "as a Legislature" and then altered the phrase to read as above.

12 In Dft Washington wrote "If this strikes" and then altered the phrase to read as above.

From Edward Church

SIR   Lisbon Saturday 12th: Octr. 1793

Yesterday the 11th. I received the following note from Coll. Humphreys, our minister Resident at this Court, but now at Gibralter.

"Dear Sir

"We have advice of a Truce between the Portugueze and Algiers, and that an Algerine Fleet has gone into the Atlantic, Pray forward the inclosed with the intelligence and believe me"

Your's

(Signed) D. Humphreys

Immediately on receipt of this very alarming news, I called together all the American Captains now in this Port, and communicated the Contents of the above Letter, with such farther information as I had a few minutes after obtained from a friendly and always well-informed Portugueze Gentleman—which was, that on the 5th. instant an Algerine Fleet consisting of eight armed Ships had been seen by a Portugueze Frigate (just arrived) sailing out of the Mediterranean, there were 4 Ships carrying 44, 36, 30 and 28 Guns—3 Xebecs 20, 24 and 26 Guns—and one Brigantine of 22 Guns. Their Signals to the Portugueze and English are said to be an English Jack at the fore-top-gallant-mast head, and a Flag with blue and white, or blue and yellow Stripes, at the main top gallant mast Head.

Early this morning I waited on his Excellency Luiz Pinto de Souza Minister and Secretary of State for foreign Affairs, on the subject of this unexpected Event, and the unfortunate situation in which it had placed not only the American Captains now here, but our nation at large, whose injury seems to have been particularly meditated in this negociation.

The Minister received me with great politeness, and anticipating the cause of my visit, informed me that he was at the moment of my arrival occupied in writing to me on the subject, but was better pleased to see me, as he could more fully and particularly explain the nature of this business to me viva voce, than by letter, and assured me that he would candidly communicate to me how far the Court of Portugal were concerned, or chargeable for the mischiefs resulting from this Truce, to all those Powers not at peace with Algiers; he declared that it was as unexpected to the Court of Portugal, as it could be to us, and if it was not quite so unwelcome, yet it was by no means agreeable to their Court, who never intended to conclude either a Peace or Truce with the Dey without giving timely notice to all their friends that they might avoid the dangers to which they might otherwise be unavoidably exposed by trusting to the protection of the Portugze. Ships of war stationed in the Mediterranean. He acknowledged that the Court of Portugal had about 6 months past, expressed to the Courts of England and Spain, a desire of their friendly co-operation to induce a disposition in the Dey towards the establishment of a firm and lasting peace with her most faithful Majesty, but having appointed no person directly or indirectly to negociate in behalf of her Majesty, they considered the business as only in embryo; but the british Court zealous over-much for the happiness of the two nations Portugal and Algiers, in order to precipitate this important business, very officiously authorized Charles Logie the british Consul-General and Agent at Algiers, not only to treat, but to conclude for and in behalf of this Court, not only without any Authority, but without even consulting it. A Truce was accordingly concluded between the Dey and the british Agent (for twelve months) in behalf of her most faithful Majesty, for the performance of which on the part of her majesty the British Court is Guarantee. The Condition is, that this Court shall pay to the Dey one third as much as he receives annually from the Court of Spain. When this Court received information of this proposed condition, from Mr. Walpole the british Envoy to this Court, They informed him, that however desirous they might be of a Peace with Algiers, they were so far from being disposed to submit to such a condition, that it was the determination of her most faithful Majesty not to pay one farthing, but in the interval, the truce was signed by the self-constituted Agent Mr. Logie. The Minister Mr. Pinto farther informed me that this Court had ordered an Augmentation of the number of armed Ships on the Meditn. Station, so little was their expectation of a peace or truce with Algiers, and intimated that the Algerines would probably ere long be less at liberty to cruise than at present, and mentioned less than a month; but though I have great confidence in his Sincerity, and in the good wishes and disposition towards us of many of the Portugze. Nobility, and of their sincere hatred of the English—yet the Prince is young, weak, and obstinate, and can, and probably will determine as his own Caprice, or Martin de Mello may direct. The Conduct of the British in this business leaves no room to doubt, or mistake their object, which was evidently aimed at us, and proves that their envy, jealousy, and hatred, will never be appeased, and that they will leave nothing unattempted to effect our ruin—as a farther confirmation, it is worthy of remark, that the same british Agent obtained a truce at the same time between the States of Holland and the Dey for six months, whereby we and the Hanse Towns are now left the only prey to those Barbarians. This last Truce has in all probability cost the English very dear, as the Algerines had profited much by Captures from the Dutch since the commencement of the late hostilities between the two Nations. This will I fear give a fatal stroke to the advantages which we might otherwise have derived from our Neutrality.

I am at this place interrupted by intelligence from a staunch friend to America, who has his information from the fountain-head—it has greatly shocked me. I have reason to fear that there is an infernal combination in Europe against us, France excepted, and that we have no other hope or resource but in our own strength.

Monday 14th. I have just received a letter from Gibralter of the 8th. with orders to charter a Vessel to carry the intelligence to you, Copy of which letter I send herewith. At this moment a Swedish Vessel arrives. On the 9th. in Lat: 38. 13. She was boarded by an Algerine Frigate, at a small distance She saw another which had just captured 4 Americans, 2 Brigs, 1 Ship, and 1 Schooner, and one Genoese Ship. She was informed of the Truce and that it was for 12 Months with both Holland and Portugal. I have forwarded letters by Expresses wherever I thought it necessary to notify our Citizens of their danger. We are betrayed and many, many of our Countrymen will fall into the cruel Snare. I send you a list of Those in this Port. I have chartered a Ship this moment for £800 Stlg. to carry my Dispatches, She sails to morrow. They will be delivered to you by Mr. Livingston to whom refer you for farther particulars which in my great hurry I may omit; I have not slept since Receipt of the news of the hellish plot—pardon me for such Expressions. Another Corsair is in the Atlantic. God preserve Us.

News is just arrived ℔ Post, that the French have retaken Toulon—have repulsed the Duke of Brunswick with great Slaughter; and that the Prince de Cobourg is in great danger of a total defeat, being hemmed in, by a very powerful Army which he dares not attack, Cetera desunt. I have chartered the Vessel to go, and return with a Cargo of Wheat or Flour to this Port or Cadiz for £800 Stlg., her freight back will go far to pay the expence of her hire. God grant her a safe and speedy Passage. Small hopes now of a peace with Algiers. It is currently reported here, that 3 or 4, some say 2, and some but one—of the Algerine Frigates now cruising against Us were a late present from the british King, but for this I have no other Authority than common report. If it should be thought that I have chartered the Vessel at a high price, I wish the Government to be informed that all the protected Ships demand at least double since the confirmation of this Algerine News, and I have been rather favoured in the Contract which I have made, and therefore hope no blame will fall on me, but that I shall be enabled by the Government to fulfill my Engagement.

Upon farther enquiry I am sorry to inform you, that the letter containing the above french news, comes from doubtful Authority.

It is a matter of Certainty, which I have received from undoubted Authority, though contradicted by the Minister Luiz Pinto, and at present a great Secret, that One of the present Portugze. Ministers is in this execrable plot, a plot loudly and publickly execrated by this Nation. I asked if it was Martinio de Mello?, and was answered that all his consequence and his pecuniary Resources were derived from the Meditn. fleet, or Algerine War, and of course no suspicion could justly fall on him. Was it the Secy. Lz. Pinto? My Informant only knew at present that one of the four Ministers had been privy to the whole transaction, but could not fix it, but could and would tell me very soon, at present he seemed disposed rather to suspect the first Minister, the Marquis Ponte-de-Lima, because he was the inveterate Enemy of Martinho de Mello, whom my Author heard say on a former occasion to an Ambassador on his taking leave of the Court to go to Algiers to negociate a peace, Sir! the Ships attend you, you will therefore proceed without delay on your Embassy, but remember what I have said, and what I now repeat, as of the greatest consequence, (meaning to himself), if You succeed in making a peace you will do well, but if you should not succeed you will do much better. The relation of These circumstances tho' trivial in themselves, may possibly enable you to form a more adequate idea of this Court than I should be able to give you, it is with this view I trouble you with them.

One of the Frigates now cruising under Algerine Colors was a present from the King of Spain, but not very lately—and one is certainly a *very late* present from the british King. I write in great haste, and perturbation of mind, yet hope and believe I have omitted nothing in my power to communicate for the public good and safety, to promote which, I pray you to believe me ever most firmly and sincerely devoted. If by the harshness of some of my expressions I should appear to you to be more strongly prejudiced against the british, or british politicks, than my Countrymen in general, I trust it is only because I know them better; Few of my Countrymen having been so much conversant with them for 30 years last past, the Interval of the late war excepted, and Fewer perhaps have observed and studied them so much. I am convinced they were making large strides again in America, and would probably ere long have possessed an influence there which sooner or later would have proved our ruin, but Heaven I hope has timely interposed, and doomed them to fall into the pit which they were digging for us, and that great good will ultimately be derived to us from this great evil. It is greatly to be deplored that so many of our Citizens must be doomed to perpetual Slavery, but better so, than the whole nation, of which there seemed to be not a little danger.

I keep this letter open to make such additions as occasions may offer till the moment the Vessel weighs Anchor, She has nothing to do but to take in Water.

I send you by this Opportunity a large Packet of Letters from Coll. Humphreys which doubtless contain the most important intelligence. I am Sir with the highest esteem & regard Yor. mo: hble & mo: obedt. Servt.

EDWD. CHURCH

RC (DNA: RG 59, CD); at head of text: "No. 2"; at foot of text: "The Honble. The Secrety. of State for the U.S. of America"; notation on verso by Church: "Important & Alarming News, sent by Express"; with brackets penciled in text by TJ and accompanying penciled notes by him: (at head of text) "Edward Church Consul of the US. at Lisbon to T. [J.]" and (on verso) "two copies & press copies of the parts within the [ ] for Congress to Morrow"; endorsed by TJ as received 11 Dec. 1793 and so recorded in SJL. Dupl (same); in a clerk's hand, signed by Church; at head of text: "(Copy)"; notation on verso by Church: "Duplicate of a Lettr. ℔ the Maria Capt. Ande. Ol. Kock from Edwd. Church"; with penciled note by Taylor on verso: "These are the letters respecting the chartered vessel [. . .] in his report on the algerine [during?] [. . .] [Congress?]"; endorsed by TJ as received 22 Dec. 1793. Tr (DNA: RG 46, Senate Records, 3d Cong., 1st sess.); with omissions corresponding to TJ's instructions on RC; note at foot of text by TJ referring to documents submitted as an addendum to his 14 Dec. 1793 Report on Algiers and Morocco: "Department of State to wit. The preceding letters are true copies from those remaining in the office of this department. Th: Jefferson." Enclosures: (1) David Humphreys to Church, Gibraltar, 6 Oct. 1793, stating that he has just received intelligence that the Algerines and the Portuguese have concluded a twelve-month truce, in consequence of which four Algerine frigates, three xebecs, and one twenty-gun brigantine passed through the Straits of Gibraltar into the Atlantic last night, "probably to cruize against the American Flag"; that Church should immediately communicate this news to all American ship commanders in Lisbon, now and in the future, as well as to any American consul or agent with whom he corresponds, especially to John M. Pintard on Madeira; and that Church should forward by the earliest opportunity to any American port the accompanying letter to the Secretary of State (Dupl in DNA: RG 59, CD, in Nathaniel Cutting's hand, signed by Humphreys, with "(Duplicate.)" at head of text; Tr in same, with notation on separate sheet by Church: "2d. Copy of Colo. Humphs's. Lettr. of 6 Octr. 93. fm. Gibralter 1st. forwarded ℔ the Maria Capt. Andre Ol. Kock"). (2) Humphreys to Church, 8 Oct. 1793, stating that he was reaffirming the news of the Algerine-Portuguese truce and the sailing of the Algerine fleet into the Atlantic contained in No. 1; that this morning a fine Algerine corsair, reportedly equipped with twenty-six guns, came from the east to Gibraltar Bay and then proceeded through the Straits of Gibraltar; that he should immediately charter a fast-sailing neutral vessel with an American master or mate as pilot to convey to any American port the enclosed dispatches to the Secretary of State about these alarming circumstances; that this pilot, in addition to informing all American ships he meets at sea of the Algerine presence in the Atlantic, should upon arrival in the United States request the magistrates to forward the dispatches by express to their destination; that Church should consult with the pro-American Mr. Bulkeley about chartering the vessel; and that he should also entrust the pilot with No. 3 (Tr in same, in Church's hand, with a 22 Oct. 1793 notation by him: "2d. Copy of a Letter from Colo. Humphreys dated Gibralter 8 Octr. 1793, sent pr. the City of Altona Capn. Pasche—the first was forwarded ℔ the Maria Capn. Andre Ol Kock—Recd. Via Faro on Monday 14th. Octr. at Noon. The

Ship Maria was ready to sail on Wednesday Morng, but the Wind was contrary; on Thursday morning at 6 oClock She was underway, and proceeded out of the Tagus—the Second Express goes To morrow morning wind & weather favouring, wth. Duplicates of Advice &ca. &ca. E.C."; Tr in same). (3) Humphreys to "all Governors, Magistrates, Officers Civil, Military & others concerned, in the United States of America," 8 Oct. 1793, requesting them as quickly as possible to give a universal alarm to all American citizens engaged in navigation, especially with southern Europe, of the danger of capture by the Algerines in consequence of the Algerine-Portuguese truce and the passage of a fleet of Algerine cruisers through the Straits of Gibraltar into the Atlantic during the night of 5 Oct. (Tr in same; in Humphreys's hand). (4) Nathaniel Skinner to Church, Cadiz, 8 Oct. 1793, requesting Church to forward an enclosure of the utmost importance to America by the first vessel, there being no vessels sailing from Cadiz, and stating that according to a just arrived express four Algerine frigates, three xebecs, and two brigs passed Gibraltar on their way westward on the morning of 6 Oct. (RC in same; with notation by Church: "Recd. ℣ Post Fryday 18 Octr. 1793"). (5) Charter Party for the *Maria*, Lisbon, 15 Oct. 1793, whereby Kantzon & Company chartered the Swedish ship *Maria*, Captain Andrew O. Kock, for a direct voyage in ballast from Lisbon to New York or Philadelphia, whence it was to return to Lisbon in a voyage not to exceed fifty days with a "full Cargo of Wares or Mer-

chandise" for which Kock was to receive £800 sterling for freight (plus £40 sterling if he was ordered to unload at Gibraltar), in addition to other specified expenses (Tr in DNA: RG 217, MTA, No. 6074, in English, with Kantzon & Company and Kock as signatories, and with witnesses and notarizations, all in a clerk's hand; Tr in DNA: RG 59, CD, in Portuguese, with notarization). (6) List of American Vessels in the Port of Lisbon, 15 Oct. 1793, listing thirteen ships; with subjoined note stating that the schooner *Violet*, Captain Babson, sailed for Boston on 7 Oct. and probably escaped, that the brig *Betsey*, Captain Joshua Atkins, sailed for Boston on the 9th, and that the bark *Henry* of Newburyport, Captain Roberteau, arrived here this morning from Virginia via Falmouth without seeing any Algerines (MS in DNA: RG 59, CD, entirely in Church's hand; see also Enclosure No. 1 listed at Church's second letter to TJ, 22 Oct. 1793). Letter and Enclosures Nos. 1-3 enclosed in Bartholomew Dandridge, Jr., to TJ, 11 Dec. 1793; letter included in an addendum to Report on Morocco and Algiers, 14 Dec. 1793; Enclosure No. 5 enclosed in TJ to Alexander Hamilton, 12 Dec. 1793.

MARTIN DE MELLO: Martinho de Melo e Castro, the Portuguese Minister of Marine (Fortunato de Almeida, *História de Portugal*, 6 vols. [Coimbra, 1922-29], v, 301). CETERA DESUNT: "The rest is missing."

TJ submitted this letter and the first three of its enclosures to the President on 11 Dec. 1793 (Washington, *Journal*, 266).

From Alexandre Maurice d'Hauterive

New York, 13 Oct. 1793. Duty obliges him to forward the enclosed letter and sheets, received by sea with the envelope missing in an open packet addressed to him, but which apparently belong to TJ, whose name and titles appear at the foot of the letter.

RC (MHi); 1 p.; in French; in a clerk's hand, signed by Hauterive; at head of text: "Le citoyen hauterive à Mr. thomas Jefferson Secretaire d'état au département des affaires étrangeres"; endorsed by TJ as received 9 Nov. 1793 and so recorded in SJL. Enclosure: Grand & Cie to TJ, 24 June 1793.

TJ wrote a brief note from Germantown on 10 Nov. 1793 thanking Hauterive for the "packet he was so kind as to forward to him which was very interesting to him" (PrC in DLC).

From John Bowman

Dear Sir   Chs: town 14 Octr: 1793

Several Months ago I enclosed to You a small sealed packet, containing a rough draught of a steam Engine, by Mr. Lucas, a most ingenious and Worthy Man. He purposed to soon afterwards send on a Model of that Engine, but the urgency of our more intelligent planters for his aid in relief of our former heavy labour in clearing out the Rice Crops has kept him in uninterrupted hurry. I now enclose for him an accurate drawing and description of the Engine in Question. He is about the immediate Construction of One of them for Me, and if necessary to his obtaining a patent, a working Model can be shortly sent forward to whatever place You shall appoint. I am confident, Sir, that Your attention to this Matter will redound to the advancement of Many Useful Arts in the United States. After which it were needless to add, that besides my share of satisfaction in the Public Welfare, the benefit of One of the best and most ingenious Men I have ever known, will from my attachment to him founded on a Nine Years Knowledge of him, give Me much pleasure.

Mrs. Bowman and Miss Lynch join Me in All good wishes to You and Family. I am with much Esteem Dear Sir Yr. most Obedt. Servt.

J. Bowman

RC (DLC); addressed: "The honble Thomas Jefferson"; endorsed by TJ as received 4 Nov. 1793 and so recorded in SJL, which erroneously dates it 11 Oct. 1793. Enclosures not found.

John Bowman (1746-1807), a native of Scotland who immigrated to Georgia via Charleston in 1769 and subsequently became a wealthy South Carolina planter, served several terms in the upper and lower houses of the South Carolina legislature between 1788 and 1799. He was the sole low-country planter to oppose the federal Constitution at the state ratifying convention in 1788, a year after Jonathan Lucas, Sr., built him a water mill to beat rice at Peach Tree, his plantation on the Santee River. Lucas also built mills powered by wind and tide, but he was not awarded a patent for his steam engine (Walter B. Edgar and others, eds., *Biographical Directory of the South Carolina House of Representatives*, 5 vols. [Columbia, S.C., 1974-], III, 82-3; "A Lucas Memorandum," *South Carolina Historical Magazine*, LXIX [1968], 193).

Bowman's letter of several months ago is not recorded in SJL, and neither it nor the contents of the small sealed packet have been found.

From James Monroe

Dear Sir   Octr. 14 1793

The fatigue of my late journey and some concerns which require immidiate attention will deprive me of the pleasure of being at Monticello till after the arrival of Mr. Madison which will be on Wednesday— Unless the funeral of his brother should detain him longer, which however is not expected. I send you the Fredbg. paper containing the proceeding there, which terminated in a recommendation to the counties to take the subject up. It commenc'd in an invitation by Jas. Mercer, Man Page and others, the most respectable inhabitants in that part of the State, to the inhabitants of the district to convene for the purpose of discussing some topics of general concern. Edwd. Stevens who was at that time in town with some associates of the same party took the recommendation up, and (he being in the chair) address'd the inhabitants of Culpepper against the meeting—similar efforts were made elsewhere, which together with the short notice given, and the real difficulty in assembling people from parts so distant, prevented a numerous meeting. The majority therefore was with the town and its dependants. This will account for the issue. Those of character, such as Page &ca. withdrew their names from the committee, and Mercer was retained by his seat in the chair only. The weight of the republican characters awed the sects, tories, and their assistants into silence or I believe a most loyal proceeding would have been exhibited to the publick. The resolves I have no copy of but they will be published in the paper. I am affecy. yr. friend & servt

JAS. MONROE

RC (DLC); endorsed by TJ as received 14 Oct. 1793 and so recorded in SJL.

James Madison's BROTHER Ambrose died on 3 Oct. 1793 (Brant, *Madison*, III, 385).

The 30 Sep. 1793 INVITATION BY JAS. MERCER, Mann Page, and other Republicans to the "Yeomanry within the Fredericksburg District" to meet in Fredericksburg on 7 Oct. to "take into consideration the present state of American affairs, and to declare their opinions thereon," appeared in the 3 Oct. 1793 issue of the *Virginia Herald, and Fredericksburg Advertiser*, next to the proceedings of a 2 Oct. meeting in Fredericksburg of INHABITANTS OF CULPEPPER chaired by Federalist Edward Stevens. The latter assembly, denouncing the call for a district meeting as "highly improper" because inadequate notice had been given, the theme was too broad and vague, and county meetings were more convenient to the citizenry, called instead for a full meeting of Culpeper County yeomen later in October to consider the Proclamation of Neutrality. Convening on 7-8 Oct., the district meeting tabled a set of Republican motions, accepted a committee report which roundly stated that "there is not the slightest ground" for

suspecting the national executive of exercising its authority unconstitutionally and suggested that meetings were needed only to attest to public confidence in the constituted authorities, and ended by recommending that those in attendance promote county meetings "to take into consideration the subjects which agitate the public mind." The lengthy set of Republican RESOLVES, bypassed by the meeting but subsequently PUBLISHED in Richmond, praised President Washington, emphasized the continuing validity of American treaties with all nations, condemned any assertion that the Proclamation of Neutrality suspended any obligations under the treaty of alliance with France as a dangerous attempt to introduce British theories of executive prerogative, acknowledged that if Edmond Charles Genet's unconfirmed threat to appeal to the American people was correctly reported it was "truly alarming and reprehensible" but suggested that the motives of those publicizing his misconduct would not bear close scrutiny, and urged that recriminations against the French minister not be allowed to damage the alliance with France (*Virginia Gazette, and General Advertiser*, 16, 23 Oct. 1793).

From Henry Remsen

Octr. 14. 1793.

H. Remsen's respectful compliments to Mr. Jefferson—and sends him the enclosed papers. The accounts from Philada. by this day's mail are no better than they were the last week, when the mortality was exceedingly great indeed. We have heard of the death of Mr. Jon: Sargent, Mr. V. Berckel, Mr. Franks and Mr. Rittenhouse, tho' respecting the latter the account does not come so strait, and is therefore not so generally credited.

RC (MHi); addressed: "Thomas Jefferson Esqui[re] Secretary of State of the [. . .] Monticello—[. . .] To be forwarded from Philadelphia by the Richmond post"; postmarked; endorsed by TJ as received 9 Nov. 1793 and so recorded in SJL.

From John Hopkins

SIR   Richmond October 15th 1793

I received your favor of the 10th. too late to Comply with its Contents by the post last Monday, but I now enclose you two Statements of the different species of Stock standing on the Books of my Office, to the Credit of William Short esquire—of the Quarterly amount of Interest payable thereon, and the payments thereof which have been made by me, in Conformity to a power of Attorney from Mr. Short, in favor of Mr. James Brown of this City.

It will then be perceived that although you have a general power from Mr. Short to transact his business, yet the one alluded to in favor of Mr. Brown was made for the special purpose of receiving the Interest as it accrues on the public Stock belonging to Mr. Short, which power is filed in my office, as a voucher for the payment—and which is the only mode authorizing such payment. So long as the Stock in question remains on the Books of Virga., the Interest will be payable here—and not in Philadelphia, but it can be removed from hence to the Books of the Treasury, when required, in which case the accruing Interest will be paid there. I have the honor to be most respectfully Sir Your very obedient Servant   JNO: HOPKINS

RC (DLC: Short Papers); at foot of text: "Thomas Jefferson esq"; endorsed by TJ as received 24 Oct. 1793 and so recorded in SJL. Enclosures: Statements of Short's holdings in United States securities, 15 Oct. 1793, detailing various categories of debt totaling $35,197.12 issued to James Brown in trust for Short and quarterly interest totaling $2,221.09 paid to Brown on this account before and after their transfer to Short's name on 29 Apr. 1793 (MSS in same, with second statement filed at 30 Nov. 1791; in a clerk's hand, each certified and signed by Hopkins).

From John M. Pintard

Madeira, 15 Oct. 1793. He encloses copies of his 8 and 9 Oct. letters. Since then he has conferred with the governor, the result of which is in the enclosed statement No. 3. He also encloses paper No. 1, his letter to Captain Goddard, and No. 2, Goddard's certified deposition, copies of all three of which he transmitted to Humphreys. He has always endeavored to get on well with the government of this country, but the governor is a stubborn man who will go to any length to revenge himself on anyone he takes a dislike to. Although he is vulnerable to injury by the governor in his commercial capacity, that will never prevent him from carrying out his consular duties. P.S. He will attend to TJ's 21 Mch. circular, which he received via Lisbon a few days ago.

Tr (DNA: RG 59, CD); 1 p.; in a clerk's hand, unsigned; at head of text: "The Honble. Thomas Jefferson Esqr."; at foot of text: "(Copy)." Recorded in SJL as received 19 Dec. 1793. Enclosures: (1) Pintard to Captain Lemuel Goddard, Funchal, 5 Oct. 1793, and Goddard to Pintard, n.d., the first requesting Goddard to send any letters for him by the visit boat or by the first boat coming ashore, the second stating that Goddard was sending six letters by the bearer and hoping to see Pintard soon, and giving his compliments to Mrs. Pintard (Trs in same; at foot of texts: "Copy"; with notation on verso of the first: "No. 1"). (2) Deposition by Goddard, Funchal, 8 Oct. 1793, stating, in his capacity as commander of the American brigantine *Washington* of Baltimore, which had arrived from Lisbon and anchored off Funchal on 5 Oct. 1793, that after having sent his boat ashore to request two boats to tow him in, the boat returned with a letter from the merchant to whom he was addressed as well as a letter from Pintard requesting any letters addressed to him to be sent ashore by the first boat; that upon being approached by a large boat and a small boat, he sent ashore by the latter a bundle of letters directed to Charles Alder & Company, all the letters directed to Murdock, Fearns & Company, and six letters directed to Pintard, three of which Goddard had received from the American consul at Lisbon, who had requested him to take particular care of them because they dealt with consequential matters (Tr in same; at foot of text: "Copy"). (3) Statement by Pintard, n.d., affirming that last July, having been informed by Joseph Fenwick of heavy freight charges on American ships, he chartered a ship for Bordeaux, which the governor here refused to allow to sail until a vessel arrived from Lisbon that was daily expected; that in response to his question as to who would pay him demurrage and damages for the detention of a ship it was costing him £65 sterling a month to charter, the governor very laconically stated that he might get paid wherever he could; that in consequence of an application by David Humphreys, whom he had immediately notified of his plight, the Portuguese court issued orders to the governor to make full satisfaction to him, sending them by the *Washington*, Captain Goddard; that after these orders and various letters to him and to the mercantile firms mentioned in No. 4 had been sent ashore by boat, the governor placed him under house arrest for thirty-eight hours for receiving letters from the Lisbon vessel "before she was Vissited"—an action, despite his many years on Madeira, he had never realized was a crime and that he found extraordinary because the mercantile firms which had received letters from the same ship under the same circumstances had not been punished; that, according to the governor, the Portuguese government approved of his detention of the chartered vessel but ordered him to pay demurrage out of the royal coffers, an order which clearly mortified him; and that he left it to the United States government to decide whether the governor was justified in imprisoning him (MS in same; in Pintard's hand). (4) Pintard to TJ, 8 and 9 Oct. 1793. Letter and enclosures enclosed in Pintard to TJ, 29 Oct. 1793.

TJ submitted this letter to the President on 19 Dec. 1793, and Washington returned it the same day (Washington, *Journal*, 271).

From Eli Whitney

RESPECTED SIR New Haven Oct. 15th 1793

It was my intention to have lodged in the Office of State a description of my machine for ginning Cotton, immediately after presenting my petition for an exclusive property in the same; but ill health unfortunately prevented me from completing the description untill about the time of the breaking out of the malignant fever in Philadelphia. This so interrupted communication and deranged business of every kind, that I thought it best not to send my description till the disorder had in some measure subsided. But as the sickness, which I hoped would be of short continuance, still prevails, and as I am unwilling to delay any longer, I herewith enclose and forward it, together with a short description designed to form the schedule annexed to the patent.

It has been my endeavour to give a precise idea of every part of the machine, and if I have failed in elegance, I hope I have not been deficient in point of accuracy.

If I should be entitled to an exclusive privilege, may I ask the favour of you, Sir, to inform me when I may come forward with my model and, receive my patent. I am, Sir, with the highest respect your most obedient and very humble Servant, ELI WHITNEY

FC (CtY: Whitney Papers); entirely in Whitney's hand; addressed: "The Honble. Thomas Jefferson Esq. Secretary of State for the United States of America"; endorsed by Whitney.

Whitney, whose PETITION to TJ for a patent on his cotton gin was dated 20 June 1793, dispatched this letter no earlier than 28 Oct. 1793, the date he had the enclosures notarized. The patent Whitney received— dated 14 Mch. 1794 and based on the three enclosures submitted with this letter as well as the model he later sent to Philadelphia— granted him exclusive rights to the invention for fourteen years beginning 6 Nov. 1793, the date TJ received the documents.

The three documents printed below, which secured for Whitney's cotton gin a place in American technological, social, and economic history that can scarcely be overestimated, had their origins in the Patent Act of 1793. For a brief period after it took effect, inventors were required to supply a long description and a drawing, to be retained by the office of the Secretary of State, as well as a short description to form part of the patent itself. As TJ had hoped, this re-

quirement placed the responsibility of describing inventions on patent recipients rather than the government. The requirement of two descriptions was soon dispensed with, though not before Whitney's application, and inventors were allowed to submit a single specification and drawing, copies of which were annexed to the patent issued to them (P. J. Federico, "Records of Eli Whitney's Cotton Gin Patent," *Technology and Culture*, I [1960], 168-76; TJ to Edmund Randolph, 17 Mch. 1793, and enclosure).

The destruction of Whitney's patent by a fire at his New Haven workshop in 1795, and the loss of the government's file copy of the patent and its supporting documents, as well as the requisite model, by a Patent Office fire in 1836, led to confusion in the literature on this invention. One historian, encountering the short description in a copy of the patent he received from the Patent Office and the long description in federal court records, confused the latter with the former and alleged that Whitney's patent had been improperly abridged in order to give him credit for a subsequent improvement to his machine (Daniel A. Tompkins, *Cotton and*

Cotton Oil [Charlotte, N.C., 1901], 12-16, 444-62).

The most reliable manuscript source for these documents consists of certified copies made from the originals in possession of the government for a court case in 1804 (DNA: RG 21). Another set, twice removed from the originals, was made in 1841, as part of efforts to reconstruct early patent records after the 1836 fire, from a different set of certified copies transcribed in 1803 (DNA:

RG 241). Drafts and file copies retained by Whitney (CtY: Whitney Papers) form a third nucleus of texts. Although an untitled publication of the three documents by the Patent Office in 1959 drew on the first two sources, it did not indicate specifically where they differed. The long and short descriptions printed below are the first texts to be based on a collation of all three manuscript sources.

ENCLOSURES

I

Long Description of the Cotton Gin

A Description of a New Invented Cotton Gin: or Machine for cleansing[1] and separating Cotton from its seeds.

This Machine may be described under five divisions, corresponding to its five principal parts: Viz: 1. The Frame, 2. The Cylinder; 3 The Breastwork; 4 The clearer, and 5 The Hopper.

I. The frame, by which the whole work is supported and kept together, ought to be made of well seasoned timber, so that it may be firm and steady, and[2] never become loose in the joints. Scantling four inches by three, will perhaps be stuff, of as suitable size as any. The frame should be of a square or parallelogramic form, the width must answer to the length of the Cylinder and the height and length may be proportioned as circumstances shall render convenient.

In the drawing annexed, Fig. 1, is a section of the Machine. A represents the cylinder, B The Breastwork, C, The clearer and D: The Hopper.

II. The Cylinder is of wood: its form is perfectly described by its name, and its dimensions may be from six to nine inches diameter, and from two[3] to five feet in length. This cylinder is placed horizontally across the frame, in such manner as to give room for the clearer on one side of it, and the Hopper on the other, as in fig. 1. Its height, if the machine is worked by Hand should be about three feet four inches: otherwise it may be regulated by convenience. In the cylinder is fixed an Iron axis so large as to turn in the lathe without quivering. The axis may pass quite thro' the cylinder or consist only of gudgeons, driven[4] with cement into each end. There must be a shoulder at, b. Fig. 2. on each side the bearing or box to prevent any horizontal variation in the Cylinder. The bearings of the axis, or those parts which rest on the boxes must be rounded in a lathe, so that the centre of the axis may coincide with the center of the cylinder. One end of the axis should extend so far without the frame as to admit the winch, by which it is turned, to be connected with it at C. and so far at the other end as to receive the whirl designed for putting the clearer in motion. The brass boxes, in which the axis of the cylinder runs, consist each of two parts; c, and, d. Fig. 7. The lower part d, is sunk into the wood of the frame to keep it firm and motionless; and the upper part, c, is kept in its place by 2 small Iron bolts, H, H, headed on the lower end at, H. These bolts are inserted into the under side of the rail or scantling of the frame and continued up through both parts of the box. A portion of the bolts, as H, a, should be square, to prevent them from turning. The upper part of the box, c, is screwed down close, with a nut on the end of each bolt. At, e, is a perforation for conveying oil to the axis.

After the cylinder, with its axis is fitted and rounded with exactness, the circular part of its surface is filled with teeth set in annular rows. The spaces d, e, f, g, h, Fig. 2 between the rows of teeth must be so large as to admit a cotton seed to turn round freely in them every way: and ought not to be less than seven sixteenths of an inch.

The spaces k, l, m, n, &c, Fig. 1, between the teeth, in the same row, must be so small as not to admit a seed or a half seed. They ought not to exceed one twelfth of an inch, and I think about one sixteenth of an inch the best.

The teeth are made and set in the following manner: Take common Iron wire* about No. 12. 13 or 14: draw it about three sizes less, without nealing, in order to stiffen it. Cut it into pieces four or five feet in length and streighten them. Then with a machine, somewhat like that used for cutting Nails, cut the wire into pieces about an inch long. In the jaws of this machine at, o, Fig. 10. are fixed the two pieces of steel, d, d,[5] which are pressed together; as may be observed from the figure, by the operation of a compound lever. These pieces of steel are so set in, that upon being pressed together, their approaching surfaces, meet only on the side next to, d, d, leaving between them a wedge like opening, which enlarges as the distance from the place of contact increases. On the side, d, d, about an inch distant from the place of contact, is fixed a guage. The wire is inserted on the side opposite, d, d, and thrust thro' to the guage. Then on forcing down the lever[6] the wire is separated, leaving that end of the wire next the side, d, d, cut smoothly and and transversely off, and the end of the other part flatted like a wedge. The flatted end is then thrust forward to the guage and the same operation is repeated. In this manner the teeth are cut of equal length, with one end flatted and the other cut directly off. Flatting one end of the wire is beneficial in two ways: 1, The flatted ends of the teeth are driven into the wood with more[7] ease and exactness: and 2, it prevents them from turning after they are set. To prevent the wires from bending while driving, they are holden with pliers the jaws of which ought to be about half an inch in width, with a corresponding transverse groove in each jaw. Thus holden, the teeth are, with a light hammer, driven, one by one, into the cylinder, perpendicular to its axis. Then with a tool, like a chissel or common screw Driver each tooth is inclined directly towards the tangent to that point of the circle, into which it is set, till the inclination is such that the tooth and tangent form an angle of about 55 or 60 Degrees. If this inclination be greater, the teeth will not take sufficient hold of the Cotton, if it be less there will be more difficulty in disengaging the Cotton from the teeth, after it is separated from the seeds.

When the teeth are all set they should be cut of an equal length. In order for this take a crooked gage Fig. 8 having two prongs q. r.; the curvature of which corresponds with that of the cylinder. This gage is merely a crooked fork, the thickness of whose prongs or tines, as represented between s. and t. Fig. 9 equalizes the length of the teeth, and is applied to the cylinder, with one tine on each side of an annular row. With a pair of cutting pliers, cut the teeth 1.2.3. &c off even with the gage, then slide it along to 6.7.8. &c. and so proceed till you have trimmed all the teeth to an equal length. This done put the cylinder into a lathe and with a file bring the teeth to a kind of angular point, resembling a wire flatted and cut obliquely. After the teeth are brought to a proper shape, smooth them with a polishing file and the cylinder will be finished.

---

* Steel wire would perhaps be best if it were not too expensive.

Remark. Though the dimensions of the cylinder may be varied, at pleasure, yet it is thought that those described are the best, being more easily made and kept in repair, than those of a larger size. The timber should[8] be quarter stuff, i.e. a quarter of the Trunk of the Tree, otherwise it will crack in seasoning. It must also be of wood of an equal density such as beech, maple, black birch &c. In oak and many other kinds of wood, there are spaces between the grains which are not so hard as the grains themselves: and the teeth driven into those spaces would not stand sufficiently firm, while the grains are so hard as to prevent the teeth from being driven without bending.

III. The breastwork Fig. 11. and B. Fig. 1. and Fig. 2. is fixed above the cylinder, parallel and contiguous to the same. It has transverse grooves or openings 1.2.3.4 &c through which the rows of teeth pass as the cylinder revolves: and its use is to obstruct the seeds while the Cotton is carried forward through the grooves by the teeth. That side of the breastwork next the cylinder should be made of brass or Iron, that it may be the more durable. Its face or surface a.x. Fig. 1. ought to make an angle with the tangent x.z. less than 50 Degrees. A tooth in passing from k up to the breastwork B. fastens itself upon a certain quantity of Cotton, which is still connected with its seeds. The seeds being too large to pass through the breastwork are there stopped, while the cotton is forced thro' the groove[9] and disengaged from the seeds. Now if the point of the tooth enters the groove before the root or that part next the cylinder, it carries through all which it has collected in coming from k; but if the root of the tooth enter the groove before the point, part of the Cotton fastened on it, will slide off: and this latter case is preferable as it helps to give the Cotton a rotary motion in the hopper. The thickness of the breastwork, or the distance from a. to i. Fig. 1. should be about $2\frac{1}{2}$ or 3 inches, in proportion to the length of the cotton. It should be such that the cotton which is carried through by the teeth may be disconnected from that which is left in the hopper before it leaves the grooves; otherwise that which is carried partly through the breastwork will by the motion of that with which it is connected in the hopper become so collected and knotted at i, as to obstruct and bend the teeth.*

The under part of the breastwork next the cylinder, ought, as has before been observed, to be made of iron or brass. It may be cast either in a solid piece and the openings for the passage of the teeth cut with a saw and files: or in as many parts as there are spaces between the several rows of teeth in the cylinder and in form of Fig. 12. and the pieces set, by means of a shank or tenon,[10] in a groove running lengthwise along the wooden part of the breastwork.

The breastwork, described, if properly constructed, will it is thought answer every valuable purpose. But I shall mention one of a different construction which I have used with success, and is made in the following manner. Form a breastwork of the same shape and dimensions as the one before described, entirely of wood. Place a bar of wood one inch below the cylinder and parallel to it. Then with straps or ribs of Iron, brass or tin plate connect the breastwork of wood with the bar below. The ribs or straps must be so applied as to sit close to the surface of the cylinder between the wooden breastwork and the bar, and of a width that will permit them to work freely between the annular rows of teeth.[11] That end of each strap which is fastened to the breastwork should divide widthwise into two parts, one of which should pass along the lower surface of the breastwork and the other run up its front. In Fig. 14.B. is the wooden

_____

* If the[12] perforation about $\frac{3}{16}$ of an inch be made thro' the breastwork at the upper part or end of each groove, the metal part need not be more than $\frac{3}{8}$ of an inch thick.

breastwork: D. the bar below the cylinder; the dotted circle b.b. the cylinder; e.e. the strap; c. the place where the strap divides; and a.a.a. wood screws or nails with which the strap is made fast to the bar and breastwork.

IV. The clearer, C, Fig. 1. is constructed in the following manner. Take an iron axis perfectly similar to that described as extending through the cylinder, except that it need not be so large nor fitted for the application of a winch. Frame together crosswise at right angles two pieces of timber of suitable size and of a length about equal to the diameter of the cylinder, so as to make the four arms equal in length, and insert the axis thro' the centers of two crosses or frames of this kind. Let their distance from each other be one third of the length of the cylinder and make them fast on the axis. The arms of the[13] two crosses are then connected by four pieces, of the same length of the cylinder:[14] equidistant from the axis, and parallel to the same, and to each other. In each of the parallel pieces, on the outside or side opposite the axis, a channel is made lengthwise for the reception of a brush. The brush is made of Hogs bristles, set in a manner somewhat similar to that of setting the[15] reeds in a Weavers Sleigh. Between two strips of wood about $\frac{1}{8}$ of an inch in thickness and half an inch in breadth, is placed a small quantity of bristles; then a strong thread or twine is wound round the sticks, close to the bristles: then another quantity of bristles is inserted &c. till a brush is formed, equal in length to the cylinder.* The bristles on the side a.a. Fig. 6. are smeared with pitch or rosin and seared down with a hot iron even with the wood, to prevent them from drawing out. On the other side they are cut with a chisel to the length of about an inch from the wood. A brush of this kind is fixed in each of the before mentioned channels.

The boxes as well as axis of the clearer, are like those of the cylinder. The clearer is placed horizontal with the cylinder, parallel to it and at such a distance, that while it revolves the ends of the bristles strike with a small degree of friction on the cylinders surface. Its use is to brush the cotton from the teeth after it is forced through the grooves and separated from its seeds. It turns in a direction contrary from that of the cylinder, and should so far outrun[16] it, as completely to sweep its whole surface.†

A clearer with two brushes may be made by simply screwing upon the axis the board K. Fig. 4. and another similar board on the opposite side, which leaves spaces for the insertion of the brushes s.s. The clearer may also be formed of a cylinder with grooves running lengthwise in it for the reception of the brushes; or in any other way, which may be found[17] convenient.

The number of brushes in the clearer is not material; but[18] let it be observed that the distance from, e, to e, Fig. 1. between the brushes, must be at least 4 or 5 inches; otherwise the cotton will wind up round the clearer. The surface of the clearer moving much faster than that of the cylinder, the brushes sweep off the Cotton from the teeth. The air put in motion by the clearer, and the centrifugal force of the cotton disengage it from the brushes. Note, It is best to set the brushes in the grooves in such a manner, that the bristles will make an angle of about[19] 20 or 25.° with the diameter of the clearer, in the direction e,o, Fig. 1. By that means the Bristles fall more perpendicularly on the teeth, strike them more forcibly, and clear[20] off the cotton more effectually.

---

* Perhaps nailing these[21] straps[22] together would be better[23] than winding them with twine.

† The brushes may be fixed in a stock which is moveable by screws so as to bring them nearer or carry them farther from the cylinder.

The clearer is put in motion by the cylinder, by means of a band and whirls. These whirls are plain wheels of solid wood about $2\frac{1}{2}$ or 3. inches thick. Their periphery is a spherical surface swelling at the center, and sloping off at the edges. To give them the proper shape, take a perfect globe of the same Diameter as your intended whirl; inscribe upon it a circle dividing it into two equal parts: then cut the globe on each side, parallel to the plane of this circle, and at the distance from it, of half the thickness of your whirl. On these whirls runs a leather band, the breadth of which answers to the thickness of the whirls. The band may be broader or narrower and the whirls thicker or thinner in proportion as the resistance to be overcome is greater or less. The reason for giving the whirls this shape is to secure them the better from being unbanded. A band of this kind always inclines to the highest place on the whirl, and is much less liable to be cast off from the work, when it runs on a spherical surface, than when it runs in a groove in the periphery of the whirl.

The whirls are four in number, and must be so arranged as to make their central planes coincident. The whirl E, Fig. 3. is fixed upon the end of the axis of the cylinder without the frame, and the button A. Fig. 5. is screwed on with the screwdriver B. to keep the whirl in its place. L is put upon the axis of the clearer in the same manner. P.Q. whose axes are pivots made fast in the frame, are false whirls added for two purposes. 1, to make the clearer turn in a contrary direction from the cylinder; 2, for the purpose of doubling the band more completely round the small whirl L. so as to bring a greater portion of the whirls surface into contact with the band, increase the friction and consequently turn the whirl more forcibly. The first of these purposes might be accomplished by the addition of one false whirl, but the second not so fully without two. The dotted line, w.v. represents the band. The diameters of the whirls E.L. should be so proportioned as to produce a proper degree of velocity in the clearer. The [24] axis of the whirl Q is fixed in a plate of Iron, which is moveable in a groove in the side of the frame, and the band is made tighter or looser by moving the plate. [25] This arrangement of whirls produces the same movement as a cogwheel and pinion, with much less friction and expence, and without the ratling noise, which is always caused by the quick motion of Cog-wheels.

V. One side of the Hopper is formed by the breastwork, the two ends by the frame, and the other side is moveable so that as the quantity of Cotton put in at one time, decreases, it may slide up nearer the cylinder, and make the Hopper narrower. This is necessary in order to give the seeds a rotary motion in the hopper, by bringing them repeatedly up to the cylinder till they are entirely stripped of the cotton. D. Fig. 1 is a section of the moveable part of the hopper. The part from H. to I. should be concave on the side next the breastwork, or rather it should be a portion of a hollow cylinder. Between H. and y. is a crate of wire thro' which the sands and the seeds as soon as they are thoroughly cleansed, fall into a receptacle below. The crate may be either fixed in the frame or connected with the moveable part of the hopper. The wires of which the crate is made should be large and placed perpendicular to the cylinder, that the cotton may turn the more easily in the hopper.

A few additional remarks will sufficiently shew the construction, use and operation of this machine.

The cotton is put into the hopper I.D.H.k.a.u.s. Fig. 1. in as large a quantity as the cylinder will put in motion. Some of the seeds become stripped sooner than others. If it be black seed Cotton, the seeds being smooth, will most of them fall through the crate as soon as they are clean, but a considerable part of the green seeds which are thus denominated from being covered with a kind of green coat, resembling Velvet will continue in the hopper. It will not answer therefore to supply it gradually as the quantity in it diminishes, because the seeds will soon grow cumbrous and by their constant intervention prevent the teeth from attaching themselves to the Cotton so fast as they otherwise would: but one hopper full must be finished, the moveable part drawn back, the hopper cleared of [26] seeds and then supplied with Cotton anew. There is a partition y.w. under the cylinder, on the left hand of which or the side beneath the hopper, the seeds fall, and the clean cotton on the other side. There may be a receptacle for the clean cotton in the frame: but it is best to have an opening through the wall or partition into a contiguous room, then place the end of the machine against this opening and let the cotton fly into a close room; [27] or it may fall through an opening in the floor into a room below. This machine may be turned by Horses or Water with the greatest ease. It requires no other attendance than putting the Cotton into the hopper with a basket or fork, narrowing the hopper when necessary and letting out the seeds after they are clean. One of its peculiar excellencies is, that it cleanses the kind called green seed Cotton, almost as fast as the black seed. If the machinery is moved by water it is thought it will diminish the usual labour of cleaning the green seed cotton at least forty nine fiftieths.

The foregoing is a Description of the machine for cleansing Cotton, alluded to in a Petition of the Subscriber, Dated Philadelphia June 20th. 1793, and lodged in the Office of the Secretary of State alledging that he the Subscriber is the Inventor of said Machine, and signifying his desire of obtaining an exclusive property in the same.   ELI WHITNEY
Signed in presence of
Chauncey Goodrich Counsellor at law Hartford.
John Allen Counsellor at law Litchfield.

State of Connecticut Ss. City of New Haven

I Elizur Goodrich Esqre. Alderman for said City, and Not. Public, by lawful authority admitted and sworn, residing in said City, and by law authorized to administer Oaths, Do hereby certify, declare and make known to whom it doth or may concern: That at said City on this Twenty Eighth day of October one thousand seven hundred and ninety three, Eli Whitney of the County of Worcester in the Commonwealth of Massachusetts, now resident in said City, personally appeared before me, the said Alderman and Notary, and made solemn Oath, that he does verily believe that he the said Whitney is the True inventor and Discoverer of the machine for Ginning Cotton, a Description whereof is hereto annexed by me the said Alderman and Notary by my Seal Notarial, and that he the said Whitney verily believes that a Machine of similar construction hath never before been known, or used.

In Testimony whereof I the said Alderman and Notary, have hereunto set my Hand and Seal at the City aforesaid on the Day above said.   ELIZUR GOODRICH Alderman & Not. Public

L.S.

Tr (GEpFAR: RG 21, U.S. Circuit Court, District of Georgia, Savannah, Mixed Cases); copy made from lost original, with appended printed form, dated 27 Apr. 1804 and signed by Secretary of State James Madison, certifying, with reference to the patent and its annexed short description (Enclosure III below), as well as to the long description, with its accompanying drawing (Enclosure II below), that "the annexed Drawings and Writings are True Copies, duly compared with the originals, and with authentic Records thereof in my office." Tr (DNA: RG 241, Restored Patent Specifications); copy made 2 May 1841 from lost Tr containing certification by

Madison of 25 Nov. 1803, the text being subjoined to the certification; with copying errors and variations in wording, punctuation, and paragraphing, only the most important being noted below. FC (CtY: Whitney Papers); with copying errors, omissions, and other variations in wording, only the most important being noted below. MS (same); entirely in Whitney's hand; undated, but probably predating lost original, notwithstanding Whitney's later notation (see below), being shorter, less detailed, and varying in structure and many important particulars—perhaps the most significant being a footnote to the section describing the teeth of the cylinder in which Whitney allowed for substitutes that included "Teeth set in right lines like a number of saws put into one frame"—none of which have been noted below; at head of text: "Description of a Machine Invented by Eli Whitney of the Commonwealth of Massachusetts in the United States for the purpose of Ginning Cotton or seperating the Staple from the Seeds; and opening and preparing it for manufactures; also for preparing Sheep's Wool, hair and other materials for manufacturing"; with notation added later by Whitney: "This paper is dated Oct. 28 1793 and was written before the patent was obtained. EW." For the substitution of saw teeth in the gins of Whitney's competitors, who claimed that this alteration created an original invention, Whitney's contention in his successful patent infringement suits that he had conceived of the use of saw teeth before deciding on the wire teeth

specified in the patent, and his later use of saw teeth in the gins he manufactured, see Ralph W. Thomas, "Historical Society Finds Original Eli Whitney Cotton Gin," New Haven Colony Historical Society, *Journal*, VIII, No. 3 (1959), 24.

[1] FC and Tr in RG 241: "cleaning."
[2] Preceding two words omitted in FC.
[3] FC: "three."
[4] Tr in RG 241: "drawn."
[5] FC here adds "Fig. 13."
[6] Tr in RG 241: "levers."
[7] Word omitted in Tr in RG 241.
[8] FC here reads "not be a larger portion of a tree than."
[9] FC: "grooves."
[10] FC here adds "left for that purpose on the upper part."
[11] Tr in RG 241: "steel."
[12] FC and Tr in RG 241: "a."
[13] Preceding three words omitted in FC.
[14] Preceding seven words omitted in FC.
[15] Word omitted in FC and in Tr in RG 241.
[16] FC: "out-turn."
[17] Word omitted in Tr in RG 241.
[18] Word omitted in Tr in RG 241.
[19] Word omitted in Tr in RG 241.
[20] FC: "clean."
[21] Tr in RG 241: "three."
[22] FC: "strips."
[23] Remainder of sentence omitted in FC.
[24] Tr in RG 241: "This."
[25] FC here adds "in the groove."
[26] FC: "cleansed of the."
[27] FC: "into the room."

II
Drawing of the Cotton Gin

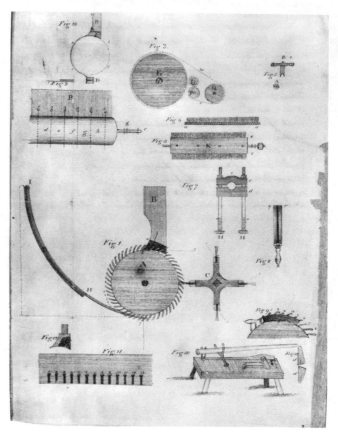

Tr (GEpFAR: RG 21, U.S. Circuit Court, District of Georgia, Savannah, Mixed Cases); copy made from lost original, with minor copying errors as evidenced by the omission of several reference points in Enclosure I above; certified by Secretary of State James Madison on 27 Apr. 1804 (see note to Enclosure I above).

A drawing made at the Patent Office on 18 Mch. 1845 and signed by Commissioner of Patents Henry L. Ellsworth (DNA: RG 241, Restored Patent Drawings), a reconstructed model made around the same time, and subsequent plates based on the reconstructed drawing vary significantly from the drawing reproduced above and were not based on Whitney's drawing, but were derived instead from the long description (see Enclosure I above) and from examination of an actual cotton gin or one of the early models then in possession of the Whitney family (P. J. Federico, "Records of Eli Whitney's Cotton Gin Patent," *Technology and Culture*, I [1960], 172-3, 175-6n; F. L. Lewton, "Historical Notes on the Cotton Gin," Smithsonian Institution, *Annual Report* [1937], 555-8).

[248]

III

Short Description of the Cotton Gin

A Short Description of the Machine invented by the Subscriber[1] for Ginning Cotton.[2]

The principal parts of this machine are, 1. The Frame. 2d. The cylinder. 3 The breastwork. 4 The clearer, and 5, The Hopper.

1st. The frame by which the whole work is supported and kept together, is of a square or parallelogramic form and proportioned to the other parts as may be most convenient.

2. The cylinder is of wood; its form is perfectly described by its name, and its dimensions may be from six to nine inches diameter, and from two to five feet in length.[3] This cylinder is placed horizontally across the frame, leaving room for the clearer on one side, and the Hopper on the other. In the cylinder is fixed an Iron axis which may pass quite through, or consist only of gudgeons driven into each end.

There are shoulders on this axis, to prevent any horizontal variation, and it extends so far without the frame as to admit a winch at one end, by which it is put in motion, and so far at the other end as to receive the whirl by which the clearer is turned. The surface of the cylinder is filled with teeth, set in annular rows,[4] which are at such a distance from each other as to admit a cotton seed to play freely[5] in the space between them. The space between each tooth in the same row, is so small as not to admit a seed, nor a half seed to enter it. These teeth are made of stiff Iron wire; driven in[6] the wood of the cylinder.[7] The teeth are all inclined the same way and in such a manner, that the angle, included between the tooth and a tangent drawn from the point into which the tooth is driven, will be about 55 or 60 Degrees.[8] The gudgeons of the cylinder run[9] in brass boxes, each of which is in two parts, one of which is fixed in the wood of the frame, and the other is confined down[10] upon the[11] Axis with screws.[12]

III. The breastwork is fixed above the cylinder, parallel and contiguous to the same, It has transverse grooves or openings thro' which the rows of teeth pass as the cylinder revolves and its use is to obstruct the seeds while the cotton is carried forward through the grooves by the teeth. The thickness of the breastwork is two and half or three inches, and the under side of it is made of iron or brass.

IV. The clearer is placed horizontal with and parallel to the cylinder. Its length is the same as that of the cylinder, and its diameter is proportioned by convenience. There are two, four or more brushes or[13] rows of bristles, fixed in the surface of the clearer in such a manner that the ends of the bristles will sweep the surface of the[14] cylinder. Its axis and boxes are similar to those of the cylinder. It is turned by means of a band and whirls; moves in[15] contrary direction from the cylinder, by which it is put in motion and so far outruns it, as to sweep the cotton from the teeth as fast as it is carried through the breastwork. The periphery of the whirls is spherical and the band a broad strap of Leather.

V. One side of the hopper is formed by the breastwork, the two ends by the frame,[16] and the other side is moveable from and towards the breastwork, so as to make the hopper more or less capacious.

The cotton is put into the hopper, carried through the breastwork by the teeth, brushed off from the teeth by the clearer and flies off from the clearer, with the assistance of the air,[17] by its own centrifugal force. The Machine is turned by Water, Horses or in any other way, as is most convenient.

There are several modes of making the various parts of this machine, which, together with their particular shape and formation are pointed out and[18] explained[19] in a Description with Drawings, attested as the act directs,[20] and lodged in the Office of the Secretary of State.   ELI WHITNEY[21]
Signed in presence of
Chauncey Goodrich
    Councillor at Law Hartford
John Allen
    Councillor at Law Litchfield

Tr (GEpFAR: RG 21, U.S. Circuit Court, District of Georgia, Savannah, Mixed Cases); copy made from lost original; undated, but presumably notarized on 28 Oct. 1793 with Enclosure I; subjoined to and forming part of Tr of 14 Mch. 1794 patent granting exclusive rights to run fourteen years from 6 Nov. 1793, George Washington and Secretary of State Edmund Randolph being signatory and countersignatory, with certification by Attorney General William Bradford, all in a clerk's hand; at head of text: "The Schedule referred to in these Letters Patent and making part of the same containing a Description in the words of the said Eli Whitney himself of an improvement in the mode of Ginning Cotton"; certified by Secretary of State James Madison (see note to Enclosure I above). Tr (DNA: RG 241, Restored Patent Specifications); undated; copy made 2 May 1841 from lost Tr of 14 Mch. 1794 patent and containing copy of certification by Madison of 26 Nov. 1803. Dft (CtY: Whitney Papers); undated; heavily emended text in Whitney's hand and signed by him, the emended text through the first sentence of second section being recopied fair on a separate sheet and the top of another (see note 3 below); at head of text, possibly being partly in Whitney's hand: "The true Copy. Phl. 8 March 94"; with notation in an unidentified hand describing the lost original: "(The schedule is written on parchment which is seperate from the Patent and connected with the Patent by a ribbon the ends of which are brought under the seal)." First printed in *American Farmer*, IV (1823), 380-1, with minor variations in wording and the addition of symbols and some amplifying language to key the text to accompanying illustrations of the model.

[1] Preceding four words interlined in recopied portion of Dft (see note 3 below),

where Whitney had first written the same words below this heading.
[2] In canceled portion of Dft (see following note) this heading reads: "A ⟨General⟩ Short Description ⟨of Whitney's new invented Cotton Gin⟩ of a machine for ginning cotton without refferences to the Drawings." In recopied portion of Dft the following notation by Whitney is circled: "a description whereof is given in the words of the said A.B. himself in the schedule hereto annexed, and is made a part of these Presents."
[3] Emended Dft to this point recopied fair by Whitney on a separate page and (as recorded in note 21 below) keyed by him to replace the canceled text, which has only slightly variant wording except for heading given in preceding note.
[4] In Dft Whitney here canceled "[. . .] the distance of about half an inch from each other. The [space?] between [each tooth?] in the same row is about one fourteenth of an inch."
[5] In Dft Whitney here canceled "every way."
[6] Dft and Tr in RG 241: "into."
[7] In Dft Whitney here canceled "and of an equal length."
[8] In Dft Whitney here canceled "[. . .]. After the teeth receive their inclination they are brought to an equal length and pointed."
[9] In Dft Whitney first wrote "This Cylinder runs" before revising the sentence to begin as above.
[10] Word interlined in Dft.
[11] In Dft Whitney here canceled what appears to be "top."
[12] In Dft Whitney here canceled "Remark."
[13] Preceding two words interlined in Dft.
[14] Preceding three words interlined in Dft.

15 Dft and Tr in RG 241 here add "a."

16 Word interlined in Dft in place of what appears to be "Clearer."

17 Preceding clause interlined in Dft.

18 In Dft Whitney here canceled "discussed."

19 In Dft Whitney here interlined and canceled "by the inventor."

20 Preceding clause interlined in Dft in place of "(*Dated Sept.* AD One thousand seven hundred and ninety three).

21 In Dft remainder of text is written on second separate page, as described in note 3 above.

From Jean Pierre Blanchard

MONSIEUR   Philadelphie ce 16 8bre. 1793

Je ne m'attendais pas en quittant l'Europe a ce qui m'arrive aujourdhui dans ce continent. Heureux dans tous mes voyages, je n'avais garde de prévoir le sort funeste qui m'était reservé a Philadelphie: Après bien des traveaux et des succès, il ne me reste plus que l'honneur et la vie et je vois avec douleur que je ne puis conserver l'un Sans détruire l'autre, car si je quitte Philadelphie, ainsi que j'aurais dû prudemment le faire il y a longtems, de petites dettes criardes que j'ai été forcé de contracter, feront beaucoup de bruit, on ne se persuadera pas que mon intention est de ne faire de tort a qui que ce Soit: Si je reste, le danger est d'autant plus émminent que j'ai des terreurs paniques de la maladie qui continue ses ravages.

Je m'adresse donc à vous, Monsieur, sans rougir et avec d'autant plus de confiance que seul dans ce pays vous savez apprécier les artistes et leurs malheurs: Je vous supplie Monsieur de déterminer Monsieur le Général Washington a me faire un prêt de 400 dollars, je m'engagerai sur mon honneur de les rendre avant le printems prochain, époque à laquelle je quitterai l'amérique, après en avoir visité les principales villes, pour retourner en Europe. Ayez s'il vous plait la bonté Monsieur d'observer a Monsieur le Président que c'est la prémiere fois que je me trouve obligé a faire un emprunt et qu'Etranger dans ce pays je ne puis absolument m'adresser a nulle autre personne, car ce n'est qu'après voir bien reflechi, consideré et consulté, que je fais cette demande.

Je signerai l'obligation telle qu'il vous plaira me la faire passer et y ferai honneur dans Son tems.

Je ne doute pas Monsieur, que vos momens ne soyent prétieux, mais néamoins j'espere qu'a cause des arts que vous aimez a protéger, vous daignerez prendre ma lettre en considération en apuyant ma demande auprès de Monsieur le Président.

Le tems est pressant Monsieur, jamais position n'égala la mienne; ce n'est que la cruelle alternative ou je Suis qui me determine a prendre le seul et dernier party qui me reste.

Qui aurait jamais pu Se persuader qu'après tant de traveaux et de

Succès couronnès en Europe, je serais reduit, un jour, a faire un tel emprunt en Amérique? C'est le sort qui le veut il faut Si Soumettre, j'espere que je serai plus heureux dans les autres villes du continent: je viens de joindre a mes opérations de Phisique et de mécanique, un Automatte qui imite parfaitement la nature, fait diverses fonctions de l'homme avec sa même agilité et souplesse, je ne doute pas que cette piece, unique dans son genre avec mon Carosse curieux et l'aërostation ne fassent beaucoup d'effet dans les autres villes ou je me propose d'aller sitôt que j'aurai reçu l'honneur de votre réponse Sans laquelle je reste dans le plus grand embaras et ne puis prendre aucun party. Je suis avec beaucoup de respect Monsieur Votre très humble et très obeissant serviteur   BLANCHARD

RC (DLC); endorsed by TJ as received 9 Nov. 1793 and so recorded in SJL.

For Blanchard's aeronautical activities in Philadelphia, see note to Caspar Wistar, Jr., to TJ, [9 Jan. 1793].

From Peter Walsh

Cadiz, 16 Oct. 1793. On the 10th his house of Dominick Terry & Company received an 8 Oct. letter from Humphreys at Gibraltar advising of a twelve-month Algerine Portuguese truce and the sailing of an Algerine fleet on the evening of the 5th westward past the straits for a suspected cruise against American shipping, information which it immediately communicated to the masters of the 19 American vessels here. It was not in the firm's power to comply with Humphreys's direction to charter immediately at government expense a neutral vessel to bring this news to America, but it did advise him that they would charter the fast-sailing American brig *Two Sisters*, commanded by Captain Alcors Sheffield and owned by John Jackson of New York, if Humphreys promised on behalf of the government that the insurance of 1,500 "Hard Dollars" required by Sheffield for himself and his mate, Abel Bunker, would be paid in America. Humphreys replied on 14 Oct. that he could not promise, but gave assurances that he would use his influence with the government to respond generously in the event of damages to any vessel carrying to America his original dispatches to the Secretary of State about the Algerine fleet. Because of this assurance, as well as his confidence that his country would protect him and his crew if they were captured by the Algerines on this perilous mission and compensate Jackson justly for losses, Sheffield has agreed to sail in the morning with Humphreys's dispatches, if he can get out. There is no doubt Sheffield will elude the Algerines and perform a useful service for his country. As yet there has been no news of any American vessels being taken, and he hopes there will be few such captures. A schooner from Boston and a brig from Virginia arrived here on 10 and 11 Oct. without seeing or hearing anything about the Algerines. In line with Humphreys's advice, vessels now here will be cautious about leaving. He has arranged with the master of the tower to hoist an alarm signal whenever an American vessel comes in sight and requested masters of all neutral vessels to inform every American ship they meet at sea about the Algerine danger, the only measures it is in his power to take. On 20 Sep. a Spanish frigate brought here, on suspicion of carrying French-owned cargoes, the *Rooksby* of Portsmouth, New Hampshire, and the *Greenway* of Boston, both bound from Bordeaux to St. Thomas. The suspicion being proved, the ships are expected to be condemned, but he hopes to get them freed and the freights paid, though both masters are still confined on their ships and townspeople forbidden to speak with them. He has informed Carmichael about these two ships and hopes that Yznardi when he arrives will be able to redress the many disadvantages under which American vessels now labor.

Dupl (DNA: RG 59, CD); 3 p.; in a clerk's hand, with dateline, part of complimentary close, internal address, and signature by Walsh; at foot of text: "Honble: Ths: Jefferson Esqr:—Philada:"; endorsed by Edmund Randolph as received 23 Jan. 1794. Missing RC recorded in SJL as received 18 Dec. 1793.

Peter Walsh, a British merchant and member of the mercantile firm of Dominick Terry & Company of Cadiz, had spent more than three years in the United States and become an American citizen. Walsh had met TJ during a visit to New York in 1790 and may have worked at that time with his brother Philip to promote American trade with Spain and solicit the appointment of their brother John, the senior member of the firm, as American consul at Cadiz. After his retirement as President, TJ ordered wine from Walsh, who by then was living in Cette (Knox, *Barbary Wars*, I, 51; Jacob Vernes to TJ, 3 Nov. 1789; Samuel Smith to George Washington, 2 Mch. 1790, DLC: Washington Papers, Applications for Office; Vol. 17: 250, 254n, 255n, s.v. "Welsh"; TJ to Walsh, 27 Mch. 1811; Walsh to TJ, 10 Oct. 1811).

TJ submitted this letter to the President on 18 Dec. 1793 and received it back the same day (Washington, *Journal*, 269).

From Peter Walsh

Cadiz, 17 Oct. 1793. In addition to what he wrote this morning by the *Fair Hebe*, two American brigs and a schooner have just arrived with the *Nancy*, Captain Butler, a ship bound from New York to Barcelona that managed to evade Algerine capture by means of its superior sailing in shallow waters, but Butler fears that the Algerines captured an American sloop. "Humanity Shudder's for the fate of those who may have the misfortune to fall into the hands of the Pirates."

RC (DNA: RG 59, CD); 1 p.; unaddressed; endorsed by TJ as received 18 Dec. 1793 and so recorded in SJL. Printed in Knox, *Barbary Wars*, I, 52.

TJ submitted this letter to the President on 18 Dec. 1793 and received it back the same day (Washington, *Journal*, 269). For Walsh's first letter of this date as well as his later letters to the Secretary of State not received by TJ, see Appendix I.

To George Washington

DEAR SIR   Monticello Oct. 17. 1793.

I was the day before yesterday honored with your favor of the 7th. inst. by post[1] and yesterday I received that of the 11th. by express from Colo. Carrington. I will take care to be at Germantown by the 1st. of the month. As the ploughing thro the roads of the month of January would be disagreeable with my own horses, I shall send them back from Fredericksburg, for which place I will set out tomorrow (Friday) sennight, in order to take the stage from thence of Monday the 28th. This of course will deprive me of the honor of waiting on you at Mount Vernon, but perhaps I may have that of seeing you on the road.

I have carefully considered the question Whether the President may call Congress to any other place than that to which they have adjourned themselves, and think he cannot have such a right unless it has been given him by the constitution or the laws, and that neither of these has given it. The only circumstance [2] which he can alter, as to their meeting, is that of *time* by calling them at an *earlier day* than that to which they stand adjourned, but no power to change the place is given. Mr. Madison happened to come here yesterday, after the reciept of your letter. I proposed the question to him, and he thinks there was particular caution intended and used in the diction of the Constitution to avoid giving the President any power over the place of meeting; lest he should exercise it with local partialities.

With respect to the Executive, the Residence law has fixed our offices at Philadelphia till the year 1800. and therefore it seems necessary that we should get as near them as we may with safety.

As to the place of meeting for the legislature, were we authorized to decide that question I should think it right to have it in some place in Pensylvania, in consideration of the principles of the Residence bill, and that we might furnish no pretext to that state to infringe them hereafter. I am quite unacquainted with Reading, and it's means of accomodation. It's situation is perhaps as little objectionable as that of Lancaster, and less so than Trenton or perhaps Wilmington. However I think we have nothing to do with the question, and that Congress must meet in Philadelphia, even if it be in the open feilds, to adjourn themselves to some other place.—I am extremely afraid something has happened to Mr. Bankson, on whom I relied for continuance at my office. For two posts past I have not received any letter from him, nor dispatches of any kind. This involves new fears for the duplicates of those to Mr. Morris. I have the honor to be with sentiments of the most perfect esteem & attachment, Dear Sir Your most obedt & most humble servt

Th: Jefferson

P.S. Mr. Randolph's and Mr. Trumbul's letters are returned.

RC (DNA: RG 59, MLR); endorsed by Washington. PrC (DLC). Tr (Lb in DNA: RG 59, SDC). Enclosures: see those listed at Washington to TJ, 11 Oct. 1793.

Washington had solicited advice from the Cabinet and James Madison as to whether he could constitutionally CALL CONGRESS TO ANY OTHER PLACE than Philadelphia (see

Fitzpatrick, *Writings*, xxxiii, 107-9, 121-7, 130-1; and the responses in Madison to Washington, 24 Oct. 1793, Madison, *Papers*, xv, 129-31; Hamilton to Washington, 24 Oct. 1793, Syrett, *Hamilton*, xv, 373-6; and Edmund Randolph to Washington, 24 Oct., 2 Nov. 1793, Charles F. Jenkins, *Washington in Germantown* [Philadelphia, 1905], 81-5, 119-31). Secretary of War Henry Knox shared the opinion of Hamilton and Randolph that the President could assemble the legislature elsewhere if extraordinary necessity so dictated, and Washington apparently had similar views, but on 2 Nov. 1793, opting to follow the course recommended by Randolph, the President decided to take no action unless Congress failed to meet in Philadelphia on the appointed day, thus leaving the way open for his interposition. The decision proved to be a sound one, for conditions in the capital had improved sufficiently by December to enable Congress to meet there on the stated day (TJ to Madison, 2 Nov. 1793).

[1] Preceding two words interlined.
[2] Word interlined in place of "case in."

To Richard Hanson

Sir   Monticello Oct. 18. 1793.

Your favor of the 7th. inst. was brought me by our last post. The bonds you received on the sale of negroes, those of Mr. Ronald for my Cumberland lands which you have also received, and those for my Elk hill lands, will, according to my calculation completely discharge my bonds to Mr. Jones, both as to sum and time, to within less than an hundred pounds of the last paiment. The Elk hill bonds are in possession of Mr. Daniel Hylton, on whom I now inclose you an order for them. The omission of this order has been owing to the impossibility of turning one moment during the last summer to my own affairs. I shall return here to live the beginning of January, and will take the first good weather afterwards to meet you at Mr. Eppes's to settle the equivalence of the bonds. I leave this for Philadelphia this day sennight. I am Sir Your very humble servt   Th: Jefferson

PrC (DLC); at foot of text: "Mr. Richard Hanson." Tr (ViU: Edgehill-Randolph Papers); 19th-century copy. Enclosure: TJ to Daniel L. Hylton, 18 Oct. 1793.

Hanson's favor of the 7th. inst., recorded in SJL as received from Petersburg on 15 Oct. 1793, has not been found.

To Daniel L. Hylton

Dear Sir   Monticello Oct. 18. 1793.

The bonds of Banks and Taylor which you were so kind as to take for my Elkhill lands, are destined to discharge bonds of mine to Mr. Jones of Bristol for Farrel & Jones, according to an agreement existing between Mr. Richard Hanson, attorney for Mr. Jones, and myself. Be pleased therefore to deliver the said bonds to Mr. Hanson, taking his receipt for them on the back of this order, which will oblige Dear Sir Your friend & servt   TH: JEFFERSON

PrC (DLC); at foot of text: "Mr. Daniel Hylton." Tr (ViU: Edgehill-Randolph Papers); 19th-century copy. Enclosed in TJ to Richard Hanson, 18 Oct. 1793.

SJL records 18 letters exchanged by TJ and Hylton between 3 Feb. 1794 and 28 Dec. 1798, none of which have been found.

To Martha Jefferson Carr

DEAR SISTER   Monticello Oct. 19. 1793.

I recieved your letter in which you were so kind as to inform me what kinds of supplies might be useful to our sister Marks, and I meant when I should make a purchase of stores for myself in Philadelphia to bring here, to have got some for her also. But the infectious fever which took place there, drove us all away very suddenly, and made it too dangerous to go into the city to purchase: so that I came away without having got any thing for myself. I have therefore thought it would be best to give her a credit with some merchant near her to furnish whatever *she* may call for. But knowing no merchant in her neighborhood, or whether there may be any, I inclose you a lctter of credit for her, in hopes you will direct it to some merchant most likely to carry my wishes into a friendly execution. Knowing nothing of the influence of her husband over her, or of his dispositions, I leave to you to take any precautions, for her or myself, which your better knowlege of circumstances may dictate.

I satisfied Mr. Myers on the subject of your order. Mr. Eppes who has the management of a very large execution for Mr. Wayles's executors, has given me hopes that I shall be able soon to furnish what the present state of your family might find convenient. I rejoice to hear you are likely to become our neighbor. I hope in January to be fixed here myself. My love to your family and am Dear Sister Your affectionate brother   TH: JEFFERSON

PrC (CSmH); at foot of text: "Mrs. Carr." Tr (ViU: Edgehill-Randolph Papers); 19th-century copy. Enclosure: Letter of Credit to Anna Scott Jefferson Marks, 19 Oct. 1793: "I promise to pay to the bearer hereof, on or before the 15th. day of April next, the price of any goods he may have delivered in consequence hereof to Mrs. Anna Scott Marks, on her own order or on that of Mrs. Martha Carr; the account of the same being certified to be just by either of them"

(PrC in DLC, signed by TJ; Tr in ViU: Edgehill-Randolph Papers, 19th-century copy; not recorded in SJL).

Mrs. Carr's LETTER was dated 8 May 1793 (see note to TJ to Mrs. Carr, 14 Apr. 1793). Her brief ORDER of 10 Oct. 1793 asked TJ "to pay to Mr. Myers the Sum of fifty five Pounds Eightteen shillings and two pence" (RC in Vi: Carr-Cary Papers; at foot of text: "Thomas Jefferson

Sec. of State"; with subjoined note in TJ's hand: "Oct. 14. 1793. Accepted to be paid in Richmd. the last day of November next Th: Jefferson"; recorded in SJL as received 14 Oct. 1793, with the notation "by Myers. order").

Earlier this year TJ had honored Mrs. Carr's 2 Feb. 1793 bill of exchange on William Austin for £10.5 Virginia currency or $34.16 (MS in same; consisting of second set of exchange, in Austin's hand, signed by Mrs. Carr; at foot of text: "Thomas Jeffer-

son Esqr. Philadelphia"; with subjoined note by TJ: "Mar. 9. 1793. Accepted to be paid the 4th. of April. Th: Jefferson"; with note on verso by Austin assigning the payment to the Philadelphia mercantile firm of Lott & Higbee; endorsed by TJ: "Carr Martha"). See also MB, 9 Mch., 5 Apr. 1793; and TJ to Mrs. Carr, 14 Apr. 1793.

A letter from Mrs. Carr of 9 May 1794, recorded in SJL as received from "Bear castle" on 17 May 1794, has not been found.

From Edmond Charles Genet

MONSIEUR

New york le 19. 8bre 1793
L'an 2e de la Republique

J'ai pressé autant que je l'ai pu le consul de Philadelphie de me rendre sur le william et la fanny les comptes que vous reclamez. Les affaires multipliées du Consulat avaient retardé la confection de ce travail, et la mort du Consul l'avait encore reculé.

Je viens enfin de recevoir les pièces relatives à cette affaire et[1] j'ai l'honneur de vous les transmetre. Ce sont de simples extraits des procedures par lesquelles, ainsi que vous le verrez, il conste que les prises ne sont point disputables sous le rapport de la violation du territoire, vu qu'il resulte des pieces legales deposées à la chancellerie du Consulat de Philadelphie, que la saisie a eu lieu bien au delà de cette ligne indéfinie qui forme la limite de la juridiction americaine.

Dft (DLC: Genet Papers); in a clerk's hand, unsigned; above salutation: "Le C. Genet à Mr jefferson." Tr (AMAE: CPEU, XXXIX). Recorded in SJL as received 4 Nov. 1793. Enclosures not found, but see TJ to Genet, 8 Nov. 1793, note 10.

[1] Preceding word inserted and remainder of sentence written in the margin.

To Anna Scott Jefferson Marks

DEAR SISTER

Monticello Oct. 19. 1793.

Absence from my country, and unceasing occupations, have prevented me from attending not only to my own concerns, but to those of my friends, and have kept me equally uninformed of both. Without any particular acquaintance with your situation, I have thought it might not always be possible for you to command supplies of those comforts which habit and constitution may have rendered necessary to you. I have therefore hoped you would not deny me the gratification of being useful to you under any difficulties to which you may be liable, and being quite unacquainted in your neighborhood, not knowing what stores are there or whether any, I have inclosed a letter of credit for the present to my sister Carr desiring any person into whose hands she shall put it, to furnish you any thing you may call for, and to apply to me for paiment. I shall consider your free use of this as a proof of your affection and confidence, and assure you it will give me great pleasure. I shall return here in January, no more to leave this place, and when our little family shall once more be together your company will make us all happy, and most particularly him who is with constant & sincere love, Dear Sister Your affectionate brother   TH: JEFFERSON

PrC (DLC); at foot of text: "Mrs. Anna S. Marks." Tr (ViU: Edgehill-Randolph Papers); 19th-century copy.

SJL records 24 letters exchanged by TJ and Mrs. Marks between 8 May 1795 and 11 Jan. 1825, and 13 letters exchanged by TJ and Hastings Marks, her husband, between 1 Dec. 1795 and 12 July 1806, none of which have been found.

From Thomas Paine

Paris,[1] 20 Oct., 1793.

I wrote you by Captain Dominick who was to sail from Havre about the 20th of this month. This will probably be brought you by Mr. Barlow or Col. Oswald. Since my letter by Dominick I am every day more convinced and impressed with the propriety of Congress sending Commissioners to Europe to confer with the Ministers of the Jesuitical Powers on the means of terminating the War. The enclosed printed paper will shew there are a variety of subjects to be taken into consideration which did not appear at first, all of which have some tendency to put an end to the War. I see not how this War is to terminate if some intermediate power does not step forward. There is now no prospect that France can carry revolutions into[2] Europe on the one hand, or that the combined powers can conquer France on the other hand. It is a sort of defensive War on both sides. This being the case, how is the War to close? Neither side will ask for peace though each may wish it. I believe that England and Holland are tired of the War. Their Commerce and Manufactures have suffered most exceedingly—besides[3] this, it is for[4] them a War without an Object. Russia keeps herself at a distance.

I cannot help repeating my wish that Congress would send Commissioners, and I wish also that yourself would venture once more across the ocean, as one of them. If the Commissioners rendezvous at Holland they would[5] know what steps to take. They could call Mr. Pinckney to their councils, and it would be of use, on many accounts, that one of them should come over from Holland to France. Perhaps a long truce, were it proposed by the neutral powers, would have all the effects of a Peace, without the difficulties attending the adjustment of all the forms of Peace. Yours affectionately,   THOMAS PAINE

MS not found; text reprinted from Moncure D. Conway, ed., *The Writings of Thomas Paine*, 4 vols. (New York, 1894-1906), III, 134. Another printing, in Foner, *Paine*, II, 1333-4 (derived from a MS identified as being in DLC: TJ Papers, though the Editors know of no other evidence corroborating this location), includes the salutation "Dear Sir" as well as variations in paragraphing, capitalization, spelling, and wording, only the last being noted below.

Recorded in SJL as received 31 Mch. 1794. Enclosure not identified.

MY LETTER BY DOMINICK: Paine to TJ, 10 Oct. 1793.

[1] Word not in Foner.
[2] Foner: "through."
[3] Foner: "and besides."
[4] Foner: "to."
[5] Foner here adds "then."

From David Meade Randolph

DEAR SIR   Presq: Isle 20th. October 1793

My return home was delayed 'till a few days past. Upon going to the Custom House, I found that your box had been entered by Mr. Patrick Hart of Richmond. The collector informed me that it was the design of Mr. Hart to forward it by the first safe opportunity—consequently I had been deprived of the pleasure of executing your commission—nor should you now be troubled with this scrawl, but to assure you of the prompt services at all times, by your obliged Hume. Sert:

D M RANDOLPH

RC (MHi); endorsed by TJ as received 12 Nov. 1793 and so recorded in SJL.

From Benjamin Bankson

SIR   Philadela. Monday, October 21st., 1793.

Your several Letters of the 3d. instant I did not receive until last Saturday (the 19th), the business committed to me shall be expedited with all the dispatch in my power.

I had the honor to forward you by last Monday's post a number of Letters and the Leyden Gazette—a fever which I had at that time and which continued upon me for several days prevented my writing.

The Fever has considerably abated—this I had yesterday from the Committee having the charge of the sick at Bush-hill and Doctr. Duffield the principal Physician there. In addition to Freneau's paper I send you herewith Brown's Evening post for the last week—some information relative to the prevailing disorder may be collected from them. Fenno has not printed a paper these three weeks.

Crosby is still absent—nor can I form a conjecture when he will return. I yesterday received a Letter from Mr. Taylor—not a syllable when he will return. Mr. Blackwell and Pfeiffer I know nothing of—I assure you, Sir, I experience great inconvenience from being left alone. This being the period to which I am limited as to the transmission of Letters to you, I shall retain those I may receive hereafter, unless otherwise instructed. I have the honor to be with great respect, Sir Your most Obedt servt   B. BANKSON

RC (MHi); at foot of text: "Mr. Jefferson"; endorsed by TJ as received 9 Nov. 1793 and so recorded in SJL.

An undated letter from Bankson to TJ recorded in SJL as received on 7 Nov. 1793 has not been found.

From James Currie

DR SIR   Octr. 21st. 1793

Not expecting the pleasure of seeing You down here, I take the liberty of writing you a line to inform I received Your polite letter dated Schyllkill inclosing the attorney's report to you of the state of my Suit vs. Griffin and am much Obligd. by your friendly intention to have it brought to an end before you leave Philadelphia again. After Your return from Monticello, there are 3 pipes or HHds. of Lisbon Wine of Yours in Jas. Brawn's cellar in Richmond—as you took a memorandum to send for some of the same kind of Wine for me, I should be glad to know if any of that Wine now here is what you intended for me. With best respects to all my friends at Monticello I am Sir Very Respectfully yr most Ob H Serv   JAS CURRIE

RC (MHi); endorsed by TJ as received 24 Oct. 1793 and so recorded in SJL.

From Edmond Charles Genet

M.   New york le 21. 8bre. 1793. l'an 2e. de la Repe. françoise

Vous avés porté des plaintes sur la Conduite du Vice Consul de la Republique françoise à Boston relativement à une prise faite par le Roland furieux batiment armé dans ce port. Je vous envoye sa Justification. Elle est imprimée. Agréés mon respect.

Dft (DLC: Genet Papers); unsigned; above salutation: "Le Cit Genet Ministre plenipotentiaire &c à Mr Jefferson &c"; with note in margin: "Mr. Pichon traduira la Justification de duplaine pour moi." Recorded in SJL as received 4 Nov. 1793. Enclosure not found.

From Christopher Gore

SIR   Boston Octr 21. 1793

I submitted to the grand jury for this district, a bill against Mr. Duplaine, for resisting and obstructing the Depy. marshal, in the execution of a writ, issuing from the Circuit Court of the United States. In addition to the evidence already transmitted to you, in my letter of the 10th. ult., a witness swore before the jury that he saw written orders, signd by Duplaine, commanding the Captain of the frigate Le Concorde, to take possession of the vessel replevied, and detain her against all persons. Eleven of the jury were for making the presentment, but more cou'd not be convinced of its legality—they agreed that the facts were prov'd; but doubted of the law. In one stage of the business, there was a prospect that the jury wou'd consult the court, as to the law—at this time, I stated the facts to judge Blair, and judge Lowell. They entertain'd no doubts, but that the opposition was illegal, whither the writ coud have been supported or not. The Jury, however, did not chuse to consult the court, and rejected the bill.

The jury return'd two bills one against five American Citizens, who were on board the Roland privateer, for a misdesmesnes in committing hostilities against nations with which the U.S. are at peace—and one against John Juttau a frenchman, and chancellor to the consulate for fitting out, and equipping the Roland as a privateer in the harbor of Boston. These bills were not returnd into court till thursday evening. On friday morning the prisoners were arraign'd, and requested that their cause might not be tried till saturday—this request was granted by the court. On saturday the judges did not think there was sufficient time for the trial, and judge Blair being obliged to quit Boston this day, to attend a circuit court in N. Hampshire, they gave notice that these causes cou'd not be tried the present term. The council for the Defendants told the court they were just going to move for a continuance—the Defendants were recogniz'd, with sureties, to appear the next term and answer the indictments found against them. With the greatest respect, I am, sir, Your very obed. servt   C. GORE

RC (DNA: RG 59, MLR); at foot of text: "Thomas Jefferson Esqr Secry. of State"; endorsed by TJ as received 4 Nov. 1793 and so recorded in SJL. Enclosed in TJ to George Washington, 5 Nov. 1793.

From Edward Church

Lisbon Tuesday 22nd Octor. 1793

On Saturday the 19th. Instant, the Vessels belonging to the Hanseatic Towns were ordered to be in readiness to sail the 25th. under Convoy of Two Portugueze Frigates, ordered by her Majesty to Convoy them to a certain Latitude. One of the Articles of the Truce with Algiers which was communicated to me on the 12th. Instt. by Luiz Pinto the Minister for foreign Affairs, expressly restricted the Portugueze from affording protection (without exception) to any one Nation, Nevertheless the Consul and Agent for the Hanseatic Towns, petitioned for a Convoy, and strongly Urged a right founded on a prior Treaty of a very ancient date existing between the two Nations, this was generally understood to be the principle upon which the Convoy was granted, and was so publickly declared by the Agent, but I had strong reasons to believe that this Government were by no means pleased with the conditions of the truce, or the manner in which it had been negociated _for_ and not _by_ this Nation, and that tho' they did not think proper formally to disavow and reject it, yet that they wou'd not be displeased if a plausible pretence shou'd offer to break it. I was also convinced that a great Majority, if not the whole Nation, were extremely offended for various reasons, they conceived it intended not only to throw on them the odium of the manifest treachery in the business, but that it was also aimed at their Navy, which was now an object of their particular attention, and which for want of some employment, wou'd again sink into neglect, which they suppose to have been one object of the English in so eagerly precipitating this Truce. Upon the presumption that such was the general opinion, and my knowledge that the Spanish Ambassador when at Court on the 15th. Instt. had been treated rather roughly by all the Nobility present when he congratulated the Prince on the happy event of the Truce; I wrote a letter to the Minister yesterday, of which transmit you a Copy per this opportunity, and as I have been diligent, in my Enquiries prior to my writing, and am particularly favoured with the interest and support of two very distinguished Personages here, who have honored me with some particular attentions, I am greatly flattered with hopes of Success; if I find there is a prospect of a speedy and favorable Answer, it is probable I may detain the Vessel a day or two in order to Convey such intelligence which will be so very important and acceptable to the United States.

I have taken the liberty to draw on you the 19th. Instt. for one hundred and fifty pounds Sterling in favor of Messrs. Jacob Dohrman & Co. as a compensation for their Chartering a Ship at a price which they had before refused, for altering her destination agreeable to my request, and for suffering the Vessel to go with only two thirds the Quantity of Salt which She would otherwise have carried, in order that the Vessel might sail faster, so as to deliver, the duplicates of my dispatches with all possible speed. This bill I trust will be duly honored, though I had no special orders, as I conceived the object of too great consequence to trust to one conveyance, and therefore hope my conduct will meet your approbation. With perfect esteem & Respect I have the honor to be Sir Yor. mo: faithful & obedt. Servant   EDWD. CHURCH

P.S. I cannot give a stronger proof of the Sincerity of the disgust and disappointment of this Court on account of the Truce with Algiers, than that the Spanish and British Ministers were unsuccessfully opposed to the granting Us a Convoy, this comes from the best Authority, even Martinho de Mello favoured Us in this instance—in short the British have lost ground by this left-handed policy, and the general opinion that I do not love them over-much is now no small recommendation of me; I think this would not be an unfavorable moment to propose a commercial Treaty upon a broad and liberal Basis—the advantages could not fail in every view to preponderate in our favor. I wish this may be taken into immediate and serious consideration as our Commerce with this Country holds out very many advantages to the U.S. if under proper regulations.

RC (DNA: RG 59, CD); in a clerk's hand except for complimentary close, signature, and postscript; above postscript: "The Secretary of State for the United States of America"; with notation by Church in part: "No. 1."; endorsed by TJ as received 22 Dec. 1793 and so recorded in SJL. Dupl (same, MD); in a clerk's hand, signed by Church; lacks postscript; at head of text: "(Duplicate)"; endorsed by Edmund Randolph as received 14 Jan. 1794. Tr (DNA: RG 46, Senate Records, 3d Cong., 1st sess.); contains postscript. Enclosures: (1) Church to Jacob Dohrman & Company, 15 Oct. 1793, stating that, having been informed of their reluctance to charter a Danish ship for a speculative voyage to Baltimore because of a cost differential of about £100 sterling, he wishes them to charter the ship immediately and change its destination to New York or Philadelphia so that it can leave this week with important duplicate dispatches for the United States government; and that he undertakes on behalf of that government to pay them £100 ster-

ling on demand in Lisbon upon learning that the dispatches have been safely delivered to the Secretary of State and if, in contrast to the recommendation he plans to make in his letter to that official, the money is not paid in America. (2) Jacob Dohrman to Church, Lisbon, 15 Oct. 1793, stating that, because the freight charged by the Swede or the Dane was so high, he would only charter the ship, change its destination to New York, and "take charge" of a messenger to deliver the dispatches there if Church agreed to pay him £150 sterling and gave him a bill for the payment of that sum to his firm in Lisbon, after delivery of the dispatches, at the then current exchange in London. (3) Church to Dohrman, 15 Oct. 1793, accepting his terms, and, should the Secretary of State refuse to pay the bill of exchange because Church was acting under the exigency of the situation rather than special authority, promising to indemnify him fully on receipt of the protest. (4) Dominick Browne to Church, Oporto, 15 Oct. 1793, stating that, in accordance with

Church's favor of 11 Oct., he warned the only two American ship captains now here—Isaac Rea, master of the snow *Phenix* from Salem, and Charles Dickinson, master of the ship *Patty and Julia* from New London—of the danger posed to United States shipping by the recent truce between Algiers and Portugal and that both agreed not to proceed until Church's further orders; that the schooner *Fayette*, Captain Wyatt, and the brig *Rozanna*, Captain Hooker Baxtor, had left port on 11 Oct. bound for Boston; that, although he knows of no American ships in Viana do Castelo, Caminha, or Aveiro, he will immediately transmit Church's instructions to these ports; that last week the *Oporto*, an English letter of marque from Liverpool, Captain Hamilton, arrived here with an American ship, the *Birmingham*, William Foster master, bound from Baltimore to Amsterdam, which it captured on suspicion that it was destined for a French port; and that the captain and three of the crew of the *Birmingham* were sent to Liverpool, the mate and one sailor were brought here and then allowed to return to America, and three free black sailors were being held against their will on the *Oporto*; with subjoined description of the *Birmingham*'s cargo (Trs in DNA: RG 59, CD, with No. 4 in Church's hand and endorsed by him as received 20 Oct. 1793; Trs in DNA: RG 46, Senate Records, 3d Cong., 1st sess.). Letter and enclosures enclosed in addendum to Report on Morocco and Algiers, 14 Dec. 1793, Bartholomew Dandridge, Jr., to TJ, 23 Dec. 1793, and George Washington to the Senate and the House of Representatives, 23 Dec. 1793.

TJ submitted this letter and its enclosures to the President on 23 Dec. 1793 (Washington, *Journal*, 271-2).

From Edward Church

SIR   Lisbon 22d. Octr. 1793. P.M.

I wrote you this morning that I had written to his Excelly. Luiz Pinto Minister &ca. &ca. I herewith send a Copy of my Letter, and at the same time have the pleasure to inclose a most favourable, friendly, and pleasing answer from his Excellency, which I have this moment received, and which you will immediately see the necessity of communicating by expresses to all parts[1] of the Union, that our Merchants may not be exposed to the heavy premium of a supposed desparate risk. I have also the pleasure to inform you from good authority, through a secret but direct channel, that a remonstrance was yesterday presented to the Prince by some of the highest and most influencial of the Nobility, wherein they state, that the late Truce has greatly dishonoured this Nation, that to ratify it would be to render the disgrace indelible, or even to accede to a Peace or Truce on the terms once offered by this nation, which were to withdraw their Ships from the Mediterranean but to pay nothing—they say it is now beneath the dignity of the Crown to accept the Offers of Peace from that nation (supposing a Peace admissible with those Piratical *Infidels*) upon any other terms than a full indemnification for all expences in maintaining their Naval Armament for about ten years in the Mediterranean for the protection of their Commerce against the hostilities of that nation—and declare that it would be far better, and more honourable for the Nation to maintain eternal War against them, than to consent to a peace or truce on any other terms; this is the present state of this English Portugze: Truce, which from present appearances promises no duration. It is also whispered, but not from equal authority, that orders are gone to the Portugze. fleet in the Streights not to suffer any Vessels captured by the Algerines to be carried into Algiers, if it should appear that[2] they were bound to or from any Port belonging to the Dominions of Portugal. I enquired concerning the truth of this report from one who is very able, and on all possible occasions perfectly disposed to give me every information which he thinks may concern me to know. His answer was—Our fleet in the Mediterranean have no Authority that I know of, from this Court, to know or believe any thing about a peace or truce with Algiers, if they have any such information it is from a different Quarter.

I have it from *good Authority*, that there has been a very severe action between the French, and the whole force of Sardinia, collected and commanded by the King in person, the battle is said to have been long and bloody, but the latter were finally routed, and pursued, with very great slaughter, both on the field of Action, and in the pursuit. The King of Sardinia was on his March towards Nice near which he expected to meet the french and intended to give them battle, but the french advanced about four leagues from Nice, when the abovementioned action ensued. This Court seems to be very much alarmed at a report circulating in the Palace, that the King of Prussia proposes to withdraw his forces from the field of action, and to retire to his own dominions in peace, various causes are assigned for this extraordinary and unexpected Maneuvre—it is certain that the report has made a very considerable impression on this Court, which encourages me to hope it is not without some foundation.

There are 16 American Vessels now in this Port, I have requested them to get ready for Sea as fast as possible when the Convoy will be ordered to attend them. There are about 30 Ships from the Hanseatic Towns now here, They are ordered to be ready on the 25th. We have no orders yet. I am Sir with all due consideration & respect Yor. mo: hble & mo: obedt. Servant   EDWD. CHURCH

RC (DNA: RG 59, CD); at foot of text: "The Secretary of State for the United States of America"; with notation by Church in part: "No. 2. . . . P.M."; endorsed by TJ as received 22 Dec. 1793 and so recorded in SJL. Dupl (same); in a clerk's hand, signed by Church; with several variations, only the most important of which are noted below; at head of text: "(Duplicate)"; contains postscript virtually identical to the one in Church's first letter of this date; endorsed by Edmund Randolph as received 14 Jan. 1794. Tr (DNA: RG 46, Senate Records, 3d Cong., 1st sess.); lacks postscript. PrC of another Tr (DLC); consists of extract of second paragraph in TJ's hand with his additional commentary subjoined; see TJ to Robert Gamble, 22 Dec. 1793. Enclosures: (1) Enclosure No. 6 listed at Church to TJ, 12 Oct. 1793, but with note of 20 Oct. on verso stating that on that day there arrived, both after voyages of seven weeks, the schooner *Alice* or *Elsy* of Boston from North Carolina and the brigantine *Betsy* of Portsmouth from Virginia, the last of which reported that thirteen ships were ready to sail at approximately the same time—eleven for Cadiz and two for Lisbon. (2) Church to Luís Pinto de Sousa Coutinho, 21 Oct. 1793, stating that, having been unable to obtain a personal interview with him on 19 Oct., he now writes to request his intercession with the Queen to obtain for American ships and citizens in Portugal the same naval protection against Algerine corsairs on the Portuguese coast that has been granted to citizens of the Hanseatic Towns; that, despite the absence of a commercial treaty between the United States and Portugal, an agreement the American government has long sought in order to strengthen the ties between the two countries, American citizens and ships deserved this favor because they came to Portugal on the assumption that the Portuguese Mediterranean fleet would continue to protect them against the Algerines and because of the importance of American trade to Portugal; that, despite the indication Pinto gave during their 12 Oct. meeting that the Algerine truce forbade the Queen to give protection to any nation at war with Algiers, this restriction had already been waived for one nation and therefore could also be dispensed with for the United States; and that he has chartered a second neutral ship to bring duplicates of his dispatches to America that will be ready to sail tomorrow and on which he hopes to send Pinto's reply (Trs in DNA: RG 59, CD, in Church's hand; Trs in DNA: RG 46, Senate Records, 3d Cong., 1st sess.). Other enclosure printed below. Letter and enclosures enclosed in addendum to Report on Morocco and Algiers, 14 Dec. 1793, Bartholomew Dandridge, Jr., to TJ, 23 Dec. 1793, and George Washington to the Senate and the House of Representatives, 23 Dec. 1793.

TJ submitted this letter and its enclosures to the President on 23 Dec. 1793 (Washington, *Journal*, 271-2). It is the last consular letter TJ received from Church. See Appendix I.

[1] Dupl: "all the Ports."
[2] Preceding four words not in Dupl.

ENCLOSURE

Luís Pinto de Sousa Coutinho to Edward Church

Translation of a Note from Louis Pinto de Souza Secretary of foreign affairs at Lisbon to Edward Church Consul for the US.

Palace of Queluz 22. Octob. 1793.

In answer to the letter you addressed to me of yesterday's date on the protection and convoy which you sollicit in favor of the vessels of the US. of America which have to sail to their destinations, in danger from the Cruizers of Algiers, I am ordered[1] to inform you that her most faithful majesty, desirous of manifesting to the said states whatsoever may benefit their navigation or commerce as far as may be compatible with her own supreme justice, is very ready to give[2] her royal orders that the vessels of the said states shall[3] enjoy in their passage the same protection which she has ordered to be extended to the vessels of the Hanseatic towns until[4] the conclusion of the ratification of the truce adjusted between her M. F. Majesty and the regency of Algiers: provided nevertheless that the vessels of the US. which shall desire to shelter themselves under the protection of the said convoys, shall unite and assemble in sufficient number to merit to be convoyed; as this measure cannot be practised in favor of a few, for clear reasons which manifest themselves. I am with the greatest esteem Sir your servant

LUIZ PINTO DE SOUZA

Tr (DNA: RG 59, CD); entirely in TJ's hand, with several revisions, the most important being noted below; at foot of text: "Mr. Edward Church." Tr (same); in Portuguese; with notation by Church on separate sheet: "Copy of a Letter from the Minister of foreign affairs dated Palace of Queluz 22d. Octr. in answer to my letter of 21st. Octr. and granting a Convoy to the Citizens & Vessels of the United States—a true Copy examd. pr. E.C." Tr (DNA: RG 46, Senate Records, 3d Cong., 1st sess.); in English.

[1] Preceding two words interlined in place of "have the honor."
[2] Word interlined in place of "provide," which had been interlined in place of "expedite by."
[3] Word interlined in place of "may."
[4] Word interlined in place of "before."

Memorandums to Thomas Mann Randolph, Jr.

[ca. 22-25 Oct. 1793]

Memorandums with respect to Watson.

The waggon is to be sent for him on Monday Nov. 4. to bring his things.

He is to work in the shop near the sawpit, and he must lodge there till Claxton moves.

Then his wife is to live in Claxton's house till I return and can fix them elsewhere.

Johnny is to work with him for the purpose of learning to make wheels, and all sorts of work.

He is to do the following work, and in the order here mentioned unless any good reason should arise for changing it.

Make a pair of wheels for Tom's mule cart.

Mend or make wheels for the two oxcarts.

Make a pair of forewheels for the Phaeton.

Make 2 pr. of wheels for wheelbarrows. 3 f. diameter.

Make a set of waggon wheels.

The Phaeton wheels should be of ash, but the rest may be of the oak I bought of Gaines.

Watson is to be furnished with provisions till I come home which may be done from the Plantations at the same time with Mr. Biddle.

In rainy weather the carpenters are to be employed in splitting, planing, jointing and rounding shingles, which may be under the eye of Watson.

MS (DLC: TJ Papers, 77: 13398); undated; entirely in TJ's hand; docketed at a later date by an unidentified hand: "Th. Jefferson Instructions relative to Watson—Sepr. 92."

The docketing notwithstanding, TJ evidently left these instructions with his son-in-law after hiring David Watson on 22 Oct. 1793 and before leaving Monticello for Philadelphia three days later. Watson, a house joiner and British deserter whom TJ had employed from 1781 to 1784, and again in 1792, remained in his service until 1797 (MB, 3 Apr. 1781 and note, 19 Sep. 1792, 22 Oct. 1793, 2 Dec. 1797; note to TJ to the County Lieutenants, 26 Mch. 1781; Randolph to TJ, 7 Nov. 1793).

From Josef de Jaudenes and Josef Ignacio de Viar

MUI SEÑOR NUESTRO Nueva York 23. de Octubre de 1793.

Por la Copia Carta que acavamos de recivir de Willmington en la Carolina Septentrional, y que tenemos la honrra de incluir á V. S. en esta; se hallará V. S. informado de lo acaecido en aquel Puerto con un Bergantin Español apresado por el Corsario frances Le *Vainqueur de la Bastille.*

Este que es uno de los proscritos por la proclamacion del Presidente de los Estados Unidos, nos proporciona el reclamar contra el hecho; y pedir á consequencia que el Presidente de los Estados Unidos se sirva dar las correspondientes ordenes para que se devuelva inmediatamente el Barco, Carga, y el dinero arrestado los primeros por el consul frances, y lo ultimo por la Aduana de aquel Puerto; juntamente con los daños, y perjuicios que se estimase ha causado el acto ilegal del mencionado Corsario.

Todo lo qual se entregara al Señor Eduardo Jones Escudero, Procurador del Estado, á quien autorizamos con esta misma fecha para que obre á nombre nuestro en favor de los Interesados, y de la Nacion Española que tenemos la honrra de representar.

En el interin quedamos mui agradecidos al paso tan oportuno que tomó el oficial de la Aduana de apoderarse del Dinero que clandestinamente queria sin duda ocultar, ó salvar el Capitan de dicho Corsario.

Para este fin suplicamos a V. S. tenga á bien informar de todo al Presidente de los Estados Unidos, quien no dudamos se servirá expedir las ordenes que juzgase convenientes con la brevedad, y energia que requieren las circunstancias del hecho. Nos reiteramos á la obediencia de V. S. y rogamos á Dios gue su vida ms. as. B. l. mo. de V. S. Sus mas recondos. y obedtes. Servs.

JOSEF DE JAUDENES JOSEF IGNACIO DE VIAR

EDITORS' TRANSLATION

OUR VERY DEAR SIR New York 23 October 1793.

From the copy of the letter which we have just received from Wilmington, North Carolina, and which we have the honor of enclosing herewith, you will be informed of what has happened in that port with a Spanish brig taken as a prize by the French privateer *Le Vainqueur de la Bastille.*

This ship, which is one of those proscribed by the proclamation of the President of the United States, provides our grounds for protesting against the deed; and for requesting, consequently, that the President of the United States be pleased to issue the appropriate orders for the immediate return of the ship, its cargo, and the money sequestered, the first two by the French consul, and the last by the customs in that port, together with the damages estimated to have been caused by the illegal act of the aforesaid privateer.

All of which is to be delivered to Mr. Edward Jones, Esquire, attorney general of the state, whom we authorize as of this date to act in our name in behalf of the interested parties, and of the Spanish nation, which we have the honor to represent.

In the meantime, we are very grateful for the timely measures taken by the customs officer in taking possession of the money which the captain of the said privateer no doubt wished to hide secretly.

To this end, we beg you to communicate everything to the President of the United States, who we do not doubt will be pleased to issue such orders as he may deem appropriate with the dispatch and vigor required by the circumstances of the event. We repeat that we are at your service, and we pray to God to preserve your life for many years. Respectfully yours, your most grateful and obedient servants   JOSEF DE JAUDENES   JOSEF IGNACIO DE VIAR

RC (DNA: RG 59, NL); in Jaudenes's hand, signed by Jaudenes and Viar; at foot of text: "Sor. Dn. Thomas Jefferson"; endorsed by TJ as received 4 Nov. 1793 and so recorded in SJL. Tr (AHN: Papeles de Estado, legajo 3895 bis); attested by Jaudenes and Viar. Enclosure: H. Duplessis to Jaudenes and Viar, Wilmington, North Carolina, 6 Oct. 1793, stating that motives of humanity prompt him to inform them that five or six days ago the pretended French privateer *Vainqueur de la Bastille*, Captain Hervieux, brought into Cape Fear river as a prize a Spanish brigantine with gold and a reputedly very rich cargo bound from Cartagena to Cadiz; that while the privateer and the prize remained at the mouth of the river, a customs officer arrested Hervieux and seized a trunk containing 40,000 dollars from him after he went ashore from his skiff before declaring his prize; that the *Vainqueur de la Bastille* is one of the French ships armed at Charleston and thus proscribed by the President's proclamation; that after having been lately arrested in Charleston by order of the governor of South Carolina and released through the intervention of the French consul, who gave him a safe-conduct pass to Cap-Français to obtain a commission from the commissaries there, Hervieux captured the Spanish ship on his way to Saint-Domingue and headed back to North Carolina; that the shameful failure of state officials to seize the privateer and the prize is the subject of daily conversations here; that he does not know the name of the prize or its captain, who is imprisoned on the privateer, reportedly in chains with his crew; that they should hire the talented North Carolina Solicitor General Edward Jones to obtain the return of the prize and its cargo, but meanwhile he will continue to provide them with all necessary information about the case; and that he believes that the customs collector is writing by this post to Alexander Hamilton about the case (Tr in same; in French; attested by Jaudenes and Viar).

UN BERGANTIN ESPAÑOL: for further information on the taking of the *San Josef*, a Spanish brigantine from Carthagena, by its true captor, the *Aimée Marguerite*, see TJ to Viar and Jaudenes, 10 Nov. 1793; and Jaudenes and Viar to TJ, 26 Dec. 1793 (second letter), and enclosures. PROCLAMACION DEL PRESIDENTE: the Proclamation of Neutrality of 22 Apr. 1793 (Fitzpatrick, *Writings*, XXXII, 430-1).

From Richard Wayne

SIR   Savannah October 23d: 1793

Permit me to acknowledge the Receipt of Your Letter of the 27th. August Last Handing me the Communication to the Merchants of Savannah. It was Immediately delivered In Conformity to the Directions thereof. The Gentlemen to whom it was Directed, were, of Opinion, It wou'd meet with the quickest Circulation by having It Inserted In the Gazette, which was done Accordingly.

The Merchants of Savannah Sir, must Feel themselves obliged, by this Singular mark of Attention, Every One that I have had the Pleasure to Converse with on the Subject has Signify'd a Grateful acknowledgement thereof. On all Occasions, wherein I can be serviceable, I shall be happy to obey Your Commands. With Great Respect I am Sir You most obdt & most hu[. . .] R WAYNE

RC (DNA: RG 59, MLR); torn at seal; addressed: "The Honble. Th. Jefferson. Philadelphia"; endorsed by TJ as received 11 Nov. 1793 and so recorded in SJL.

Richard Wayne (ca. 1740-1809), a native of Yorkshire, England, established himself in Charleston, South Carolina, in 1759,

managed to escape confiscation of his estate despite Loyalist activity in 1780, and moved to Savannah in 1789, where he prospered as a merchant and rice planter (Alexander A. Lawrence, *James Moore Wayne: Southern Unionist* [Chapel Hill, 1943], 3-8, 11, 25).

From Peter Carr

MY DEAR SIR   Spring-forest. Octr. 24. 1793.

My mother desires me to intimate to you, that there are several very pressing claims against her, which she has given assurances shall be discharged in january next. By something in one of your last letters, she hoped it would have been in your power, to furnish her with the means; if it should, a line upon the subject would be satisfactory to my mother. We all here wish you a good journey and an early return. Till I see you believe me with great and sincere esteem yr. friend and H servt

P: CARR

RC (ViU: Carr-Cary Papers); endorsed by TJ as received 24 Oct. 1793 and so recorded in SJL.

To John Breckinridge

DEAR SIR   Monticello Oct. 25. 1793.

This will be handed you by Mr. Toulmin a gentleman who goes to visit your state with a view to settle in it. I have not the pleasure of a personal acquaintance with him; but from the multiplied testimonies of those who have, I am able to assure you that you will find in him a person of understanding, of science, and of great worth: and what will be an additional recommendation to you, a pure and zealous republican. Any attentions or services you can render him will oblige me, and will be a comfort to yourself also when you shall have known him of yourself. I am with great & sincere regard & respect Dear Sir Your friend & servt.   TH: JEFFERSON

RC (DLC: Breckinridge Family Papers); addressed: "Mr. Brackenridge Kentuckey." Not recorded in SJL.

John Breckinridge (1760-1806), a lawyer and native Virginian who drafted the address with which a committee of Albemarle County residents welcomed TJ home from France in February 1790, had been elected to the third Congress as a Republican in 1792, but resigned and moved to Lexington, Kentucky, where he headed the Democratic Society of Kentucky and in 1793 supported an effort, launched by Edmond Charles Genet, to open the Mississippi River through an assault on New Orleans under the command of George Rogers Clark. After holding office as attorney general of Kentucky, 1795-97, Breckinridge served in the lower house of the state legislature, 1797-1801, presiding as speaker from 1799, where he guided a modified version of TJ's Kentucky Resolutions of 1798 through the legislature. Breckinridge was also responsible for the passage by the legislature in 1799 of a second set of Kentucky resolutions inspired by TJ. He represented Kentucky in the United States Senate from 1801 to 1805, and was appointed Attorney General by TJ during the latter year, serving until his death (DAB; Adrienne Koch, *Jefferson and Madison: The Great Collaboration* [New York, 1950], 185, 187-8, 196-201, 209; Address of Welcome by the Citizens of Albemarle, [12 Feb. 1790]).

On 8 Nov. 1793 TJ wrote Breckinridge a brief letter enclosing his interim commission as District Attorney for Kentucky (RC in DLC: Breckinridge Family Papers, in Benjamin Bankson's hand, signed by TJ, addressed "John Brackenridge esquire Kentuckey," franked and postmarked; Dft in DLC, in Bankson's hand, with "⟨Hugh⟩ John Brackinridge Esqr" at foot of text and endorsement by George Taylor, Jr.; FC in Lb in DNA: RG 59, DL; not recorded in SJL). The commission bore the same date (MS in DLC: Breckinridge Family Papers, in Bankson's hand, with place, day, and month completed by TJ, and signed by Washington and countersigned by TJ, being originally made out to Hugh Brackenridge and with one occurrence of the latter name remaining uncorrected). Breckinridge declined the appointment (note to William Murray to TJ, 7 Dec. 1792).

Harry TOULMIN, a Unitarian minister who had just fled England for religious and political reasons, visited Monticello during TJ's absence in August 1793 and called upon Madison not long after, giving him a description of a threshing machine and obtaining similar letters of introduction. Toulmin settled in Kentucky, serving first as president of Transylvania Seminary and from 1796 to 1804 as secretary of state of Kentucky. TJ appointed him one of the judges of the Mississippi Territory in 1804 (DAB; Madison, *Papers*, xv, 6, 125-6, 139-40; *Terr. Papers*, v, 320-2; JEP, i, 472, 474).

To Hague & Lester

GENTLEMEN   Monticello Oct. 25. 1793.

Mr. Randolph informs me you are desirous that my goods lodged in your warehouses should be removed. I have just engaged a person to bring up the whole by water in the course of the winter; and that they may be convenient to the watermen, Mr. Randolph has engaged a store for them at Belvedere, to which place he will take immediate measures to have them removed. I am this morning setting out for Philadelphia or it's neighborhood. If you will be pleased to forward your account to me there at any time before the 1st. of January, I will immediately remit the money to Richmond. After that date it would find me here. I am Gentlemen Your most obedt. servt

TH: JEFFERSON

PrC (CSmH); at foot of text: "Messrs. Hague & Lister." Not recorded in SJL.

John Hague and John Lester (1748-1804) were Richmond merchants (CVSP, V, 560, VII, 110, 225, 238, 348; Richmond *Enquirer*, 22 Dec. 1804).

This day TJ gave his son-in-law Thomas Mann Randolph, Jr., 20 dollars to pay the cost of moving his furniture to BELVEDERE, Daniel L. Hylton's estate (MB, 25 Oct. 1793, and note). A missing letter of 21 Apr. 1794 from Hague & Company is recorded in SJL as received from Richmond on 2 May 1794. A month later TJ ordered payment to the firm of £12.19.6 "for storage" (MB, 5 June 1794).

From Edmond Charles Genet

M.   New york le 27. 8bre. 1793. l'an 2e. de la Repe. fse.

Je viens de recevoir avec votre lettre du 3. de ce mois[1] l'acte de destitution du Citoyen duplaine Vice Consul de la Republique à Boston et Je m'empresse de vous déclarer que Je n'en reconnois point la validité parceque la Constitution des Etats unis n'a point donné au Président le droit qu'il[2] paroit vouloir s'arroger aujourdhui. Elle l'a chargé Comme premier Ministre du peuple Americain d'admettre et de recevoir les Ministres des nations[3] Etrangeres accredités auprès de la grande Confederation Americaine et leurs Agens Consulaires departis[4] auprès des Etats particuliers; mais en lui Confiant cette fonction officielle elle ne lui a point donné le pouvoir de les destituer de les renvoyer ou de les suspendre lorsqu'ils ont été admis, de pareils actes ne peuvent etre éxercés M., que par le souverain de ces Agens ou par celui auprès duquel Ils resident; de la part de leur souverain leur rappel ne peut[5] être que l'éffet de sa volonté particuliere ou la suite de négociations entamées[6] avec lui pour cet objet. De la part du Souverain auprès duquel ils sont accredités leur renvoi ou leur suspension[7] ne peut être que le resultat d'un acte de Justice reguliere[8] ou d'un acte arbitraire; Si c'est un acte de Justice nationale[9] Il faut que le souverain se soit entouré de toutes les lumieres possibles sur un objet aussi important afin d'être en mesure de prouver au Souverain Etranger que son Ministre étoit indigne de sa Confiance[10] et que sa suspension[11] ou son renvoi etoient indispensables; Si c'est un acte Arbitraire Il rentre dans la Classe des actes d'agression Il devient un cas de guerre et vous savés Mr. qu'à cet égard la Constitution des Etats unis a reservé aux Représentants du peuple[12] le droit de prononcer.

Je ne me rappelle point[13] ce que les écrits poudreux de Grotius de Vatel de Puffendorff de Wiquefort[14] disent à ce sujet, J'ai oublié dieu merci ce que ces publicistes gagés par des tyrans ont écrit sur[15] les droits des nations dans un tems où elles étoient toutes dans les fers; mais les bases fondamentales de votre liberté et de la nôtre sont gravées dans ma[16] Memoire en Caracteres inéffacables; mais les droits de l'homme sont renfermés dans mon cœur avec le feu de la vie; mais J'ai Constament sous les yeux votre Constitution et la nôtre, et c'est parceque Je suis pénétré des intentions Justes est sages de ceux qui les ont dicté que Je vous demande Mr., d'inviter Mr. le President des Etats unis à faire éxaminer par la Legislature qui représente le peuple Souverain du Massachusset[17] la Conduite du Citoyen duplaine de même que J'ai demandé qu'éxamen fut fait de la mienne dans le prochain Congrès.

Dans des gouvernements Comme les nôtres les affaires politiques ne peuvent être Jugées que par les Corps politiques et si le Vice Consul duplaine a[18] manqué aux loix particulieres[19] du Massachusset ou aux loix Generales de l'union que ce gouvernement est chargé de maintenir c'est à lui à prendre Connoissance de ce[20] crime de leze nation en premiere instance et c'est à ses officiers[21] à les denoncer[22] au gouvernement federal afin que[23] l'agent Etranger qui se trouveroit avoir violé les loix du pays soit puni par son souverain S'il merite de l'être. Je suis d'autant plus fondé, Mr., à insister sur cette marche que trois fois l'avocat du gouvernement federal à Boston à éssayé d'accuser auprès de la Cour de circuit le Citoyen duplaine, que trois fois un Juré populaire et vertueux a rejetté ses moyens et qu'enfin ce Vice Consul a été acquité[24] de la maniere la plus honorable. En éffet comment auroit on pu trouver lieu à accusation contre lui[25] puisqu'il n'a agi que d'après les traités, que d'après ses Instructions que d'après les décisions du gouvernement federal communiquées à tous les Etats[26] qui confient aux Consuls françois[27] la garde même des prises supposées faites dans la Jurisdiction[28] des Etats unis,[29] et qu'il a prouvé demonstrativement qu'il n'avoit point eu l'intention de resister par la force aux ordres qui lui avoient été intimés par une autorité Judiciaire quoiqu'ils fussent contraires aux droits politiques de la nation francoise.

Dft (DLC: Genet Papers); unsigned; above salutation: "Le Cit genet &c à Mr Jefferson"; only the most significant emendations have been recorded below. Tr (AMAE: CPEU, xxxix). Tr (NN: Samuel Adams Papers); in English; undated; at foot of text in Thomas Dannery's hand: "Copy Dannery"; endorsed by Samuel Adams. Recorded in SJL as received 4 Nov. 1793.

In addition to the Washington administration, Genet also failed to convince the governor of Massachusetts that the President lacked the authority to dismiss Antoine Charbonnet DUPLAINE, the French vice-consul at Boston. Acting on instructions from Genet, Thomas Dannery, the French consul who replaced Duplaine, transmitted a translation of the above letter to Governor Samuel Adams with a covering letter requesting that Duplaine's case be "Submitted to the most Severe examination at the next Setting of the Legislature of the Commonwealth of Massachusetts. So that he may be punished by his Sovereign, if found guilty of the charge alledged against him. And that in case where he should be acquitted by that august assembly the people of his Nation should be Satisfied" (Dannery to Adams, 4 Nov. 1793, NN: Samuel Adams Papers). Despite Dannery's reiteration of this request in a subsequent letter and protest that were widely publicized in American newspapers, Adams declined to take any action in this matter (Dannery to Adams, with enclosed protest, both dated 7 Nov. 1793, listed as enclosures at TJ to Christopher Gore, 22 Nov. 1793; *The New-York Journal, & Patriotic Register*, 27 Nov. 1793; F. J. Lequoy to Genet, 8, 12 Dec. 1793, DLC: Genet Papers).

Genet also sought to win popular support for his position on Duplaine's dismissal by having the President's 10 Oct. 1793 revocation of the vice-consul's exequatur and the above letter to TJ printed in the 30 Oct. 1793 issue of the *New-York Journal, & Patriotic Register*. For TJ's reaction, see TJ to James Madison, 2 Nov. 1793, and his unsent letter to Genet printed under 15 Nov. 1793.

[1] Preceding seven words and digit written in the margin.
[2] Genet here canceled "éxerce."
[3] Preceding two words interlined in place of "et les Agens."
[4] Preceding five words written in the margin in place of "ou."
[5] Preceding four words written in the margin in place of "⟨Ils⟩ ces mêmes actes ne peuvent," though Genet inadvertently left the last two words uncanceled.
[6] Preceding two words altered by Genet from "d'une négociation."
[7] Preceding four words interlined in place of "destitution."
[8] Word interlined.
[9] Word interlined.
[10] Genet here canceled "qu'il s'est écarté."

[11] Remainder of clause altered by Genet from "étoit indispensable pour ses propres Interêts."
[12] Preceding two words interlined.
[13] Sentence to this point altered from "J'ignore M."
[14] Preceding two words written in the margin.
[15] Genet here canceled "la souveraineté des peuples."
[16] Word interlined in place of "vot."
[17] Preceding two words written in the margin, having first been canceled after "Legislature." Genet here also canceled "dans le sein du quel le Citoyen duplaine ⟨a résidé⟩ réside qu'éxamen soit."
[18] Genet here canceled "refusé d'."
[19] Word interlined.
[20] Genet here canceled "delit."
[21] Here in the margin Genet canceled "et non à des inquisiteurs à."
[22] Preceding three words interlined in place of "à vous transmettre leurs plaintes."
[23] Genet here canceled "Justice soit rendue au peuple."
[24] Remainder of sentence altered from "honorablement."
[25] Genet first wrote "auroit il pu être condamné" and then altered it to read as above.
[26] Preceding five words written in the margin.
[27] Genet first wrote "qui autorisent les Consuls même dans les cas ou des" and then altered it to read as above.
[28] Preceding three words interlined in place of "sur le territoire."
[29] Genet here initially ended the text with "Salut." After canceling it, he added "et qu'enfin Il ⟨est⟩ faut qu'il ait eu l'intention d'opposer la force aux ordres qui lui ont été intimés par l'autorité Judicaire fait qui se trouv," before altering the addition to read as above.

To Thomas Mann Randolph, Jr.

Sunday eveng. [27 Oct. 1793]

Th:J. will be obliged to Mr. Randolph to make George prick out the inclosed grains of wheat below the garden wall or wherever he thinks best. It is of the genuine *early* wheat gathered by Mr. Jones in a field here which was reaped on the 5th. of June.—So far all well. I set out in the stage between 3. and 4. in the morning. Adieu.

RC (DLC: TJ Papers, 94: 16106); partially dated; addressed: "Mr. Randolph"; endorsed by Randolph as received 29 Oct. 1793; with notation in an unidentifed hand indicating that the letter was sent from Fredericksburg. Not recorded in SJL.

Not long after TJ's departure from Monticello, the merchant Thomas Bell of Charlottesville commented on TJ's passions for architecture and farming: "Mr. Jefferson set out a few days ago to meet the president at German town and is determined to resign the first of the year—And is resolved to— play the ⟨fool⟩. You know how easy he can take down one house and build another &c.—has got a Jersey farmer and has laid off his land in 40 acre fields with his Own hands &c. in fact you can get no News out of him untill you tyer him out on farming" (Bell to John Breckinridge, 30 Oct. 1793, DLC: Breckinridge Family Papers).

From Enoch Edwards

DEAR SIR   Liverpool Octr: 28th: 1793

Since my Arival in England as I promised so I have frequently written to You and given You such Information as I thought worthy of your Attention.

I mentioned to you heretofore the Accident (a Fall Mrs: Edwards received from a Carriage) that prevented my going immediately to the Continent. We were also induced to stay 'till Fall in Consequence of a Determination Mrs: Pinckney had come to, to go with Us and tarry there 'till the Spring. In the mean time We have Made a Tour through England, into Scotland beyond the great Canal that runs across this Kingdom. We passed up the east side of the Island—but wen't into all the principle Towns—such as Norwich, Lynn, Leicester Notingham— Chesterfield—Sheffield, Wakefield Leeds York, Durham, Newcastle, Berwick, and so on to Edinburgh—at allmost all which I saw such Places, and many of such Characters as were worthy the Attention of a Stranger. Having provided myself with good Letters for the Purpose, at the last Place I saw allmost all the Leterati—among whome are many great and worthy Men, and many lovers of Aristocracy and Tyranny. On my Way from Glasgow I visited the Bishop of Landaff. He is a great and a good Man, he is so in Appearance and in Practice—and an Enthusaist in favor of America—he is as good a Practical Farmer, as Mr: Young is a writing One and better. I have also seen the Farm of the latter.

I have passed through Manchester that Nest of Democrats, and seen the Ruins of the [things?] of the best Men in Birmingham—and I expect in about three Weeks to be in London, by Way of Bristol, Bath, and through some of the interior Counties. I have aranged my Plans so that by the time I finish this Journey, I shall have been in every County in

England, and have formed usefull and agreable Acquaintances, I am therefore convinced I shall profit by making this Tour before I go to the Continent, it has furnished Me with Knowledge that I ought to be possessed of.

The Advocates of Tyrants here are highly tickled with seeing the Misunderstanding between the french Minister and our Government, they say and indeed they hope it arises from an attachment to british Politicks, they also say we now begin to have our Eyes open to discern our best Friends, and our true Interest—and they as publickly say that they are confident we wish to return into the Arms[1] of the mother Country, and among other Things they give in support of their Assertions the Writings of our Vice President—they extol our Aristocrats to the Skies, seem highly interested about who shall succeed the President—and I sincerely beleive wish to have a Finger in the Business.

They labor here to make it appear that You among some of your Friends are endeavouring to thwart the President and all the moderate Party in their laudable Designs to establish an energic Government. I have been able notwithstanding some consequential Gentlemen from our own Country I believe have ratified if not raised this Calumny—to set it right and shall be more so. I have endeavoured also to shew that We take an abstract View of the French Cause, as it stands unconnected with the unworthy Agents into whose Hands it is entrusted—and indeed it is a very painful Reflection that so noble a Revolution should be stained by such want of Magnanimity—such Inconsistency and such execrable Crimes. Yet to a Man capable of feeling or reflecting on, the, Justice of a free Government he must continue to love the Principle 'tho he ought to detest the *Abuse of the* Means.

The French on the whole[2] are victorious in all Quarters. Lions is taken, the Slaughter has been great. The Blockade of Maubeuge is raised, they are rather[3] more setled in their Determinations, and I have no Doubt but before Christmas they will again drive away all their Enemies. The Queen is executed. The imperial Minister is arested for a treasonable Correspondence with the French. It is thought his Master has been trying to make a seperate Peace with the French, and that the aresting his Minister is all a political Humbug.

He is publickly cursed here by the Friends to the War—and so is the Dutch. I beleive there is no Doubt but this Confederacy will soon be distracted and crumble to Nothing but a heavy Debt for some of them— and poor England it is thought will be favored with at least its Share.

Our Country stands charged here for makeing no Exercions in Favor of the M. la Fayette. I am not able to satisfy the Enquirers, as I know of none that have been attempted or in Contemplation to be made, I wish I could be made Use of to do him any Service. I saw him recieve his wound in the Battle of Brandy Wine—and was the first that dressed it—it would add greatly to my Satisfaction to again be any Way instrumental in contributing towards his Comfort and Relief. A Report has lately prevailed here that He is dead—but from what I can learn it must be groundless.

I have been somewhat disappointed with Respect to the Agriculture of this Country—having heard so much about it—I expected to be struck up into a Consternation at every Farm I should see—most certainly great Industry does perform Wonders in this sterrile Island, the Land in general is poor, and yet they raise great Crops, but the Cultivation does not so far exceed the good, I mean the best, farming round Philadelphia as I expected. The great Art of their farming consists in merely choaking the Earth with Manure and a judicious Rotation of Crops. I have no Doubt but what with Us the latter in time will be adopted—the great Buisness we have then first to attend to, will be how to procure in general throughout the Country a sufficient supply of Manure at a Distance from large Towns. We have many Advantages over this Country, our Land is worked with I believe half the Labor—it is not an uncommon Thing here to see a farmer ploughing with five strong Horses—and turn up no larger Furrow than has been done on my Farm with three smaller Ones—half the Quantity of Manure that they use on an Acre here will have a better Effect with Us—nor is Wages so much higher with Us as we have been made to believe. In short when we take into Consideration the Taxes and Burdens a Farmer labors under in this Country, and the Price that Wheat Beef and Pork, beares with Us, under all our disadvantages for the Want of Hands—A Farmer with Us with the same Capital will within 50 Miles of our large Towns make more Money than can be made here. I am dear Sir with very great Respect Your very obedt: Sert: ENO: EDWARDS

29th: The Report of the Emperors Minister is contradicted—but Furnes is taken by the French, and Neuport bombarded and now it is said in a Flame if not also taken.

RC (DLC); slightly torn along margin; addressed: "Thomas Jefferson Esqr: Secretary of State to the United States of America—Philadelphia"; endorsed by TJ as received 31 Mch. 1794 and so recorded in SJL, both erroneously identifying the writer as John Edwards.

In retaliation for a celebration marking the second anniversary of the storming of the Bastille, the homes of Joseph Priestley and other MEN IN BIRMINGHAM were destroyed during a riot by opponents of the French Revolution and English constitutional reform on 14-16 July 1791 (DNB).

[1] Word interlined in place of "Bosom."
[2] Preceding three words interlined.
[3] Word interlined.

From Benjamin Hawkins

Warren in N. Carolina 28th. octr. 1793

For the first time my dear sir, I have an opportunity direct for your house. Micajah Childs called on me this evening on his return to Charlottsville. I avail myself of it by his permission to send you some grape vines.

No. 1   Burgundy, called Millers Burgundy, the berries oval and black, the leaves covered with a hoary down.

2   Auvorna second Burgundy or black Morillon esteemed the best of the two for wine

3   White Frontinac, the French muscat blanc, the bunches large, the berries round and closely clustered.

4   Rhenish grape

5.   Tokay

6   Virginia I believe a native, the bunches large, the berries round, flesh coloured, the leaves large not serrated the greatest climber I have.

[*In margin next to above list:*] No. 1. 3. 4. 5. 6 planted in 1791. the 26 of march, pruned down to three eyes, in november and the year following they bore No. 1. four bunches, No. 3. three bunches, and the others one, all of which came to perfection.

7   Damson Grape, the berries large, oval purple coloured, and grow loose on the bunches, the leaves very much and deeply serrated.

8   Royal muscadine or D'arboyce a round white berry, small, the bunch large, the wood and foliage remarkably gross and strong.

9   White muscat, from Lun'el, the berries large, when ripe of an amber colour, clouded with brown or russet, a very plentiful bearer. The vine climbs very little.

10   white sweetwater

11   black sweetwater the bunches short and close.

12   Corinth

13   I take to be the black Hamburg, the berries dark, oval, not crouded.

I have been successful with all the European vines I have planted. I put cuttings with 2 or 3 eyes obliquely, in the earth, the uppermost eye about an inch under the surface that covered with roted straw and watered, I put the straw to retain the moisture.[1] The watering is repeated on the straw twice a week in the spring if it proves dry. I have had equal success from planting a single eye, with an inch of wood above and below it, an inch or two under ground covered and watered in like manner. The native grapes I find it difficult to propagate by cuttings;

You may put your cuttings in a box of earth so as to be kept barely moist 'till spring, or plant them immediately, and cover well against the frost, the latter I prefer. I put a small stick down by the eye, of every one, and if I plant in the fall I cover with earth about 6, 8, or ten inches, in the spring I reduce the earth, to the eye then cover it an inch or two as before directed.

I have been the whole summer, building mills, wishing success to French Democracy and ruin to the combination of Kings and priests. I am now though late, sowing wheat, clover and Timothy; I am planting apple and peach trees and preparing a large nursery to stock my plantations with all the variety within my reach.

We have had in some parts of this country and of Virginia opposite to me, the longest drought ever known among us, from some week in July till saturday evening, when after very very warm weather it began to rain, the wind at N. E. and cold.

I hope you have escaped the current fever of the country. I have not. I was attacked the last of august, though not dangerously. I have been freed from it but a few days. The Physician in my neighbourhood who corresponds with some in Philadelphia says the disorder is very similar, though not so virulent here as there, we have had but four instances of persons dying with it, in some miles of me, one very healthy in three days one in six and two in nine. Four fifths of all of us have been afflicted with it. We give an emetick, and some times a cathartick, then leave the patient pretty much to nature. Bark has been tryed, but I have not seen an instance of its being efficatious without the aid of snakeroot, and with that aid, it is not much to be depended on.

The rain from the N. E. continued yesterday, and last night, it began to snow, which continued till two oclock, this day, if the earth had been frozen it would have been eighteen inches deep at least, it has generally been four inches during the whole day. This change of weather will be favourable for the citizens of Philadelphia who must have been miserably afflicted. It will cleanse the city, against the meeting of Congress. I am very sincerely your friend   BENJAMIN HAWKINS

RC (DLC); endorsed by TJ as received 16 Nov. 1793 and so recorded in SJL. Enclosed in TJ to Thomas Mann Randolph, Jr., 17 Nov. 1793.

[1] Thus in manuscript.

From Edmond Charles Genet

M.   New york le 28. [i.e. 29] 8bre. 1793. l'an 2e. de la Republique.

Quand un fonctionnaire public néglige ses devoirs, quand il Commet des actes arbitraires Il merite d'être puni; à ces deux titres Je vous denonce le Juge federal du district de New york; Cet officier au mépris de nos traités au mépris des décisions du gouvernement federal que vous m'avés communiquées a enlevé des mains du Consul de la Republique dans ce port à la réquisition du Mre. Anglois[1] deux prises supposées faites dans la ligne Indéfinie de Jurisdiction et de protection des Etats unis, Savoir la Catherine d'halifax et le Guillaume Tell et au lieu de rendre un Jugement quelconque Il laisse la premiere deperir depuis plusieurs mois et ne s'empresse pas plus à[2] motiver ses procédés[3] violents à l'égard de la seconde qui lui a été remise Conformément aux Intentions de Mr. Le President[4] ainsi que vous le verrés Mr. par la lettre ci Jointe du Consul au Mal. de la Cour du district. Le Citoyen hauterive, Mr., s'est adressé au gouvernement de l'Etat de New york pour reclamer contre les voies de fait Commises par le susdit Juge et moi Mr. Je requiers les bons offices du[5] gouvernement federal pour obtenir du Congrès 1°. la reparation de l'offense faite à la République et au gouvernement federal par la punition d'un Juge qui n'a point respecté nos traités lesquels font partie des lois des Etats unis 2°. le remboursement à qui de droit[6] des pertes resultantes pour les capteurs des dites prises de l'abandon dans lequel elles ont été laissées.

Dft (DLC: Genet Papers); unsigned; at head of text: "à Copier"; above salutation: "Le Cit Genet Ministre &c à M. Jefferson secretaire d'Etat des Etats unis." FC (same); in English; misdated 28 Aug. [1793]. Recorded in SJL as a 29 Oct. 1793 letter received 4 Nov. 1793.

LE JUGE FEDERAL: Judge James Duane of the United States District Court of New York. MRE. ANGLOIS: George Hammond. LA CATHERINE D'HALIFAX: on the French capture of this prize, see Memorial from George Hammond, 11 June 1793, and note.

[1] Preceding six words written in the margin.
[2] Preceding six words interlined in place of "laisse la seconde."
[3] Genet here canceled "irreguli."
[4] Remainder of sentence written in the margin in place of "quoiqu'elles fussent contraires à nos pactes et aux décisions que vous m'aviés fait connoitre."
[5] Preceding four words written in the margin in place of "le."
[6] Preceding four words interlined.

From Edmond Charles Genet

MR.   A New york le 29 8bre 1793 l'an 2e De la R. F.
J'ai l'honneur De vous envoyer une copie De la lettre qui a été ecrite au consul De La republique française à Newyork par le directeur Des douanes De cette ville. Cette lettre contient le refus notifie par Mr. hamilton à ce directeur De faire la remise du droit de tonnage reclamée par les capitaines du convoi français. Je vous envoye cette notification ainsi que des observations que m'a adressé[1] à ce Sujet le consul français de newyork, et le procès verbal de l'assemblée tenue par les capitaines mar-

chands. Je vous enverrai Successivement les depêches que je recevrai Sans doute bientôt Sur le même objet de norfolk et de baltimore. J'aurois eu bien de la Satisfaction, Monsieur a pouvoir annoncer à la convention nationale dont toutes les lois ont été jusqu'ici favorables à votre commerce, La concession de ce leger avantage en faveur du notre. C'est avec bien du regret que je me verrai contraint de l'instruire que toutes les reclamations officielles que je vous ai faites en vertu de Ses lois et des ordres du conseil executif, pour obtenir De vous une juste reciprocité en faveur De notre commerce, n'ont eu jusqu'ici aucun Succès.

Dft (DLC: Genet Papers); in Jean Baptiste Cassan's hand, unsigned, with revision by Genet; above salutation: "Le citoyen genet à Mr jefferson." FC (same); in English. Recorded in SJL as received 4 Nov. 1793. Enclosures: (1) Benjamin Walker to Alexandre Maurice d'Hauterive, New York Custom House, 20 Oct. 1793, advising, in his capacity as Naval Officer and at the request of the ailing Collector of Customs, that by order of the Secretary of the Treasury the French merchant ships which had entered port from Saint-Domingue were to be considered in the same light as any other vessel entering "*not in distress*" and were therefore subject to the tonnage duty; that by law the duty had to be paid within ten days of entry and prior to clearing for departure and that bond had to be given for landing their cargoes in France or wherever they were bound; and that he takes this method of informing him to avoid delay, having been told by the chancellor of the consulate this afternoon when he came to communicate this news in person that Hauterive was too busy (RC in same). (2) [Hauterive], "Observations on the Decision of Mr. Hamilton relative to the reclamation of the Captains of the trading vessels which have taken refuge in the harbours of the United States," 21 Oct. 1793, stating that Hamilton's decision requiring the French merchant ships from Saint-Domingue to pay tonnage duties was contrary to the letter and the spirit of Articles 26 and 19 of the 1778 treaty of commerce between France and the United States, in the former case because it confounded these ships—which had left port hurriedly bound for France with cargoes of colonial goods, were compelled to enter American ports in "shattered condition," without papers, provisions, and water, at vast expense, and had no intention of employing their cargoes for speculative purposes—with vessels not in distress, and in the latter case because French ships forced to enter American ports "*by any urgent necessity*" were to enjoy protection, friendship, and assistance; that although the latter article mentions only the purchase of provisions and departure without impediment, a right enjoyed by vessels of all nations, it must be interpreted as conferring a distinction in favor of French trading vessels as claimed by the French captains; that the decision was also in violation of section 37 [i.e. 38] of the 1790 Tonnage Act exempting vessels forced by weather or any other necessity to enter an American harbor for which they were not bound and authorizing them to sell part of their cargoes to defray their local expenses free of all duties but storage; that the purchase and consumption of provisions in port by these ships not only repays the hospitality given to them but sufficiently rewards those inclined to "take advantage of other people's distress"; and that the American government should be dissuaded from aggravating with "an unexpected rigour" and a narrow spirit of fiscal policy the distress of French trade "by nobler sentiments, by the impression of that generous humanity so natural to every true American." (3) Proceedings of a meeting of "The Captains of commercial Vessels assembled extraordinarily at the Consulary house under the sanction and presidency of Citizen Hautrive Consul of the French Republic," n.d., claiming an exemption from the tonnage duties on substantially the same grounds as those advanced in No. 2, asserting that the rigorous severity of enforcement stood in stark contrast to the fraternal reception given to the French by the American people, and adopting three resolutions calling for their "Complaints and reclamations" to be sent to the National Convention with an account of the damages sustained from the duties so that it could provide compensation, and for Genet to forward an extract from these proceedings to the Convention for the vindication of the rights of the French nation (Trs in same; in English; with No. 3 bearing the names of nine signatories and certified by Hauterive).

For the mistaken contention, advanced in Enclosures Nos. 2-3, that section 38 of the

1790 Tonnage Act exempted from duties the cargo of the French merchant ships that had been forced by the slave revolt on Saint-Domingue to put in at American ports, see Hamilton to TJ, 30 Nov. 1793.

[1] Altered by Genet from "ainsi que la lettre que m'a ecrite."

From Edmond Charles Genet

M.   New york le 27. [i.e. 29] 8bre. 1793. l'an 2e. de la Répube.

Je crois devoir vous prévenir que J'ai délivré des Commissions de Vice Consuls de la Republique aux Cit. Pennevert et Chervi—Le premier résident à New London le second à Alexandrie. Je vous prie de vouloir bien obtenir en leur faveur[1] l'éxéquatur de Mr. le President des Etats unis. Je ne Joins point ici leurs Commissions. Il me paroit suffisant de vous assurer qu'elles sont Conformes aux autres Commissions de Vice Consuls que vous avés déjà eu la bonté de présenter à ce Chef de l'éxécutif de l'union Americaine.

Dft (DLC: Genet Papers); unsigned; at head of text: "à Copier"; above salutation: "Le Cit Genet &c à M. Jefferson &c."; the most significant emendation is recorded below. Tr (AMAE: CPEU, xxxix). Recorded in SJL as a 29 Oct. 1793 letter received 4 Nov. 1793.

[1] Sentence to this point interlined in place of a canceled passage that in its final state read "Ces Commissions, Mr., n'étant nécéssitées que par des travaux éxtraordinaires occasionnés par les prises de vaisseaux de la Republique et par le reflus dans les Etats unis d'un grand nombre de françois refugiés de St. domingue. Je ne vous ai point importuné pour obtenir en faveur de ceux qui en sont revêtus."

From John M. Pintard

Madeira, 29 Oct. 1793. He encloses copies of his 8, 9, and 15 Oct. letters and their enclosures, as well as a copy of his letter of this date to Edward Church, which will explain the particulars of his case more fully than the statement he transmitted with his 15 Oct. letter. He does not enclose the Portuguese papers mentioned in his letter to Church, which consist of a notary public's certificate that he would not take Pintard's protest against the governor for fear of that official and a certified copy of the receipt for the money he received for demurrage on his Bordeaux vessel, the latter of which is dated 21 Oct., two days before his clerk and vice-consul were examined and the governor ordered him to exhibit his books. The Portuguese government has concluded a one-year truce with the Algerines and permitted five of their corsairs to sail beyond the Straits of Gibraltar. They are cruising off Cape St. Vincent and the Rocks of Lisbon, and yesterday two vessels arrived here from Lisbon that had been boarded by them. He fears the corsairs will wreak havoc on American ships bound to Cadiz or Lisbon. David Humphreys sailed from Lisbon for Gibraltar on 16 Sep., leaving Church in charge of American affairs. He has not heard from him by either of the vessels that has arrived, but presumes he shall by the next one. The English government at Gibraltar reportedly negotiated the Portuguese-Algerine treaty or truce, which he presumes is a political maneuver by the combined powers because of their envy of rising American prosperity. Because of the advanced season, he presumes the Algerines will wait until spring before sailing beyond the Straits in swarms. He will continue to communicate such information as he receives about this matter and all others affecting the United States.

RC (DNA: RG 59, CD); 4 p.; date altered from 28 to 29 Oct. 1793; with subjoined list of enclosed papers; endorsed by TJ as received 19 Dec. 1793 and so recorded in SJL. Enclosure: Pintard to Church, 29 Oct. 1793, stating that he was grateful for the news in Enclosure No. 2 listed at Pintard to TJ, 8 Oct. 1793, but disappointed that Church was not as successful in the case of the French ship *Commerciant*, about which he had also informed Humphreys; that the Portuguese government had sent a frigate to bring the *Commerciant* and its cargo to Lisbon, while leaving its passengers and crew free to go where they pleased; that the governor of Madeira had imprisoned him in his own home for almost two days, ostensibly because he had without official authorization sent a boat to bring himself letters from the brig *Washington*, Captain Goddard, which had just arrived from Lisbon, but in reality because of the governor's mortification at the orders that ship brought from the Portuguese government for him to make compensation for the detention of the *Minerva* from 21 July to 14 Aug. 1793, when it finally left for Bordeaux; that he advised the governor, when the latter offered to make compensation strictly on the basis of his charter party with Captain Allen of the *Minerva*, that an accurate assessment of damages would have to await the arrival of news from Bordeaux, from which the *Minerva* might have to leave without a return cargo because of a late August National Convention decree forbidding the exportation of certain articles from France, a situation the ship could have avoided if it had been allowed to leave Madeira as scheduled on 21 July; that thereafter the Royal Junto here examined under oath his bookkeeper, Nathaniel [Hayward], and his vice-consul, Richard Bright, about

how the money for the charter party was paid to Captain Allen; that following this examination he complied with a written order from the governor directing him to allow a deputy of the Royal Junto and the British vice-consul to examine his books to ascertain where and how Allen was paid, but not before unsuccessfully requesting a copy of the order; that he hopes the Portuguese government will make amends to him for the despotic conduct he has endured and that the Secretary of State will provide him with written orders to protect his person from further insult; that he will not be deterred from performing his public duties by the governor's power to injure him in his private business; that no notary public would take down his protest against his imprisonment, but one did provide the enclosed notarial certificate indicating how the governor is feared here; and that he encloses a copy of the receipt he gave at the Royal Junto for the sum paid to Captain Allen, as appears by Allen's receipt transmitted to Humphreys, the former being dated 21 Oct. 1793, when the business relating to the demurrage of the *Minerva* appears to have been settled, even though his books were examined and his employees investigated two days after that (Tr in same; in a clerk's hand, signed by Pintard; at foot of text: "(Copy)"). For the other enclosures, see the enclosures listed at Pintard to TJ, 8, 15 Oct. 1793.

Pintard also wrote a brief note to TJ from Madeira on 30 Oct. 1793 transmitting copies of letters just received from Lisbon (RC in DNA: RG 59, CD; at head of text: "Honble Thomas Jefferson"; endorsed by TJ as received 19 Dec. 1793 and so recorded in SJL). The letters were David Humphreys to Pintard, Gibraltar, 6 Oct.

1793, stating that in consequence of a twelve-month truce between Algiers and Portugal, an Algerine fleet of four frigates, one brig, and three xebecs had passed through the Straits of Gibraltar last night into the Atlantic, and that Pintard should notify his countrymen of this as soon as possible; and Edward Church to the Citizens of the United States of America, Lisbon, 14 Oct. 1793, stating that Algerine corsairs carrying 22 to 44 guns sailed out of the Mediterranean on 6 Oct. 1793 and were witnessed three days later capturing four American vessels and one Genoese vessel, and that a twelve-month truce between Algiers and Portugal was signed on 12 Sep. on behalf of the Queen of Portugal by the British agent at Algiers, who about the same time signed another truce between Algiers and the Netherlands, with a 15 Oct. postscript stating that a Swedish vessel witnessed the Algerines discharge part of a cargo of grain from a captured American vessel so as to facilitate arming it as a cruiser, that ten Dutch captains taken by the Algerines since their war with the Netherlands have died of the plague in Algiers, that he does not know how many others have succumbed to the same fate, and that according to an American just arrived from Falmouth, American vessels now in England are returning in ballast because for some reason the English have chosen not to risk their property in American ships, a conduct mysterious in England but understandable here (Trs in same; with certification at foot of each text, in a clerk's hand, signed by Pintard, indicating that the originals were received on 30 Oct. 1793).

TJ submitted Pintard's 29 and 30 Oct. letters to the President on 19 Dec. 1793, and Washington returned them the same day (Washington, *Journal*, 271).

From Edmond Charles Genet

MONSIEUR

Newyork Le 30. 8bre. 1793.
L'an 2e. de la republique française.

Des Traitres viennent de livrer aux ennemis de la france une portion intéressante de St. Domingue. Quelques bons Citoÿens qui ont mieux aimé S'expatrier et abandonner leur fortune que de prêter à une puissance étrangère un Serment qu'ils ne devoient qu'a la republique française, m'ont apporté cette nouvelle. Ainsi, Monsieur, cette Colonie dans la quelle un Decret de la Convention nationale venoit d'admettre vos vaisseaux aux mêmes Conditions que les nôtres; Cette Colonie qui étoit depuis dix ans le principal aliment de votre agriculture et de votre navigation; Cette Colonie enfin qui vous fournissoit les moyens de payer vos relations avec l'Europe, Touche au moment d'être perdüe pour vous Comme pour nous.

La Prise de possession que viennent d'effectuer les anglais d'une partie de cette Isle n'est qu'une Suite du plan qui Se combine depuis deux ans entre les Colons des isles du vent et des isles Sous le vent pour Se livrer aux anglais et aux espagnols. C'est par une suite de ce plan que l'etendart de la rebellion a flotté pendant quatre mois aux isles du vent. C'est à la demande des Colons eux mêmes, C'est d'après une députation qu'ils ont eû l'impudence d'envoyer publiquement à Londres, qu'une flotte considérable avoit été envoyée par le Ministère de St. James pour mettre le siége devant la Martinique, qui ainsy que Jérémie n'existeroit

plus ni pour vous, ni pour nous, S'il ne S'y étoit Trouvé de braves patriotes qui ont Sû repousser les traitres, et les Tirans que le même interêt
avoit Coalisé.

Les hommes qui ont appellé les anglois et les espagnols dans St. Domingue Sont liés avec un grand nombre de ces mêmes Colons que par
pitié, par bonté les Etats unis ont accueillis, que par égard pour les
vertus charitables de vos Concitoyens, j'ai moi même Secouru de Concert avec eux. C'est Sur cette Terre de liberté que Se sont formés tous
les projets, que Se Sont concertés tous Les plans contre révolutionnaires
qui viennent de S'executer. C'est d'ici que Sont partis Tous les émissaires qui Sont allés Traiter avec nos ennemis et la joie que manifestent
en ce moment un grand nombre de Colons ne laisse pas de doute Sur
leur complicité.

Cette conspiration étoit liée avec l'arrivée de L'Escadre de la Republique dans les Etats unis sous la conduite de galbaud. Les Scelerats qui
avoient fait la guerre aux Citoÿens réintégrés dans les Droits de
l'homme par la loi du 4. avril, Travailloient ici, Comme dans la Colonie
à égarer cette escadre et Se flattoient de la livrer aux nombreux Contre
révolutionnaires refugiés dans vos Ports, de la ramener à st. Domingue,
et de Concourir avec elle à l'exécution des infâmes projets qui viennent
de S'effectuer. La decouverte de leur Correspondance, la saisie légale de
leurs papiers et leur fuite dans le Canada depuis que j'ai éventé leurs
forfaits[1] ne m'ont prouvé que trop la réalité de cette Conjuration
dans le renversement de la quelle J'ai été si bien secondé par le vertueux
gouverneur et le digne maire de New york. Cependant je ne suis point
au Terme de mes peines, ces hommes qui vouloient entièrement corrompre nos forces navales,[2] méditent de nouveaux Projets et Conspirent
actuellement non Seulement Contre leur patrie, mais encore Contre
votre propre indépendance et votre propre sûreté; peuplant Toutes vos
villes maritimes, ils S'efforcent d'y pervertir l'opinion publique, en la
dirigeant vers leur Sistème de royalisme, ils Se coalisent avec les
émigrés, avec les agens des ci devant princes françois, avec les anglois,
s'avoüent hautement les Sujets de ces derniers[3] ou du prétendu Louis
XVII, grossissent le parti de cette nation qui n'a pas encore perdû
l'espoir de vous reconquérir et Se rendent Les instrumens les plus actifs
du Sistème de domination universelle à la quelle aspire cette puissance
audacieuse Sur tous les Etablissemens de l'amerique.

Enfin ne pouvant modérer leur Caractère remuant et agitateur aigri
par l'infortune, Ils deviennent dangereux même pour la Sûreté, pour
l'existence morale de vos Etats du Sud. Propageant eux mêmes des
principes Contre les quels ils declament Sans circonspection, envi-
ronnés de noirs et de mulâtres qui ont gouté le fruit Savoureux de la
Liberté, ils peuvent donner[4] lieu à des mouvemens.[5] Ce sont eux qui par

la publication irrefléchie des mesures que leur rebellion a provoquées et peutêtre malheureusement provoquera encore, fournissent à vos Planteurs du Sud l'aliment des allarmes continuelles qu'ils éprouvent; Ce sont eux qui leur faisant craindre Sans cesse une insurrection parmi Leurs esclaves, refroidissent par le sentiment puissant de leur interêt, les sentimens d'amitié que leur patriotisme les portoit à avoir pour la france. C'est à Charlestown Surtout que leur prodigieuse multiplication est devenüe dangereuse tant pour vous même que pour ma patrie. C'est là qu'on les voit Se permettre audacieusement les provocations les plus indécentes et les calomnies les plus atroces contre les agens de la republique; C'est là ainsy qu'a Philadelphie et à Baltimore qu'on les voit se porter envers les fonctionnaires publics d'une patrie qu'ils ont reniée, aux menaces les plus insolentes, [6] et que leur grand nombre a jusqu'ici assuré l'impunité de leurs attentats.

La france votre amie apprendra Sans doute avec peine que de tels hommes Soient non seulement Tolérés, mais encore qu'ils tiennent des assemblées publiques à Charlestown, à Baltimore, à Philadelphie, à Newyork et qu'ils y repandent impunément des journaux remplis d'invectives et de Calomnies contr'elle et Contre Ses délégués. Sans doute je n'ai pas droit d'exiger contr'eux des mesures répressives, mais je puis au moins exprimer le voeu du representant de la nation française. Il me paroit indispensable autant pour votre tranquillité [7] que pour les interêts de la france que le gouvernement féderal prenne dans Sa Sagesse des mesures promptes pour faire avorter les Complots que je viens de lui dénoncer et pour éviter autant qu'il Se pourra que le sol de la Liberté ne Soit point Souillé par la Lave que le volcan de st. Domingue y a jetté et qui ne peut y repandre que le poison de l'aristocratie et du Royalisme. Pourquoi ces hommes dangereux choisissent-ils de préférence le Territoire de la liberté Si ce n'est pour la Compromettre ou Conspirer Contr'elle? S'ils ne vivifient ni votre commerce, ni votre agriculture, S'ils ne peuvent que vicier votre éxistence morale et politique et diviser votre fédération en deux parts, pourquoi ne seroient ils pas à l'avenir envoyés Sur les Terres des rois vos voisins dont ils S'avouent les esclaves? L'Espagne leur offre la molesse de ses villes; l'orgueil anglois leur tend les bras; ils ont à leur porte des Compagnons de Servitude et des rivaux [8] en barbarie, et c'est icy qu'ils portent leurs pieds liberticides et corrupteurs! [9] Pardonnéz, Monsieur, à l'indignation qui m'opresse, à l'amour de ma patrie qui m'isole peutêtre de la Sensibilité; mais la Saison des Tempéramens n'existe plus; Le régime de la Liberté veut des hommes, on en exclut Comme à sparte tout ce qui ne promet pas de l'être; la gazette de la Caroline du Sud repand des bruits et des Soupçons; une Coalition atroce fait dénoncer [10] nos républicains comme des

Conspirateurs et nos magistrats comme des brandons incendiaires. C'est votre intervention que je réclame, Monsieur; vous que j'avertis si Souvent des vrais rapports de notre esprit avec les autres peuples; vous à qui j'ai notifié officiellement le Décret d'avril qui dément des Calomnies trop accreditées parmi vous. Les grandes destructions par Toute la france Sont dües à des resistances étonnantes; nous étions déterminés à ne composer avec aucun principe reconnu pour vrai. Le tumulte fut grand, parceque les abus étoient monstrueusement accumulés; mais où ont ils vû ces Calomniateurs insensés, que nous veuillions forcer les revolutions dans le sein des peuples et introniser nos Principes à la lueur des incendies et avec le Couteau des assassins? Où ont-ils vû que Les républicains français ayent meprisé les loix et méconnu Les autorités? Il est Temps, Monsieur, que vous préveniés la formation d'un autre Coblentz dans votre Sein; il est Temps que la nation française soit connüe à fond et vengée des insultes de ces émigrés pervers rejettés du monde entier; il est Temps que vous mettiéz en vigueur des loix que vos Legislateurs ont faites pour empêcher que l'intrusion des émigrés étrangers ne devienne un fardeau pour la société, car bientôt les patriotes de 1775 ne seront plus rien dans le paÿs qu'ils ont créé, l'arbre de la Liberté dont Les racines ont été arrosées de leur Sang ne Couvrira plus de Son ombre que Ses plus cruels ennemis. Ferméz vos ports à Tous ces hommes vils qui viennent Chéz vous pour y jouir des bienfaits d'un régime qu'ils ont Trahi dans leur Patrie et qu'ils Trahiraient également icy lorsque les évenemens qui s'accumulent vous auront mis dans la nécéssité de prendre part à la Lutte de la Liberté Contre la Tirannie. Cette époque, Monsieur, marquée par la destinée qui Se joüe des mesures que prennent les foibles humains pour éviter des maux souvent réels, mais plus Souvent illusoires S'approche chaque jour. La liberalité et le desinteressement[11] de nos procédés envers vous, la Circonspection de nos Demandes, la politique que vous avéz observé n'ont Conduit à rien; vous êtes Compris dans la Conjuration des tirans et votre ancien maitre Se repait déja de l'idée de tirer de vous un vengeance éclatante. Des avis que je crois Certains m'instruisent que le gouvernement Brittanique ayant appris la défaite de Gardner à la Martinique a resolu de faire une seconde tentative Sur cette Colonie. Les ordres sont déjà donnés à plusieurs vaisseaux et à plusieurs régimens de se tenir prêts à partir pour cette destination. D'autres expéditions Secretes Se préparent. L'ordre est donné de Lever des troupes dans le Canada, dans l'acadie et dans toutes les possessions anglaises du nord de l'amérique. Plusieurs officiers envoyés par le Lord *Dorchester* et par *Simpcoe* parcourent vos Etats pour observer vos mouvemens ou constater votre état d'indéfence; les Espagnols agissent de leur Côté et Tout annonce que les

Cours de Londres et de Madrid Sont déterminées à vous attaquer Sans ménagement ou à vous impôser des Conditions Si humiliantes, que Le peuple américain ne sauroit jamais y Souscrire.

Dans cet état des Choses il est de mon devoir de vous représenter qu'il n'est pas probable que le nombre de bons Citoyens qui ont jusqu'ici défendû nos Colonies puisse résister à toutes les forces tant intérieures qu'exterieures qui les menacent et que ces possessions précieuses que les loix de la Convention nationale ont rendües aussi intéressantes pour votre Commerce que pour le nôtre touchent au moment d'être perdües pour vous Comme pour nous. La république française a le droit d'espérer dans une pareille Circonstance que la garantie que vous avéz promise à cet égard ne sera pas entierement illusoire et que vous vous empresseréz de l'effectuer par des secours directs par des diversions ou bien enfin par des demonstrations imposantes [12] avec le même Zêle qu'elle défendra votre indépendance Si elle est attaquée. Vos engagemens et le partage fraternel que nous faisons avec vous de ces sources fécondes de richesses vous font un devoir de vous montrer. [13] Votre navigation vous en impose la nécéssité et votre interêt doit vous presser de vous entendre promptement avec nous Sur les mesures à prendre en Commun, puisque le danger pèse également Sur nous et Sur vous. La neutralité dont nous aurions souhaité nous mêmes que votre pavillon fut revêtu [14] n'est qu'un vain mot qui n'abuse plus la Crédulité publique; vous êtes dans un état de guerre [15] indeterminé bien plus dangereux qu'un état de guerre déclarée. L'angleterre ne veut point que votre commerce prospere tandis que le sien languit, elle ne veut point que ses matelots qui deviennent plus rares de Jour en Jour trouvent sur vos vaisseaux un azyle contre la presse; Elle insulte en Conséquence le signe de votre souveraineté sur toutes les mers. Elle prend [16] impunément vos vaisseaux, ou y presse vos matelots; elle excite au nord [17] les indiens contre vos Citoÿens; tandis que les Espagnols les arment contre eux au Sud, ces deux puissances [18] vous font une guerre Sanglante Sous le nom de ces Sauvages, elles font avorter ou prolongent avec perfidie [19] toutes les négociations que vous entaméz pour rétablir la paix avec eux, la première retient impudemment au mépris des Traités garantis par la france, des forts qui leur servent à alimenter ces barbares; et toutes deux attaquent en amérique les posséssions de la france que la religion des traités vous force de défendre Sans qu'il Soit necéssaire même que nous vous en requérions. Tous ces faits doivent vous convaincre qu'il ne vous reste plus que deux partis à prendre et que vous devéz vous courber sous le poids de vos anciens fers; passer humblement Sous les *fourches caudines* que les Rois d'angleterre et d'Espagne vous préparent, vous jetter dans les bras liberticides de ces Vampires politiques, au prix de votre honneur, ou bien Si l'esprit de 1775 n'a point encore fui de cette Contrée, avertir votre souverain qu'il est temps qu'il Se lève avec majesté, qu'il est temps que votre Jeunesse aille prendre dans vos arsenaux les armes que leurs pères y ont déposées avec leurs lauriers impérissables pour[20] défendre s'il le faut avec la france[21] la liberté et l'indépendance des peuples le bonheur du genre humain.[22]

Dft (DLC: Genet Papers); in a clerk's hand, unsigned, with revisions by Genet; above salutation: "Le Citoÿen Genet Ministre plenipotentiaire de la republique françoise près des Etats unis, à Mr. Monsieur Jefferson Secretaire d'Etat des Etats unis"; only the most significant emendations are noted below. Recorded in SJL as received 7 Nov. 1793.

UNE PORTION INTÉRESSANTE DE ST. DOMINGUE: for the landing of a British expeditionary force of 600 men under the command of Lieutenant Colonel John Whitelocke at the port of Jéremie on 20 Sep. 1793, which marked the beginning of a five-year British occupation of Saint-Domingue, see Geggus, *Slavery*, 105-8. UN DECRET DE LA CONVENTION NATIONALE: see the enclosure listed at Genet to TJ, 30 Sep. 1793. LA LOI DU 4. AVRIL: a reference to the National Convention's 4 Apr. 1793 decree freeing French soldiers imprisoned on galleys for desertion prior to the French declaration of war on Austria on 20 Apr. 1792 (*Archives Parlementaires*, 1st ser., LXI, 295). LE DÉCRET D'AVRIL: see the enclosure listed at Genet to TJ, [24] Sep. 1793 (first letter). UN AUTRE COBLENTZ: under the leadership of Louis XVI's brothers, the Comte d'Artois and the Comte de Provence, the Rhineland city of Koblenz was the principal gathering point for French émigrés plotting to overthrow the revolutionary regime in France (Jacques Godechot, *The Counter-Revolution: Doctrine and Action, 1789-1804* [New York, 1971], 155-60). LA DÉFAITE DE GARDNER À LA MARTINIQUE: see note to Fulwar Skipwith to TJ, July 1793. LA GARANTIE QUE VOUS AVÉZ PROMISE: a reference to Article 11 of the 1778 treaty of alliance with France whereby the United States agreed to guarantee French possessions in America. The British invasion of Saint-Domingue led Genet to invoke this obligation despite his previous assurances to TJ that France would not do so. Although Alexander Hamilton and Edmund Randolph subsequently advised the President to inform Congress of Genet's invoca-

tion of this article, apparently on the basis of TJ's reading of the French minister's letter at an 8 Nov. 1793 Cabinet meeting, Washington ignored their advice and TJ made no response to Genet's demand (Miller, *Treaties*, II, 39; Memorandum of Conversations with Edmond Charles Genet, 26 July 1793; Notes of Cabinet Meetings on Edmond Charles Genet and the President's Address to Congress, [18 Nov. 1793]; George Washington to the Senate and the House of Representatives, [2 Dec. 1793], and note; Randolph, "Heads of subjects to be communicated to congress; some at the opening, others by messages," filed at end of November 1793 in DLC: Washington Papers; Syrett, *Hamilton*, XV, 429).

[1] Remainder of sentence written in the margin by Genet in place of "depuis que j'ai désabusé nos marins Sur Galbaud et Ses Complices, ne m'ont prouvé que Trop évidemment la réalité de cette Conjuration dans le renversement de laquelle j'ai été Si bien Secondé par le verteux gouverneur et Les dignes magistrats de New york."

[2] Clause altered by Genet from "L'escadre est Sauvée, mais ces hommes qui vouloient la perdre."

[3] Remainder of clause written in the margin by Genet.

[4] Preceding three words altered by Genet from "ils donnent."

[5] Genet here canceled "qui Se sont manifestés dans quelques uns de ces Etats."

[6] Word interlined by Genet in place of "dangereuses."

[7] Word written in the margin by Genet in place of "sûreté."

[8] Word interlined by Genet in place of "Confrères."

[9] Exclamation point inserted by Genet.

[10] Altered by Genet from "une Conspiration atroce venge sa defaite de New york en dénonçant."

[11] Preceding four words interlined by Genet in place of "generosité."

[12] Preceding seven words interlined by Genet, who first wrote "preparatifs" for "demonstrations."

[13] Preceding sentence altered by Genet from "Vos engagemens vous font un devoir de cette garantie," to which he first added "qui doit être la Condition sine qua non de" in the margin and canceled it, and then substituted "vous reveiller au bruit des chaines" for "cette garantie" and canceled it.

[14] Sentence to this point written in the margin by Genet in place of "La neutralité dont vous voudriéz vous couvrir."

[15] Remainder of sentence interlined by Genet in place of "véritable quoiqu'elle ne soit encore déclarée."

[16] Sentence to this point and sentence preceding it interlined and written in the margin by Genet in place of "Votre pavil-lon est insulté sur toutes les mers, nos en-nemis communs prenent."

[17] Genet here canceled "et au sud."

[18] Preceding thirteen words interlined by Genet in place of "Ils."

[19] Clause to this point altered by Genet from "ils ont fait avorter."

[20] Genet here interlined and then canceled "faire respecter la paix ⟨dont le peuple americain voudroit⟩ que les Etats unis vou-droient conserver ou."

[21] Preceding seven words interlined by Genet in place of "avec nous."

[22] Genet here canceled the remainder of the text, which he sent to TJ in the form of the following document.

Note from Edmond Charles Genet

[ca. 30 Oct. 1793]

Note particuliere.

Les français du Canada, des Illinois, de la nouvelle Orléans n'atten-dent que l'Instant où les américains prendront une attitude digne d'un peuple libre pour s'unir à eux et pour Consacrer[1] ce vaste Continent au Culte de la Divinité qui regnera bientôt sur le monde entier. Les adresses cijointes les ont instruits des dispositions de la france,[2] des agens Surs les ont repandus parmi eux et l'on peut assurer que s'ils voyoient[3] paroitre Sur les frontieres tracées par leurs Tirans les 15 étoiles américaines unies aux Trois couleurs du peuple françois,[4] leurs fers Seroient brisés, l'angleterre et l'Espagne punies et l'humanité Vengée.

RC (DLC); undated; in a clerk's hand, unsigned; endorsed by TJ as a "private note" received 7 Nov. 1793 and so recorded in SJL. Dft (DLC: Genet Papers); consists of canceled portion of last paragraph of Genet to TJ, 30 Oct. 1793, in a clerk's hand with revisions by Genet and with "Note particuliere" written in the margin by him. FC (same). Enclosure: see enclosure print-ed at Josef Ignacio de Viar and Josef de Jau-denes to TJ, 27 Aug. 1793. Other enclosure printed below.

Genet wrote this private note in a bid to obtain American support of his officially au-thorized plans for subverting Spanish rule in Louisiana and British rule in Canada.

The Girondin ministry that sanctioned these ventures had instructed the French minister to seek American support for them in return for recognizing the right of the United States to navigate the Mississippi and holding out the possibility of adding Canada to the American Union, though there is no evidence that Genet ever ap-prised TJ of the latter point (Turner, *CFM*, 204). Genet had recently sent an obscure emissary named Mezieres to spread revolu-tionary propaganda among French settlers in Canada and dispatched a small naval squadron from New York to capture the is-lands of St. Pierre and Miquelon, destroy the British fishery at Newfoundland, and encourage the French inhabitants of Acadia to resist British rule—a mission these ships never carried out, preferring instead to return to France (Maude H. Woodfin, "Citizen Genet and his Mission" [Ph.D. diss., University of Chicago, 1928], 428-34). For the steps Genet had also taken to end Spanish control of Louisiana, see Editorial Note on André Michaux's proposed western expedition, at 22 Jan. 1793; TJ to Isaac Shelby, 28 June 1793, and note; and Josef Ignacio de Viar and Josef de Jaudenes to TJ, 2 Oct. 1793, and note. There is no evidence that TJ ever informed the President or the Cabinet of the French minister's note.

[1] Altered in Dft by Genet from "que cet instant pour s'unir à eux et à nous et pour consacrer de Concert."

[2] Altered in Dft by Genet from "de nos dispositions."

[3] Preceding nine words altered in Dft by Genet from "notre Escadre a dû les avoir porté dans cet instant aux Canadiens. J'ose vous assurer que lorsquils verront."

[4] Remainder of sentence written in margin of Dft by Genet in place of "Le nouveau monde Sera libre," for which he had first substituted and then canceled "⟨l'affranchissement du⟩ le nouveau monde."

ENCLOSURE

Edmond Charles Genet's Address to Canada

Les FRANCAIS LIBRES a leurs freres Les CANADIENS.

Lorsque nous gémissions sous un gouvernement arbitraire nous ne pouvions que plaindre votre sort, regretter les liens qui nous unissaient à vous, et en murmurant en secret des trahisons dont vous aviés été les victimes nous n'osions pas plus que vous lever nos têtes courbées sous le joug de la servitude, une stérile indignation de la conduite criminelle de nos rois envers vous etait le seul hommage que nous pussions vous rendre.

Mais aujourd'hui nous sommes libres, nous sommes rentrés dans nos droits, nos oppresseurs sont punis, toutes les parties de notre administration sont régenerées et forts de la justice de notre cause, de notre courage et des immenses moyens que nous avons préparés pour terrasser tous les tirans; il est enfin en notre pouvoir de vous venger, et de vous rendre aussi libres que nous, aussi indépendans que vos voisins les Americains de Etats-Unis. Canadiens, imités leur exemple et le notre, la route en est tracée, une résolution magnanime peut vous faire sortir de l'état d'abjection ou vous êtes plongés. Il dépend de vous de réimprimer sur vos fronts cette dignité premiere que la nature a placé sur l'homme et que l'esclavage avait effacée.

L'homme est né libre; par quelle fatalité est il devenu le sujet de son semblable? Comment a pu s'operer cet étrange bouleversement d'idées, qui a fait que des nations entieres se sont volontairement soumises a rester la propriété d'un seul individu? C'est par l'ignorance, la mollesse, la pusillanimité des uns, l'ambition, la perfidie; les injustices, &c, des autres. Mais aujourd'hui que par les excès d'une domination devenüe insupportable des peuples entiers, en s'élevant contre leurs oppresseurs ont révélé le secret de leur foiblesse et dévoilé l'iniquité de leurs moyens, combien ne sont elles pas coupables les nations qui restent volontairement dans des fers avilissans et qui effrayées du sacrifice de quelques momens de repos, se livrent à une honteuse inertie et restent volontairement dans la servitude. Tout autour de vous vous invite à la liberté; le païs que vous habités a été conquis par vos peres. Il ne doit sa prosperité qu'a leurs soins et aux votres, cette terre vous appartient, elle doit etre indépendante. Rompés donc avec un gouvernement qui dégénere de jour en jour et qui est devenu le plus cruel ennemi de la liberté des peuples. Partout on retrouve des traces du despotisme, de l'avidité, des cruautés du roi d'Angleterre. Il est tems de renverser un trone ou s'est trop longtems assise l'hypocrisie et l'imposture, que les vils courtisans qui l'entouraient soient punis de leurs crimes ou que dispersés sur le globe l'opprobre dont ils seront couverts atteste au monde, qu'une tardive mais éclatante vengeance s'est operée en faveur de l'humanité.

Cette révolution nécessaire, ce chatiment inévitable se prépare rapidement en Angleterre. Les principes républicains y font tous les jours de nouveaux progrés et le nombre des amis de la liberté et de la France y augmente d'une maniere sensible; mais n'attendés point pour rentrer dans vos droits l'issue de cet événement, travaillés pour vous, pour votre gloire, ne craignés rien de George III, de ses soldats, en trop petit nombre pour s'opposer avec succés à votre valeur, sa foible armée est retenue en Angleterre autour de lui par les murmures des Anglais, et par les immenses préparatifs de la France, qui ne lui permettent pas d'augmenter le nombre de vos bourreaux. Le moment est favorable et l'insurrection est pour vous le plus saint des devoirs, n'hésités donc pas et rappellés aux hommes qui seraient asses laches pour refuser leurs bras et leurs armes a une aussi généreuse enterprise l'histoire de vos malheurs. Les cruautés exercées par l'Angleterre pour vous faire passer sous son autorité. Les insultes qui vous ont été faites par des agens qui s'engraissaient de vos sueurs. Rappellés leur les noms odieux de Murray et d'Haldimand; les victimes de leurs ferocités. Les entraves dont votre commerce a été garotté; le monopole odieux qui l'énerve et l'empeche de s'aggrandir; les traites perilleuses que vous entreprenés pour le seul avantage des Anglais: Enfin rappellés leur qu'etant nés Francais vous serès toujours enviés, persecutes par les Rois Anglais et que ce titre sera plus que jamais, aujourd'hui, un motif d'exclusion pour tous les emplois.

En effet des Français traiteraient leurs concitoyens en freres et se soucieraient moins de plaire au despote Anglais qu'a rendre justice aux Canadiens, ils ne s'attacheraient pas a plaire aux rois, mais à leurs freres: Ils renonceroient plutot à leurs places que de commettre une injustice: Ils préféreraient aux pensions, qui leur seraient accordés la douce satisfaction d'etre aimés et estimés dignes de leur origine. Ils opposeraient une vigoureuse résistance aux decrets arbitraires de la cour de Londres; de cette cour perfide qui n'a accordé au Canada une ombre de constitution que dans la crainte qu'il ne suivit l'exemple vertueux de la France et de l'Amerique; qu'en secouant son joug il ne fonda son gouvernement sur les droits imprescriptibles de l'homme.

Aussi quels avantages avés vous retirés de la constitution qui vous a été donnée depuis six mois que vos representans font assemblées vous ont ils fait present d'une bonne loi? ont ils pu corriger un abus? ont ils eu le pouvoir d'affranchir votre commerce de ses entraves? non, et pour quoi? parceque tous les moyens de corruption sont employés secretement et publiquement dans vos elections pour fait pencher la balance en faveur des Anglais.

Canadiens, vous avés en vous tout ce qui peut constituer votre bonheur, eclairés, laborieux, courageux, amis de la justice, industrieux, qu'aves vous besoin de confier le soin de vous gouverner a un tiran stupide, à un roi imbecille dont les caprices peuvent entraver vos déliberations et vous laisser sans loi pendant des années entieres. N'est il pas aussi ridicule de confier a un pareil homme placé à l'autre extremité du globe le soin de veiller à vos plus chers interets, que de voir un cultivateur Canadien aller se placer aux sources du Missouri pour mieux diriger son habitation.

Les hommes ont le droit de se gouverner eux mêmes, les loix doivent être l'expression de la volonté du peuple manifestée par l'organe de ses representans, nul n'a le droit de s'opposer à leur éxécution, et cependant on a osé vous imposer un odieux *veto* que le roi d'Angleterre ne s'est reservé que pour empêcher la destruction des abus et pour paraliser tous vos mouvemens: voila le présent que de vils stipendiés ont osé vous présenter comme un monument de bienfaisance du gouvernement Anglais. On à comparé très ingenieusement le pouvoir légis-latif à la tête d'un homme qui conçoit et le pouvoir executif[1] aux bras du même homme qui éxecute, si les bras se refusent à ce que la tête a jugé necessaire au bien du corps entiér, privé de secours il devient malade et il meurt.

Canadiens, il est tems de sortir du sommeil lethargique dans lequel vous etes plongés, armés vous, appellés à votre secours vos amis les Indiens, comptés sur l'appui de vos voisins et sur celui des Francais. Jurés de ne quitter vos armes que lorsque vous serés délivrés de vos ennemis, prenés le ciel et votre conscience a temoin de l'equité de vos résolutions et vous obtiendrés ce que les hommes énergiques ne reclament jamais en vain, la liberté et indépendance.

Resumé des avantages que les Canadiens peuvent obtenir en se délivrant de la domination Anglaise.

1. Le Canada sera un Etat libre et Independant.

2. Il pourra former des alliances avec la France et les Etats Unis.

3. Les Canadiens se choisiront un gouvernement, ils nommeront eux mêmes les membres du corps legislatif et du pouvoir éxécutif.

4. Le veto sera aboli.

5. Toutes les personnes qui auront obtenu le droit de citoyen du Canada pouront etre nommées à toutes les places.

6. Les corvées seront abolies.

7. Le commerce jouira de la liberté la plus etenduë.

8. Il n'y aura plus de compagnie privilegiée pour le commerce des fourures, le nouveau gouvernement l'encouragera.

9. Les droits seigneuriaux seront abolis les lots et ventes, droits de mouture, de peage, reserve de bois, travaux pour le service des seigneurs, &c. &c. seront également abolis.

10. Seront également abolis tous les titres héréditaires, il n'existera plus ni lords, ni seigneurs, ni nobles.

11. Tous les cultes seront libres. Les prêtres catholiques nommés par le peu-ple comme dans la primitive eglise jouiront d'un traitement analogue a leur utilité.

12. Les dimes seront abolies.

Il sera établi des Ecoles dans les paroisses et dans les villes: Il y aura des imprimeries, des institutions pour les hautes sciences, la medicine, les mathe-matiques, il sera formé des interpretes qui reconnus de bonnes mœurs seront encouragés à civiliser les nations sauvages et a etendre par ce moyen leur com-merce avec elles.

Text reprinted from [Edmond Charles Genet], *Les Francais Libres A Leurs Freres Les Canadiens* [Philadelphia, 1793] (DLC: Rare Book and Special Collections Divi-sion); with alteration by TJ noted below and several obvious printer's errors silently corrected; notation, possibly by TJ, par-tially cut away at top of first page: "1793."

See Sowerby, No. 3243. Another copy is in AMAE: CPEU, xxxix.

[1] Word as corrected by TJ from "legis-latif." An unidentified contemporary hand made the same correction in the AMAE copy of the pamphlet.

From Thomas Mann Randolph, Jr.

Dear Sir   Monticello Oct: 31. 1793

Altho I know your time is allready so completely taken up, with important public concerns, that you are obliged to neglect your own private matters, allmost totally, I cannot refrain from asking a small part of it, for an affair of very considerable consequence, to myself and my family. I have mentioned to you before, tho perhaps I never related the particulars, that the[1] land in Henrico, given me by my father, was under an incumbrance. It was mortgaged in December 1787 to Mr. Herman Le Roy, then of New-York, now a resident in Philada., to secure the discharge of two bonds of £860.3.4. sterling each, the one payable on the 1st. Feb: 1788, the other on the same day of the year 1789. The sum of £.1169.16.6. current money, was paid by David Ross to the draft of my father in favor of Alexander Donald, then acting for Mr. Le Roy, on and immediately before, the 9. May 1789, in discharge of one of the bonds. Nothing, as far as I can learn, has been paid on the other: it remains still undischarged, with all the interest which has accrued. With respect to this other bond, and the interest due on it, I am somewhat uneasy in the present condition of my father; he[2] is rendered by disease incapable of managing his affairs, there is no great hope of his recovery, and in consequence a considerable derangement is likely to ensue. My purchase in Albemarle having put the means of indemnification, in my own hands,[3] I am[4] desirous of making some arrangement with Mr. Le Roy immediately, to take on myself the payment of the bond undischarged, and provide for the release of my land. You will oblige me much by proposing to him, and executing in my name some agreement to this purpose. Perhaps it might suit him to receive the whole sum at once, on a day,[5] not nearer than eighteen months from the first of March next: this would be highly convenient to me, as I could make provision by the sale of[6] my property of a certain species. It is more probable that he may prefer installments: in this case I will undertake to raise a sum of 500.£.[7] in the course of the winter; the fund, a parcel of Wheat of very good quality, by estimation 2000 bushels, now on the land of Varina and ready for market. I hope he will not insist on short intervals: I am ready however to make any sacrifice compatible with the preservation of my Estate. It will give me great satisfaction, in any case, to have the old mortgage cancelled, and to give my own bonds, secured by a new mortgage on the same land. Be kind enough to remember me to Mr. Le Roy whom I had the pleasure of seeing, and the honor of visiting frequently, at New-York, in 1789. He will confer an important favor on me by saying, whether in his opinion it would be to my advantage to ship wheat, this winter or next spring, to New-York, and by naming someone there, who is in the way of taking consignments of grain.[8] I am Dear Sir Your most sincere & affectionate friend

TH: M. RANDOLPH

RC (MHi); addressed: "Thomas Jefferson Secretary of State Philada."; endorsed by TJ as received 9 Nov. 1793 and so recorded in SJL. PrC of Tr (ViU: Edgehill-Randolph Papers); extract in TJ's hand with alterations by him noted below; at head of text: "Extract of a letter from T. M. Randolph junr. to Th: Jefferson Oct. 31. 1793"; enclosed in TJ to Herman LeRoy, 11 Nov. 1793. Tr (same); 19th-century copy of preceding text; misdated 31 Dec. 1793.

Varina, the 950 acres of LAND IN HENRICO County deeded to Randolph at his marriage by his father, labored under a much larger INCUMBRANCE than either he or his father-in-law TJ realized, and was already the target of a lawsuit by the elder Randolph's creditors. TJ's advice at this point and more substantial assistance in 1800 saved the estate for over three decades, but Randolph never paid off the mortgage and finally lost the property in 1825 (TJ to Herman LeRoy, 11, 17 Nov. 1793; TJ to Randolph, 17 Nov. 1793; Gaines, *Randolph*, 29, 44, 76-7, 148, 155-6). PURCHASE IN ALBEMARLE: Edgehill.

[1] PrC of Tr begins with this word.
[2] In PrC of Tr TJ replaced this word with "who" and omitted the final two clauses of the sentence.
[3] Sentence to this point omitted in PrC of Tr.
[4] In PrC of Tr TJ here inserted "therefore."
[5] Preceding three words omitted in PrC of Tr.
[6] Remainder of sentence in PrC of Tr: "other property."
[7] In PrC of Tr TJ here inserted "Virga. currcy."
[8] PrC of Tr ends here.

From Edmond Charles Genet

A New york le 2 9bre 1793
MONSIEUR   L'an 2e De la rep. francaise.

Une Denonciation très grave a été faite contre le consul de la republique à charlestown; telle est Son importance qu'elle a troublé la tranquillité dans vos etats du Sud. La même Denonciation S'étend à plusieurs militaires arrivés de St. domingue dans la baye de charlestown, et tel a eté l'effet de l'accusation portée contr'eux qu'ils Sont restés deux jours dans cette baye privés des objets de première nécessité et que l'entrée de la ville et même leur débarquement Sur la terre ferme leur ont été refusés. Ces militaires Sont des hommes qui ont fui de St. domingue pour ne pas porter Serment à des traitres ou à des tyrans, et dont la plupart ont versé leur Sang dans la derniere guerre pour la conquête[1] de votre liberté. J'ai été instruit qu'à la tete de ces dénonciateurs,[2] étoient les nommés moput, faurés l'ainé, calman, le chair, le ris, Mondesir.

Le consul français, et les militaires dont je viens de vous parler Sont accusés d'avoir voulu renverser les lois intérieures de vos etats du Sud, et comme un tel fait est un crime capital non seulement envers le gouvernement des etats-unis mais encore envers celui de la france,[3] je demande qu'il Soit fait Sur cette accusation une enquete solemnelle, et que les coupables, S'il en existe, Soient livrés à toute la rigueur des lois. Mais je demande en même tems qu'on livre les denonciateurs aux memes lois, Si ceux qu'ils ont accusés Sont reconnus innocents. J'ecris à ce Sujet[4] au consul accusé et je lui mande qu'il est très essentiel et que Son devoir l'oblige de Se justifier publiquement d'une accusation à la quelle on a donné le plus grand eclat et dont l'effet a été de causer dans le public une allarme générale.

Le fait suivant vous donnera quelques lumieres Sur cette affaire, et pourra peut-être vous faire juger Du veritable but de cette Dénonciation. Dans le moment de l'allarme qu'elle donna[5] le nommé dubosq se presenta chez le gouverneur de charleston pour lui proposer d'enregimenter les français refugies dans cette ville et il lui offrit leurs Services pour le maintien de la tranquillité. Ce Sage Gouverneur ne Se trompa pas Sur la nature perfide de cette Demarche, et il refusa cette offre, en disant que les milices du pays lui Suffisaient parfaitement pour faire respecter le bon ordre. Cette démarche vous fera Sans doute prejuger quel étoit[6] le veritable but et les veritables auteurs de l'allarme qui S'est répandue à charleston. C'est ainsi que nos emigrés de coblentz parvinrent à obtenir à se former en compagnies Sous le pretexte des insurrections imaginaires que le voisinage des français causait dans l'électorat de treves, et que l'effet de cette[7] aveugle condescendance des magistrats de cet electorat, a été la guerre universelle qui agite l'europe. Cette Similitude de tactique entre les emigrés de coblentz et les refugies de charleston me paroit etre un nouveau et[8] grand motif de fixer enfin votre attention Sur cette foule immense de renegats à leur patrie, d'etrangers à tous les pays qui S'agittent Sur le Sol de la liberté pour la detruire, pour renverser votre indépendance et qui Sont les vrais perturbateurs, les hommes vraiment dangereux pour votre Sureté intérieure.

On m'a dénoncé les nommés bouteille et carvin comme faisant équiper en ce moment à charleston un fort batiment Sur lequel ils doivent embarquer beaucoup de monde dont le projet est d'aller S'emparer de l'isle de la tortue distante du cap de Sept lieues, et d'y egorger tous les français qui resteront fideles à leur patrie. Je vous prie de vouloir bien instruire de cette denonciation le gouverneur de Charleston.[9]

Dft (DLC: Genet Papers); in Jean Baptiste Cassan's hand, unsigned, with salutation and part of address in Genet's hand and revisions by Cassan and Genet; above salutation: "Le citoyen genet M. &c à M. jefferson S. d'E. des Et. U."; only the most important emendations have been recorded below. Recorded in SJL as received 7 Nov. 1793.

The source and nature of the DENONCIATION of Michel Ange Bernard de Mangourit, the French CONSUL at Charleston, have not been identified. At this time Mangourit was involved in efforts to recruit American volunteers in South Carolina and Georgia for French expeditions against East and West Florida (Richard K. Murdoch, "Citizen Mangourit and the Projected Attack on East Florida in 1794," JSH, XIV [1948], 522-31).

[1] Word interlined by Cassan in place of "defense."

[2] Sentence to this point altered by Cassan from "A La tete des dénonciateurs."

[3] Here "qui a declaré qu'elle ne se mêlerait en aucune maniere Des guerres in-[téressan]t des ⟨pays⟩ peuples etrangers" is canceled.

[4] Remainder of paragraph written in the margin by Cassan in place of "au gouverneur de La caroline Du Sud et au consul accusé; je mande à l'un combien il me paroit essentiel que, dans une affaire qui a eu autant d'eclat, les coupables ou les calomniateurs soient punis, et j'ecris à l'autre que

Son devoir l'oblige De Se justifier publiquement d'une accusation qui a causé tant d'allarme dans le public."

[5] Cassan here canceled "la multitude de colons qui peuplent charleston envoya."

[6] Preceding three words interlined by Cassan in place of "juger ainsi qu'à moi."

[7] Preceding four words interlined by Cassan in place of "cette foiblesse."

[8] Preceding two words interlined by Cassan.

[9] Genet here canceled the remainder in Cassan's hand—"je vous le répéte, Monsieur, il est tems que le gouvernement des etats-unis prenne des mesures Sur les faits d'etrangers qui habitent Son Sol; une plus longue indifference me fait craindre des Suites qu'il Sera difficile d'arrêter Si on ne Se détermine à les prévenir"—as well as "énnemis de la liberté qui viennent pour en polluer le culte dans leur sien," a passage he had substituted in the margin for "qui habitent Son Sol."

To James Madison

DEAR SIR   Germantown Nov. 2. 1793.

I overtook the President at Baltimore, and we arrived here yesterday, myself fleeced of seventy odd dollars to get from Fredericksburg here, the stages running no further than Baltimore. I mention this to put yourself and Monroe on your guard. The fever in Phila. has so much abated as to have almost disappeared. The inhabitants are about returning. It has been determined that the President shall not interfere with the meeting of Congress. R. H. and K. were of opinion he had a right to call them to any place but that the occasion did not call for it. I think the President inclined to the opinion. I proposed a proclamation notifying that the Executive business would be done here till further notice, which I believe will be agreed. H. R. Lewis, Rawle &c. all concur in the necessity that Congress should meet in Phila. and vote there their own adjournment, if it shall then be necessary to change the place. The question will be between N. York and Lancaster. The Pensylva. members are very anxious for the latter, and will attend punctually to support it as well as to support Muhlenburg and[1] oppose the appointment of Smith (S.C.) speaker, which is intended by the Northern members. According to present appearances, this place cannot lodge a single person more. As a great favor I have got a bed in the corner of the public room of a tavern: and must so continue till some of the Philadelphians make a vacancy by removing into the city. Then we must give from 4. to 6 or 8. dollars a week for cuddies without a bed, and sometimes without a chair or table. There is not a single lodging-house in the place.—Ross and Willing are alive. Hancock is dead.—Johnson of Maryld. has *refused*. Ru. L. and Mc.l. in contemplation. The last least.—You will have seen Genet's letters to Moultrie and to myself. Of the last I know nothing but from the public papers; and he published Moultrie's letter and his answer the moment he wrote it. You will see that his inveteracy against the President leads him to meditate the embroiling him with Congress. They say he is going to be married to a daughter of Clinton's. If so, he is afraid to return to France. Hamilton is ill, and suspicions he has taken the fever again by returning to his house. He of course could not attend here to-day, but the Pr. had shewed me his letter on the right of calling Congress to another place. Adieu.

RC (DLC: Madison Papers); unsigned. PrC (DLC); faded dateline recopied in ink by TJ.

The PROCLAMATION with which TJ proposed NOTIFYING THAT THE EXECUTIVE BUSINESS WOULD BE DONE HERE TILL FURTHER NOTICE was probably the missing "draught of proclmn." recorded in SJPL between entries of 11 Oct. and 5 Nov. 1793; no such proclamation seems to have been issued. H. R. LEWIS: Alexander Hamilton, Edmund Randolph, and William Lewis, former District Attorney for Pennsylvania and former federal judge for the eastern district of that state. With Thomas Johnson having REFUSED to take TJ's place as Secretary of State, Edward Rutledge, Robert R. Livingston, and James McClurg were now IN CONTEMPLATION for this office (Notes of a Conversation with George Washington, 6 Aug. 1793). The letter of Edmond Charles Genet to TJ of 27 Oct. 1793 appeared in THE PUBLIC PAPERS of New York and Philadelphia before it reached the Secretary of State. The French minister had already PUBLISHED South Carolina governor William MOULTRIE'S LETTER to him of 5 Sep. 1793 expressing concern at published reports of Genet's threatened appeal from President Washington to the people "on some point relating to a prize" and asking for "an exact relation of what did happen in your dispute, if any you have had." Genet also published his own ANSWER of 15 Oct. 1793 promising to refute the "falsehoods" of which he stood accused by addressing himself to Congress "through the medium of the executive of the United States, to ask the severest examination of all my official measures, and of every particular step which may be supposed to have been an attempt, upon the established authority of the American Republic"—an examination which he was confident would show that, while he had not hidden his distress that Washington had made himself "accessible to men whose schemes could only darken his glory," he had not forgotten the respect he owed to the American head of state (New York *Diary; or Loudon's Register*, 22, 30 Oct. 1793; *Federal Gazette and Philadelphia Daily Advertiser*, 24 Oct., 1 Nov. 1793). For Hamilton's 24 Oct. 1793 LETTER ON THE RIGHT OF CALLING CONGRESS TO ANOTHER PLACE, see note to TJ to Washington, 17 Oct. 1793.

[1] Preceding three words interlined.

To Thomas Mann Randolph, Jr.

DEAR SIR   Germantown Nov. 2. 1793.

After having experienced on my journey the extremes of heat, cold, dust and rain, I arrived here yesterday. I found at Baltimore that the stages run no further North, and being from that circumstance thrown into the hands of the harpies who prey upon travellers, was pretty well fleeced to get here. I think from Fredericksburg here with a single servant cost me upwards of seventy dollars. Before this change in the weather the fever had very much abated in Philadelphia, and at this time it has almost entirely disappeared, insomuch that the inhabitants are very many of them returning into the city. This is very necessary for our accomodation here, as this place is so full that I have been able to obtain a bed in a corner of the public room of a tavern only, and that as a great favor, the other alternative being to sleep on the floor in my cloak before the fire. In this state I am awaiting till some of the Philadelphians may take courage to go into the city, and make a vacancy here. Nothing will be done by the President as to the meeting of Congress. It is imagined that knowing he is here, they will rendesvous here, and after settling informally to what place they will remove, they will go into the feilds of the city and pass a regular vote. The pure blacks have been found insusceptible of the infection, the mixed blood has taken it. What is more singular is that tho' hundreds have been taken with the disease out of Philadelphia, have died of it after being well attended, yet not a single instance has occurred of any body's *catching* it *out of Philadelphia*. The question for the session of Congress will lie between Philadelphia New York and Lancaster.—Freneau's paper is discontinued. I fear it is the want of money. He promises to resume it before the meeting of Congress. I wish the subscribers in our neighborhood would send on their money.—My love to my dear daughters & am with sincere esteem Dr. Sir Your's affectionately   TH: JEFFERSON

P.S. Mr. Hollingsworth at the Head of Elk thinks he can immediately send me on a good overseer in the place of Rogers. I authorised him to allow exactly the same as to Biddle. Consequently on his arrival I must get you to give him orders on Watson and Colo. Bell for the same necessaries which I had furnished to Biddle.

RC (DLC); at foot of text: "Mr. Randolph"; postscript in margin; endorsed by Randolph as received 29 Nov. 1793. PrC (DLC); faded dateline recopied in ink by TJ. Tr (DLC); 19th-century copy.

To Richard Dobson

Sir Germantown Nov. 3. 1793.

In my letter of Aug. 30. I asked the favor of you to furnish me a statement of the paiments made on my bill of exchange and bond and of the balance due, and to have the same lodged at Monticello, where I proposed being during the month of October, that I might give definitive directions for the payment of it. Not having received it while there, I have now to ask the favor of it's being lodged there at any time before the beginning of January when I shall return there, to remain, and will then take measures for the discharge of it. I am Sir Your very humble servt   TH: JEFFERSON

PrC (DLC); at foot of text: "Mr. Richard Dobson"; faded date recopied in ink by TJ. Tr (ViU: Edgehill-Randolph Papers); 19th-century copy.

According to SJL, TJ and Dobson exchanged 15 letters between 22 Jan. 1794 and 13 June 1796, none of which have been found. Shortly before the latter date TJ finally discharged the obligation Dobson was collecting on behalf of his father, John Dobson (MB, 4 Dec. 1791 and note, 22 May 1796).

To Walter Boyd

DEAR SIR   Philadelphia Nov. 5. 1793.

The bearer hereof, Mr. Lear, proposing to establish himself in commerce in the new city of Washington, he now sets out to visit such parts of Europe as he supposes may furnish him either articles or connections in the mercantile line useful for his position. He is well known as late Secretary to President Washington, and I can assure you that he is a person of great understanding, discretion, activity and of the most perfect integrity. Having for him a very high esteem, which an acquaintance of considerable intimacy has proved him to merit, I take the liberty of asking for him your kind attentions and services, and particularly your introduction of him to any persons in such branches of commerce or manufactures as may suit his object.—Should your views of goodness be extended to the family of your late brother near Bladensburgh, Mr. Lear's position within half a dozen miles of them will render him a very convenient channel of transmission, and I pledge myself to you that there is not a man on earth who will deal out any kindnesses you may meditate for them with more discretion and true paternal good faith than him. I beg leave to assure you of the continual esteem & attachment of Dear Sir Your most obedt. & most humble servt   TH: JEFFERSON

PrC (DLC); at foot of text: "Mr Boyd." Tr (ViU: Edgehill-Randolph Papers); 19th-century copy. Enclosed in TJ to Tobias Lear, 5 Nov. 1793.

From Angelica Schuyler Church

My dear Sir   Nov: 5th. 93.

I have heard very melancholy accounts from Philadelphia occasioned by a fever and in consequence am extremely anxious for you and my young friend Polly: I hope that you have both escaped the power of its destructive influence.

Accept of my good wishes, for your health, and be so good as to write me a line to say that your family have enjoyed security from this disease. Adieu   A Church

RC (MHi); endorsed by TJ as received 31 Mch. 1794 and so recorded in SJL.

From Tench Coxe

Sir   Treasury Department Revenue office Novr. 5th. 1793

I have the honor to inform you that a distribution of the first parcel of the Sea-letters, which was sent to my office after that of the Secretary of the Treasury ceased to be attended, was immediately made, in the best manner of which my defective information of the preceding distributions, admitted. The greater part of the Second parcel was treated in a similar Manner, and the remainder I have directed to be delivered into the office of the Secretary of the Treasury to whom the requisite communication has been made. It appears from the letters of Acknowledgement that the Supplies arrived very opportunely at several of the Custom houses. With great respect, I have the honor to be Sir; Your most obedt. Servant   Tench Coxe Commissioner of the Revue.

RC (DLC); at foot of text: "The Secretary of State." Recorded in SJL as received 8 Nov. 1793.

To Delamotte and Others

Dear Sir   Philadelphia Nov. 5. 1793.

The bearer hereof, Mr. Lear, proposing to establish himself in commerce in the new city of Washington, he now sets out to visit such parts of Europe as he supposes may furnish him either articles or connections in the mercantile line useful for his position. He is well known as the late Secretary of President Washington, and I can further assure you that he is a person of great understanding, discretion, activity, and of the most perfect integrity. Having for him a very high esteem, which an acquaintance of considerable intimacy has proved him to merit, I take the liberty of recommending him, not only to the ordinary protection and[1] aids of your office, but to any other attentions or services you can render him, assuring you they will be considered as particular favors conferred on Dear Sir Your most obedt & most humble servt   TH: JEFFERSON

RC (Gilder Lehrman Collection, on deposit NNP); at foot of text: "M. la Motte." PrC of another RC (DLC); at foot of text: "M. Cathalan" and (above it in ink) "Dumas La Motte Fenwick"; with minor variations. Tr (ViU: Edgehill-Randolph Papers); 19th-century copy; follows PrC. Enclosed in TJ to Tobias Lear, 5 Nov. 1793.

According to SJL, Delamotte, the American consul at Le Havre, wrote private letters to TJ of 6 Oct. 1793 (recorded as received 20 Feb. 1794) and 27 Oct. 1793 (recorded as received 2 Feb. 1794), neither of which has been found.

[1] TJ here canceled "good."

To Edmond Charles Genet

SIR   Germantown Nov. 5. 1793

I shall be late in acknowledging the receipt of your several letters written since my departure from Philadelphia, not having received any of them till the 24th: ult: and most of them only the last night. I have already laid some of them before the President and shall lay the others successively before him at as early moments as the pressure of business will permit. [1]

That of September 30. with the decree of the national convention of March 26. 1793. on the subject of a treaty of commerce was laid before him yesterday, and will be considered with all the respect and interest which its object necessarily requires. In the mean time, that I may be enabled to present him a faithful translation of the decree, I take the liberty of returning the copy to you with a prayer that you will have it examined by your original, and see whether there is not some error in the latter part of the 2d. article, page 2. where the description of the cargo to be reexported from the Islands is so unusual as to induce me to suspect an error in the copyist. Having to return the decree for reexamination, I take the liberty of doing the same by the letter covering it, as in the first lines of the 7th. page the sense appears to me incomplete, and I wish to be able to give it with correctness.

I am able at present to acknowledge the receipt of your letter of October 29. desiring Exequaturs for Messrs. Pennevert and Chervi, but not inclosing their original commissions. It[2] is of indispensable necessity that these originals be produced to the President and copies of them filed of record in my office; because occasions may sometimes occur where authentic copies of them may be required, which cannot be furnished but after an exhibition of the *original itself*. An exhibition of a copy and a copy from that, would not be received as evidence by our Courts in any case where it should be called for.

I must therefore trouble you to send me the originals. I have the honor to be with sentiments of respect Sir, Your most obedient & most humble servant

PrC (DLC); in a clerk's hand, unsigned; dateline added in ink by TJ; at foot of first page in ink by TJ: "Genet." Dft (DLC: TJ Papers, 94: 16121); entirely in TJ's hand; undated and unsigned; only the most significant revisions are recorded below; with penciled notation on verso by TJ: "to be copied & press copied." FC (Lb in DNA: RG 59, DL). Recorded in SJPL. Enclosures: Genet to TJ, 30 Sep. 1793, and enclosure. Printed without last two paragraphs in *Correspondence*, 22; French translation without last two paragraphs printed in *Correspondance*, 27-8.

TJ submitted this letter to the President on 7 Nov. 1793, and Washington approved and returned it the same day (Washington, *Journal*, 248).

[1] In Dft TJ here canceled the start of a new paragraph: "Those of Oct. 1 and 29. on the subject of the duties required on the vessels of St. Domingo."

[2] Before this word in Dft TJ canceled "The rule."

To Edmond Charles Genet

SIR   Germantown November 5th. 1793

I have the honor to inclose you the copy of a letter from Mr. Moissonier Consul of France at Baltimore to the Governor of Maryland, announcing that Great Britain is about to commence hostilities against us, and that he purposes to collect the Naval force of your Republic in the Chesapeak and to post them as a Van-guard to derange the[1] supposed designs of the enemy.

The bare suggestion of such a fact, however improbable, renders it a duty to enquire into it; and I shall consider it as a proof of your friendship to our nation, if you have it in your power and will be pleased to communicate to me the grounds of Mr. Moissonier's assertion, or any other respectable evidence of such an intention on the part of Great Britain.

In the mean while as we have[2] reason to believe it unfounded[3] as they have in no instance as yet violated[4] the sovereignty of our country[5] by any commitment of hostilities even on their enemies within[6] our jurisdiction,[7] we presume with confidence that Mr. Moissonier's fears are groundless. I have it therefore in charge to desire you to admonish Mr. Moissonier against the parade[8] he proposes of stationing an advanced guard in the bay of Chesapeak, and against any hostile array, which under the profession of defensive operations may[9] in fact generate those offensive. I flatter myself,[10] Sir, that you will be so good as to join the effect of your authority to that of our government to prevent measures on the part of[11] this Agent of your republic[12] which may bring on

[303]

disagreeable [13] consequences. I have the honor to be with great respect, Sir Your most obedient & most humble servant

PrC (DLC); in Benjamin Bankson's hand, unsigned; with correction in ink by TJ (see note 5 below); at foot of first page: "The Minister plenipoy of France." Dft (DLC); entirely in TJ's hand, unsigned; at head of text: "to be copd. & press copd."; at foot of text: "Mr. Bankson at the Secretary of State's office Philadelphia." Tr (DNA: RG 46, Senate Records, 3d Cong., 1st sess.). FC (Lb in DNA: RG 59, DL). Tr (DLC: Genet Papers). Tr (MHi); 19th-century copy. Tr (DLC: Genet Papers); in French. Recorded in SJPL. Enclosure: F. Moissonnier to Governor Thomas Sim Lee, Baltimore, 23 Oct. 1793, asserting that Great Britain is preparing to attack the United States in accordance with the liberticide system of the European cabinets, regretting that Maryland is not taking defensive actions because French interests will surely be the first victim of the state's carelessness if it does not put into condition the forts guarding the entrance to Chesapeake Bay, which contains the riches of the commerce of Saint-Domingue and the only hope of the French nation, and advising that meanwhile, in pursuance of Genet's orders, he was going to form all French maritime forces in the Chesapeake into a vanguard sufficiently formidable to derange if possible the projects of their common enemies (RC in DNA: RG 59, LGS, in French, with penciled marginal notation by TJ: "to be copied & press copied"; PrC of Tr in DLC; Tr in Lb in DNA: RG 59, DL; Tr in DLC: Genet Papers; Tr in MHi, 19th-century copy; Tr in DNA: RG 46, Senate Records, 3d Cong., 1st sess., in English). Letter and enclosure printed in *Message*, 89-90; translation of enclosure printed in ASP, *Foreign Relations*, I, 182.

Governor Lee had transmitted Moissonnier's letter with a covering letter to Secretary of War Henry Knox recommending that it be submitted to the President and pointing out that he had taken no action other than to acknowledge its receipt (Lee to Knox, 25 Oct. 1793, MdAA: Letterbooks of Governor and Council).

TJ submitted this letter to the President on 7 Nov. 1793, and Washington approved and returned it the same day (Washington, *Journal*, 248).

[1] In Dft TJ here canceled "designs."
[2] In Dft TJ here canceled "every."
[3] In Dft TJ here canceled "and ⟨to be perfectly satisfied that no hostilities⟩ to be assured that they."
[4] In Dft TJ first wrote "that having in no instance violated" and then altered it to read as above.
[5] Preceding five words interlined in ink by TJ in place of "our rights."
[6] Preceding five words interlined in Dft in place of "within our bays or."
[7] In Dft TJ here canceled "⟨they have⟩ we have no grounds to expect that they will ⟨do it⟩ violate them, or attempt any act of hostility by any attempt on our or your vessels ⟨within⟩ in the bay of Chesapeak."
[8] In Dft TJ first wrote "this parade of an advanced guard which" and then altered it to read as above.
[9] In Dft TJ here canceled "become the."
[10] In Dft TJ here canceled "therefore."
[11] In Dft TJ here canceled "Mr. Moissonier" in the interlineation recorded in the following note.
[12] Preceding ten words interlined in Dft in place of "manoeuvres."
[13] In Dft TJ here canceled "circumstances."

To Tobias Lear

DEAR SIR   Germantown Nov. 5. 1793.

Your favor of Oct. 10. reached me at Monticello only the night before my departure; that of Nov. 1. last night. I have thrown upon paper very roughly such notes as my memory enables me to make, for my papers are not at present at this place. I also inclose letters to such acquaintances of mine as I think may be most useful to you. There are none to London, because I have none there, and you will easily get them from everybody; and only one to Dumas, at Amsterdam, because Mr. Greenleaf will so perfectly introduce you there. I could only have given you letters to the V. Staphorsts & Hubbard, with whom Mr. Greenleaf is particularly connected. I have[1] given you none to political men in Paris, because all my friends there have been turned adrift in the different stages of the progression of their revolution. I add my sincere wishes for your success and safety, and assurances of perfect esteem & attachment from Dear Sir your friend & servt   TH: JEFFERSON

P.S. I retire decidedly the 1st. day of January next.

RC (Mrs. Francis R. Stoddard, New York City, 1945); at foot of text: "Mr. Lear." PrC (DLC). Tr (Viu: Edgehill-Randolph Papers); 19th-century copy. Enclosures: (1) TJ to William Boyd, 5 Nov. 1793. (2) TJ to Delamotte and Others, 5 Nov. 1793. (3) TJ to Ferdinand Grand, 5 Nov. 1793, consisting of the first three sentences in No. 1 nearly verbatim and a concluding sentence requesting him "to present my respect to your son and your ladies" (PrC in DLC, at foot of text: "M. Grand"; Tr in ViU: Edgehill-Randolph Papers, 19th-century copy). Other enclosure not found.

Lear's letter of 1 NOV., recorded in SJL as received from New York on 4 Nov. 1793, enclosed a representation from Captain Welsh of the brigantine *Maria* about the capture and plunder of his ship near "the Caps" by the French frigate *Médée* and its recapture by a British letter of marque (not found, but summarized in Washington, *Journal*, 245).

[1] TJ here canceled "only to add my sin."

From Joseph Nourse

Treasury Department, Register's Office, 5 Nov. 1793. On behalf of the Secretary of the Treasury, he requests an estimate of the sums needed "to defray the Expences of your Department" for 1794 for the purpose of forming a general estimate to be submitted to Congress at its next meeting.

FC (DNA: RG 53, Register's Estimates and Statements); 1 p.; unsigned; at foot of text: "Honourable Thos. Jefferson Esquire Secretary of State"; consists of circular letter sent to TJ, various officials in the Departments of Treasury and War, and the secretary of the Senate and the clerk of the House of Representatives. Recorded in SJL as received 8 Nov. 1793.

To George Washington

Tuesday Nov. 5. 1793.

Th: Jefferson with his respects to the President sends for his perusal some of the letters which had been accumulating at his office, and which he received yesterday. He will wait on the President to-day to translate the Spanish papers sent by Mr. Short, as also with some other letters in foreign languages.

Th:J. sends to the President a supply he received yesterday of paper, of which the President will be pleased to take any proportion he may have occasion for. He sends him wafers also and wax, and could furnish him copying ink, but he believes the President has no press here.— Th:J. did not understand yesterday whether any meeting was desired to-day or at any other particular time.

RC (DNA: RG 59, MLR); endorsed by Washington. Tr (Lb in same, SDC). Not recorded in SJL. Enclosures: (1) William Carmichael and William Short to TJ, 15 Aug. 1793, and enclosures. (2) Short to TJ, 20 Aug. 1793, and enclosure. (3) Thomas Pinckney to TJ, 27 and 28 Aug. 1793, and enclosures. (4) David Humphreys to TJ, 1 Sep. 1793. (5) Elias Vanderhorst to TJ, 1 and 3 Sep. 1793. (6) Ezra Fitz Freeman to TJ, 5 Sep. 1793, enclosing No. 7 (not found, but recorded in SJL as received from "N.W. territy." on 4 Nov. 1793; see Washington, *Journal*, 245). (7) Petition of Abraham Freeman to Washington, Northwest Territory, 5 Sep. 1793, relating that in 1791 his son Dr. Clarkson Freeman of New Jersey had turned himself in upon being accused of aiding in the counterfeiting of public securities of the United States; that Abraham Ogden, the federal attorney for New Jersey, had taken down his evidence and promised him a pardon in exchange for his testimony at the trials of his accomplices, who were accordingly captured and indicted; and that even after his associates subsequently escaped from prison before trial, Freeman spent six months in the Newark prison but, tired of waiting for his promised pardon, escaped to Canada, from which he now greatly desires to return; giving as an additional reason for compassion that Isaac Freeman, another of the petitioner's sons, had been murdered by hostile Western Indians in 1792 while attempting to negotiate a peace treaty under a flag of truce in the service of the United States; and accordingly requesting a pardon for Clarkson Freeman (Tr in DNA: RG 59, Petitions for Pardon; endorsed by George Taylor, Jr., and bearing his later notation that it was enclosed in an 18 Nov. 1795 letter from Ogden to Secretary of State Timothy Pickering). (8) Stephen Moylan to TJ, 19 Sep. 1793. (9) Christopher Gore to TJ, 21 Oct. 1793. (10) Tobias Lear to TJ, 1 Nov. 1793 (see note to TJ to Lear, 5 Nov. 1793).

Although TJ recorded the receipt of all of these enclosures in SJL under 4 Nov. 1793 and sent them to Washington a day later, they are listed in the President's journal as having been received from and returned to TJ on the 4th, there being no entry for the following day (Washington, *Journal*, 245).

From William Frederick Ast

SIR   Richmond Virginia the 6. Novr. 1793.

I am ashamed that I have let so many Year's pass without doing myself the honor to write to You. Persuaded of Your kindness and when You consider the hurry and bustle I have been in these Six years with my business and the Trouble the Revolution in France caused me I hope You will be so good to pardon my Silence and not attribute to neglect.

You know that I settled and established a Mercantile house at L'Orient where I did in the beginning excellent business—but the Revolution taking place I lost a good deal by the Exchange falling so uncommonly lowe. I took in 2 partners Mr. Bingham an Englishman and Mr. [Maurar?] an American—and carried on business there till last October when the Mob at L'Orient rose and cutt a very respectable Merchants Mr. Gerard's head off under pretence that he was going to ship arms to Germany. The Mob threatened to set fire to his house and as it was but 4 doors from ours and we were so to say under the same roof we thought best to leave that Country and particularly as we saw the Manner in which the British Court went on we conjectured almost with a Certainty that the two Nations would be at war and as we were in the line to sell British Manufactures we foresaw that we could not do much longer business there: we resolved therefore to go to this Country where we arrived safe with our Goods in good Condition and have established Mercantile houses at this place, Norfolk, and Petersburgh under the firm of Ast, Bingham & Co.

Necessity has often given rise to many usefull Inventions—which is the Case now with me. When we arrived in this Country we wanted to be secure on account of Accidents by fire. We wrote to England for £15000. Sterg. Insurance on our Goods in our Stores at Richmond Petersburgh and Norfolk. We were not a little surprized when we received the Insurance Account which was at 31/6. Sterg. ℔ £[100. with pol]icy 13/6. and $\frac{1}{4}$ pCt. Brokerage and Commission amounting [to £2]74. 8.s. 6.d. Sterling for one Years Insurance! This struck [me?] so much and determined me to see to find out ways [or?] means to insure here and if possible on more moderate terms to keep at least the Money in this Country. I have been fortunate enough to succeed and found out a plan which after I had examined it thoroughly I find is far more favorable than my Expectation was at first setting out. It is of such a nature that it is by far preferable to any Insurance Company. It has advantages which no Insurance Company can have. The Expence will I believe seldom or ever be more than $\frac{1}{37}$th. part what we and others are obliged to pay to the British. You see by the above Account that we are obliged to pay £274. 8.s. 6.d. Sterling or 1219 Dollars $66\frac{2}{3}$ Cents ℔ Anm. to England when according to my plan we should only have to pay, for £15000. Sterg. or 66666 dollars $66\frac{2}{3}$ Cents—33 Dollars 33 Cents *here* —and very probably on an Average of 30 Years not so much—and still must we run the risk of the London fire Insur[ers?] breaking—when it is impossible for my plan to fail—let the Accidents be as frequent as ever remembered. There is no funds required to lay Idle for the payment of Losses. You know as there is not much Money in this Country this suits it [very?] well. An Invention of this Sort which tends to promote Commerce Manufactures and secure the Husbandman from being ruined by that destructif Element—deserves a generous Annuity. I ask only one

Cent for each hundred Dollars insured ℔ Annum to be paid me each Year as an Annuity for Life by those that insure—and sure no body will refuse me so trifling a premium to sleep easy on account of Losses by fire. I [cou?]ld ask more, for I am sure it deserves more, but I wis[h for the g]ood of the Citizens of the United States that such a salut[ary pla]n might take place as soon as possible.

As it is for the good of the whole Nation and all may benefit by it, I consider it as a National Concern and intend to lay the inclosed Petition before Congress as it will be necessary (in Order that by the Publication making a public Affair and Monument of it that each Citizen may benefit by it) to grant me a patent to secure the Annuity to me as long as I live—and one half to be reversible on the Life of my wife if I should die before her as long as she lives. I must request therefore that Congress passes the inclosed provisional Decree before I lay the plan before them.

I consider You Sir as my friend and Protector. I should therefore be infinitely obliged to You if You would be so good to tell me how I must do to obtain the Provisional Decree and patent.

I know Your Patriotism and am persuaded that You will do all in Your power so that this Salutary plan may be put into execution as soon as possible—it not only will keep great Sums each Year in this Country but rescue many families from utter distress—sure a plan so interesting as this, Congress will not hesitate a Moment to adopt as it cannot be put to soon into execution, in particular as it will cost the public nothing at all but only those that benefit by it pay—and also as I offer it at so small a premium.

I should be glad to know when and where Congress sitts and if I might have the honor to wait on You at Your Country Seat near Charlottesville if You should be there shortly.

I would take it as a particular favor if You would [. . .] to indulge me soon with an answer.

I have an other plan in Contemplation on Insurance [of?] Ships and Goods ℔ Sea which will likewise keep a great deal of Money in this Country—and as I know the greatest part of the ingines used in the Manufactories in England I may produce many usefull plans in this Country [yet?] and be worse for England's Commercial Interest than 25 Men of War.

If possible I should likewise be glad to know when You think I could lay the petition before Congress. I have the honor to subscribe myself very respectfully Sir Your most obedient most humble Servant

WILLIAM AST

RC (MHi); at foot of first page: "The Honble. Thomas Jefferson Esqr."; mutilated, with some words conjectured from similar passages in enclosure; minimum punctuation supplied; endorsement by TJ torn away. Recorded in SJL as received 12

Nov. 1793. Enclosure: Petition of William Frederick Ast to the "Citizen Representatives" of Congress, Richmond, 6 Nov. 1793, describing his fire insurance plan in much the same terms as the covering letter; estimating that the scheme would save participants more than thirty-six times what it would cost in England and keep 500,000 dollars a year in the country while benefitting every citizen rather than a tiny fraction of them; stipulating that before he would reveal its details, Congress must grant him a patent and enact "a provisional Decree" mandating that a committee of Congress be appointed to examine the plan he will sub-mit, that if the United States or any state adopts this or a similar plan the life annuity he required was to paid "at the End of each Year in each Capital Town in each State by those who insure," and that a properly detailed decree was to be enacted after the plan was adopted; warning that if anyone subsequently presented a similar plan he would claim it as his property because he is certain no one thought of it before him; and concluding that the "Nature of my plan is that it must be made a Public Matter of" (MS in MHi, entirely in Ast's hand and signed by him; mutilated; endorsed by TJ).

To John Bowman

[SIR]   Germantown Nov. 6. 1793

Your favor of the [14th.] covering a drawing [. . .]¹ engine came to [hand?] two days [ago]. That which you mention [having?] forwarded several months ago, never has been received. [. . .]² the papers in my office but to entitle Mr. Lucas to a patent several more circumstances are necessary, such as the payment of [30. dollars?] into the treasury, a particular affidavit &ca. for all which [I refer him to?] the last act of Congress on the subject, which specifies the mode of proceeding. A model of the machine is also [required?]. I [shall?] be happy to give him every facility which the [law?] perm[its] to [. . .] as well to encourage an ingenious man, as to bring [. . .]³ pronounced useful by so good [. . .].⁴ There have been several applications already for pat[ents] for steam engines but none of them I think would stand in the way of this [one].

I am happy in having this occasion of renewing acquaint[ance with] you and of repeating my respects to Mrs. Bowman and Miss Lynch with assurances to yourself of the esteem & respect [. . .] Your most obedt & most humble servt   TH: JEFFERSON

PrC (MHi); very badly faded; at foot of text enhanced in ink: "Mr Bowman."

¹ Estimated three or four words illegible.

² Estimated four words illegible.
³ Estimated three words illegible.
⁴ Estimated four or five words illegible.

To Brown Folger

SIR   Germantown, November 6th. 1793.

It was not till the 14th. of Octo: that I received your favor of the 1st. of that month, which I have communicated to the President on my arrival here, and I am sorry it is not in my power to say that your property taken on board an English ship by a French Privateer can be reclaimed by us. By the 14th. article of our Treaty with France we have established the principle that enemy vessels make enemy goods, and only two months after the declaration of war is allowed for property embarked before the declaration. After that period the article declares that notice of the declaration shall be presumed, and the goods be lawful Prize. Yours having been taken long after that time, we are precluded by the treaty from reclaiming them. We have therefore only to regret that you should suffer by a principle established by treaty between the two nations, and according to which we have uniformly acted on both sides. I am, Sir, &c: TH: JEFFERSON

FC (Lb in DNA: RG 59, DL); at head of text: "Mr. Brown Folger—Boston."

Brown Folger (1744-96), a Nantucket sea captain residing in Britain, commanded the English whaling ship *Harpooner* of Bristol, which was captured by the French privateer *Marseillaise* of Le Havre and carried into Boston at the end of August 1793 (*Vital Records of Nantucket, Massachusetts, to the Year 1850*, 5 vols. [Boston, 1925-28], I, 471; Nancy S. Adams, ed., "Keziah Coffin Fanning's Diary," *Historic Nantucket*, IV, no. 4 [1957], 46; Thomas Barclay to Robert R. Livingston, 14 Dec. 1782, DNA: RG 360, PCC; Boston, *Columbian Centinel*, 31 Aug., 2, 5 Oct. 1793).

Folger's FAVOR of 1 Oct. 1793, recorded in SJL as received from Boston on 24 Oct. 1793 rather than THE 14TH., has not been found, but according to the summary in the journal of the President, to whom TJ submitted the letter on 2 Nov. 1793 and who returned it the same day, Folger "Begs Mr. Jefferson's attention to his case" and "Wishes to obtain $\frac{1}{10}$ part of the Cargo as his due," having "Complained to the french Consul without obtaining redress" (Washington, *Journal*, 243).

For the 14TH. ARTICLE of the 1778 treaty of commerce with France, see Miller, *Treaties*, II, 14-15.

To Henry Knox

DEAR SIR   Germantown Nov. [6. 1793.]

I have received from the representatives of Spain here information that the French privateer the Vainqueur de la Bastille one of those unlawfully constituted in these states, and therefore ordered to depart, has taken and brought into a port of North Carolina a Spanish brigantine bound from Carthagena to Cadiz, richly laden with money and merchandize, that Hervieux the commander proceeding to Wilmington in his boat with a trunk of 40,000 dollars, the same had been seised by the

Customhouse officer for having broken bulk without an entry, that the crew of the Spanish vessel were in irons on board the Privateer. Having laid this information before the President, he charges me to communicate it to you that proper instructions may be given to the Governor for executing the decisions of the government in[1] cases of this description. Circumstances seem to indicate that there is not a moment to be lost on the occasion. I have the honor to be with great esteem & respect Dr. Sir your most obedt & most humble servt.   TH: JEFFERSON

PrC (DLC); at foot of text: "The Secretary at war"; faded. FC (Lb in DNA: RG 59, DL); dated 6 Nov. 1793. Enclosed in

TJ to George Washington, 6 Nov. 1793.

[1] PrC and FC: "of."

To Henry Knox

DEAR SIR   Germantown Nov. 6. 1793.

As it is possible that the measures complained of by the representatives of Spain as meditated to be pursued by La Chaise and others for attempting hostilities from Kentuckey against the Spanish settlements, may require the employment of military force by the Governor of Kentucky, I have the honor to inclose you my letter to the Governor, stating the facts handed me by the Spanish gentlemen, and submit to yourself whether instructions from yourself to him may not be necessary with respect to the use of military force if necessary. My letter gives none on that subject. I have the honor to be with great esteem & respect Dear Sir Your most obedt. servt   TH: JEFFERSON

P.S. Be so good as to forward my letter with your own.

PrC (DLC); at foot of text: "The Secretary at War." FC (Lb in DNA: RG 59, DL). Enclosure: TJ to Isaac Shelby, 6 Nov. 1793. Enclosed in TJ to George Washington, 6 Nov. 1793.

To David Rittenhouse

DEAR SIR   Germantown Nov. 6. 1793.

You will recieve herein inclosed the bill of lading and invoice for between 9. and 10. tons of copper shipped by Mr. Pinckney on board the Pigou for the use of the mint, for the reception and charges of which you will be pleased to give proper orders.

It has been understood that Mr. Wright our engraver is dead. If this be the fact, will you be so good as to recommend for the office such person as you think best qualified to execute it? I hope Mrs. Rittenhouse and yourself have enjoyed good health during the late trying season, and am with great & sincere esteem Dr. Sir Your friend & servt

TH: JEFFERSON

RC (Elizabeth S. Abbot, Philadelphia, 1954); addressed: "David Rittenhouse esq. Philadelphia. corner 7th. & Arch str." PrC (DLC). FC (Lb in DNA: RG 59, DL). Enclosures not found, but see Joshua Johnson to TJ, 24 Aug. 1793.

Rittenhouse's missing reply of 12 Nov. 1793 is recorded in SJL as received from Philadelphia on 14 Nov. 1793.

To Isaac Shelby

SIR   Germantown Nov. 6. 1793.

I have received from the representatives of Spain here information of which the following is the substance. That on the 2d. of October four Frenchmen of the names of Lachaise, Charles Delpeau, Mathurin and Gignoux, set out in the stage from Philadelphia for Kentuckey, that they were authorized by the Minister of France here to excite and engage as many as they could, whether of our citizens or others, on the road or within your government, or any where else, to undertake an expedition against the Spanish settlements within our neighborhood, and in event to descend the Ohio and Missisipi and attack New Orleans where they expected some naval cooperation: that they were furnished with money for these purposes and with blank commissions to be filled up at their discretion. I enclose you the description of these four persons in the very words in which it has been communicated to me.

Having laid this information before the President of the US. I have it in charge from him to desire your particular attention to these persons, that they may not be permitted to excite within our territories or carry from thence any hostilities into the territory of Spain. For this purpose it is more desirable that those peaceable means of coercion should be used which have been provided by the laws, such as the binding to the good behaviour these or any other persons exciting or engaging in these unlawful enterprizes, indicting them, or resorting to such other legal process as those learned in the laws of your state may advise. Where these fail or are inadequate, a suppression by the militia of the state has been ordered and practised in the other states.   I hope that the citizens of Kentuckey will not be decoyed into any participation in these illegal enterprizes against the peace of their country, by any effect they may expect from them on the navigation of the Missisipi. Their good sense will tell them that that is not to be effected by half-measures of this kind, and that their surest dependance is on those regular measures which are pursuing and will be pursued by the general government, and which flow from the United authority of all the states. I have the honor to be with great respect and esteem Your Excellency's Most obedt. & Most humble servt.   TH: JEFFERSON

PrC (DLC); at foot of first page: "H.E. the Governor of Kentuckey"; with three descriptions in TJ's hand subjoined, consisting of enclosure to Josef de Jaudenes and Josef Ignacio de Viar to TJ, 2 Oct. 1793. Tr (DNA: RG 46, Senate Records, 3d Cong., 1st sess.). Tr (Lb in same, TR). FC (Lb in DNA: RG 59, DL). Tr (Pierce N. Gaines, Fairfield, Connecticut, 1964); signed at foot of text: "Nn: Jones Clk. W. Off." Enclosed in TJ to Henry Knox, and TJ to George Washington, both 6 Nov. 1793.

Three days later Henry Knox enclosed this letter with letters of his own to Shelby and Governor Arthur St. Clair of the Northwest Territory, in which, in addition to instructing St. Clair to consider TJ's letter as if written to himself, he authorized both officials to employ military force in order to prevent the projected French expedition against Louisiana (ASP, *Foreign Relations*, I, 458).

To Josef Ignacio de Viar and Josef de Jaudenes

GENTLEMEN   Germantown, Novemr. 6th. 1793.

I received on the 4th. instant, your favor of Octo. 23d. informing me that the French privateer the Vainqueur de la Bastille, one of those clandestinely armed in the United States, had taken and carried into North Carolina a vessel of your nation. It is hoped that the instructions heretofore given to the Governors of the several States will have effected the immediate restitution of the vessel and cargo. For greater caution however the Secretary at war is charged to write to the Governor of North Carolina on this special subject, and there is every reason to rely that (the facts being as has been represented to you) the vessel and her cargo will be restored. This is all the Executive can do: for by our laws, damages can only be awarded against an individual by a Court of Justice, to which the injured party must apply for that purpose. I have the honor to be with sentiments of respect & esteem, Gentln: &c:

                                   TH: JEFFERSON

FC (Lb in DNA: RG 59, DL); at head of text: "Messrs. Viar & Jaudenes." Tr (AHN: Papeles de Estado, legajo 3895 bis); in Spanish; attested by Jaudenes and Viar. Enclosed in TJ to George Washington, 6 Nov. 1793.

INSTRUCTIONS HERETOFORE GIVEN TO THE GOVERNORS: see Cabinet Opinion on Prizes and Privateers, and note to Rules on Neutrality, both 3 Aug. 1793.

To Josef Ignacio de Viar
and Josef de Jaudenes

GENTLEMEN   Germantown Nov. 6. 1793.

It was not till the 24th. of October that I received your favor of the 2d. of that month, informing me that the four Frenchmen therein named and described had set out from Philadelphia for Kentuckey furnished with money, commissions, and instructions to procure some hostile enterprize from our territories against those of Spain. I took the first opportunity of laying the same before the President and was in consequence charged by him to communicate it to the Governor of Kentuckey, with instructions to prevent any such enterprize by such peaceable means as the laws have provided if sufficient, but if insufficient to suppress it by the military force of his state: and I flatter myself that these measures will have the desired effect. The laws of our country do not permit us to seize the papers of individuals until they shall have done some act which subjects their persons to be arrested. For this reason no order can be given to violate the secrecy of their papers. I have the honor to be with great esteem & respect, Gentlemen your most obedient & most humble servt   TH: JEFFERSON

PrC (DLC); at foot of text: "Messrs. Viar & Jaudenes." FC (Lb in DNA: RG 59, DL). Tr (AHN: Papeles de Estado, legajo 3895 bis); in Spanish; attested by Jaudenes and Viar. Enclosed in TJ to George Washington, 6 Nov. 1793.

To George Washington

Nov. 6. 1793.

Th: Jefferson has the honor to inclose several letters for the perusal of the President.—When he wrote to the Governor of Kentuckey, on a former intimation from the Spanish representatives, there was no probability that the intervention of military force would be requisite, and as far as illegal enterprizes could be prevented by the peaceable process of law, his writing was proper. It is proper now, so far as the same means may suffice. But should military coercion become necessary, he submits to the President whether a letter from the Secretary at war should not go, Th:J. having avoided any order of that kind in his letter.

RC (DNA: RG 59, MLR); endorsed by Bartholomew Dandridge, Jr. Tr (Lb in same, SDC). Not recorded in SJL. Enclosures: (1) TJ to Henry Knox, 6 Nov. 1793. (2) TJ to Isaac Shelby, 6 Nov. 1793. (3) TJ to Josef Ignacio de Viar and Josef de Jaudenes, 6 Nov. 1793 (two letters).

WHEN HE WROTE TO THE GOVERNOR OF KENTUCKEY: see TJ to Isaac Shelby, 29 Aug. 1793.

George Washington to the Trustees of the Germantown Academy

GENT. [ca. 6 Nov. 1793]

The readiness with which the Trustees of the school of Germ. to. tender the buildings under their charge for the use[1] of Congress is a proof of their zeal for furthering the public good. And doubtless the other inhabitants actuated by the same motives will feel the same dispositions to accomodate if necessary[2] those who assemble but for their service and that of their fellow citizens.

Where it may be best for Congress to remain will depend on circumstances which are daily unfolding[3] themselves, and for the issue of which we can but offer up our prayers to the sovereign[4] dispenser of life and health.

His favor too on our endeavors, the good sense and firmness of our fellow citizens and fidelity in those they employ will secure to us a permanence of good government.

Dft (DLC: TJ Papers, 94: 16096); in TJ's hand, undated, but prepared no earlier than 6 Nov. 1793 (see note below); written on verso of a detached sheet bearing docketing in a clerk's hand for an unrelated letter of Thomas Sim Lee to [Henry Knox], 25 Oct. 1793. Recorded in SJPL between 11 Oct. and 5 Nov. 1793. The letter as sent by Washington, still undated, followed TJ's Dft with minor changes in wording and punctuation, but added this concluding paragraph: "If I have been fortunate enough, during the vicissitudes of my life, so to have conducted myself, as to have merited your approbation, it is a source of much pleasure; and shou'd my future conduct merit a continuance of your good opinion, especially at a time when our Country, and the City of Philada. in particular, is visited by so severe a calamity, it will add more than a little to my happiness" (Fitzpatrick, *Writings*, XXXIII, 148-9).

Treasury Comptroller Oliver Wolcott, Jr., and Pennsylvania Governor Thomas Mifflin had inquired in October 1793 about the availablity of the Germantown Academy (technically still the Public School of Germantown) for use by Congress and the Pennsylvania legislature, respectively. The trustees of the Academy voted on 2 Nov. 1793 to give the President on behalf of Congress the right of first refusal and set the rent for the building at $300 a session, with a $60 abatement if Congress made certain repairs. On the morning of 6 Nov. a committee of five trustees headed by Henry Hill personally submitted a letter to Washington formally tendering the invitation (*A History of the Germantown Academy*, 2 vols. [Philadelphia, 1910-35], I, 120-4; Washington, *Journal*, 247). The President ultimately found it unneccessary to accept the offer.

[1] Preceding nine words interlined in place of "contribute as far as depends on them to the accommodation."

[2] Preceding two words interlined.

[3] Word interlined in place of "developing."

[4] Above this word TJ canceled "supreme."

From George Hammond

Sir   Lansdown near Philadelphia 7th: Novr. 1793

In a letter, which I had the honor of addressing to you on the 6th. of September, I acquainted you with my having received information, that in the course of the last five or six weeks, antecedent to that date, a privateer, named the Industry, had been illegally fitted out in the port of Baltimore. As you never controverted my assertion, nor required from me any evidence to substantiate it, I concluded either that you regarded my assurance as a sufficient proof of the existence of the fact, or that you were yourself possessed of other testimony, by which it was confirmed. You will therefore, Sir, judge of the surprize and concern, with which I learnt that this privateer, having captured a British ship, attempts have been made, to invalidate the evidence of its illegal equipment, and thereby to retard or prevent the restoration of the prize it had made. The principal circumstances of this transaction, I shall endeavor to relate with as much brevity as possible; and shall rely on the justice of the executive government of the United States for speedy and substantial redress.

This privateer was one of two vessels which, in consequence of a positive requisition from the Secretary of war, a member of the executive Council of Maryland (named Kelty) was appointed to examine, and to endeavor to discover whether the information, that had been given to the Secretary of war, of this vessel's arming for hostile purposes, in the port of Baltimore, had been well-founded. The intelligence obtained by that person, (Kelty) on his arrival at Baltimore, was certainly deemed sufficient to warrant the immediate forcible seizure and dismantling of this vessel: Although, on the following day, he was induced to restore her, to allow her to be refitted, and to proceed to sea, with a more complete equippment, than any former privateer of a similar description had ever received.

Within a few days after the departure of the Industry from Baltimore she captured the British ship Roehampton, and sent her into that port as a prize. On the arrival of the Roehampton, Mr. Thornton, his Majesty's Vice-Consul for the state of Maryland, esteemed it his duty to ascertain the fact of the illegal equippment of the privateer the Industry: And unquestionable evidence was obtained—that material alterations had been made in her form, solely for hostile purposes; and that she had received additions to her force much beyond the measure of her former strength. A requisition was therefore made to the Governor of Maryland, accompanied by depositions of these facts, and on the authority of this testimony which placed the privateer in a predicament similar to that of the vessels proscribed by the Presidents instructions, the release

[316]

of the Roehampton was demanded. The Governor, in his answer of the 18th. of September, refused all interference on the ground—that this evidence ought to have been produced, when the owner of the vessel was present to controvert it—that it was now taken in a manner generally supposed illegal—and that even if admitted in its fullest extent, it did not appear sufficient to authorize his interposition. In the mean time, in order to prevent the precipitate sale of the vessel, and that no measures might be left untried for its recovery, a suit was instituted on behalf of the British owners in the Admiralty Court. It was presumed from the new point of view in which the circular instructions had placed all questions of this nature, that the Judge of that court might be induced to vary his former decision—or that at least in a cause which involved a breach of the law *prior* to any capture, and within the territory and judicial cognizance of the United States, an enquiry demanded by the owners might be instituted to invalidate or to establish their assertions. The Judge however continued in the opinion that the Admiralty Court had no jurisdiction, and, as a consequence of that sentiment, refused to hear the evidence which was offered. The suit was dismissed: and, as the last resource, application was once more made to the Governor for the provisional detention of the Roehampton, until the determination of the executive government could be obtained. The testimonies already adduced were thought to be sufficient grounds for this requisition at least, even if they had been considered as inadequate to procure her entire restitution. But this request was also refused, because "no testimony was offered in addition to that, which in the Governor's letter of the 18th. of September did not seem to him sufficient to authorize an interference": when in reality no other could be produced than such as the same letter had pronounced to be 'generally supposed illegal.' After these repeated ineffectual attempts to preserve the Roehampton to her original proprietors, that vesel was of necessity abandoned, was immediately exposed to sale by the French agent, and purchased by a citizen of the United States.

On the propriety of the conduct observed by the Governor of Maryland it is not my intention to offer any animadversions, but I shall content myself with submitting to you, Sir, that evidence which he has thought proper to reject, but which, as contained in the depositions inclosed, will I doubt not appear to the wisdom of the federal executive government to contain as complete a body of proof, as can be expected, of the privateer the Industry having received in the port of Baltimore such repairs, and such augmentation of force (nearly double to her original equippment) as could be intended solely for the purpose of offensive hostility—and consequently she falls under the description of privateers proscribed by the President's instructions.

After this statement of facts it only remains for me to express my hope, that the executive government of the United States will adopt such measures, as may be the most efficacious, for procuring the recovery of the ship Roehampton from the American citizen to whom, after having been illegally captured, it has been sold, under the authority of a tribunal possessing no legal authority—and for restoring it to its real owners, subjects of Great Britain.

Before I conclude this letter, it is necessary for me to observe that the delay which has arisen in submitting to you the subject of it, has been occasioned by my separation from the members of the executive government, (resulting from the melancholy situation of Philadelphia) by my ignorance of your actual residence, and by my desire of accompanying it, by any oral communication, through which it may be elucidated, or the decision upon it expedited. I have the honor to be with sentiments of great respect Sir Your most obedient humble Servant

GEO. HAMMOND

RC (DNA: RG 59, NL); in a clerk's hand, signed by Hammond; at foot of first page: "Mr Jefferson"; endorsed by TJ as received 7 Nov. 1793 and so recorded in SJL. Tr (PRO: FO 5/1). Tr (Lb in DNA: RG 59, NL). Enclosures: (1) Deposition of Warren Lisle Nicoll, Baltimore, 15 Sep. 1793, stating that the schooner *Industry* arrived in Baltimore with the French fleet from Cap-Français with no more than four guns mounted on its deck, which lacked waist and quarter boards and was surrounded by a low gunnel and railing; that the blacksmith John McClarity told him about having made iron work for some carriages for the ship and about several cannon being brought to and mounted on it; that King, the plumber, informed him about having made a considerable quantity of lead bullets for the schooner; that a considerable number of sweeps of twenty-two or twenty-three feet long were altered and shortened for rowing purposes and, according to McClarity, were sold to the captain by Christian Draybourge of Baltimore; and that the schooner left the shipyard with fourteen guns mounted. (2) Deposition of Benjamin Baker, Baltimore, 12 Sep. 1793, stating, as a ship carpenter, that the schooner *Industry* was brought to his wharf and shipyard sometime between 6 and 12 Aug. 1793 mounting either four or six guns; that thereafter the ship's waist was planked up and port holes cut in it; that about six gun carriages were made for it by French work-

men in his yard; that trucks for the carriages were made by a Baltimore turner named Myers; that ring bolts and other iron work for the carriages and port holes were made at a blacksmith's shop in his yard; that the upper works done on the ship at his yard were only needed for armaments; that when the *Industry* left his yard after two weeks of work it had mounted four six-pounders, eight four-pounders, and two howitzers; and that the captain declared in his hearing that it was not a privateer (Trs in same, in Edward Thornton's hand, No. 2 being undated, with his notations at foot of No. 1 that the original sworn before him had been forwarded to Governor Thomas Sim Lee, and at foot of No. 2 that an attested copy had been sent to Governor Lee and that the original had been sworn and signed before Justice of the Peace Presbury and forwarded to Phineas Bond; Trs in same, MLR, endorsed by Henry Knox, No. 2 being partially dated; Trs in PRO: FO 5/1, No. 2 undated; Trs in Lb in DNA: RG 59, NL, No. 2 undated). (3) Deposition of John McClarity, Baltimore, 21 Oct. 1793, stating that he made for the privateer *Industry* at the wharf where it lay iron work for four gun carriages, four iron cranes for the sweeps, stanchions for the waist and quarter nettings, and clamps for two howitzers fixed at its stern; that Draybourge sold a number of sweeps for which the deponent made cranes; that he made twenty pound weight of langrage for the *Industry*; and that his bill for all this work was settled by a Baltimore merchant named Vouchez. (4) Deposition of Benjamin King, Baltimore, 21 Oct. 1793, stating, as a plumber, that he sold to the captain of the privateer *Industry* a quantity of sheet lead, about sixty pound weight of leaden bullets, and a vice; and that his bill was settled by the Baltimore merchants Zacharie, Coopman & Company. (5) Deposition of Michael Ballard, Baltimore, 21 Oct. 1793, stating, as a tin-man, that he made for the privateer *Industry* some ladles and 144 cannisters filled with pieces of old iron; and that his bill was paid by Zacharie, Coopman & Company (MSS in DNA: RG 59, NL, in Thornton's hand, signed by the deponents, with No. 5 subjoined to No. 4; Trs in PRO: FO 5/1; Trs in Lb in DNA: RG 59, NL).

The REQUISITION FROM THE SECRETARY OF WAR was a 6 Aug. 1793 letter in which Henry Knox instructed Governor Thomas Sim Lee of Maryland to suppress "two french Privateers fitting out at Baltimore, the one a Brig to mount fourteen Guns, and the other a Virginia Pilot boat" (W. H. Browne and others, eds., *Archives of Maryland*, 72 vols. [Baltimore, 1883-1972], LXXII, 345). For the investigation carried out pursuant to this letter in Lee's absence by Maryland councillor John Kilty, see enclosure listed at TJ to Hammond, 14 Nov.

1793. The INSTRUCTIONS of the President forbidding the original arming or equipping of any belligerent ships in American ports for military service are contained in Rules on Neutrality, 3 Aug. 1793. Governor Lee's ANSWER OF THE 18TH. OF SEPTEMBER informed Edward Thornton, the British vice-consul at Baltimore, that although he did not comply with Thornton's request for the release of the *Roehampton* because of his failure to prove that the *Industry* "had made any material military equipments in Baltimore," he had forwarded copies of the vice-consul's letter and supporting depositions to Knox and left it up to the President to resolve the case (MdAA: Letterbooks of Governor and Council). The 2 Oct. 1793 letter in which Governor Lee denied Thornton's request for the PROVISIONAL DETENTION OF THE ROEHAMPTON after the United States District Court in Maryland had declined to take jurisdiction over the case is in same. A TRIBUNAL POSSESSING NO LEGAL AUTHORITY: the French consular admiralty court in Baltimore in which F. Moissonnier, the French vice-consul for Maryland, had condemned the *Roehampton* as a lawful prize (TJ's second letter to Zebulon Hollingsworth, 14 Nov. 1793).

TJ submitted this letter and its enclosures to the President, who returned them this day (Washington, *Journal*, 248).

Memorial from George Hammond

The undersigned, his Britannic Majesty's Minister plenipotentiary to the United States, has the honor of submitting to the Secretary of State the accompanying deposition; from which it appears that on the 6th. ulto., the British brigantine Pilgrim from Nanticoke in Maryland bound to Barbadoes was captured by the French Xebeck privateer, le Sans Culotte of Marseille, at the distance of two miles and a half or three miles at the farthest, from the American shore and consequently within the jurisdiction of the United States.

It is necessary to remark that the original of this deposition was transmitted by his Majesty's Vice-Consul for the state of Maryland to the Governor of Maryland under the hope that the interposition of that officer might have retarded, at least until the determination of the federal executive government might have been known, the sale of the Pilgrim. The Undersigned is entirely ignorant whether the influence of the Governor of Maryland were exerted for this purpose or not; but, even admitting that it were, it was ineffectual, since on the 19 ulto. (within less than a week after its arrival in the port of Baltimore) the brigantine Pilgrim was publicly sold under the authority of the pretended tribunal of the French Consul at Baltimore. The Undersigned will reserve for a future occasion more general representations on the subject of the mischiefs which have flowed from the tacit permission that this government has granted to the establishment of these French Consular tribunals within its territory. For the present knowing (to use the expressions of the Secretary of States letter of the 15 of May) that "their judicial acts are not warranted by the usage of nations, by the stipulations existing between the United States and France nor by any laws of the land" he shall consequently consider the condemnation in this instance by the French Consular tribunal at Baltimore, "as a mere nullity" and shall therefore confine himself to the requisition that, if the executive government of the United States esteems the facts advanced in the annexed deposition to be well-founded it will immediately pursue the necessary measures for effecting the restitution of the brigantine the Pilgrim to her owners who are subjects of his Britannic Majesty.

Lansdown near Philadelphia   (signed) GEO: HAMMOND
7th of November 1793

Tr (PRO: FO 5/1). Recorded in SJL as received 7 Nov. 1793. Enclosure: Deposition of Peter Walstrum, Edward Matthias, and John Stay, Baltimore, 11 Oct. 1793, stating, as master, mate, and mariner of the *Pilgrim*, that after leaving Nanticoke on 30 Sep. 1793 bound for Barbados, and after the pilot left the ship at Watts Island in Chesapeake Bay on 5 Oct., this brigantine was captured as a prize by the xebec *Sans Culotte* of Marseilles during the afternoon of 6 Oct., "in five fathoms water at not more than two miles and a half or three miles at most from the shore," and brought into Baltimore on the evening of 11 Oct. (Tr in same; with subjoined copies of 16 Oct. 1793 notarization by George P. Keeports of Baltimore County and 31 Oct. 1793 attestation by Edward Thornton that the original was submitted to Governor Thomas Sim Lee).

In response to a protest by Edward Thornton, the British vice-consul at Baltimore, Governor Thomas Sim Lee of Maryland had sent a copy of the enclosed DEPOSITION to F. Moissonnier, the French vice-consul at Baltimore, requesting him to take possession of the *Pilgrim* and prevent its sale until the President had ruled on the legality of its capture. At the same time Lee assured Thornton that even if his overture to Moissonnier arrived too late, the British vice-consul could still take advantage of the procedures recently established by the Washington administration for obtaining restitution for prizes illegally captured by the French. After Moissonnier informed Lee that the *Pilgrim* had already been sold, the governor obtained a deposition from him on the legality of the capture and forwarded it to Secretary of War Henry Knox for submission to the President (Lee to Thornton, 18 Oct., to Moissonnier, 18, 25 Oct., 5 Nov., and to Knox, 5 Nov. 1793, MdAA: Letterbooks of Governor and Council).

TJ this day submitted this memorial and its enclosure to the President, who returned them the same day (Washington, *Journal*, 248).

From George Hammond

SIR   Lansdown 7th November 1793

You will perceive that the original of Baker's deposition, a copy of which accompanies My public letter of this date, is in the possession of Mr. Bond; but as that Gentleman is at some distance at present, and as my means of communication with him are neither facile nor frequent, I have not judged it expedient to wait the obtaining of it, but should you wish to receive it, it shall be transmitted to you with as little delay as possible. I have the honor to be, very respectfully, Sir, your obedient humble Servant   GEO. HAMMOND

RC (DNA: RG 59, NL); at head of text: "*Private*"; at foot of text: "Mr Jefferson"; endorsed by TJ as received 7 Nov. 1793. Tr (Lb in same).

Notes on the *Roehampton* and the *Pilgrim*

[7-14 Nov. 1793]

Sep. 6. Hammond. the Industry within 5. or 6. weeks past armed in Baltimore

12. Baker's deposition that Industry was brought to Baltimore wharf int. 6th. and 12th. Aug.

15. Thornton. that the Industry about 10. days ago captured and sent the Roehampton

Nicole's deposition that the Industry came to Baltimore with Fr. fleet from Cape Francois. she had 4. guns mounted.

18. T. S. Lee to Thornton. that a member of council examined her, found she was a privateer and therefore restored her.

Bournonville. that the Industry was armed at St. Domingo.

Oct. 13. Thornton. that the Roehampton is sold.

Nov. 7. Hammd. that on requisition from Secy. at War, Kelty examined her.

sold under authority of Fr. Consular tribunal. [1]

Aug. 6. to 12th. Industry came to Balt. with Fr. fleet from St. Domingo. had 4. guns. and commission. [2]

Secy. at war ordered examination

Kelty examined—found her a privateer, no material equipments discharged her [this report wanting]

Sep. 6. Mr. Hammond's first information to me that she had been equipped 4. or 5. W. [3]

about this day she took and sent to Baltimore the Rochampton

15. Thornton applies to Govr.—takes new evidence[4]
the Rochampton arrested and discharged by Admiralty.
18. Bournonville reclaims, saying the Industry armed in St. Domingo.
the Rochampton is sold under authority of Fr. Consulr. tribunal.

[*on verso:*]

Roehampton
that she stands on the ground of *augmentation*
restn. never promised on this ground
impracticable to draw line.

Kelty's report
aided by Brit. Consul.
sufficient excuse for not *reducing* her then
on sending in prize new testimony hunted up.
this cannot by retrospection censure the former proceedings.
we attend to it however so much as
to have directed legal examination
if it shall be found true will instruct all governors if she shall enter any port, to *reduce* her.

———

Pilgrim.
refer to Atty. of district to enquire if within limits?
has she been condemned?
has she been sold?

MS (DLC: TJ Papers, 95: 16290); written entirely in TJ's hand on both sides of a small sheet; undated; brackets in original. Recorded in SJPL between 7 and 8 Nov. 1793: "Notes of Roehampton. Pilgrim."

TJ's entry in SJPL notwithstanding, these notes could have been written at any time between 7 Nov., when TJ received George Hammond's letter and memorial on the cases of the ROEHAMPTON and the PIL-GRIM, and 14 Nov. 1793, when he dealt with these matters in letters of that date to Hammond and Zebulon Hollingsworth.

[1] TJ here left a blank space equal to about five lines of text.
[2] TJ here canceled a new line reading "Sep. 6. Mr. Hammd. complained to me."
[3] Sentence interlined.
[4] Sentence interlined.

From Thomas Mann Randolph, Jr.

DEAR SIR   Monticello Nov: 7: 1793.

I have inclosed and addressed to you today the papers you left with Patsy except the pamphlet (No. 21. The political state of Europe: July.) which I take the liberty to keep till the next post that I may have the satisfaction of reading it: I did not see these papers till today. I have inclosed allso three letters, one found among the papers mentioned, one on the table in the dining room, and one which I have just received, addressed to yourself.

We have had much wet weather since you left us which has greatly brightened our prospects of Wheat another year. There has not been rain enough however to render the river navigable. Biddle is very active and well contented in his situation: in 4 or 5 days he takes the reins in his own hands. Watson has arrived and is at work as you ordered. The man whom you left ill has had a hard time of it, his disorder having terminated in a general swelling which I have no doubt is dropsical: Gilmer being confined with his legs, and his assistant absent constantly he has had no medical aid: by much attention we have placed him, I am in hopes, out of danger, the swelling having abated considerably and an alarming palpitation of the heart, produced I think by obstruction from water, subsided. There has been no other sickness.

We are all in perfect health and happy when we can forget the risk you are runing.

Martha and Maria remind you of their love. I am Dr. Sir your most sincerely affectionate friend & hble Servt.   TH: M. RANDOLPH

RC (ViU: Edgehill-Randolph Papers); endorsed by TJ as received 16 Nov. 1793 and so recorded in SJL. Enclosure: Benjamin Hawkins to TJ, 28 Oct. 1793. Other enclosures not identified.

Report on the Proceedings of the Southwest Territory

The Secretary of State having received from the Secretary of the territory South of the Ohio a report of the Proceedings of the Governor of that territory from Mar. 1. to Sep. 1. 1793. has examined the same and
    Reports to the President
                That he finds nothing therein which will require his immediate agency.   TH: JEFFERSON
                                                                Nov. 7. 1793.

RC (DNA: RG 59, MLR); addressed: "The Pr[. . .]"; endorsed by Bartholomew Dandridge, Jr. PrC (DLC). Tr (Lb in DNA: RG 59, SDC). Recorded in SJPL: "Report on proceedgs. S.W. of Ohio." Enclosures: (1) Journal of the Proceedings of Governor William Blount of the Southwest Territory, 13 Mch.-15 June 1793 (Tr in DNA: RG 59, SWT, in the hand of Daniel Smith; Tr in Lb in DNA: RG 76, Yazoo Land Claims; printed in *Terr. Papers*, IV, 453-7). (2) Act of the Governor and Judges of the Southwest Territory, 13 Mch. 1793, requiring that persons holding fines, fees, and taxes from court cases, the probate of deeds, the registration of land grants, and the issuing of licenses pay them to territorial secretary Daniel Smith, and that the secretary, court clerks, and county registers give bond for payment of the same (Tr in DNA: RG 59, SWT, in Smith's hand; printed in *Terr. Papers*, IV, 242-3). (3) Daniel Smith to TJ, Knoxville, 1 Sep. 1793, enclosing Nos. 1-2, the latter "on a separate paper, it being, as is conceived, to be laid before Congress" (RC in DNA: RG 59, SWT, at foot of text: "Thomas Jefferson Esquire Secretary

of State"; Tr in Lb in DNA: RG 76, Yazoo Land Claims; recorded in SJL as received 7 Nov. 1793; printed in *Terr. Papers*, IV, 305).

The President received this report on 8 Nov. 1793 (Washington, *Journal*, 249). See also TJ to George Washington, [7 Nov. 1793].

From William Short

DEAR SIR   Sn Lorenzo Nov. 7th. 1793

I had the pleasure of recieving by Mr. Blake your friendly letter of July 11th.—and answered it by one of a size so enormous that I should not have had courage to have sent it but for the recollection of your being now retired to private life. Although I have not since been so happy as to hear from you, and of course know nothing more of my affairs in Mr. Browne's hands than there mentioned, still I indulge myself in the hope of their being safe, and it is a most pleasing hope after what had passed.

I wrote you the useless efforts I had made to obtain Cortez's letters. I begin now to entertain hopes that you will recieve them by Mr. Blake (who has been delayed here beyond all expectations by the reasons mentioned to the Sec. of State) and who will probably set off in eight days. The book is not be found anywhere for sale, and the Archbishop of Toledo had distributed all he had. Mr. Carmichael met with him accidentally some days ago—he promised him that he would endeavor to procure a copy from a person who he believed had one he could spare— and if so he will send it by Mr. Blake. Mr. Blake will carry you also a copy of my last letter of the 7th. of October.

I could not avoid mentioning there perhaps in too warm terms the manner in which I have been treated by government, and the impression it had made on me. I have only now left vain and sterile regrets at not having followed your friendly advice of abandoning the career I had been in, and which I foolishly continued in the vain hope of being in the end employed in such a grade abroad as would enable me to return to my country in the manner I chose, and not in a low grade after so long service, which under a government that is supposed to admit of no preference but such as is founded on merit, could not but leave an idea as to me, of want both of capacity and merit—and particularly as the person at the head of the department was considered as the person best acquainted with the measure of my worth in every respect, and as it would not naturally be supposed that he was to take no part whatever in the regulations and appointments of his department. When I consider therefore that the President has been, contrary to the uniform tenor of his conduct in other respects, so ready to give credit to what was reported as to my conversations at the Hague, I suppose he must have had from the beginning some disposition not to be quite so impartial as to me as I might have expected—and when this is connected with the silence of the person the most in the way of knowing me, and most naturally in the way of saying whether I was proper for the employment I wished in France (without pretending to condemn this as I am fully persuaded no person whatever is a better judge of what is the proper conduct of the head of a department) I cannot complain of any thing but my own fatality. I have given up all hopes now of being employed in any other than subordinate grades since I am sure I shall never again have so well grounded an expectation as I have had hitherto. I shall probably be unknown to your successor, who will of course and with reason remain indifferent as to my advancement—or opposed to it—and if he should be even indifferent I have no right or pretensions to expect it from the President, after the disposition he has already shewn towards me. And as to remaining in the subordinate, unsettled, and precarious state in which I have been from the month of June 1790. so as really never to know whether or where I was to be employed for any three months to come, I am so sick of it, and have felt it so prejudicial to the state of my mind, and my own feelings as to be unable to continue it longer—besides being absolutely destructive of those literary pursuits which I had begun at Paris, and which might be carried on with great facility, with diplomatick business provided one was so established as to be able to take arrangements and have access to one's books. From the epoch abovementioned I have never ventured to take arrangements for having the books and publications I wanted sent me regularly from America, because I have at no one time known whether before the first were sent, I might not be removed from where I was and perhaps on my return to America—and yet my fatal stars have dragged me on from day to day until now. And now I am as little certain as ever as to my future destiny except so far as it depends on myself. If my fortune is saved from the hands of Mr. Browne, it will enable me to live with my moderate wants independently wherever I may chuse it, and restore to me that calm and tranquility, and that freedom from vain hopes which I have never enjoyed (though I have no body but myself to blame) since I have been in the diplomatick career. After having thus lost the best part of my life I have now nothing else left—after so many years spent therein and at my age I have been only in subordinate and precarious capacities, such as are given by other countries to inferior people, and when I return to America shall carry with me this badge of demerit and incapacity. After such a publick testimonial of the inferior opinion entertained of my by those whose approbation I sought after with so much zeal, as that of the chiefs of our government, and who are certainly very competent judges, I have no right to expect that a different one will be entertained by any other part of my country. I give up all idea of publick life in future and shall content myself to live retired and forgotten, which is the only line for which I was made, and which I shall regret to the end of my days having not adopted, instead of accepting the Residence of the Hague. How much humiliation I should have saved myself—and although it was not a little to have been supplanted in the manner and by the person I was there, it would have ended there and I should have been now a settled farmer in my own country not dependent for my ease or quiet on the will of any body. But I beg pardon, for thus yielding to my feelings. My letters whenever I recollect that it is to a friend to whom I can unbosom myself I am writing, are a constant *Renovare dolorem*. It is a long chapter and would never end if I were not to do violence to myself. At present it can answer no purpose to give you so much *ennui*, and yet I insensibly yield to it in my letters.

There are circumstances which delicacy has ever prevented my mentioning and which had I known before my arrival here would have prevented me absolutely from accepting the joint commission here, as I suppose they would have prevented its being formed, had they been known to you. From the time of my arrival here when they became known to me, it was too late for repentance, and I have from that time found myself in a situation by no means agreeable, and which on particular occasions is insupportable. I hoped the joint commission would not have so long a duration and have therefore borne with it. After finding from the circumstance of the uncertainty in which our business was here, that there was little prospect of its being terminated, I proposed and Mr. Carmichael assented to write advising that the joint commission should be put an end to and the business be confided to the permanent agent here. I am so wearied out with living thus uselessly and expensively to government, in Spanish dirty filthy taverns from day to day, and under the circumstances above alluded to, that I had rather submit to any thing than continue it. I have not thought myself at liberty by any means to leave this place without either terminating the business or recieving permission from government to leave it. Otherwise I should have done it long long ago. It would have been less expensive to have kept a Minister Plenipotentiary here than to have had us both and he would certainly have been much more in the way of rendering service. I hope that our joint commission will be put an end to as we desired. It is both expensive, humiliating and useless—expensive because we are two—humiliating because we are not considered as the representatives of a sovereign power, and useless because the character we are in, excludes us from all communication that can be relied on with the minister whose will would be unopposed in this business and who would understand it much sooner and better than any other if properly explained to him.

I am so sensible of the advantage and propriety of having a Minister Plenipotentiary here that I could not avoid touching on it in a late letter to the Sec. of State. This shews that I do it without interest and merely from the consideration abovementioned for my letter would prevent my being appointed even if the President had not already shewn that he did not think me proper for such grades—and that they were to be reserved for those better known or approved by him. Whoever he chuses to name is a matter of indifference to me—but it is with great deference to his better knowlege, much to be desired for the interests of both countries that one should be named and as soon as possible; and it is much to be lamented, perhaps not to be repaired, that this was not done when our joint commission was formed; it would have been still better if it had been done years ago, and this I would pawn my life to shew you to demonstration in one hours conversation. I have discharged my duty in stating it at different times as far as could be done by letter—and as to the rest I have nothing more to do, and will care as little as I can care where the interests of my country are concerned.

The present moment is particularly critical on account of the new system adopted in this war. Several of our vessels are unjustly siezed and brought into the ports of Spain, and our sailors ill treated and use-lessly so. This is a delicate business and should be managed with activ-ity and dignity. Much must depend on the manner of its being treated. I hope it will not be forgotten by our government that I have nothing to do with it, and as it would be improper do not meddle in any way. I mention this that if the mode of its being managed should be approved by government I may have no pretensions to any share in that approba-tion, and if not approved that I may have no part of the blame. My being here might perhaps involve me in this business in the eyes of the public unless thus expressed.

I have written to you at different times on the subject of the payments to France formerly committed to me. I hope those letters got to your hands before you left Philadelphia, and that you will have been so good as to have given any explanations that you may have thought necessary. They were dated April 5th. and June 23d.

We are quite ignorant here of every thing that passes in America except what we learn accidentally. I hope the permanent agent will take measures, which would be very possible to a permanent agent, to re-cieve more full and more regular information—for it is certainly necessary if not essential to his forming a proper judgment in many cases on the line he ought to pursue. This letter will be inclosed to the Sec. of State. I will thank you to let me know in what manner I should address and forward your letters. I hope I shall have the real pleasure of hearing from you when you have leisure—for be assured my dear Sir, that in whatever situation of life I may be—and however dissatisfied with myself or others, I shall ever remain your sincere friend,   W Short

RC (DLC); at head of text: "*Private*"; at foot of first page: "Mr. Jefferson &c &c &c"; endorsed by TJ as received 31 Mch. 1794 and so recorded in SJL. PrC (PHi: Gilpin Collection).

One of a size so enormous: Short to TJ, 7 Oct. 1793. The employment I wished in France: a reference to Short's unfulfilled ambition to succeed TJ as American minister to France. It was in the month of June 1790 that Short received his regular commission as American chargé d'affaires at Paris (Short to TJ, 14 June 1790). Supplanted in the manner and by the person: a reference to Gouverneur Morris's appointment in 1792 as American minister to France. Renovare dolorem: "renewal of pain." I proposed and Mr. Carmichael assented to write: see William Carmichael and William Short to TJ, 6 June 1793. Late letter to the Sec. of state: Short to TJ, 16 Oct. 1793 (see Appendix I).

To George Washington

[7 Nov. 1793]

Mr. Smith supposes the bill he incloses must be laid before Congress. On a former suggestion of the same kind, Th:J. being able to find nothing which rendered it necessary, consulted the Attorney General, who was of opinion it was not necessary, but promised [to][1] make more diligent enquiry. The result will now be asked of him by Th:J.

RC (DNA: RG 59, MLR); undated, but endorsed by Bartholomew Dandridge, Jr., as a 7 Nov. 1793 letter from the Secretary of State. Tr (Lb in same, SDC); dated 7 Nov. 1793. Not recorded in SJL.

The suggestion of Daniel smith and the bill he enclosed are described in Enclosures Nos. 2-3 listed at TJ's Report on the

Proceedings of the Southwest Territory, 7 Nov. 1793. For the former suggestion of the same kind, see Report on the Proceedings of the Southwest Territory, 19 June 1793, and note, and Edmund Randolph to TJ, 25 July 1793.

[1] Word supplied.

To Certain Foreign Ministers
in the United States

Sir   Germantown Nov. 8. 1793.

The President of the United States thinking that[1] before it shall be finally decided to what distance from our sea shores the territorial protection of the United States shall be exercised, it will be proper to enter into friendly conferences and explanations with the powers chiefly interested in the navigation of the seas on[2] our coasts, and relying that convenient occasions may be taken for these hereafter, finds it necessary in the mean time,[3] to fix provisionally on some distance for the present government of these questions. You are sensible that very different opinions and claims have been heretofore advanced on this subject. The greatest distance to which[4] any respectable assent among nations has been at any time given, has been the extent of the human sight, estimated at upwards of 20. miles, and the smallest distance I believe, claimed by any nation whatever is the utmost range of a cannon ball, usually stated at one sea league. Some intermediate distances have also been insisted on, and that of three sea-leagues has some authority in its favor. The character of our coast, remarkable in considerable parts of it for admitting no vessels of size to pass near the shores, would intitle us in reason to as broad a margin of protected navigation as any nation whatever. Reserving however the ultimate extent of this for future deliberation the President gives instructions[5] to the officers acting under his authority to consider those heretofore given them as restrained for the present to the distance of one sea-league or three geographical miles from the sea shores. This distance can admit of no opposition as it is recognised by treaties between some of the Powers with whom we are connected in commerce and navigation, and is as little or less than is claimed by any of them on their own coasts. For the jurisdiction of the rivers and bays of the United States[6] the laws of the several states are understood to have made provision, and they are moreover as being landlocked, within the body of the United States.

Examining by this rule the case of the British brig Fanny, taken on the 8th: of May last, it appears from the evidence that the capture was made four or five miles from the land, and consequently without the line provisionally adopted by the President as beforementioned.[7] I have the honor to be with sentiments of respect and esteem, Sir your most obedient and most humble servant

PrC (DLC); in a clerk's hand, unsigned; with dateline and "Mr. Hammond" at foot of first page inserted in ink by TJ. PrC (DLC); in a clerk's hand, unsigned; at foot of first page: "Mr. Van Berckell"; lacks next-to-last sentence. PrC (DLC); in a clerk's hand, unsigned; at foot of first page in ink by TJ: "Viar & Jaudenes"; lacks next-to-last sentence. Dft (TJ Papers, 94: 16140); entirely in TJ's hand, unsigned and undated; abbreviated text based on Dft of TJ to Edmond Charles Genet, 8 Nov. 1793 (see notes 4-6 below), only the most significant emendations being recorded below; at head of text: "Mr. Hammond Van Berckel Viar & Jaudenes"; at foot of text: "the Min Pleny. of France"; with note at foot of text referring to this Dft and the Dft of TJ to Edmond Charles Genet, 8 Nov. 1793: "these two draughts were shewn to the Atty Genl. & approved with one alteration. The fair copies were shewn to Colo. Hamilton & Genl. Knox before dinner at Bockeus's inn Germantown & approved"; on verso: "to be copied & press copied and returned by the rider this afternoon." PrC of Tr (DNA: RG 59, MD); in a clerk's hand; at foot of first page: "Mr. Genet, Mr. Hammond, Mr. Van Berckel & Messrs. Viar & Jaudenes." FC (Lb in DNA: RG 59,

DL); at head of text: "The Minister pleni. of Great Britain"; at foot of text: "☞ A copy of the above (omitting the last paragraph) was addressed to Mr. Van Berckel, Resident from the United Netherlands—and Messrs. Viar & Jaudenes, Commissioners from Spain." Tr (Lb in PRO: FO 116/3). Tr (AHN: Papeles de Estado, legajo 3895 bis); in Spanish; attested by Jaudenes and Viar; lacks next-to-last sentence. Recorded in SJPL. Enclosed in TJ to George Washington, [16 Nov. 1793].

With this letter and TJ's letter of the same date to Edmond Charles Genet, the United States became the first country officially to proclaim the three-mile limit for its maritime jurisdiction. For the antecedents of this historic proclamation, see George Hammond to TJ, 5 June 1793, and note. The process by which this provisional definition of the three-mile limit became a fixed part of American policy by the mid-nineteenth century is described in Philip C. Jessup, *The Law of Territorial Waters and Maritime Jurisdiction* (New York, 1927), 3-7, 49-54.

After obtaining Cabinet and presidential approval of the draft of this letter, TJ submitted three copies of the final version to the President on 16 Nov. 1793, and Washington returned them the same day (Cabinet Opinions on Various Letters, [23 Nov. 1793]; Washington, *Journal*, 248, 251, 252).

[1] In Dft TJ here canceled "the line of territorial protection."
[2] Preceding three words interlined in Dft.
[3] Preceding four words interlined in Dft.
[4] Remainder of this sentence and the next two sentences through "navigation" represented in Dft by "&c—."
[5] Remainder of this sentence and the next sentence through "claimed" represented in Dft by "&c—."
[6] At this point in Dft TJ wrote "&c—" and canceled "—stated in a paper inclosed to me by the representative of France extends the distance from 14. to 16. miles. But this witness not having been examined in the forms required by the law I have desired," at which point the Dft ends. Next to this canceled passage he wrote "qu." in the margin. See also Genet to TJ, 19 Oct. 1793.
[7] Preceding sentence omitted in texts sent to Van Berckel and Viar and Jaudenes.

To Edmond Charles Genet

SIR   Germantown Nov. 8. 1793.

I have now to acknowledge and answer your letter of September 13. wherein you desire that we may define the extent of the line of territorial protection on the coasts of the United States observing that Governments and jurisconsults have different views on this subject.

It is certain that heretofore they have been much divided in opinion as to the distance from their sea-coasts to which they might reasonably claim a right of[1] prohibiting the commitment of[2] hostilities. The greatest distance to which any respectable assent among nations has been at any time given has been the extent of the human sight, estimated at upwards of 20 miles, and the smallest distance I believe[3] claimed by any nation whatever is the utmost range of a cannon ball, usually stated at one sea-league. Some[4] intermediate distances have also been insisted on, and that of three sea-leagues has some authority in its favor. The character of our coast remarkable in considerable parts of it for admitting no vessels of size to pass near the shores would entitle us in reason to as[5] broad a margin of protected navigation as any nation whatever. Not proposing however at this time, and without a respectful and friendly communication with the powers interested in this navigation, to fix on the distance to which we may ultimately insist on the right of protection, the President[6] gives instructions to the officers acting under his authority to consider those heretofore given them as[7] restrained for the present to the distance of one sea-league or three geographical miles from the sea shores.[8] This distance can admit of no opposition as it is recognised by treaties between some of the Powers with whom we are connected in commerce and navigation, and is as little, or less than is claimed by any of them on their own coasts.

Future occasions will be taken to enter into explanations with them as to the ulterior extent to which we may reasonably carry our jurisdiction. For that of the rivers and Bays of the United States the laws of the several states are understood to have made provision,[9] and they are moreover as being land-locked within the body of the United States.

Examining by this rule the case of the British brig Fanny taken on the 8th. of May last, it appears from the evidence that the capture was made four or five miles from the land; and consequently without the line provisionally adopted by the President as before mentioned.[10] I have the honor to be with sentiments of respect and esteem Sir, Your most obedient and most humble servant

PrC (DLC); in a clerk's hand, unsigned; with dateline, and "Mr. Genet" at foot of first page, inserted in ink by TJ. Dft (DLC); entirely in TJ's hand, unsigned; with date added in a different ink; only the most significant emendations are recorded below; for a notation by TJ relating to this text, see note to TJ to Certain Foreign Ministers in the United States, 8 Nov. 1793. Tr (DNA: RG 46, Senate Records, 3d Cong., 1st sess.). FC (Lb in DNA: RG 59, DL). Tr (DLC: Genet Papers). Tr (DLC: John Trumbull Letterbook). Tr (DLC: Genet Papers); in French. Tr (DLC: Genet Papers; draft translation of preceding Tr. Tr (AMAE: CPEU, xxxix); in French. Recorded in SJPL. Printed in *Message*, 91-2. Enclosed in TJ to George Washington, [16 Nov. 1793].

After obtaining Cabinet and presidential approval of the draft of this letter, TJ submitted a copy of the final version to the President on 16 Nov. 1793, and Washington returned it the same day (Cabinet Opinions on Various Letters, [23 Nov. 1793]; Washington, *Journal*, 248, 251, 252).

[1] In Dft TJ here canceled "protecting vessels."

[2] In Dft TJ here canceled "all."

[3] Preceding two words interlined in Dft.

[4] Word interlined in Dft in place of "The."

[5] In Dft TJ here canceled "great."

[6] In Dft TJ here canceled "has determined."

[7] In Dft TJ here canceled "extending."

[8] In Dft TJ here canceled "For the jurisdiction of the rivers and bays, the laws of the several states are understood to have made provision."

[9] Remainder of sentence added in the margin of Dft.

[10] In Dft TJ here canceled "He considers the capture." Below it he also canceled the following paragraph: "With respect to the British ship William, taken on the 3d. of May last, the testimony as to the place of seizure varies from 2 to 5. miles from the sea-shore. The information of a certain Peter Dalton stated in the paper inclosed in your letter of Oct. 19. extends the distance from 14. to 16. miles. But his evidence not having been given before a magistrate

legally qualified to place him under the solemnity of an oath and bound to cross examine him, I am to desire that his evidence, if it is to be insisted on may be taken in legal form, and forwarded ⟨to me⟩ for the consideration of the President." Before canceling this paragraph TJ wrote "qu." next to it in the margin.

From Tobias Lear

DEAR SIR   New York November 8th: 1793

Accept my grateful acknowledgements and best thanks for your kind letter of the 5th. instant; which, together with the minutes of a Route and the letters enclosed, came to my hands Yesterday.

As a sincere friend, and truly wishing your personal happiness, I cannot but be pleased with your determination to retire from your public station; because I know that a mind like your's can find more solid enjoyment in the private walks of life than any public station, however elevated or flattering, can give it. But as a Citizen of this Country, and as one who has its best interests very much at heart, I shall exceedingly regret that event. And I know when I express this sentiment for myself, that I speak the language of a large proportion of the honest and good Citizens of this Country.

I hope, my dear Sir, that I shall never wantonly forfeit the good opinion which you have been pleased to entertain of me—and to express to your friends.

I have taken my passage on board the American Ship Fanny, which is bound to Glascow, and is expected to sail on the 10th.; but I think it likely she may be detained a day or two longer. Should anything occur to you in which I can render you service while I am in Europe, you will please me in letting me know it. Letters directed to me to the Care of our Consul at London will find me. Wishing you every happiness that the reflections of an honest and independent mind can give—I am, Dear Sir, with sincere attachment & respect, Your friend & Servt

TOBIAS LEAR

RC (ViW: Tucker-Coleman Collection); endorsed by TJ as received 11 Nov. 1793 and so recorded in SJL.

From George Taylor, Jr.

DEAR SIR   New York Nov. 8. 1793. $\frac{1}{2}$ past 11 AM.

Your favor of the 3rd. instant I have had the honor to receive a few moments ago. Ever willing to fulfil my duty to the utmost of my power, I shall take immediate steps for complying with your desire to take arrangements for resuming the Business of the office. To this end I shall set off with my little family in the first days of the next week.

From the present state of the weather and of the disorder in Philadelphia, communicated thro' the medium of the public prints, it would seem rather imprudent to risk a residence in that City. I should therefore give a preference to Germantown for the present, tho' the expense should be greater than my circumstances will afford; being convinced that on this occasion Congress will readily allow any extraordinary expenses necessarily incurred in prosecuting the public Business.

I shall immediately forward a copy of your letter to Mr. Blackwell, who I am informed is on Long Island. As to the other Gentlemen, I am totally ignorant of their places of Residence. I have not received a line from Mr. Bankson since the 7. of Octr. last tho' I have written three letters to him since that date.

Apprehensive that I may miss this days post I must close. With every sentiment of Respect and sincere Regard, I have the honor to be Dr. Sir, Your mo. ob. & Mo. humble servt.   GEO: TAYLOR JR.

RC (DLC); at foot of text: "Mr Jefferson"; endorsed by TJ as received 11 Nov. 1793 and so recorded in SJL.

TJ's FAVOR OF THE 3RD. INSTANT is not recorded in SJL and has not been found.

From James Currie

Richmond Novr. 9th. 1793

I take the liberty of troubling you with this line by Mr. Greenup just to remind you of (as soon as matters of more consequence will permit) my affair with Griffin, to have it if possible brought to a speedy and favorable issue, being much afraid that some Chicanery has, or will be, practised, to defraud me of justice ultimately I conceive Your particular enquiry [. . .] which you was kind enough in your last letter to promise me should take place in regard to the former and future management of it. Colo. T.M.R. lays dangerously ill at Colo. Harvies here and I believe Will soon leave us. This assembly of Delegates have Approved, the Presidents Proclamation, the senate has not confirmed their Vote so the matter stands at present. With my most cordial Wishes for your future happiness I am With the most sincere Regard Dr Sir Your M Obt H Serv   JAMES CURRIE

RC (MHi); one word illegible; endorsed by TJ as received 6 Dec. 1793 and so recorded in SJL.

By a 77-48 roll call vote on 1 Nov. 1793 the Virginia House of DELEGATES passed a

resolution which APPROVED THE PRESIDENTS PROCLAMATION of Neutrality as "a politic and constitutional measure, wisely adopted at a critical juncture, and happily calculated to preserve to this country the inestimable blessings of peace," but a week later the SENATE rejected it. A House resolution praising Governor Henry Lee's efforts to put the Proclamation into effect met a similar fate in the Senate (JHD, Oct.-Dec. 1793, p. 31; Virginia Senate Journal, Oct.-Dec. 1793 [Richmond, 1794], 8, 11).

To James Madison

Germantown. Nov. 9. 93.

The stages from Philadelphia to Baltimore are to be resumed tomorrow. The fever has almost disappeared. The Physicians say they have no new subjects since the rains. Some old ones are still to recover or die, and it is presumed that will close the tragedy. The inhabitants, refugees, are now flocking back generally; this will give us accomodation here. The Pr. sets out tomorrow for Reading, and perhaps Lancaster to return in a week. He will probably remain here till the meeting of Congress, should Philadelphia become ever so safe, as the members may not be satisfied of that point till they have time to inform themselves. Toulon has surrendered to Engld. and Spain. Grand Anse in St. Domingo to England. The British have recieved a check before Dunkirk, probably a great one, but the particulars cannot yet be depended on. It happened about the 10th. of September. When Monroe and yourself arrive here, come to Bockeus's tavern (sign the K. of Prussia). I will have engaged beds there for you for your temporary accomodation. Adieu.

RC (DLC: Madison Papers); unsigned. PrC (DLC).

From James Philip Puglia

SIR   Philadelphia Coomb's Alley no. 8 Novr. 9th. 1793

Wiewing with sorrow the large number of victims in all ranks and professions fallen by the late distressing desease, I suppose that some vacancies have taken place amongst the persons employed in public Offices. In this conception I take the liberty of adressing your Honour with the offer of my best services in that line, wishing (if agreeable and possible) to be admitted as a Clark in your Office.

I had several times the honour of presenting my self to you Sir, and did some translation by your command: I do not presume it to be any merit in my favour for deserving your generous protection, however should I luckily obtain it, I shall incessantly endeavour to preserve it by discharging my duty with honour and activity.

I inclose my proposal which you may intirely rely upon—for the *Three languages* I mean the Spanish, French, and Italian. I was the Book-keeper of the late Partnership of Willing, Morris and Swanwick

from whom information may be had respecting my Caracter &c. Mr. George Meade can give it likewise, and (if required) I am confident that several other respectable Merchants will favour me with their recomendations. May this letter attain your kind remembrance, wishing to know when and where I am to appear on your return to this City; meanwhile I constantly pray the Almighty for your health, exaltation and happiness. With the greatest respect I am Sir Your most obedient humble Servant JAMES PH. PUGLIA late Sworn
Interpreter of the Spanish Language for the
Commonwealth of Pennsylvania

RC (DLC: Washington Papers, Applications for Office); at foot of text: "Honble. Thomas Jefferson Esquire Secretary of the United States German town"; endorsed by TJ as received 11 Nov. 1793 and so recorded in SJL; endorsed by a clerk: "Jas. Ph. Puglia wants employment." Enclosure: Puglia's Proposal for Employment, Philadelphia, 31 Oct. 1793, stating that he is an able bookkeeper and accountant and "speaks and writes correctly three of the principal European languages," that he has given his employers entire satisfaction, and that he can produce recommendations of his "caracter, secrecy and activity" (MS in same; in Puglia's hand).

James Philip Puglia (1760-1831), a Genoa-born author, language teacher, and translator who formed an undying hatred for Spanish despotism when his career as a merchant at Cadiz ended with imprisonment in 1787, emigrated to Philadelphia in 1790, took the oath of allegiance to the United States a year later, and held an appointment as Pennsylvania's Spanish interpreter from August 1792 to April 1793. His earlier work doing TRANSLATION BY YOUR COMMAND is not otherwise documented, but the State Department hired him to translate another Spanish document in December 1793. TJ was one of the few subscribers to *El Desengaño del Hombre* (Philadelphia, 1794), Puglia's pioneering, Enlightenment-based critique of Spain's system of government, which was underwritten largely by French minister Edmond Charles Genet as part of his efforts to undermine Spanish rule in America, and subsequently condemned by the Mexican Inquisition. Puglia wrote a pro-Federalist pamphlet in 1795, but followed it with two pseudonymous attacks on Federalist William Cobbett a year later, and in 1808 he sent TJ copies of two unpublished and unperformed plays including "The Embargo," a defense of Jeffersonian trade policy. Reduced to a marginal existence and impoverished, Puglia committed suicide a decade after publishing, among other works, a Spanish translation of Thomas Paine's *The Rights of Man* (Merle E. Simmons, *Santiago F. Puglia, An Early Philadelphia Propagandist for Spanish American Independence* [Chapel Hill, 1977]; *Pa. Archs.*, 9th ser., I, 438, 566; Vol. 17: 375; Sowerby, Nos. 2333, 4600).

To Henry Remsen

DEAR SIR   Germantown Nov. 9. 1793.

I am returned to this place about a week ago, the President having concluded to fix the Executive here till the meeting of Congress or till we shall see whether Philadelphia becomes safe. It is believed to be so now, insomuch that the refugee inhabitants are flocking into it. It is said there are no new subjects in the hands of the Physicians since the great rains. Some of those before infected are still sick. I therefore think it probable that Congress will find it safe to sit there. We expect that knowing the President to be here it will be an evidence to them that this place is safe, that they will therefore gather here, consult informally together as to the place of their session, and having made up their minds on that point, will go into the feilds of Philadelphia (if they think the Congress house not safe) and there adjourn by a vote. Their next meeting having been fixed by a joint vote (which is a law as to this matter) it is understood that they cannot be a legal body, till they shall legally change the place.

I am to acknolege the receipt of your favors of Oct. 1. 7. 14. and to thank you for your care of the letters, and the box containing my model of the threshing machine. About this machine I am most anxious, as it is most precious to my future occupation as a farmer. I will therefore pray you to send it by some American vessel going to Richmond, and not to any other place in Virginia, because were it landed at Norfolk, or any where else, I know from experience the certainty of losing it. Great pains have been taken by Mr. Pinckney to procure the model and get it out to me, and it has cost 13. guineas. I will bear in mind the price of the inkpot and send it by the first person I see going to New York. In the mean time should we go into Philadelphia and you should fulfill your purpose of visiting that place I shall be very happy to see you should I be still there as I shall be to the close of the year. I am with great and sincere esteem Dr. Sir Your friend & servt   Th: Jefferson

P.S. Be pleased to direct the box to the care of Colo. Robert Gamble merchant Richmd.

RC (Gilder Lehrman Collection, on deposit NNP); endorsed by Remsen in part: "Decr. 4. Sent the Model by the Ellice Capt. Weymouth to Richmond." PrC (DLC); at foot of text in ink: "Mr. Remsen." Tr (DLC); 19th-century copy.

From Edward Rutledge

Dear Sir   Charleston, Novr. 9th. 1793.

I have been requested by the Gentlemen who have signed the within memorial, to place it under your Protection, and I do so, with the greatest chearfulness, because I know full well, that the sole motive by which they were actuated, was, Humanity. The People of St. Domingo, came to our Shores, in such Numbers, and in so destitute a Condition, and the Funds of our Citizens were so unequal to their comfortable Support, that the Memorialists, who are Respectable Merchants, and among the foremost in relieving the distressed, prevailed on poor Thompson (who felt as they did, for the Wretched) to take the Command of a small Vessel, and sail for the Island of St. Domingo, expressly for the Purpose, which is mentioned in the Dispatch.

I know you too well to doubt of your Assistance, if it can be effectually applied. The Method I must leave to yourself. With Sentiments of real Affection I am my dear Sir, your Sincere & obliged Friend

ED: RUTLEDGE

Dupl (DLC); in a clerk's hand, signed by Rutledge; at head of text: "*Duplicate*"; at foot of text: "The Honble. T. Jefferson Esqr. &ca. &ca." Recorded in SJL as received 2 Dec. 1793. Enclosure: Memorial of James & Edward Penman & Company, North & Vesey, and Jennings & Woddrop to George Washington, Charleston, 9 Nov. 1793, alleging that out of compassion for the impoverished refugees from Saint-Domingue in their city and with the additional goal of determining whether conditions in the colony would permit other vessels to be sent there safely, on 18 Aug. 1793 they had sent the American schooner pilot boat *Trial*, commanded by American citizen Archibald Thompson, with a cargo of rice, flour, and pork, to Saint-Domingue with instructions to call at Saint Marc and Port-au-Prince and to load any property offered in relief of the refugees in South Carolina but to refrain from breaking any laws or otherwise offending the ruling powers, a

caution also expressed to their agent at Port au Prince, James Grant Forbes & Company; reporting that no direct intelligence of the *Trial* has been received for some time, but a recent open letter from New Providence advises that the Commissioners have seized the vessel and confined Thompson and Forbes at Port au Prince on "*Suspicion* of *intending* to bring off Property for Persons here"; asserting their ignorance of having broken any law, treaty, or proclamation and defending their right as American citizens to trade for themselves and others with a French port that had always been open to American vessels; and requesting the government to obtain the release of Thompson, Forbes, and the vessel and its cargo, with damages (MS in ViW: Tucker-Coleman Collection; margin frayed).

On 3 Dec. 1793 TJ submitted the enclosure to the President, who returned it the same day (Washington, *Journal*, 263-4).

To Peter Carr

DEAR SIR   Germantown Nov. 10. 1793.

I received your's of Oct. 24. a little before bed-time of the same evening, and being to set out early the next morning it was impossible for me to answer it. It was the less material, as I had written some days before, and left in the hands of Mr. Jefferson a letter to my sister on the same subject. I had before imagined that the present state of her family would render it convenient to receive now the money which had remained so long in my hands, and which I imagined was till then a convenient occasional resource for bad crops, unexpected calls &c. I therefore destined to discharge it out of the proceeds of an execution of Mr. Wayles's representatives against the estate of Colo. Cary, which should have been received in February last. Mr. Eppes has thro' the summer been giving me constant expectations from Carter Page of receiving a good part of the money. I flatter myself it cannot fail to be recieved in time for the demands you speak of. I have no speedier resource for it, as all others at my command will be requisite to clear me out here.

We may soon ask you how you like your new course of life. The account I received of your debut in Albemarle was flattering for you, and very grateful to me. I think you have your fortune in your own power, and that nothing is necessary but the will to make it what you please. Your father's plan of a laborious and short course, rather than a languid and long one, was certainly the wisest. I wish you may adopt the same, no one on earth being more anxious for your success than Dear Sir Your's affectionately   TH: JEFFERSON

RC (ViU: Carr-Cary Papers); at foot of text: "Mr. P. Carr." PrC (DLC).

To the District Attorneys

SIR   Germantown Nov: 10. 1793.
    The war at present prevailing among the European Powers producing sometimes captures of vessels in the neighbourhood of our sea coast, and the law of nations admitting as a common convenience, that every nation inhabiting the sea coast may extend its jurisdiction and protection some distance into the sea, the President has been frequently appealed to by the subjects of the belligerent Powers for the benefit of that protection. To what distance from the coast this may be extended, is not precisely ascertained, either by the practice or consent of nations, or the opinions of the jurists who have written on the subject. The greatest distance to which any respectable assent seems to have been given, is the extent of the human sight, estimated at something more than 20. miles. The least claimed by any nation is the utmost range of cannon shot, usually stated at one sea league, or 3 sea-miles, which is a very small fraction less than $3\frac{1}{2}$ statute or american miles. Several intermediate distances have been insisted on under different circumstances, and that particularly of 3 sea leagues, has the support of some authorities which are recent. However as the nations which practice navigation on our coasts are interested in this question, it is thought prudent not to assume the whole distance which we may reasonably claim until some opportunity shall occur of entering into friendly explanations and arrangements with them on the subject. But as in the mean time it is necessary to exercise the right to some distance, the President has thought it best, *so far as shall concern the exercise of the executive Powers*, to take the distance of a sea league, which being settled by treaty between some of the belligerent Powers, and as little as any of them claim on their own coasts, can admit of no reasonable opposition on their part.

The executive officers are therefore instructed to consider a margin of one sea league on our coast as that within which all hostilities are interdicted for the present, until it shall be otherwise signified to them. The rivers and bays as being landlocked are of course by the law of nations and I presume by the laws of most of the states, within the body of the United States, and under the same protection from hostilities.

As the question whether a capture has been made within these limits is a question of fact, to be decided by witnesses, it becomes necessary to take measures for the examination of these witnesses in the different states where captures may happen: and the laws of the Union having as yet made no provision for this purpose, the President considers the Attornies of the several Districts as the persons the most capable of discharging the office with knowledge, with impartiality and with that extreme discretion which is essential in all matters wherein foreign nations are concerned. I have the honor therefore, Sir, to inclose you a paper expressing the desire of the President on this subject. You will see by that, that whenever a capture is suggested to have been made within the limits above mentioned, so far as they are within your state, the Governor, to whom the first application will be made, is desired to give you notice thereof, whereupon it is hoped you will proceed as the paper points out. The representatives here of the different Powers are informed of this arrangement and desired to instruct their Consuls to facilitate the proceedings as far as shall depend on them; and it is unnecessary for me to suggest what your own judgment and disposition would dictate, that the same object will be promoted by a certain degree of respect to which the Consuls are entitled, and a just and friendly attention to their convenience. I have the honor to be with sentiments of respect Sir, Your most obedt. servt.   TH: JEFFERSON

RC (PHi: Rawle Papers); in a clerk's hand, signed by TJ; at foot of first page: "William Rawle Esqr. Attorney for the District of Pennsylvania." RC (DeHi); in a clerk's hand, signed by TJ; at foot of first page: "George Read Junr. Attorney for the District of Delaware." PrC (Gilder Lehrman Collection: Henry Knox Papers, on deposit NNP); with TJ's signature added in ink. PrC (same); in a clerk's hand, signed by TJ in ink; at foot of first page: "Pierpoint Edwards Esqr. Attorney for the District of Connecticut." PrC (same); in Benjamin Bankson's hand; lacks last page; at foot of first page: "Ricd. Harrison Esqr. Attorney for the District of New York." PrC (same); in Bankson's hand, signed by TJ in ink; at foot of first page. "Abraham Ogden Esqr. Attorney for the District of New Jersey."

PrC (DNA: RG 59, MD); in a clerk's hand, signed by TJ in ink; at foot of first page: "Zebulon Hollingsworth, Attorney for the District of Maryland." PrC (DLC); in a clerk's hand, unsigned; at foot of first page: "⟨*William Lithgow Esqr Attorney for the District of Maine*⟩"; added in ink beneath it: "⟨*William Channing Esqr. Attorney for the District of Rhode Island*⟩"; inserted in ink by TJ in the margin at head of text: "Samuel Sherburne N.H. Christopher Gore M. Pierpoint Edwards C. Richard Harrison N.Y. Abraham Ogden N.J. Wm. Rawle Pensylva. George Reade jr. Del. Zebulon Hollingsworth Maryld. Alexander Campbell Virga. Wm. Hill N. Cara. Thomas Parker S. Carola. Matthew McAlister Georgia." FC (Lb in DNA: RG 59, DL); with list of addressees beneath enclosure. Letter and enclosure enclosed in TJ to George Washington, [16 Nov. 1793]; texts addressed to William Rawle and George Read, Jr., enclosed in TJ to Henry Knox, 15 Nov. 1793 (second letter).

After obtaining Cabinet approval of a draft of this letter, and presumably its enclosure, TJ submitted copies of the final versions to the President on 16 Nov. 1793, and

Washington returned them the same day (Cabinet Opinions on Various Letters, [23 Nov. 1793]; Washington, *Journal*, 251, 252).

A letter from Abraham Ogden of 19 Nov. 1793, possibly a reply to TJ's letter, is recorded in SJL as received from Newark, New Jersey, on 21 Nov. 1793, but has not been found.

ENCLOSURE

Instructions to the District Attorneys

That the Governors be requested to give to the district attornies information of any arrest made of vessels captured within the limits of the United States, or of their jurisdiction as provisionally declared by the President for the government of the executive officers. That the attornies be instructed, immediately upon the receipt of such information to apply to the principal agent of both parties who may have come in with the prize and to the Consuls of the nations interested, where any such are at the Port, or within convenient distance, and ascertain whether they will name arbiters for deciding whether the capture were made within the limits aforesaid. That the Governors be authorized to restore in case the arbiters should report in favor of the captured vessel, or to remove the arrest if they should report against her. That in case the parties or Consuls should not agree to appoint referees, the Attorneys shall give notice to them of the time and place, when and where he will be, in order to take the depositions of such witnesses as they may cause to come before him, and that he transmit to the Executive the depositions so taken.

If from peculiar circumstances, the attornies cannot attend for the above purpose he may substitute some other gentleman of the law, in whose impartiality he has absolute confidence, or if no gentleman of the law be convenient, then such other person most competent as may be had.

PrC of Tr (DLC: TJ Papers, 94: 16162); undated; in a clerk's hand, unsigned. PrC of Tr (DNA: RG 59, MD); undated; in Benjamin Bankson's hand. FC (Lb in same, DL); undated.

To Foreign Ministers in the United States

SIR   German-town, Novr. 10th. 1793

As in cases where vessels are reclaimed by the Subjects or Citizens of the belligerent powers as having been taken within the jurisdiction of the United States, it becomes necessary to ascertain that fact by[1] testimony taken according to the laws of the United States, The Governors of the several States to whom the applications will be made in the first instance, are desired immediately to notify thereof the Attornies of their respective districts. The Attorney is thereupon instructed to give notice to the principal Agent of both parties who may have come in with the prize, and also to the Consuls of the Nations interested, and to recommend to them to appoint, by mutual consent, arbiters to decide whether the capture were made within the jurisdiction of the United States, as[2] stated to you in my letter of the 8th. inst. according to[3] whose award the Governor may proceed to deliver the Vessel to the one or the other party. But in case the parties or Consul shall not agree to name arbiters, then the Attorney, or some person substituted by him, is to notify them of the time and place when and where he will be, in order to take the depositions of such Witnesses as they may cause to come before him, which depositions he is to transmit for the information and[4] decision of the President.

It has been thought best to put this business into such a train as that the examination of the fact may take place immediately and before the witnesses may have again departed from the United States, which would too frequently happen, and especially in the distant States, if it should be deferred[5] till information is sent to the Executive, and a special order awaited to take the depositions.

I take the liberty of requesting that you will be pleased to give such instructions to the Consuls of your Nation as may facilitate the object of this regulation. I urge[6] it with the more earnestness, because as the Attornies of the districts are for the most part engaged in much business of their own, they will rarely be able to attend more than one appointment, and consequently the party who should fail from negligence or other motives to produce his Witnesses at the time and place appointed, might lose the benefit of their testimony altogether.[7] This prompt procedure is the more to be insisted on as it will enable the President by an immediate delivery of the Vessel and Cargo to the party having title, to prevent[8] the injuries consequent on long delay. I have the honor to be with great respect, Sir, Your most obedient & most humble servant

PrC (DLC); in Benjamin Bankson's hand, unsigned; at foot of first page: "Mr. Genet." PrC (DLC); in Bankson's hand, unsigned; at foot of first page: "Mr. Hammond." PrC (DLC); in Bankson's hand, unsigned; at foot of text: "Messrs. Viar & Jaudenes." PrC (DLC); in Bankson's hand, unsigned; at foot of first page: "Mr. Van Berckel," with "Mr. Genet Mr. Hammond & Messrs. Viar & Jaudenes" inserted in ink by TJ. Dft (DLC); entirely in TJ's hand; only the most significant emendations are recorded below; in margin at head of text: "4. copies viz for M. Genet Mr. Hammond Mr. Van Berckel Messrs. Viar & Jaudenes. with the press copies"; at foot of text: "Nov. 11. this draught was shewn to Mr. H. K. & R. and approved." Tr (DNA: RG 46, Senate Records, 3d Cong., 1st sess.); addressed to Genet. FC (Lb in DNA: RG 59, DL); at head of text: "The Minister pleni: of France"; at foot of text: "Addressed also to Mr. Hammond, Minister pleni: of Great Britain Mr. Van Berckel, Resident from the United Netherlands & Messrs. Viar & Jaudenes, Spanish Commissioners." Tr (Lb in PRO: FO 116/3). Tr (DLC: Genet Papers); in French. Tr (same); in French; draft translation of preceding Tr; in margin at head of text in Edmond Charles Genet's hand: "Pour les consuls de Baltimore Philadelphie New york Boston Charleston Norfolk," with check marks next to the first four cities. Tr (AHN: Papeles de Estado, legajo 3895 bis); in Spanish; attested by Jaudenes and Viar. Recorded in SJPL. The text addressed to Genet is printed in *Message*, 92-3. Enclosed in TJ to George Washington, [16 Nov. 1793].

After obtaining Cabinet and presidential approval of the draft of this letter, TJ submitted a copy of the final version to the President on 16 Nov. 1793, and Washington returned it the same day (Cabinet Opinions on

Various Letters, [23 Nov. 1793]; Washington, *Journal*, 248, 251, 252).

[1] In Dft TJ here canceled "legal."
[2] In Dft TJ here canceled "declared by the President for."
[3] Preceding two words interlined in Dft in place of "on."
[4] Preceding two words interlined in Dft.
[5] Preceding two words interlined in Dft in place of "is."
[6] Word interlined in Dft in place of "sollicit."
[7] Word interlined in Dft in place of "for ever."
[8] Word interlined in Dft in place of "avoid."

To Edmond Charles Genet and George Hammond

SIR   Germantown Nov. 10. 1793.

I have the Honor to inform you that the District Attorney of Maryland is this day instructed to take measures for finally settling the case of the British brig Coningham captured by the French privateer the Sans Culottes of Marseilles, and reclaimed as taken within the jurisdiction of the United States, in which he will proceed as I had the honor of stating to you in my letter of Nov. 10. I have that of being with respect and esteem, Sir, Your most obedient and most humble servant

PrC (DLC); in the hand of George Taylor, Jr., unsigned; at foot of text: "The Minister plenipo. of the Republic of France." PrC (DLC); in Taylor's hand, unsigned; at foot of text: "The minister Plenipoy. of Great Britain." FC (Lb in DNA: RG 59, DL); at head of text: "The Minister pleni: of France"; at foot of text: "Addressed also to Mr. Hammond, Minister plenipoteny. of Gr. Britain."

TJ obtained Cabinet approval of the substance of this letter, as well as Edmund Randolph's approval of a draft, before dispatching texts of the final version to the British and French ministers. He followed the same procedure with respect to a letter he wrote this day to Genet and Hammond, identical to the one printed above but dealing with the capture of the British brig *Pilgrim* by the same privateer (PrC in DLC, in Taylor's

hand, unsigned, at foot of text: "The Minister Plenipoy. of France"; PrC in DLC, in Taylor's hand, unsigned, at foot of text: "The Minister Plenipoy. of Great Britain"; FC in Lb in DNA: RG 59, DL; at head of text: "The Minister pleni: of France"; at foot of text: "Addressed also to Mr. Hammond, Minister pleni: of Great Britain"). See Cabinet Opinions on Various Letters, [23 Nov. 1793].

In response to allegations by British Vice-Consul Edward Thornton that the *Conyngham*, a British brig from Londonderry, captured and brought into Baltimore early in October 1793, had been taken within three miles of the American shore, Governor Thomas Sim Lee of Maryland prevailed upon French Vice-Consul F. Moissonnier to take custody of the ship until the President had determined the legality of its capture. Lee then referred the case to the

President and Secretary of War Henry Knox, pointing out to the former the need to define the limits of the nation's maritime jurisdiction so as to facilitate the task of the state governors in dealing with disputed prize cases. In April 1794, after an investigation by District Attorney Zebulon Hollingsworth, Edmund Randolph, TJ's successor as Secretary of State, restored the *Conyngham* to its captors for lack of persuasive evidence that it had been seized within the three-mile jurisdiction established by the Washington administration on 8 Nov. 1793 (Lee to Thornton, 9, 11, 15 Oct., 27 Nov. 1793, to Moissonnier, 11, 15, 25 Oct., 5, 27 Nov. 1793, 12 Apr. 1794, to Washington, 11, 15 Oct. 1793, to Knox, 5 Nov., 2, 20 Dec. 1793, 12 Apr. 1794, and to Hollingsworth, 27 Nov. 1793, all in MdAA: Letterbooks of Governor and Council; *Counter Case*, 580-1, 612-13).

TJ did not actually write to the DISTRICT ATTORNEY OF MARYLAND for another four days (TJ to Hollingsworth, 14 Nov. 1793).

To Henry Knox

Nov. 10. 1793.

Th: Jefferson presents his compliments to General Knox, and sends him some papers received last night by the President from the Govr. of North-Carolina, respecting the money and vessel taken from the Spaniards by the sloop l'Amée Marguerite (formerly the British sloop Providence prize to the Vainqueur de la Bastille, armed in the US.). It would seem from this as if both vessels should be given up.

PrC (DLC). Enclosures: (1) Richard Dobbs Spaight to George Washington, New Bern, 21 Oct. 1793, stating that he was extremely mortified to learn in September from the collector of Wilmington that the privateer *Vainqueur de la Bastille*, Captain François Henri Hervieux, and its prize, the British sloop *Providence*, had come to the bar of Cape Fear river, where Hervieux had armed the sloop with guns from the privateer, and that after both ships had cruised off Wilmington the *Vainqueur de la Bastille* returned there; that in pursuance of the Secretary of War's 16 and 21 Aug. 1793 instructions he immediately directed the major of the New Hanover militia to order the *Vainqueur de la Bastille* to leave port, to deny the use of Wilmington to that or any other privateer fitted out in the United States, and to take possession of any prizes brought there by such privateers so that they could be delivered either to their former owners or to the consul of the nation to which they belonged; that on 15 Oct. he received Nos. 2 and 6 from Colonel Benjamin Smith of Brunswick County and Major Thomas Wright of New Hanover describing the frustration by "some evil disposed persons in Wilmington" of their efforts to take possession of a Spanish brig that had recently been brought there as a prize by the *Aimée Marguerite*, commanded by Hervieux, and Hervieux's refusal to obey Smith's order to leave port on the grounds that his privateer was in distress and could not put to sea until his crew recovered and his ship was repaired; that since No. 4 convinced him that the *Aimée Marguerite* was genuinely in distress he ordered Smith and Wright to allow it to remain at Wilmington until it had been refitted for sea; that since the Spanish brig was on the high seas with eight guns and a crew of twenty to thirty men and since North Carolina lacked an armed vessel, he merely instructed them to secure it for its original owners if it returned to port; that he has instructed Wright to order the marshal to keep possession of a chest from the Spanish brig reportedly containing 30,000 to 40,000 dollars, which had been given to the marshal by the revenue officers who seized it from Captain Cook's revenue cutter, on which Hervieux had put it before being informed that an effort would be made to deprive him of his prize; that he wishes to know what to do with the *Aimée Marguerite* now that it is lying at a Wilmington wharf dismasted and unrigged and with no one on board to comply with an order for it to leave port; that the case being a national one he expects the federal government to reimburse North Carolina for its expenditures on ammunition, pay, and subsistence for the militia called out to execute the President's orders; that he will instruct Wright to punish the New Hanover militia according to state law for the disobedience described in No. 6; and that he encloses Nos. 2-6 so that Washington will be fully acquainted with the case (FC in Nc-Ar: Governor's Letterbooks and Papers). (2) Smith to Spaight, Belvidere, 11 Oct. 1793, stating that Hervieux had refused to comply with his order that the *Aimée Marguerite* leave Wilmington, where it had arrived the week before, for reasons explained in No. 3; that he failed to take possession of the armed Spanish brig captured by Hervieux, which arrived at Wilmington a few days later, because of "the extraordinary conduct of some of the Inhabitants of Wilmington," about which he hopes the governor will be informed fully, and because of Captain Cook's inability to come to his aid; that he wishes to know what to do about the armed Spanish brig, which "lies within sight of land some leagues from the Bar and outside thereof"; and that he was enclosing Nos. 3-5 (No. 5 being a substitute by Hervieux for No. 3). (3) Hervieux to Smith, Wilmington, 7 Oct. 1793, stating that he was unable to comply with Smith's order of this date for the immediate departure of the *Aimée Marguerite* on the grounds that it had come there in distress and was entitled as a ship belonging to a friendly allied nation to make necessary repairs before putting out to sea, because the condition of the ship and crew described in No. 4 had to be corrected first, and because of the seizure by customs collectors or other federal officials of a trunk containing his commission, dispatches from the French consul to the French Commissioners at Saint-Domingue, various ship papers, and 30,000 to 40,000 dollars belonging to himself and some of his crew had to be returned before the vessel could proceed on its intended voyage from Charleston to Cap-Français, lest otherwise he appear "totally unavowed and unauthorized." (4) Certificate of Nathaniel Hill and Others, Wilmington, 4 Oct. 1793, stating that the *Aimée Marguerite* came here in distress, with all but two of its crew unfit for duty because of intermittent fevers and with various parts of the ship in urgent need of repair in order to make it seaworthy again. (5) Hervieux to Smith, [7 Oct. 1793], reiterating at somewhat greater length the substance of No. 3 and adding that he would be willing to obey Smith's commands as soon as the *Aimée Marguerite* was made seaworthy and his papers and effects were returned, "supposing your interference duly authorized by the Government of your Country." (6) Wright to Spaight, 12 Oct. 1793, stating that, having received on 5 Oct. a letter from Spaight about the arrival of the *Aimée Marguerite* with a Spanish prize and accompanying copies of letters from the Secretary of War, he decided to act upon the former even though it was not addressed to him; that he obtained the assistance of the revenue cutter and asked the militia officers to have twenty-five men ready to aid him on 7 Oct., but only four militia men obeyed orders to this effect, many others "declaring they would not render any assistance in such a case"; that a "Gentleman of Wilmington" warned Hervieux beforehand of Wright's intention to seize the Spanish brig, which led Hervieux to send it out to sea, where it now lay eight miles south of the bar; that unless Spaight issues a proclamation reproving such conduct and recognizes the need for raising a volunteer company it will be impossible to enforce neutrality here; that Hervieux gave Captain Cook of the revenue cutter custody of a chest from the Spanish brig supposedly containing about 30,000 dollars, which Cook seized in accordance with acts of Congress and handed over to the marshal; that efforts by Hervieux's lawyers to have the chest restored to him have failed and an appeal has been made to the federal judge; that in accordance with Spaight's orders he has felt obliged to state that since the chest is part of the prize and its former owners are confined, it should be made subject to the orders of the Spanish consul; and that he wishes to know how the state plans to pay for the expenses involved in his actions prior to reimbursement by the federal government (Trs in same).

On the previous day the President had sent TJ the above enclosures "for his perusal & consideration" (Washington, *Journal*, 250).

To Martha Jefferson Randolph

Germantown Nov. 10. 1793.

I wrote, my dear Martha, by last week's post to Mr. Randolph. Yesterday I received his of Oct. 31. The fever in Philadelphia has almost entirely disappeared. The Physicians say they have no new infections since the great rains which have fallen. Some previous ones are still to die or recover, and so close this tragedy. I think however the Executive will remain here till the meeting of Congress, merely to furnish a rallying point to them. The refugee inhabitants are very generally returning into the city. Mr. T. Shippen and his lady are here. He is very slowly getting better. Still confined to the house. She well and very burly. I told her of her sister's pretensions to the fever and ague at Blenheim. She complained of receiving no letter. Tell this to Mrs. Carter, making it the subject of a visit express, which will be an act of good neighborhood.—The affairs of France are at present gloomy. Toulon has surrendered to England and Spain. So has Grand Anse and the country round about in St. Domingo. The English however have received a check before Dunkirk, probably a smart one, tho the particulars are not yet certainly known. I send Freneau's papers. He has discontinued them, but promises to resume again. I fear this cannot be till he has collected his arrearages. My best regards to Mr. Randolph. Accept my warmest love for yourself and Maria, compliments to Miss Jane, kisses to the children, friendly affections to all. Adieu Your's   TH:J.

RC (NNP); at foot of text: "Mrs. Randolph"; endorsed by Mrs. Randolph. PrC (DLC). Tr (DLC); 19th-century copy.

MISS JANE: very likely Mrs. Randolph's sister-in-law Jane Cary Randolph—the best friend of MARIA Jefferson—who did not marry until 1795, rather than TJ's niece Jane Barbara Carr Cary (as suggested in note to TJ to Thomas Mann Randolph, Jr., 12 Oct. 1792), who had married Wilson Cary in 1782 and was widowed by February 1793 (Wilson Miles Cary to TJ, 4 June 1784, and note; Martha Jefferson Randolph to TJ, 27 Feb. 1793; TJ to Dabney Carr, 24 Sep. 1794; MB, notes to 20 Apr. 1778, 6 June 1805; Monticello Association, *Collected Papers*, I [1965], 172; same, *Annual Report* [1925], 13).

To Josef Ignacio de Viar and Josef de Jaudenes

GENTLEMEN   German-town Nov. 10. 1793.

Since the date of my letter of the 6th. inst. I have received from the Governor of Kentuckey an answer to my letter of Aug. 29. written in consequence of your's to me of Aug. 27. of which I informed you by one of the same date with that to the Governor. A copy of this answer I have now the honor to inclose you; trusting it will give you satisfaction as to the enterprizes proposed to be excited in that country.

Letters were recieved yesterday from the Governor of North Carolina, confirming the information you were pleased to convey to me in your's of Oct. 23. of a Spanish vessel having been captured and carried into that state, with a considerable sum of money. It would appear from the Governor's letter that the capture was made, not by the Vainqueur de la Bastille, but by the Aimée Margueritte (formerly the British sloop Providence) manned by the former crew and captain of the Vainqueur de la Bastille, and it seems conjecturable that this sloop was armed and commissioned in the US. in which case she is of the character of the proscribed vessels, and her prizes will be restored if in our ports and power. The money (about 34,000 Dollars) is secure and will be kept so till we can learn with certainty the true character of the capturing vessel. The Governor had ordered a party down in a boat to take possession of the prize also, but some of their partisans in Wilmington contrived to get down in the night, warn the vessel, and she slipt her cable and got down out of the river, and at the date of the Governor's letter, was lying in the open sea. Having no means of getting possession of her in that position, he was adopting those which might secure her if she returned into port. These proceedings have all been in consequence of general orders from the President extending to every port in the US. and to every party to the present war. Still however we shall be always ready to superadd particular instructions in all the particular cases which shall be made known, as is done in the present case. I have the honor to be with great esteem, gentlemen your most obedt. & most humble servt.

TH: JEFFERSON

PrC (DLC); at foot of first page: "Messrs. Viar & Jaudenes." FC (Lb in DNA: RG 59, DL). Tr (AHN: Papeles de Estado, legajo 3895 bis); in Spanish; attested by Jaudenes and Viar. Enclosure: Isaac Shelby to TJ, 5 Oct. 1793. Enclosed in TJ to George Washington, [16 Nov. 1793].

LETTERS . . . RECIEVED YESTERDAY: see the enclosures listed at TJ to Henry Knox, 10 Nov. 1793. GENERAL ORDERS FROM THE PRESIDENT: see Cabinet Opinion on Prizes and Privateers, and note to Rules on Neutrality, both 3 Aug. 1793.

From Tench Coxe

Chesnut Street Novr. 11th 1793

Mr. T. Coxe requests that Mr. Jefferson will do him the honor to inform him, whether it appears by the records of the Department of State that a commission, as *Inspector of the Revenue* for the port of Balte., has been transmitted to Danl. Delozier, lately appointed *Sur-*

veyor of that port. Mr. Coxe can not find that such a commission has ever been received by the officer, or by the Treasury. In the confusion produced by the late Malady in Philada. it is possible it may not have occurr'd that two Commissions were necessary. The late Mr. Ballard held both, and it has been almost our universal course in the appointments to those two offices in the other ports.

RC (DLC); endorsed by TJ as received 12 Nov. 1793 and so recorded in SJL.

On 23 Aug. 1793 the Department of State sent the Treasury Department an interim commission for Daniel DELOZIER as surveyor, but not as revenue inspector, for the district of Baltimore. Following his confirmation by the Senate, on 28 Jan. 1794 commissions for both offices passed the Great Seal (Memorandum Book of the Department of State, 23 Aug. 1793, 28 Jan. 1794, DNA: RG 360, PCC).

To Edmond Charles Genet

Germantown Nov. 11. 1793.

Th: Jefferson presents his respectful compliments to Mr. Genet and sends him Mr. Cassan's Exequatur, with the original commission. Mr. Genet's letter of Oct. 15., covering it, had been sent on by post to Virginia while Th:J. was on his way to this place, and did not get to his hands till the day before yesterday.

PrC (DLC). Enclosures: (1) Genet's Commission to Jean Baptiste Cassan as French vice-consul in Pennsylvania and Delaware, 17 Oct. 1793 (Tr in Lb in DNA: RG 360, PCC, in French; Dft in DLC: Genet Papers, in Genet's hand). (2) Exequatur for Cassan, 11 Nov. 1793 (FC in Lb in DNA: RG 59, Exequaturs; with George Washington and TJ as signatory and countersignatory).

Genet's LETTER OF OCT. 15, recorded in SJL as a letter of 16 Oct. received from New York 9 Nov. 1793, has not been found, the only surviving text being an uncompleted draft in Genet's hand consisting of a 16 Oct. 1793 dateline and the name of addressee (Dft in DLC: Genet Papers; beneath dateline: "Le Cit Genet &c à M. Jefferson"; at head of text: "Consulats").

From Edmond Charles Genet

M.   New york. le 11. 9bre. 1793. l'an 2e. de la Republique.

Les fonds qui se trouvoient à la disposition de la République fse. pour l'année 1793. étant épuisés par les traites des Colonies qui y ont été imputées, par les dépenses considerables[1] qu'occasionne le séjour des Vaisseaux de la Republique dans les ports des Etats unis, par les secours que J'ai fait donner[2] aux réfugiés du Cap, par les approvisionnements de tous Genres que J'ai envoyés dans les Colonies fses. de l'amerique[3] Enfin par les dépenses diverses de la légation et de l'administration qui m'est confiée, Je vous prie de vouloir bien éxposer à Mr. le Président des Etats unis que Je me trouve forcé pour faire face à mes engagements et pour subvenir à nos besoins les plus pressants de tirer sur les sommes qui seront dues à la france dans les années 94. et même[4] 95.[5] en attendant que le Congrès ait pris en Consideration le mode de remboursement que J'ai été chargé de proposer au gouvernement federal. Nos fournisseurs se contenteront de ces délégations pourvu qu'elles soient acceptées par la tresorerie des Etats unis[6] pour être payées à leur échéance.[7]

Dft (DLC: Genet Papers); unsigned; above salutation: "Le Cit Genet &c à M. Jefferson secretaire d'Etat des Etats unis"; only the most significant emendations are recorded below. Tr (AMAE: CPEU, XXXIX); certified by Genet. Tr (same, Supplément, XX); certified by Genet. FC (DLC: Genet Papers); in English. Tr (DNA: RG 46, Senate Records, 3d Cong., 1st sess.); in English. Recorded in SJL as received 12 Nov. 1793. Printed with variations and translation in *Message*, 29 (App.), 96; translation printed in ASP, *Foreign Relations*, I, 185.

[1] Word written in the margin.
[2] Preceding five words interlined in place of "qu'exigent la misere et."
[3] Genet here canceled "et de l'Inde."
[4] Word omitted in *Message*.
[5] Remainder of sentence written in the margin.
[6] Remainder of sentence substituted for "et comme Je ne doute point."
[7] *Message*: "leurs échéances."

To Herman LeRoy

DEAR SIR   Germantown Nov. 11. 1793.

I take the liberty of inclosing you the extract of a letter from my son in law Mr. Thos. Randolph, son of Colo. Randolph of Tuckahoe, on a subject in which I cannot but feel great interest. Previous to his marriage with my daughter, a proper settlement was agreed between Colo. Randolph and myself to be made by us both on the young couple, and the particular lands fixed on. Mine were accordingly conveyed, as were his also, being his tract of land in Henrico called Varina. He told me at the time that they were under a mortgage not yet entirely cleared off, I think he said there were about £500. still to pay, and he obliged himself to pay it off and clear the lands. It was not till very lately that I learned not only that it was not done, but that a suit in equity was commenced for the sale of the lands. It falls now on Mr. Randolph to clear off the remainder of the debt, his father being become incapable of business, and it would seem by his letter to be much larger than his father understood it to be. You will percieve by the inclosed letter the propositions he makes for the paiment. In proposing to pay the whole sum at once, if required, and at the time he mentions, which is to be done by the sale of property, I am afraid he has not calculated a sufficient time for the collection of the money in addition to the credit he must give. If instalments are preferred by you, he names the first, but not the others; in fact they must depend on your indulgence both as to sum and time. If the fact were to be that an early receipt of the whole money should not be very material to you, on condition that the interest should be regularly paid up, and such an instalment of principal as should be bringing it in with certainty in a given time, the greatest indulgence I would ask for him, or wish him to receive, would be to be permitted to pay a thousand dollars a year towards interest and principal till the whole should be paid off. However this must depend on your convenience and goodness, and I shall feel as a favor done to me personally any indulgence you can shew which may save the property of a person whose interests are become mine, and who is brought into this predicament by no fault of his own. I know that it is his wish to set apart the whole profits of this plantation of Varina to clear off the mortgage, and to live on the profits of his other possessions. I know too that this plantation in favorable years would enable him to pay off the instalments of two years in one; but in an unfavorable year, one instalment of 1000. Dollars would be as much as it could pay, from the profits, probably, and he would be obliged, if a greater instalment were agreed on, to make it up by a sale of capital. However, Sir, the terms must rest altogether with yourself; any favor you can shew him will be gratefully felt by us both, and I will thank you to enable me as early as convenient to inform him what he must prepare for; and at the same time to recommend to him a person to whom he might consign his wheat, and in whose hands you would take the money. I would observe, that his instalments being to be raised by the sale of wheat, the last day of March annually would be the earliest day which would give him an opportunity of getting the best prices, which are generally in March. I am with great esteem Dr. Sir Your most obedt. servt   TH: JEFFERSON

RC (Facsimile in Sotheby's, Auction No. 6761, 13 Dec. 1995, Lot 185); addressed: "Mr. Herman Le Roy New York"; endorsed by Le Roy as received 12 Nov. 1793 and answered a day later. PrC (ViU: Edgehill-Randolph Papers). Enclosure: Extract of Thomas Mann Randolph, Jr., to TJ, 31 Oct. 1793.

Herman LeRoy (1758-1841), a New York merchant and partner in the firm of LeRoy & Bayard, from which TJ borrowed a small sum of money in 1790, was a charter subscriber to the Society for Establishing Useful Manufactures and subsequently became a director of the Bank of New York and the father-in-law of Daniel Webster (TJ to LeRoy & Bayard, 3 Apr. 1790; Syrett, *Hamilton*, IX, 25, XXVI, 206n; Charles M. Wiltse and others, eds., *The Papers of Daniel Webster: Correspondence*, 7 vols. [Hanover, N.H., 1974-86], II, 387, IV, 30n).

From William Short

Dear Sir   Sn Lorenzo Nov. 11th. 1793

On reading over again my last letters of Oct. 7th. and Nov. 7th. I apprehend they may have conveyed an idea I did not intend. With the same absence of all kind of reserve, which has ever prevailed when I have been writing to you, I think it necessary to correct any error which may have been conveyed, and to express more clearly not my wishes but my idea. It might be concieved perhaps from these letters that I would not *accept*[1] *the place of minister resident*[2] if *appointed* here as seemed to be the intention of the *president. Under my* present circumstances *I would accept* it but *my remaining* in it would depend on circumstances. I should rather *be appointed to it* than *nothing* even if I were to *refuse* because I might avoid the *mortification of appearing to be turned away* after *having been* so long in the *career* as in other countries *insure advancement* in this *line.* If the *salary* be the only *objection to* put the word *plenipotentiary* instead of *resident in the letter of credence I should prefer* the former even with the *salary of the* latter. *I would do* as well as *I could with that salary* and it would certainly be *better with the former than the* latter *character.* If this *country be considered* of any importance at present as to the *United States or to be so* at any time to come rest assured *a minister plenipotentiary* should be *sent here* whatever be his *salary. One week's residence here would* impress this on you more fully than all I can say. Had one been *sent here when our commission was first formed the issue* might have been very *different. Had it been* done so long ago as the year 1790. there can *scarce be a doubt of it.* The indelible character of this *court is such* that the *easiest* things cannot be *done here without time* and in return *much may be done* with it if *properly employed.* The present *connections of this court with England are certainly unfavorable in the extreme to the United States but these connections* from the nature of things cannot *last always and the United States should begin* now to take their *measures here with a view thereto and if* I do not mistake it is well worth *their attention to* take so *trifling a* step as to change a *single word* in a letter *of credence* which would be highly pleasing to *this court* for a *variety of reasons.*

Although I hardly suppose *you will mention* these things to the *president at your* present distance from *him yet I can't* help mentioning them to you. *If it were not for my* peculiar situation *I should say much more with respect to the business of the United States here.* I am my dear Sir, as I shall ever remain, your sincere friend & servant   W Short

RC (DLC); written partly in code (see note 1 below); at head of text: *"Private"*; at foot of first page: "Mr. Jefferson. Monticello"; contains minor encoding inaccuracies; endorsed by TJ as received 31 Mch. 1794 and so recorded in SJL. PrC (DLC). FC (DLC: Short Papers); entirely *en clair*; with lacuna and marginal note (see notes 1-2 below).

¹ This and subsequent words in italics were written in code by Short and have been deciphered by the Editors using par-

tially reconstructed Code No. 10, the decipherment being verified against the FC. In the FC Short inserted brackets before this word and the complimentary close, and wrote in the margin next to the first one: "From hence this letter was cyphered partially—the original and press copy sent."
² Remainder of sentence omitted in FC.

From Henry Cooper

St. Croix, 12 Nov. 1793. He encloses an executed consular bond and refers TJ to John Wilcocks of Philadelphia, who is well acquainted with his sureties. He will shortly provide the promised estimate of this island's trade with the United States and such observations as will be useful, and hopes TJ has avoided the "dreadful calamity" in Philadelphia.

RC (DNA: RG 59, CD); 1 p.; at foot of text: "The Honble The Secretary of State for the United States"; endorsed by TJ as received 21 Dec. 1793 and so recorded in SJL. Enclosure not found.

Memorial from Lucas Gibbes and Others

To the Honorable Thos. Jefferson Secretary of State to the United States of America.

The Memorial of Alexander S. Glass a citizen of the State of New York Thomas Mason, John Housman John Herdman William Mashiter Lucas Gibbes, Giles Mardenbro, and Henry Gibbes of the Island of St. Bartholomew, and Subjects of the King of Sweden Sheweth to your Honor

That your said Memorialists are the Owners of the Sloop Betsey and her Cargo, unjustly taken on the Coast of North America on the twenty sixth day of June last by Pierre Arcade Johanné, commander of the armed Schooner called the Citizen Genet, a vessel illegally fitted out at Charleston in the United States of America, and one of those proscribed by the President, for which said Sloop Betsey and her Cargo your memorialists have duly libelled in the District Court of the District of Maryland, where a decision has been had, that the said Court had no jurisdiction nor could hold plea of the same, And upon an appeal therefrom to the Circuit Court for the District of Maryland the same decree was affirmed and the appeal dismissed as by the records of the said proceedings under the Seal of the said Court herewith Exhibited to your Honor will appear.

Your memorialists therefore finding that they cannot obtain restitution of their property by the Judgment or a decree of any of the Courts of Judicature of the United States, they not being competent to take cognizance of the same, are constrained to apply to your Honor for your interposition, and to pray your Honor to take their case into consideration and to order the restoration thereof to them in such manner as to your Honor shall seem proper.

Philadelphia 12. Novr. 1793.
Lucas Gibbes for Self and the other Libellants

RC (DNA: RG 59, NFC); in a clerk's hand, with dateline and signature by Gibbes. Enclosure: Record of the proceedings of the United States District and Circuit Courts of Maryland in the case of Alexander S. Glass and Others v. the Sloop *Betsey* and Cargo and Captain Pierre A. Johanene, 16 July to November term 1793 (Tr in same, MLR; with subjoined copies of 29 Oct. and 9 Nov. 1793 attestations of the District and Circuit Court proceedings by

Philip Moore, clerk of the courts; filed with separate sheet bearing Moore's 14 May 1798 attestation as clerk of the District Court of Maryland). Enclosed in Richard Söderström to TJ, 16 Nov. 1793.

For the final disposition of the case of the sloop betsey by the United States Supreme Court, see note to Lucas Gibbes and Alexander S. Glass to TJ, 8 July 1793.

From Edmond Charles Genet

New York le 13. 9bre 1793.
Monsieur   l'an 2e de la République

Conformement à votre demande J'ai l'honneur de vous transmettre ci joints les[1] Commissions de Vice Consul qui ont été délivrées aux Citoyens *Pennevert* et *Chervi*, le premier residant à N. London, le Second à Alexandrie. Je Serai très reconnaissant Si vous voulez les mettre à même d'entrer en fonction en leur faisant obtenir l'Exequatur de Monsieur le Président des Etats Unis.

J'ai aussi l'honneur de vous rappeler que le Citoyen Cassan que j'avais promu à l'intérim du Consulat de Philadelphie[2] devenu vacant par la mort du Cn. Dupont ne reçoit point l'Exequatur que je vous ai demandé depuis long tems. Je vous prie Monsieur de vouloir bien le lui faire avoir au plutot, les circonstances exigeant que le Consul de Philadelphie entre en fonction. Si Sa Commission que je vous ai transmise, se trouve égarée, je pourrai vous en faire passer une nouvelle.

Dft (DLC: Genet Papers); in a clerk's hand, unsigned, with revisions by Genet; at head of text in Genet's hand: "Expedié"; above salutation: "Le Ministre Plénipotentiaire de la Republique fse à Monsieur jefferson." Tr (AMAE: CPEU, xxxix). Recorded in SJL as received 14 Nov. 1793. Enclosures not found, but see those listed at Genet to TJ, 21 Dec. 1793 (second letter).

¹ Sentence to this point altered by Genet

from "Je vous transmets ci joints les Originaux des."

² Altered by Genet from "du Vice Consulat de N. London."

To George Hammond

SIR   Germantown Nov. 13. 1793.

In a letter which I had the honor of addressing you on the 19th. of June last, I asked for information when we might expect an answer to that which I had written you on the 29th. of May was twelvemonth, on the articles still unexecuted of the treaty of peace between the two nations.

In your answer of the next day, you were pleased to inform me that you had forwarded the letter of the 29th. of May 1792. in the course of a few days after it's date, and that you daily expected instructions on the subject; that you presumed these had been delayed in consequence of the very interesting events which had occurred in Europe, and which had been of a nature so pressing and important as probably to have attracted the whole attention of your ministers, and thus to have diverted it from objects more remote, and that might perhaps have been regarded as somewhat less urgent.

I have it again in charge from the President of the United States to ask whether we can now have an answer to the letter of May 29. beforementioned? I have the honor to be with great respect Sir, your most obedient & most humble servt.   TH: JEFFERSON

PrC (DLC); at foot of text: "The Minister Pleny. of Gr Britain." Tr (DNA: RG 46, Senate Records, 3d Cong., 1st sess.). FC (Lb in DNA: RG 59, DL). Tr (Lb in PRO: FO 116/3). Printed in *Message*, 106. Enclosed in TJ to George Washington, [16 Nov. 1793].

After obtaining Cabinet approval of the substance of this letter, TJ submitted the final version to the President on 16 Nov. 1793, and Washington returned it the same day (Cabinet Opinions on Various Letters, [23 Nov. 1793]; Washington, *Journal*, 252).

To Charles Homassel

SIR   Germantown Nov. 13. 1793.

Mr. Derieux, my neighbor in Virginia, having received information that some goods were sent for him from France to this port, authorized Mr. Vaughan to receive and sell them. He afterwards learnt they had been sent to you, and now understands they were sold by you. It is very important to him to receive the money, but more pressingly so to know the clear amount of the sales, that he may by that clear amount regulate his engagements. Not knowing to what place Mr. Vaughan retired on the late disorder in Philadelphia, I ask the favor of you to enable me if you can to inform Mr. Derieux of the nett amount of the whole sum which will be coming to him from the sale of the said goods. I am Sir Your very humble servt   TH: JEFFERSON

PrC (DLC); at foot of text: "Mr. Homassel." Tr (ViU: Edgehill-Randolph Papers); 19th-century copy.

Charles Homassel was a merchant at 118 South Front Street (Hardie, *Phila. Dir.*, 66).

To John Hopkins

SIR   Germantown Nov. 13. 1793.

Your favor of the 15th. of October with the statements of the different species of stock standing on the books of your office to the credit of William Short esquire, came to hand on the 24th. of the same month, being the eve of my departure for this place. Finding that Mr. Short has stock also at New York, I have thought it best to bring the whole to one place, and that, all circumstances considered, Philadelphia will be the best place of deposit. Having therefore lodged in the Treasury office there the original power of attorney under which I act for Mr. Short, and of which, for your justification I send you a copy authenticated by the Secretary of the treasury, I have now to ask the favor of you to do what is necessary and proper to be done on your part for transferring all Mr. Short's stock on your books to those of the treasury at Philadelphia. Should the certificates be in the hands of Mr. Brown, will you have the goodness to ask for them and to forward them or any other papers to me which may be necessary to complete the operation here with as little delay as possible? Your attention herein will oblige Sir Your most obedt. servt   TH: JEFFERSON

PrC (DLC); at foot of text: "Mr. Hopkins, Commr. of loans, Richmd." Tr (ViU: Edgehill-Randolph Papers); 19th-century copy. Enclosure not found.

To Patrick Kennan

SIR   Germantown Nov. 13. 1793.

I have duly received your favor of Sep. 19. with the copy of your account shewing the amount of stock which you hold for Mr. Short, as also a balance of 50.17 D. cash and a further sum of 109.83 D. the quarter's interest then due. Finding that Mr. Short possesses stock in Richmond also, and concluding it best to bring the whole to Philadelphia, I have lodged in the Treasury office there the original power of attorney under which I act for Mr. Short, and of which, for your justification, I send you a copy authenticated by the Secretary of the treasury, and have now to ask the favor of you to apply to the office of the Commissioner of loans at New York, and to have the necessary acts done there and forwarded here, for transferring the said stock from the books of that office to those of the general office here, with as little delay as possible, and to remit to me the two sums of cash abovementioned in safe paper, on the receipt of which I will send you a sufficient voucher. I am with esteem Sir Your most obedt. servt   TH: JEFFERSON

PrC (DLC); at foot of text: "Mr. Patrick Kennon. New York." Tr (ViU: Edgehill-Randolph Papers); 19th-century copy. Enclosure not found.

To Robert Morris

SIR   Germantown Nov. 13. 1793.

I am instructed by the President of the US. to forward to you the inclosed petition from Ezra Fitz Freeman, on behalf of his son Clarkson Freeman, and to ask the favor of your information of the circumstances of the case of the said Clarkson Freeman therein referred to, and your opinion on the different considerations weighing for and against the pardon therein prayed for. I have the honor to be with great respect Sir Your most obedt. & most humble servt   TH: JEFFERSON

PrC (DLC); at foot of text: "The honble Robert Morris the District judge of the US. for N. Jersey." FC (Lb in DNA: RG 59, DL).

Robert Morris (ca. 1745-1815), a prominent New Jersey lawyer, was the first chief justice of the state supreme court, 1777-79. In 1790 George Washington appointed him judge of the United States District Court for New Jersey, a post he held until his death (DAB; JEP, I, 63-4).

TJ evidently confused Abraham Freeman, the author of the PETITION, with EZRA FITZ FREEMAN, whose letter transmitted it to TJ. Both documents were enclosed in TJ to George Washington, 5 Nov. 1793.

TJ submitted this letter to the President on 16 Nov. 1793, and Washington returned it the same day (Washington, *Journal*, 252).

To William Moultrie

S<small>IR</small>   Germantown Nov. 13. 1793.

In a letter of the 2d. instant which I have recieved from Mr. Genet, Minister Plenipy. of the republic of France here, is the following paragraph.

'I have received a charge against two persons of the name of Bouteille and Carvin, as equipping at this time in Charleston a strong vessel, on which they are to embark a number of people whose object is to go and possess themselves of Turtle island, distant from the Cape seven leagues, and there to put to death all the French who shall remain faithful to their country. I pray you to be so good as to inform the Governor of Charleston of this accusation.'

The same line of Conduct being proper for us between parties of the same nation engaged in civil war, as between different nations at war with each other, I have it in charge from the President of the US. to draw your Excellency's attention to the information above stated, and to express his confidence that you will exert the powers with which you are invested to prevent every preparation of hostilities which shall be attempted to be made and carried on from any part of your state against countries or people with which we are at peace. And I will ask the favor of any information you may be able to give me of the fact above stated, and it's issue. I have the honor to be with great respect, your Excellency's most obedt. & most humble servt   T<small>H</small>: J<small>EFFERSON</small>

PrC (DLC); at foot of text: "H. E. Governor Moultrie." FC (Lb in DNA: RG 59, DL). Enclosed in TJ to George Washington, [16 Nov. 1793].

After obtaining Cabinet approval of the substance of this letter, TJ submitted the final version to the President on 16 Nov. 1793, and Washington returned it the same day (TJ to Washington, [16 Nov. 1793]; Washington, *Journal*, 252).

From William Short

D<small>EAR</small> S<small>IR</small>   Sn. Lorenzo Nov. 13. 1793

A letter from Mr. Donald informs me you had written to him that you were to leave Philadelphia the 1st. of Jany. As this is much later than you had mentioned to me it gives me some hope the President will be able under the present important circumstances both foreign and domestic to induce you to prolong the epoch of your resignation. There certainly never could be a time when it were more necessary for you to sacrifice your own wishes for retirement and tranquillity to those of the publick.

My late private letters to you have been Oct. 7th. Nov. 7th. and Nov. 11th. In them I said nothing of the delay in not having sent my account stated as usual up to the 1st. of July last, because I did not suppose my letters would find you at Philadelphia. I mentioned it in my letter to Mr. Hamilton. As I was in constant hopes of my present situation here coming to an end in a short time I thought it would be better to comprize the expences thereof to the end in the same account. In the mean time the sums paid me on account of my standing salary and those expences are regularly sent by the bankers to the Sec. of the treasury and the particular articles of expence with their vouchers shall be sent at the close of the joint[1] commission here. In the charges I make for these expences I follow of course the rule prescribed by you as to those allowed when sent on a particular[2] commission to Amsterdam.[3]

You will have seen by our joint letters and mine separately the *awkward situation*[4] in which I have been *since my arrival in this country* finding it impossible to advance under *our joint commission* and not knowing how to retire from hence. I had hoped that long ere this *the president would have terminated our joint commission* one way or another. It has been from the beginning infinitely disagreeable from various causes and particularly those with respect to which I have forced myself to be silent though perhaps in this *my delicacy* pushed me further than *was consistent*[5] *with duty.* Government must certainly have *been ignorant of them* though I cannot concieve how this can have been the case for so long a time.

I think it proper to mention here that *Gardoqui*[6] *told us* outright in a late *conference that the king* desired to form an *alliance with the United States*[7] *offensive and defensive* or if that was not agreeable *defensive.* His idea was to purchase this *alliance by yielding us our rights* as to limits and navigation and commercial advantages.[8] *He begged us and with* much warmth to communicate *this desire of the king* immediately to the *president and farther that* it was the desire of the *king*[9] *that ministers plenipotentiary* should be *named by the two countries* to reside with each other. In whatever light the *United States chuse to* consider this *overture or* in whatever light *they chuse to consider Spain*[10] they should lose not a moment in sending a *minister plenipotentiary here* for various reasons. The disadvantage of not having had *one here is [demonstrable]*[11] and particularly in the present crisis of *Europe and the* situation of our navigation[12] and commerce *in Spain* under the new system it is and will be severely felt.[13]

In the beginning of the war a considerable[14] number of Danish vessels were stopped by the armed vessels and detained[15] in the ports of this country[16] under the same pretext with ours. The Danish minister obtained their release a long time ago—and a promise, which has been fully kept that the cruisers belonging to private people should not be allowed[17] to stop or bring in any other. He obtained also damages for those[18] which by chicane were not immediately released after the orders recieved in the ports[19] to that effect. It would have taken *an chargé des affaires*[20] *three times as long to have obtained* the same[21] even if *he had succeeded at last.*[22]

The answer from the *duke is in* statu quo. *Carmichael* returned here the day before yesterday but he had such a *nervous trembling in the hand* with which he is much afflicted[23] *like our* friend *Paradise*[24] that he could not notwithstanding every effort *he made sign his name to* the letter I had written to the *duke* [*to*][25] *remind* him of the *delay.* Still he persisted in *returning* last evening to *Madrid and I* was obliged therefore as *he had desired* disagreeable as such a step is and in such a case *to imitate his hand and sign it for him.* Your friend & servant   W: SHORT

RC (DLC); written partly in code (see note 4 below), with minor anomalies; at head of text: "*Private*"; at foot of first page: "Thos. Jefferson—&c &c &c."; endorsed by TJ as received 31 Mch. 1794 and so recorded in SJL. PrC (DLC). Dft (DLC: Short Papers); heavily emended *en clair* text, only the most significant revisions being recorded below.

MY LETTER TO MR. HAMILTON: Short to Alexander Hamilton, 17 Oct. 1793 (Syrett, *Hamilton*, XV, 368). RULE PRESCRIBED BY YOU: see TJ to Short, 28 July 1791 (second letter). For a discussion of the Spanish overture for an ALLIANCE WITH THE UNITED STATES, which Short and William Carmichael never officially reported to the American government and which therefore was never acted on, see Bemis, *Pinckney's Treaty*, 190-4. THE DUKE: Manuel Godoy Alvarez de Faria, Duque de la Alcudia, the Spanish minister in charge of foreign affairs.

[1] Preceding two words interlined in Dft in place of "my."
[2] Preceding three words interlined in Dft in place of "on a separate."
[3] In Dft Short inserted a bracket at the beginning of the following paragraph and wrote next to it in the margin "from hence cyphered in part."
[4] These and subsequent words in italics were written in code by Short and have been deciphered by the Editors using partially reconstructed Code No. 10, the deci-

pherment being verified against the Dft.
[5] Preceding two words interlined in Dft in place of "such duty required."
[6] Preceding two words interlined in Dft in place of "what we shall write about more fully by Mr. Blake."
[7] Remainder of sentence interlined in Dft in place of "He had no objection it should be offensive and defensive—but was he authorized to go that length—we told him our full powers were not to that effect and referred him to them." Above the first half of this canceled passage Short interlined and then canceled "and if the [. . .] kind. He asked essentially whether we were the."
[8] Preceding sentence interlined in Dft.
[9] Dft: "the wish of H.M."
[10] Remainder of sentence interlined in Dft in place of "believe me it is for their interest that a Min. Ple. should be sent here immediately."
[11] Word supplied from Dft, being incorrectly enciphered by Short.
[12] Word interlined in Dft in place of "vessels."
[13] In Dft Short here canceled "If you think that European ministers are as far removed from prejudices as the Prest. and yourself and that they do business in the same manner with you, as you do with foreign agents without regard to the agent or the grade and have minds sufficiently enlarged to consider the country, you are much mistaken."
[14] Word interlined in Dft in place of "great."

[15] Preceding two words interlined in Dft in place of "of this country—and others."

[16] Remainder of sentence interlined in Dft.

[17] Remainder of sentence interlined in Dft in place of "⟨in future⟩ to ⟨detain⟩ stop or detain any other on any similar pretext whatever."

[18] Word interlined in Dft in place of "a few."

[19] Preceding fifteen words interlined in Dft in place of "those which had been detained after the order given for their release, under the."

[20] Preceding four words interlined in Dft in place of "an inferior character," the first word being "a."

[21] Remainder of sentence interlined in Dft in place of "and perhaps he would not have succeeded at last." After it Short also canceled an incomplete sentence: "You will know whether our vessels have been."

[22] In Dft Short here canceled the following paragraph (some of the intermediate cancellations being restored): "Notwithstanding we have not yet received the answer from Ministry on the subject of Mr. Blake's despatches Mr. C. ⟨returned to Madrid the 5th. inst.⟩ ⟨refused to wait longer⟩ left this place the 5th. inst. to return to Madrid. ⟨I wished before his departure at least to write a second letter to the Duke which he declined.⟩ ⟨He said he would return here when necessary.⟩ He returned here the day before yesterday ⟨alone⟩ on account of the gala of yesterday. I prepared a letter for us to send to the Duke reminding him of the delay of Mr. Blake and our anxiety to despatch him—but a nervous trembling in the hand with which Mr. C. is often afflicted in the same manner that Paradise was, disabled him absolutely from signing the letter in the morning notwithstanding every effort he made—he hoped he should be able to sign it after dinner and ⟨therefore desired me to meet him at his lodging for that purpose and at⟩ if he should not desired I would imitate his writing and sign it for him as he had determined to return to Madrid. By his request I went to meet him at his lodging ⟨immediately⟩ after dinner ⟨as he determined to set out immediately after and to my great⟩ and to my astonishment found he had sat off for Madrid, so that I was obliged either to sign the letter for him, or not send it. I therefore signed it notwithstanding my aversion ⟨to the step⟩ to do it which I expressed to him. ⟨I see at present no probability of Mr. Carmichaels returning here, and as it is necessary that we should be together for our joint commission I find myself obliged to follow him to Madrid, notwithstanding the court and all the corps diplomatique who have business with them are still here—and notwithstanding my own idea often repeated to Mr. C. of the propriety of our remaining here.⟩ I hope our last letter to the Duke will procure us an answer soon so as to enable us to despatch Mr. Blake. Notwithstanding the ⟨possibility⟩ manifest propriety of our waiting here for the answer, yet as it is necessary that we should be together to act under our joint commission, and as Mr. C. has persisted in quitting the sitio and going to fix himself at Madrid I find myself under the necessity of following him there against my inclination. The court and all the corps diplomatique who have business with them are still here. And it is possible our answer may be such as to oblige us to return here for further explanation."

[23] Short here canceled "in the extreme."

[24] In Dft Short first wrote "like Paradise was" and then altered it to read as above.

[25] Word supplied from Dft, being incorrectly enciphered by Short.

To William Frederick Ast

SIR   Germantown near Philadelphia Nov. 14. 1793.

Your favor of the 6th. inst. conveys to me the first information of your establishment in this country, in which I wish you every success. With respect to the application you propose to Congress on the subject of insurances, I am not able to say what may be it's effect. We are little habituated to these speculations here, and therefore the less likely to estimate their true value. Instead however of asking a provisional decree, which is not consonant with our usage, I would advise you to propose, in your petition, the communication of your plan to such committee of their house as they shall appoint. These will of course be persons of confidence, and on their report the house will act. I would also recommend to you to have your petition drawn by some gentleman of the law, who is acquainted with our forms, since it is of considerable advantage to good ideas to be presented to those for whom they are intended in a dress to which they are accustomed. As I mean shortly to retire to Virginia and shall chiefly be connected with Richmond in such matters of business as a farmer may have, I shall hope an opportunity of renewing my acquaintance with you there, unless your movements should sooner lead you into the neighborhood of Monticello, where I shall be very happy to see you. Accept assurances of my attachment.

TH: JEFFERSON

PrC (DLC); at foot of text: "Mr. William Ast."

It is not known whether Ast reworked his APPLICATION on INSURANCES to incorporate TJ's suggestion that he request its reference to a congressional COMMITTEE, but on 27 Jan. 1794 his petition "praying the aid and patronage of Congress to a discovery he has made, for securing property against fire," was read in the House of Representatives and referred to a committee of five headed by William Branch Giles. Ast's attempt to interest Congress in his plan failed on 12 Feb. 1794, when the committee's report was read and tabled (JHR, II, 49, 61).

To Giuseppe Ceracchi

DEAR SIR   Philadelphia Nov. 14. 1793.

I have received the favor of your letter of May 27. from Münich, and it was not till then that I knew to what place or through what channel to direct a letter to you. The assurances you recieved that the monument of the President would be ordered at the new election, were founded in the expectation that he meant then to retire. The turbid affairs of Europe however, and the intercessions they produced prevailed on him to act again, tho' with infinite reluctance. You are sensible that the moment of his retirement, kindling the enthusiasm for his character, the affections for his person, the recollection of his services, would be that in which such a tribute would naturally be resolved on. This of course is now put off to the end of the next bissextile: but whenever it arrives, your title to the execution is engraved in the minds of those who saw your works here. Your purpose with respect to my bust is certainly flattering to me. My family has entered so earnestly into it that I must gratify them with the hope, and myself with the permission to make a just indemnification to the author. I shall be happy at all times to hear from you, and to learn that your successes in life are as great as they ought to be. Accept assurances of my sincere respect & esteem.

TH: JEFFERSON

PrC (DLC); at foot of text: "Mr. Ciracchi, at Münich."

Ceracchi's LETTER OF MAY 27 was actually dated 27 Mch. 1793.

To Robert Gamble

Germantown Nov. 14. 1793.

Th: Jefferson presents his compliments to Colo. Gamble and takes the liberty of putting under cover to him a letter to Mr. Mewbern of Richmond, with a request to have it handed him if be arrived from London, or if not, to let it lie by, till his arrival. Th:J. thinks he must be arrived as he sailed from London Aug. 30. He has the pleasure to inform Colo. Gamble that after the great rains which fell the first three or four days of this month, not a single new infection of the yellow fever took place, that those then ill of it are either dead or recovered, and that there is the most respectable assurance that there is not at this time a single subject remaining under that disorder. The refugee inhabitants have been returning into the city ever since the rain, without incurring any accident. Some who had returned before the rains caught the disease. It is probable that in the course of this week and the next[1] 99. out of 100. of those who had left the city, will be returned into it. As the members of Congress, coming from a distance, may be uninformed of the real state of things, the President will probably remain here (tho' he has been into the city) to form a point of union for them to assemble at and decide on their own view of things.

PrC (DLC). Tr (ViU: Edgehill-Randolph Papers); 19th-century copy. Enclosure: TJ to William Mewbern, 14 Nov. 1793.

All but the first two sentences of this letter, slightly modified to omit Gamble's name, appeared in the *Virginia Gazette, and Richmond and Manchester Advertiser*, 25 Nov. 1793, with a heading describing it in part as an "Extract of a letter from Thomas Jefferson . . . to a gentleman of this city."

[1] Preceding three words interlined.

From Edmond Charles Genet

M.   New york le 14. 9bre. 1793. l'an 2e. de la R.

Etant accablé d'affaires au moment ou J'ai eu l'honneur de vous expédier le decret de la Convention nationale du 26. mars dernier, Il m'a été impossible d'en revoir la copie ainsi que celle de la note qui l'accompagnoit. Je vous suis obligé de m'avoir renvoyé ces pièces, J'ai verifié et rectifié[1] les fautes qui vous ont frappé et Je m'empresse de vous les faire repasser sous ce pli. J'ai cru devoir y Joindre la Copie d'une lettre circulaire que Je viens d'écrire aux Consuls de la Republique pour leur donner Connoissance des nouvelles dispositions de la Convention nationale relativement au Commerce des Etats unis et aux devoirs qu'elles leur imposent.[2]

Ce Decret, Monsieur, presente aux americains des avantages inappréciables: ils peuvent[3] d'après cette loi porter dans nos colonies une cargaison des produits de leur peche de leurs salaisons ou de leur agriculture, acheter des denrées coloniales avec le produit de cette cargaison et completter leur chargement au moyen du fret qui est en ce moment très abondant et très cher dans toutes nos îles, Se rendre avec ce chargement en france et faire leur retour dans les etats-unis avec des marchandises françoises. Je ne crois pas qu'il y ait de Speculation qui puisse être plus[4] lucrative pour eux. Cette loi vous accorde en outre une faveur que l'arret de 1784 vous refusait; c'est celle De pouvoir porter Directement dans les etats-unis une quantité de Sucre et de cafe Suffisante pour votre consommation; cette quantité a été evaluée par le comité de commerce De la convention nationale[5] au cinquantieme du tonnage pour le café et au dixième pour le Sucre.

Tous ces avantages qu'on paroit même disposé à accroitre Si on obtient des etats-unis une juste reciprocité en faveur du commerce francais me paroissent bien propres à[6] exciter toute la Sollicitude du gouvernement fedéral Sur le Sort de nos colonies. Je vous prie de mettre le plutot possible Sous les yeux de Monsieur le president le decret et la note cy jointes et d'obtenir le plus promptement possible Sa decision[7] soit sur la garantie que j'ai deja reclamée pour nos colonies Soit Sur le mode de négociation du nouveau pacte[8] que je Suis chargé de proposer aux etats-unis[9] et qui ne feroit qu'une seule famille de nos deux nations.

Dft (DLC: Genet Papers); in the hands of Genet and Jean Baptiste Cassan, unsigned; above salutation: "Le Cit Genet &c à M. Jefferson &c."; only the most significant emendations are recorded below. Tr (AMAE: CPEU, xxxix); with minor variations. Recorded in SJL as received 15 Nov. 1793. Enclosures: Genet to TJ, 30 Sep. 1793, and enclosure. Other enclosure not found. Translation printed in *Correspondence*, 21-2; printed in French in *Correspondance*, 26-7.

[1] Preceding two words written in the margin by Genet.

[2] Genet here canceled "Je dois vous présenter ici, Mr., une reflexion interessante d," as well as the following paragraph: "Vous avés eu sans doute Connoissance par les papiers publics, M., de la Capitulation du mole et de Jeremie; Elle a été dictée par les Anglois et elle contraste trop avec les principes d'après les quels la France veut regler ses relations commerciales et Coloniales avec vous pour qu'il soit nécéssaire de vous representer combien la prosperité de la navigation de l'agriculture et du négoce des Etats unis depend de nos succès et de la Conservation de nos possessions dans cette partie du monde."

Except where indicated, the remainder of the text is in Cassan's hand.

[3] Remainder of clause interlined or written in the margin by Cassan in place of "porter dans les colonies une cargaison de morue, de boeuf ou de farine et."

[4] Cassan here canceled "avantageuse."

[5] Preceding nine words interlined or written in the margin by Cassan.

[6] Remainder of sentence interlined by Cassan in place of "interresser le gouvernement fedéral au Sort de nos colonies."

[7] Remainder of sentence through "nouveau" interlined by Cassan in place of "Sur le mode de negociation du nouveau traité commercial."

[8] Word interlined by Genet in place of "traité."

[9] Remainder of text in Genet's hand.

From Edmond Charles Genet

M.   New york. le 14. 9bre. 1793. l'an 2e. de la Republique fse.

J'ai reçu l'exequatur de la Commission de Consul dont le Citoyen dannery a été revêtu[1] et Je l'ai fait passer sur le champ à ce fonctionnaire public. Je presenterai au Conseil éxécutif de la République, M., les réflexions Judicieuses que vous faites sur l'attribution des fonctions Consulaires,[2] qui se trouvent en effet reduites par les Commissions de nos Consuls à l'arrondissement seul[3] des villes de leur résidence[4] ce qui n'est certainement point l'intention du Conseil. Je mettrai également sous ses yeux l'observation que vous faites relativement à l'adresse de nos Commissions Consulaires et Il adoptera dans Sa sagesse[5] les changements dont cet objët paroitra susceptible[6] d'après le texte l'esprit et les bases[7] de votre Constitution. Cependant comme elle ne s'explique nullement à cet égard et que les fonctions attribuées au President des Etats unis relativement à la reception des Ministres Etrangers[8] ne paroissent être que celles que remplissent dans les Cours les premiers Ministres vis à vis de leurs pretendus Souverains savoir de vérifier[9] purement et simplement les pouvoirs des agens Etrangers accrédités auprès de leurs maitres[10] et irrevocables par eux lorsqu'une fois ils sont admis. Je souhaiterois M., pour mieux fixer les idées du Conseil françois sur cette question Intéressante que vous eussiés la bonté de l'éclairer de vos lumieres et de celles de vos Savants Collegues, que Je transmettrois fidelement à mes superieurs.

Dft (DLC: Genet Papers); unsigned; above salutation: "Le Cit Genet &c à M. Jefferson. &c"; only the most significant emendations are recorded below. Tr (AMAE: CPEU, xxxix); with one variation (see note 3 below). FC (DLC: Genet Papers); in English. Tr (DNA: RG 46, Senate Records, 3d Cong., 1st sess.); in English. Recorded in SJL as received 15 Nov. 1793. Printed with translation in *Message*, 29-30 (App.), 93; translation printed in ASP, *Foreign Relations*, I, 184.

RÉFLEXIONS JUDICIEUSES: see TJ to Genet, 2 Oct. 1793.

[1] Genet here canceled "par Le Conseil éxécutif de la Republique."

[2] Altered from "de ce Consul."

[3] Word omitted in AMAE Tr and *Message*.

[4] Altered from "de la ville de Boston."

[5] Genet here canceled "d'après le texte même de votre Constitution et même s'il le Juge convenable d'après le Commentaire qui en a été fait par les Savants auteurs du federaliste."

[6] Genet here canceled "⟨*Je dois cependant*⟩ Il n'y aurait probablement point eu d'erreur à cet égard si votre Constitution s'étoit éxprimée d'une maniere plus."

[7] Preceding five words interlined in place of "même."

[8] Preceding seven words written in the margin.

[9] Preceding three words written in the margin in place of "et d'admettre."

[10] Remainder of sentence written in the margin.

From Edmond Charles Genet

M.   New york le 14. 9bre. 1793. l'an 2e. de la Republique fse.

J'ai reçu la lettre que vous m'avés fait l'honneur de m'écrire le 8. 9bre. pour me communiquer le principe établi provisoirement par le gouvernement federal pour fixer la Jurisdiction maritime et la ligne de protection des Etats unis. Je transmettrai ce memoire, M., au Conseil éxécutif de la République et J'en donnerai communication à nos Consuls en leur recommandant de se Conformer provisoirement aussi aux dispositions qu'il renferme lorsqu'ils seront requis d'autoriser la vente de quelque propriété françoise acquise légalement[1] sur mer par le droit de la guerre. Si cette ligne M. avoit été arbitrée[2] plutôt nous aurions évité beaucoup d'écritures de debats et de procedures.

Je vous suis très obligé d'avoir remis en liberté la fanny et Je me borne à rappeller à votre souvenir ce pauvre Guillaume Tell ainsi que la Catherine d'halifax le william &c. &c.

Dft (DLC: Genet Papers); unsigned; above salutation: "Le Cit genet &c à M. Jefferson &c."; only the most significant emendations are recorded below. Tr (AMAE: CPEU, xxxix). FC (DLC: Genet Papers); in English; with translator's error in last sentence. Recorded in SJL as received 15 Nov. 1793.

[1] Word interlined.
[2] Word interlined in place of "tracée."

From Edmond Charles Genet

M.   New york le 14. 9bre. 1793. l'an 2e. de la Republique

Il devient éxtrêmement instant que vous ayés la bonté de me faire savoir promptement Si Je puis tirer par anticipation sur les prochains remboursements de la dette des Etats unis envers la france; Nos agens instruits que les fonds qui avoient été mis à la disposition de la Republique en 1793[1] se trouvoient épuisés ont suspendu leurs fournitures et leurs entreprises Jusqu'à ce qu'ils soient assurés que les délégations sur la dette[2] que Je ferai à leur profit en vertu de mes pouvoirs seront acquitées à leur écheance. Comme vous vous faites sans doute une Juste idée de toutes les branches de service qui souffriront tant que cette autorisation ne me sera point parvenue Je suis persuadé M. que vous me[3] seconderés avec Zêle dans cette négociation. Deux mille matelots et soldats que Je soutiens sont à la veille de manquer de pain, les réparations de nos vaisseaux sont arrêtées, des éxpéditions indispensables de subsistances pour nos Colonies et pour france sont suspendues et[4] le gouvernement federal sans avancer un seul des payements fixés par la loi peut par deux mots signés de vous ou du secretaire de la tresorerie[5] remettre tout en activité en attendant que le Congrès ait pris en Consideration le mode general de remboursement que J'ai été chargé de vous communiquer et qui pourra seul me mettre en mesure d'approvisionner au moins la france pour la Campagne prochaine si elle n'a pu l'être pour celle ci. Les longues nuits les brumes et les grosses mers de l'hiver seront favorables à nos transports en rendant moins probables les chances facheuses auxquelles les principes odieux de l'angleterre éxposent les batiments neutres et surtout ceux des Etats unis.

Dft (DLC: Genet Papers); unsigned; with day altered to "14"; above salutation: "Le Cit Genet &c à Mr Jefferson &c."; only the most significant emendations are recorded below. Tr (AMAE: CPEU, xxxix); certified by Genet. Tr (same, Supplément, xx); certified by Genet. FC (DLC: Genet Papers); in English. Tr (DNA: RG 46, Senate Records, 3d Cong., 1st sess.); in English. Recorded in SJL as received 15 Nov. 1793. Printed with translation in *Message*, 29 (App.), 96-7; translation printed in ASP, *Foreign Relations*, i, 185-6.

[1] Preceding word and digits written in the margin.

[2] Genet first wrote "entreprises Vous pouvés Juger de l'embarras ou me" and then altered it to read as above.

[3] Remainder of sentence altered from "seconderiés avec le Zêle que vous m'avés témoigné dans plusieurs circonstances pour les Interêts de la République et pour fixer vos idées à cet égard Je vous dirai en peu de mots que près de deux mille hommes que Je soutiens ici vont se trouver."

[4] Genet here canceled "les mots suivants signés par vous ou par le secretaire de la tresorerie peuvent remettre tout en activité."

[5] Preceding twelve words written in the margin.

From Edmond Charles Genet

A Newyork le 14 9bre 1793 L'an 2e De la republique fe.

Je Suis chargé, Monsieur, de vous communiquer les pieces cy jointes qui ont été trouvées dans le portefeuille d'un anglais. Vous y verrez que les moyens qu'employe le gouvernement de St. james pour anéantir la liberté de la france sont les mêmes que ceux qu'il employait, il y a quinze ans, pour etouffer la votre: vous y verrez calculés avec ce Sang froid qui n'appartient qu'a des hommes endurcis aux forfaits, tous[1] les moyens de corrompre,[2] d'affamer, d'incendier, d'empoisonner, d'assassiner. De tels hommes peuvent-ils encore trouver des partisans Sur une terre où la liberté et toutes les vertus domestiques et Sociales Sont honorées!

La découverte de cette conspiration a provoqué deux grandes mesures dont le succès a été[3] au delà de toute attente. Par la première, la convention a annullé tous les assignats à effigie royale qui avaient été accaparés avec l'or de l'angleterre,[4] et qui Servaient à payer les troubles interieurs; par la Seconde, elle a prohibé l'exportation de tous les objets de nécessité tant de vetement que de nourriture, et elle a fait vendre à petits lots et en meme tems tous les immenses magazins qu'on avait accumulés pour exciter, par la rareté des objets necessaires, des Soulevemens parmi le peuple. Depuis ce tems, le peuple français est bien habillé, les rebelles de la vendee ne recevant plus de Solde Se Sont Soumis et nos armées ne restent plus dans un état d'inactivité.

Je dois vous informer avant de finir cette depêche que je viens d'etre instruit mais non officiellement,[5] que la convention nationale, après avoir acceuilli avec la bienveillance la plus marquée une Deputation des capitaines americains qui lui avaient fait des reclamations relatives au decret qui prohibait l'exportation des marchandises françaises, les a exemptés des dispositions de ce decret. Vous voyez, Monsieur, que toutes les demarches de la france envers les etats-unis Sont autant de preuves de l'amitie qu'elle porte aux americains, et du desir qu'elle a de resserrer de plus en plus les liaisons qui unissent les deux peuples: j'aime à me promettre que le gouvernement[6] americain S'empressera de Seconder l'execution de ce voeu en terminant le plus promptement possible le nouveau pacte commercial que je Suis charge de negocier avec lui.

Dft (DLC: Genet Papers); in Jean Baptiste Cassan's hand, unsigned; above salutation: "Le citoyen genet à Mr jefferson S. E. E. U."; only the most significant emendations are recorded below. FC (same); in English. Recorded in SJL as received 15 Nov. 1793. Enclosures not found.

DEUX GRANDES MESURES: the National Convention's 23 May and 6 June 1793 decrees providing for the substitution of republican emblems and figures in place of the head of Louis XVI on ASSIGNATS; and the Convention's 15 Aug. 1793 decree prohibiting the exportation from France of OBJETS DE NÉCESSITÉ, including most foodstuffs and certain articles of clothing and merchandise, an edict that followed in the wake of its sweeping 26 July 1793 decree against speculation and profiteering, which among other things provided for the confiscation and sale of LES IMMENSES MAGAZINS QU'ON AVAIT ACCUMULÉS and withheld from the market (Archives Parlementaires, 1st ser., LXV, 220-1, LXVI, 99, LXIX, 550-1, 594-5, LXXII, 190-1). In response to the complaints of UNE DEPUTATION DES CAPITAINES AMERICAINS, who pointed out that the exportation measure threatened to deprive neutral ships trading with France of their customary return cargoes, the Convention decreed on 3 Sep. 1793 that such ships could carry away from France any goods whose exportation was forbidden by the 15 Aug. decree as long as they had been loaded before the promulgation of that decree and set forth certain conditions under which some of these goods could thereafter be exported in neutral ships. Eight days later, however, the Convention restricted the exportation of goods loaded on neutral ships before the promulgation of the 15 Aug. decree to the exceptions enumerated in the 3 Sep. 1793 decree (same, LXXIII, 263-4, 350, 690; ASP, *Foreign Relations*, I, 373-4).

¹ Word interlined.
² Word written in the margin in place of "Diviser," also written in the margin.

³ Remainder of sentence interlined in place of "tel qu'on Se l'était promis."
⁴ Remainder of clause interlined.
⁵ Preceding three words written in the margin.
⁶ Word interlined in place of "peuple."

From Edmond Charles Genet

M.   New york. le 14. 9bre. 1793. l'an 2e. de la Repe. fse.

Je crois devoir vous communiquer la copie d'une lettre que Je viens d'écrire au procureur gal. des Etats unis pour lui demander que M. Jay et Mr. King l'un premier Juge et l'autre senateur des Etats unis qui ont publié dans les gazettes un libelle contre moi soient traduits à la Cour federale. Je n'ai rien négligé Jusqu'à présent pour démentir les impostures perfides¹ auxquelles ces Messieurs n'ont point rougi de mettre leur nom. C'est dans cette vue que J'ai osé écrire² au President des Etats unis,³ c'est dans cette vue que mes amis ont sommé dans plusieurs papiers M. Jay et M. King de présenter les preuves de leur assertion; mais la réponse que vous avés été chargé de me faire, M., ayant été aussi indécise⁴ que le Silence de ces Messieurs a été profond, Il ne me reste plus que les voies Juridiques pour confondre ceux qui m'ont outragé comme délégué du peuple francois et comme individu. Cette satisfaction sera la plus agréable que Je puisse obtenir car Je n'ai Jamais aspiré qu'à l'estime des hommes libres et vertueux de quelque nation qu'ils puissent être. Il m'est bien pénible sans doute de voir aujourdhui la Calomnie s'attacher à me poursuivre et la religion d'un peuple que Je revere surprise⁵ ainsi que celle de son premier magistrat; mais aussi quelle Jouissance n'aurai-je point lorsque la vérité seule forcera ceux qui méconnoissent dans cet instant et mes intentions et mes principes à rendre hommage à mon courage à mon inebranlable patriotisme et à la pureté de ma conduite.

Dft (DLC: Genet Papers); unsigned; above salutation: "Le Cit Genet Ministre plenipotentiaire de la Repe. fse à M. Jefferson secretaire d'Etat des Etats unis"; only the most significant emendations are recorded below. FC (same); misdated 12 Nov. 1793. FC (same); in English; with dateline, address, and salutation in Genet's hand. Recorded in SJL as received 19 Nov. 1793. Enclosure: Genet to Edmund Randolph, 14 Nov. 1793, requesting the Attorney General to take steps to prosecute "at the ensuing Federal Court" Chief Justice John Jay and New York Senator Rufus King for certifying to the public in the enclosed New York newspaper "as a Declaration of mine what is utterly and totally false"—a calumny that has injured both himself and the country he represents (FC in same; in English; in a clerk's hand, unsigned, with dateline by Genet; addressed: "To the Attorney General of the United States").

The LIBELLE was a statement by John Jay and Rufus King in the 12 Aug. 1793

New York *Diary; or Loudon's Register* and other newspapers vouching for the accuracy of a report from Philadelphia that Genet had "said he would appeal to the People from certain decisions of the President"—a reference to an incident that had occurred during the controversy over the French minister's outfitting of the *Little Sarah* as a privateer in Philadelphia early in July 1793 (Syrett, *Hamilton*, xv, 233; Cabinet Opinions on the *Little Sarah*, 8 July 1793, and note). Randolph responded to the enclosed letter by informing Genet of his willingness to discuss the subject of it when the French minister returned to Philadelphia (Randolph to Genet, 19 Nov. 1793, DLC: Genet Papers). Genet later arranged to have his letter to TJ, the enclosed letter to the Attorney General, and Randolph's reply published in the 27 Nov. 1793 issue of the *New-York Journal, & Patriotic Register* with this statement: "☞ The

Printers throughout the United States, who have published Messrs. Jay and King's certificate, are requested to do the same for the above communications." For further information on this affair, see Proposed Public Statement on Edmond Charles Genet, [ca. 16 Dec. 1793].

Genet's 13 Aug. 1793 letter to the PRESIDENT is printed as an enclosure to George Washington to TJ, with Jefferson's Note, 15 Aug. 1793.

[1] Word interlined.
[2] Altered from "J'ai écris."
[3] Genet canceled a marginal note keyed for insertion here: "ayant pris autrefois une pareille liberté avec des Rois des Imperatrices et des Princes régnants qui loin de s'en facher m'ont répondu avec bonté."
[4] Word interlined in place of "ambigue."
[5] Altered from "la religion du peuple Soumise."

To George Hammond

SIR   Germantown Nov. 14. 1793.

I have to acknowledge the receipt of your letter of the 7th. instant, on the subject of the British ship Roehampton, taken and sent into Baltimore by the French privateer the Industry, an armed Schooner of St. Domingo, which is suggested to have augmented her force at Baltimore before the capture.[1] On this circumstance a demand is grounded[2] that the prize she has made shall be restored.

Before I proceed to the matters of fact in this case, I will take the liberty of calling your attention to the rules[3] which are to govern it. These are—

Ist. That restitution of prizes has been made by the Executive of the United States only in the two cases 1. of capture, within their Jurisdiction, by[4] armed vessels originally[5] constituted such without the limits of[6] the united States; or 2d. of[7] capture, either within or without their jurisdiction, by armed vessels, originally constituted such within the limits of the[8] United States, which last have been called proscribed vessels.

IInd. That all military equipments[9] within the ports of the United States are forbidden to the vessels of the Belligerent powers,[10] even where they have been constituted vessels of war[11] before their arrival in our ports; and where such equipments have been made before detection, they are ordered to be suppressed when detected,[12] and the vessel reduced to her original condition. But if they escape detection altogether, depart and make prizes, the Executive has not undertaken to restore the prizes.

With due care, it can scarcely [13] happen that military equipments of any magnitude shall escape discovery. [14] Those which are small may sometimes, perhaps, escape, but to pursue these so far as to decide that [15] the smallest circumstance of military equipment to a vessel in our ports shall invalidate her prizes through all time, would be a measure of incalculable consequences. And since our interference must be governed by some general rule, and between great and small equipments no practicable line of distinction can be drawn, [16] it will be attended with less evil on the whole to rely on the efficacy of the means of prevention, that they will reach with certainty equipments of any magnitude and the great mass of those of smaller importance also: and if some should in the event, escape all our vigilance, to consider these as of the number of cases which will at times baffle the restraints of the wisest and best guarded rules which human foresight can devise. And I think we may safely rely that since the regulations which got into a course of execution about the middle of August last, it is [17] scarcely possible that equipments of any importance should escape [18] discovery.

These principles shewing that no demand of restitution lies on the ground of a mere military alteration or an augmentation of force, I will consider your letter only as a complaint that the orders of the President prohibiting these, have not had their effect in the case of the Industry, and enquire whether, if this be so, it [19] has happened either from neglect or connivance in those charged with the execution of these orders. For this we must resort to facts which shall be taken from the evidence furnished by yourself, and the British vice Consul at Baltimore, and from that which shall accompany this letter.

About the beginning [20] of August the Industry is said to have [21] arrived at Baltimore with the French fleet from St. Domingo. [22] The particular state of her armament on her arrival is lately questioned, but it is not questioned, that she was an armed vessel of some degree. The Executive having received an intimation that two vessels were equipping themselves at Baltimore for a cruise, a letter was on the 6th. of Augt. addressed by the Secretary of war [23] to the Governor of Maryland, desiring an inquiry into the fact. In his absence, the Executive Council of Maryland charged one of their own Body, the honorable Mr. Kilty, with the inquiry. He proceeded to Baltimore, and after two days examination found no vessel answering the description of those which were the object of his inquiry. He then engaged the British Vice Consul in the search, who was not able, any more than himself to discover any such vessels. Captain Kilty, however, observing a Schooner, which appeared to have been making some equipments for a cruise, to have added to her guns, and made some alteration to her waist, thought these circumstances merited examination,[24] though the rules of August had not yet appeared. Finding that his inquiries excited suspicion, and fearing the vessel might be withdrawn, he had her seized, and proceeded in the investigation.[25] He found that she was the Schooner Industry, Captain Carven, from St. Domingo, that she had been an armed vessel for three years before her coming here,[26] and as late as April last had mounted 16 Guns; that she now mounted only 12. and he could not learn that she had procured any of these or done any thing else, essential to her as a privateer, at Baltimore. He therefore discharged her, and on the 23d. of August, the Executive Council made the report to the Secretary at war, of which I enclose you a copy.

About a fortnight after this (Sep. 6.) you added to a letter on other business a short paragraph saying that you had 'lately received information that a vessel named the Industry had within the last 5 or 6 weeks been armed, manned, and equipped in the port of Baltimore.' The proceedings before mentioned having been in another department, were not then known to me. I therefore could only communicate this paragraph to the proper Department. The separation of the Executive within a week after prevented any explanations on the subject: and without them[27] it was not in my power either to controvert or admit the information you had received. Under these circumstances I think you must be sensible, Sir, that your conclusion from my silence, that I regarded the fact as proved, was not a very necessary one.

New inquiries, at that time, could not have prevented the departure of the privateer, or the capture of the Roehampton: for the privateer had then been out some time. The Roehampton was already taken and was arriving at Baltimore; which she did[28] about the day of the date of your letter. After her arrival, new witnesses have come forward to prove[29] that the Industry had made some military equipments at Baltimore before her cruise. The affidavits taken by the British Vice Consul are dated about 9 or 10 days after the date of your letter and[30] arrival of the Roehampton: and we have only to lament that those witnesses had not given their information to the Vice Consul[31] when Mr. Kilty engaged his aid in the inquiries he was making, and when it would have had the effect of our detaining the privateer till she should have reduced herself to the condition in which she was when she arrived in our ports, if she had really added any thing to her then force. But supposing the testimony just and full (tho' taken ex parte, and not under the legal sanction of an oath) yet the Governor's refusal to restore the prize, was perfectly proper; for, as has been before observed, restitution has never been made by the Executive, nor can be made[32] on a mere clandestine alteration[33] or augmentation of military equipment, which was all that the new testimony tended to prove.

Notwithstanding, however that the President thought the information[34] obtained on the former occasion had cleared this privateer from any well grounded cause of arrest, yet that which you have now offered opens a possibility[35] that the former was defective. He has therefore desired new inquiry to be made before a magistrate legally authorized to administer an oath, and indifferent to both parties, and should the result be that the vessel did really make any military equipments in our ports, instructions will be given to reduce her to her original condition, whenever she shall again[36] come into our ports.

On the whole, Sir, I hope you will percieve that on the first intimation, thro' their own channels, and without waiting for information on your part, that a vessel was making military equipments at Baltimore, the Executive took the best measures for inquiring into the fact in order to prevent or suppress such equipments—that an Officer of high respectability was charged with the inquiry, that he made it with great diligence himself,[37] and engaged similar inquiries on the part of your Vice Consul, that neither of them could find that this privateer had made such equipments, or of course that there was any ground for reducing or detaining her; that at the date of your letter of Sep. 6. (the first intimation received from you) the Privateer was departed, had taken her prize, and that prize was arriving in port; that the new evidence taken 10 days after that arrival can produce no other effect than the institution of a new[38] inquiry, and a reduction of the force of the privateer, should she appear to have made any military alterations or augmentation, on her return into our ports, and that in no part of this procedure is there the smallest ground for imputing either negligence or connivance to any of the officers who have acted in it. I have the honor to be, with much respect Sir, Your most obedient and most humble servant,

PrC (DLC); in the hand of George Taylor, Jr., unsigned, with dateline and minor corrections added in ink by TJ; at foot of first page: "The minister plenipoy. of Great Britain." Dft (DLC: TJ Papers, 94: 16214-15); heavily emended text in TJ's hand, undated and unsigned, with two marginal notes by Alexander Hamilton (see notes 6 and 35 below); only the most significant revisions are recorded below; notations at foot of text: (by Edmund Randolph) "I think the draught very proper E. R." (by Hamilton) "approved A H" and (by TJ) "the fair copy was sent to Genl. Knox, at his house with a request to forward it to Mr. Hammond if he

approved of it" (but see TJ to Henry Knox, with Jefferson's Note, 15 Nov. 1793). FC (Lb in DNA: RG 59, DL). Tr (Lb in PRO: FO 116/3). Recorded in SJPL. Enclosure: Extract of James Brice to Henry Knox, Annapolis, 23 Aug. 1793, stating, in his capacity as president of the Maryland Council and acting governor during Thomas Sim Lee's absence, that the Council authorized one of its members, John Kilty, to proceed to Baltimore in order to investigate the reported fitting out there of two French privateers as mentioned in Knox's 6 Aug. letter to Lee; that after two days of fruitless inquiries Kilty enlisted the help of British Vice-Consul Edward Thornton, who was also unable to find any evidence of them; that during an inspection from the public barge of all the vessels in Baltimore harbor, which also failed to detect the privateers, Kilty observed a schooner at a Fell's Point wharf mounting twelve guns that could not be the Virginia pilot boat noted by Knox because of its size and its having arrived with the fleet from Saint-Domingue; that after a limited investigation designed to prevent alarm Kilty ascertained that the schooner was preparing for a cruise, having apparently increased its guns and altered its waist since its arrival, though he could not learn where it had procured the additional cannon; that Kilty returned to Fell's Point to conduct a final investigation in order to determine whether he would be justified in detaining the schooner for violating what he understood to be the ban on all military equipment in American ports, the federal government's regulations on this subject not yet having appeared; that Kilty had the schooner seized by Deputy Marshal Jacob Graybill in the absence of its captain and officers after learning that news of his intended investigation was being brought to the ship; that after instructing Graybill to prevent the schooner from leaving the wharf Kilty conducted an unrestricted investigation which failed to reveal that the ship had taken on any guns or equipment in Baltimore that were essential to it as a privateer; that upon leaving the schooner to return to Baltimore and find its captain, Kilty prevented a "considerable body" of Frenchmen with a leader and drum at their head from taking possession of the ship after informing them that it was being detained by authority; that the next morning Jean Baptiste Carvin, the captain and owner, angrily demanded an explanation of the seizure from Kilty, who pointed to the increase in the number of its guns as the principal reason; that Carvin produced papers from Saint-Domingue officials showing that the schooner, the *Industry*, had carried guns for the past three years and that on 11 Apr. 1793 it mounted sixteen guns and had a crew sufficient for privateering, as well as a commission or license for cruising under which prizes went to the government while the captors received a reasonable gratification; that Carvin asserted that he had obtained no guns and no military equipment except for a few spare rammers while in Baltimore and

that the extra guns he had mounted there had been brought in his hold; that Carvin admitted purchasing some cordage and cleaning the schooner's bottom in Baltimore and asked if all the armed vessels now in the harbor were not therefore also liable to detention; that being unable to disprove Carvin's assertions and wishing to avoid heavy charges to the public for the detention, Kilty had the French vice-consul verify the papers presented by Carvin and then ordered Graybill to release the *Industry* (PrC of Tr in DLC, in a clerk's hand; Tr in Lb in DNA: RG 59, DL; FC in MdAA: Letterbooks of Governor and Council, also containing a section dealing with Kilty's report on another letter from Knox about alleged preparations in Baltimore for an expedition against Saint-Domingue). Enclosed in TJ to George Washington, [16 Nov. 1793].

The REGULATIONS in question are contained in Rules on Neutrality, 3 Aug. 1793. For the EVIDENCE furnished by Hammond and the BRITISH VICE CONSUL AT BALTIMORE, Edward Thornton, see the enclosures listed at Hammond to TJ, 7 Nov. 1793 (first letter). Henry Knox's letter of the 6TH. OF AUGT. to Governor Thomas Sim Lee of Maryland is described in note to same. A MAGISTRATE LEGALLY AUTHORIZED: see TJ to Zebulon Hollingsworth, 14 Nov. 1793 (second letter).

After obtaining the approval of Alexander Hamilton and Edmund Randolph for the rough draft of this letter, TJ submitted a text of the final version to the President on 16 Nov. 1793, and Washington returned it the same day (Washington, *Journal*, 252; Cabinet Opinions on Various Letters, [23 Nov. 1793]).

[1] In Dft TJ here canceled "whereon you require" and inserted a period before these words.

[2] In Dft TJ first wrote "On that circumstance you ground a demand" and then altered it to read as above.

[3] Word interlined in Dft in place of "principles."

[4] In Dft TJ here canceled "vessels."

[5] Word interlined in Dft.

[6] Altered by TJ in Dft from "as such *out of*" in response to Hamilton, who wrote the preceding four words in the margin under his comment "substitute for perspicuity."

[7] Digit interlined and preceding word written over "to" in Dft.

[8] Preceding three words interlined in Dft.

[9] Preceding two words underscored in Dft.

[10] Preceding seven words interlined in Dft in place of "by the Executive even to armed vessels constituted such."

[11] Preceding three words interlined in Dft in place of "such."

[12] In Dft TJ first wrote "have not been discovered till made, they are to be suppressed" and then altered it to read as above."

[13] Sentence to this point interlined in Dft in place of "For since the regulations which got into a course of execution about the middle of August last, it can scarcely ever."

[14] Word interlined in Dft in place of "detection."

[15] Preceding eight words interlined in Dft in place of "say that where a vessel shall have made even."

[16] Remainder of paragraph through "regulations" interlined in Dft in place of a heavily emended passage that in its final state read: "the measure attended with the least evil on the whole is to rely on the efficacy of the means adopted for preventing and suppressing such equipments, that they will reach with certainty those of any magnitude, and the great mass of those of the smaller kind also. And if some should in event escape all our vigilance, to consider these as of the number of cases which will at times escape the restraints of the wisest and best guarded rules which human wisdom can ever devise. And I think we may safely rely that since the regulations."

[17] In Dft TJ here canceled "believed to be."

[18] In Dft TJ here canceled "notice."

[19] Preceding five words interlined in Dft in place of "this."

[20] Preceding two words interlined in Dft in place of "second week in."

[21] In the margin of the Dft TJ here canceled "Baker's affidavit." See Enclosure No. 2 listed at Hammond to TJ, 7 Nov. 1793.

[22] In Dft TJ here canceled "armed for war in the character of an armed vessel."

[23] Preceding five words interlined in Dft.

[24] Word interlined in Dft in place of "enquiry."

[25] Preceding two words interlined in Dft in place of "his enquiries."

[26] In Dft TJ first wrote "been for three years past an armed vessel" and then altered it to read as above.

[27] In Dft TJ here canceled "I had nothing to write to you."

[28] Paragraph to this point in Dft written in the margin in place of a passage that in its final state read: "New enquiries at that time could not have prevented the departure of the privateer or the capture of the Roehampton, for the Privateer had now been out some time and the capture had already taken place. The Roehampton armed at Baltimore on or about."

[29] Sentence to this point interlined in Dft in place of "On this event the British Consul has been able to find testimony."

[30] Preceding six words interlined in Dft in place of "the."

[31] In Dft TJ first wrote "lament that the testimony has not been found" and then altered it to read as above.

[32] Preceding four words interlined in Dft.

[33] In Dft TJ first wrote "on a bare alteration" and then altered it to read as above.

[34] Word interlined in Dft in place of "testimony [. . .]."

[35] At this point Hamilton wrote in the margin of the Dft "suppose probability."

[36] In Dft TJ first wrote "should she again" and then altered it to read as above.

[37] Word interlined in Dft.

[38] In Dft TJ here canceled "and more formal."

To Patrick Hart

SIR   Germantown near Philadelphia, Nov. 14. 1793.

Understanding that there was a box containing an Orrery for me at the Custom-house at the Hundred, I had asked the favor of Mr. David

Randolph to take it out and pay the duty, which I suppose small, as the machine cost but about $2\frac{1}{2}$ guineas. He writes me word that before he received my letter, you had been so kind as to liberate it from the custom house, with a view of sending it on to me. The object of this letter is to return you many thanks for this kind attention, and instead of forwarding it to me here, to ask you to be so good as to deliver it to Mr. Randolph my son in law, to be forwarded to my own house in Albemarle where I shall be within a few weeks. Be pleased at the same time to let either him or me know what you have been so good as to pay on it, and it will be immediately replaced. With repeated thanks for the civility, I am with esteem, Sir Your most obedt. servt. TH: JEFFERSON

PrC (DLC); at foot of text: "Mr. Patrick Hart." Tr (ViU: Edgehill-Randolph Papers); 19th-century copy.

To Zebulon Hollingsworth

SIR   Germantown, Nov. 14th. 1793.

The British brig Coningham having been taken by the French privateer the Sans Culottes of Marseilles within the limits of our jurisdiction as is alledged, I am to desire you to take measures for bringing the case to final settlement according to the general rules laid down in the Letter I had the honor of addressing you on the 10th. inst. By a Letter of the present date I notify the two Ministers of the reference now made to you, relying that they will instruct their Consuls to pay requisite attention to it. I have the honor to be with Esteem & Respect, Sir, Your most Obedt. servt.

PrC (DLC); in a clerk's hand, unsigned; at foot of text: "Zebulon Hollingsworth Esq. Attorney for the District of Maryland at Baltimore." Dft (DLC); entirely in TJ's hand; written on the same sheet as Dft of second letter to Hollingsworth of this date below; with note at foot of page referring to both: "these forms shewn to the Atty Genl. and approved. Nov. 15." FC (Lb in DNA: RG 59, DL). Recorded in SJPL. Enclosed in TJ to George Washington, [16 Nov. 1793].

After obtaining Cabinet approval for the substance of this letter and Edmund Randolph's approval for the rough draft, TJ submitted a text of the final version to the President on 16 Nov. 1793, and Washington returned it the same day (Washington, *Journal*, 252; Cabinet Opinions on Various Letters, [23 Nov. 1793]).

To Zebulon Hollingsworth

SIR   Germantown, Novemr. 14th. 1793.

After much remonstrance with Mr. Genet against the usurpations by the French Consuls, of jurisdiction unpermitted by the laws or treaties of the United States—and especially against their assuming to exercise admiralty jurisdiction[1] to try and condemn vessels, and that too in cases where others besides french Citizens were interested—finding that instead of repressing, he sanctioned the proceedings, I gave notice by letter of Sept. 7. to the several Consuls of that nation, that the Exequaturs of such of them as should repeat the usurpation after that date, would be immediately revoked.

It being now suggested that M. Moissonnier has since that date undertaken to[2] try and condemn as lawful prizes the British Ship Roehampton taken by the French privateer the Industry; and the British brig Pilgrim taken by the French privateer the Sans Culottes of Marseilles, and to order their sale,[3] I am to ask the favor of you to inquire into these facts with the circumspection which may be necessary to prevent that alarm which might lead them to a concealment of them, and to procure for me the most unquestionable evidence of them, if they be true. The most conclusive would be copies of the proceedings or at least of the sentences, authenticated under M. Moissonier's own hand if to be procured.[4] I have the honor to be with esteem & respect Sir, Your most obed servt.

PrC (DLC); in a clerk's hand, unsigned; at foot of text: "Zebulon Hollingsworth Esqr. Attorney of the U.S. for the district of Maryland at Baltimore." Dft (DLC); entirely in TJ's hand; subjoined to Dft of first letter to Hollingsworth of this date above and referred to in the note at foot of text recorded there; with penciled marginal note by TJ: "to be sent by the return of the rider." FC (Lb in DNA: RG 59, DL). Recorded in SJPL. Enclosed in TJ to George Washington, [16 Nov. 1793].

After obtaining Cabinet approval for the substance of this letter and Edmund Randolph's approval for the rough draft, TJ submitted a text of the final version to the President on 16 Nov. 1793, and Washington returned it the same day (Washington, *Journal*, 252; Cabinet Opinions on Various Letters, [23 Nov. 1793]).

[1] In Dft TJ first wrote the remainder of the clause as "and to condemn vessels and under that semblance of law to ensnare our citizens into purchases of them" before altering it to read as above.

[2] In Dft TJ here canceled "condemn and authorize the."

[3] Clause interlined in Dft in place of "and to authorize other sales."

[4] In Dft TJ canceled a marginal note he had keyed for insertion here: "If the Pilgrim has not been sold I shall be obliged to you."

To David Howell

DEAR SIR   Germantown Nov. 14. 1793.

I have duly received your two favors of Octob. 3. and 4. with that signed by Messrs. Brown and others. I have communicated the contents to the President, and added my own testimony, derived from former acquaintance, to the recommendations of those gentlemen. No appointment is as yet made, and the President is absent on a short tour. In this as in every other pursuit, I sincerely wish you success, and shall be greeted with the tidings of it in the retirement into which I mean to withdraw at the close of the present year. It will be the second time my bark will have put into port with a design not to venture out again; and I trust it will be the last. My farm, my family and my books call me to them irresistably. I do not know whether you are a farmer, but I know you love your family and your books, and will therefore bear witness to the strength of their attractions. Accept assurances of my constant esteem & respect.   TH: JEFFERSON

RC (Benjamin Cowell, Wrentham, Massachusetts, 1944); at foot of text: "David Howell esq. Providence." PrC (DLC).

To William Mewburn

SIR   Germantown near Philadelphia Nov. 14. 1793.

Mr. Donald of London, in a letter of Aug. 30. informs me you had been so kind as to take charge of a telescope for me. Not knowing whether you are yet arrived, and apprehending, if you were, that you might forward the glass on to this place, I take the liberty of lodging the present letter at Richmond, to desire you, instead of sending it on here to deliver it to Mr. Randolph my son in law whenever he may happen to be in Richmond, or to his order. Any duty or other charge which may have been paid on it shall be thankfully repaid as soon as made known. Returning you many thanks for the obliging office you have done, I remain with esteem Sir Your most obedt. servt.   TH: JEFFERSON

PrC (DLC); at foot of text: "Mr. Mewbern." Tr (ViU: Edgehill-Randolph Papers); 19th-century copy. Enclosed in TJ to Robert Gamble, 14 Nov. 1793.

William Mewburn of Mewburn & Company, previously a partner in the defunct firm of William Mewburn & Company, was a Richmond merchant dealing in textiles and other English goods who had just returned from a buying trip to Great Britain (Richmond *Virginia Gazette, and General Advertiser*, 20 Nov. 1793).

TJ's letter makes clear that Alexander Donald's missing LETTER OF AUG. 30. did not accompany the TELESCOPE entrusted to Mewburn, as the Editors mistakenly inferred in note to Donald to TJ, 10 Mch. 1793.

To Oliver & Thompson

GENTLEMEN   Germantown Nov. 14. 1793.

The present is to acknolege the receipt of your favor of the   inst. on the injuries you have received in the case of your ship Cincinnatus. It shall be duly attended to. I have reason to expect immediately some other matter, which by increasing the mass will give it more weight. I have the honor to be Gentlemen Your most obedt. servt

TH: JEFFERSON

PrC (DLC); at foot of text: "Messrs. Oliver & Thompson." FC (Lb in DNA: RG 59, DL).

Oliver & Thompson's missing FAVOR of November 1793, recorded in SJL as received from Baltimore on 9 Nov. 1793, was submitted by TJ to the President with its enclosure on the day of receipt and returned the same day. Washington described the letter as concerning "the detention &c. of their ship Cincinnatus taken by a british privateer and carried to New Providence requesting that measures may be taken to procure them redress for sd. detention expences &c. & enclosing the protest of the Captain of said ship, in wch. the case is fully stated" (Washington, *Journal*, 250).

From Thomas Mann Randolph, Jr.

DEAR SIR   Monticello Nov: 14: 1793.

The anxiety we allways feel in your absence has become quite painfull from our having failed every post since your departure, to recieve tidings of you. We impute it to obstructions in the communication, and trust that we shall enjoy the pleasure of knowing that you are well, next tuesday.

I have just received a melancholy summons to attend my Father, who, I am much afraid, from what I learn, cannot hold out much longer. As this painfull office may detain me some days in Richmond, where he still is, it is possible there may be some service which I can render you there. Had I forseen this I should have waited a little that your furniture might be moved under my own eye: I did indeed wait some days with a view to save the second moving of the most delicate packages by puting them at once in the boats, as there was a sufficient number to bring all such at one trip and I expected daily to see them leave Milton. They missed a tolerable good tide which happened soon after your departure. On this I took measures to have the whole moved to Belvedere without loss of time. Henderson has been some days busy in fiting out his boats and will certainly I think dispatch four the first flood.

I have not yet received accounts of the removal but have no doubt that every thing is safely lodged in Mr. Hyltons Store before this.

We have had no indisposition, except a pimple on the lip of Maria, since you left us.

The colored part of the family is doing well: the man who was ill with the flux has allmost recovered. I am Dr. Sir your most sincere friend & hble Servt. TH: M. RANDOLPH

P.S. Your horse Tarquin has mended so much that I must beg to have the preference at 120 Drs. if you are determined to part with him.

RC (ViU: Edgehill-Randolph Papers); endorsed by TJ as received 23 Nov. 1793 and so recorded in SJL.

To Edmond Charles Genet

Nov. 15. 1793. Germantown.

Th: Jefferson with his respectful compliments to Mr. Genet has the honor to inform him that his letter of the 3d. inst. on the subject of an advance of money, came to hand on the day the President had set out on a journey to Reading. That of yesterday on the same subject, is received this day. Both shall be laid before him on his return.

RC (AMAE: CPEU, Supplément, xx). PrC (DLC).

Genet's LETTER OF THE 3D. INST. was actually dated 11 Nov. and received on 12 Nov. 1793, THE DAY the President SET OUT

(Washington, *Journal*, 251). TJ correctly referred to the letter, the first to deal with Genet's request for a new ADVANCE on the American debt to France, in a related reply to Genet (see TJ's first letter to Genet, 24 Nov. 1793).

To Edmond Charles Genet

SIR [15-22 Nov. 1793]

Your publication in the newspapers in the form of a letter to me of the date of Oct. 27. reached me thro' that channel soon after it's date. It had before been known to the Pr. in the same way. It was not necessary therefore to communicate to him the MS. copy I had the honor of receiving from you afterwards. Nor did I suppose an answer expected.[1]

You had found my name and office convenient as a formality to prefix to your letter, and had had the politeness usual with authors in such cases to send me a letter. Since however I am now informed by your letter of   that you desire an answer I shall observe that[2] agents who are to exercise their functions in a foreign country need the authority first of their own nation, and next of that within whose territory they are to act. If either of these refuse their authority the agent can not commence his functions, if either withdraw his authority after having given it, he can no longer proceed in them, for nothing renders the authority once granted irrevocable either on the part of the nation sending or of that receiving him, nor more on the part of the one than the other.[3] You are[4] right therefore when you say that this[5] 'authority of suspension cannot be exerted but by the sovereign of the agent or by the one to which he is sent.' The sovereignty in your country and ours is in the people.[6] Unable to collect themselves on every occasion of correspondence with foreign nations, they have appointed certain organs to exercise their authorities in this case. In this country the President is[7] delegated to exercise that power, and not the legislature of a particular state as you have imagined. That a power to prevent[8] the action of a foreign agent resides in the nation to which he is sent might be proved from the practice of your own nation in the case of some of our consuls, but we should be answered with phrases about tyrants and despots. It might be proved by writers of the most received authority, but we should be told they are worm-eaten, or hired. It will be acknoleged that you have never troubled us with quotations from Grot. Puff. Vattel or any other authority[9] antient or recent.[10] Had you endeavored to learn from these respected authors[11] what the rest of the world have thought of the different positions you have thought proper to advance, you would have found them entirely against you. Nor could indeed any other authority be quoted for them but the exalted source from whence they have flowed. Those who have not right on their side sometimes think they save appearances by resorting to ridicule. But men of sense reason while others are contented to laugh.   Had the constitution of our country thought proper to leave[12] their correspondence with foreign nations to the legislatures of the several states, none would have exercised it with more intelligence or integrity than the respectable body to whom you propose an appeal on the present occasion. But that[13] duty being consigned to the Executive of the general government, those who have ever read the constitution will wonder at the proposition, and will certainly not augur very well of the capacity of it's author to teach us lessons on that instrument.

Dft (DLC: TJ Papers, 94: 16122); undated and unsigned; with line drawn through top half of first page (see note 3 below); in the margin at head of text: "not sent." Entry in SJPL under 5 Nov. 1793: "draught of one not sent."

This document consists of TJ's unsent draft reply to Genet's second LETTER of 14 Nov. 1793 requesting a further explanation of the President's authority for the accreditation of foreign officials. Despite the date assigned in SJPL, TJ must have drafted this response sometime between 15 Nov. 1793, when he received the French minister's letter, and 22 Nov. 1793, when he wrote a reply informing Genet that he was not authorized to discuss with him the President's constitutional authority to receive or interdict foreign agents.

[1] TJ here canceled "not having before been" and left several lines blank before writing the next sentence.
[2] TJ here canceled "when you state that the agent of a foreign nation depends."
[3] Text to this point lined out by TJ.
[4] TJ here canceled "perfectly."
[5] TJ here canceled "suspension."
[6] TJ here canceled "They have in both appointed certain organs for exercising."
[7] TJ here canceled "to exercise."
[8] TJ first wrote "the power of preventing" and then altered it to read as above.

From Edmond Charles Genet

M.   New york le 15.[1] 9bre. 1793. l'an 2e. de la Republique

J'ai recu la lettre que vous m'avés fait l'honneur de m'écrire le 5. 9bre.

Le Citoyen Moissonnier a donné à mes instructions un sens plus déterminé que celui que J'y avois attaché. Je[2] ne lui ai point écrit que l'angleterre alloit immediatement[3] fondre sur vous;[4] mais connoissant par votre histoire par la notre et par d'autres notions[5] plus particulieres encore toute la haine dont[6] ce gouvernement honore vos principes et les notres, Connoissant les traités secréts qui unissent les cours liguées contre les peuples libres; sachant que nos succès pouvoient seuls reprimer les projets de vengeance que nourrit perpetuellement dans son sein votre ancien tyran; voyant que quelques revers effacés depuis[7] pouvoient l'éxciter à accelerer l'éxécution de ses desseins J'avois préscrit à ce Vice Consul:

1°. de se concerter avec le Commandant de nos forces navales dans la Chesapeak pour faire remonter à Baltimore tous les batiments du Commerce[8] qui se trouvoient dans la rade ouverte et[9] peu sure de Norfolk.

2°. de faire mouiller suivant l'usage[10] à l'avant Garde du Convoi les batiments armés.

3° d'établir une police severe dans la rade pour prevenir le desordre et mettre nos[11] propriétés à l'abri des entreprises incendiaires[12] assés familieres à nos ennemis communs.

4°. de Sonder le gouvernement local du Maryland[13] pour savoir si l'on ne pourroit point mettre en état les forts qui font partie de la défense de Baltimore.

Le Cit. Moissonnier animé d'un patriotisme très pur a mis sans doute un peu de chaleur dans cette derniere demarche mais Je ne vois point, M., qu'il ait merité l'admonition dont vous parlés et que les mesures prises pour la sureté de la rade puissent compromettre en aucune maniere la paix des Etats unis. Dieu veuille que vous en Jouissiés longtems avec honneur de cette paix si douce et si heureuse;[14] c'est le voeu bien sincère de vos amis c'est le mien. Mais Je ne vous dissimulerai pas plus aujourdhui qu'autrefois que ce n'est point l'objet le plus certain de mes ésperances. Avant d'avoir le bonheur de servir un peuple libre[15] J'ai eu le malheur d'être employé par une cour et de résider dans plusieurs autres; J'ai été sept années chef de Bureau à vlles. [16] [Versailles] sous les ordres de Vergennes, J'ai passé une année à Londres [17] deux à Vienne une à Berlin 5 en Russie et Je suis trop initié dans les mysteres de ces cabinets pour ne point trembler du sort qui menace l'amérique si la Cause de la liberté [18] ne triomphe point partout car partout où il y a un trone Je vous garantis que vous avés un énnemi. Tous les Princes vous regardent comme nos maitres d'école; Presque tous ne voyant encore en vous que des rebelles qui doivent tôt ou tard être chatiés. Presque tous ont Juré votre perte aussi bien que la notre et croyés que George III n'est entré dans leur ligue qu'à ce prix. Vos temperaments, vos menagements, [19] ne feront point changer ce systême [20] et si les Ministres qui resident auprès de vous vous tiennent un autre langage, ce n'est que pour mieux vous tromper; Ils triomphent de La securité dans la quelle ils vous plongent au moment où leurs cours vous insultent par tout éxcépté sur vos côtes ou ils savent que nous avons des forces; [21] mais leur ton changera tandis que le notre restera toujours le même vrai et sincère.

Dft (DLC: Genet Papers); in Genet's hand, unsigned, with revision by a clerk (see note 6 below); with altered date; above salutation: "Le Cit Genet &c à M. Jefferson &c"; only the most significant emendations are recorded below. FC (same); in English. Tr (DNA: RG 46, Senate Records, 3d Cong., 1st sess.); in English. Recorded in SJL as received 18 Nov. 1793. Printed with translation in *Message*, 30 (App.), 90-1; translation printed in ASP, *Foreign Relations*, I, 183.

[1] Reworked from "14."
[2] Genet here canceled "lui avois préscrit de faire remonter à Baltimore, les bâtiments du Commerce qui se trouvoient à Norfolk dans une rade ouverte et peu sure, de" and wrote the remainder of the sentence through "nourrit" in the margin.
[3] Word interlined.
[4] Preceding four words italicized in *Message*.
[5] *Message*: "des notions."
[6] Preceding two words interlined in place of "perfidie des."
[7] Preceding two words interlined by clerk in place of "éssuiés alors par nos armes." Here in the margin "mais éffacés

depuis par d'éclatants succès" is also canceled.
[8] Preceding two words interlined.
[9] Genet here canceled "forain."
[10] Preceding three words written in the margin, after which Genet canceled "en cas d'attaque imprevue."
[11] Preceding two words interlined in place of "faire avorter les projets."
[12] Remainder of sentence inserted.
[13] Preceding two words written in the margin.
[14] Remainder of sentence written in the margin.
[15] Remainder of clause in *Message*: "je fus employé par une cour, et je résidai dans plusieurs autres."
[16] Preceding two words interlined.
[17] Preceding four words written in the margin.
[18] Word interlined in place of "france."
[19] Genet here canceled "vos dissimulations."
[20] Genet here canceled "J'en ai la certitude Je le signerois de mon sang. Ces vérités pourront."
[21] Clause altered from "La securité dans la quelle ils vous plongent est pour eux un triomphe."

From Edmond Charles Genet

M.   New york le 15.[1] 9bre. 1793. l'an 2e. de la Repe.

Je viens d'être instruit que des traites que J'avois delivrées aux fournisseurs de la Republique sur la tresorerie des Etats unis n'y ont point été admises les fonds qui étoient à notre disposition pour le mois de 9bre. étant dit on épuisés et les fonds pour l'année 1794. n'étant point encore faits. Je ne m'attacherai point à vous peindre le tort prodigieux que ce refus de payement fait à notre credit et à notre service, un instant de reflexion vous en convaincra; mais Je vous observerai seulement que l'assertion de la trésorerie n'est point fondée. Il est possible que mes traites sur 9bre. éxcedent le montant du Capital sec[2] qui devoit nous être remboursé dans ce mois; mais il est démontré à mes yeux qu'elles sont de beaucoup inferieures au montant du Capital y Compris les Interêts échus et non payés Jusqu'à ce Jour. D'ailleurs, M., quand ce fait n'éxisteroit point la situation pécuniaire des Etats unis est elle assés gênée et notre situation politique est elle assés précaire pour que la tresorerie se soit refusée même à admettre un excedent de quelques milliers de dollars sur le mois de 9bre.?

J'attends avec impatience M., votre réponse sur cet objet veritablement[3] important et Je charge le Cit. Bournonville auquel Je vous prie de vouloir bien la confier[4] de me la faire parvenir par un éxprès.

Dft (DLC: Genet Papers); unsigned; with altered date; above salutation: "Le Citoyen Genet &c à M. Jefferson &c."; only the most significant emendations are recorded below. Tr (AMAE: CPEU, xxxix); with one minor variation; signed by Genet. Tr (same, Supplément, xx); with one minor variation; certified by Genet. FC (DLC: Genet Papers); in English; misdated 11 Nov. 1793. Recorded in SJL as received 18 Nov. 1793.

[1] Altered from "14."
[2] Word interlined in place of interlined "seul."
[3] Word interlined.
[4] Preceding nine words interlined.

To Edmond Charles Genet and George Hammond

SIR   Germantown Nov. 15. 1793.

I have the honor to inform you that the district Attorney of Pennsylvania is this day instructed to take measures for finally settling the cases of the British ship William, captured by the French privateer the Citoyen Genet, and reclaimed as taken within the Jurisdiction of the United States, in which he will proceed as I had the honor of stating to you in my letter of November 10. I have that of being with respect & esteem Sir, Your most obedient and most humble servant

PrC (DLC); in the hand of George Taylor, Jr., unsigned, with day and year added in ink; at foot of text: "The Minister Plenipoy. of France." PrC (DLC); in Taylor's hand, unsigned, with day and year added in ink; at foot of text: "The minister plenipoy. of Gt. Britain." FC (Lb in DNA: RG 59, DL); at head of text: "The Minister pleni: of France"; at foot of text: "Addressed also to The Minister pleni. of Great Britain." Enclosed in TJ to George Washington, [16 Nov. 1793].

After obtaining Cabinet approval for the substance of this letter and Attorney General Edmund Randolph's approval of the draft, TJ submitted the final version of both texts to the President on 16 Nov. 1793,

and Washington returned them the same day (Washington, *Journal*, 252; Cabinet Opinions on Various Letters, [23 Nov. 1793]).

On 14 Nov. 1793 William Gray, Jr., a merchant in Salem, Massachusetts, wrote a letter to TJ that is recorded in SJL as received 3 Dec. 1793. Although Gray's letter is missing, it undoubtedly concerned the case of his brig, the *William*, which was stopped at sea on 19 Oct. 1793 by the CI-TOYEN GENET, which plundered it of property worth about £350 lawful money, beat its captain, and put four Bermudian sailors aboard (DNA: RG 123, United States Court of Claims, French Spoliation Case Files, Case No. 11).

To Henry Knox, with Jefferson's Note

Nov. 15. 1793.

Th: Jefferson, with his respects to Genl. Knox, has the honor to inclose for his examination and amendment a letter to Mr. Hammond on the subject of the Roehampton, which has already been examined and approved by the Secy. of the Treasury and Atty. genl. Should Genl. Knox propose no amendment, Th:J. will be obliged to him to stick a wafer in the cover, and send it on to the post office. Should he think it of any consequence to send a copy to Govr. T. Lee, in order to explain to him and the council[1] the reason of the new enquiries to be made into the condition of the Industry, Genl. Knox's clerk shall have the press copy retained here, to take a copy from.

[*Note by TJ:*]

After writing the above and inclosing the letter to Mr. H. it was recollected that Genl. Knox was to set out this day Friday for Trenton. This note was therefore opened and the letter sent to Mr. Hammond, to avoid the delay which would be occasioned.

RC (DLC); addressed: "The Secretary at war"; with note by TJ at foot of text. Recorded in SJPL.

LETTER TO MR. HAMMOND: TJ to George Hammond, 14 Nov. 1793.

[1] Preceding three words interlined.

To Henry Knox

Nov. 15. 1793.

Th: Jefferson has the honor to inclose to Genl. Knox press copies of his letters to the Attornies of Pensylva. and Delaware. Also the original of Mr. Kilty's report.

RC (Gilder Lehrman Collection: Knox Papers, on deposit NNP); addressed: "The Secretary at War." Not recorded in SJL. Enclosures: (1) Enclosure to TJ to George Hammond, 14 Nov. 1793. (2) Texts of TJ to the District Attorneys, 10 Nov. 1793, addressed to William Rawle and George Read, Jr.

Notes on Alexander Hamilton and the French Revolution

Nov. 15. 93. E.R. tells me that Ham. in conversation with him yesterday said 'Sir, if all the people in America were now assembled and to call on me to say whether I am a friend to the French revolution, I would declare that *I have it in abhorrence.*'

MS (DLC); entirely in TJ's hand; written out of sequence as the initial entry on the first side of the first of two sheets containing "Anas" entries for 8, 18, 21, and 23 Nov. 1793, those of 8 and 18 Nov. being printed under the latter date. Recorded in SJPL: "15. to 23. Notes. Hammond.— Genet—speech to Congress.—renvoi of Genet. fortificns—military academy." Included in the "Anas."

HAM.: clearly Alexander Hamilton, despite TJ's later expansion of the abbreviation in SJPL.

To William Rawle

SIR   Germantown Nov. 15. 1793.

You will doubtless recollect the case of the British ship William, taken by the Privateer Citoyen Genet, before the 5th. of June and within the limits of our Jurisdiction, as was alleged. On this allegation she was libelled in the district Court of Pennsylvania, and discharged by the Judge on the ground of incompetence of Jurisdiction. It then became the duty of the Executive to interpose. The British minister exhibited affidavits taken exparte which gave reason to believe that the capture was made within our jurisdiction, and the french minister was desired to shew cause against it, the vessel being in the mean time put into the Hands of the French Consul, on an assurance that she should be forth-coming to answer the determination of the President. The French Minister has now given in contrary evidence, but taken ex parte also. The limits of Jurisdiction having been provisionally settled for Executive cases, and the mode of taking regular testimony as stated in the letter I had the honor of writing you on the 10th. instant, I have now to ask the favor of you to proceed with respect to the ship William according to what was provided in that letter for such cases generally. By a letter of the present date I notify the two ministers of the reference now made to you, relying that they will instruct their Consuls to pay requisite attention to it. I have the Honor to be with great esteem Sir, your most obedient and most humble servant   Th: Jefferson

RC (PHi: Rawle Papers); in the hand of George Taylor, Jr., signed by TJ; at foot of text: "Wm. Rawle Esqr Atty. of the U.S. for the District of Penna." PrC (DLC); unsigned, with day and year added in ink. FC (Lb in DNA: RG 59, DL). Enclosed in TJ to George Washington, [16 Nov. 1793].

After obtaining Cabinet approval for the substance of this letter and Attorney General Edmund Randolph's approval of the draft, TJ submitted the final version to the President on 16 Nov. 1793, and Washington returned it the same day (Washington, *Journal*, 252; Cabinet Opinions on Various Letters, [23 Nov. 1793]).

A letter from Rawle to TJ of 22 Nov. 1793, recorded in SJL as received the same day, has not been found.

From Edmond Charles Genet

M.   New york le 16. 9bre. 1793. l'an 2e. de la Repe. fse.
  Quand l'Interêt et l'amitié unissent étroitement deux peuples Il est du devoir de leurs agents de n'avoir rien de caché entre eux. Pénétré des obligations que m'impose cette maxime Je vous ai Confié depuis que Je suis ici M., mes instructions mes vœux et mes projets et vous devés vous rappeller que lorsqu'une des erruptions du Volcan de St. domingue a fait refluer dans vos ports les forces déstinées à la défense de cette Isle et le Convoi qui devoit passer en france Je vous ai communiqué pour votre information et celle du President des Etats unis les mesures que Je me proposois de prendre pour mettre le convoi en sureté[1] reparer nos vaisseaux reorganiser nos forces et les employer de la maniere la plus utile en attendant qu'elles fussent en état d'inspirer plus de Confiance au Commerce ou qu'une nouvelle Escorte lui eut été envoyée. Après avoir surmonté des obstacles sans nombre après avoir totalement déjoué la Conspiration de Galbaud et changé l'esprit de nos marins[2] Je suis parvenu, M., au but que Je m'étois proposé, nos Vaisseaux au moyen des payments[3] que la tresorerie m'a faits ont été mis dans le meilleur état possible et le Contre Amiral Sercey dans lequel aux préjugés de la Couleur près J'avois reconnu de la fidelité et du talent est sorti avec deux Vaisseaux de ligne deux belles fregattes et deux Corvettes pour aller entreprendre des operations dont vous trouverés le plan dans les Instructions No. 1. mais malheureusement un homme que J'ai connu trop tard[4] a fait avorter par ambition ou par[5] l'étroitesse et la méchanceté de

son esprit ainsi que vous le verrés par le rapport No. 2.[6] un projet que le patriotisme le plus pur avoit conçu. Cet homme est Bompart, Il s'étoit distingué sur l'Embuscade dans un combat contre le Boston, et J'avois cru devoir lui faire donner le Commandement du Jupiter vacant par la demission du Contre Amiral Cambis; mais, ennivré de son premier Succès, persuadé qu'en france il seroit couvert de Lauriers, mécontent de l'amérique ou cependant il avoit été comblé de bontés[7] et entrainé par d'autres sentiments peu délicats[8] Il a abandonné le premier une entreprise à la quelle il avoit acquiescé dans un Conseil de Guerre; s'est separé de l'Escadre a fait route pour france[9] et a donné le signal de l'insurrection aux autres Vaisseaux dont les Equipages ont forcé les Commandants à le suivre. Cette défection M., est très facheuse, mais elle ne laisse cependant point les côtes des Etats unis sans défense et notre Commerce sans protection. Quatre[10] fregattes plusieurs corvettes et[11] d'autres batiments armés mouillent encore dans vos ports. J'en destine une partie à escorter en france quelques batiments fins voiliers chargés de farine de munitions navales[12] et de denrées coloniales. J'employerai les autres à faciliter nos Communications avec les Antilles à chatier les corsaires des Bermudes et de la Providence et à faire respecter ainsi que nous y sommes tenus par les traités le pavillon du peuple Americain[13] qui reçoit tous les Jours de nouveaux outrages. Agréés mon respect.

Dft (DLC: Genet Papers); unsigned; at head of text: "Expe"; above salutation: "Le Cit Genet Ministre &c à Mr. Jefferson &c."; only the most significant emendations are recorded below. Recorded in SJL as received 19 Nov. 1793. Enclosures: (1) Genet, "Mémoire pour servir d'Instruction au Contre Amiral Sercey Commandant les forces Navales de la République francoise en Amerique," n.d., recalling his decision, after the French naval forces repulsed from Saint-Domingue had taken refuge in American harbors, not to send them back to France, but instead to use them to carry out the vast political operations confided to him and to recoup the loss of one of France's most prized possessions; stating that this unexpected arrival of the French fleet, in which intrigues have now been suppressed, the zeal of the crews restored, and order reestablished, combined with the weakness of Spanish forces in the south and of British forces in both north and south, has made the French "les maitres des mers d'amerique"; and communicating a plan of operations in which he directs Sercey to leave the southern expeditions against the brigands of New Providence and the timid Spanish to the *Embuscade*, the *Astrée*, the *Mouche*, and the *Expedition*, whose repair will be completed in two weeks, and to sail with the first favorable wind in command of a squadron consisting of the *Eole*, the *Jupiter*, the *Concorde*, the *Précieuse*, the *Perdrix*, the *Cerf*, the *Important*, the *Cornelia*, and the *Columbia*, together with a company of dragoons and 300 volunteers from Saint-Domingue, the objectives of which were to attack the British fisheries at Newfoundland, capture St. Pierre and Miquelon, intercept the rich convoys descending the St. Lawrence, assault Halifax, demand that its governor release the St. Pierre and Miquelon prisoners, sound the dispositions of the French Acadians, and diffuse among them French revolutionary propaganda, including the principles of the French constitution, French patriotic songs and pamphlets, and Genet's own address to the French inhabitants of Canada, Sercey to be assisted in these propaganda activities by Citizen Mezieres, a young Canadian and secretary to Genet, who was to serve as political agent (Dft in same; consisting of 13 pages in Genet's hand; filed at end of September 1793). (2) Rear Admiral Sercey to Genet, on board the *Eole*, 16 Oct. 1793, enclosing a copy of the *procès-verbal* addressed to him by Captain Bompard and the answer of the assembled captains; and stating that, despite his representations, Bompard sailed for France, thereby inspiring the crew of the *Eole* to demand that Sercey follow his example, and that although he was obliged to yield to force, once in France he would establish Bompard's guilt in provoking an insurrection so detrimental to the French Republic (Tr in same; in English; conjoined to No. 3; with note at head of text: "Défection de l'Escadre. Yesterday morning the French advice boat the cerf commanded [by] the Citizen Labourdonnaye entered this port and delivered to Citizen Genet, Minister Plenipotentiary of the French Republic, the following dispatches"). (3) Extract of unidentified correspondent to Genet, on board the *Eole*, 16 Oct. 1793, stating that Bompard alone gave the signal for insurrection; that yesterday Bompard sent to the *Eole* a *procès-verbal* signed by himself and some masters of the *Jupiter*, who, like their comrades on the *Embuscade*, were aggrieved by Genet's failure to make them officers; that without prior notice Bompard informed the assembled officers that the *Jupiter* was badly rigged, that Genet's intended expedition would only benefit the Americans, that augmenting American power would merely increase American ingratitude, and that they would be unable to sell any prizes they might capture because the English had found ways to have them all restored, wherefore the *Jupiter* would sail immediately to France to be repaired and then to serve the French Republic; that Sercey communicated the *procès-verbal* to the captains of the *Concorde* and the *Précieuse*, who condemned Bompard and promised to follow Sercey's orders; that after refusing a request to remain with the fleet Bompard

hoisted the flag on the *Jupiter*'s mainmast to announce his insurrection; that Bompard's action inspired the hitherto obedient crew of the *Eole* to demand that Sercey follow Bompard's example; that Sercey failed to dissuade the crew, who wanted to return to France after an absence of four years; that in the absence of a formal written statement of opposition from the crew Sercey and his officers decided to pursue the intended expedition; that when the crew became aware of Sercey's decision on the morning of the 16th they drew up a formal opposition forcing Sercey to return to France; and that the writer hopes Americans will attribute the failure of the expedition only to the lassitude of the crews, counterrevolutionary efforts to undermine their morale in Saint-Domingue and America, and the insurrectionary acts of Bompard (Tr in same; in English; subjoined to No. 2).

For a discussion of Genet's abortive naval OPERATIONS against Canada, see Ammon, *Genet Mission*, 120-5.

[1] Preceding five words interlined.
[2] Preceding fifteen words written in the margin.
[3] Genet here canceled "à terme."
[4] Genet here canceled in the margin "un homme que J'avois comblé d'éloges et."
[5] Preceding three words written in the margin.
[6] Preceding nine words and digit written in the margin.
[7] Clause to this point written in the margin.
[8] Preceding two words interlined in place of "secrets."
[9] Preceding five words written in the margin.
[10] Word interlined in place of "trois."
[11] Genet here canceled "des corsaires."
[12] Preceding three words interlined.
[13] Remainder of sentence inserted.

From Edmond Charles Genet

New york. le 16. 9bre. 1793. l'an 2e.
Un navire americain[1] qui avoit été chargé par le Ministre des affres. Eteres.[2] de m'apporter des depêches et des Imprimes ayant ete visité par des Corsaires anglois a[3] sacrifié mes lettres et n'a pu me remettre que[4]

les Imprimés. J'ai choisi parmi ces derniers les pièces qui pouvoient le plus vous interesser. Je vous prie d'accepter celles dont il me reste des doubles et de me rendre quand vous en aurés pris connoissances celles que J'ai renfermées sous une bande particuliere. Parmi les premieres vous trouverés plusieurs éxemplaires En francois et en anglois[5] de la nouvelle Constitution du peuple françois qui a réuni tous les ésprits comblé les vœux et réalisé les ésperances de tous les Citoyens vertueux de tous les hommes[6] veritablement pénétrés des principes sublimes[7] de l'égalité.

Dft (DLC: Genet Papers); unsigned; above salutation: "Le Cit Genet &c à Mr Jefferson &c." Recorded in SJL as received 19 Nov. 1793. Enclosures not found.

For the NOUVELLE CONSTITUTION adopted by the National Convention on 24 June 1793, see John H. Stewart, ed., *A Documentary Survey of the French Revolution* (New York, 1951), 454-68.

[1] Word interlined.
[2] Preceding six words written in the margin.
[3] Genet here canceled "suivant l'us."
[4] Genet here canceled "brochures et les Memoires que."
[5] Preceding five words written in the margin.
[6] Altered from "de tous les hommes de bien de tous les Citoyens vertueux et."
[7] Word interlined.

To John Kean

Germantown Nov. 16. 1793.

Th: Jefferson presents his compliments to Mr. Kean and congratulates him sincerely on his and Mrs. Kean's having escaped the dangers of the season.

Thinking it possible that the members of Congress (retaining the horrors of the yellow fever which prevail at a distance) may remove to Lancaster, and on so short notice as to prevent Th:J. from settling his affairs in Philadelphia, he thinks it best to do that while he has time, and for that purpose it would be convenient for him to command his salary of the present quarter. He therefore begs the favor of Mr. Kean to put the note which accompanies this into the proper channel for discount; and if he will be so kind, when it is decided on, as to send a line of information for Th:J. to his office on Market street, he will be much obliged to him.

Will the form of this note render an order from Mr. Taylor requisite to authorize Th:J. to recieve the money?

RC (NN: Ford Collection); addressed: "Mr. Kean Cashier of the Bank of the US." PrC (DLC). Tr (ViU: Edgehill-Randolph Papers); 19th-century copy. Enclosure: Promissory note to George Taylor, Jr., 18 Nov. 1793, for 875 dollars payable at the Bank of the United States sixty days after date for value received (PrC in DLC, subjoined to PrC of TJ to Taylor, 16 Nov. 1793; Tr in ViU: Edgehill-Randolph Papers, 19th-century copy, subjoined to Tr of TJ to Taylor, 16 Nov. 1793). Letter and enclosure enclosed in TJ to Taylor, 16 Nov. 1793.

TJ recorded on 19 Nov. 1793 that the Bank of the United States gave him a credit for $865.82 in exchange for his note (MB, 19 Nov. 1793).

From Richard Söderström

SIR   Philadelphia Nover. 16: 1793.

The enclosed Copy of a Letter to me dated the 26. May from Sir Fried: Sparre Grand Chancellor of Sweden I recieved in the end August, and Should have had the honor of transmitting you the same long before now, if Sickness and a great deal of business had not prevented me, for which reasons, and as no business to this Country has since occured respecting the Danish Government, you will I hope excuse the delay. I am informed that the president of the United States has established some Rules for European Consuls to govern them in Cases of Captured Vessels being brought in to this Country by the Nations at War. If so I shall esteem it a particular favor if you will be so obliging as to furnish me therewith, to enable me to make such arrangements respecting the same agreeable to the instructions I have recieved.

On the 12: Instant I presented to General Knox a Memorial of Lucas Gibbes and others relative to the Captured Sloop Betzy. Said Memorial I know ought first to have been presented to you, but being unwilling to oppose the wish of the Memorialists and their Council, and in order to gain time if possible I delivered it to Said Gentleman from whom I obtained an answer. This proceeding I request you to pardon, though it was not done through ignorance of the proper mode, but as mentioned before to oblige those people. I at the time offered to General Knox to have the Memorial altered, and to deliver it to you with a letter, which he told me in the present circumstances was unnecessary; Nevertheless I now take the liberty of forwarding you a Copy thereof regularly directed. I am very unhappy in finding that a decision of this business is unavoidably so long delayed, however I hope in the end to get such Satisfaction that will pay for the delay. With respect I have the Honor to remain Sir Your most Obd: hble. Sert   RICHD: SÖDERSTRÖM

RC (DNA: RG 59, NFC); at foot of text: "The Honble. Thos: Jefferson"; endorsed by TJ as received 19 Nov. 1793 and so recorded in SJL. Enclosures: (1) Grand Chancellor Fredrik Sparre to Söderström, Stockholm, 28 May 1793, stating that since Denmark now had the same interests as Sweden with respect to commerce and neutrality toward France, the King wished him to act in concert with the Danish consul at Philadelphia and to communicate to him all the steps he may have to take in consequence of Sparre's 5 Mch. circular letter; that if there was no Danish consul in Philadelphia, he was to attend to the interests of Denmark with the same zeal he had shown for those of Sweden, especially since the King has been informed that the King of

Denmark had issued similar orders to Danish consuls in ports without a Swedish consul; and that he encloses for his further instruction a copy of the ordinance published at the King's order by Admiral General, the Count of Ehrensvärd, concerning actions to be taken for the convoy provided for the Swedish merchant marine (Tr in same; in French; with Söderström's 16 Nov. 1793 attestation subjoined). (2) Memorial from Lucas Gibbes and Others, 12 Nov. 1793.

To George Taylor, Jr.

Germantown Nov. 16. 1793.

Th: Jefferson presents his compliments to Mr. Taylor. Thinking it possible that the members of Congress, retaining the horrors of the yellow fever which prevail at a distance, may remove to Lancaster, and on so short notice as to prevent Th:J. from settling his affairs in Philadelphia, to which place he should not return again, Lancaster being so far on his way home,[1] he thinks it best to do that while he has time, and for that purpose it would be convenient for him to command his salary of the present quarter. As the rules of the bank require an endorser he begs the favor of Mr. Taylor to endorse the inclosed note for him, and to put it under cover to Mr. Kean, with the note directed to him, and to send it to him immediately.

Th:J. has received Mr. Wythe's money, on which fund he will furnish office expences here.

PrC (DLC); with enclosure to TJ to John Kean, 16 Nov. 1793, subjoined. Tr (ViU: Edgehill-Randolph Papers); 19th-century copy; with enclosure to TJ to Kean, 16 Nov. 1793, subjoined. Enclosures: TJ to Kean, 16 Nov. 1793, and enclosure.

[1] Preceding two clauses interlined.

From Volney

paris 16 9bre 1793

J'ai l'honneur de rappeller à Monsieur jefferson le souvenir d'une personne pour qui le Sien est lié à des tems et à des événémens qui en ont consacré l'intérêt. Je le prie d'agréer un petit ouvrage qui du moins aura le merite de ne pas le distraire longtems de Ses occupations Multipliées. Si cette bagatelle obtenait son suffrage, Si des élémens de ce genre, developpés Sur plusieurs Sujets avaient des Succès en amérique, j'aurais doublement à regretter d'avoir vû M'echapper le Voyage philosophique que le conseil M'avait chargé d'y executer.   C. VOLNEY

RC (DLC); endorsed by TJ as received 31 Mch. 1794 and so recorded in SJL. Enclosure: C. F. C. Volney, *La Loi Naturelle; ou catéchisme du Citoyen Français* (Paris, 1793). Constantin François Chasseboeuf Volney (1757-1820), the noted French Idéologue, linguist, orientalist, historian, and geographer, became for a few years one of

TJ's close acquaintances and regular correspondents. Having acquired a lifelong interest in classical languages while attending the colleges of Ancenis and Angers, Volney moved to Paris in 1775 in order to study medicine, and through the friendship of Pierre Jean Georges Cabanis, a fellow Idéologue whose work TJ later admired, became a member of the circles around Baron d'Holbach and Mme. Helvétius, whose philosophical materialism became one of the keynotes of his intellectual life. After making his mark with a short work on Herodotian chronology, Volney spent the years 1783-85 in Egypt and Syria, mastering Arabic and carefully observing the customs and habits of the people. On the basis of this experience he published *Voyage en Syrie et en Égypte*, 2 vols. (Paris, 1787), a work that made him famous throughout Europe and that TJ purchased in its second edition soon after publication (Sowerby, No. 3950). Volney met TJ in Paris and later was instrumental in providing him with a plan by an unidentified author for the use of naval force against Algiers that favorably impressed the Secretary of State (Vol. 18: 406-7, 416-22). Volney's strong support of the French Revolution as a member of the States General and the National Assembly led to his most famous work, *Les Ruines; ou Méditation sur les Révolutions des Empires*, 2 vols. (Geneva, 1791), an eloquent attack on political despotism and revealed religion which so strongly impressed TJ that he later secretly collaborated with Joel Barlow in preparing an English translation of it (Sowerby, No. 1277). Arrested for debt on the same day

he enclosed in this letter the PETIT OU-VRAGE that continued his attack on revealed religion and called for a scientifically-based system of morality, Volney was forced to postpone the VOYAGE PHILOSOPHIQUE he had been planning under the aegis of the French government to observe conditions in the United States. It was not until October 1795 that Volney was able to begin a private visit to the United States, in the course of which he made an extended tour that included parts of the South and the cis-Mississippi West in 1796, spending three weeks visiting TJ at Monticello, a journey that led to the publication of his *Tableau du Climat et du Sol des Etats-Unis d'Amérique*, 2 vols. (Paris, 1803), a pioneering study of American geology and climatology (Sowerby, No. 4032). During his American sojourn Volney exchanged twenty letters with TJ, who suspended the correspondence after Volney, whom Federalists wrongly suspected of being a French agent, sailed for France in June 1798, fearing arrest under the Alien Act. TJ resumed the correspondence after his inauguration as President, exchanging fourteen letters with Volney on political and scientific subjects over the next five years, by which time Volney had become an influential figure in French intellectual and political life through his close association with Napoleon (DSB; Jean Gaulmier, *Un Grand Témoin de la Révolution et de l'Empire: Volney* [Paris, 1959]; Gilbert Chinard, *Volney et l'Amérique d'après des documents inédits et sa correspondance avec Jefferson* [Baltimore, 1923]).

To George Washington

[16 Nov. 1793]

Th: Jefferson with his respects to the President has the honor to inclose for his information the following letters written in consequence of the two last consultations preceding his departure. There being quadruplicates of most of them, the trouble of looking over them will be proportionably diminished to the President.

Nov. 8. four letters to the foreign ministers on the *extent* of our jurisdiction
10. Circular to the district-attornies on the *same* subject and on the mode of settling the cases which arise.

do. four letters to the foreign ministers on the mode of settling the cases which arise of captures within our jurisdiction

*do. to Messrs. Viar and Jaudenes, covering answer of Govr. of Kentuckey as to military enterprizes projected there, and the information of the Govr. of N. Carolina as to the Spanish prize carried in there.

†13. to Mr. Hammond on the inexecution of the treaty.

†   to Govr. Moultrie. on Mr. Genet's suggestion of military enterprises projected.

*   to Judge Morris, inclosing Fitz Freeman's petition.

14. to Mr. Hammond on the Roehampton and Industry.

to the District Atty. of Maryland on the brig Coningham.

to do. on the condemnation of the Roehampton and Pilgrim by the Fr. Consul

15. to do. of Pensylva. on the Ship William.

to Mr. Genet. on same subject

to Mr. Hammond on same subject.

*these are on subjects not referred to our consultation.

†these were in consequence of determinations at our consultations, but the letters, being in plain cases, were not communicated for inspection to the other gentlemen, after they were written.

there are some other letters agreed on, but not yet copied.

RC (DNA: RG 59, MLR); undated; endorsed by Bartholomew Dandridge, Jr.: "From the Secy. of State 16. Nov: 1793." PrC (DLC: TJ Papers, 94: 16216). Tr (Lb in DNA: RG 59, SDC). Recorded in SJPL under 14 Nov. 1793, but see Washington, *Journal*, 251-2.

To Eli Whitney

SIR   Germantown Nov. 16. 1793.

Your favor of Octob. 15. inclosing a drawing of your cotton gin, was received on the 6th. inst. The only requisite of the law now uncomplied with is the forwarding a model, which being received your patent may be made out and delivered to your order immediately.

As the state of Virginia, of which I am, carries on houshold manufactures of cotton to a great extent, as I also do myself, and one of our great embarrasments is the clearing the cotton of the seed, I feel a considerable interest in the success of your invention, for family use. Permit me therefore to ask information from you on these points, has the machine been thoroughly tried in the ginning of cotton, or is it as yet but a machine of theory? what quantity of cotton has it cleaned on an average of several days, and worked by hand, and by how many hands? what will be the cost of one of them made to be worked by hand? Favorable answers to these questions[1] would induce me to engage one of them to be forwarded to Richmond for me. Wishing to hear from you on the subject, I am Sir Your most obedt. servt   Th: Jefferson

P.S. Is this the machine advertised the last year by Pearce at the Patterson Manufactory?

RC (CtY: Eli Whitney Papers); addressed: "Mr. Eli Whitney New-Haven Connecticut"; franked, stamped, and postmarked. PrC (DLC). Tr (ViU: Edgehill-Randolph Papers); 19th-century copy.

TJ had written William PEARCE on 15 Dec. 1792 inquiring about his machine for cleaning cotton.

The personal interest TJ manifested in Whitney's cotton gin typified the widespread expectations generated by reports of the machine. It was later related that, when the patent was taken out at the Department of State, "Mr. Jefferson, who was then at the head of that Department, and who will be admitted a competent Judge, declared his opinion, that it was the most useful and important invention which had then been recorded in that office" (Decius Wadsworth to Joshua Coit, Savannah, 12 Dec. 1797, CtY: Whitney Papers, Letterbook of Miller & Whitney).

TJ's interest in such a device dates back at least to the 1770s, when he had purchased crude hand cotton gins. Although TJ apparently never acquired one of Whitney's machines, in 1806 he ordered some sheet iron for a cotton gin, talked thereafter of raising cotton, and sometimes ordered or tried to order seed, but there is virtually no evidence that he did so successfully (MB, 18 Dec. 1776, and note, 18 Aug. 1777, 18 Sep. 1779; Betts, *Farm Book*, 247, 250, 361).

[1] TJ here canceled "might."

From Edmond Charles Genet

M   New york. le 17. 9bre. 1793. l'an 2. de la Repe.

J'ai reçu la lettre que vous m'avés fait l'honneur de m'écrire le 10 de ce mois sur les formalités a observer de la part de nos Consuls lorsqu'ils auront a prononcer sur la validité de prises reclamées comme ayant été[1] faites dans la Jurisdiction des Etats unis. Je leur transmettrai cette pièce, M., et Je vous la renvoye afin que[2] vous ayés la bonté d'y apposer votre signature.

Dft (DLC: Genet Papers); unsigned; above salutation: "Le Cit Genet &c à Mr Jefferson &c." FC (same); in English. Recorded in SJL as received 20 Nov. 1793. Enclosure: TJ to Foreign Ministers in the United States, 10 Nov. 1793.

[1] Preceding four words written in the margin.
[2] Preceding four words interlined in place of "et Je vous prie en Conséquence de vouloir bien y apposer."

To Mary Jefferson

Germantown Nov. 17. 1793

No letter yet from my dear Maria, who is so fond of writing, so punctual in her correspondencies! I enjoin as a penalty that the next be written in French.—Now for news. The fever is entirely vanished from Philadelphia. Not a single person has taken infection since the great rains about the 1st. of the month, and those who had it before are either dead or recovered. All the inhabitants who had fled are returning into the city, probably will all be returned in the course of the ensuing week. The President has been into the city, but will probably remain here till the meeting of Congress to form a point of union for them before they will have had time to gather knolege and courage. I have not yet been in, not because there is a shadow of danger, but because I am afoot.— Thomas is returned into my service. His wife and child went into town the day we left them. They then had the infection of the yellow fever, were taken two or three days after, and both died. Had we staid those two or three days longer, they would have been taken at our house. I have heard nothing of Miss Cropper. Her trunk remains at our house. Mrs. Fullerton left Philadelphia. Mr. and Mrs. Rittenhouse remained there but have escaped the fever.—Follow closely your music, reading, sewing, house-keeping, and love me as I do you, most affectionately.

Th: Jefferson

P.S. Tell Mr. Randolph that General Wayne has had a convoy of 22. waggons of provision and 70. men cut off in his rear by the Indians.

PrC (DLC); at foot of text: "Miss Maria Jefferson." Tr (MHi); 19th-century copy.

TJ employed THOMAS Lapseley as his personal coachman from 17 May to 17 Sep. 1793, and hired him briefly as temporary office keeper for the State Department in mid-November (MB, 17 May, 17 Sep., 14 Nov., 6 Dec. 1793). Although an early newspaper report indicated that in the 17 Oct. 1793 attack near Fort St. Clair on a CONVOY supporting the army of Major General Anthony Wayne 22. WAGGONS and 70. MEN had been lost, Wayne soon reported that the engagement resulted in the loss of seventy horses, with twenty-four men killed or missing and the wagons and their contents recovered largely undamaged (Lexington *Kentucky Gazette*, 26 Oct., 2 Nov. 1793; ASP, *Indian Affairs*, I, 361; Washington, *Journal*, 260-1).

To Herman LeRoy

DEAR SIR   Germantown Nov. 17. 1793.

I have duly received your favor of the 13th. and learn from it a very different state of things from what either my son in law or my self were apprised of. However, tho' the debt be much greater than I had under-

Mortality Table on the Yellow Fever Epidemic

Eli Whitney's Model of his Cotton Gin

Jefferson's Notes on Alexander Hamilton and on Two Cabinet Meetings

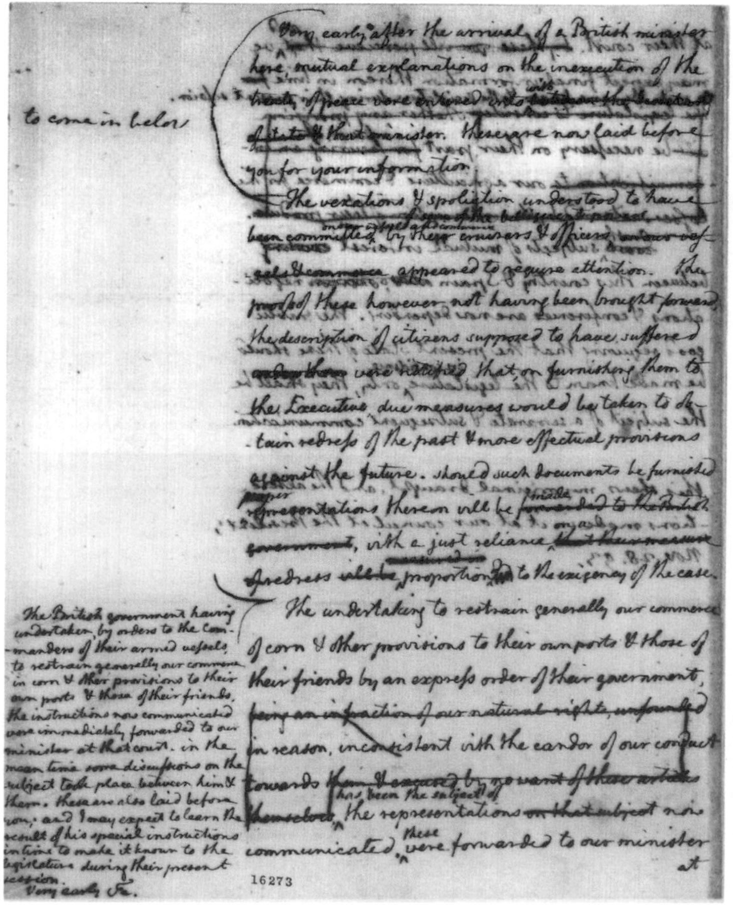
Page from Jefferson's First Draft of George Washington's

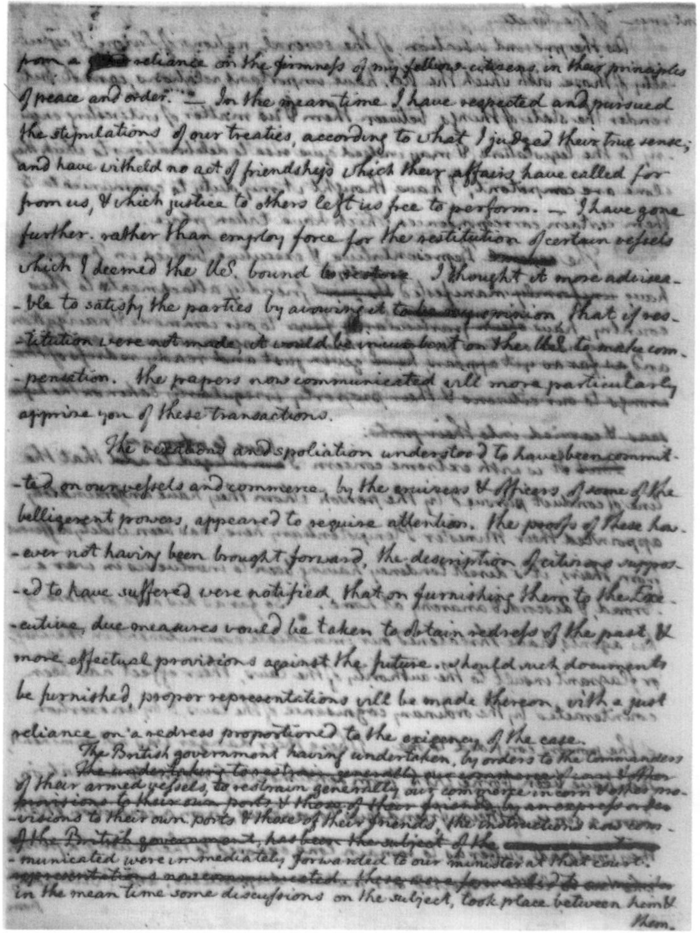
Page from Jefferson's Second Draft of George Washington's

A
MESSAGE

OF THE

PRESIDENT

OF THE

UNITED STATES

TO

CONGRESS

RELATIVE

TO

FRANCE AND GREAT-BRITAIN.

DELIVERED DECEMBER 5, 1793.

WITH THE PAPERS THEREIN REFERRED TO.

TO WHICH ARE ADDED

THE

FRENCH ORIGINALS.

PUBLISHED BY ORDER OF THE HOUSE OF REPRESENTATIVES.

PHILADELPHIA:
PRINTED BY CHILDS AND SWAINE.

M,DCC,XCIII.

Title Page of Pamphlet Containing Selections from
Jefferson's Correspondence with Edmond Charles Genet,
George Hammond, and Thomas Pinckney

Page from the First State of Jefferson's Report on Commerce
substituted after 13 Apr. 1792

Page from the First State of Jefferson's Report on Commerce
completed before 26 Aug. 1791

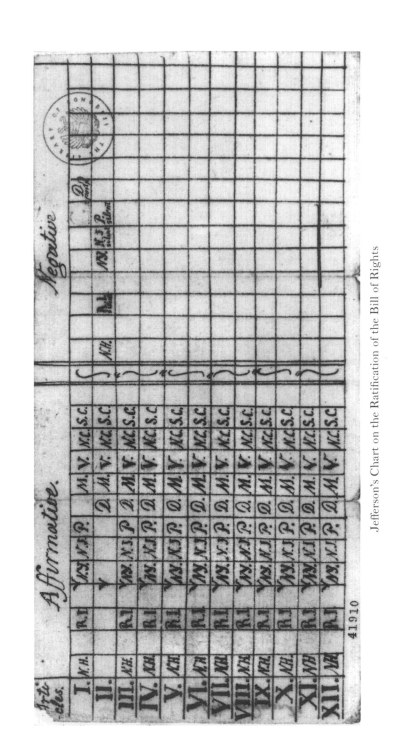

Jefferson's Chart on the Ratification of the Bill of Rights

The Great Clock at Monticello

stood, the coupling of Dover in the mortgage is a more than proportionate increase of the security. All I have therefore to wish at present is that the proceeds of the protested bill may be first applied in diminution of the debt, and Dover be applied before Varina be called on, in which case the latter will be safe, as Dover will sell for the double of the residue of the debt, after the proceeds of the protested bill shall have been applied to it's diminution. In the mean time I advise my son in law to consign his wheat to you, and to proceed in providing all the monies he can in your hands, to remain there as his separate property, subject to be hereafter declared by him to have been a paiment at the time in exoneration of Varina specially, or to any other order of his. This appears to me his safest course, relying at the same time on your indulgence by directing your agent to draw his paiments from the protested bill and Dover as far as they will go, and before he proceeds to levy them on Varina. I am with great regard and with my most friendly respects to Mr. Bayard, Dear Sir Your most obedt servt   TH: JEFFERSON

RC (PHi: Sprague Collection); at foot of text: "Mr. LeRoy." PrC (MHi). Tr (ViU: Edgehill-Randolph Papers); 19th-century copy.

LeRoy's FAVOR OF THE 13TH., recorded in SJL as received from New York on 15 Nov. 1793, has not been found.

To James Madison

Germantown. Nov. 17. 1793.

I have got good lodgings for Monroe and yourself, that is to say, a good room with a fire place and two beds, in a pleasant and convenient position, with a quiet family. They will breakfast you, but you must mess in a tavern; there is a good one across the street. This is the way in which all must do, and all I think will not be able to get even half beds.—The President will remain here I believe till the meeting of Congress, merely to form a point of union for them before they can have acquired information and courage. For at present there does not exist a single subject in the disorder, no new infection having taken place since the great rains the 1st. of the month, and those before infected being dead or recovered. There is no doubt you will set in Philadelphia and therefore I have not given Monroe's letter to Seckel. I do not write to him, because I know not whether he is at present moving by sea or by land, and if by the latter, I presume you can communicate to him.— Wayne has had a convoy of 22. waggons of provision and 70. men cut off 15 miles[1] in his rear by the Indians. 6. of the men were found on the spot scalped, the rest supposed taken. He had nearly reached Fort Hamilton. R. has given notice that he means to resign. Genet by more and more denials of powers to the President and ascribing them to Congress, is evidently endeavoring to sow tares between them, and at any event to curry favor with the latter to whom he means to turn his appeal, finding it was not likely to be well received[2] with the people. Accept, both of you, my sincere affections.

RC (DLC: Madison Papers); unsigned; at foot of text: "Mr. Madison." PrC (DLC).

In a private letter to the President written a week earlier, Attorney General Edmund Randolph had hinted that he might have to RESIGN because he feared that the yellow fever epidemic would reduce his law practice in Philadelphia and force him to return to Virginia. Randolph also confessed to the President "some difficulty in asking from the Secretary of State access to the public archives" without revealing his plan to write "a history and review" of Washington's administration (Randolph to Washington, 10 Nov. 1793, DLC: Washington Papers).

[1] Preceding two words interlined.
[2] Preceding three words interlined in place of "succeed."

To Thomas Mann Randolph, Jr.

DEAR SIR   Germantown Nov. 17. 1793.

Immediately on the receipt of your letter of Oct. 31. I extracted what was necessary from it and wrote to Mr. LeRoy. His answer has produced a state of things with which you are probably unacquainted; which however, tho it presents a much broader scene, may present also more security for you, than that which we had understood to exist. The debt from Colo. Randolph to Mr. LeRoy and others is in fact about £5000. A protested bill of D. Ross's for £2000. has been delivered to LeRoy, to be applied towards paiment, when recovered. Besides this, Dover as well as Varina are mortgaged for the whole. The protested bill is in suit, but[1] it's proceeds will not be waited for if the mortgaged subjects can sooner be pushed to judgment and sale. This presents a critical, tho, if well-managed, a safe process of things, the object of which should be to retard the proceedings on the mortgage, so that those on the protested bill may get a-head, and be first applied. The interest which the marriage settlement of Varina has vested in the parties to it, authorizes them to become parties to the suit as plaintiffs, or to be made so as defendants. But which of the two will produce the greatest delay, I am unable to say. If the protested bill was once fairly ahead, I should have no hesitation to advise their entering the field at once[2] as plaintiffs stating their interest, that it is on the double consideration of marriage, and of a counter-settlement, and praying the Chancellor to decree the application, first[3] of the protested bill (if it is recovered in time) and next of Dover, in discharge of the debt and in exoneration of the marriage settlement, at least as far as they would go; and we know they would be sufficient. There is no doubt the Chancellor would give us such a decree: but if the Protested bill is not sufficiently ahead, perhaps we might give it more time by putting off the cross-bill as long as we may without losing the effect of it towards stopping the sale. To decide on this it appears necessary that you should procure

a copy of the mortgage or mortgages (for if the lands are separately mortgaged for separate portions of the debt, it changes the case.)

a copy of the bill of foreclosure.

a certificate of the steps which have already been taken in the suit, and it's present state.

a certificate of the present state of the action against Ross on the Protested bill, and an estimate from some judicious lawyer of the utmost length of time to which Ross can stave off *actual paiment*.

These you will probably be able to obtain by the time I come home, when, if there be no danger in waiting so long, we will consult what is to be done.

I inclose you Mr. LeRoy's letter. Should you consign your wheat to him, I would advise you to do it on the express condition, that he shall hold the money in his hands as your separate property, subject to be declared hereafter by yourself to have been a paiment, at the time, in set-off against the effects of the mortgage on Varina, or to be otherwise subject to your order at your pleasure. In this way you may go on making your payments for Edgehill so as to protect Varina, as far as they will go, even if the other mortgaged estate should not be a sufficient shield. I received yesterday your favor of the 7th. Present my love to my dear Martha and accept assurances yourself of my sincere affection.

TH: JEFFERSON

P.S. I inclose you a letter from Mr. Hawkins and ask your attention to the subjects of it till I come home.

RC (DLC); at foot of first page: "Mr. Randolph." PrC (CSmH). Enclosures: (1) Herman LeRoy to TJ, 13 Nov. 1793 (see note to TJ to LeRoy, 17 Nov. 1793). (2) Benjamin Hawkins to TJ, 28 Oct. 1793.

[1] TJ here canceled "there will be no relaxation in the."
[2] Preceding two words interlined.
[3] Word interlined.

From James Currie

HBLE SIR   Richmond Novr. 18th. 1793

I very lately did myself the honor of addressing you wherein I sollicited your own very particular and pointed attention to my affair vs. Griffin. I have only further on this head to inform you that he G. last Henrico Court, has rendred in a schedule of his Estate, and taken The Oath of Insolvency. I have never seen him being sick at that time I could not be out as usual. I thought proper to give you (as my particular friend) this information, that you may Order and have done whatever (if you please) my now situation requires. I wish Mr. Bartons or his Successor's agency may not (I hope it will not) make a very essential difference to me in this business. I hope youll excuse my so frequently intruding upon you in this affair and believe me always, with the most respectfull deference—Dr Sir yr most Ob H Serv   JAS. CURRIE

RC (MHi); endorsed by TJ as received 26 Nov. 1793 and so recorded in SJL.

From Philip Mazzei

MOST DEAR SIR   Pisa, 18 9bre, 1793.

I received your last, dated 7 Jany. 1792, in Warsaw, and answer'd it the 23d. of May, inclosed to Mr. Short in Paris. I sent him a copy of it in Holland, on the 11th. of Feby. last, and a second copy, with some additions, I directed to you, via London, the 19th. of May. Mr. Short moved so rapidly from one Country to another (by what I have understood) that I doubt whether any one of my letters ever reached him. I never received an answer from him, nor do I Know where he now is. Hoping however, that my second copy, via London, is come to hand, I shall not for the present repeat the contents of it. This is only meant to inform you, that I have been obliged to have recours to our Friends Vansstaphorst in Holland for assistance in my distressed situation, and that they have been so good as to lend me 2,251:13:–: florins, Holland Currency; in consequence of which, I beg you to remit to them whatever sum, or sums of money you may collect from any Kind of the little property I have still remaining in America, as I have offered it to them for their security, having nothing else so certain[1] to offer. I hope soon to hear from you, and remain for ever, most Dr. Sr., your most Ob. and most Affe. Fr. [& Serv.]   PH. M.

Dft (DLC: Mazzei Papers); at foot of text: "Ths. Jefferson Esqre"; two words illegible. Recorded in SJL as received 10 June 1794.

Mazzei's letters to TJ of the 11TH. OF FEB. and the 19TH. OF MAY 1793, recorded in SJL as received from Pisa on 23 Jan. 1796 and 6 Sep. 1793, respectively, and the missing Dupl and Tripl of his 23 May 1792 letter recorded in SJL as received on the same dates, have not been found. In regard to these letters, Mazzei wrote the following note on the address cover of TJ's letter to him of 7 Jan. 1792:

"Jefferson,   7 Genn:
rispta.   23 Maggio   } 1792
la copia   11 Febbr.   1793
2da. copia 19 Maggio 1793 ₱ Braccini, ₱ Londra.
In questa confermo il contenuto nella sopradda.; parlo della missione ai pirati Affri-

cani, che potrebbe riuscire, perché io non potrei esservi sospetto; gli chiedo dei materiali per un 2do. supplemento, pensando io di stampar l'originale del mio libro, e qual che ora costituisca il carattiere di cittadino, e l'escluda; gli chiedo; suoi ordini per servirlo di qui, e che mi mandi dei semi di *Squackes* piccoli di più sorte.

18 9bre 1793
La copia è qui inclusa." The Editors supply the following translation:

"Jefferson, 7 Jan.
Answer 23 May   1792
Copy 11 Feb. 1793
2d. copy 19 May 1793 ℔ Braccini,
℔ London.

In this letter I confirm the contents of the aforesaid letter; I discuss the mission to the African pirates, which could well succeed, because I could not be suspected; I ask him for materials for a second supplement, since I am thinking of printing the original of my book, and what now constitutes the character of a citizen, and what excludes it; I ask him for his orders so that I may serve him from here, and that he send me the seeds of several sorts of small squashes.

18 Nov. 1793
The copy is enclosed here." Concerning Mazzei's book, see Howard R. Marraro, "Unpublished Mazzei Letters to Jefferson," WMQ, 3d ser., I (1944), 381n.

[1] Preceding two words interlined.

Notes of Cabinet Meetings on Edmond Charles Genet and the President's Address to Congress

[18 Nov. 1793]

Nov. 8. 93. At a Conference at the President's where I read several letters of Mr. Genet, on finishing one of them, I asked what should be the answer? The Presidt. thereupon took occasion to observe that Mr. Genet's conduct continued to be of so extraordinary a nature that he meant to propose to our serious consideration Whether he should not have his functions discontinued and be ordered away? He went lengthily into observations on his conduct, to raise against the Executive 1. the people, 2. the state governments 3. the Congress. He shewed he felt the venom of Genet's pen, but declared he would not chuse his insolence should be regarded any further than as it might be thought to affect the honor of the country. Hamilton and Knox readily and zealously argued for dismissing Mr. Genet. Randolph opposed it with firmness, and pretty lengthily. The Presidt. replied to him lengthily, and concluded by saying he did not wish to have the thing hastily decided but that we should consider of it, and give our opinions on his return from Reading and Lancaster. Accordingly

Nov. 18. We met at his house. Read new volumes of Genet's letters received since the President's departure, then took up the discussion of the subjects of communication to Congress. 1. The Proclmn. E.R. read the statement he had prepared. Hamilton did not like it, said much about his own views, that the Presidt. had a right to declare his opinion to our citizens and foreign nations that it was not the interest of this country to join in the war and that we were under no obligation to join in it, that tho' the declaration would not legally bind Congress, yet the Presidt. had a right to give his opinion of it, and he was against any expln. in the speech which should yeild that he did not intend that foreign nations should consider it as a declaration of neutrality future as well as present, that he understood it as meant to give them that sort of assurance and satisfaction, and to say otherwise now would be a deception on them. He was for the Pres's using such expressions as should neither affirm his right to make such a declaration to foreign nations, nor yeild it. R. and myself opposed the right of the Presidt. to declare any thing future on the qu. shall there or shall there not be war? and that no such thing was intended, that H's construction of the effect of the proclmn. would have[1] been a determination of the question of the *guarantee* which we both denied to have intended, and I had at the time declared the Executive incompetent to. R. said he meant that foreign nations should understand it as an intimation of the Pr's opinion that neutrality would be our interest. I declared my meaning to have been that foreign nations should understand no such thing, that on the contrary I would have chosen them to be doubtful and to come and bid for our neutrality. I admitted the Presidt. having received the nation at the close of Congr. in a state of peace, was bound to preserve them in that state till Congr. should meet again, and might proclaim any thing which went no farther.   The Pres. declared he never had an idea that he could bind Congress against declaring war, or that any thing contained in his proclmn. could look beyond the first day of their meeting, his main view was to keep our people in peace, he apologized for the use of the term neutrality in his answers, and justified it by having submitted the first of them (that to the merchants wherein it was used) to our consideration, and we had not objected to the term. He concluded in the end that Colo. H. should prepare a paragraph on this subject for the speech, and it should then be considered.—We were here called to dinner.

After dinner the *renvoi* of Genet was proposed by himself. I opposed it on these topics. France the only nation on earth sincerely our friend.— The measure so harsh a one that no precedent is produced where it has not been followed by war—our messenger has now been gone 84. days, consequently we may hourly expect the return and to be relieved by their revocation of him. Were it now resolved on, it would be 8. or 10. days before the matter on which the order should be founded could be selected, arranged, discussed, and forwarded. This would bring us within 4 or 5 days of the meeting of Congress, would it not be better to wait and see how the pulse of that body, new as it is, would beat—they are with us now, probably, but such a step as this may carry many over to Genet's side.—Genet will not obey the order. &c &c. The Presidt. asked me what I would do if Genet sent the accusation to us to be communicated to Congr. as he threatened in the letter to Moultrie? I said I would not send it to Congr. but either put it in the newsp. or send it back to him to be published if he pleased. Other questions and answers were put and answered in a quicker altercation than I ever before saw the President use.—Hamilton was for the *renvoi*, spoke much of the dignity of the nation, that they were now to form their character, that our conduct now would tempt or deter other foreign ministers from treating us in the same manner, touched on the Pr's personal feelings— did not believe Fr. would make it a cause of war, if she did we ought to do what was right and meet the consequences &c. Knox on the same side, and said he thought it very possible Mr. Genet would either declare us a department of France, or levy troops here and endeavor to reduce us to obedience.—R. of my opinion, and argued chiefly on the[2] resurrection of popularity to Genet which might be produced by this measure, that at present he was dead in the public opinion if we would but leave him so.   The Presidt. lamented there was not an unanimity among us, that as it was we had left him exactly where we found him. And so it ended.

MS (DLC); entirely in TJ's hand; written in one sitting below the "Anas" entry for 15 Nov. 1793 on both sides of the first of two sheets also containing "Anas" entries for 21 and 23 Nov. 1793. Included in the "Anas."

For earlier occasions on which the Cabinet considered proposals that French minister Edmond Charles Genet HAVE HIS FUNCTIONS DISCONTINUED AND BE ORDERED AWAY, see Notes of Cabinet Meeting on Edmond Charles Genet, 23 July, 1 Aug. 1793.

With the first session of the third Congress scheduled to convene on 2 Dec. 1793, the President and Cabinet here TOOK UP DISCUSSION OF THE SUBJECTS OF COMMUNICATION to that body, focusing chiefly on the presentation and justification of actions taken by the administration under the policy of neutrality it had declared in the expanded European war. Attorney General Edmund Randolph's missing STATEMENT on the President's 22 Apr. 1793 Proclamation of Neutrality and the rival PARAGRAPH prepared by Hamilton at Washington's behest after this meeting are described in Notes of Cabinet Meeting on the President's Address to Congress, 21 Nov. 1793, and note. For the earlier Cabinet debate over the form the Proclamation should take and the continued validity of the United States GUARANTEE of the French West Indies stipulated in the 1778 treaty of alliance, see Cabinet Opinion on Washington's Questions on Neutrality and the Alliance with France, [19 Apr. 1793], and note; and Editorial Note on Jefferson's opinion on the treaties with France, at 28 Apr. 1793.

The President had used THE TERM NEUTRALITY in his May 1793 answer TO THE MERCHANTS of Philadelphia (see James Madison to TJ, [22 Aug. 1793], and note). OUR MESSENGER: William Culver. On Genet's 15 Oct. 1793 LETTER TO MOULTRIE, see note to TJ to Madison, 2 Nov. 1793).

[1] TJ here canceled "precluded."
[2] TJ here canceled "advantage this."

Memorandums to George Taylor, Jr.

Notes for Mr. Taylor. Nov. 18. 1793.

Mr. Chapman to be engaged, by the day, letting him know that the job will probably be only of from 2. to 4. weeks.

Some one to come here immediately. It may be any one of the gentlemen who would rather be here than in Philadelphia; or if none of them would prefer it, it may be Mr. Chapman or any other hired person.

Mr. Taylor will be pleased to undertake the translating all the French letters of Mr. Genet which made part of the Appendix to the letter to G. Morris, sending me every afternoon his rough translations of the preceding 24. hours, which I will examine and return to him to be fair copied,[1] unless we should have time to copy them here. I have the originals here to examine them by.

It is extremely desireable that the recording my letters would go on constantly, because they must be brought up to the last day of December next by that day, and we cannot work doublehanded on that. The gentleman hitherto employed in that (I believe it was Mr. Bankson) should resume it, and not be called off for any thing else.

Three others must be immediately set to work on the letters and Appendix to Mr. Hammond. Consequently there is a necessity to engage another besides Mr. Chapman, and even two if it can be done. If one of them should understand French well, it would be a favorable circumstance.[2]

This done, the instructions to Carmichael and Short will be to be copied twice, and all before Congress meets.

The person who comes here must bring a provision of copying paper and letter paper. The quality of the last sent me is excellent, but it must be cut down to the regular office-size. I send a sample of the paper. The size-board is in the office.

800. sea letters to be printed and sent here.

The office to be whitewashed in the course of this week.

Send me by the return of the rider the date of Fulwar Skipwith's appointment to the Consulship of Martinique &c.   Th:J.

PrC (DLC). Tr (DLC); 19th-century copy; with lacunae.

TJ's directions to the chief clerk in the Department of State concerned the copying of documents that the President submitted to Congress on 5 and 16 Dec. 1793 with his messages on American relations with France, Great Britain, and Spain (ASP, *Foreign Relations*, I, 141-288; on the documents for France and Great Britain, see note to Edmond Charles Genet to TJ, 16 May

1793). TJ's drafts of Washington's messages are printed below under 2 and 14 Dec. 1793. For the unprecedented expansion of the Department's clerical staff at this time to handle these and other major copying assignments, see Vol. 17: 356-7n.

LETTER TO G. MORRIS: TJ to Gouverneur Morris, 16 Aug. 1793. RECORDING MY LETTERS: the copying of TJ's official correspondence as Secretary of State into departmental letterbooks. APPENDIX TO MR. HAMMOND: the enclosures listed at TJ to George Hammond, 29 May 1792. INSTRUCTIONS TO CARMICHAEL AND SHORT: Report on Negotiations with Spain, 18 Mch. 1792.

[1] Remainder of paragraph interlined.
[2] Sentence interlined.

From George Taylor, Jr.

Phila. 18. Nov. 1793

G. Taylor Jr. presents his respectful compliments to the Secy. of State. Has the honor to inform him that agreeably to his note of to day he has engaged Mr. Chapman, who cannot conveniently leave the City. That he has examined the letters and reports yet to be recorded, and finds that they will each require one person to be employed at least to the last of December next. That Mr. Bankson has resumed the former and Mr. Blackwell who arrived here on Saturday is engaged at the latter and is now upon the long letter to Mr. Hammond. The documents to which G. T. proposes giving to Mr. Chapman to morrow. The Dr. is now employed copying the letter to Messrs. Short and Carmichael. That a Mr. Jonathan Smith, who can be recommended by Mr. Kean Cashier of the Bank of the US. but at any rate will engage temporarily only having applied for a berth in the Treasury, will in case the Secretary of State should think proper to employ him, go out to morrow. That should the Secy. think it expedient to take Mr. Blackwell off the reports for the present he has not the least objection to go to Germantown. That the office is nearly all cleansed. That the only Credences or powers of Mr. Genet (3 in number) in his possession are herewith sent. None of them seem to give to him those of Consul General. That the date of Fulwar Skipwith's Commission as Consul at Martinique is the 7. June 1790. That G. T. has not been able to translate any of the documents to day, but will begin on them to night.

Mr. Bankson wishes to have the Secy. of States letters for July last. Please excuse haste as the rider is waiting.

RC (DLC); endorsed by TJ as received 18 Nov. 1793.

LONG LETTER TO MR. HAMMOND: TJ to George Hammond, 29 May 1792. THE DR.: George Pfeiffer, a clerk in the Department of State who held an M.D. degree from the College of Philadelphia (Sowerby, No. 938). LETTER TO MESSRS. SHORT AND CARMICHAEL: Report on Negotiations with Spain, 18 Mch. 1792.

To Edmond Charles Genet

Germantown Nov. 19. 1793.

Th: Jefferson has the honor to present his respects to Mr. Genet and to acknolege the receipt by the hands of a Courier, of his letter of Nov. 12. and two others of Nov. 16. which shall be immediately communicated to the President.

PrC (DLC). FC (Lb in DNA: RG 59, DL).

The LETTER OF NOV. 12. was actually

Genet's 14 Nov. 1793 letter about John Jay and Rufus King, which according to SJL TJ received this day along with Genet's letters OF NOV. 16.

From Edmond Charles Genet

M.   New york. le 18. [19] 9bre. 1793. l'an 2e.

Le sort des Colonies francoises dans les Antilles est tellement lié avec les intérêts politiques et Commerciaux de la france et des Etats unis que J'ai regardé comme un de mes devoirs depuis que Je suis ici[1] d'instruire et mon gouvernement et le votre de la situation de ces possessions importantes. Je vous ai communiqué précedemment toutes les notions qui étoient parvenues à ma Connoissance, Je vous transmets aujourdhui un tableau que Je crois éxact de l'état actuel des Isles Sous le vent et du vent. J'y Joins la copie d'une lettre circulaire que J'écris aux Consuls relativement aux émigrés de St. domingue et celle d'une autre lettre que J'ai adressée à une prétendue assemblée de Colons qui s'est formée à Philadelphie à l'instar de celles de Charles Town et de Baltimore. Je souhaite vivement, M., que ces differentes pieces fixent les idées du gouvernement federal sur l'événement de St. domingue qui n'est point un des phénomenes les moins remarquables de notre revolution. Le peuple nouveau qui se forme dans cette Isle pourra devenir un ami utile ou un voisin dangereux[2] et mon amitié pour les Etats unis me préscrit de vous avertir qu'il est très important qu'ils prennent à son égard un système dicté comme celui que nous suivrons vraisemblablement envers lui par la philosophie et par l'Empire des circonstances. Ce peuple quoique très Jeune encore, M., connoit ses droits.[3] Il a Juré de les défendre; Il sera sensible aux bons procédés et punira ceux qui l'outrageront; aussi, Je ne saurois vous dire combien J'ai été alarmé sous ce dernier rapport en apprenant qu'une députation tricolore envoyée par les hommes libres de la partie du Nord de St. domingue avoit été[4] scandaleusement insultée et maltraitée en débarquant à Philadelphie par des réfugiés qui se sont permis même d'enlever à bord du Vaisseau de la République ou elle étoit embarquée des papiers officiels à l'adresse de la Convention nationale et du Conseil éxécutif. Ils ignoroient sans doute les malheureux qu'une rage aveugle a portés à cet attentat que quatre cent mille noirs avoient fait le serment[5] de faire éxpier à toute l'éspece blanche qui restoit encore dans leur Isle la plus legere offense que recevroient leurs représentants de la part des hommes de Cette couleur. Mais heureusement M., que ces députés qui m'étoient adressés sont venus chercher auprès de moi un azyle; Je les ai reçus consolés, Je les ai assurés que le gouvernement seviroit[6] contre les coupables, Je me suis assuré qu'ils n'instruiroient point leurs commettants de ce qui leur étoit arrivé et par cette conduite Je crois avoir servi ma patrie et la vôtre. Agréés mon respect.

Dft (DLC: Genet Papers); unsigned; above salutation: "Le Cit Genet &c à Mr Jefferson &c"; with marginal note on first page: "4 pieces Jointes Le rapport &c."; only the most significant emendations have been recorded below. This was probably the letter of 19 Nov. 1793 on the "state of the colonies" that was recorded in SJL as received 20 Nov. 1793 and that TJ evidently answered in his second letter to Genet of 24 Nov. 1793. A letter of 18 Nov. 1793 from Genet, recorded in SJL as a "supplement to that of Nov. 19." received on 21 Nov. 1793, has not been found. Enclosures: (1) Genet to the Minister of Foreign Affairs, 15 Nov. 1793, describing the progress of the slave revolt and the conflict between revolutionary and counterrevolutionary French settlers on Saint-Domingue, which climaxed with the proclamation liberating slaves in August and the British capture of Môle Saint Nicolas and Jéremie in September 1793; urging French support for the emerging free-labor system on Saint-Domingue on the grounds that France would benefit economically from continued trade with the island and militarily from the support of ex-slaves grateful for the freedom granted them by French authorities; predicting that the British would be driven out of Saint-Domingue if the National Convention supported the freed slaves and their two most important leaders in the struggle against the occupying forces; asserting that in the end Americans would accept the new order of things on Saint-Domingue, though for the moment public opinion was split along sectional lines, with Northerners willing to trade with Saint-Domingue and Southerners fearful that its example might spark a slave revolt in their own region; discussing the activities in the United States of émigré colonists from Saint-Domingue, half of whom were opponents of the French Revolution and the other half patriots who opposed racial equality; describing the more favorable situations of St. Lucia, Martinique, and Guadeloupe; noting that General Victor Collot had twice solicited his recall by the Minister of Marine because of the realization that his prospects for promotion were greater in Europe during the war than in America; and concluding that the same problem was responsible for unrest among French naval officers in America and for the defection of the squadron that had recently left New York (RC in AMAE: CPEU, XXXIX, in French, consisting of 24 pages in a clerk's hand, signed by Genet, with his note at head of text: "Rapport sur la Situation des colonies françaises de l'Amérique"; FC in DLC: Genet Papers, in English, dated " November 1793" and lacking one sentence). (2) Genet to French Consuls in the United States, 11 Nov. 1793, instructing them to take legal action against those traitorous French refugees from Saint-Domingue who, according to reports in newspapers and from Michel Ange Bernard de Mangourit, the consul at Charleston, sought to discredit French diplomatic and consular officials by propagating atrocious lies that they were conspiring to instigate slave revolts and destroy property in the United States—falsehoods that are reminiscent of the efforts of French émigrés at Koblentz, Spires, and Brussels to undermine the French Republic, that are belied by the general calm prevailing in France's East and West Indian colonies, the sole exception of Saint-Domingue being the direct result of the actions of its treasonous refugees, and that are contrary to the National Convention's 6 Apr. 1793 decree enjoining Frenchmen to respect the governments of other countries (MS not found; English text printed in the New York *Diary; or Loudon's Register*, 25 Nov. 1793). Other enclosure not found.

For the incident at Philadelphia involving the DÉPUTÉS from Saint-Domingue who were on their way to Paris to confer with the National Convention, see the enclosure listed at TJ to Genet, 24 Nov. 1793 (second letter).

[1] Preceding five words interlined.
[2] Genet here canceled "et sous ce dernier rapport Je ne négligerai rien."
[3] Genet here canceled "et ceux de la france."
[4] Genet here canceled "odieusem."
[5] Altered from "que cent milles noirs ⟨qui ont élus ces députés ont fait le serment⟩ se sont promis."
[6] Genet here canceled "sans doute."

To John Ross

DEAR SIR   Germantown Nov. 19. 1793

I sincerely congratulate you on your resurrection. On the faith of the newspapers I really lamented you dead for several days. I hope Mrs. Ross and all your family have enjoyed good health during the afflictions of the city.

Not knowing what date was inserted in my note for the 100.D. you were so kind as to give me for it, nor where to seek the note, as nobody has come to seek me about it, I inclose you a check for the sum on the bank of the US. with many thanks for the friendly accomodation. With my best respects to yourself and Mrs. Ross I am Dear Sir Your friend & servt   TH: JEFFERSON

PrC (DLC); at foot of text: "John Ross esq." Tr (ViU: Edgehill-Randolph Papers); 19th-century copy. Enclosure not found.

A letter from Ross of 22 Nov. 1793, recorded in SJL as received from Philadelphia on 25 Nov. 1793, has not been found.

From George Taylor, Jr.

Philadelphia Nov. 19th. 1793.

G. Taylor Junr. has the honor to inform the Secretary of State that he has inquired respecting the House occupied by the late Mrs. House, now by a Mrs. Dunn, and is told by persons who remained in the City, but cannot give it as authentic, that two Gentlemen have died in it, supposed of the fever. That on this occasion, and being informed that some Nurses of the sick are in possession of several beds, imprudently given them by the friends of deceased persons, which may cause a general terror as to those used in boarding Houses—he is led, from pure motives of sincere gratitude and affection to offer for the acceptance of

Mr. Jefferson a Room and bed in his House, should Mr. Jefferson come into the City.

G. Taylor would beg the favor of Mr. Jefferson to take charge of the letter addressed to the Attorney General of the U.S. sent by the rider yesterday, not being able to prevail on him to deliver it himself, as it contains a paper of consequence which Mr. R. delivered G. T. in Sept. last. G. T. hopes the nature of the case will plead his excuse for this trouble.

RC (DLC); endorsed by TJ as received 19 Nov. 1793. The letter to ATTORNEY GENERAL Edmund Randolph has not been found.

From William Davies

SIR   Broadway near Petersburg Nov 20, 93

The compensation, which I am to receive from the Commonwealth of Virginia for my service as Commissioner for settling her account with the United States, is by contract dependent to a certain degree upon the result of that business; the Executive having engaged to add to my stipulated wages in case of a favorable termination of it. I have flattered myself that, considering the large proportion of the aggregate balance, which by act of Congress is allotted to Virginia, being more than a fifth of the whole, I have been successful in my endeavors, and the State benefitted by the result. I have hitherto been prevented from making my application to the Executive, as I had not any official authority to determine, what is the precise balance struck by the General Board. With a view to obtain this information, I have taken the liberty to apply to you, to whose office the report was made. I know not how far I am justifiable in hoping I shall receive from you an answer, which may prove favorable to my wishes. You have had some knowledge of the difficulties of the business in itself, exclusive of those, which were occasioned by the mismanagement of those, who were charged with the preparation of it, before I was engaged in it, and I have my hopes that you have formed a favorable opinion of my own conduct and attention with respect to it, so far as your opportunities of observation have enabled you to judge. I have the honor to be, sir, with most respectful esteem, Your very obedient servant   WM. DAVIES

RC (DLC); at foot of text: "Mr. Jefferson"; endorsed by TJ as received 3 Dec. 1793 and so recorded in SJL.

From Patrick Kennan

SIR   New York November 20 1793

Yours of the 13th. inst. from Germantown I received in course of Post. By the A/Ct. rendered the balance in my hands was $50.17 the further Sum received for the Quarters Interest is 59.66. D. which altogether makes $109.83 for which I here inclose you a draft @ 3 d/s on Messrs. Elliston & John Perot. You also have here inclosed, Certificates vizt. 1 for 2800. D. 6 per Cents, 1 for 2356. D. 3 ℔Cents, and 1 for 2150 D. Deferred Debt, all of which please own receipt of, and with respect I remain Sir Your most obdt. hue Servt   PATR. KENNAN

Int. on $2800 of 6 ℔Cents. 1 Qr. is $42.0
Do. on   2356   3 ℔Cent. 1 Qr. is 17.66 Dolrs. 59.66.
     Balance due ℔ A/Ct. rendered £20.1.4 is   50.17
                                              $109.83

RC (MoSHi: Bixby Collection); endorsed by TJ as received 21 Nov. 1793 and so recorded in SJL. Enclosure: Kennan's account current with Alexander Donald for William Short, and with TJ for Short, New York, 20 Nov. 1793, with entries for 18 Aug. 1792–20 Nov. 1793 and subjoined list of three certificates forwarded to TJ (Tr in DLC: Short Papers; in Kennan's hand and signed by him; endorsed by Short as a copy received from Kennan at New York in January 1803). Other enclosures not found.

TJ replied in a brief letter of 8 Dec. 1793 acknowledging receipt of the three financial instruments enclosed by Kennan, Nos. 521, 523, and 524, respectively, all issued by the loan office of New York (PrC in DLC, at foot of text: "Mr. Patrick Kennon N. York"; Tr in ViU: Edgehill-Randolph Papers, 19th-century copy).

To John Mason

DEAR SIR   Philadelphia Nov. 20. 1793.

Being now returned to the neighborhood of Philadelphia, and business resumed in that place, I will pay on sight Mr. Fenwick's draught: be pleased to accompany it with your own for the little disbursements made for me about the box of books &c. or if you prefer it, write me the amount of the whole, and I will remit you a bank post-note on the collector of George town by the return of the post which brings your letter. I am with great esteem Dr. Sir Your most obedt. servt

                                              TH: JEFFERSON

PrC (DLC); at foot of text: "Mr. John Mason." Tr (ViU: Edgehill-Randolph Papers); 19th-century copy.

SJL records a letter from Mason of 11 Sep. 1793, received from Georgetown on 14 Sep. 1793, and another letter written by

Mason in Baltimore on 19 Sep. 1793 and received in that city by TJ the same day, neither of which has been found. A letter from TJ to Mason of the latter date, described as being on "personal business matters," is not recorded in SJL and has not been found (Ritter-Hopson Galleries Catalogue, 24-25 May 1932, Lot 195).

To Richard Söderström

SIR   Germantown Nov. 20. 1793.

I received last night your favor of the 16th. No particular rules have been established by the President for the conduct of Consuls with respect to prizes. In one particular case, where a prize is brought into our ports by any of the *belligerent* parties, and is reclaimed of the Executive, the President has *hitherto* permitted the Consul of the Captor to hold the prize until his determination is known. But in all cases respecting a neutral nation, their vessels are placed exactly on the same footing with our own, entitled to the same remedy from our courts of justice and the same protection from the Executive, as our own vessels in the same situation. The remedy in the courts of justice, the only one which they or our own have access to, is slower than where it lies with the Executive; but it is more complete, as damages can be given by the courts but not by the Executive.   The President will gladly avail himself of any information you can at any time give him where his interference may be useful to the vessels or subjects of his Danish Majesty, the desire of the US. being to extend to the vessels and subjects of that crown, as well as to those of his Swedish majesty the same protection as is given to those of our own citizens. I have the honor to be with much respect Sir your most obedt. servt   TH: JEFFERSON

PrC (DLC); at foot of text: "Mr. Soderstrom Consul of Sweden." FC (Lb in DNA: RG 59, DL).

From Robert Gamble

SIR   Richmond, Novemr. 21. 1793

I have your favor of the 14th. Covering a letter to Mr. Mewburn, Which is delivered him to Night (he is returned some Weeks past).

It is with great pleasure I hear from you that the dreadful disease Which raged in Philadelphia has subsided. I wish the President may not have risked too much, by going in to the City so soon. Melancholly would public affairs appear to our Citizens, at this important Crisis; Should he be be taken from the Helm of Government. Shall we have no hopes of your Continuing in office? Many of your friends yet flatter themselves you will at [last?] postpone your resignation.

Since the day after I came to Richmond I have been confined to my Room and Bed by Sickness—And now I not able to sit up. This to a poor *Country-born Merchant* is a great difficulty at this particular season of the year. However, I trust that I feel gratitude to God, that I am in a fair prospect of recovery.

I have the pleasure to inform you that the Honble. John Brown is recovered from his sickness in Staunton and will be able to attend Congress early in the session.

The fellow Who brought your Wine (in cases) from Baltimore having been paid the freight *there*—did not call on my young man here— And therefore Stored them at Rockets. I believe all is safe. I understand you have more goods with the same people (Hague & Liester)—And now as I hope to be able in a few days to attend to business—I will select some Careful Waggoner by whom I can forward the Wine &c. either to Monticello or Colo. Bells at Charlotsville Safe. I am with sentiments of Esteem and respect Your Mo. Ob Hu st.   Ro: GAMBLE

RC (DLC); one word doubtful; addressed: "Honble Thomas Jefferson Esqre Secretary of State German Town"; stamped and postmarked; endorsed by TJ as received 28 Nov. 1793 and so recorded in SJL.

From Edmond Charles Genet

M.   New york. le 21. 9bre. 1793. l'an 2e. de la Repe. fse.

J'ai reçu les notes que vous m'avés fait l'honneur de m'écrire pour m'informer que les procureurs des districts de la Pensylvanie et du Maryland[1] étoient chargés de prendre des mesures pour arranger définitivement suivant le mode que vous m'avés fait Connoitre[2] les differents qui se sont élevés relativement à des prises reclamées comme ayant été faites dans la Jurisdiction des Etats unis. J'en instruirai les Consuls auxquels la garde provisoire de ces sortes de prises a été confiée par le gouvernement federal suivant toutes les règles de la Justice[3] et Je ne doute point qu'ils ne se prêtent à toutes les dispositions renfermées dans votre lettre du 10. de ce mois dont Je leur donnerai connoissance aussitôt que vous aurés eu la bonté de me la renvoyer revêtue de votre Signature.[4] Mon empressement et le leur, à concourir à toutes les vues du gouvernement federal me donne lieu de penser, M., que les procureurs de district qui se sont permis de s'emparer des prises contestées[5] dont la garde provisoire appartient aux Consuls recevront l'admonition d'être plus circonspects à l'avenir et que prealablement aux arrangements proposés les prises en Cause seront remises aux Consuls.

Dft (DLC: Genet Papers); unsigned; at head of text: "Exp."; above salutation: "Le Citoyen Genet &c à M. Jefferson &c."; only the most significant emendations are recorded below. Tr (AMAE: CPEU, XXXIX). FC (DLC: Genet Papers); in English; misdated 21 Sep. 1793. Recorded in SJL as a letter of "(Oct. for) Nov. 21" received 25 Nov. 1793.

LES NOTES: TJ to Genet and George Hammond, 10 and 15 Nov. 1793.

[1] Preceding six words interlined.
[2] Preceding nine words written in the margin.
[3] Preceding seven words interlined.
[4] Genet here canceled "Agréés mon respect."
[5] Word interlined.

To Jacob Hollingsworth

SIR   Germantown near Philadelphia Nov. 21. 1793.

When I passed your house last, you told me you thought there would be to be bought there red clover seed, fresh and cheap. I take the liberty to inclose you a twenty dollar bill and to beg the favor of you to lay it out for me in as much fresh clover seed as it will buy, and to give the seed in charge to the overseer whom you shall be so good as to employ for me, to be carried on with him.   Not having yet heard from you on that subject I am apprehensive you have found more difficulty than you expected. Lest the terms should have escaped your memory, I was to give Saml. Biddle 120. dollars a year, and 5. or 600. ℔ of fresh pork. When he arrived there, as it had been too far to carry heavy things and to save him the expence of buying, I had made for him a half a dozen chairs, table, bedstead and such other things as my own workmen could make. He carried his own bedding and small conveniencies.   This is sufficient to serve as a guide with the person now to be employed. I am with esteem Sir Your most obedt. servt   TH: JEFFERSON

PrC (DLC); at foot of text: "Mr Jacob Hollingsworth." Tr (ViU: Edgehill-Randolph Papers); 19th-century copy.

On 6 Jan. 1794 Hollingsworth refunded 94 cents in change from this purchase to TJ at Elkton on his return to Monticello (MB, 6 Jan. 1794).

Notes of Cabinet Meeting on the President's Address to Congress

Nov. 21. We met at the President's. The manner of explaining to Congress the intentions of the Proclmn. was the matter of debate. E.R. produced his way of stating it. This expressed it's views to have been 1. to keep our citizens quiet. 2. to intimate to foreign nations that it was the Pr's opinion that the interests and dispositions of this country were for peace. Hamilton produced his statement, in which he declared his intention to be to say nothing which could be laid hold of for any purpose, to leave the proclamation to explain itself. He entered pretty fully into all the argumentation of Pacificus, he justified the right of the Presidt. to declare his opinion for a *future neutrality*, and that there existed no circumstances to oblige the US. to enter into the war on account of the guarantee, and that in agreeing to the proclmn. he meant it to be understood as conveying both those declarations, viz. neutrality, and that the casus federis on the guarantee did not exist. He admitted the Congress might notwithstanding declare war notwithstanding these declarations of the Presidt. In like manner they might declare war in the face of a treaty, and in direct infraction of it. Among other positions laid down by him, this was with great positiveness, that the constn. having given power to the Presidt. and Senate to make treaties, they might make a treaty of neutrality, which should take from Congress the right to declare war in that particular case, and that under the form of a treaty they might exercise any powers whatever, even those exclusively given by the constn. to the H. of representatives. R. opposed this position, and seemed to think that where they undertook to do acts by treaty (as to settle a tariff of duties) which were exclusively given to the legislature, that an act of the legislature would be necessary to confirm them, as happens in England when a treaty interferes with duties established by law.—I insisted that in giving to the Pres. and Senate a power to make treaties, the constn. meant only to [1] authorize them to carry into effect by way of treaty any powers they might constitutionally exercise. I was sensible of the weak points in this position, but there were still weaker in the other hypotheses, and if it be impossible to discover a rational measure of authority to have been given by this clause, I would rather suppose that the cases which my hypothesis would leave unprovided, were not thought of by the Convention, or if thought of, could not be agreed on, or were thought on and deemed unnecessary to be invested in the government. Of this last description were treaties of neutrality, treaties [2] offensive and defensive &c. In every event I would rather construe so narrowly as to oblige the nation to amend and thus [3] declare what powers they could agree to yeild, than too broadly and indeed so broadly as to enable the Executive and Senate to do things which the constn. forbid.—On the question Which form of explaining the principles of the Proclmn. should be adopted? I declared for R's. tho' it gave to that instrument more objects than I had contemplated. K declared for H's.   The Presidt. said he had had but one object, the keeping our people quiet till Congress should meet, that nevertheless to declare he did not mean a declaration of neutrality in the technical sense of the phrase, might perhaps be crying *peccavi* before he was charged. However he did not decide between the two draughts.

MS (DLC); entirely in TJ's hand; partially dated; written on the second and third sides of two sheets containing "Anas" entries for 8, 15, 18, and 23 Nov. 1793, those of 8 and 18 Nov. being printed under the latter date. Included in the "Anas."

Attorney General Edmund Randolph had already read his WAY OF STATING the purpose of the Proclamation of Neutrality at the Cabinet meeting held three days earlier (Notes of Cabinet Meetings on Edmond Charles Genet and the President's Address to Congress, [18 Nov. 1793], and note). Hamilton's alternate STATEMENT (MS in DLC: Washington Papers; Dft in DLC: Hamilton Papers) is conflated in Syrett, *Hamilton*, xv, 430-1, with language on financial matters that he also prepared for the President's annual address (MS in DLC: Washington Papers). Randolph's view that an ACT OF THE LEGISLATURE WOULD BE NECESSARY TO CONFIRM treaty provisions which affected tariffs or otherwise impinged on the prerogatives of the lower house was confirmed when Congress debated the Jay Treaty in 1796 (DeConde, *Entangling Alliance*, 134-9; Wilfred E. Binkley, *President and Congress*, 3d rev. ed. [New York, 1962], 53-5). Washington ultimately used neither of the competing drafts in his address. Instead, to satisfy TJ's concern that the earlier versions gave the Proclamation of Neutrality MORE OBJECTS THAN I HAD CONTEMPLATED, Randolph prepared

more carefully circumscribed language stating that the Proclamation had been intended only to "admonish my fellow-citizens, of the consequences of a contraband trade, and of hostile conduct towards any of the parties; and to obtain, by a declaration of the existing legal state of things, an easier admission of our right to the immunities, belonging to our situation." This wording was incorporated almost verbatim into Washington's annual address to Congress on 3 Dec. 1793, unlike the rest of Randolph's draft, which stated that certain unspecified stipulations of the treaties with France did not conflict with the Proclamation and had accordingly been honored, that compensation had been promised for certain prizes taken by French privateers illegally commissioned in the United States, and that Congress might wish to consider banning the sale of French prizes in American ports, assigning specific penalties to foreign consuls who exercised admiralty jurisdiction in the United States, extending the jurisdiction of American courts to encompass belligerent prize cases, bolstering America's defenses, and defining the limits of the maritime jurisdiction of the United States (undated draft paragraphs by Randolph in DLC: Washington Papers; Fitzpatrick, *Writings*, xxxiii, 164).

[1] TJ here canceled "permit."
[2] TJ here canceled "of allia."
[3] TJ here canceled "interpose."

To Edmond Charles Genet

SIR   Germantown Nov. 22. 1793.

In a letter which I had the honor of writing to you on the 12th. of July I informed you that the President expected that the Jane of Dublin, the Lovely lass and Prince William Henry, British vessels taken by the armed vessel Citoyen Genet, should not depart from our ports until his ultimate determination thereon should be made known. And in a letter of the 7th. of August I gave you the further information that the President considered the US. as bound pursuant to positive assurances, given in conformity to the laws of neutrality to effectuate the restoration of, or to make compensation for prizes made subsequent to the 5th. day of June by privateers fitted out of our ports: that consequently he expected you to cause restitution to be made of all prizes taken and

[413]

brought into our ports subsequent to the said 5th. of June by such privateers, in defect of which he considered it as incumbent on the US. to indemnify the owners of such prizes, the indemnification to be reimbursed by the French nation.

This determination involved the brig Jane of Dublin taken by the armed vessel citoyen Genet on the 24th. of July, the brig Lovely Lass taken by the same vessel on the 4th. of July, and the brig Prince William Henry taken by the same vessel on the 28th. of June: and I have it in charge to enquire of you, Sir, whether these three brigs have been given up, according to the determination of the President, and if they have not, to repeat the requisition that they be given up to their former owners. I have the honor to be with great respect, Sir, your most obedt. & most humble servt   Th: Jefferson

PrC (DLC); at foot of text: "The Min. Pleny. of France." Tr (DNA: RG 46, Senate Records, 3d Cong., 1st sess.). FC (Lb in DNA: RG 59, DL). Tr (DLC: John Trumbull Letterbook). Tr (DLC: Genet Papers); in French. Tr (same); in French; draft translation of preceding Tr. Tr (AMAE: CPEU, xxxix); in French; at foot of text:

"Pour Copie conforme." Printed in *Message*, 95.

For approval of this letter by the Cabinet and the President, who this day received and returned it to TJ with his sanction, see Cabinet Opinions on Various Letters, [23 Nov. 1793]; and Washington, *Journal*, 255, 256.

To Edmond Charles Genet

Sir   Germantown Nov. 22. 1793.

In my letter of Oct. 2. I took the liberty of noticing to you that the commission of Consul to M. Dannery ought to have been addressed to the President of the US. He being the only channel of communication between this country and foreign nations, it is from him alone that foreign nations or their agents are to learn what is or has been the will of the nation, and whatever he communicates as such they have a right and are bound to consider as the expression of the nation, and no foreign agent can be allowed to question it, to interpose between him and any other branch of government under the pretext of either's transgressing their functions, nor to make himself the umpire and final judge between them. I am therefore, Sir, not authorized to enter into any discussions with you on the meaning of our constitution in any part of it, or to prove to you that it has ascribed to him alone the admission or interdiction of foreign agents. I inform you of the fact by authority from the President. I had observed to you that we were persuaded that in the case of the Consul Dannery, the error in the address had proceeded from no intention in the Executive Council of France to question the functions of the President, and therefore no difficulty was made in issuing the commmission. We are still under the same persuasion. But in your letter of the 14th. inst.[1] you *personally* question the authority of the President, and in consequence of that have not addressed to him the commissions of Messrs. Pennevert and Chervi. Making a point of this formality on your part, it becomes necessary to make a point of it on ours also; and I am therefore charged to return you those commissions, and to inform you that, bound to enforce respect to the order of things established by our constitution, the President will issue no Exequatur to any Consul or Vice consul not directed to him in the usual form after the party from whom it comes has been apprised that such should be the address. I have the honor to be with respect Sir your most obedt. & most humble servt.

TH: JEFFERSON

PrC (DLC); with dateline added in ink; at foot of first page: "Mr. Genet." Tr (DNA: RG 46, Senate Records, 3d Cong., 1st sess.). FC (Lb in DNA: RG 59, DL). Tr (DLC: Genet Papers); in French; draft translation. Tr (AMAE: CPEU, xxxix); in French; at foot of text: "Pour copie conforme." Enclosures not found. Printed in *Message*, 93-4.

YOUR LETTER OF THE 14TH. INST.: Genet's second letter to TJ of that date. HAVE

NOT ADDRESSED TO HIM THE COMMISSIONS: see Genet to TJ, 13 Nov. 1793.

For approval of this letter by the Cabinet and the President, who this day received and returned it to TJ with his sanction, see Cabinet Opinions on Various Letters, [23 Nov. 1793]; and Washington, *Journal*, 255-6.

[1] Preceding six words and digits interlined in place of "since."

To Edmond Charles Genet

SIR

Germantown Nov. 22. 1793.

Immediately on the receipt of your favor of the 2d. inst. informing me of a conspiracy among the refugees from the French colonies now at Charleston, to undertake an expedition from thence against the said colonies, I communicated the information to the Governor of S. Carolina, with a desire that he would prevent every enterprize of that nature.

The other matters contained in the same letter belong of course to the ordinary cognisance of the Judiciary, which is open to the parties interested without any interposition of the Executive. I have the honor to be with great respect Sir your most obedt & most humble servt

TH: JEFFERSON

PrC (DLC); at foot of text: "The Min. Pleny of France." FC (Lb in DNA: RG 59, DL).

For the letter to the GOVERNOR OF S. CAROLINA, see TJ to William Moultrie, 13 Nov. 1793.

To Christopher Gore

Sir   Germantown Nov. 22. 1793.

In the inclosed gazette is a paper purporting to be a Protest of the Consul Dannery against the revocation of the Exequatur of Mr. Duplaine issued by the President. Before the President proceeds to consider what notice such a protest would call for from him, he thinks it requisite to be assured that the paper is genuine. I have therefore to ask the favor of you to endeavor to procure *authentic* proof of the paper, and to transmit it to me. Whether the original has been deposited with the Lieutenant governor, or in any court, from whence either that or any copy of it can be obtained certified, or whether there be no other means of procuring evidence of it but the calling on Mr. Dannery to avow or disavow it, you will be best able to decide. I have the honor to be with respect Sir Your most obedt & most humble servt.   Th: Jefferson

PrC (DLC); at foot of text: "Mr. Gore." FC (Lb in DNA: RG 59, DL). Enclosure: Boston *Independent Chronicle*, 11 Nov. 1793, which contained (1) Thomas Dannery to Governor Samuel Adams of Massachusetts, Boston, 7 Nov. 1793, stating that Edmond Charles Genet refused to accept the validity of the President's revocation of Antoine Charbonnet Duplaine's interim vice-consular exequatur and wished the Massachusetts legislature to investigate the crime of which Duplaine stood accused, as well as the motives for his dismissal and the legal forms that should have been followed in his case, so that the French Republic can punish him if necessary; and (2) Protest by Dannery, 7 Nov. 1793, setting forth fifteen reasons why he considered the presidential revocation of Duplaine's exequatur to be an arbitrary and unwarrantable dismissal of a French official and why therefore only his own consular appointment sufficed to deprive Duplaine of his official functions.

TJ obtained Cabinet and presidential approval for the substance of this letter before sending it to Gore (Cabinet Opinions on Various Letters, [23 Nov. 1793]). For the official response in Massachusetts to Dannery's PROTEST, see note to Edmond Charles Genet to TJ, 27 Oct. 1793.

Gore presumably replied to this letter in one of 4 Dec. 1793, recorded in SJL as received from Boston on 12 Dec. 1793 but not found.

From George Hammond

Sir   Lansdown 22nd November 1793

I have the honor of acknowledging the receipt of your letter of the 8th. curt:, relative to the distance from the sea shore, in which the territorial protection of the United States shall be exercised.

I shall be at all times ready to enter into any friendly conferences and explanations upon this subject; and in the mean time it becomes my duty to acquiesce in any regulations, which the government of the United States may judge proper to establish, with regard to the extent of its own jurisdiction. I have the honor to be, with sentiments of great respect, Sir, Your most obedient humble servant   GEO. HAMMOND

RC (DNA: RG 59, NL); in a clerk's hand, signed by Hammond; at foot of text: "Mr Jefferson"; endorsed by TJ as received 22 Nov. 1793 and so recorded in SJL. FC (Lb in PRO: FO 116/3). Tr (Lb in DNA: RG 59, NL).

TJ this day submitted to the President this and the following four letters from the British minister, and Washington returned them the same day (Washington, *Journal*, 256).

From George Hammond

SIR   Lansdown 22nd November 1793

I have the honor of acquainting you that, in consequence of the requisition contained in your letter of the 10th: curt:, I have communicated the subject of it to his Majesty's different Consuls in the United States; and have directed them to pursue such measures as may be the best calculated for facilitating the object of the regulation, to which your letter refers. I have the honor to be, with sentiments of great respect, Sir, Your most obedient humble Servant   GEO. HAMMOND

RC (DNA: RG 59, NL); in a clerk's hand, signed by Hammond; at foot of text: "Mr Jefferson"; endorsed by TJ as received 22 Nov. 1793 and so recorded in SJL. FC (Lb in PRO: FO 116/3). Tr (Lb in DNA: RG 59, NL).

From George Hammond

SIR   Lansdown near Philadelphia 22. Nov: 1793

I have the honor of acknowledging the receipt of your two letters of the 10th. of November, informing me that the district Attorney of the State of Maryland has been instructed to take measures, for finally settling the cases of the British brigs, Conyngham, and Pilgrim, captured by the French privateer the Sans Culottes of Marseille, and reclaimed, as taken within the jurisdiction of the United States; and that he is therein to proceed in the manner stated in your letter of the same date.

I have also received a similar communication of the 15th. of November, relative to the instructions given to the district Attorney of Pennsylvania, to take measures for finally settling the case of the British ship William, captured by the French privateer le Citoyen Genet, and reclaimed also as taken within the jurisdiction of the United States.

I have consequently communicated the subjects, of the two former letters to his Majesty's Vice-Consul for the State of Maryland, and of the latter to his Majesty's Consul-general for the middle and Southern

States: And I have farther instructed those Gentlemen to pursue the measures that may be the best calculated for facilitating the objects of these several enquiries. I have the honor to be with sentiments of great respect, Sir, Your most obedient humble Servant GEO. HAMMOND

RC (DNA: RG 59, NL); in a clerk's hand, signed by Hammond; at foot of first page: "Mr Jefferson"; endorsed by TJ as received 22 Nov. 1793 and so recorded in SJL. Tr (Lb in same).

From George Hammond

SIR   Lansdown 22nd November 1793

In answer to your letter of the 13th. curt:, I have the honor of informing you that I have not yet received such definitive instructions, relative to your communication of the 29th. of May 1792, as will enable me immediately to renew the discussions upon the subject of it, which have been for some time suspended. I can however repeat with confidence my conviction, that the continuance of the cause, to which I alluded in my letter of the 20th. of June last, and no other, has protracted this delay to the present period. I have the honor to be, with sentiments of great respect, Sir, Your most obedient, humble Servant,

GEO. HAMMOND

RC (DNA: RG 59, NL); in a clerk's hand, signed by Hammond; at foot of text: "Mr Jefferson"; endorsed by TJ as received 22 Nov. 1793 and so recorded in SJL. FC (Lb in PRO: FO 116/3). Tr (DNA: RG 46, Senate Records, 3d Cong., 1st sess.). Tr (Lb in DNA: RG 59, NL). Printed in *Message*, 106-7.

From George Hammond

SIR   Lansdown November 22nd: 1793

I have had the honor of receiving your letter of the 14th. curt:, upon which, as it announces the *fixed* determination of this government not to restore the British ship Roehampton, it is unnecessary for me, to offer many observations, or to enter into a minute examination of the reasoning or the facts by which that determination is justified.

I cannot however avoid remarking that although your position may be well founded—"that it would be a measure of incalculable consequences, to decide, that the *smallest* circumstances of military equipment to a vessel in" your "ports should invalidate her prizes through all time"—it may also be a measure of incalculable mischief to the general commerce of friendly powers (excepting that of France) trading with the United States, if the *largest* circumstances of military equipment, superadded to French privateers, in your ports, provided they elude the vigilance of the officers appointed to watch over proceedings of this nature, shall not be considered by this government as sufficient to invalidate prizes brought into its ports by vessels under this predicament. In the present case the facts are, that the Schooner Industry, according to the deposition of Benjamin Baker of Baltimore (at whose wharf and ship-yard she lay during her additional equipment) had no more than *four or six* cannon mounted when she was brought to his wharf—that, when she left it, "she had *four six pounders, eight four pounders and two howitzers completely mounted*"—and that from Mr. Kelty's report it appears that he himself was convinced that she had added to the number of her guns, and had made alterations of a warlike nature, but as he could not learn whence these additional cannon had been procured, he did not deem himself justifiable in refusing his assent to the authenticity of the documents produced by the Captain of the vessel, or in detaining her any longer.

The privateer Industry was therefore allowed to depart from Baltimore under an augmentation of force, more than double to that of *her original appearance* in that port: And to which augmentation I have reason to believe that her subsequent capture of the ship Roehampton is, in a great measure, if not entirely, to be imputed. I have the honor to be with sentiments of great respect, Sir, Your most obedient humble Servant   GEO. HAMMOND

RC (DNA: RG 59, NL); in a clerk's hand, signed by Hammond; at foot of first page: "Mr: Jefferson"; endorsed by TJ as received 22 Nov. 1793 and so recorded in SJL. FC (Lb in PRO: FO 116/3). Tr (Lb in DNA: RG 59, NL).

From Apollos Kinsley

SIR   New York Nov 22nd 1793

I have the honour to Inform you that the Machine for Makeing bricks, for which I receivd a patent, has been made, on a large scale and has been tryd and found to answer well; so far and we can jude by the tryal it has had—I have reference to that with the horizontal wheel—the other has not yet been tryd—I found it nesessary to alter the construction of the *charger* which forces the mortar in to the moulds. Instead of a piston *fixed* at the end of the plank which moves up and down I have applyd an Iron plate which moves into the box as the plank *decends*, and drives the mortar before it into the moulds, when the plank rises to take a second charge, the Iron plate flys out of the box horrizontally through a mortis In the plank and the plank rises without raising the mortar above the Iron plate—when the plank is raised the Iron plate moves in to the box again by means of a wait. I have mad this further alteration—that instead of moveing the charger down by a Skrew—I have loaded it with a wait which will conform to the different quantitys of mortar taken into the box—that wait is raised by a rope which winds round the perpendicular shaft—which rope is held by a hitch to the shaft, and is let loos when the wait decends. The principles on which the machine is now constructed are the same as the model in your posession though some of the move ments are efected in a different way—the reason of my troubleing your Honour with this, is, to beg the favour of you to Inform me whither those alterations can be secured to me by haveing them recorded in your Office, as improvements on my former patent, or whither it will be necssary for me to apply for a nother paten. I will if necssary send a model and specification of the present construction. I expect this Letter will be deliverd to your Honour by J. Greenleaf Esqr. who is concernd with me in the property of the Patent. If you will be so kind as to inform him what will be necssary for me to do to secure the above improvements he will Inform me. I have the honour to be Sir your most Obedient & most Humb Servt   APOLLOS KINSLEY

PS I have never Seen the Machine constructed by Mr. Brower but have been Informed that some parts of it were much like mine—especially like some of the improvements, which were all[1] made before he constructed his machine. My workmen informed me that he lost no oppertunity of examining my Machine when I was not present. I hope the Law will not permit him to reap the advantage of experriments which I have made at the expence of *all my* Property and *much* time.

RC (DNA: RG 59, MLR); addressed: "Honble Thomas Jefferson Esq Philadelphia"; endorsed by TJ as received 9 Dec. 1793 and so recorded in SJL.

Apollos Kinsley (ca. 1766-1803), a Massachusetts-born physician and inventor, attended medical classes at Columbia College from 1791 to 1793 without taking a degree. In 1795 he moved to Hartford, Connecticut, where he supervised a brickmaking operation that failed to achieve financial success, was the first American to use the cylinder printing press, and reportedly experimented with steam engines and constructed a working model of a locomotive. Kinsley subsequently returned to New York City, where John Stevens subsidized his attempts to develop an improved steam engine for pumping water (Newton C. Brainard, "Apollos Kinsely," Connecticut Historical Society, *Bulletin*, XXVI [1961], 12-20; Milton H. Thomas, comp., *Columbia University Officers and Alumni, 1754-1857* [New York, 1936], 180).

Kinsley's 1 Feb. 1793 patent for his MACHINE FOR MAKEING BRICKS was supplemented with another of 20 Dec. 1794 "for an improvement in tempering Mortar, & moulding the same into Bricks." His rival, Samuel BROWER of New York, had received a patent "for manufacturing brick & pantile" in August 1793 (*List of Patents*, 8, 9; Washington, *Journal*, 99, 228, 323).

[1] Word interlined.

From Henry Knox

My dear Sir   Philadelphia 22 Nov 1793.

General Stewart declines accepting the Appointment of Inspector for the port of Philadelphia and would have done the same with the naval office had it been offered to him. He says that he made the application at the instance of his father in Law, who is now convinced that the acceptance of the office would injure his commercial pursuits.

I enclose you a letter from the Governor of Maryland, enclosing the copy of A deposition relatively to the capture of the brigs Cunningham and Pilgrim. I am my dear Sir respectfully your humble Servant

H Knox

RC (DLC); at foot of text: "Mr Jefferson"; endorsed by TJ as received 22 Nov. 1793 and so recorded in SJL. PrC (Gilder Lehrman Collection: Knox Papers, on deposit NNP); endorsed in ink by Knox. Enclosure: Thomas Sim Lee to Knox, Annapolis, 5 Nov. 1793, enclosing a copy of a deposition respecting the capture of the brigs *Conyngham* and *Pilgrim* recently forwarded to him for the President's consideration by F. Moissonnier at Baltimore, and relaying the French vice-consul's promise that further testimony, if needed, will be furnished once the *Sans Culottes* returns and his hope that in the interim no decision against the legality of the capture will be made (Dft in MdAA: Maryland State Papers, in a clerk's hand, with revisions, complimentary close, and signature by Lee; FC in MdAA: Letterbooks of Governor and Council). The enclosed deposition has not been found, but it probably offered testimony that the vessels had been in international waters when they were captured (see Lee to Knox, 25 Oct. 1793, MdAA: Maryland State Papers; Moissonnier to Lee, 23 Oct. 1793, MdAA: Scharf Collection).

Walter STEWART soon reconsidered and in December accepted appointment as surveyor and inspector of revenue for the PORT OF PHILADELPHIA after coming to an understanding with Treasury Secretary Alexander Hamilton that he could relinquish his COMMERCIAL PURSUITS gradually (Syrett, *Hamilton*, xv, 416-17, 425, 444). The President accordingly nominated him on 9 Dec. 1793 and he won Senate confirmation a day later (JEP, I, 140, 141). His commission is dated 10 Dec. 1793 (MS, owned by Lloyd W. Smith, Morristown, New Jersey, 1946; printed form with blanks filled by a clerk; signed by Washington and countersigned by TJ). Blair McClenachan was Stewart's FATHER IN LAW (PMHB, XLVII [1923], 275).

On 22 Nov. 1793 TJ submitted this letter and its enclosures to the President, who returned them the same day (Washington, *Journal*, 256).

Materials for the President's Address to Congress

Notes   [ca. 22 Nov. 1793]
                                             Text.

Cases where individuals (as Henfield &c) organize themselves into military bodies within the US. or participate in acts of hostility by sea, where *jurisdiction attaches to the person.*

The Constitution having authorised the legislature exclusively to declare whether the nation, from a state of peace, shall go into that of war, it rests with their wisdom to consider

What is the present legal mode of *restraint*? Binding to the good behavior? Military restraint? Or what?
Or can the act only be *punished* after it is committed?

Whether the restraints already provided by the laws are sufficient to prevent individuals from usurping, *in effect*, that power, by taking part, or arraying themselves to take part, by sea or by land, while under the jurisdiction of the US. in the hostilities of any one nation against any other with which the US. are at peace?

Vessels originally constituting themselves cruizers here, or those so constituted elsewhere and augmenting their force here, may they be seized and detained?
By what branch of the government? e.g. the Polly or Republican at N.Y. the Jane at Philada. the Industry at Baltimore.
Their Prizes. May they be restored? e.g. the Lovely lass, Pr. Wm. Henry, Jane of Dublin, the Spanish prize &c

Whether the laws have provided with sufficient efficacy and explicitness, for arresting and restraining their preparations and enterprizes, and for indemnifying their effects?

Captures within our waters, by whom to be restored?
e.g. the Grange, the William, the Providence, the William Tell &c.

Whether within the territory of the US. or those limits on it's shores to which reason and usage authorize them to extend their jurisdiction and protection, and to interdict every hostile act, even between hostile nations, the partition of the National authority between the civil and military organs is delineated with sufficient precision to leave no doubt which of the two is justified, and is bound, to interpose?

Cases of the Betsey, an American vessel and Swedish cargo.
The Maxwell, vessel and cargo Swedish.

Whether either and Which of them is authorized to liberate our own property, or that of other peaceable nations, taken on the high-seas and brought into our ports?

Merely an intimation to establish all these cases with the Judiciary.

Whether all such of these interferences as may be exercised by the judiciary bodies with equal efficacy, with more regularity, and with greater safety to the rights of individuals, citizen or alien, are already placed under their cognisance, so as to leave no

For a specification of some of these duties see Jay's & Wilson's charges. Are they all sufficiently provided with specific punishments?

Offences against the Law of Nations. Genet's conduct is one. By that law the President may order him away.

Has the law provided for the efficacy of this order?

room for diversity of judgment among them, no necessity or ground for any other branch to exercise them, merely that there may not be a defect of justice or protection, or a breach of public order?

And Whether the duties of a nation at peace towards those at war, imposed by the laws and usages of nature, and nations,[1] and such other offences against the law of nations as present circumstances may produce are provided for by the municipal law with those details of internal[2] sanction and coercion, the mode and measure of which that alone can establish?

[*Upside down at foot of text:*]

Other subjects[3]

_____

Proclamation.
Report of balances between the states.
Western Indians
Creeks.
Provision of arms *made*, and to be made.

_____

Subsequent. Genet's conduct
England. Inexecution of treaty.
Interception of our provisions.
Spain. Boundary and navigation of Missisipi.
Protection of Southern Indians.

MS (DLC: Washington Papers); in TJ's hand; undated, but prepared no later than 23 Nov. 1793 and recorded in SJPL under 22 Nov. 1793 as "Materials for speech to Congress"; with list of topics upside down at foot of verso; bears check marks, probably added by Edmund Randolph, next to each paragraph of text and each item in list of topics; endorsed by Washington. PrC (DLC: TJ Papers, 95: 16291-2); partially blurred and clipped; at head of text by TJ in ink: "Materials for President's speech to Congress"; lacks check marks.

At some point during an ongoing series of Cabinet meetings to prepare for the forthcoming meeting of Congress, the President had evidently requested that each Cabinet member prepare outlines of the topics and language to be included in his annual address. TJ's submission—consisting of a column of suggested text for the portions of the address dealing with neutrality issues and a parallel column of notes identifying the specific problems each paragraph was addressing, together with a subjoined list of other topics meriting congressional notification—is conjecturally assigned to this date on the basis of SJPL. Washington, Alexander Hamilton, Edmund Randolph, and Henry Knox each prepared undated proposals that differed in detail and emphasis. Two of the suggestions, the President's call for the establishment of a military academy to teach artillery and engineering and the recommendations by Hamilton and Knox for fortifying major harbors, aroused TJ's opposition in subsequent Cabinet meetings (Fitzpatrick, *Writings*, XXXIII, 160-1; Syrett, *Hamilton*, XV, 429-30; Randolph, "Heads of subjects to be communicated to congress; some at the opening, others by messages," DLC: Washington Papers; Knox's submission, entirely in the form of draft language, is in same, both being filed at the end of November 1793). These documents must have been completed prior to 23 Nov. 1793, when the Cabinet, meeting in Hamilton's absence, considered and emended a consolidated outline the Attorney General had compiled from them, all of which bear check marks presumably made by Randolph while preparing this comprehensive synopsis (Randolph, "Heads of Matter, to be communicated to congress, either in the speech, or by message, as collected from the notes of the President, and the other gentlemen," DLC: Washington Papers). At this meeting Randolph was assigned the task of drafting the President's annual address (Notes of Cabinet Meeting on the President's Address to Congress, 23 Nov. 1793, and note; Notes of Cabinet Meeting on the President's Address and Messages to Congress, 28 Nov. 1793, and note). The final version of the address did not use TJ's language on problems associated with the neutrality crisis. Nor did it adopt his suggestion about the need to delineate more precisely the PARTITION OF THE NATIONAL AUTHORITY BETWEEN THE CIVIL AND MILITARY ORGANS beyond recommending that Congress regulate the jurisdiction of Federal courts in cases concerning the validity of prizes and property brought by belligerents into American ports and that, if such cases were to remain the province of the executive rather than the judiciary, a law would be desirable authorizing the President "to have facts ascertained by the Courts, when, for his own information, he shall request it." However, the address did touch on all of the OTHER SUBJECTS listed by TJ (Fitzpatrick, *Writings*, XXXIII, 163-9).

JAY'S & WILSON'S CHARGES: see TJ to Gouverneur Morris, 26 Aug. 1793, and note. For the SUBSEQUENT messages to Congress, see George Washington to the Senate and the House of Representatives, [2], [14] Dec. 1793.

[1] TJ first wrote "of nations" and then reworked the phrase to read as above.
[2] Word interlined.
[3] These words cut off in PrC.

Memorandum to George Taylor, Jr.

The following commissions wanting

\- + Arthur Livermore Attorney for the District of New Hampshire. [1]

\- + Robert Scott (Phila.) to be Engraver to the Mint.

\- + Robert Denny to be Collector for the district of Annapolis x

\- + Wm. Mc.Pherson Naval officer for the District of Philada. x

+ Walter Stewart Surveyor of the district of Philada. and Inspector of the revenue for the port of Philada. [2]

\- + William Barker 2d. Mate ⎱	Collector [3] ⎱	*exactly* copied from one from the Secy. of the Treasury. If it is not understood, explanations must be asked at his office. [4]
\- + Matthew Cozens 3d. Mate ⎰	Charleston	
Note dates of Com.	and capt. of Cutter. ⎰	

Th:J. returns the blanks, as we are now near enough to obtain commissions from the office.[5]

Nov. 22. 93.

RC (DNA: RG 59, Miscellaneous Records Relating to Appointments); in TJ's hand, with notations and query by Taylor recorded below; addressed: "Mr. Taylor." Not recorded in SJL.

William McPherson's commission as NAVAL OFFICER of the port of Philadelphia is illustrated in Appendix III. All of the commissions passed the Great Seal on 23 Nov. 1793 except for those of WALTER STEWART (Memorandum Book of the Department of State, 23 Nov. 1793, DNA: RG 360, PCC). For the delay in commissioning Stewart, see Henry Knox to TJ, 22 Nov. 1793, and note. The memorandum FROM

THE SECY. OF THE TREASURY is not recorded in SJL and has not been found.

[1] This entry interlined.
[2] In margin next to this entry Taylor wrote "these not received from Mr. [J?]."
[3] Above this column Taylor wrote "recommended by."
[4] Below this entry Taylor wrote "all the above dated at Germantown 23. Nov. 1793."
[5] Underneath this sentence Taylor wrote to Treasury Department clerk John Meyer: "Mr. Meyer is requested to explain this memorandum as to *Barker* and *Cozens* and to signify the dates for their Commissions."

From George Washington

DEAR SIR   22d. Novr. 1793.

I think Colo. Humphrey's in one of his letters to you, refers to his to me, for some article of News. I see nothing therein that we have not had before; but send it nevertheless, for your perusal.

Can any thing be said, or done, respecting the Marquis de la Fayette? I send the letter that you may give it another perusal. I send a letter also from a French Gentleman in New York offering his Services as Engineer &ca. We may want such characters! A civil answer therefore may not be amiss to give him, although he cannot be employed *now*, nor never indeed[1] he is well qualified.

Are resignations deposited in the Office of State? If they are I send one just received. Yours always   GO: WASHINGTON

RC (DLC); at foot of text: "Mr. Jefferson"; endorsed by TJ as received 22 Nov. 1793. FC (Lb in DNA: RG 59, SDC); with minor variations, the most important being noted below. Recorded in SJPL. Enclosures: (1) David Humphreys to Washington, 13 Sep. 1793, dealing with the President's reelection and burden of correspondence, the surrender of Toulon, various reported military setbacks to France, the approaching embarkation of Portuguese troops to Spain, the need to preserve American neutrality, the unlikelihood of war between England and the United

States, and the Reverend Close's efforts to obtain the latest and best constructed English plow for Washington (RC in DLC: Washington Papers). (2) Lafayette to the Princesse d'Hénin, 15 Mch. 1793 (presumably the text Washington received from John B. Church, not found, but on which see TJ to Church, 11 Dec. 1793, and note; an extract is printed as the enclosure to Angelica Schuyler Church to TJ, 19 Aug. 1793). Other enclosures not found.

ONE OF HIS LETTERS TO YOU: David Humphreys to TJ, 13 Sep. 1793. For the

plight of the MARQUIS DE LA FAYETTE, see   [1] FC: "never unless."
note to TJ to Gouverneur Morris and
Thomas Pinckney, 15 Mch. 1793.

Cabinet Opinions on Various Letters

[23 Nov. 1793]

At sundry meetings of the heads of departments and Attorney General from the 1st. to the 21st. of Nov. 1793. at the President's several matters were agreed upon as stated in the following letters from the Secretary of state. To wit:

Nov. 8. Circular letter to the representatives of France, Gr. Brit. Spain and the U. Netherlands, fixing provisorily the extent of our jurisdiction into the sea at a sea-league.

10. Circular do. to the district attornies, notifying the same, and committing to them the taking depositions in those cases.

Same date. Circular to the foreign representatives, notifying how depositions are to be taken in those cases.

The substance of the preceding letters were agreed to by all, and the rough draughts were submitted to them and approved.

Nov. 14. to Mr. Hammond, that the US. are not bound to restore the Roehampton. This was agreed by all, the rough draught was submitted to and approved by Colo. Hamilton and Mr. Randolph. Genl. Knox was absent on a visit to Trenton.

10. letters to Mr. Genet and Hammond, and the 14. to Mr. Hollingsworth for taking depositions in the cases of the Coningham and Pilgrim

15. do. to Genet, Hammond and Mr. Rawle for depositions in the case of the William

14. do. to Hollingsworth to ascertain whether Mr. Moissonier had passed sentence on the Roehampton and Pilgrim.

These last mentioned letters of the 10th. 14th. and 15th. were as to their substance agreed on by all, the draughts were only communicated to Mr. Randolph and approved by him.

Nov. 13. to Mr. Hammond. Enquiry when we shall have an answer on the inexecution of the treaty. The substance agreed by all. The letter was sent off without communication, none of the Gentlemen being at Germantown.

22. to Mr. Genet. Returning the commissions of Pennevert and Chervi because not addressed to the President.

same date. to do. enquiring whether the Lovely lass, Prince William Henry, and Jane of Dublin have been given up, and if not, requiring that they be now restored to owners.

These were agreed to by all as to their matter, and the letters themselves were submitted before they were sent to the President, the Secretary of War[1] and the Attorney General,[2] the Secretary of the Treasury absent.

same date. to Mr. Gore for authentic evidence of Dannery's protest on the President's revocation of Duplaine's Exequatur. The substance agreed to by all. The letter sent off before communication.

TH: JEFFERSON
H KNOX
EDM. RANDOLPH
ALEXANDER HAMILTON

MS (DLC: Washington Papers); in TJ's hand, signed by TJ, Knox, Randolph, and Hamilton; undated; endorsed by Washington. PrC (DLC); with "Nov. 23. 1793" and initials of signatories added by TJ in ink at foot of text; contains variation recorded in note 2 below. Recorded in SJPL under 22 Nov. 1793: "proceedgs. of heads of dep. durg. absence of Presidt."

[1] TJ first wrote "Secretaries of the Treasury and War" and then altered it to read as above; he made this change in ink on PrC.

[2] Remainder of sentence inserted later; in PrC TJ added a separate sentence in ink: "Colo. Hamilton absent."

From Christopher Gore

SIR   Boston Novr. 23. 1793

I, yesterday, receiv'd your favor of the 10th. inst. with the inclosed order, of the President. Shoud any case happen, where an interference shall be necessary, on my part, to effect the purpose of the order, I will endeavor to comply with its direction, in the manner pointed out in your letter. I am, Sir, with great respect, your obed servt   C. GORE

RC (DNA: RG 59, MLR); at foot of text: "Thomas Jefferson Esqr."; endorsed by TJ as received 2 Dec. 1793 and so recorded in SJL.

From John Hopkins

SIR   Richmond Novr. 23d. 1793

I am favored with your Letter of the 13th. desiring a transfer of all the Stock standing on the Books of my Office, to the credit of William Short esquire, might be made to the Treasury of the United States. In Compliance with that request therefore, you will find the Certificates of

Transfer in this enclosure. Mr. Brown requested me to ask the favor of your transmitting to him an acknowledgment of your receipt of them, of which I also shall be glad to be informed. I have the honor to be with perfect respect Sir Your most Ob Servant   JNO: HOPKINS

RC (DLC: Short Papers); at foot of text: "The Honble Thomas Jefferson"; endorsed by TJ as received 2 Dec. 1793 and so recorded in SJL. Enclosures not found, but see TJ to James Brown, 8 Dec. 1793.

On 8 Dec. 1793 TJ wrote Hopkins a brief ACKNOWLEDGMENT of receipt of a list of stocks identical to that included in his letter of the same date to James Brown (PrC in DLC, at foot of text: "Mr. John Hopkins"; Tr in ViU: Edgehill-Randolph Papers, 19th-century copy).

Notes of Cabinet Meeting on the President's Address to Congress

Nov. 23. At the President's. Present K. R. and Th:J. Subject, the heads of the speech. One was, a proposition to Congress to fortify the principal harbors. I opposed the expediency of the general government's undertaking it, and the expediency of the President's proposing it. It was amended by substituting a proposition to adopt means for enforcing respect to the jurisdiction of the US. within it's waters.—It was proposed to recommend the establishment of a military academy. I objected that none of the specified powers given by the constn. to Congress would authorize this. It was therefore referred for further consideration and enquiry. K. was for both propositions. R. against the former, but said nothing as to the latter. The Presidt. acknowledged he had doubted of the expediency of undertaking the former, and as to the latter, tho' it would be a good thing, he did not wish to bring on any thing which might generate heat and ill humor. It was agreed that Rand. should draw the speech and I the messages.

MS (DLC); entirely in TJ's hand; partially dated; written on the third side of two sheets containing "Anas" entries for 8, 15, 18, and 21 Nov. 1793, those of 8 and 18 Nov. being printed under the latter date. Included in the "Anas."

The basis of discussion at this Cabinet meeting, from which Secretary of the Treasury Alexander Hamilton was absent due to illness (Washington, *Journal*, 257), was

Attorney General Edmund Randolph's consolidated outline of topics for the President's annual SPEECH to Congress distilling the essence of earlier outlines and drafts prepared by Washington and members of the Cabinet. For these documents and the sources of the proposals to FORTIFY THE PRINCIPAL HARBORS and establish a MILITARY ACADEMY, see note to Materials for the President's Address to Congress, [ca. 22 Nov. 1793]).

To Edmond Charles Genet

Sir   Germantown Nov. 24. 1793.

I laid before the President of the US. your two letters of the 11th. and 14th. instant on the subject of new advances of money, and they were immediately referred to the Secretary of the treasury within whose department subjects of this nature lie. I have now the honor of inclosing you a copy of his report thereon to the President in answer to your letters, and of adding assurances of the respect & esteem of Sir Your most obedt. & most humble servt   Th: Jefferson

RC (AMAE: CPEU, Supplément, xx); at foot of text: "The Min. Pleny. of the Rep. of France." PrC (DLC). Tr (DNA: RG 46, Senate Records, 3d Cong., 1st sess.). FC (Lb in DNA: RG 59, DL). Tr (AMAE: CPEU, xxxix); in French; certified by Genet. Enclosure: Alexander Hamilton's Report to George Washington, 23 Nov. 1793, recommending rejection of Genet's request in his 11 and 14 Nov. 1793 letters to TJ for permission to draw in advance on the 1794 and 1795 payments due on the American debt to France on the grounds that the United States had already made advance payments to France equal or almost equal to the payments due in 1794, that American law authorized discharging the principal of that debt only through loans, and that it was necessary to have on hand sufficient funds to meet the scheduled 1 June 1794 payment on the American debt in the Netherlands lest American credit in Europe be ruined; and stating, in view of the differences between Genet and the Treasury Department about the state of the account between the United States and France, that he would immediately proceed to adjust the account (Tr in AMAE: CPEU, Supplément, xx, in the hand of George Taylor, Jr.; PrC in DLC; Tr in DNA: RG 46, Senate Records, 3d Cong., 1st sess.; Tr in Lb in DNA: RG 59, DL; Tr in Lb in DLC: Washington Papers; Tr in AMAE: CPEU, xxxix, in French, certified by Genet; printed in Syrett, *Hamilton*, xv, 406-7). Letter and enclosure printed in *Message*, 97-8.

To Edmond Charles Genet

Sir   Germantown Nov. 24. 1793

I am to acknoledge the receipt of your letter of the 19th. instant, and to thank you for the information it conveys of the present state of the French islands in the West Indies. Their condition must always be interesting to the US. with whom nature has connected them by the strong link of mutual necessities.   The riot which had been raised in Philadelphia some days ago, by emigrants from St. Domingo, had before excited the indignation and attention of the government, both local and general. It is with extreme concern they now learn that the respectable strangers whom you mention, were brought into danger by it, and certainly no endeavors will be wanting to bring the offenders to condign punishment. I have the honor to inclose you a proclamation which had been issued immediately by the Mayor of Philadelphia, and to assure you that the efforts he is using, will receive from the general government every aid they can give, to make a signal example of those who have thus violated that protection which the laws of the US. extend to all persons within their pale. I have the honor to be with great respect Sir Your most obedt. & most humble servt   TH: JEFFERSON

PrC (DLC); at foot of text: "The Min. Pleny. of France." FC (Lb in DNA: RG 59, DL). Enclosure: Proclamation by Mayor Matthew Clarkson, Philadelphia, 8 Nov. 1793, declaring that the "daring outrages which were committed yesterday and this day, on board the ship Rebecca, Benjamin Wyatt, master, just arrived from Cape Francois, by a number of Frenchmen, who from their dress might have been taken for gentlemen, are scarcely to be paralelled. With premeditation, they assembled to sacrifice a passenger on board the said ship to their vengeance, for crimes which they alledged he had committed in the island of Saint Domingo; and with the basest treachery, after decoying him upon the deck of the vessel out of his cabin, by specious promises, attacked him with swords, sticks and fists, and knocked him overboard, and while in the water attempted to accomplish the assassination by throwing stones and other things upon him, by which he hath received many dangerous wounds in his head and body, and would there inevitably have perished had not a number of the citizens, at the peril of their lives, come to his rescue"; asserting that this "insult offered to our laws, by a set of men to whom an asylum from fire and sword hath been so recently offered, indicates the basest ingratitude; and not content with what had just been perpetrated, many of them had the superlative audacity to assemble at the city-hall, where the wounded person had been brought for safety, and there insolently uttered threats of their future murderous intentions"; and calling upon witnesses "for the public honor and the safety of themselves and fellow citizens, to point out every person who was concerned in the breach of the peace," and "in the mean time vigilantly to attend to the conduct of persons so capable of insulting the laws of hospitality" (*Federal Gazette and Philadelphia Daily Advertiser*, 9 Nov. 1793).

From James Madison

DEAR SIR   Fredg. Novr. 24. 93

I have your 3 letters. The last of the 17th. fell into my hands here when I arrived on friday night. Col. Monroe was a day before me. Accept our thanks for your provision in our behalf at Germanton. We set off in 5 Minutes in a machine we have procured here, and which we shall keep on with till it fails us, or we can do better. I hope we shall be with you by sunday evening, or monday morning. Giles and Venable being before us, they will give you the intelligence from Richmond. The inclosed paper contains a scrap which may be of later date. If the Senate rejected as we understand, the vote relating to the procln., the answer of the Govr. *jointly* to the Committee of the two houses is a curious one. Yrs. affy.   J. M. JR

RC (DLC); addressed: "Thomas [. . .] Post"; endorsed by TJ as received 2 Dec. 1793 and so recorded in SJL. Enclosure not identified.

The action in question by the Virginia SENATE is described in James Currie to TJ, 9 Nov. 1793, and note. The difference of opinion within the General Assembly was highlighted again on 15 Nov. 1793 when the House committee notifying Governor Henry Lee of his reelection lauded Lee's efforts in behalf of the Proclamation of Neutrality while that of the Senate said nothing on the subject. Nonetheless, in his ANSWER Lee thanked the legislature for its "commendation of my prompt and decided support of the President's Proclamation" and praised the document as well-intentioned, constitutional, and beneficial (Richmond *Virginia Gazette, and General Advertiser*, 20 Nov. 1793; JHD, Oct.-Dec. 1793, 69b).

To —— Myers

SIR   Germantown Nov. 24. 1793.

According to my engagement I now inclose you 186. Doll. thirty six cents = £55–18–3 Virginia currency to be passed to the credit of Mrs. Carr. You will readily perceive that your endorsement on the inclosed bank note will make it cash to any person wishing to remit to Philadelphia. The Custom house officers particularly take up these notes by a general arrangement. I am Sir Your most obedt. servt

TH: JEFFERSON

PrC (DLC); at foot of text: "Mr. Myers." Tr (ViU: Edgehill-Randolph Papers); 19th-century copy.

For TJ's ENGAGEMENT to pay the debt of his sister Martha Jefferson CARR to Myers, see note to TJ to Mrs. Carr, 19 Oct. 1793. The firm of "Mo & Jo A Myers" responded from Goochland on 2 Dec. 1793 with a brief acknowledgment that the BANK NOTE had been received and "pass'd to your credit with us, being for the amount of your acceptance of Mrs. Martha Carr's draft on you for

the above sum, which you have herewith transmitted" (RC in ViU: Carr-Cary Papers; at head of text: "Thomas Jefferson Esqre."; endorsed by TJ as received 18 Dec. 1793 and so recorded in SJL). Neither Myers has been positively identified, nor is it certain to which one TJ was writing; for Virginia merchants with the same surname and initials, see Joseph R. Rosenbloom, *A Biographical Dictionary of Early American Jews, Colonial Times through 1800* (Lexington, Ky., 1960), 126-8.

To Thomas Mann Randolph, Jr.

DEAR SIR   Germantown Nov. 24. 1793.

I received yesterday your favor of the 14th. Mine of the 2d. ought to have been then at hand, and since that those of the 10th. and 17th. All will have informed you of my health, and being here. I am happy that you think Tarquin will suit you, and insist on your acceptance of him. This is no sacrifice to me, because my sole motive for having thought of parting with him was that he is unnecessary for me, as I must keep carriage horses, which will do to ride. I insist also as a condition, that you feel yourself perfectly free to part with him whenever he ceases to answer your end or you can by parting with him have your ends better answered. From this moment then he is yours, and I am much happier in it than to have turned him over to any other person.—I am sorry you have so much trouble with my furniture. However I shall soon be able to relieve you from my drudgery. I inclose you a letter to Mr. Stewart, open, that you may see it's contents, and give the necessary directions to Mr. Biddle to[1] go or send for the sheep when notified that they are ready. I think it important they should be fetched before the snows.—I am sincerely sorry to hear of the situation of Colo. Randolph. It has been to be apprehended for some time. Should he leave you an executor, it may merit mature consideration whether you will consult your ease or interest in undertaking to act. My love to my dear Martha and Maria, and am Dear Sir affectionately your's   TH: JEFFERSON

RC (DLC); at foot of text: "Mr. Randolph"; endorsed by Randolph as received 5 Dec. 1793. PrC (DLC). Tr (ViU: Edgehill-Randolph Papers); 19th-century copy.

Enclosure: TJ to Archibald Stuart, 24 Nov. 1793.

[1] Preceding three words interlined.

To Archibald Stuart

DEAR SIR   Germantown Nov. 24. 1793.

When I had the pleasure of seeing you at Monticello you mentioned to me that sheep could be procured at or about Staunton, good and cheap, and were kind enough to offer your aid in procuring them. Reflecting on this subject, I find it will be much better to buy and drive them now, before they have young ones, and before the snows set in, than to wait till the spring. I therefore take the liberty of inclosing you a 40. Doll. bank post note, which I will beg the favor of you to lay out for me in sheep, taking time between the purchase and delivery, to give notice to Mr. Randolph at Monticello to have them sent for, the letter to be directed to him, or in his absence to Samuel Biddle overseer at Monticello. Your endorsement on the post note will transfer and make it payable *to bearer*, and consequently will be cash to any body at Staunton or Richmond who wishes to remit to Philadelphia; or the custom house officer at Richmond will always be glad to give cash for it.—What apology must I make for so free a call on you? And what thanks and apology for the use I made of your friendly offer as to the potatoes? But I am again a new beginner in the world, and it is usual for *old* settlers to help *young* ones. France is triumphant in the North. Her rebellion also subsides. The affair of Toulon is against her as yet; but I suspect it is not over.—The yellow fever is entirely vanished in Philadelphia, and all the inhabitants returned to it. The President remains here merely to form a point of union for the members of Congress, who may arrive uninformed of the safety of Philadelphia: but nobody doubts that they will immediately go from hence to sit in Philadelphia. I shall be within striking distance of you by the 15th. of January. Accept assurances of my respect & affection   TH: JEFFERSON

RC (ViHi); addressed: "Archibald Stewart esq. Attorney at law Staunton"; franked. PrC (DLC). Tr (ViU: Edgehill-Randolph Papers); 19th-century copy. Enclosed in TJ to Thomas Mann Randolph, Jr., 24 Nov. 1793.

To George Washington

Nov. 24. 93.

Th: Jefferson with his respects to the President returns the inclosed. He will mention M. de la Fayette to Mr. Pinckney in a letter he is now about to write, to go by the William Penn on Thursday.

The other paper was inserted in Brown's paper of Friday, probably by the Governor.

RC (DNA: RG 59, MLR); addressed: "The President of the US."; endorsed by Washington. Tr (Lb in same, SDC). Not recorded in SJL. Enclosures: (1) Lafayette to the Princesse d'Hénin, 15 Mch. 1793 (see Enclosure No. 2 listed at Washington to TJ, 22 Nov. 1793). (2) Commissioners of the City and County of Philadelphia to Governor Thomas Mifflin, 14 Nov. 1793, stating that the building they had been directed to prepare for Congress's accommodation would be ready for the next regularly scheduled congressional session, "except the Gallery, which, on account of the Malignant disorder and scarcity of Carpenters, we could not compleat" (Tr in DNA: RG 59, MLR, endorsed by Washington; text printed in *Federal Gazette and Philadelphia Daily Advertiser*, 22 Nov. 1793).

From Eli Whitney

RESPECTED SIR   New Haven Nov. 24th. 1793.

I received your favor of the 16th. inst. yesterday and with pleasure take the earliest opportunity to answer your enquiries concerning my machine for cleaning cotton.

It is about a year since I first turned my attention to constructing this machine, at which time I was in the State of Georgia. Within about ten days after my first conception of the plan, I made a small, though imperfect model. Experiments with this encouraged me to make one on a larger scale. But the extreme difficulty of procuring workmen and proper materials in Georgia, prevented my completing the larger one, untill some time in April last. This though much larger than my first attempt, is not above one third so large as the Machines may be made, with convenience. The cylinder is only two feet two inches in length and six inches diameter. It is turned by hand and requires the strength of one man to keep it in constant motion. It is the stated task of one negro to clean fifty Wt. (I mean fifty pounds after it is seperated from the seed) of the green seed cotton Per Day. This task he usually completes by one oClock in the afternoon. He is paid so much Per lb. for all he cleans over and above his task, and for ten or fifteen Days successively he has cleared from sixty to Eighty Wt. Per day and left work every day before sunset. The machine cleaned fifteen hundred weight in about four weeks, which cotton was examined in N. York, the quality declared good and sold in market at the highest price.

I have, sir, been thus particular in relating the experience I have had of the performance of this Machine, that you may be the better able to judge of its utility and success.

I have not had much experience in cleaning the Black-seed cotton. I only know that it will clean this Kind considerably faster than it will the green-seeded, but how much I cannot say.

After the workmen are acquainted with the business, I should judge, the *real* expence of one which will clean a hundred Wt. Per Day, would not exceed the price of ten of those in common use.

I shall have another person concerned with me in carrying on the business after the Patent is obtained. We have not yet determined at what price we shall sell the machines, it will however be so low as to induce the Purchaser to give them a preference to any other. We are now erecting one on a large scale, to be turned by horses, for our own use, and I do not think it will be in our power to make any for sale this winter.

This, sir, is not the machine advertised by Pearce at the Patterson Manufactory. I never saw a machine of any kind whatever for ginning cotton, untill several months after I invented this for which I have applied for a Patent. Some time last spring, I saw it mentioned in a Savannah News-Paper that Mr. Pearce of New Jersey had invented a machine for ginning cotton, but there was no mention made of the construction. I have since understood that his improvement was only a multiplication of the small rollers used in the common gins. This is every thing I know concerning the machine to which I suppose[1] you allude in your Postscript.

I think the machine is well calculated for family use. It may be made on a very small scale and yet perform in proportion to its size. I believe one might be made within the compass of two cubic feet, that would cleanse all the cotton which any one family manufactures for its own use. The machine itself does considerable towards carding the cotton, and I have no doubt but by leaving out the clearer and adding three or four cylinders, covered with card-teeth, it would deliver the cotton completely prepared for spinning. You will be able to form a more perfect idea of the machine from the model, which will be so complete as to perform the opperation of seperating the cotton from the seed.

It is my intention to come to Philadelphia within a few weeks and bring the model myself; but per[haps] it will not be in my power, in which case I s[hall] send forward the model with an order for the patent. I am Respected Sir your very humbl. Servt.   ELI WHITNEY

RC (MHi); torn at seal; addressed: "The Hon. Thomas Jefferson Esq. Secretary of State for the United States"; stamped and postmarked; endorsed by TJ as received 6 Dec. 1793 and so recorded in SJL.

ANOTHER PERSON CONCERNED WITH ME: Phineas Miller (note to Miller to TJ, 27 May 1793).

[1] Preceding two words interlined.

From Charles Carter

DR SR   Fredbg 25 Novr 93

By the Death of Doctr. Hutchison my Son Charles, is thrown out of the line of his Medical pursuit, having paid 100 Guineas as a Fee, which being lost he is unable to get in to any other Family. He proposes to go into some line, that at the same time, will not only support him, but enable him to attend the Lectures and receive private instruction. He is I hope qualified to fill any Clerks place, with propriety. Mr. Bernard Webb can inform you of his abilities. I shall esteem it great favor, if you can recommend him, to some person who may be in want, of such a young Man. As he depends intirely on his own industry for support your patronage will be a means, of advancing him, and will be greatfully acknoleged as favor conferd on Dr. Sr Yr Affe Friend & very Hb St

CHS CARTER

RC (MHi); endorsed by TJ as received 10 Dec. 1793 and so recorded in SJL.

From Edmond Charles Genet

MONSIEUR   New york Le 25. 9bre 1793 L'an 2e &c

J'ai eu l'honneur de vous prévenir que Je mettrois successivement Sous vos yeux, Les differentes pétitions qui me seroient adressées par les Captaines des navires du commerce francais En relache dans les Ports des Etats unis; Je vous ai deja communiqué celle des Capitaines qui se trouvent a New york. Je vous En adresse trois autres aujourd hui qui me viennent des Capitaines de Baltimore Et qui paroissent mériter la sollicitude du Gouvernement federal.

FC (DLC: Genet Papers); in a clerk's hand, unsigned; above salutation: "Le Cn Genet a Mr. Jefferson secre d'Et. des E.U."; at foot of text: "Translated." FC (same); in English. Recorded in SJL as received 26 Nov. 1793. Enclosures not found.

From Edmond Charles Genet

Mr.   NewYork le 25 9bre 1793 l'an 2e de la République

Je vous demande pardon si mes dépêches Se précipitent avec tant de rapidité entre vos mains: Mais les événemens Se prononcent tellement tous les jours que je puis à peine les Suivre et vous les dénoncer.

Mes dépêches précédentes vous ont présenté des plaintes sur les menées des émigrés nouveaux qui inondent votre continent; j'ai essayé de démasquer à vos yeux leurs profondes et doubles intrigues; je vous ai dénoncé leurs insultes aux agens français et les dangers personels que ces agens courent tous les jours entourés de ces furieux.

Aujourdhui j'ai à vous avertir de faits bien caractérisés et si je n'obtiens pas une justice, j'aurai du moins fait mon devoir, et mon cœur et ma patrie n'auront rien à me reprocher.

On m'annonce de Baltimore que *deux cents* Colons S'embarquent de la Chesapeak pour jérémie*; Les presses contre révolutionnaires françaises de Philadelphie avertissent que deux batimens vont prendre des passagers pour le Môle**; ainsi, Monsieur ce ne sont plus les bons offices d'un allié que la France est dans le cas de réclamer du Gouvernement fédéral; c'est de ne pas aider à nous détruire que j'ai à vous conjurer; c'est à vous prier de ne pas conspirer à la perte d'une Colonie que vous devriez défendre, que se bornent mes tristes devoirs.

Avec quelqu'acharnement[1] que l'on se *soit obstiné à me peindre dans des libelles*, *que* je méprise, comme l'ennemi du Peuple Americain et de Son Gouvernement et comme aspirant à vous entraîner dans la guerre, vous savez, Monsieur[2] avec quelle moderation je vous ai rappelé les obligations qui vous étaient imposées. En cela même, j'ai la conscience intime de n'avoir été influencé ni par nos succès ni par nos revers; Mais[3] je n'ai que cédé à des actes provisoires qui cachant une contradiction manifeste sous une modestie apparente avouent l'impuissance de nous défendre, et usurpent[4] cependant Le droit de nous laisser attaquer.

J'ai entre les mains les preuves d'une Conspiration qui a éclaté en Septembre dernier par la reddition du Mole; et les pièces originales ci Jointes[5] prouvent qu'elle était concertée depuis les premiers jours de 1793. et Signée des lors de noms qui ne Se sont démasqués[6] qu'en Septembre dernier. Les Conspirateurs adroitement cachés, se reclamaient de la République à l'instant où ils traitaient avec le Ministère anglais, afin que par cette double intrigue ils puissent renverser les vrais amis du peuple français et mener à sa fin Leur trame honteuse. Ces fils partiels qui se découvrent aujourd hui n'étaient que des projections ac-

---

* Sur un Vaisseau appartenant à M.M. Zachari et Coopman.

** L'un est le navire la delaware, cape. james Art, armateur james Shoemaker. L'autre est la goelete Betsy hannah cape. Clanachan, M.M. Reed et Soder armateurs.

cessoires de la Conspiration d'un grand traître célebre l'année dernière,[7] aujourd hui affaissé Sous les remords et les mepris du monde. Le Peuple Français, Monsieur, a déjoué toutes ces intrigues, et s'il fallait des preuves ultérieures de sa sagesse, de sa ferme volonté d'être libre, et de la stabilité de son Gouvernement, vous les trouveriez dans cette lutte glorieuse qu'offre la campagne actuelle où au milieu de grands revers d'eclatantes victoires et de conspirations atroces le Colosse du Peuple Francais S'élève[8] majestueusement et[9] fait trembler tous ses énnemis.

Voilà l'ami Sous l'aile duquel l'Amérique bravera les Despotes[10] qui partagent leur haine entre elle et nous. C'est cet ami[11] qui au milieu des mesures générales de rigueur que lui arrachent les circonstances, ne cesse pas un moment de Se souvenir de vous pour vous en excepter; les demandes que je vous fais en son nom, Monsieur, se bornent à ce que vous veuillez ne pas Souffrir qu'on forge sur votre territoire des poignards pour l'assassiner.[12]

Je vous prie en Conséquence, Monsieur, de représenter à Monsieur le Président des Etats Unis.

1° que la Sureté individuelle de nos Consuls est menacée à Charleston et à Baltimore, et qu'on met peu d'activité à les protéger.

2° que deux cens Emigrans Coloniaux S'embarquent à Baltimore et Sont peut être partis pour se joindre aux traîtres de jérémie; que deux autres bâtimens armés sans doute par nos ennemis S'annoncent à Philadelphie dans les Gazettes Contrerévolutionnaires pour porter des passagers du meme genre au Môle St. Nicolas.[13] Que je sais en outre de Science certaine que des batimens americains portent depuis long tems des provisions et des munitions de guerre dans ces deux places rébelles et enfin que des Emissaires d'hommes que quelques uns de vos ministres accueillent se sont rendus dans cette ile depuis longtems la proye de mille artificieux conspirateurs,[14] pour y négocier des insurrections,[15] et la ruine des interets commerciaux de ma patrie; et que c'est sur votre territoire que tout cela se fait, que c'est chez vous enfin que se trouve le centre des intrigans desolateurs de nos possessions d'outremer.

Je vous prie, Monsieur, d'obtenir une réponse définitive du chef Suprême du Gouvernement Féderal sur ces deux[16] chefs,[17] afin que par la première occasion, j'instruise le Gouvernement Français de mes démarches à cet égard et de leur effet.

Je prendrai d'ailleurs la liberté de vous proposer une mesure que je ne puis adopter qu'avec votre autorisation, et qui obvierait et aux Subterfuges des traitres et aux moyens coërcitifs qui peuvent vous manquer. Ce serait de donner l'ordre aux Vaisseaux armés de la République d'arrêter tout batiment américain destiné pour l'isle St. domingue qui n'aurait pas un Passeport signé de moi, ainsi je previendrais l'introduction d'ennemis qui peuvent échapper à votre[18] vigilance, et nous épargnerions à vos citoyens des Séductions et des dangers. Je vous prie de me faire connaitre l'intention de Monsieur le Président sur cette dernière proposition.

Dft (DLC: Genet Papers); in a clerk's hand, unsigned, with revisions by Genet; above salutation: "Le Ministre Plénipotentiaire de la République française à Monsieur jefferson Secretaire d Etat des Etats Unis"; only the most significant emendations are recorded below. Tr (DNA: RG 46, Senate Records, 3d Cong., 1st sess.); in English; misdated 29 Nov. 1793. Recorded in SJL as received 26 Nov. 1793. Printed with translation, with variations and errors, in *Message*, 30-1 (App.), 99-100; translation printed in ASP, *Foreign Relations*, I, 187. Enclosures not found.

In response to this letter Secretary of War Henry Knox requested the governors of Pennsylvania and Maryland to investigate Genet's charge that counterrevolutionary French refugees from Saint-Domingue in Philadelphia and Baltimore were preparing military expeditions against JÉRÉMIE and MÔLE Saint Nicolas. For the results of these inquiries, see TJ to Genet, 6 Dec. 1793, and note.

For the British capture of Môle Saint Nicolas and its strategic French naval station on 22 Sep. 1793, with the cooperation of local French naval officers and the support of French settlers concerned about the radicalization of the slave revolt on Saint-Domingue, see Geggus, *Slavery*, 64-78. Genet published one of the PREUVES D'UNE CONSPIRATION in the form of a letter, written to him from Baltimore on 14 Oct. 1793 by Citizen Genton, the former mayor of Môle Saint Nicolas, describing what he considered to be the town's treasonable surrender to the British (*New-York Journal, & Patriotic Register*, 23 Nov. 1793).

¹ Remainder of this clause and the next clause italicized in *Message*.

² Remainder of sentence interlined by clerk in place of "à quoi jusqu'ici Se sont bornées mes demandes quoique mes instructions me prescrivissent de leur donner plus de latitude."

³ Word omitted in *Message*.

⁴ Preceding eight words altered by Genet from "Se réclament d'un pouvoir Supérieur à elles pour nous défendre, prennent."

⁵ Preceding two words written in the margin by Genet.

⁶ *Message*: "ne sont démarqués."

⁷ Altered by Genet from "autrefois célebre."

⁸ *Message*: "relève."

⁹ Remainder of sentence interlined by Genet in place of "terrasse l'Europe qui l'afflige, et écrase les insectes qui s'attachent à Ses entrailles pour les dévorer."

¹⁰ Remainder of sentence interlined by Genet in place of "frémissans, et recueillera les débris de leurs systemes trop horriblement atroces et dénaturés pour pouvoir subsister long tems."

¹¹ Genet here canceled "généreux."

¹² The following passage is here canceled: "Je ne sais jusqu'où peuvent se porter mes demandes sur d'autres objets que je ne puis passer sous Silence quelque Soit le fruit de mes demarches. Des Gazettes françaises Contre révolutionnaires noircissent mon pays Sous vos yeux et calomnient impunément son représentant. Mille vagabonds avec un morceau de masque sur la figure s'y disputent l'honneur de me déchirer. Je vous laisse à determiner S'il me Serait permis d'aller jouer dans vos tribunaux la farce ridicule de les attaquer tous à la fois. Je vous prie de me dire quel est le Secours que je puis attendre du Gouvernement Fédéral contre ces nouveaux ennemies du Peuple Français. La liberté de la presse est un droit Sacré pour lequel nous avons combattu trois ans, je ne me deshonorerai point jusqu'à demander que l'on y porte atteinte; je me borne à vous dire qu'en France où nos Citoyens peuvent censurer toutes les actions du Gouvernement, les Ministres étrangers sont respectés.

"Je ne vous rappelerai point ce qui a été accordé dans d'autres tems à mes predécesseurs sur le même objet; Dans ce tems ils parlaient au nom d'un homme qui pouvait prétendre à des faveurs, je m'exprime au nom d'un Peuple auquel on dispute même la Stricte justice.

"Je me résume."

¹³ Remainder of paragraph inserted at the foot of page and in the margin by the clerk in place of: "3° qu'il est tems que les presses françaises de Philadelphie n'insultent plus au Gouvernement Fédéral qui a reconnu la République française et Son Représentant, au Peuple français qu'elles outragent, et à son Représentant qu'elles

Calomnient Sans qu'il puisse S'en venger par les voies ordinaires."

¹⁴ *Message*: "mille artifices aux conspirateurs."

¹⁵ *Message*: "instructions."

¹⁶ Word interlined by Genet in place of "trois."

¹⁷ *Message*: "deux objets."

¹⁸ *Message*: "notre."

From Robert Morris

SIR   New Brunswick Novr 25th: 1793.

On the evening of the 16th. instant I was honoured with yours of the 13th. enclosing the petition of Benjamin Freeman in behalf of his son Clarkson Freeman, and signifying the Presidents instructions thereon.

In complyance therewith I beg leave to inform

That Doctor Clarkson Freeman was apprehended (with difficulty and danger to the officer, as I understood,) in the beginning of March 1791 on a charge of being concerned with several others in counterfeiting a public security of the United States, and of uttering the same, knowing it to be so forged and a counterfeit, and was committed to the gaol of Essex county wherein he was apprehended.

He was removed by Habeas Corpus to the Circuit court of the United States held at Trenton for New Jersey District in April 1791, where he was indicted for forging, and uttering, knowing to be forged a public security of the United States purporting to be a final settlement. The District Attorney not bringing him to trial, and he appearing to be charged in Essex county on a process in a civil suit out of the Supreme court of the State, towards the close of the court on motion of the District Attorney he was remanded on his indictment to the gaol of Essex County there to be safely kept untill discharged by due course of Law. From thence he made his escape about the middle of the following August and is reported to have gone to Canada. I think I have heard that the Gaoler had unsuccessfully pursued him thither; The Gaoler, by his escape in the civil suit, being liable for a very considerable sum.

From the several depositions that I saw Clarkson Freeman appeared to be one of the most active and mischevous, in this State, of a gang of villains who, by forging and uttering counterfeit certificates, in a short time defrauded eight or nine of the inhabitants of certificates to the amount of upwards of seven thousand dollars.

He appeared to be about twenty four years of age and his demeanor in court indicated him impudent, hardened and incorrigible, which was corroborated by almost every account I heard of his behaviour at and after the time he was apprehended. He was reported not to want abillities nor knowledge in his profession equal to his standing; to have acquired by marriage something considerable for a low bred man, and to have been before guilty of many little thefts, for some of which he was early expelled the Medical society of this State.

I do not know of any person apprehended on his testimony, nor was there any such confined in this District after the rising of the court at which he was indicted. Amasa Parker was the only person then in custody, or since apprehended, besides Clarkson Freeman and Henry Smith, against whom an indictment was found. Smith had been previously pardoned, and Parker was in custody on a civil suit a long time before C: Freeman was taken, and was committed as a criminal on the testimony of the said Henry Smith, one of the gang, who was taken up in Philadelphia and there made a confession before, or about the time C. Freeman was taken.

The only considerations that I have knowledge of under which C: Freeman can set up any pretence for a pardon, are

1st. An engagement of Abraham Ogden Esquire Attorney for the United States in this District, the copy of which transmitted to me is as follows.

"Memorandum

"Clarkson Freeman being confined in goal at Newark Essex county State of New Jersey upon a warrant issued by John Chetwood Esquire one of the Justices of the Supreme court of the State of New Jersey against him the said Clarkson for counterfeiting the public securities of the United States or uttering counterfeit public securities of the United States knowing them to be counterfeit; He the said Clarkson sent for me as the Attorney of the United States for the district of New Jersey in order to make a voluntary confession of his guilt in the premisses Whereupon in the presence of his Counsel Elisha Boudinot Esqr. I informed him, that I had it not in my power to give him any assurance of pardon in consequence of his proposed confession—nor would I give him any such assurance if it was in my power. But if he thought it prudent to make an unconditional voluntary confession that I would transmit that confession to the Chief Justice of the United States with the most favourable representation of the circumstances attending such confession. At the same time I informed him that the charge against him affected his life. It was understood nevertheless by his attorney aforesaid and me that the confession aforesaid would not be made use of to work the conviction of the said Clarkson if the Government of the United States refused or neglected to make use of the said Clarkson as a witness against his accomplices or others whom he accused.

Newark 7th. March 1791.   Signed   Abrm: Ogden Atty. &c."

Copy

2d. He made a confession, which by a letter from Mr. Ogden to me of the 21st: March 1791, he had not then signed.

3d. He was introduced by the District Atty. as a Witness to the

Grand Jury while they were investigating the forgeries and frauds of himself and his accomplices, and also to the Court on the trial of Amasa Parker on an indictment, as one of the accomplices in that villany.

Amasa Parker was acquitted on that indictment through defect of proof.

In the room of the old doctrine of approvement, which was attended with difficulty, and perhaps unnecessary danger to the approver and is now out of use; A practice has prevaild in cases of extensive combinations of villany, that where an accomplice makes a true and full disclosure as well as of his own guilt as of the guilt of all concerned with him, which is accepted by the court, and he is thereupon admitted a witness, and, if required, testifies accordingly both to the grand jury and in court on the trial of his accomplices, and appears on the whole to act a fair and candid part—The Court will generally recommend him to Government for a pardon, will defer his trial, and even bail him, although indicted, to give him an opportunity of obtaining it.

Against C: Freemans pretensions on these grounds are

1st. That there was no need of his confession: Henry Smith, one of the gang, having by his confession made a pretty full disclosure, thereupon received a pardon from the President, and been detained as a witness if necessary. But Henry Smiths confession does not appear to have reached the District Attorney untill the 20th: of August 1791.

2d. The District Attorney had no authority to engage a pardon to C: Freeman, or make any contract with him that would equitably entitle him thereto without the consent of the Court, which does not appear to have been given. Although this may be considered a legal objection, yet it would lose much of its weight in an equitable view, if it appeared that C: Freeman, through the confidence he reposed in the district Attorneys power to engage a pardon, had been deceived into a full disclosure that would have worked his own conviction—As it would be unworthy the dignity of Government to take advantage of the mistake of its own officer, and a confession so obtained, if it did not opperate his pardon, would not be suffered by the court to be used against him on his trial: But this from the face of the contract appears not to be the case; Nor is the part of his confession which I have seen a full disclosure of his guilt, but rather an artful evasion thereof and an extenuation of his conduct.

3d. His want of candour in procrastinating the signing his confession from the seventh untill on, or after the twenty first of August,[1] a delay sufficient to have given notice to his unapprehended accomplices to make their escape, and none of them, that I have heard of, were afterwards taken.

4th: The want of truth and candour in his confession and subsequent testimony; which appeared by comparing them with parts of Henry Smiths confession and evidence corroborated by testimony from Witnesses of undoubted credit, And I understood that the grand jury on examining him considered his answers so false and evasive that they entirely rejected his testimony.

5th. His fresh crime in breaking gaol and escaping; whereby he violated the spirit of the contract with the District Attorney on his part, and excluded himself from any benefit under the above mentioned Usage; as he thereby deprived Government of the power of using his testimony against his accomplices, in case it was deemed expedient to do so. The pretence of unnecessary confinement set forth in the petition is no palliation of this; as, if he had an equitable claim to a pardon on the foregoing considerations, or any other, the court on application would have bailed him, that he might with more ease and effect have solicited it. Previous to his examination on the trial of Amasa Parker he was questioned by the prisoners counsel touching his interestedness, and thereon declared, under oath, that he was not an evidence on condition of a pardon, and that he had no promise of a pardon from any body.

Add to this a circumstance, which, although it ought not to weigh if he was equitably entitled to a pardon, yet is worthy of consideration where that equity does not exist, or is forfieted by the act of the party; to wit, That some of the grand jury and other respectable inhabitants attending the court expressed dissatisfaction that C: Freeman was not tried, the public opinion appeared to be much against him, and he was viewed by the people in general with abhorrence.

Moreover, some of the persons defrauded are men who stand fair in the public estimation; One of them, in addition to the loss of three thousand dollars, I understood was criminally proceeded against for selling one of the counterfiet certificates before he discovered the fraud. C: Freeman was the immediate perpetrator of the fraud on most of them. It would unnecessarily outrage the feelings of these men and their friends to learn that Government had pardoned an offender so base and detestable in their eyes.

However strongly the feelings of humanity may plead for saving the forfiet life of a fellow creature, whose death is not necessary for an example, or for the public safety: Or where the circumstances are such that the public forget the criminal in commiseration of the man—In my opinion, nothing short of strict justice, political necessity, or a litteral performance of contract should opperate to pardon and restore from a state of voluntary banishment to the community with² the rights and privileges of a citizen a person so young and so depraved, so hardened and senseless of shame, so prone to and capacitated for mischief, and so odious in the public estimation as Clarkson Freeman appeared to be.

The foregoing contains every information that my memory, or a careful examination of my papers enables me to give relative to the object of the Presidents inquiry, with such observations as have occurred to me to have opperation respecting the pardon petitioned for. I have been the more minute as I supposed Mr. Ogden must have had more powerful motives for defering C: Freemans trial than I am fully informed of. I have understood there were some communications between Judge Duane and Mr. Ogden respecting him, the object of which I do not recollect to have fully heard. Having no oppertunity of personally acquiring information from Mr. Ogden, I forwarded to him a copy of the Petition, Signifyed the Presidents desire thereon, and requested his information of such facts as I had not an opportunity to be informed of. I have waited several days for an answer but yet have none. If I receive any I will forward it. With great respect I am Sir Your very humble Servant

ROBT MORRIS

RC (DNA: RG 59, MLR); at foot of text: "The Honble Thomas Jefferson Secretary of State"; endorsed by TJ as received 28 Nov. 1793 and so recorded in SJL. Enclosed in TJ to George Washington, 29 Nov. 1793.

BENJAMIN FREEMAN: that is, Abraham Freeman. In his 7-8 Mch. 1791 confession CLARKSON FREEMAN described his associates' system of COUNTERFEITING by procuring valid public securities of the United States with small face values, erasing the amounts on them and substituting larger numbers, and exchanging the altered papers for valid instruments (DNA: RG 59, MLR; see also William Lewis to George Washington, 7 Mch. 1791, Abraham Ogden to Chief Justice John Jay, 10 Mch. 1791, and Jay to Washington, 11 Mch. 1791, in same).

Before returning this letter to TJ on 29 Nov. 1793, the President commented that it "represents said Freeman's conduct very unfavorably" (Washington, *Journal*, 260).

[1] Thus in manuscript, an apparent slip of the pen for "March."
[2] Preceding three words interlined.

From Richard Graham

SIR   Dumfries November '26 179[3]

I wished much to have waited on you on your Way to Philadelphia but was then in Fredericksbg. and being engaged with Genl. Weedon on the Sunday you spent there, did not hear of your being in Town until next Morning, After Your departure in the Stage. That disapointment induces me to take the liberty to write to you on a Subject in which the Western parts of America are much interested, And eventually perhaps the whole United States, I therefore trust that you will excuse this freedom.

Being pretty deeply interested in Landed property in the State of Virginia on the Ohio River, in the State of Kentucky, and in the N.W. Territory, I have been in that Country for upwards of two Years last past, making Settlements on some of my Lands—and Arrangements for Settling two of my Sons there. On my first going down the Ohio River, I made it my business to get every information respecting their Trade down the Missisipi, And found that it is cloged by the Spanish Government at New Orleans with a duty of 15 ℔Ct. on all produce taken down, and 6 ℔Ct. on all the Money brought from thence—which is equal to 21 ℔Ct. This of itself is too much for any trade to bear, but what is still worse, their Officers having no fixed mode of Valuing the produce they are entirely Arbitrary, and have valued Tobacco So high at times, as ten dollars ℔Ct. because that has been a price allowed by the King for their own Tobacco when Ours would not bring above four dollars by this means, our people were Actually paying a duty of $37\frac{1}{2}$ ℔Ct. in place of the Nominal duty of 15 ℔Ct, grievances of such Magnitude, the people who have settled on the Western Waters under a full expectation of having a free Navigation on the Missisipi, cannot, nor will not, long submit to. The Democratic Society in Kentucky, (who in fact include the whole State,) have already begun to enter into resolves on that subject.

Wishing for a temporary relief in this business until something permanent is settled between the United States and Spain, I have been corresponding with a capital House in Trade in London who assure me, that leave can be obtained through the present interest of the British Court with the Court of Spain for a few Ships Annually to go to New Orleans free from Duty to take in Only the produce of Kentucky and the Country on the Ohio. This with some other business, induces me to go to Europe this Winter where I have high expectations of geting Some thing done in this business provided it meets with the Approbation of the President and yourself, otherwise I would not wish to take any step in it. I had the honor to See the President before he last left Mount Vernon, and had it in idea to have mentioned this Subject, but declined, apprehending that it might go to him more properly through you. I have no doubt of geting introduced to Mr. Pitt by the interest of the Marquis of Graham who is now Master of Horse, a great favorite at Court, and particularly intimate with Mr. Pitt. Some of my conections in England have influence with the Marquis, and with Mr. Wilberforce who is also intimate with the Minister. This, together with a line from you, to our Resident at the Court of London, to lend me his Aide would I think bring about the business.

As I have some expectation of Sailing from hence about the Middle of next Month, I hope before that time, to have the honor of hearing from you. I am with due respect Sir Your Most Obedt. Servt.

RICHD. GRAHAM

RC (DNA: RG 59, MLR); dateline clipped; endorsed by TJ as received 2 Dec. 1793 and so recorded in SJL.

Richard Graham (d. 1796), a Scottish merchant and land speculator who had settled at Dumfries, Virginia, by the 1750s, served on local committees of correspondence and safety prior to the Revolution and as justice of the peace and sheriff of Prince William County afterwards (VMHB, XIX [1911], 95; WMQ, 1st ser., V [1897], 248, XVIII [1909], 94; CVSP, IV, 596, VI, 697 VIII, 54; Clayton Torrence, comp., *Virgin-*

ia Wills and Administrations, 1632-1800 [Richmond, 1930], 177).

MARQUIS OF GRAHAM: James Graham, third Duke and sixth Marquis of Montrose (DNB).

On 3 Dec. 1793 TJ submitted this letter and its enclosure to the President, who returned them the same day (Washington, *Journal*, 264).

From Josef Ignacio de Viar and Josef de Jaudenes

MUI SEÑOR NUESTRO   Nueva York 26. de Noviembre de 1793.

Hemos Recivido las dos estimadas de vmd. de 10. del Corriente Junto con la Copia de Carta del Governador de Kentucky, y nos prometemos que las providencias, que quedaba en tomar dicho Señor tendran el deseado effecto.

Quedamos informados igualmente de las que havia dado, y estaba en dar el Governador de la Carolina del Norte con Respecto à la Presa Española, y el Corsario Frances, pero sentimos el decir, que tal vez por alguna dilacion en la practica de ellas se havia huido dicho Corsario.

Tenemos escrito al señor Dn. Eduardo Jones para que en caso que se halle con algunas ocupaciones precisas que le impidan la practica de las mas vivas diligencias sobre el Asunto, confiera desde luego todos nuestros Poderes à persona de su mayor Satisfaccion. Por todo damos à vmd. las mas atentas gracias, y quedamos pidiendo à Dios guarde à vmd. muchos años. B l Mo. de vmd Sus mas attos. y Segros. Servidores.

JOSEF IGNACIO DE VIAR   JOSEF DE JAUDENES

EDITORS'   TRANSLATION

OUR VERY DEAR SIR   New York 26 November 1793.

We have received your two esteemed letters of the 10th. of this month along with a copy of the letter from the Governor of Kentucky, and we are confident that the measures the said gentleman has agreed to take will have the desired effect.

We likewise take note of the measures taken and in the process of being taken by the Governor of North Carolina with respect to the Spanish prize and the French privateer, but we regret to say that perhaps because of some delay in taking action the aforesaid privateer had escaped.

We have sent a letter to Mr. Edward Jones to the effect that in case he finds himself so busy that he is prevented from making the most vigorous efforts in this matter, he should of course convey our authority to a person entirely satisfactory to him. We give you most hearty thanks for everything, and we pray God to protect you for many years. Respectfully yours, your most attentive and assured servants,

JOSEF IGNACIO DE VIAR   JOSEF DE JAUDENES

RC (DNA: RG 59, NL); in Viar's hand, signed by Viar and Jaudenes; at foot of text: "Sor Dn. Thomas Jefferson Secreto. de Estado de los Estados unidos"; endorsed by TJ as received 27 Nov. 1793 and so recorded in SJL. Tr (AHN: Papeles de Estado, legajo 3895 bis); attested by Jaudenes and Viar.

The other letter from TJ DE 10. DEL CORRIENTE was addressed to the foreign ministers in the United States.

Viar and Jaudenes also wrote a brief letter to TJ this day acknowledging his 8 Nov. 1793 letter to certain foreign ministers in the United States and expressing satisfaction with the President's decision on American maritime limits announced in it (RC in DNA: RG 59, NL, in Viar's hand, signed by Viar and Jaudenes, with "Sor Dn. Thomas Jefferson Secreto. de Estado de los Estados Unidos" at foot of text, being endorsed by TJ as received 27 Nov. 1793 but recorded in SJL as an undated letter; Tr in AHN: Papeles de Estado, legajo 3895 bis, attested by Jaudenes and Viar).

From Josef Ignacio de Viar and Josef de Jaudenes

MUI SEÑOR NUESTRO [26 Nov. 1793]

Despues de las varias favorecidas de V.S. (á que no hemos tenido la honrra de contextar todavia, atendiendo á que no requerian una inmediata atencion, mientras pedian ésta diferentes asuntos urgentes que nos rodean) hemos recivido informes desde Wilmington relativos á la presa española ilegalmente hecha por los Franceses.

Adjuntas tenemos la honrra de remitir á V.S. Copias.

Por su contenido vendrá V.S. en conocimiento de la mala fee con que se han conducido los franceses comprehendidos en el hecho; y la imperdonable negligencia del Governador, ó Milicia de aquel Estado.

Luego que recivamos los Documentos correspondientes para provar la ultima, nos será indispensable recurrir al Presidente de los Estados Unidos por medio de V.S. protestando contra quien huviese sido la causa en la Carolina Septentrional por una parcial morosidad de que se escapase la consabida presa; áno ser que las eficases medidas, y ordenes posteriores del poder executivo del Governador de la Carolina meridional ó del Juez que correspondiese, produzcan el tan justo como deseado fin de que se entregue la presa á nuestros apoderados.

A este intento pedimos á V.S. informe al Presidente de los Estados Unidos de todo, para que con sus sabias disposiciones allane las dificultades que ofrece este hecho, y que pudieran ocasionar algun disgusto involuntario. Nos reiteramos á la obediencia de V.S. subscriviendonos los mas obedtes. y recondos. Servs. Q. B. L. M. de V.S.

JOSEF DE JAUDENES JOSEF IGNACIO DE VIAR

EDITORS' TRANSLATION

OUR VERY DEAR SIR [26 Nov. 1793]

Since your kind favors (to which we have not had the honor to reply, in view of the fact that they did not require immediate attention, whereas this was indeed required by various urgent matters besetting us), we have received reports from Wilmington concerning the Spanish prize illegally taken by the French.

We have the honor to transmit copies to you, enclosed herewith.

From their contents you will become aware of the bad faith with which the French involved in the deed have conducted themselves; and the unpardonable negligence of the Governor, or the militia, of that state.

As soon as we receive the relevant documents to prove the latter charge, it will be indispensable for us to resort to the President of the United States through you by way of protesting against whoever was responsible in North Carolina, through calculated dilatoriness, for the escape of the said prize; unless the efficient measures and subsequent orders from the executive authority of the Governor of South Carolina or the appropriate judge should produce the result, as just as it is desired, of having the prize returned to our representatives.

With this object in view, we beg you to inform the President of the United States of everything, so that with his wise measures he may iron out the difficulties that this deed presents and that might produce some kind of unintentional unpleasantness. We repeat ourselves at your service as we subscribe ourselves your most obedient and grateful servants. Most respectfully yours,

JOSEF DE JAUDENES   JOSEF IGNACIO DE VIAR

RC (DNA: RG 59, NL); undated, but presumably written on the same date as the preceding letter, both being received by TJ on the same day; in Jaudenes's hand, signed by Jaudenes and Viar; at foot of text: "Sor. Dn. Thomas Jefferson &ca."; endorsed by TJ as received 27 Nov. 1793 and so recorded in SJL. Enclosures not found.

From Charles Williamson

SIR   Bath Ontario County 26. Novr. 1793

I have the Honor to enclose You an Affadavit made before me as a Magistrate of this County. The Outrage complained of being attended with the most distressing consequences to some of the complainants who are Citizens of the United States—and not only highly alarming to the Settlers on this Frontier, but a Gross insult to this Goverment—I think it my Duty as a Magistrate to request You will do me the Honor of laying it before His Excellency the President of the United States.

The Individuals who have suffered by this unwarrantable exertion of Local Power on the Part of the British Look up with confidence to the Executive Officers of the Goverment of the United States for that redress which every good citizen feels himself entitled to.

I beg leave to say that in whatever light this transaction may be viewed by those who reside in situations inaccessible to the under strappers of an Arbitrary Power—it is here viewed as a Precedent of the most dangerous Nature (as the British may with the same propriety seize Stores on any part of the County of Ontario, where they are accessible to their depredations) and as a most shameful and Gross insult to the Goverment under which we Live, and I make no doubt will make the same impression on the breast of every American.

As a Magistrate I have done my Duty in making this Statement, which I have done with the more confidence as before this transaction Came before me I was personally acquainted with Mr. Rankin whom I regard as a Man of Honor and Truth. But as a Man that feels for the Dignity of this Goverment, and as an Extensive Proprietor in this County If such insults are submitted to, and the British Governors are permitted to Exercise a Jurisdiction within the County of Ontario, by no means even connected with the districts round the Forts they with-Hold from the United States—I beg leave to ask Whether on approaching Lake Ontario, within the bounds of the County of Ontario, and within the limits of the United States, are my settlers to consider themselves under the Protection of a Goverment that will secure them from Authorised Robberys and insults—And to secure that Protection must they cringe and Fawn on some underlin revenue Officer of Upper Canada. I have the Honor to be with the Greatest respect Sir Your most obt. and very humble Sert.
CHAS. WILLIAMSON

RC (DNA: RG 59, MLR); at foot of text: "The Honble. Thomas Jefferson Esqr"; endorsed by TJ as received 13 Dec. 1793 and so recorded in SJL; with penciled notes by TJ on verso: "copies to be taken & sent Genl. Chapin at [. . .] between [. . .]." PrC of Tr (same). Enclosure: Deposition of George Rankin, Bath, Ontario County, New York, 26 Nov. 1793, stating that he and three other men in two boats had passed the British garrison at Oswego in New York territory about 20 Aug. with a a cargo of castings, iron, tar, and gin worth about $500 and subsequently unloaded about half of their goods at the Eighteen Mile Creek and the rest at a spot about a dozen miles from the British garrison at Niagara, both of which landing points were within the jurisdiction of Ontario County; that he then went to Toronto and obtained permits to bring the goods within the British lines but that in his absence they were seized under the direction of a revenue officer of Upper Canada; that he then applied to a sheriff in Upper Canada for a writ of replevin but was refused because the seizure had taken place within American jurisdiction; that to his knowledge prior to the seizure his goods had never left American jurisdiction; that at Niagara he had seen his goods advertised for sale as contraband property and believes they were sold as such by the advertiser McKnab, whom he thinks is a revenue officer of Upper Canada; and that Mr. Lafferty and James McDonald, the chief owners

with himself of the shipment, were duly named in the permits and are so circumstanced that the seizure will materially hurt them (MS in same, in a clerk's hand, signed by Rankin and attested by Williamson as a Judge of the Court of Common Pleas of Ontario County; PrC of Tr in same, in a clerk's hand).

Charles Williamson (1757-1808) was a Scotsman whose colorful career had included service as a British army officer, capture at sea and imprisonment in Boston on his way to join Cornwallis's army, and a secret mercantile journey to Constantinople. He came to western New York in 1792 to promote a 1,200,000 acre tract of land purchased from Robert Morris by a group of investors headed by Sir William Pulteney, and during a decade there he took American citizenship and served four terms in the state assembly. After returning to Britain in 1803 he acted as an informal advisor to the British government, took an interest in the schemes of Aaron Burr and Francisco de Miranda, and died while carrying a message from Castlereagh to the Spanish West Indies (DAB; Arthur C. Parker, "Charles Williamson: Builder of the Genesee Country," Rochester Historical Society, *Publication Fund Series*, VI [1927], 1-34).

On 13 Dec. 1793 TJ submitted this letter and its enclosure to the President, who returned them the same day (Washington, *Journal*, 267). Although TJ's penciled

notes on this letter indicate that the OUT-
RAGE COMPLAINED OF here was referred to
General Israel Chapin, the American agent
to the Iroquois at Canandaigua, for further
information, TJ evidently did not correspond with Chapin directly and the matter
remained unresolved when he left office
(Washington, *Journal*, 32; TJ to George
Clinton, 30 Dec. 1793).

To Angelica Schuyler Church

Germantown Nov. 27. 1793.

I have received, my very good friend, your kind letter of Aug. 19.
with the extract from that of La Fayette, for whom my heart has been
constantly bleeding. The influence of the United States has been put
into action, as far as it could be either with decency or effect. But I fear
that distance and difference of principle give little hold to Genl. Washington on the jailors of La Fayette. However his friends may be assured
that our zeal has not been inactive. Your letter gives me the first information that our dear friend Madame de Corny has been, as to her fortune, among the victims of the times. Sad times indeed! and much lamented victim! I know no country where the remains of a fortune could
place her so much at her ease as this, and where public esteem is so
attached to worth, regardless of wealth. But our manners, and the state
of society here are so different from those to which her habits have been
formed, that she would lose more perhaps in that scale.—And Madame
Cosway in a convent! I knew that, to much goodness of heart, she joined
enthusiasm and religion: but I thought that very enthusiasm would
have prevented her from shutting up her adoration of the god of the
Universe within the walls of a cloyster; that she would rather have
sought the *mountain-top*. How happy should I be that it were *mine* that
you, she and Mde. de Corny would seek. You say indeed that you are
coming to America. But I know that means New York. In the mean
time I am going to Virginia. I have at length been able to fix that to the
beginning of the new year. I am then to be liberated from the hated
occupations of politics, and to sink into the bosom of my family, my
farm and my books. I have my house to build, my feilds to form, and to
watch for the happiness of those who labor for mine. I have one daughter married to a man of science, sense, virtue, and competence; in whom
indeed I have nothing more to wish. They live with me. If the other
shall be as fortunate in due process of time, I shall imagine myself as
blessed as the most blessed of the patriarchs. Nothing could then withdraw my thoughts a moment from home, but the recollection of my
friends abroad. I often put the question Whether yourself and Kitty will
ever come to see your friends at Monticello? But it is my affection, and
not my experience of things, which has leave to answer. And I am deter-

mined to believe the answer; because, in that belief, I find I sleep sounder and wake more chearful. En attendant, god bless you; accept the homage of my sincere & constant affection.   Th: Jefferson

RC (Peter B. Olney, Old Saybrook, Connecticut, 1950); addressed: "Mrs. Angelica Church London" and "to the care of mr Pinckney." PrC (DLC). Tr (MHi); 19th-century copy.

To Thomas Pinckney

Dear Sir   Germantown Nov. 27. 1793.

My last letters to you were of the 11th. and 14th. of Sep. since which I have received yours of July 5. 8. Aug. 1. 15. 27. 28. The fever which at that time had given alarm in Philadelphia, became afterwards far more destructive than had been apprehended, and continued much longer, from the uncommon drought and warmth of the autumn. On the 1st. day of this month the President and heads of the departments assembled here. On that day also began the first rains which had fallen for some months. They were copious, and from that moment the infection ceased, no new subject took it, and those before infected either died or got well, so that the disease terminated most suddenly. The inhabitants who had left the city, are now all returned, and business going on again as briskly as ever. The President will be established there in about a week: at which time Congress is to meet.

Our negociations with the NorthWestern Indians have completely failed, so that war must settle our difference. We expected nothing else, and had gone into the negociations only to prove to all our citizens that peace was unattainable on terms which any one of them would admit.

You have probably heard of a great misunderstanding between Mr. Genet and us. On the meeting of Congress it will be made public. But as the details of it are lengthy, I must refer for them to my next letter when possibly I may be able to send you the whole correspondence in print. We have kept it merely personal, convinced his nation will disapprove him. To them we have with the utmost assiduity given every proof of inviolate attachment. We wish to hear from you on the subject of M. de la Fayette, tho we know that circumstances do not admit sanguine hopes.

The copper by the Pigou, and the Mohawk is received. Our coinage of silver has been delayed by Mr. Coxe's inability to give the security required by law.

I shall write to you again immediately after the meeting of Congress. I have the honor to be with sentiments of great esteem & respect Dear Sir Your friend & servt   Th: Jefferson

RC (Gilder Lehrman Collection, on deposit NNP); at foot of first page: "Mr. Pinckney"; endorsed by Pinckney. PrC (DLC). FC (Lb in DNA: RG 59, DCI). Tr (ViW); 19th-century copy; lacks name of signatory.

From Thomas Pinckney

[DEAR] SIR   London 27. Nov. 17[93]

I thought we might secure the enjoy[ment of our neut]ral rights by our commercial arrange[ments; the lat]e treaties of Great Britain render that calculation [very uncerta]in but the disclosure[1] of their intention not to cede [the posts] seems to render our taking a part in the war inevitable a[s] it will now be *inst politic*[2] and popular:[3] when I retire from hence I wish to spend 6 or 8 months in france for the benefit of my children, as it is not probable that the war will be carried on within our country; I request your friendly information whether circumstances to which I may be a stranger will render that step improper. I remain Dear Sir Your faithful & obedient servant   THOMAS PINCKNEY

Tr (DLC); in the hand of George Taylor, Jr.; entirely *en clair*; parts of the first seven lines torn away supplied in brackets from decipherment in RC; with explanatory note for encoding error (see note 2 below); at head of text: "(private)"; at foot of text: "Mr. Jefferson." RC (DNA: RG 59, DD); written in code, except for notes at head and foot of text, salutation, dateline, complimentary close, and signature; with interlinear decipherment by George Taylor, Jr., and Daniel Brent (see note 1 below). PrC (DLC); with one word deciphered by Taylor (see note 3 below); endorsed by TJ as received 31 Mch. 1794 and so recorded in SJL. Dupl (DNA: RG 59, Duplicate Diplomatic Dispatches); written in code. PrC (ScHi: Pinckney Family Papers). Tr (Lb in DNA: RG 59, DD); entirely *en clair*, with encoded passages in brackets.

[1] With the exceptions noted above, the RC is deciphered interlinearly to this point by George Taylor, Jr., the remainder by Daniel Brent, both this decipherment and the Tr being verified by the Editors against partially reconstructed Code No. 16.

[2] Thus in manuscript and so encoded in RC and Dupl. Taylor explained Pinckney's coding error in a note he subjoined to the text: " in   st poli ti   c.
        640. 1565. 450. 1350. 1112

the cyphers for *deemed* the word probably

        deem ed

meant are 647. 1515."

[3] Word deciphered interlinearly by Taylor in ink on PrC at DLC.

From George Washington

[27 Nov. 1793]

Enclosed is another Specimen of Mr. Genets Indecent conduct towards the Executive Government of the U. States.

RC (DLC: TJ Papers, 95. 16271); undated, but probably written the same day TJ received it; addressed on cover sheet of an unidentified letter from TJ: "Mr. Jefferson—Secy. of State"; endorsed by TJ as received 27 Nov. 1793. Enclosures: (1) Governor George Clinton to Edmond Charles Genet, New York, 21 Nov. 1793, stating that, having been informed by Genet's 11 Nov. 1793 letter that the *Carmagnole*, the vessel undergoing repairs at the East River wharf, was fitted out as a privateer in the Delaware, he is certain that the French minister will agree to have it divested of all warlike equipment in conformity with the enclosed copy of Secretary of War Henry Knox's 15 Nov. 1793 letter to the governor, written in response to one from Clinton to the President, announcing that Genet had withdrawn commissions granted to certain privateers fitted out in American ports. (2) Genet to Clinton, New York, 23 Nov. 1793, stating that, having received No. 1 and its enclosure, he considered the governor's requisitions concerning the schooner *Columbia*, formerly known as the *Carmagnole*, to be part of the same system designed to disunite America from France and deliver her into English power that had bedeviled his mission from the first; that the orders given to Clinton were contrary to France's treaties with the United States, the federal government's practice of allowing British packets and merchant ships to arm for defense in American ports, and the bonds of friendship and mutual interest between the people of the two republics; and that since the *Columbia* was intended to serve as an advice boat with the French islands which the United States is bound by treaties to guarantee and by economics to take an interest in, he would order the consul and French commodore of the road to conform themselves to everything the governor thinks proper to direct. (3) Clinton to Washington, 24 Nov. 1793, stating that he had recently received 12 and 13 Nov. 1793 letters from Knox in answer to his of 8 Sep. 1793; that a review of his correspondence with Genet enclosed in that letter shows that he sought the departure of the privateers *Petite Démocrate* and *Carmagnole* in conformity with the presidential desire expressed in Knox's 16 Aug. 1793 letter that in cases like this force should only be used as a last resort; that the *Petite Démocrate* left New York harbor without augmenting its military equipment, as far as he could tell, while the *Carmagnole*, the subject of his 15 Nov. 1793 letter, still remains; and that he transmits Nos. 1 and 2 and wishes to be informed of any further action he is expected to take before he sets out shortly for Albany to meet with the legislature, a trip which may last until the spring (Trs in DNA: RG 46, Senate Records, 3d Cong., 1st sess.). Enclosures printed in *Message*, 98-9.

On the previous day the President had submitted these enclosures to Henry Knox with a request that he "prepare such answer to the Govs. letter as may seem proper." On the same day Washington approved a letter by Knox informing Governor Clinton that as a French privateer illicitly fitted out in the Delaware the *Carmagnole* was to be denied asylum in American ports in conformity with Knox's 16 Aug. 1793 letter to the governor, but that if the ship divested itself of all warlike equipment it would be allowed to make "any repairs not belonging to a vessel of war" in accordance with Knox's letters to the same official of 12 and 15 Nov. 1793 (Knox to Clinton, 26 Nov. 1793, DLC: Washington Papers; Washington, *Journal*, 250-1).

From Joseph Mussi

SIR   Philada. 28. Novr. 1793

Mr. Crosby having Communicated to me your desire to be accomodated in my house, give me leave to assure you sir that your Coming will afford me great deal of pleasure. My appartements are furnished in the Italian Stile, as you have seen; I have an excellent Cook from Milan, and you Shall have accomodations to your own wishes, both for appartements, and table. I am preparing a good bed for you, and Shall be glad to know when you intend to be here. I remain with sentiments of true esteem Sir your most obedt. Servant   JOS. MUSSI

RC (ViW: Tucker-Coleman Collection); at foot of text: "Thomas Jefferson Esqr. Germantown"; endorsed by TJ as received 28 Nov. 1793 and so recorded in SJL.

Joseph Mussi (d. ca. 1832), probably a native of Milan, was a Philadelphia merchant at 230 High Street in whose HOUSE TJ lodged from 30 Nov. 1793 until he left the city on 5 Jan. 1794. Mussi's sales to TJ in the 1790s included wine, vinegar, olive oil, Italian marble, and red clover seed (Hardie, *Phila. Dir.*, 104; Mussi's will, 10 Aug. 1830, admitted to probate 4 Jan. 1832, City Archives of Philadelphia; TJ to Martha Jefferson Randolph, 1 Dec. 1793; MB, 4 Jan. 1794, 4 Dec. 1796; TJ to Mussi, 17 Sep., 20 Nov. 1794; Mussi to James Hoban, 12 Dec. 1793, DNA: RG 42, PBG).

To John Nancarrow

DEAR SIR   Germ[antown] Nov. 28. 1793.

Having been sensible that Mrs. Nancarrow and yourself were proposing to incommode yourselves out of merely friendly dispositions to me, and that I could not avoid embarrassing you more than I could be easy under, I received yesterday with great satisfaction the offer of commodious apartments which I have not hesitated to engage, because it relieves me inasmuch as it relieves you from the inconveniences which your friendship disposed you to encounter. Accept for Mrs. Nancarrow and yourself my sincere thanks for this proof of your goodness, and assurances of the esteem of Dear Sir Your friend & servt

TH: JEFFERSON

PrC (DLC); faded; date enhanced in ink by TJ; at foot of text: "Mr. Nancarrow." Tr (ViU: Edgehill-Randolph Papers); 19th-century copy.

Notes of Cabinet Meeting on the President's Address and Messages to Congress

Nov 28. We met at the President's.

I read over a list of the papers[1] copying to be communicated to Congress on the subject of Mr. Genet. It was agreed that Genet's letter of Aug. 13. to the President, mine of Aug. 16. and Genet's of Nov. to myself and the Atty. Genl. desiring a prosecution of Jay and King should not be sent to the legislature: on a general opinion that the discussion of the fact certified by Jay and King had better be left to the channel of the newspapers, and in the private hands in which it now is than for the Presidt. to meddle in it, or give room to a discussion of it in Congress.

E.R. had prepared a draught of the Speech. The clause recommending fortifications was left out, but that for a military academy was inserted. I opposed it, as unauthorised by the constn. H. and K. approved it without discussion. E.R. was for it, saying that the words of the constn. authorising Congress to levy taxes &c *for the common defence*, might comprehend it. The President said he would not chuse to recommend any thing against the constitution, but if it was *doubtful*, he was so impressed with the necessity of this measure, that he would refer it to Congress, and let them decide for themselves whether the constn. authorized it or not. It was therefore left in.[2] I was happy to see that R. had, by accident, used the expression 'our republic' in the speech. The President however made no objection to it, and so as much as it had disconcerted him on a former occasion with me, it was now put into his own mouth to be pronounced to the two houses of legislature.

No material alterations were proposed or made in any part of the draught.

After dinner, I produced the draught of messages on the subject of France and England, proposing that that relative to Spain should be subsequent and secret.

H. objected to the draught in toto. Said that the contrast drawn between the conduct of France and England[3] amounted to a declaration of war. He denied that Fr. had ever done us favors, that it was mean for a nation to acknolege favors, that the dispositions of the people of this country[4] towards France he considered as a serious calamity, that the Executive ought not by an echo of this language to nourish that disposition in the people. That the offers in commerce made us by France were the offspring of the moment, of circumstances which would not last, and it was wrong to receive, as permanent, things merely temporary. That he could demonstrate that Gr. Br. shewed us more favors than France. In complaisance to him I whittled down the expressions without opposition, struck out that of 'favors antient and recent' from France, softened[5] some terms and omitted some sentiments respecting Gr. Br. He still was against the whole, but insisted that at any rate it should be a secret communication, because the matters it stated were still depending. These were 1. the inexecution of the treaty 2. the restraining our corn commerce to their own ports and those of their friends. Knox joined Hamilton in every thing. Randolph was for the communications, that the documents respecting the 1st. should be given in as public, but that those respecting the 2d. should not be given to the legislature at all but kept secret. I began to tremble now for the whole, lest all should be kept secret. I urged especially the duty now incumbent on the Presidt. to lay before the legislature and the public what had passed on the inexecution of the treaty, since Mr. Hammond's answer of this month might be considered as the last we should ever have; that therefore it could no longer[6] be considered as a[7] negociation pending. I urged that the documents respecting the stopping our corn ought also to go: but insisted that if it should be thought better to witholed them, the restriction should not go to those respecting the treaty: that neither of these subjects was more in a state of *pendancy*,[8] than the recall of Mr. Genet, nevertheless no scruples had been expressed. The Presidt. took up the subject with more vehemence than I have seen him shew, and decided without reserve that not only what had passed on the inexecution of the treaty should go in as public (in which H. and K. had divided in opinion from R. and myself) but also that those respecting the stopping our corn should go in as public (wherein H. K. and R. had been against me). This was the first instance I had seen of his deciding on the opinion of one against that of three others, which proved his own to have been very strong.

MS (DLC); entirely in TJ's hand; partially dated; written on same sheet as "Anas" entry for 1 Dec. 1793. Recorded in SJPL under 28 Nov.-1 Dec. 1793: "Notes of discussions on address to Congress. & messages." Included in the "Anas."

TJ's LIST OF THE PAPERS being prepared for transmission to Congress has not been found, but see note to Genet to TJ, 16 May 1793; and Washington to the Senate and the House of Representatives, [2 Dec. 1793], and note. For Genet's LETTER OF AUG. 13 TO THE PRESIDENT, see enclosure to George Washington to TJ, with Jefferson's Note, 15 Aug. 1793. For the French minister's letters DESIRING A PROSECUTION OF JAY AND KING, see Genet to TJ, 14 Nov. 1793 (sixth letter), and note. Attorney General Edmund Randolph's final DRAUGHT OF THE SPEECH of 3 Dec. 1793 by the President to Congress has not been found, but the address as actually given presumably followed it closely (Fitzpatrick, *Writings*, XXXIII, 163-9). Despite TJ's opinion that the proposal for a MILITARY ACADEMY WAS UNAUTHORISED by the Constitution, the address included a query whether America's defensive capabilities might be improved by affording "an opportunity for the study of those branches of the Military art, which can scarcely ever be attained by practice alone" (same, 166). The hint bore fruit in a statute of 9 May 1794 that authorized thirty-two Cadets to receive military training in the newly-created Corps of Artillerists and Engineers (*Annals*, IV,

1444; Edward S. Holden, "Origins of the United States Military Academy, 1777-1802," in *The Centennial of the United States Military Academy at West Point, New York, 1802-1902*, 2 vols. [Washington, D.C., 1904], I, 210, 212). The annual address included references to the United States as a "Republic" having a "Republican Government" (Fitzpatrick, *Writings*, XXXIII, 166). For the FORMER OCCASION when Washington had objected to this usage, see Notes of a Conversation with George Washington, 23 May 1793; and note to Washington to the Provisional Executive Council of France, [24 May 1793]).

For the revisions to the DRAUGHT OF MESSAGES about FRANCE AND ENGLAND, see Washington to the Senate and the House of Representatives, [2 Dec. 1793], and note. For THAT RELATIVE TO SPAIN, see first message of same to same, [14] Dec. 1793. Secretary of the Treasury Alexander Hamilton tried again to persuade the President that GR. BR. SHEWED US MORE FAVORS THAN FRANCE and that the portion of the message notifying Congress of Britain's failure to comply fully with the Treaty of Paris and its interference with American commerce SHOULD BE A SECRET COMMUNICATION, but this effort was equally unsuccessful (Washington to TJ, 1, 2 Dec. 1793; and TJ's first letter to Washington, 2 Dec. 1793). HAMMOND'S ANSWER OF THIS MONTH: Hammond to TJ, 22 Nov. 1793 (fourth letter).

[1] TJ here canceled what appears to be "propos."

[2] Remainder of paragraph added subsequently, partly in left margin.
[3] TJ here canceled "was."
[4] TJ here canceled "in favor."
[5] TJ here canceled "the language."

[6] Preceding two words interlined in place of "never."
[7] TJ here canceled "thing."
[8] Reworked from "dependancy."

To Certain District Attorneys

SIR   Germantown, November 29, 1793.

The Minister Plenipotentiary of France, complains that the Consuls of his Nation are exposed to insults, and their persons to danger from the numerous French Refugees, chiefly of the Islands, who are in and about the places of their residence, and are understood to be ill-disposed to the government of France, and those in authority under it. The Consuls are liable to the ordinary laws of the country and entitled to their protection, as other strangers are; yet, from respect to the Sovereign whose commission they bear, a more attentive enforcement of the laws of protection is due to them, than to other strangers. I presume that the laws of all the states have provided proper punishment for breaches of the peace *committed*; I presume that in all the states some [measur]e of *prevention* against threatened danger, equivalent to that of bind[ing] to the peace or good behaviour in the English law, has been provided. I am therefore to ask the favor of you to inform the Consul of France, residing in your state, that the federal government, respecting his nation, and attentive to the safety of those employed by it here, will put into activity all the means of protection for his person which the laws have provided; that you will be so good as to explain to him what these provisions are, and how he is to proceed to avail himself of them in case of need, and that you will in the same, and all other cases, take any measures which they authorize to prevent or to punish breaches of the peace, or good behaviour towards him, which are characterized and forbidden as such by the laws. I have the honor to be, with great esteem and respect, Sir, Your most obedient servant,   TH: JEFFERSON

RC (PHi: William Rawle Papers); printed form, signed by TJ; parts torn away supplied in an unidentified hand; addressed by Benjamin Bankson: "William Rawle Esquire Attorney of the United States for the District of Pennsylvania Philadelphia"; endorsed by Rawle: "Recd. Dec. 2d. Dec 3d. Called at the French Consuls—who was out of town communicated the contents to Mr. Bournonville ye Secretary." FC (DLC); in Bankson's hand, unsigned; at head of text in unidentified hand: "To U.S. Attornies"; at foot of text:

"⟨*Christopr. Gore*   *Mass*
Richd. Harrison   *N. York*
William Rawle   *Esqrs. Pennsya.*
Zebulon Hollingsworth   *Mayd.*
Thomas Parker   *So. Carolina*
Attornies of the U.S.⟩"; endorsed in pencil by George Taylor, Jr. FC (Lb in DNA: RG 59, DL); addressed to Gore, Harrison, Rawle, Hollingsworth, and Parker.

MINISTER PLENIPOTENTIARY OF FRANCE, COMPLAINS: see Edmond Charles Genet to TJ, 25 Nov. 1793 (second letter).

From Edmond Charles Genet

M.   New york. le 29. 9bre. 1793. l'an 2e. de la Repe. fse.

Il n'est point en mon pouvoir d'ordonner aux batiments[1] françois qui ont reçu des lettres de marque[2] dans les ports des Etats unis en vertu de nos traités en vertu de mes Instructions les plus precises de restituer les prises qu'ils ont été autorisés à faire sur nos énnemis; mais J'ai prescrit depuis longtems[3] à tous nos Consuls de n'opposer et de ne laisser opposer aucune resistance à la force morale, de la Justice des Etats unis si elle croit pouvoir se mêler des affaires relatives aux prises, ou du gouvernement s'il persiste dans[4] le systême contre le quel Je n'ai cessé de lui faire les représentations les plus fondées.

Il n'est pas en mon pouvoir non plus, Mr., de consentir à ce que les Indemnités que votre gouvernement propose de faire payer[5] aux propriétaires des susdites prises soient au compte de la france[6] premierement parceque l'on ne doit d'Indemnité que lorsque l'on a occasionné quelque dommage en faisant usage d'un droit que l'on n'avoit point tandis que nos traités et mes instructions me prouvent que nous étions[7] pleinement autorisés à armer dans vos ports. Secondement parceque d'après notre Constitution comme d'après la votre l'éxécutif n'a point l'appropriation arbitraire des fonds de l'Etat et que le Conseil éxécutif de france et ses délégués ne pourroient consentir au remboursement des Indemnites en question que lorsque le Corps législatif auroit d'abord renoncé sous sa responsabilité vis à vis du peuple[8] au droit que J'ai été éxpréssement chargé de maintenir et accordé ensuite les sommes répétées par nos énnemis et qui leur ont été[9] promises par Mr. le Président.[10]

Dft (DLC: Genet Papers); unsigned; at head of text: "Exp. Bis"; above salutation: "Le Cit Genet &c à Mr. Jefferson &c."; only the most significant emendations have been recorded below. Tr (AMAE: CPEU, XXXIX). FC (DLC: Genet Papers). FC (same); in English. Tr (DNA: RG 46, Senate Records, 3d Cong., 1st sess.); in English. Tr (DLC: John Trumbull Letterbook); in English. Recorded in SJL as a letter about the "Lovely Lass, Pr. W.H. & Jane" received 2 Dec. 1793. Printed with translation in *Message*, 32 (App.), 95-6; translation printed in ASP, *Foreign Relations*, I, 185.

The Washington administration's decision to order the restitution of PRISES captured after 5 June 1793 by French privateers fitted out in American ports and to seek INDEMNITÉS from the French government for any compensation the United States paid to the owners of such prizes was communicated in TJ to Genet, 7 Aug. 1793. See also Thomas, *Neutrality*, 188-205.

[1] Sentence to this point interlined or written in the margin in place of "⟨Je n'ai point ordonné et Je n'ordonnerai point aux armateurs⟩ Il n'⟨est⟩a point été et il n'est point encore en mon pouvoir."

[2] Preceding five words interlined in place of "⟨fait de⟩ été armés."

[3] Preceding two words written in the margin.

[4] Altered from "les déterminations."

[5] Altered from "gouvernement ⟨s'est engagé⟩ propose de faire ⟨toucher⟩ payer par la france."

[6] Preceding six words interlined in place of "si la restitution ne pouvoit point en être faite. Mes Instructions."

[7] Word interlined in place of "sommes."

[457]

⁸ Preceding eight words interlined.   ¹⁰ Genet here canceled "En Conse-
⁹ Preceding four words interlined in quence M., si."
place of "si genereusement."

To George Washington

Nov. 29. 93.

Th: Jefferson has the honor to inclose to the President some letters brought by the Rider yesterday afternoon, and which he found on his return home in the night.

RC (DNA: RG 59, MLR); endorsed by Bartholomew Dandridge, Jr. Tr (Lb in same, SDC). Not recorded in SJL. Enclosures: (1) Thomas Pinckney to TJ, 25 (two letters) and 27 Sep. 1793. (2) Robert Morris to TJ, 25 Nov. 1793.

To Edmond Charles Genet

SIR   Philadelphia Nov. 30.¹ 1793.

I have laid before the President of the US. your letter of Nov. 25. and have now the honor to inform you that most of it's objects being beyond the powers of the Executive, they can only² manifest their³ dispositions⁴ by acting on those⁵ which are within their powers. Instructions are accordingly sent to the district attornies of the US. residing within States wherein French Consuls are established, requiring them to inform⁶ the Consuls of the nature of the provisions made by the laws for preventing⁷ as well as punishing injuries to their persons, and to advise and assist them in calling these provisions into activity whenever the occasions for them shall arise.

It is not permitted by the law to⁸ prohibit the departure of the Emigrants to St. Domingo, according to the wish you now express⁹ any more than it was to force them away according to that expressed by you in a former letter. Our Country is open to all men to come and go peaceably when they chuse; and your letter does not mention that these emigrants meant to depart, armed and equipped for war. Lest, however, this should be attempted, the Governors of the States of Pennsylvania and Maryland, are requested to have particular attention paid to the vessels named in your letter and to see that no military expedition be covered or permitted¹⁰ under¹¹ colour of the right which the passengers have to depart from these States.

Provisions not being classed among the Articles of Contraband in time of war, it is possible that American vessels may have carried them to the ports of Jeremie and la Mole, as they do to other Dominions of the belligerent powers: but if they have carried arms also, these, as being contraband, might certainly have been stopped and confiscated. In the letter of may 15. to Mr. Ternant, I mentioned, that in answer to the complaints of the British Minister,[12] against the exportation of arms from the U.S.[13] it had been observed that the manufacture of arms was the occupation and livelihood of some of our Citizens; that it ought not to be expected[14] that a war among other nations should produce such an internal derangement of the occupations of a nation at peace, as the suppression of a manufacture which is the support of some of its citizens: but that if they should export these arms to nations at war, they would be abandoned to the seizure and[15] confiscation[16] which the Law of nations authorized to be made of them on the high Seas. This letter was handed to you, and you were pleased in your's of may 27. expressly to approve of the answer which had been given. On this occasion therefore we have only to declare that the same conduct will be observed which was announced on that.

The proposition to permit all our vessels destined for any port in the french West India islands to be stopped unless furnished with passports from yourself, is so far beyond the powers of the Executive, that it will be unnecessary to enumerate the objections to which it would be[17] liable. I have the honor to be, with great respect Sir, Your mo. obedient and Most humble servant   TH: JEFFERSON

PrC (DLC); in the hand of George Taylor, Jr., and partly overwritten in ink by him, signed by TJ; at foot of first page: "Mr. Genet." Dft (DLC); entirely in TJ's hand; altered date and other significant emendations are recorded below; endorsed by Taylor. Tr (DNA: RG 46, Senate Records, 3d Cong., 1st sess.). FC (Lb in DNA: RG 59, DL). Recorded in SJPL. Printed in *Message*, 101.

INSTRUCTIONS . . . TO THE DISTRICT ATTORNIES: TJ to Certain District Attorneys, 29 Nov. 1793. A FORMER LETTER: Genet to TJ, 30 Oct. 1793. COMPLAINTS OF THE BRITISH MINISTER: second Memorial from George Hammond, 8 May 1793.

[1] Month and day interlined in place of "Dec. 1." in Dft.

[2] In Dft TJ here canceled "shew their desire of."

[3] In Dft TJ here canceled "good."

[4] Remainder of sentence interlined in Dft in place of "towards the French nation by going as far as the laws permit."

[5] In Dft TJ here canceled "wherein the laws."

[6] Word interlined in Dft in place of "advise."

[7] In Dft TJ here canceled "the protection."

[8] In Dft TJ here canceled "prevent."

[9] In Dft TJ first wrote the sentence to this point as "The departure of the Emigrants to St. Domingo, which you wish to have prevented is not permitted by law" and then altered it to read as above.

[10] Preceding two words interlined in Dft.

[11] In Dft TJ here canceled "the pretext of a peaceable."

[12] This and the preceding clause interlined in Dft in place of "informing him that the British Min. had made representations."

[13] In Dft TJ here canceled "we informed him that" and above it interlined "I mentioned to."

[14] Preceding six words interlined in Dft in place of "we could not consent."

[15] Preceding two words written in the margin of Dft.

[16] Remainder of sentence interlined in Dft in place of "and seizure which might happen to them on the sea."

[17] Preceding two words interlined in Dft in place of "is."

From Edmond Charles Genet

M.   New york. le 30. 9bre. 1793. l'an 2e. de la Repe. fse.

J'ai reçu la lettre que vous m'avés fait l'honneur de m'écrire le 24 de ce mois.[1] Je suis on ne peut pas plus sensible aux mesures prises par le gouvernement federal pour faire punir les miserables qui ont violé envers les députés que St. domingue envoye dans le sein de la Convention nationale de france la protection que les lois des Etats unis accordent a tous Ceux qui se trouvent dans leur enceinte et Je ne saurois trop reclamer le secours des bons offices du gouvernement federal et du gouvernement local pour que cette affaire soit suivie avec la plus grande attention par les tribunaux chargés d'en connoitre. Elle tient, M., à une trame bien noire[2] que l'honneur de votre patrie est interesse à devoiler. L'attroupement d'emigrés françois qui[3] s'est porté à l'attentat qui est l'objet de mes plaintes étoit dirigé par un nommé[4] Talon agent de nos traitres reçu parmi vous. Ce vil suppot du despotisme est lié avec le Senateur Morris,[5] Il avoit envoyé de concert avec lui des émissaires contrerevolutionnaires. L'un d'eux l'abbé Colin a été découvert et[6] arreté; Les Commissaires m'envoyoient par les députés[7] les[8] preuves de cette Conspiration, Talon l'a scu et n'a rien négligé pour s'emparer de leurs papiers; après avoir rempli ce but il a eu assés d'influence pour faire sortir de prison le nommé Lubedeur[9] qui avoit été un de ses instruments et dont la police s'étoit emparé.

Je Joins ici, Mr., la déposition du fait relatif à la Mission de l'abbé Colin et une Gazette contrerevolutionnaire françoise imprimée à Philadelphie qui celebre la generosité prétendue avec laquelle Talon a fait sortir de prison le scelerat qui venoit de violer vos lois et celles des nations.

Dft (DLC: Genet Papers); unsigned; at head of text: "Exp. Bis"; above salutation: "Le Cit Genet &c à M. Jefferson &c." FC (same); with one omission. Recorded in SJL as received 2 Dec. 1793. Enclosure: Louis Pierre Dufay, "Note relative à Collin et a Talon," n.d., stating, in his capacity as one of the deputies to the National Convention from the northern part of Saint-Domingue, that Collin arrived last August at Cap-Français with a letter from Talon to Polverel offering Polverel a substantial sum of money if he agreed to treat in confidence with Collin about implementing a plan whereby Robert Morris and some associates would exchange 400,000 acres of land owned by Morris in Georgia for the produce of Saint-Domingue, which they proposed to bring to America; that Polverel met with Collin and, after ascertaining that he was aware of the contents of Talon's letter, asked him if he had anybody in Saint-Domingue empowered to negotiate this affair, to which Collin replied in the negative, adding that the authors of the plan intended to send an agent to the island soon;

that Polverel responded negatively when Collin asked if Talon himself could come to Saint-Domingue; that after conferring with Sonthonax, Polverel instructed Collin to leave the island in three days; and that Polverel then went to Saint Marc, where he publicly revealed Talon's proposal and his own conversation with Collin, and encouraged the friends of France to foil this plan on the grounds that it would work to the disadvantage of the French Republic by giving Americans a monopoly over colonial produce, injuring French trade with Saint-Domingue, and above all by encouraging émigré colonists and those intending to imitate them (MS in same; in Dufay's hand, with his signed authentication stating that he regarded it as his duty to communicate this note to Genet). Other enclosure not found.

Antoine Omer TALON had been introduced to TJ earlier in the year (see Thomas

Pinckney's second letter to TJ, 12 Mch. 1793, and note). COLIN: Collin de Sévigny, a French refugee priest in Philadelphia who had formerly been archdeacon of the cathedral chapter at Toul (Childs, *French Refugee Life*, 41, 170).

[1] Sentence substituted for "Je vous prie d'avoir la bonté de Joindre la piece ci."
[2] Here Genet canceled "dont les fils ont été."
[3] Preceding four words altered from "que Je vous ai deno."
[4] Preceding two words interlined.
[5] Here in the margin Genet canceled "qui a recelé s."
[6] Preceding two words interlined.
[7] Preceding three words written in the margin.
[8] Genet here canceled "copies."
[9] Preceding three words interlined in place of "sous son Cautionnement." Name left blank in FC.

From Alexander Hamilton

SIR   Treasury Department November 30th 1793

I have taken the opinion of the Attorney General on the case of the St. Domingo vessels, mentioned in your letter of the 2d. of September last, which confirms that which I had before entertained, and on further reflection continue to entertain . . . namely that those vessels do not fall within the meaning of the 38th. Section of the collection Law respecting vessels that put into our Ports from distress or Necessity; and of course are liable by law to the payment of the duty of Tonnage; from which it is not within the compass of Executive Discretion to relieve them, whatever circumstances of hardship may exist. A copy of the opinion of the Attorney General is herewith transmitted.

The law appears manifestly to contemplate cases of distress or necessity from causes which compel a vessel, being on a voyage for another port to change her destination for a port of the united States; not the case of a vessel which, induced by a civil insurrection to quit a foreign port, finds it most convenient to make a voyage to the united States.

I return enclosed the letter from the Vice Consul of Virginia; and have the honor to be with respect Sir Your obedient Servant

ALEXANDER HAMILTON

RC (DLC); in a clerk's hand, signed by Hamilton; ellipsis in original; at foot of text: "The Secretary of State"; endorsed by TJ as received 2 Dec. 1793. Enclosure: Edmund

Randolph to Hamilton, Germantown, 15 Nov. 1793, stating, in response to Hamilton's 9 Nov. 1793 letter received the day before, that, disagreeable as it was "for the cause of humanity," the French ships in question should not be exempted from tonnage duties under the Collection Act of 1790, "the cause of their quitting the Island of St. Domingo; not being the Species of necessity contemplated by that act" (Tr in DLC; in a clerk's hand; endorsed by George Taylor, Jr.; printed in Syrett, *Hamilton*, xv, 398). Other enclosure not found, but see note to TJ to Hamilton, 12 Sep. 1793.

For the letter to the ATTORNEY GENERAL that elicited the enclosed opinion, see Syrett, *Hamilton*, xv, 394. TJ's LETTER to Hamilton was actually dated 12 Sep. 1793.

From Josef de Jaudenes and Josef Ignacio de Viar

MUI SEÑOR NUESTRO   Nueva York 30. de Novre. de 1793.

Corrovorando la buena disposicion de nuestros Governadores de Luisiana y Sn. Agustin hacia conservar la paz con los Estados Unidos, y los Indios fronterizos, segun lo hemos manifestado á V.S. repetidas vezes anteriormente; tenemos la honrra de pasar á manos de V.S. ahora Copia de Carta que nos escrive el ultimo Governador, y del Expediente que en ella nos incluye; y asimismo otra Copia de un Capitulo de la que hemos recivido del primero.

De todo su contenido pedimos á V.S. informe al Presidente de los Estados Unidos, á fin de que pueda convencerse mas de raiz de los hechos que en muchas ocaciones hemos insinuado, y pueda reiterar sus sabias disposiciones al tan deseado intento de preservar la buena harmonia, y amistad que felizmente reina entre ambas Naciones.

Asi esperamos suceda, y en el interin nos repetimos á la obediencia de V.S. y tenemos la honrra de subscrivirnos con el maior respeto, y estimacion los mas obedtes. y reconocidos Servidores de V.S. Q. B. S. M.

JOSEF DE JAUDENES   JOSEF IGNACIO DE VIAR

RC (DNA: RG 59, NL); in Jaudenes's hand, signed by Jaudenes and Viar; at foot of text: "Sor. Dn. Thomas Jefferson &ca." Tr (AHN: Papeles de Estado, legajo 3895 bis); attested by Jaudenes and Viar. Recorded in SJL as received 2 Dec. 1793. Enclosures: (1) Juan Nepomuceno de Quesada to Jaudenes and Viar, St. Augustine, 12 Sep. 1793, stating that he was transmitting the enclosed documents to counteract a rumor being spread in East Florida that some of its inhabitants, supposedly inspired either by their government or by Mr. Panton (a Pensacola merchant involved in the Indian trade with the Spanish court's approval), had requested the Indian nations by letter to kill four white men settled among them; and that it was imperative for the executive power of the United States to take action to prevent border dissensions between East Florida and Georgia from destroying the peace and harmony that Spain wished to enjoy with the United States (Tr in DNA: RG 59, NL, in Spanish, attested by Jaudenes and Viar; Tr in DNA: RG 46, Senate Records, 3d Cong., 1st sess., in English). (2) Decree by Quesada, 31 Aug. 1793, ordering John Hambly to make a declaration about whatever knowledge he may have acquired during his last visit to the Indian nations on the king's business about a rumor that letters had been sent from East Florida asking those Indians to kill some white men settled among them, some with children. (3) Declaration by John Hambly, 31 Aug. 1793, stating as a Protestant through public interpreter Miguel Iznardy that, while staying at the house of Santiago Burgués during his visit to the Indian nations, Burgués repeatedly told him that he had seen a letter in which James Seagrove had requested Chief Juan Canard to arrange the deaths of Burgués, George Barnet, Noah Harald, and George Welbank, who were settled among those nations, so that Seagrove could thereby recover the property the Indians had taken from his brother, Robert Seagrove, and obtain that of the intended victims; that Seagrove had assured the chief that carrying out this plan would save the lives of four Indians demanded by the Americans for the murder of four of their countrymen and lead Seagrove to appoint him as commissioner of the Lower Creeks; that Burgués thought Seagrove had written this letter because Jacob Allen had told Seagrove that Burgués was responsible for Robert Seagrove's losses; that Burgués did not know whether anyone in East Florida had conveyed Seagrove's letter to the chief; that the chief confirmed Burgués's report about the letter without revealing who delivered it; and that he himself believed that it was delivered by George Galphin, who had been in the chief's house a few days before. (4) Declaration by Jacob or James Allen, 31 Aug. 1793, stating as a Protestant through Iznardy that, while recently visiting the Indian nations, he was told by Chief Pen of the Lachuas that Pen had heard from Hambly that Chief Canard of the Chiahas had received a letter in which Seagrove asked him to kill Galphin, Welbank, and Burgués with his son and an Indian named Mecaticochiske; that this request apparently stemmed from Seagrove's anger over the murders in Georgia and the plundering of Robert Seagrove's store by some Indians and white men, supposedly led by the intended victims; that he believed Seagrove was capable of writing such a letter but was not told by Pen whether Seagrove had offered Canard a reward or employment for the proposed murders; that, with respect to the Indians lately killed at St. Marys river,

David Cornell was killed on the spot and Cornell's companion apparently murdered; and that Mr. Hammond, a resident on the American side of that river, told Allen that two members of the company located on that coast informed him they had declared before a justice of the peace in Savannah that they had murdered the Indians by order of Mr. Randolph, their commander. (5) Certification by Public Notary Jose de Zubizarreta, 2 Sep. 1793, stating that he was present when the governor discussed the points at issue with Chief Pen through an interpreter during the chief's last visit to St. Augustine. (6) Certification by Zubizarreta, 2 Sep. 1793, stating that, being present when Pen conversed with Quesada through an interpreter during the chief's last visit to St. Augustine, Pen then said that he knew by hearsay of letters asking the Indians to kill some white men settled there, that he did not know the motive for it, that it was exclusively the work of Americans resentful of the slaughters perpetrated in their view under the leadership of the intended victims, and that neither he nor any other chief had killed the white men in question. (7) Decree by Quesada, 4 Sep. 1793, ordering authentic duplicate copies of Nos. 2-6 to be made (Trs in DNA: RG 59, NL, in Spanish, consisting of six consecutive pages with copies of Zubizarreta's certifications of each enclosure and final 7 Sep. 1793 attestation, the whole attested by Jaudenes and Viar; Trs in DNA: RG 46, Senate Records, 3d Cong., 1st sess., in English). (8) Extract of Baron de Carondelet to Jaudenes and Viar, New Orleans, 15 Oct. 1793, stating that Pedro Olivier had prevented four groups of Creeks from different parts from invading Georgia in retaliation for a Georgian attack on a Creek town on the Spanish side of the Oconee river by threatening to leave their nation and deprive them of Spanish protection; that a few days later the Creeks were obliged to renew hostilities because of a Georgian attack on the small town of Hoethletiaga, forty-five miles from Cusseta, which killed four Indians, wounded three, and led to the capture of four women, three girls, and a boy; and that he cannot refuse the resultant petitions of Hallowing King, who came here asking for protection, arms, and ammunition for the Creeks in conformity with their treaty with Spain, lest the Georgians, who are the aggressors, drive

[463]

them from their country into Spanish territory (Tr in DNA: RG 59, NL, in Spanish, attested by Jaudenes and Viar; Tr in DNA: RG 46, Senate Records, 3d Cong., 1st sess., in English).

TJ submitted this letter and its enclosures to the President on 10 Dec. 1793, and Washington returned them the same day (Washington, *Journal*, 265).

CONTEMPORARY TRANSLATION

Sir   New York November 30th. 1793

Corroborating the good disposition of our Governors in Louisiana and Saint Augustine towards preserving peace with the United States and the indians of the Frontiers, As we have repeatedly Manifested to you on former Occasions— we have now the honor of transmitting to you a Copy of a letter written to us by the latter Governor, and of the document which it enclosed As also a Copy of an extract of a letter which we have received from the former. We request you to Acquaint the president of the United States with their Contents, that he may be thoroughly Convinced of the Facts that in many occasions we have Suggested, And that he may renew his wise dispositions for the Object so desireable of preserving the good harmony And Friendship which happily exists between the two Nations. We hope it may be so, mean while we have the honor to Subscribe ourselves with the greatest respect Sir Your most Obedient And Affectionate Servants   JOSEPH DE JAUDENES   JOSEPH IGNACIO DE VIAR

Tr (DNA: RG 46, Senate Records, 3d Cong., 1st sess.). Tr (Lb in same, TR).

From John F. Mercer

Dr Sir   West River near Annapolis Nov. 30th. 1793.

I have taken the liberty to request you to inform me the state of Philadelphia as to health at present and whether Congress are to set there. If I can attend with any tolerable safety I shall do it but, the probability of being exposed in Taverns or lodging Houses to infected furniture added to a number of melancholy domestic circumstances, urge me to decline a trust which some delicate circumstances coud otherwise induce me to discharge for a time. With every sentiment of respect & friendship I am Dr Sir Yr. O H Ser.   JOHN F MERCER

RC (ViW: Tucker-Coleman Collection); endorsed by TJ as received 6 Dec. 1793 and so recorded in SJL.

From Thomas Mann Randolph, Jr.

Dear Sir   Richmond Nov: 30. 1793.

The news of my fathers death must have reached you before this thro' the ordinary channels. Having been detained a day or two longer at

Monticello than I expected when I wrote to you I did not arrive time enough to have any hand in the drawing of his will which was done by Colo. Harvie alone. As might have been expected from him, (the beggary of the younger children being likely to be more irksome to his family than the clamors of the Creditors,) a very good provision is made for them, while moneys advanced during his illness for necessary expences will probably never be recovered. My Brother and myself are appointed Executors of the will and not guardians of the children; an unaccountable and mortifying omission since we being by Nature pointed out for this trust and by custom regarded as the most proper persons for it, it wears the appearance of a suspicion of inability. We know well that my father himself would not have left them in other hands and suspect strongly from this and many other circumstances that he was when the will was signed allmost insensible. The office being an invidious, dangerous and difficult one I cannot yet prevail on myself to accept it. I should esteem your advice as a singular favor. I shall not determine untill your arrival in Virginia. If the interests of the children do not absolutely require it I shall certainly decline.

I expected on my coming to Richmond to find your furniture at Mr. Hyltons. To my astonishment no part of it had been moved from Rockets alltho I had given orders very soon after your departure for it. The person to whom I gave this charge (Mr. Leister himself) meeting with Mr. James Brown the day he received my letter communicated it to him and was advised to leave every thing in its actual situation, which he accordingly did.

Hendersons boats will be down today or tomorrow I expect and will take off a considerable part. They were stoped on their way by a sudden fall of the water: a heavy rain fell the day before yesterday which must have enabled them to proceed.

I have just heard from Monticello: Martha Maria and the two little ones are perfectly well.

I begin to be anxious to hear something from Mr. Le Roy being now directly answerable for the amount of one of my fathers bonds to him. I am Dear Sir Your most faithfull & affectionate friend

TH: M. RANDOLPH

RC (ViU: Edgehill-Randolph Papers); endorsed by TJ as received 10 Dec. 1793 and so recorded in SJL.

The DEATH of TJ's old friend Thomas Mann Randolph, Sr., occurred on 20 Nov. 1793. His 5 Nov. 1793 WILL named John HARVIE, Jr., the son of TJ's guardian and the father of the elder Randolph's young wife Gabriella, as the guardian of his minor children, and Thomas Mann Randolph, Jr., and his BROTHER William as executors of his estate (*Virginia Gazette, and Richmond and Manchester Advertiser*, 25 Nov. 1793; Gaines, *Randolph*, 32, 38).

From Richard Söderström

SIR   Philadelphia Nover. 30. 1793.

    Consistently with what I esteem my duty, I have the honor of enclosing you a translated Copy of a letter dated Algiers 7: Augst: 1793. from the Consul General of Sweden in that Country to me, (which I recieved a few days ago).[1] Permitt me to request the favour of you, in acknowledging the receipt of it, to furnish me with Such an answer as you may think can with propriety be given to it. I have the honor to be with the greatest respect Sir Your most Obd: and most Hle. Servt:

RICHD: SÖDERSTRÖM

RC (DNA: RG 59, NFC); at foot of text: "The Honle. Thos: Jefferson, Secrety. of State for the united States of America"; endorsed by TJ as received 30 Nov. 1793 and so recorded in SJL. Enclosure: A. Skjöldebrand to Söderström, Algiers, 7 Aug. 1793, asking him to deliver the enclosed letter containing a plea by ten Americans for their deliverance from a slavery of six years, several of whom have fought for their country and do not know of anything it has done to free them from languishing in chains and a raging plague; that a few days ago he saw two die, a fate the others envy; and that if Congress approves he will assume responsibility for ransoming the survivors from captivity (Tr in same; in Söderström's hand with his 30 Nov. 1793 attestation subjoined). Letter and enclosure enclosed in TJ to George Washington, 30 Nov. 1793, and returned by the President the same day (see Washington, *Journal*, 260).

No written ANSWER by TJ to the Swedish consul's letter has been found.

[1] Closing parenthesis supplied.

To George Washington

Nov. 30. 1793.

    Th: Jefferson presents his respects to the President and incloses him some letters just received.

    Mr. Pinkney's and Mr. Morris's information relative to the doing and undoing the decrees of the National assembly, in the case of the ship Lawrence and some other expressions in Mr. Morris's letter seem to render it proper to lower the expression in the message purporting the *just and ready redress of wrongs* on the high sea afforded by that government, which Th:J. will accordingly attend to.

RC (DNA: RG 59, MLR); addressed: "The Pres[. . .]"; endorsed by Bartholomew Dandridge, Jr. Tr (Lb in same, SDC). Not recorded in SJL. Enclosures: (1) Gouverneur Morris to TJ, 25 June 1793. (2) Richard Söderström to TJ, 30 Nov. 1793, and enclosure.

THE MESSAGE: George Washington to the Senate and the House of Representatives, [2 Dec. 1793].

From Patrick Hart

SIR   Richmond 1st Decr. 1793

I had the honor to receive in course Your favor of the 14th. Ulto. I shall forward the Orrery by the Boat [from?] Milton which is now down to Mr. John Watson with directions to deliver it to Mr. Randolph. It will at all times afford me pleasure to have it in my Power to render You any service this way & am with due respect Sir Yr obt. Servt.   PAT HART

RC (DLC); one word illegible; at foot of text: "The Hble Thos. Jefferson Esqr"; endorsed by TJ as received 10 Dec. 1793 and so recorded in SJL.

Notes of a Conversation with John Beckley

Dec. 1. 93. Beckley tells me he had the following fact from Lear. Langdon, Cabot and some others of the Senate, standing in a knot before the fire after the Senate had adjourned, and growling together about some measure which they had just lost, 'ah! said Cabot, things will never go right till you have a President for life and an hereditary Senate.' Langdon told this to Lear, who mentioned it to the President. The Presidt. seemed struck with it and declared he had not supposed there was a man in the US. who could have entertained such an idea.

MS (DLC); entirely in TJ's hand; written on same sheet as "Anas" entry for 28 Nov. 1793. Recorded in SJPL under 28 Nov.-1 Dec. 1793: "Presidt. for life & hereditary Senate." Included in the "Anas."

To Martha Jefferson Randolph

MY DEAR MARTHA   Philadelphia Dec. 1. 1793.

This place being entirely clear of all infection, the members of Congress are coming into it without fear. The President moved in yesterday, as did I also. I have got comfortably lodged at the corner of 7th. and Market street.—Dr. Waters is returned; not well, but better. Still always Hectic. He and Mrs. Waters are just gone to housekeeping for the first time. Mrs. Trist is also returned to town and means to take a small house and 3. or 4. boarders. Mr. Randolph, the Atty. Genl. having removed to German town during the fever, proposes not to return again to live in the city. Mrs. Washington is not yet returned.—So much for small news. As to great, we can only perceive in general that the French are triumphing in every quarter. They suffered a check as is said by the D. of Brunswick, losing about 2000. men, but this is nothing to their numerous victories. The account of the recapture of Toulon comes so many ways that we think it may now be believed.—St. Domingo has expelled all it's whites, has given freedom to all it's blacks, has established a regular government of the blacks and coloured people, and seems now to have taken it's ultimate form, and that to which all of the West India islands must come. The English have possession of two ports in the island, but[1] acting professedly as the patrons of the whites, there is no danger of their gaining ground.—Freneau's and Fenno's papers are both put down for ever. My best affection to Mr. Randolph, Maria and friends. Kisses to the little ones. Adieu affectionately

Th:J.

RC (NNP); at foot of text: "Mrs. Randolph"; endorsed by Mrs. Randolph. Tr (ViU: Edgehill-Randolph Papers); 19th-century copy; with lacunae.

[1] TJ here canceled "refusing to restore."

From George Washington

Dear Sir   Philada 1st. Dec 1793.

Is there no clue to Mr. Morris' meaning respecting Monsr. Merlino? The next paragraph of his letter is[1] enigmatical to me,[2] from the want of my recollecting perfectly[3] the subjects alluded to. What are the orders given him which he will implicitly obey, and which were, according to his account,[4] received so very[5] opportunely? Has not a letter of his of subsequent date to that laid before me yesterday, acknowledged the receipt of the Plans of the Federal City.

There can be no doubt since the information which has come to hand from our Ministers at Paris and London of the propriety of changing the expression of the Message as it respects the Acts of France. And if any bad consequences (which I declare[6] I see no cause to apprehend) are likely to flow from a *public* communication of matters relative to G. Britain it might be well to revise the thing again in your *own* mind, before it is sent in;—especially as the Secretary of the Treasury has, more than once declared, and has offered to discuss and prove,[7] that we receive more substantial benefits (favors are beside the question with any of them, because they are not intended as such) from British regulations with respect to the Commerce of this Country than we do from those of France; antecedant I mean,[8] to those of very recent date. We should be very cautious *if this be the case*[9] not to advance any thing that may recoil; or take ground we cannot maintain well.[10] Yours always

Go: Washington

[468]

RC (DLC); endorsed by TJ as received 1 Dec. 1793. Dft (DNA: RG 59, MLR); with emendations and variations, only the most important of which are noted below; at head of text: "The Presidt. of the U.S—to the Secy of State"; docketed by Washington. FC (Lb in same, SDC); wording follows Dft. Recorded in SJPL.

MONSR. MERLINO had been mentioned in Gouverneur Morris to TJ, 25 June 1793. The NEXT PARAGRAPH of this letter AL- LUDED to TJ's 12 Mch. 1793 instruc- tions to Morris to accept those currently in power in France as its legitimate rulers and resume payments on the American debt to that country. No letter from Morris ac- knowedging THE RECEIPT OF THE PLANS OF THE FEDERAL CITY has been found. The INFORMATION concerning French depreda- tions on American ships carrying property belonging to France's enemies contained in Morris's dispatch, and in Thomas Pinckney

to TJ, 27 Sep. 1793, led to last-minute revi- sions in TJ's draft of the President's MES- SAGE on relations with France and Great Britain (TJ's first letter to Washington, 2 Dec. 1793; Washington to the Senate and the House of Representatives, [2 Dec. 1793], and note).

[1] In Dft Washington here canceled "also."
[2] Preceding two words interlined in Dft.
[3] In Dft Washington first wrote "recol- lection of" and then altered the phrase to read as above.
[4] Preceding four words interlined in Dft.
[5] Word interlined in Dft.
[6] Dft: "still declare."
[7] Preceding two words interlined in Dft in place of "the point."
[8] Preceding two words interlined in Dft.
[9] Preceding five words interlined in Dft in place of "therefore."
[10] Dft: "cannot support."

From Joel Barlow

DEAR SIR   Paris 2 Dec 1793.

We have but just learnt the news of the peace between the Portu- guese and the Algerines, and of the sortie of the latter from the mediter- ranean to cruse against the Americans. You doubtless must have had the information much sooner, as it seems to have been known to Col. Humphreys on the 7th. October. We have already heard of the capture of five American ships off cape St. Vincent's. One of the crews escaped to the Portuguese shore, the others are gone into slavery.

I suppose you will have no doubt but the whole of this business is a manoeuvre of the English, to prevent our provisions coming to France, and at the same time to injure America. I dont know how long we are to bear the complicated insults of that government without manifesting any look of resentment. At the same time it appears to me that no power on earth has the means of opposing the hostilities of Great Britain at so cheap a rate as we have. We have no treaty of commerce[1] with that goverment. It can therefore be no breach of faith to impose such duties on their manufactures as shall prevent their importation. Such a mea- sure would overturn their whole system in a much shorter time than any other circumstance could do. Their war with France, as it cut off a con- siderable portion of their trade, was severely felt in their manufacturing towns, and gave a great shock to the government for a few months at first. But this, like most other evils, has become more supportable by habit. If the American Government were to impose an additional Impost of 50 percent, or any other sum that should amount to a total prohibition, on all English and Irish manufactures (perhaps declaring in the law that this duty should be continued till the algerines should make peace with us) it would open the eyes of the people of England, it would force the government to respect the American flag, it would soon establish a peace with Algires, and it would probably be among the most powerful[2] means of forcing a peace with France.

Another measure has been mentioned by some of the American merchants and captains here, who have desired me to suggest it to you. The French are at this moment extremely interested in supporting the freedom of our commerce with them. They have probably some ships of war now lying in the American ports. It is supposed that this government would lend us a 50 gun ship and three or four frigates, if it could be done in a manner not to involve this nation in a war with the Algerines, and perhaps even this is an event not to be feared by the French. It would not be difficult for America to man these ships and send them to protect her trade on the coast of Portugal, Spain and France.

Without these measures, or some others as effectual, our commerce with Europe and even to the west Indies will be almost totally cut off the next year. It is probable that the Algerine force will be greatly augmented. There is no doubt but some English vessels will be employed as algerine corsaires, that English Officers and seamen will be and are now on board of the Algerine ships, that some of them will be early in the spring crusing in the English Channel and even on the coast of America, and that the English, dutch and spanish ports, both in Europe and America will be open to their prizes.

Should any of your Anglified gentry in the American government be disposed to doubt of these probabilities, or to say that the English cabinet will not descend to the last degree of meanness and wickedness to enable these Pirates to injure us and france, let them reflect on the measures that cabinet pursued to drag the nation into the present war against France; let them call to mind the manner in which Tuscany was brought into the coalision, the insults on the port of Genoa, the protection given to the counterfeiters of French paper money which is now fabricated in great quantities in London, the mode of getting possession of Toulon, the declarations made to the courts of Denmark and Sweden, and the perpetual hostilities excited against us among the savage tribes in America.

I cannot but think that a prohibition of British and Irish manufactures in the united States would immediately bring that cabinet to reason with respect to us. It would probably also produce a national bankruptsy and a revolution in favour of liberty. At the same time a naval force to oppose the Algerines ought not to be neglected.

You will excuse, my dear sir, the crudity of my ideas and the liberty I take in exposing them to you on a subject you understand so much better than myself. If I should suggest any thing which had not occured to you before, it may render a service to my country, as it would furnish weapons to one who has the best inclination as well as abilities to use them.

I have still no doubt of the eventual triumph of the French republic. I hope my Last letter to you, as likewise several written about the same time (octobre) by Mr. Paine have arrived. The means we there[3] suggested for overtures of peace I still believe might be effectual. Yours respectfully   JOEL BARLOW

RC (DLC); endorsed by TJ as received 20 Jan. 1795 and so recorded in SJL, which also records the receipt of a missing Dupl on 10 June 1794.

Barlow's LAST extant LETTER to TJ is that of 8 Mch. 1793.

[1] Preceding two words interlined.
[2] Barlow here canceled "motives."
[3] Barlow here canceled "proposed."

To George Washington

Dec. 2. 1793.

Th: Jefferson with his respects to the President has the honor to send him the letters and orders referred to in Mr. Morris's letter, except that of the 8th. of April, which must be a mistake for some other date, as the records of the office perfectly establish that no letters were written to him in the months of March and April but those of Mar. 12. and 15. and Apr. 20. and 26. now inclosed. The enigma of Mr. Merlino is inexplicable by any thing in his possession.

He incloses the message respecting France and Great Britain. He first wrote it fair as it was agreed the other evening at the President's. He then drew a line with a pen through the passages he proposes to alter, in consequence of subsequent information (but so lightly as to leave the passages still legible for the President) and interlined the alterations he proposes. The *overtures* mentioned in the first alteration, are in consequence of it's having been agreed that they should be mentioned in general terms only to the two houses. The numerous alterations made the other evening in the clause respecting our corn trade, with the hasty amendments proposed in the moment had so much broken the tissue of the paragraph as to render it necessary to new mould it. In doing this, care has been taken to use the same words as nearly as possible, and also to insert a slight[1] reference to Mr. Pinckney's proceedings.

On a severe review of the question Whether the British communications should carry any such mark of being confidential as to prevent the legislature from publishing them, he is clearly of opinion they ought not. Will they be kept secret if secrecy be enjoined? Certainly not, and all the offence will be given (if it be possible any[2] should be given) which would follow their complete publication. If they could be kept secret, from whom would it be? From our own constituents only, for Gr. Britain is possessed of every tittle. Why then keep it secret from them? No ground of support for the Executive will ever be so sure as a complete knowlege of their proceedings by the people; and it is only in cases where the public good would be injured, and *because* it would be injured, that proceedings should be secret. In such cases it is the duty of the Executive to sacrifice their personal interests (which would be promoted by publicity) to the public interest. The negociations[3] with England are at an end. If not given to the public now, when are they to be given? And what moment can be so interesting? If any thing amiss should happen from the concealment, where will the blame *originate* at least? It may be said indeed that the President *puts it in the power* of the legislature to communicate these proceedings to *their constituents*; but is it more their duty to communicate them to *their constituents*, than it is the President's to communicate them to *his constituents*? And if they were desirous of communicating them, ought the President to restrain them by making the communication confidential? I think no harm can be done by the publication, because it is impossible England, after doing us an injury, should *declare war* against us merely because we tell our constituents of it: and I think good may be done, because while it puts it in the power of the legislature to adopt peaceable measures[4] of doing ourselves justice, it prepares the minds of our constituents to go chearfully into an acquiescence under these measures, by impressing them with a thorough and enlightened conviction that they are founded in right. The motive too of proving to the people the impartiality of the Executive between the two nations of France and England urges strongly that while they are to see the disagreeable things which have been going on as to France, we should not conceal from them what has been passing with England, and induce a belief that nothing has been doing.

Th: Jefferson

RC (DNA: RG 59, MLR); endorsed by Washington. PrC (DLC); right margin of first two pages frayed; partially overwritten in a later hand. Tr (Lb in DNA: RG 59, SDC). Not recorded in SJL. Enclosures: (1) TJ to Gouverneur Morris, 12, 15 Mch., 20, 26 Apr. 1793. (2) 2d Dft of Washington to the Senate and the House of Representatives, [2 Dec. 1793].

[1] TJ here canceled "mention."
[2] Word interlined in place of "it."
[3] Word interlined in place of "proceedings."
[4] Word interlined in place of "means."

From George Washington, with Jefferson's Note

Dr Sir   Phila 2d. Decr 1793.

I am very well satisfied with the train things are in. You will recollect that the Proclamation,[1] Rules and other things are referred to in the Speech. I shall depend upon there being got ready at your Office. Yours &ca   Go: Washington

[*Note by TJ:*]
Answer to note of this day[2] respecting publication of proceedings with Gr. Britn.

RC (DLC); in Washington's hand, with note by TJ at foot of text; addressed: "Mr. Jeffer[. . .]"; endorsed by TJ as received 2 Dec. 1793. Recorded in SJPL.

[1] Word interlined.
[2] Preceding three words interlined by TJ.

THE SPEECH: see note to Materials for the President's Address to Congress, [ca. 22 Nov. 1793].

To George Washington

Dec. 2. 93.

Th: Jefferson with his respects to the President has the honor to inclose him three copies of the Proclamation and of the Rules.

Having only heard the speech read, he cannot recollect it perfectly enough to decide by memory what documents it requires from his office, and therefore is obliged to ask of the President if any more be requisite?

RC (DNA: RG 59, MLR); addressed: "The Presid[. . .]"; endorsed by Bartholomew Dandridge, Jr. Tr (Lb in same, SDC). Not recorded in SJL. Enclosures: (1) Proclamation of Neutrality, 22 Apr. 1793 (Fitzpatrick, *Writings*, XXXII, 430-1). (2) Rules on Neutrality, 3 Aug. 1793.

Washington's annual SPEECH to Congress of 3 Dec. 1793 was also accompanied by Secretary of the Treasury Alexander Hamilton's circular letter of 4 Aug. 1793 transmitting the second enclosure listed above to the customs collectors (ASP, *Foreign Relations*, I, 140-1; TJ to Henry Knox, 11 Aug. 1793, and note).

George Washington to the Senate and the House of Representatives

GENTLEMEN OF THE SENATE   [2 Dec. 1793]

As the present situation of the several nations of Europe, and especially of those with which the US. have important relations, cannot but render the state of things between them and us matter of interesting enquiry to the legislature, and may indeed give rise to deliberations to which they alone are competent, I have thought it my duty to communicate to them certain correspondences which have taken place.

The[1] Representative and Executive bodies of France have[2] manifested generally a friendly attachment[3] to this country, have[4] given advantages to our commerce and navigation, and have made overtures for placing these advantages on permanent ground. A decree however of the National assembly, subjecting vessels laden with provisions to be carried into their ports, and making enemy goods lawful prize in the vessel of a friend, contrary to our treaty, tho revoked at one time as to the US. has been since extended to their vessels also, as has been recently stated to us. Representations on this subject will be immediately given in charge to our minister there,[5] and the result shall be communicated to the legislature.[6]

It is with extreme concern I have to inform you[7] that the proceedings of[8] the person whom they have unfortunately appointed their Minister Plenipy. here have breathed nothing of the friendly spirit of the nation which sent him. Their tendency on the contrary has been[9] to involve us in war abroad,[10] and discord and anarchy at home. So far as his acts, or those of his agents, have threatened our immediate commitment in the war,[11] or flagrant insult to the authority of the laws, their effect has been counteracted by the ordinary cognisance of the laws, and by an exertion of the powers confided to me. Where their danger was not imminent, they have been borne with,' from sentiments of regard to his nation, from a sense of their friendship towards us,[12] from a conviction that they would not suffer us to remain long exposed to the action of a person who has so little respected our mutual dispositions, and, I will add, from a reliance on the firmness of my fellow-citizens in their principles of peace and order.[13]—In the mean time I have respected and pursued the stipulations of our treaties, according to what I judged their true[14] sense; and have witheld no act of friendship which their affairs have called for from us, and which justice to others left us free to perform.—I have gone further. Rather than employ force for the restitution of certain vessels which I deemed the US. bound to restore, I thought it more[15] adviseable to satisfy the parties by avowing it to be my opinion, that if restitution were not made, it would be incumbent on the US. to make compensation. The papers now communicated will more particularly apprize you of these transactions.

The vexations and spoliation understood to have been committed, on our vessels and commerce, by the cruizers and officers of some of the belligerent powers,[16] appeared to require attention. The proofs of these however not having been brought forward, the description of citizens supposed to have suffered were notified, that on furnishing them to the Executive, due measures would be taken to obtain redress of the past, and more effectual provisions against the future. Should such documents be furnished, proper[17] representations will be made[18] thereon, with a just reliance on a redress proportioned[19] to the exigency of the case.

The British government having undertaken, by orders to the Commanders of their armed vessels, to restrain generally our commerce in corn and other provisions to their own ports and those of their friends, the instructions now communicated were immediately forwarded to our minister at that court. In the mean time some discussions on the subject, took place between him and them. These are also laid before you; and I may expect to learn the result of his special instructions in time to make it known to the legislature during their present session.[20]

Very early after the arrival of a British minister here, mutual explanations on the inexecution of the treaty of peace were entered into with[21] that minister. These are now laid before you for your information.[22]

On the subjects of mutual interest between this country and Spain,[23] negociations and conferences are now depending. The public good requiring that the present state of these should be made known to the legislature in confidence[24] only, they shall be the subject of a separate and subsequent communication.

2d Dft (DLC: TJ Papers, 95: 16278-9); entirely in TJ's hand; undated, but begun sometime after the Cabinet meeting of 28 Nov. 1793 and completed before it was enclosed in TJ to Washington, 2 Dec. 1793 (first letter); consisting of three pages on which, in order to facilitate the President's review, TJ copied his language from Dft as it stood after Cabinet review and then, canceling lightly, entered substitute language and other emendations (see notes 2, 4, and 20 below), some of them lacking in the PrC (see notes 1, 3, 4, and 7 below), with the first page having a small slip bearing substitute language pasted on so as to create a flap replacing parts of the second and third paragraphs seamlessly (see notes 1 and 10 below). PrC (same, 16308-10); dated in ink by TJ at head of text: "Dec. 5. 93."; consisting of text prior to attachment of small slip to first page of 2d Dft and lacking salutation and some emendations in the text replaced by the slip; partially overwritten in a later hand. Dft (same, 16272-3); entirely in TJ's hand, with his subjoined note written at a different time: "This shews my original draught, and the alterations made in it at our council at the President's Nov. 28. 93."; undated, but written between 23 and 28 Nov. 1793 and bearing three sets of emendations: those present in the PrC and therefore made prior to the submission to the Cabinet on 28 Nov. 1793 (see notes 13, 15, and 23 below), those probably made at the 28 Nov. 1793 Cabinet meeting (see notes 4, 11-14, 17, 19-21, and 24 below), and those presumably added on 1 or 2 Dec. 1793 (see notes 4, 16, 18, 20, and 22 below). PrC (same, 95: 16274-5, 91: 15611, 95: 16276); undated; lacks subjoined note and most of the emendations in Dft; partially overwritten in a later hand. Recorded in SJPL under 5 Dec. 1793. The text Washington sent to Congress, which was addressed to the "Gentlemen of the Senate, and of the House of Representatives," followed TJ's final draft with only insignificant differences in spelling, punctuation, and capitalization, and one minor variation in wording (DNA: RG 46, 3d Cong., 1st sess.; Fitzpatrick, *Writings*, XXXIII, 170-3).

With this presidential message, the first of three on foreign affairs drafted by TJ for the first session of the third Congress that began on 2 Dec. 1793, Washington disclosed the startling news that his administration had requested France to recall its minister plenipotentiary, Edmond Charles Genet, for repeated failures to respect American neutrality and sovereignty as well as manifold lapses in diplomatic decorum. In preparing the message, TJ sought to preserve cordial ties with France, but the evolution of the drafts reveals that his efforts to shield the French cause were first diluted by Cabinet opposition and then weakened more seriously by the arrival of news of actions taken by France which undercut American neutral rights.

On 23 Nov. 1793, when Washington and the Cabinet considered an outline of topics for the President's annual address to Congress that had been consolidated by Attorney General Edmund Randolph from their earlier outlines and drafts, they decided to reserve the thorniest issues involving American relations with France, Great Britain, Spain, and the Barbary states for special messages. With respect to France, Randolph's notations indicate that the Cabinet advised the President to inform Congress of Genet's invocation—in his 30 Oct. 1793 letter to TJ—of the clause in the 1778 treaty of alliance with France guaranteeing its possessions in America, French proposals for a new commercial treaty, Genet's ministerial conduct, proposed compensation for certain prizes captured by French armed vessels, and the maritime jurisdic-

tion of the United States. The President was also counseled to touch on British retention of certain posts on the American frontier in defiance of the Treaty of Paris and British interception of American vessels carrying provisions to France or French-occupied ports under the 8 June 1793 additional instructions of George III to the commanders of British warships and privateers. At this meeting the Cabinet assigned the task of preparing the messages to the Secretary of State (Notes of Cabinet Meetings on Edmond Charles Genet and the President's Address to Congress, [18 Nov. 1793]; Notes of Cabinet Meeting on the President's Address to Congress, 21, 23 Nov. 1793; Materials for the President's Address to Congress, [ca. 22 Nov. 1793], and note; Randolph, "Heads of Matter, to be communicated to congress, either in the speech, or by message, as collected from the notes of the President, and the other gentlemen," DLC: Washington Papers; Thomas Pinckney to TJ, 5 July 1793, and note).

TJ composed the initial draft of the message on France and Great Britain between 23 and 28 Nov. 1793. He adopted the indirect course of transmitting relevant documents on the newly-defined limit on American maritime jurisdiction with papers relating to French prizes without explicitly mentioning the subject, and he omitted mention altogether of Genet's attempt to induce the United States to honor the guarantee clause in the treaty of alliance. The core of the draft was devoted to balancing the revelation of Genet's misdeeds by highlighting France's generally friendly behavior toward the United States and emphasizing British violations of the Treaty of Paris and American neutral rights.

When the Cabinet considered the draft on 28 Nov. 1793, Secretary of the Treasury Alexander Hamilton immediately objected to it "in toto," arguing that the contrast TJ had drawn between the two belligerents was tantamount to "a declaration of war" on Great Britain. Even though TJ toned down some of the language commending France and chastising Britain, Hamilton then attempted, with the support of Secretary of War Henry Knox, to undermine TJ's effort to maintain a balance between French and British transgressions by proposing that British violations of the peace treaty and interference with American trade be dealt with in a separate and secret communication to Congress, inasmuch as these matters were still under negotiation. Although Randolph supported mention of these issues in the message, he favored withholding from Congress altogether the documents on British trade violations. To TJ's great relief, however, the President took the unusual step of overruling a majority of his advisors and insisted that papers on British as well as French abuses be communicated with the message (Notes of Cabinet Meeting on the President's Address and Messages to Congress, 28 Nov. 1793).

At this juncture, the arrival of news from Europe led to a weakening of the language, still generally favorable to France, that emerged from the Cabinet meeting. On 28 and 30 Nov. 1793 TJ received dispatches from the American ministers to Great Britain and France containing the unwelcome tidings that France had reversed itself and decided not to honor its treaty obligations to respect the neutrality of American ships carrying enemy property or bringing neutral merchandise to enemy ports (Gouverneur Morris to TJ, 25 June 1793, and note; Thomas Pinckney to TJ, 27 Sep. 1793, and note). TJ submitted both letters to Washington and advised him that he now intended to modify the part of the message crediting France with "just and ready redress" of illegal depredations. The President approved the suggestion the following day and asked TJ to reconsider the desirability of making public the papers relating to Britain in light of Hamilton's continuing insistence that the United States enjoyed greater commercial benefits from that nation (TJ to Washington, 30 Nov. 1793; Washington to TJ, 1 Dec. 1793).

On 2 Dec. TJ accordingly sent Washington a new draft that introduced French infringements on American neutral trade and included a reworked paragraph on spoliation indicating that more than one of the warring powers had been involved in ravaging American shipping. Despite the setback to his efforts to depict England as the principal culprit in disrupting American trade, the forceful arguments in TJ's covering letter ultimately persuaded the wavering President that the message should discuss British as well as French misbehavior and enclose unconditionally documents relative to both nations. Three days later Washington sent Congress the message as TJ had finally reworked it (TJ's first letter to Washington, 2 Dec. 1793; Washington to TJ, with Jefferson's Note, 2 Dec. 1793; JS, II, 7-8; JHR, II, 9-10).

For the PAPERS NOW COMMUNICATED on American relations with France and on British interference with OUR COMMERCE IN CORN and INEXECUTION OF THE TREATY OF PEACE, see ASP, Foreign Relations, I, 142-88, 188-243, respectively; see also note to Genet to TJ, 16 May 1793, on the publication of the papers by order of the House of Representatives. The sets of documents transmitted to Congress were apparently collated at a Cabinet meeting on 4 Dec. 1793 (Bartholomew Dandridge, Jr., to TJ, 4 Dec. 1793). On that day TJ also prepared certifications of these documents, with that for his correspondence with Genet reading: "Department of State—to wit. I hereby certify, That the preceding Copies and translations, beginning with a letter of May 22d. 1793, and ending with one of November 29th. 1793, are from originals, or from authentic copies in the Office of the Department of State. Given under my Hand this fourth day of December 1793. Th: Jefferson" (MS in DNA: RG 46, Senate Records, 3d Cong., 1st sess., in the hand of George Taylor, Jr., signed by TJ). TJ's certification of the documents on Great Britain varied only in vouching for "Copies beginning with a Letter of Novr. 29th., 1791, and ending with one of Septr. 25th. 1793, and the paper it inclosed" (MS in same, in Benjamin Bankson's hand, signed by TJ). For the DESCRIPTION OF CITIZENS who were NOTIFIED of the need to furnish documentation to the executive concerning maritime depredations, see Circular to American Merchants, 27 Aug. 1793, and note. The SEPARATE AND SUBSEQUENT COMMUNICATION on Spain is printed under 14 Dec. 1793.

[1] Text on small slip begins with this word. In text underneath TJ here canceled "several." Emendation not in PrC.

[2] In text underneath the small slip TJ here canceled "uniformly." He had circled this word in the Dft after making its PrC.

[3] Preceding four words altered from "the most friendly attachments" in text underneath the small slip. Emendation not in PrC.

[4] In text underneath the small slip TJ reworked the remainder of the sentence—altered from "given particular advantages"

after the PrC was made—from "shewn particular favor to our commerce and navigation and as far as yet appears, have given just and ready redress of the wrongs to our citizens and their property irregularly taken on the high seas, and carried into their ports." He made the necessary cancellations lightly for the purpose of presentation to Washington, having copied both sentence endings from the Dft, where the reworked one given in the text printed here, containing two minor variations, was inserted in the margin and the original ending was altered at the 28 Nov. 1793 Cabinet meeting by TJ's interlineation of "as far as yet appears have."

5 On the small slip TJ first wrote "also, as we learn very recently. To the representations made on the subject by our minister, others will be immediately given him in special charge," and then revised the passage to read as above.

6 Preceding two sentences lacking from text underneath the small slip and from earlier versions.

7 In text underneath the small slip TJ first copied "But it is with extreme concern I am obliged to add" from Dft and then revised the phrase to read as above. Emendation not in PrC.

8 The preceding two words appear only on the small slip. Text underneath and all other texts: "line of conduct pursued by."

9 The preceding nineteen words appear only on the small slip. The text underneath and all other texts read "has been widely different from theirs, it's direct tendency having been," except that Dft ends with "tendency being."

10 Text on small slip ends with the first syllable of this word.

11 In Dft TJ canceled "without" here, and "within" at the end of the next clause. Emendations not in PrC.

12 Preceding two words added in margin of Dft in place of "and favors, ancient and recent." Emendation not in PrC.

13 In Dft TJ here canceled "and on the continuance of that confidence which they have so long reposed in me, and which could not be withdrawn in a case where I can have no views but to pursue their best interests, according to the best of my ⟨abilities and⟩ judgment." Except for the cancellation of bracketed words, emendation not in PrC.

14 Word interlined in Dft in place of "real." Emendation not in PrC.

15 In Dft TJ here canceled "expedient."

16 In Dft TJ first wrote, with respect to the British, "committed by their cruizers and officers, on our vessels and commerce," and then revised the phrase to read as above. Emendation not in PrC.

17 Word interlined in Dft. Emendation not in PrC.

18 Word interlined in Dft in place of "forwarded to the British government." Emendation not in PrC.

19 In Dft TJ first wrote "that their measure of redress will be proportioned," then altered the phrase to read "on a redress measured in proportion," and finally revised it to read as above. Emendations not in PrC.

20 TJ interlined this paragraph in place of one that he lightly canceled for purposes of presentation to Washington: "The undertaking to restrain generally our commerce of corn and other provisions to their own ports and those of their friends, by an express order of the British government, has been the subject of the representations now communicated. These were forwarded to our minister at their court; and we may expect final information thereon in time to make the same known to the legislature during their present session." TJ had copied both paragraphs from the Dft, the interlined one being there inserted in the margin. In the Dft he had originally written the canceled paragraph as follows: "The undertaking to restrain generally our commerce of corn and other provisions to their own ports and those of their friends by an express order of their government, being an infraction of our natural rights, unfounded in reason, inconsistent with the candor of our conduct towards them, and excused by no want of these articles themselves, the representations on that subject now communicated, were forwarded to our minister at their court. By these you will perceive that we may expect final information thereon in time for the legislature to consider whether any provision will be necessary on their part for securing an indemnification to our agriculture and commerce for the losses sustained by this interception of their produce." After making the PrC, and most likely at the 28 Nov. 1793 Cabinet meeting, TJ substituted "in favor of" for "for securing an indemnification to" and then reworked the paragraph before copying it to the 2d Dft and canceling it there.

21 Word interlined in place of "between

the Secretary of state and." The same emendation is in Dft but lacking in its PrC.

²² In Dft this paragraph appeared two paragraphs earlier; in the margin next to it TJ wrote: "to come in below." Emendation not in PrC.

²³ In Dft TJ first wrote "Some subjects of mutual interest existing between this country & Spain also, whereon," and then revised the phrase to read as above.

²⁴ Preceding two words interlined in Dft. Emendation not in PrC.

From Edmond Charles Genet

M.   New york. le 3. Xbre.¹ 1793. l'an 2e. de la Repe. fse.

Je sais très bien que l'éxécutif des Etats unis est le Canal Constitutionnel des Communications qui ont lieu entre les Etats unis et les autres nations aussi est ce sous les yeux du Président que Je vous ai prié par une note officielle de mettre les Commissions de Vice Consul que J'ai délivrées en vertu de nos conventions en vertu de mes pouvoirs aux Citoyens Chervi et Pennevert à l'effet d'obtenir son exequatur.

Je ne Conçois point ce que l'on² peut éxiger de plus. Cependant³ pour vous prouver que bien loin de tenir à la pointille des formalités Je desire les applanir autant qu'il est en mon pouvoir Je vous serai veritablement obligé de vouloir bien me définir *Grammaticalement* puisque toute discussion constitutionnelle vous est interdite Ce que le gouvernement federal entend par le mot *adresse* qui présente plusieurs sens,⁴ et dont aucun ne me paroit applicable au point en discussion.

Une Commission Consulaire est un pouvoir délégué par le Souverain d'un pays à un agent particulier qu'il envoye dans un autre Etat pour y remplir avec l'agrément du gouvernement de cet Etat ou d'après des Conventions qui en font un droit certaines fonctions Judiciaires notariales, administratives et autres vis à vis de ceux de ses concitoyens qui peuvent s'y trouver.

Dans les Pays ou le souverain qui envoye un Consul entretient des Ministres ou d'autres representants leur devoir est de notifier au gouvernement du Souverain auprès du quel ils resident la nomination de ce Consul, de lui donner Communication de sa Commission et de le requerir de lui delivrer un exequatur qui n'est autre chose qu'un certificat qui atteste que verification faite des titres dudit Consul ils se sont trouves [en]⁵ regle.

Dans les pays ou le souverain qui envoye un Consul n'entretient point de Ministre cct agent est ordinairement muni d'une⁶ lettre particuliere par laquelle le gouvernement le Ministre⁷ ou l'éxécutif de son Souverain Informe le gouvernement le Ministre ou l'éxécutif de celui dans les Etats duquel il doit resider de sa nomination et des fonctions qui lui sont confiées.

Je ne vois point, M., qu'il y ait en éffet d'autre formalité à remplir et Je ne sais véritablement ce que l'on entend par l'adresse en question. Si c'est une Suscription elle est déplacée sur une Commission qui ne peut être adressée qu'à celui qui en est revêtu. Si c'est une requisition la notification officielle en tient lieu.[8]

Si c'est une accreditation particuliere elle denature la mission des Consuls et les convertit en agents politiques ainsi que cela se pratique dans quelques petits Etats. Au surplus, M., s'il y a quelqu'erreur dans les Commissions consulaires délivrées par le Conseil èxécutif de france elles sont fondées sur l'usage. Je me suis fait représenter des copies des Commissions données par le[9] ci devant Roi à ses consuls en Amerique et J'ai reconnu qu'elles étoient Conformes à celles de la Republique ainsi qu'à celles des Consuls[10] de toutes les puissances. Il n'est soyés en bien persuadé Jamais entré dans[11] les vues de la france libre de se mêler en aucune manière de votre gouvernement ni de Contester à M. le President la plus petite[12] partie de sa prerogative. Mais il est de mon devoir de veiller à tout ce qui peut avoir rapport aux Interêts et à la dignité du peuple françois et de demander l'éxplication des innovations auxquelles on éxige qu'il se soumette et aux quelles il n'est point en mon pouvoir d'adherer quand elles n'ont point été définies par la Constitution quand aucun éxemple ne les Justifie. Les éxceptions seules offensent les loix générales ne blessent personne.

Dft (DLC: Genet Papers); unsigned; with altered date; above salutation: "Le Cit Genet &c à M. Jefferson &c."; heavily emended text, only the most significant emendations being recorded below. Tr (AMAE: CPEU, xxxix); with minor variation. FC (DLC: Genet Papers). FC (same); in English. Recorded in SJL as received 5 Dec. 1793.

NOTE OFFICIELLE: see Genet to TJ, 13 Nov. 1793.

[1] Altered from "2. 9bre."
[2] Remainder of paragraph interlined or written in the margin in place of a passage which in its final form reads "éxige de plus et Je vous serai en Conséquence obligé de vouloir bien me définir 1°. en quoi doit Consister, selon le gouvernement federal, la formalité à laquelle on prétend que J'ai manqué ainsi que le Conseil èxécutif de france."

[3] Genet here canceled "comme ⟨J'ai le plus grand desir d'engager le gouvernement francois à faire tout ce qui pourroit lui être⟩ vous ⟨êtes⟩ avés été chargé de me ⟨dire⟩ déclarer positivement que l'on ne."
[4] Genet here canceled "et ⟨comment nos Commissions doivent être⟩ quelle doit être selon lui la redac."
[5] Supplied from AMAE Tr and FC in French.
[6] Genet here canceled an interlined "Commission plus detaillée ou d'une."
[7] Preceding two words interlined.
[8] Genet here canceled "si elle ne se trouve point dans le corps de la Commission et rectifie."
[9] Genet here canceled "Souverain."
[10] Preceding two words interlined.
[11] Genet here canceled "mon ésprit ni dans."
[12] Preceding three words interlined in place of "le moindre de ses droits."

From Alexander J. Dallas

SIR   Phila. 4 Decr. 1793

In a Supplement to the Daily Advertiser (a Gazette published in New York) dated the 2d. of December 1793, I find the following assertion, under the signatures of Mr. Hamilton and Mr. Knox: "That such of [the] particulars mentioned (in a statement made by Mr. [Jay] and Mr. King) as respect Mr. Jefferson, including the information *to him from Mr. Dallas* of Mr. Genet's having [said], *that he would appeal from the President to the [Peop]le*, were communicated to Mr. Hamilton and [. . .]." [1]

As this statement [does not] [. . .] with my recollection of the fact, I pray you to inform [me] as soon as you conveniently can, how far it is authorised by you. I am, with great esteem, Sir, Your most obed Sert

A. J. DALLAS

RC (DLC); at foot of text: "To Mr. Jefferson"; torn.

The partly paraphrased ASSERTION of 29 Nov. 1793 is printed from the 3 Dec. 1793 issue of the New York *Daily Advertiser* in Syrett, *Hamilton*, xv, 418-19. For a discussion, see Proposed Public Statement on Edmond Charles Genet, [ca. 16 Dec. 1793], and note.

[1] Estimated one line missing, which may have read, in whole or part, "Mr. Knox by Mr. Jefferson."

From Bartholomew Dandridge, Jr.

4. Decr 93

Bw. Dandridge has the honor to inform the Secy. of state that Congress adjourn at 1 o'Clock to day, so that no message can now go. By the President's order B.D. also informs the Secy. that the Presidt. wishes, if practicable, a meeting may be had with the Gentlemen—in order that the papers intended to have been sent to day, may go to Congress as early tomorrow as possible.

FC (DNA: RG 59, MLR); at foot of text: "The Secy. of State"; docketed by Dandridge. FC (Lb in same, SDC).

For the PAPERS, see note to George Washington to the Senate and the House of Representatives, [2 Dec. 1793].

From Edmond Charles Genet

M.   New york. le 4. xbre. 1793. l'an 2e. de la Repe. fse.

J'ai reçu la lettre que vous m'avés fait l'honneur de m'écrire le 30. du mois dernier. Les mesures que le gouvernement federal a prises pour mettre autant que les lois du pays le permettent les Consuls de la République à l'abri des insultes des émigrés et réfugiés françois me paroissent satisfaisantes et Je vous prie d'en recevoir mes remerciements. Je vois avec peine que vous n'avés point éxactement compris le sens de mes lettres du 25. 9bre. et du 30. 8bre. Je sais que votre pays est ouvert à tous les hommes pourvu qu'ils y arrivent et qu'ils en sortent paisiblement aussi ne vous aije point proposé comme vous paroissés l'avoir compris d'expulser les aristocrates nombreux qui s'y sont introduits.[1] Je vous ai seulement insinué Mr. plutot comme ami de la liberté que comme Ministre public qu'il seroit peut être utile pour le maintient de vos droits de[2] restreindre la prodigieuse importation de Royalistes d'aristocrates[3] qui a lieu depuis quelque tems et qui n'apportent ici que leur nullité leur orgueil[4] et leur haine pour les gouvernemens Populaires. Je ne vous ai point demandé non plus[5] de vous opposer au départ des réfugiés de St. domingue qui croiroient pouvoir retourner dans la partie fidele de ce département sans s'éxposer à un inconvenient très grave; Mais Je vous ai requis, M., d'empêcher l'éxpédition des batiments qui devoient partir publiquement[6] de vos ports pour se rendre dans deux places rebelles qui ont eu la bassesse de se livrer[7] aux Anglois d'après une convention criminelle[8] faite avec eux dans le mois de fevrier dernier.

Je vous laisse à Juger Mr. Si[9] la trahison a aussi des droits aux faveurs de votre neutralité[10] et si la pudeur et la politique doivent permettre à vos citoyens d'aller alimenter les rebelles de Jeremie et du Mole.

Dft (DLC: Genet Papers); in Genet's hand, unsigned, with revision by a clerk (see note 5 below); above salutation: "Le Cit Genet &c à M. Jefferson &c."; only the most significant emendations are recorded below. FC (same). Recorded in SJL as received 6 Dec. 1793.

CONVENTION CRIMINELLE: on 25 Feb. 1793 about sixty émigré Saint-Domingue planters in London, concerned about the spreading slave revolt on that island, approved a list of propositions for submission to the British government under which they would transfer their allegiance to George III until the future of the colony was determined at a general peace in return for British protection and commercial and political concessions (Geggus, *Slavery*, 58-60, 395-7).

[1] Genet here canceled "et de retenir ceux qui croiroient pouvoir se rendre sans un inconvenient très grave pour eux dans la partie fidele de St. domingue."

[2] Genet here canceled "mettre en vigeur une de vos."

[3] Preceding four words written in the margin.

[4] Remainder of sentence interlined by clerk in place of "et leur ésprit d'intrigues liberticides."

[5] Genet here canceled "d'arreter."

[6] Word written in the margin.

[7] Preceding seven words altered from "se sont livrées."

[8] Word written in the margin.

[9] Genet here canceled "la Rebelli."

[10] Genet here canceled "et si en admettant même ce" and wrote the remainder of the text in the margin.

To Jacob Hollingsworth

S<small>IR</small>   Philadelphia Dec. 4. 1793.

I received last night your favor of the 2d. inst. informing me you had employed Eli Alexander to superintend my business; on the terms proposed, finding him the same furniture which I supplied to Mr. Biddle and paying his travelling expences there, and that he will set out by the 15th. inst. I agree to the terms, confiding that he will make his travelling expences reasonable. He had better go by water to Richmond, from whence there are waggons returning nearly empty to Charlottesville which is two miles from my house. My son in law, Mr. Randolph, who lives there, will put him in possession of his charge, and give him the necessary information till I arrive, which will probably be within a week or ten days after him. I count to be there myself by the 12th. of January, so that no particular instructions need be given him at this time. I inclosed you by post on the 21st. of November a bank bill of 20. dollars to be laid out in red[1] cloverseed to be sent by him. I hope it got safe to your hands, tho' omitted to be mentioned in your letter. With many thanks for your trouble I am Sir Your most obedt. servt

T<small>H</small>: J<small>EFFERSON</small>

PrC (DLC); at foot of text: "Mr. Jacob Hollingsworth." Tr (ViU: Edgehill-Randolph Papers); 19th-century copy.

Hollingsworth's F<small>AVOR OF THE</small> 2D. <small>INST</small>., recorded in SJL as received from Elkton, Maryland, on 3 Dec. 1793, has not been found.

From Samuel Livermore

Philadelphia, 4 Dec. 1793. The President has informed him that a commission has been sent to New Hampshire appointing his son United States district attorney for that state. While the appointment was intended for his eldest son, Edward St. Loe Livermore, the commission was mistakenly made out to his youngest son Arthur. By the President's direction he has informed both sons of the mistake and now relates his order that a corrected commission be issued.

RC (DNA: RG 59, MLR); 2 p.; at foot of text: "The Hon Mr Jefferson"; endorsed by TJ as received 4 Dec. 1793 and so recorded in SJL.

Samuel Livermore (1732-1803), a Massachusetts native who graduated from the College of New Jersey, moved to New Hampshire and began a long career as a lawyer and officeholder, including service as state attorney general before and during the Revolution, chief justice of the state superior court, 1782-90, delegate to the Continental and Confederation congresses, 1780-82 and 1785-86, and member of the United States House of Representatives, 1789-93, and Senate, 1793-1801, with two terms as president *pro tempore* of the latter (D<small>AB</small>).

TJ had sent the commission to Arthur

Livermore on 23 Nov. 1793 in a brief covering letter from Germantown (PrC in DLC, in the hand of George Taylor, Jr., unsigned, with "Arthur Livermore Atty. New Hampshire" at foot of text, the day of the month and endorsement being added in ink by Taylor; FC in Lb in DNA: RG 59, DL; not recorded in SJL). The President nominated Edward St. Loe Livermore as District Attorney for New Hampshire on 14 Feb. 1794, and the Senate confirmed him three days later (JEP, I, 148).

From John Mason

SIR   George Town 4th. Decr. 1793

In due course I was honoured with your Letter of 20th. Ulto.

It is from our Connection with that City quite as convenient, to receive in Philadelphia at present as here, and not to trouble you with remitting, we send now to our Friends Messrs. Joseph Anthony & Son who will present it—F. M. & Cos. Draft on you for 205 Ds. 42 Cts.

We have written to our Friend in Baltimore for the amount of the little Charges in this Country when we ascertain will forward them in same way.

By next Post Sir the house who are now preparing the papers relative, will take the Liberty of addressing you in your Official Character on the Subject of a Ship and Cargoe we have lately had seized and condemned in a most extraordinary Manner at St. Christophers. With great Respect I have the honour to be Sir Your most Ob Hble St

J MASON

RC (DLC); at head of text: "Thomas Jefferson Esqr."; endorsed by TJ as received 10 Dec. 1793 and so recorded in SJL.

A day after he received this letter TJ accepted Fenwick, Mason & Company's draft for a wine shipment, drawn on JOSEPH AN-THONY & SON at thirty days' sight, and paid it just before leaving Philadelphia early in 1794 (MB, 11 Dec. 1793, 3 Jan. 1794). The missing letter from THE HOUSE of 6 Dec. 1793 is recorded in SJL as received from Georgetown on 10 Dec. 1793.

From James Monroe

DEAR SIR   Decr. 4. 1793.

I find the establishment of the charge against Mr. G: will depend principally upon what you heard Mr. Dallas say. This latter will deny that he ever said any thing like what the certificate states. Jay and King heard it from Hamilton and Knox, these latter from Mifflin and I am told that[1] there is a difference between those Gentlemen and Mifflin, and likewise between him and Dallas as to what they respectively stated. So that the fact will be disproved against them, unless the circumstances they are able to adduce are supported by you. If they procure from the President your report to him will not this transfer the business from them to him. I have just heard the above and transmit it for your information.   JAS. MONROE

RC (DLC); endorsed by TJ as received 4 Dec. 1793 and so recorded in SJL.

CERTIFICATE: the 29 Nov. 1793 statement by Alexander Hamilton and Henry Knox on the French minister's threat during the *Little Sarah* affair in July 1793 to appeal from the President to the American people (see note to Proposed Public Statement on Edmond Charles Genet [ca. 16 Dec. 1793]). YOUR REPORT: Memorandum of a Conversation with Edmond Charles Genet, 10 July 1793.

¹ Monroe here canceled "Mifflin says he never stated it."

From Henry Remsen

DR. SIR   New York Decemr. 4. 1793

I have had the Honor to receive your favor of the 9th. Ult:, and this day I have sent the model by the Ellice Capt. Weymouth bound to Richmond, having addressed it to the care of Coll. Robt. Gamble agreeable to your direction. The Captain has promised to attend to it's safety on the passage, and deliver it immediately after his arrival.

I am happy to learn that the Congress and Executive of the U.S. may meet in Philadelphia free from apprehension. Did any trace of the late disorder remain, it would intimidate many of them, and give occasion perhaps to much discussion respecting a proper place for their sessions. I learn that the City of Washington is encreasing fast, and will be, when once it assumes the appearance it is intended it should have, the handsomest in America, or even in Europe. Mr. Greenleaf a wealthy man of this place, has purchased a great number of lots there, and appropriated a large sum for building on and otherwise improving them. He purposes also to erect the Brick-machine invented by a Dr. Kingsland or Kingsley, from whom he has purchased the one half of the patent. A few such enterprizing men will make any new town grow. I shall always be happy to be honored with your commands and subscribe myself with grateful respect & esteem Dr. Sir Your most obedt. & h'ble servt.

HENRY REMSEN

RC (DLC); at foot of text: "Thomas Jefferson Esqr."; endorsed by TJ as received 6 Dec. 1793 and so recorded in SJL.

The BRICK-MACHINE of Apollos Kinsley was patented on 1 Feb. 1793 (*List of Patents*, 9).

To Zebulon Hollingsworth

SIR   Philadelphia Dec. 5. 1793.

Notwithstanding the sale of the Pilgrim it may be of importance to possess evidence of the place of her capture. I am therefore to ask the favor of you to have the evidence taken according to the general[1] rules heretofore communicated to you, and to send the same to me. I have the honor to acknolege the receipt of your letters of Nov. 26. and 30. & to be with great respect Sir your most obedt. servt   TH: JEFFERSON

PrC (DLC); at foot of text: "Mr. Zebulon Hollingsworth." FC (Lb in DNA: RG 59, DL).

GENERAL RULES: see TJ to the District Attorneys, 10 Nov. 1793, and enclosure. The letters of NOV. 26. AND 30. 1793 from

Hollingsworth, the District Attorney for Maryland, written from Baltimore and recorded in SJL as received 28 Nov. and 3 Dec. 1793, respectively, have not been found.

[1] Word interlined.

To Edmond Charles Genet

SIR   Philadelphia. Dec. 6. 1793.

In consequence of the notice given to the Governor of Pensylvania of the apprehensions that a number of the emigrants of St. Domingo might be returning hence to the island in a hostile form, enquiries were set on foot, the result of which I have the honor to inclose for your information; and am with respect Sir Your most obedt. & most humble servt   TH: JEFFERSON

PrC (DLC); at foot of text: "the Min. Plen. of the republic of France." FC (Lb in DNA: RG 59, DL). Enclosures: (1) Thomas Mifflin to George Washington, Philadelphia, 2 Dec. 1793, stating that he was submitting Nos. 2 and 3 in reply to Henry Knox's letter concerning Genet's suggestion that French refugees were about to embark from this port for Jérémie or Cape St. Nicolas Môle on the ship Delaware and the schooner Betsey (RC in DNA: RG 59, MLR, in a clerk's hand, signed by Mifflin; PrC of Tr in DLC, in a clerk's hand; Tr in Lb in DNA: RG 59, DL). (2) Mifflin to Nathaniel Falconer, Master Warden of the port of Philadelphia, 29 Nov. 1793, directing him, in conformity with the President's request, to ascertain the truth of Genet's allegations that French refugees in Philadelphia were preparing to embark for Jérémie or Cape St. Nicolas Môle on the Delaware,

Captain Art, owned by James & Shoemaker, and the Betsey, Captain McClanachan, so that their departure can be prevented if they are planning a military expedition. (3) Falconer to Mifflin, 29 Nov. 1793, stating that Jacob Shoemaker assured him that the Delaware was bound for Cape St. Nicolas Môle and that, though it expected to carry a number of passengers, so far only one had signed up; that he had asked Shoemaker and Captain Art to bring him any Frenchman who signed up as a passenger so that he could ascertain the purpose of his voyage; that Reed & Ford, the owners of the Betsey, assured him that it had been chartered by a French gentleman who intended to sail only to Guadeloupe to bring back his property from there, accompanied by some passengers bound for the same destination; and that he will continue to monitor these two ships and notify Mifflin if he discovers anything like armament on them (Trs in DNA: RG 59, MLR, attested by Alexander J. Dallas; PrCs of other Trs in DLC, in a clerk's hand; Trs in Lb in DNA: RG 59, DL).

Reacting to allegations in Genet's second letter to TJ of 25 Nov. 1793 that French refugees in Philadelphia and Baltimore were preparing to launch counterrevolutionary military expeditions against Saint-Domingue, the President had instructed Secretary of War Henry Knox to request the governors of Pennsylvania and Maryland to investigate this matter. Washington submitted the enclosures listed above to TJ on 2 Dec. 1793 so that he could inform the French minister of the results of the investigation in Philadelphia (Washington, *Journal*, 262). Later in the month Governor Thomas Sim Lee dispatched to Knox a report by the collector of customs at Baltimore pertaining to the activities of French refugees in that port, not found, and assured him that "nothing shall be omitted which may be necessary for preventing military expeditions of the nature alluded to" (Lee to Knox, 9 Dec. 1793, MdAA: Letterbooks of Governor and Council).

To Edmond Charles Genet

SIR   Philadelphia Dec. 6. 1793.

Your letter of the 15th. of Nov. on the subject of your bills refused paiment at the Treasury, was duly laid before the President and referred to the department of the treasury, a copy of the report from which I have now the honor to inclose you, and am with great respect Sir Your most obedt. & most humble servt   TH: JEFFERSON

RC (AMAE: CPEU, Supplément, xx); at foot of text: "The Min. Pleny. of the republic of France." PrC (DLC). FC (Lb in DNA: RG 59, DL). Enclosures: (1) Alexander Hamilton to George Washington, Treasury Department, 2 Dec. 1793, stating, with respect to Genet's 15 Nov. 1793 letter to TJ, that the Treasury had not admitted the bills of exchange totaling 14,000 dollars that he had drawn, and that were predicated on the fund put at his disposal in November 1793, because of a clerical error, since rectified, in registering one of these bills for 40,000 dollars, a mistake which temporarily created the impression that he had overdrawn, and that it had not admitted the funds which would be at the disposal of France in January 1794 because there was no previous arrangement or notice; that, as shown by No. 2 below, the Treasury had agreed to make 1,500,000 livres payable to Genet on 3 Sep. 1793, minus the deduction of 94,506.10½ dollars for the payment of bills drawn on the administration of Saint-Domingue, and 1,000,000 livres payable to him on 5 Nov. 1793; that Genet should not have drawn on the necessary fund of interest because the Treasury had not authorized him to do so and because he had been informed that the advances made to him exceeded the sums due according to the stipulated course of payment of the American debt to France; that the Treasury could not approve unauthorized drawings upon it without impropriety and inconvenience; and that it was reasonable to expect that Genet, being as close as New York, would not have exceeded the limit agreed upon without the Treasury's prior consent. (2) Hamilton to Genet, 24 July 1793, stating, in response to Genet's 19 July 1793 letter to him, that although the United States had already paid more than was due on its debt to France, the amount of the excess being undetermined because of the failure to establish a rule for liquidating payments made in France according to the current exchange rate, the Treasury would be ready to pay on account of that debt 1,500,000 livres at $18\frac{15}{100}$ cents per livre on 3 Sep. 1793, deducting therefrom 94,506.10½ dollars it had made itself responsible for paying (on the basis of expectations given by Jean Baptiste Ternant and confirmed by Genet) to the holders of certain bills of exchange drawn on the administration of Saint-Domingue, and 1,000,000 livres at the same rate of exchange on 5 Nov. 1793, the bills drawn on these funds to be presented at the Treasury for recording and paid according to the order of presentation (Trs in AMAE: CPEU, Supplément, xx; PrCs in DLC; Trs in Lb in DNA: RG 59, DL; printed in Syrett, *Hamilton*, xv, 124, 436-7).

Edmund Randolph's Opinion on Sureties for Mint Officers

THE ATTORNEY-GENERAL OF THE U. S. TO THE SECRETARY OF STATE

The fifth section of the act, establishing a mint, directs, that the assayer, chief coiner, and treasurer, previously to entering upon the execution of their respective offices, shall each become bound to the U. S. with one or more sureties, in the sum of 10,000 dollars, with condition for the faithful and diligent performance of the duties of his office. With this requisition the persons, who are commissioned, as assayer and chief coiner, have not, it seems, as yet complied. Can they then execute their offices? is your question. I answer that they cannot; because the bond is a preliminary to the *execution*. I recollect a subtle doubt, which was once raised upon a law, inflicting a penalty of five hundred pounds upon a justice, who should presume to execute the office of justice, before he took an oath. It was contended, that if he chose to submit to the penalty, he might proceed in the functions, and his acts would notwithstanding be valid. If this were law, (which, however, I disbelieve) it was certainly the ultimate point, to which the law can in such cases be extended. But between that instance, and the situation of the assayer and chief coiner, the interval, is so great, as to Afford no protection to the latter from the former. In the former, there is a far greater appearance of recognizing a right to execute, than in the latter, to which that right is impliedly denied.   EDM: RANDOLPH

Decr. 6. 1793.

RC (DNA: RG 59, Letters from and Opinions of the Attorney General); addressed: "The Secretary of State"; endorsed by TJ.

Randolph quoted nearly verbatim the FIFTH SECTION OF THE ACT of 2 Apr. 1792 ESTABLISHING A MINT, omitting only the requirement that the sureties be approved by the Secretary of the Treasury (*Annals*, III, 1351).

Cabinet Opinions on Edmond Charles Genet and James King

At a meeting of the heads of departments and Atty. Genl. at the President's on the 7th. of Dec. 1793.

Mr. Genet's letter of Dec. 3. questioning the right of requiring the address of Consular commissions to the President was read. It is the opinion that the address may be either to the US. or to the President of the US. but that one of these shoud be insisted on.

A letter from James King was read, dated Philadelphia Nov. 25. 1793. complaining of the capture of his schooner Nancy by a British privateer and carried into N. Providence, and that the court there has thrown the onus probandi on the owners, to shew that the vessel and cargo are American property. It is the opinion that Mr. King be informed that it is a general rule that the government should not interpose individually,[1] till a final denial of justice has taken place in the courts of the country where the wrong is done; but that, a considerable degree of information being shortly expected relative to these cases, his will be further considered and attended to at that time.

The Secretary of state informed the President that he had received a number of applications from Mr. Genet on behalf of the refugees of St. Domingo who have been subjected to tonnage on their vessels and duties on their property on taking asylum in the ports of this country, into which they were forced by the misfortunes of that colony. It is the opinion that the Secretary of state may put the petitions into the hands of a member of the legislature in his private capacity to be presented to the legislature.

Th: Jefferson
Edm: Randolph Alexander Hamilton
H Knox

MS (DLC: Washington Papers); in TJ's hand, signed by TJ, Hamilton, Knox, and Randolph; endorsed by Washington.

TJ conveyed the substance of the Cabinet's opinion about Edmond Charles Genet's LETTER OF DEC. 3. in his 9 Dec. 1793 reply to the French minister. LETTER FROM JAMES KING: see note to TJ to King, 7 Dec. 1793. Representative William Vans Murray of Maryland was the MEMBER OF THE LEGISLATURE to whom TJ subsequently submitted the issue of exempting from the payment of tonnage duties French ships that had come to the United States as a result of the destruction of Cap-Français during the slave revolt on Saint-Domingue in June 1793. On 7 Mch. 1794 Congress passed a law remitting such duties for all French ships which could prove they had taken refuge in the United States in consequence of that event (Annals, IV, 1418-19; TJ to Genet, and TJ to George Washington, both 15 Dec. 1793).

[1] Word interlined.

Estimate of State Department Expenses

Estimate of the Expenses of the Department of State, at Home; for one year, commencing 1st. January 1793.

	Dollrs.	
The Secretary of State's salary	3,500	
One Chief Clerk's do.	800	
3 Clerk's—(an additional one will probably be requisite) say	} 2,000	
Clerk for foreign Languages' salary	250	
Office keeper and messenger's do.	250	6,800
Stationary of all kinds	240	
Firewood	200	
	Cts	
Office rent	266,67	
newspapers from the different States abt. 20 @ 4 dollrs.	80.	
Gazettes from, and Gazettes sent to Am. Ministers abroad	25.	
Laws of the 1 Session of the 3d. Congress, to be published in 5 newspapers. at about 100 dollrs. each	} 500	
Printing an edition of the Same, to be distributed according to law	} 700	
For Binding	50	2,061.67
Deficiencies in the appropriation of the present year		
for Extra Clerks employed preparing documents laid & to be laid before Congress say	} 600	
For an index to the Laws of the 2d. Congress	200	800
		9.661.67

Department of State
Decr. 7. 1793.   TH: JEFFERSON

PrC (DLC); in the hand of George Taylor, Jr., signed by TJ; with "1793" added by Taylor in ink in heading and dateline. Recorded in SJPL.

This document was compiled for Alexander Hamilton's use in preparing a report submitted to the House of Representatives on 23 Dec. 1793 concerning the federal government's revenue estimates for 1794 (Syrett, *Hamilton*, xv, 552-5, 558, 561).

To James King

SIR Philadelphia Dec. 7. 1793.

Your letter tho' dated the 25th. of November was delivered to me only the day before yesterday. I have this day laid it before the President, and I have to observe to you that the rule by which all governments conduct themselves in cases where injury has been done by individuals of one to individuals of the other government, is to leave the injured party to seek redress in the courts of the other. If that redress be finally denied after due application to the courts, it then becomes a subject of national complaint. I do not undertake to say that it is the general practice, and much less shall I say it is just to throw the onus probandi on the owners: but it is said to be the practice of some nations. However I only mention these general matters that you may not fail to take all the measures depending on yourself for the saving your property. I expect shortly to be possessed of a considerable mass of cases which are supposed entitled to public interference; these will be submitted to the President and some general principles and plan adopted for general remedy: and I will take care that your case shall then have due attention paid. I am Sir your most obedt servt TH: JEFFERSON

PrC (DLC); at foot of text: "Mr. James King. Phila. Watkins' alley No. 2." FC (Lb in DNA: RG 59, DL).

James King (1751-1832), a well-established Philadelphia merchant who had held a contract with the Secret Committee of Trade during the Revolutionary War, moved about this time from 2 Fetter Lane, where he was located before the yellow fever epidemic, to 89 Sassafras Street, where he transacted business the following year (Hardie, *Phila. Dir.*, 78; same, [Philadelphia, 1794], 83; Genealogical Society of Pennsylvania, *Publications*, VII [1920], 282; Paul H. Smith and others, eds., *Letters of Delegates to Congress, 1774-1789*, 22 vols. [Washington, D.C., 1976-], III, 184-5, IV, 155, 207, 485).

King's letter to TJ of the 25TH. OF NOVEMBER, written in Philadelphia and recorded in SJL as received 5 Dec. 1793, has not been found. For the Cabinet's prior approval of the substance of TJ's reply to him, see Cabinet Opinions on Edmond Charles Genet and James King, 7 Dec. 1793.

To John F. Mercer

DEAR SIR Philadelphia Dec. 7. 1793.

I received yesterday your favor of Nov. 30. and can assure you that the city is understood universally to be entirely clear of infection, not a single person having the yellow fever at this time, and that this has been believed to be the case near three weeks. The members of Congress here are entirely without apprehension. Still I have not learnt how a stranger is to know into what houses he may venture, as not having had the disease at all. In fact the members have ventured into both taverns and lodging houses, where they have had it. Francis's hotel near the Indian Queen has never had it, therefore you may safely land there. Mrs. Trist intends to take a small house and a few of her acquaintances: but I believe she has not got a house yet. In the one she formerly occupied, a person died of the fever: but Mr. Giles and Mr. Venable are there, and Stockdon has lived in the very room where the person died for a considerable time. You will have seen the speech and message and therefore I need say nothing of the interesting matters before Congress. My respects to Mrs. Mercer. Accept yourself my affectionate regard.

TH: JEFFERSON

PrC (DLC); at foot of text: "Mr. Mercer." Tr (MHi); 19th-century copy.

To James Brown

DEAR SIR   Philadelphia Dec. 8. 1793.

I have duly recieved your favor of Nov. 25. as also a letter from Mr. Hopkins covering certificates of stock of the property of Mr. Short, of the following descriptions and amount, to wit,

No. 535. Ð 1 093.89 six per cents
    898. Ð15,342.18 do.
    899. Ð 7,504.42 deferred   from the loan office of Virginia
    900. Ð11,256.63 three per cents

Mr. Hopkins also transmitted me an account of interest received by you from Mr. Short amounting to Ð 2,221.09. Being uninformed of the transactions between yourself and Mr. Short, I am unable to judge whether that sum or any part of it stands as a balance with you in his favor, or has been absorbed by corresponding sums to his debet. Mr. Short's desire being to convert all his sums of interest as fast as they arise into principal stock, I have only to observe that any balance which may remain in your hands if paid at your convenience, shall be converted according to the desires of Mr. Short.

I thank you for your interesting yourself for me with Mr. Hague & Lister. I had left it in charge with Mr. TM Randolph to have my furniture removed. I expect to be settled at Monticello by the middle of January, and shall take the earliest opportunity of going to Richmond to see about several matters which my business here has obliged me too much to neglect. I am with great esteem Dear Sir your friend & servt

TH: JEFFERSON

RC (FMU); at foot of text: "Mr. James Brown." PrC (DLC). Tr (ViU: Edgehill-Randolph Papers); 19th-century copy.

Brown's missing FAVOR OF NOV. 25. is recorded in SJL as received from Richmond on 2 Dec. 1793.

To James Currie

Dear Sir   Philadelphia Dec. 8. 1793.

I have now to acknolege the receipt of your favors of Oct. 21. Nov. 9. and 18. The second of these reached me only two days ago. You will remember that I employed Mr. Sarjeant to take care of your suit against Griffin on Barton's retirement. You will have seen Sargeant's name among the victims of the Yellow fever, tho' it may not have been known to you to be the same person. On my first visit from Germantown (where I was some time after my return) to this place I engaged Mr. Ingersoll to take up your business, enquired with him into the state in which Mr. Sargeant left it, and found that by the suspension of proceedings during the yellow fever, the answers to the interrogatories filed by Sargeant, could not be obtained till the 3d. of January. I shall be here till the 6th. or 8th. of January; and consequently long enough to examine the answers, and suggest to Mr. Ingersol any cross-questions which they may need, and my knolege of the subject enable me to state. This he thinks the only important service I can render in it. I have not seen him since the receipt of your information that the defendant has taken shelter under the insolvent law: but I do not think that can affect property *here*, and consequently not subject to that law.   One of the pipes of wine mentioned in your letter of Oct. 21. is for you. I gave you notice of this so long ago as my letter of June 4. (I believe it was in that letter, for I have not my letters by me) only mentioning to you that, as your commission was given impromptu, if you had on further consideration thought otherwise, you were perfectly free, as it would be entirely equal to me to keep it; and indeed if you did not wish it for yourself, I would rather not cede it to any other person. You are still as free as ever on the subject; but observe that if you take it it will be better not to broach it these two years, as nothing but full age can give it a right to take the place of Madeira.

Ever since February last I have been in the expectation of receiving one third part of a very large execution of Mr. Wayles's executors against Colo. Cary's estate. I am made to believe it cannot be longer frustrated. It has been and is my constant intention to pay out of this the balance of my bond to you. On my return home, I shall take an early occasion of going to Richmond to see about this and some other matters, and in the mean time should paiment be made, I will give directions to have it put into your hands. My best respects to Mrs. Currie & am with great esteem Dr. Sir Your friend & servt   Th: Jefferson

PrC (DLC); at foot of text: "Dr. Currie."

To J. P. P. Derieux

DEAR SIR   Philadelphia Dec. 8. 1793.

I have not been inattentive to your matter since my return. I sent your letter to Mr. Vaughan, and I wrote one to Mr. Homassel. The merchants were at that time much dispersed. I inclose you Mr. Homassel's answer. All are now returned to the city, and I hope these two gentlemen will settle and liquidate your affair. They shall not want my sollicitations to do it. My respects to Mrs. Derieux and am with esteem Dear Sir Your friend & servt   TH: JEFFERSON

PrC (DLC); at foot of text: "Mr. Derieux."

Charles HOMASSEL'S ANSWER of 16 Nov. 1793, recorded in SJL as received from New York on 20 Nov. 1793, has not been found.

To Robert Gamble

DEAR SIR   Philadelphia Dec. 8. 1793.

I think I mentioned to you either verbally or by letter that I had the model of a threshing machine arrived at New York which I set great store by, and had taken the liberty of directing to be forwarded to Richmond to your address. My friend at New-York now writes me that he has sent it by the Ellice Capt. Weymouth bound for Richmond. Will you be so good as to receive it and hold it till the order of Mr. Randolph, as I expect it is too delicate to be moved in a waggon. I shall be myself at Monticello by the 14th. of January, when, should no safe opportunity have occurred of forwarding it thither, I shall be able to make one. I am with great esteem Dr. Sir Your most obedt. servt   TH: JEFFERSON

PrC (DLC); at foot of text: "Colo. Gamble." Tr (ViU: Edgehill-Randolph Papers); 19th-century copy.

FRIEND AT NEW-YORK: Henry Remsen.

To Richard Graham

SIR   Philadelphia Dec. 8. 1793.

I have received and laid before the President your letter of Nov. 26. and after due acknolegements for the offers of service you have made, I have to observe that the measures already taken by the Executive of the US. for the establishment of their right to the navigation of the Missisipi, would not at all comport with those you are pleased to propose in your letter.

I should have been happy if my longer stay in Fredericksburg would have given me the pleasure of seeing you, being with great regard Sir Your most obedt servt   TH: JEFFERSON

PrC (DLC); at foot of text: "Mr. Richard Graham." FC (Lb in DNA: RG 59, DL).

From Robert Morris

SIR   New Brunswick Decr. 8th. 1793.

On the fifth instant I received the enclosed from the Attorney of the United States for this District, and forward it for the Presidents further information of the case of Clarkson Freeman.

It appears from it that a pardon to him is already filled up, and resting in Mr. Ogdens hands. The opperation of it, under all the circumstances, will necessarily become a question before the Court, if he should ever be apprehended.

From the evidence that came to my knowledge, I did not consider Clarkson Freeman a necessary, or proper selection for the purposes mentioned by Mr. Ogden, and I should now doubt the policy of promulgating the existence of the pardon, least it should induce him to return within the jurisdiction of the United States; leaving which, I should have advised to have been made a condition of a pardon under any circumstances to so finished a villain. With the greatest respect I am Sir Your very humble Servt.   ROBT MORRIS

RC (DNA: RG 59, MLR); at foot of text: "The Honble. Thomas Jefferson Secretary of State." Recorded in SJL as received 10 Dec. 1793. Enclosure: Abraham Ogden to Morris, Newark, 29 Nov. 1793, stating in reply to his letter of 20 Nov. 1793 that after receiving the blank presidential pardon the Attorney General had sent on 21 Mch. 1791 for use in prosecuting the "Gang of Counterfeit Villains" he selected Freeman to testify against his accomplices; that although neither the original agreement nor Freeman's subsequent conduct entitled him to unconditional clemency, he inserted Freeman's name in the pardon because his confession had given information and evidence useful in several of the trials and he was listed as a witness in Parker's indictment; that prior to Freeman's escape he had refused to deliver the pardon until the government had fully availed itself of his testimony against his accomplices and because

he was still under civil process in the New Jersey Supreme Court for large debts; and that after Freeman fled he had also refused to deliver the pardon to Freeman's friends because his escape left the sheriff of Essex County liable for very large sums, for which he was being duly prosecuted, and he hoped to aid him in recovering Freeman by letting the sheriff avail himself of his commitment under federal authority (Tr in DNA: RG 59, Petitions for Pardon; Tr in same, MLR, undated). Morris's letter of 20 Nov. 1793 had asked whether Ogden had additional reasons for leniency than his original contract with Freeman's attorney (Tr in same, MLR).

TJ submitted this letter and its enclosure to the President on or before 14 Dec. 1793, when he returned them (Washington, *Journal*, 268).

To Mann Page

DEAR SIR Philadelphia Dec. 8. 1793.

I owe you a letter which should have been written by your servant from Fredericksbg., whom you were so kind as to send for me when I was there. But I had passed the day at Chatham, was returning about dusk, shivering, and snowing, when I met your servant in the streets. I desired him to apologize to you for my not writing, by telling you the place and state in which he found me, and I left Fredericksbg. the next morning an hour before day. I shall endeavor to repair all this in person about the 2d. week in January, when I shall be at Fredericksburg on my way home. I have directed horses to meet me there on the 12th. and whatever time can intervene between my reaching Fredericksbg. and the 12th. I will certainly have the pleasure of passing with you if you should be at home. I inclose you a newspaper which contains some interesting things. Our information from France is very chaotic. We can only distinguish that they have gained three important victories on the side of Flanders, and those said to be gained over them are very problematical. Their enemies however still hold Toulon.—I am one of those who believe in the impossibility of the resurrection of monarchy in France and of another campaign by the combined powers. Congress have not yet fully assembled, nor by any vote shewn their complexion. We hope it will be patriotic and republican, but not in the stile of republicanism of the 1st. and 2d. Congress. Your brother is not yet arrived. My best respects to Mrs. Page, and am dear Sir with great affection & respect Your friend & servt. TH: JEFFERSON

PrC (DLC); at foot of text: "Mann Page esq."

To Thomas Mann Randolph, Jr.

DEAR SIR Philadelphia Dec. 8. 1793.

This was my day of course for writing to Maria, but business obliges me to postpone her till the next Sunday,[1] which I have the better right to do as I have not yet received a letter from her.—I inclose you a second letter received from Mr. Leroy in reply to a second which I wrote to him. I thought it not amiss to cultivate his good dispositions as these might facilitate the sheltering your property under the wings of the protested bill and of Dover.—The resignation of my office will take place on the last day of the year. I suppose it will then take me a week to settle my affairs here; and consequently that I may be at Fredericksburg by the 12th. of January. On that day therefore I would wish horses to arrive for me at Fredericksburg. If the roads should be still tolerably good, and Mr. Carr's chair at Monticello, I will thank him for the use of it. But if the roads are deep, I shall do better on horseback. We shall need two horses besides that on which the person who brings them is to return.— A person of the name of Eli Alexander is engaged for me at Elk, as overseer on the East side of the river. He will set out this day week. I am to furnish him the same conveniences which I did to Mr. Biddle. Be pleased therefore to desire the latter to have made immediately a bedstead and table, and to bespeak half a dozen chairs of Fitch, also to have the house in which Rogers lived, put into habitable[2] condition. I mean as soon as I can to remove the Overseer's residence up to Hickman's. The other small utensils which were furnished to Mr. Biddle, may be got from the stores after Alexander's arrival, which will probably be but a few days before mine. He had better employ his force at Shadwell as much as he can till I come, because I mean to reform the feilds at the upper place this winter.

Congress have met, but have not begun business. Freneau's and Fenno's paper's are both discontinued. The former however will be resumed, I am told, by Swaine, one of the former printers of it. If it is, I think it will be well executed. Our information from France is so chaotic that we cannot well distinguish facts: but on the whole we know certainly of three important victories obtained by them on the side of Flanders, and those said to have been obtained over them are problematical. Toulon is still in the hands of their enemies.

I sincerely condole with you on the death of Colo. Randolph. We have had together the intimacy of brothers from 5. or 6. years of age, and the affection of brothers. No body deplored more the tormenting state of mind into which he had been latterly reduced and tho' from the accounts of his health I had for some time viewed his end as approaching, I still learn the actual event with great sensibility.—My love to my dear children, esteem to our common friends at Monticello, kisses to the little ones, and accept my best affections for yourself.

Tʜ: Jᴇꜰꜰᴇʀꜱᴏɴ

RC (DLC); addressed: "Thomas M. Randolph esq. at Monticello near Charlottesville"; endorsed by Randolph as received 18 Dec. 1793. PrC (CSmH). Tr (ViU: Edgehill-Randolph Papers); 19th-century copy. Enclosure: Herman LeRoy to TJ, 26 Nov. 1793 (recorded in SJL as received from New York on 27 Nov. 1793, but not found). Enclosed in TJ to Randolph, [8-9 Dec. 1793].

UPPER PLACE: Lego.

[1] First syllable interlined.
[2] Word interlined in place of "tolerable."

To Thomas Mann Randolph, Jr.

TH:J. TO MR RANDOLPH [8-9 Dec. 1793]

I forgot in the inclosed to mention that my Model of the threshing machine is at length sent by the Ellice Capt. Weymouth bound from New York to Richmond, addressed to Colo. Gamble. I have written to him to hold it subject to your order. Knowing nothing of the size or construction of the model, I am not able to say whether it may not be too small or too delicate to trust by a waggon, or how else it should come. I have therefore thought it best to give you the trouble of deciding that, as in some of your trips to Richmond you may perhaps have a view of the bulk, and of the structure also if it can be done easily. Your's affectionately TH:J.

RC (DLC: TJ Papers, 95: 16337, 93: 16013-a); undated; addressed: "Thomas M. Randolph esq. at Monticello near Charlottesville"; franked, stamped, and postmarked 9 Dec.; endorsed by Randolph as received 18 Dec. 1793. PrC (same, 95: 16323). Tr (ViU: Edgehill-Randolph Papers); 19th-century copy; filed at 18 Feb. 1793. Not recorded in SJL. Enclosure: TJ to Randolph, 8 Dec. 1793.

From Joseph Yznardi, Jr.

SIR NewYork 8 Decr. 1793

I was duly honoured with your Letter of the 7th. Septr. and the following post, with one for Messrs. Carmichael and Short; of which, as I adviced you in my respects of 25 Augt.; I intended to have been the Bearer: a severe indisposition, which confined me to my room for three weeks, prevented me. I forward it on immediately by a safe conveyance.

I came on here to embark for Cadiz, and had taken my passage in the Ship Montgomery, to sail in two days, and now receive the very disagreeable intelligence, comunicated by Mr. Church, from Lisbon. In this situation; I dare not venture in the said vessell, and thinking that you will have some dispatches, to send to Lisbon, or Madrid, if so, with your advice, I will charter the vessell that came as express, and take charge of any thing, to be delivered at any of the abovementioned places.

The Spanish Chargé des affaires Mr. Jaudenes, has comunicated to me, that if the united States, would apply to him, he would engage that the Spanish Court; would immediately interfere, in behalf of this Country, for a peace with these Savages, indeed more, he informed me "he would engage to establish Peace": how far this Gentleman may be able to effect it, I realy cannot say; but I think it my duty, to comunicate it to you, and at the same time to offer myself, to go to Madrid, and thence to algiers, in any Capacity the President may please to point out.

[498]

If any thing should be determined upon, with your advice I will immediately proceed to Pha. to take the necessary instructions; and at any rate I shall be much obliged to you, for an answer as soon as convenient, as I wish to go as soon as possible, to my post; and for which purpose I shall immediately take up the above mentioned Vessell. I have the honor to be with due respect Sir Your most obedient and most Humble Servant   JOSEPH YZNARDI JUNR.

P.S. Mr. Jaudenes goes on, this day to Pha.

As soon as I receive from Cadiz, a true statement of the affairs relative to the two Ships from Bourdeax, I will communicate it to you; You may relye my Father, will have done the utmost in his power in their favor.

RC (DNA: RG 59, CD); endorsed by TJ as received 12 Dec. 1793 and so recorded in SJL.

TJ submitted this letter to the President on 13 Dec. 1793, and Washington returned it the same day (Washington, *Journal*, 267).

From James Arthur

SIR   Philadelphia December 9th 93

I wish to inform you that i have Secured Some of the Best mechanicks on the Continent in the mashiene making line for water or weft Spining of Cotton or worsted. Like wise i think we Can make a cotton Gin that will feed it Self to go by water or horse which i conceive will Be of greate utility to the Sotherin States. I could wish to Spend this winter in this town to Prove the Buisness. I am so well Convinced of the abilityes of my Self and three others which is in this place that i will Engage to make a mashiene of evry Sort for the weft and a mule one water frame and the Preporation for the whole for three thousand five hundred Dollars or Receive nothing if the are not the Bes Plans that are now Entroduced in Europe. I conceive this is an oportunity that merits the publick atention as there is a sertainty of Establishing the Buisness at a small expence if the mechanicks meet with Encouragement Speedyly. The have had good Encouragement to go to the westindia ilands But i have Detained them until i have made trial what Can Be Done in america. I have laid a plan to prevent imposition as the have been Entrodused heretofore that is to have Evry mashiene made for a Certain Sum of money. I have made the prises which the are agreeable to Do them for. A line Directed to No. 198 South front street will be atended to By Sir Yours   JAMES ARTHUR

RC (DNA: RG 59, MLR); minimal punctuation supplied; addressed: "Mr Thomas Geferson Secretary of the United States"; endorsed by TJ as received 9 Dec. 1793 and so recorded in SJL.

To Edmond Charles Genet

Sir   Philadelphia, December 9th. 1793.

I have to acknowledge the receipt of your letter of the 3rd. instant, which has been duly laid before the President.[1]

We are very far from admitting your principle, that the government on either side has no other right, on the presentation of a consular commission, than to certify that, having examined it, they find it to be according to rule. The governments of both nations have a right,[2] and that of your's has exercised it, as to us, of[3] considering the character of the person appointed; the place for which he is appointed, and other material circumstances; and of taking precautions as to his conduct, if necessary;[4] and this does not defeat the general object of the convention, which, in stipulating, that Consuls shall be permitted on both sides, could not mean to supersede reasonable[5] objections to particular persons, who might at the moment[6] be obnoxious to the nation to which he was sent,[7] or whose conduct might render him so at any time after. In fact every foreign agent, depends on the double will of the two governments,[8] of that which sends him and of that which is to permit the exercise of his functions within their Territory; and when either of these wills[9] is refused or withdrawn, his authority to act within that territory[10] becomes incomplete. By what member[11] of the government the right of giving or withdrawing permission,[12] is to be exercised here, is a question on which[13] no foreign Agent can be permitted to make himself the Umpire. It is sufficient for him, under our government that he is informed of it by the Executive.[14]

On an examination of the Commissions from your nation among our records, I find,[15] that before the late change in the form of our government, foreign agents were addressed, sometimes to the United States, and sometimes to the Congress of the United States, that body being then Executive as well as Legislative. Thus the Commissions of Messrs. L'Etombe, Holker, Dannemours, Marbois, Crevecoeur, and Chateaufort, have all this clause, "Prions et requerons nos très chers et grands Amis et Allies, les Etats Unis de l'Amérique septentrionale, leurs Gouverneurs, et autres officiers &c. de laisser jouir &c. le dit Sieur &c. de la charge de notre Consul" &c. On the change in the form of our Government,[16] foreign Nations, not undertaking to decide to what member of the new Government[17] their Agents should be addressed, ceased to do it to Congress, and[18] adopted the general address to the United States[19] before cited. This was done by the government of your own Nation, as appears by the Commissions of Messrs. Mangourit and La Forest, which have in them the clause before cited. So your own Commission was, not as M. Gerards, and Luzerne's had been "A nos très

chers &c. le President et Membres du Congrès general des E. Unis"
&c. but "A nos très chers &c. les Etats Unis de l'Amerique" &c. Under
this general address, the proper member of the government was included, and could take it up. When,[20] therefore, it was seen in the Commissions of Messrs. Dupont and Hauterive, that your Executive had
returned to the ancient address, to Congress, it was conceived to be an
inattention, insomuch that I do not recollect[21] (and I do not think it
material enough to inquire) whether I noticed it to you either verbally
or by letter. When that of Mr. Dannery was presented with the like
address, being obliged to notice to you an inaccuracy of another kind, I
then mentioned that of the address, not calling it an *innovation*, but[22]
expressing my satisfaction, which is still entire, that it was not from any
design in your Executive Council.[23] The Exequatur was therefore sent.
That they will not consider our notice of it as an innovation, we are
perfectly secure.   No government can disregard formalities more
than ours. But when formalities are attacked with a view to change
principles, and to introduce an entire independence of foreign agents on
the nation with whom they reside, it becomes material to defend formalities. They would be no longer trifles if they could in defiance of the
national will, continue a foreign Agent among us, whatever might be
his course of action. Continuing, therefore, the refusal to receive any
Commission from *yourself* addressed to an improper Member of the
government, you are left free to use either the general one, To the
United States, as in the Commissions of Messrs. Mangourit and la Forest before cited,[24] or that[25] special one, To the President of the United
States. I have the honor to be, with respect, Sir, Your most obedient,
and most humble servant,

PrC (DLC); in the hand of George Taylor, Jr., unsigned; at foot of first page: "M.
Genet. minister plenipy. &c." Dft (DLC);
entirely in TJ's hand, unsigned; with only
the most important variations being noted
below. FC (Lb in DNA: RG 59, DL). Recorded in SJPL.

There is no evidence that TJ informed
Genet by letter of the irregularities in the
consular commissions of DUPONT AND HAU-
TERIVE (see note to Genet's first letter to
TJ, 22 May 1793). For THAT OF MR. DAN-
NERY, see TJ to Genet, 2 Oct. 1793.

For the Cabinet's prior approval of the
substance of this letter, see Cabinet Opinions on Edmond Charles Genet and James
King, 7 Dec. 1793.

[1] In Dft TJ here canceled two unfinished paragraphs:

"Before the late change which took place
in our form of government foreign agents
were addressed sometimes to the US. sometimes to the Congress of the US. the latter
being then the Executive as well as the legislative body. Recurring to our records as far
as they respect your nation, I observe that
      "As to the question of right."
      Next to these paragraphs TJ wrote in
the margin:
"Congress. Gerard
            Holker. Oster. Dannemours
            Luzcrne.

                        Dupont. Hauterive
      US. L'Etombe. Holker. D'annemours.
            Marbois. Crevecoeur.
            Chateaufort.
            ————
      Ternant.
            Mangourit. La Forest.
      Genet."

² In Dft TJ here canceled an interlined passage that reads "necessarily understood tho not expressed in the convention."

³ In Dft TJ here canceled "examin."

⁴ Remainder of sentence written in the margin of Dft.

⁵ Word interlined in Dft.

⁶ Preceding three words interlined in Dft.

⁷ In Dft TJ here canceled "or might become so during his residence with them."

⁸ Remainder of clause interlined in Dft.

⁹ Preceding three words interlined in Dft.

¹⁰ In Dft TJ here canceled "ceases."

¹¹ Word interlined in Dft in place of "branch."

¹² Sentence to this point interlined in Dft in place of "whether that right."

¹³ Preceding five words interlined in Dft in place of "by this or that branch of government can only."

¹⁴ Sentence interlined in Dft, "under our government" being interpolated.

¹⁵ Sentence to this point in Dft altered from "Examining this question by the precedents found in our own records I have to observe."

¹⁶ In Dft TJ here canceled "most" and an interlined "some."

¹⁷ Altered in Dft from "decide what branch of the government."

¹⁸ Preceding seven words interlined in Dft.

¹⁹ Preceding four words interlined in Dft.

²⁰ In Dft TJ here canceled "more lately."

²¹ In Dft TJ here canceled "whether I thought it was."

²² Preceding six words interlined in Dft.

²³ Remainder of text of Dft interlined and written perpendicularly in the margin in place of a heavily emended passage that in its final form appears to read: "and therefore sent the Exequatur. Whether the innovation you are pleased to charge on us was on the address of these last commissions or in our notice of them we are not afraid to leave to the good sense and the good dispositions of the Xve. Council of France: nor have we a doubt of their correcting the error as soon as it shall have been suggested to them. And to shew that we are not punctilious even with you who have thought proper to question a formality that you may build on the [charge?] of it an independence on the Presid. of the US. you are left free to adopt the address before cited."

²⁴ Preceding two words interlined in Dft in place of "or that to the Presidt. of the US."

²⁵ In Dft TJ here canceled "more."

To John Barker Church

SIR   Philadelphia Dec. 11. 1793.

The President has received your letter of Aug. 16. with it's inclosures. It was with deep concern that he learnt the unhappy fortunes of M. de la Fayette, and that he still learns his continuance under them. His friendship for him could not fail to inspire him with the desire of relieving him, and he was sure that in endeavoring to do this he should gratify the sincere attachments of his fellow-citizens. He has accordingly employed such means as appeared the most likely to effect this purpose; tho', under the existing circumstances, he could not be¹ sanguine in their obtaining very immediately the desired effect. Conscious however that his anxieties for the sufferer flow from no motives unfriendly to those who feel an interest in his confinement, he indulges their continuance, and will not relinquish the hope that the reasons for this severity will at length yeild to those of a more benign character. I have the honor to be with great respect Sir your most obedient & most humble servt

TH: JEFFERSON

RC (Peter B. Olney, Old Saybrook, Connecticut, 1950); at foot of text: "Mr. Church." PrC (DLC). FC (Lb in DNA: RG 59, DL). Enclosed in TJ to Thomas Pinckney, 12 Dec. 1793.

John Barker Church (1748-1818) was a member of Parliament whose wife, Angelica Schuyler Church, was Alexander Hamilton's sister-in-law and TJ's faithful correspondent. After going bankrupt as a London grocer in 1774, allegedly because of losses incurred in stock speculation and gambling, Church moved to America and (under the assumed name of John Carter) grew wealthy during the Revolutionary War as a supplier to Continental and French troops. Returning to England in 1783, Church aligned himself with the Whigs, befriending the Prince of Wales and Charles James Fox and representing Wendover in Parliament from 1790 to 1796. In addition to opposing the war with France throughout his parliamentary career, Church became involved in an abortive effort, shortly before he gave up his seat in Parliament in 1796, to help arrange the escape from Prussian captivity of the Marquis de Lafayette, whom he had known since the War for Independence. Moving with his family to New York in 1797, Church engaged in a variety of speculative ventures and fought a duel with Aaron Burr, before finally returning to England for good in 1814 after his wife's death (Thorne, *Parliament*, III, 441-3).

In his LETTER OF AUG. 16 to the President, Church had enclosed a 15 Mch. 1793 letter from Lafayette to the Princesse d'Hénin (another text of which is printed as an enclosure to Angelica Schuyler Church to TJ, 19 Aug. 1793) and declared that Lafayette's friends had no hope of effecting his liberation from Prussian captivity "but by the Interference of your Excellency and the Government of the United States" (NIC). See also TJ to Gouverneur Morris and Thomas Pinckney, 15 Mch. 1793, and note.

[1] TJ here canceled "very."

From Bartholomew Dandridge, Jr.

December the 11. 1793.

By the Presidents order Bw. Dandridge has the honor to transmit the enclosed papers relating to the truce between Portugal and Algiers, to the Secretary of State and to inform the Secretary that the President wishes him to prepare such information respecting the same as may be necessary to be made public—and as considerable expence has been incurred in the conveyance of said intelligence to the Goverment of the US. to consider what communication shall be made thereupon to Congress.

RC (DLC); at foot of text: "The Secretary of State"; mistakenly endorsed by TJ as received 10 Dec. 1793, a day before he recorded receipt of the enclosures in SJL. Dft (DNA: RG 59, MLR). FC (Lb in same, SDC). Enclosures: (1) David Humphreys to TJ, 6 and 8 Oct. 1793. (2) Edward Church to TJ, 12 Oct. 1793, and Enclo-

sures Nos. 1-3 listed there. For other letters that might have been returned by Dandridge, see Washington, *Journal*, 266.

For TJ's COMMUNICATION to Congress, see Report on Morocco and Algiers, 14 Dec. 1793.

To William Davies

DEAR SIR   Philadelphia. Dec. 11. 1793.

I duly received your favor of Nov. 20. The paper of which you desire a copy not being in my office, I have inclosed you an authentic printed copy: authentic, I say, because by the public printer and by order of the House of Representatives.

Of the difficulties of the business in which you were engaged here I have been fully sensible; and I have no doubt that your most zealous and assiduous exertions were employed to surmount them. Yet not having (as you are sensible) been in any manner in the way of being acquainted with what was going on, I am altogether incompetent to give any evidence or information on the subject, other than my general presumption founded on a knowlege of your attention and industry with which the government of our state is perfectly acquainted. I have the honor to be with great respect Sir Your most obedt. humble servt

TH: JEFFERSON

PrC (DLC); at foot of text: "Colo. Wm. Davies." Enclosure: *Report of the Commissioners for the Settlement of the Accounts between the United States and the Individual States, Stating Balances. Read 5th December, 1793* [Philadelphia, 1793]. See Evans, No. 47246.

From Alexander Hamilton

Decr. 11. 1793

Mr. Hamilton presents his Compliments to Mr. Jefferson. He has a confused recollection that there was something agreed upon with regard to prizes about which he was to write to the Collectors but which his state of his health at the time put out of his recollection. If Mr. Jefferson recollects it Mr. H. will thank him for information.

RC (DLC); addressed: "The Secretary of State"; endorsed by TJ as received 11 Dec. 1793.

SOMETHING AGREED UPON: see Hamilton to TJ, 18 Dec. 1793, and note.

Report on Edmond Charles Genet and Gouverneur Morris

The President doubtless recollects the communications of Mr. Ternant expressing the dissatisfaction of the Executive council of France with Mr. Morris our minister there, which however Mr. Ternant desired might be considered as informal: that Colo. Smith also mentioned that dissatisfaction, and that Mr. LeBrun told him he would charge Mr. Genet expressly with their representations on this subject; and that all further consideration thereon lay over therefore for Mr. Genet's representations.

Mr. Genet, some time after his arrival (I cannot now recollect how long, but I think it was a month or more) coming to my house in the country one evening, joined me in a walk near the river. Our conversation was on various topics, and not at all of an official complexion. As we were returning to the house, being then I suppose on some subject relative to his country (tho' I really do not recall to mind what it was) he turned about to me, just in the passage of the gate, and said 'but I must tell you we all depend on you to send us a good minister there, with whom we may do business confidentially, in the place of Mr. Morris.' These are perhaps not the identical words, yet I believe they are nearly so; I am sure they are the substance, and he scarcely employed more in the expression. It was unexpected; and, to avoid the necessity of an extempore answer, I instantly said something resuming the preceding thread of conversation, which went on, and no more was said about Mr. Morris. From this I took it for granted he meant now to come forward formally with complaints against Mr. Morris, as we had been given to expect, and therefore I mentioned nothing of this little expression to the President. Time slipped along, I expecting his complaints and he not making them. It was undoubtedly his office to bring forward his own business himself, and not at all mine to hasten or call for it; and if it was not my duty, I could not be without reasons for not taking it on myself officiously. He at length went to New York, to wit, about the of   without having done any thing formally on this subject. I now became uneasy lest he should consider the little sentence he had uttered to me as effectively, tho' not regularly, a complaint. But the more I reflected on the subject the more impossible it seemed that he could have viewed it as such; and the rather because, if he had, he would naturally have asked from time to time 'Well, what are you doing with my complaint against Mr. Morris?' or some question equivalent. But he never did. It is possible I may at other times have heard him speak unfavorably of Mr. Morris, tho' I do not recollect any particular occasion: but I am sure he never made to me any proposition to have him recalled. I believe I mentioned this matter to Mr. Randolph before I left Philadelphia: I know I did after my return: but I did not to the President, till the reciept of Mr. Genet's letter of Sep. 30. which from some unaccountable delay of the post never came to me in Virginia, tho I remained there till Oct. 25. (and received there three subsequent mails) and it never reached me in Philadelphia till Dec. 2.

The preceding is the state of this matter, as nearly as I can recollect it at this time, and I am sure it is not materially inaccurate in any point.

TH: JEFFERSON

Dec. 11. 1793.

MS (DNA: RG 59, MLR); entirely in TJ's hand. PrC (DLC); partly overwritten in a later hand. Tr (Lb in DNA: RG 59, SDC). Entry in SJPL: "Report to Presidt. on complaint agt. G. Morris." Enclosed in TJ to George Washington, 22 Dec. 1793.

This report to the President was prompted by the belated arrival in Philadelphia nine days before of Edmond Charles Genet's 18 Sep. 1793 letter to TJ, which among other things discussed the French government's wish for the recall of Gouverneur Morris as American minister to France, a wish Washington finally granted in May 1794 when he appointed James Monroe to replace him (Ammon, *Monroe*, 112-14).

COMMUNICATIONS OF MR. TERNANT: see

TJ to Washington, 20 Feb. 1793, and enclosure. COLO. SMITH . . . MENTIONED THAT DISSATISFACTION: see Notes on Conversations with William Stephens Smith and George Washington, 20 Feb. 1793. Since Genet arrived in Philadelphia on 16 May 1793, TJ's CONVERSATION with him would have taken place about the middle of June 1793. Genet WENT TO NEW YORK about 5 Aug. 1793 (Ammon, *Genet Mission*, 112; Turner, *CFM*, 236-7). TJ LEFT PHILADELPHIA on 17 Sep. 1793 (MB, 17 Sep. 1793). GENET'S LETTER OF SEP. 30.: since it made no mention of Gouverneur Morris and reached TJ well before DEC. 2., TJ must have meant the 18 Sep. 1793 letter from Genet cited above.

From St. George Tucker

DEAR SIR   Williamsburg, Decr: 11th: 1793.

This Letter will be delivered to you by my son in law John Randolph, who has resided in philadelphia for some time, with intent to avail himself of the instruction and friendship of the Attorney General of the United States, in the pursuit of his professional studies, and in his entry into life: I have some reason to apprehend that some degree of misunderstanding has subsisted between them lately, which, together with Mr. Randolph's removal from phila. renders the benefits which I flattered myself my son would derive from his patronage at least doubtful. The season of the year is such that I am unwilling to press his immediate return to Virginia: might I presume so far on your Attachment to those of your native country, who wish to improve themselves, as to sollicit your friendship and advice to him? I know, Sir, that I am not authorised to make this request upon any other footing. Permit me then to place it upon that ground, and to assure you that it is equally dictated by my Anxiety for the advancement of my son, & by that esteem with which I have the honor to be, Sir, Your very obedt: hble Servt.

S: G: TUCKER

RC (MHi); endorsed by TJ as received 22 Dec. 1793 and so recorded in SJL.

JOHN RANDOLPH of Roanoke, Tucker's stepson, who was later to become TJ's floor leader in Congress and then one of his bitterest political enemies, had returned to Philadelphia after his participation in a duel led to his departure from the College of William and Mary earlier this year. Neither this nor a period in 1790-92 under the INSTRUCTION of ATTORNEY GENERAL Edmund Randolph proved productive, with the younger man later accusing his kinsman of inattention to his legal training and embezzlement of his funds (William C. Bruce, *John Randolph of Roanoke, 1773-1833*, 2 vols. [New York, 1922], I, 74-6, 123-5). REMOVAL FROM PHILA.: Edmund Randolph remained in Germantown after the end of the yellow fever epidemic (TJ to Martha Jefferson Randolph, 1 Dec. 1793).

To Alexander Hamilton

SIR   Philadelphia Dec. 12. 1793.

Colo. Humphries having charged Mr. Church our Consul at Lisbon to send us information of the truce between Algiers and Portugal by an Express vessel, he engaged one under Swedish colours to come here with his letters. She is now lying at New York at our expence. Thinking it material to save as much of the expence as we can, by permitting her to be freighted back to Lisbon to which place she is to return, I mentioned to the President that the officer at the head of the customs at New York would be the most proper person to take charge of her. It is with his approbation that I inclose you the Charter-party, stating the terms on which she has been engaged; with a desire that you will give the necessary orders to that officer to do with the vessel what is best for the public interest. I have the honor to be with great respect Sir your most obedt servt   TH: JEFFERSON

PrC (DLC); at foot of text: "The Secretary of the Treasury." FC (Lb in DNA: RG 59, DL). Enclosure: see Enclosure No. 5 listed at Edward Church to TJ, 12 Oct. 1793.

Hamilton sent the enclosed CHARTER-PARTY in a 16 Dec. 1793 letter instructing

John Lamb, the collector of customs at New York, to "pay to the Captain one half of the freight as stipulated in the said Charter party, and . . . endeavor to procure for him a frieght back to Lisbon" (Syrett, *Hamilton*, XV, 460).

To Robert Leslie

SIR   Philadelphia Dec. 12. 1793.

I have received with great satisfaction your two letters of July 10. and Sep. 26. and particularly the last stating your present situation. I have no doubt that the public will be benefited as well as yourself by your present leisure and opportunity of pursuing your inventions. I wish this may reach you in time to make a little change in watch you were to make for my daughter, but which I now destine for myself, that is, to put a second hand on the wheel which stands nearly between the 6. aclock mark and the center of the watch. I do not know it's name. I prefer this method because it does not add a single wheel to the works, it only enlarges a pivot.

My large clock could not be made to go by Spurck. I ascribed it to the bungling manner in which he had made it. I was obliged to let him make the striking movement anew on the common plan, after which it went pretty well, the time part with three fifty sixes, and the striking part with a fifty six and a twenty eight.—The little balance clock he could not make go at all. He told me so before hand, so that I did not receive it. It was no disappointment, as the great clock renders all chamber clocks unnecessary.

No directions can yet be given to make experiments on the pendulum rod, because Congress have as yet come to no decision.—Direct to me in future 'at Monticello Virginia' and by the way of Richmond, because I leave my office the last day of this month, and become a farmer at home. Wishing you every possible success I am with esteem Sir Your most obedt servt   TH: JEFFERSON

P.S. Dec. 17. The original of the preceding went by the George Barclay. This duplicate goes by the Pigou. It is to guard against the risk of the first miscarrying, and also to add a desire that the watch may have a stop conveniently placed for stopping her at any moment. Your's with esteem   TH: JEFFERSON

PrC (DLC); at foot of letter: "Mr. Robert Leslie Watch maker No. 12. Aldersgate street or No. 4. Merlin's place near the New river head"; at foot of separate sheet containing postscript: "Mr. Lesley." Tr

(ViU: Edgehill-Randolph Papers); 19th-century copy, with postscript on separate sheet. Enclosed in TJ to Thomas Pinckney, 12 Dec. 1793.

To Thomas Pinckney

DEAR SIR   Philadelphia Dec. 12. 1793.

The George Barclay has fallen down the river before I had notice she was about to sail: I have therefore only had time to send out and get the inclosed bill of Mr. John Vaughan on Messrs. Bird, Savage & Bird of London for £13–13 the amount of the model of the threshing machine you were so kind as to send me. It is gone on from New York to Virginia without my having seen it. Accept many thanks for having procured it.

The communications between G. and us, which I mentioned in my last public letter, are now printing. You shall receive them by the first conveyance after they are done.—We heard yesterday of the truce effected between Algiers, Portugal and Holland. I am with great & sincere esteem Dr. Sir Your friend & servt TH: JEFFERSON

P.S. I trouble you with letters to Messrs. Van Staphorsts, to Mr. Church, and Mr. Leslie.—I leave this the 1st. day of January.

P.S. Dec. 17. The original of the preceding went by the George Barclay. This duplicate goes by the Pigou. It is to inclose a second of the bill for 13. guineas lest the first should miscarry: as also another letter to Mr. Leslie. Many assurances of esteem. Your's

TH: JEFFERSON

RC (CtY); at head of text: "Private"; addressed: "Thomas Pinckney esquire Minister Plenipotentiary of the US. of America at London. Great-Cumberland place"; endorsed by William A. Deas; lacks second postscript, supplied from PrC. PrC (DLC); with second postscript on separate sheet. Tr (ViU: Edgehill-Randolph Papers); 19th-century copy with second postscript on separate sheet. Enclosures: (1) TJ to John Barker Church, 11 Dec. 1793. (2) TJ to Robert Leslie, 12 Dec. 1793, and its postscript. Other enclosures not found.

COMMUNICATIONS BETWEEN G. AND US: the correspondence between TJ and Edmond Charles Genet submitted to Congress by the President on 5 Dec. 1793 and subsequently printed in *Message*.

From Jacob Hollingsworth

SIR   Elkton 13 Decbr 1793

Yours of 21 Novbr. I Received with twenty Dollars for to Buy Clover Seed, and yours of 4 Decbr. with Directions for Mr. Alaxander who will go agreable to appointment, and Respecting the Cloverseed I Can supply you with and Send it by Mr. Alaxander at Nine Dollars a Bushil and no Less. Its of the Last years Seed which I think Eaqual to New, perhaps the New will be Cheaper but as it will not be thrashed untill Jany. or Febry. it will be too Late for your purpose; If you Chose I will forward two Bushils by Mr. Alaxander, your answer Respecting it, Oblige Very Huml. Servt JACOB HOLLINGSWORTH

NB Mr. Alaxander has taken Directions from your Last Letter and his Traviling Expensis is to be Made as Reasonable as Posable.

JH

RC (MHi); endorsed by TJ as received 16 Dec. 1793 and so recorded in SJL.

From Joseph Leacock

DEAR SIR   Philada. Decmr. [13?][1] 1793

Having some time last Summer heard you Express an intention of burning the wood off your Lands in Virginia and making it into Pot-ash, immediately, on returning to my home I gave you the best instructions in my power by Letter, respecting the process, and found an answer to my Letter left at the house of Mr. Cross, Letitia-Court Market Street soon after, with an invitation to call on you when convenient. With pleasure I should have done so had I but gained further knowledge to communicate. That was my wish, and every enquiery was made of foreigners, Russians, Polanders, germans &c., respecting the mode persued in their Countrys, but was not fortunate enough to meet with any one who knew much about it, which was the reason of my not intruding on your precious time. I Expect you have made a beginning, and I am certain if you have attempted to make pot-ash, that 'tis good. You made Critical Enquiery touching every particular of the process, therefore, Mr. Jeffersons penetration and retentive memory cannot fail Exelling in the work. Indeed, the making good pot-ash is but a simple affair. Strong clear Lyes Evaporated in kettles to the consistence of brown sugar, and then, (*after* all the Lyes are thus thick'ned) these salts are to be melted with an intense heat in a covered Kettle and the fire continued till the vegitable oil and all the blackness is banished, after which 'tis to be laded out into iron coolers made warm, and this is the whole mistery.

I am acquainted with a very good German artist in this City, who probably would Engage to conduct the buissiness for you Sir, on favourable conditions, this man has a wife and 4 Children, and should it be your wish to see the man I will inform him.

I beg leave at this time, to impart my distressed condition in this world to a gentleman of Philanthropy and feeling, with humble hope his commisserating heart will administer some relief to an almost despairing mortal, struggling with an afflicted body in the sixtieth year of Life, friendless and in want. The raging Calamity in this City proved a grievous thing to me. The little income of my office in the best of times barely supported me, and, not having had any pot ash to Inspect many months because of the malady in the City, really, I am in a manner starving. The winter has come on me unprepared to withstand its rigour. I am indebted for the rent of my little appartment, not in my power to discharge, and what will be my fate God only knows! Should my Landlord seize the bed that I sleep on and all my little matters, and force me out into an unfeeling-world in the dead of winter, I must certainly perish! 'Tis not in my power to provide decent cloathing or Even daily comforts for my body. This grievous necessity has forced me to Entreat you Sir, to compassionate and help me, and your benevolence will not be lost in a happier Life hereafter. Would but your kindness enable me to live till the Spring, business will then support me. I am dear Sir, your distressed petitioner & huml. Servt.   JOSEPH LEACOCK

PS. Should what I have wrote happily Exite the benevolence of Mr. Jefferson, I entreat a line may be left at Mr. Cross's, sealed up. The sensibility of Mr. Jeffersons disposition is such, as to persuade me this Letter will be destroyed after perusal, least it might be read by others.

RC (DLC); partially dated; endorsed by TJ as received 13 Dec. 1793 and so recorded in SJL.

Leacock had corresponded with TJ in the autumn of 1792, not LAST SUMMER

(Leacock to TJ, 13, [23] Nov., 10 Dec. 1792; TJ to Leacock, 24 Nov. 1792).

[1] Date supplied for space left blank in manuscript.

From Thomas Mifflin

SIR   Philadelphia 13 Decr. 1793.

In consequence of the information, which you gave me, relative to the imprisonment and detention of the French sailors, in the Gaol of Philadelphia, I have written to the Chief Justice of this State, and the Minister of France; copies of which are inclosed. As soon as answers are received, they shall, likewise, be communicated. I am, with great esteem, Sir, Your most obedt Servt.   THO MIFFLIN

RC (MH: Simes Collection); in Alexander J. Dallas's hand, signed by Mifflin; at foot of text: "To Thomas Jefferson Esqr. Secretary of State"; endorsed by TJ as received 13 Dec. 1793 and so recorded in SJL. FC (PHarH: Secretary's Letterbooks). Enclosures: (1) Mifflin to Chief Justice Thomas McKean, 13 Dec. 1793, stating that, having been informed by TJ of complaints that last summer some French sailors were imprisoned and detained after having been committed on a warrant issued by McKean at the instance of the French consul, he wishes the chief justice to investigate this matter and inform him "what Steps have been, and will be taken with respect to the Committment, Confinement, Trial or discharge of the Prisoners." (2) Mifflin to Edmond Charles Genet, 13 Dec. 1793, stating that, complaints having been made about the imprisonment and detention of French sailors

committed last summer by warrant of Chief Justice McKean at the instance of the French consul, he transmits a copy of No. 1 and gives assurances that he and McKean will pay the utmost attention to any proposition Genet has to make on this subject (Trs in DNA: RG 59, MLR, certified by Deputy Secretary James Trimble; FCs in PHarH: Secretary's Letterbooks).

On 3 Dec. 1793 a group of French sailors petitioned the President for their release from prison in Philadelphia, where they had been arrested for desertion and held for three months by order of François Dupont, the French consul—a predicament arising from their refusal to enlist in a legion Edmond Charles Genet was raising in New York because it would have violated the oath they had sworn before the municipality of Brest not to abandon the armed ship on which they were serving, their being disarmed and denied provisions by the French minister in retaliation, and their having felt obliged to leave their ship and go to Philadelphia (M. Maurice and others to [Washington], 3 Dec. 1793, DNA: RG 59, MLR; in French). The President referred the appeal to TJ (Washington, *Journal*, 267). See also Mifflin to TJ, 20 Dec. 1793.

From Jean Pierre Blanchard

MONSIEUR   a l'hotel D'oeller's ce 14 Xbre. 1793

Il m'interesse beaucoup, pour l'ordre de mes affaires, de Savoir Si vous avez reçu une lettre que j'eus l'honneur de vous adresser il y a environ Six semaines.

Comme les plus grands personnages de l'Europe ne m'ont jamais négligé leur reponse, votre silence, Monsieur, me fait augurer que ma lettre (a la verité d'un stile tout a fait neuf pour moi) aura été interceptée. Je suis avec respect Monsieur Votre très humble Serviteur

BLANCHARD

de plusieurs academies &c &c

RC (MHi); endorsed by TJ as received 14 Dec. 1793 and so recorded in SJL.

UNE LETTRE: Blanchard to TJ, 16 Nov. 1793.

To William Rawle

SIR   Philadelphia Dec. 14. 1793.

I have to acknolege the receipt of your favor of the 9th. inst. and in answer thereto to observe that where the witnesses who deposed on the former occasion can be procured, it would be proper they should be reexamined: where they cannot be procured, the depositions formerly taken may be sent to the Executive to give such weight to them as shall be thought proper. The arbitration being declined by the agent for the owners of the vessel, you will be so kind as to proceed to have the depositions taken either by yourself, or, as you have a delicacy about that, by such other person as you shall appoint. I am with esteem Sir your most obedt. servt   TH: JEFFERSON

PrC (DLC); at foot of text: "Mr. Rawle." FC (Lb in DNA: RG 59, DL).

The letter of the 9TH. INST. from Rawle,

recorded in SJL as received 12 Dec. 1793 but not found, undoubtedly concerned the case of the *William* (see TJ to Rawle, 15 Nov. 1793).

Report on Morocco and Algiers

The Secretary of State having duly examined into the Papers and documents of his Office relative to the Negotiations proposed to be undertaken with the Governments of Morocco and Algiers, makes thereupon to the President of the United States, the following

Report.

The Reports which he made on the 28th. of Decemr. 1790, on the trade of the United States in the Mediterranean to the House of Representatives, and on the situation of their Citizens in captivity at Algiers to the President, having detailed the transactions of the united States with the governments of Morocco and Algiers from the close of the late war to that date, he begs leave to refer to them for the state of things existing at that time.

1791 Mar. 3: Act.C.17 On the 3d. of March 1791, the Legislature passed an Act appropriating the sum of 20,000 Dollars, to the purpose of effecting a recognition of the Treaty of the United States with the new Emperor of Morocco, in consequence whereof Thomas Barclay, formerly Consul General for the United States in France was appointed to proceed to Morocco in the character of Consul for the United States, to obtain a recognition of the Treaty; and on the 13th. of May in the same year the following Letter was written to him.

[*Texts of Official Instructions for Thomas Barclay, 13 May 1791, and Confidential Instructions for Thomas Barclay, 13 May 1791, printed above, Vol. 20: 397-9, 400, and here omitted.*]

A Letter was at the same time written to Francisco Chiappe a person employed confidentially near the Emperor, who had been named Consul there for the United States by Mr. Barclay on his former mission, and appeared to have acted with zeal for our interest. It was in these words.

[*Text of TJ to Francisco Chiappe, 13 May 1791, printed above, Vol. 20: 400-1, and here omitted.*]

To this was added a Letter to Col. Humphreys our Resident at Lisbon, through whom it was thought proper to require that the draughts of money should pass. It was in the following words.

[*Text of TJ to David Humphreys, 13 May 1791, printed above, Vol. 20: 406, and here omitted.*]

On Mr. Barclay's arrival in Europe he learned that the dominions[1] of Morocco were involved in a general Civil war, the subject of which was the succession to the Throne, then in dispute between several of the Sons of the late Emperor: nor had any one of them such a preponderance as to ground a presumption that a recognition of the Treaty by him would ultimately be effectual. Mr. Barclay therefore took measures for obtaining constant intelligence from that country, and in the meantime remained at Lisbon, Cadiz or Gibralter, that he might be in readiness to take advantage of the first moments of the undisputed[2] establishment of any one of the brothers on the Throne, to effect the objects of his mission.

Tho' not enabled at that time to proceed to the redemption of our captive Citizens at Algiers, yet we endeavoured[3] to alleviate their distresses by confiding to Col. Humphreys the care of furnishing them a comfortable sustenance, as was done in the following letter to him.

[*Extract of TJ to David Humphreys, 13 July 1791, consisting of first two paragraphs, complimentary close, and signature, printed above, Vol. 20: 624-5, and here omitted.*]

On the 8th. of May[4] 1792, the President proposed to the Senate the following questions.

"If the President of the United States should conclude a Convention or Treaty with the Government of Algiers for the ransom of the thirteen Americans in captivity there, for a sum not exceeding forty thousand dollars, all expenses included, will the Senate approve the same? Or is there any, and what greater or lesser sum, which they would fix on as the limit beyond which they would not approve the ransom?"

"If the President of the United States should conclude a Treaty with the Government of Algiers for the establishment of peace with them at an expense not exceeding twenty-five thousand dollars paid at the signature, and a like sum to be paid annually afterwards during the continuance of the Treaty, would the Senate approve the same? Or are there any greater or lesser sums which they would fix on as the limits beyond which they would not approve of such Treaty?"

"Go. Washington"

These questions were answered by the following resolution of the Senate,[5] of May 8th. 1792.

"In Senate, May 8th. 1792."

"Resolved, That if the President of the United States shall conclude a Treaty with the Government of Algiers, for the establishment of a peace with them, at an expense not exceeding forty thousand dollars paid at the signature, and a sum not exceeding twenty-five thousand dollars, to be paid annually afterwards, during the continuance of the treaty, the Senate will approve the same. And in case such treaty be concluded, and the President of the United States shall also conclude a Convention or Treaty with the Government of Algiers, for the ransom of the thirteen American prisoners in captivity there, for a sum not exceeding forty thousand dollars, all expenses included, the Senate will also approve such Convention or Treaty."

"Attest."

"SAM. A. OTIS. Secy."

In order to enable the President to effect the objects of this Resolution, the Legislature by their Act of May 8th. 1792 C. 41. §3. appropriated a sum of fifty thousand dollars to defray any expense which might be incurred in relation to the intercourse between the United States and foreign Nations.

Commissions were hereupon made out to Admiral Paul Jones for the objects of peace and ransom, and a third to be Consul for the United States at Algiers. And his instructions were conveyed in the following Letter.

[*Texts of TJ to John Paul Jones, 1 June 1792, and "Rough estimate not contained in the letter," printed above, Vol. 24: 3-9, note, and here omitted.*]

Mr. Pinckney then going out as our Minister Plenipo. to the Court of London, it was thought best to confide the Letter to him—to make him the channel of communication, and also to authorize him, if any circumstance should deprive us of the services of Admiral J. P. Jones, to commit the business to Mr. Barclay,[6] who it was hoped would by this time[7] be completing the object of his mission to Morocco. The letter was therefore delivered to him, and the following one addressed to himself.

[*Text of TJ to Thomas Pinckney, 11 June 1792, printed above, Vol. 24: 59, and here omitted.*]

The letter mentioned as addressed to Mr. Barclay was in these words.

[*Text of George Washington to Thomas Barclay, 11 June 1792, printed above, Vol. 24: 66-7, and here omitted.*]

By a Letter of July 3d. the following arrangements for the payment of the monies was communicated to Mr. Pinckney, to wit:

[*Extract of TJ to Thomas Pinckney, 3 July 1792, consisting of first sentence, complimentary close, and signature, printed above, Vol. 24: 153, and here omitted.*]

On Mr. Pinckney's arrival in England he learned the death of Admiral J. P. Jones. The delays which were incurred in conveying the papers to Mr. Barclay on this event will be best explained in Mr. Pinckney's own words extracted from his letter of December 13th. 1792, to the Secretary of State. They are as follows:

[*Extract of Thomas Pinckney to TJ, 13 Dec. 1792, consisting of the fifth paragraph, printed above, Vol. 24: 736-7, and here omitted.*]

In the meantime Mr. Barclay had been urged to use expedition,[8] by the following letter, from hence.

[*Extract of TJ to Thomas Barclay, 14 Nov. 1792, consisting of second paragraph, printed above, Vol. 24: 619, note, and here omitted.*]

Mr. Barclay had received the papers, had made preparations for his departure for Algiers, but was taken ill on the 15th. and died on the 19th. of January 1793, at Lisbon. This unfortunate event was known here on the 18th. of March, and on the 20th. and 21st. the following letters were written to Mr. Pinckney and Col. Humphreys.

[*Texts of TJ to Thomas Pinckney, 20 Mch. 1793, and TJ to David Humphreys, 21 Mch. 1793, printed above, Vol. 25: 410-11, 420-1, and here omitted.*]

Captain Nathaniel Cutting was appointed to be the Bearer of these Letters and to accompany and assist Col. Humphreys as Secretary in this Mission. It was therefore delivered to him, and his own Instructions were given in the following Letter.

[*Text of TJ to Nathaniel Cutting, 31 Mch. 1793, printed above, Vol. 25: 470-1, and here omitted.*]

But by a vessel which sailed on the day before from this port to Lisbon directly, and whose departure was not known till an hour before, the following Letter was hastily written and sent.[9]

[*Text of TJ to David Humphreys, 30 Mch. 1793, printed above, Vol. 25: 468-9, and here omitted.*]

Captain Cutting took his passage in a vessel bound for London which sailed about the 13th. or 14th. of April, but he did not leave England till the 3d. of September, and on the 17th. of that month Col. Humphreys embarked from Lisbon for Gibralter, from whence he wrote the Letter herewith communicated, of October the 8th. last past[10] informing us of the truce of a year concluded between Algiers and Portugal, and from whence he was to proceed to Algiers.

These are the circumstances which have taken place since the date of the former reports of December 28th. 1790. and, on consideration of them it cannot but be obvious that whatever expectations might have been formed of the issue of the mission[11] to Algiers at it's first projection, or the subsequent renewals to which unfortunate events gave occasion, they must now be greatly diminished, if not entirely abandoned. While the truce with two such commercial Nations as Portugal and Holland[12] has so much lessened the number of vessels exposed to the capture of these Corsairs, it has[13] opened the door which lets them out upon our commerce and ours alone; as with the other nations navigating the Atlantic they are at peace. Their first successes will probably give them high expectations of future advantage, and leave them little disposed to relinquish them on any terms.

A circumstance to be mentioned here is that our Resident and Consul at Lisbon have thought instantaneous warning to our commerce to be on it's guard, of sufficient importance to justify the hiring[14] a Swedish vessel to come here express with the intelligence;[15] and there is no fund out of which that hire can be paid.

To these details relative to Algiers it is to be added as to Morocco, that their internal war continues, that the succession is not likely soon to be settled, and that in the meantime their vessels have gone into such a state of decay as to leave our commerce in no present danger for want of the recognition of our treaty: but that still it will be important to be in readiness to obtain it the first moment that any person shall be so established in that Government as to give a hope that his recognition will be valid.

Th: Jefferson

Dec. 14. 1793.

MS (DNA: RG 46, Senate Records, 3d Cong., 1st sess.); in Benjamin Bankson's hand, signed and dated by TJ; with texts of documents quoted in extenso and previously printed in this edition being replaced by bracketed directive comments by the Editors; several quotation marks supplied. Dft (DLC: TJ Papers, 95: 16357-9); consists of six pages in TJ's hand, unsigned, except for correction by Bankson (see note 4 below); undated, but fols. 16357-8 written before 11 Dec. 1793 and fol. 16359 added later (see below); with directive comments by TJ indicating where the texts of documents were to be inserted in the narrative; only the most important emendations are recorded below. Tr (Lb in DNA: RG 233, House Records, 3d Cong., 1st sess., TR). Recorded in SJPL between 18 and 20 Dec. 1793: "Report on proceedings with Barbary powers. & Message." Enclosed in George Washington to the Senate and the House of Representatives, [14-16 Dec. 1793]. Enclosures: (1) David Humphreys to TJ, 26 Sep., 8 Oct. 1793. (2) Edward Church to TJ, 12 Oct. 1793. For other documents TJ later submitted to Congress as an addendum to this report, see enclosures listed at Bartholomew Dandridge, Jr., to TJ, 23 Dec. 1793.

TJ's report originated in a decision made by the President shortly before the current legislative session began to submit to Congress, "either in the Speech at the opening of the Session, or by Messages thereafter, as shall be thought best," information relating to a variety of foreign and domestic issues, including the "impediments which have taken place in the intended Ransom of our Citizens, captives in Algiers, and treaty with the Barbary States" (Memorandum of Matters to be Communicated to Congress, [November 1793], Fitzpatrick, *Writings*, XXXIII, 160). The draft of the report suggests that TJ composed this document at different times (see note 9 below). He evidently wrote the first four pages dealing with the abortive American diplomatic missions to Morocco and Algiers sometime before 11 Dec. 1793, the day he received and submitted to the President letters and enclosures from David Humphreys and Edward Church containing the first official news of the recent truce between Algiers and Portugal, and was instructed by Washington to prepare for Congress such of these documents "as might be necessary" (Washington, *Journal*, 266). He then apparently added two final pages about this ominous diplomatic development in the Mediterranean, as well as the concluding paragraph on the Moroccan treaty, and had copies made for the legislature of the three enclosures listed above. In contrast to many other reports by TJ that the President submitted to Congress, the legislature did not have this one printed because of Washington's insistence in the covering message to both houses drafted by TJ that certain parts of the report be kept confidential (Washington to the Senate and the House of Representatives, [14-16 Dec. 1793]).

TJ's REPORTS of the 28TH. OF DECEMR. 1790 on American trade in the Mediterranean and American captives in Algiers are in Vol. 18: 423-9, 430-5. For the 1786 TREATY of amity with MOROCCO and its confirmation by the Moroccan emperor in 1795, see Miller, *Treaties*, II, 185-227. Thomas BARCLAY had negotiated this treaty during his FORMER MISSION to Morocco. RESIDENT AND CONSUL AT LISBON: David Humphreys and Edward Church.

[1] Word interlined in Dft in place of "empire."

[2] Word interlined in Dft.

[3] Remainder of sentence written perpendicularly in margin of Dft.

[4] Altered in Dft from "10th. of Apr." by Bankson.

[5] Remainder of sentence left blank in Dft.

[6] Remainder of sentence interlined in Dft in place of "as it was known by this time that the succession to the emperor of Marocco was not likely to be very soon settled."

[7] In Dft TJ here canceled "nearly completed."

[8] Preceding three words interlined in Dft.

[9] Paragraph interlined in Dft, the remainder of the text being written in a different ink on a sheet of a different type of paper.

[10] Preceding two words not in Dft.

[11] Remainder of this clause and next clause interlined in Dft in place of "of Col. H. to Algiers."

[12] In Dft TJ here canceled "withdrawn such a proportion."

[13] In Dft TJ here canceled "greatly enlarged the field into which they may move, and has in a particular manner."

[14] Altered in Dft from "have thought the expediency of giving to our commerce instantaneous notice ⟨to our commerce⟩ to be on their guard was of sufficient importance to hire."

[15] In Dft TJ here canceled "that hire is to be paid."

To George Washington

Dec. 14. 1793.

Th: Jefferson has the honor to inform the President that the Spanish papers are now all ready. He sends him a set for his examination and will send two others Monday morning. He also sends the draught of the message he would propose, with the blank filled up which had been left in it. Whenever the President is satisfied about it, either with or without amendments, Th:J. will have copies made out.

The Algerine papers will not be ready till tomorrow when they shall be submitted to the examination of the President.

RC (DNA: RG 59, MLR); endorsed by Bartholomew Dandridge, Jr. Tr (Lb in same, SDC). Not recorded in SJL. Enclosures: (1) Papers on American relations with Spain submitted to Congress by the President on 16 Dec. 1793 (ASP, *Foreign Relations*, I, 247-88). (2) George Washington to the Senate and the House of Representatives, [14] Dec. 1793.

ALGERINE PAPERS: TJ's Report on Morocco and Algiers, 14 Dec. 1793, which the President submitted to Congress two days later.

George Washington to the Senate and the House of Representatives

GENTLEMEN OF THE SENATE & OF
THE HOUSE OF REPRESENTATIVES

United States
December. [14]¹ 1793.

The situation of affairs in Europe, in the course of the year 1790. having rendered it possible that a moment might arrive favorable for the arrangement of our unsettled matters with Spain, it was thought proper to prepare our representative at that court to avail us of it. A confidential person was therefore dispatched to be the bearer of instructions to him, and to supply by verbal communications any additional information of which he might find himself in need. The government of France was at the same time applied to for it's aid and influence in this negociation. Events however took a turn which did not present the occasion hoped for.

About the close of the ensuing year, I was informed through the representatives of Spain here, that their government would be willing to renew at Madrid the former conferences on these subjects. Tho' the transfer of scene was not what would have been desired, yet I did not think it important enough to reject the proposition; and therefore, with the advice and consent of the Senate, I appointed Commissioners plenipotentiary for negociating and concluding a treaty with that country on the several subjects of boundary, navigation and commerce, and gave them the instructions now communicated. Before these negociations however could be got² into train, the new troubles which had arisen in Europe had produced new combinations among the powers there, the effects of which are but too visible in the proceedings now laid before you.

In the mean time some³ other points of discussion had arisen with that country, to wit, the restitution of property escaping into the territories of each other, the mutual exchange of fugitives from justice, and above all the mutual interferences with the Indians lying between us. I had the best reason to believe that the hostilities threatened and exercised by the Southern Indians on our border were excited by the Agents of that government. Representations were thereon directed to be made, by our Commissioners, to the Spanish government, and a proposal to cultivate with good faith the peace of each other with those people. In the mean time, corresponding suspicions were entertained, or pretended to be entertained on their part, of like hostile excitements by our agents to disturb their peace with the same nations. These were brought forward by the representatives of Spain here, in a stile which could not fail to produce attention. A claim of patronage and protection of those Indians was asserted, a mediation between them and us, by that sovereign, assumed, their boundaries with us made a subject of his interference, and at length, at the very moment when these savages were committing daily inroads on our frontier, we were informed by them that 'the continuation of the peace, good harmony, and perfect friendship of the two nations was very problematical for the future unless the US. should take more convenient measures and of greater energy than those adopted for a long time past.'

If their previous correspondence had worn the appearance of a desire to urge on a disagreement, this last declaration left no room to evade it, since it could not be conceived we would submit to the scalping knife and tomahawk of the savage, without any resistance. I thought it time therefore to know if these were the views of their sovereign, and dispatched a special messenger with instructions to our commissioners which are among the papers now communicated. Their last letter gives us reason to[4] expect very shortly to know the result.—I must add that the Spanish representatives here, perceiving that their last communication had made considerable impression, endeavored to abate this by some subsequent professions which being also among the communications to the legislature, they will be able to form their own conclusions.

Dft (DLC: TJ Papers, 96: 16458-9); entirely in TJ's hand; partially dated (see note 1 below). Enclosed in TJ to Washington, 14 Dec. 1793. The text of the message that Washington sent to Congress, dated 16 Dec. 1793, with the day completed by the President, was otherwise identical in wording to TJ's Dft (DNA: RG 46, Senate Records, 3d Cong., 1st sess.; Fitzpatrick, *Washington*, XXXIII, 186-8).

TJ drafted this message to cover the documents on American relations with Spain that the President submitted to Congress on 16 Dec. 1793 (ASP, *Foreign Relations*, I, 247-88).

OUR REPRESENTATIVE AT THAT COURT: William Carmichael. CONFIDENTIAL PERSON: David Humphreys (Bemis, *Pinckney's Treaty*, 152-3). INFORMED THROUGH THE REPRESENTATIVES OF SPAIN HERE: see Report on Negotiations with Spain, 22

Dec. 1791. COMMISSIONERS PLENIPOTENTIARY: William Carmichael and William Short. INSTRUCTIONS NOW COMMUNICATED: see Report on Negotiations with Spain, 18 Mch. 1792. REPRESENTATIONS WERE THEREON DIRECTED: see TJ to Carmichael and Short, 3 Nov. 1792. WE WERE INFORMED BY THEM: see Josef de Jaudenes and Josef Ignacio de Viar to TJ, 18 June 1793. SPECIAL MESSENGER: James Blake. INSTRUCTIONS TO OUR COMMISSIONERS: TJ to Carmichael and Short, 30 June 1793. THEIR LAST LETTER: Carmichael and Short to TJ, 29 Sep. 1793.

[1] Supplied for space left blank in manuscript.
[2] TJ here canceled "under way."
[3] Word interlined.
[4] Sentence to this point interlined in place of "and I."

George Washington to the Senate and the House of Representatives

GENTLEMEN OF THE { SENATE
{ HOUSE OF REPR.   [14-16 Dec. 1793]

I lay before you a Report of the Secretary of state on[1] the measures which have been taken on behalf of the US. for the purpose of obtaining a recognition of our treaty with Marocco, and for the ransom of our citizens and establishment of peace with Algiers.

While it is proper our citizens should know that subjects which so much concern their interests and their feelings have duly engaged the attention of their Legislature and Executive, it would still be improper that some particulars of this communication should be made known. The confidential conversation stated in one of the last letters sent herewith, is one of these. Both justice and policy require that the source of that information should remain secret. So a knolege of[2] the sums meant to have been given for peace and ransom, might have a disadvantageous influence on future proceedings for the same objects.

Dft (DLC: TJ Papers, 95: 16362); entirely in TJ's hand; undated. Recorded in SJPL between 18 and 20 Dec. 1793: "Report on proceedings with Barbary powers. & Message." Enclosure: Report on Morocco and Algiers, 14 Dec. 1793, and enclosures. The text of the message that Washington sent to Congress, in the hand of Benjamin Bankson and dated 16 Dec. 1793, with the day completed in Washington's hand, was otherwise identical in wording to TJ's Dft (DNA: RG 46, Senate Records, 3d Cong., 1st sess.; Fitzpatrick, *Washington*, XXXIII, 185-6).

Despite TJ's notation in SJPL, he probably composed this draft sometime between 14 Dec., when he promised to submit to the President on the following day certain papers relating to his report on Morocco and Algiers, and 16 Dec. 1793, when Washington submitted the message to Congress (see TJ to Washington, 14 Dec. 1793).

CONFIDENTIAL CONVERSATION: see Edward Church to TJ, 12 Oct. 1793.

[1] Preceding eight words interlined.
[2] Sentence to this point interlined.

To Joseph Yznardi, Jr.

SIR   Philadelphia Dec. 14. 1793.

I received on the 12th. inst. your favor of the 8th. The Swedish vessel chartered to bring us the intelligence respecting the Algerines is given in charge to the Collector of the customs at New York, with instructions to dispose of her to the best advantage of the public according to her charter party. By that she is to return to Lisbon.—I think Mr. Jaudenes, in engaging to establish peace between us and Algiers, would find the engagement a difficult one to fulfill within the limits we prescribe in point of price.—Duly sensible of your zeal in expressing a willingness to go to Algiers, you will probably have seen lately in the public papers that Colo. Humphreys was already dispatched on that mission.—Wishing you a speedy and safe return to your own country, and making to you my last official compliments (my purpose being to retire within a few days) I have the honor to be with esteem, Sir Your most obedt servt   TH: JEFFERSON

PrC (DLC); at foot of text: "Mr. Yznardi." FC (Lb in DNA: RG 59, DCI).

To Jean Pierre Blanchard

SIR   Philadelphia Dec. 15. 1793.

At the date of your letter of Oct. 16. I was in Virginia. It was sent to that country after me, while I was on my return to this, and came back to me at German town Nov. 9. and it was not till three weeks afterwards that we removed to this place. As you expressed in the letter an impatience to leave Philadelphia on account of the danger of the infectious fever, I took for granted that you had done it before I received your letter, considering the delay which had happened. Your letter of yesterday is the first notice to me that you were still here.—The application to the President which you desire me to make is entirely foreign to my *official* relations with him, and other considerations prevent me from becoming, as a *private* individual, the channel of such a sollicitation.—I wish that my own resources were such as that I might from them have accomodated you with the sum you desire. But I am about to leave this place within a few days, and on summing up my affairs I find my engagements so much more than I had expected as to place me under real difficulty to provide for them.—I feel very sincere concern for the embarrasments of your situation and regret my own inability to relieve them being with respect & attachment, Sir Your most obedt. humble servt   TH: JEFFERSON

PrC (DLC); at foot of text: "Mr. Blanchard." Tr (ViU: Edgehill-Randolph Papers); 19th-century copy.

To Edmond Charles Genet

SIR   Philadelphia Dec. 15. 1793.

In answer to the several letters you have done me the honor of writing on the subject of tonnage and duties demanded at the Custom houses on the vessels and goods of the fugitives from St. Domingo, I have to inform you that the opinion being that the terms of the law did not authorize the Executive to dispense with those demands, I have taken the proper measures for having the subject submitted to the Legislature, who are competent to the giving an exemption by passing a special law if they shall think the nature of the case calls for it. I have the honor to be with great respect Sir Your most obedt & most humble sert

TH: JEFFERSON

PrC (DLC); at foot of text: "The Min. Pleny. of the Republic of France." FC (Lb in DNA: RG 59, DL). Tr (DLC: Genet Papers); in French; with revisions by Genet.

SEVERAL LETTERS: Genet to TJ, 1, 29 Oct. (second letter), 25 Nov. (first letter) 1793.

For the Cabinet's prior approval of the substance of this letter, see Cabinet Opinions on Edmond Charles Genet and James King, 7 Dec. 1793.

From Christopher Gore

SIR   Boston December 15. 1793

I receiv'd your favor of the 29th. ult. on the 14. instant, and immediately communicated to Consul Dannery, the intentions of Government toward him, and my own desire to comply with such their intentions— to which he replied this day.

I take the liberty to enclose you copy of my letter, and his answer— and am, sir, with the greatest respect your most obed. servt

C. GORE

RC (DNA: RG 59, MLR); at foot of text: "Thos Jefferson Esqr Secry of State"; endorsed by TJ as received 23 Dec. 1793 and so recorded in SJL. Enclosure: Gore to Thomas Dannery, 14 Dec. 1793, stating that, in consequence of Edmond Charles Genet's complaint that French consuls are exposed to insult and personal danger from hostile French refugees, chiefly from the West Indies, he has been directed by TJ to

advise that the federal government will use all legally authorized means to protect representatives of the French nation in the United States; and that he will be happy to discuss them with Dannery (Tr in same; in Gore's hand; at foot of text: "Copy"). Other enclosure not found.

YOUR FAVOR: see TJ to Certain District Attorneys, 29 Nov. 1793.

To Mary Jefferson

MY DEAR MARIA   Philadelphia Dec. 15. 1793

I should have written to you the last Sunday in turn, but business required my allotting your turn to Mr. Randolph, and putting off writing to you till this day. I have now received yours and your sister's letters of Nov. 27, and 28. I agree that Watson shall make the writing desk for you.—I called the other day on Mrs. Fullerton, and there saw your friend Sally Cropper. She went up to Trenton the morning after she left us, and staid there till lately. The maid servant who waited on her and you at our house, caught the fever on her return to town and died.—In my letter of last week I desired Mr. Randolph to send horses for me to be at Fredericksburg on the 12th. of January. Lest that letter should miscarry I repeat it here and wish you to mention it to him. I also informed him that a person of the name of Eli Alexander would set out this day from Elkton to take charge of the plantations under Byrd Rogers, and praying him to have his accomodations at the place got ready as far as should be necessary before my arrival. I hope to be with you all about the 15th. of January no more to leave you. My blessings to your dear Sister and little ones; affections to Mr. Randolph and your friends with you. Adieu, my dear. Your's tenderly　　　　Th: Jefferson

RC (ViU photostat); at foot of text: "Maria Jefferson." Tr (ViU: Edgehill-Randolph Papers); 19th-century copy.

The LETTERS OF NOV. 27. AND 28. from Mary Jefferson and Martha Jefferson Randolph are not recorded in SJL and have not been found.

Certificate for Raphaelle Peale

Department of State

The purpose of Mr. Peale's voyage being merely to collect subjects of Natural history for the valuable Museum of his father at Philadelphia, unconnected with every other object, I hereby certify that fact, in addition to the preceding passport, and recommend the said Rafaelle Peale to the aid and patronage of all the lovers and protectors of science wheresoever he may have need of them. Given under my hand at Philadelphia aforesaid this 15th. day of December 1793.

Th: Jefferson

MS (PPAmP: Peale-Sellers Papers); in TJ's hand; with subjoined 17 Dec. 1793 note by Governor Thomas Mifflin of Pennsylvania stating that he "chearfully joins in the above recommendation"; both certificates written on verso of 14 Dec. 1793 printed passport for "Rafaelle Peale" (see Appendix III).

Raphaelle Peale (1774-1825), the eldest son of the Philadelphia painter and museum proprietor Charles Willson Peale, had a varied and largely unsuccessful career as a naturalist, taxidermist, painter of portraits and miniatures, silhouette cutter, inventor, and poet, but is now recognized as the first important American painter of still lifes, a genre to which he turned in later years as his precarious health declined (DAB; Nicolai Cikovsky, Jr., Linda Bantel, and John Wilmerding, *Raphaelle Peale Still Lifes* [Washington, D.C., 1988]). His VOYAGE took him to Cayenne, French Guiana, where he obtained a wildcat and possibly a toucan, but he must have abandoned his ambitious plans for a trip northward to Mexico, for he was apparently back in Philadelphia by 24 Apr. 1794, when his father gave up painting portraits in favor of him and his brother Rembrandt Peale (Lillian B. Miller and others, eds., *The Selected Papers of Charles Willson Peale and his Family*, 3 vols. in 4 [New Haven, 1983-　　], II, pt. 1, p. 78-9, 91).

To George Washington

Dec. 15. 1793.

Th: Jefferson has the honor to return to the President the letter of Mr. Rumaine praying to be relieved from duties on the wrecks of fortune with which he escaped from St. Domingo. Th:J. has put the letter of the same person to himself, with those of Mr. Genet into the hands of Mr. Murray, to make them the foundation of a bill of relief.

RC (DNA: RG 59, MLR); addressed: "The President of the US."; endorsed by Bartholomew Dandridge, Jr. Tr (Lb in same, SDC). Not recorded in SJL. Enclosure: Either Jean Louis Du Rumaine to Washington, or Du Rumaine to Washington and Congress, Edenton, North Carolina, 15 Nov. 1793, requesting Congress to grant him a remission of the tonnage duty he paid here after being obliged in July 1793 to flee with his wife from Saint-Domingue because of the slave revolt there (RCs in DNA: RG 59, MLR).

Du Rumaine's 15 Nov. 1793 letter to TJ, recorded in SJL as received 2 Dec. 1793, has not been found. BILL OF RELIEF: see note to Cabinet Opinions on Edmond Charles Genet and James King, 7 Dec. 1793.

From Brown, Benson & Ives

SIR   Providence, Decemr. 16. 1793.

We had the honour to address you the 18th. of April last in reply to your esteem'd favour of the 5th. of the same Month on the subject of our Complaint relative to the Detention of our Brig Commerce at Port au Prince. It was then our intention to Prosecute our Claim for Damages but the Amount 'tho very great We could never estimate—on that particular suffice it to say that Capt. Munro depress'd by his sufferings and the Injury We sustain'd sicken'd and Died—his Death was an irreparable loss. We now Sir, beg leave to solicit your attention to the Papers Which Accompany this Letter—they Contain a detail of the Capture of our Ship Hamilton Capt. Rodman by a French Privateer on the 4th. of April last on her passage from Lisbon to Petersburg loaded principally on frieght also an Authenticated Statement of the loss we sustain'd in Consequence of such Capture, and as the same ship and Commander sail'd yesterday for Bourdeaux, We Conceiv'd it advisable to address a Letter to Mr. Fenwick the American Consul at that Port Coppy of which We have the honour to Inclose. We have also transmitted him our Letter of Attorney to Prosecute our Claim, but as We observe with ineffable satisfaction the Disposition of Goverment to Protect the Commerce of our Country and to resent the many unprovok'd insults to our suffering Trade and being Confident that their interference will be the most efficacious Means to enforce our Claim, you will Permit us to re-

[525]

quest an early applycation of the Inclosures which may Cooperate with our Proceedings in the business, or that available Measures may be adopted by Goverment independent of any attempts of our own, either of which we submit to its Wisdom, and only beg leave to suggest that perhaps the latter would be most eligible as our Ship on her present Passage is subject to interruption which may Procrastinate if not prevent the arrival of our Dispatches to Mr. Fenwick. We think Proper to add that before Capt. Rodman left England where he was sent after his recapture by the British Frigate Juno, he exhibited a Claim for the frieght Money by which Considerable expence was incur'd and at the date of our last advices from London the Cause was Pending in Doctors Commons and the Issue Uncertain as appears by the inclos'd Letter from Mr. Auldjo and a Coppy of one address'd to him from the Proctor Mr. Farquhar. Should more explicit information or any other Proofs we can obtain be Necessary you will do us the favour to Acquaint us. We Cannot Conclude this address without recurring to the grateful Sentiments with which your Prompt and Obliging attention impress'd us in the Case of the Brig Commerce. We ardently hope that the Dignity and the interests of our Country may ever be asserted by such enlighten'd Charecters as guide and Direct its important Councils in this truly Critical and interesting Period. We are Sir with great Consideration & Esteem, Your very Obedt. Friends   BROWN BENSON & IVES

RC (DLC: Causten-Pickett Papers); at foot of text: "The Honl. Thomas Jefferson Esq—Philadelphia"; endorsed by TJ as received 26 Dec. 1793 and so recorded in SJL. Enclosures not found.

A letter to TJ of 16 Dec. 1793 from "Brown & Francis & others," recorded in SJL as received 26 Dec. 1793 from Providence, has not been found.

From Edmond Charles Genet

MONSIEUR   Phil. le 16. xbre 1793 l'an 2e de la Rep fse

J'ai l'honneur de vous accuser la reception de votre lettre en date du 9 de ce mois. Je me conformerai aux dispositions qu'elle contient et à ses derniers résultats qui me présentent une alternative que je saisis avec empressement puis qu'elle me met en mesure de satisfaire le Gouvernement Federal sans déroger à mes devoirs, position infiniment agreable pour moi et à laquelle je ne serais point parvenu si j'eusse adhéré à vos premieres décisions qui m'assujétissaient à des formes auxquelles je ne pouvois consentir sans me compromettre.

Je n'ai jamais cru Monsieur en disputant sur une forme nouvelle m'ériger en arbitre suprême,[1] et entreprendre de donner plus ou moins de liberté aux agens Consulaires de la nation française dans les E.U. Je n'ai jamais imaginé que les E.U., que le Congrès eussent plus de prise sur eux que le Président; l'independance de leurs fonctions sur laquelle j'ai insisté ne tient point à la nature des Corps politiques ou des individus et je ne me suis attaché à ce point la que parce qu'il ne m'était pas possible de reconnaitre une liaison idéale que vous paraissiéz avoir eu l'intention d'établir entre une prérogative reconnue et une innovation qui ne l'est pas, non plus que ce double principe de dependance pour les agens politiques des nations dans la généralité que vous lui donnez menace d'arracher aux puissances le plus beau de leurs droits à l'une des plus anciennes et des plus sacrée des fonctions publiques toute sa dignité et à des usages consacrés par des siècles le cachet législatif que tous les peuples leur ont accordé. Agréez mon respect.

Dft (DLC: Genet Papers); in a clerk's hand, unsigned, with revision by Genet; above salutation: "Le Ministre de la Rep. Fse. à Mr jefferson." FC (same); in English. Recorded in SJL as received 16 Dec. 1793.

[1] Word interlined by Genet.

From Edmond Charles Genet

M.   Philadelphie[1] le 16. xbre. 1793. l'an 2e. de la Repe. fse.

Je vous prie de mettre sous les yeux du President la requisition ci Jointe que Je viens d'adresser au procureur general des Etats unis et de vouloir bien l'engager à préscrire à ce Magistrat d'entamer le plus promptement possible une procedure qui Interesse éssentiellement l'honneur de la france et le mien.

Dft (DLC: Genet Papers); unsigned; above salutation: "Le Cit Genet Ministre plenipotentiaire de la Repe. fse. à M. Jefferson secretaire d'Etat." Recorded in SJL as received 17 Dec. 1793. Translation printed in *Federal Gazette and Philadelphia Daily Advertiser*, 24 Dec. 1793.

For the context of this letter and its enclosure, see note to Proposed Public Statement on Edmond Charles Genet, [ca. 16 Dec. 1793].

[1] Interlined by Genet in place of "New York."

ENCLOSURE

Edmond Charles Genet to Edmund Randolph

MONSIEUR   Philadelphie.[1] le 16. xbre 1793 l'an 2e de la République fse.

Une nouvelle publication de Messieurs Jay et King dont vous trouverez un exemplaire ci joint m'oblige de recourir encore à votre Ministère. Vous verrez par cet écrit que ces M.M. ont aggravé Singulièrement leurs offenses envers la France, envers Son délégué 1⁰² en associant à leur calomnie Messieurs Knox et Hamilton l'un Secretaire de la guerre, l'autre Secretaire des Finances; 2° en faisant entendre que nous cherchions à nous immiscer dans les affaires intérieures des Etats Unis, ce qui est absolument faux.[3]

De la part de Simples Citoyens de pareilles assertions[4] ne fixeraient point mon attention; mais étant émanées du premier juge et d'un Senateur des E. U. elles méritent une censure publique, et j'espère qu'elles feront partie de l'accusation que je vous prie itérativement de porter à la Cour Suprème des Etats Unis contre M.M. Jay et King, ainsi que contre tous ceux qui ont eu part aux Calomnies que l'on a répandues avec perfidie dans la vue Seule de nuire aux interêts de la France en attaquant[5] celui qui est chargé de la défendre et qui met sa gloire à remplir ce devoir en dépit de tous les dégouts dont on l'abreuve chaque Jour.

Je vous Serai obligé, Monsieur, de vouloir bien me communiquer par écrit vos intentions relativement à mes differentes réquisitions et m'éclairer de vos lumières dans la procédure importante que je Sollicite. Je vais demander au Chef du Pouvoir Exécutif des E. U. par l'entremise du Secrétaire d'Etat de vous recommander de poursuivre cette affaire[6] avec toute l'activité possible, l'honneur de nos deux Républiques exigeant qu'elle Soit promptement terminée.

Dft (DLC: Genet Papers); in a clerk's hand, unsigned, with revisions by Genet, two being made after FC was prepared (see notes 3-4 below); at head of text: "Le Ministre Plénipotentiaire de la République française à Monsieur Randolph Procureur Général des Etats Unis." FC (same); in English; consisting of translation, with some revisions by Genet, reflecting Dft as finally emended, except for two minor variations. Enclosure: John Jay and Rufus King, "To the Public," New York, 26 Nov. 1793, reprinting their report of 12 Aug. 1793 avowing their assertion that Genet had declared he would appeal to the people from certain decisions of the President; affirming the accuracy of the charge and stating that during the *Little Sarah* episode in Philadelphia on 6 July 1793 Genet had angrily declared to Alexander J. Dallas that he "would appeal from the President to the People"; that Genet's letter to the President merely denied that he had made this statement to Washington; that Dallas reported the threat to Governor Mifflin and TJ; that despite TJ's expectation, founded on what he considered to be an intimation from Genet in an interview of 7 July 1793, the *Little Sarah* left port before Washington's return; and that they derived this information from Alexander Hamilton and Henry Knox; with subjoined statement of Hamilton and Knox, Philadelphia, 29 Nov. 1793, corroborating the above statements and indicating that the particulars relating to Mifflin were received from him and those relating to TJ, including the information he obtained from Dallas, were communi-

cated by him (New York *Daily Advertiser*, Supplement, 2 Dec. 1793). Translation with two minor revisions printed in *Federal Gazette and Philadelphia Daily Advertiser*, 24 Dec. 1793.

Responding to Genet in a letter of 18 Dec. 1793, Randolph declined his request to prosecute John Jay and Rufus King in the Supreme Court for the CALOMNIES of which Genet accused them on the grounds that he was authorized by law to conduct only those cases before that tribunal to which the United States was a party and that he believed the case "will not sustain the prosecution" contemplated, but pointed out that other lawyers could advise him on ways to bring it before the Court without the Attorney General's intervention; with a postscript of 20 Dec. 1793 indicating that a letter from TJ since received on the subject of Genet's request did not alter his opinion (DLC: Genet Papers).

[1] Interlined by Genet in place of "New York."

[2] This and next digit below interlined by Genet.

[3] Genet here canceled a passage that, as revised by him, read: "3° enfin en Se rendant eux mêmes coupables d'un crime Semblable à celui dont ils osent m'accuser, par des vœux qui tendent à insinuer que la Constitution vraiment Républicaine que la France vient de Se donner, que tous Ses citoyens ont ⟨juré de défendre jusqu'à la Mort⟩ acceptée, ne présente point encore Selon eux l'image d'un bon Gouvernement

et n'est point propre par conséquent à faire notre bonheur."

[4] Altered by Genet from "de pareilles opinions," with "accusations mensong" and "impostures" interlined and canceled successively above "opinions."

[5] Remainder of paragraph substituted by Genet for "leur défenseur."

[6] Preceding two words interlined by Genet.

Proposed Public Statement on Edmond Charles Genet

[ca. 16 Dec. 1793]

A Question whether Mr. G. has threatened to appeal from the Pr. to the people of the US. has excited considerable attention, has been thought worthy of calling forth the evidence of[1] the highest officers of the government[2] and to justify the disclosure of the private[3] consultations of the Exve. The performance of an official duty having connected me with the matter in question, I have[4] been vouched in affirmation of the charge.[5] It is with much[6] regret that I find my self made use of for any thing[7] in so disagreeable an altercation, but considering it's present ground, silence on my part might beget surmises which would not be just. I had conversations on Sunday the 7th. of July with Mr. Genet and Mr. Dallas as has been stated in the public papers. I had a private consultation with the Secrs. of the Treasury and war on the Monday to decide what should to be done in the event of the L.D's attempting to depart[8] and it was than I made my communication to them.[9] The Pr. returned on the Wednesday, and on that day I committed the same communications[10] to writing in a Report to him.[11] I did this when the transactions were fully in my mind, and particular considerations[12] led me to detail with more minuteness than usual every circumstance which I thought[13] worthy[14] notice. I could not then[15] foresee the[16] altercation which has now arisen, nor consequently[17] give to the statement any aspect respecting it. My only object was to give[18] to the Pr. a circumstantial and faithful relation of what he had a right to know. And I did it with a sacred regard to truth.[19] I have since heard the same matter spoken of on different[20] occasions and by different persons insomuch that I should fear to attempt from[21] memory alone to distinguish at this time[22] what I have heard from one what from another, what on one occasion or what on another. I think it therefore safest to give the whole report, without the suppression of a tittle.[23] It contains many things which relate not at all to the present question, and some which it will be obvious were never expected to be made public. Were these however now omitted it might be imagined that[24] the aspect of what would remain might be sensibly affected by it.[25] I chuse then to throw myself on the indulgencies of those who may read it, rather than to incur their suspicions, and therefore give a verbal copy of the whole report as follows.

MS (DLC: TJ Papers, 96: 16460); entirely in TJ's hand; undated; heavily emended, only the most significant revisions being noted below. Recorded in SJPL between 16 and 18 Dec. 1793: "draught of paragraph contemplatd. to have been put in papers."

TJ's unusual proposed public statement —intended as a preface to his publication of the memorandum of a conversation with Edmond Charles Genet that he had prepared for the President on 10 July 1793 —was a response to Federalist exploitation of one of the French minister's worst blunders: the threat he made on the evening of 6 July 1793 to Alexander J. Dallas, the staunchly Republican secretary of Pennsylvania, during the *Little Sarah* affair to "appeal from the President to the people" (for a discussion of this episode, see note to Cabinet Opinions on the *Little Sarah*, 8 July 1793). After reporting the threat to Governor Thomas Mifflin of Pennsylvania, Dallas apprised TJ of it the next day. Moreover, on the basis of information received in conversations with TJ and Mifflin, Alexander Hamilton and Henry Knox quoted a slightly variant version of Genet's offending remark in an 8 July 1793 report to the President on the case of the *Little Sarah*, which TJ read before it was submitted to Washington, in which they warned that Genet's defiance reflected a sinister design by the French minister to undermine popular confidence in his administration (Syrett, *Hamilton*, xv, 76; see also Hamilton to Rufus King, 13 Aug. 1793, same, 239-42; [Hamilton and Knox], Statement to John Dunlap, *Dunlap and Claypoole's American Daily Advertiser*, 17 Dec. 1793; "To the Public," same, 18 Dec. 1793). TJ also cited Genet's statement to Dallas in his memorandum to the President two days later, though he tried to minimize its seriousness by emphasizing that the French minister had not repeated the threat during their lengthy discussion of the *Little Sarah* affair on 7 July 1793. Although Genet later denied ever having made such a threat, it was consistent with his previously expressed opinion to TJ

that he had a right to "appeal from the Executive to Congress, and from both to the people," and TJ seems never to have doubted that Genet uttered the remark (TJ to James Monroe, 28 June 1793; TJ to James Madison, 1 Sep. 1793).

The Secretary of State's involvement in this chain of events became a public issue as a result of a bold counterstroke that Genet launched against his chief Federalist critics in mid-November 1793. In a letter to TJ enclosing one to Edmund Randolph, both of which he took care to have published, Genet denounced as uttterly false the charge that he had threatened to appeal from the President to the people—an accusation Chief Justice John Jay and Senator Rufus King had made against him in an otherwise circumspect joint statement published in a 12 Aug. 1793 issue of a New York newspaper—and called upon the Attorney General to have the two Federalists prosecuted for libel (Genet's sixth letter to TJ, 14 Nov. 1793, and note; New York *Diary; or Loudon's Register*, 12 Aug., 22 Nov. 1793). Jay and King retaliated early the following month with a rebuttal that described in print for the first time the exact circumstances under which Genet had made his threat and the transmission of it from Dallas to Mifflin and TJ—a statement which they acknowledged was based upon information they had received from Hamilton and Knox, and which in fact drew very heavily on an account of the events in question that Hamilton had provided to King more than three months before. Jay and King accompanied their rebuttal with a supporting certificate in which Hamilton and Knox attested that Mifflin and TJ had both informed them of Dallas's report about Genet's threat soon after it was made (Jay and King, "To the Public," 26 Nov. 1793, New York *Daily Advertiser*, Supplement, 2 Dec. 1793; Statement by Hamilton and Knox, 29 Nov. 1793, Syrett, *Hamilton*, xv, 418-19; see also Hamilton to King, 13 Aug. 1793, Jay and King to Hamilton and Knox, 26 Nov. 1793, Jay to Hamilton, 26 Nov. 1793, King to Hamilton, 26 Nov. 1793, and Hamilton and Knox to Jay and

King, 27 Nov. 1793, same, 239-42, 411-14, 416).

It was at this point, in an effort to discredit the French minister's Federalist critics by giving his own version of his disputed meeting with Genet, that Dallas made the existence of TJ's memorandum to the President a matter of public record for the first time. In his statement, which he issued apparently after conferring with Genet in New York and certainly after consulting with TJ in Philadelphia, Dallas denied that Genet had threatened to appeal from the President to the people in any seditious sense—though he conceded that Genet had spoken of "publishing his correspondence with the officers of government, together with a general narrative of his proceedings"—and suggested that TJ's memorandum had erred in citing him as an authority for the threat (Dallas, Statement to the Public, 7 Dec. 1793, *Dunlap and Claypoole's American Daily Advertiser*, 9 Dec. 1793; Dallas to TJ, 4 Dec. 1793; King, *Life*, I, 464). Instead of quelling the controversy, however, Dallas's intervention elicited a public statement from Hamilton and Knox, unsigned but clearly emanating from the highest circles of the American government and initially interpreted in some quarters as the work of TJ himself, in which they not only reiterated Jay and King's more extended account of Genet's threat to appeal to the American people, but also quoted without authorization the section of TJ's memorandum to the President asserting that Genet had made this threat to Dallas ([Hamilton and Knox], Statement to John Dunlap, *Dunlap and Claypoole's American Daily Advertiser*, 17 Dec. 1793; "To the Public," same, 18 Dec. 1793).

With two such diametrically opposed versions of Genet's remark to Dallas now in the public record, TJ reluctantly set aside his intense aversion to public controversy and prepared the above statement for publication as a preface to his memorandum to the President. Despite the memorandum's damaging admission that Dallas had in fact informed the Secretary of State of Genet's threatened appeal to the American people, TJ in his prefatory remarks tried to put the best face possible on Genet's expressions. His notation in SJPL and internal evidence suggest that he probably drafted the statement shortly before the appearance on 17

Dec. 1793 of Hamilton and Knox's pseudonymous rejoinder to Dallas's public defense of Genet. But in the end, for reasons he never explained, he chose to withhold it from the press. By remaining silent, however, TJ may have inadvertently encouraged Genet to continue his quest for legal redress against the Chief Justice and the Senator from New York, who, unbeknownst to TJ at the time, made a concerted effort to obtain a copy of his 10 July 1793 memorandum in preparation for their defense (see TJ to Edmund Randolph, 18 Dec. 1793, and note).

L.D.: *Little Democrat*, the anglicized form of the French name given to the *Little Sarah* after it was converted to a privateer.

[1] Preceding three words interlined.

[2] TJ here canceled "to bear testimony to it."

[3] Word interlined in place of "secret."

[4] Preceding ten words substituted for a passage in which TJ first wrote "having implicated me in the transaction, I have," replaced it with "made me a witness in the occasion," and finally substituted "necessarily ⟨made⟩ given me a part," canceling each interlineation in turn.

[5] Preceding three words interlined in place of "of the question."

[6] Word interlined in place of "extreme."

[7] Preceding nine words interlined in place of "enter ⟨mix⟩," which TJ had interlined in place of "find myself ⟨mixed⟩ meddle." TJ may have inadvertently left the last three words in the text uncanceled.

[8] Remainder of sentence interlined.

[9] TJ first wrote "communicated to them what had passed" and then altered it to read as above.

[10] Preceding three words interlined.

[11] TJ here canceled "a full detail of what had passed."

[12] Word interlined in place of "circumstances of the moment."

[13] Word interlined in place of "could recollect as."

[14] TJ here canceled "any" and an interlined "the least."

[15] Sentence to this point interlined in place of "I did this when it was impossible to."

[16] TJ here canceled "question."

[17] Preceding two words interlined in place of "to."

[18] Preceding nine words interlined in

place of "hue which might reflect on that, and under no other view than that of giving."

¹⁹ Sentence interlined.

²⁰ Word interlined in place of "so many."

²¹ Preceding eight words interlined in place of "⟨that my memory⟩ I could not trust to my."

²² Preceding three words interlined.

²³ TJ first wrote "without altering a tittle of it" and then revised it to read as above.

²⁴ TJ here canceled "their suppression."

²⁵ Sentence interlined in place of "Had these been omitted it mt. have been thought that tho' the parts given forth were in the very words of the report and consequently not stated with a view to the present case, yet that it has been [gar?]bled with an eye to it," with "could have no eye" interlined and left uncanceled above "consequently."

Report on Commerce

I. FIRST STATE OF THE REPORT ON COMMERCE, [BEFORE 23 AUG. 1791-AFTER 13 APR. 1792]

II. SECOND STATE OF THE REPORT ON COMMERCE, [BEFORE 5 FEB.-AFTER 23 FEB. 1793]

III. FINAL STATE OF THE REPORT ON COMMERCE, [16 DEC. 1793]

IV. THOMAS JEFFERSON TO THE SPEAKER OF THE HOUSE OF REPRESENTATIVES, 16 DEC. 1793

V. THOMAS JEFFERSON TO THE PRESIDENT OF THE SENATE, 16 DEC. 1793

EDITORIAL NOTE

Jefferson's report on commerce was his last effort as Secretary of State to achieve his longstanding goal of fundamentally reordering the new republic's political economy by lessening American economic dependence on Great Britain and fostering closer commercial ties with France. Based upon almost two decades of study and practical experience, it reflected Jefferson's vision of the United States as a virtuous agrarian republic in which the acquisition of new foreign markets for surplus agricultural production, in addition to territorial expansion, would postpone indefinitely the social degeneration and political corruption to which republics had been subject throughout history.

The report accordingly took aim at what Jefferson perceived as two threats to American agrarian republicanism. One was British mercantilism and its premise—disseminated widely in Lord Sheffield's 1783 *Observations on the Commerce of the American States* and reiterated forcefully in Lord Hawkesbury's 1791 *Report of the Lords of the Committee of Privy Council . . . on The American Trade*—that American reliance on Britain's superior manufactures and credit justified the continuance of various restrictions on American trade and shipping. The other was Hamiltonian fiscalism, with its tacit assumption that temporary acquiescence in the British navigation system was necessary to ensure the smooth flow of Anglo-American trade and the resultant import duties that were essential for maintaining the nation's public credit. With these targets in view, Jefferson's report combined an incisive account of the privileges accorded and the restrictions imposed on American trade with a bold program of commercial discrimination that was calculated to win more favorable treatment for it in the international marketplace (for the antecedents to the report, see Merrill D. Peterson, "Thomas Jefferson and Commercial Policy, 1783-1793," wmq, 3d ser., xxii [1965], 584-610; Doron S. Ben-Atar, *The Origins of Jeffersonian Commercial Policy and Diplomacy* [New York, 1993], 17-133; Stanley Elkins and Eric McKitrick, *The Age of Federalism* [New York, 1993], 378-81; and Jefferson's earlier reports on various aspects of American commerce in Vols. 18: 301-3, 565-70, 19: 121-39, 206-22).

The chain of events that led to the submission of the report to Congress just two weeks before Jefferson's resignation as Secretary of State began almost three years earlier. On 23 Feb. 1791, in response to a message from the President nine days earlier describing British rejection of American overtures for a commercial treaty, the House of Representatives referred to Jefferson a committee report recommending a navigation act aimed at British trade and shipping and directed him to prepare a report for Congress on the state of American commerce with other nations and the means for improving it. Jefferson prepared most of the first state of the report during the recess between the adjournment of the first Congress on 3 Mch. and the convening of the second Congress on 24 Oct. 1791. He drew upon his studies of American trade, official and unofficial information supplied by then Assistant Secretary of the Treasury Tench Coxe, and the House committee's recommendations for commercial retaliation against the British. He also solicited the views of certain Philadelphia merchants, to whom he variously submitted all or parts of the largely unrevised first state of the report late in August 1791, and continued to work on the text at Monticello during the next two months. Although Jefferson later suggested that he completed this state of the report before the second Congress convened, he continued to revise it during and perhaps even after this body's first session, which lasted until 8 May 1792. The most significant revision he made in this or any other state of the report was replacing two pages in which he had cautiously advocated federal encouragement of household manufactures with two others in which he clearly stipulated that this was a state responsibility (see illustration). Jefferson very likely made this change in the aftermath of Alexander Hamilton's 5 Dec. 1791 report on manufactures, whose call for federal support of a wide range of manufacturing he abhorred on constitutional and social grounds (Document i below; jhr, i, 377-8, 388; nsp, vii, 408; Coxe to TJ, 4, 5 Mch., 15 Apr., 30 June, [ca. June], 19 July 1791; Thomas FitzSimons to TJ, 23 Aug. 1791; TJ to John Ross, 26 Aug. 1791; Ross to TJ, 27 Aug. 1791; George Clymer to TJ, 1 Sep. 1791; TJ to the Speaker of the House of Representatives, 20 Feb. 1793).

Jefferson did not submit the first state of the report to Congress. As early as December 1791 Hamilton convinced him that it would be advisable to delay submission of the document in order to avoid jeopardizing negotiations for the relinquishment of the western posts held by Britain in violation of the Treaty of Paris. In the following month, moreover, Jefferson learned of Spanish willingness to conclude a commercial treaty with the United States—five months after he had become aware of the French Legislative Assembly's call for a new trade agreement. In view of the possibility of such dramatic changes in American commerce, Jefferson secured House approval in March 1792 to defer submission of the report until the next session of Congress (William Short to TJ, 6 June 1791; Josef de Jaudenes and Josef Ignacio de Viar to TJ, 27 Jan. 1792; Memoranda of Consultations with the President, [11 Mch.-9 Apr. 1792]; TJ to the Speaker of the House of Representatives, 22 Mch. 1792, and note). In addition to the motives he articulated, Jefferson withheld the report for two other reasons. Federalist control of the second Congress made it unlikely that any legislative action would result from his recommendations for commercial retaliation against Britain, and the discriminatory policies toward American shipping and tobacco that the Legislative Assembly had adopted in 1791 weakened his argument that the French treated American trade more favorably than the British.

Despite the failure to achieve a commercial treaty with Spain or a new commercial treaty with France, Jefferson also withheld the second state of the report from Congress. With a few minor exceptions, this text was initially identical to the first state of the report as Jefferson had revised it. But in February 1793 he variously submitted all or parts of this document to Tench Coxe, the President, and the British, French, Spanish, and Dutch ministers. After revising the text in response to Coxe's suggestions, he secured Washington's approval of the document as it stood and then made further revisions on the basis of the foreign ministers' comments and his own ideas. These revisions essentially involved matters of detail that left the general thrust of the report untouched. In the same month, however, Jefferson obtained House approval to delay submission of the report until the newly elected third Congress met later in 1793, in part no doubt because he learned that Edmond Charles Genet was coming to America with authority to conclude a new French-American trade treaty, and in part because he feared that releasing the report at this time would engender British interference in American peace talks with the Western Indians. He probably also hoped that the new Congress would be controlled by Republicans sympathetic to his proposals for commercial discrimination against Britain (Document II below; Notes on Conversations with William Stephens Smith and George Washington, 20 Feb. 1793, and note; TJ to the Speaker of the House of Representatives, 20 Feb. 1793, and note).

Jefferson's submission of the final report to Congress on 16 Dec. and a supplementary report to the House on 30 Dec. 1793 was the prelude to a sustained Republican legislative assault on the British navigation system. With a few slight exceptions, the former document was identical to the second state of the report as Jefferson had revised it, and thus did not reflect any of the changes in European commercial policy resulting from the French declaration of war on Britain in February 1793. Submitted to the Senate by Vice-President John Adams on 18 Dec. and to the House by Speaker Frederick Augustus Muhlenberg on 19 Dec. 1793, the report was published late in 1793 by order of the House (JS, II, 12; JHR, II, 18; Evans, No. 26339). The circumstances under which Jefferson released it seemed to be more favorable for the accomplishment of his objectives: Republicans narrowly controlled the House, though not the Senate; popular hostility to Britain was rising because of its seizures of American ships trading with France and its mediation of an Algerine-Portuguese truce that injured American shipping; and popular support for France remained strong, despite the fiasco of the Genet mission and French captures of American merchant vessels. Within this context British minister George Hammond correctly perceived that the report had an "avowed undisguised tendency . . . to recommend a closer connexion with France, and to inculcate the expediency of a direct system of commerical hostility with Great Britain" (Documents III-V below; Hammond to Lord Grenville, 22 Feb. 1794, PRO: FO 5/4).

On 3 Jan. 1794, three days after Jefferson retired from office, James Madison launched the Republican drive to implement the report's legislative recommendations by submitting eight resolutions to the House. The first resolution generally stated the desirability of a more rigorous policy of commercial discrimination, the next six called for specific discriminatory measures clearly aimed at British trade and shipping, and the last provided that compensation to American citizens for losses caused by foreign countries acting in violation of international law be paid from additional duties levied against those countries. Led by Madison, Republicans argued that the resolutions would improve the terms of American trade with Britain and other countries, end the corruption of American government and society caused by undue British economic influence, help resolve Anglo-American diplomatic differences, and strengthen American relations with the French sister republic. With the aid of data secretly supplied by the Secretary of the Treasury, the principal Federalist spokesman, William Loughton Smith of South Carolina, countered with a blistering attack on the anti-British thrust of Jefferson's report. Examining every aspect of American commerce with France and Britain covered by the report, Smith argued that in the vast majority of cases British policies were more favorable to the United States than those of the French. Federalists also contended that Madison's resolutions would devastate the thriving American economy, provoke a commercial and possibly even a shooting war with Britain, exacerbate Anglo-American diplomatic disputes, and destroy public credit. After weeks of debate, during which opinion in the House remained so closely divided that Republicans could barely pass Madison's prefatory resolution, the House agreed on 5 Feb. to postpone debate on the remaining resolutions until 3 Mch. 1794. Republicans hoped that in the interval news of fresh British provocations would strengthen support for Madison's proposals. Instead the arrival during this interval of news of British seizures of about 250 American ships in the West Indies and Lord Dorchester's incendiary speech to the Western Indians created a war crisis of such gravity that commercial discrimination now seemed like a tepid response to British aggression. Congress accordingly took no further action on Madison's resolutions and turned its attention to sterner measures, while the President dispatched Chief Justice John Jay on a mission to England that resulted in a treaty which prohibited commercial discrimination against Britain for a decade, thus dooming Jefferson's hope of radically reshaping the American political economy (*Annals*, IV, 158-9, 174-209, 226-48, 256-349, 352-66, 395-410, 413-32; Madison, *Papers*, XV, 147-8, 167-71, 182-202, 204, 206-8, 210-43, 247-8; Syrett, *Hamilton*, XIII, 395-436; Hammond to Lord Grenville, 22 Feb. 1794, PRO: FO 5/4; Elkins and McKitrick, *Age of Federalism*, 381-96; Bemis, *Jay's Treaty*, 353).

I. First State of the Report on Commerce

[before 23 Aug. 1791-after 13 Apr. 1792]

The Secretary of state, to whom was referred by the house of Representatives the Report of a committee on the written message of the President of the U.S. of the 14th. of Feb. 1791. with instruction to report to Congress the nature and extent of the privileges and restrictions of the commercial intercourse of the U.S. with foreign nations, and the measures which he should think proper to be adopted for the improvement of the commerce and navigation of the same, has had the same under consideration, and thereupon makes the following

REPORT.

The nations with which the U.S. have their chief commercial intercourse are Spain, Portugal, France, Great Britain, the United Netherlands, Denmark and Sweden, and their American possessions: and the articles of Export which constitute the basis of that commerce [1] with their respective amounts are

	Dollars
Bread-grains, & meals to the amount of [2]	7,649,887
Tobacco	4,349,567
Rice	1,753,796
Wood	1,263,534
salted fish	941,696
pot & pearl-ash	839,093
salted meats	599,130
Indigo	537,379
horses & mules	339,753
whale oil	252,591
flax seed	236,072
tar, pitch & turpentine	217,177
live provisions	137,743
ships	
foreign goods	620,274 [3]

To descend to articles of smaller value than these would lead into a minuteness of detail neither necessary nor useful to the present object. [4]

Our Navigation depending on the same commerce will appear by the following statement of the tonnage of our own vessels, entering in our ports, in one year, [5] from those several nations, and their possessions. [6] This was from Oct. 1789. to Sep. 1790 inclusive, as follows.

Spain	19,695 tons
Portugal	23,576
France	116,410
Gr. Britain	43,580
United Netherlds.	58,858
Denmark	14,655
Sweden	750.

Of our Commercial objects, Spain recieves favorably our [7] Salted fish, Wood, Ships, Tar, pitch and turpentine. [8]

They do not discourage our Rice, Pot and Pearl ash, Salted provisions or Whale oil. But these articles being in small demand at their markets, are carried thither but in a small degree. [9]

Tobacco, Indigo, and Bread grains are not recieved there. Nor are Meals, for their own consumption: but, for the use of their Colonies, Meals were heretofore admitted favourably. Lately, however, we are told that duties of from [10] half a dollar to 2. dollars the barrel are imposed on all foreign flour re-exported to their colonies; the duties being so proportioned to the current price of their own flour, as that both together are to make the constant sum of 9. dollars per barrel. [11]

Themselves and their colonies are the actual consumers of what they recieve from us.

Our Navigation is free with the kingdom of Spain; foreign goods being recieved there in our ships on the same conditions as if carried in their own, or in the vessels of the country of which such goods are the manufacture or produce.

Portugal recieves favourably [12] our Grain and Bread, Salted fish, and other Salted provisions, Wood, Tar, pitch, and turpentine.

For Flax-seed, Pot and Pearl-ash, tho not discouraged, there is little demand.

Our Ships pay 20. per cent on being sold to their subjects, and are then free bottoms.

Foreign goods (except those of the E. Indies) are recieved on the same footing in our vessels as in [13] any others, that is to say, on general duties of from 20. to 28. per cent: and consequently our Navigation is unobstructed by them. [14]

Themselves and their Colonies consume what they recieve from us.

These observations [15] extend to the Azores, Madeira and the Cape de Verd islands. [16]

France recieves favorably our Bread grains, and meals, [17] Rice, Wood, Pot and Pearlashes.

A duty of 5. sous the kental is paid on our Tar, pitch and turpentine. Our Whale oils pay 6. livres the Kental, and are the only foreign whale oils admitted. Our Indigo pays 5. livres the Kental, their own two and a half. But a difference of quality, still more than a difference of duty prevents it's seeking that market.

Salted beef is recieved freely for exportation; [18] but if for home-consumption, it pays 5 livres the kental. Other Salted provisions pay that duty in all cases, and Salted fish [19] the prohibitory one of 20. livres the kental.

Our ships are free to carry thither all foreign goods, except those of the E. Indies, [20] except tobaccos not of our own growth: and they participate with theirs the exclusive carriage of our whale oils and tobacco.

Under [21] their former government our tobacco was under a monopoly, but paid no duties; and our ships were freely sold in their ports and converted into national bottoms. The present government, since the last session of Congress, has[22] taken[23] from our ships this privilege. They[24] emancipated tobacco from it's monopoly, but subjected it to duties of 18. livres 15 sous the kental, carried in their own vessels, and 25. livres carried in ours; a difference more than equal to the freight of the article.

They and their colonies consume what they recieve from us.

Great Britain recieves favorably our Pot and Pearl ash, Indigo, Flax seed, Wood, Tar, pitch and turpentine.[25]

Our Tobacco, for their own consumption, pays 1/3 sterl. the pound, custom and excise, besides heavy incidental expences. And Rice, in the same case, pays 7/4 sterl. the hundred weight; which rendering it too dear as an article of[26] food, it is consequently used in very small quantity.

Our whale oils and Bacon are under prohibitory duties, and Salted fish and all other Salted provisions are prohibited. Our Grains, Meals and Bread are prohibited also,[27] unless in times of such scarcity as may raise the price of Wheat to 50/ sterl. the quarter and other grains and meals in proportion.[28]

Our Ships, even when purchased by their own subjects, are not permitted to be made free bottoms.

The vessels of no nation can carry thither any thing which is not of the production or manufacture of the country to which they belong; nor can ours, according to a late decision, carry even our own productions, unless they have been actually built within the U.S.[29]

The greater part of what they recieve from us is re-exported to other countries,[30] and consequently their profits thereon are intercepted between us and the consumers.

The United Netherlands prohibit our pickled beef and pork, meals and bread of all sorts, and lay a prohibitory duty on spirits distilled from grain.

All other of our productions are recieved on varied duties, which may be reckoned, on a medium, at about 3. per cent.

They consume but a small part of what they recieve, and consequently, as to the great mass, they intercept, between us and the consumer, a portion of the value equal to[31] the charges attending an intermediate deposit.

Foreign goods, except some West India[32] articles are recieved in the vessels of any nation.

Our Ships may be sold and naturalized there with exceptions of one or two privileges which scarcely lessen their value.

Denmark[33]

Sweden recieves favorably our Grains and Meals, Salted provisions, Indigo and Whale oil.

They subject our Rice to duties of 1.6 Dollars the hundred weight carried in their own vessels, and of 2.25 Dollars the hundred weight carried in ours or any others. Being thus rendered too dear as an article of common food, little of it is consumed with them. Of our tobaccos they are considerable consumers but levy[34] heavy duties on them also; their duties of entry town duties and excise being 4.38 Doll. the hundred weight, if carried in their own vessels, and of 40. per cent on that additional if carried in our own or any other vessels.

They prohibit altogether our Bread, Fish, Pot and Pearl ashe, Flax seed, Tar, pitch and turpentine, Wood (except oak-timber and masts) and all foreign manufactures.

Under so many restrictions and prohibitions, our Navigation with them is reduced almost to nothing.[35]

With our Neighbors, an order of things much harder presents itself. The extraordinary circumstances of the moment in which the inhabitants of this hemisphere became acquainted with those of the other, placed them in a predicament which still continues, and which is as new in the moral as in the physical world. The reciprocal rights and duties established by the laws of nature between neighbor nations, to supply by mutual exchange the wants of the one with the redundancies[36] of another, rights and duties well recognised and practised in other parts of the[37] earth, are suspended for the inhabitants of this; and their existence is directed, not to their own happiness, but to that[38] of their Antipodes. To these laws are submitted the native descendants, as well of the conquerers, as of the conquered people.[39]

Spain and Portugal refuse, to those parts of America which they govern, all direct intercourse with any people but themselves. The commodities in mutual demand, between them and their neighbors, must be carried to be exchanged in some port of the governing[40] country, and the transportation between that and the subject state must be in a domestic bottom.[41]

France and Great Britain admit their West India possessions to recieve directly our maize, rice, vegetables, fresh provisions, horses, wood, tar, pitch and turpentine. France prohibits our other bread-stuff to her possessions: Great Britain admits it. France admits our fish on a duty of 5.^{tt} the kental,[42] and our salted provisions (except pork). Great Britain prohibits both. Our vessels are free to carry our own commodities to the French West Indies, and to bring away rum and melasses[43] But we are not permitted to carry our[44] own produce to the British West Indies. Their[45] vessels alone may take[46] from us, and bring in exchange rum, melasses, sugar, coffee, cocoa-nuts, ginger and pimento. There are indeed some freedoms in the island of Dominica, but under such circumstances as to be little used by us.[47] To the British continental colonies, and to Newfoundland every thing is prohibited. Their governors however, in times of distress, have power to permit a temporary importation of certain articles, in their own bottoms, but not in ours.[48]

In the West India islands[49] of the United Netherlands, Denmark[50] and Sweden[51] vessels and commodities are freely recieved, subject to duties, not so heavy as to have been complained of.

To sum up these restrictions, so far as they are important
1. in Europe.

Our breadstuff is prohibited in England and Spain, except, as to Spain, Meals for re-exportation.[52]

Our Tobaccoes are heavily dutied in England, Sweden, and France, and prohibited in Spain and Portugal.

Our Rice is heavily dutied in England and Sweden, and prohibited in Portugal.

Our Fish and salted Provisions are prohibited in England, and under prohibitory duties in France.

Our Whale oils are prohibited in England and Portugal.

And our Vessels denied naturalization in Engld. and[53] France.

2. in the West Indies.

All intercourse is prohibited with the possessions of Spain and Portugal.

Our salted Provisions and Fish are prohibited by England.

Our salted Pork and Bread-stuff (except Maize) are[54] prohibited by France, and our salted Fish heavily dutied.

3. in the article of Navigation

Our own carriage of our own tobacco is heavily dutied in France and Sweden.

We can carry no article, not of our own production, to the British ports in Europe:

Nor even our own produce to her American possessions.[55]

Such being the restrictions on the Commerce and Navigation of the U.S. the question is in what way they may best be removed, modified, or counteracted?

As to Commerce, two methods occur, 1. by friendly arrangements with the several nations with whom these restrictions exist; or 2. by the separate act of our own legislatures for countervailing their effects.

There can be no doubt but that[56] friendly arrangement is the most eligible. Instead of embarrassing Commerce under piles of regulating laws, duties and prohibitions, could it be relieved from all it's shackles in all parts of the world, could every country be employed in producing that which nature has best fitted it to produce, and each be free to exchange with others mutual surplusses for mutual wants, the greatest mass possible would then be produced of those things which contribute to human life and human happiness; the numbers of mankind would be increased, and their condition bettered. [57] In such a state of things Agriculture would be doubly eligible to us, as to the profits of our labour, it would add the profits of a greater portion of our lands, which must lie idle and unprofitable [58] in proportion as we [59] betake ourselves to arts and manufactures.

Would even a single nation begin with the U.S. this system of free commerce, it would be adviseable to begin it with that nation; since it is only [60] one by one that it can be extended to all. If [61] the circumstances of either party should [62] render it expedient to levy a revenue by way of impost on commerce, it's freedom might be modified in that particular by mutual and equivalent measures, preserving it entire in all others.

Some nations not yet ripe for free commerce in all it's extent, might still be willing to mollify it's restrictions and regulations for us, in proportion to the advantages which an intercourse with us might offer. Particularly they may concur with us in reciprocating the duties to be levied on each side, or in compensating any excess of duty by equivalent advantages of another nature. Our commerce is certainly of a character to entitle it to favor in most countries. The commodities we offer are either Necessaries of life; or Materials for manufacture; or convenient subjects of Revenue: and we take in exchange either Manufactures when they have recieved the last finish of art and industry; or mere Luxuries, [63] which we might do without, or furnish to ourselves. Such a Customer [64] may reasonably expect welcome, and friendly treatment every where: [65] a Customer too whose demands, increasing with their wealth and population, must very shortly give full employment to the whole industry of any nation whatever, in any line of supply it [66] may get into the habit of calling for from them. [67]

But should any nation, contrary to our wishes, suppose it may better find it's advantage by continuing it's system of prohibitions, duties and regulations, it behoves us to protect our citizens and their commerce [68] by counter-prohibitions, duties and regulations also. A free commerce is [69] not to be given in exchange for restrictions and vexations: nor is it [70] likely to produce a relaxation of them.

Our Navigation involves still higher considerations. As a branch of Industry it is valuable, but, as a means of Defence, indispensable. [71]

It's value as a branch of Industry is enhanced by the dependance of so many other branches on it. For tho', in times of peace, other nations may carry our produce to market for us (if it be desireable that other nations should carry for us) yet when those nations are[72] at war with each other, if we have not within ourselves the means of transportation, our produce must be exported in belligerent vessels at the increased expence of war freight and insurance, and the articles which will not bear that must perish on our hands.

But it is as a Means of[73] Defence that our Navigation will admit neither neglect nor forbearance. The position and circumstances of the U.S. leave them nothing to fear on their land-board, and nothing to desire beyond their present rights. But on their Sea-board they are open to injury, and they have there too a Commerce which must be protected. This can only be done by possessing a respectable body of citizen-seamen.[74]

Were the Ocean, which is the common property of all, open to the industry of all, so that every person and vessel should be free to take employment wherever it could be found, the U.S. would certainly not set the example of appropriating to themselves exclusively any portion of the common stock of occupation. They would rely on the enterprize and activity of their citizens for a due participation of the benefits of the seafaring business, and for keeping the marine class of citizens equal to[75] their object. But where a particular nation shall grasp[76] at undue shares, and more especially where[77] they sieze on the means of the U.S. to convert them into aliment for their own strength, and withdraw them entirely from the support of those to whom they belong, defensive and protecting measures become necessary on the part of the state[78] whose marine resources are thus invaded; or it will be disarmed of it's defence, it's productions will lie at the mercy of the nation which has possessed itself exclusively of the means of carrying them,[79] it's commercial independance is gone, and political must follow commercial influence. The carriage of our own commodities, if once established in another channel, cannot be resumed in the moment we may desire. If we lose the seamen[80] whom it now occupies, we lose the present means of marine defence, and time will be requisite to raise up others when any[81] disgrace or losses shall bring home to our feelings the error of having abandoned them. The materials for maintaining our due share of navigation are ours in abundance. And as to the mode of[82] using them, we have only to adopt the principles of those who thus put us on the defensive, or others equivalent and better adapted[83] to our circumstances.

The following principles appear perfectly just; and being founded in reciprocity, can give no cause of complaint.[84]

1. Where a nation imposes high duties on our productions, or prohibits them altogether, it will[85] be proper for us to do the same by theirs; selecting at first those articles of manufacture which we take from them

in greatest quantity, and which at the same time we could the soonest furnish to ourselves, or obtain from other countries; imposing on them duties, lighter at first, but[86] heavier and heavier afterwards as other channels of supply should[87] open;[88] the proceeds of the duties on such manufactures to be applied[89] to the importation of the manufacturer himself, and in aid[90] of those employed in the same line at home. The oppressions on our agriculture in foreign ports would[91] thus be made the occasion of promoting arts and manufactures at home[92] and of relieving ourselves[93] from a dependance on the councils and conduct of others.[94]

2.[95] Where a nation refuses to recieve in our vessels any productions but our own, we should[96] refuse to recieve in theirs any but their productions. The bill reported by the committee is well framed to effect this.

3.[97] Where a nation refuses to consider any vessel as ours which has not been built within the U.S. we should refuse to consider as theirs any vessel not built within their territory.[98]

4.[99] Where a nation refuses us the[100] carriage[101] of our own productions to certain[102] countries under their subjection,[103] we should refuse to them the carriage of the same productions to the same countries;[104] and perhaps even to any others. And that this restriction might bring no inconvenience on the agriculture of our country, it might be proper to begin by leaving the present moderate tonnage duty on the vessels of that nation for the first year, doubling it the second, trebling it the third quadrupling it the fourth[105] and prohibiting them afterwards from the carriage of such productions altogether.

It is true we must expect some inconvenience in practice from the establishment of discriminating duties. But in this, as in so many other cases, we are left to chuse between two evils. These inconveniencies are nothing, when weighed against the loss of wealth and loss of force which will follow our perseverance in the plan of indiscrimination. When once it shall be percieved that we are either in the system or the habit of giving equal advantages to those who extinguish our commerce by duties and prohibitions, and commit encroachments on our navigation, as to those who treat both with liberality and justice, liberality and justice will be converted[106] into duties and prohibitions. It is not to the moderation and justice of others we are to trust for fair and equal access to market with our productions, or for our due share in the transportation of them; but to our own means of independance, and the firm will to use them. Nor do the inconveniencies of discrimination merit consideration.[107] Not one of the nations before mentioned, perhaps not a commercial nation on earth, is without them. In our case, one distinction alone will suffice, that is to say, between nations who favor our productions and navigation, and those who do not favor them. One set of moderate duties, say the present duties for the first, and a fixed advance on these as to some articles, and prohibitions as to others, for the last.

Still it must be repeated that friendly arrangements are preferable with all who will come into them; and that we should carry into such arrangements all the liberality and spirit of accomodation which the nature of the case will admit. [108]

Proposals of friendly arrangement have been made [109] by the present government to that of Great Britain, as the message states: but being already on as good a footing in right, [110] and a better in fact, than the most favoured nation, they do not discover [111] any disposition to have it meddled with.

Like proposals of friendly arrangement should be made to those [112] other nations with whom we have such commercial intercourse as may render arrangements [113] important. In the mean while it will [114] rest with the wisdom of Congress to determine whether, as to those nations, they will not surcease ex parte regulations, on the reasonable presumption that they will concur in doing whatever justice and moderation dictate should be done.

MS (DLC: TJ Papers, 68: 11914, 11916-17, 11915, 11919-22, 11924, 11918, 11926, 11925); in TJ's hand, unsigned and undated, except for marginal clerical note made by George Taylor, Jr., when copying Document II below; consisting of 22 pages, some unnumbered, on eleven unwatermarked sheets, possibly copied in whole or part from an earlier missing draft or drafts, and 2 pages on one watermarked sheet (fol. 11925) constituting replacements for p. 19-20 that TJ prepared after 13 Apr. 1792 in consequence of Alexander Hamilton's 5 Dec. 1791 report on manufactures (see note 107 below), this substitution being part of the third group of revisions described below, all of the pages following TJ's customary form for drafts. TJ's extensive revisions, virtually all of which are recorded below, fall into three groups based on internal evidence: those he made when first writing the MS, which have been incorporated into the text as printed above (see notes 1, 10, 12, 24, 37, 75, 81-2, and 102 below); those he made at indeterminate dates (some almost certainly between 23 Aug. and 24 Oct. 1791), these being written in pencil (see notes 3-4, 41, and 63 below) and ink (see notes 2, 4, 6-7, 9, 11, 13-23, 26-8, 31-4, 36, 38-40, 46, 48, 54, 56-61, 65-71, 73, 79, 83-5, 89, 94, and

perhaps 95, 97, and 99 below), though the state of the partially revised text as it stood ready for submission at the beginning of the first session of the second Congress on 24 Oct. 1791 is now indeterminable (see TJ to the Speaker of the House of Representatives, 22 Mch. 1792, 20 Feb. 1793); and those he made after an 11-13 Apr. 1792 exchange of correspondence with George Hammond on British trade policy, these also being written in pencil (see notes 91, 100, and 103-4 below) and ink (see notes 8, 25, 29-30, 42-4, 47-9, 51-3, 72, 74, 76-8, 80, 87-8, 90, 92, 96, 101, 104-14 below). *The text printed above reflects the state of the MS as it presumably existed when Thomas FitzSimons returned it to TJ on 23 Aug. 1791 and before TJ made the last two groups of revisions* (see FitzSimons to TJ, 23 Aug. 1791). Recorded in SJPL under 22 Mch. 1792 (the date TJ first proposed deferring its submission): "Rept. Th:J. on commerce of US. with foreign nations." The following fragments, notes, calculations, and documents are related to or were employed by TJ in the preparation of this state of the report:

MS 1: DLC: TJ Papers, 69: 11895, a 2-page MS in TJ's hand; undated; consisting of an outline for the section of p. 1-11 of MS dealing with American trade with the seven countries and their colonies specified therein; recto endorsed by TJ: "foreign commerce."

MS 2: DLC: TJ Papers, 69: 11896; a 1-page MS in TJ's hand; undated, but written on or after 21 June 1791; consisting of notes on those parts of Joseph Fenwick to TJ, 22 Mch. 1791, dealing with certain French trade duties and the French prohibition on the naturalization of foreign-built ships, elements of which appear on p. 4-5 of MS.

MS 3: DLC: TJ Papers, 59: 10188; a 1-page MS; undated; consisting of a small slip containing two lines written in an unidentified hand describing Dutch duties on distilled spirits, with annotations added by TJ consisting of the first and the last seven lines printed below, the whole forming notes for section of p. 7 of MS on this subject:

"duties in Holland on distilled spirits

Eau de Vie–*de Vin*–11 f 10–les 30 Viertels

Do   –*de grain*–35 f–128 Mingles

the above is taken from Ricard's treaty on commerce.

the Mingle is the English quart
the Viertel is the gallon and a half
from this it appears that the duty on distilled grains is intended for a prohibition; that on brandy for a duty on consumption."

MS 4: DLC: TJ Papers, 69: 11901; a 1-page MS in TJ's hand written on a fragmentary address cover of an unidentified letter to him; undated; consisting of three passages (the first and third being canceled) on American trade with Denmark and with the French, British, and Danish West Indies that appear in somewhat variant form as revisions on p. 8, 10, and 11 of MS, except for a sentence on the British West Indies which TJ canceled on p. 10 of MS (see notes 33, 44, and 48 below).

MS 5: DLC: TJ Papers, 69: 12003-4; a 2-page MS in an unidentified hand; undated; endorsed by TJ: "Sweden. duties"; consisting of a small sheet of notes on Swedish duties on tobacco and rice, with notes on exchange by TJ written lengthwise on verso, that were incorporated into p. 8 of MS:

		Rix D.S.R.	
Tobacco ℔ 100^{tt}	Duty of	3.16.3	
	Town dues	3.6	
		3.19.9	
40 ℔ Ct. additional by American Ships		1.18.3	4.38.0
	Excise		31.3
	Rix Dolls.		5.21.3

Rice ℔ ^{tt}	Duty of	8	
	Town dues	$\frac{2}{3}$	$8\frac{2}{3}$
40 ℔ Ct. additional			$3\frac{1}{3}$
		R.	0.1.0

Dutys as regulated in Sweden

[*on verso:*]
The additional tax of 40 ℔ Ct. uppon the Tobacco will amount to abought 14 Rix Dolls. ℔ Hogsd.

[*Notes by TJ:*]

f s   d
the Rx dollar of account of Sweden is 2–13–11 of Holland.
the Dollar of Spain is   2–10
then 1 Rx Dollar =1.07375 of Spain
_____

f s   d   s
but the Rx Dollar actual money of Sweden is 2–13–8 = 53.5
  RxD D
then 1 = 1.07
  RxD
then 3–19–9

    31–3 RxD.   D
4– 3–0 = 4.0625 = 4.346.

See also note 23 to Document II below.

MS 6: DLC: TJ Papers, 69: 11902; a 1-page MS in TJ's hand written on a fragmentary address cover of an unidentified letter to him; undated; consisting of passages on sugar maple trees, French proposals for a new commercial treaty, British reexports of American products, and British restrictions on the American carrying trade that in somewhat variant form were inserted as revisions on p. 19-20, 21, 7, and 20 of MS, respectively, the last being part of the two pages TJ later substituted for the original p. 19-20 of MS. In its final state the section on sugar maple production reads: "These trees too exist in sufficient numbers in the U.S. not only to furnish their own consumption but a surplus for foreign markets whenever the necessary labour shall be employed on them. And this surplus will be proportionably augmented as the habit shall prevail of planting these trees on every farm either in orchards or along the roads as is now done of fruit trees for the houshold use of the farmer. The process of making the Sugar is so light as to be performed by women and children and comes on at a time."

MS 7: DLC: TJ Papers, 69: 11897; a 1-page MS in TJ's hand; consisting of the following preliminary notes for the section of p. 19 of MS dealing with the encouragement of American manufacturing:
"to select particular manufactures
> e.g. woolen. because may be carried on domestically
> > cotton. linen. may be done by machines.
> masters of vessels to be authorised to receive any manufacturers who offer and to bring them

⎯⎯⎯

√ it would have been better to have adhered to agriculture because lands cheap.
> when employed in manufactures we lose profits of our lands.
√ but the jealousies and fluctuations of Europn. councils leave it unsafe to depend on them."

MS 8: DLC: TJ Papers, 59: 10107; a 1-page MS in James Madison's hand; consisting of an undated "Abstract of Duties which have accrued on the Tonnage of Foreign & Domestic Vessels from Sepr. 1. to Decr. 31. 1790 [i.e. 1789]," being a table of eleven states (Rhode Island and North Carolina were not yet in the Union) showing that 100,733.44 tons of foreign shipping

and 199,832 tons of American shipping had together paid duties of 62,356.77 dollars; with notations added by TJ: (below title) "the foreign at 50. cents, the Domestic @ 6. cents" and (next to totals for foreign and domestic tonnage) "tons"; endorsed by TJ: "Tonnage." An undated Dft (DLC: Madison Papers) contains variations, including "1789" in the title and "Treasy. Dept. May 10. 1790 A. H." at the head of text (see Syrett, *Hamilton*, VI, 414).

MS 9: DLC: TJ Papers, 57: 9832-3; a 2-page MS supplied by Tench Coxe; in a clerk's hand with note by Coxe on verso; consisting of an undated estimate of the value in the American market of American imports and exports, with related charges, for the period 1 Oct. 1789-[30?] Sep. 1790, showing 27,000,083.22 dollars for imports and 30,680,282 dollars for exports; at head of text: "A Sketch"; endorsed by TJ: "Imports & Exports."

[1] TJ here canceled "arranged in the order."

[2] TJ altered this line to read "Bread-Stuff, that is to say grains, meals & breads to the annual amount of," adding "annual" at a different sitting.

[3] Here in the margin TJ penciled the total "19,737,692."

[4] Here in the margin TJ inserted a new paragraph as follows, adding the two gross figures later in pencil (the second one not totaling correctly):

"The proportions of our exports which go to the Nations beforementioned, and to their dominions respectively are as follows.

	Dollars
To Spain & it's dominions	2,005,907
Portugal & it's domns.	1,283,462
France & it's domns.	4,698,735
Gr. Brtn. & it's domns.	9,363,416
the Unitd. Nethds. & domns.	1,963,880.
Denmark & its domns.	224,415
Sweden & its domns.	47,240
	19,587,055

Our Imports from the same countries are

Spain	335,110
Portugal	595,763
France	2,068,348
Gr. Britain	15,285,428
Unitd. Netherlds.	1,172,692
Denmark	351,364
Sweden	14,325
	19,803,030

These imports consist⟨ing⟩ mostly of Articles on which industry has been exhausted. ⟨Their amount⟩ ⟨is⟩ ⟨shews the measure of the value of our commerce to those countries so far as depends [. . .].⟩"

[5] TJ canceled these three words in connection with the revision described in the following note.

[6] TJ interlined "in one year, that is to say" in place of the next two words and changed the period to a comma.

[7] TJ here interlined "Bread-stuff."

[8] Sometime after 13 Apr. 1792 TJ here added "On our meals however, as well as on those of other foreign countries when reexported to their colonies, they have lately imposed duties of from half a dollar to two dollars the barrel, the duties being so proportioned to the current price of their own flour, as that both together are to make the constant ⟨price⟩ sum of nine dollars per barrel," writing "as . . . countries" in the margin at a different sitting.

[9] In response to Thomas FitzSimons's Notes on Jefferson's Draft Report on Commerce, [23 Aug. 1791], printed below in the supplement to the present volume, TJ here added "⟨Latterly indeed⟩ Their demand for ⟨our⟩ rice ⟨has been⟩ however is increasing."

[10] TJ here canceled "5 dimes to."

[11] TJ altered this paragraph to read: "Neither Tobacco, nor Indigo, are recieved there. Our commerce is permitted with their Canary islands under the same conditions."

[12] Word written by TJ over "freely," erased.

[13] TJ here interlined "their own or."

[14] TJ here interlined a paragraph reading "Tobacco, Rice and Meals are prohibited," interlining the first three words later in the same sitting.

[15] TJ interlined "regulations" in place of this word.

[16] In response to Thomas FitzSimons's Notes on Jefferson's Draft Report on Commerce, [23 Aug. 1791], printed below in the supplement to the present volume, TJ here changed the period to a comma and added "except that in these meals and rice are received freely."

[17] Preceding four words altered by TJ to "Bread-stuff."

[18] Word altered by TJ to "re-exportation."

[19] TJ here interlined "is made lately to pay."

[20] TJ interlined "which may be carried in their own or any other vessels" in place of this clause.

[21] TJ interlined "During" in place of this word.

[22] TJ here interlined and canceled "lately."

[23] TJ interlined "first National assembly took" in place of the preceding ten words.

[24] TJ here canceled "have."

[25] Sometime after 13 Apr. 1792 TJ altered this paragraph to read: "Great Britain recieves our Pot and Pearlashes free while those of other nations pay a duty of 2/3 the kental. There is an equal distinction in favor of our bar iron, of which article however we do not produce enough for our own use. Woods are free from us, whilst they pay some small duty from other countries. Indigo and flaxseed are free from all countries. Our Tar and Pitch pay 11d. sterl. the barrel. From other alien countries they pay about a penny and a third more."

[26] TJ here interlined "common."

[27] Paragraph to this point altered by TJ to read "Our Salted fish and Salted provisions in general are prohibited. Our bacon and whale oils are under prohibitory duties: so are our Grains, Meals and Bread as to internal consumption."

[28] TJ here interlined and canceled "When the price is below that however they permit them to be ⟨warehoused⟩ stored duty free in their ports for re-exportation."

[29] Sometime after 13 Apr. 1792 TJ replaced this paragraph with the two that follow:

"While the vessels of other nations are secured by standing laws, which cannot be altered but by the concurrent will of the three branches of the British legislature, in carrying thither any thing which is produced or manufactured in the country to which they belong, our vessels, with the same prohibition of what is foreign, are further prohibited by a standing law (12 Car. 2. 18. §. 3.) from carrying thither domestic productions and manufactures. A subsequent act indeed has authorised their Executive to permit ⟨or to refus⟩ the carriage of our own productions in our own bottoms, at it's sole discretion: and the permission has been given from year to year by proclamation; but subject every moment to be withdrawn on that single will, in which event our vessels having any thing on board stand interdicted from the entry of all British ports. The disadvantage of a tenure which may be so suddenly discontinued was experienced by our merchants on a late occasion, when an official notification that this law would be strictly enforced gave them just apprehensions for the fate of their vessels and cargoes dispatched or destined to the ports of Gr. Britain. It was privately believed indeed that the order of that court went further than their intention, and so we were afterwards officially informed: but the embarrasments of the moment were real and great, and the possibility of their renewal lays our commerce to that country under the same species of discouragement as to other countries where it is ⟨in like manner⟩ regulated by a single ⟨veto⟩ legislator: and the distinction is too remarkable not to be noticed that our Navigation is excluded from the security of fixed laws, while that security is given to the Navigation of others.

"Our vessels pay in their ports 1/9 sterl. per ton, light and Trinity dues more than is paid by British ships, except in the port of London where they pay the same as British."

In the first paragraph TJ interlined "having any thing on board" and after "distinction is too remarkeable" heavily canceled about fifteen lines of text written in the margin consisting of one clause with another interlined as a partial substitute for it. The first clause appears to read "not to be noticed that whilst the commerce of other countries enjoys [. . .] that the [. . .] and limited Government a despotism has been established for the regulation of ours singly." The interlined substitute clause appears to read "⟨our navigation [. . .] commerce is excluded from the security of fixed laws while that of other nations⟩ ⟨security of fixt laws⟩ ours has been submitted to the will of a single person while it is ⟨which has⟩ given to that of no other nation."

[30] Sometime after 13 Apr. 1792 TJ altered the rest of this paragraph to read "under the useless charges of an intermediate deposit and double voyage. ⟨And the consumers⟩ From tables published in England, and composed, as is said, from the books of their Customhouses, it appears that of the Indigo imported there in the years 1773. 4. 5. one third was reexported, ⟨of the Rice five sevenths and of the tobacco five sixths. The other years of the same tables were years of war, and therefore are not

noticed⟩ and from a document of ⟨higher⟩ authority we learn that of the rice and tobacco imported there before the war four fifths were reexported. We are assured indeed that the quantities sent thither for reexportation since the war are considerably diminished: yet less so than reason and national interest would dictate. The whole of our grain is re-exported ⟨unless⟩ when wheat is below 50/ the quarter and other grains in proportion." Above the last line TJ penciled a phrase that is now illegible. A draft of the next-to-last sentence is in MS 6.

Next to the paragraph he revised and the two succeeding unrevised ones TJ wrote the following table perpendicularly in the margin sometime after 13 Apr. 1792 and then lined it out:

"1773.4.5.	Indigo. bb.	Rice. kentals	Tobacco. bb.
Imported	5,904,403	1,472,305	299,697,342
Exported	1,847,944	1,059,623	249,658,524
	4,056,459	412,782	50,038,818

"Sheffeild's tables No. 3." There is a subtraction error in the column for rice.

[31] TJ interlined "absorbed by" in place of the preceding two words.

[32] Word altered by TJ to "East-India."

[33] For lack of information TJ left about half a page blank after this word and then, based in part on Benjamin Bourne to TJ, [after 26 Aug. 1791], printed below in the supplement to the present volume, added "takes a duty of about a half penny sterl. the pound on tobacco and 3/6 sterl. the Kental on rice carried in their own vessels and half as much more if carried in ours, and they lay prohibitory duties on Indigo and corn." See also John Ross to TJ, 26 Aug. 1791. A draft of this revision is in MS 4.

[34] Sentence to this point altered by TJ to "They consume some of our tobaccos which they take circuitously thro' Great Britain; levying."

[35] TJ left a blank space equal to about three lines of text between this and the next paragraph.

[36] TJ interlined "superfluities" in place of this word.

[37] TJ here canceled "world."

[38] TJ altered this passage to read "and the existence of Americans is made to have for it's object not their own happiness, but that."

[39] Preceding two words altered by TJ to "people conquered."

[40] TJ interlined "dominant" in place of this word.

[41] Next to this word in the margin TJ penciled "qu. as to the Havanna."

[42] Sometime after 13 Apr. 1792 TJ altered the preceding sentence and the one to this point to read "France prohibits our other bread. Our fish and salted provisions (except pork) are received in the Fr. islands on a duty of 3ᵗᵗ the kental." At the same time he canceled the remainder of the sentence.

[43] Sometime after 13 Apr. 1792 TJ here interlined "only."

[44] Sometime after 13 Apr. 1792 TJ crossed out the paragraph to this point and substituted three paragraphs in the margin:

"France by a ⟨proc⟩ standing law ⟨*⟩ permits her West India possessions to recieve directly our ⟨maize, rice,⟩ vegetables, fresh provisions, horses, wood, tar, pitch and turpentine, rice and maize and prohibits our other bread stuff: but a suspension of this prohibition ⟨being⟩ having been left to the Colonial legislature, in times of scarcity, the prohibition ⟨is⟩ has been suspended from time to time. ⟨*Gr. Britain admits all the above articles into her islands by a proclamation of her Executive limited always to the term of a year, but which has hitherto been renewed from year to year.*⟩ ⟨*Colonial arret of May 9. 1789.*⟩

"Our fish and salted provisions (except pork) are received in their islands under a duty of 3 livres the kental, and our vessels are free to carry our own commodities thither, and to bring away rum and melasses.

"Gr. Britain admits in her islands our vegetables, fresh provisions, horses, wood, tar, pitch and turpentine, rice, and bread stuff, by a proclamation of her executive limited always to the term of a year, but hitherto renewed from year to year. She prohibits our salted fish and other salted provisions. She does not permit our vessels to carry thither our." A variant of this revision is in MS 4.

[45] TJ interlined "her" in place of this word, canceled the preceding five words, and inserted a period after "produce."

[46] TJ here first interlined "them" and then interlined "it" in its place.

[47] Sometime after 13 Apr. 1792 TJ

wrote the following sentence in the margin for insertion here and then canceled it: "Our citizens cannot reside as Merchants or Factors within any of the British." See the following note.

[48] TJ wrote the following paragraphs in the margin for insertion here, the first sometime after 13 Apr. 1792 and the second at an earlier time:

"Our citizens cannot reside as Merchants or Factors within any of the British plantations.

"In the Danish-American possessions a duty of 5. per cent is levied on our Corn, corn-meal, rice tobacco wood, salted fish, indigo, horses mules and live stock, and of 10. per cent on our flour, salted pork and beef, tar, pitch and turpentine." A draft of the second paragraph is in MS 4. See also TJ to John Ross, 26 Aug. 1791.

[49] Sometime after 13 Apr. 1792 TJ interlined "American possessions" in place of the preceding three words.

[50] Word canceled by TJ.

[51] Sometime after 13 Apr. 1792 TJ here interlined "all."

[52] Sometime after 13 Apr. 1792 TJ altered this paragraph to read "Our breadstuff is at most times under prohibitory duties in England and considerably dutied on reexportation from Spain to her colonies."

[53] Sometime after 13 Apr. 1792 TJ here interlined "of late in."

[54] Remainder of paragraph altered by TJ to read "recieved under temporary laws only by France, and our salted Fish pays a weighty duty."

[55] TJ here left blank a space equal to about nine lines of text and began the next paragraph at the top of p. 13.

[56] TJ here interlined "of these two."

[57] TJ canceled the remainder of the paragraph after making the alterations recorded in the next two notes.

[58] Word altered by TJ to "unproductive."

[59] Remainder of sentence altered by TJ to "withdraw from that to other employments." Next to this sentence TJ penciled a note in the margin of which only "[. . .]t [. . .]ssedly con-" survives on the next page.

[60] TJ canceled this word and interlined it after "one by one."

[61] TJ interlined "Where" in place of this word.

[62] Word canceled by TJ.

[63] TJ canceled the remainder of this sentence.

[64] Here and below in this sentence TJ altered the preceding two words to "Customers."

[65] Altered by TJ to "at every market."

[66] TJ interlined "they" in place of this word.

[67] TJ interlined "it" in place of this word.

[68] TJ altered this passage to read "citizens their commerce and navigation."

[69] Sentence to this point altered by TJ to "Free commerce and navigation are."

[70] TJ interlined "are they" in place of these two words.

[71] TJ altered this passage at different times to "a resource of Defence, essential."

[72] Sometime after 13 Apr. 1792 TJ altered the sentence to this point to read "In times of peace, it multiplies competitors for employment in transportation, and so keeps that at it's proper level; and in times of war, that is to say, when those Nations who may be our principal carriers, shall be."

[73] TJ interlined "resource for" in place of these two words.

[74] Sometime after 13 Apr. 1792 TJ here added "and of Artists and establishments in readiness for ship building" by writing it over a largely illegible penciled passage that seems to have been of the same import.

[75] TJ here canceled "the purposes."

[76] Sometime after 13 Apr. 1792 TJ altered this passage to read "But if particular nations grasp."

[77] Sometime after 13 Apr. 1792 TJ interlined "if" in place of this word.

[78] Sometime after 13 Apr. 1792 TJ interlined "nation" in place of this word

[79] TJ revised the rest of this sentence to read "and it's Politicks must be influenced by those who command it's commerce."

[80] Sometime after 13 Apr. 1792 TJ here interlined "and artists."

[81] Word canceled by TJ.

[82] Preceding two words reworked by TJ from "means."

[83] TJ interlined "fitted" in place of this word.

[84] TJ revised this paragraph to read "The following principles being founded in reciprocity appear perfectly just, and to offer no cause of complaint to any nation."

[85] TJ interlined "may" in place of this word.

[86] For the text TJ later substituted beginning here, see note 107 below.

[87] Sometime after 13 Apr. 1792 TJ interlined "shall" in place of this word.

[88] Sometime after 13 Apr. 1792 TJ here interlined in pencil "This will operate as a bounty to encourage the [immigration?] of the Manufacturer himself to this country where he may make [his?] [. . .]."

[89] TJ here interlined "if such should be the construction of the constitution."

[90] Sometime after 13 Apr. 1792 TJ interlined "to the encouragement" in place of the preceding two words.

[91] Sometime after 13 Apr. 1792 TJ penciled "will" above this word and inserted an ampersand at the beginning of the sentence.

[92] Sometime after 13 Apr. 1792 TJ added a period here, canceled the rest of the sentence, and inserted a slightly variant version of the rest of the sentence before "promoting."

[93] TJ interlined and canceled "that" above this word.

[94] TJ here added "The manufactures of cotton, wool and leather might first be singled out."

[95] Written by TJ over "3."

[96] Sometime after 13 Apr. 1792 TJ interlined "may" in place of this word.

[97] Altered by TJ to "2."

[98] Paragraph crossed out by TJ. See note 46 to Document II below.

[99] Altered by TJ to "3."

[100] Sometime after 13 Apr. 1792 TJ canceled the preceding three words and interlined "restrains" in pencil above them.

[101] Sometime after 13 Apr. 1792 TJ here interlined "even."

[102] TJ here canceled "parts of their."

[103] Sometime after 13 Apr. 1792 TJ interlined in pencil, apparently for insertion at this point, three partly illegible lines that begin "we should lay an equivalent restraint on their carriage of the same articles to the same countries because these countries [. . .]." Under the first two of these lines he interlined in pencil two other lines of text that are illegible.

[104] Sometime after 13 Apr. 1792 TJ canceled the next part of this paragraph, consisting of "and perhaps . . . leaving," and wrote in the margin for insertion here: "And if they prohibit us from bringing thence the productions of those countries for our own consumption, such produc-

tions should ⟨*be*⟩ either be prohibited or the more heavily dutied when brought by them, and the increase of duty be employed to the encouragement of the same or equivalent productions at home. Thus an increase of duties on rum and melasses brought from countries from whence we are not free to bring them, might be applied to encourage our own distilleries and breweries, and thus enlarge the home-demand for the produce of our agriculture; still leaving on their present footing the other channels of foreign supply, perhaps encouraging, by lighter duties, the importation of small wines as another raw material for our distilleries.—So also, Sugar, circuitously permitted us from some of the places of it's growth, and in foreign bottoms only from others, should be more highly dutied from those places, and the increase of duty be applied to encourage it's production at home. It may be affirmed, on sufficient ⟨*enquiry*⟩ experiment, that the Sugar from the Sugar-Maple tree is equal in quality to that from the Cane, when made with equal skill and care, may be produced in sufficient quantity from the trees now existing in the U.S. not only for their whole consumption, but to furnish considerable supplies to foreign markets. The process too is so light as to be performed by women and children, and that at a season when other works do not press. It is highly important that we emancipate ourselves from difficulties as to an article which, from a luxury, has become almost a necessary of life to our citizens in general, and which nature has so liberally dealt out to us at home.

"Subsidiary to these measures in defence of our Navigation may be the refusing the carriage of our productions, to *all places*, to those who refuse to recieve them *in our bottoms* at *any place*, where they will recieve them in *their own*. And that this restriction may bring no inconvenience on our Agriculture, it may be proper to begin by leaving."

Below this revision—after canceling the paragraph recorded in note 98 above and renumbering the other paragraphs—TJ penciled the following paragraph in the margin: "4. Where a nation refuses permission to our merchants and factors to reside in any part of their dominions we should refuse permission to theirs to reside in any part of our dominions." A draft of the

discussion of sugar maple production is in MS 6.

[105] Sometime after 13 Apr. 1792 TJ canceled "doubling . . . fourth" and interlined "advancing it from year to year in a given ratio for a second third and fourth years."

[106] Sometime after 13 Apr. 1792 TJ here interlined "by all."

[107] In place of p. 19-20, consisting of text from note 86 above to this point, TJ sometime after 13 Apr. 1792 substituted two pages with the following text, writing the next-to-last paragraph in the margin and making the revisions in the other paragraphs at different times: "vier and heavier afterwards as other channels of supply open. Such duties ⟨*operating as incentives on*⟩ having the effect of indirect encouragement to domestic manufactures of the same kind may induce the manufacturer to come himself into these states, where cheaper subsistence equal laws and a vent of his wares free of duty may ensure him the highest profits from his skill and industry. And here it would be in the power of the state-governments to co-operate essentially by opening the resources of encouragement which are under their controul, ⟨*and*⟩ extending them liberally to artists in those particular branches of manufacture for which their soil, climate, population and other circumstances have matured them, and fostering the precious efforts and progress of houshold manufacture by ⟨*a still more special patronage, guided*⟩ ⟨*unerringly*⟩ ⟨*steadily to it's object*⟩ some patronage suited to the nature of it's objects guided by the local informations they possess and guarded against abuse by their presence and attentions. The oppressions on our agriculture in foreign ports would thus be made the occasion of relieving it from a dependance on the councils and conduct of others, and of promoting arts, manufactures and population at home. ⟨*The manufactures of cotton, wool and leather might first be singled out.*⟩

"2. Where a nation refuses permission to our merchants and factors to reside within certain parts of their dominions, we may if it should prove expedient, refuse residence to theirs in any and every part of ours.

"3. Where a nation refuses to receive in our vessels any productions but our own, we may refuse to recieve in theirs any but their productions. The bill reported by the

Committee is well framed to effect this object.

"4. Where a nation refuses to our vessels the carriage even of our own productions to certain countries under their subjection, we may refuse to theirs the carriage of the same or any other of our productions to the same or any other countries. And here justice and friendship would dictate that those who have no part in imposing the restriction on us should not be the victims of measures adopted to defeat it's effect. But that these should be pointed to the dominant country itself, by prohibiting their vessels from the carriage of our productions to the dominant country, and to all others where our own or those of any other nation may freely carry them. And that this restriction might bring no inconvenience on the agriculture of our country it might be proper to begin by leaving the present moderate tonnage duty on their vessels for the first year, advancing it from year to year, in a given ratio, till time should have been afforded for a sufficient increase of the means of transportation by ourselves and other nations, when absolute prohibition might take place.

"The establishment of some of these principles by Gr. Britain alone has already lost us in our commerce with that country and it's possessions, between eight and nine hundred vessels of near 40,000 tons burthen, according to ⟨*⟩ statements from official materials in which they have confidence. This involves a proportional loss of seamen, shipwrights, and shipbuilding, and is too serious a loss to admit forbearance of some effectual remedy. ⟨*pa. 17.⟩

"It is true we must expect some inconvenience in practice from the establishment of discriminating duties. But in this, as in so many other cases, we are left to chuse between two evils. These inconveniencies are nothing, when weighed against the loss of wealth and loss of force which will follow our perseverance in the plan of indiscrimination. When once it shall be perceived that we are either in the system, or the habit, of giving equal advantages to those who extinguish our commerce and navigation by duties and prohibitions, ⟨and commit encroach-

ments on our navigation,⟩ as to those who treat both with liberality and justice, liberality and justice will be converted by all into duties and prohibitions. It is not to the moderation and justice of others we are to trust for fair and equal access to market with our productions, or for our due share in the transportation of them; but to our own means of independance, and the firm will to use them. Nor do the inconveniencies of discrimination merit consi." Two variants of the fifth paragraph of this revision are in MS 6.

[108] TJ here inserted the following paragraph sometime after 13 Apr. 1792, writing the sentences at different times: "France has, of her own accord, proposed Negociations for improving, by a new treaty on fair and equal principles, the commercial relations of the two countries. But her internal disturbances have hitherto prevented the prosecution of them to effect, tho we have had repeated assurances of a continuance of the disposition." A variant of the first sentence in MS 6 reads: "France has ⟨set the example of⟩ of her own accord propos⟨ing⟩ed negociations for a new treaty ⟨of commerce⟩ wherein ⟨that freedom⟩ the advantages of commerce ⟨which was⟩ extended to her in ⟨the⟩ our former ⟨one⟩ treaty on other ⟨motives⟩ considerations, may ⟨be compensated to us by equal advantages [. . .]⟩ now be measured back to us on such ⟨fair and⟩ equal principles as may improve the commercial relations of the two countries."

[109] Sometime after 13 Apr. 1792 TJ here interlined "on our part."

[110] Sometime after 13 Apr. 1792 TJ interlined "law" in place of this word.

[111] Sometime after 13 Apr. 1792 TJ altered this passage to read "have not as yet discovered."

[112] Sometime after 13 Apr. 1792 TJ altered the sentence to this point to read: "We have no reason to conclude that friendly arrangements would be declined by the."

[113] Sometime after 13 Apr. 1792 TJ interlined "them" in place of this word.

[114] Sometime after 13 Apr. 1792 TJ interlined "would" in place of this word.

II. Second State of the Report on Commerce

[before 5 Feb.-after 23 Feb. 1793]

The Secretary of State, to whom was referred by the House of Representatives the Report of a committee on the written message of the President of the United States of the 14th. of February 1791, with instruction to report to Congress the nature and extent of the privileges and restrictions of the commercial intercourse of the United States with foreign Nations, and the measures which he should think proper to be adopted for the improvement of the commerce and navigation of the same, has had the same under consideration, and thereupon makes the following

REPORT.

The nations[1] with which the United States have their chief commercial intercourse, are Spain, Portugal, France, Great Britain, the United Netherlands, Denmark and Sweden, and their American possessions: and the Articles of Export which constitute the Basis of that Commerce, with their respective Amounts, are, Bread stuff, that is to say,

	Dollars.
Breadstuff,[2] Grains, meals, and Bread, to the annual amount of	7,649,887
Tobacco	4,349,567
Rice	1,753,796
Wood	1,263,534
Salted fish	941,696
Pot & pearl Ash	839,093
Salted Meats	599,130
Indigo	537,379
Horses and Mules	339,753
Whale Oil	252,591
Flax seed	236,072
Tar, Pitch and Turpentine	217,177
Live provisions	137,743
Ships	
Foreign goods	620,274

To descend to Articles of smaller value than these would lead into a minuteness of detail neither necessary nor useful to the present object.

The proportions of our exports, which go to the Nations beforementioned, and to their Dominions respectively are as follows.

	Dollars.
To Spain & it's Dominions	2,005,907
Portugal & it's Dominions	1,283,462
France & it's Dominions	4,698,735
Great Britain & it's Dominions	9,363,416
The United Netherlands & their[3] Dominions	1,963,880
Denmark & it's Dominions	224,415
Sweden & it's Dominions	47,240

Our Imports from the same countries are

Spain[4]	335,110
Portugal	595,763
France	2,068,348
Great Britain	15,285,428
United Netherlands	1,172,692
Denmark	351,364
Sweden	14,325

These imports consist mostly of articles on which industry has been exhausted.

Our *Navigation* depending on the same Commerce, will appear by the following statement of the Tonnage of our own Vessels, entering in our ports, from those several nations, and their possessions, in one Year, that is to say, from October 1789 to September 1790, inclusive, as follows.

Spain	19,695 Tons
Portugal	23,576
France	116,410
Great Britain	43,580
United Netherlands	58,858
Denmark	14,655
Sweden	750

Of Our Commercial objects, Spain receives favorably our Breadstuff, Salted Fish, Wood, Ships, Tar, Pitch, and Turpentine. On our Meals, however,[5] when re-exported to their Colonies, they have lately imposed Duties of from half a Dollar to two dollars the Barrel, the Duties being so proportioned to the current price of their own Flour, as that both together are to make the constant sum of nine Dollars per Barrel.

They do not discourage our Rice, Pot and Pearl Ash, Salted provisions, or whale oil: but these Articles, being in small demand at their Markets, are carried thither but in a small degree. Their demand for

Rice, however, is increasing. Neither Tobacco, nor Indigo are received there.[6]

Themselves and their Colonies are the actual consumers of what they receive from us.

Our Navigation is free with the Kingdom of Spain; foreign Goods being received there in our Ships on the same Conditions as if carried in their own, or in the Vessels of the Country of which such Goods are the manufacture or produce.

PORTUGAL receives favorably our Grain and Bread, Salted fish, and other Salted provisions, Wood, Tar, Pitch, and Turpentine.

For Flax-seed, Pot and Pearl-ash, though not discouraged, there is little demand.

Our Ships pay 20 per cent, on being sold to their Subjects, and are then free bottoms.

Foreign goods (except those of the East Indies) are received on the same footing in our vessels, as in their own, or any others; that is to say, on general Duties of from 20 to 28 per cent and, consequently our Navigation is unobstructed by them.

Tobacco, Rice, and Meals are prohibited.

Themselves and their Colonies consume what they receive from us.

These Regulations extend to the Azores, Madeira, and the Cape de Verd Islands, except that in these, Meals and Rice are received freely.

FRANCE receives favorably our Bread-stuff, Rice, Wood, Pot and Pearl ashes.

A duty of 5 Sous the Kental[7] is paid on our Tar, Pitch, and Turpentine. Our Whale Oils pay Six Livres the Kental, and are the only foreign Whale Oils admitted. Our Indigo pays 5 Livres the Kental; their own two and a half: but a difference of quality, still more than a difference of duty prevents it's seeking that market.

Salted Beef is received freely for re-exportation; but if for home-consumption, it pays 5 Livres the Kental. Other *salted* provisions pay that Duty in all cases, and Salted Fish is made lately to pay the prohibitary one of 20 Livres the Kental.

Our Ships are free to carry thither all foreign goods, which may be carried in their own or any other Vessels, except Tobaccos not of our own growth: and they participate with theirs the exclusive carriage of our whale oils.[8]

During their former government our Tobacco was under a monopoly, but paid no duties; and our ships were freely sold in their ports and converted into national bottoms. The first national assembly took from our Ships this privilege. They emancipated Tobacco from it's monopoly, but subjected it to duties of 18 Livres 15 sous the Kental, carried in their own Vessels, and 25 Livres, carried in ours; a difference more than equal to the freight of the Article.

They and their Colonies consume what they receive from us.

GREAT BRITAIN receives our Pot and Pearl ashes free, while those of other nations pay a duty of 2s./3d. the Kental. There is an equal distinction in favor of our bar-iron; of which Article, however, we do not produce enough for our own use. Woods are free, from us, whilst they pay some small duty from other Countries. Indigo and Flaxseed are free, from all Countries. Our Tar and Pitch pay 11d. sterling the Barrel. From other alien countries they pay about a penny and a third more.

Our Tobacco, for their own Consumption, pays 1/3 Sterling the pound, custom and excise, besides heavy incidental expenses,[9] and Rice, in the same case, pays 7/4 sterling the hundred weight; which, rendering it too dear as an Article of common food, it is consequently used in very small quantity.

Our salted fish and salted provisions, in general, are prohibited.[10] Our[11] Bacon and whale oils are under prohibitory duties: so are our Grains, Meals, and Bread, as to internal consumption, unless in times of such scarcity as may raise the Price of wheat to 50/– sterling the quarter, and other grains and meals in proportion.

Our Ships, even when purchased by their own Subjects, are not permitted to be made free bottoms.[12]

While the vessels of other nations are secured by standing Laws, which cannot be altered but by the concurrent will of the three Branches of the British Legislature, in carrying thither any thing which is produced or manufactured in[13] the Country to which they belong;[14] our vessels, with the same prohibition of what is foreign, are further prohibited by a standing law (12. Car. 2. 18. §. 3) from carrying thither[15] domestic productions and manufactures. A subsequent Act, indeed, has authorized their Executive to permit the carriage of our own productions in our own bottoms, at it's sole discretion: and the permission has been given from year to year by Proclamation; but subject every moment to be withdrawn on that single will, in which event, our Vessels having any thing on board, stand interdicted from the Entry of all british ports. The disadvantage of a tenure which may be so suddenly discontinued, was experienced by our Merchants on a late occasion, when an official notification that this law would be strictly enforced, gave them just apprehensions for the fate of their Vessels and cargoes dispatched or destined to the ports of Great Britain. It was privately believed, indeed, that the order of that Court went further than their intention, and so we were, afterwards, officially informed:[16] but the embarrassments of the moment were real and great, and the possibility of their renewal lays our commerce to that Country under the same species of discouragement as to other Countries, where it is regulated by a single Legislator: and the distinction is too remarkable not to be noticed, that our navigation is excluded from the security of fixed Laws, while that security is given to the navigation of others.

Our Vessels pay in their ports 1/9 sterling per ton, light and Trinity dues, more than is paid by British Ships, except in the port of London, where they pay the same as British.

The greater part of what they receive from us, is re-exported to other Countries, under the useless charges of an intermediate deposit and double voyage. From Tables published in England, and composed, as is said, from the Books of their Custom-houses, it appears that, of the Indigo imported there in the years 1773,–4,–5, one third was re-exported, and from a document of Authority, we learn that of the Rice and Tobacco imported there before the War, four fifths were re-exported. We are assured, indeed, that the Quantities sent thither for re-exportation since the war, are considerably diminished: yet less so than reason and national interest would dictate. The whole of our Grain is re-exported when wheat is below 50/. the Quarter, and other Grains in proportion.

THE UNITED NETHERLANDS prohibit our pickled Beef and Pork, Meals and Bread of all sorts, and lay a prohibitory duty on Spirits distilled from Grain.

All other of our productions are received on varied duties, which may be reckoned, on a medium, of about 3 per cent.

They consume but a small part of what they receive,[17] and, consequently, as to the great mass, they intercept, between us and the Consumer, a portion of the value[18] absorbed by the charges attending an intermediate deposit.

Foreign goods, except some East India articles, are received in the vessels of any Nation.

Our Ships may be sold and naturalized there, with exceptions of one or two privileges which scarcely[19] lessen their value.

DENMARK takes a Duty of about a half penny sterling the pound on Tobacco and about 3/6 sterling the Kental on Rice carried in their own Vessels, and half as much more if carried in ours, and they lay prohibitory duties on Indigo and Corn.[20]

SWEDEN receives favorably our Grains and Meals, Salted provisions, Indigo and Whale oil.

They subject our Rice to duties of 1.6 Dollars the hundred[21] weight carried in their own vessels, and of 2.25 Dollars the hundred weight[22] carried in ours, or any others. Being thus rendered too dear as an Article of Common food, little of it is consumed with them. They consume some of our Tobaccos, which they take circuitously through Great Britain; levying heavy duties on them also; their duties of entry, town duties, and Excise, being 4.34 [23] Dollars the hundred weight, if carried in their own vessels, and of 40 per cent on that additional, if carried in our own or any other Vessels.

They prohibit altogether our Bread, Fish, Pot and Pearl ashes, Flax seed, Tar, Pitch, and Turpentine, Wood (except oak timber and masts) and all foreign manufactures.

Under so many restrictions and prohibitions, our navigation with them is reduced almost to nothing.

With our neighbors, an order of Things much harder presents itself. [24] The extraordinary circumstances of the moment in which the Inhabitants of this Hemisphere became acquainted with those of the other, placed them in a predicament which still continues, and which is as new in the moral as in the physical World. The reciprocal rights and duties established by the laws of nature between neighbor nations, to supply by mutual exchange the wants of the one with the superfluities of another, rights and duties well recognised and practised in other parts of the Earth, are suspended for the inhabitants of this; and the existence of Americans is made to have for it's object not their own happiness, but that of their Antipodes. To these laws are submitted the native descendants, as well of the Conquerers, as of the people conquered.

SPAIN and PORTUGAL refuse, to those parts of America which they govern, all direct intercourse with any people but themselves. The Commodities in mutual demand, between them and their Neighbors, must be carried to be exchanged in some port of the dominant country, and the transportation between that and the subject State must be in a domestic bottom.

FRANCE by a standing law, permits her West India possessions to receive directly our Vegetables, fresh [25] Provisions, Horses, Wood, Tar, Pitch, and Turpentine, Rice and Maize, and prohibits our other Bread stuff: but a suspension of this prohibition having been left to the Colonial Legislature, in times of scarcity, [26] the prohibition has been suspended from time to time.

Our Fish and salted Provisions (except Pork) are received in their Islands under a Duty of 3 [27] Livres the Kental, and our Vessels are free to carry our own [28] commodities thither, and to bring away Rum and Molasses.

GREAT BRITAIN admits in her Islands our Vegetables, Fresh [29] Provisions, Horses, Wood, Tar, Pitch and Turpentine, Rice, and Breadstuff, by a Proclamation of her Executive limited always to the term of a Year, but hitherto renewed, from Year to Year. She prohibits our salted Fish and other salted Provisions. She does not permit our Vessels to carry thither our own produce. Her Vessels alone, may take it from us, and bring in exchange, Rum, Melasses, Sugar, Coffee, Cocoa-nuts, Ginger, and Pimento. There are, indeed some freedoms in the Island of Dominica, but under such circumstances as to be little used by us. To the British continental Colonies, and to Newfoundland, every thing is prohibited.[30] Their Governors, however, in times of distress, have power to permit a temporary importation of certain Articles, in their own Bottoms, but not in ours.

Our Citizens cannot reside as merchants or Factors within any of the British Plantations.[31]

In the Danish-American possessions a duty of 5 per cent is levied on our corn, corn-meal, Rice, Tobacco, Wood, salted Fish, Indigo, Horses, mules, and Live stock, and of 10 per Cent on our Flour, salted Pork and Beef, Tar, Pitch and Turpentine.

In the American Possessions[32] of the United Netherlands and Sweden, all vessels and commodities are freely received,[33] subject to duties, not so heavy as to have been complained of.[34]

To sum up these restrictions, so far as they are important.
1. In Europe.

Our Breadstuff is at most times under prohibitory duties in England, and considerably dutied on re-exportation from Spain to her Colonies.

Our Tobaccoes are heavily dutied in England, Sweden and France, and prohibited in Spain and Portugal.

Our Rice is heavily dutied in England and Sweden, and prohibited in Portugal.

Our Fish and salted Provisions are prohibited in England, and under prohibitory duties in France.

Our Whale Oils are prohibited in England and Portugal, and our Vessels denied naturalization in England, and of late in France.
2. In the West Indies.

All intercourse is prohibited with the Possessions of Spain and Portugal.

Our salted Provisions and Fish are prohibited by England.

Our salted pork and Bread-stuff (except maize) are received under temporary Laws only, by[35] France, and our salted fish pays[36] a weighty duty.
3. In the Article of Navigation.

Our own carriage of our own Tobacco is heavily dutied in[37] France and Sweden.

We can carry no article, not of our own production, to the British ports in Europe.

Nor even our own produce to her American possessions.

Such being the restrictions on the Commerce and Navigation of the United States, the question is, in what way they may best be removed, modified, or counteracted?

As to Commerce, two methods occur. 1. By friendly arrangements with the several Nations with whom these restrictions exist: or 2. By the separate act of our own Legislatures for countervailing their effects.

There can be no doubt but that of these two, friendly arrangement is the most eligible. Instead of embarrassing Commerce under piles of regulating Laws, Duties, and Prohibitions, could it be relieved from all it's shackles in all parts of the World, could every country be employed in producing that which nature has best fitted it to produce, and each be free to exchange with others mutual surplusses, for mutual wants, the greatest mass possible would then be produced of those things which contribute to human life and human happiness; the numbers of mankind would be increased, and their condition bettered.

Would even a single nation begin with the United States this System of free Commerce, it would be advisable to begin it with that nation; since it is one by one only that it can be extended to all. Where the circumstances of either party render it expedient to levy a revenue by way of impost on Commerce, it's freedom might be modified in that particular by mutual and equivalent measures, preserving it entire in all others.

Some nations not yet ripe for free commerce in all it's extent, might still be willing to mollify it's restrictions and regulations for us, in proportion to the advantages which an intercourse with us might offer. Particularly they may concur with us in reciprocating the Duties to be levied on each side, or in compensating any excess of duty by equivalent advantages of another nature. Our Commerce is certainly of a character to entitle it to favor in most countries. The Commodities we offer are either Necessaries of life; or Materials for manufacture; or convenient Subjects of Revenue: and we take in exchange, either manufactures when they have received the last finish of Art and Industry; or mere Luxuries. Such Customers may reasonably expect welcome, and friendly treatment at every market: Customers too, whose demands, increasing with their wealth and population, must very shortly give full employment to the whole Industry of any nation whatever, in any line of supply they may get into the habit of calling for from it.

But should any nation, contrary to our wishes, suppose it may better find it's advantage by continuing it's System of prohibitions, duties, and regulations, it behoves us to protect our Citizens their Commerce and navigation, by counter-prohibitions, duties, and regulations also. Free Commerce and navigation are not to be given in exchange for restrictions and vexations: nor are they likely to produce a relaxation of them.

Our Navigation involves still higher considerations. As a Branch of Industry, it is valuable; but, as a resource of Defence, essential.

It's value, as a Branch of Industry is enhanced by the dependence of so many other Branches on it. In times of [38] Peace it multiplies competitors for employment in transportation, and so keeps that at it's proper level; and in times of war, that is to say, when those nations who may be our principal carriers shall be at war with each other, if we have not within ourselves the means of transportation, our produce must be exported in belligerent vessels at the increased expense of war freight and insurance, and the articles which will not bear that must perish on our hands.

But it is as a resource for Defence that our Navigation will admit neither neglect nor forbearance. The position and circumstances of the United States leave them nothing to fear on their land-board, and nothing to desire beyond their present rights. But on their Sea-board, they are open to injury, and they have there too, a Commerce which must be protected. This can only be done by possessing a respectable body of Citizen-seamen, and of artists and establishments in readiness for ship-building.

Were the Ocean, which is the common property of all, open to the Industry of all, so that every person and vessel should be free to take employment wherever it could be found, the United States would certainly not set the example of appropriating to themselves, exclusively, any portion of the common stock of occupation. They would rely on the enterprise and activity of their Citizens for a due participation of the Benefits of the seafaring Business, and for keeping the marine class of Citizens equal to their object. But if particular Nations grasp at undue shares, and more especially if they seize on the means of the United States to convert them into aliment for their own strength, and withdraw them entirely from the support of those to whom they belong, defensive and protecting measures become necessary on the part of the Nation whose marine resources are thus invaded; or it will be disarmed of it's defence; it's productions will lie at the mercy of the nation which has possessed itself exclusively of the means of carrying them, and it's politicks must[39] be influenced by those who command it's commerce. The carriage of our own commodities, if once established in another Channel, cannot be resumed in the moment we may desire. If we lose the Seamen and Artists whom it now occupies, we lose the present means of marine defence, and time will be requisite to raise up others when disgrace or losses shall bring home to our feelings the Error of having abandoned them. The materials for maintaining our due share of navigation are ours in abundance. And as to the mode of using them, we have only to adopt the principles of those who thus put us on the defensive, or others equivalent and better fitted to our circumstances.

The following principles, being founded in reciprocity appear perfectly just, and to offer no cause of complaint to any nation.

1. WHERE a nation imposes high Duties on our productions, or prohib-

its them altogether, it may be proper for us to do the same by theirs, selecting at first those articles of manufactures which[40] we take from them in greatest quantity, and which, at the same time we could the soonest furnish to ourselves, or obtain from other Countries; imposing on them duties, lighter at first, but heavier and heavier afterwards as other channels of supply open. Such duties having the effect of indirect encouragement to domestic manufactures of the same kind, may induce the manufacturer to come himself into these States, where cheaper Subsistence, equal Laws, and a vent of his wares free of duty may ensure him the highest profits from his Skill and Industry. And here it would be in the power of the State Governments to co-operate essentially by opening the resources of encouragement which are under their controul, extending them liberally to Artists in those particular Branches of manufacture, for which their Soil, Climate, Population and other Circumstances have matured them, and fostering the precious efforts and progress of household manufacture by some patronage suited to the nature of it's objects, guided by the local informations they possess and guarded against abuse by their presence and attentions. The oppressions on our agriculture in foreign ports would thus be made the occasion of relieving it from a dependence on the councils and conduct of others, and of promoting arts, manufactures, and population at home.

2. WHERE a nation refuses permission to our Merchants and Factors to reside within certain parts of their Dominions, we may, if it should prove[41] expedient, refuse residence to theirs in any and every part of ours.[42]

3. WHERE a Nation refuses to receive in our Vessels any productions but our own, we may refuse to receive in theirs[43] any but their[44] productions. The Bill reported by the Committee is well framed[45] to effect this object.[46]

4. WHERE a nation refuses to our Vessels the carriage even of our own productions to certain Countries under their[47] subjection, we may refuse to theirs the carriage of the same or any other of our productions to the same or any other Countries. And here Justice and Friendship[48] would dictate that those who have no part in imposing the restriction on us should not be the victims of measures adopted to defeat it's effect: but that these should be pointed to the dominant Country itself by prohibiting their Vessels from the carriage of our productions to the dominant country, and to all others where our own or those of any other nation may freely carry them. And that this restriction might bring no inconvenience on the agriculture of our Country, it might be proper to begin by leaving the present moderate Tonnage Duty on their Vessels for the first Year, advancing it from Year to Year, in a given ratio, till time should have been afforded for a sufficient increase of the means of trans-

portation by ourselves and other Nations, when absolute prohibition might take place. [49]

The establishment of some of these principles by Great Britain alone has already lost us in our commerce with that country and it's possessions, between eight and nine hundred Vessels of near 40,000 Tons burthen, according to statements from official materials, in which they have confidence. This involves a proportional loss of Seamen, Shipwrights, and Shipbuilding, and is too serious a loss to admit forbearance of some effectual remedy.

It is true we must expect some inconvenience in practice from the establishment of discriminating duties. But in this, as in so many other cases, we are left to chuse between two evils. These inconveniencies are nothing, when weighed against the loss of wealth, and loss of force, which will follow our perseverance in the Plan of indiscrimination. When once it shall be perceived that we are either in the System, or the Habit, of giving equal advantages to those who extinguish our commerce and navigation by Duties and Prohibitions, as to those who treat both with liberality and justice, liberality and Justice will be converted by all into Duties and Prohibitions. It is not to the moderation and Justice of others we are to trust for fair and equal access to market with our productions, or for our due share in the transportation of them; but to our own means of independence, and the firm will to use them. Nor do the inconveniencies of discrimination merit consideration. Not one of the nations beforementioned; perhaps, not a commercial Nation on Earth, is without them. In our Case, one distinction alone will suffice, that is to say, between Nations who favor our productions and navigation, and those who do not favor them. One set of moderate Duties, say the present Duties, for the first, and a fixed advance on these as to some Articles, and prohibitions, as to others, for the last.

Still it must be repeated that friendly arrangements are preferable with all who will come into them; and that we should carry into such arrangements all the Liberality and Spirit of accommodation which the nature of the Case will admit.

France has, of her own accord, proposed Negotiations for improving, by a new Treaty on fair and equal principles, the commerical relations of the two Countries. But her internal disturbances have hitherto prevented the prosecution of them to effect, though we have had repeated assurances of a continuance of the disposition.

Proposals of friendly arrangement have been made on our part by the present government to that of Great Britain, as the Message states: but being already on as good a footing in Law, and a better in Fact, than the most favored nation, they have not as yet, discovered any disposition to have it meddled with.

We have no reason to conclude that friendly arrangements would be declined by the other nations with whom we have such commercial intercourse as may render them important. In the meanwhile, it would rest with the wisdom of Congress to determine whether, as to those nations, they will not surcease ex parte regulations, on the reasonable presumption that they will concur in doing whatever Justice and moderation dictate should be done.

MS (DLC: TJ Papers, 69: 11981-91); consisting originally of fair copy of Document I above—incorporating most of the revisions noted there—transcribed by George Taylor, Jr., on 21 numbered pages in the customary form for TJ's drafts; with one emendation by Taylor and many others by TJ, as noted below, some being suggested by Tench Coxe, including a slip bearing revised language pasted down over part of p. 18, the verso of fol. 11989 (see note 49 below) and others by foreign ministers in the United States, thereby transforming it into draft of Document III below; with penciled notations in the margin, eight by Taylor identifying four sets of extracts enclosed in TJ's circular to the foreign ministers of 13 Feb. 1793, and one by George Washington (see below); undated, but transcribed by Taylor sometime before 5 Feb. 1793, when TJ received Coxe's suggestions, and completed by TJ sometime after 23 Feb. 1793, when he received the last of the replies from the foreign ministers. *The text as printed above reflects the state of the MS before TJ submitted it to Coxe for review and before he revised it in light of Coxe's extensive list of queries and suggested changes* (see enclosure to Coxe to TJ, 5 Feb. 1793; and the revisions inspired by him in notes 1-2, 4, 7, 9-15, 17-18, 20-2, 24-31, 33, 35-39, 42, 45, and 47-9 below). TJ submitted the amended MS to the President on 10 Feb. 1793; two days later, after inserting a note in the margin, the President returned it with a general statement of approval (TJ to Washington, 10 Feb. 1793; Washington to TJ, 12 Feb. 1793; and note 24 below). On 13 Feb. 1793 TJ submitted extracts from the revised MS to the foreign ministers (Circular to Foreign Ministers in the United States, 13 Feb. 1793, and enclosures). The French, British, and Spanish emissaries responded with observations that led TJ to make additional changes in the MS, presumably after receiving F. P. Van Berckel's obser-

vations on 23 Feb. 1793, though the latter did not result in any revisions (George Hammond to TJ, 15 Feb. 1793; Josef Ignacio de Viar and Josef de Jaudenes to TJ, 15 Feb. 1793; Jean Baptiste Ternant to TJ, [16 Feb. 1793], Van Berckel to TJ, 22 Feb. 1793; and notes 6, 8, and 16 below). TJ made still more alterations at different times (see notes 5, 19, 32, 34, 40-1, 44, and 46 below). All of the foregoing revisions are reflected in the final report, but two other alterations TJ made in the MS and subsequently erased do not appear in that text (see notes 17 and 43 below). In amending this state of the report TJ also employed the following rough notes for the revision of the section on p. 6 concerning the British exclusion of American-built ships from the carrying trade between Great Britain and the United States (see text at note 12 below), and for other intended revisions he did not make there or on p. 8:

"page 6.

* qu. our ships when purchased and navigated by their own subjects cannot be employed in their trade with us, while the ships of other countries so purchased and navigated may be employed in their trade with those countries

√ duty on fish imported.

[. . .] to be [changed?] for a permission to islanders alone

pa.8. Ireland.

* the navigation act §.1. admits into the American trade, two descriptions of vessels

1. vessels built and belonging to America &c and navigated lawfully

2. vessels belonging to English and navigated lawfully.

our vessels, bought by British, were covered by both these descriptions with other nations it makes it sufficient that the vessel *belongs* to England or such other country

The Proclamation restrains it to
1. British built ships owned by Brit. subjects and navigated &c.
2. American built ships owned and navigated by Americans.
Consequently American built ships owned by British, are excluded

14. Car. 2. c. 11. §.6 no foreign built ship shall be deemed British
27. G. 3. c. 19. (Nodin 3.) importations restrained.
1. to Brit. or British built ships legally navigated
2. to ships of country produc[ing?] them, legally navigated
and declares no ships deemed *British* but such as are *British built*.

6. Anderson 818."

MS (DLC: TJ Papers, 233: 41597); consisting of one page entirely in TJ's hand; undated, but written at three different times, the section for p. 8 lengthwise over apparently unrelated calculations. For another document TJ may have used in revising this state of the report, see Memorandum from Tench Coxe, [before 5 Feb. 1793], printed below in the supplement to the present volume.

[1] TJ interlined "countries" in place of this word in response to Tench Coxe.
[2] Word altered to "Bread" by TJ in response to Tench Coxe.
[3] Word interlined by Taylor.
[4] TJ added "and it's dominions" after all the countries listed in this table except the United Netherlands, where he added "and their dominions," in response to Tench Coxe.
[5] TJ here interlined "as well as on those of other foreign countries."
[6] TJ here added "Our commerce is permitted with their Canary islands under the same conditions" in response to Josef Ignacio de Viar and Josef de Jaudenes.
[7] TJ here interlined "or nearly $4\frac{1}{2}$ cents" in response to Tench Coxe.
[8] TJ here added "and tobaccos" in response to Jean Baptiste Ternant.
[9] TJ here lined out "incidental" and interlined "of collection" in response to Tench Coxe.

[10] TJ altered the preceding sentence to read "Our salted fish and other salted provisions except Bacon are prohibited" in response to Tench Coxe.
[11] TJ canceled this word as part of the revision recorded in the previous note.
[12] TJ altered this paragraph to read "Our Ships, though purchased and navigated by their own Subjects, are not permitted to be used even in their trade with us" in response to Tench Coxe.
[13] TJ altered the preceding seven words to read "any produce or manufacture of," apparently in response to Tench Coxe.
[14] TJ canceled the next two words and here interlined in their place "which may be lawfully ⟨imported⟩ carried in any vessels, ours," apparently in response to Tench Coxe.
[15] TJ here interlined "all and any of our," apparently in response to Tench Coxe.
[16] Sentence to this point altered by TJ to read "The Minister of that court indeed frankly expressed his personal conviction that the words of the order went farther than was intended, and so he, afterwards, officially informed us" in response to George Hammond.
[17] After interlining "proportion" in place of "part" earlier in the sentence, TJ here changed the comma to a period, canceled the next seven words, and interlined "The residue is partly forwarded for consumption in the inland parts of Europe and partly reshipped to other maritime countries. On the latter portion," all in response to Tench Coxe. This interlineation is based on an erased and largely illegible marginal note that TJ marked for insertion in this paragraph.
[18] Clause to this point altered by TJ to "so much of the value as is" in response to Tench Coxe.
[19] TJ interlined "somewhat" in place of this word.
[20] At least partly in response to Tench Coxe, TJ altered this paragraph to read "Denmark lays considerable duties on our tobacco and Rice carried in their own Vessels, and half as much more if carried in ours, but the exact amount of these duties is not perfectly known here. They lay such as amount to prohibitions on our Indigo and Corn."
[21] TJ interlined "16 mills the pound" in place of the preceding three words and digits in response to Tench Coxe.

[22] TJ interlined "40. per cent additional on that, or $22\frac{4}{10}$ mills" in place of the preceding four words and digits in response to Tench Coxe. In the margin alongside the changes recorded in this and the preceding note TJ wrote "1. skilling pr. ℔."

[23] Based on MS 5 listed at Document I above, TJ here wrote in the margin:
"RxD. sk
    4–3– pr 100 ℔.
  RxD   D
    1. = 1.07."

[24] TJ lined out the remainder of this paragraph. In the margin he wrote "qu. whether this should be inserted or not?" Below this George Washington wrote in pencil: "It ought to be well considered in its consequences." Although Tench Coxe had questioned the paragraph, he recommended that it be modified rather than deleted.

[25] TJ interlined "live" in place of this word in response to Tench Coxe.

[26] TJ interlined "it was formerly suspended occasionally, but latterly without interruption" in place of the remainder of this sentence in response to Tench Coxe.

[27] TJ here interlined "colonial" in response to Tench Coxe and wrote in the margin "(about 37. cents)."

[28] TJ altered the preceding five words to read "as free as their own to carry our" in response to Tench Coxe.

[29] TJ interlined "live" in place of this word in response to Tench Coxe.

[30] TJ altered the preceding sentence to read "In the British continental Colonies, and in Newfoundland all our productions are prohibited, and our vessels forbidden to enter their ports" in response to Tench Coxe.

[31] TJ here added "this being expressly prohibited by the same statute of 12 Car. 2. c.18. commonly called their Navigation act" in response to Tench Coxe.

[32] TJ interlined "islands" in place of this word.

[33] TJ altered the preceding clause to read "our vessels and produce are received" in response to Tench Coxe.

[34] TJ here added "but they are heavier in the Dutch possessions on the continent."

[35] TJ interlined "in the dominions of" in place of this word in response to Tench Coxe.

[36] TJ here interlined "there" in response to Tench Coxe.

[37] Remainder of sentence altered by TJ to "Sweden, and lately in France" in response to Tench Coxe.

[38] TJ here interlined "general" in response to Tench Coxe.

[39] Word reworked by TJ to "may" in response to Tench Coxe.

[40] TJ here interlined "first burthening or excluding those productions which they bring here in competition with our own of the same kind; selecting next such manufactures as" in place of the preceding eight words.

[41] TJ here interlined "be thought" in place of this word.

[42] TJ here added "or modify their transactions" in response to Tench Coxe.

[43] TJ here interlined an erased and illegible passage of about five words.

[44] TJ here interlined "own."

[45] Sentence to this point altered by TJ to read "The 1st. and 2d. clauses of the Bill reported by the Committee are well formed" in response to Tench Coxe.

[46] TJ wrote the following paragraph in the margin for insertion here: "4. Where a nation refuses to consider any vessel as ours which has not been built within our territories, we should refuse to consider as theirs any vessel not built within their territories." He then remembered the next paragraph. See note 98 to Document I above.

[47] TJ altered the remainder of the sentence to read "domination we might refuse to theirs of every description the carriage of the same productions to the same Countries" in response to Tench Coxe.

[48] TJ altered the preceding part of this sentence to read "But as Justice and good neighborhood" in response to Tench Coxe.

[49] In response to Tench Coxe TJ here first added "—Moreover, it is of course understood that the reciprocation of this principle should be confined to cases where a disadvantageous balance of commerce with the dominant nation gives us a just [claim?] to equivalent advantages with it's colonies, and where it is right [and?] necessary that we should check an evil ourselves for which no qualification can be obtained from the other party." He then lined out, also in response to Coxe, "defeat . . . prohibiting" in the second sentence of this paragraph and pasted over the remainder of it, including his addition, a slip on which he wrote "defeat it's effect, it may be proper to confine the restriction to vessels owned

or navigated by any subjects of the same dominant power, other than the inhabitants of the country to which the said productions are to be carried. And to prevent all inconvenience to the said inhabitants, and to our own, by too sudden a check on the means of transportation, we may continue to admit the vessels marked for future exclusion, on an advanced tonnage, and for such length of time only, as may be supposed necessary to provide against that inconvenience."

III. Final State of the Report on Commerce

[16 Dec. 1793]

The Secretary of State, to whom was referred by the House of Representatives the Report of a Committee on the written Message of the President of the United States, of the 14th. of Feb: 1791, with instruction to report to Congress the nature and extent of the Privileges and Restrictions of the commercial Intercourse of the United States, with foreign Nations, and the Measures which he should think proper to be adopted for the improvement of the Commerce and Navigation of the same, has had the same under consideration, and thereupon makes the following

REPORT,

The countries with which the United States have their chief commercial intercourse, are SPAIN, PORTUGAL, FRANCE, GREAT BRITAIN, the UNITED NETHERLANDS, DENMARK, and SWEDEN, and their American possessions: and the Articles of Export which constitute the Basis of that Commerce, with their respective Amounts, are

	Dollars.
Bread-stuff, that is to say, Bread Grains, Meals, and Bread, to the annual Amount of	7,649,887
Tobacco	4,349,567
Rice	1,753,796
Wood	1,263,534
Salted fish	941,696
Pot & Pearl Ash	839,093
Salted meats	599,130
Indigo	537,379
Horses and Mules	339,753
Whale Oil	252,591
Flax seed	236,072
Tar, Pitch, and Turpentine	217,177
Live Provisions	137,743
Ships	
Foreign Goods	620,274

To descend to Articles of smaller value than these would lead into a minuteness of detail neither necessary nor useful to the present object.

The proportions of our EXPORTS, which go to the Nations before-mentioned, and to their Dominions, respectively, are as follows.

To Spain and it's Dominions	2,005,907
Portugal and it's Dominions	1,283,462
France and it's Dominions	4,698,735
Great Britain and it's Dominions	9,363,416
The United Netherlands and their Dominions	1,963,880
Denmark and it's Dominions	224,415
Sweden and it's Dominions	47,240

Our IMPORTS from the same Countries are

Spain and it's Dominions	335,110
Portugal and it's Dominions	595,763
France and it's Dominions	2,068,348
Great Britain and it's Dominions	15,285,428
United Netherlands and their Dominions	1,172,692
Denmark and it's Dominions	351,364
Sweden and it's Dominions	14,325

These imports consist mostly of Articles on which industry has been exhausted.

Our *Navigation* depending, on the same Commerce, will appear by the following statement of the Tonnage of our own Vessels, entering in our Ports, from those several Nations, and their possessions, in one Year, that is to say, from October 1789, to September 1790, inclusive, as follows.

Spain	19,695 Tons
Portugal	23,576
France	116,410
Great Britain	43,580
United Netherlands	58,858
Denmark	14,655
Sweden	750

Of our commercial objects, SPAIN receives favorably, our Bread stuff, Salted Fish, Wood, Ships, Tar, Pitch, and Turpentine. On our Meals, however, as well as on those of other foreign Countries when re-exported to their Colonies, they have lately imposed Duties, of from half a Dollar, to two Dollars the Barrel, the Duties being so proportioned to the current price of their own Flour, as that both together are to make the constant sum of nine Dollars per Barrel.

They do not discourage our Rice, Pot and Pearl Ash, salted provisions, or whale oil: but these Articles, being in small demand at their markets, are carried thither but in a small degree. Their demand for Rice, however, is increasing. Neither Tobacco nor Indigo are received there. Our commerce is permitted with their Canary islands under the same conditions.

Themselves, and their Colonies are the actual consumers of what they receive from us.

Our Navigation is free with the Kingdom of Spain; foreign Goods being received there in our Ships on the same Conditions as if carried in their own, or in the vessels of the Country of which such Goods are the manufacture or produce.

PORTUGAL receives favorably our Grain, and Bread, Salted fish, and other salted provisions, Wood, Tar, Pitch, and Turpentine.

For Flaxseed, Pot and Pearl Ash, though not discouraged, there is little demand.

Our Ships pay 20 per Cent, on being sold to their subjects, and are then free bottoms.

Foreign goods (except those of the East Indies) are received on the same footing in our Vessels, as in their own, or any others; that is to say, on general Duties of from 20 to 28 per cent, and, consequently, our Navigation is unobstructed by them. Tobacco, Rice, and Meals, are prohibited.

Themselves, and their Colonies consume what they receive from us.

These Regulations extend to the Azores, Madeira, and the Cape de Verd Islands, except that in these, Meals and Rice are received freely.

FRANCE receives favorably our Bread stuff, Rice, Wood, Pot and Pearl-ashes.

A duty of 5 Sous the Kental, or nearly $4\frac{1}{2}$ Cents, is paid on our Tar, Pitch, and Turpentine. Our whale-oils pay six Livres the Kental, and are the only foreign whale oils admitted. Our Indigo pays 5 Livres the Kental; their own two and a half: but a difference of quality, still more than a difference of duty, prevents it's seeking that market.

Salted Beef is received freely for re-exportation; but if for home-consumption, it pays 5 Livres the Kental. Other salted provisions pay that Duty in all cases, and salted fish is made lately to pay the prohibitory one of 20 Livres the Kental.

Our Ships are free to carry thither all foreign Goods, which may be carried in their own or any other Vessels, except Tobaccos not of our own growth: and they participate with theirs the exclusive carriage of our whale oils, and Tobaccoes.

During their former Government our Tobacco was under a monopoly, but paid no Duties; and our Ships were freely sold in their ports and converted into national bottoms. The first national assembly took from our Ships this privilege. They emancipated Tobacco from it's monopoly, but subjected it to duties of 18 Livres 15 Sous the Kental, carried in their own Vessels, and 25 Livres, carried in ours; a difference more than equal to the freight of the Article.

They and their Colonies consume what they receive from us.

GREAT BRITAIN receives our Pot and Pearl Ashes, free, while those of other nations pay a Duty of 2s./3d. the Kental. There is an equal distinction in favor of our Bar-iron; of which Article, however, we do not produce enough for our own use. Woods are free, from us, whilst they pay some small duty from other Countries. Indigo and Flax-seed, are free, from all countries. Our Tar and Pitch pay 11d. sterling the Barrel. From other alien Countries, they pay about a penny and a third more.

Our Tobacco, for their own Consumption, pays 1/3 sterling the pound, custom and excise, besides heavy expenses of collection: and Rice, in the same case, pays 7/4 sterling the hundred weight; which, rendering it too dear, as an Article of common food, it is consequently, used in very small quantity.

Our salted fish and other salted provisions, except Bacon, are prohibited. Bacon and whale-oils are under prohibitory duties: so are our Grains, Meals, and Bread, as to internal consumption, unless in times of such scarcity as may raise the price of wheat to 50/.— sterling the Quarter, and other Grains and meals in proportion.

Our Ships, though purchased and navigated by their own subjects, are not permitted to be used, even in their trade with us.

While the vessels of other nations are secured by standing Laws, which cannot be altered, but by the concurrent Will of the three Branches of the British Legislature, in carrying thither any produce or manufacture of the Country to which they belong, which may be lawfully carried in any Vessels, ours, with the same prohibition of what is foreign, are further prohibited by a standing law (12. Car. 2. 18. §.3.) from carrying thither all and any of our own[1] domestic productions and manufactures. A subsequent Act, indeed, has authorized their Executive to permit the carriage of our own productions, in our own bottoms, at it's sole discretion: and the permission has been given from year to year by Proclamation; but subject every moment to be withdrawn on that single will, in which event, our Vessels having any thing on board, stand interdicted from the Entry of all british Ports. The disadvantage of a Tenure which may be so suddenly discontinued, was experienced by our Merchants on a late occasion,* when an official notification that this law would be strictly enforced, gave them just apprehensions for the fate of their Vessels and Cargoes dispatched or destined to the Ports of Great Britain. The Minister of that Court indeed frankly expressed

*Apr. 12. 1792.[2]

his personal conviction that the words of the order went farther than was intended, and so he afterwards, officially informed us: but the embarrassments of the moment were real and great, and the possibility of their renewal, lays our Commerce to that Country, under the same species of discouragement as to other Countries, where it is regulated by a single Legislator: and the distinction is too remarkable not to be noticed, that our Navigation is excluded from the Security of fixed Laws, while that Security is given to the navigation of others.

Our Vessels pay in their ports 1/9 sterling per ton, light and Trinity dues, more than is paid by British Ships, except in the port of London, where they pay the same as British.

The greater part of what they receive from us, is re-exported to other Countries, under the useless charges of an intermediate deposite, and double voyage. From Tables published in England, and composed, as is said, from the Books of their Custom-houses, it appears that of the Indigo imported there in the Years 1773,–4,–5, one third was re-exported; and, from a document of Authority, we learn, that, of the Rice and Tobacco imported there, before the War, four fifths were re-exported. We are assured indeed, that the quantities sent thither for re-exportation since the war, are considerably diminished, yet less so than reason and national interest would dictate. The whole of our Grain is re-exported when wheat is below 50/. the Quarter, and other Grains in proportion.

THE UNITED NETHERLANDS prohibit our pickled Beef, and Pork, Meals and Bread of all Sorts, and lay a prohibitary duty on Spirits distilled from Grain.

All other of our productions are received on varied duties, which may be reckoned, on a medium at about 3 per cent.

They consume but a small proportion of what they receive. The residue is partly forwarded for consumption in the inland parts of Europe and partly re-shipped to other maritime Countries. On the latter portion They intercept, between us and the consumer so much of the value as is absorbed by the charges attending an intermediate deposite.

Foreign goods, except some East India Articles, are received in Vessels of any Nation.

Our Ships may be sold and naturalized there, with exceptions of one or two privileges, which somewhat lessen their value.

DENMARK lays considerable duties on our Tobacco and Rice, carried in their own Vessels, and half as much more, if carried in ours; but the exact amount of these duties is not perfectly known here. They lay such as amount to prohibitions on our Indigo and corn.

SWEDEN receives favorably our Grains and meals, Salted Provisions, Indigo, and whale oil.

They subject our Rice to duties of 16 mills the pound weight, carried in their own Vessels, and of 40 per cent additional on that, or $22\frac{4}{10}$ mills, carried in ours, or any others. Being thus rendered too dear as an Article of common food, little of it is consumed with them. They consume some of our Tobaccos, which they take circuitously through Great Britain; levying heavy duties on them also; their duties of Entry, Town duties, and Excise, being 4.34 Dollars, the hundred weight, if carried in their own Vessels, and of 40 per cent on that additional, if carried in our own or any other vessels.

They prohibit altogether our Bread, Fish, Pot and Pearl ashes, Flaxseed, Tar, Pitch, and Turpentine, Wood (except oak timber and Masts) and all foreign manufactures.

Under so many restrictions and prohibitions, our Navigation with them is reduced almost to nothing.

With our neighbors, an order of Things much harder presents itself.

SPAIN and PORTUGAL refuse, to those parts of america which they govern, all direct intercourse with any people but themselves. The Commodities in mutual demand, between them and their neighbors, must be carried to be exchanged in some port of the dominant Country, and the transportation between that and the subject-State must be in a domestic bottom.

FRANCE by a standing Law, permits her West India possessions to receive directly our Vegetables, Live Provisions, Horses, Wood, Tar, Pitch, and Turpentine, Rice, and Maize, and prohibits our other Bread stuff: but a suspension of this prohibition having been left to the Colonial Legislatures, in times of scarcity, it was formerly suspended occasionally, but latterly without interruption.

Our Fish and salted Provisions (except Pork) are received in their Islands under a Duty of 3 colonial Livres the Kental, and our vessels are as free as their own to carry our commodities thither, and to bring away Rum and Molasses.

GREAT BRITAIN admits in her Islands, our Vegetables, live Provisions, Horses, Wood, Tar, Pitch, and Turpentine, Rice, and Bread stuff, by a Proclamation of her Executive limited always to the term of a Year, but hitherto renewed from year to year. She prohibits our salted Fish and other salted Provisions. She does not permit our Vessels to carry thither our own produce. Her Vessels alone, may take it from us, and bring in exchange, Rum, Molasses, Sugar, Coffee, Cocoa-nuts, Ginger, and Pimento. There are, indeed, some freedoms in the Island of Dominica, but, under such circumstances, as to be little used by us. In the British continental Colonies, and in Newfoundland, all our productions are prohibited, and our Vessels forbidden to enter their ports. Their Governors, however, in times of distress, have power to permit a temporary importation of certain articles, in their own bottoms, but not in ours.

Our Citizens cannot reside as merchants or Factors within any of the British Plantations, this being expressly prohibited by the same Statute of 12 Car. 2. c. 18, commonly called the navigation act.

In the DANISH-AMERICAN POSSESSIONS, a duty of 5 per cent is levied on our corn, corn-meal, Rice, Tobacco, Wood, salted fish, Indigo, Horses, Mules, and Live stock, and of 10 per cent on our Flour, salted-Pork, and Beef, Tar, Pitch and Turpentine.

In the AMERICAN ISLANDS of the UNITED NETHERLANDS and SWE-DEN, our Vessels and produce are received, subject to duties, not so heavy as to have been complained of: but they are heavier in the Dutch possessions on the contintent.

To Sum up these Restrictions, so far as they are important.
1st. In Europe.

Our Breadstuff is at most times under prohibitory duties in England, and considerably dutied on re-exportation from Spain to her Colonies.

Our Tobaccoes are heavily dutied in England, Sweden, and France, and prohibited in Spain, and Portugal.

Our Rice is heavily dutied in England and Sweden, and prohibited in Portugal.

Our Fish and salted Provisions are prohibited in England, and under prohibitory duties in France.

Our Whale Oils are prohibited in England and Portugal.

And our vessels are[3] denied naturalization in England, and of late in France.
2d. In the West Indies.

All intercourse is prohibited with the possessions of Spain and Portugal.

Our salted provisions and Fish are prohibited by England.

Our salted pork, and Bread stuff (except maize) are received under temporary Laws only, in the dominions of France, and our Salted-fish pays there a weighty duty.
3rd. In the Article of Navigation.

Our own carriage of our own Tobacco, is heavily dutied in Sweden, and lately in France.

We can carry no Article, not of our own production to the British ports in Europe.

Nor even our own produce to her American possessions.

Such being the Restrictions on the Commerce and Navigation of the United States, the Question is, in what way they may best be removed, modified, or counteracted?

As to Commerce, two methods occur. 1. By friendly arrangements with the several Nations with whom these Restrictions exist: Or, 2. By the separate Act of our own Legislatures for countervailing their effects.

There can be no doubt, but that of these two, friendly arrangement is the most eligible. Instead of embarrassing Commerce under piles of regulating Laws, Duties, and Prohibitions, could it be relieved from all it's shackles in all parts of the world, could every Country be employed in producing that which Nature has best fitted it to produce, and each be free to exchange with others mutual surplusses, for mutual Wants, the greatest mass possible would then be produced of those Things which contribute to human life and human happiness; the numbers of mankind would be increased, and their condition bettered.

Would even a single Nation begin with the United States this System of free Commerce, it would be advisable to begin it with that nation; since it is one by one only, that it can be extended to all. Where the Circumstances of either party render it expedient to levy a Revenue, by way of impost, on Commerce, it's freedom might be modified, in that particular, by mutual and equivalent measures, preserving it entire in all others.

Some Nations, not yet ripe for free Commerce, in all it's extent, might still be willing to mollify it's restrictions and regulations for us, in proportion to the advantages, which an intercourse with us might offer. Particularly they may concur with us in reciprocating the Duties to be levied on each side, or in compensating any excess of duty, by equivalent advantages of another nature. Our Commerce is certainly of a Character to entitle it to favor in most Countries. The Commodities we offer, are either necessaries of life; or materials for manufacture; or convenient Subjects of Revenue: and we take in exchange, either manufactures, when they have received the last finish of Art and Industry; or mere Luxuries. Such Customers may reasonably expect welcome, and friendly treatment at every market: Customers too, whose demands, increasing with their wealth, and population, must very shortly give full employment to the whole Industry of any Nation whatever, in any line of supply they may get into the habit of calling for from it.

But should any Nation, contrary to our wishes, suppose it may better find it's advantage by continuing it's System of Prohibitions, Duties, and Regulations, it behoves us to protect our Citizens, their Commerce and Navigation, by Counter-prohibitions, Duties, and Regulations also. Free commerce and navigation are not to be given in exchange for Restrictions, and Vexations: nor are they likely to produce a relaxation of them.

Our Navigation involves still higher considerations. As a Branch of Industry, it is valuable; but, as a resource of Defence, essential.

It's Value, as a Branch of Industry, is enhanced by the dependence of so many other Branches on it. In times of general Peace it multiplies Competitors for employment in transportation, and so keeps that at it's proper level; and in times of war, that is to say, when those nations who may be our principal Carriers shall be at war with each other, if we have not within ourselves the means of transportation, our produce must be exported in belligerant vessels at the increased expense of war-freight and Insurance, and the Articles, which will not bear that, must perish on our hands.

But it is as a resource for Defence that our Navigation will admit neither neglect nor forbearance. The position and Circumstances of the United States leave them nothing to fear on their land-board, and nothing to desire beyond their present rights. But, on their sea-board, they are open to injury, and they have there too, a Commerce which must be protected. This can only be done by possessing a respectable Body of Citizen-seamen, and of Artists and Establishments in readiness for ship-building.

Were the Ocean, which is the common property of all, open to the Industry of all, so that every person and vessel should be free to take employment wherever it could be found, the United States would certainly not set the example of appropriating to themselves, exclusively, any portion of the common stock of occupation. They would rely on the enterprise and activity of their Citizens for a due participation of the Benefits of the seafaring Business, and for keeping the marine class of Citizens equal to their object. But if particular nations grasp at undue shares, and more especially, if they seize on the means of the United States to convert them into aliment for their own strength, and withdraw them entirely from the support of those to whom they belong, defensive and protecting measures become necessary on the part of the nation whose marine resources are thus invaded; or it will be disarmed of it's defence; it's productions will lie at the mercy of the nation which has possessed itself exclusively of the means of carrying them, and it's politics may be influenced by those who command it's Commerce. The carriage of our own Commodities, if once established in another Channel, cannot be resumed in the moment we may desire. If we lose the Seamen and Artists, whom it now occupies, we lose the present means of marine Defence, and time will be requisite to raise up others, when disgrace or losses shall bring home to our feelings the Error of having abandoned them. The materials for maintaining our due share of navigation, are ours in abundance. And, as to the mode of using them, we have only to adopt the principles of those who thus put us on the defensive, or others equivalent and better fitted to our Circumstances.

The following principles, being founded in reciprocity, appear perfectly just, and to offer no cause of complaint to any Nation.

1. WHERE a Nation imposes high Duties on our productions, or prohibits them altogether, it may be proper for us to do the same by theirs, first burthening or excluding those productions which they bring here, in

competition with our own of the same kind; selecting next such manufactures, as we take from them in greatest quantity, and which at the
same time we could the soonest furnish to ourselves, or obtain from
other Countries; imposing on them duties, lighter at first, but heavier
and heavier afterwards, as other channels of supply open. Such duties
having the effect of indirect encouragement to domestic Manufactures
of the same kind, may induce the Manufacturer to come himself into
these States, where cheaper subsistence, equal laws, and a vent of his
wares, free of duty, may ensure him the highest profits from his skill and
Industry. And here, it would be in the power of the State-Governments
to co-operate, essentially, by opening the resources of encouragement
which are under their controul, extending them liberally to Artists in
those particular Branches of manufacture, for which their Soil, Climate,
Population, and other Circumstances, have matured them and fostering
the precious efforts and progress of *household* manufacture by some patronage suited to the nature of it's objects, guided by the local informations they possess and guarded against abuse by their presence and attentions. The oppressions on our agriculture in foreign ports would
thus be made the occasion of relieving it from a dependence on the
Councils and conduct of others, and of promoting Arts, Manufactures,
and Population, at home.

2. WHERE a nation refuses permission to our Merchants and Factors to
reside within certain parts of their Dominions, we may, if it should be
thought expedient, refuse residence to theirs in any and every part of
ours, or modify their transactions.

3. WHERE a Nation refuses to receive in our vessels any productions but
our own, we may refuse to receive, in theirs, any but their own productions. The first and second clauses of the Bill reported by the Committee, are well formed to effect this object.

4. WHERE a Nation refuses to consider any Vessel as ours, which has
not been built within our territories, we should refuse to consider as
theirs, any vessel not built within their territories.

5. WHERE a Nation refuses to our Vessels the carriage even of our own
productions, to certain Countries under their domination, we might refuse to theirs, of every description, the carriage of the same productions
to the same Countries. But as Justice and Good neighborhood would
dictate that those who have no part in imposing the restriction on us
should not be the victims of measures adopted to defeat it's effect, it may
be proper to confine the restriction to Vessels owned or navigated by
any subjects of the same dominant power, other than the Inhabitants of
the Country to which the said productions are to be carried. And to
prevent all inconvenience to the said Inhabitants, and to our own, by too

sudden a check on the means of transportation, we may continue to admit the Vessels marked for future exclusion, on an advanced tonnage, and for such length of time only, as may be supposed necessary to provide against that inconvenience.

The establishment of some of these principles by Great Britain, alone, has already lost us in our Commerce with that Country and it's possessions, between eight and nine hundred Vessels of near 40,000 Tons burthen, according to statements from official materials, in which they have confidence. This involves a proportional loss of Seamen, Shipwrights, and Shipbuilding, and is too serious a Loss to admit forbearance of some effectual Remedy.

It is true we must expect some inconvenience in practice, from the establishment of discriminating duties. But in this, as in so many other cases, we are left to chuse between two Evils. These inconveniencies are nothing, when weighed against the loss of wealth, and loss of Force, which will follow our perseverance in the Plan of indiscrimination. When once it shall be perceived that we are either in the System, or the Habit, of giving equal advantages to those who extinguish our Commerce and Navigation by Duties and Prohibitions, as to those who treat both with Liberality and Justice, Liberality and Justice will be converted by all into Duties and Prohibitions. It is not to the Moderation and Justice of others, we are to trust for fair and equal access to market with our productions, or for our due share in the transportation of them; but to our own means of independence, and the firm will to use them. Nor do the inconveniencies of discrimination merit consideration. Not one of the nations beforementioned; perhaps, not a commercial Nation on Earth, is without them. In our case, one distinction alone will suffice; that is to say, between Nations who favor our productions and Navigation, and those who do not favor them. One set of moderate Duties, say the present Duties, for the first, and a fixed advance on these, as to some Articles, and Prohibitions as to others, for the last.

Still it must be repeated that friendly Arrangements are preferable with all who will come into them; and that we should carry into such Arrangements all the Liberality and Spirit of accomodation which the nature of the Case will admit.

France has, of her own accord, proposed Negotiations for improving, by a new Treaty on fair and equal principles, the commerical relations of the two Countries. But her internal disturbances have hitherto prevented the prosecution of them to effect, though we have had repeated assurances of a continuance of the disposition.

Proposals of friendly arrangement have been made on our part, by the present Government, to that of Great Britain, as the Message states:

but, being already on as good a footing in Law, and a better in Fact, than the most favored nation, they have not, as yet, discovered any disposition to have it meddled with.

WE have no reason to conclude that friendly arrangements would be declined by the other Nations, with whom we have such commercial intercourse as may render them important. In the meanwhile, it would rest with the Wisdom of Congress to determine whether, as to those Nations, they will not surcease exparte Regulations, on the reasonable presumption that they will concur in doing whatever Justice and Moderation dictate should be done.   TH: JEFFERSON

Tr (DNA: RG 46, Senate Records, 3d Cong., 1st sess.); undated; being a fair copy of Document II above, incorporating revisions noted there, in the hand of George Taylor, Jr., signed by TJ, with minor clerical corrections by both, and several emendations by TJ (see notes below), consisting of 18 unnumbered pages as submitted, with foliation added later by an unidentified hand. FC (Lb in DNA: RG 59, SDR); dated 16 Dec. 1793. Tr (Lb in DNA: RG 233, House Records, 3d Cong., 1st sess., TR); undated; with two clerical errors. Tr (Lb in DNA: RG 46, Senate Records, 3d Cong., 1st sess., TR); undated. Recorded in SJPL under 16 Dec. 1793: "Report on our foreign commerce." Enclosed in Documents IV and V.

The STATEMENT OF THE TONNAGE was the "General Statement of the Tonnage of Vessels entered into the United States, from foreign ports, between the 1st day of October, 1789, and the 30th day of September, 1790, together with the Coasting and Fishing Vessels," which Tench Coxe had prepared in the Department of the Treasury on 15 Apr. 1791 and sent to TJ on that day, and which Alexander Hamilton submitted to the Senate in November 1791 (Coxe to TJ, 15 Apr. 1791, and note; NSP, IX, 407-10).

LATELY IMPOSED DUTIES: a reference to the Spanish royal ordinance of 27 Jan. 1791 setting forth the duties to be imposed on "all foreign flour that may be embarked either for Carraccas, the Islands, or the Kingdoms of Santa Fe" (Tr in DLC, consisting of translation in a clerk's hand of "Spanish Decree respecting flour," endorsed by TJ: "Spain"; PrC in DLC).

A SUBSEQUENT ACT: the April 1783 act of Parliament that authorized the regula-

tion of American trade with Great Britain by orders in council (Bemis, *Jay's Treaty*, 29-30). For the LATE OCCASION in question, see George Hammond to TJ, 11 Apr. 1792, and note. TABLES PUBLISHED IN ENGLAND: the tables on British trade statistics published in an unpaginated appendix to John Baker Holroyd, Lord Sheffield, *Observations on the Commerce of the American States*, 6th ed. (London, 1784), Table III being the one containing the data on INDIGO IMPORTED THERE (see Sowerby, No. 3616). The DOCUMENT OF AUTHORITY was the lengthy abstract of the January 1791 report of a committee of the Privy Council on British trade with the United States written by Lord Hawkesbury that TJ had received from William Temple Franklin on 20 Sep. 1791, p. 7 of which contained the information given above about RICE AND TOBACCO (see Vol. 18: 269-70n).

TJ collected two specimens of the authority of royal governors to PERMIT A TEMPORARY IMPORTATION OF CERTAIN ARTICLES produced in the United States into British colonies—the proclamations of 18 May 1791 by Lieutenant Governor John Parr of Nova Scotia and Governor Thomas Shirley of the Leeward Islands (Trs in DLC, in a clerk's hand; PrC of latter in DLC, endorsed in ink by TJ: "British W. Indies"). His discussion of trade with the AMERICAN ISLANDS of SWEDEN was based in part on a 9 Dec. 1790 proclamation by Vice-Governor Carl Fredrik Bagge af Söderby and the Council of St. Barthélemy setting forth the terms of trade between that Swedish colony and foreign countries, including the United States (Tr in DLC, in a clerk's hand, in French; PrC in DLC, endorsed in ink by TJ: "Sweden").

BILL REPORTED BY THE COMMITTEE: the committee report on American commercial policy submitted to the House of Representatives on 21 Feb. 1791 (NSP, VII, 408). STATEMENTS FROM OFFICIAL MATERIALS: a reference to p. 17 of the abovementioned Privy Council report. A NEW TREATY: for the French National Assembly's 2 June 1791 call for a new commercial treaty with

the United States, see note to TJ to Delamotte, 30 Aug. 1791.

[1] Word interlined by TJ.
[2] Note inserted by TJ at foot of p. 6 of MS.
[3] Word interlined by TJ.

IV. Thomas Jefferson to the Speaker of the House of Representatives

SIR   Philadelphia Dec. 16.[1] 1793

According to the pleasure of the House of Representatives expressed in their Resolution of Feb. 23. 1791.[2] I now lay before them a Report on the privileges and restrictions on the Commerce of the United States in foreign Countries. In order to keep the Subject within those bounds which I supposed to be under the contemplation of the House, I have restrained my Statements to those Countries only with which we carry on a commerce of Some importance, and to those Articles also of our produce which are of sensible weight in the Scale of our Exports; and even these Articles are sometimes grouped together according to the degree of Favor or restriction with which they are received in each Country, and that degree expressed in general terms without detailing the exact duty levied on each Article. To have gone fully into these Minutiæ, would have been to copy the Tariffs and Books of Rates of the different Countries and to have hidden under a mass of detail those general and important Truths, the extraction of which in a Simple form I conceived would best answer the inquiries of the House, by condensing material information within those limits of time and attention which this portion of their duties may justly claim. The plan, indeed, of minute details, would have been impracticable with some Countries, for want of information.[3]

Since preparing this Report, which was put into its present form in time to have been given in to the last Session of Congress, alterations of the Conditions of our Commerce with some foreign Nations have taken place, some of them independant of the War, some arising out of it.

France has proposed to enter into a new treaty of Commerce with us on liberal principles, and has in the Mean time relaxed some of the restraints mentioned in the Report.—Spain has by an ordinance of June last, established New Orleans, Pensacola and St. Augustine into free ports for the Vessels of friendly Nations, *having treaties of Commerce* with her, provided they touch for a permit at Corcubion in Gallicia, or at Alicante; and our Rice is by the same ordinance excluded from that Country.—The Circumstances of the War, have necessarily given us freer access to the West-Indian Islands, whilst they have also drawn on our Navigation Vexations and depredations of the most serious Nature.

To have endeavored to describe all these, would have been as impracticable as useless, since the Scenes would have been shifting while under description. I, therefore, think it best to leave the Report as it was formed, being adapted to a particular point of time; when things were in their Settled order, that is to say, to the Summer of 1792. I have the honor to be with the most profound respect, Sir, Your most obedt. & most hum: Servt.   TH: JEFFERSON

Tr (DNA: RG 46, Senate Records, 3d Cong., 1st sess.); in a clerk's hand, signed by TJ, with insertions by him (see notes 1-2 below); at foot of first page: "To The Speaker of the House of Representatives of the United States of America." PrC of Dft (DLC); in the hand of George Taylor, Jr., unsigned, with insertion and revisions by TJ (see notes below); variant text containing different second paragraph and lacking final two paragraphs; possibly prepared as early as February 1793 from a missing rough draft in connection with Document II. FC (Lb in DNA: RG 59, SDR). Tr (Lb in DNA: RG 233, House Records, 3d Cong., 1st sess., TR). Tr (Lb in DNA: RG 46, Senate Records, 3d Cong., 1st sess., TR). Enclosure: Document III.

[1] Month and day inserted by TJ in space left blank by clerk; in PrC of Dft TJ inserted them in ink.

[2] Date inserted by TJ in space left blank by clerk; space left blank in PrC of Dft.

[3] Remainder of PrC of Dft consists of a variant second paragraph (having two interlineations in ink by TJ in place of a canceled word and phrase) and the complimentary close, the paragraph being as follows: "Since preparing this Report, the duties on the importation of our Tobaccos into France, were reduced by their Legislative Assembly from 18.^{tt} 15s the Kental, carried in their own and 25^{tt} carried in our Vessels as stated in the report, to 10^{tt} in theirs, and 12.^{tt} 10s. in our Vessels; ⟨but⟩ and from the present Government, we receive assurances which ⟨would leave us nothing more to desire⟩ are very encouraging on the subject of our Commerce with them. The statements as to their West Indies refer to the State of Things next preceding the derangement of public Order in those Countries." TJ received news of the French decree on 18 Dec. 1792 (see Joseph Fenwick to TJ, 11 Sep. 1792, and note).

V. Thomas Jefferson to the President of the Senate

SIR   Philadelphia December 16th. 1793.

Having, according to a resolution of the House of Representatives of February 23. 1791. given in to that House a Report on the privileges and restrictions on the commerce of the United States in foreign Countries, I think it my duty to lay a Copy of it before the Senate, and have the honor of being with the most perfect respect Sir Your most obedient and Most humble Servt.   TH: JEFFERSON

RC (DNA: RG 46, Senate Records, 3d Cong., 1st sess.); in a clerk's hand, signed by TJ; at foot of text: "The President of the Senate." PrC (DLC); unsigned. FC (Lb in DNA: RG 59, DL). Tr (Lb in DNA: RG 46, Senate Records, 3d Cong, 1st sess., TR). Enclosures: Documents III and IV.

From Richard Söderström

SIR   Philadelphia Decr: 16: 1793.

Having Certified that P: S: Oxholm and Bd: Wallington are Subjects of the King of Danmark I request the favor of you to accompany my Certificate with one from you that I am what I have styled myself Vizt.—Consul of Sweden and Agent for the Court of Danmark. I have the Honor to be with the greatest respect Sir Your most Obd: and very Humble Sert: RICHD: SÖDERSTRÖM

RC (DNA: RG 59, NFC); at foot of text: "The Honble. Thos: Jefferson, Secrety. of State for the United States of America"; endorsed by TJ as received 16 Dec. 1793 and so recorded in SJL.

From Samuel Ward & Brothers

SIR   New York 16 Decemr. 1793

We are now fitting for sea at Newport a ship of fine size and which might very readily be equipd as a thirty two gun frigate. The dimensions are as follows—viz—

100 feet keel 32 feet 8 Inches beam 14 feet lower hold 6 feet 10 Inches between decks—and built with composition bolts ready to take a sheathing of copper.

If the United States should have any occasion for such a vessel we will dispose of this one with the utmost chearfulness. We have the honour to be Sir Your most obedt. Servts

SAM WARD & BROTHERS

The ship will be ready to sail about the 10th. of January.

Brown & Francis of Providence have a fine ship now fitting for the Indies which is to sail in all this month. She is as large as our ship or larger. Those gentlemen possess smaller ships in which they could send their cargo to India and from their well known public spirit there is no doubt they would readily dispose of this ship to the States if the public service should require it.

RC (DNA: RG 59, MLR); in the hand of Samuel Ward; at foot of first page: "Mr Jefferson"; endorsed by TJ as received 17 Dec. 1793 and so recorded in SJL.

To Thomas Willing

Dec. 16. 1793.

Th: Jefferson presents his respectful compliments to the President of the bank of the US. Being now to make up his annual account of the expenditure of the fund of 40,000 ₴ for the legislature, he begs the favor of the President to have him furnished with a copy of the account of the Secretary of state on the bank books, down to the present day, to serve so far as a Voucher.

RC (Facsimile in Walter Burks Autographs & Coins Catalogue, Spring 1989, Lot 122). Not recorded in SJL.

Thomas Willing (1731-1821), a prominent Philadelphia merchant and officeholder since before the Revolution, was a principal of the firm of Willing, Morris & Swanwick—the final incarnation of a partnership with Robert Morris that extended over nearly four decades—and served as the first president of the Bank of the United States from 1791 to 1807. He had been president of the Bank of North America from 1781 to 1792 (DAB; Burton A. Konkle, *Thomas Willing and the First American Financial System* [Philadelphia, 1937]).

From Edmond Charles Genet

M.   Philadelphie le 17. xbre. 1793. l'an 2e. de la Repe. fse.

J'ai reçu la lettre que vous m'avés fait l'honneur de m'écrire le 6. de ce mois et Je m'empresse de vous éxprimer toute la reconnoissance que m'inspire les informations qu'elle renferme.

Dft (DLC: Genet Papers); unsigned; at head of text: "Exp."; above salutation: "Le Cit Genet &c à M. Jefferson &c"; at foot of text in a clerk's hand: "Translated." FC (same); in English. Possibly recorded in SJL as a garbled entry for a letter of this date from Genet about "St. Domo. tonnage" received 16 Dec. 1793.

To Jacob Hollingsworth

SIR   Philadelphia Dec. 17. 1793.

I received yesterday your favor of the 13th. and accept willingly the offer of the clover seed at the price you mention. I hope Mr. Alexander will be setting out by the time you recieve this, as the place he is to overlook must be suffering much for want of him. I am with esteem Sir Your most obedt. servt   TH: JEFFERSON

PrC (DLC); at foot of text: "Mr. Jacob Hollingsworth, Elkton." Tr (ViU: Edgehill-Randolph Papers); 19th-century copy.

To Edmond Charles Genet

SIR   Philadelphia Dec. 18. 1793.

I have laid before the President your letter of the 16th. instant, and in consequence thereof have written to the Attorney General of the US. a letter of which I have the honor to inclose you a copy, and to add assurances of the respect with which I am Sir Your most obedt & most humble servt   TH: JEFFERSON

RC (DLC: Genet Papers); at foot of text: "The Min. Pleny. of the Republic of France." PrC (DLC). FC (Lb in DNA: RG 59, DL). Enclosure: TJ to Edmund Randolph, 18 Dec. 1793. Letter and enclosure enclosed in TJ to George Washington, 18 Dec. 1793. Both printed in *Federal Gazette* and *Philadelphia Daily Advertiser*, 24 Dec. 1793.

The President approved a draft of this letter and returned it to TJ this day (Washington, *Journal*, 269).

From Alexander Hamilton

SIR   Treasury Department Decemr. 18th. 1793

I am to acknowledge the receipt of an extract of a letter from you to Mr. Hammond of the 5th. of September 1793.

As a preliminary however to the Instructions to be given to the Collectors, it will be necessary that you inform me, whether Mr. Hammond has assented to the proposed arrangement as well as the number and names of the prizes that come within the description. I have the Honor to be with great respect Sir Your Most Obedient Servant

                                    A HAMILTON
                                    Secy of the Treasy

RC (DLC); in a clerk's hand, signed by Hamilton; at foot of text: "Thomas Jefferson Esquire Secretary of State"; endorsed by TJ as received 19 Dec. 1793 and so recorded in SJL.

In his 19 Dec. 1793 circular to the customs COLLECTORS, Hamilton set forth the procedures for ascertaining the "losses by detention, waste or Spoliation" which had been suffered by British ships captured between 5 June and 7 Aug. 1793 by French privateers armed and equipped in American ports and then restored (Syrett, *Hamilton*, xv, 550-1). TJ had described these procedures in his 5 Sep. 1793 letter to George Hammond, and the British minister had ASSENTED to them in his reply of the following day.

From Josef de Jaudenes and
Josef Ignacio de Viar

Sir   Philada. Dec. 18. 1793.

In addition to the various papers which on different occasions we have had the honor to put into your hands relative to the affairs of the Indians our neighbors and allies, we have now the pleasure to transmit you a copy of extracts concerning this object, which we have lately recieved from the Governor of Louisiana.

It's contents will confirm to you the reason with which we ought to complain of the conduct observed by the several agents of the US. on those frontiers.

At the same time you will observe the salutary measure which the said governor proposes to put an end to such atrocities and disorders as have been committed, and, as is probable, will continue until an efficacious remedy be applied.

What is mentioned in the inclosed copy appears to have all the requisites of humanity, good faith, and sincere correspondence.

In this expectation we request you to be so good as to give information of the whole to the President of the US. to the end that these may determine what they shall judge convenient, seeing how much good may be produced by the friendly convention proposed, and how much evil by the omission of it.

We repeat assurances of the most sincere good will and greatest respect and have the honor to subscribe ourselves Sir Your most obedt. & humble servts.

JOSEPH DE JAUDENES   in the absence of JOSEPH DE VIAR
                          JOSEPH DE JAUDENES, for him

Tr (DLC); in TJ's hand; at head of text in a clerk's hand: "Translation." PrC (MoSHi: Bixby Collection). RC (DNA: RG 59, NL); in Spanish; in a clerk's hand, signed by Jaudenes for himself and for Viar; at foot of text: "Sor. Dn. Thomas Jefferson Secretario de Estado &ca."; endorsed by TJ as received 18 Dec. 1793 and so recorded in SJL. Tr (DNA: RG 46, Senate Records, 3d Cong., 1st sess.); in English. PrC (MoSHi: Bixby Collection). Recorded in SJPL. Enclosures: (1) Extract of Baron de Carondelet to Jaudenes and Viar, New Orleans, 28 Oct. 1793, stating that, as No. 2 shows, the Cherokees have put 600 to 700 men in the field to avenge the murder at Hanging Maw's of several of their chiefs and repeated hostilities by their American

neighbors; that the Americans have offered 500 pesos for the head of the important person living among the Cherokees who wrote No. 2; that in order to maintain good relations with the Cherokees he will supply a few munitions in the guise of gifts to the Indians of Pensacola and Mobile in conformity with the practices followed in regard to other Indian allies of Spain; that in Georgia the Americans have provoked a war with the Creeks by attacking the towns of Hoethletiaga on 21 Sep. and Chattahoochee on 25 Sep., killing several men and carrying off women and children in both cases; that a commissioner of American Indian agent James Seagrove, who was then engaged in peace talks in the Indian town of Oefasky, would have paid with his head for the burning of nearby Chattahoochee if he had not been protected by the White Lieutenant in Oefasky and one of Panton's agents; that by threatening to withdraw Spanish protection Pedro Olivier, the Spanish agent to the Creeks, prevented the chiefs of the upper and lower towns from carrying out a 27 Aug. decision to attack Georgia in four groups; that after the burnings of Hoethletiaga and Chattahoochee it was no longer possible to prevent the Creeks from going on the warpath; that Seagrove, now standing fast at Rock Landing, should bring new peace proposals to the Indian town of Fokepatchy; that although Americans along the border are clearly to blame for the renewal of hostilities, peace could be restored if Congress through its President directs Seagrove to meet with Olivier and suspends the running of boundaries, pending the discussion in Madrid; that if Congress orders hostilities against the Creeks to cease, Carondelet will try to convince that nation to make peace with the United States; that since he had just reestablished peace between the Creeks and Chickasaws, it was hardly just for American governors to try to foment war between Spain's Indian allies, as in the case of Lieutenant Clark, who at the beginning of the year brought arms, ammunition, and food to Chief Piomingo of the Chickasaws, a sharp contrast to Carondelet's own refusal to provide any arms or munitions to the Creeks and Chickasaws while they were fighting each other; that Jaudenes and Viar must obtain the strictest orders from Congress forbidding William Blount, James Robertson, and other American officials in the western settlements to arouse Piomingo's mischievous spirit or to send medals and patents to the other chiefs of Spain's nations, the practice Spain rigorously follows with respect to those under American dominion; and that the United States should in future refrain from sending armed troops down the Mississippi in disregard of Spain's territorial rights lest this give rise to hostilities (Tr in DNA: RG 59, NL, in Spanish, attested by Jaudenes; Tr in DLC, in English, in the hand of George Taylor, Jr.; PrC in MoSHi: Bixby Collection; Tr in DNA: RG 46, Senate Records, 3d Cong., 1st sess., in English; PrC of another Tr in MoSHi: Bixby Collection). (2) Extract of [John McDonald] to Governor Enrique White of Pensacola, Cherokees, 12 Sep. 1793, stating that the bearer Little Turkey, a Cherokee chief, was on his way to Pensacola to obtain ammunition for his distressed people; that the present dispute between the Cherokees and the Americans originated with the murder of a number of Cherokees who had assembled at Hanging Maw's under the faith of government at the solicitation of Governor Blount and other United States agents; that since then 600 to 700 Cherokees have turned out to take revenge for this and subsequent white killings of all Cherokees they could find without distinction, women as well as children; that when the Cherokees decided in council to fight they agreed that the traders should each bring them a horseload of ammunition, which the traders agreed to do; and that in his opinion the Cherokees presently needed about 14 horseloads, or 700 pounds of powder and 1,400 pounds of ball, which was probably all that would be delivered to them this winter (Tr in DNA: RG 59, NL, attested by Jaudenes; Tr in DNA: RG 46, Senate Records, 3d Cong., 1st sess.; PrC in DLC). Translations of letter and Enclosure No. 1, as well as Enclosure No. 2, enclosed in TJ to George Washington, 19 Dec. 1793, and Washington to the Senate and the House of Representatives, 23 Dec. 1793.

John McDonald, who was not identified as the author of Enclosure No. 2 in the text sent to TJ, was an Indian trader and former British agent operating among the Chickamaugua Cherokees as an agent of William Panton, head of the influential mercantile firm of Panton, Leslie & Company, which with official Spanish approval carried on an extensive trade with the Southern Indians from its bases in East and West Florida (D. C. Corbitt and Roberta Corbitt, eds., "Papers from the Spanish Archives Relating to Tennessee and the Old Southwest," East Tennessee Historical Society, *Publications*, xxxv [1963], 89, 91; William S. Coker and Thomas D. Watson, *Indian Traders of the Southeastern Spanish Borderlands: Panton, Leslie & Company and John Forbes & Company, 1783-1847* [Pensacola, 1986], ix-xii, 162-4).

To Caleb Lownes

Sir   Philadelphia. Dec. 18. 1793.

Not having yet seen the captain of the vessel to whom I had offered the transportation of my goods to Richmond, I conclude to send them by your vessels to Richmond if you chuse to take them on the terms I heretofore paid, that is to say @ 4d. the cubic foot. There are 15. boxes, containing 282. cubic feet now at Mr. Hazlehurst's ready to be delivered, marked TJ. No. 52. to 66. There are 22. boxes containing 458 cubic feet and a pipe of wine¹ about 3. miles off in the country which will come to town as soon as the weather will permit. There will be here 4. or 5. boxes, not yet ready, a number of Windsor chairs, some small parcels cubic contents not yet known. Likewise a chariot the transportation of which I am told should be 15. Dollars from hence to Richmond. If it would be² convenient to take in the articles from the country, and those still here as they are carried down to the water side,³ they shall be sent to any place you please. This would save the trouble and expence of warehousing. For those at Mr. Hazlehurst's I should expect the vessel would go to his wharf. I will prefer paying you the freight here, as with vessels depending on you I should be certain this would have no effect on the care taken of the things.

If I understood you yesterday, it is your custom to furnish nail rod to customers at 60. to 90 days credit. I suppose one ton will serve me the first quarter of the year by the end of which I shall be ready to work up two or three times as much every quarter, I will therefore be obliged to you to send a ton by these vessels to Richmond, paiable at three months. I take the longest term because on account of the slow transportation from Richmond to my house half that term will always be elapsed before it gets to hand. The rods should be proper for 8d. and 10 nails. All my effects will be to be delivered to Colo. Robert Gamble merchant in Richmd.

I shall be obliged to you for a line in answer to these particulars & am Sir your most obedt servt   Th: Jefferson

P.S. The boxes containing altogether books and furniture will require to be in the tightest vessel.

PrC (DLC); at foot of first page in ink: "Mr. Caleb Lownes." Tr (ViU: Edgehill-Randolph Papers); 19th-century copy.

Caleb Lownes (ca. 1754-ca. 1828), a Quaker iron merchant at 16 North Fourth Street and 21 South Wharves in Philadelphia, began his career as an engraver who in 1778 helped design a coat of arms for Pennsylvania that was used for almost a century before the state officially adopted it in 1875. Active in civic affairs, he became a penal reformer who in the 1790s played a leading role as a creator and administrator of the innovative state penitentiary on Walnut Street and served as secretary of the citizen's committee which cared for the sick during the 1793 yellow fever epidemic. Lownes was disowned by the Quakers for financial improprieties in 1809 and moved around 1814 to Vincennes, Indiana Territory, where he helped conduct government negotiations with the Piankashaw Indians in 1818 (Negley K. Teeters, "Caleb Lownes of Philadelphia: 1754-1828," *Prison Journal*, LXIII, No. 2 [1963], 1-12; Hardie, *Phila. Dir.*, 86; Robert L. Meriwether, W. Edwin Hemphill, Clyde N. Wilson, and others, eds., *The Papers of John C. Calhoun*, 22 vols. [Columbia, S.C., 1959-   ], II, 281, III, 72).

TJ purchased NAIL ROD from Lownes until he found him unreliable in his deliveries and switched suppliers in 1796 (TJ to James Madison, 24 Apr. 1796). This ONE TON order begins the history of the Monticello nailery. The most successful of TJ's efforts to find ways to supplement the agricultural profits of his Virginia estates, it operated more or less continuously from 1794 to 1812 and intermittently from 1815 to 1823. In its first decade it returned a handsome profit, but poor management, difficulty in obtaining payment from purchasers, and failures in the supply of nailrod eventually frustrated TJ's high hopes for the venture (MB, 3 Jan. 1794, and note; Betts, *Farm Book*, 426-53).

[1] Preceding five words interlined.
[2] TJ here canceled "more."
[3] Preceding four words interlined.

To Edmund Randolph

SIR   Philadelphia Dec. 18. 1793.

The Minister Plenipotentiary of France has inclosed to me the copy of a letter of the 16th. inst. which he addressed to you, stating that some libellous publications had been made against him by Mr. Jay, chief Justice of the US. and Mr. King one of the Senators for the state of New York, and desiring that they might be prosecuted. This letter has been laid before the President, according to the request of the Minister, and the President, never doubting your readiness on all occasions to[1] perform the functions of your office, yet thinks it incumbent on him to recommend it specially on the present occasion, as it concerns a public character peculiarly entitled to the protection of the laws. On the other hand, as our citizens ought not to be vexed with groundless prosecutions, duty to them requires it to be added, that if you judge the prosecution in question to be of that nature, you consider this recommendation as not extending to it; it's only object being to engage you to proceed in this case according to the duties of your office, the laws of the land and the privileges of the parties concerned. I have the honor to be with great respect & esteem Sir your most obedt. & most humble servt

TH: JEFFERSON

PrC (DLC); at foot of text: "The Attorney General of the US." PrC of Tr (DLC); in a clerk's hand. FC (Lb in DNA: RG 59, DL). Tr (DLC: Genet Papers). Enclosed in TJ to Edmond Charles Genet and to George Washington, both 18 Dec. 1793.

The President approved a draft of this letter and returned it to the Secretary of State this day (Washington, *Journal*, 269). TJ, however, remained unaware for at least two years that his communication to the Attorney General was partly responsible for eliciting a furious reaction from John Jay and Rufus King (Notes of a Conversation with Randolph, [after 15 Dec. 1795]). Later in the month, in order to enlist public support, Edmond Charles Genet published in Philadelphia newspapers seven letters relating to his demand that the Federal goverment prosecute the Chief Justice and the New York senator for libel for twice asserting in published statements that the French minister had threatened to appeal from the President to the American people during the *Little Sarah* affair in July 1793. Among these were the one to Randolph printed above and another of the same date from Randolph to Genet, also approved by the President, in which the Attorney General declined to prosecute Jay and King for libel but expressed confidence that Genet could find attorneys to pursue his suit (note to Proposed Public Statement on Edmond Charles Genet, [ca. 16 Dec. 1793]; enclosure to Genet's second letter to TJ, 16 Dec. 1793, and note; *Federal Gazette and Philadelphia Daily Advertiser* and *Gazette of the United States and Evening Advertiser*, both 24 Dec. 1793).

Angry at the apparent willingness of the Secretary of State and the Attorney General to allow Genet to take legal action against them, as well as at the President's seeming approval of this course, Jay and King wrote a sharply worded protest to Washington shortly before TJ retired from office on the last day of 1793. Treating TJ and Randolph with "much severity," Jay and King defended their conduct in the matter under dispute, complained about the President's sanction of the two letters in question, demanded that he require TJ to provide them with a certified copy of his 10 July 1793 memorandum on his conversation with Genet about the *Little Sarah* case, and asked for Washington's permission to publish it so that they could prove that Genet had indeed made the remark they had attributed to him and thereby defend themselves against his threatened libel suit. While Randolph urged the President to respond with a vigorous defense of the three high officials criticized by Jay and King, and while Alexander Hamilton counseled Washington to give the two irate Federalist leaders a copy of the memorandum they requested without conceding in any way the justice of their strictures against him, Henry Knox urged Jay and King to take back their letter and request a private meeting

with Washington to "heal the wound" it had opened. Although they refused to retract their letter, Jay and King did indicate their willingness to meet with the President if he invited them. At length, in a meeting with the Chief Justice arranged by the President, Washington defended himself against Jay and King's charges in their letter and expressed his belief that "nothing incorrect or unfriendly had been intended by Jefferson or Randolph" in theirs. In reply, Jay emphasized that he and King were entitled to a full disclosure of the facts about the French minister's threat to appeal to the American people and offered to give Washington the original draft of their letter to him in return for an authenticated copy of TJ's 10 July 1793 memorandum or at least of that part of it dealing with Genet's disputed remark.

In accordance with the President's acceptance of this arrangement, King on 20 Feb. 1794 delivered the draft to Washington, who allowed him to read "a paper in the President's handwriting justifying his conduct," after which Washington in King's presence burned his paper as well as the draft and the recipient's copy of the letter from Jay and King. On 3 Mch. 1794 the President met with King again and gave him a certificate containing the relevant extract from TJ's memorandum on the express condition that it was not to be published during his presidency unless "very imperious circumstances" made it necessary, and then only with his consent (Statement by King, Feb. 1794, King, *Life*, I, 476-8; Washington's Certificate to Jay and King, 3 Mch. 1794, with his condition subjoined, NjP: Andre deCoppet Collection). Jay and King did not have to make use of the certificate because Genet abandoned his plan to sue them for libel after the arrival of the four commissioners the French government had appointed to replace him, the first two of whom reached Philadelphia on the day Washington first met with King (King, *Life*, I, 478; Turner, *CFM*, 278-9, 308).

[1] TJ here canceled "comply with the duties."

To Samuel Ward & Brothers

GENTLEMEN   Philadelphia Dec. 18. 1793.

I have duly received your letter of the 16th. inst. and have communicated it to the President of the US. in order that such use may be made of your proposals as the future provisions of the legislature shall render expedient, these not having as yet furnished any grounds to act on it. I have the honor to be gentlemen Your most obedt. servt

TH: JEFFERSON

PrC (DLC); at foot of text: "Messrs. Samuel Ward & brothers. N. York." FC (Lb in DNA: RG 59, DL).

To George Washington

Dec. 18. 1793.

Th: Jefferson has the honor to submit to the President's approbation the draught of letters to Mr. Genet and the Atty. Genl. on the subject of the prosecution desired by the former to be instituted against Messrs. Jay and King.

He also incloses the form of a warrant for ₱2544.37 for the Director of the Mint for the purchase of copper.

RC (DNA: RG 59, MLR); addressed: "The Pres[. . .]"; endorsed by Bartholomew Dandridge, Jr. PrC (DLC). Tr (Lb in DNA: RG 59, SDC). Recorded in SJPL. Enclosures: (1) TJ to Edmond Charles Genet, 18 Dec. 1793. (2) TJ to Edmund Randolph, 18 Dec. 1793. (3) George Washington to Alexander Hamilton, 18 Dec. 1793: "Pay to the Director of the mint, for the purposes thereof two thousand five hundred and forty four dollars and thirty seven cents, on account" (PrC in DLC; in TJ's hand, unsigned; at foot of text: "The Secretary of the Treasury").

On this day the President returned the first two enclosures to TJ with his approval, while signing the third and sending it back to TJ for submission to the Department of the Treasury (Washington, *Journal*, 269).

From Charles Carter

DR SR   Fredbg Decr 19th 93

My son Charles will deliver this letter, who goes on in the stage, in consequence of a letter, by yesterdays post, from his Brother Walker, informing him you had a vacancy, in your Office, which he shoud fill, provided he coud go up, in a few Weeks. It gave me so much[1] satisfaction, to find my Friend would Take my son into his own imploy, that I determined he shoud proceed this day. To you my Friend I commit my Son, and flatter myself, youl find him a usefull young man, and worthy

[589]

of your Patronage. I was exceedingly concerned, to hear Chatham, say by a letter to Mansfield, you were to be in Virginia, early the next month, and it was thought you wou'd resign. But I now flatter myself, he was mistaken. With great regard and sincere thanks, for your kindness to my Son, I am Dr Sr Yr Affe & Obligd Hble St

CHS. CARTER

RC (MHi); endorsed by TJ as received 26 Dec. 1793 and so recorded in SJL.

On the day TJ received this letter he appointed Charles Landon Carter to a clerk-ship in the State Department (Memorandum Book of the Department of State, 26 Dec. 1793, DNA: RG 360, PCC).

[1] Preceding two words interlined.

From Thomas Mann Randolph, Jr.

DEAR SIR   Monticello Dec: 19: 1793

I received yesterday yours of the 8. inst: containing Mr. Le Roys letter of the 26. Nov. for the procurement and[1] communication of which I return you many thanks. It relieved me from an apprehension I had begun to entertain that the protested bill of Rosses might be in considerable part swallowed up by an open Accompt, in which case I might have suffered and an important credit, the price of Edgehill, would have been lost to my Fathers Estate. I am happy to feel that I stand on as good ground as the sufficiency of Mr. Ross alltho I do not believe it is perfectly sure.

I am still unlucky with respect to your letter containing instructions to me in this affair of the mortgage: at my request a memorandum concerning that packet was transmited to Mr. Davis by the Postmaster of Charlottesville: nevertheless it has failed to come: the new mail was delivered I suppose and brought away before the other was opened.

Your letter to Mr. Stewart was forwarded without delay. Mr. Biddle has prepared all things for the journey and will set out as soon as Mr. Stewart gives notice that the sheep are ready.

The threshing machine I shall take into particular care when I am in Richmond again, to which it cannot be long. A prospect-glass which came from Alexander Donald to you by Wm. Mewburn is lodged safe at Monticello.

We are all well. Martha and Maria both write. I am Dear Sir with the most sincere affection your friend & Servt.   TH: M. RANDOLPH

RC (MHi); endorsed by TJ as received 30 Dec. 1793 and so recorded in SJL.

THE POSTMASTER OF CHARLOTTESVILLE: Isaac Miller (MB, 2 Dec. 1794). The letters from MARTHA Jefferson Randolph and MARIA Jefferson mentioned here are not recorded in SJL and have not been found.

[1] Preceding two words interlined.

To George Washington

Dec. 19. 93.

Th: Jefferson has the honor to inclose to the President translations of papers received from Mr. Jaudenes. He submits whether it will not be proper to communicate them to Congress, as being nearly similar to those which closed the great communication on Spanish affairs. If the President thinks they should be sent in, Th:J. will have copies prepared.

RC (DNA: RG 59, MLR); addressed: "The Presi[. . .]"; endorsed by Bartholomew Dandridge, Jr. PrC (DLC). Tr (Lb in DNA: RG 59, SDC). Not recorded in SJL.

Enclosures: Josef de Jaudenes and Josef Ignacio de Viar to TJ, 18 Dec. 1793, and enclosures.

From William Frederick Ast

SIR   Richmond 20. Decr. 17[93]

Pray accept my warmest Thanks for Your kind wishes and good Counsels which Your very polite and esteemed favor of 14. Ulto. conveys to me. I shall esteem myself ever happy to cultivate so valuable an Acquaintance as Yours and use my utmost Endeavours to merit Your friendship. Should it ever lay in my power to be of Service to You I shall consider that as one of my happiest Moments.

I have finished three plans and hope to be at Philadelphia in about a fortnight hence—when I shall do myself the honor to wait upon You and shew You the same.

The first is Insurances on Houses, Goods, furniture &a. as mentioned to You before, and will, besides the Utility to the Inhabitants of the United States, keep about five hundred Thousand Dollars ℔ Annum in this Country.

The Second is Insurances on Vessels, which, besides the great Advantage it will give the Shipping of the United States over other Nations, it will keep upwards of Two Millions of Dollars ℔ Annum in this Country which [are?] now paid abroad and chiefly to the British.

The Third is Insurances on Goods and freights, which we shall do here for less Premiums a great deal more secure and keep upwards of Three Millions of Dollars ℔ Annum in this Country which now annually are paid abroad. And this last plan will besides that give a Revenue to Government of upwards of Two Millions of Dollars ℔ Annum— without laying a Tax on the Inhabitants of the United States. They are the profits which the Underwriters abroad have hitherto enjoyed.

These plans are such that they may be very readily and easily put into

Execution. I take upon my self to put them, under the Auspices of Government, into Execution and stake my Life for their Solidity.

What I mean by the Auspices of Government is Protection and Support of Laws—we don't want any Money of Government for the Execution of them.

No doubt the Members of Congress are patriots and as such they will not hesitate to adopt these plans and grant me patents which secure to me the Annuity which I ask—it is trifling to the Nation considering the Utility of my plans and the Money saved to this Country ℔ Annum. The Annuity which I ask will be paid me by those who benefit by my pl[ans.]

A few days ago I had the pleasure to see Madam Barclay and her sweet family. I mention'd that I should have the honor to write to You. She desires her best respects. I have the honor to be very respectfully Sir Your most obedient & very humble Servant   WILLIAM AST

RC (MHi); torn in several places; addressed: "The Honble. Thos. Jefferson Esqr. Secretary of State Philadelphia"; stamped and postmarked; endorsed by TJ as received 30 Dec. 1793 and so recorded in SJL.

From Edmond Charles Genet

MONSIEUR

Philadelphie le 20. xbre. 1793
l'an 2e de la République Fse.

Je reçois votre lettre du 16 de ce mois et j'ai l'honneur de remercier par votre canal le Président des Etats Unis de l'intention qu'il temoigne de mettre au grand jour une intrigue atroce dont le but a été de l'induire en erreur et de l'engager dans des démarches précipitées contre l'Exécuteur des ordres de la Nation française et de détruire par là la bonne intelligence qui règne Si heureusement entre nos deux Républiques.

Je ne saurais vous exprimer la profonde douleur avec laquelle je vois Se développer de jour en jour le fil d'une trame aussi noire, et je vous avoue qu'en qualifiant mes justes poursuites des mots "*groundless prosecutions*" vous me paraissez avoir oublié que je dois venger mon Souverain du tort que l'on a fait à Ses intérets, par cette Serie monstrueuse de mensonges, de certificats imposteurs, et de bruits absurdes au moyen desquels on a fasciné pendant quelque tems l'esprit public et peut être ebranlé l'alliance de deux Peuples que tout invite à S'aimer et à S'unir.

S'il existe un crime de Lèze Nation Monsieur, c'est bien celui dont je me plains et dont les auteurs doivent être livrés à la Loi devant laquelle j'imagine que chez vous comme chez nous tous les hommes Sont égaux.

FC (DLC: Genet Papers); in a clerk's hand, unsigned; above salutation: "Le Ministre Plenipotentiaire de la République française à Monsieur jefferson Secretaire d'Etat des E.U." Recorded in SJL as received 20 Dec. 1793. Translation printed in *Federal Gazette and Philadelphia Daily Advertiser*, 24 Dec. 1793.

The LETTRE in question was actually TJ's letter to Genet of 18 Dec. 1793.

From Edmond Charles Genet

M.   Philadelphie le 20. xbre. 1793. l'an 2e. de la Repe. fse.

J'ai l'honneur de porter à la Connoissance du gouvernement federal le fait suivant.

Tout étoit disposé à Baltimore pour le départ de quelques batiments Marchands que J'étois parvenu à faire charger de[1] marchandises nécessaires à la france;[2] Ils n'attendoient que quelques pieces d'artillerie destinées à leur défense. La frégatte qui devoit les éscorter étoit complettement armée et organisée, et Je concevois l'ésperance de voir bientôt s'effectuer cette éxpedition importante lorsqu'un incident[3] auquel Je ne me serois point attendu a tout suspendu. Mr. hollingsworth procureur gal. de l'Etat en vertu d'Instructions directes qu'il prétend avoir recues du President des Etats unis a fait suspendre sous peine de prison les travaux des ouvriers employés à la construction[4] des affuts destinés aux navires marchands et a déclaré au Vice Consul qu'il avoit ordre de s'opposer à toute éspece d'armement.

Quand cessera-t-on donc, Mr., de nous accabler d'injustices de contrarier tout ce qui peut être utile à notre patrie et d'élever sans cesse devant nous des difficultés qu'aucune loi des Etats unis qu'aucune décision même du gouvernement federal ne Justifie?

Dft (DLC: Genet Papers); unsigned; above salutation: "Le Cit Genet Mtre. &c à Mr. Jefferson secretaire d'Etat &c." Recorded in SJL as received 23 Dec. 1793.

INSTRUCTIONS . . . DU PRESIDENT: presumably the rules on neutrality previously approved by the President and the Cabinet, which forbade the original arming and equipping of belligerent vessels in American ports for offensive or defensive purposes

(Rules on Neutrality, 3 Aug. 1793, and note).

[1] Preceding four words interlined in place of "par des moyens personnels."

[2] Remainder of sentence written in the margin.

[3] Clause to this point altered from "elle n'attendoit que mes derniers ordres ⟨lorsqu'un⟩ lorsque deux incidents."

[4] Altered from "suspendre les travaux."

From Edmond Charles Genet

         Philadelphie le 20. xbre 1793.

MONSIEUR   l'an 2e. de la Repe. fse. une et Indivisible

La franchise, la Candeur,[1] et la publicité étant[2] les seules bases de la politique de la france devenue[3] libre et le secret de ceux qui dirigent ses affaires aujourdhui[4] étant de n'en avoir aucun[5] Je vous ai annoncé[6] que Je ferois imprimer non seulement ma Correspondance avec le gouvernement federal; mais aussi les instructions qui m'ont été données par le Conseil èxécutif de la Repe. fse. L'impression de ma Correspondance n'est point achevée, mais celle de la traduction de mes Instructions l'étant Je[7] m'empresse de vous en envoyer deux cents éxemplaires[8] en vous priant de requerir Mr. le President des Etats unis de vouloir bien les faire distribuer aux differents membres du Congrès et d'en donner communication officielle aux deux Chambres de ce Corps legislatif. Cette premiere partie du recueil que Je vous annonce et que Je vous ferai parvenir successivement[9] mettra les representants du peuple Americain à portée de Juger si ma Conduite politique depuis que Je reside dans les Etats unis a été conforme aux Intentions du peuple françois; cette démarche que Je dois à ma patrie, [10] étant faite laissant à vos sages législateurs le Soin de prendre sur les points qui sont en négociation entre nous les mesures que l'interêt des Etats unis leur paroitra éxiger[11] Il ne me restera plus qu'à poursuivre dans vos tribunaux les auteurs et complices de cette trame odieuse de cette serie monstrueuse de mensonges de certificats imposteurs de bruits absurdes au moyen des quels[12] on a fasciné pendant quelque tems l'esprit public[13] et induit en erreur votre premier Magistrat[14] dans la vue d'ébranler et de détruire peut être l'alliance de deux peuples que tout invite à s'aimer et à s'unir dans un moment où le danger le plus imminent[15] pese également sur l'un et sur l'autre. Agréés mon respect.   G

Dft (DLC: Genet Papers); at head of text: "Lettre qui doit servir d'avant propos à ma Correspondance"; above salutation: "Le Cit Genet &c à Mr Jefferson secretaire d'Etat des Etats unis de l'amerique." FC (same); consists of fair copy of Dft in a clerk's hand, with revisions by Genet recorded in note 12 below. Recorded in SJL as received 28 Dec. 1793. Enclosure: *Correspondence*, 1-9, consisting of "Instructions to Citizen Genet, Minister Plenipotentiary from the French Republic to the United States, from The Executive Council, and Minister of Marine," being five documents: instructions of the Provisional Executive Council of France to Genet, 4 Jan. 1793; extract of supplementary instructions from same to same, 17 Jan. 1793; Minister of Marine Gaspard Monge to Genet, 8 Feb. 1793; Minister of Marine Jean Dalbarade to Genet, 28 May 1793; and letter of credence of the Provisional Executive Council of France to Genet, 30 Dec. 1792 (for the

last, see enclosure to Genet to TJ, 16 May 1793). Translation with variations printed in *Correspondence*, [ii-iii]; printed in French from draft in *Correspondence*, [3-4].

As indicated above, Genet used this letter as a preface to his highly selective English and French editions of his diplomatic correspondence with the Secretary of State, which he introduced with redacted texts of his instructions. Though he enclosed here only the translation of the latter, in both editions Genet silently omitted all passages in the Provisional Executive Council's main instructions relating to French plans to liberate Canada and Louisiana, as well as those in the supplementary directives about French supporters in the American government and French plans for enlisting Indians to fight against the British and the Spanish. He also artfully softened sections of the supplementary instructions dealing with French privateering in the United

States and urging the need for him to show moderation and circumspection in treating with the American government (Turner, *CFM*, 201-11).

¹ Genet here canceled "l'honnêteté."
² Genet here canceled "actuelle."
³ Word interlined.
⁴ Word written in the margin.
⁵ Translation in *Correspondence*: "the mysterious secrecy of courts being entirely rejected from her councils and the only art of her public agents being that of using none."
⁶ Genet here canceled "dans ma lettre du ."
⁷ Sentence to this point written in the margin in place of "ce recueil n'est point," which Genet had first substituted in the margin for a passage that in its final form read: "Je ferai paroitre ce recueil par cahiers et mon premier soin sera de vous en envoyer un certain nombre d'éxemplaires que Je prierai le President des Etats unis de vouloir bien mettre sous les yeux du Congrès."
⁸ Translation in *Correspondence*: "I hasten to enclose to you copies of them."

⁹ Preceding seven words written in the margin.
¹⁰ Preceding six words written in the margin.
¹¹ Genet first wrote "faite abandonnant à vos sages législateurs le soin de décider cette importante question" and then altered it to read as above.
¹² Genet here canceled "comme Je ne saurois trop vous le répéter," a passage retained in the FC and canceled again there by him. In the FC Genet also altered the passage preceding it to read "de la trame odieuse, qui a été ourdie contre moi et au moyen de la quelle."
¹³ Passage from "cette trame odieuse" translated in *Correspondence* as "the odious and vile machinations that have been plotted against me by means of a series of impostures which for a while have fascinated the minds of the public."
¹⁴ Translation in *Correspondence*: "even your first magistrate."
¹⁵ Genet first wrote "s'aimer à s'unir pour resister au danger qui" and then altered it to read as above.

To Charles André Kierrulf

SIR   Philadelphia Dec. 20. 1793.

The President has referred to me the letter you wrote him inclosing a paper addressed to Congress, which I have now the honor to return to you. Your late arrival in this country is a sufficient cause of your mistaking the mode of conveying this paper to Congress, which cannot be through the President. I take the liberty of advising you to apply to some member of that body who will be able to judge of it's contents, and to do in it whatever these shall render proper. I have the honor to be Sir Your most obedt servt   TH: JEFFERSON

PrC (DLC); at foot of text: "Mr. Charles Andre Kienulf." FC (Lb in DNA: RG 59, DL).

Charles André Kierrulf, a self-described expatriate Swede then residing in Philadelphia who claimed to be a pensioner of the Empress of Russia, had written a LETTER to the President of 10 Dec. 1793 praising him in pretentious and illiterate French and enclosing a PAPER, not found, soliciting "the patronage of Congress, as a Professor of Moral Philosophy, in some public seminary of learning." Around the same time Kierrulf sent the President an undated letter requesting an interview, stating that he held republican principles and had committed no crimes, maintaining that his pension demonstrated the beneficent humanity of Catherine II in the face of political acts forced on her by Russian aristocrats, and promising to reveal more when they met (RCs in DNA: RG 59, MLR). On 7 Apr. 1794 the House of Representatives read and tabled this or a later version of Kierrulf's petition (JHR, II, 113-14).

From Joseph Leacock

DEAR SIR   [ca. 20 Dec. 1793]

Distress impelld me lately to write a few lines to you, entreating a little help from your benevolent hand to enable me to live thro this winter, when, I hope to be able (on the return of Spring) to subsist on the Emoluments of my little office. I mentioned the cause of my present distress, ie, the stop put to business by the raging Calamity. I have grown old and grievously afflicted in body, indigent and in want of daily comforts. I am dear sir, your sincere well wisher & hum servt.

JOSEPH LEACOCK

NB I have enclosed a few hasty crude thoughts respecting the Algerines.

RC (DLC: TJ Papers, 96: 16501); undated; addressed: "Thomas Jefferson Esquire"; endorsed by TJ as received 20 Dec. 1793 and so recorded in SJL.

ENCLOSURE

Joseph Leacock's Thoughts on the Algerines

Reflection—'tis but little more than a Century ere a human-creature inhabited the Country now possessed by the war like Algerines—[a?] perfect sandy desert, where, a few out Law'd banditti-Turks sat down to exist on what they might procure from the sea, by plunder. It was not long, ere they saw the advantage of an intercourse with the British Garrison of Gibralter on the opposite coast, and, having discover'd the interiour part of the Country fertile, created a hope of their becoming useful in supplying the English on their barren-rock with vegitables and fresh provisions, of which they were Entirely destitute, and, thro great industry, in a little time raised a supply, with which, they ventured to approach that Garrison in their boats, and, calling out to the sentinel in broken English "you wantee de fowl, de sheep, de green a." Ay Ay, roared out the sentinel, 'tis the very thing we require, for we poor soldiers are all dying with the scurvy, pass on, pass on, and welcome.

A hearty reception being given them by the Commander in Chief, a generous price paid for the supplys, and a cordial invitation to return as often as they pleased, soon Created a mutual intercourse, and this was the origin of that accursed connection between Britain and the Algerines! and, 'twas not long, ere Britain discover'd the benefit they might derive by Encouraging those Robbers and Employing them as their bull-dogs. For this purpose Engineers were sent to Examine the Coast for a place to fortify, and having reported the bay of

Algiers might be made impregnable, immediate orders were given to set about the work, and, this being Effected by the *generous* Britains, a mutual compact was Entered into, to aid and assist each other, and, in so Jesuitical a manner, as not to be developed. A wheel within a wheel, misterious and incomprehensible. 'Tis in the power of Britain when Ever they please, to set their Towzers on, to worry whom they please! and not satisfyd with setting the Algerines on us by water, but the savages by Land to murderd our back inhabitants!

Rouze from your Lethargy ye brave Americans, and put a stop to the Cursed combination of Despots. The bull-dogs of Algiers are let loose upon you. Let it not be said you are to be Cowed by such villians or their mean spirited abettors. Your prowess was once successfully display'd against a powerful-Nation, therefore, fear not to face a few Pyratical-slaves. Ah, but 'tis said, every enemy carried into Algiers is made a slave of! Well, be it so, you know your fate, therefore, never submit, but stick to the Rascals as long as your ship can swim, a man left alive, or a shot in the Locker. I know your spirit and address in the art of war is far superiour to theirs, and that victory and glory will be your reward. Let but a douzen stout ships well mannd, sail in concert to meet those marauders and they'l quickly take refuge in Algiers, where you may penn them up as long as you please to lay before that hornets-nest. Exert yourselves instantly, and let the world see what Americans are capable of doing when oppressed!

NB. An Englishman (who is fearful his only son is now a slave in Algiers) was heard to say "by the God that made me, could I get at Mr. Pit, I wou'd, without hesitation, blow the murderers brains out, be the consequence what it might!"

MS (DLC: TJ Papers, 96: 16502); entirely in Leacock's hand; undated; torn; closing quotation mark supplied.

From Thomas Mifflin

SIR   Philada., 20th: Decr. 1793.

I think it proper to communicate to you, the answer which I have received to the letter, that I addressed to the French Minister, relative to the case of the French Sailors that are confined in the Jail of Philadelphia, particularly as it contains a request, which I do not, at this time, think myself authorised to grant. I shall be happy, however, to know the sentiments of the General Government on the subject. I am, with great esteem, Sir, Your mo: obedt. Servt: THOMAS MIFFLIN

FC (PHarH: Secretary's Letterbooks); at foot of text: "To Thomas Jefferson, Esqr, Secretary of State." Enclosure: Edmond Charles Genet to Mifflin, 16 Dec. 1793, thanking him for his role in the arrest of the faithless deserters and for his willingness to assist in the future, and advising that he will shortly take advantage of his good offices to transport them under a secure guard to New York, where they will be placed under arrest on the *Normande* and to which port he would have brought them sooner had he not feared their presence there would create disturbances (Tr in DNA: RG 59, MLR; in French; on verso: "Copy"). Enclosed in TJ to George Washington, 21 Dec. 1793.

Notes on the Proclamation of Neutrality and the Law of Nations

Dec. 20. 1793. A doubt being entertained whether the use of the word *modern* as applied to the *law of nations* in the president's proclamation be not inconsistent with ground afterwards taken in a letter to Genet, I will state the matter while it is fresh in my mind, beginning it from an early period.

It cannot be denied that according to the general law of nations the goods of an enemy are lawful prize in the bottom of a friend, and the goods of a friend privileged in the bottom of an enemy; or in other words that *the goods follow the owner*. The inconvenience of this principle in subjecting neutral vessels to vexatious searches at sea, has for more than a century rendered it usual for nations to substitute a *conventional* principle[1] *that the goods shall follow the bottom* instead of the *natural* one before mentioned. France had done it in all her treaties; so I believe had Spain before the American revolution. Britain had not done it. When that war had involved those powers, Russia foreseeing that her commerce would be much harrassed by the British ships engaged Denmark, Sweden, and Portugal to arm, and to declare that the conventional principle should be observed by the powers at war towards neutrals, and that they would make common cause against the party who should violate it; declaring expressly at the same time that that convention should be in force only during the war then existing. Holland acceded to the convention, and Britain instantly attacked her. But the other neutral powers did not think proper to comply with their stipulation of making common cause. France declared at once that she would conform to the conventional principle: this in fact imposed no new obligation on her; for she was already bound by her treaties with all those powers to observe that principle. Spain made the same declaration. Congress gave similar orders to their vessels. But Congress afterwards gave instructions to their ministers abroad not to engage them in any future[2] combination of powers for the general enforcement of the conventional principle that goods should[3] follow the bottom, as this might at some time or other engage them in a war for other nations, but to introduce the principle separately with every nation by the treaties they were authorized to make with each. It had been already done with France and Holland, and it was afterwards done with Prussia, and made a regular part in every treaty they proposed to others. After the war, Great Britain established it between herself and France. When she engaged in the present[4] war with France, it was thought extremely desireable for us to get this principle admitted by her, and, hoping that as she

[598]

had acceded to it in one instance, she might be induced to admit it as a principle now settled by the common consent of nations, (for every nation belligerent or neutral had stipulated it on one or more occasions) that she might be induced to consider it as now become a *conventional* law of nations, I proposed to insert the word *modern* in the proclamation, to open upon her the idea that we should require the acquiescence in that principle as the condition of our remaining in peace. It was thought desireable by the other gentlemen, but having no expectation of any effect from it, they acquiesced in the insertion of the word merely[5] to gratify me.—I had another view, which I did not mention to them, because I apprehended it would occasion the loss of the word. By the antient law of nations, e.g. in the time of the Romans, the furnishing a limited[6] aid of troops, tho' stipulated, was deemed a cause of war. In latter times it is admitted not to be a cause of war. This is one of the improvements in the law of nations. I thought we might conclude by parity of reasoning that the guaranteeing a limited portion of territory, in a stipulated case, might not by the *modern* law of nations be a cause of war. I therefore meant by the introduction of that word to lay the foundation of the execution of our guarantee by way of negociation with Engld. The word was therefore introduced, and a strong letter was written to Mr. Pinckney to observe to Gr. Britain that we were bound by our treaties with the other belligerent powers to observe certain principles during this war, that we were willing to observe the same principles towards her, and indeed that we considered it as essential to[7] proceed by the same rule to all, and to propose to her to select those articles concerning our conduct in a case of our neutrality from any one of our treaties which she pleased or that we would take those from her own treaty with France, and make a temporary convention of them for the term of the present war; and he was instructed to press this strongly. I told Genet that we had done this. But instead of giving us time to work our principle into effect by negociation, he immediately took occasion in a letter to threaten that if we did not resent the conduct of the British in taking French property in American bottoms, and protect their goods by *effectual measures* (meaning by arms) he would[8] give directions that the principle of our treaty of goods following the bottom should be disregarded. He was at the same time in the habit of keeping our goods taken in British bottoms; so that they were to take the gaining alternative of each principle, and give us the losing one. It became necessary to oppose this in the answer to his letter, and it was impossible to do it soundly but by placing it on it's true ground, to wit, that the law of nations established as a general rule that *goods should follow the owner*, and that the making them *follow the vessel* was an exception depending on special conventions in those cases only where the convention had

been made. That the exception had been established by us in our treaties with France, Holland and Prussia, and that we should endeavor to
extend it to England, Spain, and other powers; but that till it was done,
we had no right to make war for the enforcement of it. He thus obliged
us to abandon in the first moment the ground we were endeavoring to
gain that is to say his ground against England and Spain[9] and to take the
very ground of Engld. and Spain against him.[10]—This was my private
reason for proposing the term *modern* in the proclamation, that it might
reserve us a ground to obtain the very things he wanted. But the world,
who knew nothing of these private reasons, were to understand by the
expression the *modern law of nations*, that law with all the improvements and mollifications of it which an advancement of civilization in
modern times has introduced. It does not mean strictly[11] any thing
which is not a part of the *law of nations*[12] in *modern* times, and therefore
could not be inconsistent with the ground taken in the letter to Genet,
which was that of the *law of nations*, and by no means could be equivalent to a declaration by the President of the specific principle that *goods
should follow the bottom*.

MS (DLC); entirely in TJ's hand. PrC (DLC). Entry in SJPL: "Note. on use of word *Modern* in the proclamn."

TJ was prompted to set down these notes by the appearance in this day's *Dunlap and Claypoole's American Daily Advertiser* of a letter from "A Farmer" to Edmond Charles Genet that took sharp exception to the in-dictment of the French minister's diplo-matic conduct in the Secretary of State's 16 Aug. 1793 letter to Gouverneur Morris, which had been printed in the same newspa-per three days before. The writer particu-larly criticized TJ's explanation to Morris, first expressed IN A LETTER TO GENET of 24 July 1793, of the Washington administra-tion's response to the French minister's charge that during the current European war the United States had abandoned the principle that free ships made free goods, under which French property carried by a neutral vessel was not lawful prize. Ques-tioning the relationship between TJ's state-ment to Morris and the phrase in the PRESI-DENT'S PROCLAMATION of Neutrality of 22 Apr. 1793 warning American citizens not to provide the belligerents with articles "deemed contraband by the *modern* usage of nations," the author wrote: "I am particu-larly diverted with his 5th point of differ-ence, and want extremely, in addition to the

learning displayed to prove that free bot-toms, do *not, now* make free goods, to know why the word modern was printed in Italics, or printed at all, in the proclamation, what occasioned an alteration of the sentiments, that *hint* was intended to convey? Or, that notable discovery that a retainer of part of the Law of Nations, was a disclaimer of the remainder?" For the wording of the Procla-mation of Neutrality, see the broadside il-lustrated in Volume 25 of this series; on its issuance, see Cabinet Opinion on Washing-ton's Questions on Neutrality and the Alli-ance with France, [19 Apr. 1793], and note.

The 9 July 1780 CONVENTION among Russia, Denmark, and Norway establishing the League of Armed Neutrality, docu-ments pertaining to the adherence of Swe-den, Portugal, and Holland to the League, and the statements supporting the League's principles by France and Spain are in James B. Scott, ed., *The Armed Neutralities of 1780 and 1800* (New York, 1918), 299-304, 318-23, 325-8, 329-30, 420-3. On 5 Oct. 1780 CONGRESS ordered the Board of Admiralty to prepare instructions directing all armed vessels commissioned by the United States to conform to the principles respecting neutral ships set forth in the convention, but on 12 June 1783 it in-structed the American peace commission-ers in Paris, "in case they should comprise in the definitive treaty any stipulations amounting to a recognition of the rights of neutral nations, to avoid accompanying them by any engagements which shall oblige the contracting parties to support those stipulations by arms" (JCC, XVIII, 905, XXIV, 394). For expressions of the PRINCIPLE that free ships made free goods in American commercial TREATIES with France, the Netherlands, and Prussia, see Miller, *Treaties*, II, 21, 70, 170-1. GREAT BRITAIN ESTABLISHED the same principle in its 1786 treaty of commerce with France (Clive Parry, ed., *The Consolidated Treaty Series*, 231 vols. [Dobbs Ferry, N.Y., 1969-81], L, 83).

TJ's STRONG LETTER to Thomas PINCK-NEY was dated 20 Apr. 1793. Genet TOOK OCCASION IN A LETTER to TJ of 9 July 1793 to make the threat described above.

¹ TJ here canceled "that free bottom."
² Word interlined.
³ Word interlined.
⁴ Word interlined in place of "late."
⁵ Word interlined.
⁶ Word interlined in place of "fixed."
⁷ TJ here canceled "do the same."
⁸ TJ here canceled "declare."
⁹ Preceding ten words interlined.
¹⁰ Preceding two words interlined.
¹¹ Word interlined.
¹² TJ here canceled "even."

From Edmond Charles Genet

Philadelphie Le 21. Décembre. [1793]
M   L'an 2e. de la République française.

J'ai reçû la Lettre que vous m'avéz fait l'honneur de m'ecrire le 6. de ce mois ainsi que le rapport du secretaire de la Tresorerie qui y étoit joint.

Il resulte de ce rapport que sur une erreur accidentelle, on a compromis les intérêts de la République françoise et le Caractère de son représentant par le refus d'accepter des traites délivrées à nos fournisseurs Sur des sommes dües à la République. Une pareille mesure méritait à ce qu'il me semble l'attention la plus serieuse et Je ne sais de quel nom appeller la négligence qui a été commise à cet égard. Il est aisé de sentir que si l'erreur a été rectifiée le tort qu'elle nous a fait n'a pas pû l'être de même. Cet évenement a fourni aux malveillans et aux Ennemis de la République un moyen puissant de nuire à Sa cause, en effrayant les négocians et en ruinant notre credit. Ces effets malheureux que les Circonstances ont encore aggravés, n'ajoutent pas peu aux desagrements qui ont été multipliés autour de moi.

Le secretaire de la Trésorerie paroit Surpris, Mr., que J'aye tiré sans l'en prévenir Sur les fonds dus à la france en janvier prochain. Je vous observerai à cet égard.

1°. que les 300,000.ᵗᵗ dûs au 1er. Janvier Sont les interêts du Prêt de 6. millions fait par la france aux Etats unis en 1783. que les remboursemens de cet emprunt ne doivent commencer qu'en 1797. et qu'en conséquence je ne vois aucun motif qui puisse arrêter le payement de l'Interêt de cette somme à l'époque stipulée Tant qu'il en Sera dû à la france une équivalente.

2°. qu'en Supposant que les payemens effectués par la Tresorerie jusqu'a ce moment cy excedassent le montant des sommes dües, J'ai toujours été fermement convaincû que ces avances aux quelles les besoins urgens de la france l'avoient forcé de recourir, Seroient imputées à l'extinction de la dette prise en totalité. Cette mesure est parfaitement d'accord avec la clause inserée dans les différens Contrats qui portent que les Etats unis pourront S'ils le jugent à propos Se liberer plutôt qu'aux époques fixées par les dits Contracts.

Ce n'est M., qu'avec douleur que je me rappelle la conduite qui a été Tenüe à notre égard relativement aux négociations dont J'étois chargé pour le remboursement de la dette des Etats unis envers la république. Je n'ai caché au gouvernement féderal aucun de nos besoins. Je lui ai remis mes Instructions il y a vû que notre République S'en reposait pour assurer une partie de sa subsistance et celle de ses Colonies Sur la fraternité de la nation Américaine, qu'elle offroit en conséquence au gouvernement féderal plusieurs moyens de s'acquitter à notre égard des devoirs de la reconnoissance en Venant à notre secours au moment du danger, qu'enfin elle lui laissoit le Choix des moyens.

Je crois inutile de vous rappeller, M., la reponse du gouvernement fédéral à mes propositions; mais Lorsque d'après cette réponse Je lui ai fait part de la nécessité où j'étois de faire usage de la seule mesure qu'il m'eut laissée en déléguant une partie de la dette américaine, un refus d'enregistrer mes délégations que l'on a eu soin de divulguer[1] est Venu entraver cette opération, Semer l'alarme et la méfiance parmi nos fournisseurs et m'ôter le pouvoir de remplir les engagemens que les dépenses Enormes dont Je suis Chargé m'avoient forcé de prendre.

Il est temps, M., de faire cesser l'Etat précaire et Tourmentant dans lequel on laisse le representant de la nation française. Je l'attends de la justice du gouvernement féderal, Je le demande au nom de la République française dont les besoins S'augmentent chaque jour, au nom des ses braves deffenseurs dont la subsistance est confiée à mes soins. Je vous Prie en Conséquence de vouloir bien mettre le plutôt possible sous les yeux de M. le Président la demande suivante.

1°. que l'Etat de situation des Etats unis envers la france, Soit presenté sous Le plus court delai possible.

2°. que Les sommes qui auront pû être avancées à la france audelà de Celles qui étoient éxigibles aux termes des Contrats Soyent attribûées à l'Extinction de la dette prise en Totalité.

3°. que provisoirement et en attendant que la situation des Etats unis envers la république soit arrêtée, le Secretaire de la Tresorerie Soit autorisé à enregistrer les délégations que je serai dans le Cas de fournir jusqu'a concurrence de 5 millions tournois, les quelles délégations Seront affectées Sur les premieres rentrees de fonds qui seront opérées en faveur de la france, aux Epoques dont il Sera Convenu.

Dft (DLC: Genet Papers); partially dated; in a clerk's hand, with revisions by Genet; above salutation: "Le Ministre de la République française à M. Jefferson Secretaire d'Etat des Etats unis"; only the most significant emendation has been noted below. Tr (AMAE: CPEU, Supplément, xx); with one minor variation; certified by Genet. Recorded in SJL as received 23 Dec. 1793.

For the Washington administration's response to Genet's complaints, see Alexan-

der Hamilton to TJ, 23 Dec. 1793, and note. JE LUI AI REMIS MES INSTRUCTIONS: see Genet to TJ, 22 May 1793 (third letter), and note. LA REPONSE DU GOUVERNEMENT FÉDÉRAL À MES PROPOSITIONS: TJ to Genet, 11 June 1793, and enclosure. JE LUI AI FAIT PART DE LA NÉCESSITÉ: see Genet to TJ, 11 Nov., 14 Nov. (fourth letter), and 15 Nov. 1793 (second letter).

[1] Preceding eight words written in the margin.

From Edmond Charles Genet

M.   Philadelphie le 21. xbre 1793. l'an 2e. de la Repe. fse.

Je Joins ici les nouvelles Commissions de Vice Consul pour les Cit. Chervi et Pennevert. Je vous prie de vouloir bien les mettre sous les yeux du President des Etats unis à l'effet d'obtenir son éxequatur. Agréés mon respect.

Dft (DLC: Genet Papers); unsigned; above salutation: "Le Cit Genet &c à M. Jefferson &c." Recorded in SJL as received 23 Dec. 1793. Enclosures: (1) Commission for Citizen Chervi as French vice-consul at

Alexandria, [18] Dec. 1793. (2) Commission for Citizen Pennevert as French vice-consul at New London, 18 Dec. 1793 (Trs in DNA: RG 59, NFC; in French; endorsed by George Taylor, Jr.).

To Josef de Jaudenes and Josef Ignacio de Viar

GENTLEMEN   Philadelphia December 21. 1793.

I have to acknowledge the receipt of your favors of November 30. and December 13. which have been laid before the President, to whom every evidence of a disposition in your agents to keep the Indians in peace gives real satisfaction. It is a conduct, which if pursued with good faith both by Spain and us, will add to the prosperity of both, and to the preservation and happiness of the Indians. The event which is said to have taken place at the Hanging Maw's, wears a complexion to meet the most entire disapprobation of the United States. It is not yet however so developed in all its circumstances as to authorize me to express their definitive judgment on it. This will be the office of the Court before whom prosecutions were immediately instituted against the persons charged with the fact.[1] I may say with safety in the mean while, that they will approve at no time of any act, which shall be either aggressive or unjust towards our Indian neighbors. I flatter myself that your residence among us, must have convinced you, that atrocities of the nature of those charged on that occasion, are not in the spirit of our Government, and must have satisfied you how groundless is the base calumny repeated by the Governor of Louisiana, of a reward of 500 dollars offered for the head of an individual *by the Americans*, if by that term he means those in authority; and if he means unauthorized individuals, it would hardly seem to justify his very general invective.

This officer undertakes too in a case of hostilities between us and the Indians to decide, that we are the aggressors, and that Spain, a neutral nation, may furnish them with arms and ammunition.

His remonstrating against the passage of our citizens along the Mississippi, even above the 31st: degree, and his appropriating to Spain, Nations of Indians inhabiting above the same limit, will not be noticed at a moment when a higher solution of those questions is expected. Till then we rely on the justice of Your Government, and your own dispositions to inculcate[2] it, that your agents will be inhibited from taking any part between us and the Indians, inconsistent with the friendship which we hope will ever prevail between us; and which we shall endeavour sincerely to cultivate by every act of justice and good neighborhood. I have the honor to be with great esteem & respect Gentlemen Your most obedient, and Most humble servant

PrC (DLC); in a clerk's hand, unsigned; at foot of first page: "Messrs: Jaudenes & Viar." PrC of Dft (DLC); in a clerk's hand, unsigned, with revisions by TJ and George Taylor, Jr. (see notes below). Tr (DNA: RG 46, Senate Records, 3d Cong., 1st sess.). FC (Lb in DNA: RG 59, DL). Tr (MHi); 19th-century copy. Tr (AHN: Papeles de Estado, legajo 3895 bis); in Spanish; attested by Jaudenes and Viar. Enclosed in George Washington to the Senate and the House of Representatives, 23 Dec. 1793.

The letter of DECEMBER 13 was actually dated 18 Dec. 1793.

[1] Preceding sentence written in ink by George Taylor, Jr., at the foot of the first page of PrC of Dft and keyed for insertion here.

[2] Word interlined in ink by TJ in PrC of Dft in place of "cultivate."

To Thomas Mifflin

SIR   Philadelphia Dec. 21. 1793.

I am honored with your's of yesterday's date relative to the French sailors in the jail of Philadelphia. The object of the original enquiry I took the liberty of making on that subject, was to know whether they were in the custody of the Executive or the Judiciary authority of the country: and being informed that it is in that of the Judiciary, the Federal Executive does not think itself authorized to interfere either as to their enlargement or detention. They take for granted the judge will do in the case what the law enjoins. I have the honor to be with great respect Your Excellency's most obedt & most humble servt

TH: JEFFERSON

RC (NjP: Andre deCoppet Collection); addressed: "His Excellency Governor Mifflin"; endorsed by Mifflin. PrC (DLC). FC (Lb in DNA: RG 59, DL). Tr (PHarH: Secretary's Letterbooks). Tr (MHi); 19th-century copy. Enclosed in TJ to George Washington, 21 Dec. 1793.

The President approved this letter and returned it to TJ on 23 Dec. 1793 (Washington, *Journal*, 272).

From Murray & Mumford

SIR   New York Decr. 21st. 1793

We are authorised by Messrs. Marshal Jenkins & Son of Hudson, to acquaint you, that if our government intend building vessels of War to defend the commerce of the United States, that they will contract to build a frigate; and will transmit the terms, on our receiving information officially at any time hereafter, that such a measure is necessary. We are very respectfully sir Yr. most obedt: servts   MURRAY & MUMFORD

RC (DNA: RG 59, MLR); at head of text: "Thomas Jefferson Esqr."; endorsed by TJ as received 24 Dec. 1793 and so recorded in SJL.

Murray & Mumford was a New York mercantile firm located at 94 Wall Street that specialized in East Indian tea. The partners, who lived at 162 William Street and 399 Pearl Street respectively, were John B.

Murray, an English immigrant, and John P. Mumford (d. 1821), who came from Newport, Rhode Island, and subsequently headed several insurance companies (William Duncan, *The New-York Directory, and Register, for the year 1794* . . . [New York, 1794], 134, 135; [Joseph A. Scoville], *The Old Merchants of New York City*, 5 vols. [New York, 1864-70], II, 107, V, 190-4).

To Benjamin Carter Waller

SIR   Philadelphia Dec. 21. 1793.

I have received your letter of Dec. 10. as I had done in due time that of Mr. Welsh, tho' I did not know that it had come from you. At that time it was my intention to have retired from office at the end of September, and meant to have taken the first opportunity of seeing Mr. Eppes the acting executor of Mr. Wayles, and to have acquired from him the information necessary to enable me to answer Mr. Welsh's letter; for a ten year's absence from Virginia has left me without knolege of the affairs of the estate. I was induced however to put off my retirement to the end of this month, and therefore have not seen Mr. Eppes. I leave this place within ten days, and shall take the earliest occasion which the season will admit of meeting with Mr. Eppes, and of settling with him arrangements relative to Mr. Wayles's debt to Mr. Welsh. In the mean while it will save time if you will be so good as to inform us whether your powers from Mr. Welsh would authorize you fully to settle this transaction, and to take measures to obtain full powers if you have them not. If you will settle it on the same terms on which the much greater claim of Farrel & Jones was settled, that is to say, dividing the principal and interest *before* and *since* the war into practicable instalments, I think I can venture to assure you there will be no difficulty in the case. The executors have uniformly denied interest *during the war* in all cases where the estate was concerned.—I shall use my best endeavors to have this matter brought to a speedy settlement on my return to Virginia, and should be enabled to propose a meeting if you will be so good as to send me an answer by post to Monticello.

My separate debt to Mr. Welsh is small. I paid him the interest up to 1785. when I saw him in London. This included interest during the war. I cannot, till I return home and look into my affairs, say any thing specific as to the balance, but the earliest attention shall be paid to it, and Mr. Welsh may be assured that I will with zeal do what I can for the speedy and just settlement and discharge of the general debt from Mr. Wayles. In expectation of hearing from you on the point beforementioned I am Sir Your most obedt. servt   TH: JEFFERSON

PrC (DLC); at foot of first page: "Mr. B. Waller." Tr (ViU: Edgehill-Randolph Papers); 19th-century copy.

Benjamin Carter Waller (1757-1820), son of Virginia General Court clerk and Williamsburg attorney Benjamin Waller, was a lawyer who served as clerk of the James City County Court, represented York County and Williamsburg in the House of Delegates, 1792 and 1799-1801, and was an active Republican at the time of the 1800 election (Robert P. Waller, "Records of the Waller Family," WMQ, 1st ser., XIII [1905], 176; CVSP, IV, 519, IX, 81, 87; Earl G. Swem and John W. Williams, *A Register of the General Assembly of Virginia 1776-1918 and of the Constitutional Con-*

ventions [Richmond, 1918], 442; Waller's will, 17 Oct. 1820, admitted to probate 20 Nov. 1820, York County Will Books, York County Circuit Court, Yorktown, Virginia).

Waller's LETTER OF DEC. 10., recorded in SJL as received from Williamsburg on 20 Dec. 1793, has not been found. THAT OF MR. WELSH: Wakelin Welch to TJ, 21 Feb. 1793. For TJ's payment on his personal debt to Welch of THE INTEREST UP TO 1785, the only recorded instance in which he INCLUDED INTEREST DURING THE WAR, see MB, 1 Apr. 1786, and note.

To George Washington

Dec. 21. 93.

Th: Jefferson with his respects to the President incloses a letter from the Governor of Pensylvania in answer to one from Mr. Genet praying him to deliver the French sailors (whom he calls *deserters*) on board a vessel to be transported to New York, there to be put on board a man of war. The Convention having directed the proceeding to be observed in this case, and the laws having directed the District judge to attend to it, Th:J. has prepared an answer to the Governor informing him that the Federal Executive has nothing to do in it, but to leave the law to take it's course.

RC (DNA: RG 59, MLR); addressed: "The Presid[. . .]"; endorsed by Bartholomew Dandridge, Jr. Tr (Lb in same, SDC). Not recorded in SJL. Enclosures: (1) Thomas Mifflin to TJ, 20 Dec. 1793, and enclosure. (2) TJ to Mifflin, 21 Dec. 1793.

To Robert Gamble

DEAR SIR   Philadelphia Dec. 22. 1793.

Tomorrow I shall have embarked on board one or more sloops bound for Richmond, my books and furniture remaining here, which will be in 50. or 60. packages and parcels. I take the liberty of addressing them to you, and shall endeavor if possible to oblige the captain to deliver them at Shockoe landing. But whether there or at Rocket's, the trouble I am obliged to ask of you is to employ drays to carry them from the water side directly up to Mr. William Hylton's at Belvedere, who has been so kind as to offer me store-room, convenient to be taken off at once by the batteau-men. Not knowing the price of drayage with you I can only guess that the inclosed bills of 10. dollars will suffice. But should it be more I will thankfully repay it on my arrival at home which will be about the middle of January.

You will have heard that a truce between Portugal and Algiers has let loose those rovers on us. As they constantly go into port about the 1st. of December, and do not come out again till late in March our vessels will be in no danger during the winter months. It will depend on Congress to decide what shall be done, and whether in time to prevent their coming out in the spring.—Our foreign affairs in general have a turbid aspect. I hope the inability of the allied powers to carry on another campaign may produce a cessation of war, and thus rid us of the dangers to which that exposes us. This session of Congress is the most interesting one I have ever seen, and I have great confidence that their measures will be wise.—Should you pass through Albemarle after my return at any time I shall always be happy to see you, and with more leisure than when you were so kind as to call last. I am with great esteem Dr. Sir Your most obedt. servt   TH: JEFFERSON

[*On separate sheet:*]
Monday morng. Dec. [23?]. The above I received from Lisbon last night.   The cold here this morning is at 13.° below [and I very] much fear the river will be blocked up and prevent the sending [. . .].

PrC (DLC: TJ Papers, 96: 16395); consists of letter only; at foot of text: "Colo. Gamble." PrC (same, 94: 16095); consists of faded and slightly torn postscript subjoined to extract in TJ's hand of second paragraph of Edward Church to TJ, 22 Oct. 1793 (second letter); at head of text: "Extract of a letter from Lisbon dated Oct. 22. 1793"; at foot of extract: "Portugal has granted a convoy to the American vessels now in her ports, to protect them [from] the Algerines." Enclosures not found.

Gamble's reply of 26 Dec. 1793, recorded in SJL as received from Richmond on 2 Jan. 1794, has not been found. SJL also records letters from TJ to Gamble of 17 Jan., 27 Mch., and 17 Apr. 1794, and letters from Gamble to TJ of 25 Jan. and 22 Apr. 1794 that were received from Richmond on 3 Feb. and 2 May 1794, respectively, none of which have been found.

To Martha Jefferson Randolph

MY DEAR MARTHA   Philadelphia Dec. 22. 1793.
    In my letter of this day fortnight to Mr. Randolph, and that of this day week to Maria, I mentioned my wish that my horses might meet me at Fredericksburg on the 12th. of January. I now repeat it, lest those letters should miscarry. The President made yesterday, what I hope will be the last set at me to continue; but in this I am now immoveable, by any considerations whatever. My books and remains of furniture embark tomorrow for Richmond. There will be as much in bulk as what went before. I think to address them to Colo. Gamble. As I retained longest here the things most necessary, they are of course those I shall want soonest when I get home. Therefore I would wish them, after their arrival to be carried up in preference to the packages formerly sent. The Nos. most wanting will begin at 67.—I hope that by the next post I shall

be able to send Mr. Randolph a printed copy of our correspondence with Mr. Genet and Mr. Hammond, as communicated to Congress. They are now in the press. Our affairs with England and Spain have a turbid appearance. The letting loose the Algerines on us, which has been contrived by England, has produced peculiar irritation. I think Congress will indemnify themselves by high duties on all articles of British importation. If this should produce war, tho not wished for, it seems not to be feared. My best affections to Mr. Randolph, Maria, and our friends with you. Kisses to the little ones. Adieu my dear Martha. Your's with all love   TH: JEFFERSON

RC (NNP); at foot of text: "Mrs. Randolph"; endorsed by Mrs. Randolph. PrC (DLC). Tr (ViU: Edgehill-Randolph Papers); 19th-century copy.

For the publication of TJ's CORRESPONDENCE with French minister Edmond Charles Genet and British minister George Hammond, see note to Genet to TJ, 16 May 1793.

To St. George Tucker

DEAR SIR   Philadelphia Dec. 22. 1793.
    I this instant recieve by Mr. Randolph your son in law your favor of the 11th. inst. Had I known the situation you mention I should have taken the liberty, without waiting for authority, to have given him any counsel which his pursuits would have required. I should continue to do it now, with greater confidence, were I to remain here, but I retire from my office the last day of this month, and to my farm within a few days after. In the mean while on finding that Mr. Randolph has only read Blackstone in the line of the law, I have advised him to devote the winter to Coke Littleton, preparing him as well as I could against the labours of the undertaking, and encouraging him by the assurance that this task accomplished, what remains of law reading will be mere amusement. Should you think any thing better can be advised him, I hope you will do it without regard to what I have proposed, having been too long out of that line to feel my self qualified to prescribe in it.   I shall hope that some of the revolutions in your orbit will produce a transit over Monticello, and give me again the happiness of seeing you there. I am with great & sincere esteem Dear Sir Your friend & servt
                                    TH: JEFFERSON

RC (DNCD); addressed: "The honble St. George Tucker Williamsburg"; franked, stamped, and postmarked. PrC (MHi). Tr (MHi); 19th-century copy.

To George Washington

Dec. 22. 1793.

Th: Jefferson has the honor to return to the President Govr. Clinton's letter. Also to send him a statement of Mr. Genet's conversation with him in which he mentioned Gouvernr. Morris. This paper Th:J. prepared several days ago, but it got mislaid which prevented it's being sent to the President.

RC (DNA: RG 59, MLR); addressed: "The President of the US."; endorsed by Bartholomew Dandridge, Jr. Tr (Lb in same, SDC). Not recorded in SJL. Enclosures: (1) George Clinton to Washington, New York, 19 Dec. 1793, enclosing duplicates of Charles Williamson's letter to him of 26 Nov. 1793 and the affidavit of George Rankin, even though Williamson states that he has transmitted the latter to TJ; soliciting redress from the United States for the injury New York sustains from the British-held military posts, which he fears might provoke a retaliation by New Yorkers that he would not be able to prevent and that might have grave national consequences; calling attention to the state's exposed frontiers, the west having Indians engaged in hostilities against the United States, with the only immediate security being the friendly disposition of the Six Nations, in which too much confidence should not be placed, and the north being critically threatened by the accession to the hostile Indian confederacy of the Caughnawauga Indians of Lower Canada, some of whom had reportedly settled under British auspices at Oswegatchie, New York, since 1783, a danger increased by the destitution of the militia in the north on account of their expectation that Congress would supply them with arms; and noting that the situation of the seaboard was not much better, the easily accessible port of New York, on which the public revenues depended so much, having no fortifications to defend it against "the insults of even a single Pirate" (RC in same, MLR; in a clerk's hand, signed by Clinton; endorsed by Dandridge). (2) Report on Edmond Charles Genet and Gouverneur Morris, 11 Dec. 1793.

From Bartholomew Dandridge, Jr.

23d. Decemr. 1793.

By the President's direction Bw. Dandridge has the honor to return to the Secretary of State the papers herewith enclosed—and to inform the Secretary that the President agrees in opinion with him that they ought to be communicated to Congress, and wishes copies may be prepared for that purpose.

RC (DLC); at foot of text: "The Secretary of State"; endorsed by TJ as received 23 Dec. 1793. Dft (DNA: RG 59, MLR). FC (Lb in same, SDC). Enclosures: (1) Edward Church to TJ, 22 Oct. 1793 (two letters), and their enclosures. (2) David Humphreys to TJ, 7 Oct. 1793.

From Alexander Hamilton

Decr. 23. 1793

The Secretary of the Treasury presents his Respects to The Secretary of State requests he will favour him with copies of all his communications to Mr. Genet in answer to applications concerning the Debt. They will be necessary to complete a Report on his last—Mr. Hamilton having acted from his knowlege of them in some instances without having them before him.

RC (DLC); endorsed by TJ as received [23] Dec. 1793 and so recorded in SJL.

The Secretary of the Treasury's 4 Jan. 1794 REPORT to the President on Genet's complaints about his department in the French minister's LAST letter to TJ of 21 Dec. 1793 is in Syrett, *Hamilton*, XV, 610-18.

From George Hammond

SIR   Philadelphia 23d December 1793

In consequence of our conversation of this morning, I have made the necessary enquiries relative to the Sloop Hope of Antigua Captain William John Richardson, and I learn that that vessel was captured, on her passage from St. Bartholomews to Norfolk, near the capes of Virginia, on the 10th. day of August last by the privateer le Citoyen Genet—was sent into this port, where she arrived on the 14th. of the same month—and on the 20th. of August was restored to her master in consequence of the orders of this government.

As this vessel appears to be strictly within the description of those, whose losses, by waste, spoliation or detention, are to be ascertained in the mode prescribed by your letter to me of the 5th. of September, I flatter myself, Sir, that you will be pleased to give the proper directions for this purpose, with as little delay as may be convenient, since it is probable that the navigation of the Delaware may shortly be closed, and the detention of this vessel, which has so long subsisted, be protracted by this circumstance to a still more distant period. I have the honor to be, with great respect, Sir, Your most obedient humble Servant

GEO. HAMMOND

RC (DNA: RG 59, NL); at foot of text: "Mr Jefferson"; endorsed by TJ as received 24 Dec. 1793 and so recorded in SJL. FC (Lb in PRO: FO 116/3). Tr (Lb in DNA: RG 59, NL).

In accordance with the terms of a 1790 act of Congress, Hammond on 9 Dec. 1793 had made out for TJ a list of his household servants for registry with the United States marshal for Pennsylvania (MS in DNA: RG 59, NL; in a clerk's hand, signed by Hammond, signed and docketed by TJ as received 10 Dec. 1793; endorsed by George Taylor, Jr.). TJ forwarded a copy of this list to the marshal on 10 Dec. 1793 with his subjoined certification that Hammond's servants were registered as required by law (PrC of Tr in same, MLR; in Benjamin Bankson's hand, unsigned; endorsed by Taylor: "Certificate—Servants of Mr Hammond sent to Marshal of Pennlva 10 Decr. 1793"). For the antecedents, see note to Edmund Randolph to TJ, 26 June 1792.

To Richard Harrison

Dr Sir   Philadelphia Dec. 23. 1793.

You were so good as to inform me some time before our late dispersion, that on considering the account rendered for my department you thought you could proceed to settle it and give a quietus. I have now prepared it down to the present day, and wish to give it in to the legislature on Thursday or Friday. I shall be happy therefore if you can assign me half an hour tomorrow or next day, and I will call at your office. I am with great esteem Dr. Sir Your most obedt. servt.   Th: Jefferson

These are my ideas of the course of accountability for the foreign fund in my department.[1]

I. The Treasurer gives his[2] order for the money on the bank of the US. in favor of the Secrety. of state, who is thereupon debited by the auditor with it. The Secretary of state gives orders on the bank, first in favor of the drawers of bills of Exchange to be remitted generally to our bankers in Amsterdam;[3] 2dly. in favor of special messengers going from hence.[4] Consequently due proofs of the remittance[5] of these bills of exchange to the bankers, and of the paiment of these special monies to messengers &c. exonerate the Secy. of state, and debit the bankers and special messengers.

II. This gives rise to a second order of accounts for the whole money, to wit, with the bankers[6] who are required to[7] render their accounts annually on the 1st. day of July, to be deposited in the Auditor's office:[8] and with the said special messengers for the sums they receive. The bankers account debits themselves with the portion of the monies remitted them (which is nearly the whole of the fund) and they[9] exonerate themselves by payments to our foreign ministers, who are debited with those paiments.

III. This begets a third order of accounts for that proportion of the money which has passed thro' the bankers hands (nearly the whole fund as before observed) to wit, with our foreign ministers, who are required to render their accounts on the 1st. of July annually to be deposited for settlement in the Auditor's office. These ministers debit themselves the sums they receive from the bankers, and balance them by credits for their salaries and other authorised disbursements. These being for the most part final expenditures, the course of accountability ceases at this stage.[10]

Note. Amsterdam having been considered here at the earlier part of this year as a depository of some risk, the remittances of the year have been made to Mr. Pinckney our minister at London, (on which place alone good bills were to be had) to be deposited by him at Amsterdam when safe. It is probable that the accounts of our bankers, acknoleging all these remittances specifically, will save the necessity of erecting any intermediate[11] account for them against Mr. Pinckney.

PrC (DLC); at foot of first page: "Mr. Harison." Dft (DLC: TJ Papers, 84: 14517); undated; consists only of incomplete (see note 10 below) and heavily emended variant text of subjoined observations, the most significant differences being recorded below; written on verso of 2d Dft of enclosure printed at TJ to George Washington, 31 Dec. 1793 (first letter).

[1] Dft to this point reads:
"Observations
"The course of accountability for the foreign funds ⟨confided⟩ appropriated to the department of state is ⟨regularly⟩ as follows."
[2] In Dft TJ here canceled "warrant."
[3] In Dft TJ here canceled "but while that city was supposed here to be in danger, they were remitted to Mr. P. in London ⟨and on which place the bills were drawn⟩ and by him to the bankers in Amsterdam when it should be safe."

[4] In Dft TJ inserted a period here after canceling "or other."
[5] In Dft TJ first wrote the remainder of this sentence as "the receipt of these bills of Exchange by the bankers (or in the late special case by Mr. P. and evidenced by their letters and of the monies by the special mission as evidenced by the bank account exonerates the Secy. of state and debits them." He then interlined and canceled "or accounts" above "letters" before altering the text to read as above.
[6] In Dft TJ here canceled "by the bankers and special messengers."
[7] Preceding three words interlined in Dft.
[8] Remainder of sentence interlined in Dft.
[9] In Dft TJ here canceled "credit them."
[10] Dft ends here.
[11] Word interlined.

From Richard Harrison

Dear Sir   Decr 23. 1793.

I shall with pleasure attend to the subject of your Accounts to morrow at any hour between 10 and 3 oClock, that may be most convenient to yourself, and am with perfect respect & esteem Dr Sir Yr. Obed hble Servt   R. Harrison

I took the liberty of mentioning to you on a former occasion that some items in your Accounts seemed to require *special Certificates*, in order to their being admitted as final expenditures.

RC (DLC); endorsed by TJ as received 23 Dec. 1793.

To William Moultrie

Sir   Philadelphia Dec. 23. 1793.

It is my duty to communicate to you a piece of information, altho' I cannot say that I have confidence in it myself. A French gentleman, one of the refugees from St. Domingo, informs me that two Frenchmen, from St. Domingo also, of the names of Castaing, and La Chaise, are about setting out from this place for Charleston with a design to excite an insurrection among the negroes. He says that this is in execution of a general plan formed by the Brissotine party at Paris, the first branch of which has been carried into execution at St. Domingo. My informant is a person with whom I am well acquainted, of good sense, discretion and truth, and certainly believes this himself. I enquired of him the channel of his information. He told me it was one which had given them many pre-admonitions in St. Domingo, and which had never been found to be mistaken. He explained it to me; but I could by no means consider it as a channel meriting reliance: and when I questioned him what could be the impulse of these men, what their authority, what their means of execution, and what they could expect in result; he answered with conjectures which were far from sufficient to strengthen the fact. However, were any thing to happen, I should deem myself inexcusable not to have made the communication. Your judgment will decide whether injury might not be done by making the suggestion public, or whether it ought to have any other effect than to excite attention to these two persons should they come into S. Carolina. Castaing is described as a small dark mulatto, and La Chaise as a Quarteron, of a tall fine figure. I have the honor to be with great respect your Excellency's most obedt. & most humble servt   TH: JEFFERSON

PrC (DLC); at foot of first page: "H. E. the Governor of S. Carolina." FC (Lb in DNA: RG 59, DL). Tr (MHi); 19th-century copy.

To William Short

Dear Sir   Philadelphia Dec. 23. 1793.

I have to acknolege the receipt of your private letters of Apr. 2. 5. June 23. and Oct. 7. of all of which due use has been and will be made. The last was put into my hands this day: and as on the last day of the month I resign my office and set out immediately, I went immediately to a Notary to have enquiries made whether ground rents could be purchased here, as this is unquestionably the best place. If they can, one fourth of your effective paper shall be invested in them, as soon as it rises to 20/. for at present it is lower than I would sell at, tho' higher than I would buy at, to wit @ about 19/. When I get home I shall be better able to judge of the expediency of vesting another fourth in the James river or Patowmac canals. I wish another fourth could be laid out in lands so clearly advantageous as not to endanger any regret on your part. But this is problematical. Could it be so, there would remain a fourth in paper: and such is the disfavor with which the public view every person holding that sort of property, that I think if I can get ground-rents, with good buildings, clear of taxes, which will yeild *equal* profit, I shall venture as the[1] friend of your favor as well as fortune to convert into them that fourth also.[2] I have received from Patrick Kennon the stock stated hereafter and 109. Đ 83 cents cash for interest. I have received from Mr. Brown the stock also stated hereafter. The Loan officer certified the interest which had been received by Mr. Brown, amounting as well as I remember to about 2000. Đ. (for I cannot at this moment turn to the paper). I have written to Mr. Brown to know if that is a balance of so much in your favor, and if it is, expressing a wish to have it vested in stock immediately: but have not yet received his answer.—This being unquestionably the best market to have stock at, I have had the certificates transferred from the books at Richmond and New-York to those at this place, where they now stand in your own name, and I shall place it under the care of an honest broker, without giving him power to alienate any capital but by express authority.—You were never more mistaken then in supposing the red lands of Albemarle not favorable for grain and grass. On the contrary there are no *highlands* in the US. equal to them for these two objects. They cannot indeed be watered; but their richness renders that unnecessary. Witness la belle gazon of J. Cole's.[3] But of this more when I have more leisure, for now all is hurry and preparation for winding up here. E. Randolph is to be my successor. Having found that my former *private* letter went safely to you through the hands of Messrs. Viar and Jaudenes, I shall confide this to the same. Accept assurances of my pure and zealous friendship.

Th: Jefferson

P.S. Do not fail if possible to get me Cortez's letters.

RC (ViW); at head of text: "Private"; endorsed by Short as received 26 Apr. 1794. PrC (DLC); at foot of first page in ink: "Wm Short."

I HAVE WRITTEN TO MR. BROWN: see TJ to James Brown, 8 Dec. 1793.

In a private letter of 24 Dec. 1793 the President informed Edmund RANDOLPH of TJ's determination to retire as Secretary of State on the last day of the year, despite Washington's wish that he continue in office until the end of the current congressional session, and asked the Attorney General for permission to place his name in nomination as TJ's successor (Fitzpatrick, *Writings*, XXXIII, 216). In reply, Randolph asked either to meet personally with Washington on 26 Dec. 1793 to discuss the matter or to write him "a candid opinion" about it (Randolph to Washington, 24 Dec. 1793, DLC: Washington Papers). In the end, the President submitted Randolph's nomination to the Senate on 1 Jan. 1794, and it was approved the following day (JEP, I, 144).

MY FORMER PRIVATE LETTER: TJ to Short, 3 Jan. 1793. CORTEZ'S LETTERS: see TJ to David Humphreys, 11 Apr. 1791 (second letter), and note.

[1] Word interlined in place of "your."

[2] TJ first wrote "the fourth proposed to be kept in paper" and then altered it to read as above.

[3] Sentence interlined.

ENCLOSURE

Certificates Received for William Short

Certificates received by Th:J. for William Short

No.	kind	principal	date of intert.	date of transfer	signer	office.	
521.	6. pr. €	2,800.	Oct. 1. 1793.	Nov. 18. 93	Jno Co[llins]	New York	recd from
523.	3.	2,356.01	do.	do.	do.	do.	Patrick
524.	deferred	2,150.	Jan. 1. 1801.	do.	do.	do.	Kennon[1]
535.	6. pr. €	1,093.89	Oct. 1. 1793.	Nov. 22. 93	Jno Hopkins	Virginia.	from J.
898	6.	15,342.18	do.	Nov. 23. 93	do.	do.	Hopkins for
899	deferred	7,504.42	Jan. 1. 1801.	do.	do.	do.	Mr Brown.[2]
900	3. pr. €	11,256.63	Oct. 1. 1793.	do.	do.	do.	

The above certificates were delivered in to the Treasury office at Philadelphia, and the following were taken in exchange, having merely the effect of transferring them from N. York and Richmd. to Philadelphia.

No.	kind	principal	date of interest	signer	office.
1464.	deferred	7,504.42	Jan. 1. 1801.	Nourse	Treasy. of US.[3]
1724.	3. pr. €	11,256.63	Oct. 1. 93	do.	do.
2424	6. pr. €	15,342.18	do.	do.	do.
6511.	deferred	2,150.	Jan. 1. 1801	do.	do.
7750	3. pr. €	2,356.01	Oct. 1. 93	do.	do.[4]
10429	6. pr. €	2,800	do.	do.	do.
10430	6. pr. €	1,093.89	do.	do.	do.[5]

P.S. The whole sum of interest received by Mr. Brown has been ₰ 2221.09 but I suspect that the 1,093.89 above stated, and also 333.33 part of the 15,342.18 have been purchased with it, and perhaps his commissions and disbursements take a part of the rest.

Dec. 31. 93. I have this day resigned. E. Randolph succeeds me.

MS (ViW); entirely in TJ's hand; with related computations by Short on verso of address cover of TJ's letter, including a table of figures Short captioned "In the hands of Mr. Jefferson." PrC (DLC). MS (DLC: Short Papers); variant text in TJ's hand probably written in part no earlier than May 1795 (see note 5 below); consists of the two tables printed above, the first being headed "A list of mr Short's Certificates received by Th:J." and the second "Dec. 17. 1793. Received from the treasury certificates in exchange for the above as follows," with entries arranged according to date of interest; contains variant glosses as noted below, but lacks TJ's other commentary and postscripts; endorsed by TJ: "Short Mr."; with related computations by Short. Tr (ViU: Edgehill-Randolph Papers); 19th-century copy.

[1] Below these four words in MS in DLC TJ wrote a second gloss: "received from him also 109.83 cash."
[2] Gloss lacking in MS in DLC.
[3] Here in MS in DLC TJ wrote this gloss: "sold."

[4] In MS in DLC TJ wrote the following gloss for this and the preceding certificate: "sold to purchase land of W. C. Carter." See Articles of Agreement with William Champe Carter, 20 Apr. 1795.
[5] In MS in DLC TJ wrote the following gloss for this and the preceding certificate: "sold to purchase Canal shares." See TJ to Short, 25 May 1795.

George Washington to the Senate and the House of Representatives

GENTLEMEN OF THE SENATE, AND OF THE HOUSE OF REPRESENTATIVES

United States
23d. December 1793.

Since the communications which were made to you on the affairs of the United States with Spain and on the Truce between Portugal and Algiers, some other papers have been received which making a part of the same subjects are now communicated for your information.

GO: WASHINGTON

RC (DNA: RG 46, Senate Records, 3d Cong., 1st sess.); in Benjamin Bankson's hand, signed by Washington. Enclosures: (1) Josef de Jaudenes and Josef Ignacio de Viar to TJ, 18 Dec. 1793, and enclosures. (2) TJ to Viar and Jaudenes, 21 Dec. 1793. (3) Enclosures listed at Bartholomew Dandridge, Jr., to TJ, 23 Dec. 1793.

TJ prepared this message after he met with the President this day and convinced him of "the propriety of laying . . . before the Legislature" the documents comprised in Enclosure No. 3 listed above (Washington, *Journal*, 271-2; ASP, *Foreign Relations*, I, 304-6).

From Jacob Hollingsworth

SIR   Elkton 24 Decber. 1793

Yours I Received and agreable to Request have Bought Clover seede two Bushels at Eighteen Dollars and this afternoon Mr. Alaxander is to set sail from Frenchtown with the seede for Richmond. He would have started sooner but was Disappointed by the post. [. . .] your very Huml Servt   JACOB HOLLINGSWORTH

RC (MHi); one word illegible; addressed: "Thomas Jefferson Esqr Post—Philada."; endorsed by TJ as received 26 Dec 1793.

According to SJL, TJ wrote letters to Hollingsworth of 15 Feb., 9 May, and 18

Sep. 1794, and received his letters of 10 Mch., 20 Apr., and 29 Sep. 1794 from Elkton on 31 Mch., 1 May, and 15 Oct, 1794, respectively, none of which have been found.

From Henry Knox

Sir   December 24. 1793.

I have the honor to transmit you, the enclosed letter, dated the 20th. inst: received this day, from the Governor of Maryland, with sundry depositions, relative to the augmentation of force alledged to have been received in the port of Baltimore by the French Privateer Schooner Industry, and the capture of the Brig Cunningham by the Sans Cullotes of Marseilles.

I have the honor also to inclose a statement respecting the pay &c. supposed to be due the Marquis de la Fayette had he not relinquished the same. I am, Sir, Most respectfully—Your obedt: Servt:

H Knox

RC (DLC); in a clerk's hand, signed by Knox; at foot of text: "The Secretary of State"; endorsed by TJ as received 25 Dec. 1793 and so recorded in SJL. Enclosures: (1) Governor Thomas Sim Lee to Knox, Council Chamber, 20 Dec. 1793, enclosing for transmittal to the President examinations into the alleged augmentation of force in the port of Baltimore by the French privateer *Industry* and the capture of the brig *Conyngham* by the French privateer *Sans Culottes* of Marseilles, the institution of which he had notified Knox in a letter of 2 Dec. 1793 (FC in MdAA: Letterbooks of Governor and Council). (2) Statement of Joseph Howell to Knox, War Department, Accountant's Office, 24 Dec. 1793, showing that the Marquis de Lafayette's pay as a major general in the Continental Army from 31 July 1777 to 3 Nov. 1783 and commutation amounted to 24,100$\frac{12}{90}$ dollars, including extra pay for an estimated year on separate command, "the precise time to be ascertained at a future period" (Tr in DNA: RG 46, Senate Records, 3d Cong., 1st sess., at foot of text: "Copy ⟨*Original on file in the war office—Jno. Stagg Junr. Chf. Clk:*⟩"; Tr in Lb in same, TR). Other enclosures not found.

To Edmond Charles Genet

Sir   Philadelphia Dec. 25. 1793.

I have the honor to inclose you the Exequaturs for Messieurs Pennevert and Chervy and to return therewith the original commissions: and am with great respect Sir Your most obedt. & most humble servt

Th: Jefferson

PrC (DLC); at foot of text: "The Min. Pleny. of the republic of France." FC (Lb in DNA: RG 59, DL). Enclosures: (1) Exequatur for Citizen Chervi as French vice-consul at Alexandria, 24 Dec. 1793. (2) Exequatur for Citizen Pennevert as French vice-consul at New London, 24 Dec. 1793 (Trs in same, Exequaturs; in a clerk's hand, with George Washington as signatory and TJ as countersignatory). (3) Enclosures listed at Genet to TJ, 21 Dec. 1793 (second letter).

A letter of 26 Dec. 1793 from Genet to TJ acknowledging receipt of the enclosed exequaturs, recorded in SJL as received on the same day, has not been found.

From Edmond Charles Genet

MONSIEUR

Philadelphie le 25. Xbre. 1793, l'an 2e.
de la Republique Française une et indivisible.

J'apprends par les rapports du Consul de la République à Charlestown, et par les papiers publics, que la Legislature de la Caroline du Sud avoit fait arrêter différentes personnes accusées d'avoir reçû de moi des Commissions à l'effet de lever une force armée dans cet Etat pour le service de la République. Sentant qu'une pareille demarche si elle était véritable offenserait la Souveraineté du peuple Américain,[1] Je m'empresse de vous affirmer,[2] Monsieur, que je n'ai autorisé en aucune manière le recrutement,[3] la formation, ou le rassemblement d'une force armée, ni d'aucun Corps[4] *sur le territoire des Etats unis;*[5] mais en même temps je suis trop franc pour vous déguiser,[6] qu'autorisé par la nation française à délivrer des brevets à ceux de vos Concitoyens qui se sentiroient animés du desir de servir la plus belle des Causes, j'en ai accordé à plusieurs braves républicains de la Caroline du Sud dont l'intention m'a parû être en s'expatriant,[7] de se rendre chéz des Tributs indiennes independantes,[8] anciennes amies et alliées de la france pour rendre, s'ils le pouvaient, de concert avec nous,[9] aux Espagnols et aux[10] Anglais, le Mal que les gouvernemens de ces deux nations[11] avoient la Lacheté de faire depuis longtems[12] à vos Concitoyens sous le nom[13] de ces sauvages de même que depuis peu[14] sous celui des Algeriens.

Je vous préviens, Monsieur, que je publierai cette déclaration[15] afin de calmer les inquiétudes et de dissiper les doutes auxquels la dénonciation faite à la Législature de la Caroline a pû donner lieu. Agréez mon respect.

GENET

Tr (DNA: RG 46, Senate Records, 3d Cong., 1st sess.); in the hand of George Taylor, Jr.; above salutation: "Le Citoyen Genet ministre plénipotentiaire de la République française près les Etats Unis. À monsieur Jefferson Secretaire d'Etat des Etats Unis." Dft (DLC: Genet Papers); unsigned; only the most significant emendations are recorded below. Tr (DNA: RG 46, Senate Records, 3d Cong., 1st sess.); English translation in Taylor's hand. Tr (Lb in same, TR). Recorded in SJL as received 26 Dec. 1793.

Genet was prompted to write this letter by the publication in this day's *Dunlap and Claypoole's American Daily Advertiser* of news that the South Carolina House of Representatives had appointed a committee earlier in the month to investigate a report that "an armed force is now levying within this state by persons under a foreign authority, without the permission, and contrary to the express prohibition of the government of the United States and of this state." On 17 Apr. 1793, just before leaving Charleston for Philadelphia and in anticipation of the outbreak of war between France and Spain, Genet had instructed Michel Ange Bernard de Mangourit, the French consul in that port, to investigate the possibility of inciting uprisings against Spanish authority in East and West Florida and New Orleans. With the aid of military commissions left behind by Genet for this express purpose, and while keeping the French minister fully informed of his actions, Mangourit spent the remainder of the year enlisting a number of South Carolinians and Georgians in proposed French expeditions against East Florida and New Orleans. Attributing responsibility to both

Genet and Mangourit for thus violating American neutrality, the South Carolina House and Senate on 6 and 7 Dec. 1793 approved a report condemning these French actions and calling upon Governor William Moultrie to suppress them. Moultrie transmitted copies of this report and related documents to the President, who submitted them to Congress on 15 Jan. 1794 with copies of Genet's letter (ASP, *Foreign Relations*, I, 309-11; Keller, "Genet Mission," 392-429).

Genet's public DÉCLARATION, informing the American people that "the minister of the French Republic, has not authorised the recruiting, formation, or assembling of any armed force or any military corps on the territory of the United States," appeared in *Dunlap and Claypoole's American Daily Advertiser*, 27 Dec. 1793.

This is the last letter from Genet that TJ received as Secretary of State. See Appendix I.

[1] Sentence to this point written in the margin of Dft in place of "et."
[2] Preceding six words altered in Dft from "Je ne perds point un instant pour vous informer."

[3] Preceding two words interlined in Dft.
[4] Preceding four words written in the margin of Dft.
[5] Preceding six words not underscored in Dft.
[6] Preceding seven words altered in Dft from "Je ne vous déguiserai point."
[7] Preceding three words interlined in Dft.
[8] Word written in the margin of Dft.
[9] Preceding four words interlined in Dft in place of "à ces."
[10] In Dft Genet here canceled "Indiens."
[11] Word interlined in Dft in place of "peuples."
[12] Preceding fourteen words interlined and written in the margin of Dft in place of "qu'ils faisoient."
[13] In Dft Genet here canceled "d'autres hordes."
[14] Preceding two words written in the margin of Dft.
[15] Preceding three words interlined in Dft in place of "rendrai cette lettre publique, l'interêt de la Republique fse. dans les États unis me paroiss."

From Bartholomew Dandridge, Jr.

26. Decemr. 1793

By the President's direction Bw. Dandridge has the honor to transmit to the Secretary of State a Resolution of the House of Representatives, just received—and to request the Secretary to furnish the several papers therein required.

RC (DLC); at foot of text: "The Secy. of State"; endorsed by TJ as received 26 Dec. 1793. Dft (DNA: RG 59, MLR). FC (Lb in same, SDC).

The substance of the RESOLUTION of 24 Dec. 1793 requesting documents on American commerce (JHR, II, 21) is given in TJ's Supplementary Report on Commerce, 30 Dec. 1793.

To George Hammond

SIR   Philadelphia, Decr. 26th. 1793.

Your letter of the 23rd. instant, desiring an ascertainment, in the mode pointed out in my letter of Septr. 5. of the losses occasioned by waste, spoliation, and detention, of the Sloop Hope, taken on the 10th. of August by the privateer le Citoyen Genet, brought into this port the 14th. and[1] restored on the 20th. in consequence of the orders of this Government, has been laid before the President.

I observed to you in the letter of Sept. 5th. that we were bound by Treaties with three of the belligerent powers, to protect their vessels on our coasts and waters, by all the means in our power: that if these means were sincerely used in any case,[2] and should fail in their effect, we should not be bound to make compensation to those nations. Though[3] these means should be effectual, and restitution of the vessel be made; yet if any unnecessary delay or other default in using them should have been the cause of a[4] considerable degree of waste or spoliation, we should probably, think we ought to make it good; but whether the claim be for compensation of a vessel not restored, or for spoliation before her restitution, it must be founded on some *default* in the Government.[5]

Though we have no treaty with Great Britain, we are in fact in the course of extending the same treatment to her, as to nations with which we are in treaty: and we extend the effect of our stipulations beyond our coasts and waters, as to vessels taken and brought into our ports, by those which have been illicitly armed in them. But still the foundation of claim from her, as from them, must be some palpable *default* on the part of our Government. Now none such is alleged in the case of the Sloop Hope. She appears to have been delivered within 6 days after her arrival in port, a shorter term than we can possibly count upon in general. Perhaps too the term may have been still shorter,[6] between *notice* to the proper Officer and restitution; for the time of notice is not mentioned. This then, not being a case where compensation seems justly demandable from us, the President thinks it unnecessary to give any order for ascertaining the degree of injury sustained.

I have stated to the President, the desire you expressed to me in conversation, that the orders proposed to be given for ascertaining damages, in the special cases described in my letter of Sep. 5., should be rendered general, so that a valuation might be obtained by the Officers of the Customs, whenever applied to by a Consul, without the delay of sending for the orders of the Executive[7] in every special case. The President is desirous not only that Justice shall be done, but that it shall be done in all cases without delay. He, therefore, will have such general Orders given to the Collector of the Customs in every state. But you must be pleased to understand that the valuation in such case,[8] is to be a mere provisory measure, not producing any presumption whatever that the case, is one of those whereon compensation is due, but that the question whether it is due or not shall remain as free and uninfluenced as if the valuation had never been made. I have the honor to be, with great respect, Sir, Your most obedient and most humble servant,

PrC (DLC); in the hand of George Taylor, Jr., unsigned; at foot of first page: "Mr. Hammond, Minister Plenipy. of Great Britain." Dft (DLC); in TJ's hand, unsigned; note at foot of text by Alexander Hamilton, with signatures subjoined: "approved—A Hamilton Edm: Randolph H Knox." FC (Lb in DNA: RG 59, DL). Tr (Lb in PRO: FO 116/3). Recorded in SJPL.

The GENERAL ORDERS . . . TO THE COLLECTOR OF THE CUSTOMS IN EVERY STATE were issued in Alexander Hamilton's circular letter of 10 Feb. 1794 (Syrett, *Hamilton*, XVI, 23-4).

On 28 Dec. 1793 the President returned a text of this letter that TJ had submitted to him (Washington, *Journal*, 275).

[1] In Dft TJ here canceled "delivered."
[2] Preceding three words interlined in Dft.
[3] Before this word in Dft TJ canceled "if."
[4] Word interlined in Dft in place of "⟨waste⟩ any."
[5] In Dft TJ here canceled the incomplete paragraph "We do in fact extend."
[6] In Dft TJ first wrote "Perhaps too it might ⟨be still⟩ have been a still shorter term" and then altered it to read as above.
[7] Word interlined in Dft in place of "President."
[8] Preceding three words interlined in Dft.

From Josef de Jaudenes and Josef Ignacio de Viar

MUI SENOR NUESTRO   Philadelphia 26. Decre. de 1793

Parte del Contenido de la Carta conque V.S. nos honrró del 21 del corrte. (aunque Contextacion a nuestras dos Ultimas) no nos permite pasar en Silencio algunas reflecciones que Se nos ofrece hacer Sobre el objeto de ella.

V.S. construie de baxa calumnia las expressiones del Governador de la Louisiana quando habla *del Galardon de Quinientos pesos ofrecido por la Cabeza de un individuo por los Americanos.*

Como por el modo de explicarse en todas las Cartas dicho Governador no deve dudarse (y nosotros lo afirmamos) que està persuadido de que el poder executivo de los Estados Unidos no autoriza las depradaciones que Se Cometen en aquellas fronteras; no nos detenemos en vindicarle Sobre este punto. Resta pues hacerlo por la voz general de Americanos.

En quanto a esta, nada es mas trivial en nuestro Idioma que hacer uso de ella para distinguirlos de los de otra nacion, Sin que Se extienda a la maioria de ella; y asi Sucede en el caso presente en que Se trata de diferenciar los Americanos Georgianos (aquienes se Ciñe la voz) de los Indios.

El otro resentimiento de V.S. por llamar a los dichos Americanos los agresores en las hostilidades presentes requiere en nuestro Concepto mui poco Comento, pues que haviendo probado tan repetidas veces nuestra buen disposicion a evitarlas, y producido Documentos incontestables de haverlas fomentado los Georgianos, y algunos de los empleados de los Estados Unidos, parece no merece el Governador citado se le calumnie por repetir con evidencia los Actos hostiles que Siguen Cometiendose en las fronteras, por los predichos empleados ē individuos.

La oposicion que hasta ahora ha hecho y premedita hacer el mismo Governador relativa al paso por el Misisipi de los Cuidadnos de los Estados Unidos, mas arriba de los treinta, y un grados de latitud, nada tiene de injusta ni extraordinaria, pues bien Save V.S. que hemos estado, estamos, y estaremos en posecion de ella mientras que por combenio ō por la fuerza no nos desprendamos del derecho que nos asiste.

Que Subministre el Governador Armas y demas peltrechos de Guerra, à las naciones de Indiones Que habitan el territorio en Question tampoco tiene cosa alguna de extravagante, y Si tendria de injusto Si no lo efectuase, pues faltaria a la buena fé de los tratados Celebrados entre España y las diferentes naciones de Indios el año de Mil Siete Cientos Ochenta y Quatro (de los Quales hemos tenido la honra de pasar a V.S. Copias anteriormente).

Resulta pues que haviendo el Governador negado a los Indios armas en unos lanzes, y en otros escaceadolas, ha manifestado Su condecendencia, y buena disposicion à favor de los estados Unidos; Accion que en vez de Ser desaprobada por el Govierno de V.S., la deviamos contemplar acrehedora al elogio y las mayores gracias.

Combenimos con V.S. que es del mayor momento el que Se conserve la buena fé y amistad de nuestra parte y de la de los Estados Unidos.

Por lo que á nosotros toca y a la nacion que tenemos la honra de representar, nada se ha omitido ni Se omitirà de quanto pueda Contribuir à tan plausible fin, como hemos prometido anteriormente y confirmamos ahora, esperanzados de que los estados Unidos executaràn lo mismo de Su parte.

En prueba de ello insinuamos el plan que al Governador de la Luisiana y à nosotros nos parecio mui Oportuno para conciliar los Animos de los Vasallos del Rey, nuestro amo, en aquellas fronteras, los Ciudadanos de los Estados Unidos, y las naciones de Indios intermedios, al que no hemos merecido Contextacion.

Suplicamos a V.S. informe al Presidente de los Estados Unidos del Contenido de esta Carta, y nos lisonjeamos que con su notoria justicia, y Superior talento adoptarà los medios que estimase mas poderosos y que produxesen el remedio temporal mas oportuno, mientras no Se consigue la Cura radical que promete la negociacion en planta en nuestra

Corte, Siempre que Se Condusca, baxo los principios de justicia reciprocidad buena fé y generosidad. Tenemos la honra de Subscrivirnos con lamas pura voluntad y profoundo respecto Señor Los mas Obtes. y recondos. Servidores Q. S. M. B.

JOSEF DE JAUDENES   JOSEF IGNACIO DE VIAR

RC (DNA: RG 59, NL); in a clerk's hand, signed by Jaudenes and Viar; at foot of text: "Sor. Don Thomas Jefferson"; endorsed by TJ as received 26 Dec. 1793 and so recorded in SJL. Tr (AHN: Papeles de Estado, legajo 3895 bis); attested by Jaudenes and Viar. Recorded in SJPL.

COPIAS ANTERIORMENTE: see Viar and Jaudenes to TJ, 7 May 1793.

CONTEMPORARY   TRANSLATION

SIR   Philadelphia Dec 26. 1793.

A part of the contents of the letter with which you honored us on the 21. instant, in answer to our two last, does not permit us to pass in silence, some reflections which occur to us on that subject.

You consider as a base calumny, the expressions of the Governor of Louisiana, when he speaks of the reward of 500 dollars offered for the head of an individual, *by the americans*. As, from the manner, in which the said Governor explains himself, in all the papers, there can be no doubt, and we affirm, that he is persuaded, that the executive power of the United States, does not authorize the depredations which are committed on those frontiers, we do not stop to vindicate him on that point. It remains then to do it, as to the general word Americans—and as to that, nothing is more usual in our idiom than to make use of it, to distinguish them from those of other nations, without extending it to the generality of them. Thus it happens in the present case, in which the object was to distinguish the Georgian americans who were intended by the word from the Indians.

Your other censure—for having called the said americans the aggressors in the present hostilities requires in our opinion very little comment—since having proved so many times our good disposition to prevent them, and having produced incontestable documents that the Georgians and some of the agents of the US. have fomented them, it appears that the said Governor does not calumniate, in repeating, on proof, the hostile acts which are committed on those frontiers, by the said agents and individuals. The opposition which the said Governor has hitherto made and intends to make to the passage along the Missisippi by the Citizens of the US. above the 31st. degree of latitude, is neither unjust nor extraordinary, since you well know that we have been, are, and will remain, in possession of it, until by agreement or force, we yield our right.

That the Govr. administers arms and war stores to the nations of Indians, who inhabit the territory in question, is as little extraordinary, and it would be unjust were he not to do it since he would fail in good faith under the Treaties executed between Spain and the different nations of Indians in the year 1784, of which we had the honor of sending you a copy on a former occasion.

It follows then that the Govr. having denied to the Indians arms on some occasions, and given them scantily in others, has manifested his favor and good disposition towards the United States, an action, which instead of being disapproved by the Govt. of the US. ought to be considered as entitling him to praise and the greatest thanks.

We agree with you, that it is of the greatest moment to preserve good faith and friendship on our part and on that of the US.

As to what depends on ourselves and the nation which we have the honor to represent, nothing has been or will be omitted, which may contribute to so pleasing an end, as we have promised heretofore, and confirm now hoping that the US. will do the same on their part.

In proof of it we mentioned the plan which to the Govr. of Louisiana and to ourselves, appeared very proper to conciliate the minds of the subjects of the King our master on that frontier—the citizens of the United States and the intermediate nations of Indians to which we have not received answer.

We pray you to inform the Presidt. of the US. of the contents of this letter, and we flatter ourselves that his well known Justice and superior understanding, will adopt the measures which he shall deem the most energetic and which may produce the most convenient temporary remedy until the radical cure shall be effected, which we may hope from the negotiation on foot, at our Court; observing the principles of reciprocal Justice, good faith and generosity. We have the honor to subscribe ourselves with the greatest esteem & most profound respect, Sir your most obt. humble servants

JOSEF DE JAUDENES   JOSEF IGNATIUS DE VIAR

Tr (DLC); translation in the hand of George Taylor, Jr. Tr (DNA: RG 46, Senate Records, 3d Cong., 1st sess.). PrC (MWA). Tr (Lb in DNA: RG 46, Senate Records, 3d Cong., 1st sess., TR). En-closed in Bartholomew Dandridge, Jr., to TJ, TJ to George Washington, both 27 Dec. 1793, and Washington to the Senate and the House of Representatives, [30 Dec. 1793].

From Josef de Jaudenes and Josef Ignacio de Viar

MUY SEÑOR NUESTRO   Philadelphia 26 Dicre. 1793

Acavamos de recevir, y ahora tenemos la Satisfacion de embiar a V.S. las pruevas requisitas al assunto del Bergantin Español nombrado San Josef y Carga, que fueron llevados a Wilmington (Carolina Septentrional) como presa de un Corsario frances, y reclamada por nuestra Carta escrito a V.S. con fecha 23 de Octubre de 1793.

Dichos Documentos declaran, y pruevan incontestablemente, que el expresado Bergantin Español fue apresado y llevado al Puerto de Wilmington (Carolina Septentrional) el dia Cinco de Agosto Ultimo, por la Balandra nombrada la Amable Margarita, la misma que fue apresada algun tiempo antes por el Conquistador de la Bastilla (Siendo uno de los Corsarios proscritos por el poder Executivo del Govo. Gl.) Su Capitan Francis Henry Hervieux, y llevado por el dicho, al referido puerto de Wilmington, en donde fue armado y abilitado por el dicho, como Corsario frances; de manera que la Captura del San Josef se puede justamente considerar como dos veces ilegal.

El Testimonio no parece haver sido tomado en la forma que V.S. nos recomendo en su Carta del 10 de Noviembre Ultimo, porque el procurador del districto de la Carolina Septentrional a tomado una parte activa contra nosotros, y a favor del apresador, por cuya razon, no juzgamos oportuno el recurir a el en esta ocasion; se hallara haver sido tomado de la manera acostumbrada; que es a decir, jurado delante de un Magistrado Autorizado para este efecto, y Certificado por un Notario publico.

Despues que V.S. havra leido este testimonio, confiamos que Se dara una Orden en nuestro favor al poder Executivo de la Carolina Septentrional para que Se nos entriegue immediatamente el dinero y qualesquiera otra propriedad tomado en el San Josef por. F. H. Hervieux y al presente en possecion del juez del almirantazgo de aquel districto.

Nos han informado con certitud que el Buque con el resto de la Carga abordo, han permitido que fuese extraido fuera de la jurisdicion de la Carolina Septentrional, no obstante las instructiones del Presidente y nuestras repetidas aplicaciones al Governador de dicho Estado, por Consiguiente no esperamos direcciones por ahora del poder Executivo de los Estados Unidos para la imediata restitucion de estos, aunque nos lisonjeamos con grande confianza, que tales direcciones no se dilataran mas tiempo que el necesario para que el Presidente obtenga la informacion que se requiere para una ocurrencia tan inprevista. Tenemos la honra de Subscrivirnos con la mas pura voluntad y profundo respecto Los mas obtes. y reconocidos Servs. Q. S. M. B.

JOSEF DE JAUDENES   JOSEF IGNACIO DE VIAR

EDITORS' TRANSLATION

OUR VERY DEAR SIR   Philadelphia 26 Dec. 1793

We have just received, and we now have the pleasure of sending to you, the requisite proofs in the matter of the Spanish brig named San Josef and its cargoes, which were brought to Wilmington (North Carolina) as a prize by a French privateer, and reclaimed in our letter to you under date of 23 October 1793.

These documents make clear, and prove irrefutably, that the said brig was captured and brought to the port of Wilmington (North Carolina) on the 5th day of August last, by the sloop called Amiable Margaretta, the same one that was captured sometime ago by the Vainqueur de la Bastille (being one of the privateers proscribed by the executive authority of the general government) her captain Francis Henry Hervieux, and brought by him to the said port of Wilmington, where it was armed and outfitted by the same as a French privateer. So the capture of the San Josef may be considered to be twice illegal.

The testimony seems not to have been taken in the form which you recommended to us in your letter of the 10th of November last because the attorney general of North Carolina has taken an active role against us in favor of the captor, for which reason we did not deem it opportune to have recourse to him on this occasion; it has been taken in the customary manner, that is, sworn before a magistrate authorized for such purposes, and certified by a notary public.

After you have read this testimony, we trust that an order will be issued in our favor to the executive authority of North Carolina for the immediate delivery to us of the money and any other property taken from the San Josef by F. H. Hervieux and at present in the possession of the admiralty judge of that district.

We have been informed with some certainty that the ship with the rest of the cargo on board has been permitted to slip out of the jurisdiction of North Carolina, in spite of the President's instructions and our repeated requests of the governor of that state. Consequently, we do not for the present expect directions from the Executive authority of the United States for immediate restitution, although we do flatter ourselves with great confidence, that such directions will not be longer in coming than is necessary for the President to obtain the information necessary for such an unforeseen occurrence. We have the honor to subscribe ourselves with the most sincere good will and profound respect, your most obedient and grateful servants, Respectfully yours,

JOSEF DE JAUDENES   JOSEF IGNACIO DE VIAR

RC (DNA: RG 59, NL); in a clerk's hand, signed by Jaudenes and Viar; at foot of text: "Sor. Dn. Thomas Jefferson"; endorsed by TJ as received 26 Dec. 1793 and so recorded in SJL. Tr (AHN: Papeles de Estado, legajo 3895 bis); attested by Jaudenes and Viar. Enclosures: (1) Affidavit of Marshal Robert Wilkings, Wilmington, North Carolina, 23 Nov. 1793, stating, as town notary public, that Edward Jones, before whom Nos. 2-6 were taken, was, as acting justice of the peace of New Hanover County, duly authorized and empowered to administer the oaths and grant the certificates thereof. (2) Affidavit of William Reddie and John Telfair, 24 Nov. 1793, stating, as Wilmington shipwrights, that about last August they were employed by Mr. Brouard, the acting French vice-consul, to repair a sloop brought as a prize to Wilmington by its captor, the privateer Vainqueur de la Bastille, commanded by Captain François Henri Hervieux, so that the sloop could mount and carry guns, for which work Hervieux gave them an order of payment on Brouard; that in September or October, at the request of Hervieux and Severin Erickson, they surveyed a sloop at Fort Johnston, which they found to be the same one they had previously repaired, which then had six carriage guns, together with swivels and muskets, and which Hervieux commanded and called his privateer; that at the same time they also observed the San Josef of Cartagena, which Hervieux and his

crew identified as a Spanish brig they had brought in as a prize; that going aboard the San Josef they found Hervieux and some sailors from the privateer Amiable Margaretta, with Hervieux holding a piece of gold said to be worth 460 dollars, which one sailor said he had found on the brig, and a handkerchief with some dollars, which a sailor had also found on the brig; and that they understood that Hervieux had brought a trunk with gold and some silver from the San Josef to the Brunswick County home of William Cook, captain of the revenue cutter, who, understanding that it contained a large quantity of these precious metals, seized the trunk for a breach of the revenue laws of the United States. (3) Affidavit of James Laroque, 24 Nov. 1793, stating, as a New Hanover County physician, that in September or October he went on board the Spanish brig San Josef of Cartagena with several other persons at the request of Captain Hervieux and satisfied himself by the conversation of Hervieux, his officers, and his crew and that of Captain Don Jaquinas de Mendenez y Marques and his officers and crew that the brig was the prize of the Amiable Margaretta; and that he spoke in Spanish to Captain de Mendenez, who asked him to request the captors to treat the captives well and informed him that the gold the brig carried belonged to the Spanish government but that the vessel and the rest of its cargo were private property. (4) Affidavit of James Robertson, 24

Nov. 1793, stating, as late commander of the sloop *Providence* of Montego Bay, Jamaica, that his sloop was captured in May or June last by Captain Hervieux, commander of the schooner *Vainqueur de la Bastille*, brought into Wilmington, and laid up for a short time, during which period Hervieux went out on a cruise with his schooner but returned to Wilmington because of sailing problems, fitted out the *Providence* as a privateer, and went to sea with it under the name of the *Amiable Margaretta*. (5) Affidavit of Robert Harley, November 1793, stating that in September or October he and others at Fort Johnston at the mouth of the Cape Fear river boarded the brigantine *San Josef*, which he had been informed was a prize of the *Amiable Margaretta*, Captain Hervieux, formerly the sloop *Providence* of Montego Bay, Jamaica, which had been brought in last June by the *Vainqueur de la Bastille*, also commanded by Hervieux; that he learned from the prize master, an American citizen, that the brig *San Josef* was captured at night off the pan of Matanzas on Cuba carrying 40,000 dollars, most of which had been brought to Wilmington by Hervieux and there seized by the customs officers for a breach of the revenue laws; that a few days ago, but after this seizure, he saw a piece of uncoined gold worth 460 dollars in the possession of an inhabitant of Wilmington who was accompanied by Hervieux and gold worth at least 1,000 dollars in the possession of two privateersmen; that after the seizure Hervieux told him that the 35,000 or 36,000 dollars taken by the revenue officers had come from the *San Josef*, on board of which at least another 1,000 dollars had been found sub-

sequent to the seizure; and that from personal observation it was clear to him that the captors were mistreating the Spanish captives. (6) Affidavit of John Deparr, 24 Nov. 1793, stating, as a mariner serving on board the privateer *Amiable Margaretta* commanded by Captain Hervieux, that on 22 Sep. 1793 the ship captured without any resistance the *San Josef*, Captain de Mendenez, bound from Cartagena to Cadiz, which was brought to Wilmington under the direction of a prize master put aboard it by Hervieux; that the considerable quantity of gold and small amount of silver found on the *San Josef* was divided among Hervieux, his officers, and his crew, with Deparr's share amounting to 600 dollars, which he allowed to be put in Hervieux's trunk along with the shares of several other mariners; that while headed for Wilmington, Hervieux, accompanied by Deparr and another mariner, lodged this trunk in the home of Captain Cook, who seized it on the ground that it was a breach of the revenue laws to land it at night; and that the money in the trunk had been taken from the *San Josef* after its capture by the *Amiable Margaretta*, which was formerly the *Providence*, a sloop from Montego Bay in Jamaica that about July 1793, after its capture by the *Vainqueur de la Bastille*, was fitted out as a privateer with equipment from the ship that had captured it (MSS in DNA: RG 59, NL; in a clerk's hand, signed by the respective deponents and Edward Jones, except for No. 1 in Wilkings's hand and signed by him).

CARTA DEL 10 DE NOVIEMBRE ULTIMO: TJ to Foreign Ministers in the United States, 10 Nov. 1793.

From Timothy Pickering

General Post Office Decr. 26. 1793.

If there be any spare copies of the Census of the Inhabitants of the UStates in the office of the Secretary of State, the postmaster General requests Mr. Jefferson to favour him with one: it being proper to attend to the population of the country in forming an opinion upon applications for new post-roads.

RC (DNA: RG 59, MLR); endorsed by TJ as received [26] Dec. 1793 and so recorded in SJL.

From Bartholomew Dandridge, Jr.

27. Decr. 1793

By the Presidents direction Bw. Dandridge sends the enclosed Letter and the papers therein mentioned, to The Secy. of State—and has the honor to inform the Secretary that the President wishes if any thing is necessary to be done in consequence thereof, the Secretary will take such steps as he may conceive to be proper.

RC (DLC); at foot of text: "The Secry. of State"; endorsed by TJ as received 27 Dec. 1793. Enclosures: (1) Jean Baptiste Cassan to Thomas Mifflin, 24 Dec. 1793, intimating that the governor should prevent the *Peggy* from departing for British-occupied Môle St. Nicolas or Jérémie with French emigrants from Saint-Domingue in order to spare France from having to exercise its right under the law of nations to seize any ship that was either carrying aid to rebels or was bound for a port under blockade or siege (Tr, consisting of extract enclosed in Alexander J. Dallas to Nathaniel Falconer, Master Warden of Philadelphia, 27 Dec. 1793, in PHarH: Secretary's Letterbooks; full text not found). (2) Alexander J. Dallas to Cassan, 26 Dec. 1793, stating, as secretary of Pennsylvania, that although the general government would not allow a military expedition against any of the belligerents to be formed on United States territory, it would allow the emigrants from Saint-Domingue to return to their homes or to go anywhere else peacefully, that he would submit Cassan's letter to the President for his instructions, and that he would inform the owners of the *Peggy* of the risks to which they will be exposed according to Cassan's letter. (3) Mifflin to George Washington, Philadelphia, 26 Dec. 1793, enclosing Nos. 1 and 2 and stating that the sentiments expressed in the latter corresponded with those contained in a recent letter he had received from Henry Knox (Trs in same). See also Washington, *Journal*, 274.

Cassan, the French vice-consul at Philadelphia, raised the issue of the *Peggy* again in a 30 Dec. 1793 letter to Governor Mifflin, who replied on the following day that the "answer" he had provided in the form of Enclosure No. 2 listed above was "the only one my official situation permits me to give." On the same day Mifflin sent the President this latest exchange of correspondence with Cassan, together with a report by Falconer on "the real destination" of the *Peggy* (Mifflin to Cassan, and to Washington, both 31 Dec. 1793, PHarH: Secretary's Letterbooks).

From Bartholomew Dandridge, Jr.

27. Decembr. 1793

By the President's direction B. Dandridge has the honor to return to the Secretary of State the translation of a Letter from the Commissioners of Spain—and to inform the Secretary that the President thinks it should be communicated to Congress—and wishes copies to be prepared for that purpose.

RC (DLC); at foot of text: "The Secretary of State"; endorsed by TJ as received 28 Dec. 1793. Enclosure: Josef de Jaudenes and Josef Ignacio de Viar to TJ, 26 Dec. 1793 (first letter).

To George Washington

Dec. 27. 93.

Th: Jefferson has the honor to inclose to the President the translation of a letter he received last night from Messrs. Viar and Jaudenes and which he supposes should be communicated to the legislature as being in answer to one communicated to them.

RC (DNA: RG 59, MLR); addressed: "The Preside[. . .]"; endorsed by Bartholomew Dandridge, Jr. Tr (Lb in same, SDC). Not recorded in SJL. Enclosure: Josef de Jaudenes and Josef Ignacio de Viar to TJ, 26 Dec. 1793 (first letter).

From Harry Innes

DR SIR   Kentucky Woodford County Decr. 28th 1793

Your polite and freindly Letter of the 23d. of May did not reach me till sometime in August. Be pleased to accept of my thanks for the freindly part you manifested respecting my Slaves who were captured by the Indians; there was a probability of recovering them; I had no hopes thro' that channel, neither am I disappointed by the Indians refusing to Treat with our Commissioners.

The campaign is ended with the expenditure of about 1.000000 of Dollars and no point gained. There must be[1] some great defect in the War department, and, from every information I incline to think the Commander in Chief is certainly in fault. He appears to be a man of very moderate abilities, vain, capricious, jealous in the extreme and a Dupe to a few who flatter him, particularly the Quarter Master General, who I am informed said over a Glass of Wine (as he passed thro' Kentucky) that he had no idea of Œconomising with the public monies; thus sir between the Comr. in Chief and the Q. M. G. the war will be prolonged, our innocent Citizens butchered and the public monies squandered.

The War at present is a source by which the extra provisions raised in this state are consumed, but the inhabitants view that market as of momentary duration and begin to be restless at the delay of the Treaty with Spain relative to the Navigation of the Mississippi; to give you an idea of this subject I now inclose you an address to the Inhabitants of the Western waters, by the Democratic society in this state, which is composed of very respectable characters, this together with a spirited Remonstrance will soon be circulated in this state the western parts of Pensylvania and Virginia; I will inclose you a Copy of the Remonstrance by the next Post, it being now in the Press. To attain this most desirable object I can with certainty assure you that Foreign aid is now offered.

We are extremely anxious relative to the deliberations of the present Congress. Most of the Inhabitants of this state are true Republicans and we begin to fear the truth of the observation of a great Patriot in Virginia "that th[is?] Government has an awful squinting at Monarchy." I respect the President but cannot approve of his mode in removing Consul Duplaine. A power by Implication is a dreadful instrument in the hands of the Executive. I fear I trespass on your patience therefore conclude with every sentiment of respect Dr sir your mo. ob. servt.

HARRY INNES

RC (DLC); slightly torn; at foot of text: "The Honble Thos. Jefferson"; endorsed by TJ as received 31 Mch. 1794 and so recorded in SJL. Enclosure: Democratic Society of Kentucky, *To the Inhabitants of the United States West of the Allegany and Apalachian Mountains* [Lexington, 1793], a broadside of an address dated 13 Dec. 1793, asserting that Americans are entitled both by natural right and by the Treaty of Paris to the free navigation of the Mississippi and that both before and after the Constitution took effect the general government failed to assert this right adequately due to negligence and the fear by eastern states that freer navigation in the west would lead many of their most industrious citizens to migrate there; urging all westerners to join in a remonstrance demanding action from the President and Congress at this critical juncture, when Spain's energies are diverted by its war with France; and proposing that corresponding societies be formed in convenient districts throughout the western country to exchange information and concert action "upon this and every other subject of general concern" (Evans, No. 46730).

COMMANDER IN CHIEF: Major General Anthony Wayne. QUARTER MASTER GENERAL: James O'Hara. For the SPIRITED REMONSTRANCE, see enclosure to Innes to TJ, 21 Jan. 1794. The FOREIGN AID being OFFERED to help open the Mississippi to American navigation was the abortive effort by French minister Edmond Charles Genet to engage George Rogers Clark to recruit an army of Kentucky volunteers to help liberate Louisiana from Spanish rule (Editorial Note on Jefferson and André Michaux's proposed western expedition, at 22 Jan. 1793; note to TJ to Isaac Shelby, 28 June 1793; Innes to TJ, 21 Jan. 1794). The GREAT PATRIOT IN VIRGINIA was Patrick Henry, who asserted in a 5 June 1788 speech at the Virginia Ratification Convention that the proposed Federal Constitution had "an awful squinting; it squints towards monarchy" (DHRC, IX, 963).

[1] Preceding two words interlined in place of "is certainly."

From Jeremiah Wadsworth

SIR   28 Xr 1793

The prices are all in New York Currency—the labor is very moderate and those who are workmen—do much more and are allowed accordingly—a little profit to the laborers—is found to be advantageous to the proprietor. Your H Svt   J WADSWORTH

RC (MHi); endorsed by TJ as received from Philadelphia on 30 Dec. 1793 and so recorded in SJL.

To George Washington

Dec. 28. 93.

Th: Jefferson has the honor to inclose to the President a copy of Mr. Genet's instructions which he has just recieved from him with a desire that they may be communicated to the legislature.

RC (DNA: RG 59, MLR); addressed: "The Presid[. . .]"; endorsed by Washington. Tr (Lb in same, SDC). Not recorded in SJL. Enclosure: see enclosure listed at Edmond Charles Genet to TJ, 20 Dec. 1793 (third letter).

From George Washington

DEAR SIR   Saturday Afternoon [28 Dec. 1793]

I have received with vexation the enclosure you have just sent me from the French Minister: and pray you to take the opinion of the Gentlemen upon the measure proper to be taken in this business. Every day, more and more discovers the intention of this Agent to perplex this Government, and to scatter thick and wide the Seeds of dissention. Yours always   GO: WASHINGTON

RC (DLC); endorsed by TJ as received 28 Dec. 1793. Recorded in SJPL.

From George Hammond

SIR   Philadelphia 29th. December, 1793

I have had the honor of receiving your letter of the 26th curt., communicating to me the President's refusal to give any order for ascertaining the degree of Injury, sustained by the Sloop Hope of Antigua, in consequence of her capture by the privateer le Citoyen Genet.

Having never entertained a doubt that this particular vessel, from the circumstances under which she was taken, would have been included in the number of those, entitled to compensation for damages resulting from waste, spoliation or detention, the present determination of the President has naturally excited in me considerable concern.

My confidence on this subject was founded on the following reasons. I have always imagined that the resolution of the *federal* government to restore vessels, captured by the privateers, fitted out in the United States, or (in some instances) to grant compensation for them, was dictated not *more* by a sense, of the necessity of avenging the insult offered to its sovereignty, and of repressing such practices in its citizens, than by the desire of affording retribution to the individuals, who might suffer injury, from the *unauthorized* depredations of American citizens, and from means of annoyance *originally* created in, and issuing from, American ports. Considering the latter part of this position to be as just as the former, I also concluded that, as this government preferred the prohibition of future asylum and the restitution of, or compensation for, any prizes they might make, to the suppression of these privateers, whilst, on their first return to its ports, they were in its power, it intended likewise to comprehend in the restitution of or compensation for the vessel, an indemnification for other damages arising from the capture. I deemed myself farther justified in forming this conclusion by the *single* passage upon this point in your letter of the 5th. of September, wherein you specify the mode to be pursued for ascertaining the amount of "losses by detention, waste or spoliation, sustained by vessels, taken between the dates of June 9th. and August 7th." Though you advert to vessels in this predicament only, yet as you assign *no reason* for this distinction, I did not infer from your silence, as to all future cases, that no compensation would be granted for waste or spoliation suffered by any vessels, that might be taken after that date, and restored to their owners. Had you stated at that time (the 5th. of September) as you have asserted in your letter of the 26th. of December, that no retribution would be allowed for waste or spoliation, except it should be proved that they resulted, from any unnecessary delay or other default on the part of the Government in restoring the vessel, and upon no other ground whatsoever, I should certainly not have applied to you for redress in the present instance, but however I might have lamented the decision should have waited until I could have received instructions from my court upon the subject.

To the principle now established in your letter of the 26th. curt. the case of the sloop Hope is certainly not applicable; for I most readily admit that no unnecessary delay in effecting her restitution occurred on the part of the government. At the same time, you will permit me, Sir, to observe, that waste and spoliation of every material of a vessel (the hull indeed alone excepted) can be committed to as great an extent in the space of a few hours as of any longer period: And that the Sloop Hope actually suffered very considerable waste and spoliation, previously to her restitution, is fully evinced by the authentic documents, which I have the honor of inclosing.

It is not my intention to urge farther this particular case for the present: But whatever may be the ultimate decision upon it, I cannot but indulge the hope that, in all future cases of a similar nature, this government may be induced to adopt the more comprehensive principle I had attributed to it—viz., to grant a compensation for all damages, from waste, spoliation or detention, that may occur to prizes made by proscribed privateers. The danger to be apprehended from these last mentioned vessels still continues to exist to a very alarming degree: Since notwithstanding the repeated assurances I have received from the *federal* government, of its determination to exclude those privateers from any future asylum in its ports, and the sincerity of its desire to enforce this determination, I have reason to infer that in *other quarters*, means have been successfully devised, either to elude its vigilance, or to render nugatory its injunctions. My inference arises from the information I have received—that the privateer le Citoyen Genêt, fitted out at Charleston, was on the 21st. of August, permitted to return to the port of Philadelphia for the *second* time, to remain there some days, and then to proceed to sea, for the purpose of commencing new depredations, which, as it appears from the public prints, she is now prosecuting in the adjacent seas—that le petit Democrat and la Carmagnole, both fitted out in the Delaware, were permitted to enter the port of New-York and to continue therein unmolested, during a great part of the months of August, September and October last—that the latter vessel is still in that port—and that the former, having sailed from thence, in company with the French fleet under the command of Admiral Sercey, and having separated from it at Sea, proceeded first to Boston, and afterwards returned for a *second* time to New-York, wherein she at present remains.

I have thought it my duty to state these last mentioned particulars, in the manner, in which they have been communicated to me, but if my information has been erroneous, it will afford me the sincerest satisfaction to have my error corrected. I have the honor to be with sentiments of great respect, Sir, Your most obedient humble Servant

GEO. HAMMOND

RC (DNA: RG 59, NL); in a clerk's hand, signed by Hammond; at foot of first page: "Mr Jefferson"; endorsed by TJ as received 30 Dec. 1793 and so recorded in SJL. FC (Lb in PRO: FO 116/3). Tr (Lb in DNA: RG 59, NL). Enclosures: (1) Two inventories by William John Richardson, master of the *Hope*, 24 Dec. 1793, listing various items that were on the ship before its capture by the *Citoyen Genet*, but not after its restoration to him, and noting damage sustained by others (MSS in DNA: RG 59, NL, in a clerk's hand, signed by Richardson, certified by Notary Public Peter Lohra, partially torn; Trs in Lb in same). (2) Writ from United States District Court Judge Richard Peters to William Allibone, John Mease, and Nathaniel Falconer, Philadelphia, 20 Aug. 1793, directing them to provide him with a report on the nature and cause of damages sustained by the sloop *Hope*, which had been captured by the *Citoyen Genet* while on a voyage from St. Barthélemy to Norfolk and brought to Philadelphia (Tr in DNA: RG 59, NL, consisting of printed form with blanks filled by District Court Clerk Samuel Caldwell; Tr in Lb in same). (3) Report by Allibone and Mease to Caldwell, 21 Aug. 1793, stating that their personal survey of the *Hope* had revealed extensive damage to the ship's stores, sails, rigging, and cargo of limes, oranges, sugar, and rum that was directly attributable to its captor (Tr in DNA: RG 59, NL, partially torn, with Nos. 2 and 3 being certified by

Caldwell as true copies of the originals in the United States District Court of Pennsylvania and endorsed: "Exemplification of

Writ & Report of Survey on the Sloop Hope of Antigua Wm. John Richardson Master"; Tr in Lb in same).

From George Taylor, Jr.

DEAR SIR   Philadelphia Decr. 29. 1793.

Learning with much regret that you are soon to leave us, and impressed with the most lively sentiments of gratitude for the manner in which you have treated me during the whole time I have had the honor to serve under your immediate direction—Sentiments which those who are acquainted with your generous mind, cannot but be penetrated with—Sentiments which if I know myself will never be effaced from my breast—my feelings will not suffer you to take your final departure without troubling you with these few lines bearing but an imperfect testimony of them—Of the effusions of I trust a faithful heart.

It is possible, Sir, that in the course of human events, in my passage through this tempestuous life, a particular Certificate, coming from you, of my conduct while under your direction, might prove of infinite service to me, and such an one as you may think I have merited, I would beg leave to solicit, independent of any general one or recommendation you may be pleased to give to your successor.

May you find in your proposed retirement, that happiness and ease, which the great and good, only, know how to value, and may those who are dear to you, long enjoy the pleasure of your Society, is the sincere prayer of he who will ever deem himself happy in executing any commands you may be pleased to honor him with, and who subscribes himself with the most profound veneration for your virtues and sincerest personal respect and attachment, Dear sir, Your most obedient and most humble servant   GEO. TAYLOR JR.

RC (MHi); at foot of text: "Mr. Jefferson"; endorsed by TJ as received 31 Dec. 1793 and so recorded in SJL.

TJ responded on 31 Dec. 1793 with a certificate recommending Taylor: "The Bearer hereof George Taylor has acted in this Department, first as Clerk, and afterwards as Chief Clerk, the whole time of my being at the Head of it. I have found him faithful in the care and administration of it's affairs, indefatigable in it's duties, able, obliging, and of the most perfect integrity: and, on retiring from the Office, it is with

great satisfaction I leave him this testimony of my sense of his conduct and merit. Given under my Hand this 31st. day of December 1793" (Tr in DLC: Washington Papers, Applications for Office, in Taylor's hand, with "Department of State, to wit" at head of text and "(copy)" at foot of text; PrC of another Tr in DLC: Madison Papers, in Taylor's hand and attested by him). Taylor probably intended to use the recommendation to lobby Congress for a higher wage. Within a week he enclosed a copy to Senator James Monroe and expressed the hope that it "may perhaps have some weight in the discussion of my salary" (Taylor to Monroe, 6 Jan. 1794, DLC: Washington Papers, Applications for Office). The appropriation for salaries at the State Department was indeed augmented in the 1794 civil list, with Taylor's annual compensation increased from $800 to $1,000 (Vol. 17: 356-7n; *Annals*, III, 1439, IV, 1419). Two years later Taylor used the certificate to good advantage when his salary was again at issue in Congress (Taylor to James Madison, 30 Jan. 1796, Madison, *Papers*, XVI, 206-7).

From Joseph Yznardi, Jr.

SIR   New York 29 Decr. 1793

I was the 17th. int. duly honoured, with your favor of the 14th. and return you my thanks for the information you give me, respecting the Swedish Vessell that came as express. I have taken my passage in her, for Lisbon (the nearest safe conveyance I can find for Cadiz,) and shall be very happy to take charge of any dispatches for that *quarter*. I observe what you say respecting Algiers, I sincerely wish Colo. Humphreys, may be successful, but in case, unfortunately it happens, on the contrary, I have only to add, that if the President, or Congress, should determine on any other plan, I shall always be ready to go there, or any where else, where my services can be of any utility to the United States. I have the honor to be, with due respect, Sir Your most Obedient & most Humble Servant   JOSEPH YZNARDI JUNR.

RC (DNA: RG 59, CD); at foot of text: "The Secretary of State of the United States of America"; endorsed by TJ as received 31 Dec. 1793 and so recorded in SJL.

To George Clinton

SIR   Philadelphia Dec. 30. 1793.

The President has received your letter on the seisure of goods in the county of Ontario by certain officers of the British government, and measures having been taken to procure a full and certain statement of the case, whenever that shall be received, he will proceed to have done in it whatever the facts shall render proper. I have the honor to be with great respect & esteem Sir Your most obedt. & most humble servt

TH: JEFFERSON

PrC (DLC); at foot of text: "H.E. Govr. Clinton." FC (Lb in DNA: RG 59, DL).

For Clinton's 19 Dec. 1793 LETTER to George Washington, see note to TJ to Washington, 22 Dec. 1793. For the MEA-SURES . . . TAKEN to substantiate reports of alleged illegal confiscations by CERTAIN OFFICERS OF THE BRITISH GOVERNMENT, see note to Charles Williamson to TJ, 26 Nov. 1793.

To Enoch Edwards

DEAR SIR   Philadelphia. Dec. 30. 1793.

I have to acknolege the receipt of your two favors of July 30. and Aug. 16. and to thank you for the information they contained. We have now assembled a new Congress, being a fuller and more equal representation of the people, and likely I think to approach nearer to the sentiments of the people in the demonstration of their own. They have the advantage of a very full communication from the Executive of the ground on which we stand with foreign nations. Some very unpleasant transactions have taken place here with Mr. Genet, of which the world will judge, as the correspondence is now in the press; as is also that with Mr. Hammond on our points of difference with his nation. Of these you will doubtless recieve copies. Had they been out yet, I should have had the pleasure of sending them to you, but tomorrow I resign my office, and two days after set out for Virginia where I hope to spend the remainder of my days, in occupations infinitely more pleasing than those to which I have sacrificed 18. years of the prime of my life; I might rather say 24. of them.—Our campaign against the Indians has been lost by an unsuccessful effort to effect peace by treaty which they protracted till the season for action was over. The attack brought on us from the Algerines is a ray from the same center. I believe we shall endeavor to do ourselves justice in a peaceable and rightful way. We wish to have nothing to do in the present war; but if it is to be forced upon us, I am happy to see in the countenances of all but our paper men a mind ready made up to meet it unwillingly indeed, but perfectly without fear. No nation ever strove more than we have done to merit the peace of all by the most rigorous impartiality to all.—Sr. John Sinclair's queries shall be answered from my retirement. I am with great esteem Dear Sir your most obedt. servt   TH: JEFFERSON

PrC (DLC); at foot of text: "Dr Edwards."

To Thomas Mann Randolph, Jr.

DEAR SIR   Philadelphia. Dec. 30. 93.

My letters to you have been of Nov. 2. 17. 24. Dec. 8. all of which I hope you have received. Yours come to hand have been of the 31st. of Oct. 7th. 14th. and 30th. of Nov. and 11th. of December.—When I wrote the last Sunday, I hoped my furniture, books &c would have been embarked and sent off the next day. But the vessel loitered till the river has frozen up, and will now prevent their going till the spring.—I mentioned in my letter an extraordinary degree of cold then indicated by the thermometer. I afterwards discovered that the thermometer was entirely false.—I must repeat and insist that you take Tarquin, and on the express condition of making the most of him whenever you have a good opportunity. I should not use him myself, because of his awkwardness in going down hill, that is to say half the time one is on him, as all is either up hill or down hill with us. I resign tomorrow. E. Randolph is to succeed me. I do not know whether I shall be able to set out on Friday. If not there will be no stage till Monday. In either case I shall pass with Mann Page the spare days between my arrival and that of my horses at Fredericksbg., for I hope some of my letters have got safe desiring them to be at Fredericksbg. on Sunday the 12th. with a petition for P. Carr's chair if it be at Monticello and the roads good. My love to all I love, and friendship to all my friends. Your's affectionately

TH: JEFFERSON

RC (DLC); addressed: "Thomas M. Randolph esq. at Monticello near Charlottesville." PrC (DLC: TJ Papers, 95: 16380). Tr (ViU: Edgehill-Randolph Papers); 19th-century copy.

Randolph's letter of the 11TH. OF DECEMBER, recorded in SJL as received from Monticello on 26 Dec. 1793, has not been found. A letter to him of LAST SUNDAY, 22 Dec. 1793, is not recorded in SJL and has not been found, but may have been a missing postscript or covering note accompanying TJ's letter of that date to Martha Jefferson Randolph.

To Edward Rutledge

DEAR SIR   Philadelphia Dec. 30. 1793.

Your favor of Nov. 9. came duly to hand with the Memorial it inclosed of Penman and others. In consequence of circular letters addressed by me to the merchants of the several states, we are now receiving statements of the vexations suffered by our commerce from the cruizers of the belligerent powers. This will be taken up with them, be made part of a general application for redress and a reformation of these practices, which will be prepared without delay. But this will be the work of my successor as tomorrow I resign the seal. It is now 18. years since you and I met in Congress, and since that time I have been only two years at home; while you my friend have been setting under your vine and fig-tree, and supposing that general talents could be excused by employing themselves in a particular sphere. I had hoped to see you pushed on this point: but it was said here, thro' a channel deemed well informed, that it would be only time lost to make the proposition to you. I believe you are happier in the line you have chosen; but you have not yet proved to me that the performance of a *certain* tour of duty in any line which the public calls for, can be rightfully declined. Should this observation produce an occasion of my hearing from you in my retirement, it will add a pleasure the more to those I promise myself in that retirement where I shall be, as I ever have been, with great & sincere esteem & respect Dear Sir Your affectionate friend & servt

TH: JEFFERSON

PrC (DLC); at foot of text: "E. Rutledge esq." Tr (DLC); 19th-century copy.

TJ's CIRCULAR to American merchants was dated 27 Aug. 1793. I HAD HOPED TO

SEE YOU PUSHED: Rutledge had been considered to succeed TJ as Secretary of State (Notes of a Conversation with George Washington, 6 Aug. 1793; TJ to James Madison, 2 Nov. 1793).

Supplementary Report on Commerce

The Secretary of State, to whom the President of the United States referred the Resolution of the House of Representatives, of December 24th, 1793, desiring the substance of all such Laws, Decrees, or Ordinances, respecting Commerce in any of the Countries with which the United States have Commercial Intercourse, as have been received by the Secretary of State, and not already stated to the House, in his Report of the 16th. instant.

Reports:

That he has had an official communication of a Decree rendered by the National Assembly of France, on the 26th. day of March last, of which the following is a translation.

Decree

Exempting from all duties the subsistences and other objects of supply in the Colonies, relatively to the United States, pronounced in the sitting of the 26th. March 1793, 2d. year of the French Republic.

The National Convention, willing to prevent, by precise dispositions, the difficulties that might arise relatively to the execution of its decree of the 19th. February last, concerning the United States of America; to grant new favors to this ally nation, and to treat it in its commercial relations with the Colonies of France, in the same manner as the vessels of the Republic—Decree as follows.

Art. 1. From the day of the publication of the present Decree, in the French American Colonies, the vessels of the United States, of the burthen of 60 tons at the least, laden only with meals and subsistences, as well as the objects of supply, announced in Art. 2d. of the arret of 30th. August 1784, as also lard, butter, salted salmon, and candles, shall be admitted in the Ports of the said colonies, exempt from all duties: The same exemption shall extend to the French vessels laden with the same articles, and coming from a foreign port.

Art. 2. The Captains of vessels of the United States, who, having brought into the French American colonies the objects comprised in the above article, wish to return to the territory of the said States, may lade in the said Colonies, independent of sirrups, rum, taffias, and French merchandizes, a quantity of Coffee equivalent to the $\frac{1}{50}$ of the tonnage of every vessel, as also a quantity of sugar equal to the $\frac{1}{10}$, on conforming to the following articles.

Art. 3. Every Captain of an American vessel, who wishes to make returns to the United States of coffee and sugar of the French Colonies, shall make it appear that his vessel entered therein with at least $\frac{2}{3}$ of her Cargo according to Art. 1st. For this purpose he shall be obliged to transmit, within twenty four hours after his arrival, to the custom house of the place he may land at, a certificate of the marine Agents, establishing the guage of his vessel, and the effective tonnage of her cargo.

The heads of the said Custom houses shall assure themselves that the exportation of the sugars and coffee does not exceed the proportion fixed by the 2d. Art. of the present Decree.

Art. 4. The Captains of vessels of the United States of America shall not pay on going from the Islands, as well as those of the Republic, but a duty of five livres per quintal of indigo, ten livres per thousand weight of Cotton, five livres per thousand weight of Coffee, five livres per thousand weight of brown and clayed sugars, and fifty sols per thousand weight of raw sugar. Every other merchandize shall be exempt from duty on going out of the Colonies.

Art. 5. The sugars and Coffee which shall be laden, shall pay at the Custom houses which are established in the Colonies, or that shall be established, in addition to the duties above fixed, those imposed by the law of 19th. March 1791, on the sugars and Coffee imported from the said Colonies to France, and conformably to the same law.

Art. 6. The Captains of vessels of the United States, who wish to lade merchandizes, of the said colonies, for the ports of France, shall furnish the Custom house at the place of departure with the bonds required of the masters of French vessels by the 2d. Art. of the law of 10th. July, 1791, to secure the unlading of these merchandizes in the ports of the Republic.

Art. 7. The vessels of the nations with whom the French Republic is not at war, may carry to the French American Colonies all the objects designated by the present Decree. They may also bring into the ports of the Republic, only, all the productions of the said Colonies, on the conditions announced in the said Decree as well as that of the 19th. February.

Copy conformable to the Original.

Genet.

That he has not received officially any copy of the Decree said to have been rendered by the same assembly on the 27th. day of July last, subjecting the vessels of the United States laden with provisions, to be carried against their will into the ports of France, and those having enemy goods on board, to have such goods taken out as legal prize.

That an ordinance has been passed by the government of Spain on the 9th. day of June last, the substance of which has been officially communicated to him in the following words, to wit,

Extract of an ordinance for regulating provisionally the commerce of Louisiana and the Floridas—dated the 9th. of June 1793.

The preamble states that the inhabitants of Louisiana being deprived of their Commerce with France (on account of the war) as allowed by the ordinance of January 1782: and his Majesty considering that they and the inhabitants of the Floridas cannot subsist without the means of disposing of their productions and of acquiring those necessary for their consumption—for that purpose and to increase the national commerce—the commerce of those Provinces and their agriculture—has directed the following articles to be provisionally observed.

The inhabitants of the abovementioned Provinces to be allowed to commerce freely both in Europe and America with all friendly Nations who have treaties of Commerce with Spain. New Orleans, Pensacola, and St. Augustine, to be ports for that purpose. No exception as to the articles to be sent or to be received. Every vessel however to be subjected to touch at *Corcubion in Gallicia, or Alicant,* and to take a permit there, without which the entry not to be allowed in the ports abovementioned.

The articles of this Commerce carried on thus directly between those Provinces and foreign nations to pay a duty of fifteen per cent importation, and six per cent exportation, except negroes who may be imported free of duty—the productions and silver exported to purchase those negroes to pay the six per cent exportation duty—the exportation of silver to be allowed for this purpose only.

The commerce between Spain and those Provinces to remain free. Spaniards to be allowed to observe the same rules and to fit out from the same ports (in vessels wholly belonging to them without connexion with foreigners) for those Provinces as for the other Spanish Colonies.

To remove all obstacles to this Commerce, all sorts of merchandize destined for Louisiana and the Floridas, (even those whose admission is prohibited for other places) may be entered in the Ports of Spain, and in like manner Tobacco and all other prohibited articles may be imported into Spain from these Provinces, to be re exported to foreign Countries.

To improve this Commerce and encourage the agriculture of those Provinces, the importation of *foreign Rice into the ports of Spain is prohibited*, and a like preference shall be given to the other productions of these Provinces, when they shall suffice for the consumption of Spain.

All articles exported from Spain to these Provinces shall be free of duty on exportation, and such as being foreign, shall have paid duty on importation into Spain, shall have it restored to the exporters.

These foreign articles thus exported, to pay a duty of three per cent on entry in those Provinces, those which are not foreign to be free of duty.

The articles exported from those Provinces to Spain to be free of duty, whether consumed in Spain or re exported to foreign Countries.

Those Spanish vessels which having gone from Spain to those Provinces should desire to bring back productions from thence, directly to the foreign *Ports of Europe*, may do it on paying a duty of exportation of three per cent.

All vessels both Spanish and foreign, sailing to those Provinces to be prohibited from touching at any other port in his Majestys American Dominions.

No vessel to be fitted out from New Orleans, Pensacola, or St. Augustine for any of the Spanish Islands or other dominions in America, except for some urgent cause, in which case only the respective Governor to give a permission, but without allowing any other articles to be embarked than the productions of those Provinces.

All foreign vessels purchased by his Majesty's subjects, and destined for this Commerce, to be exempted from those duties to which they are at present subjected, they proving that they are absolute and sole proprietors thereof.

He takes this occasion to note an Act of the British Parliament of the 28. G. 3. c. 6. which though passed before the epoch to which his report aforesaid related, had escaped his researches. The effect of it was to convert the Proclamations regulating our direct intercourse with their West Indian Islands into a standing law, and so far to remove the unfavorable distinction between us and foreign Nations stated in the report, leaving it however in full force as to our circuitous intercourse with the same Islands, and as to our general intercourse, direct and circuitous with Great Britain and all her other dominions.

TH: JEFFERSON

December 30. 1793.

FC (Lb in DNA: RG 59, SDR); with subjoined French text of decree of the National Convention of 26 May [i.e. Mch.] 1793. Dft (DLC: TJ Papers, 96: 16468); entirely in TJ's hand, unsigned and undated; consists of narrative passages only, with the directive comment "[here insert it]" marking the places where two texts were to be added. Tr (Lb in DNA: RG 233, House Records, 3d. Cong., 1st sess., TR).

The President submitted TJ's report to the House of Representatives this day, having sent him the RESOLUTION that prompted it four days before. After first tabling the report, the House then submitted it on 1 Jan. 1794 to the committee of the whole in connection with its consideration of TJ's 14 Dec. 1793 report on Morocco and Algiers. There is no mention of it thereafter in the House's journal (JHR, II, 24, 25; Bartholomew Dandridge, Jr., to TJ, 26 Dec. 1793, and note).

REPORT OF THE 16TH. INSTANT: Report on Commerce, 16 Dec. 1793. The 26 Mch. 1793 decree of the NATIONAL ASSEMBLY had been enclosed in Edmond Charles Genet to TJ, 30 Sep. 1793. The 27 July 1793 decree of the SAME ASSEMBLY is in *Archives Parlementaires*, 1st ser., LXIX, 582. See

also note to Gouverneur Morris to TJ, 20 May 1793. TJ received the extract of the ordinance of the GOVERNMENT OF SPAIN with William Short's 1 July 1793 letter. The 1788 ACT OF THE BRITISH PARLIAMENT is in Sir Thomas Edlyne Tomlins and John Raithby, eds., *The Statutes at Large, of England and Great Britain*, 20 vols. (London, 1811), XVII, 2-8.

To George Washington

SIR   Philadelphia, Decr. 30.[1] 1793.

Certain proceedings of the Ministers of the United States abroad, on behalf of M. de la Fayette rendering it necessary that I should do myself the honor of addressing you on that subject in order that the proper sanction may be obtained for what is done, I shall[2] be justified by the interest which yourself and our fellow citizens generally feel in the fortunes and sufferings of that Gentleman in suggesting something more for his future aid.

Soon after his captivity and imprisonment, and before the Ministers had received our instructions to endeavor to obtain his liberation, they were apprised that his personal restraint, and the peculiar situation of his fortune disabled[3] him from drawing resources from that, and would leave him liable to suffer for[4] subsistence, and the common necessaries of life. After a consultation by letter, therefore, between our ministers at Paris, London, and the Hague, they concurred in opinion that they ought not in such a case to wait for instructions from hence, but that his necessities should be provided for until they could receive such instructions. Different sums have been therefore either placed at his disposal, or answered on his draughts, amounting, as far as we hitherto know to about twelve or thirteen hundred Guineas. This has been taken from a fund not applicable by law to this purpose nor able to spare it: and the question is whether, and how it is to be made good? To do this, nothing more is requisite than that the United States[5] should not avail themselves of the Liberalities of M. de la Fayette, yielded at a moment when neither he nor we could foresee the time when they would become his only resource for subsistence. It appears by a statement from the War Office, hereto annexed, that his pay and commutation as a major General in the service of the United States, to the 3rd. of Nov. 1783. amounted to 24,100 dolls. thirteen Cents exclusive of ten years interest elapsed since that time, to the payment of which the following obstacle has occurred. At the foot of the original engagement by Mr. Deane, a copy of which is hereto annexed,[6] that a certain roll of officers there named, and of which M. de la Fayette was one, should be taken into the american service in the grades there specified, M. de la Fayette alone has subjoined for himself a declaration that he would serve without any *particular allowance or pension*. It may be doubted whether the words in the original French do strictly include the general allowance of pay and commutation.[7] And if they do, there is no[8] evidence of any act of acceptance by Congress. Yet, under all the circumstances of the case, it is thought that the legislature alone is competent to decide it. If they decline availing the United States of the declaration of M. de la Fayette, it leaves a fund which not only covers the advances which have been made, but will enable you to take measures for his future relief. It does it too, in a way which can give offence to nobody, since none have a right to complain of the payment of a debt, that being a moral duty, from which we cannot be discharged by any relation in which the creditor may be placed as to them. I therefore take the liberty of proposing that this matter may be submitted to the consideration of the Legislature, who will determine in their wisdom whether the supplies already furnished, or any others in future, shall be sanctioned by them, and made good in the way here suggested, or in any other which they shall deem more proper. I have the honor to be, with the most perfect respect & attachment, Sir, Your most obedient and most humble servant

TH: JEFFERSON

RC (DNA: RG 46, Senate Records, 3d Cong., 1st sess.); in the hand of George Taylor, Jr., signed by TJ; at foot of first page: "The President of the US."; with date reworked. Dft (DLC); entirely in TJ's hand; dated 31 Dec. 1793; only the most significant emendations are recorded below. Tr (Lb in DNA: RG 46, Senate Records, 3d Cong., 1st sess., TR). Not recorded in SJL. Enclosures: (1) Baron de Kalb, Lafayette, and Silas Deane, List of officers of infantry and light troops destined for service in the Continental Army, Paris, 7 Dec. 1776, showing that, among the twelve French and German officers whose ranks and initial dates of service were listed, Lafayette was to serve as a major general beginning 7 Dec. 1776; subjoined to which were statements of the same date by Deane, explaining that he had offered this rank to Lafayette, subject to congressional approval, because he would not accept a lesser one and because of the desirability of attaching such a prominent French noble to the American cause, and by Lafayette, announcing that he would serve the United States "sans aucune Pen-

sion ny traittement particulier" while reserving the liberty of returning to France when recalled by his family or his king (Tr in DNA: RG 46, Senate Records, 3d Cong., 1st sess.; with list in English and subjoined statements in French and English; Tr in Lb in same, TR). (2) Enclosure No. 2 listed at Henry Knox to TJ, 24 Dec. 1793. Letter and enclosures enclosed in George Washington to the Senate and the House of Representatives, 30 Dec. 1793.

In conformity with TJ's recommendation, Congress in March 1794 passed an act making available to Lafayette 24,424 dollars, "being the amount of the pay and emoluments of a Major General during the time he was in the service of the United States, and that the same be paid out of any moneys which may be in the Treasury, and not otherwise appropriated" (*Annals*, IV, 1428). For American efforts to succor Lafayette and speed his release from Prussian and Austrian captivity, see note to TJ to Gouverneur Morris and Thomas Pinckney, 15 Mch. 1793.

¹ Altered from "31."

² In Dft TJ here canceled "indulge."

³ In Dft TJ first wrote "his own fortune ⟨would leave him⟩ rend" and then altered it to read as above.

⁴ Preceding four words interlined in Dft in place of "as to the article of."

⁵ In Dft TJ first wrote "To do this, no new grants are necessary from the US. but

only that they" and then altered it to read as above.

⁶ Preceding clause interlined in Dft.

⁷ In Dft TJ here canceled "However it may be well conceived that the officers of the government would not undertake in a case of doubtful construction."

⁸ In Dft TJ here canceled "other."

To George Washington

SIR   Philadelphia Dec. 30.¹ 1793.

I am informed, by the Director of the Mint, that an impediment² has arisen to the coinage of the precious Metals, which it is my Duty to lay before you.

It will be recollected, that, in pursuance of the Authority, vested in the President, by Congress, to procure Artists from abroad, if necessary, Mr. Drotz, at Paris, so well known by the superior style of his coinage, was engaged for our Mint; but that, after occasioning to us a considerable delay, he declined coming: That thereupon, our Minister at London, according to the instructions he had received, endeavored to procure, there, a chief Coiner and Assayer; That, as to the latter, he succeeded, sending over a Mr. Albion Coxe, for that Office, but that he could procure no person, there, more qualified to discharge the duties of chief Coiner,³ than might be had here; and therefore did not engage one. The Duties of this last Office, have consequently been hitherto performed,⁴ and well performed by Henry Voight, an Artist of the United States; but the law requiring these Officers to give a security in the sum of 10,000 dollars each, neither is able to do it. The coinage of the precious metals, has, therefore, been prevented, for some time past, though, in order that the Mint might not be entirely idle, the coinage of copper has been going on; the trust in that, at any one point of time, being of but small amount.

It now remains to determine⁵ how this difficulty is to be got over. If, by discharging these Officers, and seeking others, it may well be doubted if any can be found in the United States, equally capable of fulfilling their duties; and to seek them from abroad, would still add to the delay; and if found either at home or abroad, they must still be of the description of Artists, whose circumstances and connections rarely enable them to give security in so large a sum: The other alternative would be to lessen the Securityship in money,⁶ and to confide that it will be supplied by the vigilance of the Director, who, leaving as small masses of metal in the hands of the Officers, at any one time, as the course of their process will admit,[7] may reduce the risk to what would not be considerable.

To give an idea of the extent of the trust to the several Officers, both as to sum, and time, it may be proper to state the course of the Business, according to what the Director is of Opinion it should be.[8] The Treasurer, he observes, should[9] receive the Bullion; the Assayer, by an operation on a few Grains of it, is to ascertain it's fineness. The Treasurer is then to deliver it to the Refiner to be melted and mixed to the standard fineness—the Assayer, here again, examining a few grains of the melted mass,[10] and certifying when it is of due fineness: the Refiner then delivers it to the Chief Coiner to be rolled and coined, and he returns it when coined,[11] to the Treasurer. By this it appears, that a few grains only, at a time, are in the hands of the Assayer, the mass being confided, for operation, to[12] the Refiner and Chief Coiner. It is to be observed that the law has not taken notice of the Office of Refiner, though so[13] important an officer ought, it should seem, to be of the President's nomination, and ought to give a Security nearly equal to that required from the Chief Coiner.[14]

I have thought it my duty to give this information,[15] under an impression that it is proper to be communicated to the Legislature, who will decide in their Wisdom, whether it will be expedient[16] to make it the Duty of the Treasurer to receive and keep the Bullion before coinage.

To lessen the pecuniary Security required from the Chief Coiner and Assayer; And

To place[17] the office of the Refiner under the same nomination with that of the[18] other Chief Officers, to fix his Salary, and require due Security.[19] I have the honor to be with the most perfect respect & attachment Sir, Your most obedient & most humble servant,

Th: Jefferson

RC (DNA: RG 46, Senate Records, 3d Cong., 1st sess.); in the hand of George Taylor, Jr., except for part of dateline, a clerical correction, and signature by TJ; at foot of text: "The President of the US." PrC (DLC); unsigned, with date completed in ink by TJ; lacks clerical correction. Dft (DLC: TJ Papers, 96: 16423-4); in TJ's hand, unsigned, except for a clerical notation by Taylor; in pencil at head of text: "Dec. 30. 1793"; in pencil at foot of first page: "to the President"; heavily revised, only the most important emendations being noted below. FC (Lb in DNA: RG 59, DL). Tr (Lb in DNA: RG 46, Senate Records, 3d Cong., 1st sess., TR). Enclosed in Washington to the Senate and the House of Representatives, 30 Dec. 1793.

director of the mint David Rittenhouse probably informed TJ of the impediment to the coinage of precious metals in one of his missing letters of 5 and 14 Dec. 1793, both recorded in SJL as received on their respective dates.

An act of 3 Mch. 1794 drafted by a Senate committee appointed to consider TJ's letter followed his suggestions in part by requiring the Treasurer to receive and keep the bullion before coinage and by lowering the pecuniary security demanded of the chief coiner and assayer to $5,000 and $1,000, respectively. This statute was silent on the call for placing the Refiner under the same nomination as other Mint officers, but one provision of an act of 3 Mch. 1795 passed as the result of an investigation of Mint procedures by a House committee during the winter of 1794-95 established the office of Melter and Refiner as a presidential appointment with a salary of $1,500 and with $6,000 required as surety (*Annals*, IV, 1418, 1528; JS, II, 27, 31, 32, 41; JHR, II, 24-5, 65, 72, 76; Taxay, *Mint*, 120-1, 127-31).

As indicated by notes 14 and 19 below, TJ considered but decided against recommending to Congress creation of a fund for redeeming silver brought to the Mint for coining by individuals, a deficiency he had helped remedy informally earlier this year (TJ to Washington, 15 Aug. 1793; Tobias Lear to TJ, 21 Aug. 1793).

¹ Month and day inserted by TJ. He completed the date in ink on PrC.

² Preceding two words, reworked from "some impediments," interlined in Dft in place of "an obstacle."

³ In Dft TJ wrote "person likely to discharge the duties of chief coiner better" before altering the phrase to read as above.

⁴ In Dft TJ at this point canceled "by Mr.   Voight an."

⁵ In Dft TJ here canceled "whether."

⁶ Preceding two words added in margin of Dft.

⁷ In Dft TJ wrote "who of course would feel himself bound to leave as small masses of metal as the course of their process will admit in their hands at any one time" before altering the phrase to read as above.

⁸ In Dft TJ substituted this sentence for "Indeed as to the Assayer the course he has of the business places but few grains of metal in his hands at a time, his duty being to ascertain the quantity of pure metal in any mass whatever, which he does by an operation on a few grains taken from it. It is the refiner who is necessarily entrusted with the mass while under the operation of [. . .], as the Treasurer ought to be for this is what the director ⟨*thinks should be the*⟩ describes as the proper course of the business."

⁹ Preceding three words interlined in Dft in place of "to."

¹⁰ Preceding four words interlined in Dft.

¹¹ Preceding two words interlined in Dft.

¹² Preceding five words interlined in Dft in place of "passing thro the hands of."

¹³ Word interlined in Dft in place of "an indis."

¹⁴ Preceding paragraph interlined and

written in the margin of Dft in place of the following heavily revised paragraphs, only the most important emendations being recorded here: "Another obstacle to the coinage arises from the following source. The laws have not enabled or authorized the mint to take in any bullion on public account. The only coinage of gold or silver therefore which can be carried on is that for individuals bringing bullion to be coined. But it is rarely convenient for them to await the operation of coining. They therefore carry away their bullion to those who will give them ready money. A deposit of a few thousand dollars of public property in the mint, ready coined, to serve merely as a basis of prompt exchange, would very greatly increase the quantities to be coined on private account: and seems to have been contemplated tho not provided by the law where it allows an half percent to be retained for prompt paiment.

"⟨*Another reason renders indeed the coinage*⟩ Without such a deposit too a separate coinage for each individual as ⟨*contemplated*⟩ directed by the law is from the nature of the operation impracticable. The bullion is to be rolled into plates, the round peices to be cut from these plates, and consequently there remains a considerable portion of corners and scraps, supposed one fifth of the whole. These may be melted over again rolled, and cut; but a like proportion will always remain and a great multiplication of work take place. This would be avoided ⟨*by the bank having a deposit of it's own to give at once in exchange, and having a sum to exchange at once with the individual*⟩ were the mint enabled to give to the individual his whole sum at once, and to carry on the process of coinage in such masses as should be found most advantageous.

"The law too authorizes the individual to receive a quantity of pure metal in coin, equal to that he gave in. As no degree of skill and care can prevent a small waste in the operation, the giving back the exact quantity is impossible unless there be some deposit ⟨*in the mint to make up this waste. As the public has thought proper to take this loss on themselves, it will of course be wearing down the amount of the deposit.*⟩ from which this waste can be made up. Such a deposit once made it's loss by waste would probably be more than supplied by the half percent retained from those who prefer prompt paiment at that price. It should ⟨*of course*⟩

therefore be provided that whenever a replenishment of the deposit shall be applied for, satisfactory statements shall be furnished of the quantity of coined metal whereon that waste has arisen to shew that it has not been greater than it ought to be from the nature of the operation.

"As the legislature alone is competent to decide whether these difficulties are such as ought to be obviated by any change in the existing laws, I think it my duty to propose that they be submitted to their consideration."

[15] In Dft TJ here canceled "of the impediments which have arisen to the execution of the laws for establishing the mint."

[16] Remainder of sentence interlined in Dft in place of "thereupon to make any change in the existing laws."

[17] Word interlined in Dft in place of "establish."

[18] In Dft TJ here canceled "higher."

[19] In Dft TJ here canceled "and to authorize some determinate sum to be deposited in the Mint on public account, to be the basis of prompt exchange, always subject to the disposal of the legislature."

George Washington to the Senate and the House of Representatives

Gentlemen of the Senate and of
the House of Representatives   United States Decr. 30.[1] 1793.

I lay before you for your consideration a letter from the Secretary of State, informing me of certain impediments, which have arisen to the coinage of the precious Metals at the Mint.

As also a letter from the same Officer relative to certain advances of money, which have been made on public account. Should you think proper to sanction what has been done, or be of opinion that any thing more shall be done in the same way, you will judge whether there are not circumstances which would render secrecy expedient.

Go: Washington

RC (DNA: RG 46, Senate Records, 3d Cong., 1st sess.); in the hand of George Taylor, Jr., signed by Washington, though presumably drafted by TJ. Enclosures: TJ to Washington, 30 Dec. 1793 (two letters).

[1] Altered from "31."

George Washington to the Senate and the House of Representatives

Gentlemen of the Senate &[1] H. of Repr.   [30 Dec. 1793][2]

I communicate to you the translation of[3] a letter received from the Representatives of Spain here in reply to that of the Secretary of state to them of the 21st. inst. which had before been communicated to you.

Dft (DLC); in TJ's hand, unsigned and undated; with dateline and part of salutation completed by George Taylor, Jr. (see notes below); endorsed by Taylor. Enclosure: Josef de Jaudenes and Josef Ignacio de Viar to TJ, 26 Dec. 1793 (first letter). The text of the message that Washington sent to Congress was identical to the wording of TJ's Dft as revised by Taylor (DNA: RG 46, Senate Records, 3d Cong., 1st sess.).

[1] Taylor here inserted "of the."
[2] Taylor here inserted "United States 30 Decr. 1793."
[3] Preceding three words interlined.

To Edmond Charles Genet

SIR   Philadelphia Decr. 31. 1793.

I have laid before the President of the United States your letter of the 20th. instant, accompanying translations of the instructions given you by the Executive Council of France, to be distributed among the members of Congress, desiring that the President will lay them officially before both Houses, and proposing to transmit successively, other papers, to be laid before them in like manner: and I have it in charge to observe, that your functions as the missionary of a foreign nation here, are confined to the transaction of the affairs of your nation with the Executive of the United States, that the communications, which are to pass between the Executive and Legislative branches, cannot be a subject for your interference, and that the President must be left to [1] judge for himself what matters his duty or the public good may require him to propose to the deliberations of Congress. I have therefore the honor of returning you the Copies sent for distribution, and of being with great respect, Sir, Your most obedient and most humble servant

PrC (DLC); in the hand of George Taylor, Jr., unsigned; at foot of text: "M. Genet Minister Plenipy. of the Repub. of france." Dft (DLC); in TJ's hand, unsigned; note at foot of text by TJ, with the signatures of the other members of the Cabinet subjoined: "submitted to the correction of the Secretaries of the Treasury & war & the Atty Genl.

Th:J. approved A Hamilton H Knox E. Randolph"; only the most significant revisions are recorded below. FC (Lb in DNA: RG 59, DL). Tr (DLC: Genet Papers); in French. Enclosure: see enclosure listed at Genet to TJ, 20 Dec. 1793 (third letter).

[1] Preceding three words interlined in Dft.

Memorandum on State Department Business

[31 Dec. 1793]

Notes.

Accounts of the Department of State.
The Domestic account to the 31st. inst. will be settled and signed.
The foreign accounts.

> my own for the foreign monies down to this moment are delivered to the Auditor, as also to the President for himself and the two houses of Congress.

The Bankers account for July 1. 1792 to July 1. 1793, is also given in to the President for himself and Congress.

Originals {
The Bankers accounts (originals) from July 1.–90 to July 1st. 93
Dumas. The contingencies of his account in part only
Humphreys.　　His accounts from his appointment to July 1–93
Morris.　　His　do.　from his appointment to July 1–93
Pinckney.　　His　do.　from his appointment to July 1–93
Short.　　His　do.　from his appointment to July 1–93
　　　　are all delivered into the Auditor.
}

Carmichael. No account from him has ever come to hand.

Copies of the Bankers accounts from July 1–90 to July 1–93. are retained in the office.

Consuls letters to be answered at the close of this Session. See a note on this in the Bundle of their letters.

The Consuls have not yet all given Bonds. This should be examined into, and those who have not, called on.

Letters to our Ministers abroad to be acknowledged. The dispersion of the Executive from Sep. to Nov. The throng of business on my return and till I quit my Office, as well as want of conveyances to some of them, place the Dept. a little in retard with them.

There is a chasm in the Bundle of Colo. Humphrey's letters from No. 34 to 44—that is from Sep. 10–91 to Feb. 11. 92. It may be seen by recurring to my letters whether any between those Nos. were acknowledged, or whether it was an error in Colo. Humphreys' numbering. Perhaps when the letters of the existing Ministers were taken from the office to be in my own keeping, these may have remained overlooked.

'Bundle of Papers to be acted on.'

Letter to be written from the President to the Queen of Portugal.

Moissonier's ⎫
Du Plaine's ⎭ cases to be considered.

Treaty of Commerce with France.

Philip Wilson's case, sent by Mr. Pinckney to be laid before Congress que:?

Wright's representatives to be paid for engraving the Medal of Govr. Lee and (that being broke in hardening) another to be engraved.

Seagrove's letters—concerning the St. Mary's river. Not worth attending to in the present and probable state of things between us and Spain.

Another relative to a trespass by some Georgians on the territory of West Florida. See my letter to the Govr. of Georgia, to which no answer is received.

Johnson's Account (Consul at London) some articles in it not allowed by the law. He wished it to be referred to Congress. Qu:?

The Hotel of the US. at the Hague. There was an ancient Order of Congress to sell it. Dumas has repeatedly pressed it on account of its ruinous condition. Nothing done in it since the present Governmt.

Smith's letters relative to laying western laws before Congress.

Williamson's complaint of a trespass by the British in Ontario County. Genl. Chapin has a copy and promised to inquire into and report the reality of the case.

Remittances to the foreign Ministers.

There remain something between 4. and¹ 5,000 dollars in the Bank of the US. of the fund due to July 1. 1793. Six months more having elapsed, the Treasury should be applied to for at least 20,000 Dollars on account of the present year; and the money now in the Bank and one half of the 20,000 D. to be called for, should be immediately remitted to our Bankers in Amsterdam, and generally about 10,000 D. every quarter, keeping beforehand in order to profit by exchange when low.

The Bundle of Spoliations might now be taken up, as most of the cases produced by the circular letter, are probably received.

In the message of the Presidt. to Congress the 2d. day, it was said that representations would be sent to the Govt. of France on their Decree of July 27. Should this wait more authentic information of the fact, or be done now de bene esse?

Medals voted by Congress—of which Govr. Lee's is one.

I will prepare and send a special statement of this business, which will require time. I have among my Paris papers some relative to this Subject, which shall be sent with the Statement.

MS (DLC: TJ Papers, 96: 16442-3); in the hand of George Taylor, Jr., unsigned, doubtless being a fair copy of a missing rough draft by TJ; undated, but assigned on the basis of internal evidence (see below). PrC (same, 16485-7).

TJ presumably had this memorandum prepared from his rough notes for the benefit of his successor as Secretary of State, evidently on the same day his account of the foreign fund DOWN TO THIS MOMENT was delivered TO THE PRESIDENT (see TJ's first letter to George Washington, 31 Dec. 1793).

The President signed the letter to the QUEEN OF PORTUGAL on 11 Mch. 1794 (see Washington, *Journal*, 290). PHILIP WILSON'S CASE: see Thomas Pinckney to TJ, 27 Aug. 1793, and note. Joseph WRIGHT'S role in engraving the medal the Continental Congress had voted Henry LEE for the capture of Paulus Hook in 1779 is described in Jefferson's notes on these medals discussed below. MY LETTER TO THE GOVR. OF GEORGIA: TJ to Edward Telfair, 22 May 1793. SMITH'S LETTERS: see Report on the Proceedings of the Southwest Territory, 7 Nov. 1793, and note. WILLIAMSON'S COMPLAINT: see Charles Williamson to TJ, 26 Nov. 1793. CIRCULAR LETTER: Circular to American Merchants, 27 Aug. 1793.

The MESSAGE OF THE PRESIDT. TO CONGRESS THE 2D. DAY was Washington's fifth annual address to Congress of 3 Dec. 1793, not the message on relations with France and Great Britain in which he alluded to the National Convention's DECREE of 27 July 1793 (Fitzpatrick, *Writings*, XXXIII, 163-9, 171; TJ's draft of the latter is printed under 2 Dec. 1793).

The SPECIAL STATEMENT TJ here prom-

ised to write on the medals the Continental Congress had voted for various officers during the Revolutionary War is printed under the conjectural date of 8 July 1792 in Vol. 16: 77-8, but that document is actually a draft of TJ's 9 Mch. 1796 letter to Richard Harrison, the Auditor of the United States.

[1] Preceding two words and digit interlined in place of "upwards of."

To George Washington

SIR   Philadelphia Dec. 31. 1793

I have the honor to enclose you a statement of the expenditure of the monies appropriated to our intercourse with foreign nations to be laid before the legislature according to the requisitions of the law.

The account of the Secretary of state commences July 1. 1792. where that rendered at the last session ended; and is brought down to this time. In the two preceding years of this appropriation, bills of exchange were given me from the Treasurer on our bankers at Amsterdam; so that the remittance of these bills to the bankers, for the credit of the Department of state constituted a separate Deposit in their hands on which the public agents abroad might draw for their salaries and other authorised expenditures. For the last year an order was given me by the Treasurer on the bank of the US., bills of Exchange were purchased by an agent employed for that purpose, and the money was paid to the Drawers by the bank, on my orders. As Amsterdam was at one time in danger of an attack, and the seat of war continued not very distant from it, it was thought safer to make the bills payable to Mr. Pinckney, our Minister in London, to be remitted by him to our bankers in Amsterdam if the place were safe.

The deposit being thus transferred to the bankers of the US. in Amsterdam, the monies pass from them into the hands of the public agents abroad, with whom the expenditures are final, being for their salaries and other authorised disbursements. The account of the bankers now rendered, from July 1. 1792. to July 1. 1793. shews the sums paid to each of these.

With these paiments the Ministers are debited, and are required annually on the 1st. day of July to state and forward their separate accounts[1] to be settled by the proper officers of the Treasury. This, with the payments to occasional Agents (generally a very small Article) completes the system of accounts for the foreign fund confided to the Department of State.

I enclose herewith Statements from the accounting Officers of the Treasury vouching my own account, begging leave only to observe that the 4,786 dollars, 67 Cents therein stated to be due from me, are the same which are stated in my account to be remaining on hand in the Bank, and which never have been taken out of it, as is vouched by the Bank book. I have the honor to be, with the most perfect respect and attachment, Sir, Your most obedient & most humble servant

TH: JEFFERSON

PrC (DLC); with signature added in ink; partially faded and overwritten in a later hand; at foot of first page: "The President of the US."; missing second page supplied from first Tr (see note 1 below). Tr (DNA: RG 46, Senate Records, 3d Cong., 1st sess.); in the hand of George Taylor, Jr., signed by TJ. PrC (DLC); with signature added in ink. PrC of another Tr (DLC); in Taylor's hand, signed by TJ. FC (Lb in DNA: RG 59, DL). Tr (Lb in same, SDC). Tr (Lb in DNA: RG 46, Senate Records, 3d Cong., 1st sess., TR). Tr (MHi); 19th-century copy. Enclosures: (1) Accounts of Department of State with Willink, Van Staphorst & Hubbard, 2 Apr. and 1 July 1793, covering the period 1 July 1792-1 July 1793 (Trs in Lb in DNA: RG 59, DL; Trs in DNA: RG 46, Senate Records, 3d Cong., 1st sess.; Trs in Lb in same, TR; the original MSS received by TJ and other copies are listed at Willink, Van Staphorst & Hubbard to TJ, 4 Apr. and 1 July 1793). (2) Enclosures to Oliver Wolcott, Jr., to TJ, 31 Dec. 1793. Other enclosure printed below.

As part of the settlement of the accounts of the Department of State during his tenure, TJ also prepared three documents pertaining to the following American diplomats: (1) Statement on William Carmichael, 26 Dec. 1793: "Mr. Carmichael has never rendered any account since I have been in the Departmt. of state. Nor have I ever received but one letter from him. I understand he affirms he has written regularly. If so his accounts may have been forwarded and miscarried with his letters" (MS in DNA: RG 59, Consular Accounts and Returns; consists of a docketing slip in TJ's hand initialed by him; at head of text: "Carmichael William"; with note at foot of text

added by an unidentified hand sometime after the 1798 law in question: "Mr. Carmichaels Accts have been settled by direction of an act of Congress"). The sole official letter TJ received from Carmichael during his tenure as Secretary of State is dated 24 Jan. 1791 (see note to Carmichael to TJ, 19 Aug. 1791). (2) Statement on C. W. F. Dumas, 26 Dec. 1793: "Mr. Dumas has not drawn up and rendered a regular account. The inclosed papers seem to be of his contingent disbursements, which being added to his salary will make up his accounts for those periods of time" (MS in same; consists of a docketing slip in TJ's hand initialed by him; at head of text: "Dumas. William"; with later note at foot of text in an unidentified hand: "irregular & incomplete—of no use"). Enclosures not found. (3) Certificate from Washington, [27] Dec. 1793: "I hereby certify that the sum of two thousand Dollars was allowed to Gouverneur Morris esq. for his expences and services on a special mission to London, previous to his appointment as Minister Plenipotentiary for the US. to France. Given under my hand this ____ day of Dec. 1793" (Dft in same, MLR, partially dated, being in TJ's hand except for completion of the blank with "27." and the insertion of Washington's initials at foot of text by Bartholomew Dandridge, Jr., who endorsed it: "Certificate given to the Secry of State 27 Decr. 93. relative to allowce. to Gour. Morris"; Tr in Lb in same, SDC, dated 27 Dec. 1793). See Washington, *Journal*, 274.

REQUISITIONS OF THE LAW: see note to TJ to George Washington, 3 Nov. 1792.

[1] Remainder of text supplied from first Tr.

Statement of the Foreign Fund Account

The Department of State (for the foreign fund) in account with the United States

1793.		Dollars	1793.		Dollars
Apr. 11.	To the Treasurer's order on the Bank of the US. for	39,500.	Apr. 11.	By orders on the bank as follows, to wit,	
				in favor of Mordecai Lewis for Gilmore's bills of exchange payable to Thos. Pinckney for £600. sterl. (as per the bank acct., and by our bankers letter of July 1. 1793).	2,600.
				in favor of Willing, Morris & Swanwick for their Exchange payable to T. Pinckney for £3000. sterl. (as per the bank acct. & banker's letters of July 1. & Aug. 15. 93.)	13,000.
			12.	in favor of Walter Stewart for his Excha: payable to T. Pinckney for £400. sterl. (as per the bank acct. and our bankers letters of July 1. & Aug. 15. 93.)	1,733.33
				in favor of Nathaniel Cutting on account of his mission to Algiers. (as by the bank acct.)	1,000.
			July 12.	in favor of James Blake on account of his mission to Madrid (as by the bank acct.)	800.
			31.	in favor of John Wilcocks for his Excha: payable to T. Pinckney for £1077.11.9[1] sterl. (as by the bank acct.)	5,000.
			Sep. 27.	in favor of John Swanwick for his Excha: payable to T. Pinckney for £1300. sterl. (as by bank acct. and Mr. Kean's letter of Nov. 4. 93.)	5,980.
			30.	in favor of John Vaughan for his Excha: payable to T. Pinckney for £1000. sterl. (as by the bank acct. and Mr. Kean's letter of Nov. 4. 93.)	4,600.
			Dec. 18.	By cash in the bank of the US. (as by the bank acct. & Mr. Kean's lre this date)	4,786.67
					39,500.

3d Dft (DLC: TJ Papers, 95: 16374-5); consists of two pages in TJ's hand, with an insertion by George Taylor, Jr. (see note 1 below); undated, but written sometime between 18 Dec. 1793, when TJ probably received John Kean's letter of that date, and 23 Dec. 1793, the date of TJ's letter to Richard Harrison about this account. 2d Dft (same, 84: 14517); entirely in TJ's hand; consists of one page with abbreviated debit and credit entries keyed to subjoined references to supporting documents; undated, but written before TJ received Kean's 18 Dec. 1793 letter, the last entry being incomplete and partially dated "Dec.   "; with Dft of postscript of TJ's 23 Dec. 1793 letter to Harrison on verso. Dft (same, 14518); entirely in TJ's hand; undated; consists of one page containing preliminary formulations of debit entry of 10 Apr. 1793 and credit entries for 11-12 Apr. 1793 only. PrC of Tr (same, 96: 16461-2); in Taylor's hand; undated. Tr (DNA: RG 46, Senate Records, 3d Cong., 1st sess.); undated. PrC (DLC: TJ Papers, 96: 16451-2). FC (Lb in DNA: RG 59, DL). Tr (Lb in DNA: RG 46, Senate Records, 3d Cong., 1st sess., TR). Tr (MHi); 19th-century copy. Enclosed in George Washington to the Senate and the House of Representatives, 31 Dec. 1793.

The letter from John KEAN to TJ of 4 Nov. 1793, recorded in SJL as received from the Bank of the United States on 7 Nov. 1793, has not been found. Kean's missing LRE. THIS DATE—that is, 18 Dec. 1793—is not recorded in SJL.

[1] Amount inserted by Taylor in blank space left by TJ.

George Washington to the Senate and the House of Representatives

GENTLEMEN OF THE SENATE, AND
OF THE HOUSE OF REPRESENTATIVES   United States Decr. 31. 1793.

I now lay before you a letter from the Secretary of State, with his account of the expenditure of the monies appropriated for our intercourse with foreign nations, from the 1st. of July 1792 to the 1st. of July 1793. and other papers relating thereto.

PrC (DLC); in the hand of George Taylor, Jr., unsigned. Tr (MHi); 19th-century copy. Enclosures: TJ to Washington, 31 Dec. 1793 (first letter), and enclosures. The text of the message that Washington sent to Congress follows the wording of the PrC (DNA: RG 46, Senate Records, 3d Cong., 1st sess.).

From George Washington

DEAR SIR   31st. Decr. 1793.

It is my wish that the result of the determination on Mr. G—ts request may go to him with your Signature, and of this date. It was for this reason I aimed at a decision on it Sunday or yesterday. Yours always

GO: WASHINGTON

RC (Edward N. Bomsey, Springfield, Virginia, 1984). DETERMINATION ON MR. G—TS REQUEST: TJ to Edmond Charles Genet, 31 Dec. 1793.

From George Washington

DEAR SIR   Tuesday 31st. Decr. 1793.

I perceive by the Gazettes, that the Philosophical Society of this City, is required to meet on friday next. I am reminded by it, to ask if the names of Buchan and Anderson have ever yet been proposed as Members? Yours always   GO: WASHINGTON

RC (DLC); addressed: "Mr. Jefferson"; endorsed by TJ as received 31 Dec. 1793 and so recorded in SJL. Recorded in SJPL.

The advertisement for the 3 Jan. 1794 meeting of the American PHILOSOPHICAL SOCIETY, which TJ did not attend, appeared in *Dunlap and Claypoole's American*

Daily Advertiser, 30 Dec. 1793. His role, if any, is undocumented, but both the Earl of BUCHAN and James ANDERSON, as well as TJ's son-in-law, Thomas Mann Randolph, Jr., were elected on 18 Apr. 1794 (APS, *Proceedings*, XXII, pt. 3 [1885], 217, 220; note to Anderson to TJ, 3 Nov. 1792).

To George Washington

DEAR SIR   Philadelphia Dec. 31. 1793.

Having had the honor of communicating to you in my letter of the last of July, my purpose of retiring from the office of Secretary of state at the end of the month of September, you were pleased, for particular reasons, to wish it's postponement to the close of the year. That term being now arrived, and my propensities to retirement daily more and more irresistible, I now take the liberty of resigning the office into your hands. Be pleased to accept with it my sincere thanks for all the indulgencies which you have been so good as to exercise towards me in the discharge of it's duties. Conscious that my need of them has been great, I have still ever found them greater, without any other claim on my part than a firm pursuit of what has appeared to me to be right, and a thorough disdain of all means which were not as open and honorable, as their object was pure. I carry into my retirement a lively sense of your goodness, and shall continue gratefully to remember it. With very sincere prayers for your life, health and tranquility, I pray you to accept the homage of the great & constant respect & attachment with which I have the honor to be Dear Sir Your most obedient & most humble servt

TH: JEFFERSON

RC (DNA: RG 59, MLR); at foot of text: "The President of the US."; endorsed by Washington. PrC (DLC). Tr (Lb in DNA: RG 59, SDC).

From Oliver Wolcott, Jr.

Sir   Treasury Department Comptroller's office Decemr. 31: 1793.

I have the honour to enclose three copies of the Statement and Report on your account, with the account of the Bank of the United States with your department, and to be with perfect respect, Sir, Your obedt. Servt.

OLIV. WOLCOTT JR.

One of the copies not being at present compleated, will be sent in the course of the morning.

RC (DLC); in a clerk's hand, signed by Wolcott; at foot of text: "Thomas Jefferson Esquire Secretary of State." Dft (CtHi: Oliver Wolcott, Jr., Papers); in Wolcott's hand, with postscript added by clerk.

ACCOUNT OF THE BANK: Statement of the Foreign Fund Account, printed at TJ to George Washington, 31 Dec. 1793 (first letter).

I

Statement of Jefferson's Account as Secretary of State

Thomas Jefferson Esquire Secretary of State in Account Current with The United States

Dr.

To Treasury Warrants, for the following warrants drawn in his favour as ℗ certificate from the Register vizt.
Warrant No. 780 dated decr: 21st: 1790 for 1,233.33

				Dolls.	Cts
605	augst. 14		500.		
1062	may 7.	1791	13,000.		
1497	jany 29:	1792	40,000		
1498		do	38,766.67		
2612	march 30th: 1793		39,500		
3006	august 1		50,000		
				183,000	

Cr.

	Dolls.	Cts.
By David Humphreys advanced him on his mission to Madrid ℗ Rect. No. 1 dated august 10th. 1790 & for which he is to be held accountable	500	
By for this amount paid Gouvr. Morris decr. 17th: 1790 in a bill of exchange drawn by the Treasurer of the U: States, on W. & J. Willink & Nicholas & J van Staphorst & Hubbard of amsterdam being in part for said Morris's services as ℗ certificate of the President of the U: States f2475 equal to ℗ Voucher No. 2	1,000	
By John B. Cutting remitted him on account in a bill drawn by the Treasurer on the persons above mentioned for f577.10 equal to ℗ Vo. 3	233	33
By W. & J. Willink & Nicholas & J van Staphorst & Hubbard of Amsterdam, Agents for the department of State, for the following remittances made to them in bills drawn by the Treasurer of the United States and which they credit in their accounts Vos. No. 4 vizt		

f99,000 remitted march 19th. 1791 equal to 40,000
32,175 may 2 (subject to the orders of Humphreys & Barclay) eql. 13,000
95,947.10 jany 23d. 1792 equal to 38,766.67
123,750 june 30th do 50,000
f350,872.10 141,766.67

Of these bills Messrs. Willinks & van Staphorst & Hubbard in their letter of the 15th. august 1793 advise the acceptance to amount of £4000 Sterlg. The remainder appearing to have been purchased at a later date, no advice of their fate is yet received.

Dollars	183,000

For sundry bills of exchange on London as ⅌ particular account herewith to amount of £7377.11.9 Sterlg. purchased and remitted from the 11th. april to 30th. September 1793 to T. Pinckney Esqr. to be by him placed in the hands of the aforesaid Agents & for which was paid ⅌ Bank book & vouchers herewith No. 4 the sum of

32,913.33	174,680	
By Nathaniel Cutting advanced him April 12th. 1793 on account of his mission to Algiers ⅌ his rect. No. 5 & for which he is to be held accountable	1000	
By James Blake advanced him July 12th. 1793 on account of his mission to Madrid ⅌ Bank book & for which he is to be held accountable	800	
By balance due from T. Jefferson Esqr.	4,786	67
Dollars	183,000	

Comptroller's Office
30th. December 1793
A. BRODIE

Treasury Department
Auditor's office Decr. 28th. 1793
Stated & Examined by
DOYLE SWEENY

Tr (DLC: TJ Papers, 96: 16434-5); with subjoined attestation by Joseph Nourse; endorsed: "No. 4736. Statement of the Account of Thomas Jefferson Esqr Secretary of State (Copy)." Tr (DNA: RG 46, Senate Records, 3d Cong., 1st sess.); with Nourse's subjoined attestation. Tr (Lb in same, TR).

Treasury Report on Jefferson's Account as Secretary of State

No. 4736   Treasury Department Auditors Office Decr. 28th. 1793
    I have Examined and adjusted an Account between the United States and Thomas Jefferson Secretary of State for monies placed in his hands, by direction of the President of the United States, in pursuance of the Several Acts of Congress "providing the means of intercourse between the United States and foreign Nations" and find that he is chargeable on Said Account

To Amount of Sundry Warrants drawn in his favor for
the purposes abovementioned from the 14 August
1790 to the 1st. August 1793 as ⅌ Statement herewith   Dollars   183.000.

    I also find that he is Entitled to the following credits vizt.
By David Humphreys for this Amount Advanc'd him on his
    Mission to Madrid as ⅌ Statement   500.
By   for this Amount paid Gouvr. Morris in
    part for his Services ⅌ Do. Statement   1.000
By John B. Cutting for this amount remitted him for which he
    is accountable ⅌ Do.   233.33.
By Wilhem & J. Willink & N. & J. Van Staphorst & Hubbard
    Agents for the Department of State at Amsterdam for this
    amount remitted to them as particulariz'd in the Statement   174.680
By Nathaniel Cutting advanced him on Acct. of his Mission to
    Algiers ⅌ Statement   1.000
By James Blake advanced him on Acct. of his Mission to
    Madrid ⅌ Statement   800.

                                                          178.213.33

Leaving a ballance due from the said Thos. Jefferson
Esqr. & for which he is Accountable being to the
Credite of the Department of State in the Bank of the
United States the Sum of   4.786.67

                                            Dollars   183.000.

As will appear from the Statement & vouchers herewith transmitted for the Decision of the Comptroller of the Treasury thereon.

                                        R. Harrison Auditor
To Oliver Wolcott Jr. Esqr
Comptr of the Treasury

                                        Treasury Department
                                        Comptrollers Office
To Joseph Nourse Esqr   Decemr 30th. 1793
Register of the Treasury   Admitted & Certified
                                        Olivr Wolcott Jr. Comptr

    Tr (DLC); in the hand of a Treasury De-   Joseph Nourse; on docketing slip: "(Copy)
partment clerk; with subjoined attestation   No 4736 Auditors Report on the Accot of
of 30 Dec. 1793 by Register of the Treasury   Thos Jefferson Esqr. Secretary of State for

rect. & expenditure of monies placed in his hands for the purpose of providing the Means of Intercourse between the United States & foreign Nations Decr. 30. 1793."

Tr (DNA: RG 46, Senate Records, 3d Cong., 1st sess.); with Nourse's subjoined attestation of 30 Dec. 1793. Tr (Lb in same, TR).

To Joseph Yznardi, Jr.

SIR   Philadelphia Dec. 31. 1793.

I have just received your favors of the 29th. inst. public and private, and being in the moment of giving in my resignation I shall only answer the last by thanking you for the order for the wine, and informing you that Richmond is my nearest port and that to which both letters and things had best be addressed for me in future. Repeating assurances of my esteem, I have the honor to be Sir Your most obedt. & most humble servt   TH: JEFFERSON

PrC (DLC); at foot of text: "Joseph Yznardi esq." Tr (ViU: Edgehill-Randolph Papers); 19th-century copy; misdated 3 Dec. 1793.

Yznardi's PRIVATE letter of 29 Dec. 1793, recorded in SJL as received from New York on 31 Dec. 1793, has not been found.

Supplementary Documents

Down to the Year 1793

To ———

I like your proposal of keeping up an epistolary correspondence on subjects of some importance. I do not at present recollect any difficult question in natural philosophy, but shall be glad to have your opinion on a subject much more interesting. What that is I will tell you. In perusing a magazine some time ago I met with an account of a person who had been drowned. He had continued under water 24 hours, and upon being properly treated when taken out he was restored to life. The fact is undoubted, and upon enquiry I have found that there have been many other instances of the same kind. Physicians say that when the parts of the body[1] are restrained from performing their functions by any gentle cause which does not in any manner maim or injure any particular part, that to restore life in such a case nothing is requisite but to give the vital warmth[2] to the whole body by gentle degrees, and to put the blood in motion by inflating the lungs. But the doubts which arose in my mind on reading the story were of another nature. We are generally taught that the soul leaves the body at the instant of death, that is, at the instant in which the organs of the body cease totally to perform their functions. But does not this story contradict this opinion? When then does the soul take it's departure? Let me have your opinion candidly and at length[3] on this subject. And as these are doubts which, were they to come to light, might do injustice to a man's moral principles in the eyes of persons of narrow and confined views it will be proper to take great care of our letters. I propose as one mean of doing it to put no name or place[4] to the top or bottom of the letter, and to inclose it in a false cover which may be burned as soon as opened. No news in town only that Sir John Cockler has given Knox £450 for his house and lots here. Orion is 3 Hours–40′ west of the sun and of consequence goes down and rises that much before him. So you must rise early in the morning to see him. The upper star in his belt is exactly in the Æquinoctial.

RC (Gilder Lehrman Collection, on deposit NNP); unsigned, but apparently complete.

This manuscript, only recently come to light, is said to have "descended in a family with connections to the Pages of Virginia" (Sotheby's, Catalogue No. 6553, 3 May 1994, Lot 60). The possibility exists that the recipient was John Page, a lifelong friend who preserved the bulk of TJ's surviving correspondence for the early 1760s. Although they had discussed ways of shielding their correspondence six months before (TJ to Page, 23 Jan. 1764), neither internal evidence nor the sparseness of TJ's papers for this period allows more confident speculation. The letter itself reflects the period in TJ's life when, as he later informed a correspondent who had raised another question about the SOUL, he was "fond of the speculations which seemed to promise some insight" into the "country of spirits" (TJ to Isaac Story, 5 Dec. 1801). It is also symptomatic of the rational investigation of traditional Christian doctrine that he carried out during the same period (*Extracts*, ed. Adams, 5-7; *LCB*, ed. Wilson, 8, 214).

[1] Preceding five words interlined in place of "none of the parts of the body are injured, but."

[2] Preceding two words written over "whole body."

[3] Preceding three words interlined.

[4] Preceding two words interlined.

Report on Parliamentary Procedure

[8 Nov.–8 Dec. 1769]

A.6.   √   Resolved that a question being once determined must stand as the judgment of the house, and cannot again be drawn into debate.[1]

A.9.   √   Ordered that the orders for the business appointed for the day be read by the clerk before any other matter be proceeded on.[2]

A.5.   √   Ordered that when a question shall arise between the greater and lesser sum or the longer and shorter time, the question shall be first put on the least sum and longest time.[3]

A.10.   √   Ordered that all bills be read and receive dispatch in[4] priority and order of time as they were brought in.[5]

D3.   √   Resolved that any person shall be at liberty to sue out an original writ or subpoena in chancery[6] in order to prevent a bar by the statute of limitations, or to file any bill in equity to examine witnesses thereupon[7] in order only to preserve their testimony, against any member of this house notwithstanding his privilege[8] provided that the clerk after having made out and signed such original writ or subpoena[9] shall not deliver the same to the party or to any other during the continuance of that privilege.

D.4.   √   Resolved that all persons who are summoned[10] to attend this house or any committee thereof as witnesses[11] in any matter depending before them be privileged from arrests[12] during[. . . .][13]

[*on verso:*]

A.13.   √   Ordered that when the house is to rise every member keep his seat till the speaker go out, and then every one in his course orderly[14] as he sits.

A.7.a.   √   Ordered that no member while another is speaking in the course of debate while any bill, order, or other matter shall be reading or opening, or[15] while the speaker is putting any question,[16] shall entertain[17] private discourse, stand up, walk into, out of, or across the house[18] or read any printed book.

A.8.b.   √   Ordered that no member who is not present when any question is put by Mr. speaker be counted on either side tho' he happen to be present at the time of the division.

A 8.a.   √   That no member shall vote on any question, in the event of which he is immediately interested.[19]

D.2.   √   That the privilege of this house shall not be allowed to any member in cases wherein he is only a trustee.[20]

D1.   √   That[21] any member may waive his privilege in matters[22] of a private nature without the leave of the house, and having so done he shall not[23] resume the same.

[. . .] 5.b. √   That[24] no person be taken into the custody of the serjeant at arms on any complain[. . . .][25]

Dft (ViU); entirely in TJ's hand; undated; consisting of a single sheet torn away at bottom, probably at a fold, resulting in two fragments arbitrarily designated by the Editors as recto and verso, and the loss of an indeterminable amount of text, one or more additional sheets presumably being lost (see below); only the most significant emendations are noted below, those made to the marginal glosses being omitted.

This draft report marks TJ's earliest surviving documentary contribution as a public official to promoting the orderly conduct of legislative business, a subject of enduring interest that culminated during his vice-presidency with the publication in 1801 of his *Manual of Parliamentary Practice*, which still helps to guide parliamentary procedure in the United States Congress today (*Parl. Writings*, ed. Howell, 435-41). The report grew out of TJ's membership on the Committee of Privileges and Elections, a standing body to which he was initially appointed by the House of Burgesses on 8 May 1769, his second committee assignment during his inaugural session as a Virginia legislator and one which seems to have inspired him to begin his first serious study of parliamentary practice (*Journal of the House of Burgesses*, May 1769 [Williamsburg, 1769], 5; Perkins, Buchanan & Brown to TJ, 2 Oct. 1769; *Parl. Writings*, ed. Howell, 4-5). On 7 Nov. 1769, during his second leg-

islative session, the Burgesses reappointed him to this committee, which was chaired by Edmund Pendleton, and charged it on the following day to "consider of the ancient Rules and standing Orders of the House, and present such as are fit to be continued, with any others which they think ought to be observed." TJ wrote his draft sometime between that date and 8 Dec. 1769, when Pendleton presented a revised and significantly reordered version of it as the committee's report to the Burgesses, who then read it and ordered that its "Orders and Resolutions be standing Orders of the House" (*Journal of the House of Burgesses*, November-December 1769 [Williamsburg, 1769], 5, 11, 124-5).

What survives of TJ's draft is considerably shorter than the report the Burgesses approved, making it impossible to determine the full extent to which the Committee on Privileges and Elections revised it. Although every section of TJ's draft except those dealing with the LONGER AND SHORTER TIME and the PRIVILEGE OF THIS HOUSE appears in the committee's report either verbatim or in revised form in the order indicated by his marginal glosses (see notes below), that report contains seventeen other sections that appear before, between, or after those in the incomplete manuscript printed here (same, 124-5).

[1] Here *Journal* adds "during the same Session."

[2] *Journal*: "*Ordered*, That each Day, before the House proceed on any other Business, the Clerk do read the Orders for taking any Matters into Consideration that Day."

[3] Paragraph omitted in *Journal*.

[4] TJ first wrote "bills receive dispatch according to" and then altered it to read as above. *Journal*: "and dispatched in."

[5] Here *Journal* adds "unless the House shall direct otherwise in particular Cases."

[6] Preceding four words interlined.

[7] In *Journal* the remainder of this clause reads "for the sole Purpose of preserving their Testimony."

[8] Preceding three words interlined.

[9] Preceding two words omitted in *Journal*.

[10] *Journal*: "every Person summoned."

[11] *Journal*: "a Witness."

[12] *Journal*: "Arrest."

[13] Remainder of recto torn away, the ascenders of another line of text being barely visible. In *Journal* the remainder of this paragraph reads: "his coming to, attending on, or going from the House or Committee; and that no such Witness shall be obliged to attend, until the Party at whose Request he shall be summoned, do pay, or secure to him, for his Attendance and Travelling, the same Allowance which is made to Witnesses attending the General Court."

[14] *Journal*: "every one to follow in Order."

[15] *Journal* omits everything in the foregoing part of this paragraph beginning with "no member."

[16] Preceding twenty words interlined in place of a heavily canceled passage. *Journal* here inserts "none."

[17] Preceding two words written over an erased passage.

[18] TJ wrote the preceding ten words over an erased passage that is illegible except for the ending "to another."

[19] Below this paragraph TJ canceled the following entry: "That the orders of the house be drawn up every day and read the next morning before any other business be done; and then entered in the journal and printed without delay." He added the last clause after writing the next paragraph. *Journal* combines the preceding two paragraphs: "*Ordered*, That no Member shall vote on any Question, in the Event of which he is immediately interested; nor in any other Case, where he was not present when the Question was put by the Speaker, or by the Chairman in any Committee."

[20] Paragraph omitted in *Journal*.

[21] *Journal* begins this paragraph with "*Resolved*."

[22] *Journal*: "in any Matter."

[23] *Journal* here adds "in that Instance."

[24] *Journal* begins this paragraph with "*Ordered*."

[25] Remainder torn away, the ascenders of another line of text being barely visible. In *Journal* the remainder of this paragraph reads: "Complaint of a Breach of Privilege, until the Matter of such Complaint shall have been examined by the Committee of Privileges, and reported to the House."

From Samuel Jordan, with Jefferson's Notes

SIR   Augst. 7. 1770

I some time Since received a letter from Colo. Randolph of Tuckahoe requesting I would inform him what I knew of his right to Leatherwood land and as you are or will be his Lawer I trouble you with it which is as follows. There was leive granted by the Council to Colo. Peter Jefferson Charles Lynch and Ambross Smith to take up fifteen Thousand Acres of Land adjoining Randolph & Co. at the Wart mountain extending toward the Branches of James's River. One third of said order was purchas'd by Colo. William Randolph of Tuckahoe of Colo. Jefferson the other two thirds Colo. Lomax purchased. By virtue of said order I directed the Survey on Leatherwood I think in 1747. Soon after it was cavited by Reid, Jones & Co. and on hearing, the Council gave it against Lomax and Randolph, and I think Lomax pray'd an Appeal. After that the Contending Parties agreed that If the Council would grant them leive to take up twenty Thousand Acres of Land on Beaver, and Reedy Creeks and some creeks below leatherwood to take place before any other order or entry where Right was not[1] that the appeal should be drop't and they the contending parties become one company [on which?] the council did grant such order, and I directed the Survey [. . .] them. Since that I know nothing but by information which is [that] Reid, Jones &c took the last Survey'd Lands for their parts and Sold them to Ennis, Rose, and Copeland and they have them in possession and that the Survey on leatherwood remains between Lomax and Randolph as if never disputed which was the reason I never mentioned the circumstance of the Cavit to Colo. Randolph. If you'll be kind enough to let me know by Mr. Nicholas or otherwise how my causes stands it will greatly oblige Sr. Yr Very Hble Servt   SAML JORDAN

[*Notes by TJ:*]

Lomax
  v.   } S. Jordan's letter.
Lomax et al

That was joint ord. conc. to Lom, Rand, Reid, Jones & al.
That was division
That those on Leatherwood (15,000 as.) left to Lom & Rand.
  the rest to Reid, Jones et al.
    who conveied to Innis, Rose, Copeld.
Aug. 14. I wrote to Jordan
  that I expected T. M. Randolph was not conce[rned?] if there was ever actual division
  that if was no division he must a[. . .]
  inclosed subpoena ad test.
  that expected would prove effects on the land.

RC (ViHi); with notes on verso by TJ; torn at seal; addressed: "To Mr. Thomas Jefferson attorney at Law Albemarle ℔ favour Mr Nicholas."

Samuel Jordan (ca. 1710-89), a planter of the Seven Islands, Buckingham County, Virginia, served as sheriff of Albemarle County, 1753-55, was presiding justice of the peace and county lieutenant of Buckingham County at its creation in 1761, represented Buckingham in the House of Burgesses, 1765-68, and served as a militia colonel in the Revolution and as an Anglican vestryman (Alexander Brown, *The Cabells and Their Kin* . . . [Boston and New York, 1895], 127-9; Edythe R. Whitley, *Genealogical Records of Buckingham County, Virginia* [Baltimore, 1984], 1, 98; William G. Stanard and Mary N. Stanard, *The Colonial Virginia Register* [Albany, 1902], 171, 174, 176, 178).

Thomas Mann Randolph, Sr., engaged TJ as legal counsel because of his fear that the supposedly friendly action of Lomax v. Innes's heirs would hurt his one-third interest in the LEATHERWOOD tract (MB, legal section, 12, 25 June, 14 Aug. 1770; TJ's Case Book, No. 423, 12 June 1770). Jordan's CAUSES, a suit brought against him by Nathaniel Terry of Halifax County, remained unsettled when TJ turned over his

law practice to Edmund Randolph in 1774 (MB, legal section, 10 Aug. 1769; TJ's Case Book, No. 369, 10 Aug. 1769).

TJ's letter TO JORDAN of 14 AUG. 1770 has not been found.

[1] Preceding four words interlined.

To Thomas Turpin

DEAR SIR   June 3. 1771.

Below I send you a state of the prices of the books you mentioned in your's as far as it is my power to judge without having seen them. Much depends on their being new, much or little worn, and also upon the editions. And besides this the prices are sometimes accidentally high or low. However I have affixed such prices as I have usually known them cost in England. If the Hawkins's pleas of the crown be in folio, a single volume, and not abused I would gladly take it myself and in that case would ask the favor of you to send it either to J. Bolling's, to Tuckahoe or to Richmond for me, with a line as to the advance, and the money shall be sent by the first opportunity. As to the rest I shall take a pleasure in procuring you a chap for them if in my power. Be pleased to tender my most sincere affections to my aunt and the family, whom with yourself I shall mostly gladly visit whenever the necessities of my business shall allow me to deviate so far from the direct road. That it should not will appear strange to you, tho' I assure you it is a truth. I am generally detained at home in preparation for the court till I have but barely time to get to it, and never pass more than one night with my sisters on the road. My returns are generally as precipitate in order to be at Albemarle court which is commonly but three or four days after the General court rises. However some opportunity it is hoped will occur, and shall be most gladly embraced by Dr. Sir Your affectionate friend & kinsman

TH: JEFFERSON

[Po]llexfen's reports 20/ sterl.
[Da]lrymple. if 8vo is 5/ —if 12mo, it is 3/
[Ha]le's history of the laws 5/
[Cok?]e's reports. £3.7.6
[Stra]nge's reports £3.
[Sal]keld's reports if 1. vol. 30/ —if 2. vols 40/ —if 3 vols £2.
[Ha]wkins's pleas of the crown if 8vo. 10/ —if one vol. folio 30/ —if 2. vols folio £2.
[Vau]ghan's reports 20/.

RC (ViU); left edge of subjoined list torn away; opposite signature in an unidentified hand: "To Col Thos Turpin Powhatan Co Va"; with calculations by Turpin at foot of text.

Turpin's letter asking for THE PRICES OF

THE BOOKS has not been found. Sir John DALRYMPLE, *An Essay towards a General History of Feudal Property in Great Britain*, appeared in three 8vo and two 12mo editions in London and Dublin, 1757-59. See also Sowerby, No. 2005.

From John Lewis

SR.   October 4—1772

Have received yours by Col. Lewis's Man, and find he has not deliver'd my mesage as I directed, should have wrote to you had I bin accquainted of his going, but happen'd to find him in his journey to you, and deliver'd this mesage—to ask you if you had taken Mr. Carrs, and Mr. Jno. Woodsons, diposisions, as I have formerly requested, being at so great distance from me which made it inconvenient. The two evidences above, are the most material in my behalf, the first to prove the tender of the last payment, with an overplush of Money to make up payment had I made any mistake in the Account, and other things that I cant at preasent recollect, the latter to prove Mayo's giving up the Creek low grounds, which was not to be meashur'd, and how he exspected the line was to go across the Creak to turn them out from the River. You have inform'd me that living and well evidences must apear at tryal, but I do indeavour to prepare against dangers, as you may see Mayo's evidences and mine in the Office, if you think it may be as safe without there apearing as with it, and will signiefie the same, shall indevour to git Mayo's consent to it. Please to answer this fully, and let me know when you exspect the Sute will be try'd. From Yr Very hble Servt   JNO. LEWIS BD.

PS [Have just?] one of the subpeanies lef that you sent me, Please let me know if that will be good, should I want another deposision.

RC (George M. Cochran, Staunton, Virginia, 1976); torn; addressed: "To Mr. Thomas Jefferson Wms Burg"; endorsed by TJ: "John Lewis To be answd, from home"; with apparently unrelated calculations by TJ on recto and verso.

John Lewis (1720-94) was born in New Kent County, moved when young to Goochland County with his father, Charles Lewis, who named his estate there "The Byrd," and subsequently became a planter

in Pittsylvania County, where he gave his own estate the same name and referred to himself as John Lewis of The Byrd to avoid confusion with others sharing this common surname (WMQ, 1st ser., x [1901], 52-3; Maud C. Clement, *The History of Pittsylvania County Virginia* [Lynchburg, 1929], 104-5, 166).

In 1768 Lewis had engaged TJ to defend him in two related legal disputes with John Mayo of Cumberland County. Both cases were unresolved and transferred to Edmund Randolph when TJ gave up his legal practice in 1774 (MB, legal section, 14 Aug., 25 Sep., 8 Nov. 1768, 2 July 1770; TJ's Case Book, Nos. 133 and 138, 14 Aug. and 25 Sep. 1768).

To Ann Eppes Harris

DEAR MADAM   Williamsburgh Apr. 26. 1773

I have applied to Mr. Waller on the subject of your bonds. He sais that Colo. Hunter when he left the country directed him not to call for the money due from yourself and son nor to do any thing further with your bonds till further orders. On being furnished by Daniel Hylton[1] with a copy of Colo. Hunter's letter [. . .] he immediately inclosed it to Colo. H[unter an]d desired his directions [. . .] for these therefore he now [. . . .][2] [to do noth?]ing till he receives them. There is a p[oint in Colo. Hun?]ter's letter which Mr. Waller did not understand, nor was I so far instructed as to be able to explain it. When I have the pleasure of seeing you you can let me into the light of it.—The Long-mountain lands are once more saved, Mr. Swann's petition being again dismissed with costs. I will send you up an execution for the costs as soon after the court as it can be made out.   I forget whether I informed yourself or your son Ned that I had got the patent made out and sealed for the lands on Otter. This secures them effectually, and on calling the caveat in June I shall hope to have costs allowed you in that also.—You desired to know when I shall be at Mr. Wayles's after the court, and promise us the pleasure of seeing you there. I cannot with great certainty fix on the day, because it is incertain when the merchants will finish their business here, which being done I shall go to Mr. Wayles's and after staying there three or four days shall proceed home. I expect however to leave this place about the 7th. of May, and Mr. Wayles's the 11th. Patty will not go up with me till after the June court, when we will infallibly do ourselves the pleasure of calling on you. Mr. Wayles has been very ill for some months past, and still continues so. He mends slowly. His physician has given us hopes that he will continue to do so, tho' he thinks it will be long before his health will be established. I am with compliments to your family Dear Madam Your affectionate friend

TH: JEFFERSON

P.S. I think Skipp Harris should lose not a moment till he gets a deed from Hall for the Long-mountain, since Swann talks of trying some other way of getting the money he sais is due out of this land. If he should get a conveiance from Hall I am afraid we should be much puzzled to set it right again.

RC (Cumberland County Circuit Court, Cumberland, Virginia); lacks address; torn at seal.

Ann Eppes Harris (d. 1787), the widow of Benjamin Harris and the sister of TJ's mother-in-law Martha Eppes Wayles, lived at Indian Camp, a 2,400-acre estate that was located in the part of Cumberland County, Virginia, soon to become Powhatan County, and had been given to her and Martha Eppes Wayles by their father Francis Eppes. Martha Wayles Skelton Jefferson—TJ's wife PATTY—had inherited the other half of Indian Camp when her mother died, although her father, John Wayles, held a life interest. After Wayles died in May 1773, TJ and his wife joined Mrs. Harris in a successful petition to the House of Burgesses to have Indian Camp partitioned, upon which the Jeffersons sold their half to Henry Skipwith in 1774 (Will of Ann Eppes Harris, [1777], and note, printed below; TJ to Jerman Baker, 22 June 1824; MB, legal section, 28 Jan. 1774, and note).

The LONG-MOUNTAIN LANDS consisted of 750 acres in Bedford County. TJ sent the writ of EXECUTION, a capias ad satisfaciendum on Thompson Swann, to Mrs. Harris on or after 9 Aug. 1773. The CAVEAT first entered by TJ on behalf of Edward and Ann Harris on 5 Apr. 1772 concerned 400 acres on Little Otter Creek in Bedford County. In neither case did TJ charge his wife's aunt for his services (TJ's Case Book, Nos. 642-3, 5 Apr. 1772). John SKIPP HARRIS evidently responded to TJ's warning by engaging him to bring suit against John Hall for 750 acres in Bedford on 2 Jan. 1774 (MB, legal section, 2 Jan. 1774; TJ's Case Book, No. 911, 2 Jan. 1774).

[1] Preceding three words interlined.
[2] Estimated five words missing.

Notes for Epitaph and Grave of Dabney Carr

[after 16 May 1773]

Inscription on my friend D. Carr's tomb-stone.

Lamented shade! [whom ev'ry][1] gift of heav'n
Profusely blest: a[2] temper winning mild;
Nor pity softer, nor was truth more bright.
Constant in doing well, he neither sought
Nor shunn'd applause. No bashful merit sigh'd
Near him neglected: sympathizing he
Wip'd off the tear from Sorrow's clouded eye
With kindly hand and taught her heart to smile.
        Mallet's Excursion.

send for a plate of copper to be nailed on the tree at the foot of his grave with this inscription

Still shall thy grave with rising flow'rs be dress'd
And the green turf lie lightly on thy breast:
There shall the morn her earliest tears bestow,
There the first roses of the year shall blow:
While angels with their silver wings o'ershade
The ground now sacred by thy reliques made.

On the upper part of the stone inscribe as follows
      Here lie the remains
        of DABNEY CARR
      Son of John & Jane Carr of Louisa county
      who was born   1744.
      intermarried with Martha Jefferson
      daur. of Peter and Jane Jefferson
            1765.
      and died at Charlottesville May. 16. 1773.
          leaving six small children.
    To his Virtue, Good sense, learning and Friendship
    this stone is dedicated by Thomas Jefferson
    who of all men living loved him most.

[Lengthwise in margin at foot of recto:]
This stone shall rise with all it's moss and speak to other years 'here lie
&c'[3] see 2. Ossian pa. 53. a fine inscription. see post

[on verso:]
1773. May. 22. two hands grubbed the grave yard 80. f. sq. = $\frac{1}{7}$ of an
acre in $3\frac{1}{2}$ hours, so that one would have done it in 7. hours, and
would grub an acre in 49. hours = 4. days.

weight of Ry. Rand's chain
3f–$\frac{1}{2}$Inch weighed 23 oz–8 dwt

---

2. Ossian. 53. Temora. b.2. This stone shall rise with all it's moss and
speak to other years 'here lies[4] gentle Carr[5] within the dark and narrow
house where no morning comes with her half opening eyes.' when thou,
O stone, shall fail $\lbrace$ and the mountain stream roll quite away!
              moulder down and lose thee in the moss of years.[6]
then shall the traveller come, and bend here perhaps in rest. when the
darkened moon is rolled over his head, the shadowy form[7] may come,
and, mixing with his dreams, remind him who is here.

      Hon. V.
     Joanni Page
    Opusculum hoc
      Amicitiae
       Pignus
    Dat, Donatque
    T. Jefferson.
      17—

MS (Dabney J. Carr, III, on deposit ViU); written entirely in TJ's hand at different times on both sides of a single sheet; with recto undated and verso beginning with entry of 22 May 1773; apparently unrelated dedication to John Page subjoined; faded; printed literally.

Dabney Carr, TJ's brother-in-law and closest friend, had died of a bilious fever on 16 May 1773. According to family tradition, in TJ's absence Carr was buried at Shadwell, but upon his return TJ had a graveyard prepared at Monticello and reinterred Carr there at a spot the two had previously chosen, which served thereafter as the Jefferson family cemetery and TJ's own burial spot (Randall, *Life*, I, 83; Malone, *Jefferson*, I, 160-1, 431). TJ was the sole executor of Carr's estate, with Thomas Mann Randolph, Sr., and David Coupland joining him as sureties in a bond for £4,000, dated 19 July 1773, pledging that he would accurately compile and present an inventory of the estate to the Goochland County Court, account for its administration, and pay the legacies stipulated in the will as far as the estate extended (MS in Vi: Goochland County Court Records; in a clerk's hand, signed by TJ, Randolph, and Coupland).

TJ had previously extracted the quotation from David MALLET's poem, "The Excursion," in his Literary Commonplace Book; he abridged but did not otherwise alter it for the inscription. The quotation in-tended for engraving on a PLATE OF COPPER was copied almost verbatim from a Literary Commonplace Book extract taken from Alexander Pope, "Elegy to the Memory of an Unfortunate Lady" (*LCB*, ed. Wilson, 131n, 132-3, 138-9).

TJ copied into his Garden Book variant versions of his notes on the labor needed to GRUB AN ACRE and on the WEIGHT of Ryland Randolph's fencing CHAIN (Betts, *Garden Book*, 40). He combined and revised for his own use two widely separated passages for the quotation from James Macpherson's epic poem "Temora," ostensibly written by the Gaelic poet OSSIAN (Macpherson, *The Works of Ossian, the Son of Fingal*, 2 vols. [London, 1765], II, 52, 100). MOULDER . . . YEARS: possibly a construct by TJ from portions of the shorter version of "Temora" (same, I, 247, 266n).

HON. V. . . . T. JEFFERSON: "To the Honorable John Page, this small work of friendship, a token, T. Jefferson gives and offers."

[1] MS faded; words supplied from *LCB*, ed. Wilson, 132.

[2] Word interlined in place of "his."

[3] Closing quotation mark supplied.

[4] TJ here canceled what appears to be "the remains of the."

[5] Remainder of sentence interlined.

[6] Alternate sentence ending interlined by TJ.

[7] Phrase reworked from "our shadowy forms."

Deed from Jane Randolph Jefferson for the Conveyance of Slaves

Whereas Peter Jefferson[1] did by his last will and testament bequeath to Jane Jefferson his wife[2] one sixth part of all his slaves during her life, with power by deed or will to appoint the same to any of his children as she should think proper, and on his death partition having been made, the several slaves hereafter named with divers others were alloted to the said Jane: and whereas Thomas Jefferson one of the children of the said Peter hath paid and assumed to pay for the said Jane divers large sums of money, which she the said Jane hath no means or prospect of repaying to him, and is also indebted to him other monies on her own proper account; and it is just that the said Jane should make to him the only recompense which it is in her power to make; Now this indenture made on the twenty ninth day of September in the year of our lord one thousand seven hundred and seventy three between the said Jane and the said Thomas witnesseth that the said Jane in pursuance of the said power and authority by the said will of her husband to her given doth by these presents appoint, give and convey unto the said Thomas and his heirs the following negro slaves to wit, Caesar, Val, Simon, Lucinda, Charlotte, Squire, Belinda, and her children not before named, Sall the elder and her children not before named, Sall the younger and her children not before named Minerva, Sarah, Cyrus[3] and the future issue of all the said slaves—some of which said slaves are in possession of the said Thomas by virtue of a lease of the same with the Shadwell plantation made to the said Thomas by the said Jane for her life, and others thereof are in the possession of the said Jane.

Provided nevertheless that nothing in this deed contained shall bar or restrain the said Jane from having and demanding during her life the hire for such of the said slaves as are in the said lease conveyed, nor from keeping during her life possession of such others as, being not under lease, are in her possession.

Provided also that it shall be lawful for the said Jane by her last will and testament duly executed in writing to appoint any of the said slaves to any other of her children, such appointee, or any other person paying to the said Thomas within one year after her death[4] all sums of money which shall then be due to the said Thomas from the said Jane and all sums for which the said Thomas shall stand engaged for her. In witness whereof the said Jane hath hereto put her hand and seal the day and year above-written.   JANE JEFFERSON

signed, sealed and ⎫ the words 'Jane   ⎫ THOS. GARTH
delivered in   ⎬ Jefferson his wife' ⎬
presence of   ⎭ being first interlined ⎭ JOSH. HUCKSTEP
also the words 'within one year after her death.'

MS (MHi); in TJ's hand, signed by Mrs. Jefferson, with seal affixed, and witnessed by Thomas Garth and Joseph Huckstep; endorsed by TJ:

"Jane Jefferson ⎫ Deed of
    to   ⎬
Thos. Jefferson ⎭ Appointmt.";

beneath endorsement in an unknown hand: "Recorded & Ed."; notation on verso by deputy clerk: "Albemarle County [. . .] This Deed was proved by the Oath of Thos. Garth & Joseph Huckstep wits. thereto & Ordered to be recorded—Teste Tucker Woodson D.C."

Jane Randolph Jefferson (1720-76), TJ's mother, was born in England, the eldest of the nine surviving children of Isham and Jane Rogers Randolph, but soon moved with her family to Virginia and lived at Dungeness plantation in Goochland County when she married Peter Jefferson in October 1739. With the exception of a period of residence at Tuckahoe plantation from about 1746 to 1752, she lived throughout her marriage and during her widowhood at Shadwell, the Albemarle County estate her husband named for the London parish where she was baptized (Malone, *Jefferson*, I, 13-15, 19-21, 26, 216, 429). This conveyance is the only document exchanged between TJ and his mother that is known to the Editors.

The will of TJ's father PETER JEFFERSON was dated 13 July 1757 and admitted to probate on 13 Oct. 1757 (Tr in Albemarle County Will Book, Albemarle County Circuit Court Clerk's Office, Char-

lottesville). TJ later said that he spent much more settling his mother's debts than he received from her or her estate (TJ to James Lyle, 7 Oct. 1791).

[1] TJ here canceled "my late husband."
[2] Preceding four words interlined in place of "me."
[3] TJ here left blank portions of two lines, which suggests that he filled in the names of the slaves after composing the rest of the document.
[4] Preceding six words interlined.

From John Hook

SIR   New Londo May 12 1774

I sent a Message to you by Mr. Steptoe offering you a small tract of Land laying between your Old and new tracts in this County, it was formerly the property of Saml. Brown, at £100 payable as follows, £40 to be paid [at the?] ensuing June or July Meeting of the Merchants in [Wil]lmsbg. and the Remainder by XMass or Aprl. 1775. Since then I have determined to write you by Mr. Ross,[1] that I may have your Answer and to have a bargain concluded if you are agreeable. Mr. Ross is Partner in the Land with me and will confirm it on our part.[2] As to the quallity of the Land if you are not aquainted with it I can give you no satisfaction as I never see it.[3] I have been offered once £75. for it and once another Piece of Land in Exchange that cost 100£ and has since sold for £11[0]. Brown was indebted to me, I feard if he sold his Land [to] any one else I should loose my Debt, this was [. . .] for buying it, I beleve it is worth more to you then to any other Person[4] on Account of its laying between your River and Forrest tract[s]. There is 282 Acres of it includeing the Patent land and two [. . .]. We will make you a Deed for the Whole. I [cannot?] conveniently lay long out of my Money[5] else [I?] do not fear but I should in one or two years be able [to sell?] it for a Much better price. I have been offerd two other small Pieces of Land I think on good terms[6] joining to this I offer you. I do[. . .] want to deal[7] in that Article but if you want [. . .] and I can be of any service to you in the Purchase I make you a tender of my best services in that way & am

Dft (Vi: John Hook Letterbook); unsigned; mutilated; at head of text. "Mr Thos Jefferson"; only the most significant emendations are recorded below.

Hook's earlier MESSAGE has not been found. On 14 May 1774 he enclosed this letter in one to his partner, David ROSS, also written from New London, in Bedford

County, Virginia, authorizing him to settle for their own purchase price of £70 if necessary and admitting that the land was "not such a bargain as I first apprehended" (Vi: John Hook Letterbook). TJ apparently declined to purchase the land.

¹ Preceding three words interlined.
² Preceding four words interlined in place of "what I offer."
³ Hook here canceled "(till last ⟨Sunday⟩ Saturday and then I only see the small

piece that is cleard. I went with a design to get one of the Neighbours to show it to me but he was from home ⟨so that⟩, I bought it of Brown for Seventy Pounds before [. . .] of it was cleard out of the Office."
⁴ Hook here canceled "being ⟨convenient to⟩ contiguous to both your [. . .] Planta-[tions]."
⁵ Hook here canceled "at this time."
⁶ Preceding five words interlined.
⁷ Word interlined in place of "specu-late."

Election Tally for the Virginia Committee of Safety

[17 Aug. 1775]

John Page ....|···|···|···|···|···|···|···|···|···|···|···|···|···|···|···| 70. √
R. C. Nicholas ....|... 8 √
R. Bland ....|·········|·········|·········|·········|······ 66 √
E. Pendleton ....|·········|·········|·········|·········|·········|·········|·········|········· 77 √
A. Cary ....|·········|·········| 26 √
D. Digges ....|·········|·········|·········|··· 42 √
C. Carter ....|·········|···· 23 √
T. L. Lee ....|·········|·········|·········|·········|·········|··· 63 √
Jo: Jones ....|·········|······ 26 √
John Nicholas .... 4 √
John Blair .... 4 √
Jas. Holt ....|······· 17. √
B. Dandridge ....|·········|·········|···· 35 √
C. Braxton ....|·········|·········|···· 38 √
J. Mercer ....|·········|·········|······· 38 √
P. Carrington ....|·········|·········|·········|·········|··· 54 √
J. Washington .. 2 √
G. Mason ....|·········|·········|·········|·········|·········|··· 72 √
J. Banister ....|·········|··· 23 √
G. Rootes ....|·········|········· 29 √
T. Lewis . 1. √
J. Harvie ....|····· 15. √
[Jo]hn Page Junr. . 1. √
[W.] Cabell ....|·········|·········|······· 39 √
[J.] Tabb ....|·········|·········|····· 36. √
[W.] Fitzhugh ...... 6 √
B. Martin ... 3 √

H. Lee .. 2 √
M. Page Junr. .. 2 √
R. Randolph .. 2 √
N. Lewis .... 4 √
J. Bowyer . 1√
J. Tazewell ..... 5 √
Jas. Madison .. 2 √
Gal: Jones ...... 6 √
Ry: Randolph . 1 √
Thomps. Mason .. 2 √
T. Whitinge .. 2 √
Theo: Bland .. 2 √
The revd. Mr. Thruston .. 2 √
I. Zane . 1 √
And: Lewis .. 2 √
Joseph Hutchings .. 2 √
Feilding Lewis .. 2 √
James Madison, junr. .. 2 √
Thomas Walker . 1 √
John Lewis Spotsylva. . 1 √
Theod. Bland junr. . 1 √
T. M. Randolph . 1 √
Davd Mason . 1 √

MS (Vi: Third Virginia Convention, Loose Papers); probably in an unidentified hand in part, with the last eight names and numerical totals added by TJ, the dots and check marks being in TJ's or another hand; undated, but assigned on basis of minutes of the Third Virginia Convention (see below); left margin partly torn away; with inverted and unrelated notation in the hand of John Tazewell, clerk of the Convention.

This is the only known manuscript in TJ's hand deriving from his activities at the Third Virginia Convention in Richmond, where he stopped on 9 Aug. 1775 on his way home from service at the Continental Congress. He was reelected to Congress and served on several committees until obtaining leave on 16 Aug. to proceed to Monticello, but he tarried one day longer, for on 17 Aug. the Convention chose him along with fellow congressmen Benjamin Harrison and Richard Henry Lee and militia commander Patrick Henry, all presumably ineligible by virtue of their other responsibilities, to count the ballots for the eleven-man Committee of Safety established to govern the colony until the next Convention met. Since the Convention's journal recorded only the names and votes of the winning eleven, this tally is significant as a comprehensive record of the balloting (William J. Van Schreeven, Robert L. Scribner, and Brent Tarter, eds., *Revolutionary Virginia: The Road to Independence*, 7 vols. in 8 [Charlottesville, 1973-83], III, 409, 418-19, 451, 456-7, 460-2).

To William Bradford

SIR   Albemarle in Virginia, April 26th. 1777.

I am constrained by the subscribers to your paper in this neighborhood to trouble you with information of the uncertainty with which they seem likely to come. The first mail came about ten days ago open and loose, and containing not more than one paper for any subscriber, and none for several. The papers which came were of three several dates. The last mail, which would have been the second, brought not a single paper. Where the failure happens, we know not; but mean to inquire. In order to do this, it will be essential that you observe our former direction in making up and *sealing* the mail, as we *suppose* that it is for want of *this* circumstance the papers are taken out *either by the riders for sale*, or by others.

Your punctual attention to this will oblige your customers here as well as, sir, your humble servant,   TH: JEFFERSON

MS not found; reprinted from John W. Wallace, *An Old Philadelphian, Colonel William Bradford, The Patriot Printer of 1776: Sketches of his Life* (Philadelphia, 1884), 327; at foot of text: "Mr. William Bradford."

William Bradford (1722-91), grandson of the famous printer of the same name in the Middle Colonies and nephew of Andrew Bradford, who founded the first newspaper in Pennsylvania, was a printer and Revolutionary soldier whose PAPER, *The Pennsylvania Journal; and the Weekly Advertiser*, was one of Philadelphia's leading newspapers for half a century (DAB).

Memorandum on Paper Money

[October 1777-January 1778]

year.	sum in circulatn.	rate	sum raised
1778.	3,125,000 £	10/	500,000
1779.	2,625,000	20/	1,000,000
1780.	1,625,000	15/	750,000
1781.	875,000	10/	500,000
1782.	375,000	5/	250,000
1783.	125,000.	2/6	125,000
1784.	000,000		3,125,000

The sums supposed to be raised yearly are on the supposition that the valuation of estates will be equal thro the whole 6 years to what they are now. But it is certain that valuation must diminish yearly, as the quantity of money in circulation diminishes. Allowance must therefore be made for this.[1]

	£
$\frac{1}{8}$ of 40,000,000 dollars is	1,500,000
Colonial emissions made & to be made before other funds come in	1,625,000
	3,125,000

It is supposed the Continental debt which is about £400,000, with the sale of the back lands may support government.

[. . .][2]

MS (ViU); entirely in TJ's hand; consists of undated fragment written on a small sheet, with text in margin partly torn away (see notes below); on verso in an unidentified hand: "Page 5—☞."

These fragmentary notes evidently relate to the efforts of TJ and George Mason during the October 1777-January 1778 session of the Virginia General Assembly to address the growing problem of the state's Revolutionary War debt. TJ arrived at the session as early as 22 Oct. 1777 and later, as a member of a committee, drafted a bill, submitted by Mason but ultimately deferred by the House of Delegates, that was intended to raise the credit of the state's paper money by establishing a land office for the purpose, among other things, of

using the proceeds from the sale of western lands in Virginia to help retire the state's public debt. Mason, for his part, drafted a tax act, approved in January, that was designed to retire Continental and state bills of credit (see Editorial Note and group of documents on bills for establishing a land office and for adjusting and settling titles, at [8-14 Jan. 1778]); Robert A. Rutland, ed., *The Papers of George Mason*, 3 vols. [Chapel Hill, 1970], I, 375-97; and JHD, October 1777-January 1778, p. 1-2). See also Selby, *Revolution*, 152-4.

[1] Remainder of text written lengthwise in the right margin.
[2] One or more lines torn away, the ascenders of a new line of text being visible.

Will of Ann Eppes Harris

[1777]

I Anne Harris of the parish of Southam and county of [1] make the following testamentary disposition of my estate.

First I give to my son Joseph and his heirs four hundred acres of the tract of land whereon I live, meaning that the parcel I some time ago conveied to him by deed shall be reckoned part of the said four hundred acres, and that the residue necessary to make up his complement be laid off adjoining to the said parcel already conveied.

I give to my son Benjamin and his heirs two hundred acres of the same tract to be laid off at the lower end thereof. I give to my son Francis Eppes and his heirs two hundred acres of the same tract to be laid off adjoining to the lands he bought of Henry Skipwith esquire. I give to my son Richard and his heirs two hundred acres of the same tract: but if he dies before age and without a child, I give the same to my sons Edward, Benjamin and Francis Eppes and their heirs equally to be divided among them in severalty. I give to such of my daughters as shall not have been married at the time of my death two hundred acres of the same tract to include my dwelling house and the outhouses thereto belonging; which two hundred acres with the houses it is my will they should hold jointly and undivided so long as they live single, and when any of them marries or dies her interest to go over to the others or other remaining alive and single, and on the death or marriage of the last of them, I will that the said two hundred acres go to all my sons and their heirs equally to be divided among them. If on a resurvey of the said tract of land there should be found more or less than twelve hundred acres, I will that the gain or loss be born by the several devisees in proportion to the quantity devised to them respectively.

I confirm to my son Joseph the negro man called Peter which I have delivered to him during my life. I give to my son Edward my negro man Caesar. I give to my son Francis Eppes my negro boy Ludlow. I give to my son Richard my negroe boy Jamey. I confirm to my daughter Mary a negro woman called Jenny and her children whom I had delivered to her during my life. I give to my daughter Anne a negro woman called Rose. I give to my daughter Martha a negro woman called Doll. I give to my daughter Tabitha a negro girl called Nancy. To my son Benjamin and my daughter Sarah I have above given no negroes specifically because they already have some under gifts from their friends, which put them on an equal footing with their brothers and sisters. My horses and the rest of my slaves I give to be equally divided among my children Edward, Benjamin, Francis Eppes, Richard, Mary, Sarah, Anne Martha, and Tabitha; omitting in this bequest my son Joseph, because independently of this my will he is better provided for than his brothers and sisters. The rest of my personal estate, in which I mean to include all emblements and crops, shall be first applied to the paiment of my debts, and the residue thereof equally divided among such of my children as shall not have been married at the time of my death. If any of my children shall die before twenty one years of age and also before marriage I will that the negroes and horses to which they are entitled under this my will shall fall into the residuum of slaves and horses and be divided with them, and that their part of the residuum of personal estate in like manner fall into the residuum of personal estate given to the unmarried children.

Lastly I appoint my sons executors of this my will hereby revoking all other wills by me heretofore made. In witness whereof I have hereto set my hand this ² day of ³ in the year of our lord one thousand seven hundred and seventy seven. ⁴

Signed by the testatrice in our
presence, which we attest and
subscribe in her presence

MS (Vi: Powhatan County Wills); partially dated; in TJ's hand, with blanks completed and year altered by Mrs. Harris and signed by her as "Ann Harris"; witnessed by William Daniel, Langhorn Tabb, Jacob Mcgehee, and Charles Worsham; with subjoined codicil in Mrs. Harris's hand similarly signed, dated, and witnessed, bequeathing to her daughter Martha the slave Bett, daughter of Doll; with subjoined notation by county clerk Abner Crump that on 15 Nov. 1787 the Powhatan County Court ordered the will recorded and appointed Mrs. Harris's son Edward executor of the estate.

[1] Space completed by Mrs. Harris with "Powhatan."
[2] Space completed by Mrs. Harris with "Fifteenth."
[3] Space completed by Mrs. Harris with "May."
[4] Word replaced by Mrs. Harris with "Nine."

From Edmund Randolph

DEAR SIR   Wmsburg Novr. 13. 1778.

Mr. Carrington, who is a defendant in the suit, brought by your Relation Jefferson vs. Reade's administrators, obtained an order at the last court, that he, as being nonresident, should give security for costs at the next Term. Will you be so good, as to inform him of this, if he is within the circle of your correspondence? Be pleased to add, that dismission is the penalty on non compliance with the order. Sincerely yours,

EDM: RANDOLPH

RC (Thomas Jefferson Memorial Foundation, on deposit ViU); with apparently unrelated notations on verso: (in an unidentified hand) "Mr Jefferson per Shifflett Bad money Retd" and (in TJ's hand) "Joyce Shifflet 125. Dollars to be exchanged. 70. bad."

Prior to giving up his legal practice in 1774, TJ had been employed by his first cousin George JEFFERSON in a suit he filed as the executor of Field Jefferson, his father, against Mary Reade, Thomas Reade, and Paul Carrington, surviving ADMINISTRATORS of Clement Reade (MB, legal section, 1 May 1773; TJ's Case Book, No. 834, 1 May 1773).

From Riedesel

SIR   Cotté 19 June 1779.

The happiness I have had in becoming acquainted with you, and the many kindnesses I received of you during your short residence at Montichelli, induces me to present you these lines, and my most perfect congratulations on your new Charge as Governor of Virginia, as much Pleasure as it is possible for this event to give you. Such on your account I feel on the occasion, having only to struggle against the great dissatisfaction of being deprived for the future of your pleasing Society, which formerly rendered our abode at Cotté so much more agreeable: Madame de Riedesel joins her congratulations to mine and sends her best Compliments and respects to Your Lady, but cannot help lamenting the loss of Her good Friend Mrs. Jefferson when she sees Montichelli.

Captain Bärlling will send your Excellency this Letter. He is sent down to Richmond by me, to take charge of the Transport of the remainder of the Baggage in that Place belonging to the German Troops under the Convention of Saratoga. I particularly recommend him to your Excellencys protection, being persuaded you will give him every necessary assistance to accomplish his Commission. I have the Honor to be, with the most perfect respect, Your Excellencys most obedient humble Servant,   RIEDESEL, *Major General*

MS not found; reprinted from *New England Historical and Genealogical Register*, XLIV (1890), 174; at foot of text: "*His Excellency Governor Jefferson.*"

COTTÉ: Colle, Philip Mazzei's estate, where Riedesel and his wife were quartered (Malone, *Jefferson*, I, 293-4). TJ's reply is dated 4 July 1779.

From John Jay

Philadelphia, 26 Sep. 1779. Encloses act of Congress of this date requesting the states to provide the allied forces in America with the men and provisions needed to drive the common enemy from the country and noting that the preamble will sufficiently explain the reason for this requisition.

RC (M-Ar: Revolutionary War Letters); 1 p.; in Henry Brockholst Livingston's hand, signed by Jay; at head of text: "(Circular)"; at foot of text: "The Honorable President Powell." Enclosure: Resolution of Congress, 26 Sep. 1779, recommending, in light of the receipt of authentic information of the arrival of a powerful French fleet commanded by the Comte d'Estaing, that the states furnish General Washington with such aid as he may require, including detachments of militia, so that allied forces would be able to "strike an important blow against the enemy" (JCC, XV, 1108).

From Arthur Lee

SIR   Paris Sepr. 28th. 1779

Give me leave to congratulate my Country on the choice of your Excellency to preside over its welfare. I always saw with very great pleasure that one of whose integrity, talents, and prudence, I had so high an opinion, stood among the foremost in support of our cause.

Your Excellency will see by the Papers I have had the honor of transmitting to Governor Henry what I have advanced, and how I am pledged for the Supplies which I am happy to hear are arrivd, except those in the Chapeur. But that loss is not above one third of what must have been paid to ensure the cost, coud I possibly have found money for it, besides the risque of never getting the insurance paid which among these People is exceedingly difficult. I find there are still some little errors against[1] the State even in the Account I last sent. But they shall be rectifyd shoud Orders be sent to pay it, before the amended Account which I have sent to my Brother, reaches you. I am no merchant, and besides it is a most tedious difficulty to obtain accurate Accounts from People here, when once they have got your money.

The combined fleets of France and Spain of 60 of the line will soon sail, in search of that of England which will amount to about 45. The Army remains still on the Sea Coast ready to embark for invading England if the Season will permit. It does not seem to me, that you pay much attention to your Marine, which I have always wishd to see upon a respectable establishment, because it will be the best protection not only of the Commerce but of the Coast of Virginia insomuch that without it the latter must be forever exposd to insult and depredation.

Capt. Harris who will have the honor of delivering this to your Excellency, has been spoken of to me by some respectable American Officers who knew him at Nantes, as a prudent and deserving Seaman, who merits the favor of the State.

I am obligd to write this in a small Letter, because it must go by post, and large ones by the appearance of importance tempt the being opend.

I shall be happy to hear from you, and have the honor of being with the greatest esteem Yr. Excellency's most Obedt. Servt.   A. LEE

FC (Lb in DNA: RG 360, PCC); in Lee's hand; at head of text: "His Excellency Thomas Jefferson Esqr. Governor of the State of Virginia."

Although Lee was serving in Paris as one of the three commissioners to France appointed by the Continental Congress in October 1776, he was writing to TJ in his capacity as commercial agent for Virginia, a position he was authorized to hold by his brother William, whom Governor Patrick Henry had appointed to exercise it in 1778 but who was unable to do so because of a diplomatic assignment to Germany he had received from Congress (William Lee to TJ, 15 Aug. 1780).

[1] Word interlined in place of "in favor of."

From Arthur Lee

SIR   Paris Ocr. 13th. 1779.

I am persuaded that when I state to you my situation, you will see the justice and necessity of contriving some immediate means of re-imbursing me the Advances I have made for the State. In consequence of these, the funds in my hands which were to support my Ambassy, are almost entirely exhausted, and Dr. Franklin refuses to supply me out of the funds in his disposal. The consequence of this is that I must either return to America and disappoint my mission, or be reduced to the most disgraceful state of want.

As my return without leave, might be construed into a criminal disobedience, especially as occasiond by such a disposal of the public funds without the orders of Congress; you must be sensible Sir, into what a perillous alternative I am committed by no funds arriving from you to re-imburse me. You see how numerous and urgent my Enemies are, and that I have the misfortune to number among them my immediate Country men in Congress. I therefore hope that you will leave no moment nor means unemployd of preventing both the public business and myself from being sacrificd to my zeal and affection for our Country.

I have only a moment to entreat you to put the marine of the State and the entrance into the Rivers in the best posture of defense that is possible, because I have undoubted intelligence that the Enemy's plan in future will be entirely to block up the Bay, and lay waste by a continual predatory war wherever they can approach. And as Admiral Rodney, who has very superior[1] abilities in this way, is appointed and will soon sail to execute this plan, I am afraid it will be ruinous to the State unless the wisest and most effectual defensive measures are adopted. I have the honor to be with the greatest respect & esteem, Yr. Excellency's &c

P.S. I must beg that the Remittances may not be made thro the House of D'Acosta because I cannot trust to their veracity or honesty.

FC (Lb in DNA: RG 360, PCC); in Lee's hand, unsigned; at head of text: "His Excellency the Governor of the State of Virginia."

Unknown to Lee, his acerbic relations with his fellow commissioners to France, Silas Deane and Benjamin FRANKLIN, had led the Continental Congress to dismiss him from this office on 27 Sep. 1779 (Louis W. Potts, *Arthur Lee: A Virtuous Revolutionary* [Baton Rouge, 1981], 179-237).

[1] Preceding two words interlined in place of "great."

From Stephen Hopkins

SIR   Hartford Octobr. 28th. 1779.

The astonishing Depreciation of the Continental Currency having already produced such great Embarresments in our Public measures as are truly Alarming and occasion'd a meeting of the States of New Hampshire, Massts. Bay, Rhode Island, Connecticut and New York in Convention at this place by their Commissioners and Agents, I am directed by them to transmit to you and to each State as far as Virginia inclusive the result of their proceedings; requesting a meeting by Commissioners in a Convention proposed to be held at Philada. on the first wednesday in January next, for the purpose of Considering the expediency of Limiting the prices of Merchandize and produce, and if they Judge such a measure necessary then to proceed to limit the prices of Articles as they think proper in their several States, in such manner as shall be adopted to their respective situations and Curcumstances, which measures this Convention flatter themselves will have a tendency to prevent the further Depreciation of the paper Currency, and thereby more effectually enable us to procure the necessary supplies for the Army, and as it will greatly tend to promote the Continuance of the limitation of prices, in those States that have already adopted such a measure, to be Inform'd as early as possible of the determination of the other States relative to the Subject, this Convention desire you will take the earliest oppertunity to lay this Letter with the Resolutions, inclosed before the Legislature or Executive Council of your State for Consideration, and transmit the result of their deliberations thereon.

STEP HOPKINS Prest

RC (MH): in a clerk's hand, signed by Hopkins; at foot of text: "Attest Hez Wyllys Secrty" and "His Excellency Thomas Jefferson Esqr. Governor of the State of Virginia." Enclosure: Proceedings of the Hartford Convention, 20-28 Oct. 1779 (Tr in DNA: RG 360, PCC; printed in *Pub. Recs. Conn.*, II, 563-71).

Both the Hartford CONVENTION, of which former Rhode Island governor and delegate to the Continental Congress Stephen Hop-kins was president, and the Philadelphia convention held in January-February 1780, which was attended by COMMISSIONERS from the four New England states, Pennsylvania, Delaware, and Maryland, failed in their efforts to deal with the problem of price inflation. See Richard B. Morris, "Labor and Mercantilism in The Revolutionary Era," in Morris, ed., *The Era of the American Revolution: Studies Inscribed to Evarts Boutell Greene* (New York, 1939), 116-20. See also *Pub. Recs. Conn.*, II, 572-9.

Board of Trade to Oliver Pollock

Board of Trade, 6 Nov. 1779. The governor has this day directed them to acknowledge the receipt of Pollock's letter to his predecessor, and they are empowered to authorize him, in case the request to the governor of New Orleans for a loan fails, to draw on Penet, D'Acosta Frères for all of the money he advanced on behalf of the states, except the 2,602 pesos and 4 reales drawn by Captain James O'Hara, about which they are completely ignorant and request an explanation in his reply so that the money can be replaced if it has been properly authorized. They enclose four letters of advice of the same tenor and date to Penet, D'Acosta Frères for his assistance in drawing and will not miss any opportunity to inform them. By this conveyance the governor will send a letter to the governor of New Orleans about a loan, by which means they hope Pollock will be reimbursed more quickly and spared the need to use the credit with Penet, D'Acosta Frères.

Tr (AGI: Papeles de Cuba, legajo 2370); 2 p.; with Jacquelin Ambler and Duncan Rose as signatories and TJ as countersignatory; consists of Spanish translation by Juan Josef Duforest forming part of examination of TJ's commission to Oliver Pollock by Spanish officials in New Orleans, 20 Apr. 1782. Enclosure: Board of Trade to Penet, D'Acosta Frères, 6 Nov. 1779 (Vol. 3: 160). Translation of letter printed in Kinnaird, *Spain*, II, 10.

TJ's accompanying letter to Governor Bernardo de Gálvez is dated 8 Nov. 1779. For Pollock's efforts to obtain compensation for the wartime debts he incurred as

Virginia's unofficial commercial agent at New Orleans during the Revolutionary War after Penet, D'Acosta Frères refused to honor the enclosed drafts, see James A. James, *Oliver Pollock: The Life and Times of an Unknown Patriot* (New York, 1937), 240-2, 269-70, 274-6, 279-80, 288, 301-5, 333-7, 343-4.

To Bernardo de Gálvez

SIR   Williamsburg January 29th. 1780.

I had the Honor of writing to your Excellency the last Month expressing hopes that by the return of Colo. Rogers we should receive information on the Subject of a Loan of Money formerly sollicited through the intervention of your Excellency by my Predecessor Governor Henry. Colo. Rogers however was unhappily surprised and killed on his return by the Indians together with about 20 others of his escort and with them we lost a valuable Cargo of Goods formerly carried for us from New Orleans to St. Lewis and then going under his care up the Ohio. I thought it necessary to Notify this unfortunate event to your Excellency, that if you should have sent by him any dispatches for this Government you might be apprised of their fate and repair the Loss by taking the trouble of transmitting duplicates. I have the Honor to be with every Sentiment of Esteem and respect Your Excellency's most Obedt. & most humble Servant   TH: JEFFERSON

RC (PWacD: Feinstone Collection, on deposit PPAmP); in a clerk's hand, signed by TJ; addressee supplied from internal evidence (see below).

The letter TJ wrote LAST MONTH to Gálvez, the governor of Louisiana, appears to have been that of 8 Nov. 1779. For the 14 Jan. 1778 request for a LOAN of 150,000 pistoles "more or less" by GOVERNOR HENRY, see H. R. McIlwaine, ed., *Official Letters of the Governors of the State of Virginia*, 3 vols. (Richmond, 1926-29), I, 227-9.

From Charles Thomson

Secretary's Office, 1 Feb. 1780. Encloses the journals of Congress to complete the state's set to 1 Jan. 1780, hereafter to be printed in monthly pamphlets regularly sent, and requests a reply to his letter of 20 Nov. 1779, the request therein not being made "by idle curiosity but a desire of promoting public Utility and the cause of America."

RC (MdAA: Red Books); 1 p.; in a clerk's hand, signed by Thomson; at foot of text: "His Excellency The Governor of Maryland"; consists of a circular letter to state executives. Enclosures: presumably the weekly journals of Congress for the period 22 Nov.-31 Dec. 1779 (JCC, XV, 1462). See Thomson to TJ, 20 Nov. 1779, for the last known occasion when he forwarded the weekly journals to TJ.

Thomson's request for a reply to his 20 Nov. 1779 letter may have been omitted from the copy sent to the governor of Virginia because TJ had already responded to the earlier letter on 31 Dec. 1779.

From Arthur Lee

Sir   Paris Feby. 7th. 1780

Sir   Paris Feby. 7th. 1780

I have the honor of enclosing you a Letter from our worthy friend Mr. Fabroni. A powerful fleet of 18 Sail of the Line and 4000 troops has just left Brest for the W. Indies to restore the superiority of this Country in that quarter. The Enemy's fleet has been successful on the coast of Spain in taking some Spanish men of war and a number of transports laden with naval stores, but as there is a superior combined fleet in quest of them we hope they will not escape. By the first opportunity I hope to have the pleasure of seeing again my native Country. I have the honor to be &ca.

FC (Lb in DNA: RG 360, PCC); in Lee's hand, unsigned; at head of text: "His Excellency the Governor of Virginia." Enclosure not found, unless it was Giovanni Fabbroni to TJ, 20 Dec. 1779.

From Samuel Huntington

Sir   Philadelphia Feby 12. 1780

Your Excellency will receive herewith enclosed an Act of Congress of the 11th. Instant authorizing the Executive Power of Virginia to examine the Accounts charged against Colo. Bland while in Command at Charlotte-Ville by the Deputy Commissary General of Purchases and Issues and make such allowances in his favour as they deem Just and proper &c from the peculiar Situation of his Command. I have the honour to be with the highest respect your Excy's hble Servt

Sam. Huntington President

RC (MHi: Washburn Collection); in a clerk's hand, signed by Huntington; at foot of text: "His Excy The Govr of Virginia." FC (Lb in DNA: RG 360, PCC); dated 11 Feb. 1780. Enclosure: Resolution of the Continental Congress, 11 Feb. 1780 (printed in JCC, XVI, 154).

To James Wood

Sir   Williamsburg Mar. 20. 1780.

This express brings some packets of letters for Generals Specht, Hamilton and Gall, which came by the Patsy, flag of truce just arrived from New York with money and stores for the Convention troops. You will please to send on the express to the two first named gentlemen. The flag is to go as far up James river as she can. When her arrival there shall be notified to you, you will be pleased to give permission to Mr. Geddes, Mr. Clarke and Mr. Hoakesley to go to the flag and receive their several charges. A proper guard of horse you will also be pleased to furnish Mr. Geddes with to carry up the money. Let him name the day on which they shall attend at the flag. I think it will be well that Mr. Geddes himself should attend with the guard thro' the whole journey up. You will of course take proper paroles of the gentlemen thus permitted to come down. Mr. Hoakesley must[1] not break his packages till they are ultimately delivered from the waggons in Albemarle, a circumstance proper to be noticed in his parole.

The Continental Board of war having referred to us to give final orders on the subject of the Convention horses you will be pleased to obtain and send us a report of the officers who keep horses, and the number kept by each. I am Sir with great esteem, your most humble servt.   Th: Jefferson

RC (Gallery of History, Las Vegas, Nevada, 1994); unaddressed, but endorsed by Wood. A catalogue extract was printed in Vol. 3: 322.

[1] Word interlined in place of "should."

To the Board of Trade

Gentlemen   Williamsburg Mar. 23. 1780.

It having been concluded that the Council shall discontinue business at this place from the 7th. of the ensuing month, and commence at Richmond on the 24th. I am desired to mention it to you as our desire that your board should make a correspondent adjournment.

I must ask the favor of you to order a vessel or vessels to be in readiness on the evening of the 7th. at the landing most convenient to this place, to receive and convey to Richmond, the presses, books, papers, and implements of the offices of council, War, Trade, Auditors, and Register and furniture of the Capitol and Palace. An armed vessel will be furnished by the board of War to receive the treasury with it's implements, and to convoy those which will contain the articles of the other offices. I have the honor to be with great respect Gentlemen Your most obedt. servt.   Th: Jefferson

RC (ViW); addressed: "The honble The Board of Trade"; with apparently unrelated mathematical notation on cover; endorsed.

The Board of Trade's reply is dated 25 Mch. 1780.

Board of War to ———

War Office, Williamsburg, 25 Mch. 1780. Sell or immediately exchange the six horses reported totally unfit for service by Captain Charles Fearer and replace them with suitable mounts. Signed by James Innes and George Lyne. Countersigned by TJ.

RC (Mrs. Earl McMillen, Atlanta, Georgia, 1963); 1 p.; in a clerk's hand except for signatures.

To the County Lieutenants of Berkeley and Certain Other Counties

SIR   Richmond April 19 1780

I have heard with much concern of the many Murders committed by the Indians in the Counties of Washington Montgomery, Green Briar and Kentucky, and in the neighborhood of Pittsburg. Hostilities so extensive prove a formidable Combination of that kind of enemy. Propositions have been made for Particular Stations of men as a present Safe guard to the Frontiers, but I own that they do not appear to me adequate to the object—all experience has proved that you cannot be defended from the Savages but by carrying the War home to themselves, and Striking decisive Blows. It is therefore my opinion that instead of Putting our Frontier Inhabitants under that fallacious Idea of Security; an Expedition must be instantly undertaken into the Indian Country.—Want of full Information of the facts which have happened—of the Particular Nations and Numbers confederated against us, put it out of my Power to direct the minute Parts of such an Expedition, or to Point it to it's Precise Object.—Such a plan laid here would probably be rendered abortive by difficulties in the Article of Provisions, ill adjusted times and places of Rendezvouse, and unforeseen events, and circumstances, which if to be explained and amended here from Time to Time the Evil will have had its course while we are Contriving how to ward it off. I can therefore only undertake to Authorise such an Expedition, and put it into a Train for Execution. For this Purpose I have desired the Co. Ls. of Washington, Montgomery, Botetourt, Rockbridge and Green Briar (the Counties Principally exposed) to meet at Botetourt C. H. on the 18 Day of the ensuing Month of May to concert an Expedition against the offending Tribes to be carried on by the joint Militia of their Counties.—I must in like manner desire you to meet the C. Ls. of Augusta, Rockbridge, Shenandoah, Frederick and Hampshire at [Shenandoah] C. H. in the 29th. Day of May for the same Purpose.—This meeting is appointed so long after that of the Officers of the South western Quarter, that they may have time to send to you the result of their deliberations—having these before you I shall not doubt but you will so concert yours as to co-operate with them in the most effectual manner—whether that be by concurring in the Same expedition or carrying on a distinct one—and of your Proceedings be Pleased to return them Information.—The Objects of your enquiry and Deliberation when you Assemble will be First—The Particular tribes who have committed Hostilities: their Number and residence. 2ndly. The Proportion of your Militia Necessary to encounter them. 3rdly. The officers who shall take command, and also proper Staff Officers. 4thly. Supplies of Provision and Ammunition. 5thly. Times and Places of Rendezvouse. When everything shall have been settled by your meeting be Pleased to send on by Express the Letters to the County Ls. of Yohogania, Monongalia, and Ohio, giving them Information of the Aid which you shall hope to receive from them. I hope you will see the Propriety of my setting this matter in motion in the Southwestern Quarter first. This has been occasioned by their Neighborhood to the Scene of danger, and their opportunity of knowing the Nations and number of the enemy, and not from any want of equal Confidence in your Zeal, Activity and wisdom. I am quite uncertain where Major Slaughter is. Probably he has by this time got to the Falls of Ohio. Any Aid he can give I trust he will do on your forwarding to him my Letter, lodged with Col. Matthews. It is my duty to affix some bounds to the Numbers to be embodied on this Occasion. On Considering the Strength of the Militia in the Cs. beforementioned and the Probable numbers of the enemy, I suppose it will not cramp your efforts when I restrain your numbers to one tenth of the Militia. Indeed I expect you will Consider a much smaller number, Perhaps the half of that, Sufficient, more especially when the difficulties of getting Provisions, and the delays Occasioned by encreased Numbers are Maturely weighed by you. The Poverty of the Treasury, moreover will require in you the Strictest attention to oeconomy. This obliges me to enjoin you to retrench every Possible article of Expence to avoid the Cumbersome Parade of regular Troops, and the long list of sinecure appointments usual in the Staff department. Consolidate together as many of those appointments as you can, and put them into active hands; There are Standing Commissaries in the Southwestern and Northwestern Quarters. The former is a Mr. Baker of Washington, the latter is in the neighborhood of Winchester, and was instructed to convey his Provisions to Pittsburg. These Persons are Quarter Masters at the same time and the Provisions laid in by them will be subject the latter to the order of your Comma. Off. the former to that of the C. O. from the Southwestern Counties. Besides this at the Particular request of Col. Donnally of Green Briar I send Him seven Thousand Pounds to Procure Provisions in His Quarter. I shall immediately order 2000 lbs. of Powder and 2000 Flints to Staunton for the general Service from which place you will call for what is Necessary for your Corps; I enclose to Col. Preston an order for Lead. It might be Premature to speake of the Terms of Peace but if events will justify it the only condition with the Shawenese should be their removal beyond the Mississipi or the Lakes, and with the other Tribes whatever may most effectually Secure their observation of the Treaty. We have been too long diverted by Humanity from enforcing good behavior by Severe Chastisement. Savages are to be Curbed by fear only: We are not in a condition to repeat Expensive Expeditions against them and I hope the Business will now be done so as not to necessitate doing it again and that instead of making Peace on their 1st Application you will only make it after such [. . .] Shall be felt and Remembered by them as long as they [. . .] a Nation. I am sir your very humble servt   TH. JEFFERSON

Tr (NcD: Journal of Danske Dandridge, 1903-1904, Bedinger-Dandridge Family Papers); 20th-century copy; at head of text: "Capt (Van) Swearingen No 15. To the Lieut of B Co (autograph letter)"; with two tears in the original noted by the copyist.

According to a letter TJ wrote to George Rogers Clark, evidently on this date, he "directed" the county lieutenants of Washington, Montgomery, Botetourt, Rockbridge, and Greenbrier to assemble part of their militia for an immediate expedition "into the Indian Country" in retaliation for "many Murders recently committed" by unidentified Indians in various parts of Virginia and Pennsylvania and asked Clark to lend his support to this enterprise (TJ to Clark, [19 Apr.] 1780). The text printed above is the only known copy of a circular

letter to the county lieutenants of Berkeley, Augusta, Frederick, Hampshire, Rockbridge, and Shenandoah, one of two groups of counties that TJ expected either to support this expedition or to mount one of their own. Although a shortage of provisions made it impossible for the county lieutenants to take offensive action against any hostile Indian tribes, a volunteer force led by Clark carried out a devastating raid on the Shawnee Indians near present-day Chillicothe, Ohio, early in August 1780, an action that TJ had advocated even before writing the above letter (TJ to Clark, 1, 29 Jan. 1780; Proceedings of Council concerning Western Defense, 8 June 1780; TJ to the County Lieutenant of Berkeley, 21 June 1780, Vol. 15: 588; Clark to TJ, 22 Aug. 1780).

To Charles Thomas

SIR   May 10. 1780.

Please to furnish Capt. Markham for the use of the brig Jefferson with twenty three fathom of seven inch rope, six coil of spunyarn, 150 ℔. seine twine, six coil of $2\frac{1}{2}$ inch rope, three coil of 2.I. do. and one coil of $3\frac{1}{2}$ I. do. six hanks of Marline six do. of Housline two coil of Hamberline.   TH. JEFFERSON

RC (PWacD: Feinstone Collection, on deposit PPAmP); at foot of text: "Capt Thomas"; with notations on verso by James Markham and Thomas Chandler about the receipt and cost of the supplies.

Captain Charles Thomas of the Virginia Navy was master of the ropewalk at War-

wick (John H. Gwathmey, *Historical Register of Virginians in the Revolution: Soldiers, Sailors, Marines, 1775-1783* [Richmond, 1938], 766).

To Philip Mazzei

DEAR SIR   Richmond May 12. 1780.

Your letter of Nov. 27. 1779 from Nantes came safely to hand on the 6th. of April last. The Fier Rodrique being not yet sailed, enabled me to answer it. Three copies of your duplicates and instructions were sent by different conveyances since you left us; so that we have great hopes they have come safe to hand: the present however being a very safe conveyance, another set will accompany this letter. Mr. Penet's house acted very prudently in refusing to supply Moebal with money on our account as he was charged with no business whatever from us. He had been an officer in our state troops, and on occasion of some disgust had resigned and left the continent. It was found most expedient after your departure to relinquish the purpose of sending Mr. Smith to Europe, and to put on you the execution of his duties, as you will perceive by the instructions. I think in the course of some conversations I had with you I mentioned it as my private opinion that if you should succeed in obtaining the loan we desired, it would be better not to agree that interest should commence until the money be actually called for. I am still strongly of that opinion and am authorized to advise you to provide for this; as it is not our purpose to draw any part of the loan from Europe in the form of money. I hope Mr. Penet's house found it convenient to furnish you the money expected from them, as no relief from hence subsequent to the receipt of your letter could reach you in time. We had been very attentive to the strengthening their hands as far as we have been able. Six hundred hogsheads of tobacco were consigned them in two ships of Mr. Haywood, and two hundred are consigned them by the Franklin which now goes under convoy of the Fier Rodrique. Besides this we have paid here on orders from Mr. Penet between thirty and forty thousand pounds, our currency.

Since my last no great change in our military affairs has come to our knolege. The enemy have posted themselves on the neck of land behind Charles town. The reinforcements under Woodford, Scott and Hogan had arrived there when our last advices came away (which was Apr. 15.). The movements of the enemy indicated an intention of proceeding by way of blockade. The town being well stored with provisions will give time for relief both by land and water. The latter would be a capital stroke, as their fleet and army would both fall. I am Dr. Sir with much esteem your friend & servt.   TH: JEFFERSON

RC (Gilder Lehrman Collection, on deposit NNP). Tr (NhD: Ticknor Manuscripts); possibly a 19th-century copy. Enclosures not found, but see Mazzei to TJ, 8 Aug. 1781.

HIS DUTIES: see note to TJ to John Adams, 21 Aug. 1777. HOGAN: Brigadier General Isaac Huger.

From Arthur Lee

SIR   L'Orient May 13th. 1780

I have the honor of sending you by Major John G. Frazer, the great Seal for the State, which I before informd you I had engraved at Paris. This is the first direct opportunity I have had since it was finished. I have the honor to be &ca

FC (Lb in DNA: RG 360, PCC); in Lee's hand, unsigned; at head of text: "His Excelly. the Govr. of Virginia."

GREAT SEAL: see note to Lee to TJ, 4 Sep. 1779.

To Arnold Henry Dohrman

SIR   Virginia, May 24. 1780.

The many Kindnesses which you have shown to our captive countrymen, whom the fortune of war has carried within the reach of your inquiries, do great honour to your humanity, and must forever interest us in your welfare. I beg leave on behalf of my countrymen[1] to assure you, that these attentions are felt with sensibility, and that any occasion which shall offer of rendering you service will be cheerfully embraced. Should future events open an intercourse between your country and ours for the exchange of productions yielded by the one and wanted by the other, your actions have pointed out the friend to whose negotiations we may safely confide our interests and necessities. I beg leave to subscribe myself with the greatest esteem and respect, sir, Yr Mo. Obt. & Mo humble Servant   THO: JEFFERSON

Tr (DNA: RG 46, Senate Records, 14th Cong., 2d sess.); at head of text: "No. 5"; at foot of text: "To Arnold Henry Dohrman Esq." and "(Copy.)"; with subjoined note: "Secretary's Office, March 7. 1818. The foregoing are truly copied from the original documents, which accompanied the petition of Rachael Dorhman. Charles Cutts." Tr (same); with text crossed out and note written at head of text: "Omit this letter it being a duplicate"; at foot of text: "(Copy)"; with one variation (see note 1 below).

Arnold Henry Dohrman (d. 1813), a Dutch-born merchant in Lisbon at the beginning of the American Revolution, was such a strong supporter of the American cause and so distinguished himself by the assistance he rendered to captive American seamen, that in June 1780 the Continental Congress appointed him unsalaried United States agent in Portugal, a post that ultimately led to the destruction of his mercantile credit. In 1787, after he arrived in Philadelelpha and petitioned for the settlement of his disordered accounts, evidently with this letter from TJ and other testimonials from prominent Americans in hand, the Confederation Congress recompensed Dohrman for his services by approving annual payments of $1,600 for his salary from the time his expenditures began and granted him a township in the Northwest Territory, which led him to settle in Steubenville, Ohio, where he died in penury. Rachel Dohrman, his widow, submitted a text of the above letter to Congress as part of her successful claim in 1817 for an annuity for herself and her eleven children (ASP, *Claims*, 508-14).

[1] Second Tr: "Country."

From the Continental Board of Admiralty

SIR   June 19th 1780

Being informed that arms and other warlike stores are preparing to be sent via the Head of Elk and Cheseapeake Bay into the State of North Carolina for its immediate defence, the board beg leave to solicit your Excellencys complyance with the enclosed requisition. The Vessels expences while upon this Service, is to be defrayed by the United states. For the Accomplishment of this Service, dispatch in fitting out the vessel will be highly necessary, that she may be in proper time on her station in the Bay, so as to protect the stores &c on their passage from the Head of Elk to Sufolk or other places of their destination. I have the honor to be with great respect your Excellencys Obedt hble servant

FRANCIS LEWIS by Order

FC (Lb in DNA: RG 360, PCC); at head of text: "His Excellency Governor Jefferson of Virginia." Enclosure not found.

To Thomas Sim Lee

SIR   Richmond June 28. 1780.

Having just received from Carolina an authentic state of things as they exist there at present, I have thought it worthy of being communicated to Congress by putting into motion our line of express riders. The sum of it is that Clinton has sailed with about 5000 men from Charlestown; but whither, is not known: that that place is garrisoned by 800 men: that they have 2500 men at Cambden; their cavalry (the number not mentioned) a little above Cambden and one regiment at the Cheraws hill on Pedee. They have never yet crossed the boundary between the two Carolinas. Genl. De Kalb is at Hillsborough with the regulars: there are 2600 militia of North Carolina actually embodied under Generals Caswell and Rutherford, and 2500 Virginia militia are now on their march to Hillsborough where they will probably be within about five days. Governor Nash is embodying 4000 militia more of his state. I expected it would be agreeable to you to know the state of things in this quarter, and at the same time thought that were you not informed of the true cause for which the line of riders is put into motion, you might have presumed a long expected event had taken place. I have the honor to be with every sentiment of esteem & respect Your Excellency's most obedient & most humble servt.   TH: JEFFERSON

RC (Mrs. Albert D. Lasker, New York City, 1964); unaddressed.

This letter was almost certainly written to Governor Thomas Sim Lee of Maryland, with whom TJ had recently concerted the establishment of a LINE OF EXPRESS RIDERS to Philadelphia (see Lee to TJ, 10, 17 June 1780; TJ to Lee, 14 June 1780). The letter being conveyed by the chain of expresses was TJ to Samuel Huntington, 28 June 1780. LONG EXPECTED EVENT: the arrival of the French fleet in America (see Huntington to TJ, 5 June 1780, and note).

To George Gibson

SIR   Richmond July 7th. 1780.

By a Letter from the Board of war on the subject of the first and second state regiments, they inform me that Congress will agree to take them on their expence if the officers shall be apportioned to the men, but decline the receiving them surcharged with Officers. The state of affairs to the south ward is such as requires great exertions from this country and renders it necessary that we avail ourselves of the services of those two Battalions. I am therefore to desire that you will have them marched to join the southern army with one set of field officers, and so many captains and subalterns as may be proportioned to the number of men; the residue of the officers will remain as supernumeraries at the expence of the state. Colo. Brent tells me he has appointed a captain and subalterns for his men being only about thirty in number. These must be annexed to your command till we can fill up both regiments and procure employment by that means for all the officers. I hope the draught now enacting by the legislature may enable us to do this. Be so good as to deliver to the continental Quarter master at Petersburg a list of the necessaries you may want and what articles he cannot get otherwise we will furnish him with as far as we have them. Tents we are utterly unprovided with, nor do I suppose he can get them, an order has been given to the Clothier to issue a hunting shirt to every souldier. I shall immediately inclose to congress the resolutions of Assembly on the subject of the rank of the officers of those two battalions for their determination. I am Sir Your very humble servt.   Th: Jefferson

RC (GU: Felix Hargrett Collection); in a clerk's hand, with complimentary close and signature by TJ; addressed by TJ: "Colo George Gibson Petersburg"; on verso by TJ: "No 12."

No such letter from the Continental or the Virginia BOARD OF WAR has been found.

From Bernardo de Gálvez

MUY SOR. MIO   [18 July 1780]

Tube el honor de recibir la muy apreciable de V. S. su fecha en Williamsbourg 8 de Noviembre de 1779. Me ha servido de una particular satisfaccion saber por ella habia V. S. sucedido en ese Gobierno por designacion de su antecesor Mr. Henry. No me lisonjean menos las fundadas esperanzas que concibe V. S. de ver quanto antes dichosamente terminadas las actuales desavenencias con la Inglaterra por medio del poderoso influxo de la Francia con quien oportunamente se ha declarado el poder del Rey mi Amo. Veo con singular complacencia las acertadas medidas, y solidos fundamentos de Poblacion, y comercio que comenzaba à hechar el Estado de Virginia. Pero empeñada mi Nacion en una Guerra costosa, y siendo esta Provincia una de las mas expuestas teniendo el enemigo à la Puerta, los inmensos, é innumerables gastos ocasionados à la Corona en este Pais con las dos Expediciones que dichosamente acabo de terminar no me permiten hacer el menor avance de dinero para librar a V. S. y a esta Provincia del embarazo en que se halla por Dn. Olivero Pollok.

Por el duplicado, y triplicado de la respuesta que llevaba el Coronel Rogers que tubo la desgracia de ser muerto en el camino por los Indios se habra V. S. instruido de los pasos que tengo dados, y de lo que tengo escrito à la Corte sobre el particular: las actuales circunstancias de la Guerra han sido naturalmente la causa de no haber aun contestado, luego que reciba alguna respuesta la dirigire por el dicho Dn. Olivero Pollock.

Deseo me proporcione V. S. ocasiones en que pueda manifestar la perfecta consideracion con que anhelo a complacerle en quanto penda de mis facultades. Dios &c.

My dear Sir   [18 July 1780]

I have had the honor of receiving your most estimable letter under date of Williamsburg, 8 November 1779. It has given me particular satisfaction to know that you had succeeded to the governorship thanks to designation by your predecessor, Mr. Henry. I am no less pleased by the well-founded hopes that you hold of seeing happily terminated, as soon as possible, the present quarrels with England through the powerful influence of France supported appropriately by the power of my master the King. I observe with exceptional satisfaction the effective measures and the solid foundations for establishing settlements and trade that the state of Virginia was beginning to engage in. But with my nation embarked upon a costly war and with this province being one of the most exposed, having the enemy at its gate, the immense and innumerable expenditures brought upon the Crown in this region by the two expeditions that happily I have just concluded do not permit me to make the slightest advance of money in order to free you and this province from the predicament in which you find yourself because of Mr. Oliver Pollock.

Through the duplicate and triplicate of the answer carried by Colonel Rogers, who had the misfortune to be killed on the road by the Indians, you will have learned of the steps I have taken, and of what I have written to the Court about this matter: the present circumstances of the war have naturally been the reason for not yet having an answer. As soon as I receive an answer, I shall send it by the aforementioned Mr. Oliver Pollock.

I wish you to provide me with opportunities to show the total esteem with which I zealously desire to oblige you in every way in which it is within my power to do so. God etc.

FC (AGI: Papeles de Cuba, legajo 2370); at head of text: "A Monsieur Thomas Jefferson, Gobernador de la Virginia en 18 de Julio de 1780." FC (same).

DOS EXPEDICIONES: a reference to the Spanish capture of Baton Rouge in September 1779 and of Mobile in March 1780 (Kinnaird, *Spain*, I, xxviii-ix).

William Armistead to Samuel Smith

Richmond, 3 Aug. 1780. Having already been serviceable to Virginia in obtaining supplies for the army and navy, Smith is requested to state the availability of certain articles in or near Baltimore and the terms on which they can be bartered for tobacco delivered either at Baltimore or the James River, to the end that these items can be procured on the most advantageous terms; with subjoined list specifying the articles needed. Signed by William Armistead. Countersigned by TJ.

RC (MH: Frederick M. Dearborn Collection); 1 p.; addressed: "Colo. Samuel Smith Baltimore"; franked; endorsed.

List of Virginia Recruiting Officers, with Jefferson's Note

[*After 28 Aug. 1780*]. Lists one captain, six lieutenants, and one major who had been entrusted by Paymaster William Russell with £6,369.17.6 between 16 Mch. and 28 Aug. 1780 "for the purpose of Recruiting Soldiers for Col. Gibsons Regiment" and who had not yet accounted for the money. Note at foot of text by TJ: "The above is proper for the Auditors alone. Th: Jefferson."

MS (Vi: Executive Department, Auditor's Office Papers); 1 p.; in a clerk's hand, except for TJ's note; endorsed: "Gibsons Officers in Acct. with the State Vaga. £6,396.17.6."

From Samuel Huntington

Philadelphia, *29 Aug. 1780*. Encloses acts of Congress of 12 and 24 Aug. 1780 for the provision of the officers and soldiers of the Continental Army, with recommendations to the states, and for the extension of the half pay approved for officers to their widows and orphans.

FC (Lb in DNA: RG 360, PCC); 1 p.; at head of text: "Circular." Enclosures: Resolutions of Congress, 14 and 24 Aug. 1780, as described above (JCC, XVII, 725-7, 772-3).

Appointment of a Commissioner of the Provision Law

SIR   VIRGINIA, IN COUNCIL, *Sept.*   ¹, 1780.

You are hereby appointed a Commissioner under the act *For procuring a supply of provisions and other necessaries for the use of the army*, but restrained specially to the procuring the articles enumerated in the said act, and live cattle, horses, waggons and their geer, for the subsistence and transporting the baggage of the militia marching from your county to Carolina. You are in the first instance, if it can be done with any convenience, to call on the continental commissaries, or on the commissioners of the same provision law appointed in each county in which you may be with the said militia, to furnish provisions for their subsistence during their stay at any place within this state, or on their march through the same. Your receipt to such Commissioners shall be to them a good voucher for the delivery of any articles you shall call on them for, notwithstanding any former orders we may have given to deliver them otherwise. If neither the said commissioners nor commissaries can furnish you with subsistence, you are in that case and in that case only, to exercise the powers hereby given you within the counties before described. When you shall have passed with the militia out of the limits of this state, or your attendance on them for the purposes of this commission shall be dispensed with by any officer having authority so to do, this commission is to determine, and you are to transmit to me by safe conveyances, duplicate lists of all the certificates or receipts you shall have given for articles hereby submitted to your seizure, specifying the name of the owner, the article seized, the price to be paid, and date of the certificate. That you may be informed of the manner in which you are to proceed, in the execution of this commission, you will receive herewith a copy of the provision law, and an extract from another act relative to the particular articles of live stock, horses, waggons and their geer; this last being the only article to which under the term *necessaries* used in the act, we mean that your power should extend. I am, Your humble servant,   TH: JEFFERSON

P. S. Waggons employed by the Commissioners of the provision law, or by others to perform publick services, should not be impressed under the power above given.

RC (Gilder Lehrman Collection, on deposit NNP); consisting of a printed form letter, signed by TJ, with blank in dateline completed in ink at a later date (see note 1 below), but obviously prepared ca. 4 Sep. 1780 with the covering letters listed below; unaddressed; with minor correction in ink in an unidentified hand; endorsed. Enclosures: (1) "An Act for procuring a supply of provisions and other necessaries for the use of the army," [21 June 1780], empowering the governor and council to appoint commissioners with broad authority to purchase at fixed prices or to impress provisions for Continental, Virginia militia, and French troops (enclosure not found, but printed in Hening, x, 233-7). (2) "Extract of the act giving farther powers to the Governour and Council, and for other purposes," [13 July 1780], extending the authority of the governor and council granted by No. 1 to certain articles for the use of the Virginia militia "or other troops that are or may be ordered into actual service from this commonwealth," as well as for provisioning the Saratoga Convention troops and their guard at Albemarle barracks, and specifying procedures for valuing and paying for the articles (printed form in Gilder Lehrman Collection, on deposit NNP; text printed in Hening, x, 311-12). Enclosed in TJ to the County

Lieutenants of Frederick and Certain Other Counties, and to the County Lieutenants of Pittsylvania and Certain Other Counties, both 4 Sep. 1780.

In consequence of the crushing defeat of General Horatio Gates's army at Camden on 16 Aug. 1780, TJ and the Virginia Council decided on about 4 Sep. 1780 to try to stem the northward advance of the victorious British army by calling into service 2,041 militia troops from certain counties and ordering them to rendezvous by 20 Oct. 1780 at Hillsborough, North Carolina, under the command of General Edward Stevens, and by sending "a power" to all of the county lieutenants from whose counties the militia would be drawn to "impress waggons, provisions and other necessaries for the subsistence and transportation of their men on their march" (Advice of Council respecting Reinforcements of Militia, [ca. 4 Sep. 1780]). The document printed above is the only known text of the letter which the abovementioned county lieutenants were deputed to use for the appointment of commissioners to carry out the duties prescribed in it and its enclosures.

[1] Here an unidentified hand completed the blank with "9th."

Certificate from the Virginia Delegates in Congress

Philadelphia, 5 Sep. 1780. Certifies that Congress has received authenticated copies of state legislative acts complying with its 18 Mch. 1780 resolutions on public finance from Maryland (12 June), New Jersey (9 June), New York (15 June), Massachusetts (5 May), and New Hampshire (29 Apr.), as well as a conditional act from Pennsylvania (1 June).

MS (Vi); 2 p.; in James Madison's hand, signed by Joseph Jones, Madison, and John Walker.

For the circumstances that prompted TJ to request the above information from the Virginia delegates, see Samuel Huntington to TJ, 20 Mch. 1780, and note, and TJ to James Madison, 26 July 1780.

To John Page

DEAR PAGE   Richmond Oct. 10. 1780.

The Pot-clay, a Cherokee chief having lately died, his friend delivered to Majr. Martin a silver badge which he said had been given by the Governor of Virginia and therefore desired should be returned to him. It's size, figure, and inscription is as below.

To give you a better idea of it I inclose a reversed impression of it on paper. To shew you how little I think you have a right to refuse publick employment from want of leisure I send you this to puzzle out, and ask the favor of you to communicate the result to your sincere friend & servt

TH: JEFFERSON

RC (CtY); note at foot of text by Page: "This was a badge given by Presidt. Madison to the Censors at College & was given by one of them to Pot-Clay"; on verso in an unknown hand: "Found among the papers of the late John Page Junr. and given to Mrs White by Mr Saunders of Williamsburg Virginia."

For the provenance of the SILVER BADGE and an expansion of its abbreviated Latin inscription, see Page to TJ, 20 Oct. 1780, and TJ to Page, 29 Oct. 1780, the latter in Vol. 15: 593.

To Timothy Pickering

SIR   In Council November 21. 1780.

On receipt of your favour by Colo. Mead we offered the office of Deputy quarter master General for the Continent in this state to a Mr. George Divers, a person qualified in every point for exercising it as we wou'd wish it to be. A peculiarity in the present situation of his private affairs has however prevented his acceptance of it. I have this day written to major Foresythe to know if he will accept it, as I believe he will discharge its dutys with great cleverness and activity. Shou'd he decline I shall really be at a loss to find one possessing in tolerable degree the several qualities necessary in that office. As soon as we can get the appointment made and accepted I will do myself the pleasure of informing you of it. That it be filled properly is becoming of daily greater consequence as the exhausture of the two Carolinas renders the southern army daily more dependent on us for subsistance, and we can subsist them plentifully if the transportation can be affected. I have the honor to be with the most perfect respect sir, Your most obedient & mo humble servant   TH: JEFFERSON

RC (Gallery of History, Las Vegas, Nevada, 1994); in a clerk's hand, signed by TJ; at foot of text in TJ's hand: "Colo Pickering."

YOUR FAVOUR: Pickering to TJ, 19 Oct. 1780. TJ's letter to Robert Forsyth THIS DAY WRITTEN has not been found.

To Robert Lawson

SIR   Richmond Nov. 23. 1780.

The last intelligence from the enemy having indicated that they were on the point of departure, and it being probable that not only the force from hence but a new embarkation is destined Southwardly Genl. Greene has recommended strongly the hastening on succours to the South. For this purpose Baron Steuben is left here. He entertains hopes of receiving more immediate support from your corps than any other we have. Should it not be inconvenient to you to take a ride here the Baron is very anxious to see and confer with you on the equipments still necessary for them. If you will do me the favor to call at my house I will send for the baron, and contribute my aid towards determining what is necessary and practicable to be done. I am Sir with great respect Your most obedt. humble servt.   TH: JEFFERSON

RC (facsimile in Sotheby Parke Bernet Catalogue, 25 Jan. 1977, Lot 164); endorsed.

POINT OF DEPARTURE: a reference to the withdrawal from Virginia of Major General Alexander Leslie's 2,200-man British invasion force, which for more than a month had been raiding various parts of the state to facilitate Earl Cornwallis's inva- sion of the Carolinas (Selby, *Revolution,* 216-21).

From Theodorick Bland

SR.   Philadelph: Decr. 17th 1780

Yr. Excellency will I hope excuse the liberty I take to Introduce to you the Marquis de La Valle and the Count de Guistine two Noblemen of distinction the latter a Brigadier in the Army of France and the for- mer a Colonel—of the House of Montmorenci—they have been intro- duced to me by the Minister of France and the Marquis de la Fayette. I doubt not but that the Civilities they will meet with from the Principal Gentlemen of our state will under your Excellencys Influence be such as their High rank, and the Zealous part they have taken in our Cause Intitles them to, and will make favorable and lasting impressions to our advantage.

Those reasons Independant of the knowlidge I have of Yr. Excellys. personal disposition to treat Merit with distinction and to extend the rights of Hospitality to its utmost limits will plead my excuse for giving you this trouble, and for assuring you that I am with perfect respect Yr. Excys. most obedt. & obliged Humbe. St.   THEOK. BLAND

Tr (DLC: Edmund C. Burnett Collection); 20th-century copy; at head of text: "S. V. Henkels—Catalogue 1078—No. 431." and "[Theodoric Bland to Gov. of Va.]."

To the Virginia Delegates in Congress

GENTLEMEN   Richmond December 18th 1780

I have made the necessary enquiry as to the place where any armed vessels, which the minister of France shoud think proper to have win- tered in our bay, might cover its trade, be safest, and have the most secure retreat. Hampton road and york town are the only ports from which a view of the entrance into the bay is commanded. No vessel can pass up it without being seen from either of these places. Hampton road is nearest to the capes by about an hour or hour and halfs sail; and so far woud be preferable for other reasons: however it is much inferior to york. Vessels do not lie in perfect security from storms in hampton road. There can be no assistance from the Land against ever so small a superi- ority of naval force. A Line of battle ship can retire no higher than within about three miles of Burwells ferry, and a frigate no higher than

James Town, without lightening: then indeed she may go above Hoods, where she woud be in perfect security. At york town as good a view of the bay is commanded tho somewhat more distant[. The har]bour is safe thro the winter. The guns mounted at that place may, by their [cooperation] save the necessity of retreating from a small superiority of [force] and if a retreat becomes necessary, there is four fathom water up to Poropo tank, twenty five miles above york, and six miles below West point, where the river is one and a half miles wide, but the channel 150 yards only, and lying close under the north shore. At that place there is a soft bar having eighteen feet water only, at high water. That depth continues then up to Cumberland on Pamunkey, and King and Queen courthouse on mattapony. At Cumberland the river is one hundred or one hundred and twenty yards wide, at King and Queen courthouse it is 250 yards wide; and both of these places are in the heart of our country. From this it appears that frigates would have a perfectly safe retreat; but that line of battle ships, or other vessels drawing more than 18 feet water woud not. At york town accommodations and refreshments may be better procured than in hampton road. So that for these reasons york town seems to be the better place. I have the honor to be with great esteem Gent. your most obedient servt

TH: JEFFERSON

RC (Vi); in a clerk's hand, with complimentary close and signature by TJ; words torn away in three places supplied on the basis of the French translation printed in Vol. 15: 598-9; endorsed: "Copie des Lettres de Mr: de la L_____."

George Muter to the Auditors

War Office, 3 Jan. 1780 [1781]. Issue a warrant for £450 to John Liggon for two months house rent for Nathaniel Nattall and ten men for the state from 4 Nov. to 4 Jan. Signed by Muter. Countersigned by TJ.

RC (Vi: Executive Department, Auditors' Office, Vouchers); 1 p.; at foot of text: "The Auditors"; endorsed: "Jno. Liggon £450 30 Jan: 1781 Army" and "Exd."

To John Woodson

SIR   Richmond Jan. 4. 1781

The Enemy having last night passed far up James River and seeming to point immediately to this place or [Peters]burg I must desire you without a moments delay to send every Man of your County able to bear Arms to rendezvous at Westham. Let them come in small detachments as they can be collected and not wait to be formed into companies. I am Sir Yr mo hb Servt.   TH: JEFFERSON

RC (Edna Byers, Decatur, Georgia, 1960); in a clerk's hand, signed by TJ; torn at fold; addressed: "To The County Lieutenant of Goochland"; with notation above this in unidentified hand: "John Woodson the person to whom this is addressed."

Colonel John Woodson (d. 1789), the county lieutenant of Goochland, was also TJ's uncle, being married to Dorothea Randolph, the sister of TJ's mother, Jane Randolph Jefferson (WMQ, 1st ser., x [1901-02], 187).

From George Weedon

DR. SIR   Hanover Court. Jany 11. 1781.

I was honor'd with your Excellency's Letter of Yesterday at this place. Two Hundred of Spotsylvania Militia will be here by the Afternoon, they are well arm'd and equipt, I had also embodied about 150 of the Stafford Militia besides a Body of Volunteers which are now on their march, those are also very well found. I had call'd on the Counties of Loudoun Fauquier Prince William, Fairfax Orange, Culpeper and King George, not knowing from the rapid advances of the Enemy how far they meant to penetrate; but on getting advice the Foe had retreated from Richmond, the whole were countermanded before they began their March except Spotsylvania and Stafford, the latter of which would march as Yesterday. I would now Submit it to your Excellency whether any of those Men that are on their way should be halted or not, and shall wait at this place for your Excellencies further directions on this Head. I must remark at the same time that the County of Caroline was call'd together Yesterday near 700 were assembled out of which we cou'd not arm fifty. The different Captains were order'd to Collect every Gun in the County to day and the Cols. promised me all the men they could Arm should be sent on as soon as possible. If your Excellency thinks proper to send back the Stafford Militia, should not those from Caroline come forwards, if you can send any Arms to meet them at this Place 2 or 300 Men might come forward from that County. I have order'd down a Waggon Load of Camp Kettles and Axes to this place for the accommodation of such as go on, and shall wait here for further directions either from your Excellency or Baron Steuben. I had sent an Express to the Baron informing him what I had done, and should also have wrote to your Excellency had I have known of your return to Richmond. I have had no answer from the Baron, but shall, I expect hear from him to day and shall conform to anything he or your Excellency may please to advise. Mr. Hunter's Work's is no doubt a grand Object as well as the Gun Factory and should the Enemy point up Potowmac would be in great danger, previous to my leaving Fredg: I wrote to all the Cols. of the Counties advising them to arrange and equip their Men as your Excellency may see by the inclosed Copy. If I go back shall make it my Business to see that this is comply'd with, and if any Fortification are to be thrown up for the defence of the Works I must beg your Excells. Authority for employing Engineers. I could have more fully advised your Excellency on the propriety of reinforcing Genl. Nelson with the whole of the Troops mention'd, had my Express to him return'd, but no doubt you are inform'd of his Numbers. Should they not be fully adequate to the Invasion or should there not be a prospect of his getting so from the Counties below, I should think those Men had better join him, if they only remain'd till he was strengthen'd from below. I am With high esteem Your Excellency's Most obt. Humbl Servt.

G WEEDON

RC (OClWHi: Robert C. Norton Collection); in a clerk's hand, signed by Weedon; addressed: "His Excellency Govr. Jefferson Richmond"; franked; endorsed. FC (RPAB: Weedon Papers); in Weedon's hand. Enclosure not found.

From Steuben

SIR   Petersburgh 13. Jany. [1781]

I have just received the inclosed from Col. Parker, and am very unhappy that till this moment I did not know of there being any Public stores at South Quay. I am now informd there is not only a Quantity of Powder, but a Number of Cannon at that place.

I have given Col. Parker the Command of the Troops, in the front, with orders, if possible to remove the Powder and Cannon out of the Enemy's reach. I am with respect Sir Your Excellencys Most Obedt Hbl Servt   STEUBEN Maj: Gen

RC (CSt); in a clerk's hand, signed by Steuben; partially dated; endorsed in part: "13 Jany 1781." Enclosure: possibly Steuben's Queries concerning Military Supplies, with Jefferson's Answers, [before 14 Jan. 1781].

From George Weedon

DEAR SIR   Fredericksburg Janry. 23d 1781

The Commissioners Appointed in the different Counties by the provision Act conceive by a Clause in the latter part of the law that their powers are at an End. I have however prevailed on them to Act till further Instructions from your Excellency can be obtained, and would thank you to forward them to me as early as possible. It may be Necessary for this department to Appoint Commissioners to all the Counties that have been Call'd on for the Protection of Potowmack and the Objects that Navigation affords. The Caroline Militia are Stationd at Port Royal with a View to Succour Potowmack, or Aid the lower Counties should the Enemy come into Rapahannock, they are pretty strong. The King George Militia are Stationd at Boyds Hole on Potowmack at which place is a good landing and about 20 Miles below Hunters works, they are 170 Strong tho' badly Armed. The Stafford Militia are Stationd at Caves Ware-Houses on Potowmack Creek, Seven Miles from hence and the Nearest Navigable Water that makes out of the River, they are 200 Strong and very well Armed and equipt. The Spotsylvania and Orange Men, make one Regiment of 330 under the Command of Colo. Towles, and Stationd in this Town. The Augusta and Rockbridge Rifle men ware Quartered at Mr. Hunters Forge, but Baron-De-Steuben writing to be reinforced have detached them to his Aid, they ware near 500 strong. In Consequence of their being sent below, have call'd on Frederick, Barkley, and Shanandoah for 300 of their best Riflemen which I have reason to believe will turn out Volunteers, and join me in a few days. The Culpeper Militia I have Ordered down to take the place of those Detached. Prince William, and Fair Fax Counties lay immediately above us and on Potowmack River, Loudoun and Fauquier County, join on the back of them. Those Counties are not Call'd into the Field, but are Arranged and lay nearby at a short warning. Should the Enemy mean to Establish themselves below, further reinforcements can be drawn from this Quarter, and their places Supply'd by Loudoun and Fauquier who can join in two days. Each County complain Sadly of their deranged Situation with respect to Arms and Accoutrements but are making the best possible Shift we can, I have only to lament that our Military defences are not equal to the Spirit of the people, which on this Occation is pleasing among all ranks.

I am honored with your Excellencies letter 21st. Inst. I fearr it will not be possible to engage many recruits without the money, as the want of that Article is Generally the cause of their enlisting. I have the honor to be with high Esteem & Regd. yr. Excellencies Most Obt. Servt.

G. WEEDON

DR. SIR

Just as I was closeing this letter, received Baron Steuben's Orders to discharge the Militia of Spotsylvania, Caroline, Stafford, King George and Orange. This shall be done as he directs, but would Submit it to your Excellency whether it would not be prudent to keep up, a defence here. The Culpeper Militia will only join to day, those I shall take the

Liberty of Arranging, and Stationing here till further Orders, and should More force be Necessary below those men can go forward. I am with Esteem & Regd. yr. Excellencies Most Obt. St.   G WEEDON

FC (RPAB: Weedon Papers); in Weedon's hand; endorsed: "To Governour Jefferson a Copy."

PROVISION ACT of June 1780: see note to Appointment of a Commissioner of the Provision Law, printed above under 4 Sep. 1780. The act had expired ten days after the start of the next legislative session, which began on 16 Oct. 1780. During that session the Virginia General Assembly reenacted the law with the stipulation that it remain in force until the end of the following meeting of the legislature (Hening, x, 233-7, 344-6).

From Edward Stevens

SIR   Pittsylvania Old Court House February 11th: 1781

With this the Letter I wrote you of the 8th. Inst. before I crossed the Dan River will be handed you. The Militia we Trust got to this place, their Arms and Accoutrements, I shall Store here as it is not possible to get them to take them any farther. They will be lodged in a Good Store House and under the imediate care of Capt. Brewer a Militia Officer of this County. I shall write to the County Lieut. desiring him to have an Eye to the Security of them till any orders from you may be received respecting them. I shall send you an Account of the numbers of them.

Before they are lodged I shall have them put in good order. The Troops will be mustered in the morning. After which I shall Discharge them, with orders to each Capt. to Keep his men together till he gets them into the County they came from.

Since writing you the 8th. Inst. I have been informed that Genl. Greene has retired to Guilford Court House, from this I suspect the Enemy had or was about to Cross the Yadkin. And if so I expect they are determined to push our Little Army, which by this time must be got together. They are not able to fight Cornwallis (without geting some great advantage). Therefore they must continue to retire if they are pushed And I incline to believe (tho' this the Genl. keeps to himself) they will File off to the Right and Cross the Dan River either at the Lower Saury Town or at Dickens Ferry or perhaps some where between the Two And then make a Stand. If this should be the case the Arms will be Lodged in a proper place, for the use of them to be had on an emergency of that Kind. I have the Honour to be With every Sentiment of respect Your Excellencies Most Obt. & very hum: Servt

EDWARD STEVENS

RC (PWacD: Feinstone Collection, on deposit PPAmP); addressed: "His Excellency Thomas Jefferson Esqr. Governor of Virginia"; franked; endorsed.

From Thomas Nelson

DEAR SIR   Williamsburg Febry. 14. 1781

I am favoured with your's of the 10th. Inst. by Mr. Prentis. I have never been informed that any Horses were left by the Enemy, except those at Westover, which were taken by Captain Selden's and Captain Hockaday's Men. Those in the Possession of Captain Hockaday's Men I ordered to be carried to Richmond for the Proprietors to claim. Farther Enquiry shall be made, and if there be any such as you mention, they shall be disposed of as you direct.

The Numbers of Militia on this Side the River are greatly reduced, as you will see by the Return, and they are chiefly such as ought to be discharged; but the Militia from the upper Counties having been ordered to the South Side of James River, I have been under the Necessity of detaining those from Hanover, New Kent, and Henrico. In a former Letter I mentioned the calling down Men from Caroline and Essex. Perhaps the latter County may be too much exposed to admit of any Assistance being drawn from it. If the People of Elizabeth City, who have thrown aside their Paroles, are not protected, they will probably experience the heaviest Vengeance of the Enemy. I am, dear Sir, with the greatest Respect, Your mo: Obedt. & hble Servt.

THOS NELSON JR. B. G.

RC (MB); in a clerk's hand, signed by Nelson; addressed: "His Excellency Thomas Jefferson Governor of Virginia Express"; franked; endorsed.

A FORMER LETTER: see Nelson to TJ, 7 Feb. 1781.

From Commissary Benjamin Harrison

SIR   South Branch of Potomack Feby. 20th 1781

I beg leave to inform your Excellency that I am a person imployed by Majr. Wm. Harrison who hath receiv'd your Instructions of the 20th Decr. for the purchase of Beef Flour and Building Boats &ca.

The Scarcity of Beef on the Western side of the Allegania Mountain has Obliged me into this and the Neighbouring Counties to procure that article and find by the Strictest examination that not one sixth part of the Quantity required can possibly be had, Either by contracts with any Gentleman or purchase made by myself.

Those reasons Induces me to address your Excellency most earnestly requesting you to consider the expences attending the keeping of that inconsiderable Quantity untill the Vigitation will admit of their being put to pasture and untill which time any more cannot be had. You may inform yourself of many other reasons why your instructions cannot be comply'd with by refering to a Letter from Mr. Harrison of the 6th Inst. Likewise I refer you to Col. Josh. Nevill for the Validity of what I now Lay before you. I purpose Desisting from the purchase of Beef untill your future pleasure respecting that Business may be known.

Only a Sufficient quantity to support the Workmen that will be necessarily imployed in Building the Boats required.[1]

Your Excellency may rely on the utmost exertions to expedite the Business Agreable to any Directions which may be Given. I have the Honor to be with Due respect your most Obt Hble Sevt

BENJ. HARRISON

RC (Vi); addressed: "To His Excellency Thomas Jefferson Esqr. Governor of the Commonwealth of Virginia" and "Handed by Col. Nevill"; endorsed in part in a clerk's hand: "Impossible to obtain the requisite quantity of beef on the Western side of the Mountain." Summarized from printed source in Vol. 4: 666.

TJ's INSTRUCTIONS OF THE 20TH DECR., which were related to George Rogers Clark's expedition against Detroit, have not been found (see TJ to Clark, 25 Dec. 1780; and William Harrison to TJ, 6 Feb. 1781).

[1] Sentence thus in manuscript.

From the Virginia Delegates in Congress

SR.   Phila: 27. Febry 1781

We have nothing new to communicate but what is contained in the inclosed paper except that a considerable Reinforcement from the Continental Army under the Command of the Marqs. la Fayette is on its march to join the Southern Army. This Force added to that now under Genl. Greene will we expect enable him to oppose Ld. Cornwallis or subdue the Traiter Arnold, to whichever object circumstances may direct his attention. Hays the Printer informs us it will be some days yet before he shall be ready to set out for Virga., that it will require he expects three Waggons to transport the printing materials, and some money advanced the Waggoners before they depart—we shall give him what assistance we can to hasten him away. Colo. Harrison desires his Compliments and says he would have written but as he leaves this City Tomorrow expects to be in Richmond as soon as the post. We are respectfully yr. Excely.'s obed Servts   JOS: JONES

THEOK. BLAND JR

Thursday is fixed for the Maryland Delegates to subscribe the Articles of Confederation.

RC (PHi: Gratz Collection); in Bland's hand, signed by Jones and Bland; unaddressed. Enclosure not identified.

From Steuben

SIR   7 oClock PM 28 feby [1781]

The Letters which Your Excellency was so Polite as to send, I have received, and shall have the Pleasure of waiting on Your Excellcy. to morrow in order to confer on matters of importance. I am with Respect & Esteem Sir Your Excellencies Most Obedient Hbl Servant

STEUBEN Majr Genl

RC (IHi); in a clerk's hand, signed by Steuben; partially dated; addressed: "His Excellency Gover Jefferson Richmond"; endorsed in part: "Feby 81."

THE LETTERS: see TJ to Steuben, 28 Feb. 1781, and note.

From Steuben

March 4th. [1781]

Un Considerable nombre des hommes delivres des Comtees comme recrues, et entierement unfit for any service, ont été deja dechargé par Collonel Davis, qui cependant a gardes Leurs noms et les comtees qui les ont délivré.

Ceux que le Capt. Gambel aurat L'honneur de presenter a Votre Exellence seront une preuve convaincanté de la déception dont des Malintentionné abusent le publique. Capt: Gambel delivrerat en meme temps un Liste des hommes et des Comtees quil les ont fournis, et comme je ne me croie pas droits d'accepter de telles hommes pour la defense de la patrie, je Lui ai ordonné de les dechargé a Richmond, apres quil les a soumis a la Consideration du Gouvernement. J'ai L'honeur.

Dft (NHi: Steuben Papers); unsigned; partially dated, possibly in a different hand; at head of text: "Gouverneur"; endorsed: "a Son Excellence Mons le Gouverneur Mar 4e. 1781." Enclosed in TJ to the Speaker of the House of Delegates, 5 Mch. 1781, presumably in the form of an English text.

From Lafayette

SIR   Elk March the 8th 1781

The detachment under My orders is to embark this Morning, and if the Bay is Clear of Privateers will proceed as far as Annapolis where I expect to Hear from our Allies.

My former letters Having exposed our Wants to Your Excellency, I Shall Content Myself with adding that a Number of large vessels, and a quantity of provisions will be very necessary for transporting and Subsisting the troops in the Course of operations.

I am to Request that Your Excellency Be pleased to forward the inclosed letters with dispatch, and Beg leave to assure your Excellency of the Highest Respect and Have the Honor to be With Your most obedient Humble Servan[t]   LAFAYETTE

RC (MHi: Wells Autograph Collection); at foot of text: "His Exy Governor jefferson of virginia"; endorsed. Enclosures not found.

MY FORMER LETTERS: Lafayette to TJ, 3 and 6 Mch. 1781.

From Steuben

MONSIEUR   Nessons Ordnary ce 22 Mars [1781]

Pour donner a Votre Exellence le detail le plus exact de La situation de nos Affaires, je Vous envoie le Collo. Senf qui en est parfaitement instruit.

J'amais Scene n'a changé si subittement que la Notre Avant hier. A six heure du soir nous etions parfaitement persuadé de L'Arrivé de la flotte de nos Allies et a huit heures nous fument Instruit que cetais L'Ennemi.

Cette circonstence m'obligea de me replier, et de mettre les trouppes dans L'Ancienne position, tant de cette que de L'autre côté du Dismal swamb.

Le Marquis de la fayette partit hier de souffolk pour Williamsbourg; Des arrangement avec le General Muhlenberg ne me permettoit que de le suivre Aujourdhui et me Voici en Route pour le joindre a Williamsburg.

Dans ce moment je Viens de recevoir une lettre du Marquis qui me Mande que la flotte francoise à partie le 8 de Road Island, et qu'un Corps de trouppes est partie de New-York pour secourir Arnold. D'apres cela la Guerre se porterat tres Vigoureusement dans peut des jours dans cette partie. Ce qui doit nous engager de continue nos préparatifs avec Vigeur. Il serat surtout necessaire de nous pourvoir des provisions, sans cependant porter des Magazins trop en avant. Je le soumet a Votre Exellence, quel seront les Moyens les plus sure, pour atteindre cet object. A moi il me semble que les Rivieres de York et James seront toujours les Voies les plus sures pour attirer nos Vivre en haut du païs avec le moins de Risque et de depenses.

Quoique le nombre des trouppes que J'ai demandé pour L'entreprise sur Portsmouth n'est pas encore complet et que le Genl. Muhlenberg n'avait que 2030 au Lieux de 2500 qu'il devait avoir, J'espere qu'avec la Milice de Chesterfield et Danviddy dont J'ai rencontrés aujourdhui des partie, Le nombre serat suffisant, pourvue que nous puissions les tenir ensemble J'usqu'a L'enouëment de la Scene, ce qui se deciderat dans peut des jour.

Je promet a Votre Exellence que je ne tiendrai pas un homme plus longtems en Campagne, qu'il ne serat absolument neccessaire.

Une chose sur laquelle je souhaite la continuation de nos preparatifs, est d'assemblé les outils neccessaires pour les batterie et tranchees: a plus forte Raison que L'Ennemi est actuellement si bien retranché a Portsmouth, qu'il n'est plus question de L'Emporter d'un coup de Main. Collonel Senf est a meme de donner a Votre Exellence la Meillieure enumeration des Articles les plus neccessaire pour cet objet.

Je saisie cette occasion pour recommander encore cet officier a Votre Exellence; Persuader que L'Etat ferat en Lui une Acquisition bien interressant. Collonel Walker m'a dit qu'il ne S'agissait que du Rang de Collonel, sur quoi L'assemblé hesite en consequence d'un Resolve du Congrès. Si Mr. Senf n'etoit deja employé dans ce rang par L'Etat de la Caroline ce Resolve du Congrès serait certainement un obstacle. Mais comme il ne s'agit point d'un nouveau appointement et qu'il ne fait que passer du service d'un Etat dans celui d'un autre, avec le meme rang et les memes Emolumens dont il jouissait auparavent, Il me semble que cette difficulté cesserat d'etre une, aussi tot qu'il plait a L'etat d'accepter ses services sous les termes que je Viens de mentionné, sans faire un nouveau Appointement. La Scene qui se prepare sur nos Cotes est un Motif de plus qui me fais de[sirer] que cet Officier fut plus fixé pour cet etat, ou ses services dans ce moment seront des plus Essentielles.

Malgré que la Presence de Mr: le Marquis, m'enleve une partie de la Correspondence avec Votre Exellence je ne manquerai pas de Vous faire part, de tout cequi se passe ici, et je Vous suplie d'etre bien persuade du parfait respect avec lequel J'ai L'honneur d'etre Monsieur De Votre Exellence le tres humble et tres obeissant ser[viteur]

STEUBEN

FC (CSt); in Steuben's hand; partially dated; unaddressed, but internal evidence establishes TJ as the intended recipient. The missing RC was probably written in English.

To William Davies?

Mar. 27. 1781.

Not having that kind of knolege of the transactions of the artificers which is acquired by personal inspection, we think it will be better that a determination on the above point should be suspended until Colo. Davies shall become so far acquainted with them as will enable him to form a judgment on the subject.   TH: JEFFERSON

RC (Paul C. Richards Autographs, Brookline, Massachusetts, 1969); unaddressed, but probably a reply to William Davies, being written on verso of the address cover of his missing letter to TJ of 27 Mch. 1781 (Vol 5: 255); cover is addressed

"His Excellency The Governor" in an unidentified hand and bears two almost identical notations in different clerical hands, one of which reads "Col. Davies' Letter To Governor Jefferson respecting Anderson's application for cooking & washing March 27. 81."

From Robert Hoakesly

SIR   Hampton Road 28 March 1781

I do myself the Honor by this Flag which Capt. Gerlach is sending On Shore to the officer commanding at Hampton to request your Excellency will be Pleased to forward to Brigd. Genl. Hamilton the five different Parcells of Letters and Papers.

I have also to Inform your Excellency that Alexr. Frazier Gregorie is on Board the Flag as mentioned in Brigadier Genl. Woodfords Letter, and should your Excellency approve of his landing you will Please to Inform his relations that they may send for him. I have the Honor to be your Excellencys Most Obedt. Hble Servt.   ROBT HOAKESLY

RC (George M. Rinsland, Allentown, Pennsylvania, 1974); above salutation: "His Excellency Governor Jefferson."

Robert Hoakesly was a British commissary of prisoners on the *General Riedesel*, a British flag vessel carrying letters, money, and supplies for the Saratoga Convention troops (Heinrich Gerlach to TJ, [27 Mch. 1781], and note; Thomas Sim Lee to TJ, 27 Apr. 1781, and note).

From James Barbour

SIR   Culpeper April 5th. 1781

I must again beg leave to Address your Excellency in behalf of a number of poor men who march'd in the Detatchment of Militia from this County the other day, if Possible to have them releived by or before the last of this month, that they may return to their homes in order to get their Corn Planted, who with their famalys must Suffer greatly if not Perish unless they can return time Enough to make Corn. I have Order'd a Sufficent number to relieve those now sent to be in readiness to march at one hours notice, and to get their Corn planted Early as I expected they would be call'd on to relieve those now sent. Your Acquiescence and Orders for a Relief if necessary from this County (by the Bearer) will much Oblige Honble. Sir with great Esteem & regard your most Obedt. Hum. Servt.   JAS. BARBOUR

RC (ViU); unaddressed.

To Thomas Walker, John Walker, and Nicholas Lewis

GENTLEMEN   In Council Apr. 5. 1781.

I take the liberty of inclosing to you a resolution of council requesting you to carry into execution the desire of Congress as to the settlement of Colo. Wood's accounts. I am with much respect & esteem Gent. Your most obedt. humble servt.   TH: JEFFERSON

RC (ViU); addressed: "Doctr. Walker John Walker Nicholas Lewis esqrs. Albemarle."

For the enclosure and the events leading up to the appointment of the addressees to settle Colonel James Wood's accounts as superintendent of the Saratoga Convention prisoners, see Samuel Huntington to TJ, 26 Mch. 1781, and note.

Contract between Thomas A. Talbot and the Board of War

War Office, Richmond, 6 Apr. 1781. Talbot agrees "to perform the Turners work for the public Laboratory" and to have his work valued by two "indifferently" chosen men, who will also value everything the public furnishes him and deduct it from his allowance. Signed by Talbot. Countersigned by TJ: "In Council Apr. 7. 1781. Approved. Th: Jefferson."

MS (Vi: Executive Department, Governor's Office, Letters Received); 1 p.; in a clerk's hand, except for Talbot's signature and TJ's countersignature; torn at top right corner; endorsed by clerk: "Talbot's engagement [. . .] by the Executive 7th April, 1781."

From Samuel Huntington

Philadelphia, 7 Apr. 1781. Encloses copies of two important letters received this morning from Governor Livingston and General Forman.

FC (Lb in DNA: RG 360, PCC); 1 p.; at head of text: "To His Excelly. General Washington"; at foot of text: "N.B. The like to the Presidents of Pennsylvania & Delaware & the Governors of Maryland & Virginia." Enclosures: (1) David Forman to Huntington, Freehold, 2 Apr. 1781, stating that he just learned from a highly reliable informant in New York that a large British expeditionary force under Sir Henry Clinton's command was preparing to set sail in order to take post at New Cas- tle, Delaware, and that he is further inclined to credit this report because of the "known disaffection of the lower parts of Delaware and Maryland States." (2) William Livingston to Huntington, Trenton, 5 Apr. 1781, stating that he has just received No. 1 and is forwarding it by express on the assumption that it contains the same reliable intelligence about the planned British expedition against New Castle as the covering letter he received at the same time from Forman (RCs in same).

To William Davies

SIR   Apr. 9. 1781.

I beleive it will be necessary for us to begin to register our people in captivity with the enemy, in order that we may be enabled on all exchanges to give preference according to *turn*: which is certainly just whether a person be exchanged as a souldier, a sailor, or a citizen. I therefore have recommended to the bearer John Wood to enter his name with you, time of captivity, denomination (that is Whether Souldier, Sailor or Citizen) whether on parole, and where. It should be noted that tho' an officer in Georgia, yet being taken not on military command, he did not make known his military character, but gave a parole as a common passenger. As a citizen too he seems not to have annexed himself to this state when he was taken. I am with much respect Sir Your most obedt. servt   TH: JEFFERSON

RC (DLC); addressed: "Colo Davies"; endorsed in part: "sent one Jno: Wood to have his name entered &c."

From George Weedon

DR. SIR   Williamsburg April 9th. 1781

I last night received the Inclosed from Captain Davenport who Acts in the lower Counties with a party of Horse. You will see by the letter the fate of the Boat Patriot, Commanded by Captain Chandler. That Officer had my positive Orders not to risque an Action on any Account, his directions ware to cruise from Warransquake Bay as low down as Newport News, to Shift his Station every Night, and upon the Appearance of any Vessels coming up James River, was to fire three Signal guns, which ware to been Answered by the Galley Stationd near Mulberry Island, upon which both ware to move up the River, and alarm the Shores and Craft as they went, Instead of which he has imprudently brought on an Action, and lost his Boat and Crew. I have sent Captain Travis up to your Excellency, and must request you will either send him down in the Jefferson, or in some other Vessell, for the Protection of Chandlers Station. I have the honor to be with much Esteem yr. most Obt. Servt.   G WEEDON

RC (ViU); addressed: "His Excellency Governor Jefferson Richmond." Enclosure not found.   For further information on the loss of the PATRIOT, see TJ's reply of 14 Apr. 1781, and note.

[717]

From the Virginia Delegates in Congress

[ca. 10 Apr. 1781]

[. . .]¹ [ap]plication [. . .],² [. . .] with no Difficulty in arbitrating [the?] dispute, as he admitted the Facts stated [as?] agreed between you; and acquiesced in the Gentleman proposed; but contrary to our Expectation we received a Letter from him a Copy of which is inclosed and also our Answer to it. You [will] see by these Letters the Turn this affair has taken; and we must wait your further Instructions. Mr. Nathan urges that he may be indulged in the Choice of Merchants to arbitrate th[e dis]pute; if you approve of his Request you will be pleased to signify [. . .] your pleasure.

Your favour of the 26th. of [March] came to hand yesterday. We shall attend to what you have mention'd therein respecting Col. Davis, and give you as speedy an Answer as possible to the [. . .]³ Packet had arrived at New York from England, bringing Advice of the Sailing of the French Fleet for America. It is very probable the Account is true. We have the Honour to be, with very great Respect Your Exccellency's most obedient Servants.   JAMES MADISON JUNR.

RC (Vi); in Meriwether Smith's hand, signed by Madison; consisting of a fragmentary and mutilated sheet; conjecturally dated on the basis of the reading in Congress on Monday, 9 Apr. 1781, of TJ's 26 Mch. 1781 letter to the Virginia Delegates and Madison's habit of writing to TJ from Philadelphia on Tuesdays (JCC, XIX, 367n; Madison, *Papers*, III, 65n). Enclosures not found.

TJ had discussed the financial claims of Simon NATHAN on Virginia in his 15 Mch. 1781 letter to the Virginia Delegates (see also Vol. 6: 321-4n). The Delegates dealt with the case of COL. DAVIS (William Davies) in their 17 Apr. 1781 letter to TJ.

¹ Estimated one or two sheets missing.
² Estimated four or five words torn away.
³ Manuscript torn; indeterminable number of lines missing.

From Samuel Huntington

Philadelphia, 29 Apr. 1781. Encloses a 20 Apr. 1781 resolution of Congress recommending that certain states make good the depreciation of monthly pay to the officers and soldiers belonging to the regiment of Colonel Moses Hazen who are considered part of their quotas in the same manner as they have done for the officers and soldiers in their respective state lines.

FC (Lb in DNA: RG 360, PCC); 1 p.; at head of text: "Governor Greene"; at foot of text: "N.B. The like to the Governors of New York, N. Jersey, Maryland & Virginia, and the Presidents of Pennsylvania & Delaware." Enclosure: Resolution of Congress, 20 Apr. 1781 (JCC, XIX, 428).

From Silas Deane

Dr. Sr.   Paris May 2d. 1781

This will be handed to you by Mr. Greive who goes to America with the Resolution of establishing himself in the United States, whose Interests, he has, (to my knowlege,) at all times zealously espous'd, and of which he has a few Days since, qualified himself a Citizen; He has an Affair of some Importance in your State, in the adjustment of which, I flatter myself, you may be of service to him, and therefore take the Liberty of recommending him, to your good offices. I have the honor to be with the most sincere respect Dr. sr. yours &c   S DEANE

FC (Lb in CtHi: Deane Papers); at foot of text: "His Excelly. Govr. Jefferson."

AN AFFAIR OF SOME IMPORTANCE: Greive was going to Virginia apparently to help Charles Bennet, the fourth Earl of Tankerville, assert his family's claim to an estate in Fairfax County that had been bequeathed to the third Earl by John Colvill (*Deane Papers*, New-York Historical Society, *Collections*, Pub. Fund Ser., XIX-XXIII [1887-91], IV, 305-6; Fitzpatrick, *Writings*, XXIV, 75; Washington, *Papers*, Confed. Ser., I, 64-6, 109-10, 120; Thorne, *Parliament*, III, 178).

To the Commander of the Essex County Militia

SIR   Richmond May 8th. 1781

The British army under Major General Phillips having landed at Brandon and meaning to press Southwardly and Lord Cornwallis being now advancing Northwardly with a Design probably of uniting their force, it behoves us immediately to turn out from every County as many men as there are arms to be found in the County in order to oppose these forces in their separate State if possible and if not to do it when combined. You will therefore be pleased with the assistance of your Captains and Subalterns to collect immediately every fire Arm in your County in any wise fit for military Service and to march so many men with these arms in their Hands to Richmond where they will receive orders to join Major General Marquis Fayette. When you shall be possessed of the Arms I think those men should be called on whose regular tour it is to go unless any should offer voluntarily in which Case the Service should be accounted to them as a Tour of Duty. The Person who receives any fire arm must be noted by you and held accountable to the Owner for its safe return in which he will not be obstructed when he shall be discharged. When the Discharge will take place we cannot undertake to say. It is fixed that no tour shall exceed two months in the field but our expectation is that the present Crisis will be over in a much shorter time, and whenever it is over they shall be discharged except the number called for by my Letter of Yesterday who will be retained to perform a full Tour.

Cavalry in a due proportion being as necessary as Infantry you will be pleased to permit and even to encourage one tenth Part of those who are to come into Duty as above required[1] to mount and equip themselves as Cavalry. They must not be received however unless their Horses be really good and fit for service. A short sword can be furnished them by the State, 'tho if they can procure a proper one with other Equipments themselves they had better do it. Their Horses and Accoutrements shall be ensured by the public against every thing but their own Negligence, and they shall be allowed Forage for them in addition to their own pay and Rations. I need not urge to you that the greatest Events hang on the Dispatch which is used in getting the militia into the Field. I am with great Respect Sir your mo. obt. Servt   TH: JEFFERSON

RC (NN: Berg Collection); in a clerk's hand, with signature and revision by TJ (see note 1 below); addressed: "To the Commanding Officer of the Militia of the County of Essex."

This letter is a variant of those addressed to various county lieutenants on the same date (see Vol. 5: 614-18).

[1] Preceding three words interlined by TJ.

From La Luzerne

MONSIEUR   A Philadelphie le 4 Juin 1781

Des causes inévitables ont empeché l'envoi de notre Seconde division pour l'epoque à laquelle on avoit projeté de l'expédier. Je ne puis entrer ici dans le détail des raisons de ce Changement dans nos mesures; mais j'en ai Fais part au Congres et ce senat, malgré le préjudice qui en résulte pour les opérations, n'a pu S'empecher de rendre justice a la sagesse et à la prudence du Roi dans le parti que S. M. a adopté. Nous attendons Cependant quelques renforts; mais ils ne sont aucunement égaux à ce que l'amitié du Roi pour les Etats-unis l'avoit engagé à Faire. Pour Suppléer à ce retard dans les mesures précédemment arretées, il leur a accordé un Subside gratuit dont la disposition a été laissé au Congres. M. Robert Morris Surintendant des Finances a ordre de songer dans l'application graduelle qu'il en Fera aux besoins de l'armée du sud. Au reste, Monsieur, quoique je ne puisse entrer dans le détail des mesures qui Seront prises pour l'assistance des Etats unis, je puis Vous assurer qu'elle Sera efficace, Que le Roi est Fermement résolu à les aider de tout son pouvoir et qu'en Faisant de leur coté les efforts capables de contenir encore quelque tems l'ennemi, ils peuvent compter Solidement

Sur une heureuse issue de la glorieuse cause qu'ils défendent. Je puis d'ailleurs vous assurer que les calamités et le danger des états méridionaux Sont un motif de plus pour S. M. de redoubler d'interet en leur Faveur, Que son affection en reçoit de nouvelles forces et que l'evenement prouvera qu'ils étoient parfaitement bien fondés à ne pas Se laisser décourager par la difficulté de la Conjoncture présente. J'ai l'honneur d'etre avec le plus Sincere et le plus respectueux attachement Monsieur De Votre Excellence Le très humble et très obéissant Serviteur.

LE CHR DE LA LUZERNE

RC (Joseph Rubinfine, West Palm Beach, Florida, 1990); in a clerk's hand, signed by La Luzerne; at foot of first page: "S. E. M. le Gouverneur Jepherson"; English translation printed in Vol. 6: 80-1.

From Harry Innes

SIR   Richmond Novr. 29th. 1781

A circumstance has lately transpired in the Western country which is likely to create great Litigation, and as I expect to be considerably employed in the investigation of the matter, I would beg leave to communicate the affair to you and request your opinion on it; I have presumed to do this under a confidence that you would have no objection to giving your opinion as you are not in any of the judicial departments. Inclosed is a State of the case. Those Surveys were cheifly made before the Year 48 at which time it is said no Depy. or Assistant Surveyor was necessary—the Law directing Assistants passed about the year 50.

I would beg leave Sir to request your opinion in another matter which concerns myself, (I mean) who has the Titles to the Leatherwood Lands—Lomax or my Fathers Representatives—as I beleive you are better acquainted with the matter than I am, shall not undertake to state it. Your favour Sir in answering the two cases here refered to you will lay me under singular obligations, besides making you any satisfaction you may require—and if an oppertunity offers of sending [an answer?] shortly to Bedford I would request you to send it to the care of your Overseer—if no oppertunity offers that way soon a Letter sent to Richmond any time during the Session to the care of Mr. Talbott would meet with a ready conveyance. I am Sir Your mo. ob.

HARRY INNES

RC (CtY: Benjamin Franklin Papers); addressed: "Thomas Jefferson Esqr. Albemarle"; one line partially clipped, with notations by TJ on address cover: "Grants of lands. Stopped by caveat Revoked by Sci. fa.

Ct. of Appeals. Writ of error
Appeal
Rehearing qu?"

Harry Innes, a Bedford County lawyer, evidently solicited TJ's advice on the CIR-

CUMSTANCE . . . IN THE WESTERN COUNTRY in order to help him decide how best to represent the legal interests of the Augusta County opponents of the land grant to James Patton described in the enclosure below. The 1749 LAW DIRECTING ASSIS-

TANTS for Virginia surveyors is in Hening, VI, 33-8.

TJ responded to Innes in missing letters of 15 Dec. 1781 and 3 Feb. 1782 (see Innes to TJ, 18 Feb. 1782, and note).

E N C L O S U R E

State of the Case, with Jefferson's Notes

James Patton late of Augusta County and others obtained an Order of Council in the Year 174   for 100.000 Acres of Land to be Located on the Western Waters in Augusta County[1] in one or more Surveys. Patton who was Agent for the Company, employed a certain John Buchannan one of the Partners to Survey the Lands, who never was either cheif or Assistant Surveyor in the said County, nor had he any Special Commission for this purpose; After the Surveys were compleated by Buchannan they were returned to Thomas Lewis the Surveyor of Augusta who Recorded them and made out the Certificates as the Law directed for the Grantees to obtain their Pattents. The works of the Land were returned to the Secretary's Office and Pattents issued on all the Surveys except 28 before the Revolution. On the passing of the Law for establishing the Land Office and the Law directing the Court of Appeals to determine the Validity of such Surveys the Representatives of Buchannan and Patton laid their Claims before the Court who Established them and Grants have Issued for the said 28 Surveys.

There are a number of People who have been Ejected off those Lands, and others who on seeing the Grants lately obtained have become Tenants to the Representatives of Patton and Buchannan, but still wish to destroy the Pattents and Grants if practicable, and claim the Lands by Occupancy under the Act of Assembly passed in May 1779 for "Adjusting and settling the Titles of Claimers to unpatented Lands under the present and former Government, previous to the establishment of the Como. Land Office."

If the Surveys are illegal will not the Lands be in the eye of the Law vacant, or will 20 Years possession give them a Title—see the above recited Act.

[*Notes by TJ:*]
Under laws before revolution a grant on a survey made by an unsworn surveyor might 1. be arrested before issuing by Caveat. 2. if injurious to the crown, might be vacated by scire facias in Conc.
1779. session 1. c. 12. confirms surveys on Western wat. *made by any county surveior commissioned by Wm. & M. coll.* founded on *ord. conc.* and made while such order was in force. All others made void.
That all claims on surveys under orders of council shall be laid before court of appeals, and by them be determined[2]
1779. sess. 2. c. 27. such surveys allowed to be laid before the then next Ct. of Appeals
Ct. of Appeals having determined cannot be brought on again.
H. of Lds. may possibly re-hear, because done before signing judgment or decree.
two methods of bringing cause before them

1. Comm. Law. by writ of Error directed to Ct. below.
2. Chancery. by petition to H. Lds. to *call it*[3] before them.
   In both cases no new evidence allowed.
We have abridged both methods by permitting party to omit the previ-ous[4] application to H. L. for writ of error or[5]

MS (CtY: Benjamin Franklin Papers); undated; in Innes's hand; with TJ's unfin-ished notes on verso.

The 1745 land grant in Augusta County to JAMES PATTON and his associates and the subsequent problems arising during the Revolutionary War from the unauthorized survey of this tract by his son-in-law, John Buchanan, are discussed in Thomas P. Abernethy, *Western Lands and the Ameri-can Revolution* (New York, 1937), 4-5, 256. The 1779 laws relating to the LAND OFFICE and to the COURT OF APPEALS and UNPATENTED LANDS are in Hening, x, 35-65. The 1779 law allowing SURVEYS to be submitted to the NEXT COURT OF APPEALS is in same, 177-80.

[1] Preceding three words interlined.
[2] Sentence added later.
[3] Above the preceding two words TJ wrote "appellare."
[4] Word interlined.
[5] TJ's notes end here.

From Thomas Mann Randolph, Sr.

MY DEAR SIR   Tuckahoe Apr 10 1782
   There seems to be Fatality attending the promise I made you, of a Supply of beer. Two days after Jupiter went up last, my Brewer went up the County to see his Wife, and I have never set eyes on him since, and of Course have had none brewed! Colo. Cary who is now here, joins me in thanks for the Paccan trees. I dont know of a Rabbit nearer this, than Shirley and Mr. Carter is just now begining a Stock.
   I am extremely Sorry for your loss by fire! One triffling circumstance or other, prevented my coming up with the Boys, and Now I am in-formed by Mr. Tucker, that the Vacation begins the first Week in May, and Continues one Month, till which time I shall be deprivd of the pleasure of waiting on you. Our best respects to Mrs. Jefferson. My dear Sir Your most Aff hum St   THOMAS M. RANDOLPH

RC (ViU); addressed: "Thomas Jefferson esqr Monticello"; with notation by TJ oppo-site address: "Lines."

From Esteban Rodríguez Miró

New Orleans, 4 May 1782. He commends the many services for the common cause made by Oliver Pollock, the agent of Congress, who is about to leave for the United States. Pollock facilitated the first successful actions by Spanish forces against the English establishments on the Mississippi, whereby the in-habitants of Natchez accepted the dominion of the Spanish king without the least opposition, and he has been obliged to sacrifice his own interests in the service of TJ and Virginia, for which he deserves TJ's esteem. He wishes God may favor American forces with success for many years.

FC (AGI: Papeles de Cuba, legajo 2370); 1 p.; in Spanish; in a clerk's hand, unsigned, but authorship attributed on the basis of Miró's 4 May 1782 letter to the President of Congress on the same subject (DNA: RG 360, PCC); at foot of text: "Exmo. Sor. dn. Tomas Jefferson."

Esteban Rodríguez Miró (1744-95), a Spanish army officer who participated in the West Florida campaigns during the Revolutionary War, was acting governor, 1782-85, and governor, 1785-91, of Louisiana, as well as intendant of the province during the last three years of his governorship (DAB).

From John Taylor, with Jefferson's Opinion on Mary Wayland

SIR   [16 Aug. 1782]

Your most Curious Council is required on the following Cases.

Case the   Adam Wayland of Culpeper County in the Virga. State, after
1st.   Lawful Marriage had 6 Children by his wife and She pregnant with the 7th.—Made a Will by which will he bequeath'd his wife one full Third part of his Estate, his wife in time of her pregnancy was Taken with the Small pox and Died— after remaining a widower Some Time he married again. The remainder of his Estate by the aforesaid Will he left to be Eaqually Divided, among (all) or as the Executors have it his Children, without nominating So much as even One of them—having a View as must be Suppos'd by that Omission of a future posterity, which According happen'd by his Second Lawful married wife, and then himself died Leaving 2 Small Children (a Son and a Daughter) without any Other will than that made in his first wifes Lifetime, which said Will was prov'd in Court, orders Issued for appraisers to appraise the Estate and Gentlemen to divide, giving the widow her Thirds And her Two Children an Eaqual part with the 6 by his first wife. The Court Granting her the Guardianship to her own Children, and to be (possess'd of their) or at least to have the Care of their Estates during their Minority, which Accordingly was Set apart and put in her possession by the Executors.

Case 2d.   The Executors by Some Council Since received Cavil with her that her 2 Children have no right to Any part of the Estate, and She Only a right to her thirds of the Lands Slaves

[724]

and mills and Only a Childs part of the movable Estate (viz.) $\frac{1}{7}$th. and Threaten to Sue her for Her 2 Childrens part and what She has received over a Childs part of the Movable Estate (or $\frac{1}{7}$th.).

Case 3rd. There is 3 Tracts of Land, one whereof the heir at Law pretends to Hold as a Gift from his father; by Marriage Contract, he neither Married the Woman, has no Deed or record from his father nor Any proof his own Oath Excepted. How are Those Lands to be Divided to do the widow Justice—She having renounc'd the will in Nine Months after Probate.

Case 4th. The Widow on the Mannor plantation Sow'd a field with wheat last fall which in april Last the Executors Came and offer'd to rent out with the Cornfield And pasture Ground, the widow warn'd them to Concern themselves with nothing Concerning the Mannor plantation, upon which they at that Time desisted Only Among themselves Judging the Quantity of wheat they thought the field might Make, but Since the wheat has been reap'd they Came and fore[warn'd?] the widows Overseer (not her) from removing the wheat out of the field, the widows Right in the mannor plantation relating to Croping, working none but hers and her Childrens people with an overseer thereon required.

Case 5th. The Executors Sent the Collector to Collect the widows and Her Childrens Taxes which She paid by the Hand of Capt. Henry Field, who on her behalf Took receipt for the Same as may appear—whether this Does not in Measure Establish hers and her Childrens property is the Case.

Case 6th. The Heir at Law has a Negroe man in his possession which he Says his father gave him, but has neither record nor witness to prove it. Your opinion in that Case is desired.

Case 7th. There is another Tract of Land, Seperate from the Other Three Adjoining Tracts, is the widow to have her Thirds Laid off in Quantity And Quality of Each Tract Seperately, or her thirds Taken off the Mannor plantation and Tracts Binding thereon and Adjoining it in One Tract, [is?] the Case required.

Monticello Aug. 16. 1782.[1]

I am of opinion that the widow is not entitled to any thing under this will.[2] That therefore she is put to claim her legal rights which are one third of the lands and slaves for life as of her dower, and a child's part, that is, one ninth of the personal estate in absolute property, the testator's debts being first paid. In allotting dower, all lands adjacent to each other are to be considered as one tract and the dower to be laid off in one parcel: but separate tracts must be separately divided.

I think that the two children born after making the will are entitled to share equally with those born before. The cases of Garbland v. Mayot 2. Ver. 105. Cook v. Cook ib. 545. and Bateman v. Roach 9. Mod. 104.[3] have so decided; and the late case[4] of Coleman v. Seymour 1. Vez. 209. admits it.[5] The particular circumstance of this case, which is of a father making provision for his children, all of whom are equally near to him, can leave no doubt but that had he been asked at his death whether he intended that his two children born after making the will should take? he would have answered affirmatively. 2 Vez. 84. and if his intention be admitted, it will be carried into execution.

Though there be no words of limitation annexed to this devise to the children they will take a fee simple, a devise of a man's 'estate' having been often determined to pass all his interest in the subject.

The tract of land which the heir at law claims under a marriage settlement must be submitted[6] to division among the children, unless the settlement be proved by witnesses or writing to have been stipulated, and the marriage take effect in consequence:[7] and even if so proved, will yet be subject to the widow's dower. The Slave in his possession and claimed as a gift,[8] will[9] be subject to dower and division; that gift not having been made by deed and of record as required by law.

The wheat which the widow sowed and reaped on the manor plantation is hers undoubtedly:[10] as the law allows her to retain possession of[11] the mansion house and plantation, without rent, till her dower shall be assigned. While she retains possession, I think her liable for the taxes leviable on it.

TH: JEFFERSON

RC (ViU); in a clerical hand, undated, unsigned, and unaddressed; with TJ's dated opinion subjoined in his own hand; on detached sheet in an unidentified hand: "Legal Opinions of Thomas Jefferson & John Taylor. 1782." Dft (DLC: TJ Papers, 233: 41736); consists of TJ's opinion only; entirely in his hand, unsigned and undated; the most significant revisions are recorded below; endorsed:

"Mrs Wayland's case.
  divests 'children' if those born
    after shall take.
  devise of 'estate' passes fee
  gift of slave under act of 1758.
Widow's Quarentine." Tr (Office of the Clerk of the Circuit Court, Madison County Court House, Madison, Virginia); copy of TJ's opinion in the hand of Richard Vawter;

at foot of text: "Copy Test Richd. Vawter"; filed with the case of John Wayland et al. v. Daniel Utz and Wife, "the Opinions of Col John Taylor & Mr Jefferson" being referred to several times therein.

Taylor, the Virginia lawyer and future agrarian political economist, was at this time devoting himself to his legal practice (Robert E. Shalhope, *John Taylor of Caroline: Pastoral Republican* [Columbia, S.C., 1980], 32). TJ's legal opinion in this case is one of six he is known to have prepared during the brief time in 1782 when he resumed his law practice, three others having been previously published in this series (Vol. 6: 145-6, 151-4, 180-2). TJ was paid 21s. 3d. the day after he wrote it (MB, 17 Aug. 1782). The opinion was closely followed six years later in the final disposition of the case of Mary Wayland, the second wife and WIDOW of Adam Wayland of Culpeper County, Virginia, whose 16 May 1775 WILL was made out while he was still married to his first wife, Elizabeth (John C. Wyllie, ed., "The Second Mrs. Wayland, An Unpublished Jefferson Opinion on a Case in Equity," *American Journal of Legal History*, IX [1965], 64-8).

[1] In Dft TJ prefaced his opinion with this paragraph: "Adam Wayland of Culpeper having three separate tracts of land, slaves and personal estate and a wife Elizabeth and 6 children and his wife enseint with another made his will bearing date May. 16. 1775. in which he bequeathed 'unto his beloved wife Elizabeth the third part of his estate and the rest of his estate to be equally divided among his children.' The wife dies during her pregnancy. The testator marries again, has two other children and dies in 1781. The eldest son holds one of the testator's tracts of land pretending a marriage contract, whereas he ⟨never⟩ can produce no proof of such contract nor did he ever marry the woman with whom his marriage was in contemplation. He has also a slave of the testator's which he sais was given but without proof. The widow was appointed guardian to her own two children. Persons were appointed by the court to divide the estate, who allotted the widow her thirds and delivered her the share of her two children. She sowed and reaped the manor plantation and has paid the taxes of it."

[2] In Dft TJ wrote in the margin next to this sentence "Swinb. 7. 11. 6. bequest to the parish in which he lived and removes after to another parish. Legacy goes to the first."

[3] In Dft TJ here canceled "are pretty clear."

[4] In Dft TJ first wrote "have decided in their favour and that" and then altered it to read as above, inadvertently canceling the last two syllables of "decided."

[5] In Dft TJ here inserted an asterisk to reference a note he wrote in the margin: "The doctrine seems to be that there are in these cases 3. times worthy of notice. 1. the time of making the will. 2. that of the death of the testator. 3. when the legacies become payable. The Chancellors have declared that these cases cannot be subjected to any general rule, but that every one must be decided on it's particular circumstances. 1. that primâ facie the time of making the will, not of the death of the testator is to be regarded. Swinb. 7.11.6. 1. P.W. 342. Northey v. Strange. S.C. Pr. Ch. 489. 1. Vezey. 295. 2. that words de futuro or circumstances may extend it to the death of the testator. ⟨Weld v. Bradbury 2 Ver. 705.⟩ Coleman v. Seymour 1. Vez. 209. 3. that the words of futurity must indeed be very express which shall carry it beyond the testator's death when the will becomes complete, to the day of paiment Musgrave v. Parry 2. Ver. 710 and 4. that express words shall be overruled which would carry it beyond that period, because it would suspend the right to property too long, or leave the divisions to be perpetually unravelled and resettled. Ellison v. Airey 1. Vez. 111. Lomax v. Holmden. ib. 295. Horsley v. Chaloner. 2 Vez. 83. econtre Weld v. Bradbury. 2. Ver. 705.

[6] In Dft TJ here canceled "to the widow's dower at any rate, and also."

[7] Remainder of sentence interlined in Dft.

[8] In Dft TJ here canceled "unless that gift can be proved by writing or by witnesses."

[9] In Dft TJ here canceled "in like manner."

[10] Remainder of text interlined in place of "but unless that plantation has been allotted to her in dower, I think she is liable to pay rent for it, in which she must be allowed for the taxes she has paid, and also for her right to a third of the land from the time of her making a legal demand of dower." TJ canceled the same passage in Dft.

[11] In Dft TJ first wrote "remain in" and then altered it to read as above.

Epitaph for Martha Wayles Jefferson

[after 6 Sep. 1782]

To the memory of
Martha Jefferson
daughter of John Wayles
born Oct. 19. 1748. O.S.
intermarried with Thomas Jefferson
Jan. 1. 1772
torn from him by death
Sep. 6. 1782.
this monument of his love [1]
is inscribed.

εἰ δὲ θανόντων περ καταλήθοντ᾽ εἰν Ἀΐδαο
αὐτὰρ ἐγὼ καὶ κεῖθι φίλου μεμνήσομ᾽ ἑταίρου.

[*on verso:*]

to be engraved on a marble slab.

MS (Thomas Jefferson Memorial Foundation, on deposit ViU); written entirely in TJ's hand on both sides of a small sheet; undated.

TJ recorded the death of his wife in an entry in one his notebooks: "My dear wife died this day at 11:45 A.M." (MB, 6 Sep. 1782; see also Malone, I, 396-7). For reports of his grief at the time and for months afterward, see Vol. 6: 199-200n. The Editors know of no evidence indicating when TJ set down this epitaph.

The lines in Greek are from the lament for Patroclus spoken by Achilles after his triumph over Hector, as given in the *Iliad*, 22.389-90: "Though the dead forget their dead in the House of Death, I will remember, even there, my dear companion" (Homer, *The Iliad*, trans. Robert Fagles [New York, 1990], 554). TJ's transcription does not depart from what was the received text. Except for minor differences in capitalization, punctuation, and the arrangement of lines, the tombstone inscription in the cemetery at Monticello followed TJ's wording exactly (Randall, *Life*, I, 383).

[1] TJ here canceled "and [. . .]."

From James Madison

MY DEAR SIR   Philada. Feby. 12th. 1783.

I acknowledged yesterday by the post your two favors of the 30th. Ult: and 7th. inst: I add this by Col: Jameson just to inform you that your letter to the Secy. of F. A. has been referred to a Committee consisting of Mr. Jones, Mr. Rutledge and Mr. Wilson, who are to confer with Mr. Morris as Agent of Marine, and report to Congs. whether any and what remedy [1] can be applied to your embarrassments. I made the first acquainted with the ideas suggested in your last letter, and he will take care to lead the attention of his colleagues and of Mr. Ms. to them as far as may be requisite and proper. Mr. Livingston was not here when your letter to him came to hand: but he is now returned. I will take occasion to check with him before the next post, and will give you the result as well as of the commitment of your letter, if any thing shall have come of it. In the mean time accept of my unfeigned regards.

J. MADISON JR

RC (DLC: George B. McClellan Papers); endorsed by Madison.

TJ's letter OF THE 30TH. ULT: was actually dated 31 Jan. 1783. For his letter TO

THE SECY. OF F. A., see TJ to Robert R. Livingston, 7 Feb. 1783.

[1] Word interlined in place of "steps."

Memorandum from James Madison

[ca. 6 Mch. 1783]

Plan proposed consists of 1st. permanent revenue. 2. abatements in favor of the States distressed by the war. 3. common mass of all reasonable expences incurred by the States without sanction of Congress. 4. territorial cessions.

Manner in which the interests of the several States will be affected by these objects:

N. Hamshire will approve the establishment of permanent revenue, as tending to support the confederacy, to remove cause of future contention, and to guard her trade from taxation by the States through which it is carried on:[1] the loans of her Citizens being under her proportion, she has not that motive. Having never been much invaded will be against abatements—for the same reason against common mass—covets a share of vacant territory.

Massts. is deeply interested in the provision for the public debts by the loans of her citizens—against abatements. The Penobscot expedition alone interests her in a common mass. The other objects do not particularly affect her.

R.I. being a weak State is interested in a permanent revenue as tending to support the confederacy and prevent future contentions; but against it as tending to deprive her of the occasion of taxing commerce of neighbouring states. Her proportion of loans does not interest her in it. Not opposed to abatements, nor against a common mass, having been long the seat of war. Anxious for territorial Cessions.

Connecticut interested in general revenue as tending to shelter her trade from taxation by N.Y. and R.I. and in Some degree as providing for loan office debts, her loans being above her proportion. Strenuous against abatements—in favor of common, having often employed militia without sanction of Congss. Since the condemnation of her title to West: claims interested in the cessions of other States.

N.Y. strongly attached to permanent revenue as tending to support the Confederacy &c—altho her Citizens are not lenders beyond her proportion yet individuals of great weight are deeply interested in the funds. Deeply and peculiarly interested in abatements—favorable to a common mass. Since the acceptance of her cession of territory interested in those of other States.

N.J. interested as a small State in the tendency of permanent revenue to Support the Confederacy &c.—and to save her commerce from taxation by Pa. and N.Y. The loans of her Citizens are not materially disproportionate altho much the seat of war not interested in abatements and[2] her expenditures have been previously Sanctioned, solicitous for territorial cessions.

Pena. deeply interested by the loans of her Citizens in a permanent revenue—as far as revenue from trade tends to restrain her from taxing that of N.J. her interest opposed to it. Not interested in abatements nor common mass, but has espoused both—urgent for vacant territory.

Delaware interested by her weakness in permanent revenue as tending to support the confederacy and—not materially by the credits of her Citizens—opposed to abatements and common mass. To the vacant territory firmly attached.

Maryland having never been the seat of war and her citizens being creditors below her proportion is no otherwise interested in permanent revenue than in the support of Confederacy &c. Against abatements—and common mass. The vacant territory is her ruling object.

Virga. in common with the S. States interested by her opulent and defenceless commerce in a permanent revenue as tending to secure the protection of the Confederacy against the maritime superiority of E. States. As it tends to discharge the loan-office debts and to restrain her from taxing the trade of N.C. justice and a liberal policy only recommend to her a permanent revenue. It is uncertain how the credit of her Citizens may stand in a liquidation of their claims on U.S.[3] Interested somewhat perhaps in abatements—particularly so in common mass—not only her excentric expenditures being enormous—but many of them which have been similar to those allowed to other States, having received no sanction of Congs. Her Cession will be considered as a sacrifice.

N. Carolina interested in permanent and general revenue as tending to prolong the protection of Confederacy against maritime superiority of E. States; and to guard her trade from taxation of Virga. and South Carolina—the loans of her Citizens are inconsiderable, but their claims for supplies must be great—in abatements and in common mass essentially interested. In the article of territory would make a Sacrifice.

S. Carolina being a weak and exposed State is interested in permanent revenue as tending to secure the protection of Confedcy. against enemies of every kind—also as to providing for debts, her Citizens having been lenders above her proportion and having besides immense unliquidated demands on U.S. As tending to restrain her taxation of trade of N.C. a Continentl. revenue not favorable to her supposed interest—in abatements and common mass she is supposed to be deeply interested, but in fact opposed to both—her sacrifice of territory would be inconsiderable.

Georgia as a feeble, opulent and frontier State peculiarly interested in whatever tends to support and prolong confederacy; also in permanent revenue by the credits of her Citizens, even those of the loan Office being beyond her proportion—in abatements and in common mass deeply interested—in article of territory would make sacrifice.

To make this plan more effectual for removing all present difficulties and occasions of future disputes, a recommendation is to be included for substituting numbers in place of the value of land as the rule of apportionment. In this all the States are interested, if proper deductions be made from the number of Slaves.

MS (DLC: TJ Papers, 11: 1913-14); entirely in Madison's hand; undated; only the most important emendations are noted below.

Madison's memorandum consists of a significantly revised version of a long footnote that he had appended to his notes of debates in the Confederation Congress for 26 Feb. 1783, which among other things concerned issues relating to a revenue plan he was preparing as a member of a committee that had been appointed five days earlier for that purpose (Madison, *Papers*, VI, 290-2, 293-4n; same, 309-11, for an analysis of the major variations between the footnote and the memorandum; and the discussion of the revenue plan in Morris, *Papers*, VII, 517-

19n). The committee presented Madison's plan to Congress on 6 Mch. 1783, and it was probably on or about this date that he submitted the memorandum to TJ, who had returned to Philadelphia from Baltimore on 26 Feb. after Congress suspended his ultimately abortive appointment as one of the commissioners to negotiate peace with Great Britain (Madison, *Papers*, VI, 309-16).

[1] Remainder of sentence interlined in place of "however," replacing the part of the interlineation through "proportion" that Madison initially wrote as the last sentence of the paragraph.
[2] Preceding five words interlined.
[3] Sentence interlined.

Deed for the Purchase of Lego

This indenture made on the Fourteenth[1] day of August[2] in the year of our lord one thousand seven hundred and Eighty Three,[3] between James Hickman and Hanah his wife of the county of Culpepper and

Thomas Garth and Judith his wife of the county of Albemarle of the one
part and Thomas Jefferson of the same county of Albemarle on the
other part witnesseth that Whereas Edwin Hickman father of the said
James was in his lifetime seised and possessed in his demesne as of fee
of and in one certain tract of land on the Rivanna river in the county of
Albemarle containing by estimation eight hundred and nineteen acres
and one quarter of an acre lying between and contiguous to two tracts
of land of the property of the said Thomas Jefferson, and being so seised
and possessed departed this life having first made his last will and testament in writing and thereby devised the said parcel of lands to his two
sons William and Thomas and their heirs equally to be divided between
them; and after the death of the said Edwin partition was made between
the said William and Thomas Hickman by certain metes and bounds,
and on such partition that moiety of the said parcel of lands which lies
to the South west upon the said Rivanna river was allotted to the said
William and his heirs to be held in severalty, and that moiety of the same
which lies to the North East under and upon the mountains was allotted
to the said Thomas Hickman and his heirs to be held also in severalty,
and after such partition made the said William Hickman and Anne his
wife by their deed indented and duly recorded in the county court of
Albemarle for the considerations therein expressed conveied their said
moiety of the said lands to the said Thomas Garth in fee-simple, and the
said Thomas Hickman died intestate whereby his said moiety descended to the said James his eldest brother of the whole blood and heir at law
and by the said James was conveied to the said Thomas Garth in fee-
simple by the deed of the said James in writing indented and recorded
in the same county court of Albemarle, but the said Hanah, wife of the
said James having not been a party to the said deed the same is deemed
insufficient to convey or bar her right of dower in the said moiety: And
whereas the said Thomas Garth and Judith his wife for and in consideration of the sum of four hundred and fifty pounds to them in hand paid
have covenanted to convey both the said moieties of land in entiertie
containing by estimation eight hundred and nineteen acres and one
quarter of an acre be the same more or less to the said Thomas Jefferson
in fee-simple [and the] said James and Hanah his wife in consideration
of the sum of five shillings to them in hand paid have covenanted to
convey and confirm to the said Thomas Jefferson in fee-simple all their
right and title in and to their said moiety of the said lands: Now this
Indenture WITNESSETH that the said James and Hanah his wife do by
these presents give grant bargain sell and confirm unto the said Thomas
Jefferson their said moiety of the said lands with all their appurtenances
and all their right and title thereto; And the said Thomas Garth and
Judith his wife do give grant bargain sell and confirm unto the said

Thomas Jefferson both the said moieties of land in entiertie with all their appurtenances: to have and to hold the two said moieties of land in entiertie to the said Thomas Jefferson and his heirs. And the said James and Hanah his wife for themselves their heirs executors and administrators do covenant and agree with the said Thomas Jefferson and his heirs that they the said James and Hanah his wife their heirs executors and administrators, their moiety of the said lands aforesaid to the said Thomas Jefferson and his heirs will for ever warrant and defend. And the said Thomas Garth and Judith his wife for themselves their heirs executors and administrators do covenant and agree with the said Thomas Jefferson and his heirs that they the said Thomas Garth and Judith his wife their heirs executors and administrators the two said moieties of land to be held in entiertie to the said Thomas Jefferson and his heirs will for ever warrant and defend. In witness whereof the said James and Hanah his wife and Thomas Garth and Judith his wife have hereto set their hands and seals severally on the day and year abovewritten

| Signed sealed and delivered by James Hickman & Thomas Garth in presence of HUMPHRY GAINES ANN GARTH RICHARD GAINES | Signed sealed and delivered by Hanah Hickman in presence of | Signed sealed and delivered by Judith Garth in presence of HUMPHRY GAINES ANN GARTH RICHARD GAINES | THOS. GARTH seal JUDITH GARTH Seal |

MS (Facsimile in Sotheby's, Catalogue No. 6761, 13 Dec. 1995, Lot 184); in TJ's hand, except for date completed by an unidentified hand (see notes 1-3 below) and signatures; with remnants of seals; torn at fold, resulting in loss of two words supplied from Tr. Tr (Albemarle County Deed Book, Albemarle County Circuit Court Clerk's Office, Charlottesville); at head of text: "Garths to Jefferson"; note at foot of text: "At a Court held for Albemarle County the fourteenth day of August MDCCLXXXIII This Indenture was Acknowledged by Thomas Garth a party thereto and Ordered to be be Recorded, Judith his wife personly appeared in Court and after being privately Examined as the Law directs Voluntarially Relinquished her Right of Dower in the Lands Conveyed by the Said Indenture Teste H Martin Dy Clk."

With this document TJ effectively completed his 1774 or 1775 acquisition of a tract adjoining his Shadwell plantation that he called Lego (notes to MB, 14 Jan. 1775, cash accounts, and 2 Aug. 1778; Malone, *Jefferson*, I, 440 and n).

[1] Word written by an unidentified hand in space left blank by TJ.
[2] Word written by an unidentified hand in space left blank by TJ.
[3] Preceding two words written by an unidentified hand in space left blank by TJ.

Notes on Resolutions of Congress

[after 4 Nov. 1783]

17[83 Jan]. 29. Chairman of Com. of whole by balot
   [Feb]. 5. Com. of whole to vote by states.
        10. Comr. for Virga. to receive proofs instead of vouchers lost
        14. Motion to postpone a proposition to take up another cannot be divided
  Mar. 7. Min. 4/6 sterl. = doll.   doll. = £5–5s without regard to variation of exchange
  Apr. 15. Commandr. in chief to make arrangements with Brit. Commr. for receiving posts.
  May. 12. Commr. in chief occupy posts when delivered, to exchange cannon and stores or transport
        15. tickets for Committees prepared at seat and carried to balot box by one delegate
        16. For. min. to charge for couriers and postage of letters.
        26. Commr. in chief to continue remonstr. with Carleton respecting negroes

MS (DLC: TJ Papers, 11: 1906); entirely in TJ's hand; undated; torn.

TJ compiled this list of resolutions of Congress sometime after he took his seat in that body at Princeton on 4 Nov. 1783, but the reason why he did so is not known. For the resolutions, see JCC, XXIV, 98, 109, 123, 131, 176, 242-3, 338, 344, 346, 363-4.

From Eliza House Trist

Dec. 13th 1783

I take particular notis of that part of your letter that relates to my intended reunion with my Husband. I fear if the chain is intirely loosened my confidence must be great if I succeed in fasting it again. It is rather too late in the day for me to attempt at conquest, I am in hopes the links are only a little rusty. If that shou'd be all I will exert my skill to restore them to their lusture.

Patsy is verry hearty. She now and then gives us a call. She seems happy much more so than I expected. When you write give her a charge about her dress which will be a hint to Mrs. H. to be particular with her. De Semitiere complains that his pupil is rather inatentive. You can be particular to these matters when you write but dont let her know you heard any complaints. I fancy the old Lady is prepareing for the other world, for she conceits the Earthquake we had the other night is only a prelude to something dreadfull that will happen.

I have this moment Received a letter from my Worthy friend *Mercer*. Have not time to write by this Post. Tell him if you please that I will not forget him and if it is not too troublesome do when you write to Mr. Madison let him know my situation and my resolution of leaving this place. When he is so good as to honor me with a letter I will write to him and not before. I am obliged to conclude and I dare say you are not sorry. I have intruded on your patienece. That is one of your virtues and I fancy before I have done with you I shall put many more to the test. Mama desires me to say a thousand things for her but they are only Repetions of her distress at parting with the best Men in the world. Your polite offer with respect to My Son, with the rest of your kindnesses are never to be erased, you may depend if he shou'd require any acts of friendship an application shall be made to you. With sincerity and truth I am Your Much Obliged friend   E TRIST

RC (NcU: Southern Historical Collection, Nicholas P. Trist Papers); consists of last three pages and address cover, being the concluding portion of the four-page letter partially printed under the conjectural date of ca. 8 Dec. 1783 in Vol. 6: 375-6; dateline below signature; minimum punctuation supplied; addressed: "Honble.

Thomas Jefferson Esqr in Congress Annapolis"; franked and postmarked; endorsed by TJ.

This letter inspired TJ's letter to his daughter PATSY advising her ABOUT HER DRESS (TJ to Martha Jefferson, 22 Dec. 1783). MRS. H.: Mary Johnson Hopkinson.

To William Whipple

SIR   Annapolis Jan. 12. 1784.

Being anxious to procure information on the subject of the black moose or Caribou which cannot be procured in any of the United states but New Hampshire I take the liberty of addressing myself to you on the foundation of the acquaintance I have had the pleasure of contracting with you, and my beleif that you will be so obliging as to lend me your assistance. Mr. Forster, your delegate here, gives me hopes it will be particularly in your power to do it through the medium of a brother of yours who he says is about to settle in that part of the country where these animals are to be found. A complete skeleton of one is what I would wish to procure: or if this cannot be got, then the horns, hoof, and such bones as would enable me to decide on it's size. I suppose that if a box were made large enough to take in the horns, that the other bones would pack under and between the antlers. A little soft hay would be necessary to prevent their rubbing. If sent to Philadelphia to the care of Mr. Samuel House I should get them safely and will chearfully pay your draught for the expence of purchase and transportation. This could be transacted through your delegates here with convenience to them. As this may take some little time will you be so good as to procure me answers which I may rely on to the questions subjoined? I have a very strong suspicion that this animal has been altogether mistaken by the naturalists of Europe. They suppose it the same with their Rein deer which is not above 3. feet high. I have been taught to beleive our black-Moose or Caribou much larger. You will pardon the liberty I take I hope in giving you this trouble, as my acquaintance in your state does not point out any other person on whose friendship I would so willingly throw myself. I am with very great esteem Dr. Sir Your most obedt. humble servt   TH: JEFFERSON

Is not the black Moose and the Caribou one and[1] the same animal?
Is not the grey Moose, the Orignal, the elk, one and the same animal, and quite different from the former?
What is the height of the black Moose at the wethers,[2] it's length from the ears to the root of the tail, and it's circumference where largest?
Has it a solid or a cloven hoof?
Has the doe horns, as well as the buck?
If she has,[3] is it true that she loses them with her first fawn and never more has any?
At what season do they shed their horns, and when recover them?
Are they a swift animal?
Do their feet make a loud rattling as they run?
Is the under part of the hoof covered with hair?
Do they sweat when hard run? or only drip at the tongue like a dog?
What is their food?
How many young do they produce at a time?
Have they ever been tamed and used for any purpose?[4]
How far Southward are they known?
Are the horns of the Elk palmated, that is to say flattening off to an edge, or are they round and pointed?
Has the elk always, or ever, a white spot a foot in diameter round the root of the tail?

RC (MH); addressed: "[Gener]al Whipple New-Hampshire"; endorsed by Whipple as answered 15 and 29 Mch. 1784, though no letter of the latter date has been found or is recorded in SJL. Not recorded in SJL.

[1] Preceding two words interlined.
[2] Preceding three words interlined.
[3] Preceding three words added in margin.
[4] Sentence interlined.

To Thomas Hutchins

SIR   Annapolis Jan. 24. 1784.

I have been recurring to your pamphlet (which I borrowed for that purpose) for the times at which the inundations begin and end in the Missouri, Missisipi, Illinois, Ohio, Wabache, but I do not find it mentioned there. Will you be so kind as to give me as accurate an account of these times as you can? Does the Tanissee overflow periodically? I suppose not.   Will you give me leave to correct an error in your pamphlet page 13. where you say that the country extending from Fort Pitt to the Missisipi and on both sides watered by the Ohio and it's branches contains at least a million of square miles. I think the Ohio in all it's parts and branches cannot water more than the fourth of that. Count the degrees in your map into which it pushes it's branches. You will find them not quite 80, but suppose them made 80 by the branch of the Tanissee which heads in S. Carola. A degree in the middle of this space would contain about 3000, or 3100 square miles and of course 80 would contain about 250,000. I think the whole United states reduced to a square would not be more than one of 900 miles each way and of course that the whole U.S. do not contain a million of square miles. Excuse my freedom. I think this an error in your pamphlet and would wish to know from you whether I see it wrong. I am with much esteem Sir Your most obedt. servt   TH: JEFFERSON

RC (IU: Illinois Historical Survey, George Morgan Papers); addressed: "capt. Thomas Hutchings Philadelphia"; franked; endorsed as received 9 Feb. 1784; at foot of text, probably by Hutchins: "900

$$\frac{900}{180,000.}"$$

YOUR PAMPHLET: Thomas Hutchins, *A Topographical Description of Virginia, Pennsylvania, Maryland, and North Carolina . . .* (London, 1778). See Sowerby, No. 525. For an analysis suggesting that TJ's concern about the ERROR in this work arose from his interest in promoting the settlement of the Northwest Territory and linking it economically with Virginia, see John Hoffmann, "Queries Regarding the Western Rivers: An Unpublished Letter from Thomas Jefferson to the Geographer of the United States," *Journal of the Illinois State Historical Society*, LXXV (1982), 15-28.

Vol. 17: 123n errs in suggesting that TJ in this letter was discussing a 1784 pamphlet by Hutchins.

From the Massachusetts Delegates in Congress

Sunday, 29 Feb. [1784]. They present their compliments to TJ and invite him to dinner on Tuesday next at 4 P.M.

RC (ViU: Mary Kirk Moyer deposit); 1 p.; in the hand of George Partridge; partially dated; addressed: "Honle Mr Jefferson"; with notations added later by TJ to record various household expenses and accounts with James Monroe while they were Virginia delegates to Congress in Annapolis, the recto bearing the endorsement "Houshold expenses" and listing undated entries for TJ and Monroe beneath a line reading "our last settlement was Dec. 31," the verso bearing undated entries for expenses TJ and Monroe each incurred alone and an undated summation of their account current to 2 Mch. 1784 (see MB, 1-2 Mch. 1784). TJ also recorded the household expenses he incurred in Annapolis, either alone or when he shared a house there with Monroe, in the following documents: (1) Account headed "Houshold expences," containing entries for "Permanent Articles," 24 Feb.-29 Apr. 1784, and "Articles of consumption," 25 Feb.-29 Apr. 1784, as well as entries pertaining to both purchased "For myself," with the former dated 24 Feb.-14 Mch. 1784 and the latter dated 2-10 May 1784. (2) Account of household expenses shared with Monroe, consisting of a narrow and fragmentary sheet bearing draft entries for [8]-13 Mch. 1784, and draft entries for 14-21 Mch. 1784 contained in No. 3 below. (3) Account with Monroe for household expenses, with entries for 14 Mch.-1 May 1784 on recto and 25 Apr.-10 May 1784 on verso (MSS in ViU: Mary Kirk Moyer deposit; entirely in TJ's hand; undated).

To Benjamin Harrison

SIR   Annapolis Apr. 16. 1784.

I wrote you by the last post that some objections had been started in debate on the justice of that part of the national debt which consists in loan office certificates. The doubt was new to me. I had always considered this to be as honest a debt as any we owed: perhaps a more tender one in most cases, as being due to daughters, to younger children, to widows &c. It proved in event to be the doubt of only two or three individuals in Congress. Every state, and every other individual establishing the demand when put to the vote.—We have obtained a reduction of the general requisitions from about four millions and a half of dollars to about two and a half. The quota of Virginia stood at about 860,000; and now stands at about five hundred and sixty or seventy thousand dollars. (I mention round numbers, not having the exact sums in my possession at present.) I can assure you this was getting as low as could be proposed without professing a bankruptcy. I hope therefore our state, heavy as this demand is, will seriously encounter it. The report sent you will have informed you she is much in arrears. The idea of adjournment is at present for about the middle or end of May. We have no foreign intelligence. I have the honour to be with very great esteem Your Excellency's Most obedt. humble servt.   TH: JEFFERSON

RC (CSt); addressed: "His Excellency Governor Harrison Richmond"; franked; endorsed.

BY THE LAST POST: presumably TJ to Harrison, 9 Apr. 1784. For the debate in Congress over LOAN OFFICE CERTIFICATES, see note to Report on Arrears of Interest on the National Debt, [5 Apr. 1784]. On 27 Apr. 1784 Congress formally approved a QUOTA of 538,693.47 dollars as Virginia's share of a requisition on the states to help pay interest arrearages on the national debt (JCC, XXVI, 309). REPORT SENT YOU: see the report cited above.

To William Whipple

Annapolis Apr. 27. 1784.

I am now to acknolege the receipt of your favor of the 15th Ult.
inclosing some hair of the Moose and the answers to my queries. There
is a confusion among the writers of natural history as to the Caribou, the
Renne, the black Moose, the grey Moose, and the Elk. It is the prevailing opinion they are but two animals. Should any further intelligence
come to you on the subject at any time I shall be obliged to you for a
communication of it wheresoever I may be. The horns and bones you
are so kind as to endeavor to procure for me would be most conveniently
received at Richmond the seat of government in Virginia. Otherwise
Philadelphia will be the most convenient.

Congress have divided the territory ceded or to be ceded to the Westward into states to comprehend from North to South two degrees of
latitude each, beginning to count from 45°. Eastwardly and West-
wardly they are divided by meridians one of which passes thro' the
mouth of the great Kanhaway, the other thro the rapids of Ohio. They
have determined to adjourn on the 3d. of June to meet in November at
Trenton. I have the honor to be with great esteem Sir Your most obedt.
humble servt   TH: JEFFERSON

RC (NhPoS: Thayer Cummings Library and Archives, John Langdon Papers); addressed: "Genl. William Whipple Portsmouth in N. Hampshire"; franked, stamped, and
postmarked.

From James Madison

Richmond, 8 May 1784. "Near a whole week has already passed without the
meeting of a house. 79 are requisite for business, of which about 60 have arrived. . . . Not a single idea can as yet be formed of the politics which will
predominate."

MS not found; extracts reprinted from Stan. V. Henkels, Catalogue No. 712, 14 Dec.
1893, Lot 199. See record entry in Vol. 7: 235.

To ——— Cabot

DEAR SIR   Ship Ceres off Scilly July 24. 1784.

I deliver to Mr. Tracy to be returned to you the copy of Don Quixot
which you were so obliging as to lend me: for which I return you many
thanks. The winds have been so propitious as to let me get through one

volume only: yet this has so far done away the difficulties of the language as that I shall be able to pursue it on shore with pleasure. I have found it a very advantageous disposal of time which could have been applied to no other use, and would have hung heavily on my hands.

It would give me great pleasure to have opportunities suggested to me of rendering you any service personally in my power, and at all times to hear from you either on private or public subjects, being with real esteem Dr Sir Your most obedt. & most humble servt

TH: JEFFERSON

RC (Facsimile in Goodspeed's Bookshop, Catalogue No. 510, 1963, Lot 126); unaddressed, but recorded in SJL as a letter to "Cabot."

The recipient of this letter was probably the prominent merchant George Cabot (1752-1823) of Beverly in Essex County, Massachusetts, the future Federalist senator and stalwart of the so-called "Essex Junto," or perhaps one of his older brothers, John and Andrew Cabot, who supervised his early career as a sea captain in the Spanish trade in the family shipping businesses before he retired from active seafaring about 1777 to take an important role in directing the clan's wartime privateering enterprises (DAB; John L. Sibley and Clifford K. Shipton, *Sibley's Harvard Graduates: Biographical Sketches of Those Who Attended Harvard College*, 17 vols. [Cambridge and Boston, 1873-1975], XVII, 344-67; Henry Cabot Lodge, *Life and Letters of George Cabot* [Boston, 1877], 26n).

For TJ's use of Cabot's COPY OF DON QUIXOT to learn Spanish, see Vol. 7: 383.

Notes on France and Great Britain

[1784-1789]

Comparative view of France and the British islands in Europe.

	France.	British islands.
Extent.	150,000 square miles	104,000 square miles.
Souls	17,000,000.	
	$5\frac{3}{4}$ acres to each person	$6\frac{3}{4}$ acres to each person.
Ecclesiastics	500,000.	
	Paris 600,000.	London. 1,000,000.
Rental	52,800,000	32,000,000.
Plate, jewels &c.	52,500,000	20,000,000
Current coin	52,500,000	20,000,000.
Paper currency	none	380,000,000.
Standing army	10,717 guards	
	133,780 French & foreign infantry.	
	28,979 do. cavalry.	
	173,476	
	9,230 Invalids for garrison duty	
Militia	62,600	
	245,306.	
Navy.		
Revenue	12,546,666£	10,213,000£
Interest of debt	2,022,222£	4,860,000
Debt		6,600,000£ in 1689: at the revolution.
		20,000,000. 1697. peace of Ryswick.
		6,748,780. 1701. Q. Anne's accession.
		50,000,000. 1714. Q. Anne's death.
		50,000,000. 1727. death of G. I.
		46,661,767. 1739. beginning of Spanish war.
		78,293,313 1748. peace of Aix la Chapelle.
		72,000,000. 1755. beginning of French war.
		140,000,000. 1763. Treaty of Paris

MS (DLC: TJ Papers, 234: 41844); entirely in TJ's hand; undated; endorsed by TJ: "France & Engld. compared."

Since precise figures on the public finances of the French monarchy did not become available until the publication of

Jacques Necker's *Compte rendu au Roi* in 1781, TJ presumably compiled this comparative view of France and Great Britain sometime during his years in France (J. F. Bosher, *French Finances 1770-1795: From Business to Bureaucracy* [Cambridge, 1970], 126).

To David Hartley

[29 Jan. 1785]

Mr. Jefferson's compliments to Mr. Hartley and sends him a copy of the act of assembly of Massachusets giving Congress the powers asked by their resolutions of Apr. 30. 1784. which act is complete. The printed leaf from the journals of the Virginia assembly contains only the beginning of the resolutions. It was inclosed him by a friend just before he left America, with information that the legislature had passed the resolutions but that the last sheet actually printed happened to contain only part of the first. In the resolutions which precede this in the same page, Mr. Hartley will see proofs of the disposition which Mr. Jefferson mentioned to him as growing in America, that is, to strengthen the hands of Congress, and to arm them with coercions sufficient to force all the states to a union of effort.

RC (ViU); undated, but apparently the letter to Hartley on the "State of American affairs" recorded in SJL under 29 Jan. 1785; note at foot of text by Hartley: "Virginia resolutions 19 May 1784"; endorsed by Hartley.

In RESOLUTIONS OF APR. 30. 1784 aimed at retaliation against British commercial restrictions, the Confederation Congress asked the states to vest it for fifteen years with the power to forbid trade with ships owned or navigated by subjects of countries lacking a commercial treaty with the United States and to prohibit foreigners, unless authorized by treaty, to import products not grown or made in the dominions of the sovereign to whom they were subject (JCC, XXVI, 321-2). The 1 July 1784 act of the Massachusetts General Court granting these powers to Congress is in *Acts and Laws of the Commonwealth of Massachusetts* [1780-1805], 13 vols. (Boston, 1890-98), 1784-85, p. 41. For the ultimate failure of the plan, see DHRC, I, 66-7. The enclosed PRINTED LEAF was probably the page from the journal of the Virginia House of Delegates containing the first part of its 19 May 1784 resolution on this subject, which was enacted into law on 8 June 1784, as well as associated resolutions of the same date concerning compliance with the revenue plan Congress had submitted to the states on 18 Apr. 1783. One of the resolutions sanctioned the ratification of an amendment to the Articles of Confederation making population instead of land the basis for apportioning common expenses of the Union (JHD, May-June 1784, p. 14; Hening, XI, 388-9, 401-2; JCC, XXIV, 257-61; Morris, *Papers*, VII, 523-4).

Memorandum from Thomas Ruston

[April 1785?]

Question by Mr. Jefferson.

If the people of America double their numbers in twenty five years, Query,

How long will it take for the increase of the Duty upon Impost to extinguish the National Debt?

In order to be able to answer this question fully three things are requisite.

1st: It is necessary to know the present state of population.

2ly: It is necessary to know the amount of the impost—and

3ly It is also necessary to know the amount of the interest to be paid on the national debt.

Suppose for instance that the number of the people is three millions.

That the amount of the impost is 6,000,000 Dol. and, that the interest to be paid on the National Debt is 6,000,000.

In this case it is to be supposed that each individual pays at the rate of two dollars a head per Annum, and

That the amount of the impost is just sufficient to discharge the interest of the National Debt. But,

According to the probable increase of population, if they double their numbers every 25 years, the next year the numbers will be 3,120,000 which at two dollars a head will make 6,240,000 Dollars. This will occasion a surplus of 240,000 Dollars to be applied to the extinction of the National Debt.

240,000 Dollars applied to the extinction of the principal of the National Debt, will at four per Cent (for the United States actually pay no more than about that sum on the aggregate of their Funds) I say an extinction of 240,000 Dollars at 4 per Ct. will also make a diminution of Interest to be paid of 9,600 Dollars.

A Similar increase of population the second year may be supposed to make a proportional increase of surplus in the produce of the impost. Thus, If there is a surplus of 240,000 Dollars the first year, there may be supposed to be a surplus of 480,000 more 9600 Dollars of the interest less to be paid.

In this way of computing therefore there will be at the end of the second year a surplus of 489,600 Dollars to be applied to the extinction of the capital, which will also occasion a diminution of the interest of 19,200 Dollars less to be paid.

This calculation is made upon the supposition that 3,000,000 of people increase at the rate of 120,000 a year which is one 25th. part, but they will not increase quite so fast the first year, for if they do they will increase faster the second year. Thus, If 3,000,000 produce 120,000 the first year, 3,120,000 may be supposed to produce 124,800 the second year. It will therefore be necessary to set the first years increase of population some what lower than one 25th., or 120,000.

So much for the method of making this calculation till the actual state of population, of revenue and of interest to be paid is more accurately known.

MS (ViW); entirely in Ruston's hand; undated; endorsed by TJ: "Ruston Dr."

Dr. Thomas Ruston (ca. 1740-1804), a Pennsylvania native who received his A.B. from the College of New Jersey in 1762 and his M.D. from the University of Edinburgh in 1765, practiced medicine in London until 1771 or 1772, when marriage to a wealthy heiress led him to pursue a business career in various parts of England before resuming his medical practice in Exeter around the end of 1777. A strong supporter of the American cause despite his residence in England during the Revolutionary War, Ruston wrote essays on American banking and finance which Benjamin Franklin so admired that he had them translated into French. In the spring of 1785 Ruston went to Paris to confer with Franklin and TJ about his return to America, and it was there that he probably wrote the memorandum printed here (see below). Later in the year he moved with his family to Philadelphia, where he gained entry to the city's elite by virtue of his wealth and became a director of the Bank of Pennsylvania, a member of the American Philosophical Society, a public advocate of a balanced national economy, and a partner with Tench Coxe and Robert Morris among others in various speculative ventures that ultimately resulted in his imprisonment for debt and fraud in 1796 and left his fortune in tatters (James McLachlan, *Princetonians 1748-1768: A Biographical Dictionary* [Princeton, 1976], 402-7; Cooke, *Coxe*, 324-30).

Although there is no record in SJL that Ruston ever corresponded with TJ, internal evidence suggests that he wrote this memorandum in response to a request the Virginian made at some point during the doctor's visit to Paris in April 1785, when they met five times and discussed American commercial policy in Europe, the only occasions on which their paths are known to have crossed there (Ruston's Diary, 5-6, 19, 26, 28 Apr. 1785, DLC: Ruston Papers). The memorandum also indicates that Ruston was generally unfamiliar with the American scene, and that he was writing before the establishment of the new federal government under the United States Constitution and the publication of census figures in October 1791, for his reference to the IMPOST almost certainly alludes to the duties which Congress on 18 Apr. 1783 requested authority from the states to levy for twenty-five years in order to help fund the public debt, a requisition that was finally defeated only in 1786 (Morris, *Papers*, VII, 523-5n).

To John Quincy Adams

May 12. 1785.

Mr. Jefferson's compliments to Mr. Adams and begs his care of the inclosed letters. Those directed to Messrs. Monroe and Hardy will make him acquainted with two very worthy gentlemen of the Virginia delegation. Should Colo. Monroe not be at New York Mr. Jefferson begs the favor of Mr. Adams to deliver his letter either to Mr. Hardy or Mr.

Charles Thomson with a request to keep it till they meet with some confidential person who will deliver it into Colo. Monroe's own hand. The letters for Virginia and Pennsylvania may be put into the post office.

The gentlemen on the whale oil business not being yet come Mr. J. sends his own letters that they may run no risk of arriving too late at Auteuil. He wishes Mr. Adams a pleasant and prosperous voiage over the Atlantic and a happy sight of his friends and native country.

The gentlemen having brought the echantillons since closing this, the bearer brings them.

RC (MHi: Adams Papers); addressed: "A Monsr. Monsr. Adams le fils"; with postscript on address cover; endorsed by Adams. Not recorded in SJL.

The INCLOSED LETTERS are identified in Vol. 8: 141-52. WHALE OIL BUSINESS: see TJ to Elbridge Gerry, 11 May 1785, and note.

To Giovanni Fabbroni

Sir   Paris May 23. 1785. Cul-de-sac Tetebout.

Mr. Mazzei having done me the favor of establishing a certain degree of acquaintance between us, I took the liberty during the late war of addressing you twice or thrice by letter. I received two letters from you during the same period. Among the agreeable circumstances which my appointment to come to Europe presented to me, one was the pleasure of being placed nearer to you, which gave a hope of hearing oftener from you. I am now fixed for some time at this court as the successor to Doctr. Franklin who has obtained leave to return into the bosom of his country to finish there a life which has been distinguished by services to mankind.

I take the liberty of presenting you with some notes giving an account of the country which once hoped to count you among it's citizens. They were written at the sollicitation of Monsr. de Marbois secretary of the French legation in America, while our country was wasting under the ravages of a cruel enemy, and whilst the writer was confined to his room by an accidental decrepitude. Less than this added to his want of talents would account for their errors and defects. Sensible of this he does not make them public, having printed a few copies only to present to particular persons. The one presented herewith is meant as a testimonial of the esteem and regard with which he has the honor to be Sir your most obedient humble servt   TH: JEFFERSON

RC (InU: U.S. History Manuscripts); unaddressed, but recipient identified from SJL entry calendared in Vol. 8: 161. Enclo-

sure: *Notes on the State of Virginia* [Paris, 1785]. See Sowerby, No. 4167; and the inscription recorded in Coolie Verner, "Mr.

Jefferson Distributes His *Notes*: A Preliminary Checklist of the First Edition," New
York Public Library, *Bulletin*, LVI (1952),
164.

The only previous surviving LETTER
from TJ to Fabbroni is that of 8 June 1778;
TJ had previously received at least three letters from him.

From John Paul Jones

SIR   Paris June 23d. 1785

After the War, I made application to Congress, for authority to return
to Europe, to settle with and receive from the Court of France, the
Prize-Money due to the Citizens and Subjects of the United-States,
who had served under my Orders on board the Squadron which his
most Christian Majesty was pleased to equip and support under the
Flag of America. Congress passed the enclosed Act for that purpose the
1st. of November 1783, agreeable to which I gave security to the Super-
intendant of Finance to transmit the Prize-Money in question to the
Treasury of the United-States, to be from thence distributed by that
Minister to the persons who are thereunto entitled; as appears by the
Certificate subjoined to the Act of Congress, and signed by the Superin-
tendant of Finance at Philadelphia Novr. 6th. 1783.

I therefore embarked for Europe immediately, and received the enclosed Commission from Dr. Franklin, as Minister Plenipotentiary of
the United-States, authorizing and directing me to transact the Business in question, dated at Passy Decr. 17th. 1783. I delivered a Copy of
those Credentials to the Marechal de Castries with a Letter on the Subject from Dr. Franklin dated at Passy the 18th. of Decr. 1783.

The Liquidation of the Prizes was a lingering and disagreeable Business, and I could not obtain the enclosed State of it signed by the Marechal de Castries 'till the 23d. of Octr. 1784.

I could not obtain a decision of the Marechal de Castries respecting
the Payment of the Prize-Money before his Letter of the 27th. of May
1785, of which I enclose a Copy: That Letter has the face of a clear and
unconditional Order for the Ordonnateur at L'Orient to pay the Prize-
Money into my Hands; But, as the Commis in the Bureau at Versailles
informed me that no explicit Orders had been sent on the subject to
L'Orient, I wrote a Letter to the Marechal de Castries the 5th. of this
Month, praying him to give such Orders as would prevent any misunderstanding from taking place between myself and the Ordonnateur of
L'Orient &c.

I have just received an Answer dated the 17th. of this Month, which
I own surprizes me very much; because the Marechal, by that Letter,
appears to retract his former decision, and asks me, as I conceive the

matter, to induce Mr. Grand to become my Security in a Business which I am transacting with the Court of France by the express command and authority of the United-States of America. As I have already given security to the United-States, I think the proposition of the Marechal de Castries for a Second Security, for what regards only the Subjects of America, is highly unreasonable; and as I cannot consent to commit the Dignity of Congress, I shall not accept the condition proposed by the Marechal de Castries. I therefore enclose a Copy of the Marechal's Letter of the 17th. and conceive it my Duty to ask your interference. I am, with great esteem and respect, Sir, Your most obedient and most humble Servant

FC (MBFM); in Jones's hand, unsigned; at foot of first page: "His Excellency Thomas Jefferson Esquire Minister Plenipotentiary of the United States at the Court of France." Enclosures: (1) Resolution of Confederation Congress, 1 Nov. 1783, authorizing Jones, in conjunction with the United States minister to France, to solicit payment and satisfaction to the officers and crews for all the prizes captured in Europe under his command and to deduct from this prize money the commission customarily allowed in such cases in full compensation for his services and expenses, provided he first gave sufficient bonds with good security for the benefit of all concerned to the Superintendent of Finance, who would distribute the prize money to those entitled to receive it (JCC, xxv, 787-8). (2) Certificate of Robert Morris, Philadelphia, 6 Nov. 1783, stating that Jones had executed sufficient bonds with good security in accordance with No. 1. (3) Commission from Benjamin Franklin, Passy, 17 Dec. 1783, authorizing Jones to carry out the terms of No. 1 (Trs in DLC: TJ Papers, 9: 1542; in TJ's hand, with No. 3 subjoined to No. 2).

(4) Charles Eugène Gabriel de La Croix, Marquis de Castries, to Jones, Versailles, 27 May 1785, stating that the muster rolls for Jones's squadron have now been completed, that he has given orders to satisfy the crews, and that Jones can contact the ordonnateur at L'Orient harbor (Tr in DNA: RG 360, PCC; in French; with marginal note in a clerk's hand: "On lui manque qu'il peut s'adresser à l'ordonnateur de L'Orient pour toucher le produit des Prises fait par son Escadre"; attested by Jones). (5) Same to same, 17 June 1785, stating that although he is ready to order payment to Jones of the prize money due to the subjects of the United States who had served in his squadron, the funds cannot be delivered unless guaranteed by one of the king's subjects, so that Jones must petition Grand, whom he will accept as guarantor (Tr in same; at foot of text: "M. Paul-Jones chez M. Grand Banquier a Paris"; with marginal note in a clerk's hand: "Le produit des Prises faites par son Escadre lui sera remis lorsqu'il fournira un Cautionnement"; attested by Jones). Other enclosure not found.

To John Paul Jones

SIR   June 24. 1785.

I had prepared a letter for you to the Count de Vergennes but I think it rather better before we resort to him that the Marechal de Castries should be again applied to and the resolution of Congress and certificate of Mr. Morris presented to his view. I therefore return you the papers left with me yesterday, and your draught of a letter inclosed this morning which is perfectly proper in all it's parts. Should this endeavor be unsuccesful I shall be ready to make an official application for you. I am with much esteem Sir your most obedt. humble servt

TH: JEFFERSON

RC (Richard C. Aldrich Family, Barrytown, New York, 1967); unaddressed, but obviously a reply to Jones to TJ, 23 June 1785. Not recorded in SJL. Enclosure: presumably Jones to Charles Eugène Gabriel de La Croix, Marquis de Castries, [ca. 24 June 1785], reminding him of his promise in a 13 May 1785 letter to pay the prize money as soon as he received the liquidation from Chandon, which was then expected without delay, and expressing hope that payment would soon be made, this being a matter he had been trying to settle in France since 1783, much to his financial cost and the prejudice of his other concerns (FC in DLC: Jones Papers; in Jones's hand; badly faded). For other enclosures, see note to preceding document.

The draft letter to French foreign minister VERGENNES was never sent and has not been found. TJ subsequently applied on Jones's behalf to the French naval minister (TJ to Castries, 10 July 1785).

To Samuel Hardy, James Madison, and James Monroe

DEAR SIR   Paris July 5. 1785.

The bearer hereof, Mr. Franklin, being about to return to America, I take the liberty of presenting him to your acquaintance. Your esteem for the character of his grandfather would have procured him a favourable reception with you: and it cannot but increase your desire to know him, when you shall be assured that his worth and qualifications give him a personal claim to it. I have taken the liberty of [. . .][1] your friendship myself, and am persuaded you will both be obliged to me for bringing you together, when you shall have had time to become known to each other. I beg you to be assured of the sincerity of my esteem, and of the respect with which I have the honour to be Dr. Sir Your friend & servant   TH: JEFFERSON

RC (NhExP: photocopy); unaddressed, but presumably one of three identical letters recorded in the 4 July 1785 SJL entry calendared in Vol. 8: 259; text obscured at crease (see note 1 below).

In a separate letter to Monroe, TJ encoded a more reserved assessment of William Temple FRANKLIN (TJ to Monroe, 5 July 1785).

[1] Estimated four or five words illegible.

To Jan Ingenhousz

SIR   Paris July 14. 1785.

Doctor Franklin left us two days ago. On his departure he charged me with the inclosed packet to be forwarded to you. His commands will justify the liberty I take of accompanying them with a line, and with assurances of the satisfaction it affords me to do this to a person to whose researches the lovers of science are so much indebted. I have the honour to be with sentiments of the highest respect Sir Your most obedient & most humble servt   TH: JEFFERSON

RC (PPAmP); endorsed by Ingenhousz.

The INCLOSED PACKET, which had been enclosed in Benjamin Frankin to TJ, 11 July 1785, consisted of Franklin to Ingenhousz, 6 July 1785 (NUtM), which in turn enclosed copies of Franklin's published papers on geology, meteorology, and light and heat (Albert H. Smyth, ed., *The Writings of*

Benjamin Franklin, 10 vols. [New York, 1905-07], VIII, 597-602; IX, 215-18, 227-30). TJ indicated in SJL that, in accordance with Franklin's wish, the packet was forwarded to Ingenhousz by the Imperial ambassador to France, Florimund Claude Charles, Comte de Mercy-Argenteau. Ingenhousz acknowledged its receipt in a letter of 28 Dec. 1786.

From Abigail Adams

DEAR SIR   Grosvenor Square London August 12 1785

I would not omit so good an opportunity as presents by Mr. Short, of continuing the correspondence which you have done me the honour to Say you consider as settled.

Your obliging favours of june 21 and july 7th were punctually deliverd, and afforded me much pleasure.

Were you to come to this Country, as I sincerely hope you will, for the sake of your American Friends[1] who would rejoice to see you; as a Husbandman you would be delighted with the rich verdure of the field, and the high cultivation of the Lands. In the Manufactory of many articles, the Country can boast a superiority over their Galician Neighbours. But when you come to consider the Man and the social affections; ease, civility, and politeness of Manners, this people suffer by[2] the comparison. They are more contracted and narrow in their Sentiments notwithstanding their boasted liberality[3] and will not allow their Neighbours half the Merrit they really deserve. They affect to despise the French, and to hate the Americans, of the latter they are very liberal in their proofs. So great is their pride that they cannot endure to view us as independant, and they fear our growing greatness.

The late Arrets of his most Christian Majesty have given the allarm here. They term them Calamitous, and say they will essentially affect

[749]

their trade.[4] If Ireland refuses the propositions with steadiness, and firmness,[5] England may be led to think more[6] justly of America. If a person was to indulge the feelings of a moment, the infamous falshoods, which are daily retailed here against America, would prompt one to curse and quit them, but a statesman would be ill qualified for his station, if he feared the sarcasm of the sarcastic, the envy of the envious, the insults of the insolent or the malice of the dissapointed, or sufferd private resentment to influence his publick Conduct. You will not I dare say envy a situation thus circumstanced, where success is very dubious, and surrounded with so many difficulties.[7] It is rather mortifying too, that Congress appear so inattentive to the situation of their Ministers. Mr. A has not received any letters of any concequence since the arrival of Col. Smith, nor any answers to the lengthy Letters he has written. Mr. Short informs us that you are in the same situation. What can have become of the said Mr. Lamb mentiond by Mr. Jay? Is he gone with all his papers directly to the Barbary powers? I suspect it, but Mr. A will not think so.

I fear Mr. Short will not have a very favourable opinion of England. Unfortunately Col. Smith set off, upon a tour a few days after his arrival, and Mr. Short having but few acquaintance will not find himself highly gratified; we have accompanied him once to the Theater, but after having been accustomed to those of France, one can have little[8] realish for the cold, heavy action, and uncouth appearence of the English stage. This would be considerd as treason of a very black dye, but I speak as an American.[9] I know not how a Siddons may reconcile me to English action, but as yet I have seen nothing that equals parissian ease, and grace. I should like to visit France once a year during my residence in Europe.

The English papers asscribe the late disturbances in the provinces of France, to the example set by the Rebellious Americans, as well as every failure of their own Merchants and Manufactories to the *Ruinous* American trade, tho perhaps two thirds[10] of them never had any intercourse with America. O! for the energy of an absolute government, aya and for the power too. How many Letters de cachet have these abusive Beings deserved?

The cask of wine you mentiond in your Letter, Mr. Adams request you to take if agreeable to you. He has written to Mr. Garvey with respect to that which is under his care. As to the House rent which you mentiond, neither you or Mr. Adams can[11] do yourselves justice unless you charge it,[12] and Mr. A is fully determined to do it. There is an other heavy expence which I think he ought to Charge this year.[13] These are[14] the Court *taxes*. Being considerd as minister in Holland, the servants applied for their perquisites which was allowd them by Mr. Lotter, tho realy without Mr. Adams's knowledge or direction. At Versailles he went through the same ceremony, and when he came to this Court all the servants and attendants from St. James came very methodically with their Books, upon which both the Names of the Ministers and the sums given were specified. [15] Upon the New Years day this is again to be repeated: and the sum this year [16] will amount to not less than [17] a hundred pounds, [18] which will be thought very extravagant I suppose; but how could it be avoided? Our Countrymen have no Idea of the expences of their Ministers, nor of the private [19] applications which they are subject to, many of which cannot be dispenced with. All the prudence and oeconomy I have been able to exercise in the year past, has not enabled me to bring the year about; without falling behind hand. I have no objection to returning to America, but I have many, against living here at a greater expence than what our allowence is: because we have 3 children in America to Educate, whose expences must be, and have been borne by our private income which for 12 years past has been diminishing by Mr. Adams's continued application to publick buisness; these are considerations sir which some times distress me. As I know you are a fellow sufferer you will excuse my mentioning them to you.

You were so kind sir as to tell me you would execute any little commission for me, and I now take the Liberty of [20] requesting you to let petit go to my paris shoemaker and direct him to make me four pair of silk shoes 2 pr. sattin and two pr. fall silk; I send by Mr. Short the money for them. I am not curious about the colour, only that they be fashonable. I cannot get any made here to suit me, at least I have faild in several atempts. [21] Col. Smith proposes visiting paris before he returns, and will be so good as to take Charge of them for me. An other article or two I have to add, a Glass for the middle of the table. I forget the French name for it. I think they [22] are usually in 3 peices. If you will be so good as to procure it for me and have it put into a small Box well packed and addrest to Mr. Adams; Col. Smith will also have the goodness to take care of it for me; and to pay you for it: I do not know the cost, as we had one at Auteuil, which belongd to the House. I have to add four *Godships*, [23] these are so saleable in Paris that I think they are to be had for Six livres a peice, but should they be double that price it cannot be thought much of for deitys. Apollo I hold in the first rank as the Patron of Musick Poetry and the Sciencies. Hercules is the next in my favour on account of his numerous exploits and enterprizing spirit. If he is not to be had, I will take Mercury as he is said to be the inventer of Letters, and God of eloquence. I have no aversion to Cupid, but as I mean to import them through the Hands of a Young Gentleman, one should be cautious of arming persons with powers; for the use of which they cannot be answerable; there cannot however be any objection to his accompanying Madam Minerva and Diana, Ladies whose company and example are much wanted in this city. If you have any command to execute here you will do a favour by honouring with them Your obliged Humble Servant   A. ADAMS

RC (DLC: C. W. F. Dumas Papers). Dft (MHi: Adams Papers); undated; incomplete; with variations and emendations, only the most important being noted below. Recorded in SJL as delivered by William Short on 23 Sep. 1785.

For the LATE ARRETS discouraging importation into France of English merchandise, see note to TJ to John Adams, 10 Aug. 1785. The PROPOSITIONS by which Prime Minister William Pitt attempted to liberalize Anglo-Irish trade regulations in return for a mandatory Irish financial contribution to imperial defense and Irish enactment of certain British commercial legislation were abandoned in the face of fears in Ireland that the scheme threatened that nation's sovereignty (Theodore W. Moody and others, eds., *A New History of Ireland*, 7 vols. [Oxford, 1976-], IV, 277-81). John LAMB was MENTIONED as a possible negotiator with the BARBARY POWERS in John Jay to the American Commissioners, 11 Mch. 1785. He did not reach Paris until 18 Sep. 1785 (Editorial Note on reports on Mediterranean trade and Algerine captives, Vol. 18: 384-90).

[1] Dft: "Friend."
[2] Dft: "fail in."
[3] Sentence to this point in Dft: "They possess in general a much greater narrowness of Sentiment."
[4] Sentence not in Dft.
[5] Dft: "with proper firmness."
[6] Dft here adds "seriously ⟨*of America*⟩— and."
[7] Sentence in Dft reads: "The Situation however is not very enviable and Success very dubious."

[8] Dft: "no."
[9] Dft lacks preceding sentence and instead reads "Indeed most of the Ammusments of this Metropolis are closed for the Season."
[10] Dft: "and every failure of every Merchant and Manufactory in this Country to their connection with America, tho it is more than probable that ⟨*more than*⟩ two thirds."
[11] Dft: "will."
[12] Remainder of sentence not in Dft.
[13] Dft here adds: "I wish you would give me your opinion of it."
[14] Remainder of sentence in Dft: "what is called Etraines."
[15] This and the preceding sentence in Dft read: "As Mr. Adams was minister at the Hague the Court Servants applied for their perquisites which were paid by Mr. Lotter. At Versailles also, Mr. Adams was obliged to do the same, at his Reception here he had also to pay the Servants and attendants who are so methodical as to bring their Books which Shews you the Sum paid and by whom."
[16] Dft: "repeated here so that in the course of ⟨*one*⟩ this year the tax."
[17] Preceding three words not in Dft.
[18] Remainder of sentence not in Dft.
[19] Dft: "numerous."
[20] Dft: "liberty to Send by Mr. Short a Louis."
[21] Dft lacks preceding sentence and instead reads "They are all for me, and the whole four pr. will not cost me more than one pr. here."
[22] Dft lacks preceding ten words and instead reads "These."
[23] Dft ends here, at the foot of a page.

To John Langdon

[11 Sep. 1785]

P.S. Since writing this letter, I receive one from Mr. Carmichael at Madrid informing me that by letters from Cadiz and Algiers he is advised that five American vessels had been captured by the Algerines. Portugal is arming powerfully against them. It seems probable that Spain will buy their peace. I am in hopes we shall be able to stop their depredations on us.

I beg leave to renew my acquaintance with Miss Langdon by sending her a Doll of the present mode, dressed in Muslin, a mode which prevailing here to an almost total exclusion of silk, has literally and truly starved a great number of people. I add to it a box in which she will find a small gentleman who will teach her a short-handed and graceful manner of going down stairs.

RC (NhPoS: John Langdon Papers); consists of entire text of TJ's 11 Sep. 1785 letter to Langdon, with postscript as given above; at foot of first page: "His Excy. J. Langdon"; endorsed by Langdon: "Answered." PrC lacking postscript printed in Vol. 8: 512-13, the bracketed passages there being conjectured correctly.

ONE FROM MR. CARMICHAEL: see William Carmichael to TJ, 2 Sep. 1785.

From Thomas Boylston

S<small>R</small>   Rouen Novr 11 1785

I arrived here Tuesday Evening. I have not as yet informed my self what price, I shall be able to realize for my Oil, but as far as I have enquired, find it will not save me harmless at any rate, except the duties charged on it be remitted. Should the Marquis de Fiat and your assistance, for that purpose prove successfull it will answer. If the terms of receiving the Cash, without being Obliged to invest some part of the amount, in French Goods, prevent its being attainable, rather than not succeed in your endeavours to have the duties remitted, I will compromise, and take one half in Cash the other in Goods, provided the whole duties are remitted. If the Marquis and you are of Opinion that Monsieur Tourlille Saugram's weight and influence, would be of service in Obtaining the remitting of the duties, I think it should be proposed to him in Order to interest him in the success of it, that the Oil cannot be sold on his terms, burdend as they are with duties, but if the duties are remitted I shall be able to treat with him on terms more to his Advantage, than I can at present, and may be an introduction to further contract another Season with him. I'm Sr wth great Regard your H S

T<small>HO</small> B<small>OYLSTON</small>

PS

If the Marquis de Fiat cannot bring the Minister to grant, what we wish and would press to Obtain Viz the whole duties please to try to Obtain part—perhaps he may be prevailed upon to indulge or grant us either

$\frac{3}{4}$ $\frac{2}{3}$ or $\frac{1}{2}$ of said Duties to be remittd. I shall be glad to be favored with a line from you, Adviseing of the progress and prospect of success if any.

The Ship was not two days ago arrived, and will be reported and not enterd on her Arrival, my Letters ordering her to report and not to be enterd has been received. This is a favorable circumstance, which may be represented to the Minister that Goverment looses nothing by granting the indulgence of the duties, as She now can depart and leave the port without paying any duties whatever, which She'll be necessitated to do, if a price or indulgence for the Cargo should not be Obtained.

It may be also mentiond that this sort of Oil does not interfere and clash with the Common Oil, its not put to the same use, therefore will not counteract the ministers design to promote the Common Whale Fishery, which only can be executed from hence, with probable success, not having Men Skilful and capable for the other Spemacety Fishery.

T BOYLSTON

Make my Compliments to the Marquis to whom I feel my self very Obliged.

Dft (MHi: Boylston Family Papers); addressed: "His Excellency Thos Jefferson Esqr Ambassador of the United States of America at Paris." Recorded in SJL as received 13 Nov. 1785.

For TJ's assistance to Boylston, see TJ to Lafayette, with Thomas Boylston's Proposal, [ca. 13 Nov. 1785]. Boylston's proposal was probably written no later than 4 Nov. 1785 (see TJ to John Adams, 19 Nov. 1785, and note).

To Giovanni Fabbroni

SIR   Paris Mar. 2. 1786.

I have for sometime deferred the honor of addressing you, in expectation that our friend Mr. Mazzei on his return from Holland, would go on immediately to Florence. He is now returned, but proposes staying here two months. I must therefore adopt an earlier conveiance to return you my thanks for the pamphlets you were so kind as to inclose to me, and from the perusal of which I received very great satisfaction. That relative to the value of lands, being particularly applicable to our plan of taxation in America, I consider as very precious, and filled with useful ideas. I hope you have before this received the book I took the liberty of sending you thro' Mr. Favi; a medley little worth your notice but of some avail to me as it has furnished me an occasion of testifying the sentiments of esteem and respect with which I have the honour to be Sir Your most obedient & most humble servant   TH: JEFFERSON

RC (Paul Francis Webster, Beverly Hills, California, 1972); at foot of text: "Mr. Fabbroni."

The pamphlet RELATIVE TO THE VALUE OF LANDS was Adamo Fabbroni, *Dissertazione sopra il Quesito Indicare le vere Teorie con le quali devono eseguirsi le stime dei terreni, stabilite le quali abbiano i pratici stimatori delle vere guide, che gli conducono a determinarne il valore* . . . (Florence, 1785).

Fabbroni had probably also enclosed two other pamphlets by his brother on "ancient things" promised in his 5 July 1785 letter to TJ: *Del Bombice e del Bisso degli Antichi Dissertazione di Adamo Fabbroni* . . . (Perugia, 1782); and *Della Farfalla Simbolo Egiziano Dissertazione di Adamo Fabbroni* . . . (Florence, 1783). See Sowerby, Nos. 816, 119, 120. BOOK: see TJ to Fabbroni, 23 May 1785, printed above.

From Thomas Robinson

SIR   No. 6. Charing Cross 25 March 1786

I have inclosd a list of a Tool Chest which 2 ft. 5 Inches long Wide and deep in proportion—With two drawers besides the upper division. I can easily accomadate the Chest to the tools you will please approve of or enlarge the Size if more is wanted. I am Sr. Your obliged Humble servt.   T. ROBINSON

RC (ViU: Margaret and Olivia Taylor deposit); addressed: "Mr. Jefferson No 14 Golden Square." Enclosure not found.

Thomas Robinson was a wholesale ironmonger in London who subsequently moved to 11 Spring Gardens (Roger Wakefield, *Wakefield's Merchant and Tradesman's General Directory for London* . . . *For*

the Year 1790 [London, 1790], 283). TJ had the purchase of a TOOL CHEST "containing small tools for wooden and iron work" in mind before leaving Paris for London (TJ to Rayneval, 3 Mch. 1786). In April 1786 he paid Robinson a total of £12.1 for the chest and its contents (MB, 4, 11 Apr. 1786).

From Martha Jefferson Carr

DEAR BROTHER   Eppington May 22. 1786.

Mr. Eppes has this morning received yours of Dec. the 11. and poor Dear Polly has been in tears, tho after much ado she is so far pacified as to wipe her eyes and set down to write to you. We have endeavoured to amuse her by every little account of what children look upon to be Luxurys, and tell her they are to be found in France, but to all She turns a deef Ear. Her avertion to going is such that I am sure no arguments will prevaile on her to give her consent, and her Apprehentions of being decoyed and carryed there will prevent I think any Scheem of that kind taking place. I did not think a child of her age capable of so warm an Affection as I find she is, by her attatchment to Mrs. Eppes, I have been with her now near a fort-night and can not Ingreatiate myself so far as to prevaile on her to accompany me on a visit to her Aunt Bolling, her constant answer is that she can not leave her Aunt Eppes. Upon the whole it is my Opinion she can not be carryed without compultion and with a child of her sensibility and timidity what may be the Consequence of such a method we must leave to your own judgment. Mrs. Eppes is Extreemly Anxous for her Improvement and pays the greatest attention to her, She is a Sweet Girl, reads and Sews prettily and dances gracefully. That good ladie is so much unhinged by the recept of yours today that she is not in a situation to write by this Oppertunity, tho Says she has once written to you very fully on the Subject and concludes that her letter has not reached you or that the Multiplicity of business you are engaged in has prevented your acknowledgeing the recept of it. I inclosed to Mr. Madison A letter to you and one to Patsy dated May 1. in which I Answered all the kind inquires contained in yours of August 22 with regard to my family. Nancy is with me and desires her love to you and Patsy as dos all the little ones of this family. Give mine to Patsy and tell her she must Excuse my not writeing to her now as I have so lately written her a long letter. I must repeat my question when Shall we see you in Virginia. Aduei my Dear Brother may happyness ever attend you, and beleive me to be with Sincere Affection Yours

M Carr

RC (Laurence L. Prince, Hilton Head Island, South Carolina, 1975). Recorded in SJL as received at Aix-en-Provence 3 May 1787.

Elizabeth Wayles Eppes probably wrote

VERY FULLY ON THE SUBJECT of Mary Jefferson's reluctance to come to France in her missing letter of 13 Sep. 1785. TJ's missing letter OF AUGUST 22 was evidently dated 20 Aug. 1785, and Mrs. Carr responded on 5 May 1786 (Vol. 15: 626-7).

To Mary Barclay

DEAR MADAM   Paris Nov. 3. 1786.

Mr. Aop applied to me on the subject of a dividend of prize money assigned to Mr. Barclay, which, as I informed him, can only be paid in America. It has since occurred to me that Mr. Barclay might perhaps have relied on this in part for your particular use during his absence. If so, and any inconvenience should arise from the disappointment, I beg you to be so friendly as to communicate it to me, as I shall take a real pleasure in accomodating you with such sums as you may have need of. In doing this I pray you to have no scruples. I shall be happy to hear how yourself and your daughter do. Indeed, on the presumption that your health is reestablished I will flatter myself with your coming to dine with us on Sunday the 5th. inst. You will meet Mrs. Barret and

Mrs. Montgomery here. The exercise will be good for your health and the company for your spirits. I am with much esteem Dr. Madam your most obedient & most humble servant TH: JEFFERSON

RC (ViHi); in TJ's left hand. Not recorded in SJL.

From J. F. Marmontel

ce 28 9bre 1786.

Mr. Marmontel va faire passer a Mde. La Marquise de la fayette L'exemplaire de La lettre que Monsieur de Jefferson veut bien Lui confier.

Mde. Marmontel Se fait une fête d'aller Voir Monsieur de Jefferson en route, puis qu'elle ne peut esperer d'avoir L'honneur de le voir à Monticello, ce qui lui feroit encore plus de plaisir. Le bon ami Mazzei prendra jour avec elle; et Mr. Marmontel Sera certainement d'une partie si agreable. Le Mari et la femme Se reunissent pour offrir leur hommage a Monsieur De jefferson.

RC (Robert R. Crout, Charlottesville, Virginia, 1985); addressed: "A Monsieur Monsieur de jefferson Ministre Plenipotentiaire des Etats unis de L'amerique en son hotel a Paris."

Jean François Marmontel (1723-99), a French poet, dramatist, novelist, literary critic, and contributor to the *Encyclopédie*, whose work TJ much admired, was a vigorous champion of the Enlightenment currently serving as permanent secretary of the French Academy (J. C. F. Hoefer, ed., *Nouvelle Biographie Générale depuis les Temps les Plus Reculés jusqu'a Nos Jours*, 46 vols. [Paris, 1855-66], XXXIII, 899-907; TJ to Robert Skipwith, 3 Aug. 1771). The LETTRE has not been identified.

From James Madison

DEAR SIR   N. York. March 18th. 1787

My endeavors to obtain for you the peccan Nuts have all been unsuccessful untill a few days ago when I received by the post about a dozen of them which I now inclose. They go by a French Gentleman in a Vessel bound for England, who will either carry them himself to Paris, or consign them to the care of Mr. Adams. I do not yet despair of being able to possess myself of the full quantity which you wished. My endeavours have been equally unsuccessful as to the seed of the Sugar Maple, notwithstanding the different plans pursued for the purpose. I have begun a letter to you of some length which I allotted for this conveyance, but the short notice I had of it, the tediousness of writing in Cypher, and several unseasonable interruptions make it doubtful whether I shall be able to finish it. If I should it will accompany this.

The fear of losing the opportunity for both induces me to send this off without delay. I remain yr. affecte. friend & Servt.

Js. MADISON JR.

RC (PWacD: Sol Feinstone Collection, on deposit PPAmP); at foot of text: "Mr. Jefferson." Recorded in SJL as received 16 June 1787.

Madison's letter OF SOME LENGTH was dated a day later.

From Mary Jefferson Bolling

Chesnut Grove May 3 1787

This letter has been long due tho hope it will be acceptable to my dear brother but must confess he has reason to accuse me with long Silence. I have waited with great impatience to receive a line from you but to my great mortificacion have always been disappointed but still could not indulge the most distant idea it was for want of that affection that I have ever flattered my self I possest nor had I ever any reason to doubt but rather supposed it was the publick had taken your attention, and your extensive correspondence hear. I hope this will find you perfectly racovered of your dislicatied rist which I am exceedingly sorry to hear of. I cannot omit thanking you for your kind condolence in a letter to my sister Carr but had it been to me what a cordial it would have been to my drooping spirits, but I must not dwell two long on this subject I shall grow malincoly, I know you feel the sorrows of the afflicted, experience has taught you to do so. I have just returnd from a visit to Epington left Mrs. Epps very much dejected at being oblige to part with dear little polley and polley as much so at being seperatied from a person so dear to her. I left polley yesterday but did not take a final leave. I intend meeting her at osborns tomorrow and shall attend her to the hundred whear she is to embark.

I hope in my next I shall have the hapiness to congratulate you on her safe arrival of which I have very few doubts the fine season and undoubtedly a very fine ship. Her accomodations on bord will be exceeding good and I am perswaided the gentlemen whose care she is in will endeavour to make her passage as agreable as it is in their powers. It is my most ardent wish that she may have a pleasant passage. We shall all be very anxtious to hear of her safe arrival. I am quite at a loss now to know what to think of your return. I have numberless conjectures on that head. You have deprived us of the only object which made your return certain, but I will not despair. Permit me Solicite your return as soon as the situation of your affairs will admit it. Your friends all long to see you. Your presence would make us exceeding happy. Mr. Bolling is very much indisposed and has been for some time, pleads his excuse for not wrighting as you know his great avertion to it desires to be remembred to you in the most affectanate manner. I must conclude with wishing you and yours may injoy every blesing that this transitory life will admit of and beleive me to be with sincear affection   MARY BOLLING

PS A few seeds and flower roots would be very accepttable. M B

RC (ViU: Mary Kirk Moyer deposit); minimum punctuation supplied; endorsed by TJ. Recorded in SJL as received 30 June 1787.

TJ sent his KIND CONDOLENCE on the deaths of Mrs. Bolling's children, Thomas Bolling and Anne Bolling Lewis, in a letter to Martha Jefferson CARR of 20 Aug. 1785 (Vol. 15: 620; see also same, 618).

From Tench Coxe

SIR   Philadelphia Septr. 15th. 1787

On the 3d. instant I had the honor to enclose you a letter (of introduction) from the hon. Js. Maddison Jr., and another from myself directed to the person, who will deliver you this. The Nature of my Object did not permit my entering at that time into any explanation of the reasons by which I had been induced to request the favor of Mr. Maddison's Letter, and at this time I think it will be most safe to leave entirely to the bearer the explanation of the plan we have been on. You will find him intelligent and strictly upright—and both his wishes and my desire will lead him to open himself completely to you. The very high veneration I feel for your Character, as well as the hope I have that you will use your weight, as far as it may be proper, in aid of our views render it extremely desirable as well as necessary that you should have our whole secret reposed in you. I will not therefore trespass on your time by any unnecessary addition to this letter, but shall only observe, that as far as I may presume upon Mr. Maddisons information concerning Me, I beg leave to recommend the bearer and his business to your Countenance, and advice, and if I may venture so far, to your influence and assistance. I have the honor of being with sentiments of the most perfect Esteem, Sir, yr. very respectful & mo. obedt. Servt.   TENCH COXE

FC (PHi: Coxe Papers); entirely in Coxe's hand; addressed: "His Excellency Thos. Jefferson Esqr Min. pleny. of the United States of America Paris."

THE BEARER was Andrew Mitchell, an Englishman recently resident in Westmoreland County, Pennsylvania, with whom Coxe had formed a partnership a month ear-

lier—one that was probably inspired by the establishment, around the same time, of the Pennsylvania Society for the Encouragement of Manufactures and the Useful Arts, in which Coxe played a central role. Their PLAN called for Mitchell to go to Great Britain and obtain models and patterns of "divers machines, moved by water, fire, horses or men for preparing and manufacturing wool, cotton, flax, hemp, metals or any other raw Materials." Although exporting such machinery from Britain was illegal, Mitchell was to spirit models to France, sell them there to the government or private individuals, and with the proceeds bring prototypes to Pennsylvania for use in constructing factories. Mitchell proved either corrupt or inept, for none of the models he later claimed to have obtained left England. There is no evidence that Mitchell reached France or that TJ received this or the following letter from Coxe (Contract between Coxe and Mitchell, 9 Aug. 1787, and Coxe to Mitchell, 21 Oct. 1787, PHi: Coxe Papers; Cooke, *Coxe*, 102-7).

From Tench Coxe

SIR   Philada. Octr. 4th. 1787

I had the honor to inclose you some time ago a letter from the hon. Jas. Maddison Jr. Esqr. of Virga. and at the same time mentioned that a little time would necessarily elapse before I could have the pleasure of explaining myself on the business, which induced me to take the liberty of troubling you. The person who presents this to you, Mr. Andw. Mitchell will take the liberty of requesting your Attention to the Objects we have in View. Apologizing for the liberty I take I have the honor of being, Sir, yr. mo. respectf. h. Servt   TENCH COXE

FC (PHi: Coxe Papers); entirely in Coxe's hand; addressed: "His Excellency Thos. Jefferson Esqr. Minister Plenipotentiary of the United States of America Paris."

From Jarnac

Vlles [Versailles] nov. the 30th 1787.

M. Jefferson's Commands have been regularly executed, and the Bishop of Adran who is gone Last thursday with the young prince of Cochinchina will Send at Least one pound of Dry rice.

Le Comte de Jarnac for more attention has given the Same Commission for to be register'd in the Navy's office, he begs M. Jefferson to be So good as to be convinc'd that Le Comte de Jarnac will be allways ready for his orders.

Here is inclos'd M. Poivre's useful work.

RC (Thomas A. Lingenfelter, Doylestown, Pennsylvania, 1994); endorsed by TJ. Recorded in SJL as received 4 Dec. 1787. Enclosure: Pierre Poivre, *Voyages d'un Philosophe, ou Observations sur les Moeurs & les Arts des Peuples de l'Afrique, de l'Asie & de l'Amérique* (Yverdon, 1768). TJ later acquired an edition published in Maastricht in 1779. See Sowerby, No. 3931.

Marie Charles Rosalie de Rohan Chabot, Comte de Jarnac (1740-1813), a brigadier general in the French army with a strong interest in the arts and natural sciences, was reputed to be the most refined member of Louis XVI's court. He left France for Ireland early in the Revolution and evidently remained in the British Isles for the rest of his life, his second wife being a daughter of a member of the Irish Parliament (*Diction-naire de biographie française*, 18 vols. [Paris, 1933-]; *Mémoires inédits de Madame la Comtesse de Genlis, sur le dixhuitième siècle et la révolution françoise, depuis 1756 jusqu'a nos jours*, 2d ed., 8 vols. [Paris, 1825], I, 337, II, 198; Marquis de Bombelles, *Journal*, ed. Jean Grassion and Frans Durif, 3 vols. [Geneva, 1977-93], II, 50n; *Lettre du Comte de Jarnac a Monsieur de Condorcet* [Dublin, 1791]).

Pierre Joseph Georges Pigneau de Béhaine, the BISHOP OF ADRAN, a titular see in Asia Minor, and Apostolic Vicar of Cochin China, who had come to France in February 1787 with Nguyen Phuoc Chan, the YOUNG PRINCE OF COCHINCHINA, had just completed negotiations for a treaty whereby the French government pledged, in return for certain territorial and commercial concessions, to assist the efforts of the prince's father, Nguyen Anh, to regain the throne of which he had been deprived by the Tay-son rebellion (Nicholas Sellers, *The Princes of Hà-Tiên (1682-1867)* ... [Thanh-Long, 1983], 77-8, 107-9).

Memorandum on Wine

[after 23 Apr. 1788]

Burgundy. The best white wines are

1. Monrachet. Made on the vineyards of Monsr. de Clermont, and the Marquis de Sarsnet. The latter is rented by M. de la Tour. This sells @ 48. sous the bottle new, and 3. livres fit for drinking.

2. Meursault. The best quality is the Goutte d'or. 6 sous the bottle new. Monsr. Parent, tonnelier at Baune is a good hand to conduct a person through these vineyards.

The best red wines of Burgundy are Chambertin, Vougeau, Romanie, Veaune, Nuys, Beaune, Pommard Voulenay. But it is only the Chambertin, Voujeau, and Veaune which are strong enough to be transported by sea—even in the most favourable seasons. They sell therefore for 48.s. the bottle new, which is 3 or 4 times the price of the others.

Champagne. The Mousseux or Sparkling is dearest because most in demand for exportation, but the Non-mousseux is most esteemed by every real connoisseur. The best is made at Aij by *M. d'Orsay, M. le Duc, M. de Villermont and M. Janson. The first gentleman makes more than all the rest. It is from him I have taken. It costs 3.ᵗᵗ the bottle when old enough for use.

The best red Champaigne is made by the Benedictines at Auvillaij. They furnish the king's table: but the red Champagne is not of first rate estimation.

* He lives at Paris. His homme d'affaires is M. Louis at Aij.

[761]

Cote rotie. This is a league below Vienne on the opposite side of the Rhone. The best red is made at Ampuys by Monsr. de la Condamine in his vineyard called Monlis, Monsr. de Leusse dans son grand tupin, Monsr. de Montjoli, M. du Vivier, and M. de Prunel.　　　The best white are at Chateau-grillé by Madame Peyrouse. They cost 12.s. the bottle new. Those which are strong enough to bear transportation, cannot be drunk till 4 years old. These wines are not in such estimation as to be produced commonly at the good tables of Paris.

Hermitage. This is made at Tains on the Rhone. The red is not very highly esteemed, but the White is the first wine in the world without a single exception. The best is made by Monsieur Meuse, M. de Loche, avocat, M. Berger avocat, M. Chanoine Monron, M. Gaillet, M. de Beausace, M. Deure, M. Chalamelle, M. Monnet and two or three others. There is so little of the White made that it is difficult to buy it unless you will buy two or three times the quantity of red at the same time. The white improves fastest in a hot situation, and must be 4. years old before it is drank. It then costs, when it can be bought, 3.ᵗᵗ the bottle.

Lunel. This is a wine resembling the Frontignan, but not quite so rich. It is near Nismes. The best is made by M. Bouquet and M. Tremoulet.

Frontignan. The best are made by Made. Soubeinan, M. Reboulle, M. Lambert, M. Thomas, M. Argilliers, and M. Audibert. The price 20 to 24.s. the bottle. I purchase always of M. Lambert, who is a physician, and the best person to apply to for information. There are two or three casks of red made in a particular vineyard, not differing at all in flavor from the white. It's scarceness makes it sought and higher priced. It is counterfeited by putting a little Alicant into the white.

Bordeaux. Red. There are 4. vineyards of first quality, viz

    1 Chateau-Margau belonging to Monsr. d'Agicourt, all under contract.

    2 la Tour de Segur belonging to M. Mirosmenil.

    3. Hautbrion belonging to M. de. Femelle and M. de Toulouse. The part of M. de Femelle is under contract.

    4. de la Fite. Belonging to President Pichard. This is in perfection at 3 years old, the three former not till four. When fit for use the[1] all cost about 3.ᵗᵗ the bottle.

    Those of the best quality, after the 4. crops before mentioned, are Rozan, belonging to Madame de Rozan (from whom I take)

Dabbadie, ou	all these, when fit for use cost from
Lionville	40.s. to 50.s. the bottle, and some-
La Rose	times 3.^{tt} I doubt whether the best
Quirouen	judge can distinguish them from
Durfort	the 4. crops unless he tastes them
	together.

[. . .]^2

[. . .] the three upp[er parishes?], viz.

     1. Sauterne, belonging to M. Salus.

     2. Prignac. The best is the President du Roy's.

     3. Barsac. The best is the President Pichard's.

          These last are more esteemed at Paris than those of Grave, and they cost from 8.s. to 24.s. the bottle according to their age.

A general observation as to all wines is that there is great difference in those of the same vineyard in different years, and this affects the price considerably.

Moselle. The best are made about 15 leagues from Coblentz on the mountain of Brownberg, adjoining the village of Dusmond: and the best crop there is that of the Baron Breidbach Burresheim. This when fit for use costs 22.s. the bottle.

There are others, towit Vialen, Crach, Bispot, Selting, Kous, Berncastle 'which are good,' but not equal to Brownberg.

Hock. There are now three wines of this character viz.

1. Hocheim	of these the Johansberg has for some years past
2. Johansberg	acquired the highest reputation. It sells at a florin
3. Rudesheim	as soon as drinkable, which is not till it is 5. years

old, and to be tolerably mild they all require a much greater age. The oldest and dearest are 5/ sterl. the bottle wholesale.

PrC (DLC: TJ Papers, 234: 41990-3); consisting of four pages entirely in TJ's hand, with footnote added in ink; undated and unaddressed; top of final page torn away (see note 2 below); endorsed in ink by TJ: "Wines."

TJ used his notes from his travel journals of 1787 and 1788 to compile this memorandum, the last entry of 23 Apr. 1788 supplying the earliest possible date of composition (Notes of a Tour into the Southern Parts of France, &c., printed at 10 June 1787; Notes of a Tour Through Holland and the Rhine Valley, printed under March 1788). Internal evidence suggests that TJ prepared the memorandum for an unidentified traveler during his remaining months in France, or shortly after his return to America.

^{1} Thus in manuscript.

^{2} Estimated five lines torn away, the missing text probably being based on the paragraph on the white wines of Bordeaux in Vol. 11: 456.

To Boyd, Ker & Company

GENTLEMEN   Paris May 9. 1788.

In conformity to the desire of Mr. Rutledge I shall desire Messrs. Berard & Co. to pay to you whatever sums of money they may have orders to remit me for the use of Mr. Rutledge. I have the honor to be with much esteem Gent. Your most obedt. & most humble servt.

TH: JEFFERSON

RC (ViU); addressed: "Messieurs Messieurs Boydker & co. rue d'Amboise No. 4."; endorsed in part: "Recu le même Jour Répone. do."

DESIRE OF MR. RUTLEDGE: see John Rutledge, Jr., to TJ, 6 May 1788.

To Martha Jefferson

Monday[1] June 16. 1788

Madame de Corney proposes, my Dear to carry you to the Opera tomorrow evening. I will therefore call for you precisely at five oclock. Be ready without fail before that hour. Know exactly at what hour they will shut your doors in the evening, and as you come down to the carriage see exactly what oclock it is by the Convent clock that we may not be deceived as to the time. Adieu. Yours' affectionately   TH. J

Kisses to Polly. She will keep your supper for you till you return tomorrow night.

Tr (ViU); 20th-century copy; at foot of text: "Mademoiselle Jefferson à l'Abbaye royale de Panthemont." Tr (Mrs. Robert Graham, Alexandria, Virginia, 1960);

20th-century typescript; lacks address and part of dateline. Not recorded in SJL Index.

[1] Word lacking in other Tr.

From John Ledyard

Hotel d'aligre rue d'orleans 4 Juilet [1788]

Mr. Ledyard presents his compliments to Mr. Jefferson. He has been imprisoned and banished by the Empriss of Russia from her dominions after having almost gained the pacific ocean. He is now on his way to Africa to see what he can do with that Continent. He is ill with a cold and fever or he would have waited on Mr. Jefferson with Mr. Edwards. He is with perfect respect & affection Mr. Jeffersons most humble & obt. Servant.

RC (NhD); partially dated, with year established from SJL Index; addressed: "A Monsieur Monsieur Jefferson Ambassadeur pour les etats uni de l'amerique."

ALMOST GAINED THE PACIFIC OCEAN: see Ledyard to TJ, 7 Feb. 1786, and note.

To Mary Jefferson

MY DEAR POLLY   Saturday [12 July 1788]

I am now writing to your aunt Eppes, and wish to inclose her something of your drawing. Bring with you tomorrow the best lesson you have done and the smallest. Or could you to-day and Monday begin, and finish something on purpose to be sent? Desire your sister to write to your aunt to-day, and to bring the letter tomorrow. Kiss her for me and kiss Kitty too. Be always good, practise your lessons a great deal and do not lose too much time on your Doll. Adieu my dear Polly. Your's affectionately   TH:J.

RC (DNCD); date established from TJ to Elizabeth Wayles Eppes, 12 July 1788; addressed: "A Mademoiselle Mademoiselle Maria Jefferson à l'Abbaye royale de Panthemont." Not recorded in SJL Index.

John Paradise's Power of Attorney to Nathaniel Burwell

Know all men by these presents that I John Paradise of James city county in the Commonwealth of Virginia, but now at Paris in the kingdom of France, do by these presents constitute and appoint Nathaniel Burwell esquire of Carter's grove in the same county and commonwealth my lawful attorney for all my property in the said commonwealth, real and personal, in possession and in action, giving to him full power for me, and in my behalf, to superintend and direct the management of my said property, to sell or otherwise dispose of all parts thereof which I could myself sell or dispose of, to receive and apply as shall be hereinafter directed the proceeds of such sales, to purchase and take conveiances for me of property of all kinds, to prosecute and defend all actions and suits in which I may be concerned in my own or in any other right, to employ such persons for the transaction of my business as he may think proper, to settle with them, and all others, all matters of account now existing, or which may hereafter exist between them and me giving to whatsoever he shall do in the premises the same force and validity as if done by myself. And I do further declare that the true intent of these presents is that the said Nathaniel Burwell shall out of the profits and proceeds of the said estates in possession and action pay to Edward Bancroft and William Anderson in the city of London and kingdom of England, or to such other person or persons as I shall appoint by letter or other writing signed by myself the sum of two hundred and forty pounds sterling money of Great Britain annually in quarterly paiments of sixty pounds sterling each to be made in the said city of London on the first days of January, April, July and October in every year ensuing the present year, which said sum being for the subsistence of my wife and myself is to be paid in preference to all other demands whatsoever: and that he shall pay all other the profits and proceeds of my said estates in possession and in action, as they shall come to his hands for the discharge of my debts contracted before the day of my departure from England in the last year together with lawful interest, taking therein such arrangements with my said creditors as to him and them shall seem reasonable, and the surplus after the said debts shall be satisfied to pay or apply as I shall direct from time to time: these presents to remain in full force during the whole time of my absence from the said commonwealth of Virginia, unless sooner revoked by deed indented, executed by myself, attested and authenticated according to the forms prescribed by the laws of the said commonwealth of Virginia for deeds executed in foreign countries. In Witness whereof I have hereunto subscribed my name and affixed my seal at Paris aforesaid this eighth day of August in the year one thousand seven hundred and eighty eight.

Signed, sealed, and
delivered in presence of } JOHN PARADISE

TH: JEFFERSON
W: SHORT
PHILIP MAZZEI

MS (Gilder Lehrman Collection, on deposit NNP); in TJ's hand, signed by Paradise, TJ, Short, and Mazzei, with Paradise's seal affixed.

TJ prepared this document as part of his ongoing effort to help John and Lucy Ludwell Paradise sort out their tangled finances (TJ to Edward Bancroft, 24 Aug. 1788).

Memorandums to William Short

[before 17 Sep. 1788]

Memorandums for Mr. Short.

According to the route you propose at present you will probably see no part of the Rhone between Lyons and Pont St. Esprit. Consequently you will not pass Tains, where the Hermitage wine is made. Should any change of plan carry you by Tains, be so good as to enquire Who makes the 1st. 2d. and 3d. best crops of White Hermitage, what have been the best years for 7. or 8. years back, and how much per quart[1] bottle the best crop of each year costs?

Do not lodge chez Revol. He is unconscionable and there is a better house.[2]

Venice. Get for me the edition of the Vocabolario della Crusca printed in 5. vols. 4to. at Venice in 1741.[3] I had rather have it unbound, but this is not very material. Qu. how it can be forwarded to me? This I must leave to your enquiry on the spot. All the seaports of Italy have communication with Marseilles where M. Cathalan would receive and forward it.

The essential part of a Maccaroni machine, is 1. an iron mortar with the bottom out, except as to a little annulur or margin thus **⌊ ⌋** 2. a round peice of metal which drops into this mortar, and is supported on the margin at bottom, as on a shoulder.

This iron is thus formed where all the black is solid.

The white represents the apertures through which the Maccaroni are forced by a screw. I would wish to have one of these irons the smallest (as to diameter) that is ever used, but with holes for Maccaroni of the common size. I have no occasion for the mortar, because we can easily make that: only I should wish to know it's depth, and the breadth of the margin left in the bottom of it.

Avignon. To buy for me 6. dozen bottles of the wine of M. de Rochegude which resembles Madeira. It is as dry, not quite so strong, and a little paler. Chuse it of the best year, not under 6. years old. I think his homme d'affaires told me it would cost 24s. a bottle, the bottle included. At Nismes, ask leave at the Cabinet de Segur to have a model made of the vase in the form of the duck, which they were so good as to permit me to have a model of in May 1787, which has been lost by the accident you are acquainted with. The best tavern there is au Petit Louvre. They gave me a good red wine at about 3. sous the bottle. I had a good servant there named Blondin. He can tell you the workman who made the model in wood of the duck-shaped vase. I paid 18. livres for it. They did not know at the Cabinet de Segur who I was; but the Secretary and the Principal may remember me from the circumstance of the Model, and from my having given them one of Dro's crowns. Be so good as to tell them from me that Congress have ordered me to have a series of Medals of the American war made, and to give sets of them to such Colleges or Cabinets as I shall think best: and that I propose to ask the Director of the Cabinet of Segur to accept a set for that Cabinet.

There is at Nismes a M. l'Abbé d'Arnal at the head of some steam mills, of very superior talents in Mechanics. I saw him also without his knowing me. He will remember me by the impertinence of my introduction to him, and by a subsequent breach of promise, which was to send him a description of the American manner of hanging the upper millstone of a grist mill. I wrote the description soon after I returned to Paris, but not being quite contented with it, I intended not to have sent it till the Marquis de la Fayette should go there, and to have explained it to him verbally, and asked him to explain it in like manner to the Abbé. As he does not go, you will be so good as to give the written description, with such further explanation as may be necessary to make it intelligible. Present my compliments also to the Abbé d'Arnal and my excuses for my failure.

MS (ICN); in TJ's hand, with marginal note by Short (see note 3 below); undated.

TJ must have composed these memorandums for Short, his private secretary in France, sometime before 17 Sep. 1788, when Short left Paris for a grand tour of southern France and Italy that lasted until the following May (George Green Shackelford, *Jefferson's Adoptive Son: The Life of William Short, 1759-1848* [Lexington, Ky., 1993], 34-40). The editions of the VO-CABOLARIO DELLA CRUSCA TJ eventually acquired are listed in Sowerby, Nos. 4806-

7, the last being the one TJ asked Short to obtain; see also TJ to Short, 21 Nov. 1788. A SERIES OF MEDALS: see Editorial Note and documents on Notes on American medals struck in France, in Vol. 16: 53-79. DE-SCRIPTION OF . . . A GRIST MILL: see TJ to the Abbé d'Arnal, 9 July 1787.

[1] Word interlined.
[2] These two sentences interlined.
[3] Next to this sentence Short wrote in the margin "Dec. 5. not to be found any where in Venise."

From Thomas Boylston

SR.   London Novb. 18th. 1788

Having just received Advice of an Edict being publishd in France, forbiding the importation of foreign Sparmacitæ Oil[1] I beg leave to apply to you for your Assistance respecting the American Ship Diana Capt.   from Boston, with a Cargo of Sparmacitæ Oil purchasd there, and Ship'd for Have de Grace, to the Address of Mess. Homberg & Homberg freres of that City.

This Cargo, was purchased, by Vertue of an agreement made at Haver Febuary last, with the foresaid Gentlemen, and Ship'd in the Diana at Boston in August last, and from thence sail'd with said Cargo for Havre   Octr. All this was done in full faith, and confidence, that the French Court (which had encouraged, and promoted the *Oil Trade* in America Ships, from America) would not take any sudden, and determinate steps to injure any Person that might engage in the prosecution of it on the foresaid faith and Credit of their Edicts, encouraging the same. Its highly reasonable, and consonant with Honor, and Justice, that an Edict shoud not be in force, and operate against a Ship and Cargo, at so great a distance as Boston, before a suitable and proper time for due notice thereof be first given.

In this case the Edict was announced in France about the last of Sept. or begining of Octr. This Cargo was purchased, in August, the Ship was loaded, and ready to sail, the first fair wind from Boston for Havre, and of Course, impossible to be informed of any design the French Court had of reversing their former Edict, granting Liberty and encourageing the Oil Trade in American Ships, from any of the United States of America.

The favor requested is that your Excellency, would undertake in behalf, of said Ship and by application to the French Court, Obtain Liberty for the said Ship, to finish her Voyage, undertaken on the faith of the Kings Edict, and to enter and sell her Cargo of Sparmacitæ Oil at Havre.

The necessity of this indulgence is very urgent. The Ship being an American built Ship, is prohibited by Act of the English Parliament comeing with her *Oil* to any Port in England to Land it, and She must return back again to Boston with it, if not Admitted into France—there is no alternitive. And surely the French Court cannot refuse a request circumstanced as this is. I'm Sr. with great Regard your most Huml. Ser.   THO BOYLSTON

PS.

I have this minute received a Letter from your Honorable Friend Mr. John Adams. He's well and wishes to see and hear of his friends among which he esteems you.

Dft (MHi: Boylston Family Papers); at head of text: "Mr. Jefferson."

For the steps initiated by TJ, even before receipt of this letter, that led the French government in December 1788 to exempt the United States from the EDICT . . . FORBID-ING THE IMPORTATION OF FOREIGN SPERMACITÆ, see TJ to Montmorin, 23 Oct. 1788, and Editorial Note and Document VI of a group of documents on the whale fishery, at 19 Nov. 1788.

[1] Sentence to this point interlined.

To Adrian Kissam

Monday Nov. 24. 1788.

Mr. Jefferson has the honour to present his compliments to Mr. Kissam and to send him a letter which has come to his hands. He wrote yesterday morning to invite Mr. Kissam to do him the favor of dining with him to-day: but the servant not finding him at his antient lodgings brought back the note, and it was not till night that Mr. Jefferson knew of this circumstance. He wishes the present may be received in time to obtain him that happiness for to-day. He dines from three to a quarter after three, and wishes much to see Mr. Kissam, and to avail himself of every occasion of proving his respect for him personally, as well as on account of the recommendation of his good friend Mr. Livingston for whom he has a very sincere attachment.

RC (William P. Wreden, Palo Alto, California, 1974); addressed: "A Monsieur Monsieur Kissam rue des postes." Not recorded in SJL Index for 1788. Enclosure not found.

Adrian Kissam (b. 1765), a New York attorney who came to France with a letter of introduction from Robert R. LIVINGSTON, received a passport from TJ in March 1789 (Edward Kissam, *The Kissam Family in America from 1644 to 1825* [New York, 1892], 32-3; Livingston to TJ, 3 Mch. 1788; Vol. 15: 486).

TJ's note of YESTERDAY has not been found.

From D'Estaing

MONSIEUR   a paris ce 14 mars 1789

Agrées je vous suplie mes remerciments de ce que vous me mettes dans le cas heureux d'éxecutter vos ordres, de rendre homage a mes sentiments pour Mr. Short et pour Mr. Rutledge, et de leur être d'une bien foible utilité. Ils n'avoient besoin que d'eux-mêmes certifiés par vous, pour avoir le droit de tout attendre de Mr. le Comte d'Albert de Rions commandant de la Marine a Toulon. Il remplace dans mon estime et dans mon coeur Mr. le Bailly de Suffren; et ce que je lui dis, de ce que je pense sur son compte, dans la lettre a cachet volant c'y jointe, n'est pas exageré; j'espere que nos Amis en penseront la même chose, et j'oserois leur en repondre comme je faisois de Mr. de Suffren, si jamais le détestable fléau de la guêrre venoit a éxister. Agrées avec indulgence, et bonté, l'assurance de l'estime, de l'attachment, et du respect avec lesquels j'ai l'honneur d'etre Monsieur Votre tres humble et tres obéissant serviteur   ESTAING

RC (NNP); at foot of text: "Mr Jefferson"; endorsed by TJ. Recorded in SJL as received 14 Mch. 1789. The enclosure, not found, is identified in TJ to William Short, 16 Mch. 1789, and note.

This letter was the Comte d'Estaing's response to TJ's request that William Short and his traveling companion, John Rutledge, Jr., be allowed to visit the docks and arsenals at Toulon (see TJ to D'Estaing, 13 Mch. 1789).

Notes on Arranging Books at Monticello

[before 26 Sep. 1789]

Manner of arranging my books at Monticello when I return
I have there about 400 sq. feet of books, and shall carry from Paris about 250 sq.f. Fix shelves from a. to b. and from c. to d. and e extending from the floor to the entablature. This will give 420 sq.f. It must be divided into 2 orders of 7.f. each. In the upper order the shelves may come from a. to the chimney. This gives 45 sq.f. more. Place 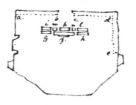 my large book case at f. the 5. small ones (bought of P.R's estate) at g.h.i.k.l. and make two small supplementary ones at m.n. This gives 156. sq. feet more: in all 621 sq.f.

Lay planks from the top of the book case to the cornice of the lower order of shelves so as to form a platform in front of the upper order of shelves. To get up to this have steps folded up into the form of a table, moveable, and in the form noted in the margin.

Making the tread to the rise as 3. to 4. and 7. steps a foot apart, the whole rise will be 5.6 feet so that one may either step from the uppermost step up on the platform 1.4f. or break the distance into two by a hanging step.

MS (MHi); entirely in TJ's hand; un-dated, but written before TJ's departure from Paris on 26 Sep. 1789.

P.R'S ESTATE: that of Peyton Randolph, from which TJ made large purchases of books and manuscripts in 1776 (MB, 10 Dec. 1776, and note).

To James Brown

DEAR SIR   Cumberland Dec. 19. 1789.

The inclosed letter being of importance I take the liberty of asking you to give it a conveyance. Should any vessel be going directly to France that would certainly be the best way of sending it. Otherwise if put under cover to your correspondents in London, and by them put into the post office *there*, it will go safely to Paris where the postage from London to Paris is always paid. If put into any post office of Great Britain except that of London it is thrown aside of course for want of postage. Pardon this additional trouble I give you and be assured of the sentiments of esteem and attachment with which I am Dear Sir Your sincere friend & humble servt   TH: JEFFERSON

RC (ViU); unaddressed, but endorsed by Brown. Not recorded in SJL. Enclosure: TJ to William Short, 14 Dec. 1789.

From Lafayette

Paris, 1 Feb. 1790. He asks TJ to be of service to M. Minguée, who is leaving for America to "faire un établissement" on the Scioto river, having served with patriotism and zeal in the national Parisian army from the beginning of the Revolution, and from whose great friend, the "Gouverneur de mon fils," he has just received new testimony in his favor. [P.S.] "I don't know, My dear friend, When this will reach You, Accept My Most afectionate Compliments, and Warm Wishes for Your Speedy Return."

RC (MdHi); 1 p; in French in a clerk's hand, with signature and English postscript by Lafayette; at foot of text: "M. Jefferson"; endorsed by TJ as received 5 Mch. 1792 and so recorded in SJL.

From Richard R. Saltonstall

New York, 5 Feb. 1790. Seeking a post in which he can acquire knowledge while supporting himself, he requests "an appointment under you" and refers to Senator William Samuel Johnson of Connecticut, who has promised to "mention me to you."

RC (DLC: Washington Papers, Applications for Office); 1 p.; unaddressed; endorsed by TJ as received 6 Apr. 1790 and so recorded in SJL.

The following letters pertain to recommendations for positions in the Department of State: (1) Zachariah Burnley to TJ, 28 Feb. 1790, recommending the appointment to a Department of State clerkship of his son, who was about 23 years of age, had been "bound" to Hollingsworth & Johnson of Richmond, and was currently living in New York with Colonel William Davies, "who I think is Imployed by Congress to settle the Accounts betwixt the diferent States" (RC in DLC: Washington Papers, Applications for Office; addressed: "To the Honourl. Thomas Jefferson Esqr."; endorsed by TJ as received 28 Feb. 1790 and so recorded in SJL). (2) Arthur Greer to TJ, Reading, 16 Mch. 1792, requesting confirmation that a State Department clerkship had become vacant and offering to come to Philadelphia with the best recommendations (RC in same; at foot of text: "The Honorable Thomas Jefferson Esquire"; endorsed by TJ as received 19 Mch. 1792 and so recorded in SJL). (3) Elias Boudinot to TJ, 31 Mch. 1792, recommending, with reference to the same opening, a 25-year-old son of "one of the Judges of our Supr. Court" (RC in DNA: RG 59, LAR; dated "Saturday afternoon"; addressed: "The Honble Mr Jefferson"; endorsed by TJ as received 31 Mch. 1792, a Saturday, and so recorded in SJL, where it is mistakenly listed as a 30 Mch. 1792 letter). None of these letters accomplished their objectives.

Memorandum on Land Dispute with John Harvie, Jr.

[after 12 Feb. 1790]

Notes on my title to 485. acres of land surveyed for me Mar. 27. 1788. and to 490. acres adjoining the same and the lands of Colo. T. M. Randolph surveyed for James Marks Nov. 29. 1783.

My titles have a double foundation.

Ist. An Order of council in the following words. 'At a council held March 11th. 1773. On the petition of Thomas Jefferson, leave is given him to survey and sue out a patent for one thousand acres of land on the South West mountains in Albemarle, between the lines of Thomas Mann Randolph, James Hickman, the said petitioner, Martin Key and William Watson. Copy John Blair Cl. Conc.'

II. Two entries in the following words. 'Oct. 21. 1774. Thomas Jefferson esqr. enters for 800. acres of land to be included by two entries of 400. acres each to adjoin the land of Thomas Mann Randolph on the South West mountains. Copy ℔ Anderson Bryan S.A.C.'

I. As to the order of council.

1. This was completely suppressed by the act. of ass. 1779. c.12.s.3. 'All orders of council or entries for land in the council books, (except so far as such orders or entries respectively have been carried into execution by actual surveys) shall be, and they are hereby declared void and of no effect.'

[Sect. 10. of this act, referred to by Mr. Harvey, respects claims for lands upon *surveys* under order of council, which it directs to be laid before the court of appeals. For the policy of the act was to abolish ipso facto all orders of council *not carried into execution by survey*, and as to those *carried into execution by survey*, to refer their merits to the court of appeals. This 10th. section therefore concerns the latter only, and not the former, consequently not my order of council.]

[Act. of ass. 1779. c.27. sect.3. Octob. session. respects also only those claims under *actual survey* which the act beforementioned of the May session of the same year had directed to be laid before the court of Appeals. Consequently this act, also referred to by Mr. Harvie, does not apply to my order of council which was not surveyed, but was completly suppressed by the former act.]

2. The act ass. 1781. c.29. sect.8. completely re-establishes my order of council in the following words. 'And whereas by the said law for establishing the land office all orders of council or entries in the council books for lands not carried into execution by actual survey, were made

void, which, so far as it respected lands on the Eastern waters, produced much injury to individuals and no utility to the public: be it therefore enacted that all orders of council and entries in the council books for lands on the Eastern waters which were in force at the passing of the said act, and which have [not] been precluded from revival by entries or surveys regularly made for the same lands since the passing of the said act, shall stand revived and re-established, and the rights accruing thereon be vested in the persons then owning the same, their heirs or other representatives: and that the said orders of council, or entries in the Council books shall stand on the footing of entries in the surveyor's books, and as such be considered to every intent and purpose, save only that where they exceed the quantity of 400. as. they shall be good for their whole quantity so far as they would have been good by authority of the said orders of council or entries in the council books before the passing of the said act.' [It is well known that an order of counc. for more than 1000. as. was void.] My order of council being thus revived I was entitled to 1000. as. if there were so much within the limits therein described, or so much as was within those limits. There proved in event to be but 485 + 490. = 975 acres. I am entitled to the whole of this.

Note. The word 'not' in the section of the act last cited was omitted in the first printed acts of the session, and the Chancellor's revisal, copying that edition, have retained the error but noted it among the errata. [1] Recourse must be had to the Rolls if disputed. In fact the absurdity of the act, without the correction, reviving only those orders which had been since taken by others under the faith of the law, and not reviving those which had not been so taken, is sufficient evidence of the intention of the legislators.

II. The entries of 1774. seem to have been intended as supplementary to the order of council both as to title and quantity.

Act. ass. 1779. c.12. sect. 2. 'Where any person, before the end of this present session of assembly, hath made a regular entry according to act of assembly, with the county surveyor for any tract of land not exceeding 400. as. upon any of the eastern waters, which hath not been surveyed or forfeited, according to the laws and rules of government in force at the time of making such entry, the surveyor of the county where such land lies, shall after advertising legal notice thereof, proceed to survey the same accordingly, and shall deliver to the proprietor a plat and certificate of survey thereof within three months: and if such person shall fail to attend at the time and place so appointed for making such survey, with chain carriers and a person to mark the lines, or shall fail to deliver such plat and certificate into the land office, according to the rules and regulations of the same, together with the Auditors certificate of the Treasurer's reciept for the composition money herein after mentioned, and pay the office fees, he or she shall forfeit his or her right and title, but upon performance of these requisitions shall be entitled to a grant for such tract of land as in other cases.'

Act. ass. 1780. c.9. gives further time.

Act ass. 1781. c. 29. sect. 7. renders the time indefinite as follows. 'And whereas by the act of Gen. ass. for adjusting and settling the titles of claimers to unpatented lands, a certain time was limited within which the surveyors of the counties on the Eastern waters should survey all lands within their counties regularly entered for before the end of the session of ass. in which the said act was passed, which time was, by subsequent acts, extended to other definitive periods and it not being in the power of the party claiming such entries to compel the surveyor to a performance of his duty, or to controul those accidents which may sometimes render such performance impracticable, it is therefore unjust that he should lose his rights on any failure of duty in the surveyor, whether wilful or involuntary: be it therefore enacted, that the surveyors of the several counties on the said Eastern waters shall proceed, with all practicable dispatch, to survey the said entries before described, and for this purpose shall proceed in notifying the party, making the survey, delivering a plat and certificate, and in all other circumstances as by the act for establishing the land office is directed in the case of surveys to be made on entries subsequent to the end of the said session of assembly; and the party interested shall be subject also to the same forfeitures of right if he fail in any thing prescribed by the same act last mentioned, to be done on his part.'

Obj. My entry of 1774. is not sufficiently special.

Ans. 'Two entries of 400. as. each to adjoin the lands of Th. M. Rand. on the S.W. mountains.' There were no vacant lands adjoining his but these, consequently no others to which this description could apply. The description designates these lands as perfectly and fully as could be required. Any other additional terms of description would have been surplusage, and the want of a surplusage never vitiates.

Obj. Colo. Randolph's entry.

Ans. I never intended to prejudice any entry which Colo. Randolph may have there. But I really doubt his having any. Without calling for his entry however I did intend to accomodate him with a part of these lands, if any of them suited him particularly. But this intention was merely voluntary, and directed personally to him as tenant of Edgehill. If he sells Edgehill, I am under no legal obligation, and feel no moral one to convey my lands to a purchaser. If Colo. R. retains Edgehill, and my title under the *entries* be alone confirmed, then he must take the surplus 175. acres in part of his entry.[2]

Refer for further explanations to my three following letters to Mr. Harvie

1790. Jan. 11.

Nov. 2

1791. Apr. 7.

MS (MHi); entirely in TJ's hand; undated, but assigned on the basis of internal and collateral evidence cited below; last five lines added at a later date; brackets in original. PrC (CSmH); lacks last five lines; endorsed in ink by TJ: "Harvie John."

In this document TJ addressed points about a disputed tract of land raised in a letter from John Harvie, Jr., of 2 Feb. 1790 that he received ten days later. Internal evidence and the existence of a press copy suggest that TJ intended the memorandum for arbitrators or, possibly, for presentation to Harvie himself in Richmond, where TJ at one point hoped they would meet to settle the disagreement (see TJ to Harvie, 2 Nov. 1790). In any event, it seems likely that TJ

completed it before he prepared his 2 Nov. 1790 answer to Harvie, which made many of the same arguments, and he certainly composed it before 3 Feb. 1791, when he received Harvie's letter of 25 Jan. 1791, to which he replied on 7 Apr. 1791 relinquishing a part of the claim being defended in the memorandum. The concluding five lines were added no earlier than 7 Apr. 1791 and probably around December 1799, when TJ composed a fuller statement of his position in this protracted and complex dispute (TJ to Harvie, 5 Dec. 1799).

CHANCELLOR'S REVISAL: see Vol. 2: 321.

[1] Preceding six words interlined.
[2] Remainder of text lacking in PrC.

From Thomas Mann Randolph, Sr.

My dear Sir   Feby. 15. 1790

The great hurry that Old Phill was in, when in Richmond, prevented my writing to you by him. I wrote a few lines to Tom, to apologize to you for not coming up to the Nuptials of our Children. The Weather seems to be very unsettled, and at present I have got a Cold which is troublesome to me. I desired Tom to Mention to you the Circumstance of a prior Mortgage on the Land at Varina which I have given him by a Deed, which my Son will shew you. The Sum of Money for which it is incumbered is only twelve hundred pounds Sterg. Mr. David Ross is now under a promise to pay £600. of it, and the Money, as I am told by his Nephew is now ready for the payment, but Mr. Ross having been at his Iron Works for some weeks past prevents my seeing him. The other payment of £600. will not become due 'till the first day of next February. Nothing but the fear of being Sick, would prevent my paying my respects to you at Monticello, and the great pleasure I should receive by being present at an Event that would give me real pleasure. I hope to have the pleasure of seeing you in Richmond, on your way to the North-ward, and I beg you will make my house your home, during your Stay there. I am Dear Sir with great Esteem and respect, Your Friend & Servt

THO. M. RANDOLPH

RC (ViU: Coolidge Deposit); addressed: "Thomas Jefferson Esqr Monticello"; endorsed by TJ as received 18 Feb. 1790 and so recorded in SJL.

This day Randolph executed a deed for the LAND AT VARINA on behalf of his son and namesake, but the PRIOR MORTGAGE and the subsequent inability of DAVID ROSS to fulfill his commitments eventually placed the land in jeopardy (TJ to Randolph, 4 Feb. 1790, and note; Marriage Settlement for Martha Jefferson, 21 Feb. 1790; TJ to Thomas Mann Randolph, Jr., 26 Feb. 1795).

Notes for the Settlement of the Estate of Jane Randolph Jefferson

[ca. February 1790]

Notes for the settlement of my mother's affairs.

There is an old account to settle between her and my father's executors, for the board of the children. In order to do this, the time when the several children left her or came of age, must be fixed.

An account with Mr. J. Bolling for the expenditure of her distributable part of my sister Jane's estate, left in his hands. He laid out a part or perhaps the whole for my mother in necessaries.

There must be some account between her and my sister Elizabeth for board &c.

Upon settlement of my sister Elizabeth's estate, my mother was entitled to a distributive share of it.

A long account of 20 year's currency with Kippen & Co. has subsisted without any settlement. The whole of this is[1] charged or chargeable to me on my assumpsit.

A long account between my mother and myself. This consists of several kinds of articles. 1st. the balance assumed[2] to Kippen & Co. beforementioned. 2. monies paid or assumed for her to other people. These will be generally found in my pocket memorandum books of the respective years. 3. Corn, meat and other necessaries furnished her. These will be found in an account stated and signed by Willm. Hickman, and Garth and Mousley's accounts, and some articles in my own memorandum books.   On the other hand I am chargeable to her for some stock (cattle) bought of her when she rented her estate to me; and for the rents of her estate. I was to give her £6 sterlg. a hand. At first there were five hands. Then little Sal came into the crop for about two years before she was drowned. Old Samson died, after which there were but 4. hands. If after furnishing the necessaries of the year and monies paid for her to others[3] any balance of that year's rent remained in my hands it is to go towards discharging so much of the interest of Kippen & Co's account.

MS (MHi); entirely in TJ's hand on both sides of a small sheet; undated.

TJ evidently prepared this and the following document in February 1790, when he was busily engaged in closing the accounts of his deceased father, mother, and sisters Jane and Elizabeth (TJ to Thomas Walker, 18, 25 Jan. 1790; TJ to John Nicholas, Sr., 20 Jan. 1790; TJ to Martha Jefferson Carr, 3 Feb. 1790; TJ to John Walker, 7 Feb. 1790; TJ to John Bolling, 8 Feb. 1790; TJ to Charles Lilburne Lewis, 22 Feb. 1790; TJ to Randolph Jefferson, 28 Feb. 1790).

[1] TJ here canceled "transferred to."
[2] Word interlined in place of "due."
[3] Preceding seven words interlined.

Notes on the Will of Jane Randolph Jefferson

[ca. February 1790]

Questions which will arise on the two residuary clauses of my mother's will.

2.[1] It is a rule in law that wills shall be so construed as to make every part stand if possible. Under this rule, shall these clauses be so construed as that the first 'I give everything else to be equally divided &c' shall relate to her personal estate which she had power to 'give' and the latter 'I make &c sole legatee of whatever else I have power to dispose of' relate to her slaves which under the will of her husband she had power to appoint only.

Or.

3.[2] It being another rule that the first clauses in deeds and the last in wills shall take place, shall the latter residuary clause take place of the former as to both slaves and personal estate?

1.[3] To whom does the word 'all' relate in the clause 'I give every thing else to be equally divided among all'? The testatrice had 6 children—but[4] in her will names only three of her children.

MS (MHi); written entirely in TJ's hand on a ragged scrap; undated; with calculations in TJ's hand on verso.

TJ's MOTHER'S WILL, which contained perplexing ambiguities despite its brevity, reads as follows: "I Jane Jefferson of the

County of Albemarle do make this my Last Will and Testament, in manner and form following, I give to my daughter Anna Scott my 2 Negroes Lucinda old Sals daughter an Belin Jacks daughter sharlott, I give to my Son Randolph, my two negroes Simon old sals Son and Sirus Little Sals Son, I give to my daughter Elizabeth all my wearing Apparel, with one good bed an furniture, Every thing Else I give to my Executor, to be Equally divided Among all, perhaps there May be Some debts I am not Apprized of, and Lastly I do Constitute my Son Thomas Jefferson my Sole Executor, and Legatee of whatever Else I have power to dispose of" (Tr in Albemarle County Will Book, II, 367, Albemarle County Circuit Court Clerk's Office, Charlottesville; entirely in the hand of county clerk John Nicholas, with John Huckstep and William Henderson listed as witnesses; undated; at head of text in margin: "Jeffersons Will"; with subjoined note attested by Nicholas: "At Albemarle October Court 1778 This Will was proved by the Oath of One Witness thereto and Ordered to be Recorded; and upon the motion of Thomas Jefferson the Executor therein named who made Oath According to Law, Certificate is granted him for obtaining a Certificate in due form, whereupon he gave bond with Security and Acknowledged it Accordingly"). The appraisal of the estate inventory is in same, 356.

[1] Digit reworked from "1."
[2] Digit reworked from "2."
[3] Digit reworked from "3."
[4] Preceding three words and digit interlined.

Notes on Executive Departments

[after 21 Mch. 1790]

Departmt.
of War . . . .
{ Regular troops
Militia
Pensioners
Posts
stores
Navy
Indian affairs

Department
of the Treasury. . . . .
{ Customs
Excises
other matters
of Revenue

Department
of State.
{

Domestic affairs {
qu. Light houses.
Custody of the seal
          records
              N.W.
subordinate govmts S.W.
Land office   Fed. terry.
Courts of justice qu.?
Weights & measures

Coinage
Post Office
Arts, Sciences.
Manufactures
Commerce. at home

Foreign affairs {
Commerce. abroad
Foreign affairs

MS (DLC: TJ Papers, 233: 41776); entirely in TJ's hand; undated.

The absence of the Department of the Navy, created in 1798, indicates that TJ drew this chart during his tenure as Secretary of State, when WAR, TREASURY, and STATE were the only existing executive departments, and other internal evidence suggests that he did so early in his tenure when the Department of State's lines of authority were still fluid.

It was undoubtedly soon after TJ took office as Secretary of State that he received from Tobias Lear, acting either at the President's behest or in response to a request by TJ, a document entitled "A List of such Officers as have been, or may be appointed by the President of the United States, by and with the advice and consent of the Senate" (MS in DLC: TJ Papers, 234: 42197-8; consisting of a three-page roster of offices in Lear's hand; undated, but written before 4 June 1790).

Marriage Certificate for
Louis Guillaume Otto and
America Francès de Crèvecoeur

New York, 13 Apr. 1790. Declaration by Father Nicolaus Burke, Pastor of St. Peter's Church, that Otto, the French chargé d'affaires to the United States, and Crèvecoeur, the daughter of St. John de Crèvecoeur, were married this day by him in a Roman Catholic ceremony in the presence of TJ and other witnesses. Signed by the groom, the bride, the bride's father, TJ and eleven other witnesses (Jeremiah Wadsworth, Jonathan Trumbull, Richard Morris, Antoine René Charles Mathurin de La Forest, Beaumanoir de La Forest, John Kean, S. Livingston Kean, Philip Livingston, William Seton, John Trumbull, and Mantel Duchoqueltz), and Burke, with subjoined signed statement by Vice-Consul General La Forest attesting that Burke was a Catholic priest.

MS (Gilder Lehrman Collection, on deposit NNP); 3 p.; in Latin, with La Forest's attestation in French; in a clerk's hand, except for signatures; endorsed in French.

From Sylvanus Bourne

New York, 19 Apr. 1790. Requests TJ to deliver officially to the President the enclosed memorial and to acquaint him with Bourne's qualifications for a diplomatic or consular appointment. His concern for the public good forbids him to solicit a particular post, but if he is appointed he will endeavor to merit the public's confidence.

RC (DLC: Washington Papers, Applications for Office); 1 p.; endorsed by TJ as received 19 Apr. 1790 and so recorded in SJL. Enclosure: Bourne to George Washington, New York, 19 Apr. 1790, requesting an appointment "in the Diplomatic or Consular System" and advising that the Secretary of State would "impart every official Communication relative to the subject of this Memorial" that his friends have induced him to present (RC in same).

The following letters also pertain to applications and recommendations for diplomatic or consular offices: (1) John M. Pintard to TJ, Madeira, 23 Jan. 1791, applying for consular appointment at Lisbon for himself or his partner Samuel Weston, a naturalized citizen of Massachusetts (RC in DLC: Washington Papers, Applications for Office; endorsed by TJ as received 7 Mch 1791 and so recorded in SJL). (2) Nathaniel Appleton to TJ, Boston, 22 Sep. 1791,

recommending his son Thomas, now on business in Paris, as consul at Lisbon (RC in same; at foot of text: "Honorable Thomas Jefferson Esqr Secretary of State"; endorsed by TJ as received 22 Oct. 1791 and so recorded in SJL). (3) Pierce Butler to TJ, "Ship Dellaware," 27 Mch. 1792, asking whether Major Franks, whose situation was far from satisfactory, could be placed on a better footing, with a postscript asking TJ at his leisure to "think of the Bristol Consul" (RC in DLC; endorsed by TJ as received 28 Mch. 1792 and so recorded in SJL). (4) Frederick Folger to TJ, Baltimore, 8 May 1792, applying for consular appointment to the Barbary States (RC in DLC: Washington Papers, Applications for Office; above salutation: "His Excellency Thomas Jefferson Esqr."; endorsed by TJ as received 2 June 1792 and so recorded in SJL). (5) Samuel Sterett to TJ, Baltimore, 31 May 1792, enclosing and endorsing No. 4 (RC in same; addressed:

"The Honble Tho. Jefferson Secretary of State Philada."; endorsed by TJ as received 2 June 1792 and so recorded in SJL). (6) Bourne to TJ, Philadelphia, 9 Jan. 1793, noting that the consular appointment at Cadiz they had discussed was impracticable under the existing consular law and asking TJ to consider him for another appointment (RC in same; at foot of text:

"The Secretary of State"; endorsed by TJ as received 9 Jan. 1793 and so recorded in SJL). (7) Thomas FitzSimons to TJ, Philadelphia, 6 Dec. 1793, recommending Michael M. O'Brien as consul in Guadeloupe (RC in same; at foot of text: "Thomas Jefferson Esqr"; endorsed by TJ as received 6 Dec. 1793 and so recorded in SJL).

To Alexander Hamilton

SIR   New York April 29th. 1790.

The amount of the last warrant for money for the contingent expences of the office for foreign affairs being laid out, I take the liberty to enclose an account of them, with the vouchers, and to request the favour of you to order a further sum of two hundred and fifty dollars for the contingent expences of the office of the Secretary of State. I have the honor to be &c.   (signed) THOMAS JEFFERSON

FC (Lb in DNA: RG 360, PCC, AL); at head of text: "To the Secretary of the Treasury." Not recorded in SJL. Enclosure not found.

Hamilton wrote a brief note to TJ from the Treasury Department on 30 Apr. 1790

enclosing a warrant he had issued in his favor for the amount requested and advising that he had submitted the ACCOUNT and VOUCHERS to "the Auditor for examination" (Tr in Lb in DNA: RG 360, PCC, AL; at head of text: "From The Secretary of the Treasury").

To Tench Coxe

Sunday. June 6. 1790.

Mr. Jefferson's compliments to Mr. Coxe: he [takes] the liberty of requesting him thro' Mr. Madison to [. . .] partake of his little dinner to-day. He shall be happy if Mr. Coxe can do it, and pardon his asking him to so unceremonious a one.

RC (PHi: Coxe Papers); upper right quadrant torn away; endorsed by Coxe. Not recorded in SJL.

The suggestion that TJ's LITTLE DINNER was probably connected in some way with

the ongoing negotiations over the residence and assumption questions has been advanced in Norman K. Risjord, "The Compromise of 1790: New Evidence on the Dinner Table Bargain," WMQ, 3d ser., XXXIII (1976), 309-14.

Petition of William Pollard to the Patent Board

Philadelphia, 29 June 1790. He represents that more than a year ago he purchased for several hundred pounds a model of Sir Richard Arkwright's "machine for Roving and Spinning of Cotton" that had been brought to this country at great risk and potentially heavy penalty, that a machine he built to small scale from the model would not work, either through poor workmanship in the model or by design, but that "having been bred in part a manufacturer and being some judge of Spinning and of yarn," he made alterations in it and has now perfected his own machine. Both the model and his own machine are ready for the board's inspection, so that they can see the "visible and material" differences between them, his own being able to work from twenty to twenty thousand spindles if adequate force is supplied. He quotes a statement from the Philadelphia *American Museum* of October 1788, "which from his knowedge of Manchester Cotton goods" he knows to be reasonable, showing that the cotton and wool spinning industry in Great Britain has more than tripled in value between 1781 and 1787 and yielded immense profits to laborers and mill and factory owners. In the southern states "young negroes and weakly and disabled Men and Women . . . at present a Burthen to their owners" may be advantageously employed in mills, as can "the poor white inhabitants in all our large towns." He believes that "to a certain extent" manufactures created with such machines can be produced as cheaply in America as England. One child from age eight to fourteen can tend thirty to fifty spindles, one adult can supervise ten children, and "no exertion of strength is required in the spinning apartment." Requesting a patent on the basis of the improvements incorporated into his machine, and wishing to encourage the use of something so important to the nation and to prove that he will not charge an extortionate rate, he will submit "to the consideration of the Board the price per spindle he shall demand," noting that Arkwright obtained five guineas per spindle during his patent and one guinea thereafter, that Kendrew & Porthouse sell a machine for spinning flax and long combed wool for twenty-four shillings sterling per spindle under a recent English patent, and that brass work costs more here than in England.

Tr (DNA: RG 241, Restored Patent Specifications); 3 p.; at head of text: "To the Honorable Thos Jefferson, Henry Knox, Edmd. Randolph Esqrs."; beneath signature: "Patent Office May 28th. 1836. The above is a true Copy of Petition and Drawing. Henry L. Ellsworth Superintendent"; at foot ot text: "Recd. & Recorded June 14, 1841."

This petition and the drawing Pollard submitted in connection with his application resulted in the issuance of a patent on 30

Dec. 1791 (Tr of drawing in DNA: RG 241, Restored Patent Drawings; undated; at head of text: "William Pollard ass. of Richard Arkwright. Spinning and Roving Cotton"; endorsed: "This is copied from a Certified Copy of a drawing attached to a Petition and Statement given by the Office, May 28 1836, in reference to the patent which was granted Dec 30 1791 and destroyed by the burning of the Patent Office"). See also Pollard to TJ, 26 June 1792, and note.

To William Temple Franklin

Tuesday July 6. 1790.

Mr. Jefferson has the honor to present his compliments to Mr. Franklin. He is here without furniture, without housekeeper and faisant très mauvaise chere. If Mr. Franklin is disengaged to-day, and will do him the favor to partake of his little meal without ceremony, it will be so much the more obliging. He dines at half past three pretty exactly.

RC (PPAmP). Not recorded in SJL.

Notes on Fresco Painting

[before 6 Aug. 1790]

Fresco painting.

The plaister is of the common composition and laid on in the common way, except the last coat which is half lime, half sand, not laid on too smooth.

If the last coat is put on early in the morning the painter can work on it all that day, and the next day, only moistening it occasionally with a brush and water.

Old plaistering can be painted, only hacking it so as to recieve a thin coat of plaister.

Schneider is a scene painter. He asks 1 dollar the sq. yard for ornamented parts let the design be what it will.

$1\frac{1}{4}$ dollar the square yard for plain blue or yellow
 because they require 3. coats. The other colours but one.

The colours are mixed with water only
 very thick

> vermilion (red), orpiment (yellow),[1] powder blue.
> patent-yellow also. The white is of lime alone
> The green is a mixture of yellow and blue.[2]

If laid on hard, it will rub up the plaister and look ill—must be laid on delicately.

The colours are very different when they are dried on the plaister, from what they appear in the pot. Therefore attention must be paid to this.[3]

Schneider would ask 2. dollars a day, and be found diet, lodging washing, colours, brushes &c:

He painted 6. square yards in about 12 hours; in which there was a landscape about 12 I. by 18.I. a pot of flowers 2.f. by 1.f. a column 5.f. high with a garland, 3 pannels of marble work, and 3. do. with border

MS (DLC: TJ Papers, 233: 41659); entirely in TJ's hand; undated, but written in two sittings (see note 3 below); endorsed by TJ: "Fresco painting."

Internal evidence suggests that TJ set down these notes around the time he employed Ignatius Shnydore to paint wall panels in his New York residence, probably no later than 6 Aug. 1790, when he paid the painter £5.12.10 for the work (MB, 6 Aug. 1790; TJ to Henry Remsen, 13, 25 Nov. 1792; Remsen to TJ, 19 Nov. 1792).

[1] This and the preceding parenthetical word interlined.
[2] Sentence interlined.
[3] Remainder of text written in a different ink.

From William Blount

SIR   Washington August 20th 1790

On the 18th Instant I had the Honor to receive your letter of the 1st. with the Inclosures. On the 24th I leave this for the ceded Territory of the United States South of the River Ohio from whence I will embrace the first Opportunity of Writing you after I have fixed my Residence. I now suppose it will not be far distant from Judge Campbell's. I am very happy to hear that friendly arrangements are like to take place with Colonel Mc.Gillivray and the Creek Chiefs, there will then be little or Nothing to apprehend from the other Tribes to the Southward. Would it not be best to direct lettres for me to the Care of the Governor of Virginia, he will have frequent Opportunities to forward them. I thank you for your Promise of a Copy of the Laws of the United States and shall be glad to receive it as early as conveniently may be. I have the Honor to be with great Respect Your most Obedient Humble Servant

WM. BLOUNT

RC (DNA: RG 59, SWT); at foot of text: "Thomas Jefferson esqr. Secretary of State"; endorsed by TJ as received 6 Oct. 1790 and so recorded in SJL.

Memorandums to Henry Remsen

[. . .][1] [fur]niture and servant arrive from Paris, either here or at Philadelphia, I will thank Mr. Remsen to do for me whatever may be necessary. If they arrive here, they may proceed to Philadelphia with the other things. Colo. Hamilton sais no duties will be demandeable for my furniture arriving. The servant with them will have an invoice to shew whether there is any thing but furniture.

The removal to be so as that every thing may be in Philadelphia by the

25th. of October, unless I direct otherwise from Philadelphia, from whence I will write as to the house they are to be deposited in.

I do not think it material to lay up wood before November.

I have nothing to do with the papers of the court of Appeals.

I am of opinion that the public papers, which, on account of their being originals, we do not trust by sea, will go as safely and with less injury by water to Amboy, thence to Bordentown by land, thence to Philadelphia by water, as they would by land altogether.

The $2\frac{1}{2}$ dozen green chairs to be sent to Richmond by Carey if he comes, or any other conveyance. They are to be addressed to Mr. James Brown merchant Richmond, for me. He will pay the freight. If no conveyance occurs, they may go with the other things to Philadelphia.

TH: JEFFERSON

Aug. 31. 1790.

P.S. Mr. Remsen is desired to pay my servants Francis and Matthew $8\frac{1}{2}$ dollars each on the last day of September.

MS (Facsimile in Charles Hamilton, Catalogue No. 57, 20 Apr. 1972, Lot 175); entirely in TJ's hand; consists of second page only, with extracts from first page supplied from catalogue (see note 1 below); at head of text according to catalogue: "*Memorandum.*"

This document was elicited by Memoranda from Remsen, [ca. 30 Aug. 1790], in Vol. 17: 379-81. Adrien Petit, the SERVANT TJ expected to ARRIVE FROM PARIS with his furniture, actually reached the United States in July 1791 (TJ to William Short, 12 Mch., 6 Apr. 1790; note to Short to TJ, 7 Nov. 1790; MB, 19 July 1791).

According to an account George Taylor, Jr., submitted to Remsen on TJ's behalf, the REMOVAL from New York included "7 Loads" of TJ's furniture that were transported from the wharf in Philadelphia to his new house at Market Street on 14 Oct. 1790 at a cost of 16/4 New York currency (MS in MHi; in Taylor's hand and signed by him; endorsed by Remsen). For Remsen's reim-bursement by TJ for this amount, which included the cartage of other goods, see Remsen's Account of Moving Expenses, [25 Nov. 1790].

[1] First page missing; the catalogue, describing it as including instructions for forwarding newspapers and mail, gives the following extracts on other subjects: "I do not know yet whether Matthew goes. With respect to Okie the doorkeeper, he may be told that the office is to be at my own house in Philadelphia, & consequently it would not be convenient for me to have a doorkeeper with a family."

"The office should be given up . . . if a tenant should offer for my house, my furniture must be removed to the office. If that also be let, ware-room somewhere must be hired."

"The letter of credit I leave for Mr. Remsen on the treasury will authorise him to receive, of my salary, what must pay . . . the expense." The "letter of credit" is TJ to Alexander Hamilton, 30 Aug. 1790.

From Samuel Clarke

Philadelphia, 2 Sep. 1790. Encloses a letter from Captain Nathaniel Cutting that will most probably advise TJ of a keg of seed rice he was given charge of by Cutting at St. Marc. At Captain Pultey's request he has lodged the rice here with the merchants James & Shoemaker subject to TJ's order.

RC (MHi); 1 p.; at foot of text: "Honorable Mr Jefferson"; endorsed by TJ as received 6 Sep. 1790 and so recorded in SJL. Enclosure: Nathaniel Cutting to TJ, 6 July 1790.

Samuel Clarke was a board merchant at 40 North Fifth Street in Philadelphia (Clement Biddle, *The Philadelphia Directory* [Philadelphia, 1791], 22).

From William Blount

26 Nov. 1790. North Carolina's militia law, which remains in force by the eighth article of the act of cession until repealed or altered by the territory's legislative authority, assigns a brigadier general to each district. John Sevier and Daniel Smith were the brigadiers for Washington and Mero districts, respectively, at the time the act was passed. Under the ordinance governing this territory, Congress appoints territorial officers above the rank of field officer. He therefore recommends that Sevier be reappointed for the district of Washington because of his "spirit judgement, experience," and that James Robertson, the colonel of Davidson County, who is "cool, brave and prudent," be appointed for the district of Mero, both men enjoying the confidence of the people. Daniel Smith is now secretary and would not accept reappointment as brigadier even if it were proper.

Tr (DNA: RG 46, Senate Records, 1st Cong., 3rd sess.); 1 p.; extract; at head of text: "Extract from a letter of Governor Blount to the secretary of State—dated 26th. November 1790." Recorded in SJL as received 23 Dec. 1790 from the "Southern territy."

On 17 Feb. 1791 Daniel Smith wrote TJ from "William Cobb's" in the Southwest Territory accepting his commission as territorial secretary "forwarded from your Office," and reporting that he had taken the requisite oaths and would soon send a copy of the governor's executive acts (RC in DNA: RG 59, SWT; at foot of text: "Thomas Jefferson Esquire Secretary of State"; endorsed by TJ as received 11 Mch. 1791 and so recorded in SJL; printed in *Terr. Papers*, IV, 46). John McNairy wrote TJ from the Southwest Territory on 7 Mch. 1791 accepting his commission as territorial judge and reporting that he had begun

to discharge his duties but that Peery, reportedly also appointed a judge, "is not come forward, nor have we any information from him" (RC in DNA: RG 59, SWT; at foot of text: "Thomas Jefferson Esquire"; printed in *Terr. Papers*, IV, 49; see Vol. 17: 293n). On 1 Sep. 1792 Smith wrote a brief note to TJ from Knoxville transmitting "another report of the acts of Governor Blount in his executive department" (RC in DNA: RG 59, SWT, at foot of text: "Thos. Jefferson Esquire Secretary of State," endorsed by TJ as received 4 Dec. 1792 and so recorded in SJL; Tr in DNA: RG 76, Yazoo Land Claims; printed in *Terr. Papers*, IV, 167). The enclosure was the Journal of the Executive Proceedings of Governor Blount of the Southwest Territory, 1 Mch.-29 July 1792, Tr in DNA: RG 59, SWT, in Smith's hand, endorsed by George Taylor, Jr.; Tr in DNA: RG 76, Yazoo Land Claims; printed in *Terr. Papers*, IV, 447-51).

From Tench Coxe

SIR   Novemr. 26th. 1790

I have the honor to inclose you a return of the piscatory articles exported from the United States in one year, one month, and ten days, excepting fourteen quarterly returns from twelve ports which have not yet been received. Among these are Boston, Newyork Charleston and five small ports of Massachusetts and Main. From the irregular Manner in which the first returns were made it was impossible to take the 30th. of September 1789 as the beginning, nor would the forms of the papers admit of a conclusion at August 1790.

On this return I beg leave to remark that about two thirds of our whole export in this branch is to the Dominions of France and that a conduct on the part of that nation similar to that of G. Britain would be almost a deadly blow to our fisheries. I am informed that a late regulation of G. Britain prohibits the importation of the produce of the fisheries, but cannot vouch for the truth of it. If unknown to you it is probably without foundation.

I do not find any mention of skins and furs, which certainly are obtained and imported, and therefore must have been blended, in the Custom house papers, with the skins and furs of land animals. I have the honor to be with the highest respect, Sir, your most obedient & most humble Servant   T. C.

It is further worthy of remark that the North Carolina returns do not begin till March nor those of Rhode Island till June. From the latter state the single quarterly return that is received, amounts to about 27,000 Dollars in Value.

Dft (PHi: Coxe Papers); above post-script: "The honorable Thomas Jefferson Esqr." Enclosure not found, but see Vol. 19: 224.

This letter and its enclosure, which had been promised in Coxe to TJ, [23 Nov. 1790], were part of his continuing effort to assist TJ in preparing his 1 Feb. 1791 report on the American fisheries (see Vol. 19: 140-237).

Memorandum to George Washington

[29 Nov. 1790]

A note of subjects, some of which the President may think proper to be mentioned to Congress.

Announce the location of the Federal seat, and measures taken in consequence of it.

The act of Independence of Kentucky, should it be authentically communicated to the President.

The ratifications of the amendments to the constitution by Jersey and Virginia (which last[1] may be expected before the meeting of Congress) which making three fourths of the states, consequently establishes them.

An Execution law is wanting to complete our compliance with the treaty of peace.

A law to regulate the exercise of jurisdiction permitted by foreign nations to our Consuls established within their dominions, and ascertaining their fees.

A law making the auxiliary provisions stipulated in the Consular convention with France.

Encouragement to American vessels and seamen. [with an eye to Gr. Britain.]

Protection to our navigation on the ocean. [with an eye to Algiers.]

The extreme want of a coin: and necessity of pursuing the establishment of a Coinage, and of uniformity in measures, weights and coins.

PrC (DLC: TJ Papers, 59: 10131); entirely in TJ's hand; undated; brackets in original. Recorded in SJPL under 29 Nov. 1790: "Subjects of speech to Congress."

In his 8 Dec. 1790 message at the opening of the third session of the First Congress, the President mentioned all of the subjects suggested by TJ except the LOCATION OF THE FEDERAL SEAT, which he chose to announce on 24 Jan. 1791 in a separate message drafted for him by TJ, and the RATIFICATIONS of the Bill of Rights by New Jersey and Virginia, the first of which Washington had already transmitted to Congress on 6 Aug. 1790 and the second of which was not in fact completed until late in 1791 (Fitzpatrick, Writings, XXXI, 164-9; President to the Senate and House of Representatives, [24 Jan. 1791], in Vol. 19: 64; JS, I, 201, 340, 361). Washington obtained a similar list of suggested topics from Secretary of the Treasury Alexander Hamilton (Syrett, Hamilton, VII, 107-8, 172-3).

In an earlier volume the Editors mistakenly identified the SJPL entry for this document as Jefferson's Draft of Items for the President's Message to Congress, which is printed conjecturally under 29 Nov. 1790 in Vol. 18: 99-100, but actually listed separately in SJPL under 3 Dec. 1790 as "paragraphs proposed for speech." Washington had elicited these two draft paragraphs in a missing letter to TJ of 3 Dec. 1790 (see Vol. 18: 100n).

[1] Word interlined.

From Michael Jenifer Stone, with Jefferson's Note

[*Philadelphia*], *23 Dec. 1790.* He presents his friend Mr. Hobson from New York, who will request a passport from this place to England for Gilbert Morewood, who intends to sail in a British vessel and seeks protection in case of war between England and Spain. Hobson says that Morewood is a United States citizen. Although he forgets the particulars, he has understood the same from information received at New York, and he presumes that Hobson can ascertain Morewood's right to citizenship. He is acquainted with and highly respects both Hobson and Morewood and knows them to be of totally unexceptionable character. He does not know if TJ has the power to act in this business, but hopes he will give Hobson such information as may facilitate Morewood's object. [*Note by TJ:*] "Mr. Remsen will be pleased to make out a passport for the above. Th: Jefferson."

RC (DNA: RG 59, Certificates of Naturalization); 3 p.; addressed: "The Honble Mr. Jefferson"; with TJ's note subjoined; notation by Henry Remsen at foot of text: "Gilbert Morewood."

Michael Jenifer Stone (1747-1812), a lawyer of Charles County, Maryland, was a member of the United States House of Representatives, 1789-91 (Edward C. Papenfuse and others, *A Biographical Dictionary of the Maryland Legislature, 1635-1789*, 2 vols. [Baltimore, 1979-85], II, 785-6).

From Nathan Read

SIR   Salem Jany. 8th. 1791.

Having improved some of the machines, for which, last winter, I solicited a Patent, and desirous, after farther improvement, of communicating others to the public; also informed that some of my supposed improvements in the distillery particularly the application of the Syphon, had been suggested several years since, to the late President of the American Academy; and not wishing for an exclusive privilege to any improvement that is not new; I must request your Excellency to solicit the Honorable Board to grant me leave to withdraw my former petitions, paying all charges that have arisen, and to present[1] the inclosed petition in which I have stated, agreable to the Order of the Honorable Board the nature and extent of the discoveries therein mentioned. I forwarded last week to Mr. Remsen Models of several machines, drafts and descriptions of which are inclosed. The model of the Boiler which I have forwarded is an improvement upon one of those I exhibited last winter. The model I refer to consists of several annular vessels placed one above another within the furnace in such a manner as to expose a very large surface directly to the fire. For annular vessels, placed in a horizontal position, I have substituted circular tubes, placed in a vertical position, within the furnace which is formed by the Boiler itself in the same manner as the other was. In the last boiler which is stronger, more simple and elegant in its construction I have paid less regard to the evaporating surface than in either of the others; finding by experiment, that the principle of evaporation suggested by your Excellency is perfectly just when applied to close vessels. I am sensible that a pipe was several years since, made use of by Mr. Rumsey for generating steam and also perceive, from the Philosophical Transactions that a tube, in the form of the worm of a Still, was used upwards of twenty years ago for the same purpose, but do not know that any other person but myself hath ever constructed a tubular Boiler, formed in such a manner as to constitute of itself a compleat furnace. It is about three years since I first projected a boiler upon this plan. How far my improvements merit an exclusive privilege the Honorable Board will judge. Should a Patent be granted, I request it may be delivered to Benja. Goodhue Esqr. who will pay Mr. Remsen all charges that have arisen or may arise in consequence of my applications. I have requested Mr. Remsen, by permission of the Honorable Board to inclose me my former petitions, and to deliver to my order several models which have too long encumbered your Office. I am with the sincerest respect your Excellency's most obedient servant   NATHAN READ

FC (MSaE: Read Papers); at foot of text: "His Excellency Gov. Jefferson." Enclosures: (1) Petition of Read to the Patent Board, Salem, 1 Jan. 1791, describing and requesting patents for four inventions: a method of distilling at reduced labor and expense that freed the resulting spirits from the noxious metallic taint found in those produced in the common way; a more efficient, compact, and portable steam boiler; a more portable steam cylinder capable of operating in a horizontal position; and a chain wheel or rowing machine operating on the principle of the chain pump and capable of impelling steamboats through the water with great speed; and requesting permission to withdraw his former petitions upon paying any fees that had already arisen (FC in same; FC in same, undated and unsigned). (2) Read's "Specification of an Improvement in the Art of Distillation," with drawings and explanatory key, "Specification of an Improved Steam Boiler," "Specification of a chain Wheel, or Rowing Machine for Impelling boats or vessels thro' the water," and "Specification of an Improved Steam Cylinder, advantageously constructed to work in an horizontal posi-

tion," with drawings (FCs in same, undated; Dfts in same, undated, consisting of last two specifications only; with accompanying draft certifications prepared for Read by Henry Remsen on 23 Apr. 1791 containing subjoined instructions for filing the specifications and Read's fair copies of the certifications).

Nathan Read (1759-1849), a Harvard graduate and apothecary in Salem, Massachusetts, was unable to raise funds to build a steamboat and turned to farming and iron manufacturing, later serving in the United States House of Representatives from 1800 to 1803 (DAB; David Read, *Nathan Read: His Invention of the Multi-Tubular Boiler and Portable High-Pressure Engine* . . . [New York, 1870]).

Read had SOLICITED patents from Congress for a variety of inventions in a petition read by the House of Representatives on 8 Feb. 1790, and evidently discussed his inventions with TJ when he delivered a letter of introduction on 22 Mch. (JHR, I, 154; Joseph Willard to TJ, 16 Jan. 1790, and note; TJ to Willard, 1 Apr. 1790, and note). After statutory authority to grant patents was transferred to the Patent Board, Read sent his FORMER PETITIONS of 14 and 23 Apr. 1790 to that body, with the earlier one seeking patents for the distilling apparatus, steam boiler, and steam cylinder described above and the later one asking for exclusive rights to the chain wheel as well as ideas for a "new and simple method of moving land carriages by the power of steam, and also of directing them principally by the same agent" and a way to use the temperature-induced contraction and expansion of metals to build self-winding timepieces and scientific apparatus (FCs and Dfts in MSaE: Read Papers). Read subsequently abandoned his efforts to patent the latter two inventions (Henry Remsen to Read, 5 Feb. 1791, and Read to Remsen, 10 May 1791, same). On 26 Aug. 1791 he was awarded one patent for his distilling improvements and another for his steam boiler, steam cylinder, and chain wheel (Trs in same, with Washington as signatory and TJ as countersignatory; List of Patents, 5).

James Bowdoin was the LATE PRESIDENT OF THE AMERICAN ACADEMY of Arts and Sciences. The reference to the PHILOSOPHICAL TRANSACTIONS is probably to Peter Woulfe, "Experiments on the Distillation of Acids, volatile Alkalies, &c. shewing how they may be condensed without Loss, and how thereby we may avoid disagreeable and noxious Fumes," Royal Society of London, *Philosophical Transactions*, LVII (1767), 517-36.

[1] Manuscript: "prevent."

Petition of Ezekiel Hall to the Patent Board

Boston, 11 Jan. [*1791-93*]. Having inherited a Boston distillery upon the death of his father Ezekiel in 1789, and with it a method invented by him in 1774 whereby "Brandy equal in quality to foreign brandy, or to brandy distilled from wine or other materials, might be produced with very great advantage, from common rum, by distillation only," he requests a patent for the process, which they have both used successfully, and will submit a full specification and comply with any other legal requirements.

MS (Gilder Lehrman Collection: Henry Knox Papers, on deposit NNP); 3 p.; in Hall's hand; partially dated; water stained and torn at seal; at head of text: "To The Hon[orable] [. . .] Jefferson Esqr secretary of State, the Honorable [Henry Knox Esqr] Secretary at War, and the Honorable [. . .] [Randolph?] Esqr Attorney General of the United States."

The presence of this petition in Henry Knox's papers suggests that the Secretary of War refrained from presenting it to the Patent Board. Hall did not receive a patent (*List of Patents*).

From James Madison

[ca. 11 Jan. 1791]

T. J. to J. M.	Dr.
To advances for him on the road to Philada.	£14–5–6
To Horse	

Credit	By 50 dollars	£18–15–

	Balance to T.J.	£4–9–6 Pa. Curry.

If the intended charge of £25. for the Horse is not cancelled by the presumptive evidence that he was not sound at the time of sending him, the balance will lie on the other side. The scruples of J. M. on this point are not affected, and are enforced by his having discovered after the death of the Horse from the servant who accompanied Mr. J. that on his return the Horse was taken very sick and drenched, and from the symptoms mentioned it can scarcely be doubted that the malady must have been the prelude of that which proved fatal. To get rid of all embarrassment on either side, J. M. thinks it essential that a common friend should hear and decide the case, and for that purpose insists that it be stated to such an one[1] by both, on the first convenient occasion. Mr. Hawkins occurs as an eligible umpire. The map and 1st. chapter of the Magazine seem to contain Pond's Western discoveries and are curious.

RC (DLC: Madison Papers); undated; endorsed by TJ:

"Madison James

⟨D

Virga curry	£25	= 83.33
Pennsylva do	4–9–6 =	11.93
		95.26⟩."

This letter must have been written between those from Madison to TJ of 10 and 12 Jan. 1791. TJ's endorsement reveals that the analysis by the Editors in the note to the latter is erroneous. As the Madison biographers contradicted there had correctly argued, TJ mistakenly added when he should have subtracted the sum Madison owed him for ADVANCES . . . ON THE ROAD to the amount he owed Madison FOR THE HORSE, and Madison's refund of $23.26 came after rather than before TJ's payment of $95.26. See also MB, 12 Jan. 1791.

The WESTERN DISCOVERIES of Peter Pond, the American fur trader and explorer, including an erroneous description of a Northwest water passage to the Pacific, were described in extracts from an anonymous letter dated Quebec, 7 Nov. 1789, and an accompanying "Map shewing the communication of the Lakes and the Rivers between Lake Superior and Slave Lake in North America," both of which appeared in the *Gentleman's Magazine*, LX (1790), 197-9, and were reprinted in the *New-York Magazine; or, Literary Repository*, I (1790), 677-80. See also Grace L. Nute, "A Peter Pond Map," *Minnesota History*, XIV (1933), 81-4.

[1] Preceding four words interlined.

To Albert Gallatin

Philadelphia. Jan. 14. 1791.

Th: Jefferson presents his compliments to Mr. Gallatin. This letter comes to him, as others have done, from Mr. Tronchin Minister for Geneva at Paris. Th: Jefferson will with pleasure on all occasions give a conveyance of Mr. Gallatin's letters through the same channel, putting them into his dispatches to our Chargé des affaires at Paris.

RC (NHi: Gallatin Papers); written on address cover of Catherine Pictet and Abraham Trembley to Gallatin, 1 Sep. 1790, which was sent from Geneva "To the Care of Mr Robert Morris Philadelphia." See Vol. 25: 93n.

From John Woodward

Bordentown, 1 Feb. 1791. In view of TJ's 1 Dec. 1790 letter, which arrived yesterday, he wishes to be informed of openings in any federal department other than the Department of State.

RC (DLC: Washington Papers, Applications for Office); 1 p.; endorsed by TJ as received 9 Feb. 1791 and so recorded in SJL.

The following letters also pertain to applications or recommendations for miscellaneous federal offices: (1) Allan B. Magruder to TJ, Georgetown, 1 Nov. 1791, reminding him of his promise to ascertain whether there were any clerical openings in the Treasury or War Departments (RC in DLC: Washington Papers, Applications for Office; endorsed by TJ as received 3 Nov. 1791 and so recorded in SJL). (2) Arthur Emmerson to TJ, Portsmouth, Virginia, 25 Nov. 1791, recommending the claims of the bearer, Thomas Wishart, and applying for the chaplain's appointment at the marine hospital there (RC in MHi; endorsed by TJ as received 29 Nov. 1791 and so recorded in SJL). (3) TJ to George Washington, 7 July 1792, enclosing David Meade Randolph's 30 June 1792 letter recommending John Waller Johnston as keeper of the Cape Henry lighthouse (RC in DNA: RG 59, MLR; addressed: "The President of the United States"; endorsed by Tobias Lear; not recorded in SJL; see also Vol. 24: 708n). (4) Daniel Gaines to TJ, Wilkes County, Georgia, 22 Nov. 1792, recommending Captain Peleg Greene as commander of an additional cutter to cruise off the coasts of Georgia and South Carolina (RC in DLC: Washington Papers, Applications for Office; endorsed by TJ as received 29 Dec. 1792 and so recorded in SJL). (5) Arthur Emmerson to TJ, Portsmouth, Virginia, 15 Dec. 1792, applying for the chaplain's appointment at the marine hospital in Washington, Virginia, and recommending Bevard Jones as steward there (RC in same; endorsed by TJ as received 1 Jan. 1793 and so recorded in SJL). (6) Samuel Sterett to TJ, Baltimore, 8 Aug. 1793, soliciting TJ's support for his letter of this date to the President applying for the surveyorship of the port of Baltimore (RC in same; at foot of text: "Tho. Jefferson, Esq."; endorsed by TJ as received 10 Aug. 1793 and so recorded in SJL).

From Tobias Lear

United States, *5 Feb. 1791*. Transmits by the President's command for deposit in the Secretary of State's office "the Return of the enumeration of the Inhabitants of Massachusetts District" made to the President by the marshal of that district.

PrC (DNA: RG 59, MLR); 1 p. FC (Lb in same, SDC).

Lear also wrote a note to TJ on 7 Mch. 1792 transmitting "a return of the inhabitants in each County and town of Kentucky" made to the President by the marshal (RC in DLC: Washington Papers, Applications for Office, endorsed by Henry Remsen as received 7 Mch. 1792; Dft in DNA: RG 59, MLR; FC in Lb in same, SDC). See also note to Report on Census, 24 Oct. 1791.

To James Brown

DEAR SIR   Philadelphia Feb. 9. 1791.

The trouble of the inclosed commission I have been willing to impose in the first place on my friend D. Hylton. If therefore he is at home, I will beg the favor of you to stick a wafer in the letter and send it to him. But as I know he sometimes takes long journies, and I am anxious to have done what I have therein desired, I must in that case ask the favour of you to do what I did not mean to trouble you with if Mr. Hylton was in the way. The letter to him is left open on purpose, and the order for the 20 hhds. of tobacco names you in the case of his absence.   I also trouble you with a letter to Capt. Colley of the brig Clermont at City point, because it contains a remittance, and I know not how 'otherwise to get the letter safely to his hands. I am with great esteem Dear Sir Your friend & servt   TH: JEFFERSON

RC (ViU); at foot of text: "Mr. James Brown." Enclosures: (1) TJ to Daniel L. Hylton, 9 Feb. 1791. (2) TJ to Nathaniel Colley, 9 Feb. 1791.

To David Ross

[6 May 1791]

[Nor] are there any alterations in the Observations but what the change of these articles in the Accounts rendered necessary. I made the change because I wished that the minds of the arbitrators should have as little embarrasment from the beginning as possible. I have now to propose to you that this matter be decided by three of the judges, and I would propose the three eldest, without knowing which they are, excepting however Mr. Wythe, whose friendship for me I would not embarras by a reference of this kind. I do not think it can be decided till I return to Virginia in September, because the papers are there which will be essential to the decision. I neither wish to attend personally, nor shall attend. Indeed I presume the whole papers must be taken into the country by the arbitrators to be examined at their leisure at their homes. In the mean time should you wish to make any new obervations on my Reply, I shall be glad to have them to consider of in time before the arbitration. I am Sir Your very humble servt.   TH: JEFFERSON

PrC (ViU: Edgehill-Randolph Papers); consists of second page only; first page printed in Vol. 20: 373, with last word omitted there being supplied here; at foot of first page: "Mr. Ross."

From Alexander Martin

SIR   North Carolina May 10th. 1791
    I have been duly favoured with your Letter of March 26th. last respecting the line that forms the eastern boundary of the Cession of this State to Congress and the private claims within the Cession which form exceptions to their general right of granting the ceded Territory. I have not by me any immediate Map of the Western Country ceded to Congress otherwise with pleasure I should transmit it for your information. The Act of cession points out the line by what mountains and water courses it is bounded, but the several distances between the stations, the direction of the mountains and Water courses through that Country the extent of Land along and between them and the quality thereof have not been laid down with precision on any regular Chart I have seen. Governer Blount who is on the spot perhaps could give you more satisfactory communication as to the military and other Claims. I have given directions to the Secretary of the State and Colo. Armstrong to make returns of all the perticular entries with the Locations in their respective offices which when made out I shall forward on immediately, there will be some difficulty in assertaining the Locations of the entered Land in Armstrongs office not being confined to perticular districts interspersed thro' that Country from 5000 to 100 Acres in a Tract. Many are on the Mississippi, the Chicasaw Bluff, Wolf River, Tenasse and its Waters and the Cumberland: the military Claims are perticularly reserved on the Cumberland The Grant to General Greene on Duck River the Waters of Tenasse. I will endeavor to give you further information shortly and shall be happy to be servicable to you in the business required of you by Congress if in my power. In the meantime I have the honor to be with very great respect & esteem Sir, Your most Obedient humble Servant   ALEX. MARTIN

FC (Nc-Ar: Governor's Letterbook); at foot of text: "The Honble. Thomas Jefferson Esquire Secretary &c." Recorded in SJL as received 1 July 1791.

LETTER OF MARCH 26TH. LAST: see note to TJ to William Blount of that date.

On 20 May 1791 Martin wrote TJ that, "not then being in the Union," North Carolina had not been sent "authenticated Copies of the Acts of the first Session of Congress," and requested that they be forwarded, remarking that "As those Acts are now to be observed by this State a full Authentication of them appears to be necessary particularly of the Act prescribing the oath to be taken to the federal Government which the officers of this State have not taken, by reason of the same not having more than a Newspaper Authenticity" (RC in DNA: RG 59, LGS; at foot of text: "The Honourable Thomas Jefferson Esquire"; endorsed by TJ as received 1 July 1791 and so recorded in SJL). TJ's response to both letters from Martin is dated 2 July 1791.

John Stevens to the Patent Board

[*10 May 1791*]. He enumerates "improvements respecting the generation of steam and the application thereof to different purposes," including two types of boilers, an improvement of Savery's machine for raising water, a method of using steam to work a "forcing pump" to supply a boiler with water, and new techniques for raising water and working bellows using steam-driven pistons which he has invented and for which he has requested patents in a petition addressed to the board.

Dft (NjHi: Stevens Family Papers); 3 p.; fragmentary text, with conclusion supplied from Archibald D. Turnbull, *John Stevens: An American Record* (New York, 1928), 111; addressed: "To the Hon: Thomas Jefferson Esquire Secretary of State Henry Knox Esquire Secretary at War and Edmund Randolph Esquire attorney General Commissioners for granting Patents"; endorsed by Stevens: "Description of Improvements &c Letter to Mr. Jefferson."

On 8 Feb. 1790 the House of Representatives had read a petition from Stevens asking Congress for a patent for "an improvement on the steam engine, which he has invented, by a new mode of generating steam" (JHR, I, 154). After the Patent Board was established Stevens sought a patent from that body. He wrote Henry Remsen, the board's clerk, from Hoboken on 20 Apr. 1791, stating that he was constructing a steam engine to propel a boat and therefore wished to know the result of his application for a patent (NjHi: Stevens Family Papers). The present list of his inventions was elic- ited by Remsen's response of 4 May 1791, explaining that the board had abandoned its efforts to decide between the conflicting claims of James Rumsey and John Fitch for a steamboat patent and "at a late meeting agreed to grant patents to them—and to all claimants of steam patents—according to their respective specifications," enclosing an incomplete patent he had drafted based on Stevens's specification, noting that the specification was silent regarding some of his claims, and requesting a "description of your several improvements" (Turnbull, *Stevens*, 109-10). Stevens duly received three patents dated 26 Aug. 1791 for these inventions (*List of Patents*, 5; Tobias Lear to TJ, with List of Patents, 30 Aug. 1791, printed below; patent for two types of steam boiler and a method of propelling boats using steam power, Tr in NjHoS, with George Washington as signatory, TJ as countersignatory, and certification by Edmund Randolph, consisting of later transcription of copy certified 10 May 1814 by James Monroe).

To Pierre Guide

[*Ed. Note*: This letter, printed in Vol. 24: 246-7 under its inscribed date of 21 July 1792, was in fact written from Monticello on 21 July 1791 and recorded in SJL under that date. Guide's letter of 28 July 1791, summarized in Vol. 20: 685, is clearly a reply to this epistle.]

Petition of Henry Voigt to the Patent Board

[*Before 10 Aug. 1791*]. He requests a patent for his "easy method of propelling Boats and other Vessels through the water by the power of Horses or cattle, whereby their strength may be applied nearly as well as that of a man at an Oar, which of course will reduce the price of inland navigation nearly as much as the labour of Horses is cheaper than that of Men."

Tr (DP: Scientific Library, Propulsion of Vessels, 1791-1810); 1 p.; undated; at head of text: "To the Honourable the Secretary of State, the Secretary at War, and the Attorney General"; with accompanying notation by Nicholas King that he copied it and the supporting documents described below in July 1811 from the originals in the Patent Office of the Department of State; and another notation in the margin by Robert Schuyler indicating that he had received these texts from the heirs of Robert Fulton in 1841.

In compliance with the 1790 patent law, on 10 Aug. 1791, in exchange for his patent, Voigt transmitted to the Secretary of State a specification for his boat propelled by "Horses or Cattle working cranks or wheels which Act on Paddles not before known or used" (Tr in DP: Scientific Library, Propulsion of Vessels, 1791-1810; subjoined to Tr of petition summarized above; conjoined with Trs of Voigt's undated "Description of a Boat or Boats to be propelled by Horses or any Cattle" and two undated drawings of the invention; first drawing reproduced in Prager, *Fitch*, 201). Voigt's patent for "Propelling boats by cattle" was dated 10 Aug. 1791 (*List of Patents*, 5).

Voigt had been employed by John Fitch to help construct his steamboat, and later this year Fitch alleged that Voigt's invention had in fact been his own idea (Prager, *Fitch*, 118, 120, 201, 203-4).

From Thomas Leiper

SIR   Philadelphia 16th August 1791

I have yours of this date, and observe the Contents.

Inclosed you have my Note in your favor for 400 dollars, payable 45 days after date. I have examined my account of Building, and cannot exactly ascertain from my own principles, what the rent should be, as there are a number of accounts unsettled, and as they have along exceeded my estimates, what I have already settled, I suppose what are to come will be in the same line.

But as you want to have the house rent, and the other buildings fixed, I will let you have the house for Two hundred and ten pounds the stable Twenty five pounds, and the Book room fifteen pounds in all Two hundred and fifty pounds annually, the rent of the Book Room and stable to commence when they are finished, the house January 7th. 1792 and this rent I know is not six per Cent. And that there may be no misunderstanding in future I will mention what other improvements I intend to make. I intend to have a stone pavement of hewn stone. The steps to the back building will be of hewn stone. The Book room will be finished with a plain wooden stair down to the Garden, a Brick wall from the Book room to the stable, Also the Brick and stone[1] of the house you mentioned in the Garden you obliging yourself to pay the Carpenters work and all other Bills. An answer to the above soon will much oblige sir your most obedient serv   TL.

P.S. I have reason to believe from what passed between Mr. Cassinovi and me I shall get more rent from him, when I informed him I had made a mistake in the leting of my houses he said he would consider it and when he takes into view that he can get $7\frac{1}{2}$ ℔ Cent for Money in our Bank and perhaps more in the National he will be sensible that 6 ℔Cent is not too much for houses. I am as above yours &c.   TL

FC (Lb in Leiper Papers, Friends of Thomas Leiper House, on deposit PPL); at head of text: "The Honble Thomas Jefferson." Recorded in SJL as a 16 Aug. 1791

letter received 15 Aug. 1791. Enclosure not found.

[1] Leiper here canceled "and Building."

From James Madison

DEAR SIR   N. Y. Augst. 16. 91.

Since I learnt that you are not to start for Virginia till the beginning of next month, I have been less in a hurry to shift myself to Philada. from this place, which I have reason to believe the more favorable of the two, at this season, to my health, as well as the more agreeable in the present state of the weather. I now propose to suspend my departure till monday next, and have therefore to ask the favor of you if this should get to hand in time, to forward any letters you may have received for me, by friday's mail.

You intimated some time ago that one of your horses was ill and might retard the journey to Virga. Mine is now recovered, and can take his place. Matthew, whom I have no desire to carry with me, will remain in Philada. till my return.

I just hear that the British packet is arrived. From the time of her passage, she can bring nothing new; nor is any thing of that sort supplied here from any other quarter. Adieu My dear Sir, Yrs. affely:

Js. MADISON JR.

RC (DLC: Madison Papers); endorsed by TJ as received 18 Aug. 1791 and so recorded in SJL.

From Thomas Mann Randolph, Jr.

DEAR SIR   Richmond August 22. [1791] 2 h. p. m.

The Satisfaction my Fathers Success gives me, makes me communicate it to you. Colo. Harvey lies dangerously ill. I am Dear Sir your affectionate friend & devoted Servant   T. M. RANDOLPH

RC (Thomas A. Lingenfelter, Doylestown, Pennsylvania, 1994); partially dated; addressed: "Thomas Jefferson Secretary of State Philadelphia"; stamped and postmarked; endorsed by TJ as received 27 Aug. 1791 and so recorded in SJL.

This note probably covered Randolph's letter to TJ written at Tuckahoe earlier this day. Thomas Mann Randolph, Sr., achieved SUCCESS in his bid for election to the Virginia Senate (see Vol. 22: 60-1).

Thomas FitzSimons's Notes on Jefferson's Draft Report on Commerce

[23 Aug. 1791]

Spain

Besides the Articles Enumerated Receives for her own Consumption a Considerable quantity of Rice.

Portugal

The prohibitions on Meals and Rice does not extend to Madeira, or the Azores, where they are Received freely.

Great Britain

Tobacco and Rice are the Articles principally Reexported.

The United Netherlands

Besides their Islands, have Colonys on the Main—Surinam, Demarara, &c. To these the produce of the US. are freely admitted—but the export is limited to Melasses, and Rum.

Negroes are admitted, for a limitted term at the port of Havana, in Vessells of any Nation and Any Article the produce of the Island of Cuba may be exported in Such Vessells. Several from Rhode Island, has been there in the present Year with Slaves from Africa—and many from Virginia and Maryland—with Slaves from those States.

In India—

The Vessells of all Nations are Admitted—at the places held by the British, and may trade there in payment of a dutie of 10 ⅌Ct. on Import and Export.

The United Netherlands exclude the Vessells of the US. from the port of Batavia, while those of the European nations are admitted.

MS (DLC: TJ Papers, 65: 11313); in FitzSimons's hand, except for the last nine words, which TJ undoubtedly copied from the missing final page, and two check marks TJ made in the left margin next to the notes on Spain and Portugal; undated; endorsed by TJ: "Mr. Fitzsimmons's notes." Enclosed in FitzSimons to TJ, 23 Aug. 1791.

For the changes TJ made to the first state of his Report on Commerce in response to FitzSimons's memorandum, see notes 9 and 16 to Document I of a group of documents on the report, printed above under 16 Dec. 1793.

From Benjamin Bourne

[after 26 Aug. 1791]

The Preceding are extracts of Letters from Capt. Benjn. Peirce of New port Rhode Island who has commanded a Ship in the Trade to Denmark for several Years and is very respectable in his line and in much repute for his Knowledge in that trade.   B BOURN

RC (DLC: TJ Papers, 236: 42322); undated, but undoubtedly written after TJ to John Ross, 26 Aug. 1791; subjoined to enclosure; endorsed by TJ: "Denmark Pierce's informn."

Benjamin Bourne, a congressman from

Rhode Island, proffered this letter and its enclosure in connection with the preparation of TJ's Report on Commerce, which was at length submitted to Congress on 16 Dec. 1793. See note 33 to Document I of a group of documents on the report, printed above under that date.

ENCLOSURE

Extracts from Benjamin Peirce's Letters on Trade with Denmark

[1791]

There have been landed in Copenhagen from American Ships 650 Hhds. of Tobacco and 1200 Tierces of Rice annually for five years—Tobacco subject to a natural duty of one half penny ⅌ ℔., and the additional duty of Aliens of one farthing ⅌ ℔.

The Rice to a natural duty of 3/6 ⅌ Cwt. and the duty of Aliens of 1/9 ⅌ Cwt.

Upon my Arrival in Denmark in the year 1785, I petitioned the Chamber of Customs to remit the extra duty which was granted in consequence of the Cargo's being the first landed in that Kingdom from an American.

In the year 1786 I again made the same request and was answered "That the

Court of Denmark had never received any official Letters from the United States and until they did, they should look upon Us as Aliens and require the duty."[1]

650 Hhds Tobacco at 1000 ℔s each, is 65000 ℔s—duty at ½ ℔.		£1354.3.4.
Duty of Aliens	£677. 1.8.	
1200 Casks of Rice @ 450 ℔s. is 54000 ℔s. at 3/6 ℔ Cwt.		945.
		2299.3.4.
Duty of Aliens	472.10.	
	1149.11.8.	

By the above statement which is moderate there is a tax on the American Merchants of £1149.11.8. sterling that the Merchants of Europe are not subject to, which enables them to undersell us in the Articles of Rice and Tobacco, the extra duty amounting to a freight; and is one sixth part of the first cost of the Tobacco and Rice.
There was landed in Copenhagen this present year (1791)—800 Hhds. Tobacco from London in British Ships.   BENJA. PEIRCE

"The Duty on Indigo I have forgot but Remember that with the aliens duty it amounts to a Prohibition, of this I will write you from Newport where my Papers are. Corn an Article of Attention, as Denmark scarcely ever produces a Sufficiency, is under the same predicament. Rum and other American Manufactures are entered for exportation and pay only a poor tax which is inconsiderable. The Demand for tobacco and Rice is increasing. To the eligible situation of Copenhagen to supply the orders of the Ports on the Baltic which would all be supplied by American Ships if the extra duty was taken off which I make no doubt would be effected by the appointment of a Consul General and official Letters from America to the Court of Denmark.

The Gentleman Mr. Clark mentioned to you is Hans Rodolph Saabye esquire of Copenhagen. He is possessed of great commercial abilities and integrity, indeed he is the first mercantile character I ever Knew and at the head of the first commercial house in the Kingdom. I believe he would Accept of the appointment of Consul General in the North of Europe, who will naturally reside at Copenhagen; I have tack'd *General* to the Consular Appointment thinking it may charm a german who, I am certain, if he Accepts, will be of Infinite service to the Commercial Interests of America."

Tr (DLC: TJ Papers, 236: 42321-2); undated; with subjoined extract in Benjamin Bourne's hand.

[1] Closing quotation mark supplied.

From Nathaniel Irish

Philadelphia, 27 Aug. 1791. Requests his commission and a certificate from Richard Peters, which he submitted to Congress in 1785 with a petition and other papers, so that he can present them to the Paymaster General's office. He will return them to TJ's office after the Paymaster General is finished with them.

RC (DNA: RG 59, MLR); 1 p.; addressed: "The Honble. Thomas Jefferson Secretary to Congress"; penciled notation by TJ below signature: "If the above papers are such as may be parted with under the rules of the office, Mr. Remsen will be pleased to deliver them, taking a receipt. Th: Jefferson"; endorsed by Henry Remsen as received 26 Aug. 1791.

From Tobias Lear, with List of Patents

Augt. 30th. 1791.

The fifteen enclosed Patents, having received the signature of the President of the United States, are, at the request of the Attorney General, transmitted to the Office of the Secretary of State by

TOBIAS LEAR
Secretary to the President
of the United States

[*Note by Lear:*]

NB. The above mentioned patents were as follows—viz.

1 to Englebert Cruse for improvements on Savery's steam engine

6 to James Rumsey—one for improvement on a mill proposed by Dr. Barker.

—One for improvement on Captn. Savery's engine for raising water by steam.

—one—for New Modes of generating steam

—One—for improvement on bellows

—one—for a discovery of propelling boats through water by the reaction of steam

and—one for a discovery for facilitating the work of mill saws—tilt-hammars, or mill stones, by conveying water in a certain manner.

2—to Nathan Read—one for improvement of a boiler in a steam engine—and

—one for improvement in the Art of distillery.

3—to John Stevens Junr.—one for applying steam to working a bellows.

—One for improvement on Savery's engine
for raising water by steam
—one for a new mode of generating steam.

1—to Jno. Fitch for improvement in a steam boat.

1—to Jams. Macomb for improvements for the use of Grist mills.

1—To Jno. Biddis & Thos. Bedwell for discovry of extracting gum
from the bark of various woods and bringing it to a consistance
of tar—to be used in tanning.

Dft (DNA: RG 59, MLR); with sub-joined note by Lear; endorsed in part: "the Secy of State." FC (Lb in same, SDC); with subjoined list of recipients omitting patent descriptions. Enclosures: for the patents to Nathan Read, the third patent to John Stevens, and the patent to John Fitch, see Read to TJ, 8 Jan. 1791, and note, Stevens to the Patent Board, 10 May 1791, and note, and Fitch to TJ, 24 July 1792, and note, in this Supplement. Other enclosures not found.

Fourteen of the FIFTEEN INCLOSED PATENTS were dated 26 Aug. 1791; that of John Biddis and Thomas Bedwell was dated 10 Aug. 1791 (*List of Patents*, 4-6).

From the University of the State of Pennsylvania

[*Philadelphia*], 20 Sep. [*1791*]. He is directed by the trustees and faculty of the University of Pennsylvania to request that "the Honble. Thos. Jefferson secretary of state and his Family" attend a public commencement for conferring degrees in arts and medicine to be held in the Presbyterian church in Mulberry St. on Thursday at 10 A.M.

RC (DLC); 1 p.; in an unidentified hand, unsigned; partially dated; addressed: "The Honble. Thomas Jefferson—secretary of state"; endorsed by TJ as received 22 Oct. 1791 and so recorded in SJL as an "Anonymous" invitation.

On 19 Sep. 1791 the trustees of the University of the State of Pennsylvania instructed a committee consisting of Jonathan Bayard Smith, John Bleakley, and Frederick Kuhl to invite a wide range of college, city, state, and federal officials to the school's COMMENCEMENT on 22 Sep. 1791 (PU-Ar: Trustees' Minutes, University of the State of Pennsylvania, 19 Sep. 1791). At the end of the month a Pennsylvania statute merged the university and the College of Philadelphia, with which it had competed since 1789, to create the University of Pennsylvania (Edward P. Cheyney, *History of the University of Pennsylvania 1740-1940* [Philadelphia, 1940], 123, 129, 150-67; *Acts of the General Assembly of . . . Pennsylvania, passed at a session, which was begun . . . the twenty-third day of August, in the year one thousand seven hundred and ninety-one* . . . [Philadelphia, 1791], 160-3).

To James Strange

[7 Oct. 1791]
for which sum of £97–14–6¾ with interest from the 19th. of April
1783. I now inclose you an order on Mr. N. Pope attorney to be paid
out of monies for which he has brought suits for me in the Henrico
District court against Robert Lewis and Samuel Woodson of Goochland, being partly on bond and partly for rent. This resource of payment
being the surest and quickest it is in my power to propose to you, I hope
it will prove agreeable to you. I shall be glad to hear from you on this
subject, at Philadelphia, for which place I set out in three or four days.
I am Sir your very humble servt   TH: JEFFERSON

PrC (ViU: Edgehill-Randolph Papers); consists of final page only; first two pages
printed in Vol. 22: 203-4; at foot of first page: "Mr. James Strange"; conjoined with the
enclosed order on Nathaniel Pope, 7 Oct. 1791 (see Vol. 22: 204n).

From David Campbell

SIR   City Tavern Philadelphia Novr 3d. 1791
    I hesitate to intrude upon you, engaged as you are in such a multiplic-
ity of public business: But suffer me to profit by your knowledge of
those books which really ought to be read. I mean a small Law and
family Library. A memorandum of such will be considered a favor.
    I communicate to you the Sentiments of intense Regard and Respect
I entertain for you, by informing that I have had my eldest son, a fine
boy, christened by the name of Jefferson, that I might have the pleasure
of hearing your name daily pronounced in my family.
    You will not consider these lines as proceeding from ostentation.
They are the pure expressions of a heart sensible of the value of a wise,
faithful, and upright Officer of Government.
    I shall leave the City about the tenth Instant. I have the honor to be,
Sir, Your Obt. Servt.   DAVID CAMPBELL

RC (MHi); endorsed by TJ as received 3   TJ replied to Campbell, a Southwest
Nov. 1791 and so recorded in SJL.   Territory judge, in a letter of 10 Nov. 1791.

From Jan H. C. Heineken

Philadelphia, 10 Nov. 1791. Having asked Frederick A. Muhlenberg to introduce to TJ "Mr. Halbach of Remschua," who has come to America to see if
his house's "very extensive manufactory of Ironmongery, arms &c." can supply

the American market, he gives assurances that his sole view in this is to encourage intercourse between the United Netherlands and the United States.

RC (DNA: RG 59, MLR); 2 p.; at foot of text: "The Honorable Th: Jefferson Esqr Philada"; with penciled note by TJ below signature: "Jan Hendrick Christian Hanck-en qu?"; endorsed by TJ as received 10 Nov. 1791 and so recorded in SJL as a letter from "Jan—the rest indecypherable."

To James Brown

DEAR SIR   Philadelp[hia 13 Nov. 1791]
I have duly recieved your [. . .] with the extracts of Mr. Short's letter[s] [. . . .] might be advantageous to transfer his pap[er] [. . .] impossible to ask the opinion of a perso[n] [. . . .] However, after having consulted with thos[e] [. . .] made up an opinion on the subject. Th[. . .] [advan]tageous to have been an original subscriber to [. . .] the commerce in that stock has now brought [. . .] real value, if they rightly conjecture the future [. . .] which it's paper may have. If the circulation sho[uld] [. . .] will be gain; if less, there will be loss; and I confess I [. . .] so possible, that I rather believe bank stock will [. . . .] I observe too that Mr. Short's idea was to subscribe at [. . .] price, and that he was not disposed to purchase at an [. . .] price. This therefore makes me the rather conclude [. . .] would not be adviseable to do it. I am with great esteem Dear Sir your most obedt. humble servt   TH: JEFFERSON

PrC (DLC: TJ Papers, 69: 11955); at foot of text: "Mr. James Brown"; right margin mutilated, with last part of each line in body of text torn away, ranging from six to eight words at head of text to one or two words at foot of text; date established by SJL and Brown's reply of 4 Dec. 1791.

In letters to TJ of 21 and 31 Oct. 1791, Brown had enclosed EXTRACTS OF MR. SHORT's correspondence about the possible purchase of stock in the Bank of the United States.

From Samuel Smith

SIR   Baltimore 13th November. 1791
Your obliging favour 9th. Inst. came to hand per post, consequently we have not had the pleasure of seeing Mr. Skipwith. On a consultation with the other Gentle. concerned, We have concluded it will be best to make our first Tryal at Martinique; should we not succeed, we shall at least possess ourselves of all the material Evedence, and get our papers all properly authenticated, that we may be ready for an immediate Tryal when it is brought before the National Assembly; but it is our wish to settle it at Martinique if possible, which obliges us to renew our request,

and the sooner you could obtain the Papers from the french Minister, the more you would oblige us, as we have a Vessel already loaded and waiting for nothing but your Answer. We have not of late heard from the Capt. of the Sloop; which leads us to beleive he has gone to France to make application for Damages; we have therefore to request that you will be so obliging as to write Mr. Short at Paris to prevent any compensation being made to him which will much oblige Your Obdt Hble Servt   SAM SMITH

RC (DNA: RG 76, France, Unbound Records); endorsed by TJ as received 15 Nov. 1791 and so recorded in SJL.

Contextual correspondence about the capture of the American sloop *Jane* and its cargo off Martinique by a French warship is printed in Vol. 22: 288-9, 302, 304-5, 317-18.

To Henry Remsen

Monday [14 Nov. 1791]

Th: Jefferson will be obliged to Mr. Remsen to have copies made out immediately of the reports in the cases of How, and Colvill for the President also of the clause which was changed in Mangnall's.

RC (PWacD photostat); date established from the reports of 14 Nov. 1791, a Monday, printed in Vol. 22: 295-300.

From Thomas Keene

SIR   Richmond Novr. 23rd. 1791

By the direction of Mr. T: M. Randolph I now enclose you the Power of Attorney, which you should have had long since—but the necessity of one witness swearing to the signature, and all living up the Country has delayed the forwarding it untill now.

Please acknowledge the receipt, & believe me to be, with great respect Dear Sir Yr Mt: Obedt. & Obliged Hble Sert:

THOMAS KEENE
of the house Warington & Keene

RC (ViW: Tucker-Coleman Collection); endorsed by TJ as received 29 Nov. 1791 and so recorded in SJL. Enclosure not found.

A missing letter from Keene to TJ of 25 Aug. 1794 is recorded in SJL as received from Richmond on 3 Sep. 1794.

From George Washington

[1 Dec. 1791]

Mr. Hammond starts three to one against you.

RC (DLC: TJ Papers, 79: 13729); un-dated; endorsed by TJ as received 1 Dec. 179[1]. Recorded in SJPL under that date.

Washington's note was a commentary on George Hammond's 30 Nov. 1791 letter to TJ on alleged American violations of the Treaty of Paris.

From Willing, Morris & Swanwick

SIR   Philada. Decr. 1. *1791*.

Enclosed We have the honour to transmit you a Letter We lately Received from Mr. De Lormerie in which he Refers us to you for Information and assistance. You will greatly oblige us by giving us any Intelligence you may have on the Subject and thereby enabling us to Render Mr. Lormerie any service immediately in our power. We have the honour to be with great Respect sir Your most hble servt

WILLING MORRIS & SWANWICK

RC (ViW); in John Swanwick's hand; at foot of text: "Honble Thos. Jefferson Esqr."; endorsed by TJ as received 1 Dec. 1791 and so recorded in SJL. Enclosure not found, but for its probable subject, see Memorandum on Deed of Lormerie, 7 Mch. 1792.

From Tench Coxe

Saturday [17 Dec. 1791]

Mr. Coxe has the honor to inform Mr. Jefferson, that the *silver* crown of six livres Tournois is worth in the French W. Indies nine livres of the Colonies and that the livre Tournois according to the par of french coins is deemed conformable with that fact—that is 30s. of the Colonies are worth 20s. of France.

Mr. C. will read the letter with care and have the honor to return it in person to Morrow.

RC (DLC: TJ Papers, 96: 16500); par-tially dated, but probably part of the se-quence of letters in Vol. 22: 405-6, 414.

LETTER: probably Walter Stewart's letter of this date to TJ (see note to Coxe to TJ, 15 Dec. 1791).

From Edmund Randolph

E. R. TO MR. JEFFERSON   Sunday [18 Dec. 1791]

1. I cannot discover any existing authority, to make the deed to Pennsylvania. Congress must be resorted to. It is probable, that the land-office is the true channel.

2. Metcalfe has undoubtedly committed murder on the high seas: and altho' other nations might lay hold of him, and perhaps punish him; it seems to be the peculiar duty of the U.S., whose citizen he is, to disclaim the act, and with adequate testimony[1] to take measures for his arrest.[2] But the proof ought, I conceive, to be invincibly strong, And of the most formal kind, to justify the seizing of him beyond sea: I mean by this, that otherwise the opprobrium of it would be ecchoed from one end of the U.S. to the other. Even the letter, howsoever authenticated, would be a basis, too unsolemn, for such a violent step.

I was just writing the above, when your servant called.

RC (DLC: TJ Papers, 80: 13909); partially dated; endorsed by TJ as received 18 Dec. 1791. Recorded in SJPL with date torn away.

DEED TO PENNSYLVANIA: see Report on Sale of Lands on Lake Erie, 19 Dec. 1791, wherein TJ followed the Attorney General's advice and recommended that Congress BE RESORTED TO in order to facilitate Pennsylvania's purchase of the land in question.

On 8 Mch. 1792 Alexander J. Dallas wrote a brief note to TJ transmitting a copy of the survey of the land purchased by Pennsylvania from the United States so that it could be "annexed to the Instrument of Conveyance, upon the footing which you suggested" (FC in PHarH: Mifflin Administration Papers, at foot of text: "To Thomas Jefferson Esqr. Secretary of State"; FC in same, Secretary's Letterbooks).

During this period TJ received two other letters dealing with land matters. On

2 Jan. 1792 Richard Harison, the District Attorney for New York, wrote a letter to TJ from Philadelphia transmitting "the Deeds and Papers, which have been in my Hands, respecting the Lands of the United States at West Point, and which, I think, should be deposited with the Public Archives in your Office" (RC in DNA: RG 59, MLR; at foot of text: "Honble. Thomas Jefferson Esqr. Secretary of State"; endorsed by Henry Remsen as received 4 Jan. 1792). On 17 Mch. 1792 Senator Oliver Ellsworth of Connecticut wrote a letter to TJ on behalf of the governor requesting authenticated copies of Connecticut's deed ceding its western claims to the United States and the act of Congress accepting it (RC in same; addressed: "The Secretary of State"; endorsed by George Taylor, Jr.; see JCC, XXXI, 654-5, for the texts in question).

[1] Preceding three words interlined.
[2] Word interlined in place of "capture."

Memorandum to James Monroe

[after 21 Dec. 1791]

I find the calculation of the *As* of Holland (which is the common measure applied by the Encyclopedie to all coins) will be so difficult to trace through the coins and weights of Holland and Spain, that no public assembly will ever understand them. Consequently it is better to rest the question altogether on the report of the Board of Treasury of Apr. 8. 1786. and the Consequent *Final decision* of Congress of

The first page of their Report contains the principles of their decision, which may be developed by the following observations.
A Troy pound of standard silver is cut, at the mint into 62. shillings.
Standard silver contains 11 oz.–2 dwt. pure metal to the pound
    that is to say 5,328. grains pure silver
    5328 grs. divided into 62/ gives 85.935 grs. to each shilling

The market price of the dollar varies from 4/4 to 4/6 sterl. This fact is familiar to all merchants and indeed to all persons, and will therefore furnish the standard of comparison the most likely to be understood and approved.

The board of treasury, and Congress, in adopting 375.64 grs. pure silver to the dollar, took almost the lowest market price, towit $4/4\frac{1}{2}$ sterl. to the dollar.

The Secretary of the Treasury in proposing 371.25 grs. makes it but $4/3\frac{7}{8}$ sterl. That is, he withdraws $1\frac{2}{3}$ penny sterl. or 5 cents out of every dollar.

It is to be observed further that

                      grs. Troy
    till 1728. the Dollar of Spain contained 394.744 pure
    from 1728 to 1772 it   contained 376.72824
    in 1772 it was depreciated to   370.95548
It is evident that when the American debt was contracted the idea of a dollar in America must have been that of the second epoch, as that of 1772. could not have been yet so much circulated here as to have reduced the public opinion to it as a standard.   This fact is from the Encyclopedie.

MS (NN: Monroe Papers); written entirely in TJ's hand on a narrow sheet; undated, but see below; verso bears calculations by Monroe related to this notation by him: "Secy. of Treasury makes 416. [. . .] wt. of 371. fine & 45. of base being $\frac{1}{8}$ alloy. He adopts the [. . .] of Spain. But that coin of Spn. contained of fine 389.18 grs. more than his."

This and the following memorandum to Senator James Monroe concern the QUESTION of the proportion of silver in the dollar being considered by Congress as part of a plan for an American coinage. In his 28 Jan. 1791 Report on the Mint, Secretary of the Treasury Alexander Hamilton had recommended that Congress adopt a dollar standard of one part alloy to eleven parts pure silver (Syrett, *Hamilton*, VII, 599-600). Although the two Secretaries were in substantial agreement on the new coinage, TJ opposed the standard Hamilton had suggested not only because it reduced the silver content to less than that proposed by the BOARD OF TREASURY on 8 Apr. 1786, adopted by the Confederation CONGRESS on 8 Aug. 1786, and confirmed in its ordinance to establish a mint on 16 Oct. 1786, but also because it ran counter to his vision of a uniform system of weights, measures, and coinage (see Vols. 18: 454-8, 20: 738; JCC, XXX, 162-3, 166; XXXI, 503-4, 876-8; Memorandum to James Madison, printed below under 12 Jan. 1792, and note).

TJ could have sent this memorandum at any time after the Senate appointed Monroe on 7 Feb. 1791 to a committee assigned to consider Hamilton's report. However, Monroe's notation on verso suggests that TJ prepared these notes after 21 Dec. 1791, when a second committee chaired by

Robert Morris, to which Monroe did not belong, reported a bill to establish a mint and regulate coinage, and before 12 Jan. 1792, when the Senate approved the final bill, which devalued the dollar even beyond the standard of one in twelve that Hamilton had proposed (JS, I, 239, 332, 359, 373-4).

In this and the following memorandum to Monroe, TJ derived the figures on the metallic content of the DOLLAR OF SPAIN from tables on weights and coins in the *Encyclopédie Méthodique. Commerce*, 3 vols. (Paris, 1783-84), III, 276, 417 (see Sowerby, No. 3579).

Memorandum to James Monroe

[after 21 Dec. 1791]

The Spanish dollar	dwt grs.	dwt
till 1728. had	11– 4 of pure metal in every 12 of mixed.	
from 1728. to 1772.	10–21	
since 1772	10–17	

Extract from the Encyclopedie.

The dollar of 1728–1772 being taken as our standard, we have this

| | grs mixed | | grs alloy | | grs mixed | | grs alloy |
| proportion | 288 | : | 27 | :: | 416 | : | 39 |

so that the dollar proposed of 416. grains should have but 39 grains alloy.

The base dollar of 1772 gives this

| | grs mixt | | grs alloy | | grs mxt | | grs alloy |
| proportion | 288 | : | 31 | :: | 416 | : | 44.77 so that |

it appears they have taken the base dollar for their standard.

Quere, whether it will not be better to let them retain their base alloy, because, if the bill passes the Senate, the extravagance of the alloy will render alteration in the lower house more probable, and also because an opposition which it is previously known will be unsuccessful, draws disreputation without doing any good.

MS (NjP: Andre deCoppet Collection); entirely in TJ's hand; undated, but see note below; addressed: "Colo. Monroe"; endorsed by Monroe.

TJ must have composed these notes after a Senate committee headed by Robert Morris reported a bill to establish a mint and regulate coinage on 21 Dec. 1791 and before the proposal passed the SENATE on 12 Jan. 1792 (JS, I, 359, 373-4).

From Willink, Van Staphorst & Hubbard

Amsterdam, 30 Dec. 1791. Having received TJ's 26 July letter about his draft of 1,000 dollars in favor of Gouverneur Morris, they paid it at the rate of 50 stivers per dollar and, as TJ directed, charged it at 2,500 florins to the Secretary of State's public account.

RC (DLC); 1 p.; in a clerk's hand, signed by both firms; at foot of text: "To Thomas Jefferson Esqr."; endorsed by TJ as received 28 Mch. 1792 and so recorded in SJL. Dupl (DLC); endorsed by TJ as received 10 Apr. 1792 and so recorded in SJL.

TJ's letter of 26 July 1791 is described in Vol. 20: 680n.

From William Vans Murray

Thursday Morng. [1791-1793] 275. So. Front.

Mr. Murray returns "The Preface to Belendenus" with many thanks to Mr. Jefferson—and begs leave to add the pamphlet which accompanies this (, as a Juvenile essay,) to Mr. Jefferson's collection of American pieces.

RC (DLC: Rare Book and Special Collections); partially dated; inserted in presentation copy of Enclosure No. 2. Enclosures: (1) [Samuel Parr], *A Free Translation of the Preface to Bellendenus; containing Animated Strictures on the Great Political Characters of the Present Time,* trans. William Beloe (London, 1788). The Latin original of Parr's work appeared with his edition of the works of the poet William Bellenden in 1787 and was published separately the next year. See Sowerby, No. 2772. (2) [William Vans Murray], *Political Sketches, inscribed to his Excellency John Adams, Minister Plenipotentiary from the United States to the Court of Great Britain* (London, 1787). See Sowerby, No. 3151.

Murray clearly wrote this and the following letter when both he and TJ were in Philadelphia, most likely at some point during 1791-93 when he was attending Congress as a representative from Maryland.

From William Vans Murray

Saturday Morng. [1791-1793]

Mr. Murray does himself the honour of sending to Mr. Jefferson a small specimen of the Hickory Juice in its own crust—he scraped it off, froth, from a Log about five inches diameter which was probably cut lately as it came a few days since from the country and was bought in Market Street. A Log of about nine inches diameter produced little or none. It may be thought a trifling auxiliary to the maple juice. As an humble observer of facts he offers it to Mr. Jefferson's reflections.

RC (ViW); partially dated; endorsed by TJ.

To George Hammond

Dec. [i.e. Jan.] 2. 1792.

Th: Jefferson presents his compliments to Mr. Hammond, who not having been here before on the New Year's day, Th:J. takes the liberty of informing him that those who chuse to pay visits of compliment to the President to-day are recieved at twelve aclock.—While on this subject he will add that the 4th. of July is another anniversary on which those who chuse it visit the President. Those are the only days of the year on which this is done; and therefore are mentioned together.

RC (MoHi); misdated (see note below); addressed: "Mr. Hammond Min. Plenipo. of Gr Britain." Not recorded in SJL.

The President was evidently receiving NEW YEAR's guests a day later than usual because the holiday fell on a Sunday in 1792. Hammond had arrived in Philadelphia in October 1791.

Memorandum to James Madison

[after 12 Jan. 1792]

Notes on the alloy of the Dollar

dwt grs.   dwt

The Spanish dollar, till 1728, had 11– 4 of pure metal to every 12 of mixed

from 1728. to 1772	10–21	
since 1772	10–17	

The above is from the Encyclopedie

	grs mixed		grs alloy		grs mixed		grs alloy
The 1st. dollar gives this proportion	288	:	16	:: 416	:	23.11 &c.
The 2d.	288	:	27	:: 416	:	39
The 3d.	288	:	31	:: 416	:	44.77

The vote in the Senate for reducing the dollar from 375.64 grs. pure metal to 371.25 is a presage of what may be expected in the other house: if an opposition to that reduction be desperate, and it's motives liable to be mistaken, would it not be better to let it pass, and to try whether the quantum of alloy may not be usefully changed thus?

grs

The dollar proposed in the bill is to contain 371.25 pure metal.
Instead of 44.75 grains alloy, add only $\underline{38.92}$ alloy
it will make the Dollar of 410.17 mixed metal
which is exactly the Unit proposed in the Report on Measures, weights and coins, viz the Ounce or cubic inch of rain water.

[813]

That Avarice which attaches itself to the *pure metal* will see some
saving also in the reduction of the *alloy*, both in the alloy saved, and
the greater worth of what remains because the more base metal you
add, the less is the worth of the[1] mass.

It will preserve this link of the general system and the possibility of
establishing it.

It will try the dispositions of the Representatives towards that
system.[2]

It will give us a coin, which instead of 25.8 dwt. of alloy in the pound
of mixed (which is that proposed in the bill and taken exactly from the
base dollar of 1772) will give us one of 22.75 dwt. of alloy only in the
pound, which is extremely near to that of the Dollar of 1728–1772,
to wit 22.5 dwt. in the pound (because 288 grs. mixd : 27 grs. alloy
:: 240 dwt. : 22.5 dwt.) and coming nearer to the alloy of our gold, of
20 dwt. in the pound, may render more probable some future attempt
to raise the pure metal so as to bring the alloy in both coins to the
same measure, when the effect on the public debt shall be out of the
question.

MS (DLC: Madison Papers); entirely in
TJ's hand; undated, but see note below.
PrC (DLC: TJ Papers, 62: 10812). Tr
(DLC: Madison Papers); undated abstract
in Madison's hand filed at the end of 1791.

TJ wrote these notes after the VOTE IN
THE SENATE on 12 Jan. 1792 approving a
bill for a mint that provided for a dollar
with a silver content lower than that originally mandated by the Confederation Congress in 1786 and proposed by Alexander

Hamilton in January 1791, and before the
House of Representatives concurred on 26
Mch. 1792, with Madison dissenting (JS, I,
373-4; JHR, I, 549; note to first Memorandum to James Monroe, [after 21 Dec.
1791], above). For TJ's earlier effort to link
the unit of coinage to his GENERAL SYSTEM,
see Report on Weights and Measures, 4
July 1790, in Vol. 16: 650-67.

[1] TJ here canceled "pure."
[2] Sentence interlined.

From William Knox

Dublin, 18 Jan. 1792. Encloses account of his expenses for obtaining recognition as consul and has forwarded an order to Henry Knox to receive the
amount in question and receipt for the same.

RC (DNA: RG 59, CD); 1 p.; at head of
text: "No. 5."; at foot of text: "The Honorable Thomas Jefferson Secretary of
State." Recorded in SJL as received 4 Apr.

1792. Enclosure: Knox's Account with the
United States, 1 Jan. 1792, with entries for
17 Nov.-17 Dec. 1791 (MS in same; in
Knox's hand; filed at 17 Nov. 1790).

Circular to the Governors of the States

SIR   Philadelphia March 1st. 1792

I have the honor to send you herein enclosed two copies, duly authenticated, of an Act concerning certain fisheries of the United States, and for the regulation and government of the fishermen employed therein; also of an Act to establish the Post office and Post roads within the United States; also the ratifications, by three fourths of the Legislatures of the several States, of certain articles in addition to and amendment of the Constitution of the United States, proposed by Congress to the said Legislatures; and of being with sentiments of the most perfect respect Your Excellency's Most obedient & most humble servant

TH: JEFFERSON

RC (Vi); in the hand of Henry Remsen, signed by TJ; at foot of text: "His Excellency The Governor of the State of Virginia." RC (MdAA); in Remsen's hand, signed by TJ; at foot of text: "His Excellency The Governor of the State of Maryland." RC (NN); in the hand of George Taylor, Jr., signed by TJ; at foot of text: "To His Excellency the Governor of the State of Pennsylvania." FC (Lb in DNA: RG 59, DL); at head of text: "To the Governors of the Several States." Not recorded in SJL. For the two enclosed acts of Congress, see *Annals*, III, 1329-41; see below for the other enclosure.

CERTAIN ARTICLES IN ADDITION TO AND AMENDMENT OF THE CONSTITUTION: the first ten amendments as passed by Congress and ratified by eleven of the fourteen states. TJ this day directed that the amendments and ratifications, as well as two amendments that were not ratified, be printed as a pamphlet for transmission to the state governors in the same manner as acts of Congress. The eleven-page booklet, enclosed in this letter, was the earliest official printing of the ratified Bill of Rights (*Congress of the United States: Begun and held at the City of New-York, on Wednesday the fourth of March, one thousand seven hundred and eighty-nine* . . . [Philadelphia, 1792],

Evans, No. 46596; Memorandum Book of the Department of State, DNA: RG 360, PCC, No. 187; Vincent L. Eaton, "Bill of Rights," *The New Colophon*, II [1949], 279-83; *Antiquarian Bookman*, VI [1950], 125; note to TJ to Christopher Gore, 8 Aug. 1791). For the steps leading to the transmission to the states of this landmark of American liberty, see Kenneth R. Bowling, "'A Tub to the Whale': The Founding Fathers and Adoption of the Federal Bill of Rights," *Journal of the Early Republic*, VIII (1988), 223-51. TJ's chart tracing state actions on the twelve amendments submitted to the states in 1789 is illustrated in this volume.

TJ dispatched this circular after receiving letters from Tobias Lear of 30 Dec. 1791 transmitting Virginia's ratification of the Bill of Rights with a covering letter from Governor Henry Lee to the President (RC in DLC, endorsed by TJ as received 30 Dec. 1791; PrC in DNA: RG 59, MLR; FC in Lb in same, SDC) and of 18 Jan. 1792 transmitting Vermont's ratification with a covering letter from Governor Thomas Chittenden to the President (RC in DNA: RG 11, Bill of Rights and Ratifications; PrC in DNA: RG 59, MLR; FC in Lb in same, SDC). Vermont's action provided the three-fourths majority required for amendments to the Constitution.

From Tobias Lear

United States, *3 Mch. 1792*. By the President's command he transmits the "return of the enumeration of the Inhabitants of South Carolina" received from the marshal there, a letter from Governor Pinckney which, if necessary, the President wishes TJ either to answer or to report to him about, and two pardons signed by the President to which the seal must be affixed. The President wishes to have a copy of the "aggregate of each description of persons" in the South Carolina return laid before the House of Representatives that meets today.

RC (DLC); 1 p.; endorsed by TJ as received 3 Mch. 1792. PrC (DNA: RG 59, MLR). FC (Lb in same, SDC). Enclosure: Charles Pinckney to George Washington, 8 Jan. 1792 (see note to Enclosure No. 2 printed at Report on Proposed Convention with Spain Concerning Fugitives, 22 Mch. 1792). Enclosed pardons not found.

The President submitted the copy of the South Carolina census return he requested from TJ to the House this day (JHR, I, 526). TJ responded to Governor Pinckney in a letter of 1 Apr. 1792.

From Tobias Lear

United States, March 13th. 1792.

By the President's command T. Lear has the honor to return to the Secretary of State the draft of a letter to the King of France, which meets the President's approbation; and to enclose the Resolution of the House of Representatives with the signature of the Speaker.

As it is possible that the Senate may come forward with a Resolution on this occasion; the President asks, if it would not be best to delay preparing the letter to the King as long as can be done with security to the present opportunity, in order to comprehend the sentiments of the senate if they should be expressed?

The Resolution of the House is dated the 10th.—the letter will therefore be dated the same, or a subsequent day.

TOBIAS LEAR
Secretary to the President
of the United States

RC (DLC); endorsed by TJ as received 13 Mch. 1792. PrC (DNA: RG 59, MLR). FC (Lb in same, SDC). Enclosures: George Washington to Louis XVI, 14 Mch. 1792, and Enclosure No. 1 listed there.

On the previous day Lear had written a brief note to TJ transmitting a text of the 10

Mch. 1792 resolution of the House of Representatives mentioned above and stating that the President "intended that T. Lear should have left the enclosed Resolution with the Secretary of State," so that its sentiments could be inserted in the reply to the French king (RC in DLC; partially dated; endorsed by TJ as received 12 Mch. 1792).

From Tobias Lear

United States, 16 Mch. 1792. By the President's command he transmits a 28 Oct. letter from Chiappe, which the President asks TJ to consider and report whatever may demand his attention. The President wishes to see TJ "some time between this and two o'clock as he can make it most convenient."

RC (DLC); 1 p.; endorsed by TJ as received 16 Mch. 1792. PrC (DNA: RG 59, MLR). FC (Lb in same, SDC). Enclosure: Giuseppe Chiappe to George Washington, Mogador, 28 Oct. 1791, enclosing a copy of his 31 Aug. letter and describing efforts by Morocco and Spain to negotiate an end to the hostilities between them (RC in DNA: RG 360, PCC; in French; in a clerk's hand, signed by Chiappe). See Vol. 20: 401n.

From Tobias Lear

United States, 16 Mch. 1792. Transmits by the President's command a copy of the Senate resolution extending the negotiation proposed at Madrid to commerce.

RC (DLC); 1 p.; endorsed by TJ as received 17 Mch. 1792. Dft (DNA: RG 59, MLR). FC (Lb in same, SDC). Enclosure: Resolution of the Senate, 16 Mch. 1792 (see note to TJ's second letter to George Washington, 7 Mch. 1792).

From Edmund Randolph

E. R. TO T. J.   Friday P. M. [after 18 Mch. 1792]

The existence of the bill is, I believe, unquestionable. I remember to have heard my uncle speak of Mr. Montagu's communication. But I possess no copy, nor can I direct you to any place, where you can obtain it.

Mr. Remsen some time ago sent a box, which for months past has been supposed to contain my papers. When I opened it, starch, instead of papers, was found to be the contents. I shall again write to him, and urge a further search in Mr. Bowne's warehouse.

RC (DLC: TJ Papers, 98: 16771-2); partially dated, being conjecturally assigned (see note below); addressed: "Mr. Jefferson Market-Street"; endorsed by TJ: "E. Randolph's notes."

MY UNCLE: probably Peyton Randolph, who was successively the king's attorney in Virginia and speaker of the House of Burgesses during the tenure of Edward MONTAGU as the colony's agent in London from 1759 to 1770 (Michael G. Kammen, *A Rope of Sand: The Colonial Agents, Brit-*

ish Politics, and the American Revolution [Ithaca, N.Y., 1968], 325). Neither the BILL nor the COMMUNICATION has been identified.

The BOX, which evidently contained records of Randolph's Virginia law practice, including the cases TJ transferred to him in 1774, was probably that discussed in Henry Remsen to TJ, 16 Mch. 1792; TJ to Remsen, 18 Mch. 1792; and Randolph to TJ, 4 July 1792. See also TJ to Robert Fleming, 11 Sep. 1792.

Notes on Cotton

[ca. 24 Mch. 1792]

Cotton.

Dunlap's paper. 1792. Mar. 24.

Nashville. 'I have made 600. ℔. of cotton on half an acre of land, but on a moderate calculation an acre will produce 1000. ℔.'

MS (DLC); entirely in TJ's hand; undated.

TJ copied from an extract in *Dunlap's American Daily Advertiser*, taken in turn from a 1 Oct. 1791 letter to the editor appearing in the 3 Mch. 1792 issue of *Bowen's Virginia Centinel & Gazette: or,*

the Winchester Political Repository, in which an unnamed correspondent writing from Cumberland in the Southwest Territory described a visit to the cotton manufactory of John Hague in Nashville on 22 Sep. 1791 and reported that the fall cotton crop would be abundant.

From Tobias Lear

United States, *31 Mch. 1792*. Transmits by the President's command letters from James Seagrove so that TJ could "take extracts therefrom for the purpose mentioned this day." The President wishes to know if the copies sent to him of the letter of George Hammond are intended to be forwarded to Seagrove by the Secretary of War.

RC (DLC); 1 p.; endorsed by TJ as received 31 Mch. 1792. Dft (DNA: RG 59, MLR). FC (Lb in same, SDC). Enclosures not found, but see TJ to George Washington, 2 Apr. 1792, and note.

Hammond's letter to TJ is dated 30 Mch. 1792.

Memorandum to James Monroe?

[before 4 Apr. 1792]

The rival propositions

I. The National assembly proposes *actual* mensuration of a *considerable portion* of a meridian (e.g. 9 degrees) *bisected* by the 45th. degree of lat. and *terminated* at each end by the sea. To[1] these 9 degrees found by *mensuration* they will add the other 81.° to be found by *calculation* on the *hypothesis* that the earth is *spheridical* in it's figure, and having thus the quarter of the circumference of the globe, they take it for their Unit, and dividing it decimally, the ten millionth part yeilds them a measure for common use very near 6. feet, their present toise.

[818]

Objections. 1. The inaccuracies of admeasurements over hills, vallies, rivers, and, in this instance, over high mountains, the Pyrenees.

2. This gives them but 9.° or $\frac{1}{10}$ of the quadrant. The other $\frac{9}{10}$ they are to obtain by calculation, founded on *hypothesis*.

3. The length of time, the apparatus, the number of Mathematicians to be employed (to wit 6. committees of 3. in each).

4. That there is but one portion of a meridian to be found on all the globe involving all the conditions they require, which is exactly the one passing through France and a small portion of Spain from Dunkirk to Barcelona.

5. If other nations adopt this unit, they must take the word of the French mathematicians for it's length, or they must send their mathematicians into that country to make the admeasurement, whenever they wish either to establish or verify their standard.

6. Spain has refused to permit the admeasurement to be made on her part of the meridian. So there is an end of it.

II. The Pendulum, and III. the Rod, vibrating seconds under the 45th. degree of latitude. The 45th. degree is assumed 1. because it's pendulum is a mean between those vibrating in equal times under the equator and pole. 2. because it is a mean between any two taken under parallels equally distant on both sides. 3. it is a mean of the pendulums for every degree added together and divided by their number. 4. it is within a convenient distance and temperature for the inhabitants of both hemispheres. 5. because a very great portion of it lies in, or bordering on, the U.S.

The Disadvantages common to both the Pendulum and Rod.

1. The variations in their length under different parallels of latitude.

Ans. This difference between 31.° and 45.° (our extremes) is but $\frac{1}{679}$ of the whole pendulum. This difference, for any parallel, can be found by a calculation, on pretty certain principles, so as to reduce it to a *very minute* part of a *very minute* difference, consequently it is insensible and may be called nothing.

2. Variations of length according to the degree of heat or cold.

Ans. This is got over by placing it in a cellar deep enough to be of the mean temperature of the earth. 20. feet deep suffices.

Advantages common to both Pendulum and Rod vibrating seconds.

1. In every country their lengths are already well known in the measures of that country, and consequently, taken as our Unit, it is already[2] the common measure of every country.

2. If an actual verification of them be required, it can be had by the aid of a common house clock, by actual experiment under any parallel whatever, only supplying by calculation the small difference resulting from the difference of parallel.

Advantages peculiar to the Pendulum.

Not a single one.

Advantages peculiar to the Rod.

1. It avoids the impracticability of measuring the pendulum. This impracticability results from the difficulty *in fact* of finding the centre of oscillation of the bob, from which center the admeasurement is to be made. It can be easily found *by calculation* in a bob of a regular form. And it is from *calculation* and not *measure* that the length of the pendulum has been generally given to very minute fractions. When you come to actual mensuration no two mathematicians will put the point of their dividers on the same point of the bob.—This fact is so certain, that it is on this difficulty, and this alone, that Whitehurst was induced to propose his theory of two Pendulums, the *ratio* between the vibrations of which should furnish[3] the standard.—But this in truth doubles the difficulty, for[4] after you have got your two pendulums to vibrate in the given *ratio*, you have then to *measure both* in order to find your standard. The error from this source in the Rod, is but the $\frac{1}{120}$ of what it is in the pendulum.

2. The aliquot part of the Rod (to wit $\frac{1}{5}$ of 58.72 I.) gives $11\frac{3}{4}$ inches for our foot, which is but $\frac{1}{4}$ of an inch different from the present foot. Whereas the aliquot part of a pendulum (to wit $\frac{1}{3}$ of 39.15 I.) gives 13. inches, which is an inch more than the present foot.—The foot is certainly the most important measure to preserve as nearly as possible.

If the Rod be agreed to as the Standard, I do not foresee any objections to the decimal arrangement reported in the

Measures of length

surface

capacity and

Weights.

except indeed the general objection of novelty and difficulty to the people, to which I need not mention the answers.

But an objection will be made to the Unit of coin, because different from what the legislature has adopted.

The Dollar of Spain   dwt   grs   dwt

        till 1728. had 11– 4 of pure metal to every 12 of mixed

    from 1728. to 1772   10–21

    since 1772.   10–17

The Dollar adopted is to have only $371\frac{1}{4}$ grs. pure metal

                         and $\underline{44\frac{3}{4}}$ grs. alloy

             which make 416   grs.

Here the alloy is nearly $\frac{1}{8}$ of the pure metal. There is not a country under the sun which has adopted so base a mixture for it's general standard. The alloy in England and France is less than $\frac{1}{12}$ of the whole mass.

To bring back our Money Unit to a coincidence with the system of measures and weights, by making the Dollar weigh one ounce of rain water, let the pure metal remain at   371.25 grs. Troy, as now.

and add, of alloy, only $\underline{38.92}$

which makes the dollar of mixed metal 410.17 grs. Troy, which is the new Ounce of rain water, as the Report proposes.

This raises our coin to a middle ground of purity between what it now is, and that of England and France. To wit

The mixed mass is to the alloy in the dollar established as   9   to 1.

                  in that I now propose $10\frac{1}{2}$ to 1.

                  in that of France and Engld.   12   to 1.

and it brings us back very near to the Spanish Dollar previous to 1772 which was the one we were generally acquainted with when we contracted our debt (for the subsequent ones could not then have come into general circulation) and was therefore the honest measure of that debt.

    That Spanish Dollar had $22\frac{1}{2}$ dwt. of alloy in the pound of mixed metal.

    The one I now propose will have $22\frac{3}{4}$ dwt. alloy in the pound instead.[5]

Note. I have not Hamilton's Report on the Mint. But I well remember that it proposed a *purer dollar than that adopted by the Senate.—But if an attempt to alter the money unit, would endanger the making any additional enemies to the general system of weights and measures, would it not be better to omit altogether, now, whatever relates to coins? If the system passes, it will be easy hereafter to engraft the Money

*It was $\frac{1}{12}$ alloy

unit into it: and an opportunity will probably arise this Session, when the change [in the?] copper coinage shall be taken up, as I think it certainly will be.

PrC (DLC: TJ Papers: 62: 10809-11); entirely in TJ's hand, with footnote added in ink; undated; last page frayed.

These notes apparently constitute TJ's reaction to a draft report of a Senate committee consisting of Ralph Izard, James Monroe, and John Langdon, which had been appointed on 1 Nov. 1791 to consider a system of weights and measures for the United States. The report adhered to TJ's call for a DECIMAL ARRANGEMENT of measures of length, surface, capacity, and weight, and proposed a money unit consisting of a dollar that was to weigh one ounce and be made up of eleven parts silver to one of copper, a standard recommended by Alexander Hamilton in his 28 Jan. 1791 Report on the Mint, one that was PURER THAN THAT ADOPTED BY THE SENATE on 12 Jan. 1792. When the committee reported to the Senate on 4 Apr. 1792, it followed the draft closely, but accepted TJ's advice that it OMIT ALTOGETHER the coinage proposal. TJ most likely prepared these notes for James Monroe, with whom he had recently communicated on related questions (Draft Senate Committee Report, [before 4 Apr. 1792], PrC of Tr in DLC: TJ Papers, 62:

10813-17, in a clerk's hand, undated; NSP, XIII, 26-7; JS, I, 335, 373-4, 420; Syrett, *Hamilton*, VII, 599-600; Memorandums to James Monroe, [after 21 Dec. 1791], above). For the outcome of this initiative to implement the substance of TJ's 4 July 1790 Report on Weights and Measures, see TJ to John Rutherford, 25 Dec. 1792, and note.

For the geographically based unit of measure proposed by the NATIONAL ASSEMBLY of France on 26 Mch. 1791, see *Archives Parlementaires*, 1st ser., XXIV, 379, 394-7; William Short's first letter to TJ, 30 Mch. 1791; and TJ's first letter to Short, 28 July 1791. TJ obtained his figures on the DOLLAR OF SPAIN from the *Encyclopédie Méthodique. Commerce*, 3 vols. (Paris, 1783-84), III, 276 (Sowerby, No. 3579).

[1] Word interlined in place of "from."
[2] Preceding three words interlined in place of "is."
[3] TJ wrote "between which should become" before altering the phrase to read as above.
[4] TJ here canceled "to find the."
[5] Remainder of text added in margin.

To Alexander Hamilton

Philadelphia, 10 Apr. 1792. Requests that a warrant be issued on the United States Treasurer for 500 dollars payable to George Taylor, Jr., "for defraying the contingent expenses of the department of State."

FC (Lb in DNA: RG 59, DL); at head of text: "To the Secretary of the Treasury." Not recorded in SJL.

Notes on John Robertson and Algerine Prisoners

John Robertson native of Scotld. taken on board the Dauphin by the Algerines in 1785.

The Ld. Provost, magistrates and common council of Glasgow applied to Govmt. to procure his manumission, but to no purpose.
His friends redeemed him for £341–12 sterl.

The above certified by the Ld. Provost under the seal of Glasgow.
He left Glasgow June 14. 1791. He left 13. of our people there.
The old Dey was not then dead.
Marine force

a 44 gun frigate rigged and ready for sea.

a 24. gun French vessel. fine vessel

a 14. gun Xebeck

4. half gallies carrying 2 large guns in the bows.

5. vessels from 34. to 16. guns in the Archipelago.

towit 1. of 34

2 of 18.

2 of 16

48. gun boats for the port. Carrying a single gun. They can go out 4. or 5. miles.

He thinks a 20 gun vessel would best their 44. on account of their ignorance. They know nothing of managing guns or any thing else. They do not trust to that at all, but to boarding.

2 frigates of 28 or 30 guns constantly cruising would suffice.

The Danes kept 4. frigates of 36. guns each, of which two were constantly cruising, and the other 2 resting. They cruised between Mahon and Algiers bay, now and then heaving in sight. This was for 2. years, during which time the Algerines never attempted to send a vessel out of their harbour, tho' their marine were stronger then than now. This was some years before he was in Algiers.

He has heard since he left Algiers that the Portuguese have taken one of their vessels. He supposes it either the 24. or 14.

A constant peace would cost 1,000,000 Doll.

He thinks the Venetians pay 25,000 Chequins = 10,000£ sterl.

The Prime minister (now Dey) said to this man that Algiers had better have peace than war with the Americans, for here sais he we have been 5 years and taken only 2 prizes: if we had been receiving a tribute we should have got more.

Our prisoners have beans and oil and vinegar for breakfast, and boiled wheat and butter for dinner and three small loaves of rye bread for the day.

A suit of cloaths once a year, viz an oznabrigs shirt, a flannel frock, jacket and trowzers, and a pair of slippers.

Obrian bit by a mad dog last summer. But doing well.

[823]

Harnet is out of his senses.

Now remain thirteen.[1]

He thinks the common man will cost 330.£ sterl. The mates double that, about treble.

Robertson will be to be found at Mrs. Innes's in Penn street near South street.

He proposes to apply to Congress.

Taken Apr. 10. 1792.

MS (DLC); entirely in TJ's hand, with last line added in a different ink.

TJ took these notes on Robertson's testimony in conjunction with his efforts to secure the release from Algerine captivity of the officers and crews of the DAUPHIN and the *Maria* (see TJ to John Paul Jones, 1 June 1792, and note). For Robertson's unsuccessful efforts to secure repayment of his ransom and traveling expenses from Congress, see JHR, I, 580-1, 586, 587.

[1] Remainder of text written lengthwise in the margin.

Notes on Headaches

Recipe for the head-ach called the Sun-pain
6. grains of Calomel taken at night, without any thing to work it off, or any other matter whatever.

Mr. Willis of Georgia has had this head-ach to a dangerous extremity, and tried bark ineffectually. A drunken Doctr. recommended the above dose of Calomel, it relieved him from the next fit. He had it some years after, and the same medecine relieved him again as quickly.

He has cured his son of it also, and was obliged to give it twice at an interval of 2. or 3 days.

He communicated it to Mrs. Broadnax a sister of Colo. Fieldg. Lewis who had the same species of head ach. It cured her.

She has communicated it to others who have tried it with never failing success.

Apr. 10. 1792.

Sep. 1. 96. A negro man had been 3 weeks laid up with the periodical head ach or eye ach: I gave him a dose of salts in the morning and in the night 3. drachms of bark. Recollecting then the above prescription I gave no more bark, but the next night gave 6 grs. of calomel. He missed his fit the next day. But note, I was not perfectly satisfied that his sickness was genuine.

MS (DLC); entirely in TJ's hand, with later entry added in a different ink; endorsed by TJ: "Receipt for Head-ach."

Dissenting Opinion on the Sinking Fund

[12 Apr. 1792?]

The Secretary of State continuing to dissent from any estimate of [the par of the sixes at more than 20/ the pound, of] the true value of the three percents[1] at more than 10/ the pound[2] [and of that of the deferred sixes at such a sum as at a compound interest of 6 per cent would produce 20/ at the term of paiment].

MS (DLC: TJ Papers, 72: 12592); written entirely in TJ's hand on a small scrap; undated; brackets in original. Presumably the second document recorded in SJPL under 31 Mch. 1792 below the entry listed in note to Alexander Hamilton to TJ, 20 Mch. [1792]: "Th:J. note respecting same subject.—our debt trebled by Hamilton." For the third document, see the undated Note on the National Debt in Vol. 24: 810.

TJ drafted this dissent in his capacity as a Commissioner of the Sinking Fund to express opposition to Alexander Hamilton's policy during the Panic of 1792 of purchasing government securities at par, rather than at their lower market value, in order to preserve public credit, a policy the Virginian evidently regarded as a prop to speculators. Although TJ and one of the other three Commissioners then in Philadelphia had questioned the legality of this policy from the time they first considered it on about 21 Mch. 1792, this impasse was broken by Chief Justice John Jay, an absentee member who advised his colleagues in a 31 Mch. opinion that the policy was legal. Despite TJ's later entry in SJPL, the resolution from which the Secretary of State dissented was probably the one adopted by the Commissioners at a meeting on 12 Apr. 1792, which authorized Hamilton to extend his current purchases of the debt in the three classes of stock by up to a total of $200,000 according to principles they had approved on 15 Aug. 1791. Consistent with TJ's opinion, the minutes of the 12 Apr. 1792 meeting record that the Secretary of State dissented from the resolution as it related to the purchase of 3 percent and deferred 6 percent stock. As TJ's opinion suggests, he had previously dissented entirely from a resolution of 4 Apr. 1792 approving Hamilton's purchase of those classes of securities "upon a computation of interest at the rate of five per centum," though he had joined in a resolution adopted on 26 Mch. 1792 authorizing the Secretary of the Treasury to begin purchases of $100,000 in funded 6 percent stock at the par value of 20 shillings in the pound. In May 1792, inspired in part by James Madison, Congress specified that henceforth the Commissioners were to purchase the debt at the lowest possible price (ASP, *Finance*, I, 235-7; Syrett, *Hamilton*, XI, 158-61, 172-3, 434; *Annals*, III, 1383; Peterson, *Jefferson*, 462-3; Forrest McDonald, *Alexander Hamilton: A Biography* [New York, 1979], 170-1, 248-50; Hamilton to TJ, 20 Mch. 1792, and note).

[1] MS: "threes percents," the second word being interlined.
[2] Preceding two words interlined.

From William Lambert

Philadelphia, 17 Apr. 1792. John Roney, a former lieutenant in the Virginia line of the Continental Army, and Michael Ford, who was trained in a merchant's counting house and writes a very good hand, both clerks to the Commissioner of Loans for Virginia who were formerly in the office of the Commissioner of Accounts for that state, regard their employment as precarious and wish to obtain posts in the executive departments of the United States. Since the Treasury and War Departments have no vacancies, he asks that they be recommended to David Rittenhouse for clerkships at the Mint when it begins operations.

RC (DLC: Washington Papers, Applications for Office); 2 p.; at foot of text: "The Honorable Thomas Jefferson, esq"; endorsed by TJ as received 17 Apr. 1792 and so recorded in SJL.

The following letters also pertain to employment at the Mint: (1) William Barton to TJ, Philadelphia, 18 Apr. 1792, requesting his support for his unsuccessful application to become Treasurer of the Mint and stating that Rittenhouse approved of his application for the post (RC in DLC: Washington Papers, Applications for Office; at foot of text: "Hon. T. Jefferson, Esq Secry. of State"; endorsed by TJ as received 18 Apr.

1792 and so recorded in SJL). (2) Rittenhouse to TJ, 26 Jan. 1793, enclosing "such certificates in favour of Henry Voight as have come to my hands" for use as he thought proper (RC in same; addressed: "Mr. Jefferson Secretary of State"; filed with certificates attesting to Voigt's good conduct and character from John Nancarrow of 16 Jan. 1793, Henry Deberger, Sr., of 21 Jan. 1793, William Will and ten others of 22 Jan. 1793, and Benjamin Rittenhouse of no date). Later in the month Voigt was promoted from interim to permanent chief coiner of the Mint (see TJ to George Washington, 9 June 1792, and note).

From Alexander Hamilton

Treasury Department, 12 May 1792. Requests that the patent for 214,285 acres, when sealed and recorded, "be delivered to the bearer The Rev. Mr. Cutler."

RC (DNA: RG 59, MLR).

For further information about the patent, see Syrett, *Hamilton*, XI, 379-80, 397n.

Edmund Randolph's Notes on Jefferson's Letter to George Hammond

[ca. 16 May 1792]

A cursory reading suggests for consideration the following hints.

√ pa. 7.   1. When the just distinction is pressed between the covenanting and recommendatory parts of the treaty, would it be improper to refer to the knowledge, which Mr. Oswald must have had of the confederation, and therefore of its incapacity to warrant our ministers to go farther upon the points recommended? [1]

pa. 23.   2. The doctrine of alienage is not free from difficulty. As it existed at common law, it could not exist relatively to those who were formerly members of the same empire: for this disability must be *born* with a man. It sprang then from the law of nations only. But when a foreigner is permitted to hold lands, and no restriction is connected with the words, giving that licence, is not an enjoyment of them by personal residence a clear consequence?

pa. 30.   3. The similitude of an act of confiscation to an office found seems correct. But to what species of office? That of intituling; which can hardly be said to give possession without entry. See Buller's nisi prius on this head. I have not consulted it; not having it with me.[2]

pa. 42.   4. Levari facias is said to affect the profits only of lands. But if the profits do not exceed the annual interest, the creditor will become the proprietor for ever, altho' he will not acquire a freehold.

√ 43. 44.   5. I do not see, that it has been thought fit to reply to Mr. H's remark on the laws, allowing a tender of property, that this was the same and no other measure, dealt out to the citizens as well as foreigners.[3]

          6. There are some positions in the answer, which militate against the attempts, now made by the debtors in Virginia; The most obvious are, that treaties under the confederation were superior to the laws of the states, and that the lawyers in Virginia have so declared. I question the universality of the latter fact.

          7. Messrs. Monro and Giles are undoubtedly mistaken in saying, that suits have been generally[4] sustained in the state-courts for british debts contracted[5] *before the war.*

√   8. Is not a peculiar asperity to be found in speaking of *murders*, *rapes*, *robberies*, *trespasses* &c. Does the subject require it?[6]

pa. 52.   9. Do we know enough of Brailsford vs. Morris from the newspaper to say, that it proves the point, for which it is quoted; or does what is published[7] absolutely reach the matter in hand?

pa. 59.   10. Can it be important to diminish the value of our debts to G. B; and if not, is it clear, that they are so much within the compass of payment? and if not clear, may not the ease of paying be retorted upon us under some future circumstances with great affect?

pa. 60.   11. The true situation of the Maryland bank-Stock is in some particulars different from your representation.[8]

          12. I once supposed, that a distinction[9] between a claim of interest on an open account or bond was maintainable. My principle was, that the penalty became the debt, from which equity would not absolve without a payment of interest. But being thrown into the arms of equity, it partakes of every subject within its cognizance, and may therefore be modified, as an open account.

√ pa. 5.   13. In examining Pagan's case, I have been led to believe, that some aid may be drawn to his antagonist, from considering, that the whole of british hostility was carried on under the colour of acts of parliament, not the law of nations. Does not this discharge us from the liberality, due to other enemies?[10]

[827]

14. I know not, what circuit court has allowed interest during the war. The case in Connecticut is the nearest; but it is too indistinctly known to be cited by me.

The above observations are too much hurried, to have any thing deserving reliance.

MS (DLC: TJ Papers, 98: 16775); in Randolph's hand, with check marks and page references added by TJ; undated; endorsed by TJ: "E. Randolph's notes."

This document, consisting of the Attorney General's comments on TJ's draft of his 29 May 1792 letter to British minister George Hammond on the disputed provisions of the Treaty of Paris, establishes that Randolph did in fact suggest a number of changes to the Secretary of State (see Vol. 23: 606n). TJ reported to the President on 16 May 1792 that the draft "is now in the hands of the Attorney general," thus indicating approximately when Randolph wrote these notes (TJ to George Washington, 16 May 1792). For the changes TJ made in the draft in response to Randolph's recommendations, see notes 1-3, 6-7, and 11 below.

BULLER'S NISI PRIUS: Sir Francis Buller, *An Introduction to the Law relative to trials at Nisi Prius* (London, 1772), the sixth edition of which (Dublin, 1791) TJ subsequently acquired (Sowerby, No. 1974). MR. H'S REMARK: see Hammond to TJ, 5 Mch. 1792. PAGAN'S CASE: see note to Hammond to TJ, 26 Nov. 1791.

[1] For the revision TJ made only in the Dft in response to this paragraph, see TJ to Hammond, 29 May 1792, note 11.

[2] For the revision TJ had previously made in response to suggestions by James Madison, see TJ to Hammond, 29 May 1792, note 25.

[3] For the revision TJ made in response to this paragraph, see TJ to Hammond, 29 May 1792, notes 54 and 60.

[4] Word interlined.

[5] Word interlined.

[6] For the revision TJ made in response to this paragraph, see TJ to Hammond, 29 May 1792, note 68.

[7] Word interlined in place of "quoted."

[8] Randolph here canceled an unfinished line: "12. Does not the st."

[9] Randolph first wrote the remainder of the sentence as "of a claim of interest was maintainable" before altering it to read as above.

[10] For the revisions TJ made in response to this paragraph and to earlier suggestions by Madison, see TJ to Hammond, 29 May 1792, note 10.

From Eliza House Trist

DR SIR   [ca. 30 May 1792]

Mr. Madison consented that Mrs. Pine Shou'd finnish a portrait of him self—which was began by Mr. Pine: The Morning he left the city he desired that I wou'd refer the Ladies to you for payment; and you will also please to receive it under your roof. I am Your &ca   E. TRIST

RC (DLC: TJ Papers, 235: 42144); undated; addressed: "Mr Jefferson"; endorsed by TJ. Recorded in SJL as received 30 May 1792.

TJ quickly asked his daughter Mary to ascertain the price of Robert Edge Pine's portrait of James MADISON, and bought it on 2 June 1792 (TJ to Mary Jefferson, [30 May 1792], and note).

Memorial from William Green

To, Thomas Jefferson, Esquire, Secretary of State. The Memorial of William Green of New York, Merchant, Most humbly Sheweth.

That your Memorialist is a Citizen of the United States of America, and hath Carried on a Trade under the Flag of the said States, to the East Indies, in which a Very large Capital is involved.

That in the Course of his dealings, he hath exported from, as well as sold therein, large quantities of East India Goods, all which he had, from time to time, imported on his own Account, directly from the East Indies, unconnected with any Foreigner, or foreign Interest.

That in the Year One thousand Seven hundred and eighty six, having occasion to make large Remittances to Europe, he exported from the Port of Newport, Rhode Island, in a Ship, solely belonging, to himself, of the burthen of Seven hundred Tons, (Coppered and Copper bolted,) called the Hydra, and Navigated according to the Laws of the United States, and in sundry other Vessels, to the Port of Ostend, in the Austrian Netherlands, Merchandize, to the Value of Near Fifty thousand pounds Sterling, which he Consigned, under certain Conditions, to John Buchannan and Robert Charnock, two British Merchants, established there, and having so done he returned immediately to his Family and establishment at Newport aforesaid.

That soon after his return to America, he received Advices, that the Conduct of his said Correspondents, John Buchannan and Robert Charnock, was extremely dishonest, and irregular; They having suffered Bills of Exchange drawn on them, on his Account, and by their Consent, to be protested, and at the same time having made away with his property, under a Feigned Sale, and rendered no proper Account thereof to his Agent in London, who is as Respectable a Merchant as any in that Capital.

That a prevailing reason with Your Memorialist, for Confiding his property to the Management of the said British Merchants, John Buchannan and Robert Charnock, was, that particular Article of the Treaty between the United States and Great Britain, whereby it is stipulated, that there should be no Legal Impediment to the Recovery of the Full Value in Sterling Money of all, Bona Fide, debts heretofore Contracted.

That the said Conduct of the said British Merchants, obliged Your Memorialist, after his Removal from Newport to New York, which took place in the Year One thousand seven hundred and eighty eight, to make a Voyage to England; to look after, and recover the said property; to Effect which; on his Arrival there, he was obliged to bring an Action against the said John Buchannan and Robert Charnock, in the Court of

King's Bench, but being invited by the said John Buchannan and Robert Charnock, to go to Ostend, under an offer of an Amicable Settlement, he was there Arrested under the Most frivolous pretences, and kept in Confinement Thirteen Months, with a View, to detain him from prosecuting the said Action, so that he was unable to bring it to Trial until Hilary Term, One thousand seven hundred and ninety, when he was Nonsuited on the following principles; which however interesting to him, appear also to have involved questions of Public Right, relative to the United States, and on the ground of these Rights, and on his Claims of Protection, in the Trade he has been Carrying on, he founds his hopes of redress, from the Wisdom and Policy of the Executive of these United States.

Your Memorialist presumes to assert, that he carried Complete Evidence into that Court, for the Conviction of the Defendants, in the said Action, in a Debt of near Thirty thousand pounds Sterling, against which, the said British Subjects, John Buchannan and Robert Charnock, who appeared in Court in their defence, put up no other plea than the following—Vizt.

That your Memorialist, although Married to a Native of these States, settled for some years, and Naturalized therein, and several of his Children being Natural born Subjects thereof, had been once reputed a British Subject, and therefore had no right to trade to the East Indies, without a Licence from the English East-India Company, and having traded there without such licence, that all your Memorialist's Bargains, with British Subjects, were null and of no Effect in Law, and that therefore They were not Legally responsible to him, for that the said William Green having trenched on the Monopoly of the said English East-India Company, by Shipping of East-India Goods, from America to Ostend, They were exempt by Law as British Subjects, from being obliged to Account with him (although he is Avowedly a Citizen of the said United States) for the whole or any part of the said property, and their Counsel therefore Moved the Court to protect the said John Buchannan and Robert Charnock in the said exemption, in which Lord Kenyon, the presiding Judge, and Lord Chief Justice of England acquiesed, and Ordered your Memorialist to be Nonsuited, and he was accordingly obliged to suffer a Nonsuit, after expending near Three thousand pounds Sterling in endeavouring to recover his Aforesaid property.

That that Judgment, which went to Annihilate, or to Confer upon British Subjects, so great a proportion of the Capital of your Memorialist, must appear the more extraordinary, when it is known, that not sixteen hours before, the said Lord Chief Justice of England, had Adjudged Your Memorialist under the very same Circumstances of an East India Trade, to pay a Tradesman of London, the Sum of Two thousand pounds Sterling and upwards, although your Memorialist was not then and never had been indebted to the said Tradesman, in that, or any other sum of Money whatever, the Circumstances of this part of the Case of your Memorialist stands thus. Your Memorialist in the year 1784, had remitted to an English Merchant resident in London the sum of Twenty thousand pounds Sterling and upwards, for Certain Mercantile Purposes; and in the following years 1786 and 1787, remitted such farther sums to the said Merchant, as to make in favor of your Memorialist, a very large Cash ballance, having which in his hands, the latter end of the last mentioned year, the said English Merchant became a Bankrupt to the Immense loss of your Memorialist, the said Tradesman, was one of Many with whom the said Merchant, whilst in Credit, had dealt, and he had bought Goods of the said Tradesman, during the said year 1784, which Goods he the said Merchant had in that very year shipped to the Order of your Memorialist, and received for the same full payment from your Memorialist; the said Tradesman's plea against your Memorialist was, that the said Merchant had not paid the whole Amount of his debt, and that your Memorialist, having derived benefit from the Goods, supplied to him, was responsible for the deficiencies of his Correspondent, the said English Merchant; in the Justice of which plea, the Court Acquiesed, and decided accordingly; and your Memorialist was of Course most unjustly Compelled as an American Merchant, to pay to him the sum of Two thousand and twenty pounds Sterling, which he had before paid to the said English Merchant, altho' in the same Term, and almost with the same breath, your Memorialist had been totally refused, any right to recover debts from British Subjects, because he had been Carrying on a Trade to the East Indies; the Proofs of this Branch of your Memorialist's Case is Contained in the affidavit of William Maxwell, sworn before Joshua Johnson Esquire, Consul of the United States for the Port of London, which Maxwell, was the only evidence produced in Court to support the plea of the said Tradesman.

Your Memorialist after having expended near Three thousand pounds Sterling as aforesaid, in the pursuit of Justice, returned home, to his Family to New York in the Month of June 1790, from which period he hath been almost Constantly employed in putting the Affairs of his Capital in America in proper Order, and in Authenticating in the best manner possible, the very great Wrongs, Injuries and Losses, which it hath been the Misfortune of your Memorialist to sustain, as a Citizen of and under the Flag of the United States.

Your Memorialist for this last mentioned purpose, went to England in the Winter of that year, in a Brigantine belonging to himself, Called the Rachel, concerning which Vessel, he hath already by Letter, made particular references: and Joshua Johnson Esquire, being about that time appointed to be Consul of the United States, for the Port of London, and your Memorialist Conceiving the said Joshua Johnson Esquire, to be vested with all the Powers usually given to Consuls, for the protection of Trade, applied to him, by Letter requesting that in his Public Capacity, he would call to his Aid, such a Number of American Merchants, as might then be in London, in order to form a Committee, to receive and authenticate Evidence, and to prepare such a Conclusive report upon the whole Circumstances of his Case, as might reasonably justify the Executive Government of the United States, in Remonstrating to the British Court, upon the Unparalell'd treatment which your Memorialist has met with, and in a solicitation of the redress of his Grievances; the result was, that Duncan Ingraham Esquire then of Philadelphia Merchant, Samuel Broome Esquire of New York Merchant, and John Brown Cutting Esquire were the Gentlemen approved of by Mr. Johnson for this Important employment.

Driven out of the Courts of Justice in England, under the before stated Circumstances, your Memorialist was left without any other resource than to put all the Important evidence, which he could have produced, to support his Plea, against the said British Merchants, John Buchannan and Robert Charnock, upon Consular Record, and he therefore entreated the Gentlemen, who attended at the Court of King's Bench, on the Trial; and who were prevented from giving evidence in the said Court, by the said Lord Chief Justice, to proceed voluntarily before the above said Joshua Johnson Esquire, and render upon Oath their true and sufficient Testimony to establish the Merits of the Case; an Authentic Copy of that body of Evidence, notarially Attested, and Certified by the said Joshua Johnson Esquire, is herewith humbly submitted to your Consideration.

Thus it appears that whilst the British Government, are frequently procuring Laws to be enacted, for the purpose of Checking and restraining the Trade of Foreigners in India, the English East-India Company, with a proper Knowledge of what is right and expedient, adapting its regulations for its dependencies, to the happiness and prosperity of its Asiatic Subjects, have opened upon the payment of a Certain Tariff, upon Imports and Exports, all their Ports in India to Foreigners of every Nation in Europe, as well as to the Ships and Vessels, and Citizens of these United States.

It was thus your Memorialist was permitted to trade in Calcutta, where his Ship the Hydra, bearing the Flag of the United States, was Admitted to a regular Entry at the Custom-House of the said City, and where the Amount of the Duties paid to the English East-India Company, by your Memorialist, upon his Imports and Exports therefrom, in that Ship, in the year 1785, amounted to the Sum of Four thousand four hundred and ninety four Pounds thirteen shillings and eleven pence Sterling; and the Trade is still carried on in the same Manner from these United States, upon the payment of similar duties, to the English East-India Company, although your Memorialist has been punished by the Sequestration of More than Two thirds of his Capital, in favor of the said British Merchants, John Buchannan and Robert Charnock; and as he himself Conceives, in Violation of every principle of Moral or political Justice, as well, of that particular Article of the Treaty, between these United States and Great Britain, which has been already quoted, and under which, Our Courts of Justice are so intirely free and open, to the Claims of every British Suitor.

Your Memorialist, with great Respect and Deference, states these Circumstances in order to shew, from whence some of these Confusions arise, which are perpetually happening on the part of the British Administration, to An Immense disadvantage, and loss to the Commerce of the Citizens of these United States.

Hence too Arises, the power of the said British Merchants, John Buchannan and Robert Charnock to withold from your Memorialist, his property, which by a Certified Account, signed by Duncan Ingraham, Samuel Broome, and John Brown Cutting Esquires, including the Interest at five per Cent arising upon their balance, Amounted on the thirty first day of December 1790, to no less a Sum than Thirty seven thousand nine hundred and forty three pounds six shillings and seven pence three farthings Sterling.

Hence too Arises, the Power of the said British Merchants, to detain in the Port of Ostend from your Memorialist, his Ship the Hydra, Coppered and Copper bolted, and of the burthen of Seven hundred Tons, ever since she sailed from Rhode-Island, in the latter end of the year 1786, and the said British Merchants, as if in Mockery, have spread the Flag of these United States, at her Mast-head, on all the usual Festivals for the space of these Five last years.

Hence too Arises, the incapacity of your Memorialist, to recover any part of the Vessel and Cargo, which he sent from the Port of Philadelphia to India, in the Spring of the year 1788, which Vessel was called the Betsey, Commanded by Edward Kirby, was loaded with one hundred and eighty Tons of Wines and Liquors; and taken jointly, is estimated at the value of Forty thousand Dollars; the Vessel was sold by order of the Consignee, after her Arrival in Calcutta, in the latter end of the same year, but your Memorialist has never received Any part of the Amount of the Sales of the said Vessel or Cargo, and British Subjects by the decision of the said Lord Chief Justice of England, being declared to be exempt in Law, from any necessity of accounting with him, or to him, for the whole, or Any part of the property, which as a Citizen of these United States, he hath embarked in the said Trade to the East-Indies; It is therefore only from the Virtue or Conscience of the said Consignee, that he has the smallest hope of obtaining any Satisfaction for the same, which Considering the present state of Mercantile Societies, and the Many thousand Leagues distance, between the two Countries, may be Considered as a Matter extremely problematical.

Hence too arises, other incapacities to which Your Memorialist is unfortunately subject, as a Citizen of these States; for, Your Memorialist having sold, or Consigned for Sale, large quantities of East-India Goods to British Merchants resident in the West-India Islands, to whom in many instances, he has given Very long and extensive Credits, Your Memorialist by this extraordinary Law doctrine of the said Lord Chief Justice of England, is debarred of All right of recovery, in any English Chief, or subordinate Court of Law, and the said Consignees or Debtors, are of Course at Liberty to pay him, or not, at their Will and Pleasure.

The Earnest and Sincere desire of your Memorialist to Avoid Any kind of Personal Litigation, with the said British Merchants, John Buchannan and Robert Charnock, hath induced your Memorialist not only before the Institution of his Action against them in the Court of King's Bench, in England, but Very frequently since that time, and when all other Means had failed, even by Public and printed Advertisements, prefixed at the Gates of the Royal Exchange of London, to offer and propose to leave the Settlement of the Amount of the Debt, which they owed to him, and the periods and extent of their payments, to the Arbitration of Any Committee of American and British Merchants, which might be mutually chosen in that City, for that purpose (Nay Your Memorialist hath also made offer, to submit it even to the Arbitration of British Merchants alone) in all the Various Ways that are attested to have been employed, by the Aforesaid Joshua Johnson Esquire, for it as little suited with the Natural Affections of your Memorialist to be longer absent from his Family in America, than indispensable Necessity required, as it was in the highest degree inconvenient and dangerous to your Memorialist, to trust his remaining property in America, during his Absence to the Management of Factors and Clerks.

The Amount of property, Virtually and Effectively, sequestered from your Memorialist by the Aforesaid Sentence of the said Lord Chief Justice of England, are as follows—Vizt.

Item 1st. a Balance upon Account due from John Buchannan and Robert Charnock, arising from the Sales of East India Goods, and other property Consigned to them, by your Memorialist from Newport Rhode Island, the latter end of the year 1786, which Balance sustained by Authentic documents, is Attested by Duncan Ingraham Esquire, Samuel Broome Esquire, and John Brown Cutting Esquire, to be on the thirty first day of December 1790, the Sum of £37943.6s.7½ d. Sterling—which in Spanish Milled Dollars @ 4/3 is   Dollars. 178,556

Item 2nd, To the Amount of a Sum of Money, which Your Memorialist was Unjustly obliged by the Sentence of the said Lord Chief Justice to pay for a pretended debt, to a Trades-man of London, one James Chapman, for a parcel of Goods, which had been supplied by him, to a Merchant of that City, who was your Memorialist's Correspondent—and to whom he made full payment for the same, several years before, but for which nevertheless, his present English Correspondent, who was his bail in the Action, was obliged to pay over again, to the said Tradesman, being the sum of £2020 Sterling which in Dollars @ 4/3, is,   9,505

Item, 3rd. To the Amount of Sundry Debts due to your Memorialist, from sundry British Merchants Residents in the West India Windward Islands, but which the Lord Chief Jus-tice of England, declares your Memorialist hath no Legal right to recover, and which are in Consequence sequestered from him: Your Memorialist Very much under-rates this Ar-ticle, to Avoid fractions at the sum of   40,000

Item, 4th. To Amount of the Value of the Brigantine Bet-sey Captain Edward Kirby Commander and of her Cargo, which Vessel sailed from Philadelphia to Calcutta in the Spring of the year 1788, and Arrived there in the Month of December of the same year, the proceeds of which Vessel and Cargo, notwithstanding all the Efforts of your Memorialist, to have the same remitted to this Country, Yet remain in the hands of the Consignees, who Are British Merchants estab-lished there and the sum whereof, is effectively sequestered from your Memorialist, under the Sanction of the aforesaid Decision of the Lord Chief Justice of England, and which is Considerably under-rated at the Sum of,   40,000

Dollars 268,061

Making the whole Amount of the present damage sustained by him, two hundred and Sixty eight thousand and sixty One Dollars.

The feeble powers of Your Memorialist Are not Adequate to resist with Any effect, the Mighty but Cruel Policy, which declares and justi-fies, the Measures of impoverishing, distressing, and discouraging the Commerce of the Citizens of these United States. Everything that was possible to be done by your Memorialist, to recover his property by Law, or in an Amicable Manner by Arbitration from the said British Merchants, has Already been done, but without any other effect, but that of Involving your Memorialist deeper and deeper, in a fruitless and expensive Struggle, whilst They, by a Combination of Circumstances, such as a large Capital of their own, a great property of Your Memorialist's which they detain in their hands, a Profligacy of Principle almost beyond Conception or Credibility; together with the powerfull protection of the Courts of Justice of England, hold him in open defiance, as a Citizen of these United States, and leave him to the inevitable Necessity of Appealing, to the humanity, Wisdom and power of the Government of these United States for Relief and Protection.

Your Memorialist therefore with All due Respect to the Government of his Country, with the firmness of a Citizen, claiming its protection, exhibits this Complaint; unfolds his Grievances; states the Facts of it; and offers the proofs; trusting and expecting; that the National Executive; apprized of the true Nature of a Mischief, that may extend far beyond the Case of your Memorialist, to points touching Important Rights, and the Interests of Many American Citizens, will consider—he beseeches You to Consider—to examine the premises—to Attend to the Prayer of his Memorial—to grant it—It is this—That the Executive will demand for him from the British Government, and insist on his Obtaining, a Just indemnification for the great Losses, and damage, which as an American Citizen and Merchant, he hath most injuriously sustained.   Philadelphia June the 11th. 1792

                                                WILLIAM GREEN

RC (DNA: RG 76, Great Britain, Unbound Records); in a clerk's hand, with dateline and signature by Green. Enclosure not found. Enclosed in Green to TJ, 11 June 1792.

From John Carey

SIR   Friday, July 13. [1792]

Having amended my proposals in conformity to the ideas you were pleased to suggest, permit me (with sincerest thanks for the favors conferred on me in the commencement of my undertaking) to enclose you a few copies, on the eve of your departure, in hopes they may come into the hands of some of your friends in Virginia. I have the honor to be, with perfect respect, Sir, your most obliged humble Servant,

                                                J: CAREY

RC (DLC: TJ Papers, 90: 15505); partially dated; endorsed by TJ as received 13 July 1792 and so recorded in SJL.

The enclosure probably consisted of COPIES of Carey's undated broadside proposing that a subscription be opened to publish *The American Remembrancer, or Proceedings of the Old Congress*, a work which was never printed (see Evans, No. 46708, which assigns the year 1793 to the broadside).

From John Fitch

24 July 1792

I Sir am sorry to live in a State that no soner becomes a Nation than it becomes depraved. The injuryes which I have Received from my Nation or rather from the first Officers of Government has induced me for a lesson of caution to future generations to record the treatment which I have received which will in a Very Few Days be sealed up and placed in the Library of Philadelphia to remain under Seal till after my Death in which Sir your candour is Very seriously called in question.

I Sir altho an Indigent Citizen feal myself upon an equal floore with the first Officers of Government therefore trust that your Exalted Station will not permit you to treat this proposal with contempt as I do not wish to take any undue advantage and should I out live you and you not haveing it in your Power to make your Defence I should think it unmanly to conceal it from you therefore offer you the perusal of all my Manuscripts for Six days on your giveing in writing your Plighted faith of honor to return them all safe in that Time and on these conditions that if you should make any observations upon them that you will furnish me with a Coppy of the same. This Sir is from a poor but an independant Citizen of the United States of America and from one who wishes to subscribe himself your most Sincear Friend   JOHN FITCH

MS (PPL: Fitch Papers); entirely in Fitch's hand; at foot of text: "Thomas Jefferson Esqr."; with subjoined note by Fitch indicating that this letter was never sent: "This I suppressed by the advice of my Friends who was unaquainted with my designes"; endorsed by Fitch.

This unsent letter reflected Fitch's profound bitterness at his failure to obtain a general patent for a steamboat and his unshakable conviction that TJ, as chair of the Patent Board, was partial to his chief rival, James Rumsey. Fitch first petitioned the board on 22 June 1790, describing how he completed the arduous efforts he began in 1785 to develop a steamboat only after receiving exclusive patents from five states, spending about $8,000 of his own money when assistance from Congress and the state legislatures was not forthcoming, and conducting countless futile experiments partly because he was totally ignorant of steam engines being developed in England; urging that interference from competitors not be allowed to undermine his invention

"under any pretense of a different Mode of Application"; and requesting a patent granting "an exclusive Right to the Use of Steam to Navigation, for a Limited time" (FC in DLC: Fitch Papers; entirely in Fitch's hand; at head of text: "To the honourable the Secretary of State the Secretary of War and the attorney General"; endorsed as received by the board a day later; printed from lost MS in William Thornton, *Short Account of the Origin of Steam Boats, written in 1810, and Now Committed to the Press* [Washington, 1814], 10-12). In at least nine ensuing petitions, the last of which was dated 14 Apr. 1791, Fitch peppered the board with arguments against granting anyone else a patent for any method of propelling boats by steam, with requests for procedural changes and expeditious action, with complaints about the financial cost of the delays to which his application was subjected, and with exhaustive documentation of his assertions that the law permitted issuance of a general patent founded on the use of fire and steam and did not require one based on a specific method, that his claim to a steamboat patent predated Rumsey's, and that the pretensions of other claimants were weak (Dfts and FCs in Fitch's hand in PPL: Fitch Papers and DLC: Fitch Papers).

The board eventually decided to award patents bearing the date of 26 Aug. 1791 to all but the last named of the five aspirants—Fitch, Rumsey, John Stevens, Nathan Read, and Isaac Briggs—and to leave a final determination on the competing claims to the courts, a decision that effectively ended serious American work on steamboats until the expiration of the rival patents in 1805 (Frank D. Prager, "The Steam Boat Interference 1787-1793," Patent Office Society, *Journal*, XL [1958], 640-1). Fitch's patent did not grant the general rights for all water transportation powered by steam that he had sought, but rather awarded rights "for applying the force of Steam to a trunk or trunks for drawing water in at the bow of a boat or vessel and forcing the same out at the Stern, in order to propel a boat or vessel through the water; for forcing a column of air through a trunk or trunks filled with water, by the force of Steam; for forcing a column of Air through a trunk or trunks out at the Stern with the bow valves closed by the force of Steam; and for applying the force of Steam to cranks and paddles for propelling a boat or vessel through the water" (Tr in NjHi: Alofsen Collection; with George Washington as signatory and TJ as countersignatory, and with subjoined 26 Aug. 1791 certification by Attorney General Edmund Randolph and 30 Aug. 1791 notation by TJ that the patent had been delivered to Fitch that day; consisting of a certified copy of 12 July 1811 authenticated by

Secretary of State James Monroe, filed with Trs of specification and drawing; for the latter, see Prager, *Fitch*, 196).

Fitch attributed the board's decision to the favoritism he believed the three members, but the Secretary of State most of all, displayed toward Rumsey at the decisive hearing on 23 Apr. 1791 (Prager, *Fitch*, 197-8). Although he chose not to confront TJ directly with his encyclopedic allegations of mistreatment, and decided against sending the letter printed here, Fitch followed through on his intention of depositing copies of his papers relating to the controversy in the Library Company of Philadelphia. Instructing the Librarian to keep them under seal for thirty years because of his "fear that the violence of the times or the parties whome they affected might be a means of haveing them destroyed," Fitch nevertheless authorized him "should Mr. Jefferson ever be aiming toward the presidents chair by all means to obtain leave to breake the seals and extract what affects the Commissioners of Congress [i.e., the Patent Board] and then seal them again." Fitch also expressed a keen desire that the same might be "done to all the scounderals that is stepping forward for more favours from their country," but always in such a manner as to ensure that they would not be able to destroy his papers (Fitch to the Librarian of the Library Company of Philadelphia, 30 July, 26 Oct. 1792, in Prager, *Fitch*, 207-9). No evidence has been found to indicate that the Librarian honored Fitch's request during TJ's elections to the presidency.

From Charles Carroll of Carrollton

Doughoragen, 9 Aug. 1792. At his request he introduces the bearer, "Mr. Cassanave," an upright and amiable gentleman who will explain his future views and schemes. He has received from him a strong letter of recommendation by Bishop Carroll reporting that several of Baltimore's principal merchants have provided similar letters and is confident that TJ will render him any services in his power. P.S. He sends his respects to Madison.

RC (NNP); 1 p.; endorsed by TJ as received 16 Aug. 1792 and so recorded in SJL.

TJ wrote two letters of introduction for Etienne Cassanave the day he received this one (TJ to William Carmichael, and to Etienne Clavière, both 16 Aug. 1792).

Petition of Jonathan Williams, Jr., to the Patent Board

Northern Liberties of Philadelphia, 20 Nov. 1792. Having been "formerly engaged in the business of refining and claying Sugar" in London, he requests a patent for a new multiaperture mold he has invented for claying and whitening refined sugar, as explained by the annexed memoir and figures. Maple sugar manufacture would benefit much by claying or whitening on the spot, which would greatly reduce the expense of transportation and enable the molasses produced by refining to remain at its point of origin, "where it is much wanted for consumption or distillation." To promote this infant manufacture, he offers to exempt from the patent the claying of sugar at the places of its growth, albeit restricting this exception to the inland country to avoid frauds involving the claying of foreign sugar, a distinction that will "operate like a bounty on american sugar" and increase its production by making it more competitive.

MS (InU: Jonathan Williams Papers); 3 p.; in Williams's hand; at head of text: "To The Honorable The Secretary of State for the Department of foreign affairs. The Secretary of State for the Department of War and The Attorney General of The United States"; endorsed by George Taylor, Jr., as received 21 Nov. 1792 and read 5 Jan. 1793, but subsequently returned to Williams for revision in light of the 23 Feb. 1793 patent act. 2d Dft (same); undated and unsigned. Dft (same); undated and unsigned. Enclosure: Williams's "Memoir," comparing the effectiveness of the existing single-aperture mold for whitening refined sugar with his multivent mold, which yields 28 ounces of additional sugar for every 98 produced under the current system at no additional expense, and presenting models in glass and clay (MS in same; undated; endorsed by Taylor as a "Specification" received 21 Nov. 1792). Enclosed drawings not found, but earlier versions are in same.

Williams announced this invention, based in part on his observations in 1784 at a sugar refinery at Bercy, near Paris, in a 17 July 1792 paper read three days later at a meeting of the American Philosophical Society (InU: Jonathan Williams Papers; see also APS, *Proceedings*, XXII, pt. 3 [1885], 206). He was issued a patent for improving "Moulds or Vessels for the purpose of claying or whitening refined Sugar" on 23 Mch. 1793 (MS in PPAmP: Penn Letters and Ancient Documents; see illustration in Appendix III; with attached copy of Williams's short description of the process, which closely follows the language of the "Memoir" described above, the verso bearing his 29 Apr. 1801 assignment of the patent to the American Philosophical Society for $1).

Directions for Building the Great Clock

[1792-1793]

The great clock.

The works are 15 I. deep, from the plate to the farthest point in the back.[1] A circle of 12 I. radius round the center of the hour circle, will barely cover the remotest point of the works.

The center of vibration of the pendulum is 7. I. above the[2] back end of the axis of the hour hand.

The arc of vibration is (at the bob[3]) 18. I.

The same arc, at 7. I. below the center, will be 3. I.

Then a toothed wheel of 2.[4] I. on the back-end of the[5] axis of the hour hand, taking in an equal wheel whose axis will be of course 2[6] I. horizontally from that of hour hand, will be clear of the vibration of the pendulum, and may turn an hour hand on the reverse face of the wall on a wooden hour plate of 12. I. radius. There need be no minute[7] hand, as the hour figures will be 6. I. apart. But the interspace should be divided into quarters and 5. minute marks. The fore and back hour-plates will not be concentric.[8]

The[9] axis of the second hand $4\frac{1}{6}$ I. from that of the hour-hand (i.e. their centers)

The radius of the second circle (i.e. length of hand) $1\frac{3}{4}$ I.

MS (DLC: TJ Papers, 233: 41588); written entirely in TJ's hand on a small sheet; undated.

THE GREAT CLOCK: a large, seven-day timepiece gracing the entrance to Monticello, with faces hanging inside the Entrance Hall and outside beneath the East Portico, that with occasional restoration has continued to operate to the present day (see illustration). TJ certainly penned these instructions for the clock before 27 Apr. 1793, when he paid $113.80 for the instrument to the Philadelphia clockmaker Robert Leslie, whose employee Peter Spurck had constructed it, and probably before 13 Nov. 1792, when he asked Henry Remsen to help obtain a gong for the device (MB, 27 Apr. 1793, and note; TJ to Remsen, 13 Nov. 1792). For the fullest treatment of the clock's construction, installation, and operation, see Silvio A. Bedini, "Thomas Jefferson, Clock Designer," APS, *Proceedings*, CVIII (1964), 165-70; for the clock as pictured in its architectural setting, see William H. Adams, *Jefferson's Monticello* (New York, 1983), 109, 110, 118-19, 196. See also Stein, *Worlds*, 376-7.

[1] Sentence interlined.
[2] TJ here canceled "point."
[3] Word interlined in place of "uttermost."
[4] Digit written over "3."
[5] Preceding three words interlined.
[6] Digit interlined in place of "4."
[7] Word interlined in place of "second."
[8] Sentence interlined.
[9] TJ here canceled "center."

Memorandum from Tench Coxe

[before 5 Feb. 1793?]

[. . .][1]

10

To abolish the drawbacks of the foreign or impost duty upon all manufactures from grain, upon butter, cheese, wet provisions, oil, whalebone, fish. (Quere, also the manufactures from wood).

11

To abolish the draw backs of the foreign or impost Duty upon all manufactures necessary in the building, equipping, or repairing of merchant

Vessels and Ships of war (or at least certain of them) such as Sail cloth Cordage, anchors, sheathing paper, gun powder, cartridge paper.[2]

12

To prohibit foreign Ships from carrying from hence to foreign ports, other than their own, any foreign goods wares or merchandize.[3]

MS (DLC: TJ Papers, 234: 42049); consisting of a one-page fragment in Coxe's hand, lacking sections 1-9, with notations by TJ recorded below; undated, but presumably written sometime before Coxe to TJ, 5 Feb. 1793.

Coxe's memorandum may have been related to the second state of TJ's Report on Commerce, printed above under 16 Dec. 1793, even though TJ did not make there the revision recorded in note 2 below.

[1] Estimated three pages missing.
[2] TJ here wrote "The objects of the 10th. and 11th. as also the duty on fish will be covered by the insertion pa. 17. line 3. of the words 'such articles as we produce ourselves.' For in proceeding to lay duties on manufactures from grain, &c. sailcloth &c. drawbacks will naturally be first withdrawn."
[3] TJ inserted a check mark at the beginning of this sentence and here wrote "Qu? We cannot expect to force them out of that principle of their navigation act which prohibits all nations from carrying productions not their own. Consequently the only effect of this measure would be to deprive ourselves of the transportation from the place of produce to this country."

To Tench Coxe

[on or before 8 Feb. 1793]

Th: Jefferson presents his compliments to Mr. Coxe. He cannot find under what authority a Swedish built ship, for instance, bought by British subjects and navigated legally, can be employed between England and Sweden.—Is it that where the law uses the terms *British*, or *British built* ships, the former means any ships *owned by British subjects*? If so, a Swedish ship bought[1] by a British subject may be employed not only between Engld. and Sweden, but Engld. and France or any other country.—The ascertainment of the fact that the *vessels of other countries* bought by British subjects, may be used in the trade with such other country, is necessary before Th:J. can make one of the statements proposed.

What indulgencies have we, our vessels, or commodities in Ireland which are not allowed in Engld.? A very material information.

P.S. On further examination I find that the stat. 14. Car. 2. c. 11. and 27. G. 3. c. 19. both declare that no ships shall be deemed *British* but such as are *British built*.

RC (CtY); undated, but conjectured on the basis of Coxe's reply of 8 Feb. 1793; addressed: "Mr. Coxe"; endorsed by Coxe. Not recorded in SJL.

[1] Word interlined in place of "owned."

Memorandum to Henry Sheaff

[after 20 Feb. 1793]

Lisbon wines. The best quality of the Dry kind is called Termo, and costs 70. dollars the pipe at about 2. years old. At 5. years old it is becoming a fine wine; at 7. years old is preferable to any but the very best Madeira. Bulkeley & son furnish it from Lisbon.

Sherry. The best dry Sherry costs at Cadiz, from 80. to 90. Dollars the pipe. But when old and fine, such as is sent to the London market it costs £30. sterling the pipe. Mr. Ysnardi, the son, Consul of the US. at Cadiz, at this time in Philadelphia, furnishes it.

The following facts are from my own enquiries in going thro' the different wine cantons of France,[1] examining the identical vineyards producing the first quality of wines, conversing with their owners, and other persons on the spot minutely acquainted with the vineyards, and the wines made on them,[2] and tasting them myself.

Burgundy. The best wines of Burgundy are

Monrachet, a white wine. It is made but by two persons, to wit Monsr. de Clermont, and Monsr. de Sarsnet. The latter rents to Monsr. de la Tour. This costs 48. sous the bottle, new, and 3. livres when fit for drinking.

Meursault. A white wine. The best quality of it is called Goutte d'or. It costs 6. sous the bottle new. I do not believe this will bear transportation. But the Monrachet will in a proper season.[3]

Chambertin, Vougeau, Veaune, are red wines, of the first quality, and are the only fine red wines of Burgundy which will bear transportation, and even these require to be moved in the best season, and not to be exposed to great heat or great cold. These cost 48. sous the bottle, new, and 3. livres old.[4]

I think it next to impossible to have any of the Burgundy wines brought here in a sound state.

Champagne. The Mousseux or Sparkling Champagne is never brought to a good table in France. The still, or non-mousseux, is alone drunk by connoisseurs.

Aij. The best is made at Aij, by Monsr. d'Orsay, who makes more than all the other proprietors of the first quality

[842]

put together. It costs 3. livres the bottle when of the proper age to drink, which is at 5. years old.

> The Red Champagne is not a fine wine. The best is made by the Benedictine monks at Auvillaij.

The wines of Burgundy and Champagne being made at the head of the Seine, are brought down that river at Havre from whence they are shipped. They should come down in the month of November, so that they may be brought over sea in the winter, and arrive here before our warm Spring days. They should be bottled on the spot where they are made. The bottle, bottling, corking and packing costs 5 sous a bottle. Capt. Cutting Consul of the U.S. at Havre a good person and well informed, to supply the wines of Burgundy and Champagne.[5]

Bordeaux red wines.

> There are four crops of them more famous than all the rest. These are Chateau-Margau, Tour de Segur, Hautbrion, and de la Fite. They cost 3. livres a bottle, old: but are so engaged before hand that it is impossible to get them. The merchants, if you desire it, will send you a wine by any of those names, and make you pay 3. livres a bottle: but I will venture to affirm that there never was a bottle of those wines sent to America *by a merchant.* Nor is it worth while to seek for them; for I will defy any person to distinguish them from the wines of the next quality, to-wit

> Rohan-Margau, which is made by Madame de Rohan. This is what I import for myself, and consider as equal to any of the four crops. There are also the wines of Dabbadie, la Rose, Quirouen and Durfort which are reckoned as good as Madame de Rozan's. Yet I have preferred hers. These wines cost 40. sous the bottle, when of the proper age for drinking.

Bordeaux white wines.

> Grave. The best is called Pontac, and is made by Monsr. de Lamont. It costs 18. sous a bottle.

> Sauterne. This is the best white wine of France (except Champagne and Hermitage) the best of it is made by Monsr. de Luz-Saluz, and costs at 4. years old (when fit to drink) from 20. to 24. sous the bottle. There are two other white wines made in the same neighborhood called Prignac and Barsac, esteemed by some. But the Sauterne is that preferred at Paris, and much the best in my judgment. They cost the same. A great

advantage of the Sauterne is that it becomes higher flavored the day after the bottle has been opened, than it is at first.

Mr. Fenwick, Consul of the US. at Bordeaux, is well informed on the subject of these wines, and has supplied the President and myself with them genuine and good. He would be a proper person to endeavor to get from the South of France some of the wines made there which are most excellent and very cheap, say 10. or 12. sous the bottle. Those of Rousillon are the best. I was not in Rousillon myself, and therefore can give no particular directions about them. At Nismes I drank a good wine, stronger than claret, well flavored, the tavern price of which was 2. sous the quart. Mr. Fenwick might perhaps be able to get these brought through the Canal of Languedoc.

A good correspondent at Amsterdam might furnish the following wines.

Moselle. The best of these is called Brownberg, being made on a mountain of that name adjoining the village of Dusmond, 15 leagues from Coblentz, to which last place it is brought and stored for sale. The best crop of Brownberg is that of the Baron Breidbach Burresheim. It costs 22. sous the bottle when old enough to drink. It is really a good wine.

Hock. There has been discovered within these 30. years, a finer wine of this quality called Johansberg, now decidedly preferred to Hock. They both cost 5/ sterl. a bottle when of the oldest and best quality. It is to be observed of the Hock wines that no body can drink them but Germans or the English who have learnt it from their German kings. Compared with the wines of more Southern climates they are as an olive compared with a pineapple.

Observe that whenever the price of wine *by the bottle* is mentioned, it means to include the price of the bottle, &c which is 5. sous. Deduct that sum therefore, and it leaves always the price of the wine.

MS (Spencer Gilbert, New York City, 1944); entirely in TJ's hand; undated, but assigned to earliest possible date on basis of internal evidence; consists of a large sheet folded to make four pages, with words torn away at folds supplied from PrC; unaddressed, but endorsed on last page by an unknown hand: "Thos. Jefferson [. . .] U.S. to Mr. H. Sheaff on French Wines." PrC (DLC: TJ Papers, 234: 41994-6).

TJ evidently intended this memorandum for Henry Sheaff, a wine merchant at 180 High Street, Philadelphia, from whom he purchased wine several times during the period from 1791 to 1794 and again from 1800 to 1804. President Washington also bought wine and spirits from Sheaff, who was a large creditor of Robert Morris and lost heavily at the time of the latter's bankruptcy in 1797-98 (Hardie, *Phila. Dir.*,

129; MB, 19 Jan. 1791, 6 July 1793, 5 Jan. 1794, 26 Sep. 1800, 6 Dec. 1804; PMHB, XXIX [1905], 398, XXXI [1907], 348; Syrett, *Hamilton*, XXI, 351; Sheaff to TJ, 27 June 1805, 16 Oct. 1815).

This document could not have been written earlier than 20 Feb. 1793, when Nathaniel Cutting and Joseph Yznardi, Jr., were confirmed as United States consuls at Le Havre and Cadiz, respectively, and probably no later than 25 Aug. 1793, when Yznardi was in Boston awaiting a ship for Spain (Memorandum on Consuls Recommended for Appointment, 18 Feb. 1793, and note; Yznardi to TJ, 25 Aug., 29 Dec. 1793). The first two sentences on SHERRY in the second paragraph follow nearly verbatim a memorandum of a con-

versation with Yznardi that TJ wrote on a small slip which begins "Ysnardi tells me that" (MS in DLC: TJ Papers, 234: 41997; entirely in TJ's hand; undated, but almost certainly written sometime in 1793; endorsed by TJ: "Sherry wine").

Missing letters from Sheaff to TJ of 23 Nov. 1791 and 25 June 1792 are recorded in SJL as received from Philadelphia on 25 Nov. 1791 and 25 June 1792, respectively.

[1] TJ here canceled "and."
[2] Remainder of sentence added.
[3] Preceding sentence interlined.
[4] Preceding sentence inserted.
[5] This and preceding paragraph inserted in TJ's small hand at the foot of the first page.

To Nathaniel Cutting

Mar. 20. 1793.

Th: Jefferson presents his compliments to Capt. Cutting, and informs him that the President counts on him in the matter spoken of. The article of money shall be arranged.

RC (Thomas A. Lingenfelter, Doylestown, Pennsylvania, 1992); addressed: "Capt Cutting"; endorsed by Cutting. Not recorded in SJL.

THE MATTER SPOKEN OF: Cutting's appointment as David Humphreys's secretary for the latter's mission to Algiers (see TJ to Humphreys, 21 Mch. 1793; TJ to Cutting, 31 Mch. 1793).

On 24 Jan. 1793 TJ had sent an invitation asking "the favor of Capt. Cutting's company to dinner with a small party of friends, on Monday next, at half after three," with postscript beneath date: "The favor of an answer is requested" (printed form in MiU-C; with date and blank spaces for recipient and day of the week completed by TJ; addressed: "Capt Cutting").

From Robert Montgomery

Liverpool, 23 July 1793. Since leaving Alicante on 26 May for a tour of England and Ireland required by his business, he has received a letter from his brother, John Montgomery of Boston, announcing the reception of his commission and instructions for the Alicante consulship, which his brother will either send by the first safe conveyance or deliver when he comes to Alicante, where he is expected shortly. He thanks Congress for this mark of confidence and will return to Alicante and assume office after the completion of his business here in a few weeks On his way here he spent a few days with our plenipotentiaries in Aranjuez, where he learned that Charles IV had decided to make New Orleans a free port on condition that all ships going there first obtain passports in Spain.

[845]

He immediately gave notice of this to Short, who had had no idea that anything like it was under consideration, and believes Short mentioned this news in a 10 June letter to TJ. In Lisbon he delivered copies of Short's letter to Humphreys and Captain Dekay of New York, taking the latter's receipt, and in Falmouth to James Barry of Baltimore, who was just about to leave. As soon as he arrives in Alicante, he will write to TJ in accordance with his instructions.

RC (DNA: RG 59, CD); 3 p.; at foot of text: "His Excellency Thomas Jefferson Esqr."; endorsed by TJ as received 24 Oct. 1793 and so recorded in SJL. For later consular letters from Montgomery not received by TJ, see Appendix I.

William Short actually notified TJ of the news about the status of New Orleans as a free port in a letter of 7 June 1793.

Appendix I

Letters Not Received by Jefferson

EDITORIAL NOTE

This appendix lists chronologically letters written to Jefferson as Secretary of State during the period covered by this volume and the first five months of 1794 that arrived after his retirement from office and were neither received nor read by him. The list includes letters addressed to Jefferson by name or title through 31 Dec. 1793 and letters addressed to him by name after that date. Each entry indicates the location of the most authoritative manuscript text and (if known) where the letter has been printed elsewhere. Letters marked with an asterisk are addressed to Jefferson by name; those not so designated are addressed only to the Secretary of State.

William Short, 5 Sep. 1793 (PrC of Tripl in DLC: Short Papers)
*James Anderson, 14 Sep. 1793 (RC in DNA: RG 59, CD)
*James Anderson, 19 Sep. 1793 (RC in DNA: RG 59, CD)
*Gouverneur Morris, 22 Sep. 1793 (RC in DNA: RG 59, DD).
    PRINTED: ASP, *Foreign Relations*, I, 372
*James Anderson, 5 Oct. 1793 (RC in DNA: RG 59, CD)
*Delamotte, 6 Oct. 1793 (RC in DNA: RG 59, CD)
James Maury, 9 Oct. 1793 (RC in DNA: RG 59, CD)
David Humphreys, 10 Oct. 1793 (RC in DNA: RG 59, DD)
*Robert Montgomery, 10 Oct. 1793 (RC in DNA: RG 59, CD)
*Gouverneur Morris, 10 Oct. 1793 (RC in DNA: RG 59, DD).
    PRINTED: ASP, *Foreign Relations*, I, 372
*Gouverneur Morris, 10 Oct. 1793 (RC in DNA: RG 59, DD).
    PRINTED: ASP, *Foreign Relations*, I, 373
*Robert W. Fox, 11 Oct. 1793 (RC in DNA: RG 59, CD)
David Humphreys, 11 Oct. 1793 (RC in DNA: RG 59, DD)
*Michael Morphy, 11 Oct. 1793 (RC in DNA: RG 59, CD)
David Humphreys, 12 Oct. 1793 (RC in DNA: RG 59, DD)
Thomas Pinckney, [12 Oct. 1793] (RC in DNA: RG 59, DD; misdated 12 Aug. 1793). PRINTED: ASP, *Foreign Relations*, I, 315 (extract)
David Humphreys, 13 Oct. 1793 (RC in DNA: RG 59, DD)
David Humphreys, 14 Oct. 1793 (RC in DNA: RG 59, DD)
David Humphreys, 15 Oct. 1793 (RC in DNA: RG 59, DD)
William Short, 16 Oct. 1793 (FC in DLC: Short Papers)
*Robert Montgomery, 17 Oct. 1793 (RC in DNA: RG 59, CD)
*Peter Walsh, 17 Oct. 1793 (RC in DNA: RG 59, CD). PRINTED: Knox, *Barbary Wars*, I, 51
David Humphreys, 18 Oct. 1793 (RC in DNA: RG 59, DD)
Elias Vanderhorst, 18 Oct. 1793 (RC in DNA: RG 59, CD)
*Gouverneur Morris, 19 Oct. 1793 (RC in DNA: RG 59, DD).
    PRINTED: ASP, *Foreign Relations*, I, 374-5
Elias Vanderhorst, 19 Oct. 1793 (RC in DNA: RG 59, CD)
*John S. Eustace, 20 Oct. 1793 (RC in DNA: RG 59, MLR)

APPENDIX I

*Gouverneur Morris, 20 Oct. 1793 (RC in DNA: RG 59, DD).
   PRINTED: ASP, *Foreign Relations*, I, 378
James Simpson, 21 Oct. 1793 (RC in DNA: RG 59, CD)
William Carmichael and William Short, 22 Oct. 1793 (Tr in DNA:
   RG 46, Senate Records, 3d Cong., 1st sess.). PRINTED: ASP,
   Foreign Relations, I, 328
William Short, 22 Oct. 1793 (Tr in Lb in DNA: RG 59, DD)
David Humphreys, 23 Oct. 1793 (RC in DNA: RG 59, DD)
John Parish, 25 Oct. 1793 (RC in DNA: RG 59, CD)
*Robert Montgomery, 27 Oct. 1793 (RC in DNA: RG 59, CD)
Edward Church, 30 Oct. 1793 (RC in DNA: RG 59, CD)
James Simpson, 31 Oct. 1793 (RC in DNA: RG 59, CD)
Benjamin H. Phillips, 2 Nov. 1793 (Dupl in DNA: RG 59, CD)
David Humphreys, 5 Nov. 1793 (RC in DNA: RG 59, DD)
James Maury, 5 Nov. 1793 (RC in DNA: RG 59, CD)
William Short, 6 Nov. 1793 (PrC in DLC: Short Papers). PRINTED:
   ASP, *Foreign Relations*, I, 413 (extract)
Robert W. Fox, 7 Nov. 1793 (RC in DNA: RG 59, CD)
James Maury, 8 Nov. 1793 (RC in DNA: RG 59, CD)
Edward Church, 9 Nov. 1793 (RC in DNA: RG 59, CD)
David Humphreys, 9 Nov. 1793 (RC in DNA: RG 59, DD)
Thomas Pinckney, 9 Nov. 1793 (PrC in ScHi: Pinckney Family Papers)
Peter Walsh, 9 Nov. 1793 (RC in DNA: RG 59, CD)
*Thomas Lloyd, [ca. 11 Nov. 1793] (RC in DNA: RG 76, British
   Spoliations)
Thomas Pinckney, 11 Nov. 1793 (RC in DNA: RG 59, DD).
   PRINTED: ASP, *Foreign Relations*, I, 315 (extract)
Thomas Pinckney, 11 Nov. 1793 (RC in DNA: RG 59, DD)
Robert W. Fox, 12 Nov. 1793 (RC in DNA: RG 59, CD)
Edward Church, 15 Nov. 1793 (RC in DNA: RG 59, CD)
David Humphreys, 16 Nov. 1793 (RC in DNA: RG 59, DD)
*Gouverneur Morris, 16 Nov. 1793 (Dupl in DNA: RG 59, DD).
   PRINTED: ASP, *Foreign Relations*, I, 399-400
David Humphreys, 19 Nov. 1793 (RC in DNA: RG 59, DD).
   PRINTED: ASP, *Foreign Relations*, I, 413
Peter Walsh, 20 Nov. 1793 (RC in DNA: RG 59, CD). PRINTED:
   Knox, *Barbary Wars*, I, 54-5
James Maury, 21 Nov. 1793 (Dupl in DNA: RG 59, CD)
William Short, 21 Nov. 1793 (PrC of Tripl in DLC: Short Papers)
   James Simpson, 21 Nov. 1793 (RC in DNA: RG 59, CD)
John Parish, 22 Nov. 1793 (RC in DNA: RG 59, CD)
David Humphreys, 23 Nov. 1793 (Dupl in DNA: RG 59, DD).
   PRINTED: ASP, *Foreign Relations*, I, 413-14
Thomas Pinckney, 25 Nov. 1793 (RC in DNA: RG 59, DD).
   PRINTED: ASP, *Foreign Relations*, I, 327-8
James Simpson, 25 Nov. 1793 (RC in DNA: RG 59, CD).
   PRINTED: Knox, *Barbary Wars*, I, 55-6
*Gouverneur Morris, 26 Nov. 1793 (Dupl in DNA: RG 59, DD).
   PRINTED: ASP, *Foreign Relations*, I, 400
Hans Rodolph Saabÿe, 26 Nov. 1793 (RC in DNA: RG 59, CD)
James Simpson, 27 Nov. 1793 (Dupl in DNA: RG 59, CD)

James Simpson, [ca. 27 Nov. 1793] (RC in DNA: RG 59, CD; conjoined to preceding letter)

*Peter Walsh, 28 Nov. 1793 (RC in DNA: RG 59, MLR)

Edward Church, 29 Nov. 1793 (RC in DNA: RG 59, CD)

*James Anderson, 1 Dec. 1793 (RC in DNA: RG 59, CD)

Edward Church, 2 Dec. 1793 (RC in DNA: RG 59, CD)

Michael Morphy, 4 Dec. 1793 (RC in DNA: RG 59, CD). PRINTED: Knox, *Barbary Wars*, I, 58-9

*Edward Church, 6 Dec. 1793 (RC in DNA: RG 59, CD)

James Maury, 6 Dec. 1793 (RC in DNA: RG 59, CD)

Edward Church, 7 Dec. 1793 (RC in DNA: RG 59, CD)

*Robert W. Fox, 7 Dec. 1793 (RC in DNA: RG 59, CD)

David Humphreys, 7 Dec. 1793 (RC in DNA: RG 59, DD). PRINTED: Humphreys, *Humphreys*, II, 191-2

*Robert W. Fox, 8 Dec. 1793 (RC in DNA: RG 59, CD)

*Gouverneur Morris, 12 Dec. 1793 (Dupl in DNA: RG 59, DD). PRINTED: ASP, *Foreign Relations*, I, 401

*Joshua Johnson, 13 Dec. 1793 (FC in DNA: RG 59, CD)

William Short, 13 Dec. 1793 (PrC in DLC: Short Papers)

James Maury, 14 Dec. 1793 (RC in DNA: RG 59, CD)

*Robert Montgomery, 17 Dec. 1793 (RC in DNA: RG 59, CD)

Thomas Pinckney, 17 Dec. 1793 (Dupl in DNA: RG 59, DD)

James Simpson, 18 Dec. 1793 (Dupl in DNA: RG 59, CD)

Philip and Anthony Filicchy & Company, 19 Dec. 1793 (RC in DNA: RG 59, MLR)

Edward Church, 20 Dec. 1793 (RC in DNA: RG 59, CD)

William Short, 20 Dec. 1793 (PrC in DLC: Short Papers)

*James Anderson, 21 Dec. 1793 (RC in DNA: RG 59, CD)

*James Swan, 21 Dec. 1793 (RC in DNA: RG 59, MLR)

*Alexander Campbell, 23 Dec. 1793 (RC in DNA: RG 59, MLR)

Thomas Pinckney, 23 Dec. 1793 (RC in DNA: RG 59, DD)

Elias Vanderhorst, 24 Dec. 1793 (RC in DNA: RG 59, CD)

David Humphreys, 25 Dec. 1793 (RC in DNA: RG 59, DD). PRINTED: ASP, *Foreign Relations*, I, 418-19 (extract)

Thomas Pinckney, 26 Dec. 1793 (RC in DNA: RG 59, DD). PRINTED: ASP, *Foreign Relations*, I, 430

William Short, 27 Dec. 1793 (PrC in DLC: Short Papers)

Thomas Pinckney, 28 Dec. 1793 (RC in DNA: RG 59, DD)

*Edmond Charles Genet, 31 Dec. 1793 (Dft in DLC: Genet Papers)

*John Kendrick, n.d. (RC in DNA: RG 59, MLR; filed at 1 Jan. 1793). PRINTED: Massachusetts Historical Society, *Collections*, LXXIX (1941), 154-6

*Thomas François Galbaud, 1 Jan. 1794 (RC in DNA: RG 59, MLR)

*Edmond Charles Genet, 1 Jan. 1794 (Dft in DLC: Genet Papers)

*Edmond Charles Genet, 1 Jan. 1794 (Dft in DLC: Genet Papers)

*Robert Montgomery, 8 Jan. 1794 (RC in DNA: RG 59, CD)

*Isaac Shelby, 13 Jan. 1794 (RC in DNA: RG 59, LGS). PRINTED: ASP, *Foreign Relations*, I, 455-6

*Gouverneur Morris, 21 Jan. 1794 (RC in DNA: RG 59, DD). PRINTED: ASP, *Foreign Relations*, I, 402-3

*Joshua Barney, 17 Feb. 1794 (RC in DNA: RG 76, British Spoliations)
*Robert Montgomery, 20 Feb. 1794 (RC in DNA: RG 59, CD)
*Gouverneur Morris, 6 Mch. 1794 (RC in DNA: RG 59, DD). PRINTED: ASP, *Foreign Relations*, I, 404-5
*Gouverneur Morris, 7 Mch. 1794 (RC in DNA: RG 59, DD, with body of letter in code; Tr in same, *en clair*). PRINTED: Sparks, *Morris*, II, 415-16
*Robert Montgomery, 29 Mch. 1794 (RC in DNA: RG 59, CD)
*Robert Montgomery, 8 Apr. 1794 (RC in DNA: RG 59, CD)
*Robert Montgomery, 22 Apr. 1794 (RC in DNA: RG 59, CD)
*Robert Montgomery, 28 Apr. 1794 (RC in DNA: RG 59, CD)
*Richard O'Bryen, 7 May 1794 (Tr of extract in DNA: RG 46, Senate Records, 6th Cong., 2d sess.)

Appendix II

Miscellaneous and Routine Papers

EDITORIAL NOTE

As Secretary of State Thomas Jefferson received and dispatched a wide range of routine letters and papers relating to appointments, acts of Congress, passports, copyrights, and patents in accordance with responsibilities Congress and the President assigned to the Department of State (see Appendix III, Editorial Note). At the beginning of this segment of the edition, Julian P. Boyd announced that the "numerous commissions, letters of transmittal of laws and their routine acknowledgments by governors, applications for office, testimonials for applicants, appeals for patent rights, and other routine records . . . will be grouped for summary treatment at the close of Jefferson's tenure of office" (Vol. 16: ix). In practice, however, Mr. Boyd printed, summarized, or noted documents in some of these categories—particularly those relating to appointments, copyrights, and patents—and his successors followed this course.

Except for commissions, which are treated in Appendix III, this appendix categorizes such routine documents, briefly describes their treatment in this and previous volumes, and provides general locational information for those not already dealt with. But readers are advised that no systematic effort has been made to locate all routine documents in each category.

Appointment Papers

Letters of Application and Recommendation

Many of the letters of application and recommendation for federal office that Jefferson received as Secretary of State, concerning for the most part consular and diplomatic positions, have been printed, summarized, or noted in previous volumes. The remainder have been summarized or noted in the supplement to this volume.

Letters about Nominations and Commissions

Two of President Washington's secretaries—Tobias Lear and Bartholomew Dandridge, Jr.—wrote routine letters informing Jefferson of Senate action on presidential nominees, transmitting commissions to him for some who had received Senate confirmation as well as for others who had declined or resigned their appointments, or asking him to have commissions prepared for others. Some of these letters from Lear have been noted in previous volumes. RCs of the remainder are in DNA: RG 59, MLR and Miscellaneous Appointment Records, while FCs of others are in same, SDC. RCs of such letters from Dandridge are in same, MLR; FCs are in same, SDC.

Letters Transmitting Commissions

Some of the routine covering letters in which Jefferson transmitted commissions to federal appointees have been noted in previous volumes. FCs of the remainder are in DNA: RG 59, DL. For reproductions of sample commissions, see Appendix III, Nos. 1-4.

Letters Accepting Office

Some of the letters in which federal appointees informed Jefferson of the acceptance of their commissions have been printed, summarized, or noted in this and previous volumes. RCs of the remainder are in DNA: RG 59, MLR, CD, LGS, and Acceptances and Orders for Commissions.

Papers Relating to the States

Letters Transmitting Acts of Congress

Under the terms of the 15 Sep. 1789 act for the safekeeping of the public records and seal of the United States, the Secretary of State was obliged to transmit to every state executive two duly authenticated printed copies of every congressional act approved by the President or passed over his veto (see Appendix III, Editorial Note). One letter in which Jefferson transmitted acts of Congress to state executives has been printed (Circular to the Governors of the States, 1 Mch. 1792, in the supplement to this volume), and another has been noted (Vol. 17: 293n). FCs of many circulars are in DNA: RG 360, AL and RG 59, DL. RCs of additional circulars of 25 June, 6 and 19 July 1790, and 11 Jan. and 16 Mch. 1793 are in R-Ar; RCs of circulars of 20 Aug. 1790 and 10 Apr. 1792 are in MHi and MdAA, respectively. For a reproduction of an authenticated act of Congress enclosed in one of Jefferson's letters, see Appendix III, No. 5.

Letters Acknowledging Acts of Congress

State executives informed Jefferson of the receipt and occasionally of the non-receipt of acts of Congress in routine letters that have not been dealt with in previous volumes. RCs of many of these letters are in DNA: RG 59, LGS and MLR.

Letters Transmitting Acts of the States

Letters transmitting acts of the state legislatures to the Secretary of State have been found for only four states, and none have been dealt with in previous volumes. In accordance with a resolution of the New Jersey legislature, James Mott, the New Jersey treasurer, wrote a number of routine letters to Jefferson enclosing copies of acts of the state legislature (RCs are in DNA: RG 59, MLR). Alexander J. Dallas, the secretary of Pennsylvania, followed the same course pursuant to gubernatorial orders and a law of the Pennsylvania legislature (an RC of one of Dallas's letter is in same; FCs of others are in PHarH: Secretary's Letterbooks). Similar letters of 17 May 1790 from Governor Edward Telfair of Georgia and 30 Aug. 1790 from Governor Pierpont Edwards of Connecticut are in DNA: RG 59, LGS and MLR, respectively.

Letters Relating to Citizenship and Passports

Documents in these related categories have generally not been accounted for in this and previous volumes. A letter from Benjamin Rush to Jefferson of 25 Jan. 1791 requesting a certificate documenting the American citizenship of a young physician preparing to travel abroad is in DNA, RG 59, Certificates of Naturalization and Proofs of Citizenship; two letters of June and July 1793 from the same source relating to natives of France and its colonies were dealt with in Vol. 26: 308. With regard to passports, letters of the following dates from Governor Thomas Mifflin of Pennsylvania request passports for citizens of that state planning to visit foreign countries: 26 Sep. and 31 Oct. 1791 (DNA: RG 59, MLR; Jefferson's 2 Nov. 1791 reply to the latter is in PHarH: Mifflin Administration Papers); 24 May 1793 (DNA: RG 59, Letters Requesting Passports); and 7 and 27 Aug. 1793 (FCs in PHarH: Secretary's Letterbooks). There is a similar letter of 12 Aug. 1793 from Alexander J. Dallas, the secretary of Pennsylvania (same). For a reproduction of a passport for an individual, see Appendix III, No. 6.

Letters Relating to Copyright

Under the terms of the 31 May 1790 Copyright Act, the "author or proprietor" of any copyrighted "map, chart, book or books" was obliged "within six months after the publishing thereof" to "deliver, or cause to be delivered to the Secretary of State a copy of the same, to be preserved in his office" (*Annals*, II, 2288). Many of the routine letters in which copyrighted works were transmitted to Jefferson for deposit in his office have been printed, summarized, or noted in previous volumes. RCs of the remainder are in DNA: RG 59, MLR.

Petitions for Patents

Under the terms of the Patent Act of 10 Apr. 1790, anyone who "invented or discovered any useful art, manufacture, engine, machine, or device, or any improvement therein, not before known or used," could submit a petition for a patent to a board consisting of the Secretary of State, the Secretary of War, and the Attorney General. Patents were to be issued only when the Secretary of State received "a specification in writing, containing a description, accompanied with draughts or models, and explanations and models, (if the nature of the invention or discovery will admit of a model)." This statute was replaced by the Patent Act of 21 Feb. 1793, which transferred the authority to grant patents from the Patent Board to the Secretary of State, to whom inventors were to submit a petition, evidence that they had sworn or affirmed that the invention was their own, and witnessed descriptions accompanied by drawings, specimens, and models as practicable (*Annals*, II, 2270-1, III, 1431-3). The original petitions to the Patent Board and to Jefferson, together with related documents, were destroyed in the

APPENDIX II

1836 Patent Office fire. Other texts of a small number of these documents—located in the papers of some of the patentees, Federal court records, and DNA, RG 241: Restored Patent Specifications—have been printed, summarized, or noted in this and previous volumes, especially in the supplement to this volume. For reproductions of sample patents, see Appendix III, Nos. 8-9.

Appendix III

Commissions, Laws, Passports, Patents, and Other Forms

E D I T O R I A L   N O T E

In his capacity as Secretary of State Thomas Jefferson countersigned, signed, or endorsed a variety of official documents of differing degrees of importance based upon the explicit or implicit authority granted to his office by five acts of Congress. Examples of some of these documents are described and illustrated below.

Diplomatic and consular commissions, exequaturs, passports, and passport certifications fell within the Secretary of State's purview by virtue of the 27 July 1789 act establishing the Department of State which required him to "perform and execute such duties as shall, from time to time, be enjoined on or intrusted to him by the President of the United States, agreeable to the Constitution, relative to correspondences, commissions, or instructions, to or with public ministers or consuls from the United States, or to negotiations with public ministers from foreign states or princes, or to memorials or other applications from foreign public ministers, or other foreigners, or to such other matters respecting foreign affairs as the President of the United States shall assign to the said department" (*Annals*, II, 2187).

The Secretary of State obtained authority over five other kinds of official documents under the terms of the 15 Sep. 1789 act for the safekeeping of the public records and seal of the United States. This act entrusted the Secretary with the custody of original laws signed by the President, or passed by Congress over his veto, and directed him to publish every "law, order, resolution, and vote" of Congress in at least three American newspapers, deliver one printed copy to every member of Congress, and transmit two "duly authenticated" printed copies to each state executive (same, 2234; see also J. H. Powell, *The Books of a New Nation: United States Government Publications, 1774-1814* [Philadelphia, 1957], 88). From this the Secretary derived his authority for signing printed laws of the United States sent to the states. The act also gave the Secretary custody of the seal of the United States and stipulated that he was to "make out and record, and shall affix the said seal to all civil commissions, to officers of the United States to be appointed by the President by and with the advice and consent of the Senate, or by the President alone. *Provided*, That the said seal shall not be affixed to any commission before the same shall have been signed by the President of the United States, nor to any other instrument or act without the special warrant of the President therefor" (*Annals*, II, 2234). In addition to making the Secretary of State implicitly responsible for countersigning civil commissions—the Secretary of War having previously been given authority to countersign military commissions by the 7 Aug. 1789 act establishing that department (same, 2214)—this section also provided the legislative authority for the Secretary of State to countersign judicial commissions and presidential proclamations. Finally the 15 Sep. 1789 act authorized the Secretary to authenticate State Department records, directing him to "cause a seal of office to be made for the said department of such device as the President of the United States shall approve" and providing that "all copies of records and papers in the said office, authenticated under the said seal, shall be evidence equally as the original record or paper" (same, 2234). The seal of office Jefferson used was identical to the seal of the United States except for the addition of "Secretary of State" (Vol. 16: xlii).

Three other acts of Congress gave the Secretary of State authority over two other kinds of official documents. The Patent Acts of 10 Apr. 1790 and 21 Feb. 1793 provided the statutory bases for the Secretary to affix the seal of the United States to patents, countersign them, and endorse them with the date of their delivery to the inventor. The 14 Apr. 1792 act regulating the consular service required the Secretary to approve the bonds that consuls and vice-consuls were obliged to post with him for the faithful discharge of their duties (*Annals*, II, 2270-1, III, 1362, 1431-2). Jefferson carried out the last responsibility by noting his approval on the verso of these bonds, which were then lodged at the Treasury.

During his tenure in office Jefferson followed three different procedures with respect to the use of seals. He had the seal of the United States affixed to commissions, exequaturs, patents, ship passports, and presidential proclamations. He had the seal of the Department of State affixed to passports for individuals and to some authentications. But he did not have any seal affixed to other authentications, letters of credence, laws of the United States, passport certifications, or consular bonds.

No systematic effort has been made to collect all documents signed, countersigned, or endorsed ex officio by Jefferson as Secretary of State. Nevertheless, originals in only two of the document categories mentioned above were not located: (1) Proclamations of the President countersigned by Jefferson (a file containing printed texts of some of Washington's proclamations and one Tr is in DNA: RG 11, Presidential Proclamations). (2) Exequaturs for consuls and vice-consuls countersigned by Jefferson (see enclosure to Jefferson's first letter to Benjamin Bankson, 3 Oct. 1793; a file containing FCs for foreign consuls and vice-consuls is in DNA: RG 59, Exequaturs). Four other categories of documents are not illustrated: (1) Letters of credence countersigned by Jefferson (see Vols. 16: 314-15, 25: 422, for examples, all such letters on behalf of ministers and agents abroad having been printed or noted in previous volumes; a file containing FCs of them is in DNA: RG 59, Credences). (2) Consular bonds endorsed by Jefferson (MSS in DNA: RG 39, Records of the Section of Surety Bonds, consisting of blank forms completed in ink as well as handwritten texts; FCs of some of these as well as others are in DNA: RG 53, Register of Official Bonds). (3) Passport certifications signed by Jefferson (a representative MS is in DNA: RG 59, MLR; issued 15 Nov. 1792 in connection with the granting of a passport to the *Canton*, Hugh Alexander Makee master). (4) Authentications signed by Jefferson (a representative MS is in DNA: RG 267, Records of the Supreme Court of the United States; issued 8 Apr. 1793 to validate transcriptions of records in the Department of State submitted in connection with United States Supreme Court, Case No. 57, William Bingham v. John Cabot; with seal of the Department of State). Two 4 Dec. 1793 authentications of transcripts of Jefferson's correspondence with Edmond Charles Genet, George Hammond, and Thomas Pinckney submitted to the Senate in December 1793 suggest that Jefferson omitted the State Department seal when certifying copies of departmental records for Congress, presumably on the assumption that his signature would suffice for the legislative branch of government (see note to George Washington to the Senate and the House of Representatives, [2 Dec. 1793]).

The numbers and captions of the documents described in the following notes correspond with the numbers and captions of the documents annexed hereto in facsimile form.

Commissions

1. *Commission for a Foreign Minister*

Philadelphia, 21 Feb. 1791. Issued to David Humphreys as minister resident to Portugal (NjP: Andre deCoppet Collection). MS in a clerk's hand; signed by Washington and countersigned by Jefferson, who also wrote "By the President"; with seal of the United States.

A file containing FCs of diplomatic commissions for foreign ministers, chargés d'affaires, and commissioners countersigned by Jefferson as Secretary of State is in DNA: RG 59, Credences. The other commissions in this file differ in varying degrees in form and substance from the one illustrated here depending upon the rank, destination, and mission of each appointee.

2. *Commission for a Consul*

New York, 7 June 1790. Issued to James Maury as consul for Liverpool (ViHi). MS in Henry Remsen's hand; signed by Washington and countersigned by Jefferson, who also wrote "by the President"; with seal of the United States.

A file of FCs of consular and vice-consular commissions countersigned by Jefferson as Secretary of State is in DNA: RG 59, Commissions of Consuls and Consular Agents. The other commissions in this file are identical in form to the one illustrated here.

3. *Commission for a Supreme Court Justice*

[Philadelphia], 4 Mch. 1793. Issued to William Paterson as associate justice of the Supreme Court (NjP: General Manuscripts: George Washington). MS in a clerk's hand; signed by Washington and countersigned by Jefferson, who also wrote "By the President"; with seal of the United States.

A file of FCs of commissions for District Court judges, Territorial Court judges, district attorneys, marshals, and another associate justice of the Supreme Court countersigned by Jefferson as Secretary of State is in DNA: RG 59, Miscellaneous Permanent and Temporary Presidential Commissions.

4. *Commission for a Naval Officer*

Germantown, 23 Nov. 1793. Temporary commission issued to William McPherson as naval officer of the port of Philadelphia (PHi). Blanks in form filled by George Taylor, Jr., who also interlined "Germantown" in place of "Philadelphia"; signed by Washington, who also added the day and month, and countersigned by Jefferson, who also wrote "By the President"; with seal of the United States.

A file of FCs of commissions for the different kinds of civil officials countersigned by Jefferson as Secretary of State is in DNA: RG 59, Miscellaneous Permanent and Temporary Presidential Commissions.

Laws of the United States

5. *Act Respecting Fugitives*

[*Philadelphia*], *12 Feb. 1793*. Printed law signed by Jefferson (MB).

The printed laws Jefferson signed as Secretary of State followed the same form as the one illustrated here with one exception. Those passed during the second session of the First Congress, which met from 4 Jan. to 12 Aug. 1790, read "(True Copy.)" instead of "Deposited among the Rolls in the office of the Secretary of State." See, for example, the 26 May 1790 Act for the Government of the Southwest Territory (OT).

Passports

6. *Passport for an Individual*

Philadelphia, 14 Dec. 1793. Issued to Raphaelle Peale (PPAmP: Peale-Sellers Papers). Blanks in form filled by Taylor; signed by Jefferson, who wrote another certification on verso (see Certificate for Raphaelle Peale, 15 Dec. 1793); with seal of the Department of State.

7. *Passport for a Ship*

Portland, 24 Aug. 1793. Issued to the *Polly*, Joshua Merrill master (MeB). Printed form, with blanks filled by Nathaniel F. Fosdick and Joseph Hooper, who both certified it; signed by Washington and countersigned by Jefferson at an undetermined date; with seal of the United States.

Concerning the various forms of ship passports countersigned by Jefferson as Secretary of State, of which the one reproduced here is the most elaborate, see notes to Opinion on Ship Passports, 3 May 1793, and Jefferson to Alexander Hamilton, 8 May 1793.

Patents

8. *Patent under the 1790 Patent Act*

Philadelphia, 29 Jan. 1791. Issued to Francis Bailey for his invention of a type punch (John H. James, Urbana, Ohio, 1946). MS in Remsen's hand; signed by Washington, countersigned by Jefferson, who also wrote "By the President," and certified by Edmund Randolph; with seal of the United States.

Another example, dated New York, 31 July 1790. Issued to Samuel

Hopkins for his improved apparatus for making potash and pearl ash (ICHi). MS in Remsen's hand; signed by Washington and certified by Randolph; endorsed on verso by Jefferson: "Delivered to the within named Samuel Hopkins the fourth day of August 1790. Th: Jefferson"; with seal of the United States. Not reproduced.

9. *Patent under the 1793 Patent Act*

Philadelphia, 23 Mch. 1793. Issued to Jonathan Williams, Jr., for his improvement of molds for claying and whitening refined sugar (PPAmP: Penn Letters and Ancient Documents). Printed form, with blanks filled by clerk and by Randolph; signed by Washington, countersigned by Jefferson, who also wrote "By the President," and later certified by Randolph; with seal of the United States (see Petition of Williams to the Patent Board, 20 Nov. 1792, in the supplement to this volume).

Commissions, Laws, Passports, Patents,
and Other Forms

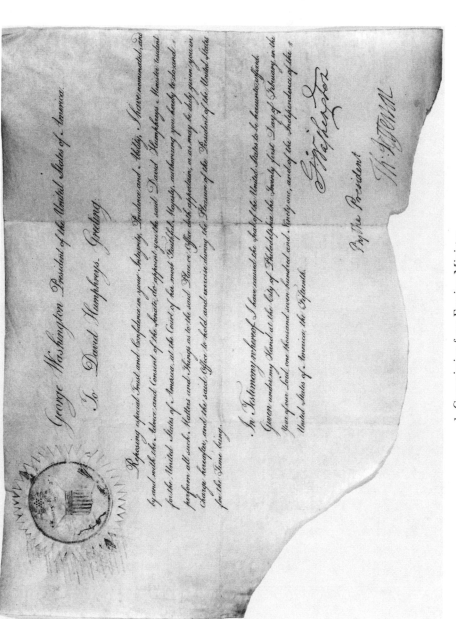

1. Commission for a Foreign Minister

2. Commission for a Consul

95

George Washington President of the United States of America. To all who shall see these Presents — Greeting.

Know Ye, That reposing special Trust and Confidence in the Wisdom, Uprightness, and Learning of William Paterson, of New Jersey, I have nominated, and by and with the Advice and Consent of the Senate, do appoint him one of the associate Justices of the Supreme Court of the United States, and do authorize and empower him to execute and fulfil the Duties of that Office, according to the Constitution and Laws of the said United States, and to have and to hold the said Office, with all the Powers, Privileges, and Emoluments to the same of Right appertaining unto him the said William Paterson, during his good Behaviour.

In Testimony whereof I have caused these Letters to be made Patent, and the Seal of the United States to be hereunto affixed.

Given under my Hand the fourth Day of March, in the Year of our Lord one thousand seven hundred and ninety three, and of the Independence of the United States of America, the Seventeenth.

Washington

By the President

3. Commission for a Supreme Court Justice

GEORGE WASHINGTON, President of the United States of America.

TO ALL WHO SHALL SEE THESE PRESENTS, GREETING.

WHEREAS the Office of a Naval Officer of the Port of Philadelphia 〃 〃 〃 〃 Discretion of William McPherson of Pennsylvania, I DO APPOINT him Naval Officer of the Port of Philadelphia 〃 〃 〃 and do authorize and empower him to execute and fulfil the Duties of that Office according to LAW; AND TO HAVE AND TO HOLD the said office, with all the Rights and Emoluments thereunto legally appertaining, unto him the said William McPherson, during the Pleasure of the President of the United States for the Time being, and until the End of the next Session of the Senate of the United States, and no longer.

IN TESTIMONY whereof I have caused these Letters to be made Patent, and the Seal of the United States to be hereunto affixed. GIVEN under my Hand, at Germantown the Twenty Ninth Day of November in the Year of our Lord one thousand seven hundred and ninety three, and of the Independence of the United States of America the Eighteenth.

G. Washington

By the President

Th. Jefferson

4. Commission for a Naval Officer

SECOND CONGRESS

OF THE

UNITED STATES:

At the Second Seffion, begun and held at the City of PHILADELPHIA, in
the State of Pennfylvania, on Monday, the fifth of November,
one thoufand feven hundred and ninety-two.

An ACT *refpecting Fugitives from Juftice, and Perfons efcaping from the Service of their
Mafters.*

Sec. 1. BE *it enacted by the Senate and Houfe of Reprefentatives of the United States of America
in Congrefs affembled,* That whenever the executive authority of any ftate in the
union, or of either of the territories north-weft or fouth of the river Ohio, fhall demand any perfon as a fugitive from juftice, of the executive authority of any fuch ftate
or territory to which fuch perfon fhall have fled, and fhall moreover produce the copy
of an indictment found, or an affidavit made before a magiftrate of any ftate or territory
as aforefaid, charging the perfon fo demanded, with having committed treafon, felony
or other crime, certified as authentic by the governor or chief magiftrate of the ftate
or territory from whence the perfon fo charged, fled, it fhall be the duty of the executive authority of the ftate or territory to which fuch perfon fhall have fled, to caufe him
or her to be arrefted and fecured, and notice of the arreft to be given to the
executive authority making fuch demand, or to the agent of fuch authority appointed
to receive the fugitive, and to caufe the fugitive to be delivered to fuch agent when he
fhall appear : But if no fuch agent fhall appear within fix months from the time of the
arreft, the prifoner may be difcharged. And all cofts or expenfes incurred in the apprehending, fecuring, and tranfmitting fuch fugitive to the ftate or territory making
fuch demand, fhall be paid by fuch ftate or territory.

Sec. 2. *And be it further enacted,* That any agent, appointed as aforefaid, who fhall
receive the fugitive into his cuftody, fhall be empowered to tranfport him or her to the
ftate or territory from which he or fhe fhall have fled. And if any perfon or perfons
fhall by force fet at liberty, or refcue the fugitive from fuch agent while tranfporting, as
aforefaid, the perfon or perfons fo offending fhall, on conviction, be fined not exceeding five hundred dollars, and be imprifoned not exceeding one year.

Sec. 3. *And be it alfo enacted,* That when a perfon held to labour in any of the
United States, or in either of the territories on the north-weft or fouth of the river
Ohio, under the laws thereof, fhall efcape into any other of the faid ftates or terrritory,
the perfon to whom fuch labour or fervice may be due, his agent or attorney, is hereby
empowered to feize or arreft fuch fugitive from labour, and to take him or her before
any judge of the circuit or diftrict courts of the United States, refiding or being within
the ftate, or before any magiftrate of a county, city or town corporate, wherein fuch
feizure or arreft fhall be made, and upon proof to the fatisfaction of fuch judge or
magiftrate, either by oral teftimony or affidavit taken before and certified by a magiftrate of any fuch ftate or territory, that the perfon fo feized or arrefted, doth, under
the laws of the ftate or territory from which he or fhe fled, owe fervice or labour to the
perfon claiming him or her, it fhall be the duty of fuch judge or magiftrate to give a
certificate thereof to fuch claimant, his agent or attorney, which fhall be fufficient warrant for removing the faid fugitive from labour, to the ftate or territory from which he
or fhe fled.

Sec. 4. *And be it further enacted,* That any perfon who fhall knowingly and willingly
obftruct or hinder fuch claimant, his agent or attorney in fo feizing or arrefting fuch
fugitive from labour, or fhall refcue fuch fugitive from fuch claimant, his agent or attorney when fo arrefted purfuant to the authority herein given or declared ; or fhall harbour or conceal fuch perfon after notice that he or fhe was a fugitive from labour, as
aforefaid, fhall, for either of the faid offences, forfeit and pay the fum of five hundred
dollars. Which penalty may be recovered by and for the benefit of fuch claimant, by
action of debt, in any court proper to try the fame ; faving moreover to the perfon claiming fuch labour or fervice, his right of action for or on account of the faid injuries or
either of them.

JONATHAN TRUMBULL, *Speaker of the
Houfe of Reprefentatives.*
JOHN ADAMS, *Vice-Prefident of the United
States, and Prefident of the Senate.*

APPROVED, February twelfth, 1793.
G°: WASHINGTON, *Prefident of the United States.*

DEPOSITED among the Rolls in the office of the Secretary of State.

Secretary of State.

---

5. Act Respecting Fugitives

To all to whom these presents shall come, GREETING.

THE Bearer hereof _Rafaelle Peale_ a native

a citizen of the United States of America, having occasion to pass into foreign countries about his lawful affairs, these are to pray all whom it may concern, to permit the said _Rafaelle Peale_

(he demeaning himself well and peaceably) to pass wheresoever his lawful pursuits may call him, freely and without let or molestation in going, staying or returning, and to give him all friendly aid and protection, as these United States would do to their citizens in the like case.

In faith whereof I have caused the seal of the Department of State for the said United States to be hereunto affixed. Done at Philadelphia, this fourteenth day of December in the year of our Lord 1793 and of the Independence of these States the Eighteenth.

Gratis.

Th. Jefferson _Secretary of State._

6. Passport for an Individual

By the President.

7. Passport for a Ship

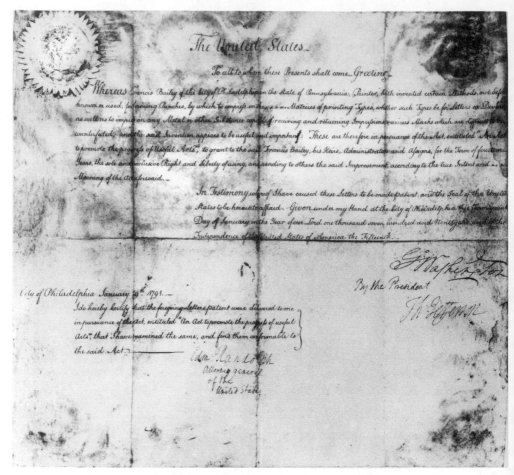

8. Patent under the 1790 Patent Act

The United States of America.

To all to whom these Letters Patent shall come:

Whereas *Jonathan Williams junior* . . . . . a citizen of the State of *Pennsylvania*, in the United States, hath alleged that he has invented a new and useful improvement *in Moulds or Vessels for the purpose of claying or whitening refined Sugar*

which improvement has not been known or used before his application; has made oath, that he does verily believe that he is the true inventor or discoverer of the said improvement; has paid into the Treasury of the United States, the sum of thirty dollars, delivered a receipt for the same, and presented a petition to the Secretary of State, signifying a desire of obtaining an exclusive property in the said improvement, and praying that a patent may be granted for that purpose: These are therefore to grant, according to law, to the said *Jonathan Williams junior* his heirs, administrators or assigns, for the term of fourteen years, the full and exclusive right and liberty of making, constructing, using, and vending to others to be used the said improvement, a description whereof is given in the words of the said *Jonathan Williams junior* himself, in the schedule hereto annexed, and is made a part of these presents.

In testimony whereof, I have caused these Letters to be made Patent, and the Seal of the United States to be hereunto affixed.

Given under my hand, at the City of Philadelphia the *twenty third* day of *March* in the Year of our Lord, one thousand seven hundred and ninety *three*, and of the Independence of the United States of America the *seventeenth*.

G. Washington

By the President

Th. Jefferson

City of Philadelphia, to wit:

I do hereby certify, That the foregoing Letters Patent, were delivered to me on the *tenth* day of *May* in the year of our Lord one thousand seven hundred and ninety *three* to be examined; that I have examined the same, and find them conformable to law. And I do hereby return the same to the Secretary of State, within fifteen days from the date aforesaid, to wit: On this *tenth* day of *May* in the year aforesaid.

Edm. Randolph
Att. Gen. of the U.S.

9. Patent under the 1793 Patent Act

INDEX

Abadie (Dabbadie), M. d': TJ evaluates
wine of, 763, 843
Acadia. *See* Nova Scotia
Acosta, M. d'. *See* Penet, d'Acosta Frères
& Cie.
Adair, James B. M.: letter to, 3-4; letter
from, 66-7; and model of threshing machine for TJ, 3-4, 66, 102-3, 173; and
case of *Jay*, 4; and Sinclair's queries on
agriculture, 66-7; plans to visit TJ, 67;
letter from cited, 67n
Adams, Abigail: letter from, 749-52; opinion of Great Britain, 749, 750; and
household finances, 750-1; commissions
TJ to make purchases, 751
Adams, John: letter to, 580; and "Camillus" essays, 6-8; nominates Prebble as
consul at Cádiz, 60n; and ransom of
American captives in Algiers, 142n;
writings of admired in England, 276;
and TJ's report on commerce, 534, 580-
1; and Barbary States, 750; expenses as
diplomat, 750-1; wine for, 750; and
seeds for TJ, 757; friendship for TJ,
769; mentioned, 67n
Adams, John Quincy: letter to, 744-5; TJ
recommends, 744-5
Adams, Samuel: and case of Duplaine,
273-4n, 416n
Adran, Bishop of. *See* Pigneau de Béhaine,
Pierre Joseph Georges
Aerial (ship): captured by British privateer, 54
Africa: Ledyard's expedition to, 764
Agicourt, M. d': vineyard, 762
agriculture: value of threshing machine to
southern states, 3-4; Sinclair's queries
on, 66-7, 637; Harriott's views on, 193;
Short's views on, 201, 204-6; and share-
cropping by slaves, 204-5; crop rotation
in British, 277; Edwards's views on
British, 277; and maple sugar manufacture, 546n
Aij, France. *See* Ay (Aij), France
Aimée (*Amée*) *Marguerite* (*Amiable Margaretta*; *Providence*) (French privateer and
British sloop): captures *San Josef*, 268-
9, 343-4, 346; renamed from *Providence*, 343-4; and restoration of French
prizes, 422, 625-8
Albany, N.Y.; military stores removed to,
47; and yellow fever, 174
Albemarle barracks: accounts respecting,
689; Convention troops held at, 689-90,
701n

Albemarle Co., Va.: resolutions on neutrality, 19n, 27; Short desires to reside
near, 205; estate of T. M. Randolph, Jr.,
294-5; fertility of soil in, 615; suitability
of cultivating grain in, 766; suitability of
cultivating grass in, 766
Albert de Rions, François Hector, Comte
d': naval command, 770
Alder, Charles, & Co.: and Pintard's arrest, 239n
Alexander, Eli: overseer for Shadwell and
Lego, 483, 497, 524, 582; TJ's instructions for, 509; departs for Richmond,
617
Alexandria, Va.: Short considers purchasing lots in, 202-3; French vice-consul at,
282
Algiers: Humphreys's mission to, 23-5,
106-7, 139-40, 152-3, 283, 636, 654,
845; relations with U.S., 60, 198n, 469-
70, 513-18, 521, 522, 596-7, 637;
Yznardi's proposed mission to, 60, 498-
9; navy, 107, 222, 283-4n, 823; piracy,
107, 135, 139-40, 187, 196-8, 199,
222-3, 224, 230-5, 252-3, 607-8, 609,
789; relations with Netherlands, 107;
plague in, 126, 284n; Portuguese naval
protection against, 196-8, 199, 222-3,
230-5, 252-3, 264-7; truce with Portugal, 196-8, 199, 222-3, 224, 230-5,
252-3, 262-7, 282-4, 469, 498-9, 503,
507, 508-9, 516-18, 607-8, 617, 619;
truce with Netherlands, 284n;
Skjöldebrand's proposed mission to,
466; Leacock's thoughts on, 596-7; relations with Gibraltar, 596-7; relations
with Great Britain, 596-7, 637; Cutting's mission to, 659-60; relations with
Portugal, 752-3; relations with Spain,
752-3; Danish naval blockade, 823; relations with Venice, 823; vessel taken by
Portugal, 823
Algiers, American captives in: ransom of,
142n, 513-18, 521, 822-4; numbers increase, 197n, 253, 284n, 469, 752-3;
additional captures, 232; plea for ransom by, 466; subsistence of, 823
Algiers, Dey of. *See* Ali Hassan, Dey of Algiers; Muhammad Ibn Uthman, Dey of
Algiers
Alicante, Spain: Humphreys visits, 153,
187, 200; and colonial trade, 579-80;
consul at, 845
Alice (ship), 266n
aliens: and peace treaty, 826-7

[873]

Blount, William (*cont.*)
  appointments, 787; journal of, 787n;
  and land grants, 796
Board of Admiralty, Continental: letter
  from, 696; and free ships and free goods,
  600-1n; and transport of military supplies, 696
Board of Agriculture and Internal Improvements, British: queries on agriculture, 66-7
Board of Treasury, U.S. *See* Commissioners of the Treasury, U.S.
Board of War, Continental: and Convention horses, 690; letter from cited, 697,
  698n
boats: building of, 710; horse-powered,
  798
Bockius (Bockeus), William: Cabinet
  meets at tavern of, 329n; Madison and
  Monroe lodge with, 334
Bolling, John (TJ's brother-in-law): aversion to writing, 758-9; and Jane Jefferson's estate, 777; mentioned, 670
Bolling, Mary Jefferson (Mrs. John Bolling, TJ's sister): letter from, 758-9; relations with Mary Jefferson, 755-6, 758;
  affection for TJ, 758; deaths in family of,
  758
Bolling, Thomas (TJ's nephew): death of,
  759n
Bompard (Bompart), Citizen: and sale of
  French prizes in U.S., 219; departure
  for France, 386-7
Bond, Phineas: and impressment of seamen, 92; and case of *Industry*, 321; and
  case of *Conyngham*, 417-18
Bonne, Corporal: and Galbaud's dispute
  with Genet, 42, 77n, 97
bookcases: of TJ, 771
books: shipment of TJ's, 152, 408, 586,
  607, 608, 637; plans for arranging at
  Monticello, 771
Bordeaux, France: exchange rate, 5; U.S.
  consul at, 9; and case of *Minerva*, 141,
  223; U.S. trade with, 149, 155; U.S.
  ships detained at, 192; and Lear's trip to
  Europe, 226n; trade with Madeira,
  239n; trade with St. Thomas, 253; and
  case of *Hamilton*, 525; TJ evaluates
  wines of, 762, 843
Bordman, William: and case of *Flora*, 50;
  letter from cited, 50n
Boston: and case of Duplaine, 6, 13, 79-80,
  82n, 260, 261; trade with Málaga, 139;
  and yellow fever, 174; trade with Lisbon, 222, 235n; trade with Cádiz, 252;
  and withdrawal from U.S. ports of

French privateers commissioned by
  Genet in U.S., 634; and exports of fish,
  788
Boston (H.M.S.): captures *Republican*,
  77n; battle with *Embuscade*, 386
Botetourt Co., Va.: and defense of west-
  ern frontier, 691, 693n; militia, 691,
  693n
Boudinot, Elias: letter from quoted, 772n;
  recommends friend for State Depart-
  ment clerkship, 772n
Boudinot, Elisha: and pardon for C. Freeman, 440, 495n
Bouquet, M.: vineyard, 762
Bourdieu, Peregrine: owner of *William
  Tell*, 46n
Bourne, Benjamin: letter from, 801; and
  TJ's report on commerce, 548n, 801-2
Bourne, Sylvanus: letter from, 781; seeks
  diplomatic appointment, 781; letter
  from cited, 782n; seeks consular appointment at Cádiz, 782n
Bournonville, Charles François: letter to,
  183-4; and tonnage duties from Saint-
  Domingue refugees, 43n, 99, 173n; and
  relief of Saint-Domingue refugees, 93;
  and case of *Citoyen Genet*, 124; and case
  of *Roehampton*, 183, 189; identified,
  184n; letter from cited, 184n; letter from
  submitted to Washington, 189; Washington approves letter to, 228; and case
  of *Industry*, 321-2; and U.S. debt to
  France, 382; and alleged threats to
  French consuls, 456n
Bouteille, M.: plan to capture Tortuga
  Island, 296, 356
Bowdoin, James: and improvements in
  distillation, 790
Bowen, Jabez: letter from quoted, 194n;
  recommends Howell for district attor-
  ney, 194n, 376
Bowen's Virginia Centinel & Gazette (Win-
  chester): extract from, 818n
Bowman, John: letter to, 309; letter from,
  236; letter from cited, 236; and Lucas's
  steam engine design, 236, 309; identi-
  fied, 236n
Bowman, Sabina Lynch Cattell (Mrs.
  John Bowman): affection for TJ, 236;
  TJ's affection for, 309
Bowne, Mr.: warehouse of, 817
Bowyer, John: receives vote for Va. Com-
  mittee of Safety, 679
Boyd, Archibald: family of, 300
Boyd, Ker & Co.: letter to, 764; and Rut-
  ledge's funds, 764
Boyd, Robert: governor of Gibraltar, 153

INDEX

Cyrus (Sirus, slave): deeded to TJ by mother, 676; bequeathed to TJ's brother, 779n

Dabbadie. *See* Abadie (Dabbadie), M. d'

D'Acosta, M. *See* Penet, d'Acosta Frères & Cie.

Dagobert de Fontenille, Luc Siméon Auguste: defeats Spanish army near Montlouis, 149

Daily Advertiser (New York): and Genet's threat to appeal from Washington to American people, 481

Dalbarade, Jean: instructions of to Genet, 594n

Dallas, Alexander J.: letter from, 481; abandons Genet, 6; and Genet's threat to appeal from Washington to American people, 481, 484, 528n, 529-32; and alleged French refugee plots in U.S., 629n; letter from quoted, 809n; and Pa. land purchase, 809n; letters from cited, 852; sends Pa. executive acts to TJ, 852; and passport requests, 853

Dalrymple, Sir John: *Essay towards a General History of Feudal Property in Great Britain*, 670-1

Dalton, Peter: and case of *William*, 331-2n

damson grape: vine sent to TJ, 278

Dandridge, Bartholomew, Jr.: letters from, 481, 503, 610, 620, 629; and commissioning of federal appointees, 39, 851; and passports for U.S. ships, 39; translator for Washington, 189; and meeting of Cabinet, 481; and Portuguese-Algerine truce, 503, 610; and TJ's report on commerce, 620; and alleged French refugee plots in U.S., 629; and British occupation of Saint-Domingue, 629; and relations with Southern Indians, 629; and relations with Spain, 629

Dandridge, Bartholomew, Sr.: elected to Va. Committee of Safety, 678

Daniel, John: master of *Laurel*, 107

Daniel, William: witnesses will, 683n

Dannemours, M. *See* Anmours (Dannemours), Charles François, Chevalier d'

Dannery, Thomas: and French right to commission privateers in U.S., 148; exequatur for, 175-6, 181, 188-89, 228, 363, 414 15, and case of *Duplaine*, 273-4n, 416, 427; and address of French consular commissions, 501; and alleged threats to French consuls, 523

Dan river: and retreat of Greene's army, 709

D'arboyce grape: vine sent to TJ, 278

Dauphin (ship): captured by Algiers, 822

Davenport, William: commands cavalry contingent, 717

Davidson, John: customs collector, 94

Davies (Davis), William: letters to, 504, 714, 717; letter from, 407; and final settlement of state accounts, 407, 504; and discharge of unfit troops, 712; and Va. public armorer, 714-15; letter from cited, 714n; and exchanges of prisoners of war, 717; appointment to Va. War Office, 718; mentioned, 772n

Davis, Col. *See* Davies (Davis), William

Davis, Augustine: and Short's diplomatic conduct, 216-17; and postal service, 590

Davis, William: master of *Catharine*, 160

Deane, Silas: letter from, 719; and Lafayette's Continental Army pay, 643-4; recommends Greive, 719

Deberger, Henry, Sr.: recommends Voigt as chief coiner of Mint, 826n

debts to British creditors: Brailsford v. Morris, 827; extent of, 827; in Va., 827

Deforgues, François Louis Michel Chemin: and French West Indies, 405n

Deism: TJ's alleged belief in, 39-40

Dekay, Capt.: correspondence with Short, 845

Delamotte, F. C. A.: letters to, 95-6, 301-2; and case of *Lawrence*, 96n; promotes commerce with France, 96n; letters to forwarded, 198-9, 200; TJ recommends Lear to, 226n, 301-2; letters from cited, 302n, 847

Delaware: Loyalist strength in, 716n; and Madison's revenue plan, 730

Delaware, President of. *See* Clayton, Joshua

Delaware (ship): and alleged French refugee expedition against Môle Saint Nicolas, 436-7, 458, 482, 486-7n

Delaware bay: and U.S. maritime jurisdiction, 105n

Delaware river: and French privateering, 78, 452n, 634; freezes, 611, 637

Del Bombice e del Bisso degli Antichi (Adamo Fabbroni): given to TJ, 754-5

Della Farfalla Simbolo Egiziano (Adamo Fabbroni): given to TJ, 754-5

Delozier, Daniel: commission for, 346-7

Delpeau, Charles. *See* De Pauw (Delpeau), Charles

Demerara, Dutch Guyana: U.S. exports to, 800

194n; recommends Howell for district attorney, 194n, 376

Francis II, Holy Roman Emperor: relations with France, 276

"Franklin": pseudonym used by John Taylor of Caroline, 7-8, 62-3

Franklin (ship): carries tobacco to France, 694

Franklin, Benjamin: and Coffyn's consular appointment, 9; refuses funds to A. Lee, 685; retires as minister to France, 745, 749; and prize money for Jones's command, 746, 747n; esteem for, 748; TJ forwards correspondence of, 749

Franklin, William Temple: letter to, 784; and TJ's report on commerce, 578n; TJ recommends, 748; TJ invites to dinner, 784

Franks, Mr.: and yellow fever, 238

Franks, David Salisbury: recommended for federal appointment, 781n

Franks, Moses: and British captures of U.S. ships, 118, 184, 190

Frazer, John G.: brings Va. seal, 695

Frederick Co., Va.: letter to county lieutenant of, 691-3; and defense of western frontier, 691-3; militia, 691-3, 708

Fredericksburg, Va.: and resolutions on neutrality, 19n, 237; TJ visits, 254, 495; horses to meet TJ at, 496-7, 524, 608, 638; militia garrison, 708

Frederick William II, King of Prussia: and war with France, 265

Freeman, Abraham (Benjamin): and pardon for C. Freeman, 306n, 355n, 439-43

Freeman, Clarkson: counterfeits public securities, 306n, 355, 439-43, 495

Freeman, Ezra Fitz: letter from cited, 306n; and pardon for C. Freeman, 306n, 355, 392

Freeman, Isaac: murder of, 306n

Free Translation of the Preface to Bellendenus (Samuel Parr): returned to TJ, 812

French language: professional translator of, 334-5

French Revolution: consular reports on (*see* Cathalan, Stephen, Jr.; Delamotte, F. C. A.; Fenwick, Joseph); execution of queen, 5, 153; Humphreys's reports on, 5; and Washington, 131; and Genet's expulsion from Russia, 133-4n; Noailles and Talon seek refuge from, 134n; G. Morris's views on, 213-14; Edwards's views on, 276; opposed in Birmingham, 277n; at L'Orient, 306-7;

Hamilton's views on, 384; mentioned, 404-6

Freneau, Philip: letter from, 227; resigns Department of State clerkship, 227. *See also National Gazette* (Philadelphia)

fresco painting: for TJ, 93; TJ's notes on, 784-5

fresh provisions: export to British West Indies, 539, 549n, 558; export to French West Indies, 539, 549n, 558. *See also* provisions

Frontignac grape, white: vine sent to TJ, 278

Frontignan, France: TJ evaluates wine of, 762

fruit trees: and U.S. farmers, 546n

Fullerton, Valeria: letter to, 124; account with TJ, 116, 124; identified, 124n; leaves Philadelphia during yellow fever epidemic, 394; TJ visits, 523

Furnes, Austrian Netherlands: captured by French, 277

furniture: storage of TJ's, 271-2, 410, 492; shipment of TJ's, 377, 431-2, 465, 586, 607, 608, 637, 786; for TJ's overseers, 411, 497. *See also* chairs; desk

furs: U.S. trade in, 788

Gaillet, M.: vineyard, 762

Gaines, Daniel: letter from cited, 794n; recommends Peleg Greene, 794n

Gaines, Hierom: TJ purchases wood from, 267

Gaines, Humphrey: witnesses deed, 733

Gaines, Richard: witnesses deed, 733

Galbaud, Thomas François: dispute with Genet, 32-4, 41-2, 75-8, 97, 123, 285, 385; letter from cited, 849

Gall, Wilhelm Rudolf von: letters for, 689

Gallatin, Albert: letter to, 794; letters forwarded to, 794

Galphin, George: and Creek hostilities with Ga., 463n

Gálvez, Bernardo de: letter to, 688; letter from, 698; and Va. loan request, 687, 688, 698-9; congratulates TJ on election as governor, 698-9

Gambel, Capt. *See* Gamble (Gambel), Thomas

Gamble, Robert: letters to, 152, 361, 494, 607-8; letter from, 409-10; and goods for Monticello, 64; and orrery for TJ, 85; and books for TJ, 152; and wine for TJ, 152, 410; and model of threshing machine for TJ, 336, 485, 494, 498; forwards letter to TJ, 361; health, 410;

594n; and compensation for French prizes, 112-13, 457; and French right to fit out privateers in U.S., 112-13, 260, 452n, 593; letters forwarded from, 112, 117; withdrawal from U.S. ports of French privateers commissioned by in U.S., 112-13, 124, 451-2; and enlistment of U.S. citizens in French service, 112n, 131, 177, 178-9, 296-7n, 619-20; letters from submitted to Washington, 123, 190; and case of *Citoyen Genet*, 124; views on U.S. Constitution, 126, 138, 272-4, 379, 414-15, 457-8, 480; diplomatic career in Europe, 128, 380-1; expulsion from Russia, 128-9, 133-4n; reproaches TJ, 128; and G. Morris's recall, 129, 504-6; publishes correspondence with TJ, 130, 134n, 450, 508-9, 531n, 593-5, 632, 649; and purchase in U.S. of provisions for France, 131, 347-8, 365; requests arms for French West Indies, 131, 134n; and U.S. debt to France, 131, 347-8, 364-5, 378, 382, 429, 457, 487-8, 601-3, 611; and French right to bring prizes into U.S. ports, 132; and new commercial treaty with U.S., 132, 164-9, 281, 302, 361-2, 366, 534; and sale of French prizes in U.S., 132, 219, 364; instructions from Provisional Executive Council, 134n, 594, 632, 649; and French policy against meddling abroad, 147; and French right to commission privateers in U.S., 148, 594-5n; and passports for French ships, 148; and French trade restrictions, 156-7, 365-7; and British trade restrictions, 157, 167; and prize of *Concorde*, 171-2; and address of French consular commissions, 175-6, 363, 414-15, 426, 479-80, 489, 500-2, 526-7; and exequaturs for French consuls, 175-6, 181, 188-9, 479-80, 489, 500-2, 526-7, 603, 618; and case of *Roehampton*, 183-4; and French captures of British ships, 183-4, 331-2, 364; and French consular appointments, 185n, 282, 302-3, 347, 352, 363, 414-15, 426; British attitude toward, 276; and case of *Catherine*, 279-80, 364; and British occupation of Saint-Domingue, 284-9, 436-7; and U.S. guarantee of French possessions in America, 284-9, 362, 452n, 599; and British impressment of seamen, 288; and British relations with Western Indians, 288; and British retention of western posts, 288; and French plan to liberate Canada, 290-3, 385-7, 594n; *Les*

Français Libres à leurs freres de la Louisiane, 290-1; *Les Francais Libres a leurs freres Les Canadiens*, 290-3, 386n; and denunciation of Mangourit, 295-7, 415, 619-20; and French plan to capture E. and W. Fla., 295-7, 619-20; marries Cornelia Clinton, 298; and alleged British plots against U.S., 303-4, 380-1; and case of *Conyngham*, 342-3, 374, 426; and case of *Pilgrim*, 342n, 426; and funds for French naval vessels in U.S., 347-8, 365; and relief of Saint-Domingue refugees, 347-8; and French reissue of assignats, 366; attempts to sue Jay and King for libel, 367-8, 527-9, 530-1n, 583, 587-8, 589, 592-3, 594; and case of *Moissonnier*, 375; and departure of French naval vessels in U.S., 385-7; and French naval operations in Caribbean, 386; and French naval protection for vessels to France, 386; dispatches from France lost, 387-8; sends French constitution to TJ, 388; and appeal from Washington to Congress, 395-6, 401, 593-5, 632, 649, 655; translation of letters of, 402; credences of, 403; rank as consul general questioned, 403; courier to TJ, 404; and mistreatment of deputation from Saint-Domingue, 404-5, 429-30, 460; report on French West Indies, 404, 405n, 429; and Saint-Domingue political situation, 404-5; and factionalism of Saint-Domingue refugees, 405n; and case of *Jane* of Dublin, 413-14, 426-7; and case of *Lovely Lass*, 413-14, 426-7; and case of *Prince William Henry*, 413-14, 426-7; and alleged threats to French consuls, 437, 456, 458, 481-2, 523; requests authority over U.S. ships to Saint-Domingue, 437-8, 459; and freedom of the press, 438-9n; and case of *Carmagnole*, 451-2; and arming of British ships in U.S., 452n; and case of *Little Sarah*, 452n, 528n; and sale of arms to belligerent nations, 458-9; correspondence with TJ certified for Congress, 477n; and payment of bills drawn on Saint-Domingue, 487-8n; and enlistment in French service of French citizens in U.S., 511-12n; and TJ's report on commerce, 534; and neutrality rules, 593; and enlistment of Indians in French service, 594n; and free ships and free goods, 598-601; and Proclamation of Neutrality, 598-601; and opening of French ports to U.S. ships, 639-41; mentioned, 6, 163, 423

INDEX

GREAT BRITAIN (*cont.*)

Public Finance
TJ compares to France, 741; proportion of alloy in silver coinage, 821

Society
described by Mrs. Adams, 749

U.S. Relations with
possibility of war, 10, 29, 32, 138, 221-2, 425n, 451, 535, 637; Federalist friendship toward Britain, 27; and alleged conspiracy against France in U.S., 41; and proposed purchase of provisions in U.S. for France, 131; blamed for Portuguese-Algerine truce, 139, 197-8n, 199, 231-4, 283, 284n, 469-71, 534, 596-7, 609, 619, 637; alleged British plots against U.S., 142, 220-1, 284-9, 303-4, 380-1; and case of Lafayette, 151; and maritime jurisdiction of U.S., 190-1; and Short's diplomatic conduct, 213-18; and G. Morris's diplomatic conduct, 218n; and British relations with Western Indians, 288, 470, 534; possible support for U.S. right to navigate Mississippi, 444; and British retention of western posts, 447-9, 533, 610, 636; impact of communications to Congress on, 454; mercantilism opposed in TJ's report on commerce, 532-3; American popular hostility toward, 535, 596-7; and British captures of U.S. ships, 535; and U.S. guarantee of French possessions in America, 599; attitude toward U.S., 750; and need to encourage American ships and seamen, 789. *See also* Grenville, William Wyndham, Lord; Hammond, George; Pinckney, Thomas

U.S. Trade with
and French trade restrictions, l-li, 33, 156-7, 158; and British trade restrictions, 6, 11, 29, 552n, 563, 577, 829-36, 841; trade statistics, 166, 548n, 557, 571, 578n; Genet condemns British mercantilism, 167; duties on U.S. imports from, 469-70, 609; and TJ's report on commerce, 532-5; and proposed U.S. navigation act, 533; rejects U.S. overtures for commercial treaty, 533, 544, 563, 577-8; tonnage of U.S. shipping to, 536, 554, 568; U.S. exports to, 536, 546n, 553-4, 567-8; duties on U.S. exports to, 538, 540, 549n, 556, 559, 570-1, 573; restrictions on U.S. shipping, 538,

546n, 564-5n; colonial trade regulations, 539, 540, 545n, 546n, 549n, 558-9, 572, 573, 578n; and reexports of U.S. products, 546n, 800; U.S. imports from, 546n, 554, 568; and British navigation acts, 547-8n, 556-7, 570-1, 642, 841; restrictions on fisheries, 788

War of First Coalition
restrictions on neutral trade, l-li, 6, 10, 33, 50, 55-8, 100-2, 123, 138, 143, 149-50, 157, 423, 451, 454-5, 468, 471-2, 475, 476-7n, 478n, 481, 489, 491; and additional instructions to British warships and privateers, 6, 33, 100-2, 115, 123, 143, 149-50, 475, 476-7n, 478n; and French trade restrictions, 33, 156-7, 158; captures Toulon, 135, 153, 155, 187, 199, 227, 334, 345, 470; siege of Dunkirk, 149, 334, 345; troops for Canada, 158; and Portuguese-Algerine truce, 197-8n, 199, 231-2, 262-3, 264-5, 469-71; and Paine's peace commission proposal, 226-7, 258-9, 471; naval operations in Caribbean, 284-5, 287, 334, 345; occupation of Saint-Domingue, 289n, 405n, 436-7, 438n, 468, 482, 629; and French plan to liberate Canada, 290-3, 386n; alleged conspiracy against France, 365-6; and French naval operations in Caribbean, 386n; loss of Toulon, 467-8; and British captures of U.S. ships, 535; and free ships and free goods, 598-601. *See also* privateers, British; privateers, French

Great Falls of the Potomac: Short desires to reside near, 207
Great Kanawha (Kanhaway) river: as boundary of new states, 739
Great Slave lake: communication with Lake Superior, 793n
Green, William (R.I.): memorial from, 829-36; claim for compensation, 829-36
Greenbrier Co., Va.: and defense of western frontier, 691, 693n; Indian depredations, 691; militia, 691, 693n
Greene, Nathanael: reinforcements for, 703, 711; at Guilford Court House, 709; land grant for, 796
Greene, Peleg: recommended as commander of cutter, 794n
Greene, Ray: appointed district attorney, 194n
Greenleaf, James: and TJ's recommendations for Lear, 226, 304-5; and Kinsley's

[902]

INDEX

INDEX

INDEX

INDEX

INDEX

INDEX

JEFFERSON, THOMAS (*cont.*)
the French constitution, 816; and
Panic of 1792, 825; and sinking fund,
825; and Ohio Company land purchase, 826; and case of William
Green, 829-36; sends acts of Congress
to governors, 852, 855; and certification of American citizenship, 853;
documents signed ex officio, 855-9

Virginia Estate
Edgehill boundary dispute, 773-6. *See
also* Elk Hill; Lego; Monticello;
Shadwell

Virginia Legislator
drafts report on parliamentary procedure, 666-8; service on Committee of
Privileges and Elections, 667n; tallies
votes for Committee of Safety, 678-9;
and paper money redemption, 680-1

Writings
"Anas," xlix-l, 32-3, 384, 394 (illus.),
399-401, 411-12, 428, 453-5, 467;
Report on Commerce, li, 394 (illus.),
532-79 (editorial note and docu-
ments); Opinion on Henry Knox's
Report on Defense, 46-7; Cabinet
Opinions on Relations with France
and Great Britain, 49-50; Report on
Weights and Measures, 154, 789,
813-14, 818-22; Report on the Pro-
ceedings of the Southwest Territory,
323; Cabinet Opinions on Various
Letters, 426-7; Cabinet Opinions on
Edmond Charles Genet and James
King, 489; Report on Edmond
Charles Genet and Gouverneur Morris, 504-6; Report on Morocco and
Algiers, 513-17; Proposed Public
Statement on Edmond Charles
Genet, 529-30; Notes on the Proclamation of Neutrality and the Law of
Nations, 598-600; Supplementary
Report on Commerce, 639-42; Report on Parliamentary Procedure,
665-7; Notes for Epitaph and Grave
of Dabney Carr, 673-4; Garden Book,
675n; Literary Commonplace Book,
675n; Election Tally for the Va. Committee of Safety, 678-9; Memorandum on Paper Money, 680-1; Epitaph for Martha Wayles Jefferson,
728; Notes on France and Great Britain, 741; Memorandum on Wine,
761-3; Notes of a Tour into the
Southern Parts of France, 763n;

Notes of a Tour Through Holland
and the Rhine Valley, 763n; Notes on
Executive Departments, 780; Notes
on Fresco Painting, 784-5; Report on
Fisheries, 788n; Notes on John Rob-
ertson and Algerine Prisoners, 822-4;
Notes on Headaches, 824; Dissenting
Opinion on the Sinking Fund, 825;
Directions for Building the Great
Clock, 839-40; Memorandum to
Henry Sheaff, 842-4. *See also Notes on
the State of Virginia*

Jefferson v. Reade's administrators: law
case of TJ, 683
Jenkins, Marshall, & Son: and ships for
U.S. navy, 605
Jennings & Woddrop: and case of *Trial*,
337n
Jenny (slave): bequeathed by Ann Eppes
Harris, 682
Jérémie, Saint-Domingue: captured by
British, 284-5, 289n, 362n, 405n, 468;
alleged French refugee expedition
against, 436-8, 458-9, 482, 486-7n,
629n
Jesse (ship): captured by *Sans Pareil*, 12
Johanene (Johanné), Pierre A.: arrest of,
78, 124; master of *Citoyen Genet*, 351
Johannisberg (Johansberg), Germany: TJ
evaluates wine of, 763, 844
John Marie Joseph Louis, Prince of Bra-
zil: influenced by Melo e Castro, 140-1;
governs Portugal, 142-3n; and Portuguese-Algerine truce, 264
Johnny. *See* Hemings, John
Johnson, Joshua: letter from, 160; and impressment, 160; and Mint, 160; account
with U.S., 651; and case of William
Green, 831, 832, 834; letter from cited,
849; mentioned, 332
Johnson, Thomas: as possible Secretary of
the Treasury, 17; refuses appointment
as Secretary of State, 298
Johnson, William Samuel: recommends
Saltonstall for Department of State post,
772
Johnston, John Waller: recommended as
lighthouse keeper, 794n
Jones, Mr.: land transactions of, 669
Jones, Bevard: recommended for hospital
stewardship, 794n
Jones, Edward: and case of *San Josef*, 268-
9, 445, 627-8n
Jones, Gabriel: and Federalist resolutions,
27-8; receives votes for Va. Committee
of Safety, 679

[917]

368-73, 387n, 418-19, 426, 445, 446-7, 457, 512, 625-8, 632-5; and French capture of Swedish ship, 25, 351-2, 389, 422; and French privateers commissioned by Genet in U.S., 25-6, 49, 73-4, 78, 79, 104, 131, 351-2, 611, 620-2, 625-8; and use of U.S. ports by French navy, 30-1, 48, 49-50, 55, 70-1, 123, 177-8, 179; and sale of French prizes in U.S., 31, 48, 132, 219, 364, 413n, 486; and use of U.S. ports by armed allied ships, 31, 55, 70-1; and French captures of prizes in U.S. territorial waters, 44-6, 49, 67-9, 103-5, 257, 279-80, 319-20, 322, 342-3, 374, 382-3, 384-5, 393, 410, 417-18, 421, 422, 426, 486, 512, 618; and British right to bring prizes into U.S. ports, 49; and threatened revocation of French consular exequaturs, 49, 51, 52-3, 83, 123, 132, 170, 375; and French right to fit out privateers in U.S., 50, 112-13, 148, 195, 261, 268-9, 310-11, 316-19, 321-2, 343-4, 346, 368-73, 418-19, 594-5n; and U.S. jurisdiction over belligerent prize cases, 55, 67-9, 131-2, 351-2, 389, 409, 413n, 422, 424n; and arming of belligerent ships in U.S. ports, 57, 422, 452n; and detention of French prizes in U.S. ports, 62, 67-9, 71, 104-5, 108, 131-2, 191, 279-80, 342-3n, 372n, 410; and French right to bring prizes into U.S. ports, 70-1, 132; and enlistment in French service of French citizens in U.S., 73-4, 511-12n; and enlistment of U.S. citizens in French service, 73, 131, 177, 178-9, 196, 261, 296-7n, 619-20; and arrest of French deserters, 75-6, 76-8, 97-8; and maritime jurisdiction of U.S., 78, 104, 105n, 171-2, 190-1, 257, 328-31, 338-40, 340-1, 364, 391-2, 393, 413n, 416-17, 422, 426, 427, 446n, 476n; and arming of French privateers in U.S. ports, 80-2n, 593, 618; and free ships and free goods, 96n, 310, 474, 477n, 598-601, 640-1, 651; and French plan to liberate Louisiana, 111-12n, 176-80, 196, 290-1, 311, 314, 392, 445, 594n, 631n; and withdrawal from U.S. ports of French privateers commissioned by Genet in U.S., 112-13, 124, 451-2, 632-5; and Genet's request for arms for French West Indies, 131, 134n; and proposed purchase of provisions in U.S, for France, 131; and Dutch capture of U.S. ship, 136; and abuse of neutral shipping by belligerent privateers, 140;

and U.S. treaty obligations, 144n; and French mistreatment of U.S. ships, 175n, 383n; and delay in pursuing belligerent ships leaving U.S. ports, 177-8, 179; and French captures of British ships, 183-4, 310, 329, 331-2; and Portuguese detention of U.S. ship, 223-4, 239, 282-3; and Spanish captures of U.S. ships, 252-3, 327, 357-8, 499; and French capture of Spanish ship, 268-9, 310-11, 313, 343-4, 346, 391-2, 422, 445, 446-7, 625-8; and alleged French refugee plots in U.S., 284-9, 295-7, 356, 372n, 392, 405-6n, 415, 436-9, 456, 458, 460-1, 481-2, 486-7, 523n, 629; and U.S. guarantee of French possessions in America, 284-9, 362, 400, 412, 452n, 476n, 599; and French plan to liberate Canada, 290-3, 385-7, 594n; and French plan to capture E. and W. Fla., 295-7, 619-20; and alleged British plots against U.S., 303-4, 380-1; Va. legislative resolutions on, 333-4, 430-1; and departure of French naval vessels in U.S., 385-7; Hamilton's views on, 399-400, 401n, 411-12; TJ's views on, 399-400, 412; E. Randolph's views on, 400, 401n, 412; Washington's views on, 400; and mistreatment of deputation from Saint-Domingue, 404-6, 429-30, 436, 460; rules on, 409, 593; and enlistment of U.S. citizens in belligerent service, 421-2; and equipment of belligerent ships in U.S., 422; and alleged threats to French consuls, 437, 456, 458, 481-2, 523; and Genet's request for authority over U.S. ships to Saint-Domingue, 437-8, 459; and sale of arms to belligerent nations, 458-9; and detention of French sailors, 510-11, 597, 607; and enlistment of Indians in French service, 594n. *See also* passports

Nevill, Joseph: and supplies for Clark's army, 711

New Castle, Del.: rumored British expedition against, 716

New England: reaction to Shays's Rebellion, 220-1

Newfoundland: abortive French naval campaign against, 177-8n, 290-1n, 386n; fisheries, 221-2; and British trade restrictions, 540, 559, 566n, 572

New Hampshire. Duplaine as vice-consul for, 185; appointment of district attorney for, 424, 483-4; and Madison's revenue plan, 729

submitted to Washington, 123; recommends Miller, 144; account with U.S., 150, 650; and Mint, 150, 158, 160, 311, 450-5, 645; and case of Lafayette, 151, 433, 643; assists Leslie, 154; and case of *Lawrence*, 158; and French trade restrictions, 158, 466, 468-9, 477n; and Paine's peace commission proposal, 227, 258-9; and Graham's offer to negotiate opening of Mississippi, 444; and British retention of Western posts, 451; and Portuguese-Algerine truce, 508-9; and J. P. Jones's mission to Algiers, 515; and U.S. guarantee of French possessions in America, 599-601; and case of P. Wilson, 650-1; letters from cited, 847, 848, 849

Pine, Mary (Mrs. Robert Edge Pine): and portrait of Madison, 828

Pine, Robert Edge: portrait of Madison, 828

Pintard, John Marsden: letter to, 95-6; letters from, 223, 239, 282-3; assists French prisoners, 96n; and case of *Commerçant*, 141, 282-3; and case of *Minerva*, 141, 223-4, 282-3; compensation for, 149; under house arrest, 223-4, 239, 282-3; letters from cited, 224n, 283n, 781n; letters from submitted to Washington, 224n, 239n, 284n; and Portuguese-Algerine truce, 234n, 282-4; seeks consular appointment at Lisbon, 781n

Pintard, Mrs. John Marsden: Goddard's affection for, 239n

Pinto de Sousa Coutinho, Luís. *See* Coutinho, Luís Pinto de Sousa

Piomingo (Chickasaw Chief): and Chickasaw-Creek war, 585n

pitch: French-Portuguese trade in, 140; export to Spain, 536, 554, 568; U.S. exports of, 536, 553, 567; duties on in France, 537, 555, 569; export to Portugal, 537, 555, 569; duties on in Great Britain, 538, 547n, 556, 570; export from U.S. to Sweden forbidden, 539, 558, 572; export to British West Indies, 539, 549n, 558, 572; export to French West Indies, 539, 549n, 558, 572; duties on in Danish West Indies, 549n, 559, 573

Pitt, William: and Graham's offer to negotiate opening of Mississippi, 444; and Portuguese-Algerine truce, 597

Pittsburgh: Indian depredations, 691

Pittsylvania Court House, Va.: arms stored at, 709

Pius VI, Pope: anecdote about, 221

plague: in Algiers, 126, 152, 284n; in Turkey, 193

Plan for establishing a Board of Agriculture and Internal Improvement (Sir John Sinclair): sent to TJ, 66-7

plateau, glass: for Mrs. Adams, 751

plows: for Madison, 63; for Washington, 425n

Plumard de Bellanger, Mme: TJ forwards letter from, 4

Plymouth, England: and case of *Jay*, 8; impressment in, 29

Pocomoke river: and Va.-Md. boundary, 54n

Poivre, Pierre: *Voyages d'un Philosophe*, 760

Poland: tenancy in, 205

Political Sketches (William Vans Murray): given to TJ, 812

Political State of Europe: owned by TJ, 322-3

Pollard, William: petition to Patent Board, 783; cotton spinning machine, 783

Pollexfen, Sir Henry: *Arguments and Reports*, 670

Pollock, Oliver: given drafts on France, 687; Va. commercial agent, 687-8, 698, 699; recommended by Miró, 723-4

Polly (ship): carries letter to TJ, 138

Polly (sloop): carries wine for TJ, 152

Polly (U.S. brig): passport for, 858

Polly (U.S. sloop and French privateer): renamed *Republican*, 422

Polverel, Etienne: and Talon's business affairs, 460-1n

Pommard, France: TJ evaluates wine of, 761

Pond, Peter: western discoveries, 793

Pontac: vineyard, 843

Ponte do Lima, Tomás Xavier de Lima Nogueira Vasconcelos Teles da Silva, Marqués de: and Portuguese-Algerine truce, 233

Pontevin, John: master of *Ambitieux*, 159n

Pope, Alexander: "Elegy to the Memory of an Unfortunate Lady" quoted by TJ, 673, 675n

Pope, Nathaniel: as attorney for TJ, 805

porcelain: figurines for Mrs. Adams, 751

pork: captured by British, 52; price of, 277; captured by French, 337n; for TJ's overseers, 411; export from U.S. to French West Indies forbidden, 549n, 572. *See also* pickled pork; salted pork

Poropotank creek, Va.: depth of water at, 705

A comprehensive index of Volumes 1-20 of the
First Series has been issued as Volume 21.
Each subsequent volume has its own index,
as does each volume or set of volumes
in the Second Series.